Nails

Nail lengths are identified by numbers from 4 to 60 followed by the letter "d," which stands for "penny."

For general framing and repair work, use common or box nails. Common nails are best suited to framing work where strength is important. Box nails are smaller in diameter than common nails, which makes them easier to drive and less likely to split wood. Use box nails for light work and thin materials.

Most common and box nails have a cement or vinyl coating that improves their holding power.

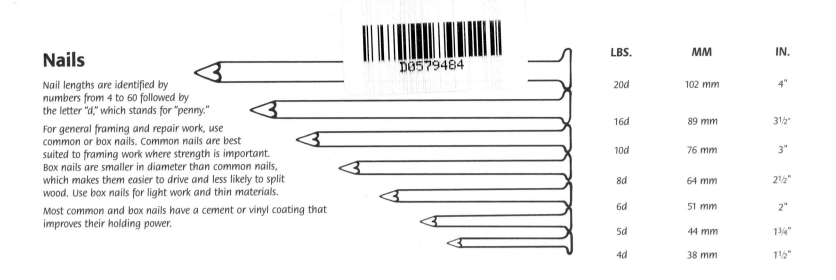

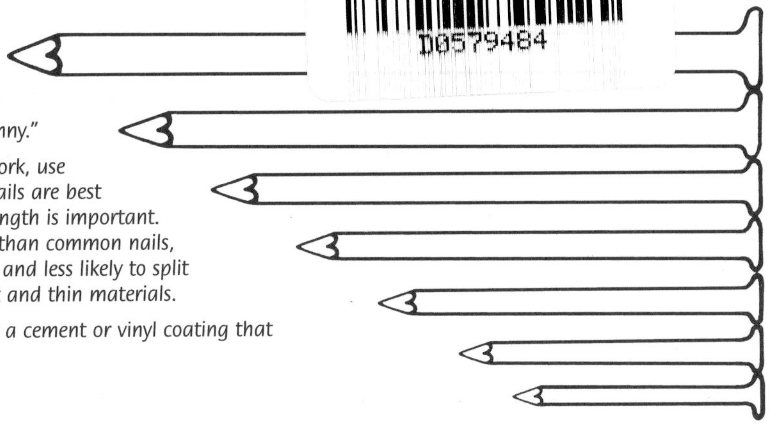

LBS.	MM	IN.
20d	102 mm	4"
16d	89 mm	3 1/2"
10d	76 mm	3"
8d	64 mm	2 1/2"
6d	51 mm	2"
5d	44 mm	1 3/4"
4d	38 mm	1 1/2"

Lumber Dimensions

NOMINAL - U.S.	ACTUAL - U.S.	METRIC
1 × 2	3/4" × 1 1/2"	19 × 38 mm
1 × 3	3/4" × 2 1/2"	19 × 64 mm
1 × 4	3/4" × 3 1/2"	19 × 89 mm
1 × 5	3/4" × 4 1/2"	19 × 114 mm
1 × 6	3/4" × 5 1/2"	19 × 140 mm
1 × 7	3/4" × 6 1/4"	19 × 159 mm
1 × 8	3/4" × 7 1/4"	19 × 184 mm
1 × 10	3/4" × 9 1/4"	19 × 235 mm
1 × 12	3/4" × 11 1/4"	19 × 286 mm
1 1/4 × 4	1" × 3 1/2"	25 × 89 mm
1 1/4 × 6	1" × 5 1/2"	25 × 140 mm
1 1/4 × 8	1" × 7 1/4"	25 × 184 mm
1 1/4 × 10	1" × 9 1/4"	25 × 235 mm
1 1/4 × 12	1" × 11 1/4"	25 × 286 mm
1 1/2 × 4	1 1/4" × 3 1/2"	32 × 89 mm
1 1/2 × 6	1 1/4" × 5 1/2"	32 × 140 mm
1 1/2 × 8	1 1/4" × 7 1/4"	32 × 184 mm
1 1/2 × 10	1 1/4" × 9 1/4"	32 × 235 mm
1 1/2 × 12	1 1/4" × 11 1/4"	32 × 286 mm
2 × 4	1 1/2" × 3 1/2"	38 × 89 mm
2 × 6	1 1/2" × 5 1/2"	38 × 140 mm
2 × 8	1 1/2" × 7 1/4"	38 × 184 mm
2 × 10	1 1/2" × 9 1/4"	38 × 235 mm
2 × 12	1 1/2" × 11 1/4"	38 × 286 mm
3 × 6	2 1/2" × 5 1/2"	64 × 140 mm
4 × 4	3 1/2" × 3 1/2"	89 × 89 mm
4 × 6	3 1/2" × 5 1/2"	89 × 140 mm

Metric Plywood Panels

Metric plywood panels are commonly available in two sizes: 1,200 mm × 2,400 mm and 1,220 mm × 2,400 mm, which is roughly equivalent to a 4 × 8-ft. sheet. Standard and Select sheathing panels come in standard thicknesses, while Sanded grade panels are available in special thicknesses.

STANDARD SHEATHING GRADE	SANDED GRADE
7.5 mm (5/16 in.)	6 mm (4/17 in.)
9.5 mm (3/8 in.)	8 mm (5/16 in.)
12.5 mm (1/2 in.)	11 mm (7/16 in.)
15.5 mm (5/8 in.)	14 mm (9/16 in.)
18.5 mm (3/4 in.)	17 mm (2/3 in.)
20.5 mm (13/16 in.)	19 mm (3/4 in.)
22.5 mm (7/8 in.)	21 mm (13/16 in.)
25.5 mm (1 in.)	24 mm (15/16 in.)

CREDITS

Associate Creative Director: Tim Himsel
Executive Editor: Bryan Trandem
Managing Editor: Jennifer Caliandro
Assisting Project Manager: Michelle Skudlarek
Senior Editor: Jerri Farris
Lead Editor: Daniel London
Editors: Rose Brandt, Karl Larson, Christian Paschke, Philip Schmidt
Technical Editors: Timothy Bro, Robert Weaver
Copy Editor: Janice Cauley
Lead Art Director: Kari Johnston
Art Directors: Gina Seeling, Kevin Walton
Mac Design Manager: Jon Simpson
Mac Designers: Keith Bruzelius, Arthur Durkee, Patricia Goar, Lynne Hanauer, Jonathan Hinz, Brad Webster
Technical Illustrators: Elroy Balgaard, Patricia Goar
Technical Photo Editors: Scott Christensen, Keith Thompson
Photo Acquisition: Angela Spann
Studio Services Manager: Marcia Chambers
Photo Services Coordinator: Carol Osterhus
Photo Team Leader: Chuck Nields
Photographers: Tate Carlson, Rex Irmen, Jamey Mauk, Andrea Rugg, Gregory Wallace
Scene Shop Carpenters: Troy Johnson, Gregory Wallace, Dan Widerski
Production Service Manager: Kim Gerber
Production Staff: Laura Hokkanen, Helga Thielen

CREATIVE PUBLISHING international

5900 Green Oak Drive
Minnetonka, MN 55343
1-800-328-3895

President/CEO: David D. Murphy
Vice President/Editorial: Patricia K. Jacobsen
Vice President/Retail Sales & Marketing: Richard M. Miller

Printed on American paper by: R. R. Donnelley & Sons Co.
10 9 8 7 6 5 4 3

Contributing Editors, Art Directors, Set Builders, and Photographers

Cy DeCosse, William B. Jones,
Gary Branson, Bernice Maehren,
John Riha, Paul Currie,
Greg Breining, Tom Carpenter,
Jim Huntley, Gary Sandin,
Mark Johanson, Dick Sternberg,
John Whitman, Anne Price-Gordon,
Barbara Lund, Dianne Talmage,
Diane Dreon, Carol Harvatin,
Ron Bygness, Kristen Olson,
Lori Holmberg, Greg Pluth,
Rob Johnstone, Dan Cary,
Tom Heck, Mark Biscan,
Abby Gnagey, Joel Schmarje,
Jon Simpson, Dave Mahoney,
Andrew Sweet, Bill Nelson,
Barbara Falk, Dave Schelitzche,
Brad Springer, Lori Swanson,
John Hermansen, Geoffrey Kinsey,
Phil Juntti, Tom Cooper,
Earl Lindquist, Curtis Lund,
Tom Rosch, Glenn Terry,
Wayne Wendland, Patrick Kartes,
John Nadeau, Mike Shaw,
Mike Peterson, Troy Johnson,
Jon Hegge, Jim Destiche,
Christopher Wilson, Tony Kubat,
Phil Aarrestad, Kim Bailey, Rex Irmen,
John Lauenstein, Bill Lindner,
Mark Macemon, Charles Nields,
Mette Nielsen, Cathleen Shannon,
Hugh Sherwood, Rudy Calin,
Dave Brus, Paul Najlis,
Mike Parker, Mark Scholtes,
Mike Woodside, Rebecca Hawthorne,
Paul Herda, Brad Parker,
Susan Roth, Ned Scubic,
Stewart Block, Mike Hehner,
Doug Deutsche, Paul Markert,
Steve Smith, Mary Firestone.

Library of Congress Cataloging-in-Publication Data

The complete photo guide to home repair : 2000 color how-to photos.
p. cm.
Includes index.
ISBN 0-86573-753-3 (hardcover)
1. Dwellings--Maintenance and repair Amateurs' manuals.
I. Creative Publishing International.
TH4817.3.C655 1999
643'.7--dc21 99-26355

BLACK & DECKER®

The COMPLETE PHOTO GUIDE TO HOME REPAIR

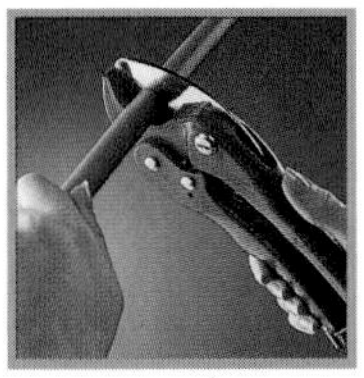

2000 Color How-To Photos

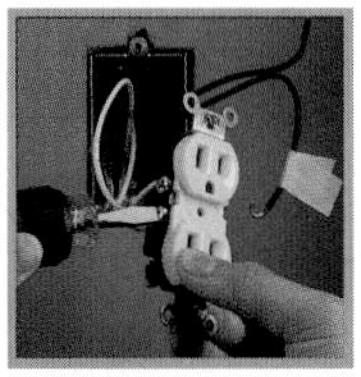
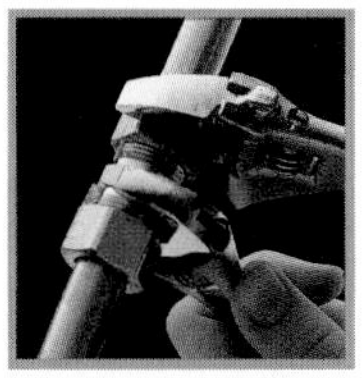

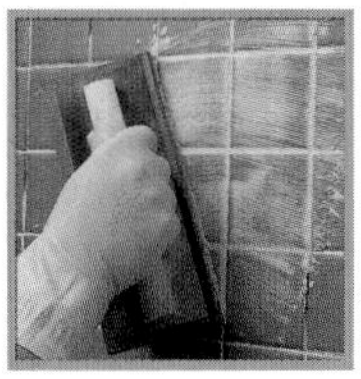

CREATIVE PUBLISHING international
MINNETONKA, MINNESOTA

CONTEN

INTRODUCTION *page 4*

INTERIOR REPAIRS *page 20*

*E*XTERIOR REPAIRS *page 180*

*S*YSTEMS REPAIRS *page 268*

The Complete Photo Guide to Home Repair

For some people, a house is just a possession, but we believe it's much more than that. After all, your house shelters your family and most of your belongings. It keeps you healthy and safe, and offers refuge from the outside world. No wonder most of us develop strong emotional ties to our homes: they provide the stage upon which our family lives are played out.

The technology found in your home was developed over many centuries of creative innovation, and the structure itself was born out of thousands of hours of work by carpenters, plumbers, electricians, and other skilled craftspeople. Doing your own home repair and maintenance work connects you to your home in a unique, tangible way, and even creates a bond between you and the members of the extended family that helped this house evolve into your home.

With *The Complete Photo Guide to Home Repair* by your side, you're now ready to give your home the loving care it needs and deserves. At first, your goal might be simply to quickly fix annoying problems that arise in your house, but you'll gradually find that systematic home repair and maintenance offers many other benefits. As you work around your home, you will:

• Learn about your home's systems and structure. Every home has its own personality, and doing your own repairs reveals the true character of your home.

• Protect your greatest investment. For most people, a home represents the largest single purchase they'll ever make, and taking care of this investment makes good business sense. In almost any housing market, a well-maintained home steadily appreciates in value.

• Contribute to the well-being of your community. Good home maintenance is contagious. Taking good care of your home encourages your neighbors to do likewise, and the results benefit everyone.

• Develop skills that can be applied to a wide variety of projects, as well as the confidence that you can, indeed, do it yourself.

The Complete Photo Guide teaches you professional techniques for hundreds of the most common home repair problems. For each project, we'll give you background information, tool and material lists, and step-by-step instructions accompanied by detailed photographs. The book is organized in four sections.

The *Introduction* provides a guide to safety, tools, and materials, and includes many valuable maintenance and repair tips. You'll find advice on storing tools and materials, and learn how to transport lumber and the other large materials often purchased at lumber yards or home centers.

Section two, *Interior Repairs*, offers both emergency repairs and long-term remedies for common problems related to each aspect of your home's interior, from the basement right up to the attic.

Section three, *Exterior Repairs*, offers the information you'll need to repair the outdoor elements of your home. It covers everything from the walkways, steps, and driveway to the roof peaks and chimney bricks.

Section four, *Systems Repairs*, addresses a wide range of plumbing and electrical repairs. You'll also learn maintenance and repair techniques for the HVAC system, including furnaces, heaters, air conditioners, and heat pumps.

At the end of the book, you'll find checklists that provide a convenient reminder of the most common maintenance and repair tasks, with page references for related projects. Using these checklists, you can easily spot potential problems and resolve them before further damage develops.

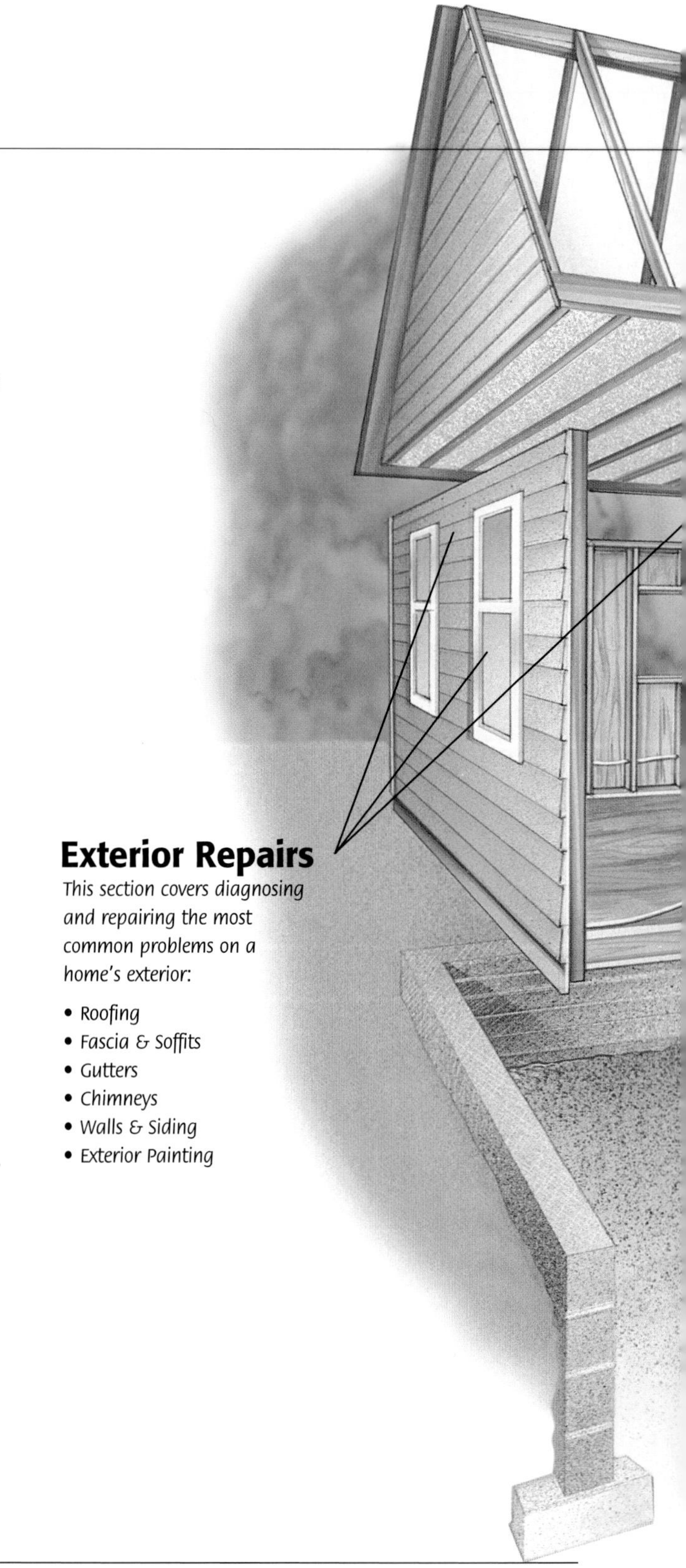

Exterior Repairs

This section covers diagnosing and repairing the most common problems on a home's exterior:

- *Roofing*
- *Fascia & Soffits*
- *Gutters*
- *Chimneys*
- *Walls & Siding*
- *Exterior Painting*

Interior Repairs

This section includes repair solutions for every room of your house. It includes information on:

•Basements •Ceilings & Walls •Painting •Floors •Windows •Cabinets •Countertops •Insulation & Weatherproofing

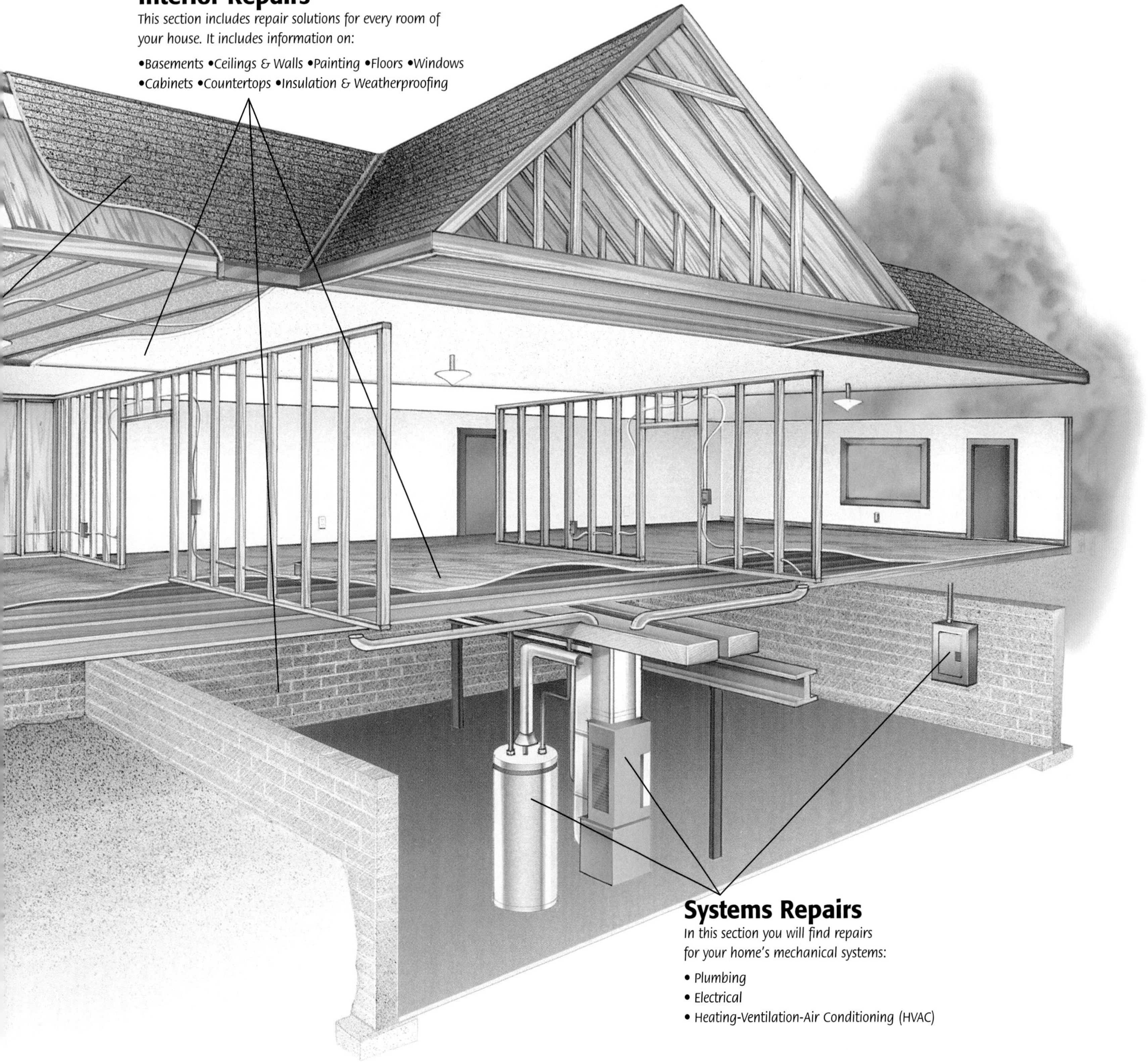

Systems Repairs

In this section you will find repairs for your home's mechanical systems:

- *Plumbing*
- *Electrical*
- *Heating-Ventilation-Air Conditioning (HVAC)*

Working Safely

Before you begin any home repair, take the time to think the project through and identify the proper safety precautions. In many cases, these precautions may be obvious, but it never hurts to ask for specific advice at your hardware store or home center. We've identified some of

Protecting Your Lungs

A dual-cartridge respirator protects against toxic vapors—like those from solvents—and toxic particles such as asbestos. Use the proper filters in the respirator cartridges, and replace them according to the manufacturer's directions.

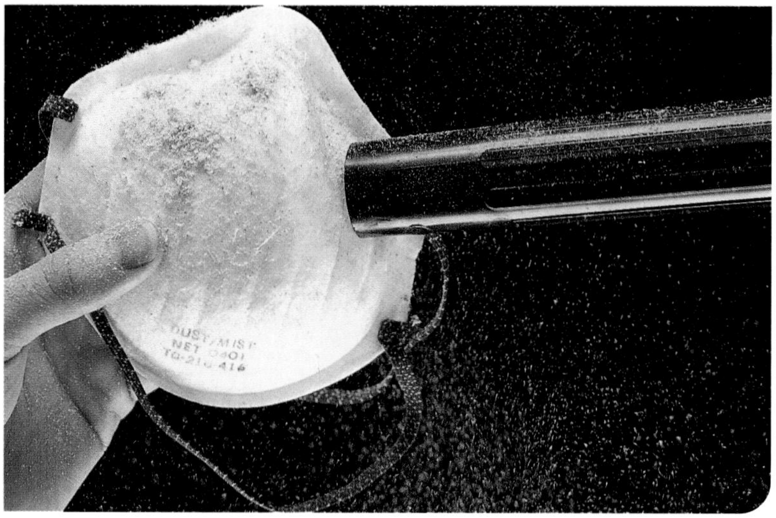

Clean lightly soiled particle filter masks with a shop vacuum. They should be thrown away when heavily soiled. Change the particle filter on a respirator mask frequently.

Stocking Safety Items

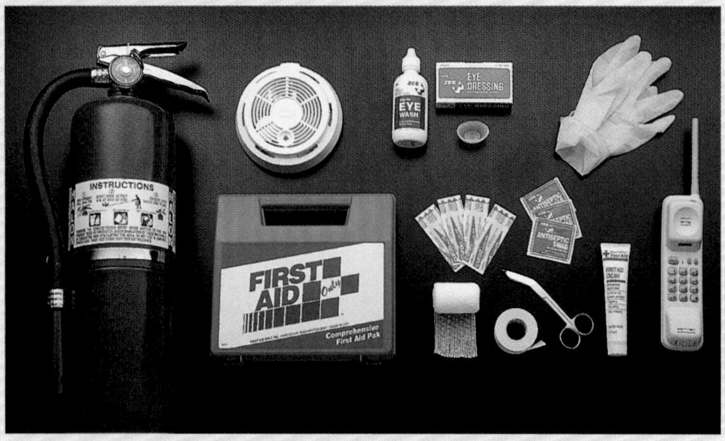

Keep a well-stocked basic first-aid kit where it can be reached easily. Include a variety of bandages, tweezers, antiseptic ointment, disposable gloves, first-aid tape, sterile gauze, and an eyewash kit. In addition to a first-aid kit, your work area should also have a fire extinguisher, smoke detector, and a telephone.

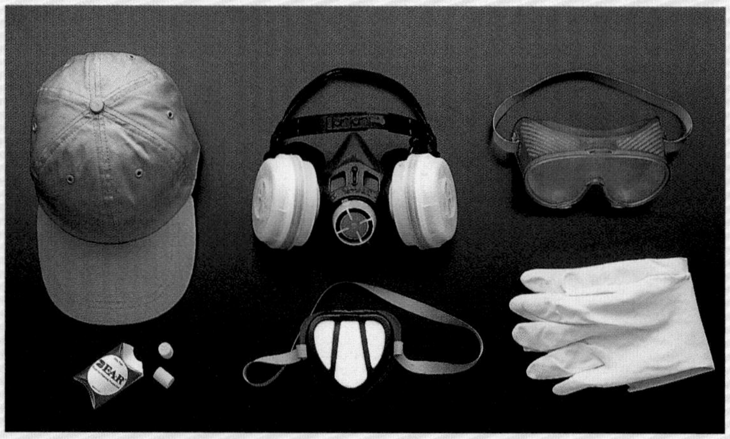

Protective equipment needed for home repair projects includes: a cap with a brim and a dust mask for sanding and painting; a respirator, safety goggles, and stripping gloves, recommended when using harsh stripping chemicals; and ear plugs, for protection from loud power tools.

the major safety concerns in this section. If the project involves hazardous materials, such as solvents or paint, gather any protective gear you will need before starting the project, and find out the safest way to dispose of leftover materials.

Store your protective gear so it can be located easily before you begin a project. Inspect the gear when you finish with it and replace it as soon as you spot signs of wear. Make sure that your first-aid kit is well stocked and that smoke detectors and fire extinguishers are working.

Protecting Your Hands

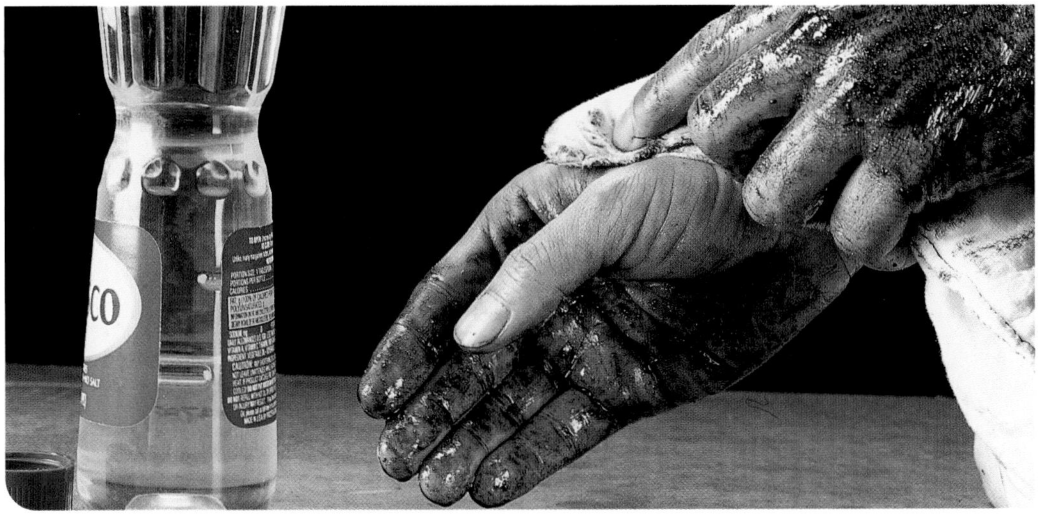

You can clean hands soiled with oil or oil-based paints and stains using ordinary salad oil. Never use kerosene, mineral spirits, or other solvents to wash skin; these hazardous materials are skin irritants and can be absorbed by the body.

Wear rubber gloves when working with solvent-based liquids.

Disposing of Hazardous Materials

Reading Labels

Check labels for proper disposal instructions, and never pour hazardous liquids into a drain system. Make a hazardous waste reminder list and post it above your utility sink. Products rated as environmental hazards by the U.S. Environmental Protection Agency carry one or more of the following warnings: *Danger!, Toxic, Harmful to Animals and Humans, Harmful Vapors, Poison, Flammable, Combustible, Corrosive, or Explosive.*

Discarding Paint

To dispose of a small amount of unwanted paint, remove the lid from the can and set it outdoors in a protected area where children and pets can't reach it. Let the paint dry completely before throwing it away. Sand or sawdust can absorb paint and speed up drying.

Place used mineral spirits in a sealed container until solid paint sediments settle. Pour off the clear solvent into a storage container for later use, and set the original container outdoors in a protected location where children and pets can't reach it. Let the residue dry completely, then throw it away with household trash.

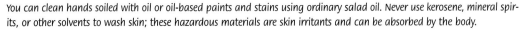

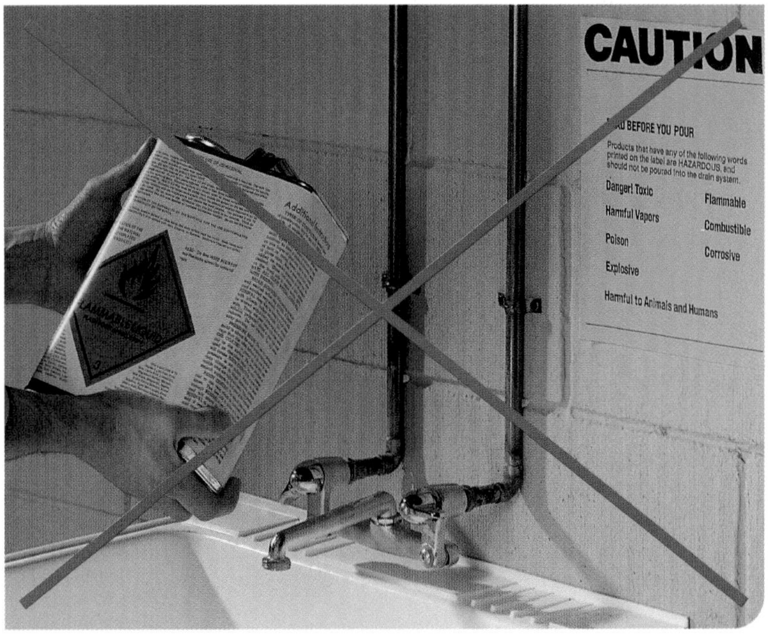

Working with Outlets & Switches

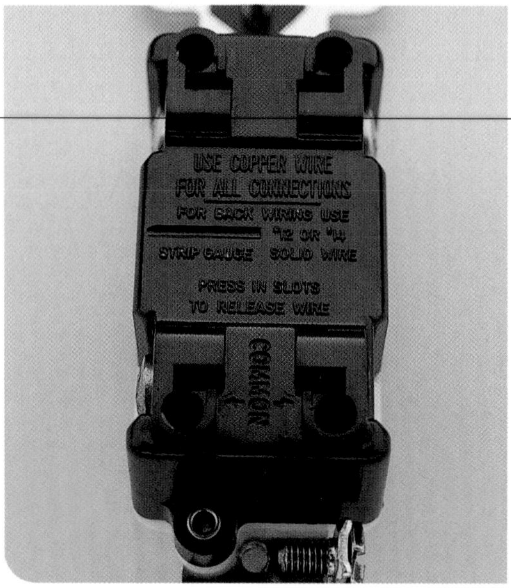

Read markings on old outlets and switches before buying replacements. Choose replacements with the same voltage and amp ratings.

Test a 2-slot receptacle for grounding by inserting one probe of a neon circuit tester in a vertical slot. Touch the other probe to the metal coverplate screw. Repeat test with other vertical slot. If the tester lights, the outlet is grounded, and a new 2-slot receptacle can be installed (page 407).

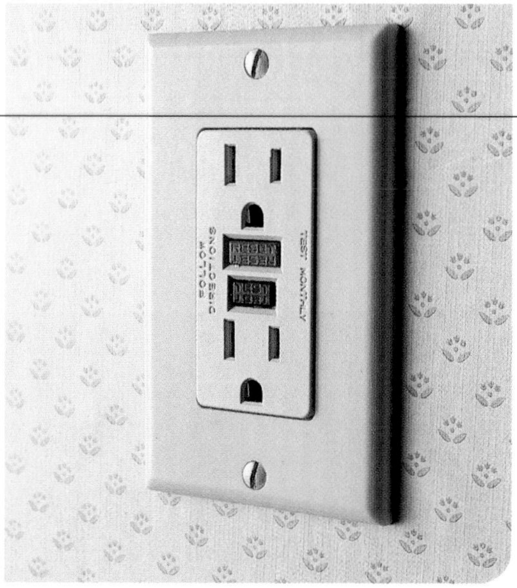

Install a GFCI (ground-fault circuit-interrupter) receptacle whenever replacing a receptacle near water or plumbing, or outside. A GFCI detects changes in current flow and quickly shuts off power to the outlet before shock can occur. Install GFCI receptacles in laundry rooms, bathrooms, kitchen, and outdoor outlets (page 408).

3-prong plugs should be used only in grounded outlets. If using a 3-prong adapter, test to make sure it is grounded. Do not alter the plug to fit a 2-slot receptacle.

Polarized plugs use prongs of different widths to maintain proper circuit continuity and protect against shock. If you have a receptacle that won't accept polarized plugs, don't alter plugs to fit the outlet. Install a new receptacle (page 407) after testing the outlet for grounding.

Protect children against the possibility of electrical shock. Place protective caps in receptacles that aren't in use.

Preventing Electrical Shock

Close the service panel door and post a warning sign over it to prevent others from turning on the power while you are making electrical repairs.

Before disconnecting an old receptacle or switch, mark the wires with small tabs of masking tape. Attach the wires to the new receptacle or switch, using the marks as a guide.

Dry your hands before plugging in or unplugging appliances. Water conducts electricity and increases the possibility of electrical shock.

Removing a Broken Light Bulb

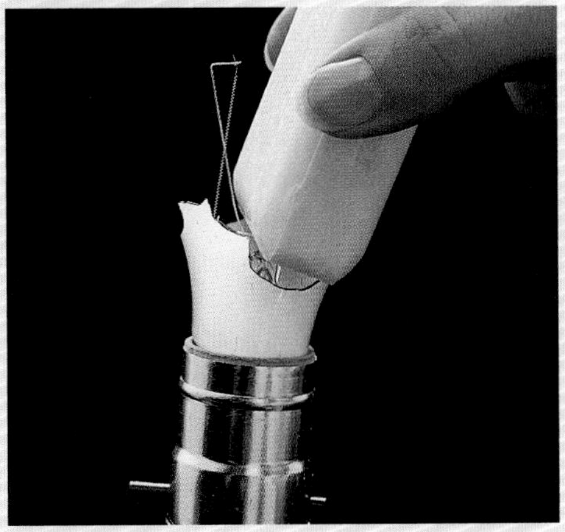

Remove a broken light bulb—after turning off the electricity or unplugging the lamp—by inserting a bar of soap, then turning counterclockwise. Discard the soap. Or, use needlenose pliers to grip the filament or the metal base of the bulb.

Choosing the Right Extension Cord

Use only heavy-duty extension cords when you need to extend the reach of large power tools. Extension cords are rated by wire gauge, watts, and amps. The smaller the wire gauge, the higher the amp and watt ratings. Make sure the ratings of the extension cord are equal to or greater than the tool ratings. For extension cords longer than 50 ft., choose the next larger wire gauge from the chart below.

Wire gauge	Watt rating	Amp rating	Typical use
#18	600	5	Power drill, jig saw, detail sander
#16	840	7	Reciprocating saw, belt sander
#14	1440	12	Router, circular saw, miter saw
#12	1920	16	Radial arm saw, large table saw

Storing Tools

Quality tools that are in good condition make home repairs easier. Store your tools properly so they will last for years.

Extension cords often become a tangled, knot-ridden mess. In addition to being a nuisance to untangle, knotted cords often develop weak

Coiling Long Extension Cords

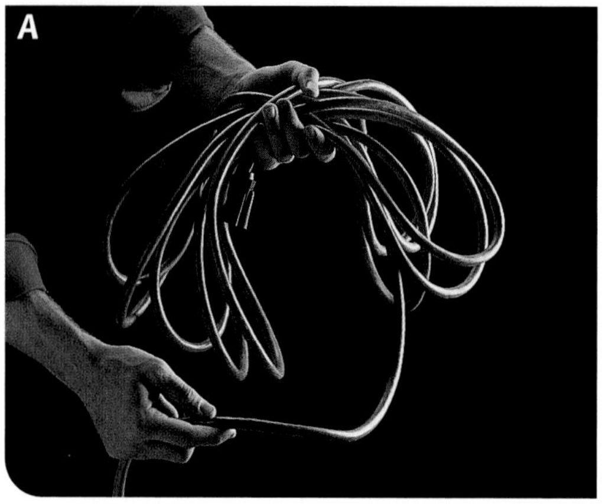

Hold the end of the extension cord in one hand. Use the other hand to loop the extension cord back and forth in a figure-eight pattern until it is completely coiled.

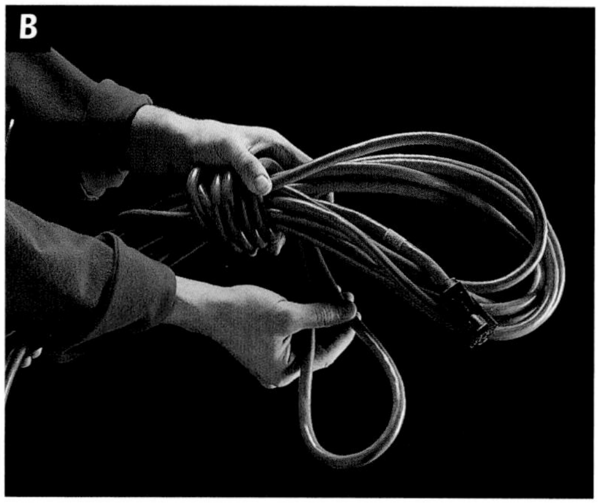

Take one of the cord loops and wrap it twice around one end of the coil.

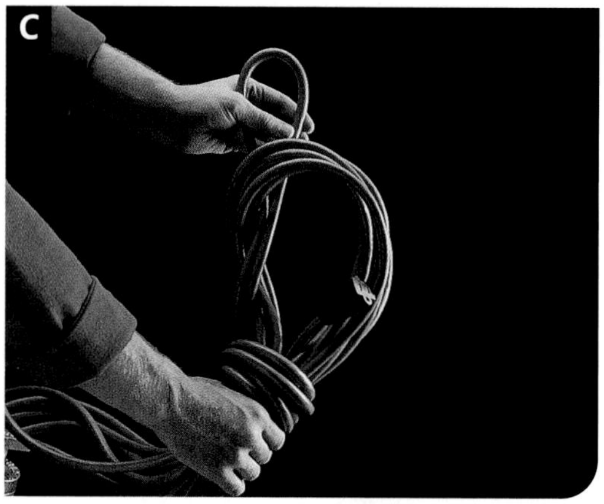

Insert the loop through the center of the coil, and pull it tight. Store the cord by hanging it from this loop.

Storing Cords

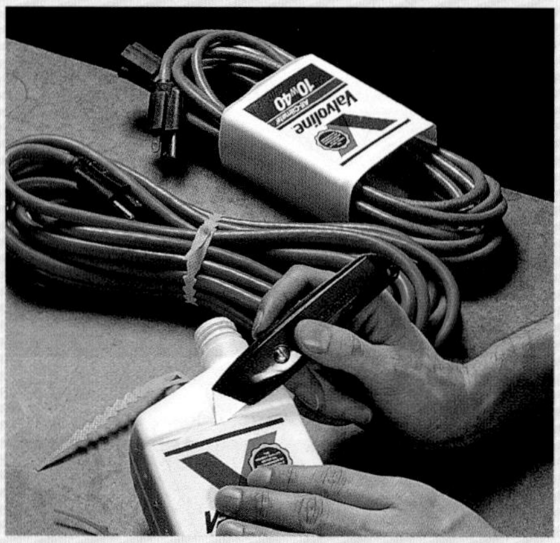

Extension cords and power tool cords often become knotted and tangled. To keep a cord neatly coiled, cut off the ends of a clean plastic motor oil bottle, and slip it over the coiled electrical cord. Or secure cords with plastic garbage bag ties.

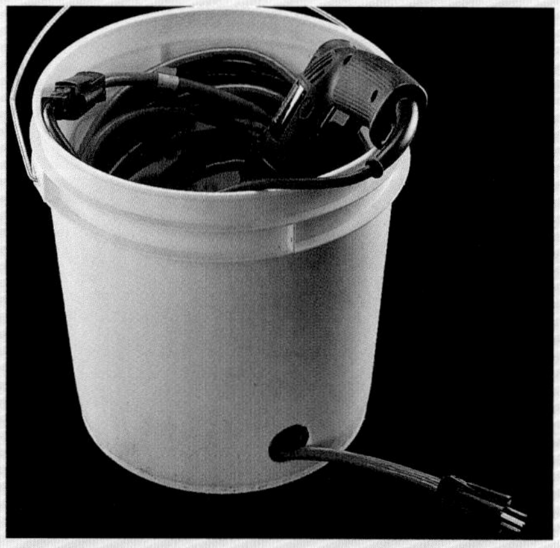

Keep extension cords tangle-free by storing them in five-gallon plastic buckets. Cut a hole in the side of the bucket near the bottom. Thread the pronged plug through the hole from the inside, then coil the cord into the bucket. The extension cord will remain tangle-free when pulled from the bucket.

Storing Power Tools

Use large, rubber-coated lag hooks to store power tools off the floor and away from dirt, moisture, and small children who might be tempted to play with them. Anchor the lag hooks securely to ceiling joists or cross blocking.

sheathing and electrical shorts. The tips collected here demonstrate methods for keeping extension cords tangle-free.

Metal power and hand tools are not immune to rust and wear. But, with a few simple storage solutions, you can discourage the development of rust and prolong the life of your tools.

Small children with curious minds and active hands are another reason tools don't last as long as they should. By taking a few precautions, you can eliminate this dangerous problem.

Preventing Rust

Use a dehumidifier to control dampness in areas where tools are stored, such as the garage or basement. High humidity can cause rust to form on tool surfaces and inside power tool motors.

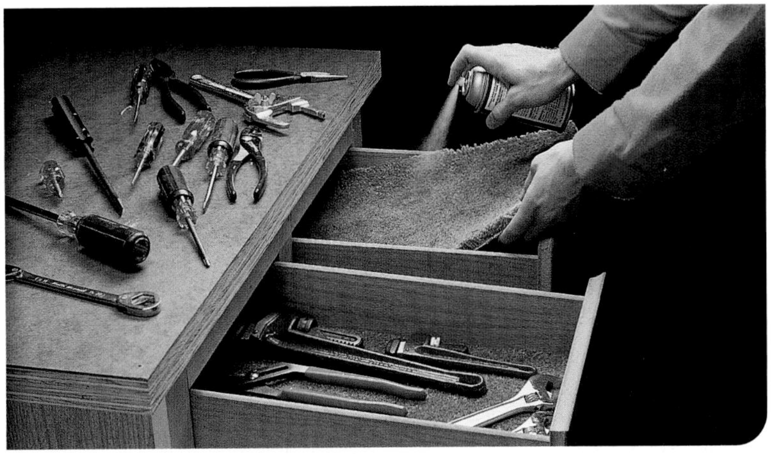

Store hand tools in a drawer lined with a piece of scrap carpet moistened with light machine oil. The carpet prevents tools from getting scratched or nicked, and the oil prevents rusting. Replace the carpet if it becomes caked with sawdust or dirt.

Safeguarding Tools

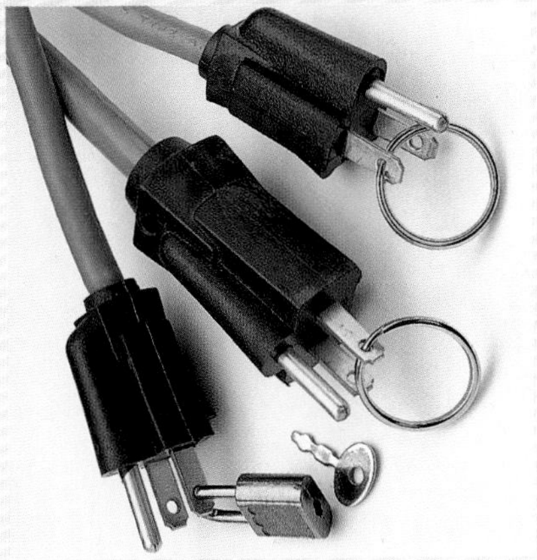

Prevent children from using power tools by inserting spring-metal key rings through the small holes on the prongs of the plug. Or, attach small, key-operated luggage padlocks to the prongs.

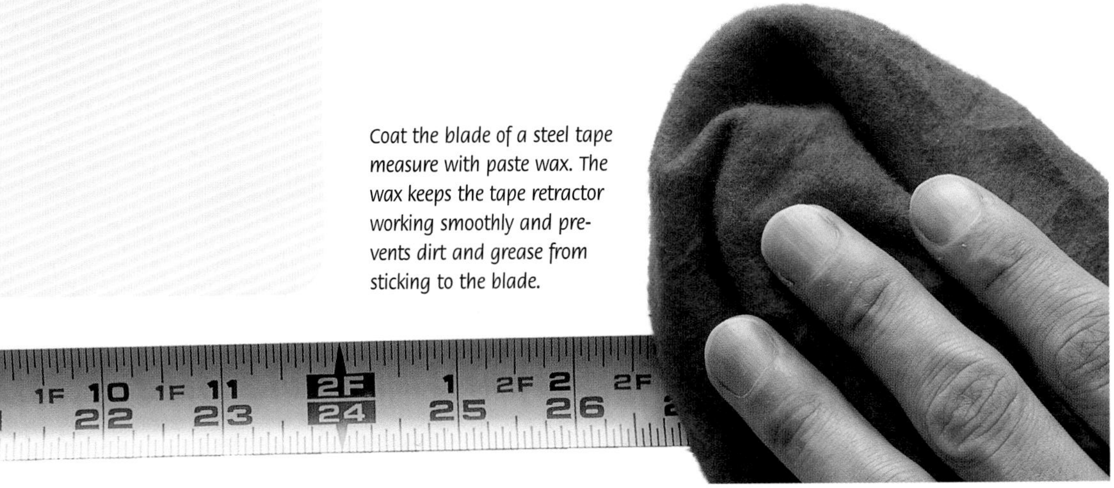

Coat the blade of a steel tape measure with paste wax. The wax keeps the tape retractor working smoothly and prevents dirt and grease from sticking to the blade.

Storing Materials

Storing materials in an organized fashion ensures that they'll be ready when you need them. Well-kept tools will give you years of service; and paints, stains, glues, and other liquids will last longer when properly stored.

Maximizing Storage Space

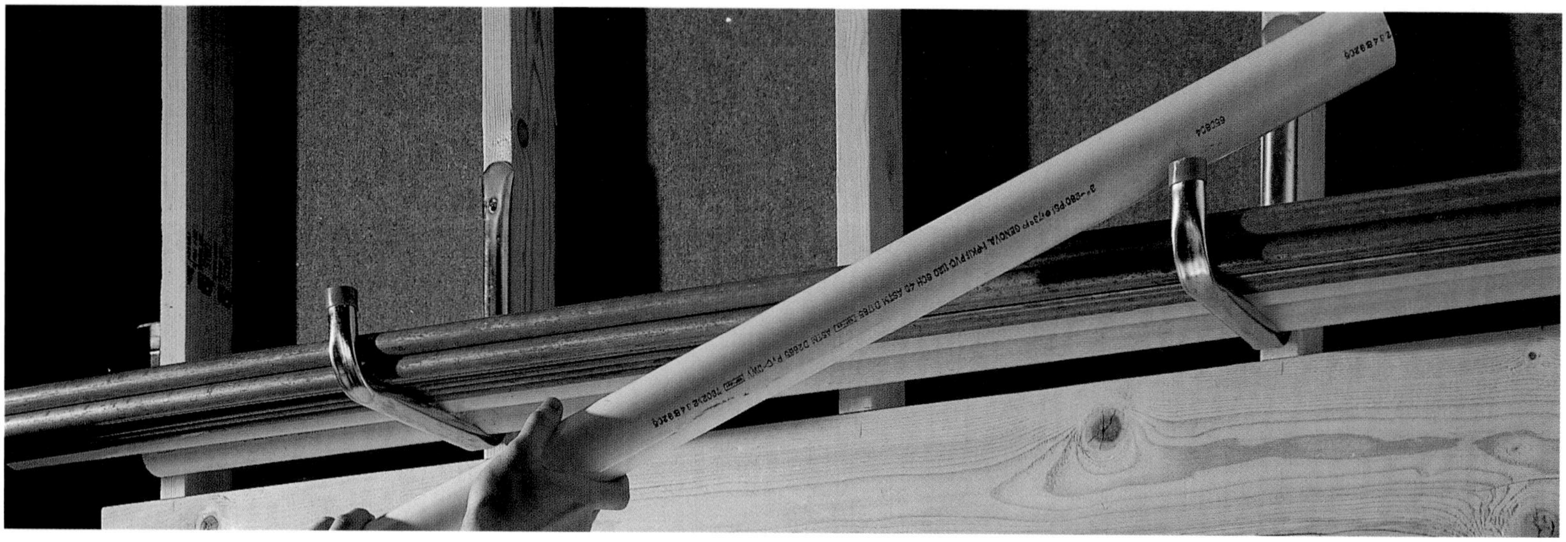

The inside wall above a garage door makes a good storage space. Use this area to store long pieces of wood molding, dimension lumber, or plumbing pipe. Attach metal or wooden support brackets to the sleeper studs or header. Metal brackets, available at any hardware store or home center, can be attached to the front of sleeper studs with long wallboard screws or lag screws. To provide adequate support, space the brackets no more than 36" apart.

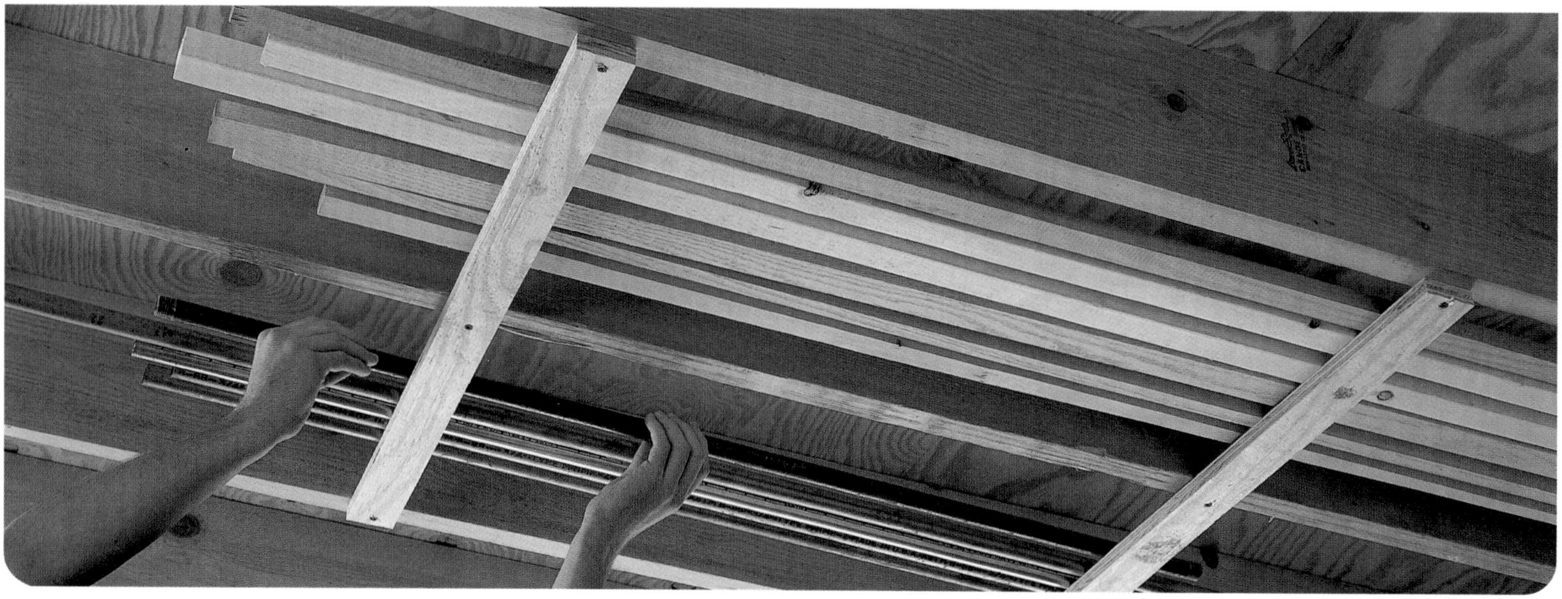

Store long materials in the space between open ceiling joists in an unfinished utility area, such as a garage or basement. Attach ¾" plywood furring strips across the joists with 2½" wallboard screws or lag screws. Space the strips no more than 36" apart to ensure adequate support. Avoid electrical cables or fixtures located between the ceiling joists. Some homeowners attach boards across the bottom of the ceiling joists to make out-of-the-way storage shelves for small cans and other shop items.

Without the proper preparation, paints and glues dry up and become useless. Leftover wood and plumbing pipe can become a jumbled mess that takes up precious workshop space.

Connectors, such as screws, washers, and nails, clutter workshop drawers and the bottom of the toolbox. The ideas illustrated below will help you organize these items so you can locate materials easily and reduce clutter.

Storing Paint & Glue

Label paint and stain containers clearly with a description of the contents and the date the material was used. Also note any special projects to which the product was applied, so that you can use it later if touch-up becomes necessary.

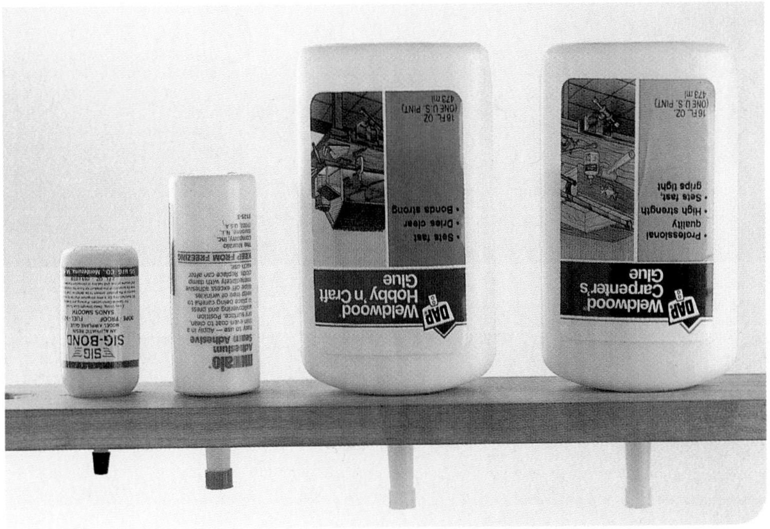

Store glue bottles upside down so the glue is ready to pour. Make a glue bottle holder by drilling holes in a scrap 1 × 4 and mounting it on a wall.

The caps that come with glues, caulks, and other shop products are easy to lose. Replace lost caps with screw-on electrical wire connectors. Wire connectors are available in many sizes at any hardware store.

Organizing Connectors

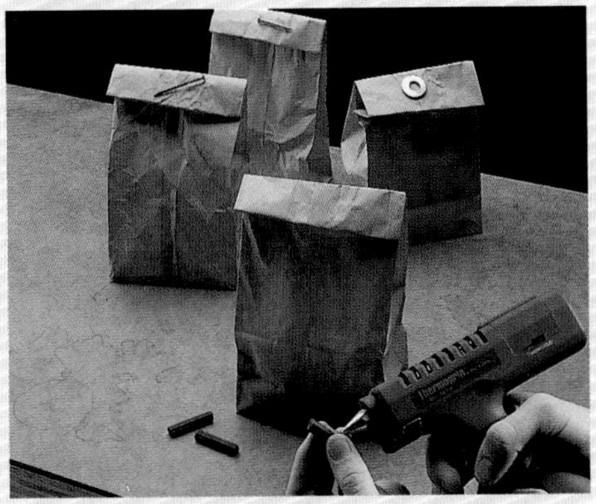

Most workshops have dozens of small containers holding screws, nails, bolts, and other hardware. To locate items quickly and easily, use a hot glue gun to stick a sample of the contents on the outside of each bag or box.

Transporting Materials

Transporting building materials from the lumberyard or home center to your home is the first step in many workshop projects—and it's one of the most difficult. Framing lumber can be tied to a roof carrier rack for travel, but sheets of plywood, paneling, or wallboard should be

Carrying Full-size Materials

To carry full-size sheets of plywood, paneling, or wallboard by yourself, tie a single length of rope, about 18 ft. long, in a loop. Hook the ends of the loop over the lower corners of the sheet, and grip the middle of the rope in one hand. Use the other hand to balance the sheet.

Cutting Materials Down

If you know the cutting dimensions for plywood, paneling, or other sheet goods, you can make transportation easier by cutting the materials to size at the lumberyard or home center. Some suppliers will cut materials free of charge.

Using Roof Brackets

A

Tie materials onto the roof of your car using inexpensive, vinyl-coated roof brackets. Use carpet scraps under the materials to avoid scratching the roof, and center the load on the roof.

B

Hook the brackets over the edge of the roof, then attach nylon packing straps or ropes to the brackets and cinch the materials in place.

delivered by truck. Your lumberyard may deliver your materials for a small additional charge.

If you transport materials on a roof carrier, make sure to tie the load securely. Materials that extend past the rear bumper should be tagged with a red flag to warn other drivers. Drive carefully and avoid sudden starts and stops. When using your vehicle to carry heavy loads, like bags of concrete or sand, allow extra braking distance.

Carrying a Load on an Auto Roof Rack

Tie a half-hitch around one end of the roof carrier bar. Pull the knot tight.

Tie a second half-hitch in the rope, and pull the knot tight. A half-hitch has good holding power, yet is easy to untie.

Pull the rope over the top of the load. If possible, wrap the rope once around the load. Tie a small slip loop in the rope.

Stretch the rope around the opposite end of the roof carrier bar.

Thread the end of the rope through the slip loop. Pull the rope firmly against the loop to cinch the load tight against the roof carrier.

Tie off the rope below the slip loop, using half-hitches. Repeat these steps at the other carrier bar.

Using Tools

Owning a variety of hand and power tools will make it possible for you to complete most of the repairs in this book. But your tools will be of little use if you don't use them correctly. Whether you are painting, drilling, or cutting, knowing which tool to use and the right way to use it will help you make repairs efficiently. The tips shown below point

Using Screwdrivers

Buy several cordless screwdrivers. Most models have removable tips that can drive either slotted or Phillips screws.

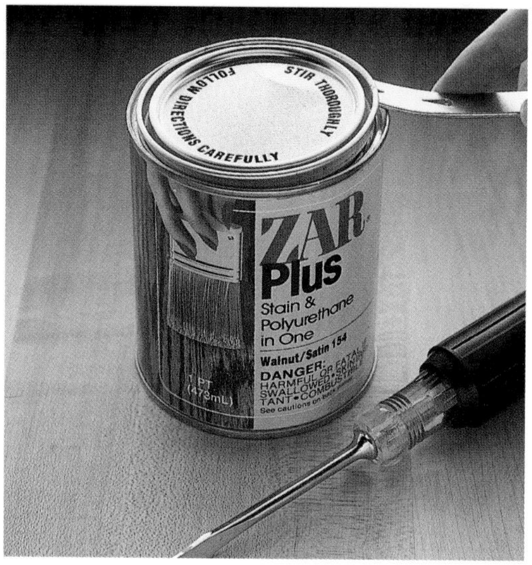

Do not use screwdrivers as chisels or pry bars. A bent screwdriver shaft or a damaged tip can cause the screwdriver to slip, damaging the workpiece or injuring you.

Keep chisels and other cutting tools sharp. Dull tools can be dangerous because they are prone to slipping.

Using Brushes

Natural-bristle brushes provide a smoother finish for many finish coats.

Synthetic-bristle brushes, such as this blend of nylon and polyester fibers, should be used for latex paints.

Inexpensive sponge brushes can be used on small paint or touch-up jobs and thrown away when the job is done.

out some common misuses of tools and offer advice for preventing damage to your tools. There are also some tool maintenance suggestions that will help prolong the life of your tools and help you use them more safely. Putting these practices to use will help ensure that you get full life from your tools.

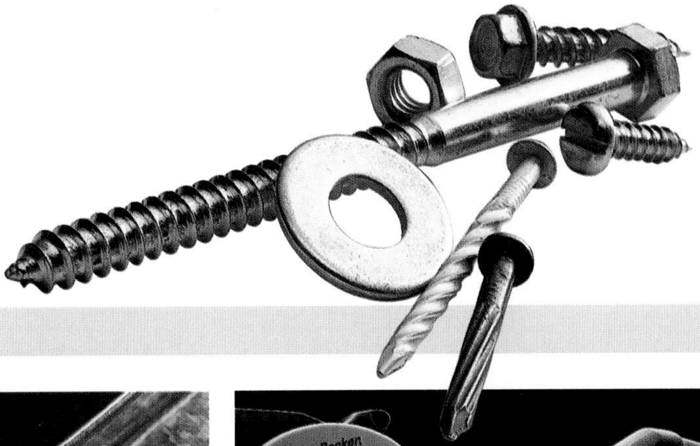

Using Drills, Saws & Hammers

Before drilling metal, make a dent with a center punch to start the hole. This will help the bit stay on target.

Use a variable-speed drill for metal and keep rpms low to drill smoothly and without dulling the bit.

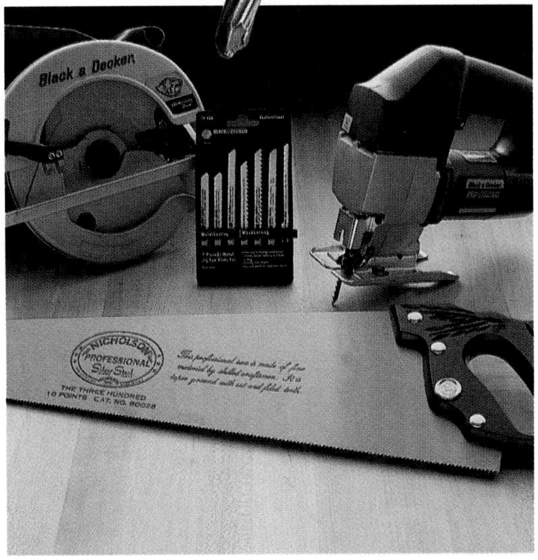

A set of saws and blades allows you to handle a wide range of tasks. The circular saw is a must for cutting heavy framing lumber; a jig saw can cut irregular shapes.

Use a hot glue gun to secure corner braces or reinforcements or to fasten small objects that might split if nailed.

Don't use a claw hammer as an all-purpose tool. It's designed only for driving and pulling nails.

Clean hammer faces with sandpaper to remove residue caused by coated nails. This reduces the number of bent nails.

Every nail type is designed for a highly specialized purpose. The broad head on a roofing nail is ideal for fastening shingles but unsightly as a finish nail on moldings and trim. Nail lengths are identified by numbers from 4 to 60, followed by the letter "d," which stands for "penny." Some specialty nails are identified by either length or gauge. Other specialty nails—like wallboard nails, siding nails, masonry nails, and flooring nails—are identified by their intended function.

Screws are categorized according to length, slot style, head shape, and

Using Nails

Angling nails as shown will provide better holding power than driving them in straight.

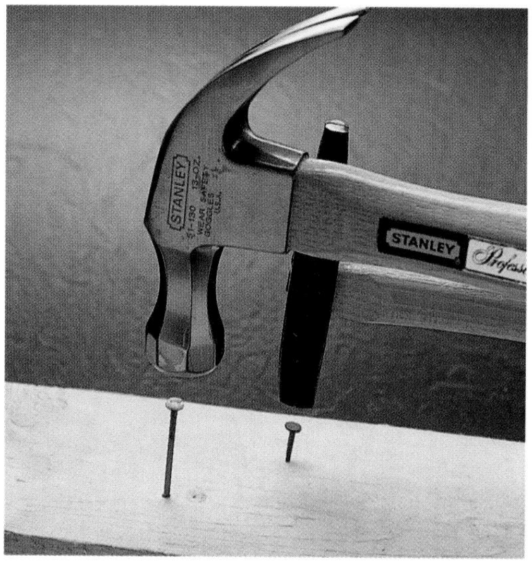

Use the right hammer for the job. The tack hammer at rear is magnetized to hold the tack, and is lightweight to avoid damaging wood.

Toenailing is one method of joining two pieces of wood when endnailing isn't possible.

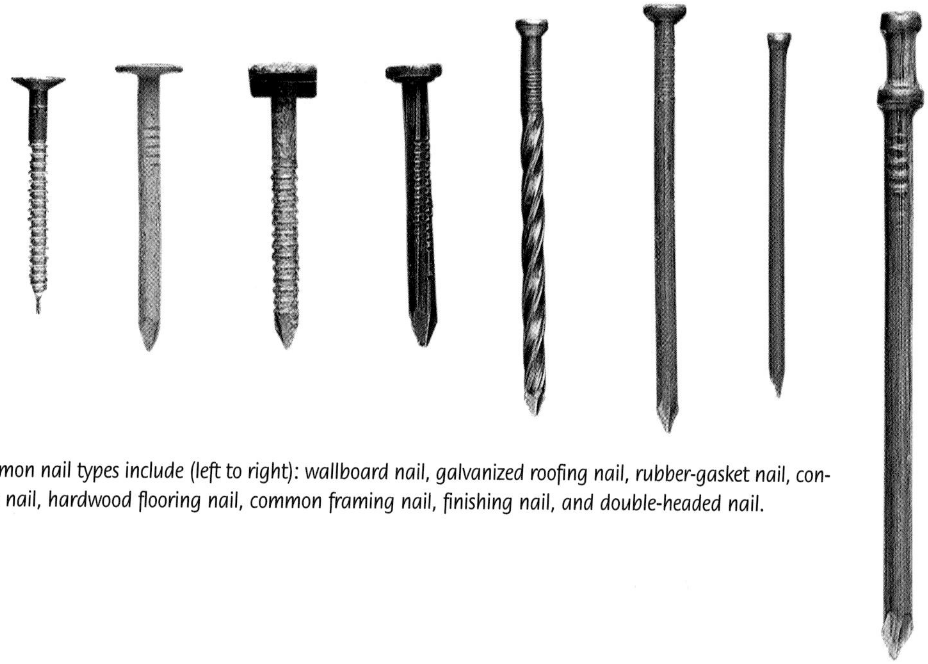

Common nail types include (left to right): wallboard nail, galvanized roofing nail, rubber-gasket nail, concrete nail, hardwood flooring nail, common framing nail, finishing nail, and double-headed nail.

To avoid splitting wood, stagger nails so they don't all enter the same spot in the wood grain.

gauge. The thickness of the screw is indicated by the gauge number; the larger the gauge number, the larger the screw. Large screws provide extra holding power; small screws are less likely to split a workpiece.

Using Screws

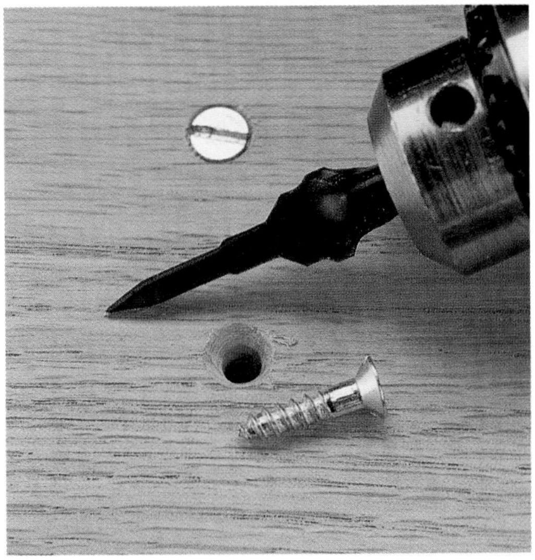

Counterbore a pilot hole and countersink the screw head using this combination drill bit.

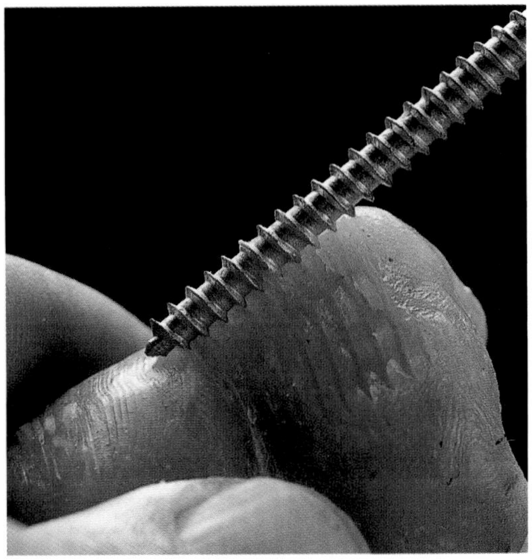

Lubricating a screw with beeswax makes for easier driving with a screwdriver or screwgun.

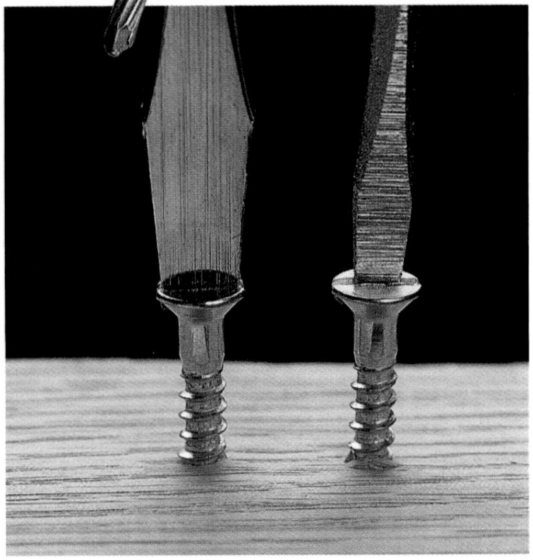

Choose a screwdriver that fits the slot in the screw head. The narrow blade of the driver at right may slip and damage the screw head or workpiece.

To drill an effective pilot hole, select a drill bit slightly smaller than the screw shank diameter.

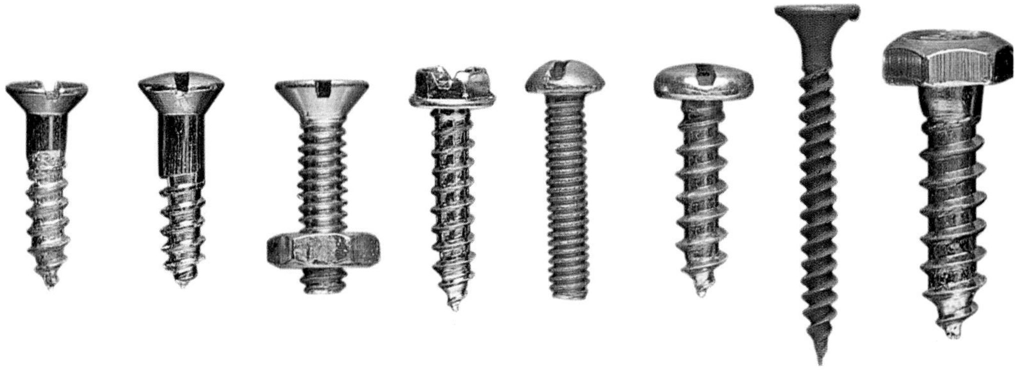

Screw types include: flat- and oval-head wood screws, machine screw with nut, screw with washer for securing fiberglass panels, machine screw, sheet-metal screw, wallboard screw, and lag screw.

INTERIOR REPAIRS

Your home's interior provides a backdrop for day-to-day activities. This chapter helps you maintain these interior elements, creating a more comfortable, attractive, and cost-efficient living space for you and your family.

Interior Repairs

The interior of your home is where you're likely to do the majority of your home repairs. Whether it's a small job—like patching a plaster wall or fixing a nagging hinge on a kitchen cabinet—or a major project like replacing a wood floor, interior repairs will have the greatest impact on the comfort and appeal of your living spaces.

This section shows you how to maintain, protect, and repair your basement, interior walls, ceilings, stairs, floors, doors, windows, cabinets, and countertops. We'll cover painting, plastering, insulating, weatherproofing, and a range of other skills you'll use again and again.

Use the maintenance schedules at the back of the book to help you establish your maintenance and repair priorities. The most common projects won't require a big budget or professional help, especially if you keep your home's interiors well maintained.

Working Safely

When doing interior repairs, use common sense and observe basic safety precautions. Here are some reminders to keep you safe and comfortable while you work.

If your project exposes electrical wiring, even just painting around a switch or receptacle—take the time to review the basic rules of electrical safety (page 395). It's easy to forget that all kinds of projects can affect the electrical wiring in your walls and ceilings. The most fundamental rule is never to work with live wires. Before you expose any electrical wiring at a fixture, switch, outlet, or receptacle, go to

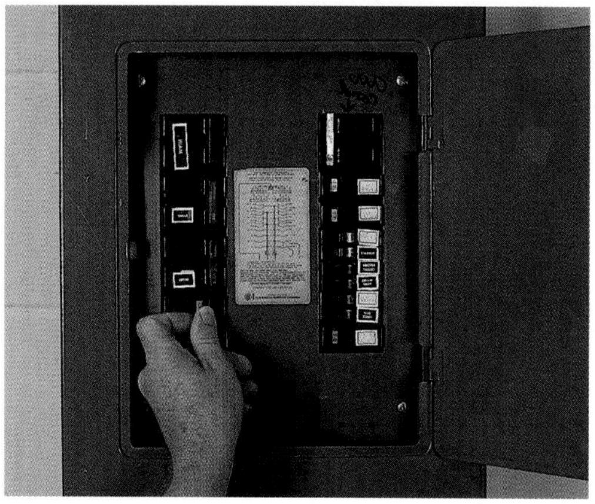

Before working with exposed electrical wiring, turn off the circuit that supplies power to that part of the house.

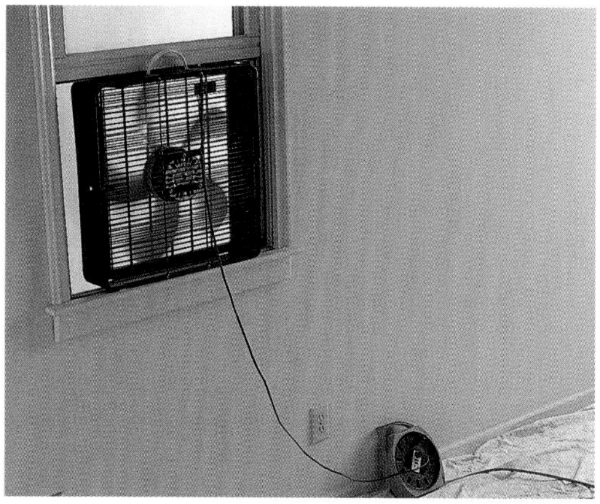

A portable window fan is an easy way to provide good ventilation for a painting or sanding job.

the main service panel and shut off the power. Once the wires are exposed, use a neon circuit tester to make sure that the power is off.

If a project involves the use of power tools, be sure you know how to use them safely before you start the job. If you're unfamiliar with a tool, practice your skills first on scrap materials, and remember to keep electrical cords away from cutting blades.

Use proper lighting and ventilation to create a safe working environment. Good ventilation is especially important for projects that produce dust or fumes, such as sanding, painting, or stripping and refinishing woodwork. A portable window fan is an ideal choice. Place it in an open window, positioned so it draws particles and fumes out of the room.

Dress properly for the project, especially when using power tools. Don't wear loose-fitting clothing, watches, or jewelry; if you have long hair, tie it back. Many projects require work gloves, eye protection, a particle mask, hearing protectors, and sturdy nonslip boots.

A well-designed tool belt is a good investment. In addition to offering convenient access to your tools, it's less likely that you'll place a tool in a potentially dangerous spot, such as on the rung of a ladder.

Helpful Hint

Before you start any major project, familiarize yourself with the procedures for shutting off the electricity, water, and fuel supply to your home.

Label the main gas and water shutoff valves clearly, and index your service panel (pages 390 to 391). These simple steps will reduce the time it takes to handle these routine precautions at the start of each new project.

Dressing for the Job

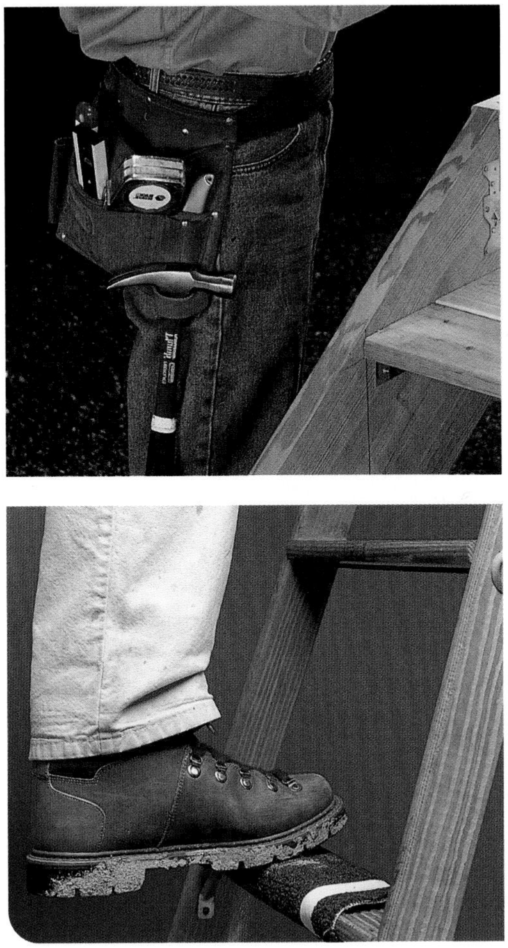

A tool belt and sturdy, rubber-soled work boots are important for safety.

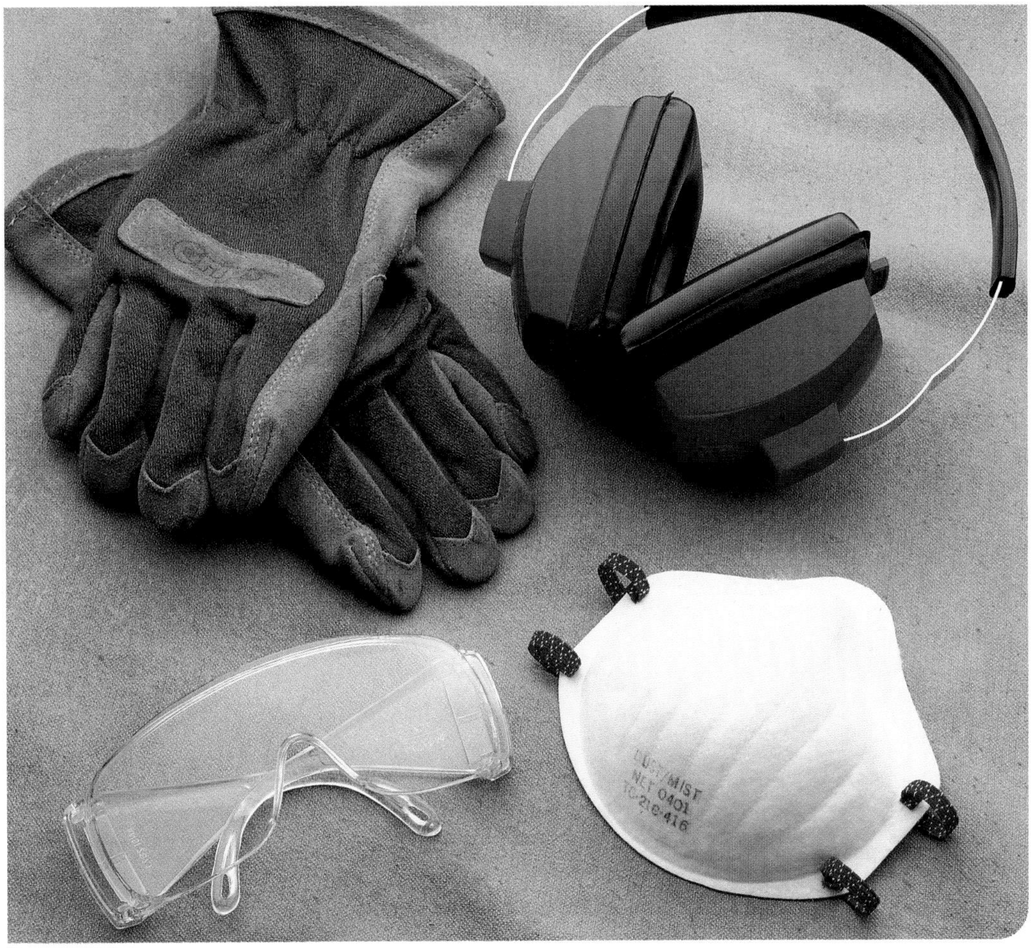

A basic set of safety gear will make all your repair and maintenance projects safer and more comfortable. The equipment shown includes: work gloves, hearing protectors, particle mask, and safety goggles.

Basements

Failing gutters, broken or leaking pipes, condensation, and seepage are the most common causes of basement moisture. To prevent damage to walls and floors, identify the source of the moisture and make appropriate repairs.

Condensation usually occurs in the summer months. It often results from an improperly vented clothes dryer. Check and adjust the dryer vent connection, or install a dehumidifier to eliminate condensation.

Seepage is water that flows from the soil around your foundation into the basement through cracks and holes. Creating a waterproof seal over these openings controls minor seepage. The best method for sealing surfaces depends on the size of the openings and the frequency of the moisture. In basements where seepage is an occasional problem, sealing openings and coating the walls with masonry sealer and paint is usually sufficient. If seepage is frequent, seal the openings, then resurface the walls with a concrete coating. If seepage continues, install a baseboard gutter and drain system to manage the problem.

Diagnosing Common Problems

Ninety-five percent of all wet basement problems occur because water pools near the foundation **(photo A).** Wet basements can usually be traced to roof gutters and downspouts that are plugged, rusted through, or not diverted away from the house. To prevent problems, repair gutters and downspouts and position them to channel water away from the foundation (pages 214 to 217, and page 31). After adjusting the downspouts and gutters, check the soil grade around the house. If necessary, regrade the soil so that it slopes away from the foundation (page 30).

Peeling paint on basement walls is caused by moisture seeping through from outside that becomes trapped between the wall and the paint **(photo B).** To identify the source of moisture on basement walls, tape a piece of foil to the wall **(photo C).** If moisture collects on the outer surface of the foil, the source likely is condensation. If moisture isn't visible on the foil, seepage is the most likely cause.

Stains can ruin the appearance of a concrete basement floor **(photo D).** Remove stains with commercial-grade concrete cleaner or one of several chemicals marketed for this purpose (page 27). To protect against stains, seal masonry surfaces with a waterproof masonry sealant (page 26).

Frozen pipes are a common problem in unheated basements and crawl spaces. Prevent pipes from freezing by insulating pipes in these areas. To thaw a frozen pipe, turn off the water supply at the main shutoff valve, then heat the pipe with a heat gun or hair dryer **(photo E).**

Walls exposed to constant moisture develop cracks and, over time, begin to crumble **(photo F).** To seal walls and prevent further damage, fill cracks and holes larger than 1/8" (page 28) and seal the walls with either masonry sealer or a concrete coating (page 26).

Basement moisture is often caused by failing roof gutters and downspouts, or an improperly graded yard.

Paint on basement walls peels off when water is trapped between the wall and the paint.

Determine the source of moisture on basement walls by taping a square of aluminum foil to a wall.

Stains on basement floors can be removed with concrete cleaner and prevented with masonry sealant.

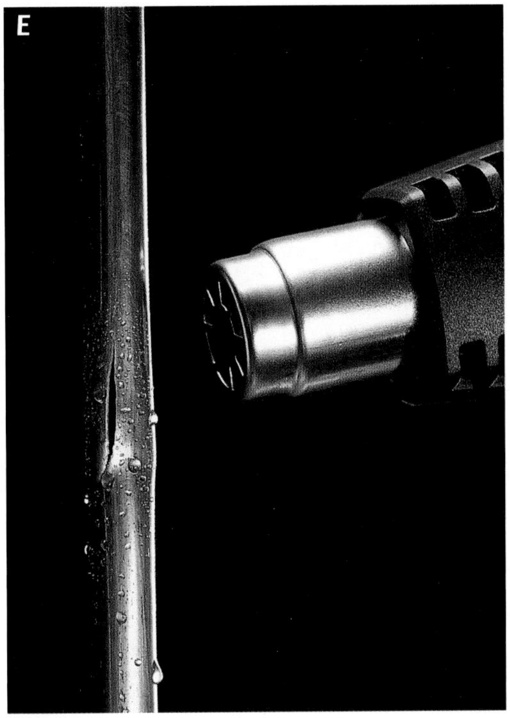

After turning off the water supply, thaw frozen pipes with a heat gun or hair dryer.

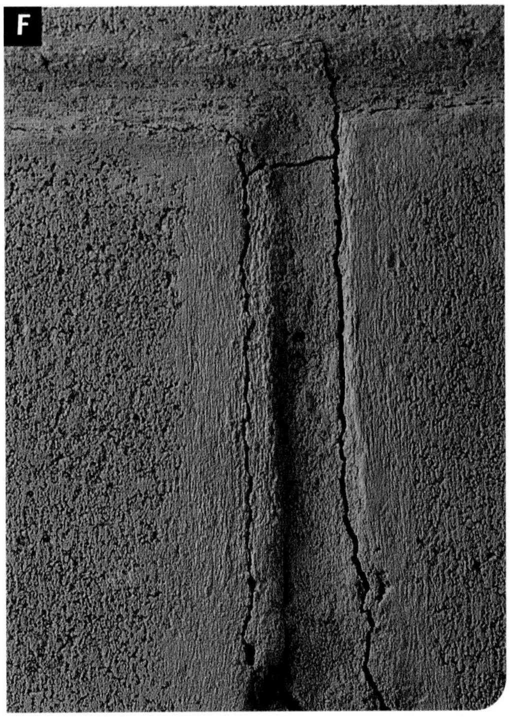

Walls exposed to constant moisture develop cracks and eventually begin to crumble.

Protecting Walls & Floors

Protecting with Sealer

Protect basement walls from moisture by sealing them with a waterproof masonry sealer. The sealer helps eliminate moisture from minor seepage.

Waterproof masonry sealer products are sold in powder form and contain cement. These products must be mixed with water and applied to damp walls.

Start by cleaning the walls with household cleaner and a wire brush. Rinse the walls clean with water and a sponge. Mix the masonry sealer with water in a large container, following the manufacturer's instructions. Stir the mixture thoroughly with heavy-duty stirrer until it's thick and pastelike.

Using a stiff-bristled paintbrush, apply the sealer to the damp walls, making sure to cover the surface—and any mortar joints in brick or block surfaces—completely **(photo A).**

Allow the sealer to dry, then apply a second coat over the first. Make sure that the sealer coverage is even and complete.

Tools: *Wire brush, heavy-duty stirrer, stiff-bristled paintbrush.*

Materials: Household cleaner, sponge, large container, waterproof masonry sealer.

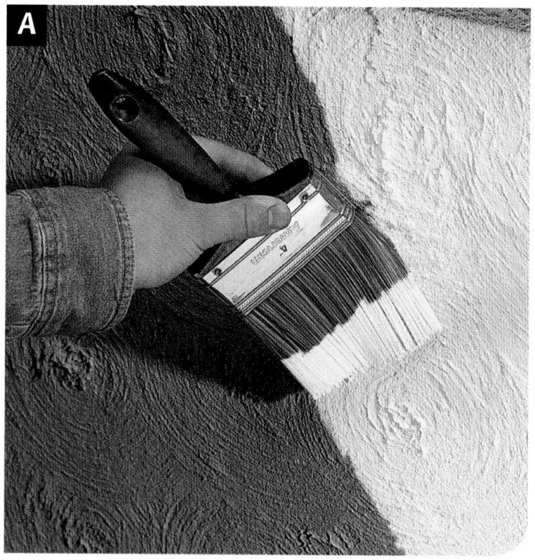

Apply sealer to damp walls with a brush.

Protecting with Concrete Coating

Resurface masonry walls that have an abundance of cracks and fissures by adding a layer of concrete coating. You'll need to fill any cracks or holes larger than 1/8" (page 28) before applying the coating.

Mix the coating by combining 1 part cement with 2 1/2 parts moist, loose mortar sand. Add water until it resembles a stiff plaster. Before applying the concrete coating, scrub the walls with a wire brush, then rinse them clean with a sponge and water. While the walls are still wet, apply a 1/4"-thick coating of the mixture to the walls with a trowel **(photo B).** Allow the coating to dry slightly, then scratch the surface with the teeth on a paint roller cleaning tool **(photo C).** After 24 hours, apply a second coating. Wait another 24 hours, then mist the wall with water twice a day for three days.

Tools: *Wire brush, sponge, concrete trowel, paint roller cleaning tool.*

Materials: *Cement, mortar sand.*

Spread a 1/4" coating of the concrete mixture on the walls with a concrete trowel.

Scratch the concrete coating with the teeth on a paint roller cleaning tool.

Protecting with Paint

Waterproof masonry paint helps keep minerals in concrete, brick, and block surfaces from leeching through paint and hardening into a white, dusty film (called *efflorescence*). Masonry paint is sold in stock colors, or you can have custom colors mixed from a tint base.

As with any other painting job, thorough surface preparation and the use of a quality primer ensures a successful finish. To prepare the walls, clean the mortar joints in brick and block walls, using a drill with a wire wheel attachment. Scrub any loose paint, dirt, mildew, or mineral deposits off the walls with a wire brush **(photo D).** Rinse the walls clean to ensure that the primer and paint adhere.

After the walls have dried, apply masonry primer with a stiff-bristled paintbrush **(photo E).** Allow the primer to dry completely. Mix the masonry paint with a paint stirrer, then apply it according to the manufacturer's directions.

Tools: *Drill with wire wheel attachment, wire brush, paint stirrer, stiff-bristled paintbrush.*

Materials: *Masonry primer, waterproof masonry paint.*

Scrub the walls with a wire brush.

Apply masonry primer to the walls before painting.

Removing Stains

Cleaning concrete floors regularly helps prevent deterioration from oils and deicing salts. For general cleaning, use a concrete cleaning product. Soak the surface to be cleaned with water before applying the product, and follow the manufacturer's application instructions. Rinse the surface thoroughly after cleaning to wash off any remaining solution.

Most concrete cleaners will not remove oil stains from floors. To clean oil stains, dampen sawdust with paint thinner and apply the sawdust over the stain. The paint thinner will break apart the stain, allowing the oil to be absorbed by the sawdust. Sweep up the sawdust with a broom when finished, and reapply as necessary **(photo F).**

To remove other common stains, consult the chart below for the best method.

Solvent Solutions for Common Brick, Block & Concrete Stains

- ***Efflorescence:*** *Scrub the surface with a stiff-bristled brush. Use a household cleaning solution for surfaces with heavy accumulation.*
- ***Iron stains:*** *Spray or brush a solution of oxalic acid crystals dissolved in water (following the manufacturer's instructions) directly to the stain.*
- ***Paint stains:*** *Remove new paint with a solution of trisodium phosphate (TSP) and water, following the manufacturer's mixing instructions. Old paint can usually be removed with heavy scrubbing or sandblasting.*
- ***Smoke stains:*** *Scrub the surface with a household cleanser containing bleach, or use a mixture of ammonia and water.*

Remove oil stains with sawdust and paint thinner.

Preventing Dampness & Leaks

Filling Holes & Cracks

The quickest method for sealing small holes in concrete is to fill them with gray-tinted latex masonry caulk. If the hole is more than 1" deep, stuff a piece of fiberglass insulation into the hole to provide a base for the caulk **(photo A).** For small holes in the mortar joints of brick and block basement walls, replace the mortar by tuckpointing the joints (page 222).

For larger holes in concrete, use latex bonding agent and a concrete patch product to make the repair. Clean the hole with a wire brush and remove the dirt and debris from the hole with a hand vacuum. Coat the edges of the hole with latex bonding liquid. Mix the concrete patcher with water, then stir in bonding liquid. Pour the mixture into the hole, and smooth it with a flexible knife **(photo B).**

The materials and methods used for repairing cracks in concrete depend on the size of the crack. For small cracks (less than 1/4" wide), you can use gray-tinted concrete caulk to effectively seal the crack. For larger cracks, use a pourable crack filler or fortified patching cement and follow the process for repairing an exterior masonry crack (page 255).

Thorough preparation of the cracked surface is essential for creating a good bonding surface. Remove loose masonry from the crack with a masonry chisel and a wire brush **(photo C).** Clean all dust and debris from the surface with a hand vacuum.

Using a caulk gun, apply latex masonry caulk to the crack **(photo D).** Smooth the masonry caulk so it completely fills the crack, using a putty knife or trowel **(photo E).**

Tools: *Caulk gun, putty knife or trowel, masonry chisel, wire brush, hand vacuum.*

Materials: *Latex masonry caulk, fiberglass insulation, latex bonding agent, concrete patcher.*

A

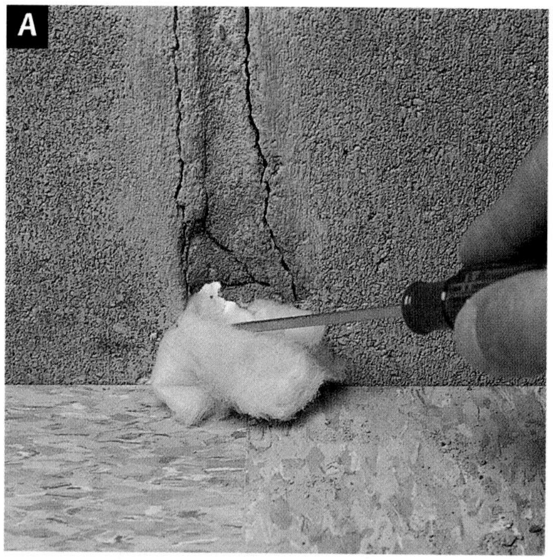

Stuff fiberglass insulation into holes more than 1" deep.

B

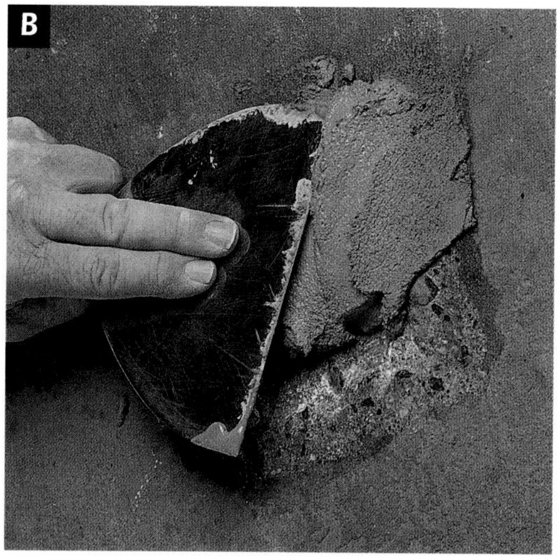

Smooth the concrete patch mixture with a flexible knife.

C

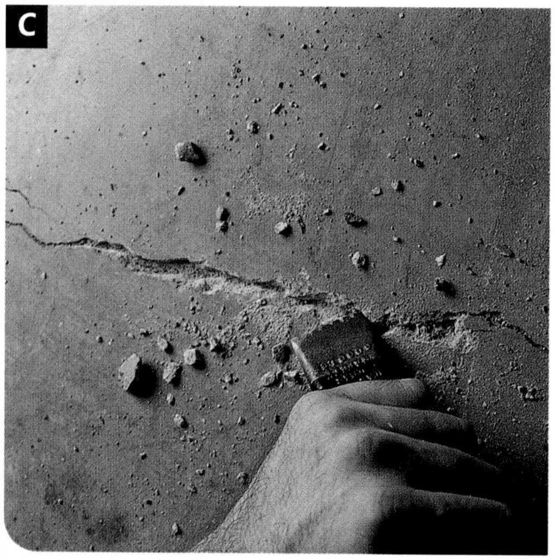

Remove loose masonry with a chisel and a wire brush.

D

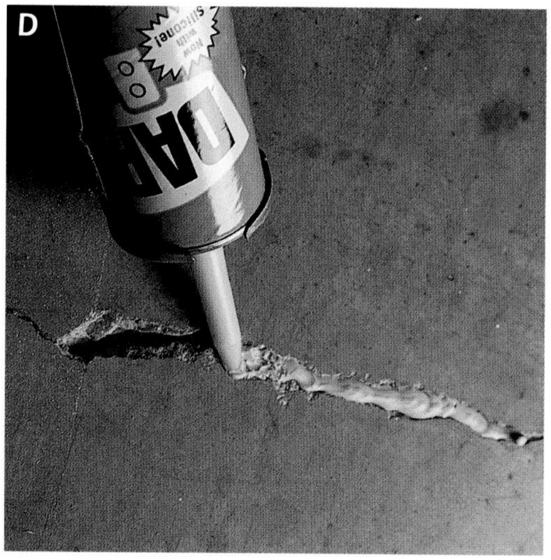

Apply latex masonry caulk to the crack.

E

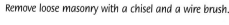

Smooth the caulk with a putty knife or trowel.

Installing an Interior Gutter/Drain

In basements where preventing moisture accumulation isn't practical or possible, install an interior gutter and drain. Interior gutters channel moisture away from the walls, directing water to a floor drain. Plan your system so that it runs along the perimeter of the wet basement walls, and leave an opening in front of each floor drain.

You'll need to prepare the walls before installing the gutter system. Brick and block walls must be relieved of the hydrostatic pressure. Drill "weep" holes at the base of the wall with a drill outfitted with a 1/2" masonry bit, spacing the holes 1 ft. apart **(photo F).** If the walls are painted or sealed, the next step is to strip a 3"-wide section between the wall and the floor down to the bare concrete. Use a drill outfitted with a metal paint-scraper wheel to remove the paint, and wear eye protection. Wipe away dust and paint residue with a damp cloth or sponge.

Place a premolded corner section from the gutter kit in each corner. Trace the position of the base of the corner section onto the floor with a marker. To cut and fit the baseboard gutter sections, lay sections end to end spanning the length of the wall between the corner outlines. Cut the sections to fit with a hacksaw.

Working with a section at a time, apply a 1/2"-high bead of adhesive along the base of the gutter. Flip the gutter back over and align the end with the corner mark on the floor. Position the gutter so that the back rests flush against the wall and the base is 1/4" out from the wall. Press the gutter gently against the floor. Caulk the seam between the gutter section and the floor **(photo G).** Install the remaining sections, leaving a 3" space between each section.

When all the sections for a wall are installed, apply a bead of adhesive to the ends of each section, except at the corners. Install a butt-joint connector between each section, sealing the butt joints.

After all the sections and butt joint connectors are installed, install the corners. Apply adhesive to the ends of the sections at the corners, then slide the corner piece into place from the top **(photo H).**

Install an end cap on all open gutter ends, except for those in front of the floor drains **(photo I).**

At the openings in front of the floor drains, lay a 1/2"-wide piece of square wood perpendicular to the gutter ends, extending toward the drain. The wood blocks should be parallel to each other. They will help guide the water channeled from the gutter openings to the drain **(photo J).**

Tools: Drill with ½" masonry bit, metal paint-scraper wheel, hacksaw, caulk gun.

Materials: Adhesive, baseboard gutter sections, butt joint connectors, corner connectors, ½"-wide wood blocks.

F
Drill weep holes 1 ft. apart at the base of wet walls.

G
Caulk the seam between the base of the gutter and the floor.

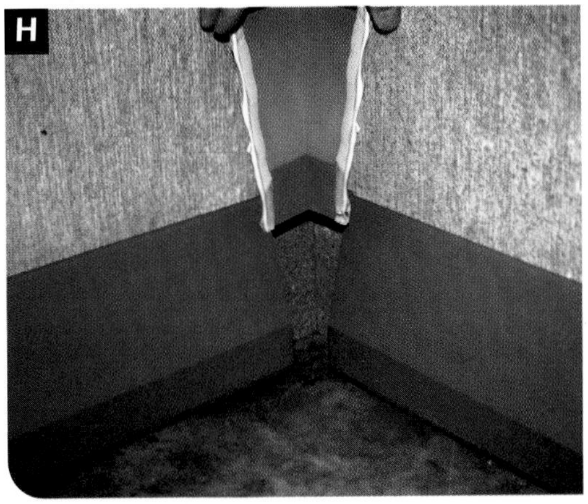
H
Install the corner pieces from the top, sliding them into place.

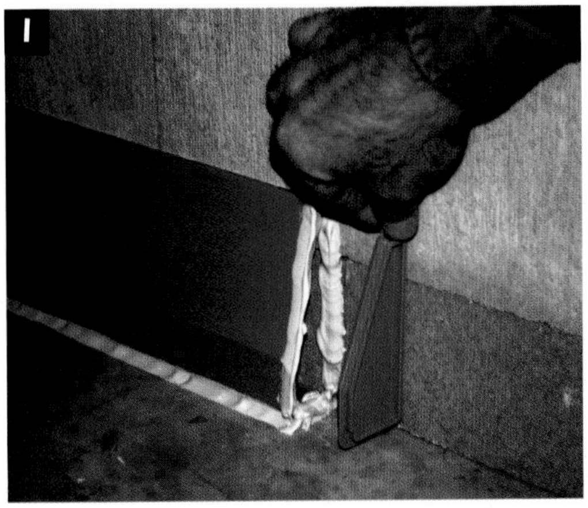
I
Install end caps on the open ends of the gutters.

J
Position the wood pieces perpendicular to the gutters.

Correcting a Foundation Grade

An improper grade can direct water toward, rather than away from, the foundation of the house and can cause water to seep through basement walls. To remedy the problem you'll need to regrade the soil so that it has a gradual slope away from the house of about 3/4" per horizontal foot. The process involves measuring the slope, then adding or removing topsoil to correct the grade. Topsoil can be purchased from and delivered by a soil contractor.

Start by driving a pair of stakes into the soil, one at the base of the foundation, and another at least eight feet out into the yard in a straight line from the first. Attach a string outfitted with a line level to the stakes and adjust the string until it's level. Measure and flag the string with tape at 1-ft. intervals.

Measure down from the string at the tape flags **(photo A).** Use these measurements as guidelines for adding or removing soil to create a correct grade. Starting at the base of the house, add soil to the low areas until they reach the desired height. Using a garden rake, evenly distribute the soil over a small area **(photo B).** Measure down from the tape markings as you work to make sure that you are creating a 3/4" per 1-ft. pitch. Add or remove soil as needed, working away from the house until the soil is evenly sloped. After you've completed an area, repeat the process to grade the next section of your yard.

Use a hand tamp to lightly compact the soil **(photo C).** Don't overtamp the soil. After all the soil is tamped, use a grading rake to remove any rocks or clumps. Starting at the foundation, pull the rake in a straight line down the slope **(photo D).** Repeat the process, working on one section at a time until the entire area around the house is graded.

Tools: *Line level, tape measure, shovel, wheelbarrow, garden rake, hand tamp, grading rake.*

Materials: *Stakes, string, tape, topsoil.*

Attach tape flags to the string at 1-ft. intervals, then measure the distance between the tape flags and the ground.

Use a garden rake to distribute the soil, checking and adjusting the slope as you work.

Lightly compact the soil in the graded area with a hand tamp.

Pull a grading rake in a straight line down the slope to remove rocks, clumps, and debris.

Extending Downspouts

Gutters are designed to channel water off your roof and and away from your home. But many gutter systems don't carry the water far enough away; excess water collects near the foundation and seeps into the basement. The problem can be corrected by extending the downspouts. The extensions disperse water farther out into the yard and away from the house.

There are several options for extending downspouts, each using different materials. The option you choose will depend on the foot traffic outside your house and your preference for the extended downspout's appearance.

The most popular option for extending a downspout is to attach a new length of downspout pipe to the existing downspout **(photo E).** Cut the new section of gutter downspout pipe from a section that matches your gutters. To make the extension, use a hacksaw to cut a 6-ft.- to 8-ft.-long section of downspout pipe **(photo F).**

Attach the new section to the downspout with a galvanized gutter elbow **(photo G).** Place a splash block at the end of the ground pipe to disperse the water onto the lawn **(photo H).**

If your downspouts are located near walkways, patios, or other high-traffic areas, there are special downspout extenders designed to work in these situations. One option is to install a roll-up sleeve to the end of the downspout. These sleeves fit snugly on the end of the downspout and automatically unroll when the gutters channel water. After the water is gone, the sleeve automatically rolls up again. Another option is to install a swing-up elbow at the base of the downspout. This elbow allows you to flip the ground pipe up when it's in the way.

Tools: *Tape measure, hacksaw.*

Materials: *Gutter downspout pipe, splash block, downspout extenders (if needed), swing-up elbows (if needed).*

Extend downspouts that empty water too close to the house.

Measure and cut a 6-ft.- to 8-ft.-long section of downspout pipe with a hacksaw.

Attach the new pipe to the downspout with a galvanized gutter elbow.

Position a splash block beneath the ground pipe.

Ceilings & Walls

Well-maintained walls and ceilings create an attractive atmosphere, conserve energy, and muffle sounds between rooms. But the wear and tear of everyday life takes a toll on walls. Corners often crack as a new home settles or an older home ages, and ceilings can be damaged by moisture, usually when water finds its way into a ceiling cavity.

Repairing holes, structural cracks, stains, and water damage to wallboard is simple. Small holes can be filled, and large areas of damage can be replaced. Plaster repairs are somewhat more involved, but can be accomplished. It's best to check the overall condition of the walls and ceilings before making any repairs. If they feel spongy, or have large bulges and cracks, hire a professional to cover or replace the entire surface.

Tools & Materials

Home centers and hardware stores carry a wide variety of products for patching, filling, and camouflaging wall and ceiling damage.

Tools that are especially useful for wall and ceiling repair include trowels, a wallboard saw, heat and glue guns, tile pliers, wallboard knives, stud finder, adhesive syringe, awl, wallcovering roller, and a utility knife.

Special materials include bonding products that improve the adhesion of patching materials as well as production sandpaper, which has an open surface that doesn't clog with dust.

Tools for wall and ceiling repair include: adhesive trowel (1), wallboard saw (2), heat gun (3), glue gun (4), tile pliers (5), wallboard knives (6), sash brush (7), stud finder (8), adhesive syringe (9), awl (10), wallcovering roller (11), utility knife (12), and grout float (13).

Materials for wall repair include joint and crack fillers, patching materials, adhesives and bonding materials, stain removers, wall anchors, caulk, grout, and sandpaper.

Removing Stubborn Stains

Most home centers and hardware stores carry a number of products intended to remove stains from painted walls. Test new products in an inconspicuous area before using them.

Apply the remover to a clean, dry cloth and rub it lightly across the stain **(photo A).**

If you can't completely remove a stain, seal the area and repaint it. White pigmented shellac will keep stains from bleeding through a new coat of paint. Apply the pigmented shellac **(photo B),** and let it dry thoroughly. Then repaint the area, feathering the new paint onto the surrounding surface.

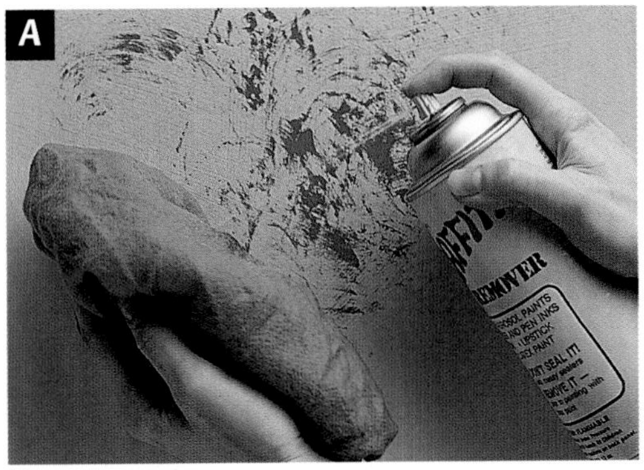

Stains sometimes can be removed with specialty products designed for painted surfaces.

Seal stubborn stains with pigmented shellac before repainting.

Removing Mildew

Before bleaching a wall, wash it with soap and water. If the stains are caused by mildew, they won't wash out with just soap and water.

To kill mildew spores, wash the wall with bleach **(photo C).** Wear rubber gloves and eye protection, and protect surrounding surfaces.

Wash the wall with a TSP (trisodium phosphate) solution, following manufacturer's directions **(photo D).** Rinse the wall with clear water.

NOTE: Never combine products containing ammonia with products containing bleach.

Wash mildew stains with bleach. Work carefully, and protect clothing as well as nearby surfaces from the bleach.

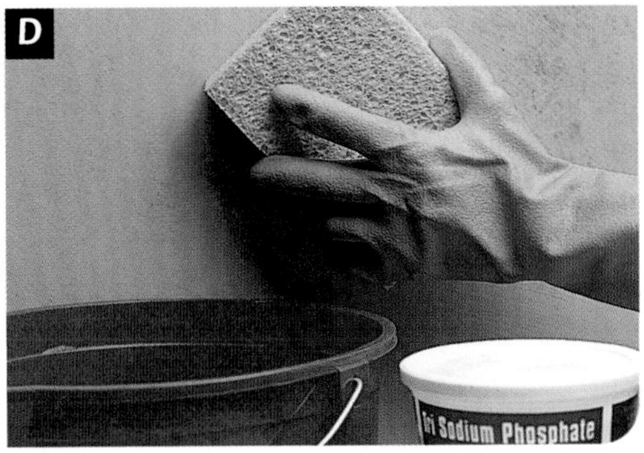

Wash again with a TSP solution, then rinse the area with clear water.

Patching Peeling Paint

Painting over peeling paint just guarantees that the paint will peel again. To permanently patch peeling paint, begin by scraping away all the loose paint, using a putty knife or paint scraper **(photo E).**

Apply spackle to the edges of the chipped paint, using a putty knife or flexible wallboard knife **(photo F).**

Let the patch dry completely, then sand the area with 150-grit sandpaper. When the patch is smooth and you can't feel any ridges along the edges, paint the patch, feathering the edges.

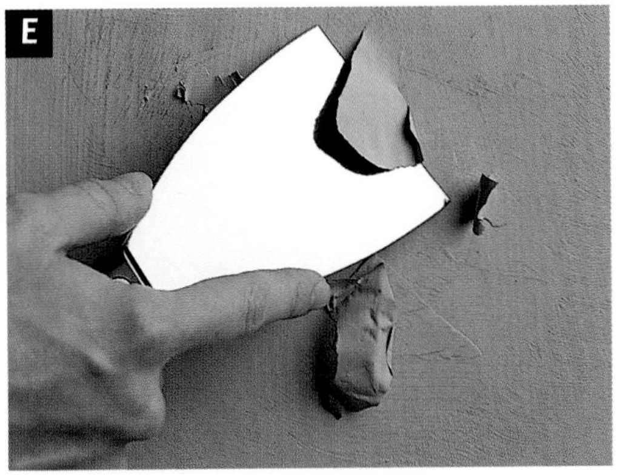

Scrape away any peeling paint, using a wallboard knife.

Fill in the chipped areas with spackle, feathering the edges onto the surrounding wall.

Repairing Plaster

Plaster walls are constructed in layers. Behind the plaster is a layer of wood, metal, or rock lath that holds the plaster in place. *Keys*, formed when the base plaster is squeezed through the lath, hold the dried plaster to the ceilings or walls.

Before you begin repairing plaster, make sure the area is generally in good shape. If the lath is deteriorated or the surrounding plaster is soft, consult a professional.

Using a latex bonding liquid ensures a good bond and a tight, crack-free patch. Bonding liquid also eliminates the need to wet the plaster and lath to prevent premature drying and shrinkage, which could ruin the repair. There are several versions of this product on the market. Read consumer literature, or ask your hardware dealer to recommend a good brand.

Tools: *Wallboard knives, paintbrush.*

Materials: *Spackle, wallboard compound, patching plaster, fiberglass wallboard tape, latex bonding liquid, sandpaper, paint.*

Filling Cracks

Scrape away any texture or loose plaster around the crack. Reinforce the crack with self-adhering fiberglass wallboard tape.

Apply spackle or wallboard compound **(photo A)** until the tape is concealed with a thin layer—a thick layer will quickly crack again.

Add a second, thinner, coat if necessary to conceal the edges of the tape. Lightly sand **(photo B),** then prime the repair area. Retexture the surface (page 35).

Cover wallboard tape with a thin layer of spackle or wallboard compound.

Sand and prime the patch. Retexture the surrounding surface, if necessary.

Filling Small Dents & Holes

To properly fill small dents and holes in plaster, you have to establish a solid base for the patch. Scrape or sand away any loose plaster or peeling paint **(photo C).**

Fill the hole with lightweight spackle **(photo D).** Apply the spackle with the smallest knife that will span the damage. Let the spackle dry.

Sand the patch lightly with 150-grit production sandpaper **(photo E).** Wipe the dust away with a clean cloth, then prime and paint the area, feathering the paint to blend the edges.

Scrape or sand away any loose plaster or peeled paint.

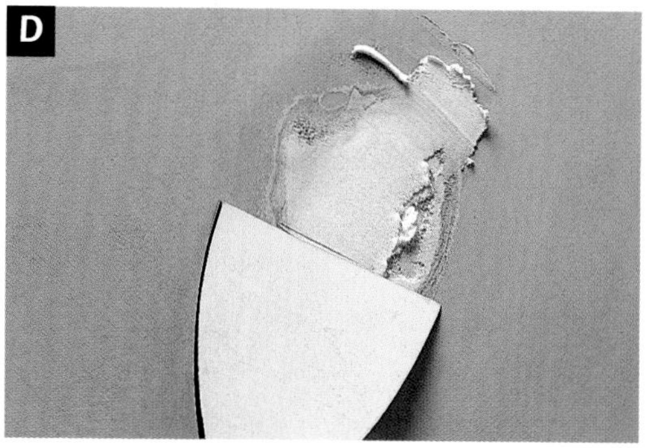

Fill the hole with lightweight spackle.

Lightly sand the patch, prime, and repaint it.

Patching Large Holes in Plaster

Before you begin patching a large hole, make sure the lath backing is solid. To create a smooth, firm edge the patch can adhere to, sand or scrape any texture or loose paint from the area around the hole **(photo F).**

Use a wallboard knife to test the plaster around the edges of the damaged area. Scrape away all loose or soft plaster **(photo G).**

Liberally apply a latex bonding liquid around the edges of the hole and over the base lath **(photo H).** The bonding liquid improves the adhesion of the plaster and helps keep it from cracking or separating as it cures.

Mix the patching plaster as directed by the manufacturer, and use a wallboard knife to apply it to the hole **(photo I).** Shallow holes can be filled with a single coat, but be careful not to fill too much at a time—thick layers tend to crack, despite the effects of the bonding liquid.

For deeper holes, apply a shallow first coat, then scratch a crosshatch pattern in the wet plaster **(photo J).** Let this coat dry, then apply a second coat of plaster. Let the second coat dry, then lightly sand the patched area.

Use texture paint or wallboard compound to re-create any surface texture **(photo K).** Depending on the texture you're trying to duplicate, you can use a roller, whisk broom, trowel, sponge, or paintbrush. Practice on heavy cardboard until you can duplicate the wall's surface. Prime and paint the area.

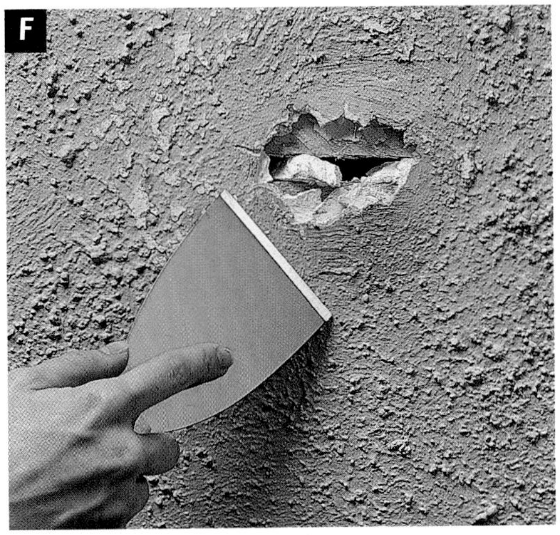

Scrape texture and any peeling paint from the area.

Remove loose or soft plaster around the edges.

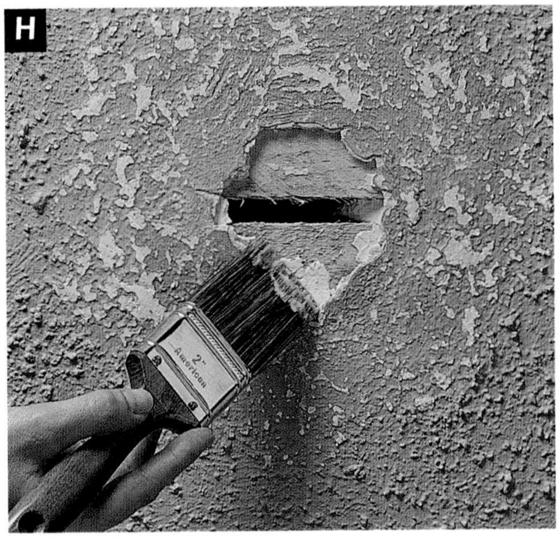

Apply a liberal coat of latex bonding liquid around the edges of the hole and the base lath.

Fill shallow holes with a single coat of plaster.

Fill deeper holes with a shallow first coat, scratching a crosshatch pattern in this wet plaster. Add a second coat.

Reproduce the surface texture, using texture paint or wallboard compound. Prime and paint the patched area.

Repairing Wallboard

Patching holes and concealing popped nails are common wallboard repairs. Small holes can be filled directly, but larger patches must be supported in some way. Many products are available, but wallboard or plywood make inexpensive, effective backing materials.

Tools: *Screw gun, hammer, wallboard knife, paintbrush, wallboard saw.*

Materials: *Wallboard screws, wallboard compound, wallboard tape, plywood scraps, sandpaper, paint repair patch (if needed).*

Resetting Popped Nails

As framing lumber dries, nails often pop away from the wall **(photo A).** Popping is also common if wallboard fasteners have been improperly applied. To avoid problems in the future, use wallboard screws for repairs—the threaded shanks resist popping.

To reset popped nails, press the wallboard tightly against the stud or joist. Holding the wallboard in place, drive a new screw about 2" from the popped nail **(photo B).** Make sure you're hitting a stud or joist, then drive the screw in until the head is slightly indented.

Scrape away any loose paint or wallboard compound, then drive the popped nail slightly below the surface of the wall **(photo C).** Fill both holes with wallboard compound. Let the compound dry thoroughly, sand if necessary, and repaint.

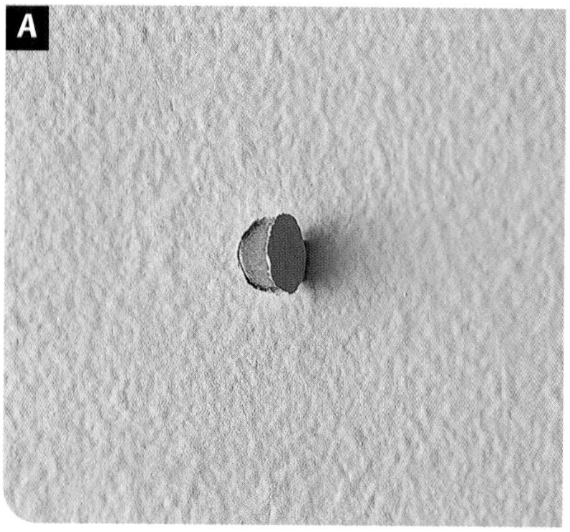

A

Popped wallboard fasteners, especially nails, are a common problem.

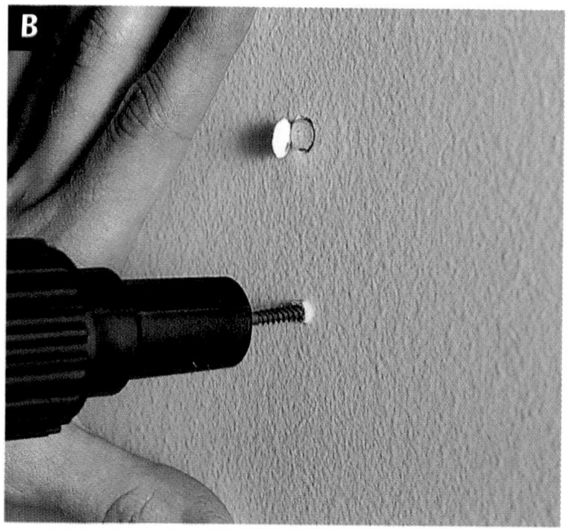

B

Press the wallboard against the stud and drive a screw about 2" from the popped nail.

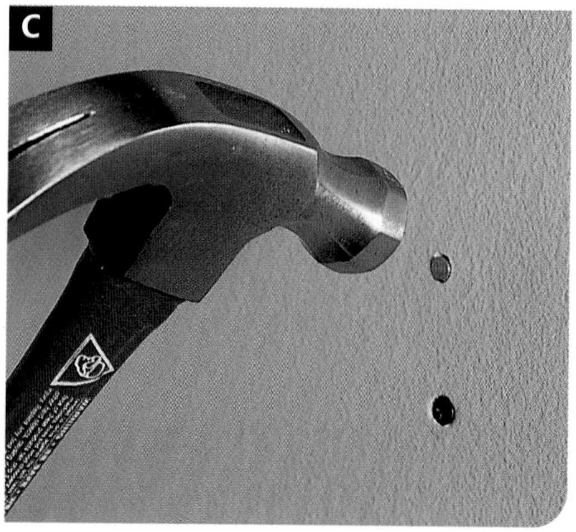

C

Drive in the popped nail, then fill the holes and touch up the paint.

Patching Small Holes

Inspect the damaged area. If there are no cracks around the edge of the hole, just fill the hole with spackle, let it dry, and sand it smooth **(photo D).**

If the edges are cracked, cover the hole with a peel-and-stick repair patch. These patches, which have a metal mesh center for strength, can be cut or shaped as needed.

Use a wallboard knife or putty knife to apply a thin layer of spackle or wallboard compound over the patch **(photo E).** Let the compound dry, add a second coat, then let the patch set until it's nearly dry.

To smooth the repair area without creating a lot of dust, use a damp sponge or wallboard wet sander **(photo F).**

When the patch is completely dry, prime and paint it, feathering the paint to blend into the surrounding area.

D

Fill smooth holes with spackle, sand, then touch up the paint.

E

Cover ragged holes with a repair patch, then apply two coats of spackle or wallboard compound.

F

Use a damp sponge or wet sander to smooth the repair area, then prime and paint.

Patching Large Holes

Outline the damaged area with a carpenter's square **(photo G).** Cut away the damaged section, using a wallboard saw or jig saw.

Install plywood or wallboard backer strips. Use a screwgun to drive $1\frac{1}{4}$" wallboard screws that will hold the wood strips in place **(photo H).** If you're using wallboard strips for backers, secure them with hot glue.

Cut a wallboard patch slightly smaller than the open area. Leaving a gap of at least $\frac{1}{8}$" around the edges of the patch gives the wallboard compound room to create a solid foundation—if the patch fits too closely, it will be difficult to blend the edges into the surface of the wall. Place wallboard tape over the cracks **(photo I),** then apply wallboard compound, and complete the repair as described above.

G

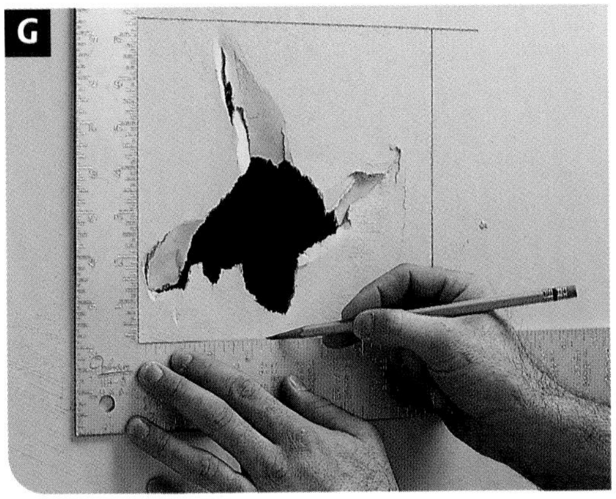

Draw cutting lines around the hole, then cut away the damaged area, using a wallboard saw.

H

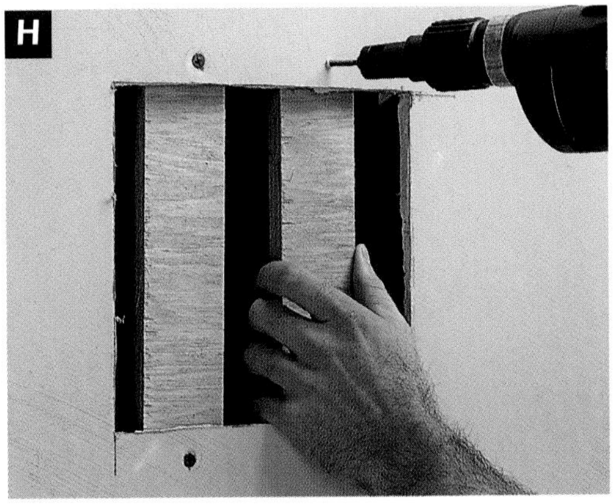

Place plywood strips behind the opening and drive screws to hold them in place.

I

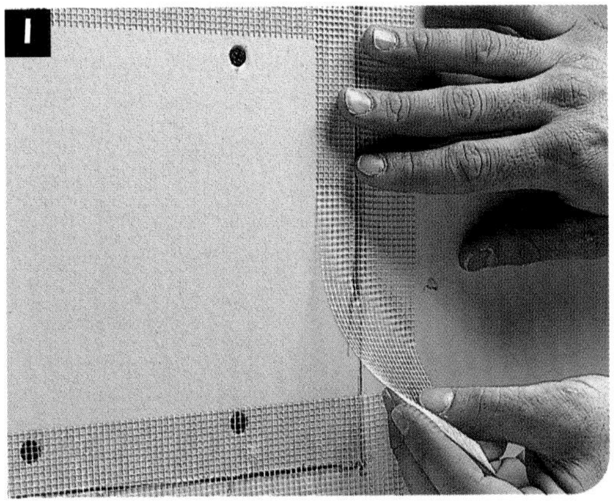

Drive screws through the patch and into the backers. Cover the joints with wallboard tape and finish with compound.

Restoring Paneling

Photo courtesy of Broyhill Furniture Industries, Inc.

Paneling is a generic term for a wood product wallcovering that comes in several different forms. Although tongue-and-groove boards can be installed as paneling, the most familiar form of paneling consists of 4 × 8 sheets of 1/4"-thick plywood with a prefinished surface.

Prefinished sheet paneling is quite durable—it often lasts for decades without needing any repairs. Generally speaking, dusting it or washing it with a damp cloth and mild soap is all the maintenance it requires.

Despite its durability, paneling occasionally requires minor repairs. Many scuff marks can be removed with a light coat of paste wax, and most small scratches can be disguised with a touch-up stick.

Manufacturers don't recommend trying to spot-sand or refinish prefinished paneling.

Replacing Paneling

The most common forms of significant damage to paneling are water damage and punctures. If paneling has suffered major damage, the only way to repair it is to replace the affected sheets.

If the paneling is more than a few years old, it may be difficult to locate matching pieces. If you can't find any at lumber yards or building centers, try salvage yards. Buy the panels in advance so that you can condition them to the room before installing them. To condition the paneling, place it in the room, standing on its long edge. Place spacers between the sheets so air can circulate around each one. Let the paneling stand for 24 hours if it will be installed above grade, and 48 hours if it will be installed below grade.

Before you go any further, find out what's behind the paneling. Building Codes often require that paneling be backed with wallboard. This is a good idea, even if Code doesn't require it. The support provided by the wallboard keeps the paneling from warping and provides an extra layer of sound protection. However, if there is wallboard behind the paneling, it may need repairs as well, particularly if you're dealing with water damage. And removing damaged paneling may be more difficult if it's glued to wallboard or a masonry wall. In any case, it's best to have a clear picture of the situation before you start cutting into a wall.

Finally, turn off the electricity to the area and remove all receptacle covers and switch plates on the sheets of paneling that need to be replaced.

To remove a damaged panel, carefully pry off the baseboard and top moldings **(photo A).** Use a wallboard or putty knife to create a gap, then insert a pry bar and pull the trim away from the wall. Remove all the nails.

Draw a line from the top of the panel to the bottom, 3" or 4" from each edge of the panel. Holding a framing square along this line, cut along it with a linoleum knife **(photo B).** If

Tools: *Wallboard knife, putty knife, flat pry bar, framing square, linoleum knife, hammer, chisel, caulk gun, rubber mallet, nail set.*

Materials: *Replacement panels, spray paint, panel adhesive, color-matched paneling nails, shims, finish nails, putty sticks, and wood filler.*

you use a fair amount of pressure, you should be able to cut the panel with one or two passes. If you have trouble cutting all the way through the panel, use a hammer and chisel to break it along the scored lines.

Insert a pry bar under the panel, beginning at the bottom **(photo C).** Pry the panel up and away from the wall, removing nails as you go. Once this center portion of the panel is out of the way, pry off the narrow pieces that remain along the edges. When all of the panel has been removed, scrape away the old adhesive, using a putty knife or chisel.

If the vapor barrier is now accessible, check it for damage and make any necessary repairs. For below-grade applications, make sure there is a layer of 4 mil polyethylene between the outside walls and the paneling.

If it hasn't been done previously, spray paint or stain the wall surfaces at the points where two panels meet. Adding a color that matches the edges or grooves of the panels camouflages the seams, particularly if the paneling shrinks or settles after installation.

Make any necessary cutouts, and test-fit the new panel, making sure the directional arrows on the back are positioned correctly. Run zigzag beads of panel adhesive from the top to the bottom of the panel, placing one bead every 16", about 2" in from each edge, and around every cutout.

Tack the panel into position at the top, using color-matched paneling nails. Following the adhesive manufacturer's directions, use shims to prop the panel away from the wall long enough for the adhesive to set up properly.

When the adhesive has set up, press the panel to the wall and lightly tap along stud lines with a rubber mallet, creating a tight bond between the adhesive and the wall **(photo D).**

Drive finish nails at the base of the panel to hold it in position while the adhesive dries. To protect the finish of the panel, drive the nails to within 1/8" of the face, then use a nail set to countersink the nails.

Replace the baseboard and trim moldings, and fill all the nail holes.

Pry off the baseboard and top moldings with a flat bar, then remove all nails.

Make cuts from top to bottom of the panel, cut 3" to 4" in from each edge.

Working from the bottom, pry the main portion of the panel off of the wall.

Apply adhesive, then tap lightly along seam to create a tight bond.

Restoring Ceramic Tile

Ceramic tile is durable and nearly maintenance-free, but like every other material in your house, it can fail or develop problems. The most common problem with ceramic tile involves damaged grout. Failed grout is unattractive, but the real danger is that it offers a point of entry for water. Given a chance to work its way beneath grout, water can destroy a tile base and eventually wreck an entire tile job. For these reasons, it's important to regrout ceramic tile as soon as you see signs of damage.

Although it doesn't happen often unless the base is damaged, a sharp blow at just the right angle can crack or break a tile. It's not difficult to replace a tile, but removing it can be somewhat delicate. By working carefully with the right tools, it's possible to get a broken tile out without creating further damage.

To avoid stains and mineral buildup on tiles, wipe down tile walls after using the bath or shower, or spray them with a product designed to eliminate mineral deposits and mildew. Using the exhaust fan during showers and baths removes moist air from a bathroom, which also helps protect tile surfaces from mold and mildew.

NOTE: Before the 1960s, ceramic tile was set in a masonry base. If your tile is of this vintage, contact a professional for repairs.

Tools: *Awl, utility knife, grout float, hammer, chisel, tile nippers, rented tile cutter or glass cutter, compass, wood file.*

Materials: *Replacement tile, tile adhesive, masking tape, grout, rubbing alcohol, silicone or latex caulk.*

Regrouting Ceramic Tile

When replacing grout in a ceramic tile wall, choose a premixed grout that's resistant to mildew and stains. Scrape out the old grout completely, leaving a clean bed for the new grout **(photo A).** An awl or utility knife works well for this. Allow plenty of time for this step—removing grout isn't difficult, but doing it well takes more time than you might think. When all of the grout is out, remove and replace any broken tiles (page 41).

Clean and rinse the grout joints, then spread grout over the entire tile surface, using a foam grout float or a sponge **(photo B).** Work the grout well into the joints. Let the grout set slightly, then tool it with a rounded object, such as a toothbrush. Wipe away excess grout with a damp cloth **(photo C).**

When the grout is dry, wipe away the residue and polish the tiles. Apply caulk (page 42). Don't use the tub or shower for 24 hours.

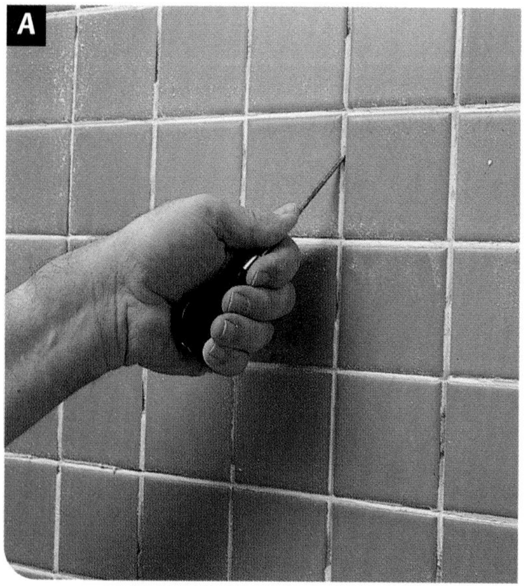

Scrape out old grout, using an awl or utility knife.

Spread grout over the tile and work it into every joint across the surface.

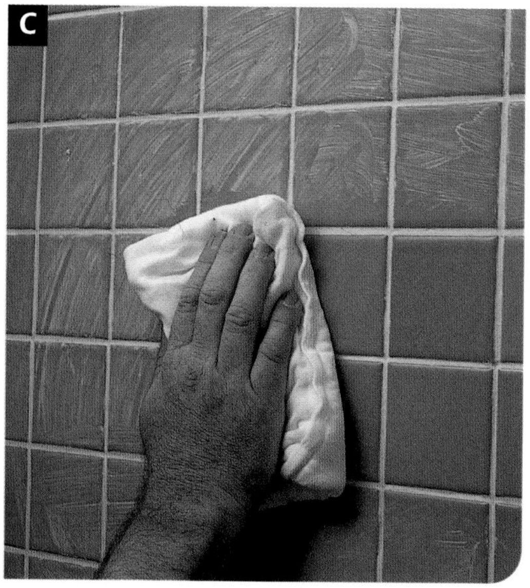

Wipe away the grout residue and polish the tiles with a soft, dry cloth.

Removing & Replacing Broken Tiles

Carefully scrape away the grout from the surrounding joints, using a utility knife or awl. Break the damaged tile into small pieces, using a hammer and chisel. Remove the broken pieces **(photo D),** then use a utility knife to scrape any debris or old adhesive from the open area.

If the tile to be replaced is a whole tile, you're ready to test-fit it in the open space. If it's a partial tile, cut a new one to match. Cutting tile with a tile cutter is a two-step process. First, score a cutting line, pressing down firmly. Next, snap the handle to quickly break the tile. If you don't have access to a tile cutter, score the tile with a glass cutter, then place it over an edge and snap down on the free side. The tile should break cleanly along the scored line. If you need to cut a curved edge, mark the curve with a compass, then use tile nippers to remove small chunks until you reach the marked lines. Smooth the cut edges with a wood file.

Test-fit the new tile and make sure it fits and sits flush with the old tile. Spread adhesive on the back of the replacement tile, then place it in the hole, twisting slightly to make sure the tile makes good contact with the wall **(photo E).** Use masking tape to hold the tile in place for 24 hours so the adhesive can dry completely.

Remove the tape, then apply premixed grout, using a sponge or grout float **(photo F).** Let the grout set slightly, then tool it with a rounded object, such as a toothbrush handle. Wipe away excess grout with a damp cloth.

Let the grout dry for an hour, then polish the tile with a clean, dry cloth **(photo G).**

Remove the grout from the surrounding joints, then break and remove the tile, using a hammer and chisel.

Test-fit the new tile, then apply adhesive to the back and press it securely onto the wall. Let it dry for 24 hours.

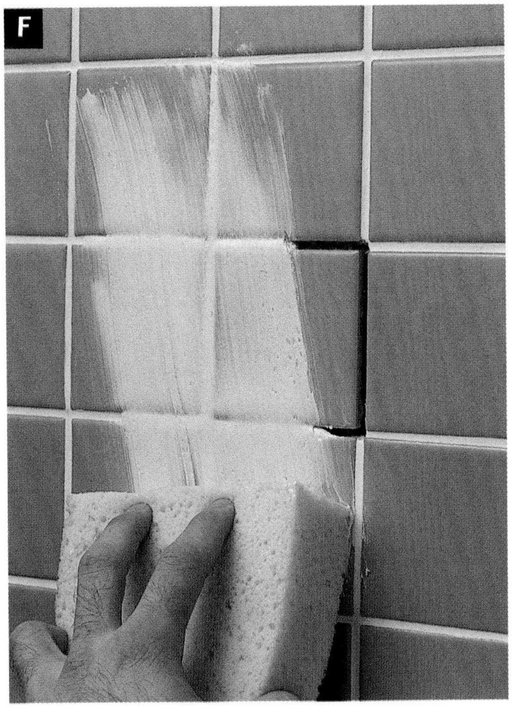

Apply premixed grout with a sponge or grout float.

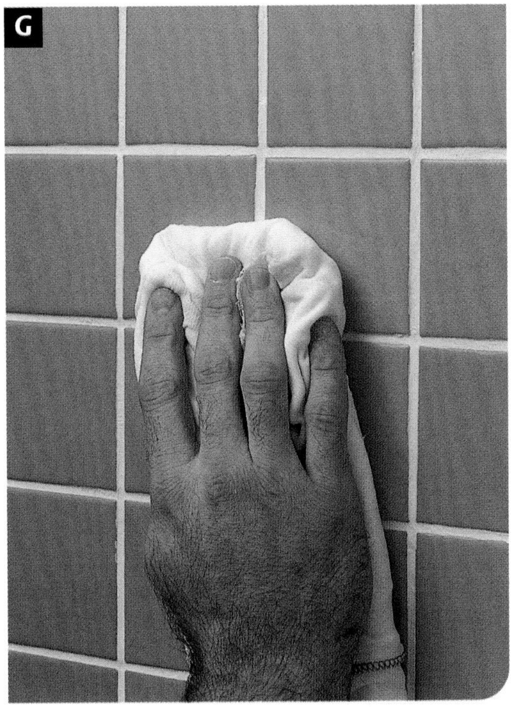

Let the grout dry, then polish the tile with a clean, dry cloth.

Recaulking a Bathtub or Shower Stall

In a tub or shower stall, the joints between ceramic tiles and where the walls meet the tub are all sealed with caulk. The caulk eventually deteriorates, leaving an entry point for water. Unless the joints are recaulked, seeping water will destroy the tile base and the wall.

To recaulk around a bathtub or shower stall, you need to start with a completely dry surface. If possible, let the tub or shower dry for a few days before starting.

Scrape out old grout or caulk with an awl or a can opener **(photo A).** Wipe soap scum from the joint with a clean, dry cloth dipped in rubbing alcohol.

Slowly fill the tub with water. Don't let water splash onto the walls or into the joints. Caulking while the tub is weighted with water eliminates the possibility that the caulk will crack the first time you fill the tub.

If a joint tends to mildew, clean it with a product that kills mildew spores (available at hardware stores and home centers). Once the joint is completely dry, fill it with silicone or latex caulk **(photo B).**

Wet a fingertip with cold water (so the caulk won't stick to your skin). Use your finger to smooth the caulk into a cove shape **(photo C).** After the caulk hardens, use a utility knife to trim away any excess.

Preformed peel-and-stick tub and tile caulk allows you to eliminate cleaning the joint and shaping wet caulk. Simply peel off the backing and press the caulk into place **(photo D).**

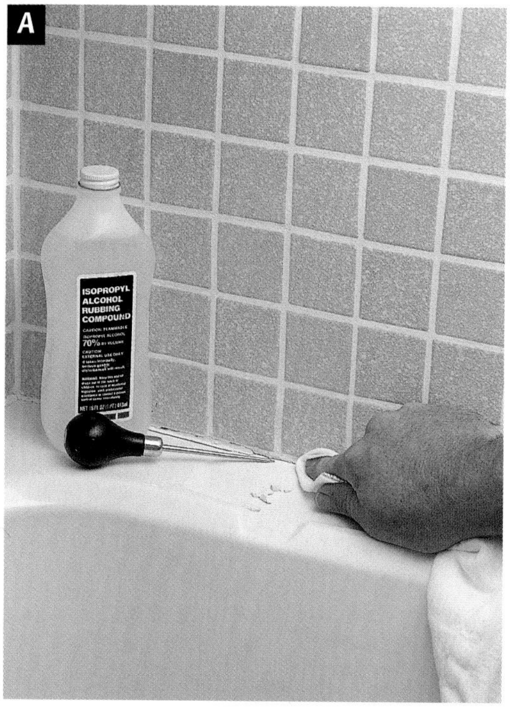

Scrape out old caulk and clean the joint.

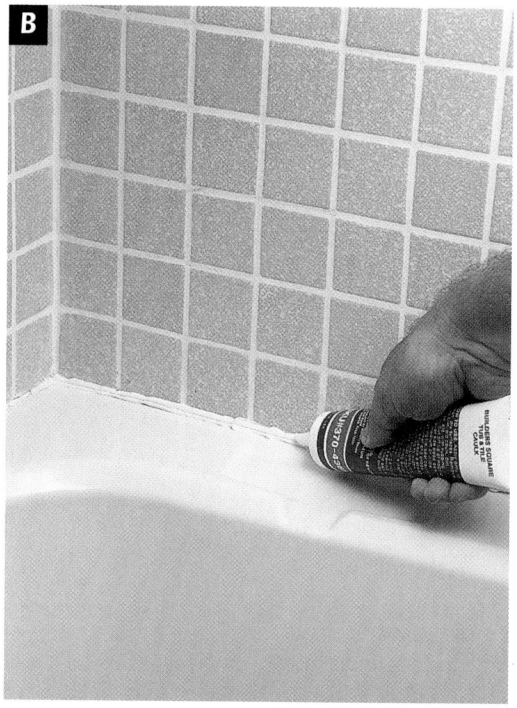

Fill the tub with water, then fill the joint with caulk.

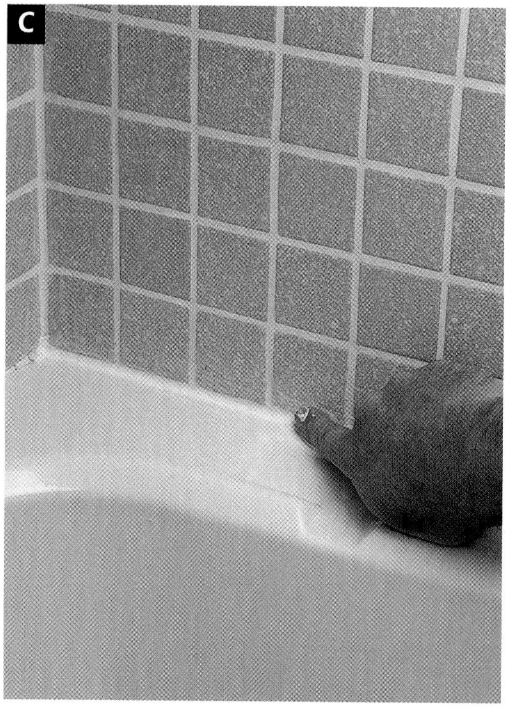

Smooth the caulk. After it hardens, trim away any excess.

Peel-and-stick tub and tile caulk is simple to use.

Replacing Wall Accessories

Towel rods, soap dishes, and other bathroom accessories can work loose from walls, especially if they weren't installed correctly or aren't supported properly.

To limit the amount of wall repair that's necessary, remove old accessories carefully. For maximum holding power, anchor new accessories to wall studs or blocking. If no studs or blocking are located in the area where you want to hang the accessories, use special fasteners **(photo E),** such as toggle bolts or molly bolts, to anchor the accessories directly to the surface of wallboard or plaster walls. To hold screws firmly in ceramic tile walls, drill pilot holes and insert plastic sleeves, which expand when screws are driven into them.

Tools: *Hammer, chisel, utility knife, notched trowel, screwdriver.*

Materials: *Replacement accessories, specialty fasteners as required, dry-set tile adhesive, masking tape, grout.*

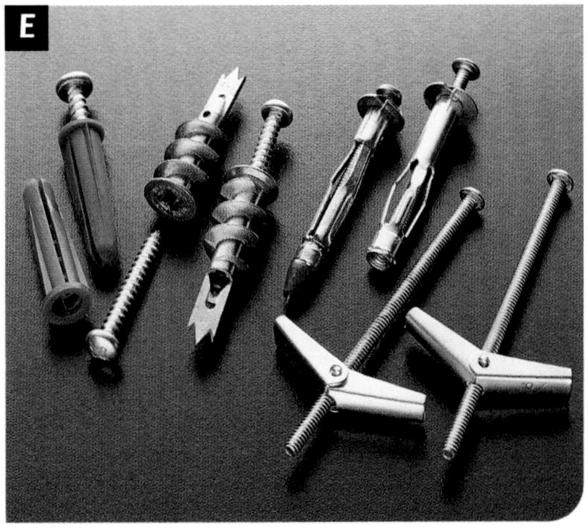

Specialty fasteners help hold wall accessories securely.

Replacing Built-in Accessories

Carefully remove the damaged accessory, using the techniques described for removing damaged ceramic tile (page 41). Scrape away any remaining adhesive or grout from the surrounding area, using a utility or putty knife.

Apply dry-set tile adhesive to the back side of the new accessory **(photo F),** then press it firmly into place.

Use masking tape to hold the accessory in place while the adhesive dries **(photo G).** Let the mortar dry completely (12 to 24 hours), then grout and seal the area (page 40).

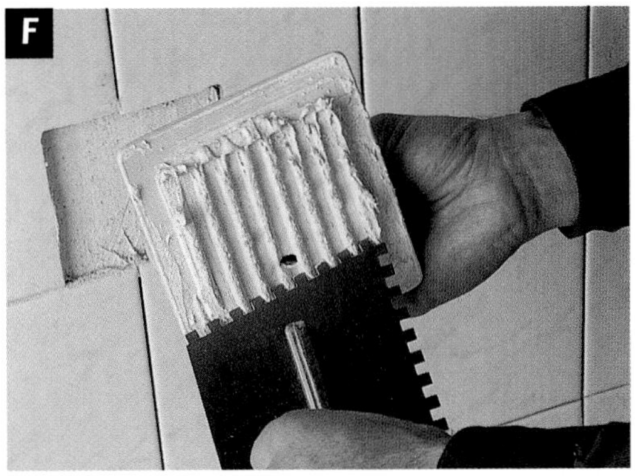

Apply dry-set mortar to the back of the accessory, using a notched trowel.

Hold the accessory in place with masking tape until the adhesive dries. Grout and seal the area.

Replacing Surface-mounted Accessories

To remove a surface-mounted accessory, lift it up and off the mounting plate **(photo H).** If the mounting plate screws are driven into studs or blocking, simply hang the new accessory. But if the screws aren't well supported, replace them with specialty fasteners, such as molly bolts or toggle bolts. On ceramic tile, use plastic anchor sleeves.

To seal out moisture and enhance the holding power of the screws in or near high-moisture areas, apply a dab of silicone caulk over pilot holes and screw tips before inserting screws **(photo I).** Let the caulk dry, then install the new fixtures on the mounting plates.

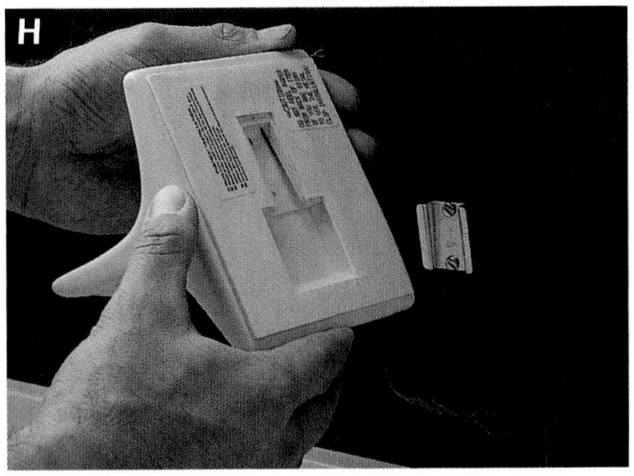

Remove surface-mounted accessories by lifting them off their mounting plates.

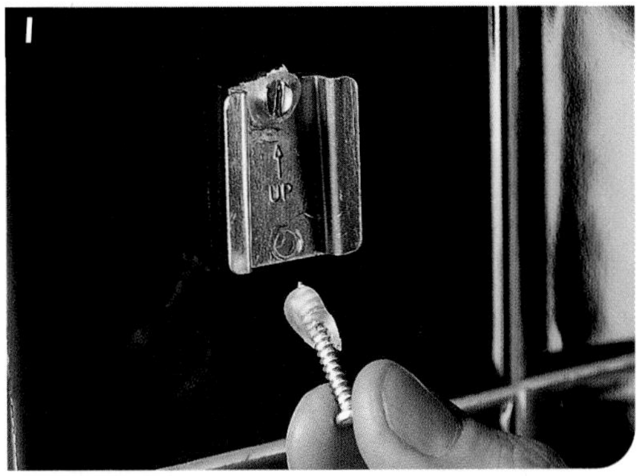

Put drops of silicone caulk over each pilot hole and screw tip, then secure the mounting plates to the wall.

Repairing Wallcovering

Very few modern wallpapers are actually made of paper. Today's wallcoverings may be made of vinyl, vinyl-coated paper or cloth, textiles, natural grasses, foil, or mylar. Vinyl and coated vinyl wallcoverings are extremely popular because they're easy to clean or repair—other types may require special handling. Grasscloth and flocked wallcoverings, for example, can't be washed or even rinsed with water.

Loosened seams and bubbles are common wallcovering problems, but both are easy to solve, as described in this section. Areas with scratches, tears, or obvious stains can be patched so successfully that the patch is difficult to spot.

Whenever you hang wallcoverings, save remnants for future repairs. It's also a good idea to record the name of the manufacturer as well as the style and run numbers of the wallcoverings. Write this information on a piece of masking tape and put it on the back of a switchplate in the room.

If you need to patch an area and don't have remnants available, remove a section of wallcovering from an inconspicuous spot, such as inside a closet or behind a door. You can camouflage the spot by painting the hole with a color that blends into the background of the wallcovering.

Tools: *Edge roller, syringe-type adhesive applicator, sponge, utility knife.*

Materials: *Wallpaper dough, adhesive, removable tape, wallcovering remnants.*

Renewing Wallcovering

Before cleaning any wallcovering, try to find out what methods are appropriate. If you have a remnant, read the back—the description there provides clues about the type of cleaning that's appropriate. *Washable* wallcoverings can be cleaned with mild soap and a sponge. *Scrubbable* versions are durable enough to be scrubbed with a soft brush.

Some stains can be removed from wallcovering with a gum eraser or wallpaper dough **(photo A),** which are available at most decorating centers and paint stores.

Loose seams tend to get caught and torn, so repair them as soon as you notice them. Lift the edge of the wallcovering and insert the tip of a glue applicator **(photo B).** Squirt adhesive onto the wall and press the edge back into place. If it's appropriate for the type of wallcovering you're working with, firmly roll the seam, then wipe away excess adhesive with a clean, wet sponge. On embossed or flocked papers, just press the seam into place with your fingers—a seam roller could crush the pattern.

Use wallpaper dough to remove stains from nonwashable wallcoverings.

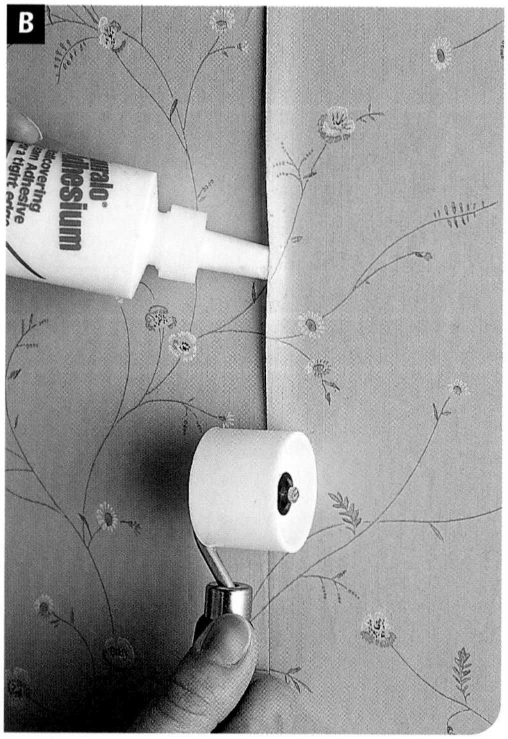

To eliminate loose seams, squirt adhesive under the edge and press the seam back into place. Roll the seam.

Patching Wallcovering

By using a technique called "double cutting," you can make a virtually undetectable patch. Start by taping a remnant of wallcovering over the damaged area **(photo C).** Using removable tape, position the patch so the pattern is precisely aligned with the existing wallcovering.

Cut through both layers of wallcovering, using a utility knife **(photo D).** Use a new blade so the cut is sharp, which helps assure a perfect pattern match. Remove the patch material, then apply water to the cut area of damaged wallcovering. Peel the damaged section away from the wall. When you're lifting the cut piece, be careful not to damage the surrounding edges.

Apply adhesive to the back of the patch and carefully position it in the hole, aligning it so that the pattern matches exactly. Gently wipe the area with a clean, wet sponge **(photo E).**

Tape a remnant of wallcovering in place, lining up the patterns precisely.

Cut through both layers of wallcovering. Remove the patch and peel away the damaged section.

Carefully reposition the patch, then remove excess adhesive with a damp sponge.

Removing Bubbles

In certain lights, bubbles in wallcovering are noticeable and unattractive. To remove a bubble, cut a slit at the edge of the bubble, using a utility knife with a new blade **(photo F).** If the wallcovering has a pattern, cut along a pattern line to help conceal the cut.

Insert the tip of a syringe-type adhesive applicator under the edge of the cut, and apply a small amount of adhesive to the wall **(photo G).** Repeat this process under the other edge of the cut. Distribute a small amount of adhesive under the entire bubbled area.

Press gently down on the wallcovering to rebond it with the wall. For papers that are compatible with water, use a clean, damp sponge. For other types of paper, clean fingers are probably the best choice. When the edges seem slightly set, carefully wipe away excess adhesive.

Cut a slit through the bubble.

Sparingly apply adhesive to the wall under the bubble.

Press the wallcovering against the wall. Wipe away excess adhesive.

Repairing Trim Moldings

There's no reason to let damaged trim moldings detract from the appearance of a well-maintained room. With the right tools and a little attention to detail, you can replace or repair them, quickly and easily.

Home centers and lumber yards sell many styles of moldings, but they may not stock moldings found in older homes. If you have trouble finding duplicates, check salvage yards in your area—they sometimes carry styles no longer manufactured. Or, try combining several different moldings to duplicate the more elaborate version.

Tools: *Flat pry bars (2), coping saw, miter saw, drill, hammer, nail set.*

Materials: *Wood scraps; replacement moldings; 2d, 4d, and 6d finish nails; wood putty.*

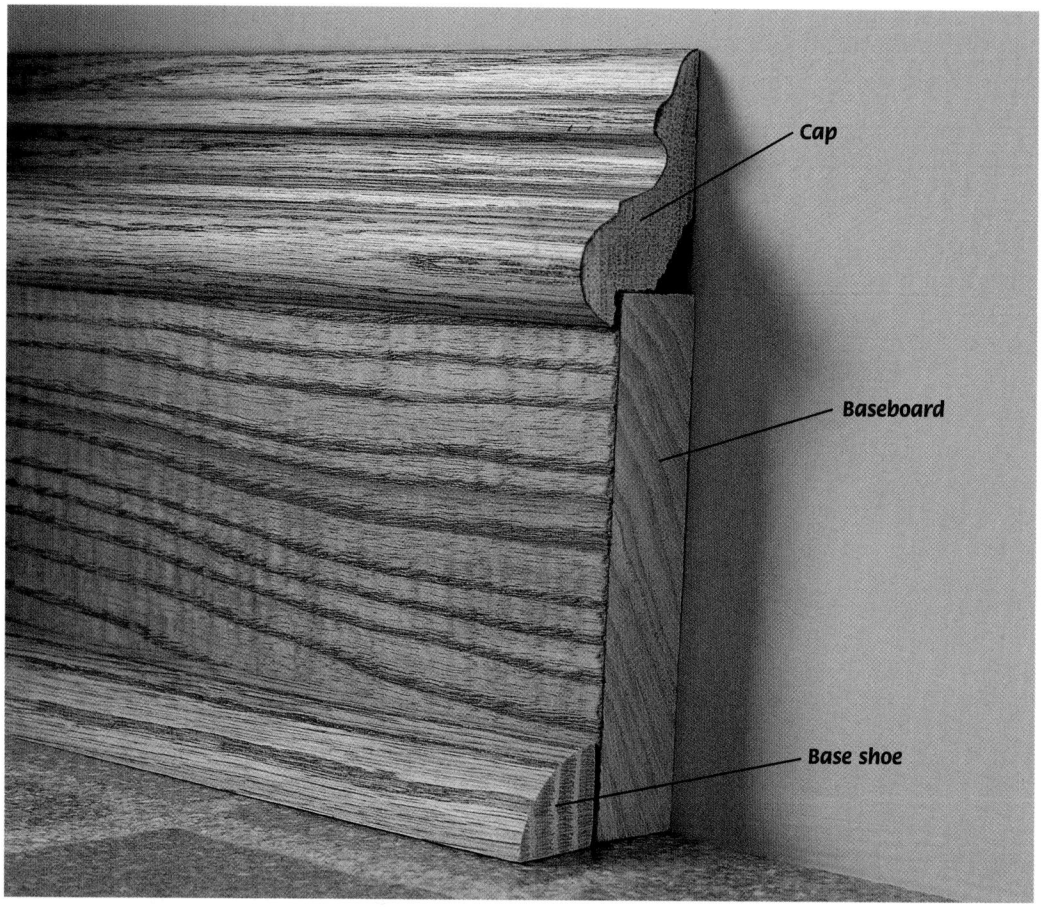

Removing a Damaged Baseboard

To remove baseboards without damaging the wall, use leverage rather than force.

Pry off the base shoe first, using a flat pry bar **(photo A).** When you feel a few nails pop, move farther along the molding and pry again.

Baseboards are typically nailed to the sole plate of the wall and into each wall stud. Use two pry bars and clean blocks of scrap wood to pull the baseboard up from the floor and away from the wall **(photo B).** Remember, even the lightest pressure from a pry bar can damage wallboard or plaster, so use a large, flat scrap of wood to protect the wall.

Insert one bar beneath the trim, and work the other bar between the baseboard and the wall. Force the pry bars in opposite directions to remove the baseboard.

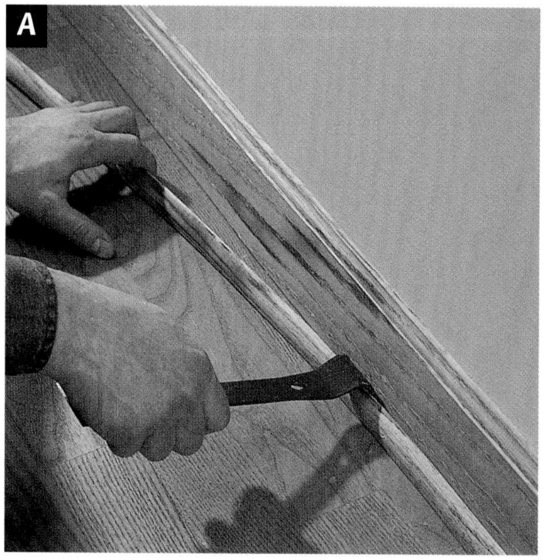

Insert a flat pry bar behind the base shoe, and pull the bar up to release the shoe.

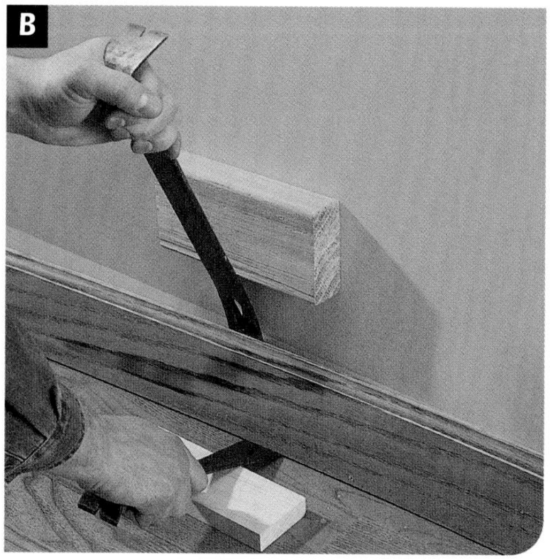

Use blocks of wood for protection and leverage as you pry the baseboard up and out.

Replacing Baseboards

To fit baseboards together at inside wall corners, carpenters use a technique known as *coping*. There are different methods for doing this, but the basic procedure is to cut the end of one baseboard piece to match the profile of another piece. It's easy to do, with a little practice, but you will need a *coping saw*, a small handsaw with a very thin, flexible blade that can twist to make curved cuts.

To install new baseboard, start along a wall that ends in two inside corners. Cut the ends of the baseboard square, and butt them against the adjacent walls at the inside corners. Drill pilot holes to prevent splitting the wood, then fasten the baseboard with two 6d finish nails, aligned vertically, at each wall stud location.

To cope the end of the return baseboard piece, cut a scrap of baseboard so the ends are perfectly square **(photo C).** Also cut the end of the workpiece square. Position the scrap on the back of the workpiece so its back face is flush with the end of the workpiece. Trace the outline of the scrap onto the back of the workpiece, using a sharp pencil. Cut along the outline with a coping saw, keeping the saw perpendicular to the baseboard face. Test-fit the coped end. Recut it, if necessary **(photo D).**

To cut the baseboard to fit at outside corners, fit the coped end into the inside corner and mark the other end where it meets the outside wall corner **(photo E).** Cut the end at a 45° angle, using a power miter saw or a hand miter box. Lock-nail all miter joints together with 4d finish nails (page 49).

Install base shoe molding along the bottom of the baseboards. Make miter joints at the inside and outside corners, and fasten the base shoe with 2d finish nails.

Whenever possible, complete a run of molding using one piece. For long spans, join molding pieces by mitering the ends at parallel 45° angles **(photo F).** This type of joint, known as a *scarf* joint, hides a gap well if the wood shrinks.

Set all nail heads below the surface, using a nail set. Then, fill the holes with wood putty.

Outline the baseboard profile onto the back of the new piece.

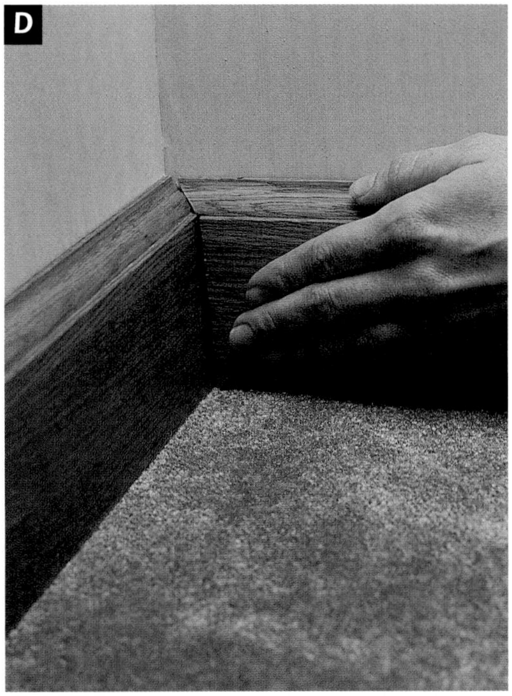

Butt the coped end against the face of the preceding piece.

Cut opposite 45° miters to fit the molding at outside corners.

Join molding pieces along a wall with a scarf joint.

Replacing Window & Door Moldings

Remove the old moldings, following the same general technique described for removing baseboards (page 46). If you're working on a window or exterior door, check the insulation around the frame, and fill any significant gaps with expandable foam or strips of fiberglass insulation.

On double-hung windows, moldings are typically installed flush with the edge of the jamb. But if you're replacing the molding around a door or a window of another style, such as a casement window, mark a setback line 1/8" from the inside edge of each jamb **(photo A).** You'll install the moldings flush with these lines.

Place a length of molding against one side jamb, flush with the setback line **(photo B).** In the case of a double-hung window, hold the molding flush with the edge of the jamb. At the top and bottom of window moldings, mark the points where the horizontal and vertical setback lines meet. On doors, mark the moldings at the top only.

Cut the ends of the molding at a 45° angle, using a power miter saw **(photo C).** Measure and cut the other vertical molding piece, using the same method.

Drill pilot holes every 12" along the vertical moldings. To attach the moldings, first drive 4d finish nails near the inside edge of the moldings and into the jambs **(photo D).** Then, drive 6d finish nails near the outside edge of the molding and into the framing members.

Measure along the setback lines between the installed moldings and cut the top and bottom moldings, mitering the ends at 45° **(photo E).** If the window or door isn't perfectly square, make test cuts on scrap pieces to find the correct angle for the joints.

Drill pilot holes and attach the moldings with 4d and 6d finish nails, as described above.

Lock-nail the corner joints by drilling a pilot hole and driving a 4d finish nail through each corner **(photo F).** Set all nail heads below the surface of the molding, using a nail set. Fill the nail holes with wood putty. Then, stain or prime and paint the molding.

Mark a setback line 1/8" from the inside face of each jamb on doors and on windows that are not double-hung.

Mark the junction of the horizontal and vertical setback lines on each vertical molding.

Cut the vertical moldings, mitering the ends at a 45° angle.

Drill pilot holes and nail the vertical moldings in place.

Measure between the inside edges of the vertical moldings to get the length of the horizontal moldings.

Drill pilot holes and lock-nail the corner joints. Set all nails with a nail set, and fill the nail holes with wood putty.

Crown Moldings

Crown molding—also called "sprung cove" molding—is used to cover the joint between wall and ceiling surfaces. Styles vary in size and complexity of design. More elaborate crown moldings may consist of separate pieces, fastened to a square nailing strip that provides backing.

All crown moldings have an upper and lower edge, along the back side, that meet the ceiling and wall squarely. Use these edges to make accurate miter cuts. The trick is to cut the molding upside down. Using a power miter saw or hand miter box, set the wall-side edge of the molding against the back fence of the saw and the ceiling-side edge against the saw base.

Restoring a Ceiling

The two greatest enemies of a ceiling are gravity and water. The sheer weight of a ceiling surface can pull fasteners loose, allowing the surface to sag. Water from a leaky roof or pipe tends to collect in those low areas, adding more weight to the surface and further weakening the material. A sure sign of a water problem is discoloration and bubbling on the ceiling surface.

Repairing a wallboard ceiling is easy. You can refasten loose panels, replace damaged spots with a patch, or replace entire panels. Plaster, by contrast, is difficult to work with, and replastering is not an option for most do-it-yourselfers. As with plaster walls (pages 34 to 35), plaster ceiling repairs are limited to filling holes or patching larger areas with wallboard. You can conceal repairs to both ceiling types with wallboard compound and a variety of texture treatments.

It's important to note that plaster is heavy, and that widespread failure of the bond between the plaster coating and a lath foundation can be dangerous. Inspect your plaster ceiling carefully before attempting any repairs. If you find large spongy areas or extensive sags, it's time to call a professional who can install wallboard over the existing ceiling or tear off the old plaster and start over.

Photo courtesy of Crestline Windows

Proper ceiling maintenance is important for the visual appeal of any room as well as for the safety of your home.

Raising a Sagging Ceiling

Although wallboard isn't as heavy as plaster, it can still be too heavy for the fasteners that hold it to the ceiling joists, especially if those fasteners are nails. While it's not likely that the panels will fall, it's common for old wallboard ceilings to sag. In other cases, the fasteners stay put, but the panels don't. The presence of round depressions, about 1" in diameter, is a telltale sign that your wallboard ceiling is drooping.

Another common cause of sagging is water. Water from above will quickly find a low spot or a joint between wallboard panels, soaking through to the visible surface in a matter of minutes. Water in joints is especially damaging because it ruins the edges of two panels at once. If you have a water problem, be sure to fix the leak before repairing the ceiling.

The solution for most sagging problems is to prop up the sagging panels, using a T-brace, and fasten the wallboard to the ceiling joists with screws. If the wallboard edges have been damaged, use broad, thin washers to provide support for the weakened material.

Raising sagging panels may cause the existing fasteners to pop through the wallboard surface. If this happens, either pull the fasteners out or drive them back in.

To make a T-brace, cut a 2 × 4 board 1/2" longer than the height of the ceiling. Cut another 2 × 4 to 4 ft. and attach it to the end of the longer one so the two are perpendicular.

Set a piece of plywood or hardboard on the floor to use as a skid for the brace and to protect the floor surface. Position the brace under the lowest point of the sagging area **(photo A).** Set the bottom end on the skid and nudge it forward until the sagging panels are tight to the joists.

Because wallboard gets its strength from its paper skin, screws hold best if they depress the paper slightly without breaking through. Ideally, the screw head should be set $1/16$" below the surface. If your drill has a variable clutch setting, try a few test screws and adjust the clutch so it engages when the screw is at the proper depth **(photo B).**

Remove any loose tape from the joint between wallboard panels. Drive the screws with washers through the center of the joint and into the ceiling joists **(photo C).** Start at the end of the damaged area and work in one direction along the joint, driving a screw every 4" or at every joist.

To fasten sagging areas that aren't along a joint, align the screws with the existing fasteners to be sure you'll hit a joist. Drive a screw 2" from each existing fastener.

When the area is securely fastened, remove the T-brace. Repeat the process to repair other sagging areas.

Scrape off any loose chips of paint or wallboard around the joint and screws, using a wallboard knife. Fill the joint and depressions made by the fasteners with wallboard compound **(photo D).**

Cover large cracks or gaps with fiberglass wallboard tape before applying the compound. If necessary, texture the area to match (page 52).

Tools: *Drill, hammer, wallboard knife.*

Materials: *2 × 4 lumber, plywood, wallboard screws, washers, fiberglass wallboard tape, wallboard compound.*

Set the T-brace across the sagging area and straighten the post to force the wallboard panels against the joists.

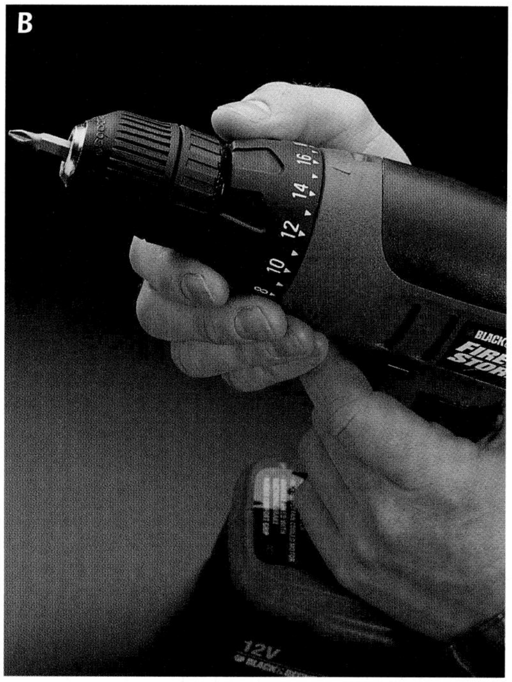

A clutch setting on a cordless drill can help you drive the wallboard screws to the proper depth.

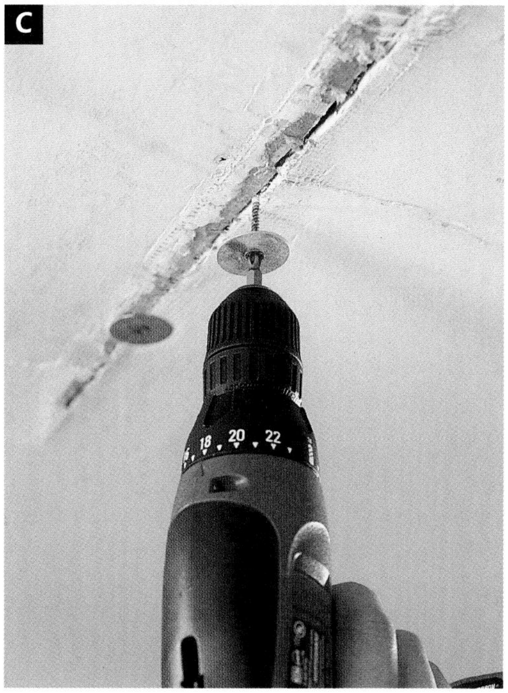

Install a screw every 4" where wallboard joints are parallel to joists. Otherwise, drive a screw into each intersecting joist.

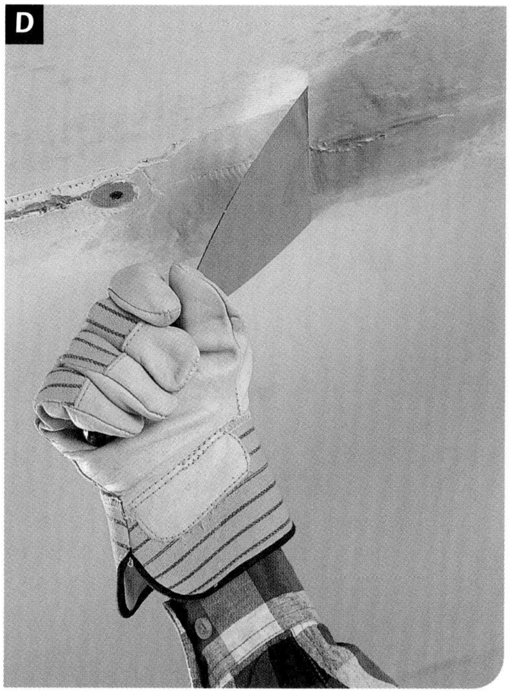

Cover the repair areas with wallboard compound. If necessary, smooth out the first coat with several thin coats.

Patching a Plaster Ceiling

Replastering damaged areas of a ceiling is a difficult job that requires special skills and experience with mixing plaster components. If your ceiling is generally in good condition, it's far easier to patch the damaged area with a piece of wallboard.

Helpful Hint

With texture paint and the right tool, you can make a patch disappear. Texture paints are available in premixed latex form or as a dry powder that you mix yourself to get the proper thickness. Use premixed paints for light stipple patterns and use powder for heavy adobe or stucco finishes.

Practice texturing on heavy cardboard until you get the pattern you want. Try these and other tools for texturing: long-nap paint roller, whisk broom, flat trowel, sponge, paintbrush.

Begin by cutting out a square or rectangular section around the damaged plaster. A patch with straight sides is easier to cut and the result will look better than if you cut the patch to fit an oddly shaped hole.

Use a framing square to mark the outline of the cutout. Then, score the surface of the plaster with a utility knife. This will help you break through the hard topcoat and will minimize any disturbance to the surrounding plaster.

Carefully chisel out the plaster, using a hammer and a masonry chisel **(photo A).**

If the plaster is installed over metal mesh, make the cutout extend from the center of one ceiling joist to the center of another so the patch will have adequate backing. If the plaster is installed over wood lath, fasten the patch directly to the lath.

Measure the dimensions of the cutout, as well as the thickness of the plaster. Cut the patch from a piece of wallboard with the same thickness as the plaster. Make the patch slightly smaller than the cutout to provide a gap for joint compound **(photo B).**

Position the patch over the cutout, and fasten it to the joists or lath with wallboard screws **(photo C).**

Cover the joints with fiberglass wallboard tape. Apply several thin coats of wallboard compound until the patch is smooth and level with the surrounding surface.

If your ceiling is textured, reproduce the effect over the patch, using a thin mixture of wallboard compound or texture paint.

Tools: Framing square, utility knife, hammer, masonry chisel, drill, wallboard knives.

Materials: Wallboard, screws, wallboard tape, wallboard compound.

A

Make a neat cutout by scoring the surface with a utility knife and chiseling out the plaster.

B

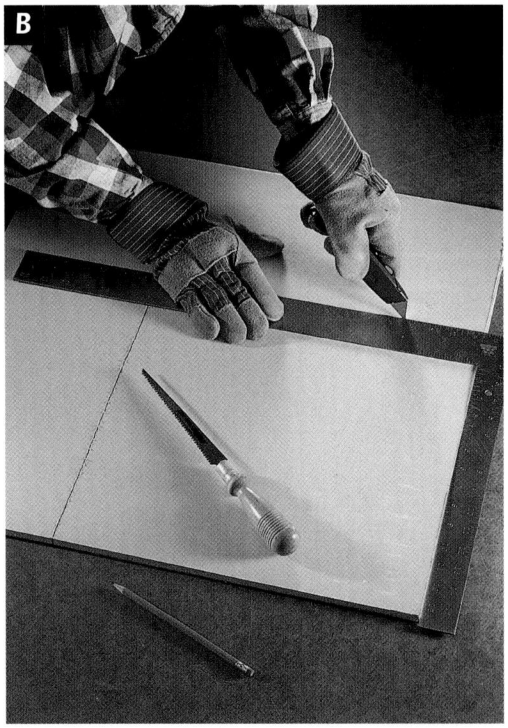

Cut the patch from a flat piece of wallboard, using a framing square and a utility knife.

C

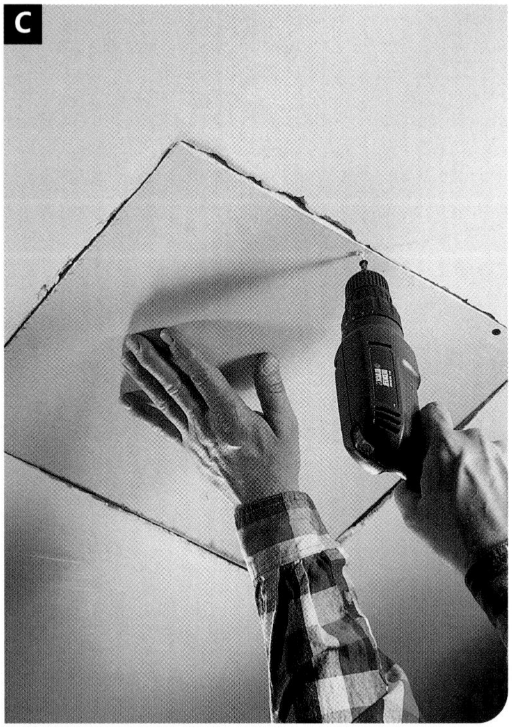

Secure the patch in place with wallboard screws. Space the screws 4" to 6" apart.

Patching a Wallboard Ceiling

Shut off all power to the area at the main service panel before cutting into the ceiling.

Use a framing square to draw a square outline around the damaged section. Then, make the cutout with a wallboard saw **(photo D).**

Cut a piece of plywood for backing. It should be narrow enough to fit into the hole and long enough to span the hole by 2" on opposite sides **(photo E).** Insert the plywood backing, and center it in the opening.

Fasten the backing with wallboard screws **(photo F).**

Cut a wallboard patch to fit the opening, and attach it by driving screws into the backing.

Tape the joints with fiberglass wallboard tape, and finish the area with wallboard compound.

Tools: *Framing square, wallboard saw, drill, wallboard knives.*

Materials: *Plywood, wallboard, screws, fiberglass wallboard tape, wallboard compound.*

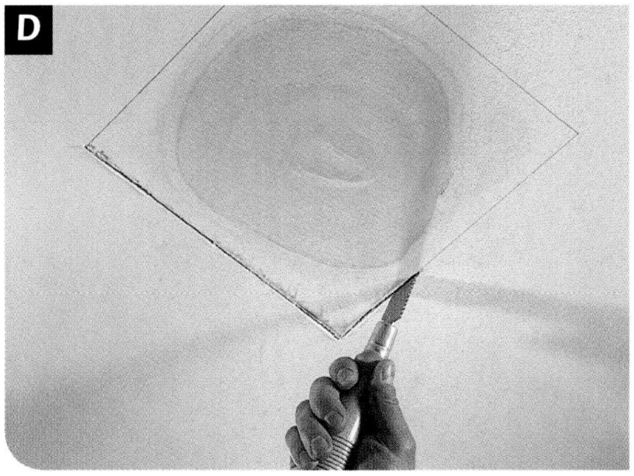

Cut out the ceiling damage with a wallboard saw.

Use a piece of plywood to provide backing for the patch.

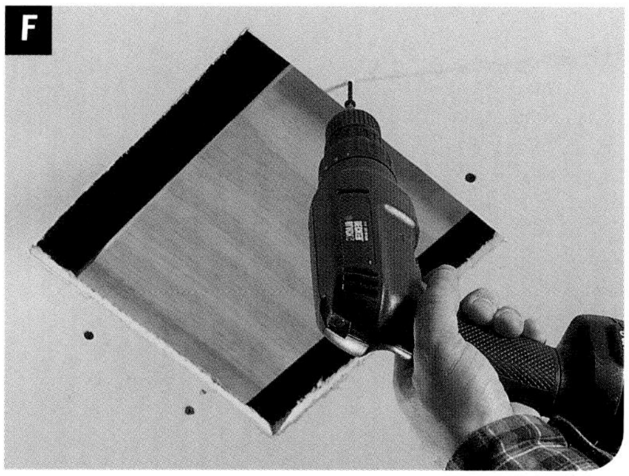

Secure the backing behind the opening with screws.

Replacing a Damaged Ceiling Tile

Acoustical ceiling tiles usually fit together with tongue-and-groove edges and attach to wood or metal furring strips nailed to the joists.

Cut out the center section of the damaged tile with a utility knife **(photo G).** Then, slide the edges away from the surrounding tiles.

Trim the upper lip of the grooved edges of the new tile, using a straightedge **(photo H).** Also remove one of the tongues, if necessary.

Apply construction adhesive to the furring strips **(photo I).** Install the new tile, tongue first, and press it into the adhesive.

To hold large tiles in place while the glue dries, make a brace with a flat board and a 2 × 4 post. Lay the board across the tile, and set the post between the board and the floor.

Tools: *Utility knife, straightedge.*

Materials: *Replacement tile, construction adhesive, board, 2 × 4.*

Cut the damaged tile into pieces with a utility knife.

Remove the upper (back side) lip of the grooved edges.

Apply construction adhesive and press the new tile into place.

Reducing Noise

The best time to soundproof is during construction, when framing is accessible and specialized soundproofing materials can be installed. You can improve soundproofing on existing doors, walls, and ceilings by adding the appropriate materials to cushion against sound transmission.

Sound transmission is rated by a system called Sound Transmission Class (STC). The higher the rating, the quieter the house. For example, loud speech can be understood through a wall rated at 40 to 35 STC. At 42 STC, loud speech is reduced to a murmur, and at 50 STC, loud speech can't even be heard.

Standard construction methods result in a rating of 32 STC. With the proper materials, you can increase the rating to 48 STC.

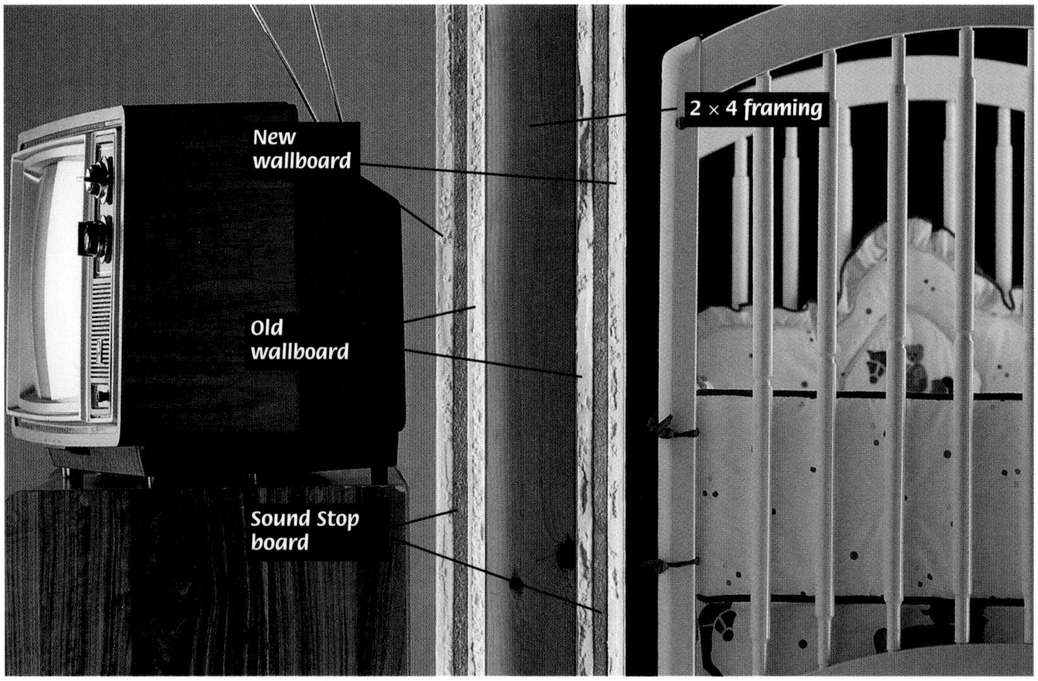

Existing walls can be soundproofed by adding layers of sound-absorbing panels and additional layers of wallboard.

Reducing Doorway Noise

A workshop or utility room door can transmit a lot of noise to the rest of the house, especially if it's a hollow-core door.

Reduce sound transmission by installing acoustical ceiling tiles to the side of the door where the most sound is produced **(photo A).** Cut the tiles to fit, using a straightedge and a utility knife. To minimize damage to the door surface, attach the tiles with dabs of hot glue or construction adhesive.

Prevent sound from escaping underneath the door by installing a door sweep **(photo B).** Use a hacksaw to cut the sweep to length, and install it so the vinyl skirt just touches the floor.

Tools: Utility knife, straightedge, glue gun, hacksaw, drill.

Materials: Acoustical ceiling tiles, construction adhesive, glue sticks, door sweep.

Acoustical tiles will absorb sound from workshop tools or utility room appliances.

A door sweep keeps sound from passing underneath doors.

Reducing Wall & Ceiling Noise

Sound travels from one room to another through cracks and air passages or by causing floor and wall elements to vibrate, creating reverberations in adjacent rooms. You can reduce noise by sealing around openings, such as doors, windows, and electrical outlets. Or, you can increase the density of your walls and ceilings by installing additional layers of wallboard, which will reduce vibrations.

A third method of reducing sound is to absorb it. Soft, porous materials, such as acoustical tile, fiberglass insulation, and Sound Stop—a fiber panel product—all absorb sound effectively.

For the best results, use a combination of these soundproofing methods to seal off, absorb, and block sound transmission throughout your house.

Seal gaps between the wall finishes and the floor with expandable foam **(photo C).** Remove door and window moldings and seal around the outside of the frames.

Stop sound transmission through electrical receptacle cutouts by installing neoprene slips behind the cover plates **(photo D).**

Adding layers to your existing wall or ceiling is the most effective way to block sound transmission between rooms. This requires you to install and finish new wallboard. If you have no experience with these tasks, consider hiring a professional for the job.

You can soundproof a wall by nailing 1/2" Sound Stop board over the existing surface **(photo E).** Use long wallboard nails and drive them into the wall studs. Then, glue 1/2" wallboard over the Sound Stop, using construction adhesive. Doing this to both sides of an insulated wall can raise the wall's STC rating to 50.

Soundproof ceilings by installing resilient steel "hat" channels over the ceiling surface, perpendicular to the existing framing **(photo F).** Space the channel 24" on center, and screw both flanges to the joists above. Attach 5/8" wallboard to the channels to increase the ceiling's STC rating to 44.

If you're finishing a basement, insulate between the floor joists with fiberglass batts, and install 5/8" wallboard over steel channels.

Remove the shoe molding and spray insulating foam along the bottom of walls to seal air passages between rooms.

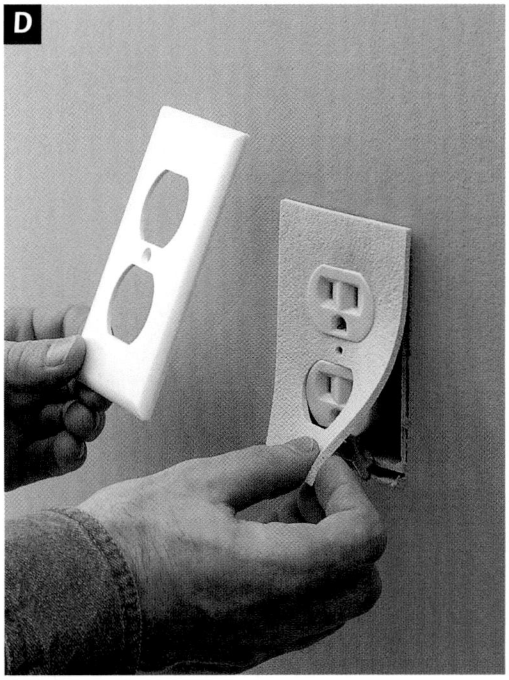

Insulate holes cut into wall surfaces for electrical outlets. Reinstall the coverplates over the neoprene seals.

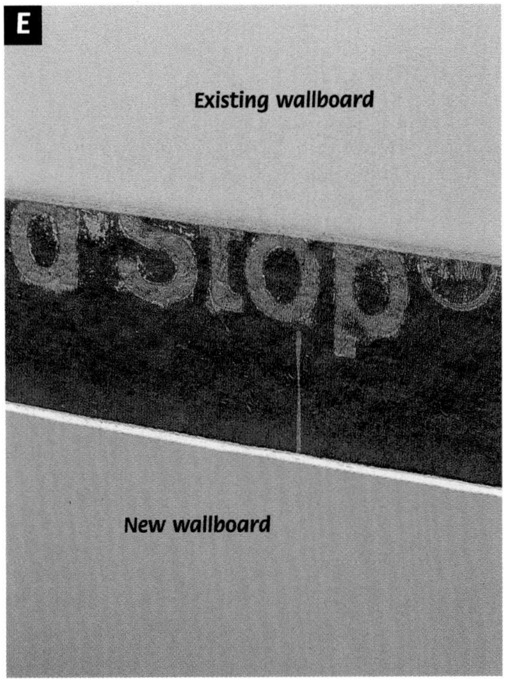

A layer of 1/2" Sound Stop board and 1/2" wallboard over your existing wall will increase the STC rating to 46 or better.

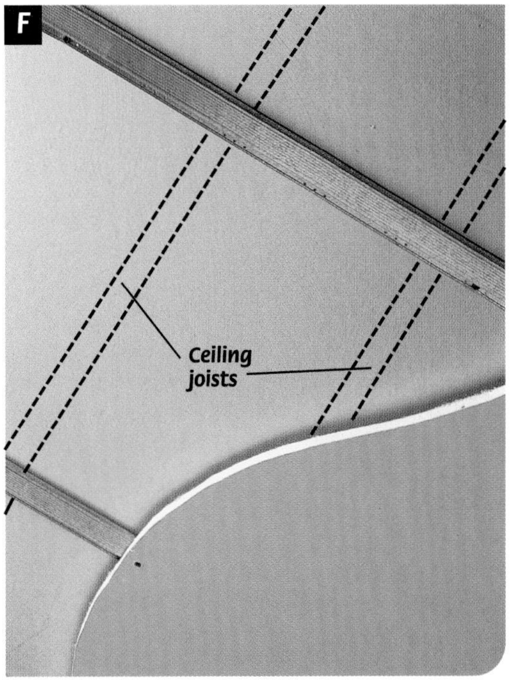

Resilient steel channels and 5/8" wallboard reduce sound vibrations passing through the ceiling from the floor above.

Painting

A new color scheme can dramatically change a room, and implementing this kind of change doesn't have to cost a fortune. Without changing expensive furniture or carpeting, you can transform an ordinary room into an an inviting living space.

The key to a successful paint job is careful attention to details. First, select a stepladder that will allow you to comfortably reach the surfaces you need to paint. If the job involves painting large, high surfaces, use a scaffold. Scaffolds make working at heights for extended periods of time safer and more convenient.

Safety is another detail that cannot be overlooked. Read the labels of all removal chemicals, primers, and paints for use and disposal instructions.

The quality of the materials and tools you use will also affect the quality of paint finishes. Buy the best quality tools and materials you can afford. Brushes and rollers will last for years if properly cleaned. With planning, you can buy only as much paint as you need.

Ladder Safety

Two quality stepladders and and an extension plank are all you need to paint most interior surfaces. With these materials you can build a simple, but sturdy, scaffold for painting high areas and ceilings. Choose tall stepladders and a strong, straight 2 × 10 plank, no more than 12 ft. long.

To build the scaffold, arrange the stepladders so they face one another with the steps to the inside. Make sure the ladder braces are locked, then run the plank through the steps of the two stepladders **(photo A).** Don't place the plank on the top step of either ladder: the upper part of the ladder can help you balance, and will keep you from stepping off the ends of the plank.

To build a scaffold on a stairway, you only need one stepladder. Run the extension plank through a step of the ladder, and place the other end on a stairway step **(photo B).** Adjust the scaffold so the plank is close to the wall. Make sure the ladder is steady, and check to see that the plank is level before stepping onto the platform.

You can purchase an extension plank from a home center, or rent one from a material dealer or rental outlet **(photo C).** When selecting a stepladder, always check the manufacturer's sticker, which is usually attached to the side **(photo D).** This sticker provides the weight ratings and the instructions for using

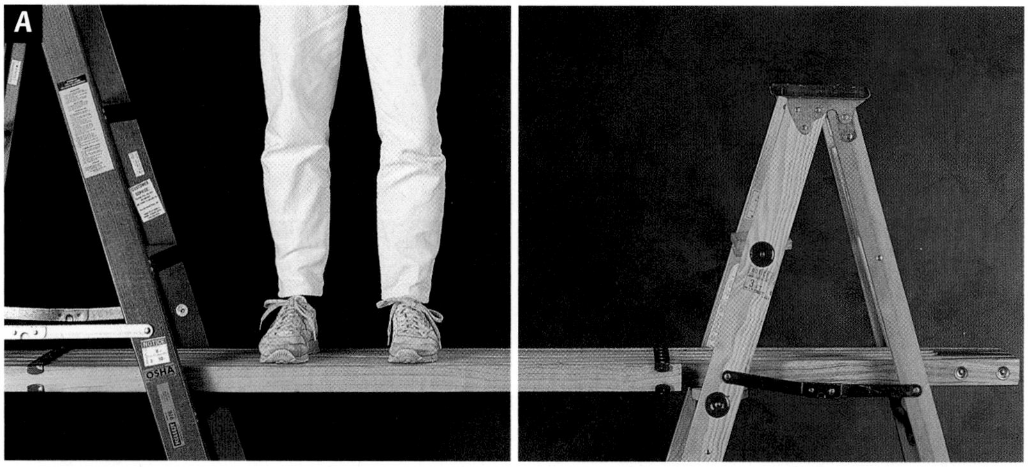

Make a scaffold for painting high areas and ceilings by running an extension plank through the steps of two stepladders.

For a stairway scaffold, run an extension plank through the step of a ladder, and place the other end on a stairway step.

the ladder correctly. Make sure to choose a ladder with a weight limit that will easily accommodate your weight, plus the additional weight of any tools or materials you plan to use while on the ladder.

The braces on a stepladder are critical for ensuring stability. Push braces completely down and make certain they're locked before you step onto the ladder **(photo E).** Also, check to see that the legs of the ladder are level and steady against the ground.

It's also important to periodically tighten the steps. Over time, the step braces can loosen. If a step is loose, tighten the nut with a wrench until it's secure **(photo F).**

Always position the stepladder between you and the area where you'll be painting. Keeping the ladder in front of you allows you to lean your body weight against the ladder for balance. Center your weight on the ladder **(photo G).** Don't stand on the top step, top brace, or on the utility shelf of the stepladder. Move the ladder often to avoid overreaching, which can cause the ladder to tip.

An adjustable ladder is often a good investment if you plan to do a lot of painting. These ladders can be purchased at home centers or rented from rental suppliers. The ladder adapts to many different work needs. It can be used as a single straight ladder, a stepladder, or as a base for a scaffold plank **(photo H).** Be sure to check the weight restrictions and read the manufacturer's directions before use.

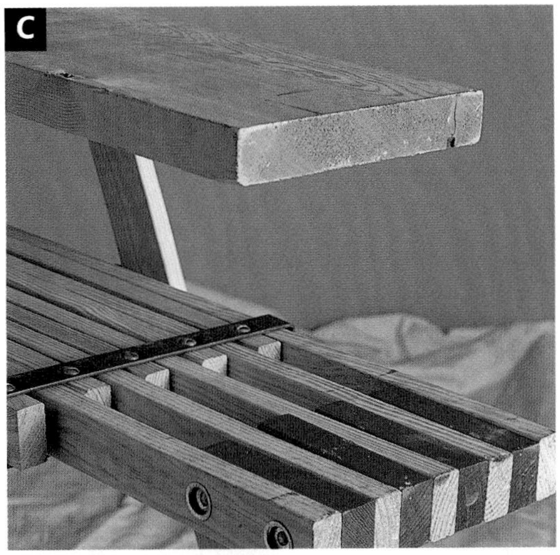

Buy extension planks from a home center, or rent them from a paint dealer or rental center.

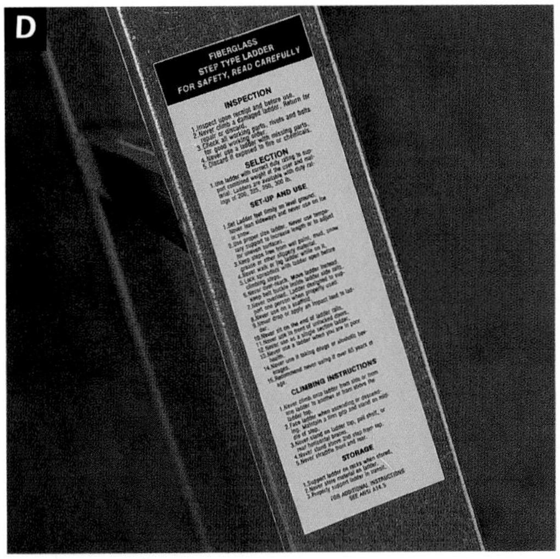

Read the manufacturer's sticker to find the weight ratings and instructions for correct use of the ladder.

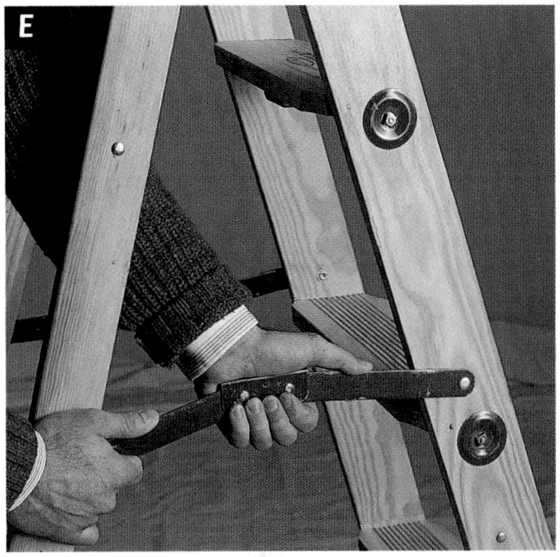

Push braces down until they are completely locked.

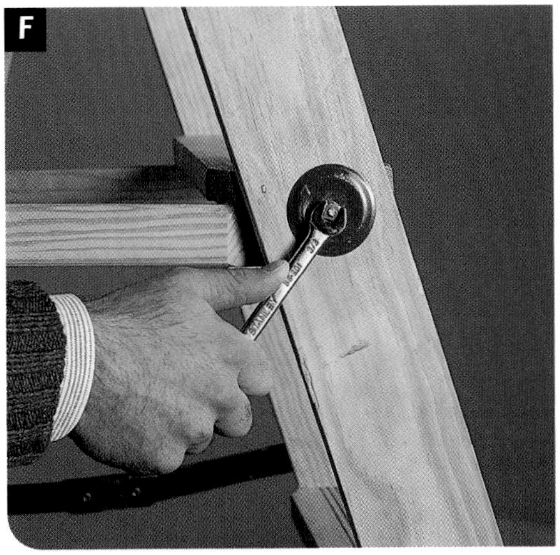

Keep steps tight by periodically checking them and tightening the braces when they need it.

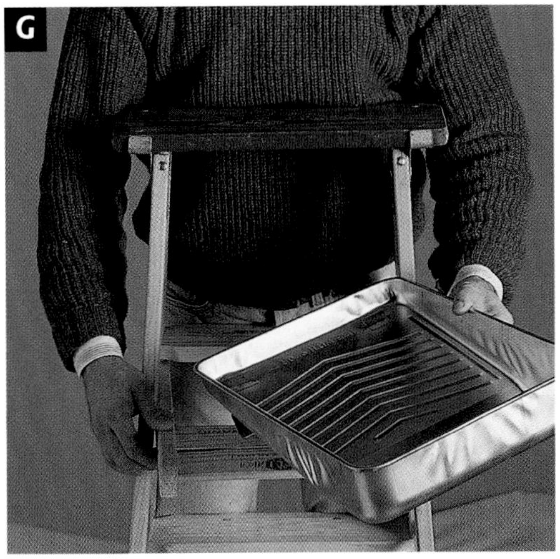

Center your weight on the ladder. Move the ladder often: don't overreach.

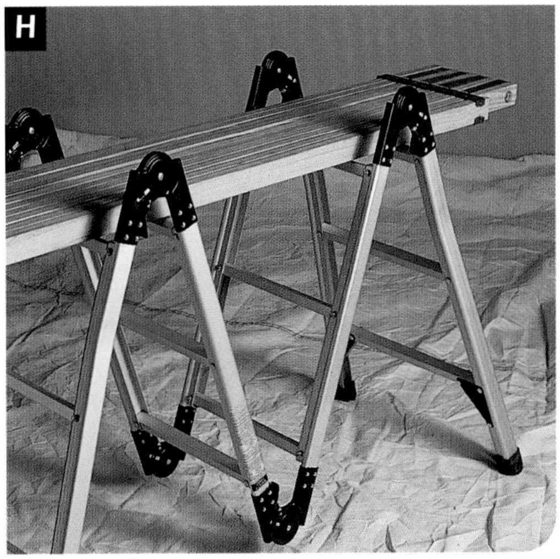

An adjustable ladder can be used as a straight ladder, a stepladder, or as a base for scaffold planks.

Safety Issues

Always read the label information on paint and solvent containers **(photo A).** Chemicals that pose a fire hazard are listed (in order of flammability) as: *combustible, flammable,* or *extremely flammable.* Use caution when using these products, and remember that the fumes are also flammable. Follow the instructions on the label for safe handling of the substance.

The warning "use with adequate ventilation" means that there should be no more vapor buildup than there would be if using the material outside. If a product label has the warning "harmful or fatal if swallowed," assume that the vapors are dangerous to breathe. Open doors and windows, and use a fan for ventilation **(photo B).** Use a respirator mask if you cannot ventilate the work area properly **(photo C).** If you can still smell paint or solvent vapors, the ventilation isn't adequate. If you are working with chemical stripper or cleaning products, or painting overhead, wear safety goggles to protect your eyes **(photo D).**

Paint chemicals don't store well. Buy only as much as is needed for the project and store them away from children. Don't use or store flammable materials, such as paint stripper, near an open flame or an appliance with a pilot light **(photo E).**

Never pour leftover paint thinner down a drain. Let used thinner stand until the solid material settles. Pour off the clear thinner and save it for reuse **(photo F).**

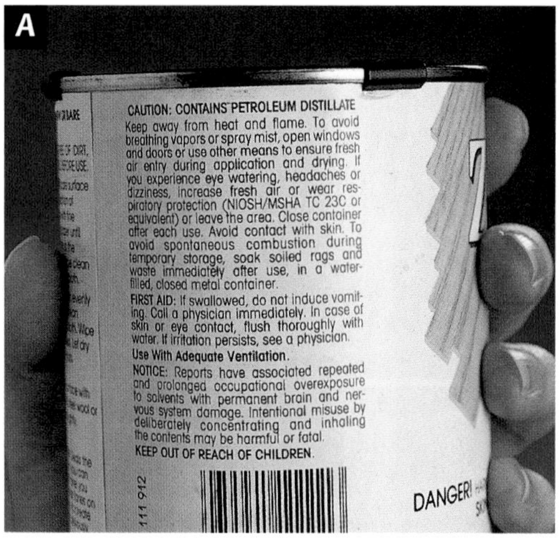

Read the label information for warnings and instructions for safe handling.

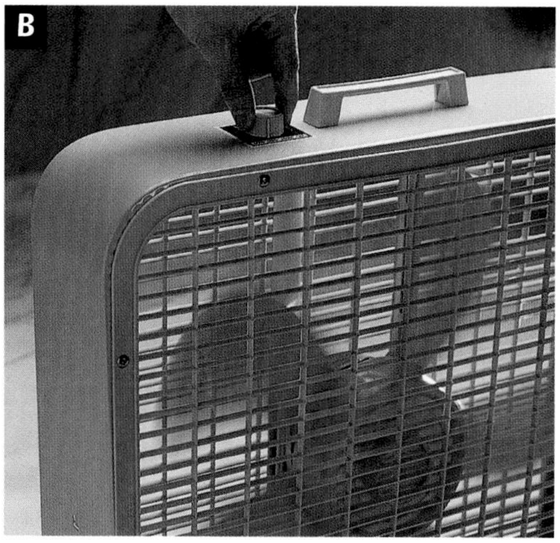

Open the windows and doors, and use a fan for ventilation.

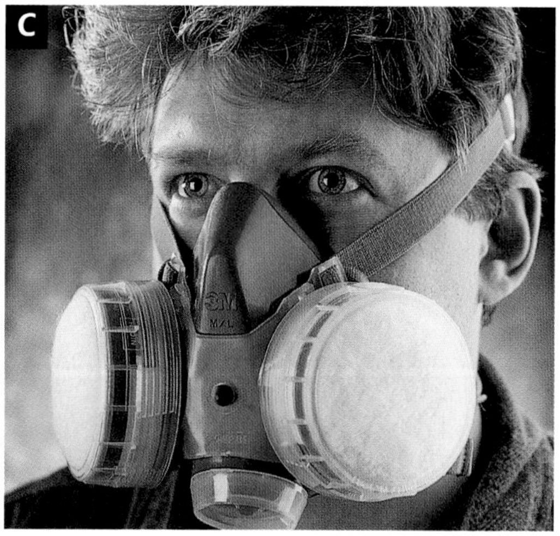

Wear a respirator mask if you cannot ventilate the work area.

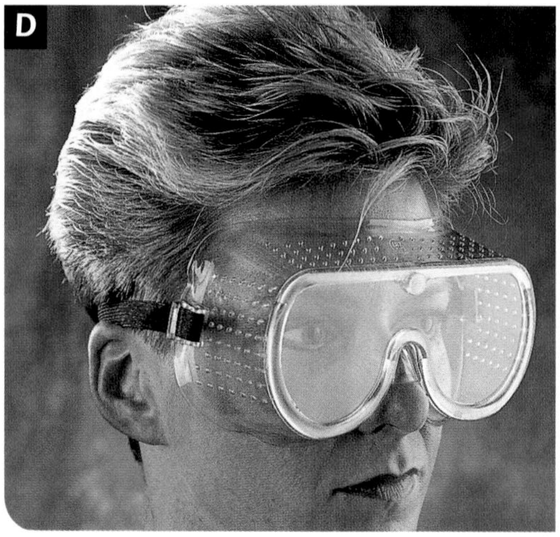

Wear safety goggles when using chemical stripper or cleaning products, or painting overhead.

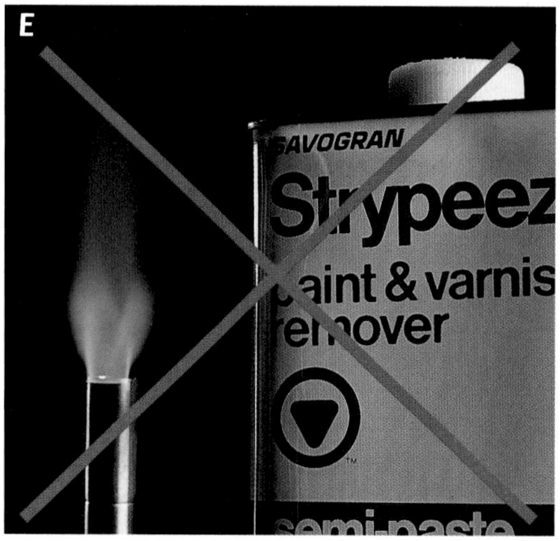

Don't use or store combustible or flammable chemicals near an open flame or an appliance with a pilot light.

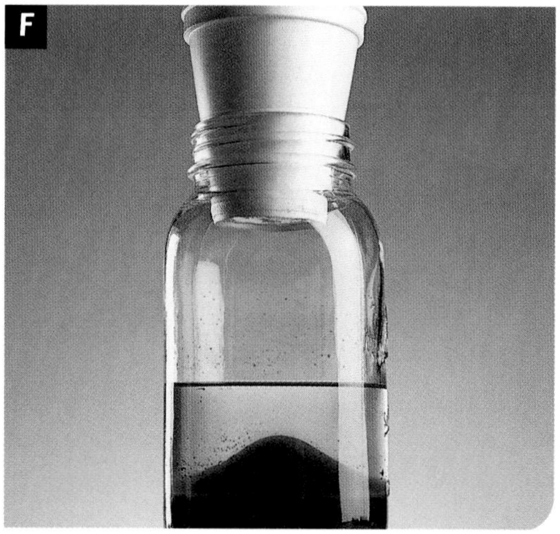

Let the solid material settle from paint thinner, then pour off the clear thinner and save it for reuse.

Tools & Materials for Preparation

You can reduce or eliminate most cleanup chores by buying the right prep tools. For example, buy plastic or paper throwaway pails for mixing patching plaster, taping compound, or spackle. When the patching compound hardens in the container, just throw it away.

Buy a variety of patching tools. You'll need a narrow putty knife for reaching into small spaces, and a wider knife or trowel that just spans the repair area when patching holes in walls or ceilings. A patching tool that overlaps both edges of the hole will let you patch with one pass of the tool, reducing tool marks and eliminating sanding. Use a sponge or wallboard wet sander to smooth plaster or wallboard compound while it's still soft, rather than waiting until it dries and becomes more difficult to sand.

Use the preparation products needed to create a smooth, clean surface on walls and ceilings before painting. Removal agents **(photo G)** help prepare surfaces for paint and wallcovering, and speed cleanup. Preparation liquids **(photo H)** allow you to quickly alter surfaces as necessary. Patching and masking products **(photo I)** are used to fill holes, patch cracks, and protect surfaces that won't be painted. Primers and sealers **(photo J)** provide a good base coat that bonds with paint or varnish finishes.

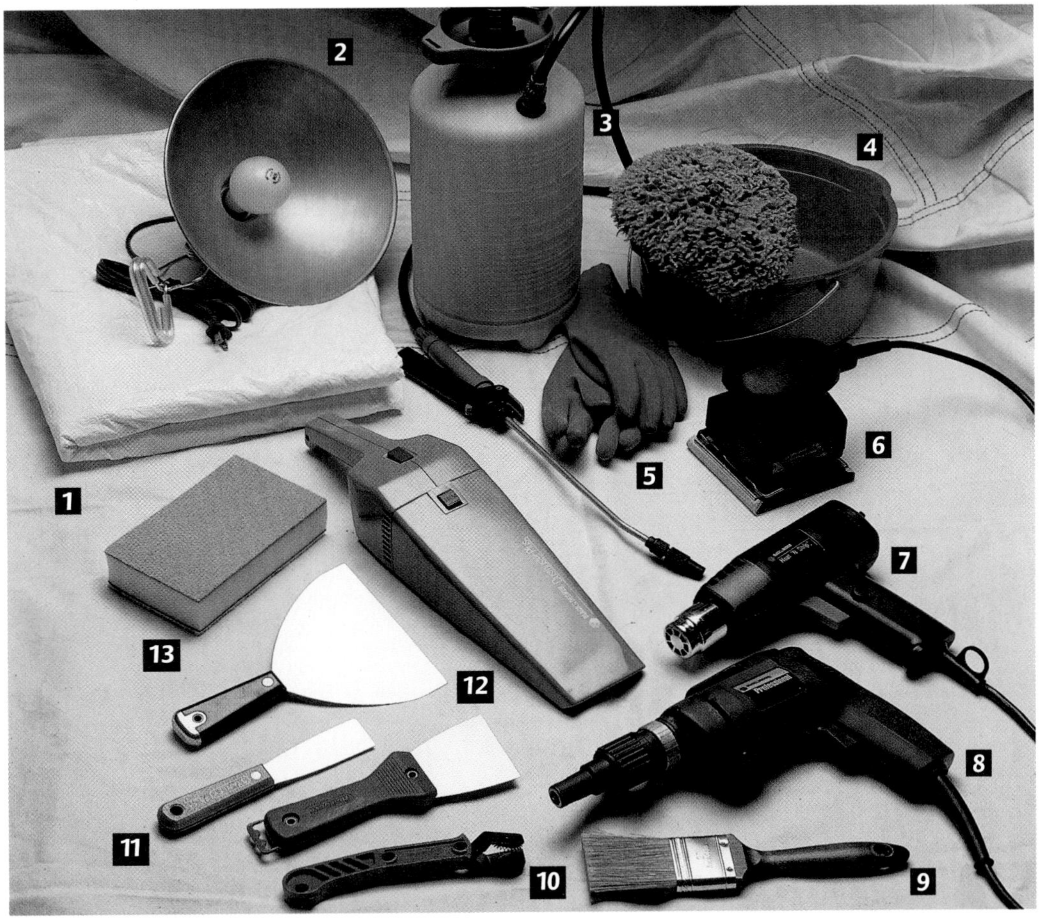

Tools and materials needed for paint preparation include: drop cloth (1), work light (2), pressure sprayer (3), natural sponge and bucket (4), rubber gloves (5), palm sander (6), heat gun (7), screw gun (8), paintbrush (9), perforation tool (10), wallboard knives (11), hand vacuum (12), and wet sander (13).

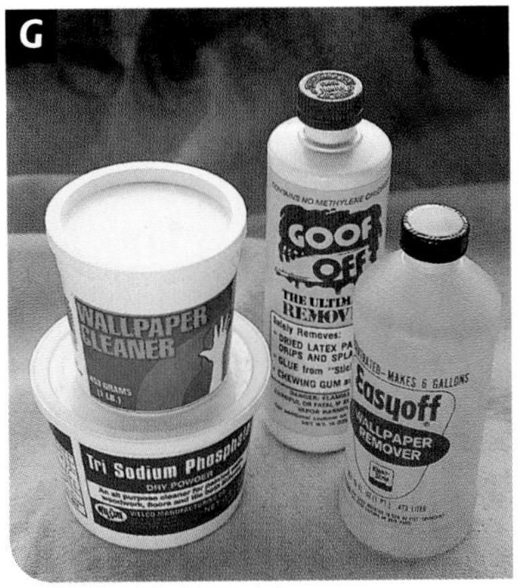

Wallpaper dough, cleanup solution, wallcovering remover, and TSP are removal agents.

Preparation liquids include paint remover, liquid deglosser, and latex bonding agent.

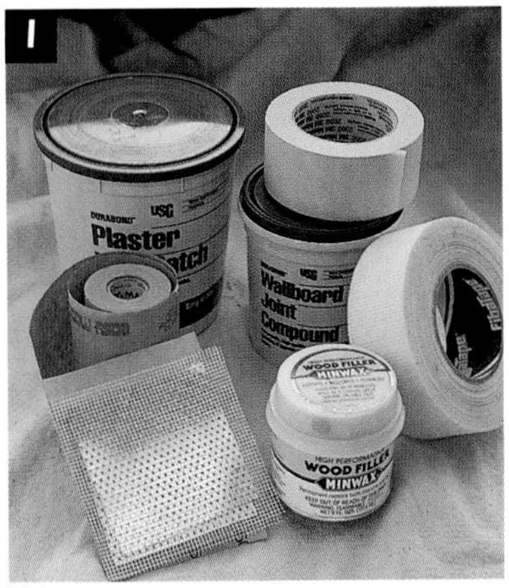

Patching and masking products protect surfaces and conceal holes and cracks.

Primer & sealers include sanding sealer, PVA primer, shellac, and alkyd wallboard primer.

Choosing Paint, Tools & Equipment

Paints are either water-base latex or alkyd-base. Latex paint is easy to apply and clean up, and is suitable for nearly every application. Some painters feel that alkyd paint has a smoother finish, but local regulations may restrict the use of alkyd-base paints.

Paints come in various sheens. Paint finishes range from flat to high-gloss enamels. Gloss enamels dry to a shiny finish and are used for surfaces that will be washed often, like bathrooms, kitchens, and woodwork. Flat paints have a nongloss finish and are used for most wall and ceiling applications.

Spend the extra money and buy high-quality paint, which will have better coverage than a bargain brand. Check the label to make sure the coverage is about 400 square feet per gallon. Bargain paints will require several coats to cover the same area. Always use a good primer over new surfaces before painting. Primer provides a durable base that keeps the finish coat from cracking or peeling.

Estimating Paint

Length of the wall or ceiling (feet) ×
Height of wall, or width of ceiling =
Surface area ÷
Coverage per gallon of chosen paint =
Gallons of paint needed

Choosing Paint

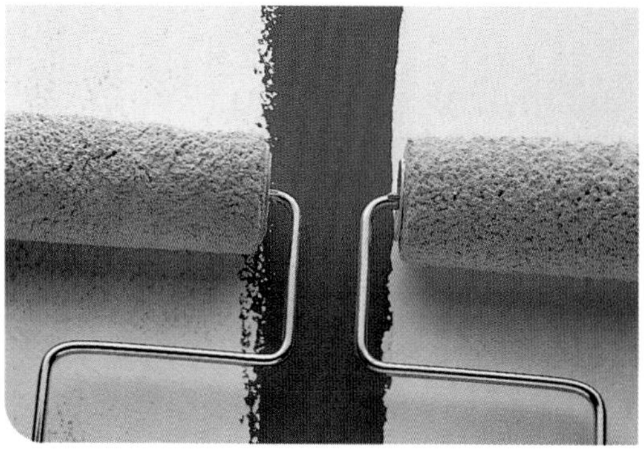

Bargain paints (left) may require two or three coats to cover the same area as one coat of a quality paint (right).

Gloss and medium-gloss enamels are best suited for woodwork and for kitchen and bathroom walls. Eggshell enamel and flat finishes are used for most other walls and ceilings.

Choosing Brushes

Choose a straight-edged 3" wall brush for cutting paint lines, a 2" straight-edged trim brush for woodwork, and a tapered sash brush for corners and window sashes. Buy brushes made of hog or ox bristles for alkyd-base paints. For latex paints, choose all-purpose brushes, which blend polyester, nylon, and sometimes animal bristles.

Buy quality brushes with a sturdy, reinforced ferrule made of noncorrosive metal. The brushes should have flagged (split) bristles and a chiseled end. Cheaper brushes have a blunt end, unflagged bristles, and a single spacer plug made of cardboard.

The three essential brushes for any paint job, from left: 3" straight-edged, 2" trim, and tapered sash.

Quality brushes have an angled tip and flagged bristles.

Choosing Rollers & Other Specialty Tools

A good paint roller is an inexpensive, time-saving tool that can last for years. Choose a standard 9" roller with a wire frame and nylon bearings. The roller should feel well balanced and should have a handle molded to fit your hand. The handle should also have a threaded end that lets you attach an extension for painting ceilings and high walls.

Roller covers are available in a wide variety of nap lengths, but most jobs can be done with 3/8" nap. Use a 1/4"-nap cover for very flat surfaces and a 1"-nap cover for rough surfaces. Select medium-priced synthetic roller covers that can be reused a few times before discarding. Bargain roller covers might shed fibers onto the painted surface and cannot be cleaned and reused. Rinse all roller covers in solvent to prevent lint.

Use more expensive lamb's wool roller covers when using most alkyd-base paints. Mohair covers work well with gloss alkyd paints, where smoothness is especially important.

Surfaces with unusual angles and contours are sometimes difficult to paint with standard rollers and brushes. Specialty tools make some painting situations easier.

Typical roller covers come in 1/4", 3/8", and 1" nap lengths.

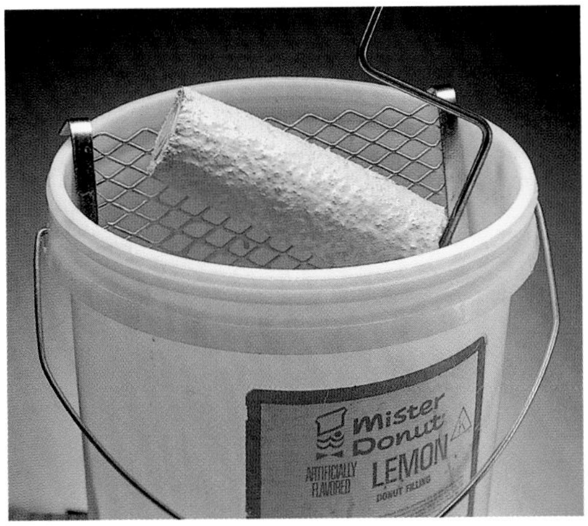

Use a five-gallon paint container and a paint screen for painting large areas faster.

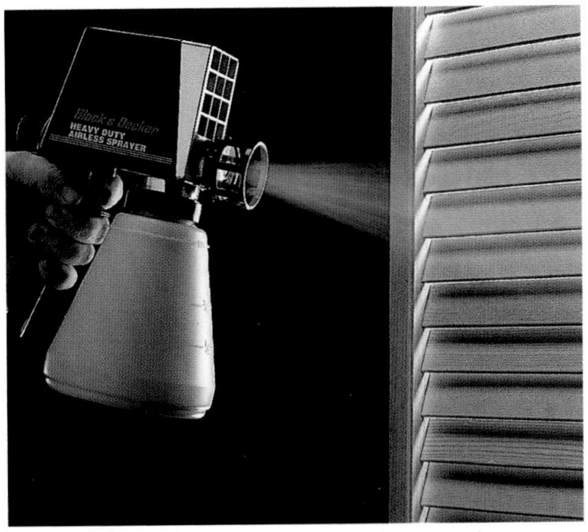

An airless paint sprayer is useful for painting large areas, or for irregular surfaces like louvered closet doors.

A bendable tool can be shaped to fit unusual surfaces, such as the fins of cast-iron radiators or window shutters.

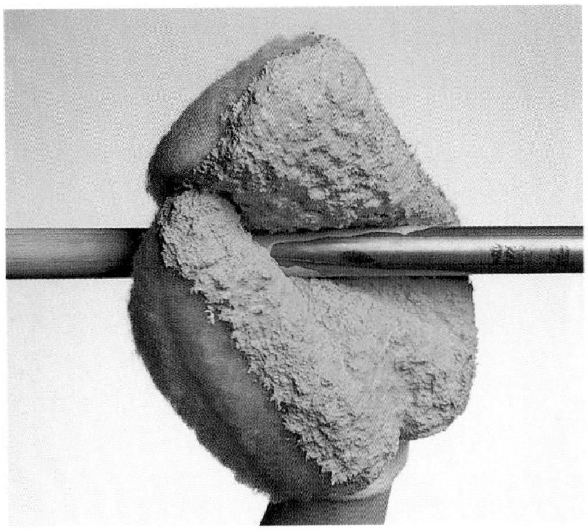

Use a paint glove to simplify painting pipes and other contoured surfaces, like wrought iron.

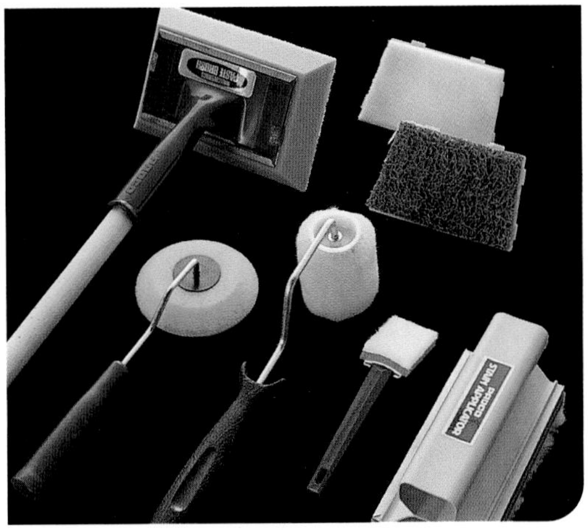

Paint pads and specialty rollers come in a wide range of sizes and shapes to fit different painting needs.

Preparing to Paint

Before painting or refinishing wood, clean, repair, and sand it. If the old paint is heavily layered or badly chipped, strip it down to the bare wood before repainting.

If you use a heat gun, take care not to let it scorch the wood or surrounding surfaces. Never use a heat gun after using chemical strippers: the chemical residue can be vaporized or ignited by the heat.

If you use a chemical paint stripper, wear protective clothing and safety gear, including eye protection and a respirator. Follow the label directions for safe use, and keep the work area well ventilated.

Tools: *Heat gun, scraper or putty knife, paintbrush, bucket, rubber gloves, safety goggles.*

Materials: *Chemical stripper, steel wool, denatured alcohol.*

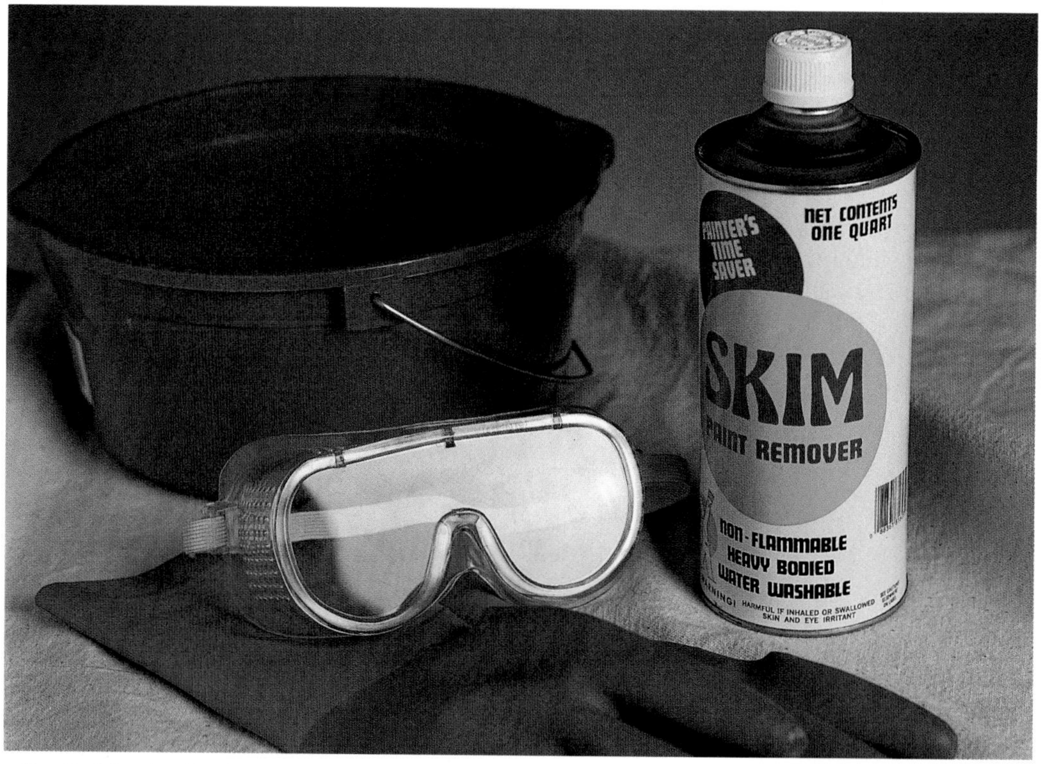

Follow the label directions for safe use of chemical strippers. Wear heavy rubber gloves and eye protection, use drop cloths, and open windows and doors for ventilation.

Removing Old Paint

To strip wood with a heat gun, hold the heat gun near the wood until the paint softens and just begins to blister **(photo A).** Overheating can make the paint gummy, or scorch the wood. Remove the softened paint with a scraper or putty knife **(photo B).** Sand away any remaining paint residue.

To strip wood with a chemical stripper, apply a liberal coat of stripper to the surface, using a paintbrush or steel wool **(photo C).** Let it stand until the paint begins to blister. Scrape away the paint with a putty knife, scraper, or steel wool **(photo D).** Rub the stripped wood with denatured alcohol and steel wool to help clean the grain. Then wipe the wood with a wet sponge or cloth dampened with solvent, as directed on the stripper label.

Soften the paint with a heat gun.

Remove the softened paint with a scraper.

Brush chemical stripper onto the wood.

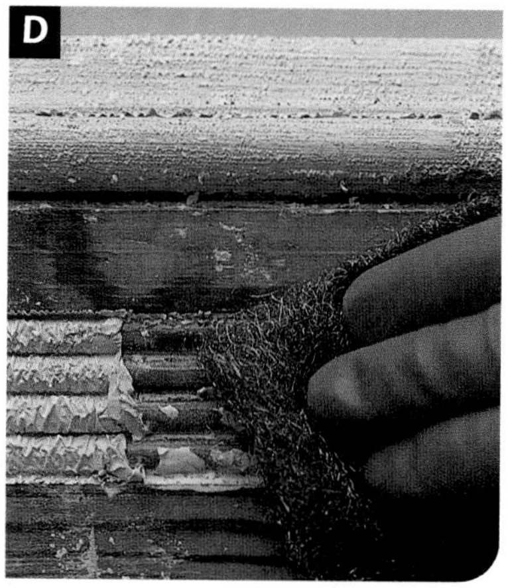

Scrape away the paint with steel wool.

Preparing Painted Woodwork

To prepare a wood surface for painting, wash it with a TSP solution, then rinse it clean with a sponge and water. Scrape away any peeling or loose paint **(photo E).** Strip badly chipped woodwork (page 62).

Use a putty knife to apply latex wood patch or spackle to any nail holes, dents, or other damaged areas **(photo F).** Allow the compound to dry.

Sand the surfaces with 150-grit sandpaper until they're smooth to the touch **(photo G).** Wipe the surface with a tack rag before priming and painting.

Tools: *Bucket, putty knife.*

Materials: *TSP, cloth, sponge, latex wood patch or spackle, 150-grit sandpaper, tack rag.*

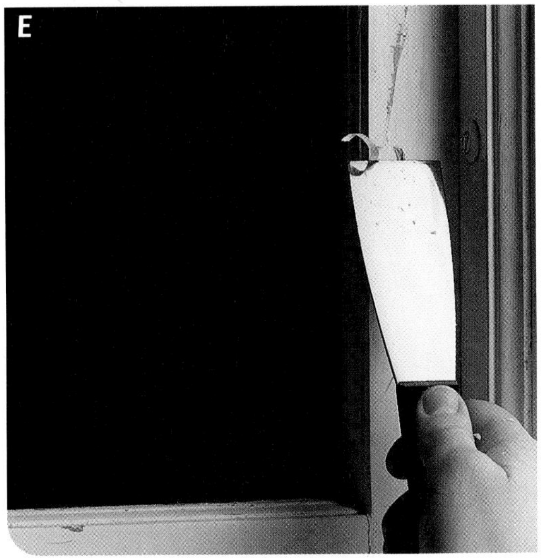

Use a putty knife to scrape off all loose paint.

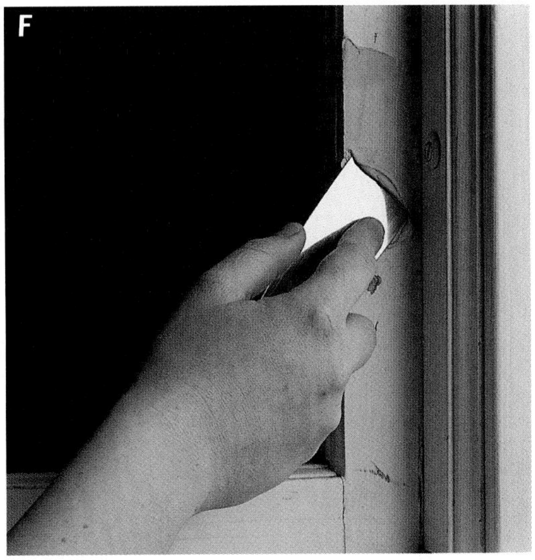

Apply wood patch to damaged areas with a putty knife.

Sand the surface smooth with 150-grit sandpaper.

Patching Varnished Woodwork

To renew varnished wood, clean it with a soft cloth and odorless mineral spirits **(photo H).** Apply a tinted wood putty to any holes and dents, using a putty knife **(photo I).** Allow the patch to dry, then lightly sand the area with 150-grit sandpaper. Wipe away dust particles with a tack rag, then restain the patched areas to match the surrounding wood. When the stain is completely dry, touch up the varnish.

Tools: *Putty knife, paintbrush.*

Materials: *Cloth, mineral spirits, tinted latex wood putty, 150-grit sandpaper, tack rag, stain, varnish.*

Clean woodwork with a soft cloth and mineral spirits.

Apply wood patch to holes and dents using a putty knife.

Cleaning Concrete

Preparation is especially important when the surface to be painted is a concrete floor, such as in a laundry room or workshop.

First, sweep and scrape off the dirt from the floor. Clean off any grease, oil, and other contaminants, using a cleaning solution. Rinse the floor well to remove all traces of the cleaning solution.

Next, etch the concrete with a muriatic acid solution. **Caution: muriatic acid is strong enough to burn skin and eyes.** Before you begin the etching process, put on the proper safety gear. You'll need chemical-resistant rubber gloves, splashproof goggles, and rubber footwear. If you can't ventilate the work area, wear a dual-cartridge respirator.

Mix a solution to etch the floor by adding one part muriatic acid to three parts water (don't add the water to the acid). Apply the solution at a rate of one gallon per 100 sq. ft. and scrub the floor with a stiff-bristled brush **(photo A).** Leave the solution on the floor until it stops bubbling. Rinse the floor thoroughly with clean water; wipe it down with a damp sponge mop to eliminate puddles. If the floor isn't dry in four hours, repeat the rinsing procedure.

After the floor is completely dry, vacuum it to remove the powder residue left by the muriatic acid solution. You can now paint the floor with an alkyd or urethane-latex floor and deck enamel.

Tools: *Broom, scraper, bucket, rubber gloves, safety goggles, rubber boots, dual-cartridge respirator, stiff-bristled brush, sponge mop, shop vacuum.*

Materials: *Cleaning solution, muriatic acid.*

Scrub the muriatic acid solution into the floor with a stiff-bristled brush.

Masking & Draping

For fast, mess-free painting, shield any surfaces that could get splattered. Remove lightweight furniture, then move heavier pieces to the center of the room and cover them with plastic. Cover the floors with 9-ounce canvas drop cloths that will absorb paint splatters.

If you're painting only the ceiling, drape the walls and woodwork with sheet plastic to prevent splatters. Press the top edge of 2"-wide masking tape or painter's tape along the top edges of the wall, leaving the bottom half of the tape unattached **(photo B).** Hang sheet plastic under the bottom half of the masking tape, draping the walls and baseboards **(photo C).**

When painting walls, mask the baseboards, window casings, and door casings with pregummed masking paper, masking tape, or painter's tape. Press one edge of the tape against the woodwork where it meets the wall **(photo D).** Leave the outside edge of the tape loose. After applying tape, run the tip of a putty knife along the inside edge of the tape to seal it against seepage **(photo E).**

If you're also painting the windows, try using a liquid masking product, rather than masking off the glass with tape. This acrylic latex product is specially formulated to prime and seal wood trim and to mask off the glazing quickly and efficiently. Paint the thick, white paste onto the trim, lapping over onto the glass.

When the masking product dries, it forms a clean, thin sheet that sticks solidly to the wood but peels away from the glass quite easily, leaving a clean, unpainted surface.

After painting, masking tape and paper should be removed just as soon as the paint is too dry to run.

Tools: *Putty knife, paintbrush, masking tape dispenser.*

Materials: *Drop cloth, sheet plastic, 2" masking tape or painter's tape, pregummed masking paper, liquid masking product.*

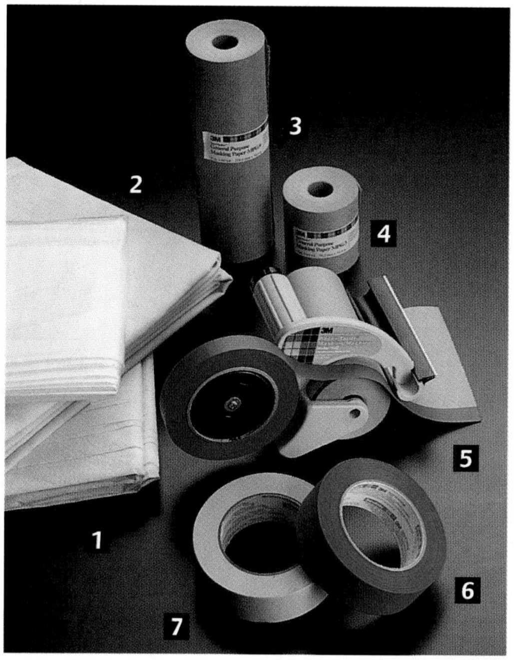

Masking and draping materials: plastic drop cloth (1); canvas drop cloth (2); masking papers (3),(4); masking tape dispenser (5); painter's tape (6); and masking tape (7).

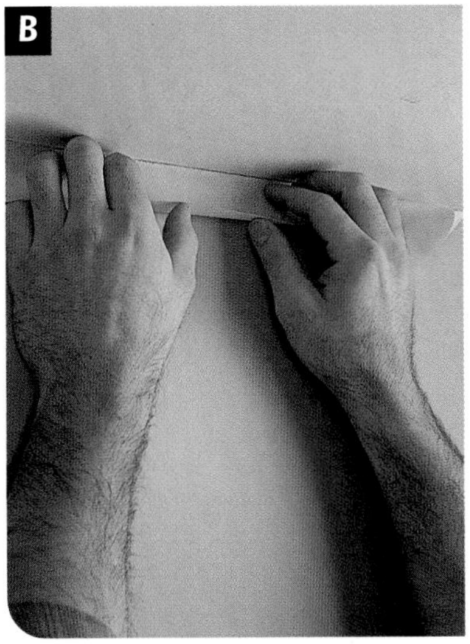

Press the top half of 2"-wide masking tape along the top edge of the wall.

Hang the sheet plastic under masking tape.

Cover the edges of all wood moldings with masking paper.

Run the tip of a putty knife along the inside edge of the masking paper to seal it.

Making Final Preparations

For professional-quality results, sand the surfaces with 150-grit sandpaper and a pad sander **(photo F).** Sanding dulls the surface so it will accept new paint. Wipe dust from the sanded surfaces with a tack rag. For woodwork, remove the dust with a tack rag, then apply a liquid deglosser with a clean cloth **(photo G).**

Vacuum dust from windowsills and window tracks **(photo H).** Before painting, clean the room thoroughly to eliminate dust that might settle on wet paint. Turn off forced-air furnaces and air conditioners so the fan won't circulate dust in the area being painted.

Tools: *Pad sander, rubber gloves, hand or shop vacuum.*

Materials: *150-grit sandpaper, cloth, tack rag, liquid deglosser.*

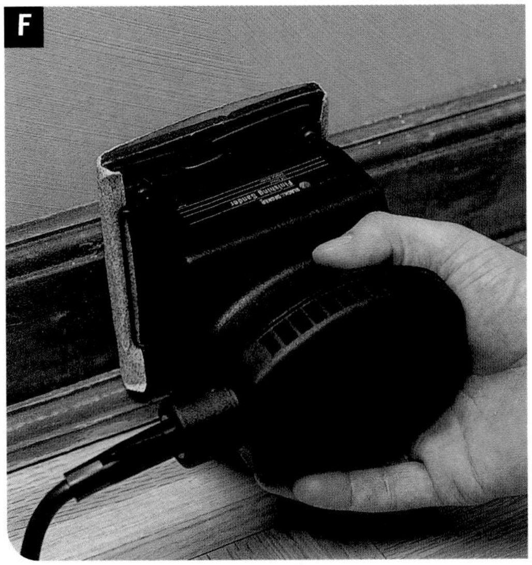

Sand the surfaces that will be painted, using 150-grit sandpaper.

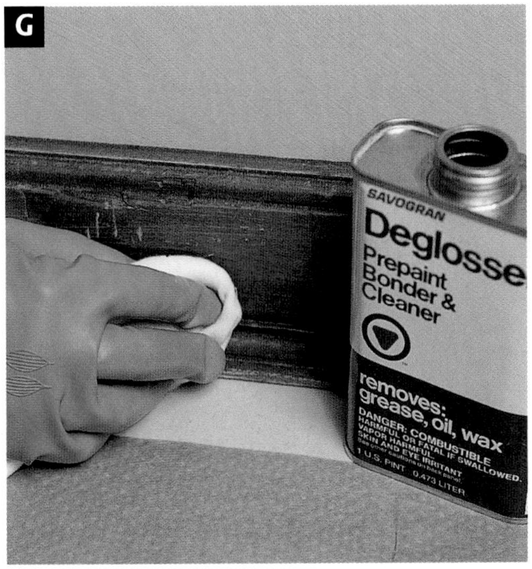

Remove dust from woodwork, then apply liquid deglosser.

Vacuum dust from windowsills and window tracks.

Applying Primers & Sealers

Primers are used to seal surfaces that will be painted. Primer is white, but it can be tinted to color-match the finish paint you plan to use **(photo A).** If you're painting woodwork, clean, patch, and strip the wood as needed (pages 62 to 63). Apply an alkyd- or latex-based primer to all bare wood and patched areas **(photo B).**

For woodwork that will be varnished, apply a clear wood sealer before varnishing. Wood often has both hard and soft grains, as well as a highly absorbent end grain. Applying a sealer helps close the wood surface so that the varnish is absorbed evenly in different types of wood grain. Unsealed wood may dry to a mottled finish when varnished.

Patched areas and wallboard seams that have been treated with patching material or wallboard compound can absorb paint at a different rate than the surrounding areas, and often show or "shadow" through the finished paint. To avoid shadowing, spot-prime these areas with a PVA primer **(photo C).**

All gloss surfaces, such as windows, trim, and doors painted with semi-gloss or gloss paints, must be roughened and primed before painting. Sand these areas with a pad sander and 150-grit sandpaper **(photo D).** Remove the dust with a tack cloth, then prime the surfaces with a quality primer. The primer provides "tooth" for the new coat of paint and prevents the finish coat from peeling off.

Seal textured surfaces, such as ceilings, with a PVA or alkyd primer. Textured ceilings and walls soak up a lot of paint, which makes it difficult to apply paint evenly. Use a long-nap roller to apply the primer and the finish coat **(photo E).**

Tools: *Paintbrush, paint roller, pad sander.*

Materials: *Alkyd- or PVA-based primer, color base, clear wood sealer, 150-grit production sandpaper.*

Tint primer with a color pigment, or ask your dealer to tint the primer.

Seal raw wood with a primer before painting or a clear sealer before varnishing.

Spot-prime minor repair areas on plaster or wallboard with PVA primer.

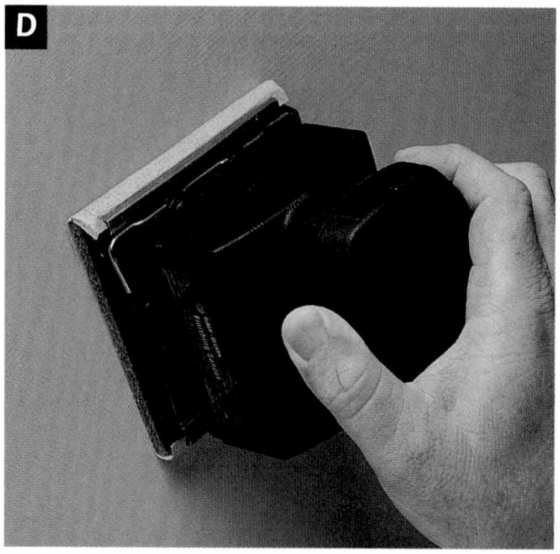

Roughen gloss surfaces with fine sandpaper, then apply a primer to the surfaces.

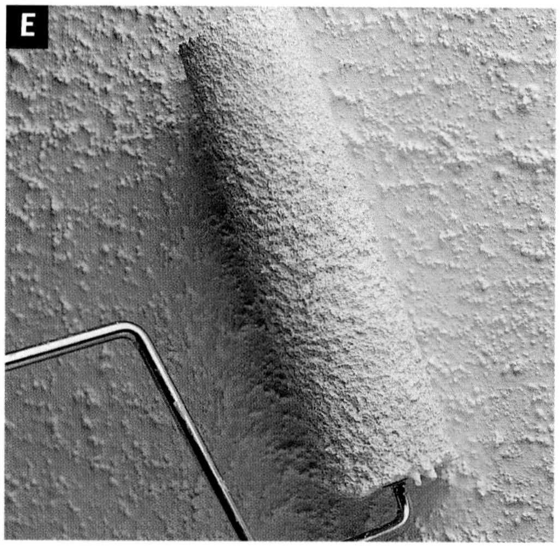

Seal textured surfaces with a PVA or alkyd primer.

Preparing Surfaces for Painting

Surface to be Painted	Preparation Steps	Primer Type
Unfinished wood.	• Sand surface. • Wipe with damp cloth to remove grit. • Apply primer.	Fast-drying oil-based or latex primers.
Previously painted wood.	• Wash surface and rinse with clear water; allow to dry. • Sand surface lightly, removing any loose paint chips. • Wipe with damp cloth to remove grit. • Apply primer to any areas of bare wood.	Fast-drying oil-based or latex primer, only on areas of bare wood.
Previously varnished wood.	• Wash surface and rinse with clear water; allow to dry. • Sand surface to degloss. • Wipe with damp cloth to remove grit. • Apply primer.	Fast-drying oil-based or latex primer.
Unfinished wallboard.	• Dust with hand broom, or vacuum with soft brush attachment. • Apply primer.	Flat latex primer.
Previously painted wallboard.	• Clean surface to remove any grease and dirt.	Flat latex primer, only if painting over dark, strong colors.
Unpainted plaster.	• Sand surfaces as necessary. • Dust with hand broom, or vacuum with soft brush attachment. • Apply primer.	Polyvinyl acrylic primer.
Previously painted plaster.	• Wash surface and rinse with clear water; allow to dry thoroughly. • Fill any cracks with spackling compound. • Sand surface to degloss. • Apply primer, if necessary.	Polyvinyl acrylic primer, only if painting over dark, strong colors.

Using a Paintbrush

Painting with a brush is a three-step process: The paint is applied, distributed, and then smoothed out. Even application eliminates runs and drips and avoids the lap marks and incomplete coverage that can result from trying to stretch paint too far.

Start by dipping the brush directly into the can, loading one-third of the bristle length. Dipping any deeper will overload the brush. Tap the bristles against the side of the can. Don't drag the brush against the lip of the can, which causes the bristles to wear.

Use the narrow edge of the brush to cut in the edges, pressing just enough to flex the bristles **(photo A).** Brush the wall corners, using the wide edge of the brush **(photo B).**

Paint the open areas inside the cut-in edges before the brushed paint dries. Paint large areas with two or three diagonal strokes. Hold the brush at a 45° angle, pressing just enough to flex the bristles. Distribute the paint with horizontal strokes **(photo C).** Smooth off the surface by drawing the brush vertically from top to bottom. Use light strokes and lift the brush from the surface at the end of each stroke **(photo D).**

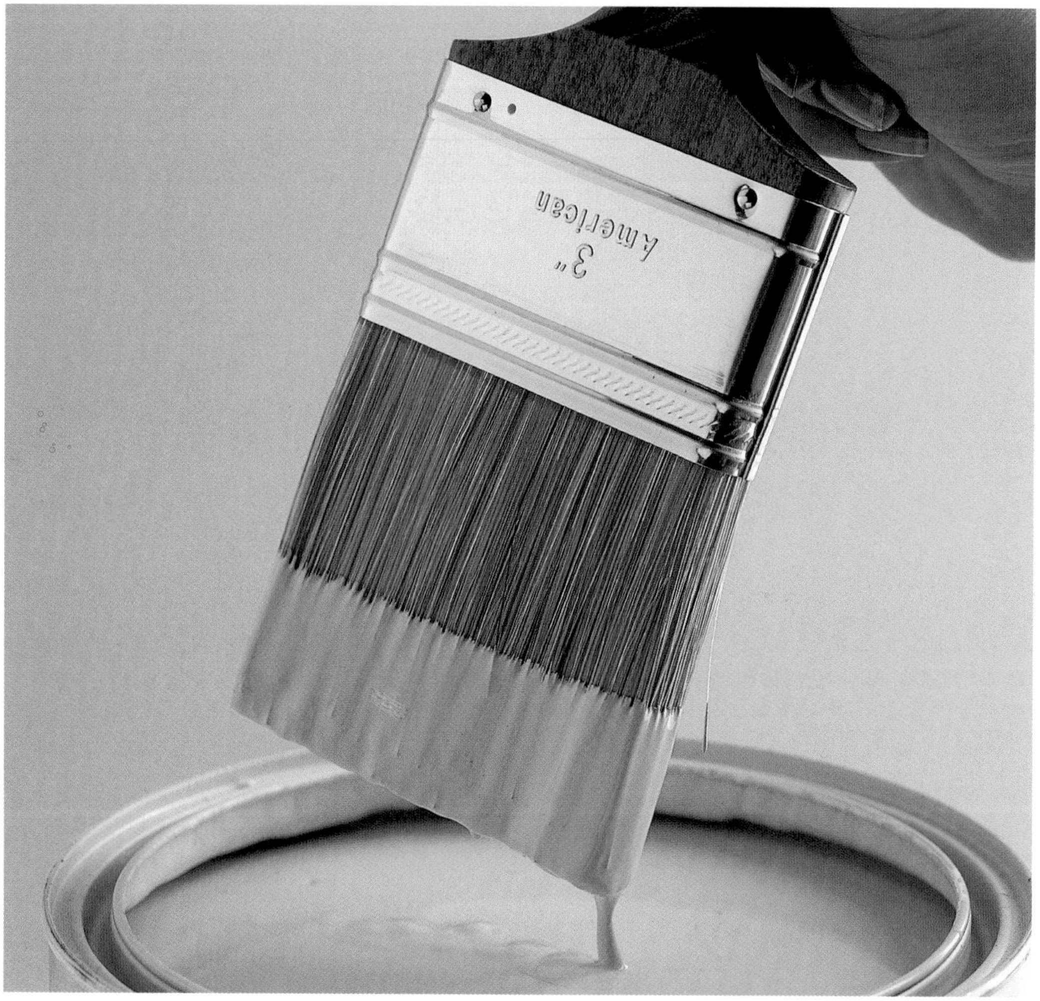

Dip the brush directly into the can, loading one-third of the length of the bristles with paint.

A

Cut in the edges using the narrow edge of the brush.

B

Cover the wall corners using the wide edge of the brush.

C

Apply the paint with diagonal strokes, then distribute it with horizontal strokes.

D

Create a smooth surface by drawing the brush vertically from top to bottom.

Using a Roller

Just as with a brush, painting with a roller is a three-step process in which the paint is applied, distributed, and smoothed.

The first step is to remove lint and open the roller fibers by priming the roller cover with water (when painting with latex) or mineral spirits (when painting with alkyd paint). Squeeze the excess liquid from the roller, then fill the paint tray reservoir with paint.

To load the roller, dip it fully into the reservoir. Using a back-and-forth motion, roll the roller over the textured ramp to distribute paint evenly on the nap. The roller should be full, but not dripping.

Make an upward diagonal sweep about 4 ft. long on the surface **(photo E).** Use slow strokes to avoid splattering. Draw the roller straight down from the top of the diagonal sweep. Move the roller to the beginning of the diagonal and roll up to complete the unloading of the roller **(photo F).**

Distribute the paint over the section with horizontal back-and-forth strokes **(photo G).** Smooth off the area by lightly drawing the roller vertically from top to bottom **(photo H).** Lift the roller and return it to the top of the area after each stroke.

Paint ceilings and walls easily without a ladder by attaching a 4-ft. extension handle to the handle of the roller.

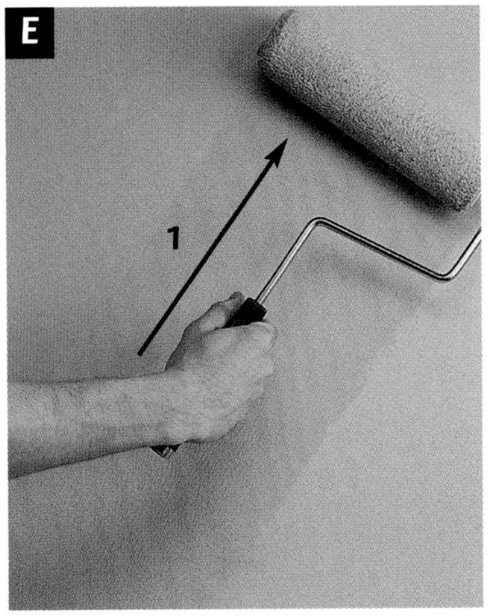

Begin with a 4-ft.-long diagonal stroke.

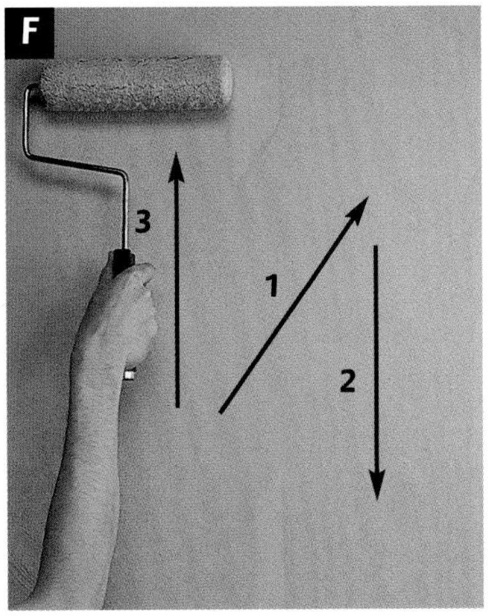

Draw the roller straight down, then roll up from the beginning of the first stroke.

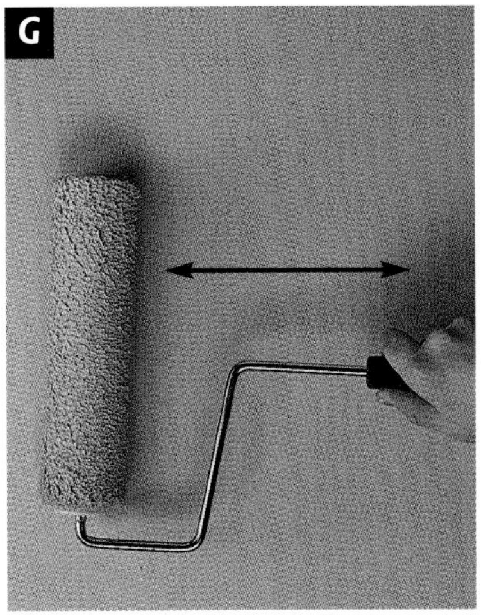

Distribute the paint with horizontal back-and-forth strokes.

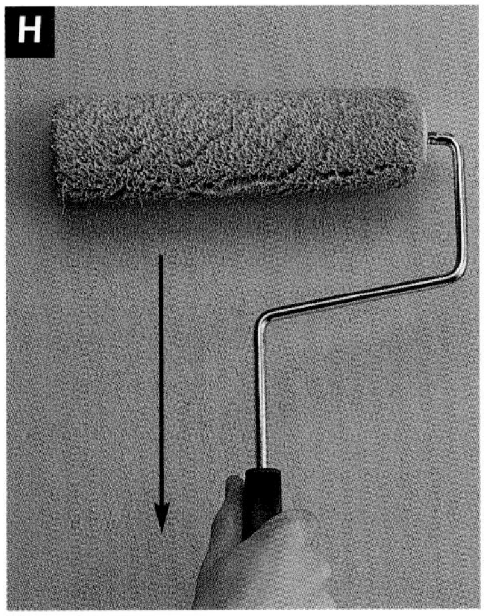

Smooth the paint with light vertical strokes, moving from top to bottom.

Painting Windows, Doors & Trim

When painting an entire room, paint the trim first. Start by painting the "inside" portions of the trim and working out toward the walls. On windows, for instance, paint the edges close to the glass first, then the surrounding face trim.

Alkyds and latex enamels may require two coats. Always sand lightly between coats, and wipe with a tack rag to remove dust so that the second coat bonds with the first.

Tools: *Stepladder, sawhorses, 3" nails, paintbrushes (3" straight, 2" trim, tapered sash, stenciling), putty knife, screwdriver, hammer, pad sander, broadknife or shielding tool.*

Materials: *paint, drop cloths, wood sealer, tack rag, 150-grit sandpaper, clean cloth.*

Painting Windows

If possible, remove double-hung windows from their frames before painting. Newer, spring-mounted windows can be released by simply pushing against the frame **(photo A).**

To create a painting stand, drive a pair of 3" nails into a wooden stepladder at a comfortable height and set the window on top of the nails **(photo B).** Or, lay the window flat on a bench or sawhorses for painting.

Using a tapered brush, begin by painting the wood next to the glass **(photo C).** Use the narrow edge of the brush, and overlap the edge of the glass by 1/16" to create a weather seal. Remove any excess paint from the glass with a putty knife wrapped in a clean cloth **(photo D).**

Paint the flat portions of the sashes next, then the case moldings, sill, and apron **(photo E).** Use slow brush strokes, and avoid getting paint between the sash and frame. Don't paint the sides or bottoms of the window sashes.

If you paint the windows in place, move them up and down several times during the drying period to keep them from sticking. Use a putty knife to avoid touching the painted surfaces **(photo F).**

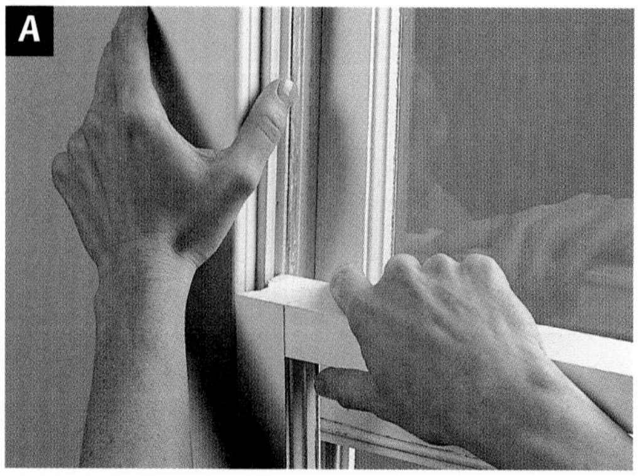

If possible, remove double-hung windows for painting.

Create a painting stand with a stepladder and 3" nails.

Begin painting next to the glass, using a tapered sash brush.

Overlap the glass slightly as you paint, then wipe off the excess.

Paint the flat portion of the sash, using slow, even strokes.

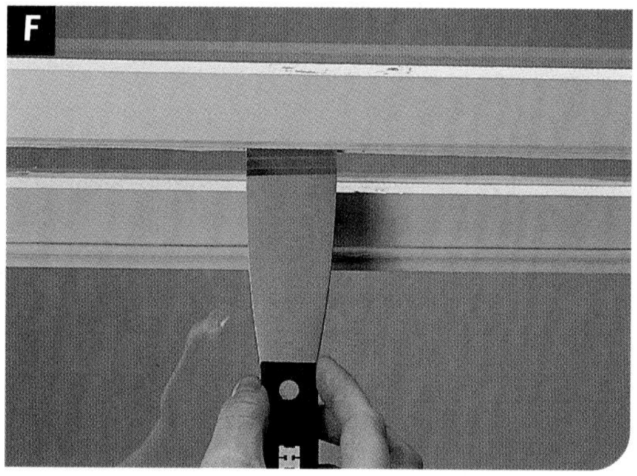

Use a putty knife to avoid touching painted surfaces.

Painting Doors

Doors should be painted quickly so all surfaces are covered before the paint begins to dry. To avoid lap marks, always paint from dry surfaces back into wet paint.

Remove the door by driving the lower hinge pin out with a screwdriver and hammer. Have a helper hold the door in place, then drive out the upper hinge pin **(photo G).** Place the door on sawhorses to paint.

On paneled doors, paint the recessed panels first, then the horizontal rails, and finally the vertical stiles **(photo H).** Let the door dry. If a second coat of paint is needed, lightly sand the door and wipe it with a tack rag to remove any residue before repainting **(photo I).** Seal the unpainted edges of the door with clear wood sealer to prevent moisture from entering the wood **(photo J).**

Remove a door by driving out the hinge pins.

Paint the door on sawhorses or a flat bench.

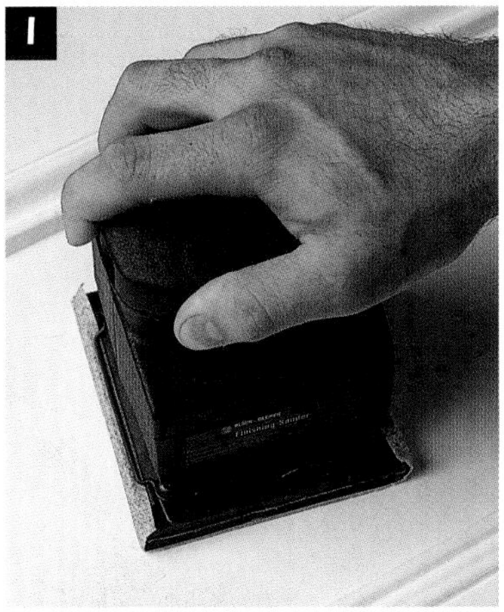

Sand between coats with 150-grit sandpaper.

Seal the unpainted edges with wood sealer.

Painting Trim

When painting trim, protect the adjacent wall and floor surfaces with a broadknife or a plastic shielding tool. On baseboards, paint the top edge first and work down to the floor **(photo K).** To prevent smearing, remember to wipe the paint off the broadknife or shielding tool each time it's moved **(photo L).** On deep, patterned surfaces, use a stiff-bristled brush or a stenciling brush to penetrate the recesses **(photo M).** Use small circular strokes and approach the recesses from several angles to achieve full coverage.

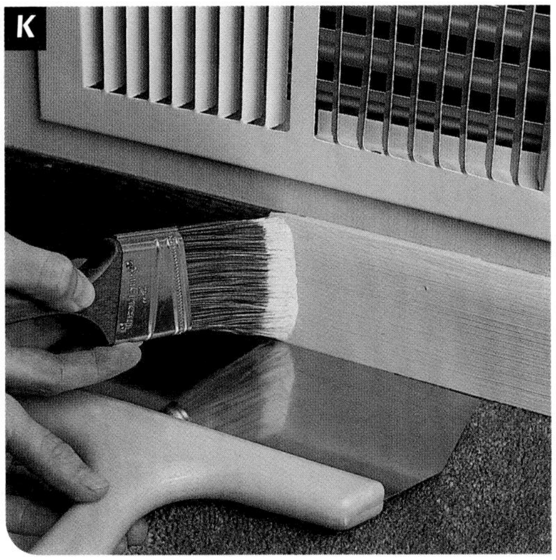

Protect wall and floor surfaces with a wide broadknife.

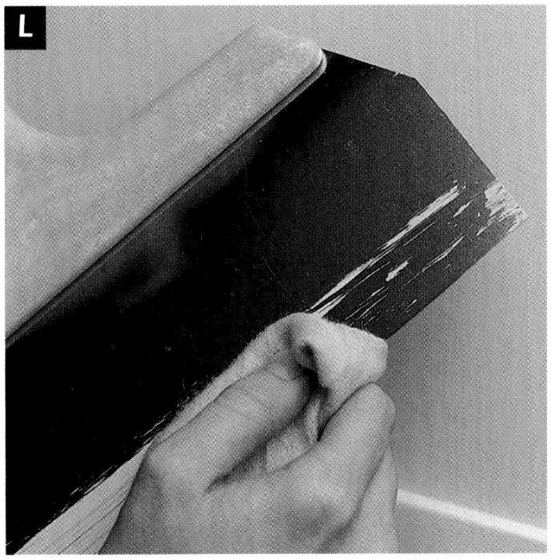

Keep the broadknife clean to avoid smearing paint.

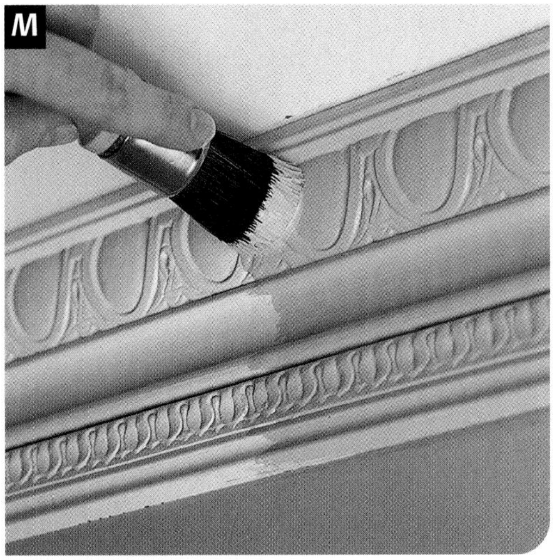

Use a stenciling brush to paint recesses in patterned trim.

Painting Cabinets

Wood, metal, and previously painted cabinets can be painted easily, but plastic laminate cabinets cannot be painted.

Cabinets receive heavy use and frequent scrubbing, so paint them with heavy-duty gloss enamel. Enamel paint is more durable than flat wall paint, and easier to clean as well. Most cabinets require two coats of paint; sand the surfaces lightly between coats with 150-grit sandpaper.

Start by emptying the cabinets and removing any shelves. Take the doors off, and remove the hardware **(photo A).** If the hardware is painted, remove the old paint by soaking the hardware in paint remover.

Wash the cabinets with a mild detergent. Rinse all traces of soap away with clean water and a sponge, then scrape away any loose paint with a putty knife. Use the putty knife and wood patch to fill any scratches, dents, or cracks **(photo B).** Let the wood patch dry.

Sand the cabinet surfaces with a pad sander and 150-grit sandpaper **(photo C).** Wipe away the sanding dust with a tack rag and spot-prime the patched areas and any bare spots with primer. If the cabinets are varnished, sand the surfaces, apply a liquid deglosser, then apply a primer before painting (page 66).

To ensure an even finish, you'll need to paint the surfaces of the cabinets in a specific order. Begin by painting the interiors in this order: back wall, top, sides, and the bottom **(photo D).** Next, use a short-nap roller to paint the outside surfaces. Working from the top down, apply the paint in smooth, even passes **(photo E).**

Paint both sides of cabinet doors to prevent warping. Using a trim brush, paint one side of the doors at a time, beginning with the inner surfaces. Paint the raised panels first, then the horizontal rails, and finally the vertical stiles **(photo F).** When the paint has dried, use the same technique to paint the other side of the doors, then paint the edges.

Paint the drawer fronts last, using a tapered sash brush **(photo G).** Let the doors and drawers dry for several days, then install the hardware and hang the doors.

Tools: *Screwdriver, pad sander, putty knife, paintbrushes (3" straight, 2" trim, and tapered sash), short-nap paint roller.*

Materials: *150-grit sandpaper, paint remover, detergent, latex wood patch, tack rag, primer, cloth, liquid deglosser, high-gloss enamel paint.*

Empty the cabinets and take the doors off the hinges.

Fill any dents, scratches, or cracks with wood patch.

Sand all of the surfaces with 150-grit sandpaper.

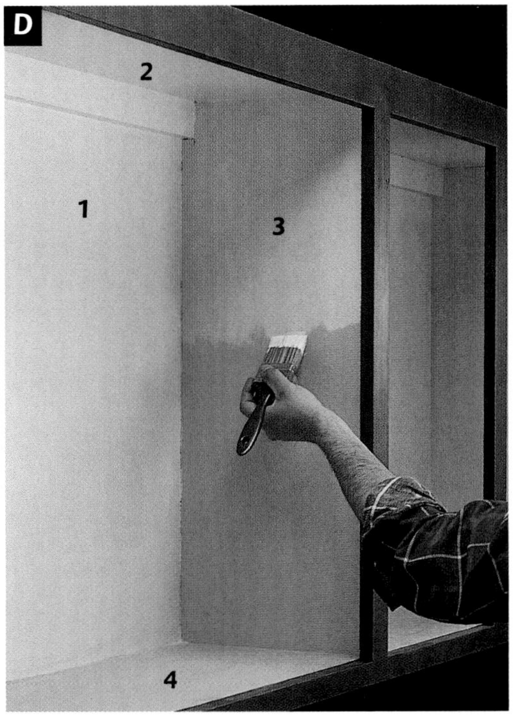

Paint the interior, starting with the back walls (1), the tops (2), the sides (3), and then the bottoms (4).

Helpful Hint: Varnishing Cabinets

If you'd like to varnish rather than paint your cabinets, you'll need to strip the wood, fill holes or scratches with wood patch, and seal the wood before varnishing (pages 62 to 63). Because of their size, stripping cabinets can be a challenge. If the cabinets aren't too large, you can unbolt them from the wall and move them to another area for refinishing. However, if removal isn't practical, you can leave the cabinets in place and refinish them one unit at a time.

Mask the area around the cabinets and cover the countertops and floor with drop cloths to protect them during the stripping process (pages 64 to 65). Start by emptying the cabinets and removing the hardware and doors. In most cases, using a heat gun first to strip the existing paint or varnish will be more efficient than starting with a chemical stripper. Remove any loose paint with a scraper before you begin stripping the wood. If you've left the cabinets in place, use a heat shield to prevent the heat gun from damaging or blistering the surfaces around the cabinets. After stripping the framework, strip the paint from the doors. Use a contoured specialty scraper to remove paint from the grooves and contoured areas. Be careful not to apply too much pressure around these areas: they're more vulnerable to scorching and gouging than flat surfaces. Use chemical stripper to spot-strip any areas that don't come clean (page 62).

After you've made the necessary repairs with wood patch, and sanded the wood, apply a clear wood sealer (page 66). Using the same technique outlined for painting cabinets (page 72), apply varnish.

Roll paint onto the exterior surfaces, working from the top to the bottom.

Paint the doors beginning with the raised panels (1), horizontal rails (2), and finishing with the vertical stiles (3).

Paint the drawer faces last, using a tapered sash brush.

Painting Ceilings & Walls

For a smooth finish on walls and ceilings, apply paint in one small section at a time. First use a paintbrush to cut in the edges, then immediately roll the section before moving on. If brushed edges are left to dry before the large surfaces are rolled, lap marks will be visible on the finished walls. Choose quality paint and tools, and work with a fully loaded brush or roller to avoid lap marks and assure full coverage (pages 68 to 69). If possible, work in natural light, which makes it easier to spot any areas you missed.

Paint ceilings with a roller outfitted with a handle extension. Wear eye protection and a cap with a brim to protect yourself against splatters. Start at the corner farthest from the entry door. Paint the ceiling along the narrow end in 3-ft. × 3-ft. sections, cutting in the edges with a brush before rolling. Apply the paint with a diagonal stroke, then distribute it evenly with back-and-forth strokes **(photo A).** For the final smoothing strokes, roll each section toward the entry wall, lifting the roller at the end of each sweep.

Paint walls in 2-ft. × 4-ft. sections. Start in an upper corner, cutting in the ceiling and wall corners with a brush. Then roll the section, making the initial upward diagonal stroke to avoid drips **(photo B).** Distribute the paint evenly with horizontal strokes, then finish with downward sweeps of the roller. Next, cut in and roll the section directly below. Continue with the adjacent areas, cutting in and rolling the top sections before the bottom sections. Roll all finish strokes toward the floor to ensure a smooth, even finish.

Tools: *Paint roller, roller extension handle, 3" straight paintbrush, safety goggles, brimmed cap.*

Materials: *Paint.*

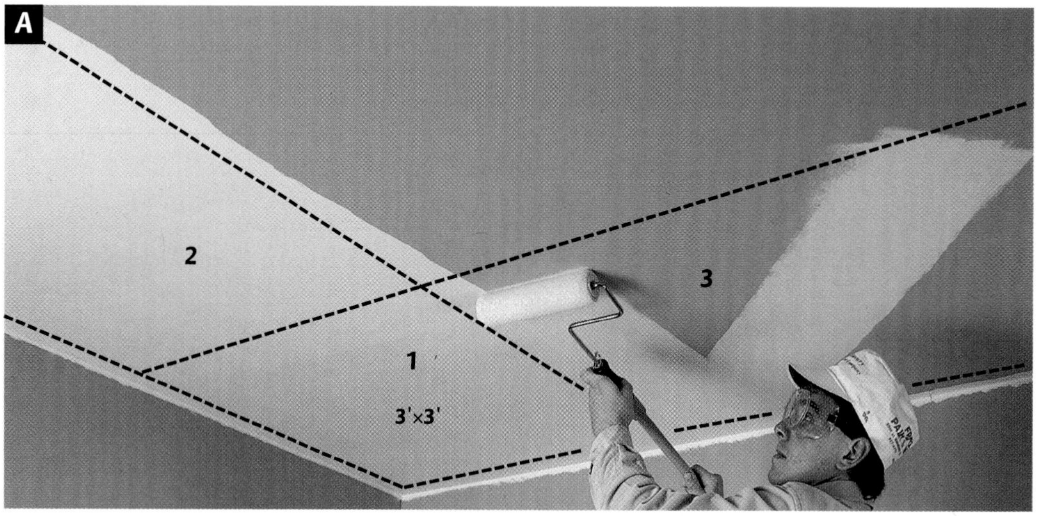

Paint ceilings with a roller handle extension, working in 3-ft. × 3-ft. sections and cutting in with a brush before rolling.

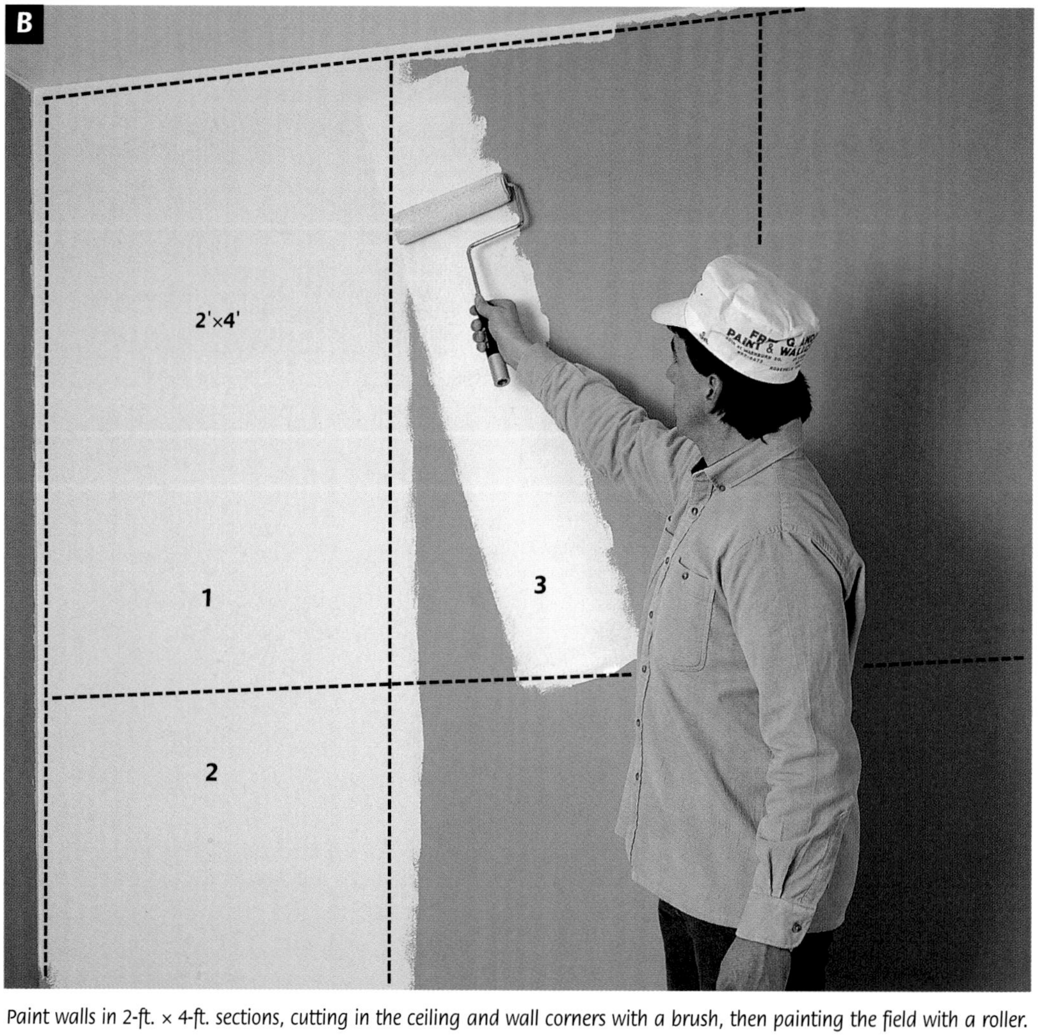

Paint walls in 2-ft. × 4-ft. sections, cutting in the ceiling and wall corners with a brush, then painting the field with a roller.

Cleaning Up

At the end of a paint job you may choose to throw away the roller covers, but the paint pans, roller handles, and brushes can be cleaned and stored for future use.

Pour leftover paint from the paint pan back into the can. Wash brushes coated with latex paint with water and a mild detergent. Comb the bristles with the spiked side of a painter's roller cleaner tool **(photo C),** which aligns the bristles so that they dry properly.

Soak brushes coated with alkyd paints in a small container of mineral spirit. Once the sediment has settled to the bottom of the container, remove the brush and let it dry before storing. Store brushes in their original wrappers, or fold the bristles inside brown wrapping paper.

If you decide to keep the roller covers for future use, scrape out excess paint with the curved side of the roller cleaner tool **(photo D).** Soak the roller in solvent, then use a roller spinner tool to remove the remaining paint and solvent. Attach the roller cover to the spinner, then hold the spinner inside a cardboard box or five-gallon pail to catch the liquid and prevent splatters. Pump the handle to force the liquid out of the roller **(photo E).** Store roller covers on end to avoid flattening their nap.

Stray paint drips can be wiped away if they are still wet. Latex paint drips can often be removed with a cloth dampened with an oil soap for wood. A putty knife or razor blade will also remove many dried paint spots on hardwood or glass.

Stubborn paint splatters can be removed from most surfaces with a chemical cleaner and a clean cloth. Before using the cleaner, test an inconspicuous area to make sure it's colorfast. Chemical cleaners are flammable and have very strong fumes; always use them in a well-ventilated area.

Tools: *Roller cleaner tool, roller spinner tool, putty knife or razor blade.*

Materials: *Liquid detergent, mineral spirits, cardboard box or five-gallon pail, cloth, oil soap, chemical cleaner.*

C

Comb the bristles with the spiked side of a cleaner tool.

D

Scrape the paint from the roller with the curved side of the cleaner tool.

E

Use a roller spinner tool to remove paint and solvent from the roller.

Floors

A floor is composed of several layers that work together to provide the required structural support and desired appearance. At the bottom of it all are the floor *joists*. Made from 2 × 8 or larger framing lumber, joists are set on their edges and spaced 16" apart. On the ground floor, joists are supported by the foundation walls or the main support beam of the house. Second-story floor joists rest on top of the load-bearing walls. Between the joists, solid blocking or *X-bridging* keeps the joists from twisting under the weight from above and allows them to "share" the load by transferring pressure from one joist to the next.

The next layer, the *subfloor*, consists of plywood sheets or 1"-thick boards that are nailed to the tops of the joists. The subfloor adds rigidity to the joists, and together they form the structural platform of the floor.

The layer that goes on top of the subfloor depends on the type of finish material. Carpet and traditional hardwood flooring are usually laid directly over the subfloor. Other finishes, such as ceramic tile and resilient vinyl products, require a smoother surface than the subfloor can provide and are usually installed over a layer known as *underlayment*. The most common underlayment is 3/8"- or 1/2"-thick plywood, which is nailed or screwed to the subfloor. The joints between the sheets are filled with a flooring compound to create a smooth surface.

The floor finish is important not only as a principle decorative element of any room but also as a protective layer that keeps moisture from damaging the floor's wood structure.

Typical Floor Problems

Flooring surfaces wear out faster than any other interior surface because they get the most wear and tear. And surface damage can affect more than just appearance. Scratches in resilient flooring and cracks in grouted tile joints let moisture into the floor's underpinnings. Hardwood floors loose their finish and become discolored. Loose boards squeak.

Underneath the finish flooring, moisture ruins wood underlayment and the damage is passed on to the subfloor. Bathroom floors suffer most from moisture problems. Subflooring can pull loose from joists—another cause of squeaks—so the floor becomes uneven and springy in affected areas.

Joist problems are less common, but their effects won't go unnoticed for long. A cracked or otherwise weakened joist may sag, causing a low spot in the floor above and placing added stress on neighboring joists, while a bulging joist will push a subfloor upward, pulling the fasteners loose and projecting a hump in the flooring surface.

A defective joist can be repaired, but problems that indicate serious structural failure require the attention of a professional. These include widespread sagging, an overstressed main beam, sunken support posts, and visible deterioration of foundation walls.

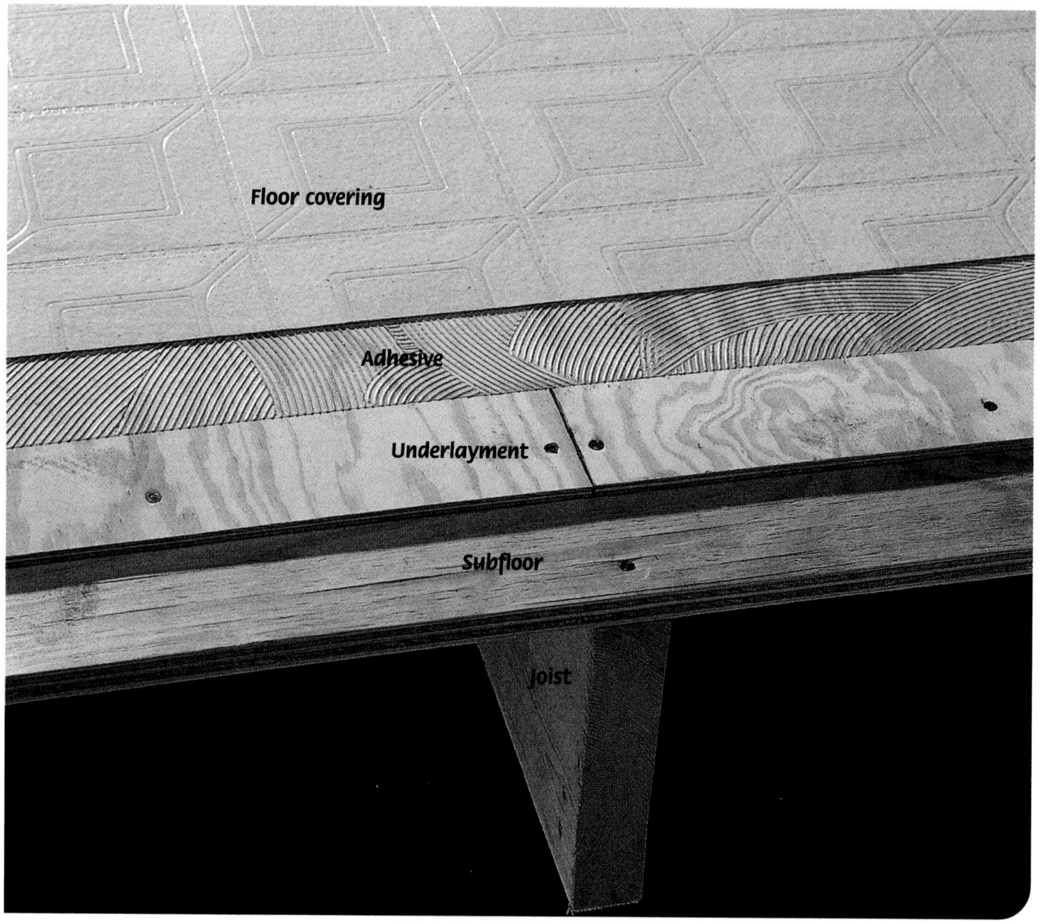

Evaluating a Floor

A careful examination of your floor can help you decide whether to repair damaged areas or to replace the flooring altogether. Often, a new covering or underlayment can be installed over the existing flooring, but first check to see how many layers are already on the floor. If there are several layers, it's best to remove them and start over. Keep in mind that the goal of any preparation for new flooring is a structurally sound, smooth, and level surface.

Inspect the adhesive bond of vinyl tiles by using a wallboard knife to pry up loose edges **(photo A).** Loose tiles in many different areas of the room may indicate failure of the adhesive, warranting a complete removal of the flooring. If tiles are secure and you want to install new tile over the old, prepare the surface with embossing leveler (page 79).

Air bubbles trapped under sheet flooring indicate that the adhesive has failed **(photo B).** In this situation, the old flooring must be removed before new flooring can be installed.

Cracks in grout joints around ceramic tile are a sign of floor movement or deterioration of the adhesive layer **(photo C).** If more than 10% of the tiles are loose, remove the old flooring. To install resilient flooring over a tiled surface, apply an embossing leveler to smooth the surface. When laying new ceramic tile over old tile, use an epoxy-based thin-set mortar for better adhesion.

Buckling in solid hardwood floors indicates that the boards have loosened from the subfloor **(photo D).** Unless you're installing a new hardwood floor, there's no need to remove the old flooring. Instead, refasten loose boards with flooring nails or screws. New carpet can go right over a well-fastened hardwood floor. New ceramic tile or resilient flooring over hardwood should be installed over underlayment laid on the hardwood flooring.

Warning: Some resilient flooring produced before 1986 contained asbestos, which can cause severe lung problems if inhaled. Cover asbestos-laden flooring with an underlayment, or hire a certified asbestos-abatement contractor to remove the flooring.

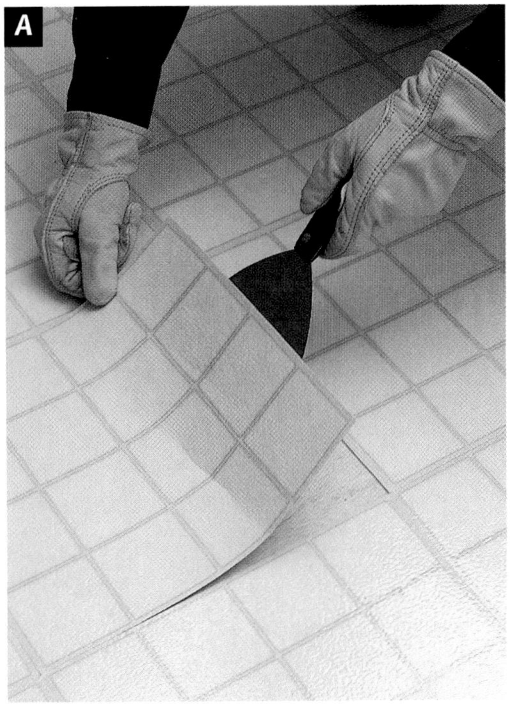

Test the condition of vinyl tiles, using a wallboard knife.

Air bubbles are a sign of adhesive failure in sheet flooring.

Grout deterioration may be caused by an unstable underlayment or failure of the adhesive layer.

Refasten loose hardwood floor boards to the subfloor before installing a new underlayment or flooring.

Tools for Floor Projects

You probably own many of the hand and power tools needed to complete most flooring projects. And those that you don't own, such as special hand tools for specific flooring installations, are usually inexpensive and easy to find. There are also many rental tools that can help make your project go smoothly.

Common power tools for flooring projects **(photo A)** include a power miter saw, circular saw and jig saw. These are needed for cutting and shaping wood flooring. A circular saw also is helpful for almost any repair. Use a power sander to touch up small areas of hardwood flooring or to smooth patches made to an underlayment. A power drill is indispensible to a flooring project, as it is to most other jobs. And a heat gun is great for working with vinyl tile. Power tools available for rent include drum sanders and edgers, for power stripping hardwood floors; and floor buffers, for polishing waxed floors.

All flooring projects call for some basic hand tools **(photo B).** The list of tools you'll need depends on the project, but any successful installation of new flooring starts with an accurate layout; be sure you have the essential measuring and marking tools, including a chalk line, framing square, level, straightedge, measuring tape, and pencil. To install vinyl flooring or any type of tile, use a notched trowel for spreading the adhesive or mortar. A floor roller is used to press flooring materials into the adhesive layer. And a stapler is handy for hanging plastic sheeting over doorways and other openings to contain dust and fumes.

The fact that flooring projects require your body to be close to your work raises important safety issues. For example, running a power saw while you are on your knees can be uncomfortable and often dangerous. Be aware of what you're cutting into and where the saw (or chisel) might go if the tool binds or slips. Wear eye and ear protection, and a respirator where appropriate. And last but not least—wear knee pads; without them, the project will seem to take a lot longer.

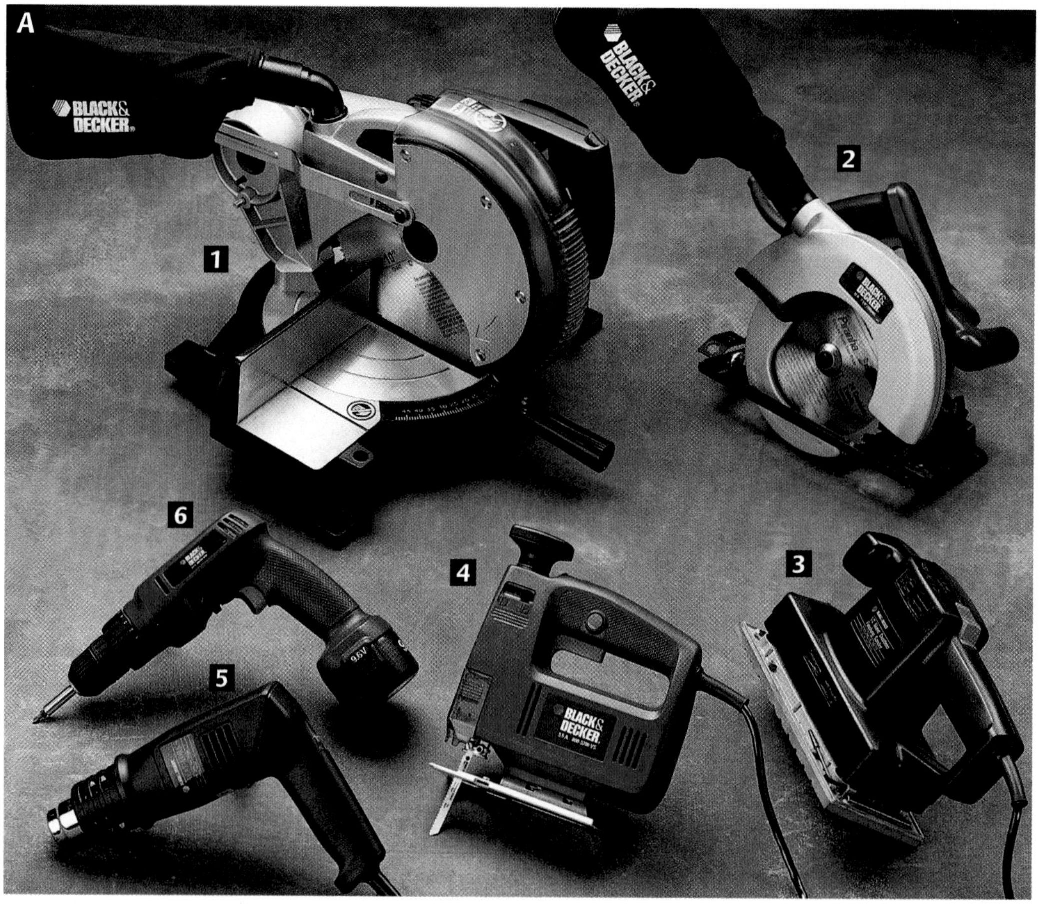

Power tools used in flooring repair and replacement projects include: power miter saw (1), circular saw (2), power sander (3), jig saw (4), heat gun (5), and cordless drill (6).

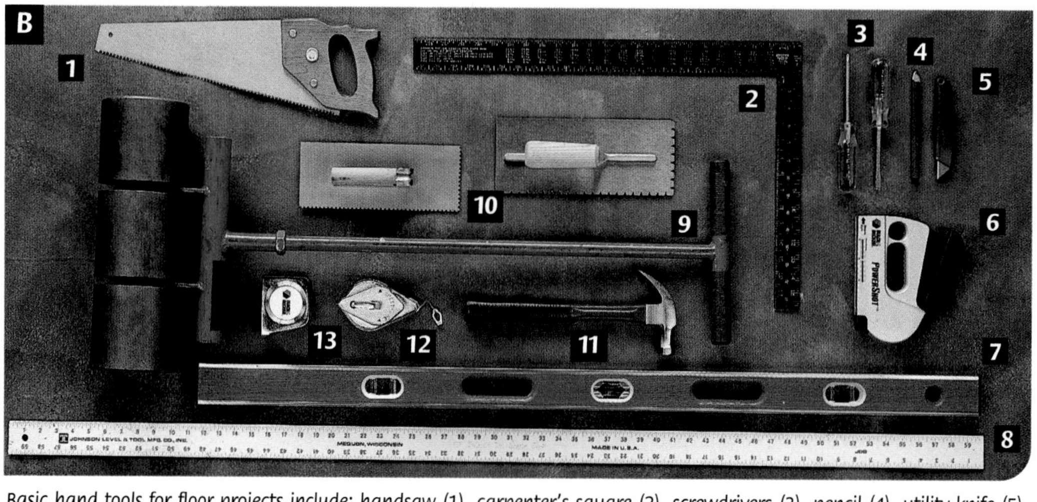

Basic hand tools for floor projects include: handsaw (1), carpenter's square (2), screwdrivers (3), pencil (4), utility knife (5), stapler (6), level (7), straightedge (8), floor roller (9), notched trowels (10), hammer (11), chalk line (12), and tape measure (13).

Preparation Tools & Materials

Preparations for new flooring installation may involve as little effort as filling in the cracks of an existing floor or as much as tearing up the old flooring and underlayment and making spot repairs to the subfloor.

If you've decided to remove the old flooring, there are a number of demolition tools to help **(photo C).** Use a hand maul and chisel to break up ceramic tile. A wallboard knife makes a handy scraper; for large scraping tasks, buy or rent a floor scraper. Pry bars are better than hammers for pulling nails and lifting boards. Use a reciprocating saw for quick, rough cuts.

If the existing floor is sound enough to serve as an underlayment, apply an embossing leveler, following the manufacturer's directions **(photo D).** This mortarlike product fills tiny indentations to create a smooth surface that will increase the life of the new flooring.

To prepare underlayment for new flooring, use a latex patching compound to fill in cracks and chips and to cover screw or nail heads **(photo E).** Also fill the seams between the sheets of new underlayment.

Undercut moldings with a handsaw to make room for the new flooring, using a scrap of underlayment and a piece of new flooring as a spacing guide **(photo F).** For ceramic tile, also allow for the height of the adhesive as well.

Always ventilate the project room whenever dust or fumes are present **(photo G).** A box fan placed in an open window and directed outside creates good air movement.

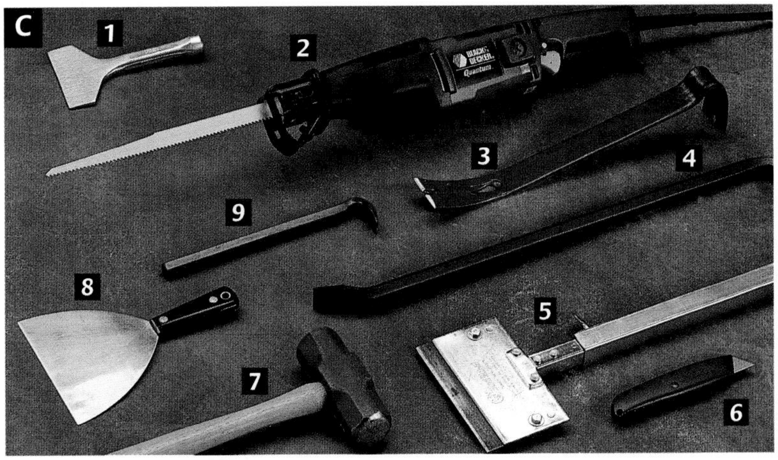

Tools for flooring removal include: masonry chisel (1), reciprocating saw (2), flat pry bar (3), crowbar (4), long-handled floor scraper (5), utility knife (6), hand maul (7), wallboard knife (8), and cat's paw (9).

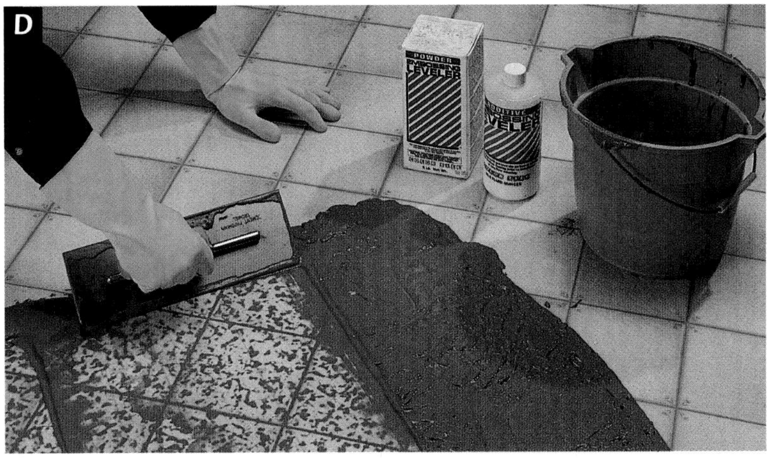

Turn old flooring into a smooth underlayment layer for new flooring by applying an embossing leveler, using a flat-edged trowel.

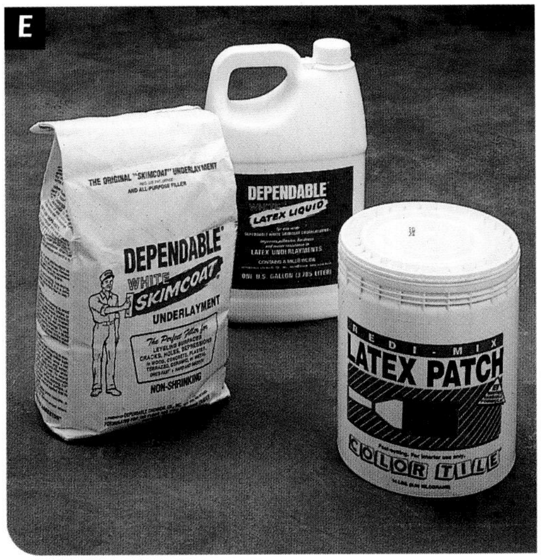

Latex patching compound fills gaps, holes, and low spots in underlayment. Apply it with a trowel or a wallboard knife.

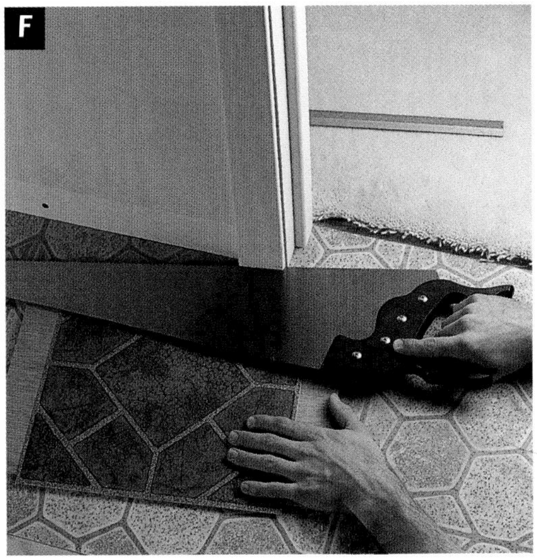

Stack the new flooring materials to use as a spacing guide, and trim door casing and other moldings with a handsaw.

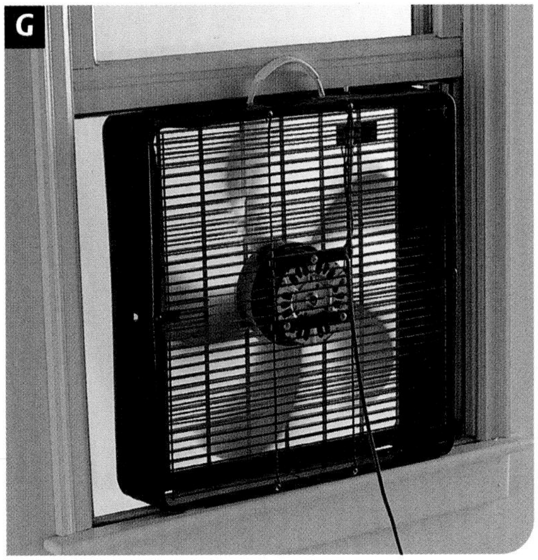

Place a box fan in an open window to help draw dust and noxious fumes from your work area.

Eliminating Floor Squeaks

Floors squeak when floorboards rub against each other or against the nails securing them to the subfloor. Other noises may be caused by water pipes rubbing against floor joists. In any case, normal changes in wood make some squeaking inevitable.

While noisy floors are a common household annoyance, they sometimes indicate serious structural problems. If an area of a floor is soft or excessively squeaky, inspect the framing and the foundation supporting the floor.

Your choice of methods for silencing squeaks depends on the type of flooring you have and whether you have access to floor joists.

Whenever possible, work on squeaks from underneath the floor. To locate the noisy areas, have a helper walk over the floor while you listen and watch from below to identify the causes. Another method is to chart squeaks from above by measuring from elements common to both floors, such as exterior walls, pipes, or heating ducts.

If the joists are covered by a finished ceiling, work on squeaks from the top side of the floor. Drive fasteners through floor boards and subfloors, or lubricate the joints between boards.

Joists more than 8 ft. long should have X-bridging or solid blocking between each pair to help distribute the weight. If these supports aren't present, install them every 6 ft. to stiffen and help silence a noisy floor.

Tools: Drill, hammer, nail set, putty knife, toothbrush, caulk gun.

Materials: Wood screws, flooring nails, wood putty, graphite powder, dance-floor wax, pipe straps, hardwood shims, wood glue, 2 × 4 lumber, construction adhesive, 16d common nails.

Securing Subfloors to Floors

Hardwood floors will squeak if they haven't been properly nailed or the nails have loosened over time and boards have pulled away from the subflooring.

If you have access to the floor joists from underneath, drive wood screws up through the subfloor and into the hardwood planks, drawing them together **(photo A).** Drill pilot holes to prevent splitting, and make sure the screws aren't long enough to break through the top of the floorboards. Determine the combined thicknesses of the floor and subfloor by measuring at cutouts for pipes.

When you can't reach the floor from underneath, surface-nail the floor boards to the subfloor with ring-shank flooring nails. Drill pilot holes close to the tongue-side edge of the board, and drive the nails at a slight angle to increase their holding power **(photo B).** Whenever possible, nail into joists. Countersink the nails with a nail set and fill the holes with tinted wood putty.

An easy way to eliminate squeaks in a carpeted floor is by using a special device to drive screws through the subfloor and into the joists **(photo C).** The device guides the screw and controls the depth. The screw has a scored shank, so once it's set, you can break the end off just below the surface of the subfloor.

A

Drive screws through the subfloor and into hardwood flooring planks to stop them from squeaking.

B

Nail down flooring planks with ring-shank flooring nails. Hide the nails by filling the holes with putty.

C

Use a floor fastening system to secure subfloors from above, especially on carpeted floors.

Reducing the Sound of Rubbing

The easiest way to eliminate squeaks in a hardwood floor is to lubricate the joints between the boards. This won't keep the boards from moving and rubbing together, but it will probably quiet them for a while.

Use mineral oil or talcum powder as a lubricant, or buy some powdered graphite from a hardware store. Graphite, commonly used for lubricating locks, comes in a small, plastic "puffer tube" with a pointed nozzle.

Start by removing dirt and deposits from the joints between the floorboards, using a putty knife or a toothbrush.

Apply a small amount of graphite powder or oil between squeaky boards. Bounce on the boards repeatedly to work the lubricant into the joint. Clean up excess powder with a damp cloth.

Dance-floor wax, available from amusement stores, is a longer-lasting lubricant that can stop squeaks. Some floor finishes are not compatible with wax, so check with the flooring manufacturer first.

Use a clean cloth to spread wax over the noisy joints **(photo D).** Then, force the wax deep into the joints, using a toothbrush.

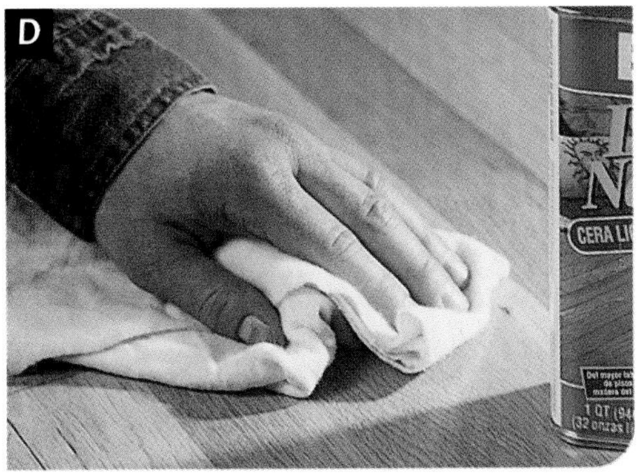

Apply dance-floor wax to squeaky joints, using a cloth and a toothbrush.

Quieting Pipe Hangers

In an unfinished basement or a crawl space, copper water pipes are usually hung from floor joists. During your investigation of a noisy floor, listen for pipes that may be rubbing against joists and other framing members. Loosen or replace wire pipe hangers to silence the noise.

Never remove a pipe hanger without installing a substitute—an unsupported pipe can vibrate or sag when heated, possibly working itself loose at a joint.

To adjust a wire hanger, pull the pointed ends of the hanger from the wood, using a hammer or a pry bar. Straighten the ends, if necessary. Lower the hanger just enough so that the pipe isn't touching the joist, making sure the pipe is held firmly so it won't vibrate.

Renail the hanger, driving the pointed end straight into the wood **(photo E).**

An alternative is to replace wire hangers with plastic split-type pipe straps. These straps spread apart so you can easily fit them around the pipe. Once installed, the plastic ring surrounds the pipe, shielding it from the joist.

Lower wire pipe hangers to prevent joists from rubbing against pipes.

Shimming Joists

Just as floorboards pull loose from subfloors, the boards or sheeting of a subfloor can separate from the joists, creating gaps. These gaps often are caused by joist shrinkage or by insufficient nailing of the subfloor. The result is a noisy or spongy spot on the floor. Where gaps are severe or where they appear above several neighboring joists, the framing may need reinforcement, but isolated gapping usually can be remedied by installing a few hardwood shims or a cleat to support the subfloor.

Fill short gaps with tapered hardwood shims. Apply a small amount of wood glue to the shim and squirt some glue into the gap. Using a hammer, tap the shim into place, just until it's snug **(photo F).** Shimming too much will only widen the gap. Allow the glue to dry before walking on the floor.

To support longer gaps, nail a cleat to the side of the joist instead of using shims. Cut a 2 × 4 or 2 × 6 to span the length of the gap. Drive several 16d common nails partially into one face of the cleat, and apply construction adhesive to the other face and to the top edge.

Position the cleat against the face of the joist with its top edge against the subfloor. Then, using one hand to force the cleat upward against the subfloor, nail the cleat to the joist.

Use wedges to fill in gaps between joists and the subfloor.

Reducing a Bulging Joist

A severely arched, or bulged, floor joist can get worse over time, eventually deforming the flooring above it. Correcting a bulging joist is an easy repair because it relies on gravity to straighten the board.

If you can see or feel a hump in a floor, check the area with a level to find the highest point **(photo A).** Move the level to different points, noting the gap between the floor and the ends of the level.

Mark the highest point of the bulge, and measure from an element that extends to the floor below, such as an exterior wall or a heating duct. Use this measurement to mark the high point onto the bulging joist from below the floor.

From the bottom edge, make a straight cut into the problem joist below the high point mark, using a reciprocating saw **(photo B).** Make the cut 3/4 of the depth of the joist.

Allow several weeks for the joist to relax and straighten, checking the floor periodically with a level. Don't load the floor above the joist with excessive weight.

When the joist has settled, reinforce it by nailing a board of the same size to the joist **(photo C).** Make the reinforcement piece at least 6 ft. long, and drive 16d common nails in staggered pairs, 12" apart. Drive a row of three nails on either side of the cut in the joist.

Tools: *4-ft. level, reciprocating saw, hammer.*

Materials: *Framing lumber, 16d common nails.*

Find the high point of the bulge, using a level.

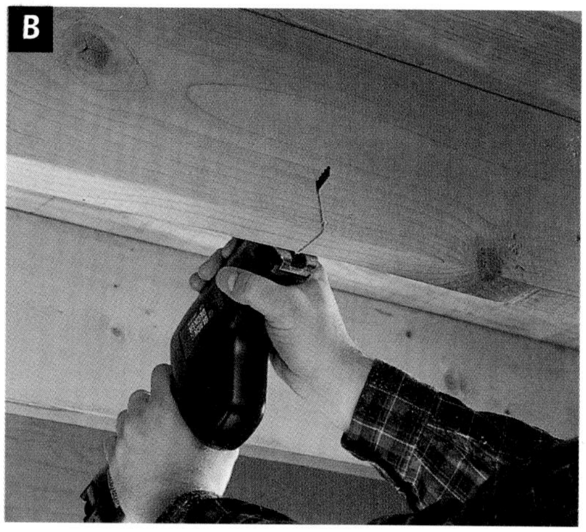

Use a reciprocating saw to cut the joist at the bulge.

Center a board over the cut and nail it to the joist.

Reinforcing a Cracked or Sagging Joist

When a floor joist is weakened by a large crack or the aging process has caused the wood to sag, often the best solution is to fasten a new joist to the damaged one to help carry the weight. This process, known as *sistering*, involves fitting the new (sister) joist next to the old one and jacking up both of them, using two foundation jack posts or hydraulic floor jacks and 2 × 4 cross beams.

Sistering is effective for repairing one or two joists in a floor. Floors with severe sagging or sloping may have undersized joists or other framing or foundation problems, requiring more extensive repair.

A crack in a joist may start from a natural defect or where notches cut to install service lines have weakened the wood **(photo D).**

Hold a 4-ft. level on the bottom edge of a joist to determine the amount of sagging **(photo E).** Note the distance between the ends of the level and the joist.

To install a sister joist, remove any blocking or bridging on the side of the damaged joist where the sister will go.

Measure the old joist and cut the sister to the same length. You may shorten the sister to get it into position, but as a general rule, keep it as long as possible. Cut the sister from the same size of lumber as the damaged joist. Use a straight board, with only a slight crown, if any. If the new joist is crowned, be sure to install it with the arch pointing up.

The sagging floor may make it difficult to position the sister joist. If so, solve this problem by notching the bottom edge of the sister joist at both ends so it will fit over the foundation or beam. Using a chisel, make the notches 1/2" deep and about 18" long.

To get the sister into position, hold it flat

Tools: *Hammer, chisel, 4-ft. level, adjustable wrench, ratchet wrench.*

Materials: *Replacement joist, metal jack posts, 2 × 4 lumber, hardwood shims, 3" lag screws with washers.*

and set the ends on the foundation sill or beam. Then, stand it upright, hitting the top of the side with a hammer, if necessary.

Make the two cross beams by nailing together pairs of 6-ft.-long 2 × 4s.

Position a jack post and cross beam near one end of the joists. Set the beam perpendicular to the joists and adjust the post to rough height. Use a level to make sure the post is plumb **(photo F).**

Raise the post by turning the threaded shaft extending from the bottom end, just enough so the cross beam is snug to the joists.

Position the second jack post and cross beam at the other end of the joists, and raise it slowly. Stop when the sister joist is flush with the subfloor.

Install tapered hardwood shims at the ends of the sister joist, between the notched portions and the foundation sill or beam **(photo G).** If possible, use two shims, with the tapered ends opposing each other, to create a flat surface. Carefully tap the shims into place with a hammer, just enough to get them snug.

With the joists flush together, release the pressure from the jacks posts.

Use 3" lag screw with washers to fasten the joists together. Drill a pair of pilot holes every 12" to 16". Drive the screws with a ratchet wrench **(photo H).**

Cut the blocking or bridging to fit and install it between the joists in the original positions.

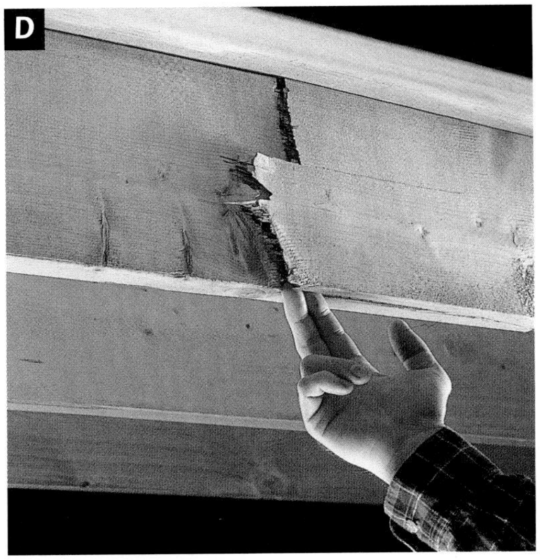

Reinforce a cracked joist before it starts to cause problems.

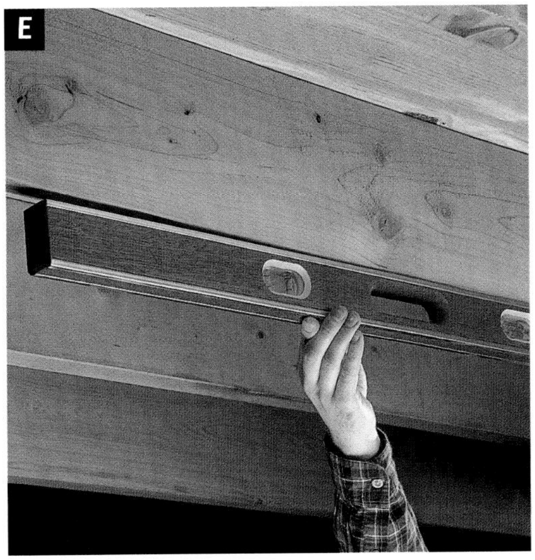

Use a level to check joists for sagging.

Make sure the jack post is plumb before raising it.

Helpful Hint

Follow these rules for notching or drilling into a joist to install service lines:

Never notch a joist in the middle ⅓ of its length. Cut notches no deeper than ⅙ of the actual depth of the joist. For example, a 2 × 12, which is 11¼" wide, can have a 1⅞"-deep notch.

Center holes between the top and bottom edges of the joist. The hole diameter can be no more than ⅓ the depth of the joist. Make holes for pipes only slightly larger than the diameter of the pipes.

With jacks supporting the joists, shim the ends of the sister.

Fasten the sister to the old joist with lag screws and washers.

Underlayment

Underlayment is a layer of sheeting screwed or nailed to the subfloor to provide a smooth, stable surface for the floor covering. Repair or replace the underlayment before installing new flooring. Use a latex patching compound to fill holes and seams in underlayment sheeting.

When replacing the underlayment, which type you choose depends in part on the floor covering you'll be installing. For example, ceramic and natural-stone floors require a rigid underlayment that resists movement, such as cement board. For vinyl flooring, use a quality-grade plywood, since some manufacturers will void the warranty if their flooring is installed over substandard underlayment. Solid wood strip flooring and carpet don't require underlayment and are often placed directly over a plywood subfloor.

Plywood is the most common underlayment for vinyl flooring and ceramic tile installations. For vinyl, use 1/4" exterior grade AC plywood. This type has one smooth side for a quality surface. Wood-based floor covering, like parquet, can be installed over lower-quality exterior-grade plywood. For ceramic tile, you can use 1/2" AC plywood. When installing plywood, leave 1/4" expansion gaps at the walls and between sheets.

Fiber/cementboard is a thin, high-density underlayment used under ceramic tile and vinyl flooring in situations where floor height is a concern.

Cementboard is used only for ceramic tile installations. It's stable even when wet, and is therefore the best underlayment to use in areas likely to get wet, such as bathrooms. Cementboard is more expensive than plywood, but if you're planning a large tile installation, it's a good investment.

Isolation membrane is used to protect ceramic tile installations from movement that could occur on cracked concrete floors.

Removing Underlayment

Before you begin the removal process, tear up a small section of flooring and see what type of fastener was used to install the underlayment. If it's secured with screws, you'll have to remove the flooring first and pull the screws, one by one, to avoid damaging the subfloor. If the underlayment is held by nails, you can remove it along with the floor covering **(photo A).** The technique is to cut the flooring into manageable pieces that can be handled easily.

Be sure to discard boards with nails in them as soon as you pull them up from the floor. Renting a dumpster for this project will save time and help you avoid painful surprises.

If your existing floor is ceramic tile over plywood underlayment, use a hand maul and masonry chisel to chip away tile along cutting lines before making cuts with a circular saw.

Warning: The following floor removal method releases flooring particles into the air. Be sure the vinyl you are removing doesn't contain asbestos (page 77).

Before cutting into the floor, prepare yourself and your saw for some unfavorable conditions. Your saw will undoubtedly meet some nails as you cut the floor into sections, so use an old saw blade, if possible, and make sure to wear eye protection and gloves. A carbide-tipped blade works best for this job.

Tools: *Circular saw, reciprocating saw, chisel, hammer, pry bar, hand maul, masonry chisel.*

Adjust the cutting depth of a circular saw to equal the combined thickness of your floor covering and underlayment. Cut the floor into sections measuring about three feet square **(photo B).**

At the ends of cuts, where you run into walls and cabinets, get as close as you can with the circular saw. Switch to a reciprocating saw to complete the cuts **(photo C).** Hold the saw so the blade is at a slight angle, sloping down to the floor. Be careful not to cut any deeper than the underlayment. To avoid damaging walls or cabinet with the plunging blade of the reciprocating saw, use a chisel to finish the last few inches of the cuts.

Once the cuts are made, use a flat pry bar and a hammer to separate the underlayment from the subfloor **(photo D).** Remove and discard the section immediately, watching for exposed nails.

When the floor covering and underlayment are completely removed, sweep the floor thoroughly. Pull any nails that are sticking out and inspect the subfloor for any areas that need repair.

Removing underlayment and floor covering together is effective with any covering that is bonded to the underlayment.

Cut the floor covering and underlayment into small squares, using a circular saw set to the correct depth.

Use a reciprocating saw to cut near walls and cabinets. Complete cuts in tight spots, using a chisel.

Remove sections of floor covering and underlayment, using a pry bar and a hammer. Pull any loose nails.

Subfloors

The subfloor is the structural layer of wood decking between the floor joists and the finished floor. Most modern subfloors are 5/8" or 3/4" tongue-in-groove plywood sheets running perpendicular to the joists. Older homes may have subfloors made of 1 × 4 or 1 × 6 boards installed diagonally. Subfloor decking is nailed directly to the joists with 8d common nails or ring-shank nails that grip wood fibers to resist pulling out.

The subfloor is an important structural element in your house because it ties together all parts of the flooring system. It keeps joists vertical and straight for maximum strength and is the foundation of the floor you walk on. For these reasons, the health of your subfloor is a critical matter.

During a flooring replacement project, take time to inspect and repair the subfloor. Removing old flooring and underlayment gives you a chance to refasten loose boards and fill in low spots of the subfloor. A solid, securely fastened subfloor minimizes floor movement and ensures that your new floor will last a long time.

Support is the central role of a subfloor. When replacing sections, be sure to install sturdy backing lumber to support the edges and hold the fasteners. It doesn't have to look pretty—it just needs to be strong.

Tools: *Drill, hammer, finishing trowel, straightedge, carpenter's square, cat's paw, circular saw, chisel, caulk gun.*

Materials: *2¼" deck screws, floor leveler, bucket, 2 × 4 lumber, 16d common nails, plywood, construction adhesive.*

Refastening & Leveling a Subfloor

After removing old flooring and underlayment, inspect the subfloor for loose seams, cracks, holes, and low spots.

Walk back and forth over the floor, listening for squeaks and feeling for soft spots indicating that the subfloor has separated from the joists. Refasten subfloor material to joists with 2¼" deck screws **(photo A).** Hammer down or pull any loose nails.

Fill dips and defects with floor leveler. Using a latex or acrylic additive, mix the leveler according to manufacturer's directions.

Spread the leveler on the subfloor with a finishing trowel **(photo B).** Fill the deepest spots first, and use the trowel to feather out the leveler at the edges.

Use a level or a straightedge to make sure the patch is level with the surrounding area **(photo C).** Add more leveler, if necessary.

Allow leveler to dry, then shave off any ridges with the edge of the trowel, or sand the area smooth.

A

Drive deck screws through subflooring and into floor joists.

B

Spread floor leveler over cracks and low spots, using a trowel.

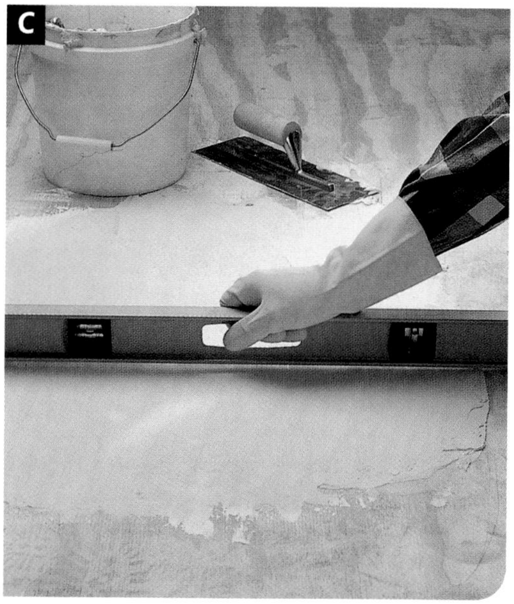

C

Check with a straightedge to ensure the patch is level.

Replacing a Section of Subfloor

When replacing decayed or damaged areas of a subfloor, check the joists underneath to make sure the damage hasn't affected them. In wet areas, such as bathrooms, where floors are highly prone to water damage, inspect subfloors carefully, especially if the wall or finished floor surfaces show signs of discoloration, cracking, or peeling. Locate the source of any damage, like leaky pipes or fixtures, and correct the problem before you replace or reinforce the damaged wood.

If your subfloor is made of dimensional lumber rather than plywood, you can use plywood to patch damaged sections. If the plywood patch doesn't reach the height of the subfloor, use floor leveler to raise its surface to the correct height.

To replace damaged sections of a subfloor, remove old underlayment, then cut out damaged areas of the subfloor decking, exposing some nailing surface on joists that border the cutout. Install 2 × 4 backing where necessary.

Mark the outline of the cutout around the damaged area, using a carpenter's square so the lines are square and straight. This will make it easier to cut and fit the patch. Make sure two sides of the cutout are centered over joists.

Pull all nails on or near the cut lines, using a cat's paw and a hammer.

Adjust the blade depth on your circular saw to the exact thickness of the subfloor. Wear eye protection when cutting the floor with a circular saw because there may be hidden nails that you've missed **(photo D).** Where lines are too close to the wall to fit the saw, complete the cuts with a wide chisel.

Remove the damaged piece. Cut two 2 × 4 blocks to fit between the joists at either end of the cutout.

Nail the blocks between the joists so their top edges are centered under the cut edges of the subfloor **(photo E).** If possible, end-nail the blocks through the joists from below the floor. Otherwise, toenail them from above. When toenailing, predrill pilot holes through the ends of the board at the correct angle.

Measure the hole, and cut the replacement piece, subtracting 1/16" from each dimension so the new piece will be slightly smaller than the hole. Use quality plywood that's the same thickness as (or slightly thinner than) the original subfloor.

Apply a small amount of construction adhesive to the joists and blocking. Position the replacement piece and fasten it to the joists and blocking with 2 1/4" deck screws, spaced about 5" apart **(photo F).**

Where subfloors have rotted from a leaky toilet, carefully cut the damaged wood from around the toilet flange **(photo G).** To provide adequate support for the subfloor patch, install 2 × 6 or 2 × 8 blocking between joists, and between the blocking pieces on either side of the toilet drain pipe.

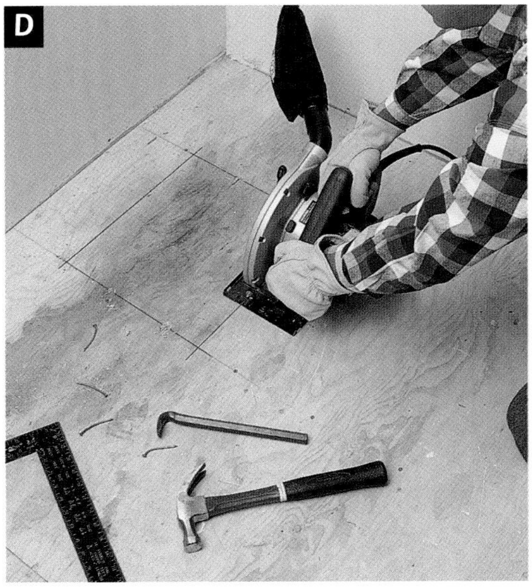

Cut out the damaged area with a circular saw.

Nail blocking to joists to support the edges of the patch.

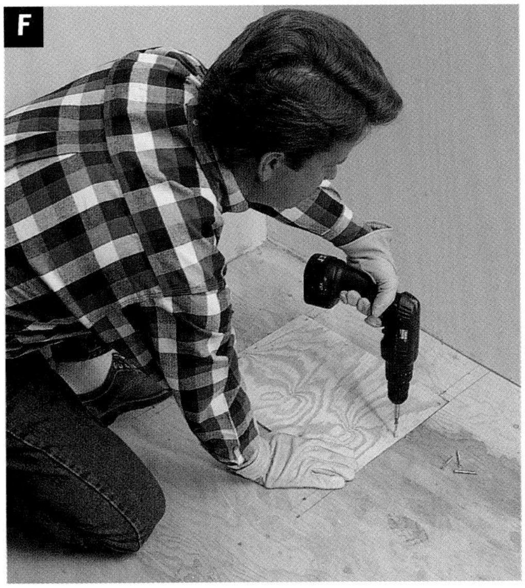

Attach the plywood patch with adhesive and deck screws.

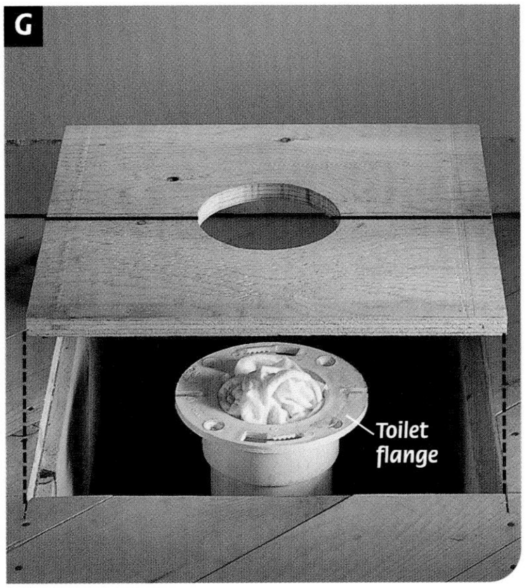

Install heavy blocking to support a patch around a toilet.

Common Floor Coverings

Vinyl Flooring

Vinyl flooring, also known as *resilient flooring,* is the least expensive floor covering, as well as the easiest to install. Because it's durable and easy to clean, vinyl flooring is often found in kitchens and bathrooms.

Vinyl flooring, available in *sheet vinyl* and *vinyl tile,* typically is glued to a plywood underlayment.

Sheet vinyl comes in 6-ft. and 12-ft. rolls and is cut to fit the floor. *Full-spread* vinyl has a felt backing that's completely covered with adhesive for installation. *Perimeter bond* vinyl has a PVC backing, and only the edges of the material are glued down.

Vinyl tile is very easy to install or replace—many styles come with peel-off adhesive backing. But because tile floors have many seams, moisture can soak between the tiles and ruin the bond.

Vinyl flooring ranges from 1/16" to 1/8" in thickness and is available in sheets or tiles.

Ceramic Tile

Ceramic tile is a hard, durable, versatile material that's available in a wide variety of sizes, patterns, and colors.

All ceramic tile is created from molded clay and baked in a kiln, but there are several different categories. *Glazed ceramic tile* is coated with a colored glaze after it's baked. Then, it's fired again to produce a hard surface layer, which is clearly visible along its edges. *Quarry tile* is an unglazed, porous tile. It's softer and thicker than glazed tile, and needs to be protected periodically with sealer. *Porcelain mosaic tile* is extremely dense, hard, and naturally water-resistant. Like quarry tile, porcelain tile has the same color throughout its thickness.

The ceramic tile typically used for floors has a textured surface, which is not as slippery as smooth glazed tile.

Ceramic tile comes in a wide variety of colors, patterns, shapes, and sizes. Thicknesses range from 3/16" to 3/4".

Hardwood

Hardwood floors look and feel warm; they're also durable and relatively easy to clean. If treated periodically with a strong urethane finish, a hardwood floor should last a lifetime.

Traditional solid hardwood planks are still the most common wood flooring product, but a growing number of wood floor products are being used in remodeling or new construction. These products, including plywood-backed flooring and parquet tiles, cost less than solid hardwood and are well suited for do-it-yourself installation.

Scratches in hardwood flooring can be filled, and the surface can be sanded down and refinished. If a small area of a hardwood plank floor is badly damaged, it's even possible to splice in new planks.

Hardwood flooring is available in laminated parquet squares as well as solid and laminated planks.

Carpet

Carpet is made of synthetic or natural fibers bonded to a mesh backing. It's a popular flooring choice for bedrooms, family rooms, and hallways.

The two basic types of carpeting are *loop-pile*, which uses uncut loops of yarn to create a textured look, and *cut-pile*, which has trimmed fibers that present a more uniform appearance. The two pile types are sometimes combined in one carpet.

Most people choose carpet for its appearance and comfort, rather than durability, but new materials are improving carpet's resistance to wear patterns and stains.

Carpet maintenance consists of reducing wear by keeping it as clean as possible and patching minor damage when necessary.

Carpet, a soft, flexible floor covering, requires little maintenance beyond regular cleaning.

Other Floor Coverings

Natural stone tiles are a beautiful but expensive floor covering. The stone itself is expensive, and so are repairs and installation. Natural stone floors require subfloors of poured mortar or cementboard, and installing or replacing subfloors and tile is a job for an experienced tile setter. Once in place, however, granite, marble, and slate tiles are incredibly durable and rarely require any maintenance other than routine cleaning.

Synthetic laminate flooring is an economical, durable alternative to hardwood. Like laminate countertops, these flooring products consist of thin layers of plastic laminate, usually patterned to resemble the color and grain of natural wood, bonded to a fiberboard core.

Synthetic laminate flooring resists scratching, and requires very little maintenance other than routine cleaning. However, installation requires a perfectly smooth subfloor, and many manufacturers provide warranties only on floors laid by registered professional installers.

Maintaining & Repairing Vinyl Flooring

Vinyl floors are popular because they're easy to clean and maintain. Today's high-quality vinyl floor coverings don't require any regular care beyond frequent sweeping and mopping.

The finish on older or lower-quality vinyl floors sometimes needs to be restored. Begin by removing the old finish. Working in small sections, apply a commercial floor stripper. Use a nylon pad and a buffer to remove ground-in dirt. Mop the floor and rinse it twice. When it's dry, fill nicks or gouges with latex filler.

Recoat the floor with an acrylic polish. In high traffic areas or areas that are extremely worn, apply one coat and let it dry overnight, then apply a second coat. To help the finish last, sweep often, put throw rugs in all doorways, and add protectors under furniture legs.

Don't place padded area rugs directly on top of vinyl floors, particularly in sunny areas. Carpet padding often contains petroleum products that can leave indelible stains on vinyl. And if you spill nail polish on vinyl flooring, don't try to clean it with nail polish remover, which can eat into the floor. Instead, try a little scouring powder or a steel wool pad.

Asphalt stains, a common problem on vinyl floors, can be removed with mineral spirits or household bleach. Dampen a rag with mineral spirits and set it on the stain, then place a piece of plastic over it to slow the evaporation. After an hour or two, wipe away the stain. Test solvents in an inconspicuous spot before using them on any flooring.

Repair methods for vinyl flooring depend on the type of floor as well as the type of damage. With vinyl tile, it's best to replace the damaged tiles. With sheet vinyl, you can fuse the surface or patch in new material.

Small cuts and scratches can be fused permanently and nearly invisibly with liquid seam sealer, a clear compound that's available wherever vinyl flooring is sold. Clean the area with lacquer thinner and a soft cloth. When it's dry, squeeze a thin bead of sealer into the scratch. For tears or burns, cut out the damaged area and glue in a patch (below).

When vinyl flooring is badly worn or the damage is widespread, the only answer is complete replacement. Although it's possible to add layers of flooring in some situations, evaluate the options carefully.

Patching Sheet Vinyl

Patching sheet vinyl requires an extra piece of matching flooring and a technique called *double-cutting*. If you don't have scraps of the flooring, lift a piece from inside a closet or under an appliance.

Place a scrap over the damaged area and adjust it until the pattern matches precisely. Tape the patch to the floor. Use a carpenter's square to outline the patch **(photo A).** If possible, draw along pattern lines, which helps conceal the seams of the patch.

Cut through both the patch and the flooring, using a utility knife. Use a new blade and hold the knife vertically while cutting.

Remove the patch and pull up the damaged section. If the flooring is perimeter-bonded, the piece will come up easily. If the flooring is fully adhered, scrape up the piece with a putty knife or razor scraper. Dissolve any remaining adhesive on the subfloor with mineral spirits, then scrape the area clean.

Spread flooring adhesive onto the subfloor. If the flooring is perimeter-bonded, lift the cut edges and spread mastic under them. Press the patch in place **(photo B),** positioning it to match the pattern exactly. Gently wipe away any excess adhesive. Cover the patch with wax paper and weigh it down with several books. Wait at least 24 hours for the adhesive to dry.

Apply a thin bead of liquid seam sealer to all the edges of the patch. The resulting repair will be nearly undetectable.

Tools: *Carpenter's square, utility knife, putty knife.*

Materials: *Scrap of matching flooring, masking tape, marker, mineral spirits, floor covering adhesive, wax paper, liquid seam sealer.*

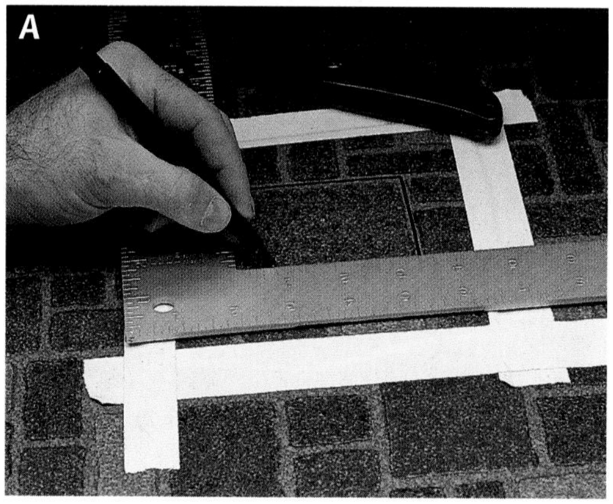

Tape a scrap of flooring into position and mark cutting lines for the patch.

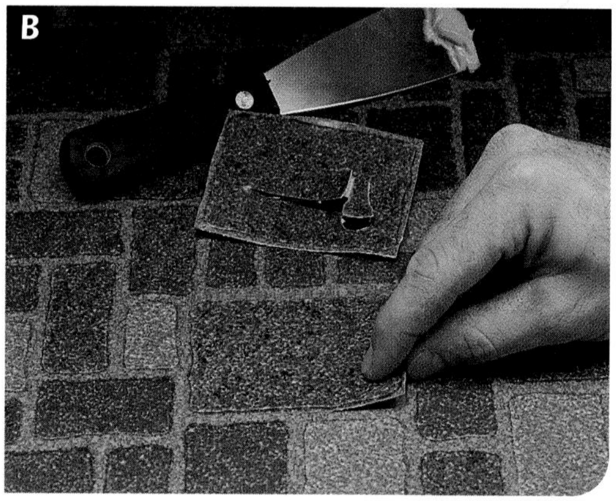

Apply adhesive and press the patch into place. After 24 hours, apply liquid seam sealer to the edges.

Replacing Sheet Vinyl

Careful removal is essential to the quality of the new installation. Removal can be very easy or rather time-consuming—depending on the type of flooring and the original installation method. Removing perimeter-bond vinyl is generally easier than removing full-spread. With any removal, keep tool blades sharp and try to avoid damaging the underlayment.

Cut the old flooring into strips about a foot wide, using a utility knife. Pull up the strips by hand **(photo C).** Cut stubborn areas into strips about 5" wide. Starting at a wall, peel up as much of the remaining flooring as possible. If any backing remains, spray a solution of water and liquid dishwashing detergent under the surface to help separate the backing from the vinyl. Use a wallboard knife to scrape up particularly stubborn patches.

Scrape up remaining flooring, using a floor scraper **(photo D).** If necessary, spray the backing with the soap solution to loosen it. Sweep up the debris, then fill a wet/dry vacuum with about an inch of water (to keep the dust down) and finish the cleanup.

Evaluate the condition of the underlayment, and remove and replace any sections that are damaged or deteriorated (page 84). Take your time—professionals say that the most important phase of installing sheet vinyl is creating a nearly perfect underlayment surface.

Using a cutting template is the best way to make sure you cut the flooring accurately. To make a template, place sheets of heavy paper along the walls, leaving a 1/8" gap **(photo E).** Cut triangular holes in the paper, using a utility knife. Fasten the template to the floor by placing masking tape over the holes.

Continued on next page

Tools: *Floor scraper, eye protection, wallboard knife, spray bottle, heat gun, wet/dry shop vacuum, flooring knife, compass, utility knife, straightedge.*

Materials: *Dish detergent, masking tape, heavy butcher's paper, vinyl flooring, felt-tipped pen.*

Cut the flooring into strips and pull up as much of the flooring as possible by hand.

Scrape up remaining vinyl and backing. Sweep and vacuum the underlayment to remove all debris.

To make a cutting template, tape pieces of paper together, creating a complete outline of the room.

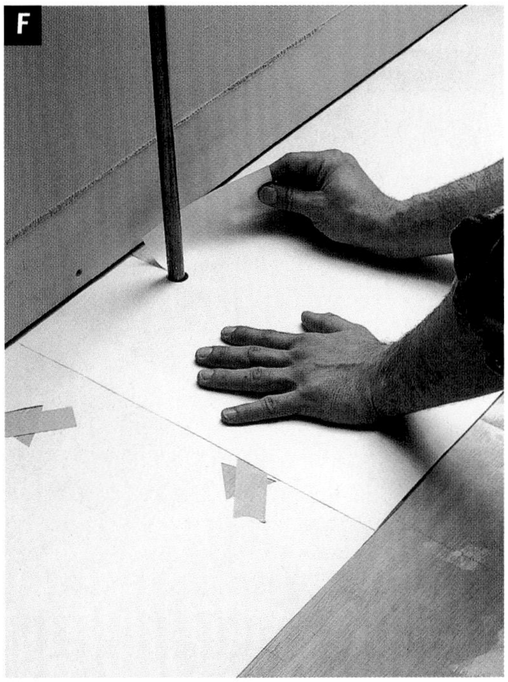

Indicate cutting lines on the template for pipes and other obstructions.

Replacing Sheet Vinyl (cont.)

Follow the outline of the room. Overlap the edges of adjoining pieces of paper by about 2", taping them together as you go.

To fit the template around a pipe, tape paper on either side. Measure the distance from the wall to the center of the pipe, and subtract 1/8". Transfer the measurement to a separate piece of paper. Use a compass to draw the pipe diameter onto the paper, then cut it out. Cut a slit from the edge of the paper to the hole, and fit the hole cutout around the pipe **(photo F).** Tape this template to the adjoining paper.

Unroll the flooring on a clean, flat surface, pattern-side-up. For multi-piece installations, overlap pieces by at least 2", creating the seams along pattern lines **(photo G).** Align the pieces until the pattern matches precisely, then tape them together with duct tape.

Tape the paper template over the flooring. Trace the outline onto the flooring, using a nonpermanent, felt-tipped pen **(photo H).**

Make the necessary cuts, using a linoleum knife or a utility knife with a new blade **(photo I).** For long cuts, use a straightedge.

Cut holes for pipes and other permanent obstructions. Then cut a slit from each hole to the nearest edge of the flooring **(photo J),** cutting along pattern lines, if possible.

Loosely roll the flooring and carry it to the installation area. Unroll and carefully position the flooring, sliding the edges beneath door casings.

Now, cut the seams for installations that require two or more pieces. Holding a straightedge tightly against the flooring, cut along the pattern lines, through both pieces **(photo K).**

Remove scraps **(photo L).** The vinyl is now positioned, and you're ready to bond it—either perimeter or full-spread.

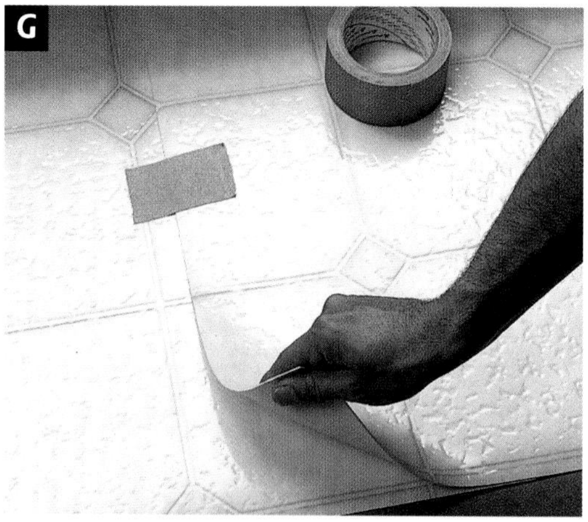

Create seams by overlapping pieces by 2", with the pattern precisely aligned.

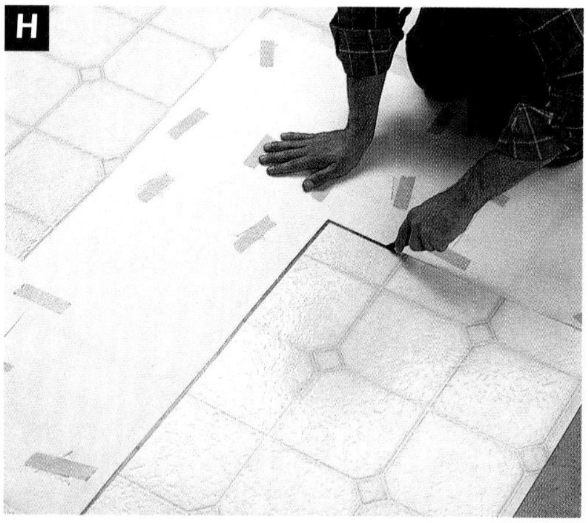

Trace the outline of the template onto the flooring.

Cut along the marked lines of the template.

Cut holes for obstructions, then make slits between the holes and the nearest edge.

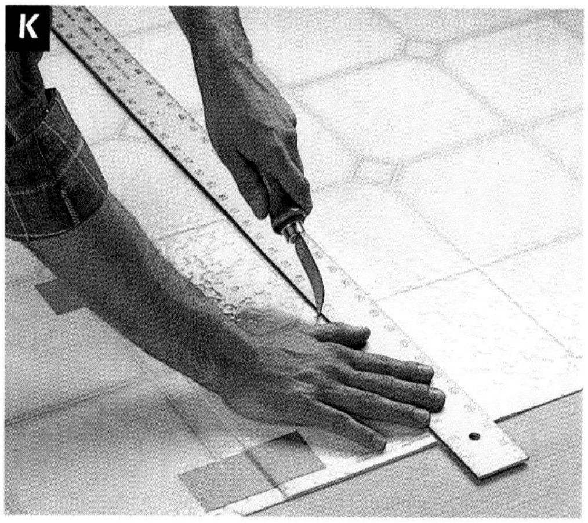

Double-cut the seams, using a straightedge as a guide for long cuts.

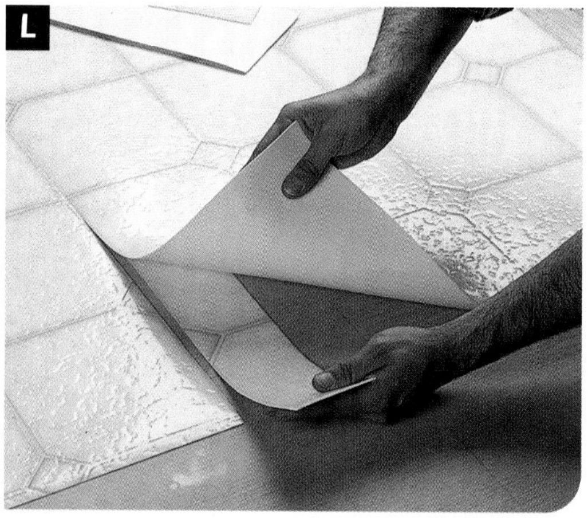

Remove the scraps and check the alignment of the seams.

Installing Perimeter Bond Sheet Vinyl

Cut and position the vinyl (pages 91 to 92), then fold back each sheet. Apply a 3" band of multipurpose flooring adhesive to the underlayment beneath the seams, using a wallboard knife or 1/4" notched trowel **(photo M).**

Lay the seam edges into the adhesive one at a time. Press the gaps together, then roll the seams with a J-roller **(photo N).** Apply adhesive at pipes or posts and around the entire perimeter of the room **(photo O).** Roll the flooring with the roller to ensure good contact with the adhesive.

Fasten the outer edges of the sheet to the floor by driving 3/8" staples every 3" around the edge. Cut and fit metal thresholds across the doorways, and replace the baseboards.

Tools: *Wallboard knife or 1/4" notched trowel, J-roller, heavy-duty stapler, hammer.*

Materials: *Multipurpose flooring adhesive, metal thresholds.*

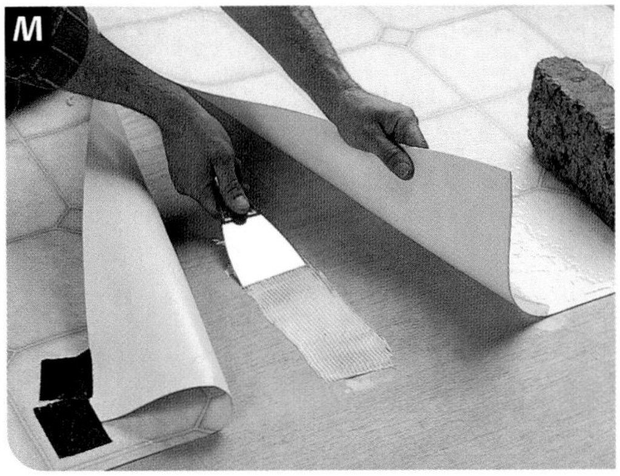

Fold back the edges and apply adhesive beneath the seams.

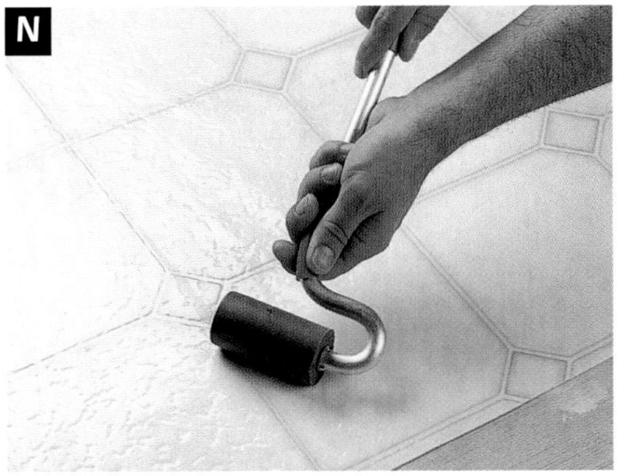

Press the edges into the adhesive and roll them down.

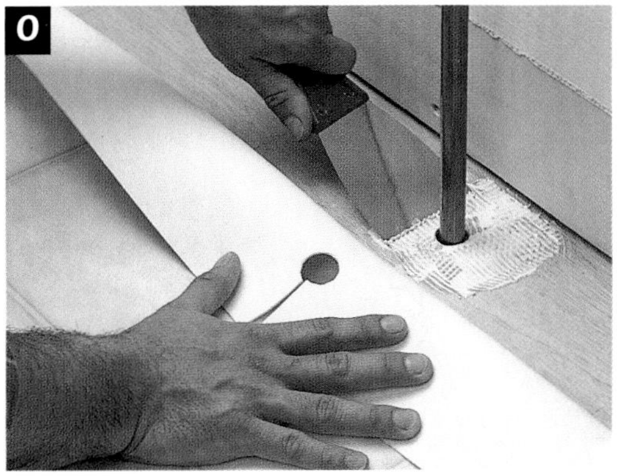

Surround obstructions and the perimeter with adhesive.

Installing Full-spread Sheet Vinyl

Cut the vinyl (pages 91 to 92), then position it in the room **(photo P).**

Pull back half of the flooring, then apply a layer of flooring adhesive over the underlayment, using a 1/4" notched trowel **(photo Q).** Lay the flooring back onto the adhesive.

To create a stronger bond and eliminate air bubbles, roll the floor with a floor roller **(photo R).** Move from the center of the room toward the edges. Fold over the unbonded section of flooring, apply adhesive, then lay and roll the area. Use a damp rag to wipe up any adhesive that oozes up around the edges of the vinyl. Cut and fit metal threshold bars across doorways, then replace the baseboards.

Tools: *1/4" notched trowel, floor roller, hammer.*

Materials: *Multipurpose flooring adhesive, metal thresholds.*

Position vinyl, sliding the edges under the door casings.

Pull back half the flooring and apply adhesive beneath it.

Roll the flooring to bond it with the subfloor.

Replacing Broken Vinyl Floor Tiles

If a few tiles are damaged, replace them. If you don't have replacements, remove tiles from a hidden area, such as inside a closet or under an appliance. Be aware that the backing of older tiles made of asphalt may contain asbestos fibers; consult a professional for their removal.

Use a heat gun to soften the underlying adhesive **(photo A).** Move the gun rapidly, being careful not to melt the tile. When the adhesive gives way, lift the tile out with a putty knife. If you don't have a heat gun, try setting a pan of ice cubes over the tile. The cold makes the adhesive brittle, allowing you to pop the tile up easily.

Apply mineral spirits to dissolve any remaining adhesive. Scrape away all the residue, using a putty knife **(photo B).**

Inspect the underlayment and repair it, if necessary. Apply new adhesive to the underlayment with a notched trowel, and position a new tile in the hole **(photo C).** Roll the tile, using pressure to create a good bond. Wipe off any excess adhesive.

Tools: *Heat gun, putty knife, notched trowel, J-roller or rolling pin.*

Materials: *Mineral spirits, flooring adhesive, replacement tile.*

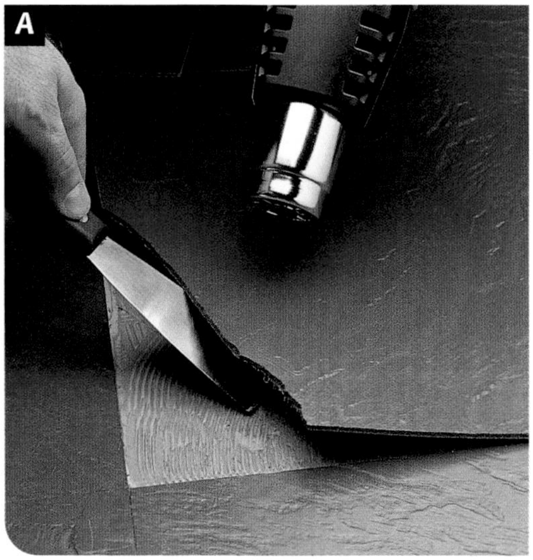

Remove the tile, using a heat gun to soften the adhesive.

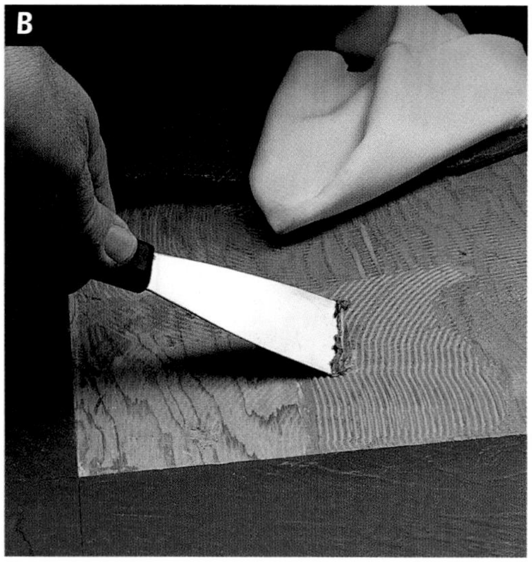

Dissolve adhesive with mineral spirits and scrape it away.

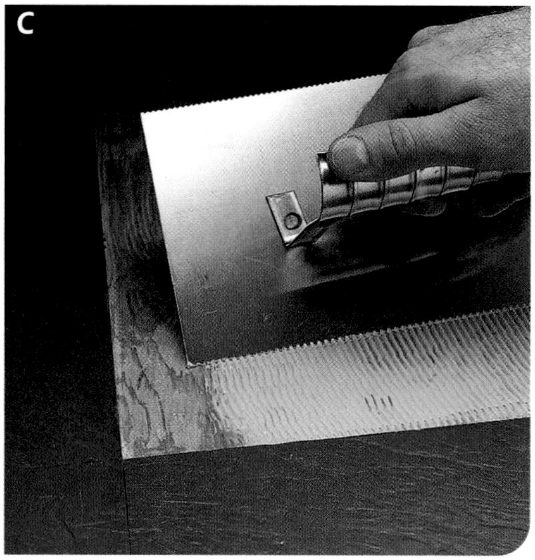

Apply adhesive and press the new tile into place.

Preparing to Install a Vinyl Tile Floor

Although it's simple to replace individual tiles, as shown above, at some point it no longer makes sense to keep repairing failing flooring. And since it's not difficult to install vinyl tile flooring, there's no reason to avoid it.

As you consider your options, inspect the existing flooring. Look for loose seams, tears, chips, air bubbles, and other areas where loose tiles may indicate widespread failure of the adhesive. Use a wallboard knife to test tiles. If tiles can be pried up easily in many different areas of the room, plan on removing all the flooring. Professionals suggest this guideline: if more than 30% of the flooring has failed, you're better off replacing the floor than trying to repair it.

Before purchasing vinyl tile, do some investigation and comparison shopping. Vinyl tile comes in self-adhesive and dry-back styles. Self-adhesive tile is easy to install, but the bond is less reliable than dry-back tile, to which you apply adhesive. And you can't use additional adhesives with self-adhesive tile.

You also need to consider how you're going to remove the existing tile and what you may find under it. Self-adhesive tiles are usually easy to remove and it's not likely that you'll create any damage in the process. So if the existing underlayment is sound, you can probably clean it up and install the new tiles directly over it.

Dry-back tiles, on the other hand, are fully secured with adhesive, and can be difficult to remove. It may be simpler just to remove the underlayment, taking the old flooring right along with it. This method makes even more sense if the underlayment is damaged or needs

Tools: *Wallboard knife, tape measure, chalk line, carpenter's square.*

Materials: Pencil.

to be replaced for some other reason.

If you are able to separate the tile from the underlayment, inspect the underlayment before you begin replacing the flooring. Solid underlayment is essential for any successful vinyl installation. Repair or replace the underlayment (page 84) or subfloor (page 86), if necessary.

Once the floor is down to a clean, solid layer of underlayment, the next step is to establish layout lines. Carefully positioning the lines will make installation easier.

Before committing to a layout, dry-fit the tiles to identify any problems. Check the tile for pattern or noticeable directional features. Tiles with an obvious grain pattern can be laid so that all the grain runs in the same direction. Or, you can use the quarter-turn method, in which the grain alternates in a checkerboard pattern.

Measure opposite sides of the room and mark the center of each side. Snap a chalk line (X) between the two marks as a reference line **(photo D).**

Measure and mark the center point of the chalk line. From this point, use a carpenter's square to establish a second line perpendicular to the first. Snap a second reference line (Y) across the room **(photo E).**

Check for square, using the "3-4-5 triangle" method. Measure and mark one reference line 3 ft. from the center point on line X. Measure and mark the other reference line 4 ft. from the center point on line Y **(photo F).**

Measure the distance between the marks **(photo G).** If the reference lines are perpendicular, the distance will measure exactly 5 ft. If not, adjust the reference lines until they are exactly perpendicular to one another and properly placed for your installation.

Snap a chalk line marking the center of the room.

Find the center point of this line and snap a second line (Y) exactly perpendicular to it.

To make sure the lines are perpendicular, measure and mark points exactly 3 ft. from the center point of line X and 4 ft. from the center point of line Y.

Measure between the marks. The distance should be exactly 5 ft. Adjust the reference lines as necessary to achieve this measurement.

Establishing Layout Lines

The marked perpendicular reference lines X and Y (page 95) form the basis for layout lines, the next step in the installation process. Begin by dry-fitting tiles along line Y **(photo A).** Shift the layout one way or the other to make it visually symmetrical or to reduce the number of cuts that will be necessary.

If you had to shift the layout, create a new line that is parallel to reference line X and runs through a tile joint near the original line. This new line (X') will be one of the layout lines you'll use when installing the tile. NOTE: To avoid confusion, use a different-colored chalk to distinguish between the original reference line and the new line.

Dry-fit tiles along the new layout line, X' **(photo B).** If necessary, adjust the layout again, as described above.

If you had to adjust the layout along line X, measure and mark a new layout line (Y') that is parallel to the reference line (Y) and runs through one of the tile joints **(photo C).** This new line forms the second layout line that you will use during the installation.

Dry-fit tiles along Y, adjusting layout line X, if necessary.

Dry fit tiles along X', adjusting layout line Y, if necessary.

If you adjusted the layout, measure and mark a new Y'.

Installing Self-adhesive Tile

Draw reference and layout lines as described above. Peel off the paper backing and install the first tile in one of the corners formed by the intersecting layout lines **(photo D).** Lay three or more tiles along each layout line in the quadrant. Rub the entire surface of each tile to bond the adhesive to the underlayment.

Begin installing tile in the quadrant, forming tight joints **(photo E).** Finish setting full-size tiles in the first quadrant, then in an adjacent one. Set the tiles along the layout lines first, then fill in the interior.

Mark cutting lines on tiles **(photo F).** Lay the tile to be cut (A) upside down on top of

Tools: *Straightedge, utility knife, tile cutter (optional), hammer.*

Materials: *Self-adhesive vinyl tile, felt-tipped pen, metal thresholds.*

Lay three tiles along each layout line in the quadrant.

Set the full-size tiles in two quadrants.

Mark tiles for cutting. NOTE: Cut tile shown inverted for clarity; tiles should be faceup for actual marking.

the last full tile. Position a 1/8"-thick spacer against the wall, then set a marker tile (B) on top of the tile to be cut. Trace a cutting line along the edge of the marker tile. NOTE: it's the uncovered portion of the cut tile that will be installed.

To mark tiles for cutting around outside corners, make a cardboard template to match the space, allowing an 1/8" gap along the walls **(photo G).** Cut the template, check its fit, then trace its outline on a tile.

Cut the tile to fit, using a straightedge and a utility knife. Hold the straightedge securely against the cutting lines to ensure a straight cut. If the tile is thick or difficult to cut, score and cut it with a tile cutter **(photo H).**

Install the cut tiles **(photo I).** You can precut all tiles, but measure the distance between the wall and the installed tiles at various points to make sure the variation doesn't exceed 1/2".

Install tile on the remaining quadrants until the room is covered. Check the entire floor, pressing loose tiles to improve their bond. Install thresholds and replace baseboards.

Make templates for the outside corners.

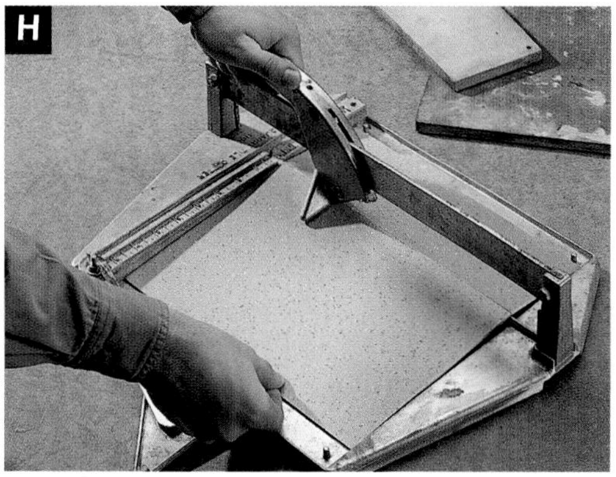

Cut the tile, using a tile cutter, if tiles are thick.

Install cut tiles next to the walls.

Installing Dry-back Tile

Measure and mark reference lines (page 95) and layout lines (page 96).

Begin applying adhesive around the intersection of the layout lines, using a trowel with 1/16" V-shaped notches. Hold the trowel at a 45° angle, and spread the adhesive evenly over the surface **(photo J).**

Spread adhesive over three quadrants of the installation area. Allow it to set according to the manufacturer's instructions, then install the tile, beginning at the intersection of the layout lines **(photo K).**

Use the techniques described above to cut and fit the tile. When one quadrant is completely tiled, spread adhesive over the remaining quadrant and set the remaining tile.

Tools: *1/16" V-notched trowel, straightedge, utility knife or tile cutter.*

Materials: *Dry-back vinyl tile, flooring adhesive, metal thresholds.*

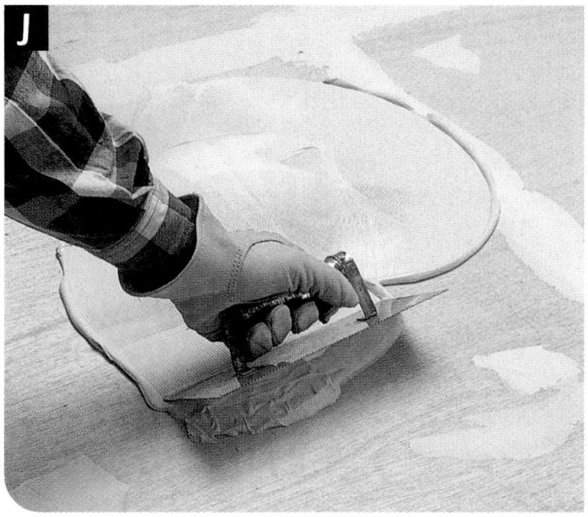

Apply adhesive to three of the marked quadrants.

Install tile in each quadrant. Then spread adhesive in the remaining quadrant and complete the installation.

Maintaining & Repairing Ceramic Flooring

Ceramic tile is one of the hardest flooring materials on the market. Its installation is fairly simple—an underlayment is put in place, then tile is set into a cement-based mortar. Finally, the spaces between tiles are filled with a thin mortar, called *grout*. Each of these elements plays a part in maintaining the integrity of the floor.

One of the fundamental requirements for a durable ceramic tile floor is a sound underlayment. Another is a continuous field—broken tiles and failed grout can expose the underlayment to moisture, which will destroy the floor.

Although there are significant differences among the various types of ceramic tile, most carry a price tag that reflects ceramic's appeal and durability. Ceramic tile doesn't generally require extensive maintenance, but it certainly makes sense to protect this investment by maintaining and repairing it as necessary.

Many ceramic tiles have a glazed surface that protects the porous clay from staining, but you should protect unglazed ceramic tile from stains and water spots by periodically applying a coat of tile sealer. Keep dirt from getting trapped in grout lines by sealing them about once a year.

Major cracks in grout joints indicate that movement of the floor has caused the adhesive layer beneath the tile to deteriorate. The adhesive layer must be replaced along with the grout in order to create a permanent repair.

Any time you remove tile, check the underlayment. If it's no longer smooth, solid, and level, repair or replace it before replacing the tile (page 85).

Regrouting a Ceramic Tile Floor

The first step may be the trickiest—you have to completely remove the old grout without damaging any of the tile. This calls for a hammer, a cold chisel, and a gentle touch. (Always wear eye protection when working with a hammer and chisel.) Holding the chisel at a slight angle, break away small sections of grout at a time. Remove loosened grout, then clean out the joints with a stiff-bristled broom or a small vacuum. Solve any underlying problems that could cause repeated failure.

Prepare a small batch of floor grout. If you're working with porous tile, include an additive with a release agent that will keep the grout from bonding to the surface of the tile.

Starting in a corner, pour the grout over the tile **(photo A).** Use a rubber grout float to spread the grout outward from the corner, tilting the float at a 60° angle to the floor, and using a figure-eight motion. Press firmly on the float to fill the joints completely.

Remove excess grout from the surface of the tile, using the grout float **(photo B).** Wipe diagonally across the joints, holding the float nearly vertical. Continue applying grout and removing the excess until you've grouted about 25 percent of the surface of the floor.

Wipe a damp grout sponge diagonally over the tile to remove excess grout, working on about 2 square feet at a time **(photo C).** Rinse the sponge between wipes. Wipe each area only once, to avoid pulling grout from the joints. Repeat until all joints are filled.

Let the grout dry about 4 hours, then buff the surface with a soft, dry cloth.

Tools: *Hammer, cold chisel, eye protection, stiff-bristled broom, bucket, rubber grout float.*

Materials: *Floor grout mix, rubber gloves, grout sponge, soft cloth.*

A — *Completely remove old grout, and clean the joints. Using a rubber grout float, spread grout over tile.*

B — *Force the grout into the joints, then use the float to remove the excess.*

C — *Wipe the joints with a damp sponge, working diagonally and covering about 2 square feet at a time.*

Replacing Damaged Tile

Remove the grout (page 98). When the joints are clean, use the hammer and cold chisel to break away the damaged tile **(photo D).** Drive the chisel down into a crack near the center of the tile, angling the piece forward and away. Work outward from the center until the tile is removed.

In bathrooms or other rooms where the floor is often exposed to water, the underlayment should be cementboard. In other types of rooms, the underlayment may be plywood. In either case, scrape away any adhesive or mortar, leaving the underlayment smooth and flat **(photo E).** If necessary, fill chips or dents in the underlayment, using an epoxy-based thin-set mortar for cementboard or a floor leveling compound for plywood.

Apply thin-set mortar to the back of the replacement tile, using a notched trowel to furrow the mortar **(photo F).** If you're replacing several tiles, use plastic spacers to ensure consistent spacing. Set the tile in position, and press down on it until it's even with the adjacent tiles.

Using a rubber mallet, gently rap the central area of the tile a few times to set it evenly into the mortar. Check the area with a level. If necessary to bring the tile level, lay a flat piece of 2 × 4 padded with carpet across several tiles, and rap it with the mallet **(photo G).**

Remove any spacers, using needlenose pliers. Clean out the wet mortar from the grout joints with a small screwdriver, and wipe the mortar from the tile surfaces **(photo H).** Let the mortar dry for 24 hours.

Matching the new grout to the existing color will blend the repair into the background. Mix some grout samples with pigment. When the samples are dry, compare colors, and adjust the pigment as necessary.

Fill the joints with grout (page 98). Apply grout sealer with a small paintbrush.

Tools: *Hammer, cold chisel, putty knife, square notched trowel, rubber mallet, level, needlenose pliers, screwdriver, grout float, paintbrush.*

Materials: *Thin-set mortar, floor leveling compound (optional), replacement tile, tile spacers, 2 × 4, bucket, grout, grout pigment, grout sponge, grout sealer.*

D

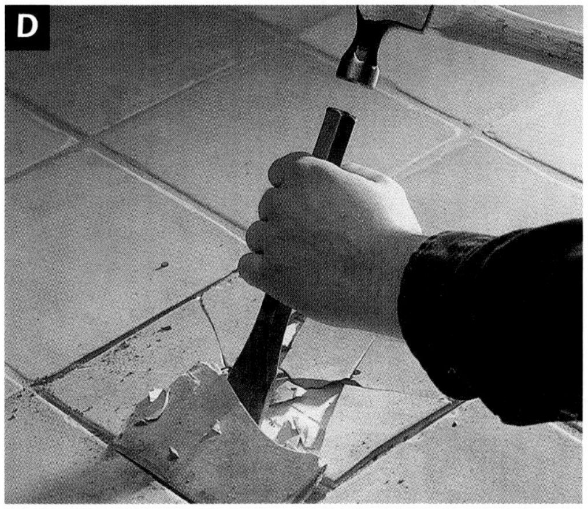

Carefully break apart and remove the damaged tile.

E

Remove any remaining mortar, scraping until the underlayment is smooth and flat.

F

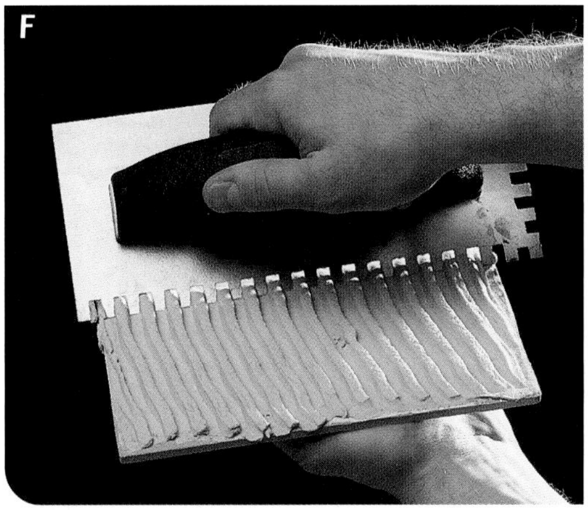

Apply thin-set mortar to the back of the replacement tile, and position it in place.

G

Use a 2 × 4 covered with carpet to set the tile flush with the surrounding tiles.

H

Remove the wet mortar from the grout joints, using a screwdriver. Then, wipe the tile clean.

Maintaining & Repairing Hardwood Flooring

Perhaps the most desirable feature of hardwood flooring is that it's a natural product. The patterns of the grain are interesting to the eye and the combinations of colors give any room a soft, inviting glow. The resilience of wood fibers makes a hardwood floor extremely durable but also susceptible to changes caused by moisture and aging.

Typically, the first thing to wear out on a hardwood floor is the finish. Even the toughest finishes deteriorate over time, leaving the wood flooring exposed to the destructive effects of light, water, and ground-in dirt. As it's tracked in on shoes, dirt is like sandpaper to your floor's finish, scratching and scraping with each step. Therefore, the best maintenance for a hardwood floor is regular and thorough cleaning. Instead of a broom, use a vacuum with a sweeper attachment to remove dirt from your floors.

To help you maintain or refinish your hardwood floor, you should know what type of finish the floor carries. If you're not certain what the finish is, try this test using a cloth or cotton swab, denatured alcohol, and lacquer thinner. In a clean, inconspicuous area of the floor, rub the alcohol in a small circle. If the floor's finish starts to come off, it's probably shellac. If the alcohol doesn't work but the thinner does, the finish is lacquer. If neither solvent works, it's a varnish, probably polyurethane. Remember the type of finish you have when purchasing cleaners and waxes.

If you have a fairly new hardwood floor, or a prefinished floor, check with the manufacturer or the flooring installer before applying any cleaning products or wax. Most prefinished hardwood, for example, should not be waxed.

Because sanding removes the wood's aged coloring, or *patina*, it's often difficult to blend a repaired area with the rest of the floor. If you're planning a major repair, consider refinishing the entire floor.

Tools: *Vacuum, buffing machine, hammer, nail set, putty knife.*

Materials: *Clean cloths, hardwood cleaning kit, paste wax, rubber gloves, oxalic acid, vinegar, wood restorer, latex wood patch, sandpaper.*

Cleaning & Renewing Hardwood

Often, a darkened, dingy hardwood floor needs only a thorough cleaning to remove dirt and built-up wax, revealing an attractive, healthy finish. Use water and soap or a cleaning solvent to remove old wax. Then, wax and buff the floor for a renewed shine.

Begin by vacuuming the entire floor to remove dirt, sand, and dust **(photo A).**

In a bucket, mix hot water and a moderate amount of dishwashing detergent that doesn't contain lye, trisodium phosphate, or ammonia. Working on 3-ft.-square sections at a time, scrub the floor with a brush or nylon scrubbing pad. Wipe up the water and wax with a towel before moving to the next section.

If the water and detergent solution doesn't remove the old wax, try using a hardwood floor cleaning kit **(photo B).** Use only solvent-type cleaners, as some water-based products can blacken wood. Apply the cleaner following the manufacturer's instructions.

When the floor is clean and dry, apply a high-quality floor wax **(photo C).** Paste wax is more difficult to apply than liquid floor wax, but it lasts much longer. Buff the floor with a rented buffing machine fitted with synthetic buffing pads.

A

Vacuum the floor to remove loose dirt and grit.

B

Clean the floor with hot water and mild detergent, or use a commercial hardwood floor cleaner.

C

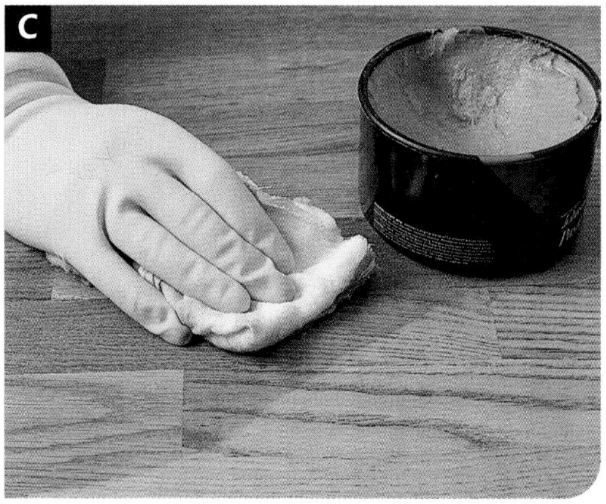

Protect and polish the floor with paste wax. Apply the wax by hand. Then, polish the floor with a buffing machine.

Removing Stains

Water and other liquids can penetrate deep into the grain of hardwood floor boards, leaving dark stains that are sometimes impossible to remove by sanding. Instead, try bleaching the wood with oxalic acid, available in crystal form at home centers or paint stores.

First, remove the floor's finish by sanding the stained area with sandpaper.

In a disposable cup, dissolve the recommended amount of oxalic acid crystals in water. Wearing rubber gloves, pour the mixture over the stained area, taking care to cover only the darkened wood **(photo D).**

Let the liquid stand for one hour. Repeat the application, if necessary.

Wash the area with vinegar to neutralize the acid **(photo E).** Rinse with water, and let the wood dry. Sand the area smooth.

Apply several coats of wood restorer until the bleached area matches the finish of the surrounding floor **(photo F).**

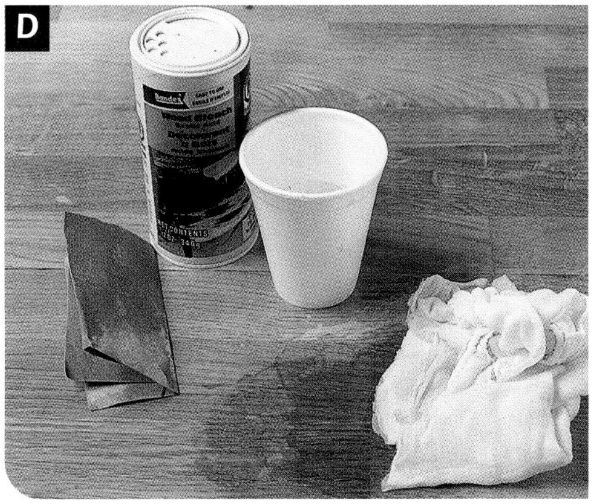

Apply a solution of oxalic acid and water to the stained area.

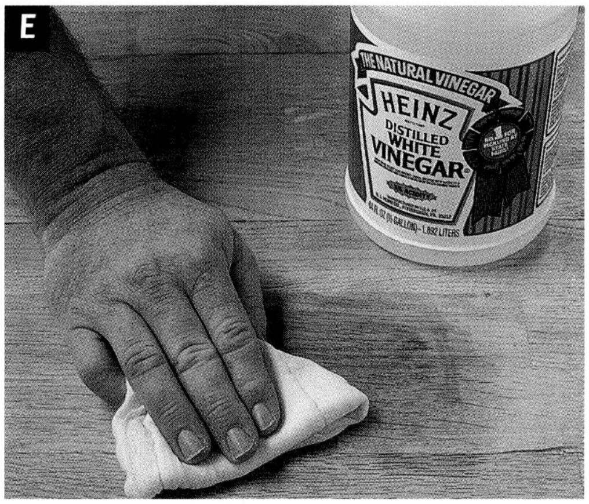

Neutralize the acid with vinegar, and rinse with water.

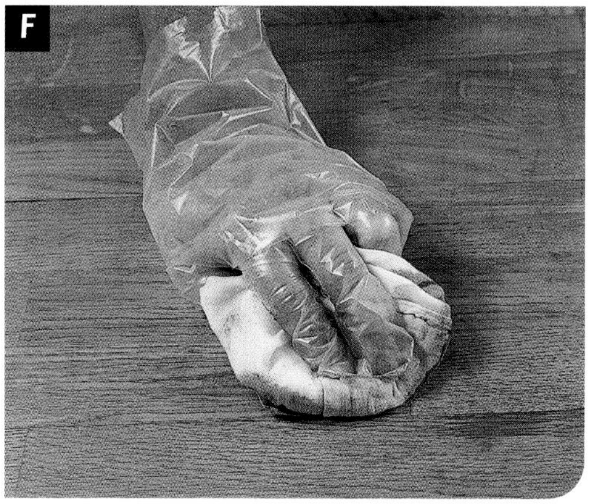

Restore the color to the bleached area with wood restorer.

Patching Scratches & Small Holes

When gouges, scratches, and dents aren't bad enough to warrant replacing a floor board, repair the damaged area with a latex wood patch. Patching compounds are available in various wood tones, so choose one that matches the color of your floor.

Before filling nail holes, first make sure the nails are securely set in the wood. Use a hammer and a nail set to drive loose nails below the surface so they won't pop back out.

Apply the wood patch to the damaged area, using a putty knife **(photo G).** Force the compound into the hole by pressing the knife blade downward until it lies flat on the floor.

Scrape excess compound from the edges, and allow the patch to dry completely.

Sand the patch flush with the surrounding surface **(photo H).** Use fine-grit sandpaper, and sand in the direction of the wood grain.

Apply wood restorer to the sanded area until it blends with the rest of the floor **(photo I).**

Press patching compound into the hole with a putty knife.

Sand the patch smooth with fine-grit sandpaper.

Coat the patch with wood restorer to match the finish.

Replacing Damaged Boards

When solid hardwood floor boards are beyond repair, carefully cut them out and replace them with boards of the same width and thickness. Replace whole boards, whenever possible. If a board is long, or part of its length is inaccessible, draw a cutting line across the face of the board, and tape behind the line to protect the section that will remain.

First, drill several overlapping holes at the ends of the board or just inside the cutting lines, using a spade bit.

Set the depth of your circular saw to cut to the exact thickness of the floor boards, and make several cuts through the middle of each board **(photo A).** Cut outward from the center until the saw cuts intersect the holes.

Chisel out the center of the board, working out to the edges **(photo B).** Don't pry or drive the chisel against any good boards.

To complete a cut in the middle of a board, square off the edge at the cutting line, using a sharp, wide chisel **(photo C).**

Cut the replacement boards to fit and install them, one at a time. Apply construction adhesive to the bottom face and in the groove of the board, and set it in place. Drill pilot holes, and drive spiral-shank flooring nails at a 45° angle through the base of the tongue and into the subfloor. Set the nails with a nail set **(photo D).**

To install the last board, chisel off the lower lip of the groove **(photo E).** Also remove the tongue on the end of the board, if necessary. Apply adhesive to the board, and set it in place, tongue first. Drive flooring nails through the top of the board at both ends and along the groove side **(photo F).** Fill the nail holes with wood putty.

Tools: *Drill, spade bit, circular saw, chisel, hammer, caulk gun, nail set.*

Materials: *Replacement boards, masking tape, construction adhesive, spiral-shank flooring nails, wood putty.*

Drill holes in the ends of the boards. Then, cut between the holes with a circular saw.

Remove the middle portion of the boards with a chisel. Then, carefully chisel away the edges.

Square off the end cuts of long boards at the cutting lines, using a sharp chisel.

Drive flooring nails through the front edges of replacement boards, and set the nails with a nail set.

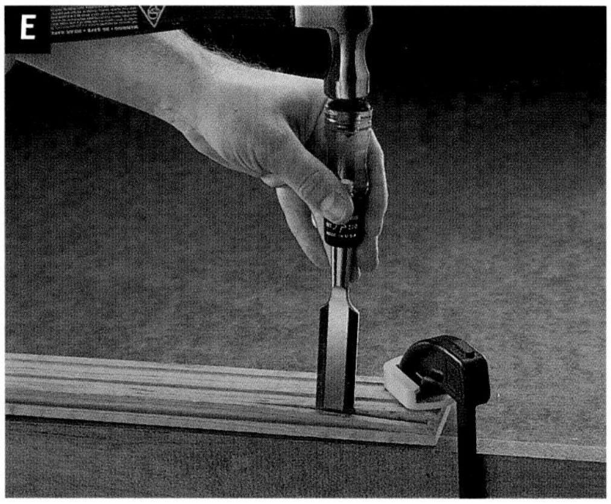

Clamp the final replacement board to your workbench, and remove the lower lip of the groove.

Surface-nail the ends and groove edge of the replacement board through predrilled pilot holes. Then, set the nails.

Refinishing a Hardwood Floor

Sanding a hardwood floor with a rented drum sander and edger will make your old floor look new. You should practice using the machines on a piece of plywood, and remember to keep the sander moving when the drum or disc is in contact with the floor. As a general rule, use the finest sandpaper that's effective for the job.

Prepare the floor by nailing down loose boards and setting nails with a nail set. Remove base shoe molding, and mask off doorways and ductwork to contain the dust during sanding. Vacuum the floor thoroughly before each sanding stage.

Start with 80-grit sandpaper, and position the drum sander about 6" from the wall. With the drum raised above the floor, start the machine and move it forward, slowly lowering the drum **(photo G).** Sand in the direction of the floorboards, to within 1 ft. of the end wall, and raise the drum with the sander in motion.

Return to your starting point and begin the second pass, overlapping the first path by one-half its width **(photo H).**

The first stage of sanding should remove most of the old finish **(photo I).** Switch to a 120-grit sandpaper and resand the entire floor. Repeat the sanding process, using finer sandpaper (150- to 180-grit) to remove scratches left by the coarser papers.

Sand along the edges using the same sequence of sandpapers used with the drum sander **(photo J).**

Scrape old finish from hard-to-reach areas. Then, hand-sand the area smooth **(photo K).**

Wipe the floor with a tack cloth to remove dust, and apply the topcoat of your choice **(photo L).** Polyurethane is a good product for a clear, durable finish.

Tools: *Nail set, hammer, drum sander, edger, vacuum, scraper, painting pad.*

Materials: *Sanding belts and discs, tack cloth, floor finish.*

Turn on the machine and begin moving forward before lowering the drum. Follow a straight path, with the grain.

Sand the next row, overlapping one-half of the first row.

Remove most of the old finish before switching to a fine-grit sanding belt. Use finer belts until floor is consistently smooth.

Sand the borders with an edger. Keep the sander moving and let the machine's weight supply downward pressure.

Use a sharp scraper to reach the tight spots. Hand-sand the area to blend with the power-sanded floor.

Apply a topcoat, using a painting pad with a pole extension. Buff the floor with a fine abrasive pad.

Chemically Stripping a Wood Floor

Stripping the finish from a floor is a good alternative to sanding if you want to retain the floor's aged glow or if the boards have been sanded before and are less than 3/8" thick. Determine what type of finish your floor has (page 100), and purchase the type of semi-paste stripper that will do the job best.

Protect baseboards and other trim with masking tape, seal interior doors, and open the windows before applying the stripper.

Wearing a respirator and rubber gloves, apply the stripper with a paintbrush **(photo A).** Cover only an area small enough to be scraped within the working time of the stripper.

Scrape off the sludge of stripper and old finish, using a nylon stripper knife **(photo B).** Move the scraper with the wood grain, and deposit the sludge onto old newspapers.

After the entire floor is stripped, scrub it with an abrasive pad dipped in a rinsing solvent, such as mineral spirits, that's compatible with your stripping product. Do not use water.

Clean residual sludge and dirt from the joints between floorboards, using a palette knife or putty knife **(photo C).**

Remove stains and discoloration by carefully sanding only the affected area **(photo D).** Use oxalic acid on deep stains (page 101).

Touch up sanded areas with wood stain **(photo E).** Test the stain before applying.

Tools: *Paintbrushes, nylon stripper knife, palette knife, sanding block.*

Materials: *Chemical stripper, masking tape, respirator, rubber gloves, rinsing solvent, abrasive pads, sandpaper, wood stain.*

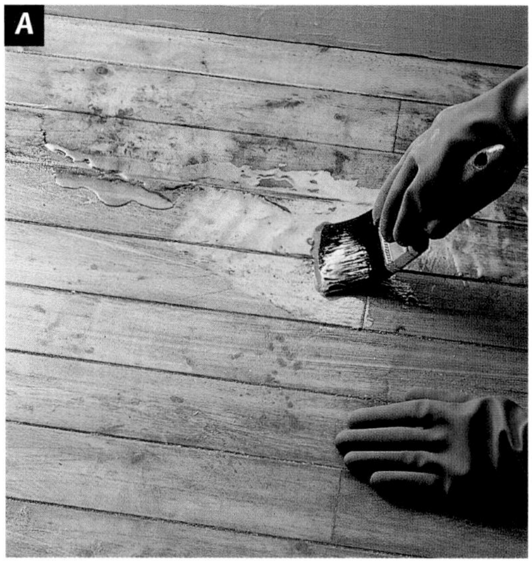

Spread the stripper over a small area with a paintbrush.

When the finish dissolves, scrape it up with a stripping knife.

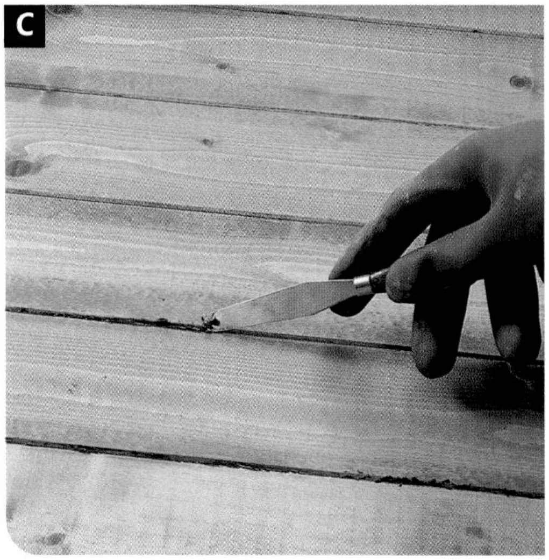

Clean the joints between boards with a palette knife.

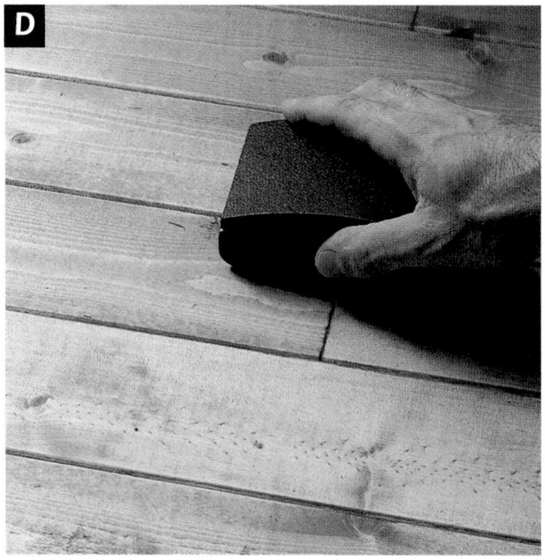

Remove surface stains by carefully sanding with the grain.

Blend sanded areas with wood stain.

Cutting & Fitting Hardwood Flooring

Installing traditional solid hardwood flooring is a difficult job that's best left to professionals. However, there are many manufactured wood flooring products now available that are designed for do-it-yourself installation **(photo F).** Popular options include fiberboard surfaced with a synthetic laminate layer that mimics the look of wood grain, and plywood planks topped with a hardwood veneer. Parquet tiles, made with hardwood strips bonded together in a decorative pattern, are also easy to install. These products are prefinished by the manufacturer and don't need to be sanded, stained, or protected.

Laminated plank flooring can be installed two different ways. One is the "floating" technique, in which the planks are edge-glued together and laid over a foam backing. This is ideal for applications over concrete slabs susceptible to moisture, such as those in basements. The other method is to glue the planks to an underlayment with flooring adhesive—a good choice for high-traffic areas. Install parquet flooring following the same methods used to install vinyl or ceramic tile (pages 94 to 99).

Because wood expands with moisture, always leave a 1/2" gap between wood flooring and walls. Hide the gaps with base molding.

Whichever flooring you choose, follow these cutting tips for a quality installation. When using a circular saw or a jig saw, always cut from the back side of the piece to prevent splintering on the top surface.

To fit the last plank along a wall, measure the distance to the last board installed, and subtract 1/2" to allow for an expansion gap. Mark the cut with a chalk line **(photo G).**

When cutting narrow planks with a circular saw, place another plank next to your workpiece to provide a stable surface for the foot of the saw **(photo H).** Also, clamp a straightedge in place to use as a cutting guide.

Make crosscuts and angled cuts with a power miter saw **(photo I).** Keep the top of the workpiece facing up to prevent splintering.

Use a coping saw or jig saw to cut curves and notches **(photo J).**

Like solid hardwood planks, manufactured flooring products have tongue-and-groove edges for a tight bond between pieces.

Use a chalk line to make straight cut lines on long planks.

A straightedge and scrap board help keep your saw in line.

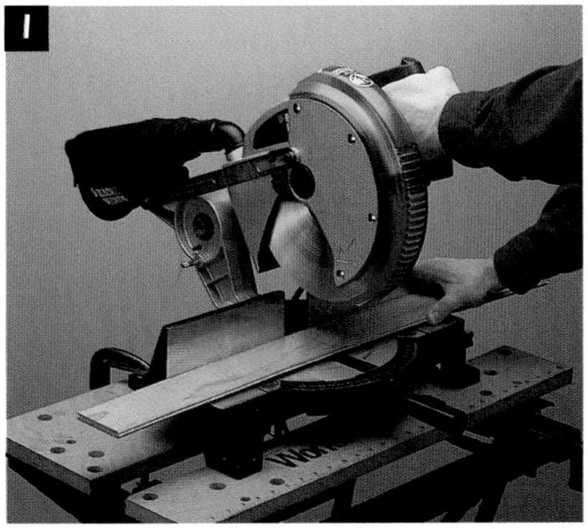

A power miter saw makes accurate straight and angled cuts.

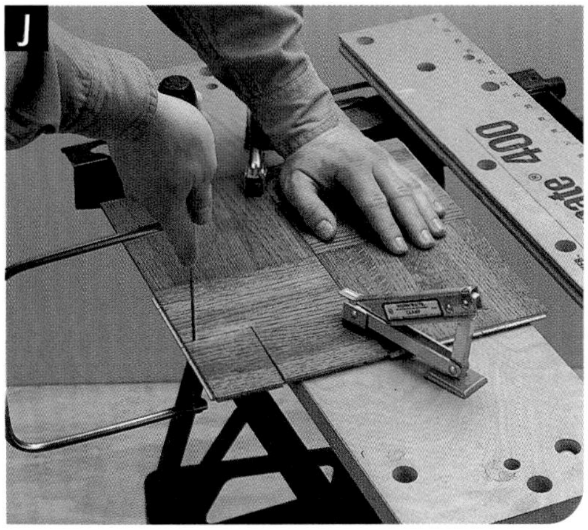

Make notches and curved cuts with a coping saw or jig saw.

Installing Wood Strip Flooring with Adhesive

A successful installation of wood strip flooring starts with a smooth, sound underlayment.

To install the first row of flooring, establish a straight layout line. Snap a chalk line parallel to the longest wall, about 30" from the wall. Work from the wall side of this line.

Apply flooring adhesive on the opposite side of the layout line, using a notched trowel **(photo A).** Spread the adhesive evenly, and don't obscure the layout line.

Install the first row of flooring with the edge of the tongues directly over the chalk line **(photo B).** Apply wood glue to the grooved end of each piece as you install it. Make sure the end joints are tight, and wipe up excess glue immediately. Leave a 1/2" gap at all walls for expansion.

To install succeeding rows, first insert the tongue edge of each strip into the groove of the preceding row, and lay the strip into the adhesive **(photo C).** Then, slide the strip over, butting the end joint with the strip next to it.

After every few rows, tap the last strip along its leading edge, using a scrap piece and a hammer, to tighten the joints between rows.

Use a cardboard template to fit boards in irregular areas **(photo D).** Cut the cardboard to size. Then, trace its outline onto the strip, and cut the strip with a jig saw.

Finish each section by rolling the floor with a heavy flooring roller to bond it with the adhesive **(photo E).** Complete this step within the working time of the adhesive.

Tools: *Measuring tape, chalk line, V-notched adhesive trowel, power saws, hammer, flooring roller (available for rent from flooring distributors).*

Materials: *Wood flooring, flooring adhesive, wood glue, cardboard.*

Apply an even layer of adhesive, using a notched trowel.

Install the first row of flooring along the layout line.

Set the long tongue edge first. Then, slide the ends together.

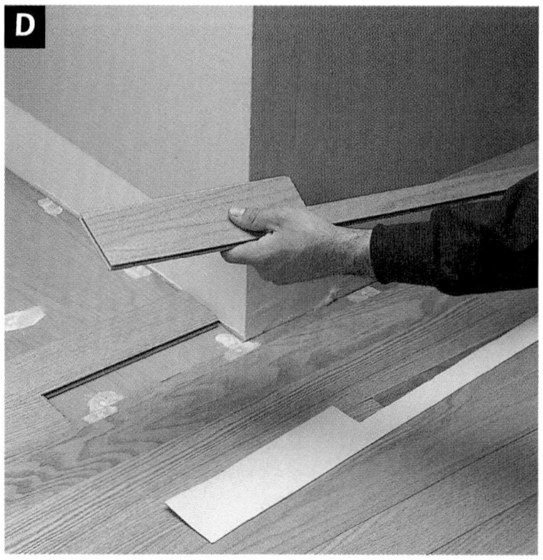

For accurate custom cuts, make a cardboard template.

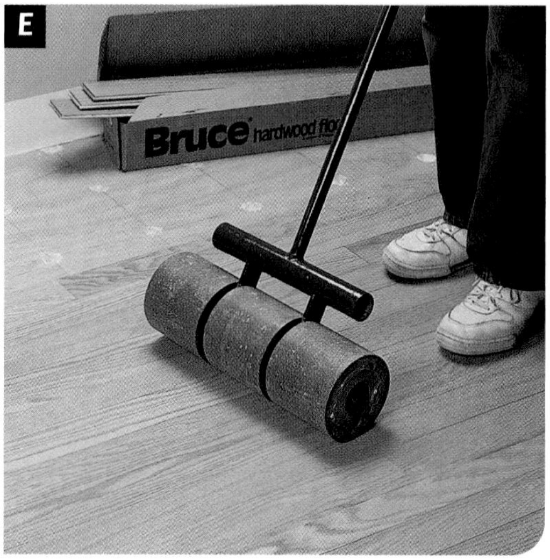

Use a flooring roller to secure the bond with the adhesive.

Installing a Floating Plank Floor

A floating plank floor is easy to install because there are no nails or adhesives securing the flooring to the subfloor. Instead, individual planks are glued together, forming a solid layer that rests on a bed of foam backing. Foam backing comes in various thicknesses, so be sure to purchase the right type for your flooring.

Because there are no fasteners, floating floors are especially appropriate over concrete slabs, which don't accept nails very well. For this application, however, you must install a vapor barrier directly over the concrete to seal off any moisture that can ruin the wood. Get a wide roll of polyethylene sheeting (4 mil, or thicker) and a roll of duct tape. Lay the plastic sheeting over the entire floor, overlapping the rows by several inches, and tape the seams. Install the foam layer over the vapor barrier.

If you're installing over a wood floor, be sure the underlayment is smooth and flat.

Roll out the foam backing, and cut it to fit with a utility knife **(photo F).** Tape the rows together, but don't overlap the seams.

Cut spacers from 1/2"-thick plywood, and place them about every 8" along the longest wall. Lay the first row of flooring, setting the grooved edges of the planks against the spacers **(photo G).** Leave the spacers in place until the job is finished.

Join the planks by gluing along the grooved edges and ends **(photo H).** Set the groove over the tongue of the preceding row, and lay it flat on the floor. Then, set a straight wood block at least 1 ft. long against the tongue of the workpiece, and tap the block with a hammer to close the joint between the planks. Use the same method for the end joints. Wipe up excess glue with a damp cloth.

Cut the end pieces to fit (page 105), and remember to leave a 1/2" expansion gap between the flooring and the walls.

Tools: *Utility knife, hammer, power saws.*

Materials: *Wood flooring, plastic sheeting, duct tape, foam backing, ½"-thick plywood, wood glue.*

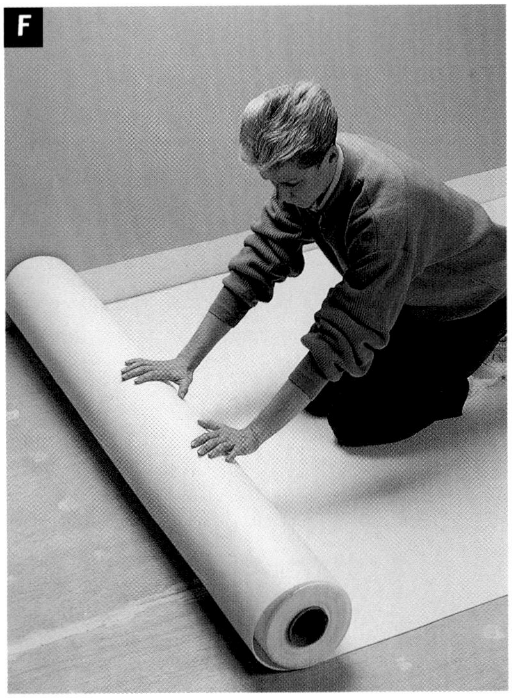

Roll out the foam backing, and tape the seams together.

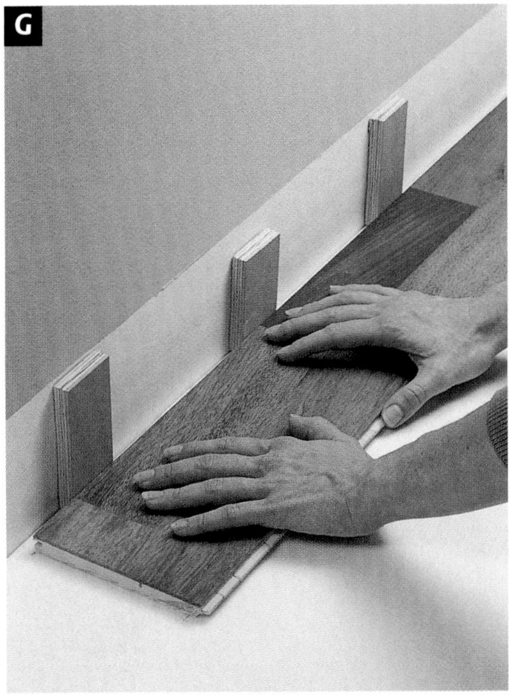

Use spacers to support the first row and to provide a gap.

Apply glue to the grooved edges and ends of each plank. Use a wood block and a hammer to tap the planks together.

Maintaining & Repairing Carpeting

Carpet, one of the most popular and versatile floor coverings available, lends color and style to a room. It also muffles sound, adds warmth, and creates a cozy effect.

The most important thing you can do to extend the life of a carpet is to keep it clean, vacuuming often and removing stains as soon as they appear. Ground-in dirt mats a carpet's pile and wears out its fibers. To prevent damage and excessive wear, place a doormat in front of each entry door.

Be wary of any cleaning method that exposes carpet to excessive moisture or leaves a soap residue, which often proves to be a magnet for dirt in the future. Ordinary glass cleaner removes stubborn stains from most types of carpet. Spray the stained area liberally, allow it to soak in for 5 to 10 minutes, then blot the area with a paper towel. If necessary, repeat the treatment. For tough stains, scrub the area, using a small scrap of carpeting.

To reduce the static electricity in carpeted rooms, spray the carpet with a solution of five parts water and one part liquid fabric softener. Apply a light mist of it onto the carpeting as you back out of the room, paying particular attention to traffic patterns. Wait about five minutes before walking on the carpet.

Walking barefoot leaves traces of the oil contained by human skin, which can attract dirt. To protect carpets, insist that your family wear socks, slippers or clean shoes indoors.

Common carpet problems include small burns or stains, loose areas, and faulty seams. All these problems can be resolved relatively easily with readily available tools and materials. The key to many repairs is having new pieces available, so save scraps any time you install new carpeting.

Tools: Cookie-cutter tool, knee kicker, 4" wallboard knife, utility knife, seam iron.

Materials: Replacement carpeting, double-face carpet tape, seam adhesive, heat-activated seam tape, boards, weights.

Repairing Spot Damage

Burns and stains are the most common carpeting problems. You can clip away the burned fibers of superficial burns, using small scissors. Patch deeper burns, as well as indelible stains, by cutting away and replacing the damaged area.

Remove extensive damage or stains with a "cookie-cutter" tool **(photo A),** which is available at carpeting stores. Press the cutter down over the damaged area, and twist it to cut away the carpet.

Using the cookie cutter tool again, cut a replacement patch from scrap carpeting. Insert double-face carpet tape under the cutout, positioning the tape so it overlaps the patch seams **(photo B).**

Press the patch into place. Make sure the direction of the nap or pattern matches the existing carpet. To seal the seam and prevent unraveling, apply seam adhesive to the edges of the patch **(photo C).**

A

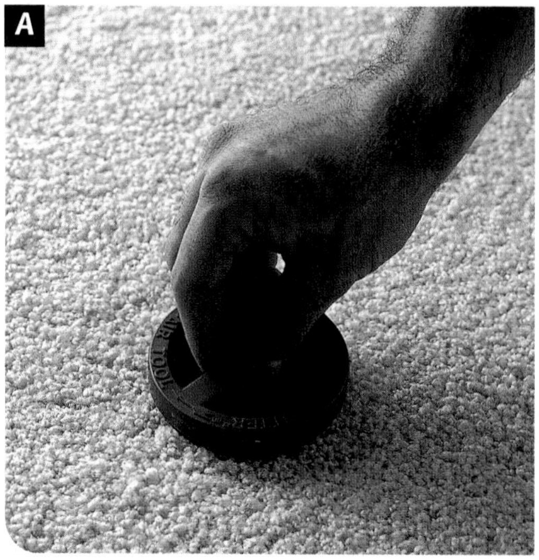

Twist the cookie-cutter tool to cut around the damaged area.

B

Use double-face carpet tape to hold the patch in place.

C

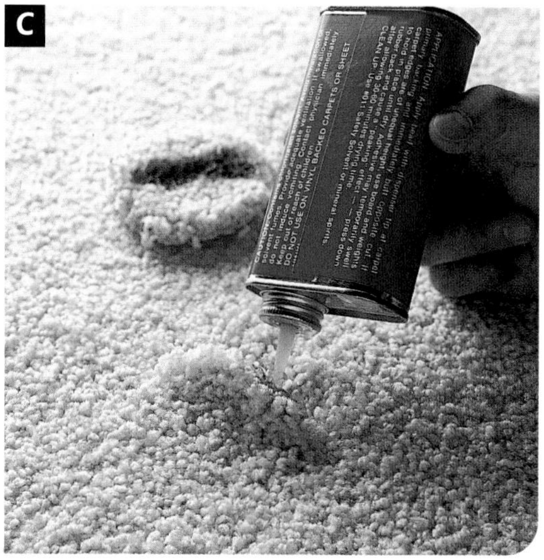

Apply seam adhesive to the seam to prevent unraveling.

Restretching Loose Carpeting

Carpeting that isn't glued down is held around the perimeter of a room by wood strips with metal pins that grip the carpet backing. To repair loose carpets, use a *knee kicker* carpet stretching tool to pull the carpet tight and reattach the edges to the strips.

Rent a knee kicker from a rental center or carpet distributor. Turn the knob on the head of the kicker to adjust the depth of the prongs **(photo D).** The prongs should extend far enough to grab the carpet backing without penetrating through the padding.

Starting from a corner or near a point where the carpet is firmly attached, press the knee kicker head into the carpet, about 2" from the wall. Thrust your knee into the cushion of the knee kicker to force the carpet toward the wall. Then, tuck the carpet edge into the space between the wood strip and the baseboard, using a 4" wallboard knife **(photo E).**

If the carpet is still loose, trim the edge with a utility knife, and stretch it again.

Set the knee kicker prongs to grab just the carpet backing.

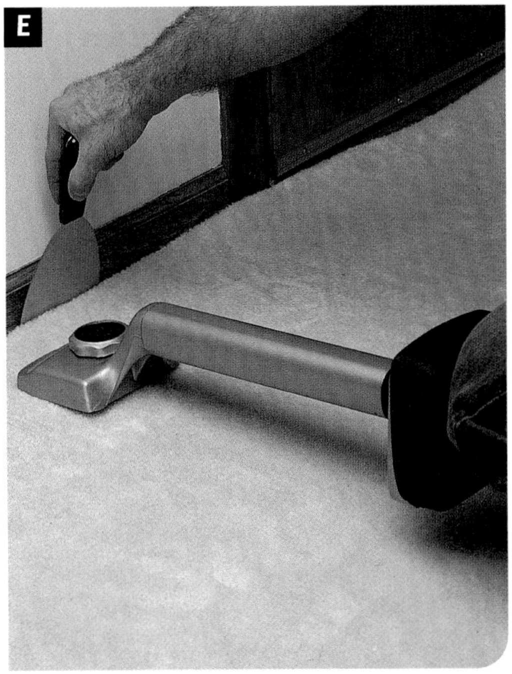

Stretch the carpet, and tuck the edge behind the strip.

Regluing Loose Seams

Most carpets are held together at the edges with heat-activated seam tape. The tape comes in rolls and has hardened glue on one face. To repair a loose seam, replace the tape and reglue the seam, using a rented seam iron.

Start by removing the old tape from under the carpet seam.

Cut a strip of new seam tape and place it under the carpet so it is centered along the seam with the adhesive facing up **(photo F).**

Plug in the seam iron, and let it heat up. Pull up both edges of the carpet, and set the hot iron squarely onto the tape. Wait about 30 seconds for the glue to melt. Then, move the iron about 12" farther along the seam **(photo G).**

Quickly press the edges of the carpet together into the melted glue behind the iron. Separate the pile to make sure no fibers are stuck in the glue and that the seam is tight.

Place weighted boards over the seam to keep it flat while the glue sets. Remember, you have only 30 seconds to repeat the process.

With the old seam tape removed, insert the new tape under the carpet edges with the glue-coated side facing up.

Once the glue melts, move the iron down, and press the edges of the carpet into the hot glue.

Stairs

Once a focal point of the architect's design and the carpenter's craft, the staircase has become quite standardized in modern home construction. Yet even today, staircases are designed and constructed following rigorous Codes and specifications. A staircase must be easy to climb and descend, with perfectly uniform steps, yet occupy as little living space as possible. And, because it joins two floors, it must withstand the movement of both—sometimes in opposite directions—as the house settles with age.

The continual pounding of foot traffic and pulling of hands take their toll on even the best built staircases and railings. And an unstable staircase is as unsafe as it is unattractive. Problems related to the structure of a staircase, such as severe sagging, twisting, or slanting, should be left to a professional. But given an understanding of the many parts of a staircase and how they are related, you can easily complete many common repairs.

A staircase starts with two or more solid boards spanning diagonally from one level to the next. These boards, known as *stringers* (or carriages), are commonly made from 2 × 12 lumber and they support the steps of the staircase. The stringers are cut either in a sawtooth pattern, providing support from below the steps, or they have grooves cut into their faces that receive the ends of the steps—known as "housed" stringers. A stringer may have a decorative skirtboard attached to one or both sides to conceal construction joints.

Each step of a staircase has two parts: the *tread*—the horizontal board that you walk on, and the *riser*—the vertical board linking each pair of treads. Treads and risers are joined with grooved joints or simple butt joints. Both parts are nailed to the stringers or, in the case of the housed stringer, held tightly in the stringer grooves by wedges driven from the underside of the staircase.

The handrail assembly that encloses open-sided stairways is called the *balustrade*, which consists of the railing, the newels, and the balusters. The newels are the large posts, either hollow or solid wood, that support the railing at the ends of the staircase and at the landing. Between the newels, the balusters support the railing from each stair tread. Round balusters fit into railing holes, while square ones attach within a continuous groove milled into the bottom of the railing. Thin pieces of wood, called *fillets*, provide support between square balusters.

Knowing the type of staircase you have and the construction of its basic parts will help you make efficient, quality repairs. If you have access to the underside of the staircase, start your investigation there. Note the location and design of the supporting stringers, as well as their general health, and examine the joints between the stair treads and risers. From the top side of the staircase, peek under carpet or remove molding to find how your stair parts are fitted together.

The most common stair problems are squeaky steps and loose balustrades. Squeaks are usually caused by movement between the treads and risers, which can be alleviated from above or below the staircase.

Balustrade remedies include reinforcing or replacing balusters, fastening loose newels, and tightening railing joints. Remember that these parts are all connected, and fixing loose balusters won't help for long if you ignore failed railing connections.

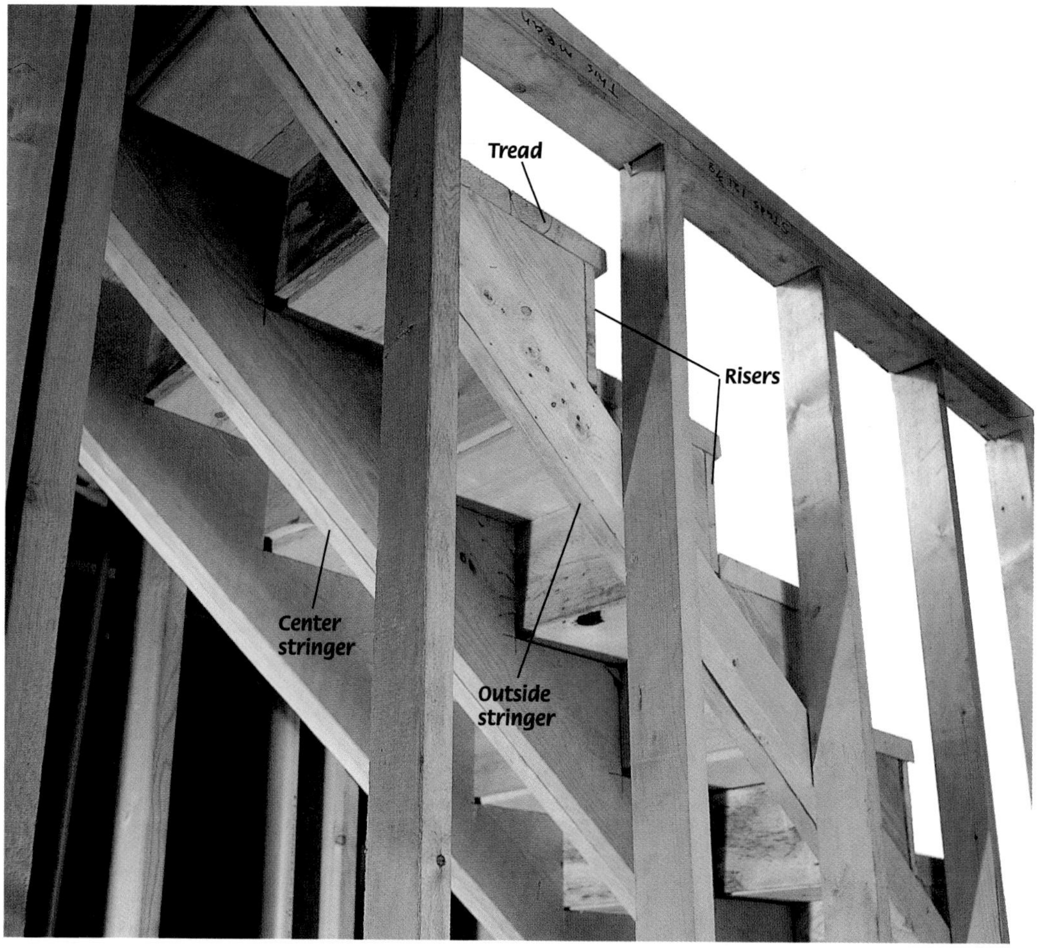

This staircase has center stringers to help support the treads. The 2 × 4s nailed between the outside stringers and the wall studs serve as spacers that allow room for the installation of skirt boards and wall finishes.

Eliminating Squeaks from Below

If possible, fix squeaking stairs from underneath the staircase—where you won't have to hide the repairs.

Glue wood blocks to the joints between treads and risers with construction adhesive **(photo A).** Once the blocks are in place, drill pilot holes and fasten them to the treads and risers with screws.

If the risers overlap the back edges of the treads, drive screws through the risers and into the treads to bind them together.

Fill the gaps between stair parts with tapered hardwood shims **(photo B).** Coat the shims with wood glue and tap them into the joints between treads and risers just until they are snug.

Tools: *Drill, hammer, screwdriver.*

Materials: *Construction adhesive, wood blocks, screws, hardwood shims, wood glue.*

Attach wood blocks to the treads and risers with adhesive.

Use shims to stop squeaking where stair parts are gapped.

Eliminating Squeaks from Above

When the underside of a staircase is inaccessible, silence noisy stairs from above with screws, shims, or molding.

Drill pilot holes and drive screws down through stair treads and into risers **(photo C).** Countersink the screws and fill the holes with putty or wood plugs.

Tap glued shims under loose treads to keep them from flexing **(photo D).** When the glue dries, cut the shims flush, using a utility knife.

Support the joints between treads and risers with quarter-round molding **(photo E).** Use finish nails and set the nails with a nail set.

Tools: *Drill, screwdriver, hammer, utility knife, nail set.*

Materials: *Screws, wood putty, hardwood shims, wood plugs, wood glue, quarter-round molding, finish nails.*

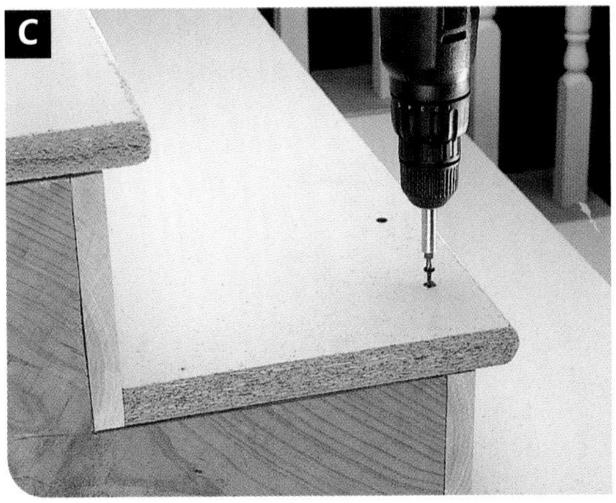

Use screws to bind loose stair treads to risers.

Tap shims under treads, using a block to prevent splitting.

Reinforce loose joints with quarter-round molding.

Tightening Balusters

Square-top balusters are fastened to stair railings with glue and finish nails, both of which can lose their grip over time. Reinforce loose balusters with screws and replace loose fillet spacers between balusters. If several neighboring balusters need repair, fasten all of them before installing the new fillets.

Start by chiseling out the fillets between the loose balusters, and pulling any loose nails.

Where fillets are removed, support the lower side of the baluster with a clamp secured to the railing.

Drill and countersink an angled pilot hole. Locate the hole so that the screw head will be concealed by the new fillet.

Secure the baluster with a wallboard or wood screw **(photo A).**

Cut the new fillets to fit snugly between the balusters, using a miter box to ensure clean angle cuts. Test-fit each fillet before attaching it. Apply glue and clamp the fillets in place.

Drill pilot holes, and drive finish nails with a tack hammer to secure the fillets to the railing **(photo B).** Set the nails with a nail set.

Tools: *Chisel, hammer, clamp, drill, miter box, tack hammer, nail set.*

Materials: *Screws, fillet stock, finish nails.*

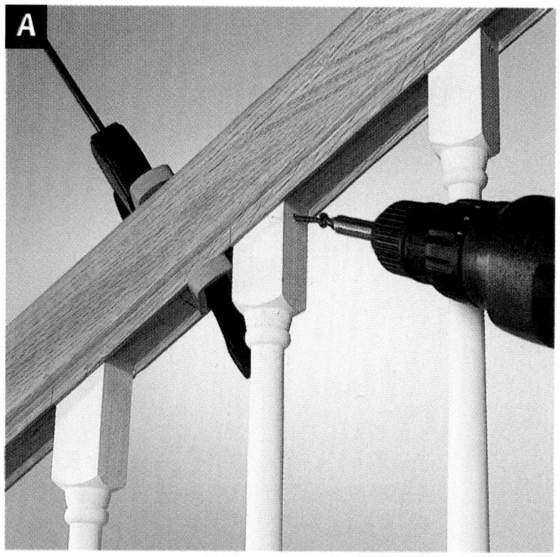

Support the baluster with a clamp, then drive a screw through the end of the baluster and into the railing.

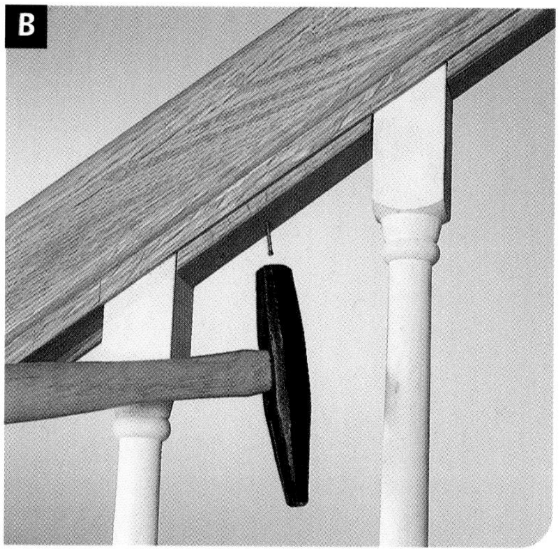

Custom-cut each fillet and glue it into the railing groove. Then, nail the fillet in place with two finish nails.

Replacing a Broken Baluster

The first step in replacing a baluster is determining how it's joined to the stair tread and railing. This will guide your methods of removal. If the base of the baluster rests on a solid section of tread, it should have a rounded dowel end that's glued into a hole in the tread. If the base rests on a seam where a piece of trim covers the end of the tread, the baluster most likely is secured with a square tenon or dovetail joint. Remove the trim—called *return nosing*—to expose the joint, and carefully knock the pin from the groove.

Balusters with rounded top ends are glued into holes bored into the underside of the railing. Remove these by pulling any nails, using channel-type pliers, and twisting the end out of the hole. To remove square-top balusters, chisel out the fillet on the higher side of the broken baluster. Where balusters use the groove-and-fillet system on both ends, chisel out the fillet on the lower side of the baluster to free the bottom end.

Follow these basic steps to replace a baluster with a rounded dowel end, and adapt your methods if your balusters are different from the ones shown here.

Using a reciprocating saw, cut completely through the damaged baluster **(photo C).** Make the cut in a plain section, leaving intact any special details you'll need to match or replicate the piece.

Protect the stair tread around the base of the baluster with masking tape. Then, clamp the jaws of a pipe wrench to the baluster, as close as possible to the tread **(photo D).** Pull the wrench firmly to twist the baluster and break the glue bond of the dowel.

If the dowel breaks off in the hole, ream the hole with a drill and spade bit the same size as the dowel end of the new baluster.

Detach the top half of the baluster from the railing. Scrape any old glue from the dowel hole and railing.

Take the baluster with you to the lumber yard. If you can't find a good match among stock balusters, have a cabinet maker create a custom duplicate.

Cut the new baluster to fit. Use a T-bevel or the old baluster to find the proper angle of the top end, and make the cut with a miter box to make sure it is straight. Test-fit the baluster before installing it.

Apply wood glue to the mating surfaces of both ends, and install the new baluster **(photo E).**

Replace fillets (above). Avoid using the railing until the glue dries.

Tools: *Chisel, hammer, channel-type pliers, reciprocating saw, pipe wrench, drill, spade bit, T-bevel, miter box.*

Materials: *Masking tape, replacement baluster, wood glue.*

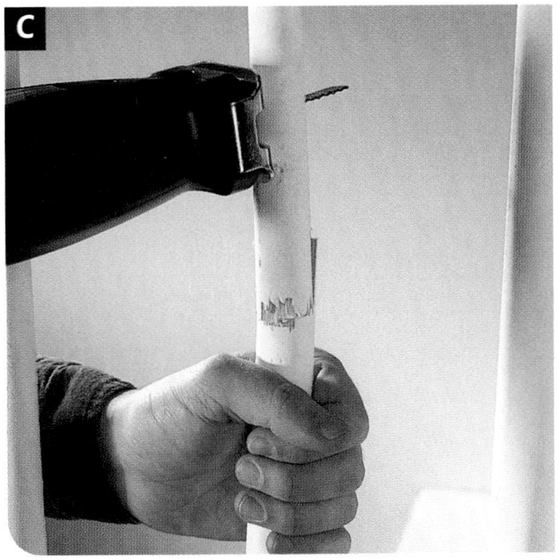

Simplify the removal of a damaged baluster by cutting it into two pieces with a reciprocating saw.

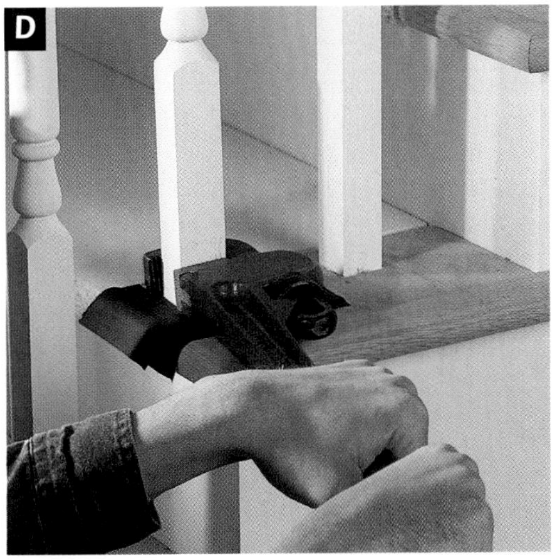

With masking tape protecting the stair tread, twist the baluster with a a pipe wrench to free the dowel joint.

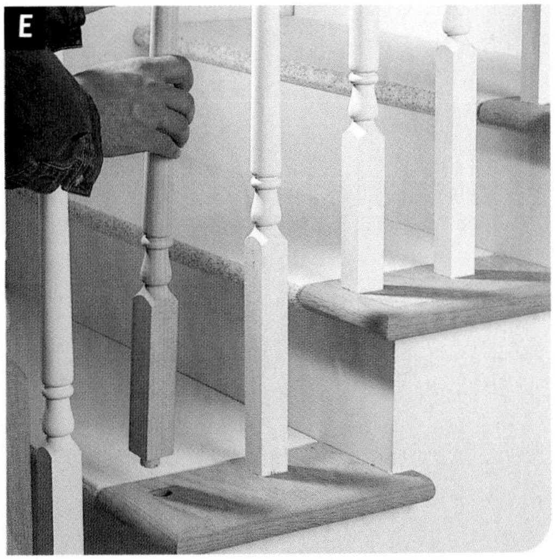

Glue both ends of the new baluster. Set the doweled end into the stair tread first, then position and secure the top end.

Tightening Railings

Where railings connect to newel posts or other sections of railing, the joints are secured internally with special hanger bolt hardware and glue **(photo F).** The hanger bolt has a threaded metal shaft, half with coarse threads and half with machine threads. The coarse end is driven into one piece of railing or the newel post, and the machine end is inserted in a hole drilled into the end of the other railing piece. A large hole drilled up through the bottom of the railing provides access to the machine threads where a star nut is tightened to pull the pieces together. The access hole is concealed by a wood plug.

If these connections have become loose, and gaps show between railing parts, clean and reglue the joints, and tighten the hanger bolts.

Begin by locating the plug in the access hole on the underside of the railing. It should be 1" to 2" from the joint.

Remove the plug by drilling several holes with a 1/4" bit, taking care to avoid the hardware **(photo G).** Knock out the plug with a small chisel.

Loosen the star nut by tapping the points with a nail set or screwdriver and a hammer. Do not completely unscrew the star nut from the bolt.

Scrape off the old glue and any dirt from the mating surfaces of the joint, using a chisel, sandpaper, or a piece of wire.

Apply a thin layer of wood glue to both surfaces, using a string to spread the glue.

Tighten the star nut to close the joint by tapping the points in the opposite direction.

To make a replacement plug, cut a thin section from a wood dowel that matches the railing and has the same diameter as the access hole. Glue the plug in place, and sand it flush with the surface.

Tools: Drill, chisel, hammer, nail set.

Materials: Sandpaper, wire, string, wood glue, wood dowel.

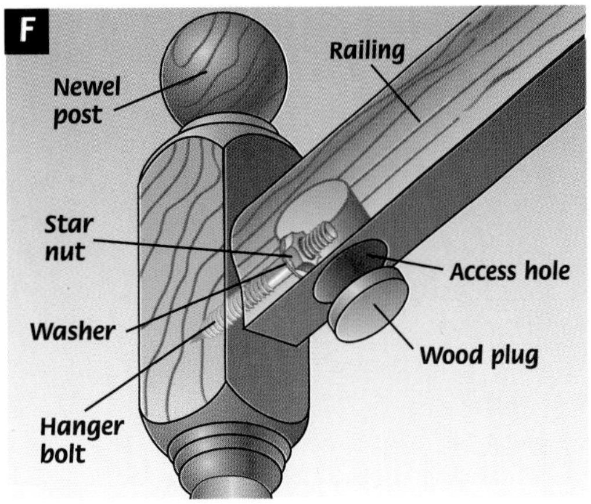

Hanger bolts hold railing parts together and attach railings to newel posts. Star nuts and glue keep the joints tight.

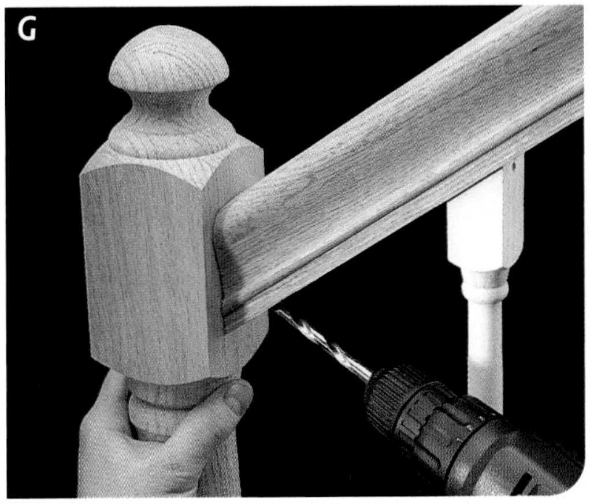

Remove the access hole plug on the bottom side of the railing by drilling small holes, then breaking it out with a chisel.

Replacing a Broken Tread

A broken stair tread is especially hazardous because it's easy to forget until you stumble over it in the dark or a guest trips on it. Replace a broken or severely weakened step as soon as possible. The difficulty of this job depends on the construction of your staircase and whether you can reach the underside of the stairs. In any case, it's better to replace a damaged tread than to repair one, because a patch could create an irregular step that surprises someone who's unfamiliar with it.

If you have a staircase with housed stringers, where the ends of the treads are secured in grooves cut into the stringers, you must gain access to the underside of the damaged step. Remove wall finishes, if necessary, and replace the tread by chiseling out the wedges that hold it tight in the grooves. Replacing a tread in most other staircases can be done from above, but having access to both sides helps with prying up the old tread and fastening the new one.

Before tearing out the broken tread, carefully remove any decorative elements attached to the tread. Pull up carpeting and roll it out of the way, and remove trim pieces on or around the edges of the tread.

Remove the balusters by detaching the top ends from the railing and separating the joints in the tread (page 112).

Some partially carpeted staircases have a decorative hardwood cap inlaid into each tread. Remove these with a flat pry bar, taking care to pry from underneath the cap to avoid marring the exposed edges **(photo A).**

The next step is pulling up the tread **(photo B).** If possible, hammer upward from underneath to separate the tread from the risers and stringers. Otherwise, use a hammer and a pry bar to work it loose, pulling nails as you go.

Once the tread is out of the way, scrape the exposed edges of the stringers to remove old glue and wood fragments.

Measure the length for the new tread and mark it with a combination square so the cut end will be square and straight **(photo C).** If the tread has a milled end for an inlay, cut from the plain end. Cut the new tread to size, using a circular saw, and test-fit it carefully.

Apply a bead of construction adhesive to the exposed tops of the stringers **(photo D).** The adhesive will strengthen the bond between the tread and stringer and will cushion the joint, preventing the parts from squeaking.

Set the tread in place. If you have access to the step from underneath, secure the tread to the riser above it by driving screws through the riser and into the back edge of the tread **(photo E).** To fasten it from the top side, drill and countersink pilot holes and drive two or three screws through the tread and into the top edge of each stringer. Also drive a few screws along the front edge of the tread and into the riser below it. Fill the screw holes in the tread with wood putty or plugs.

Reinstall any decorative elements, using finish nails **(photo F).** Set the nails.

Reinstall the balusters and replace the fillets, if necessary.

Tools: *Flat pry bar, hammer, combination square, circular saw, drill, nail set, caulk gun.*

Materials: *Stair tread, construction adhesive, screws, wood putty, finish nails.*

Remove trim and other finishing elements from the tread.

Remove the tread and pull out any remaining nails.

Use a square to mark the cutting line on the new tread.

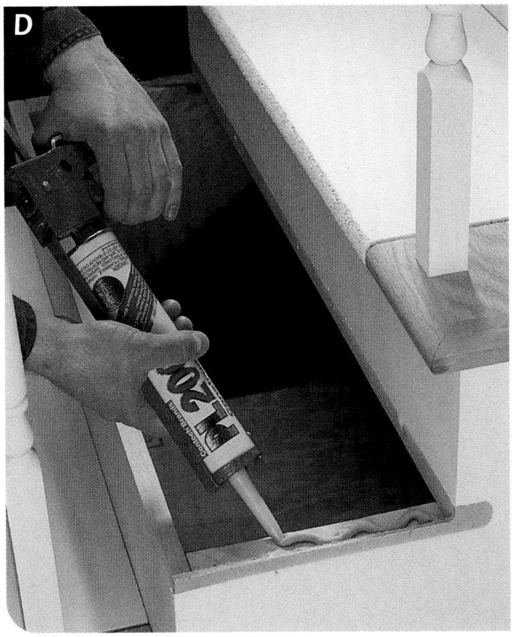

Apply a bead of construction adhesive to the stringers.

Screw through the riser to secure the back edge of the tread.

Reattach the tread inlay or trim with finish nails.

Reinforcing Newel Posts

Solid wood newel posts are bolted or screwed to the floor, the first stair tread, or the stair stringer. Some newels have bases that are bolted to a joist underneath the floor. If these fasteners are inaccessible, you can reinforce a loose newel by securing it to the stair stringer with a lag screw **(photo G).**

To locate a pilot hole for the screw, inspect the newel base for wood plugs that conceal existing fasteners. Avoiding the plugs, locate the hole near the middle of the base section.

Using a 3/4" spade bit, drill a counterbore into the post, about 3/4" deep. Be sure to aim the hole toward the stringer.

Drill a 7/32"-dia. pilot hole through the center of the counterbore and into the stringer. Then, widen the pilot hole through the newel only, using a 5/16" bit. This will prevent the screw shank from splitting the wood.

Fit a 3/4"-dia. washer to a 5/16"-dia. × 4"-long lag screw. Drive and tighten the screw with a socket and ratchet wrench **(photo H).**

Plug the counterbore with a 3/4"-dia. wood dowel that matches the wood of the newel.

Cut a 2" section of dowel and glue the end into the counterbore. After the glue dries, trim the dowel with a handsaw and sand it flush with the surface of the newel. Stain or paint the area to match.

Tools: Drill, ratchet wrench, handsaw.

Materials: 5/16" × 4" lag screw with 3/4" washer, 3/4"-dia. wood dowel, wood glue.

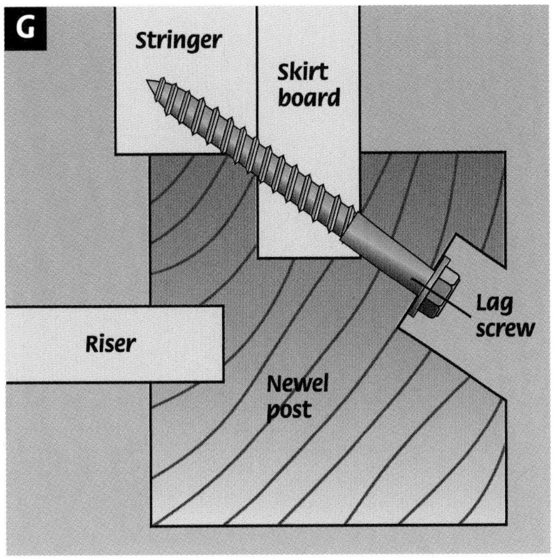

The lag screw should penetrate a solid portion of the newel and extend well into the stringer that supports the staircase.

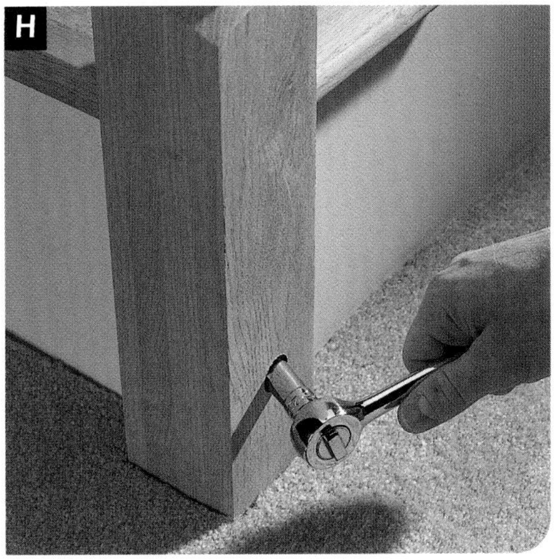

Use a ratchet wrench to drive the lag screw. Don't overtighten the screw, as this may split the wood.

Doors

Doors are so highly visible and get so much use in our homes that it's easy to take them for granted. Yet few elements are expected to serve such diverse, important, and demanding functions.

On the one hand, doors must allow easy passage in and out of the house; on the other, they need to repel unwanted intruders and pests. On the outside, they must withstand storms, wind, bitter cold, and searing heat. On the inside, they experience relatively constant temperature and humidity. We expect them to last for decades, while offering an attractive front to every visitor.

Your home probably has many different types of doors, and each is likely to need attention from time to time. Common repairs range from simple adjustments to complete replacement of a door. Each different door type has certain types of problems that you're likely to encounter.

Entry doors are those that connect indoor living spaces to the outdoor world. Because they're directly exposed to the elements, they experience a wide range of problems. Over time, you may find it necessary to repair or replace locksets (pages 120 to 121), adjust latchbolts and hinges (page 122), straighten warped wood (page 123), repair rot damage (page 124), or even completely replace an entry door (pages 129 to 130).

When an entry door is drafty, it can be due to either missing or faulty weatherstripping, or to inadequate insulation around the door frame. The simplest approach is to add or replace the weatherstripping (pages 132 to 133) and see if the problem improves. If it doesn't, you need to remove the casing moldings and fill all the open spaces between framing members with fiberglass insulation.

Your entry doors may be protected by *storm doors*, which improve the insulating value of entry doors while shielding them against the elements. Storm doors have their own maintenance needs (pages 134 to 135), including hinge and latch adjustments, and window track repairs.

Passage doors are the interior doors that define the boundaries for individual rooms and provide privacy. Common repairs on standard passage doors include repairing latches (page 119), aligning latchbolts and strike plates and tightening hinges (page 122), and freeing doors that stick in their frames (page 123). Passage doors may need to be trimmed off when new flooring is installed (page 125) or refinished when you redecorate (page 126). Finally, passage doors may need to be replaced (page 128), either because they're damaged or because their style is outdated.

Sliding doors, which can either be entry doors or interior passage doors, are relatively free of problems, but you'll need to periodically clean the tracks, clean and lubricate the rollers, and adjust the doors (page 118).

Similarly, the bi-fold doors that are commonly used on closets and other utility spaces will need to be inspected and maintained (page 119).

Tools for Repairing Doors

As a rule, door repair projects don't require any specialized equipment: all you need for most jobs is a basic set of carpentry tools and woodworking supplies.

A cinder block comes in handy when you're trying to straighten a door that's been warped by excess moisture.

Clear wood sealer is used to keep damaging moisture from penetrating the edges of a door in the first place.

Penetrating spray lubricant has many uses, such as lubricating hinges that squeak and locksets that stick.

Hammers and screwdrivers of various sizes are used in almost all door projects.

Chisels of various widths are essential woodworking tools that are needed when installing a security lock, repairing damaged wood, or replacing a threshold.

Sandpaper and a wood plane are especially useful for refinishing doors and trimming them to size.

Other useful tools include short dowels, for filling holes behind loose hinges, and a utility knife, which has many uses, including scoring marked lines before cutting.

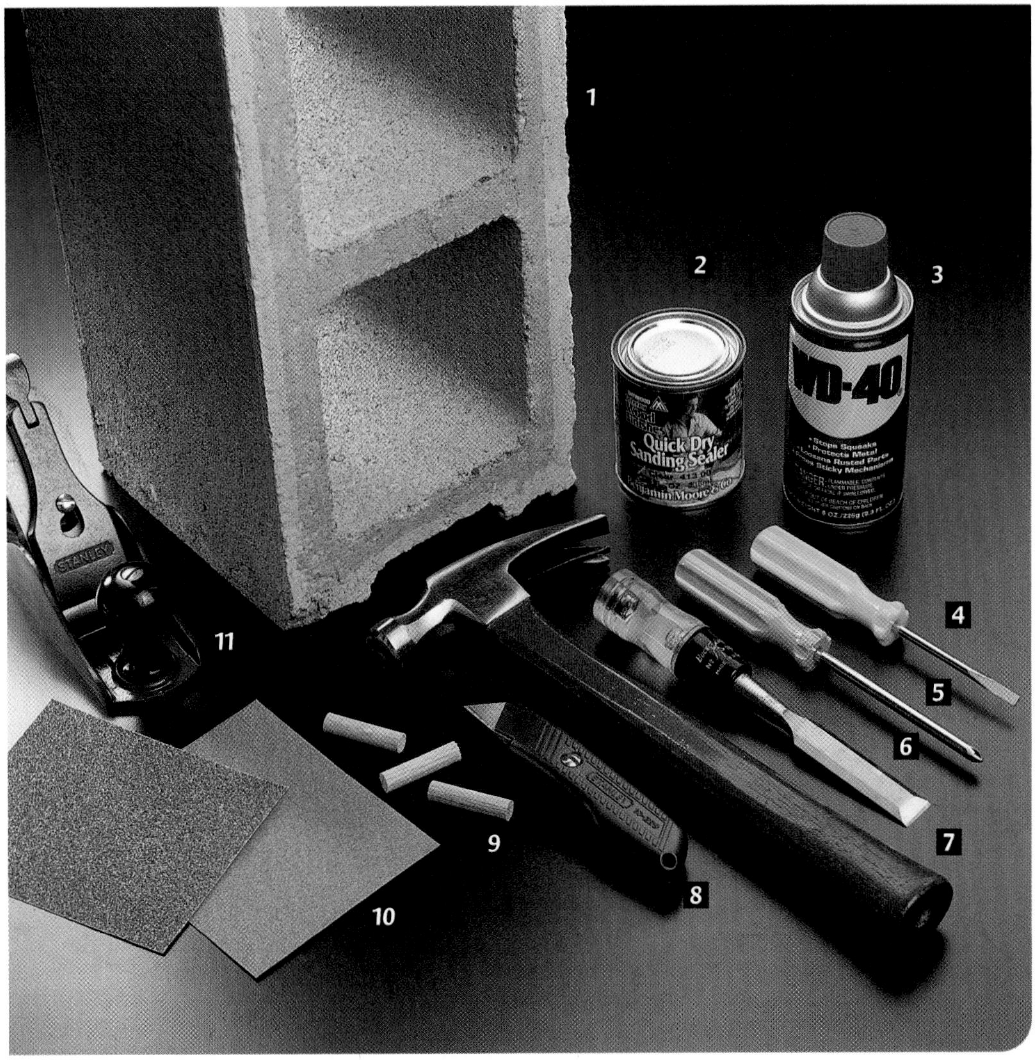

The tools and materials needed to repair doors include: cinder block (1), sealer (2), spray lubricant (3), standard screwdriver (4), Phillips screwdriver (5), chisel (6), hammer (7), utility knife (8), dowels (9), sandpaper (10), and plane (11).

Maintaining & Repairing Doors

Almost all problems with door hardware are caused by a lack of lubrication. The best way to unstick a door is to spray the moving parts with a spray lubricant and wipe them down. Here are some other tips that will help you handle door problems with ease:

Clean the tracks on sliding doors with a hand vacuum and a toothbrush. You'll find that the tracks of sliding doors, in particular, tend to accumulate dirt that can interfere with the workings of the door.

Clean the rubber weatherstripping around a door by spraying it with a cleaner and wiping away the dirt.

Lubricate locksets and hinges once a year by taking them apart and spraying them with a spray lubricant. When installing a new lockset, lubricate it first.

Graphite powder is a good solution for a sticking door lock. If you don't have any graphite powder on hand, shavings from a soft-leaded pencil work just as well.

Transfer graphite to a key for the lock by rubbing the pencil lead up and down and all around the key. Once there's a good graphite buildup on the key, put it in the lock and move it in and out, then open and close the lock several times. The sticking problem should disappear right away.

To remove a stubborn hinge pin, insert the top of a nail into the hole from the bottom of the barrel. Tap the nail with a hammer to force the pin up and out of the hinge.

Maintaining a Sliding Door

We tend to ignore sliding doors until they begin sticking or hopping out of the track. However, the best time to maintain a sliding door is before problems begin.

Regular maintenance, including vacuuming and applying powdered graphite or silicone spray, can keep a door sliding smoothly.

However, if a sliding door starts to have problems, begin the maintenance process by checking its adjustment: stand back and examine the door. There should be a uniform gap along the bottom and the top of the door. If the gap isn't even, note which side is too high so you'll know which way to adjust it later.

Next, clean and lubricate the doors. Remove the dirt from the tracks with a hand vacuum or a toothbrush and a damp cloth **(photo A).**

Check the rollers. If there are any bent or worn parts, replace them. Spray lubricant on the rollers **(photo B).**

Next, check the metal track that forms the threshold. If it's bent, straighten it out: lay a thin wooden block in the track, place one foot on it, and hammer the bumps in the threshold against the block to flatten them.

Finally, if the gap above and below the door is uneven, correct the adjustment. If the side with the adjusting screw is too high, turn the screw counterclockwise. If that side is too low, use a flat pry bar to raise the door while you turn the adjusting screw clockwise **(photo C).**

Tools: *Toothbrush or damp cloth and hand vacuum, flat pry bar, screwdriver, wooden block.*

Materials: *Spray lubricant, replacement parts (if needed).*

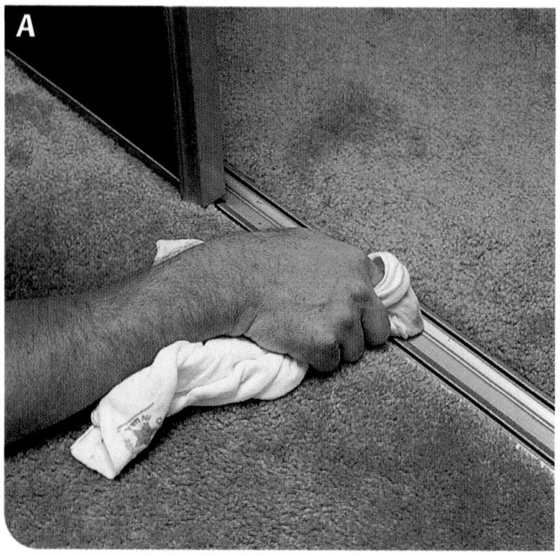

Clean the tracks to remove any accumulated dirt.

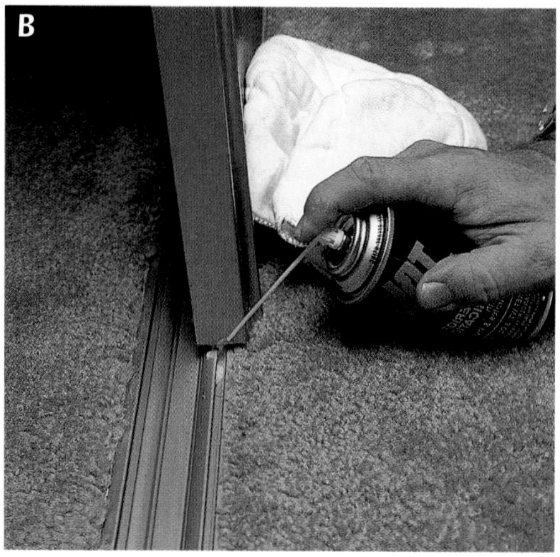

Lubricate the rollers and replace any faulty parts.

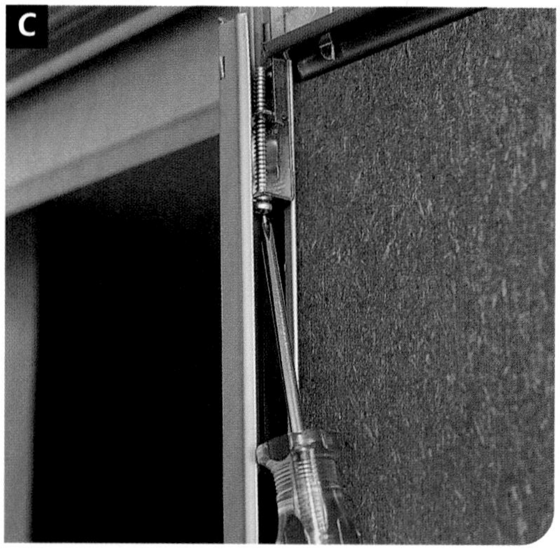

Adjust the mounting screw, if necessary.

Maintaining a Bi-fold Door

To lubricate and adjust a bi-fold door, start by closing the door and checking the alignment. The gap between the closed doors should be uniform from top to bottom.

Next, open and remove the doors. Wipe the tracks down with a clean rag to remove any accumulated dirt.

Spray the track, the rollers, and the pins with a spray lubricant **(photo D).**

If the gap between the closed doors isn't even, adjust the top pivot blocks with a screwdriver or wrench **(photo E).** Some door models also have adjustable pivot blocks at the bottom edge of the door **(photo F).**

Adjust the pivot blocks and reinstall the doors, then check the alignment again. Keep adjusting and checking until the gap between the closed doors is even.

Tools: *Clean rag, screwdriver or wrench.*

Materials: *Spray lubricant.*

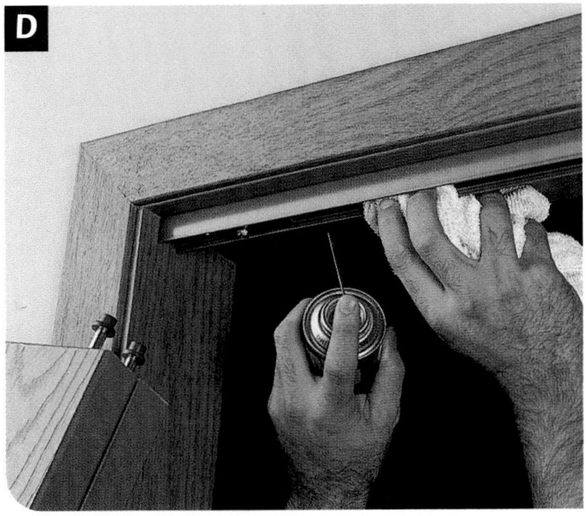

Spray the tracks, the rollers, and the pins with lubricant.

If the alignment of the door is off, adjust the top pivot block.

If the door has a bottom pivot block, adjust it as well.

Repairing a Sticking Door Latch

A sticking latchbolt **(photo G)** is usually caused by built-up dirt and insufficient lubrication. To free it, clean and lubricate the lockset (page 120).

Also make sure that the connecting screws on the lockset aren't too tight. An overly tight screw may also cause the latchbolt to bind.

If the latchbolt is misaligned with the strike plate, it won't fit into the strike plate opening **(photo H).** Check the door for loose hinges first. If the problem persists, align the strike plate and latchbolt (page 122).

Another cause of latchbolt problems is warping caused by humidity or water penetration. Use a straightedge to see if the door is warped **(photo I)** and straighten it if necessary (page 123).

To fix a sticking latchbolt, clean and lubricate the lockset.

A misaligned latchbolt won't fit into the strike plate opening.

Use a straightedge to check the door for warping.

Repairing a Lockset

Modern locksets operate by extending a latchbolt through a faceplate into a strike plate set in the door frame **(photo A).** The latchbolt is moved back and forth by a spindle or a connecting rod operated by a thumb latch, door lever, or keyed cylinder.

Most lockset problems are easy to solve; you simply need to remove the lockset and lubricate the inner mechanism with an all-purpose spray lubricant.

For example, if a doorknob or a key binds when it's turned, the problem probably lies in the spindle and latchbolt mechanism. Cleaning and lubricating the moving parts should correct the problem.

To clean an older passage lockset **(photo B),** loosen the handle setscrew and remove the handles and the attached spindle. Loosen the faceplate screws and pry the lockset from the door. Remove the lockset cover or faceplate, and spray a lubricant on all the parts. Wipe away the excess lubricant and reassemble the lockset.

If the handle of an older passage lockset keeps falling off the spindle, rotate the handle to a different position on the spindle and retighten the setscrew.

To clean a modern passage lockset **(photo C),** remove the handles (which are held in place by connecting screws or a spring catch). Loosen the retaining screws to remove the faceplate and the latchbolt shaft. Spray lubricant on all parts. Wipe away the excess lubricant and reassemble the lockset.

To clean a security lock **(photo D),** loosen the connecting screws to remove the inside and outside cylinders. Loosen the retaining screws to remove the faceplate and the latchbolt shaft. Spray solvent/lubricant on all the parts. Wipe away the excess lubricant and reassemble the lockset.

If a door still won't latch after you've cleaned and lubricated the lockset, check to see if there are any problems with the wood, the hinges, the strike plate, or the door frame.

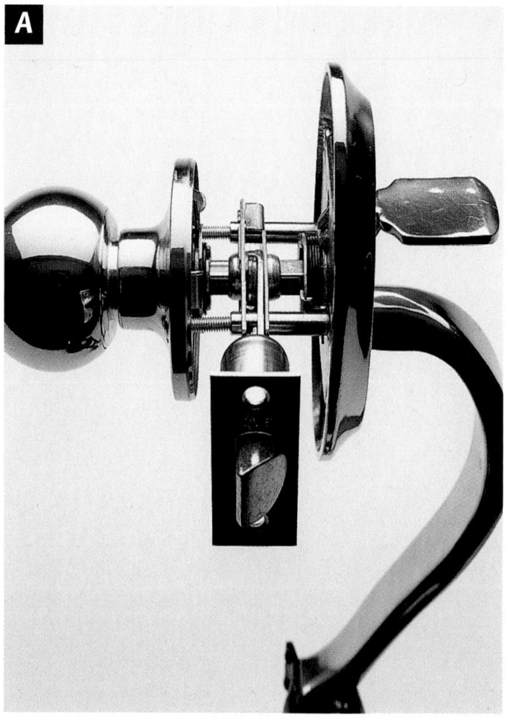

The working parts of a lockset operated by a thumb latch.

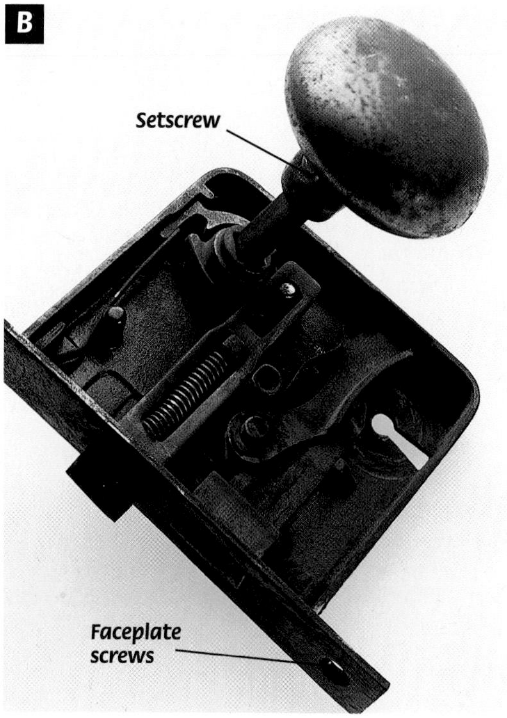

Older passage locksets can still be found in many homes.

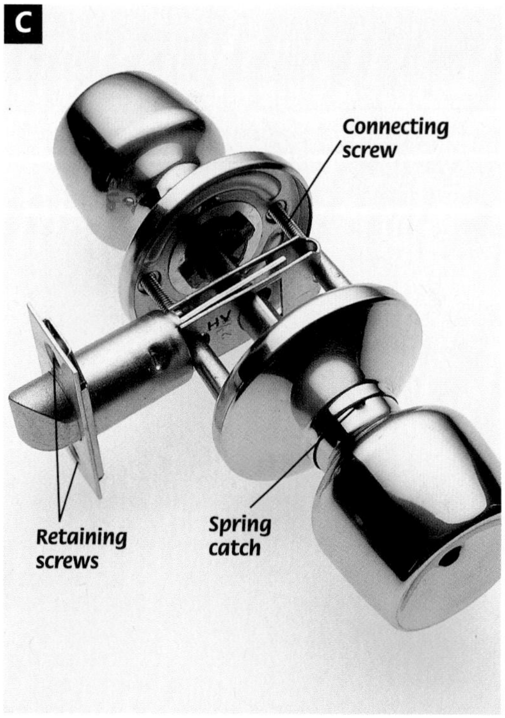

The working parts of a modern passage door lockset.

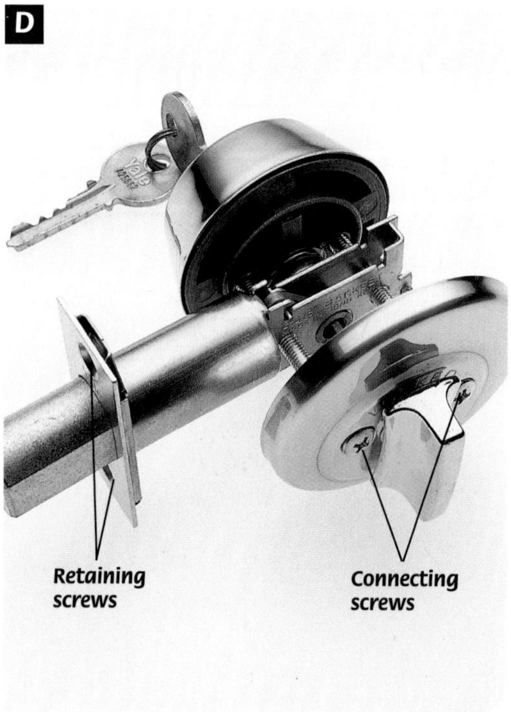

The working parts of a security lock.

Installing a Security Lock

Security locks have long bolts called *dead bolts* that extend into the door jamb and are operated by a keyed mechanism. Since a dead bolt offers added protection from break-ins, installing a security lock may qualify you for a reduction in your homeowner's insurance.

The first step in installing a security lock is to locate the proper height of the lock on the door. Next, tape the cardboard template onto the door **(photo E).** Use a nail or an awl to mark the center points of the cylinder and the latch bolt holes.

Bore the cylinder hole, using a hole saw and a drill **(photo F).** To avoid splintering the door, drill through one side until the hole saw pilot just comes out the other side. Remove the hole saw and complete the hole from the opposite side of the door.

Use a spade bit and a drill to bore the latch bolt hole from the edge of the door into the cylinder hole **(photo G).** Keep the drill perpendicular to the door edge while drilling.

Insert the latch bolt into the edge hole. Insert the lock tailpiece and the connecting screws through the latch bolt mechanism **(photo H),** and screw the cylinders together. Close the door to the point where the latch bolt meets the door jamb.

Score the outline of the strike plate on the door frame with a utility knife, using the hardware as a template. Chisel the outline of the mortise **(photo I),** holding the tool bevel-side-in. Tap the butt end lightly with a mallet until the chisel reaches the proper depth.

Make a series of parallel cuts 1/4" apart across the mortise, holding the chisel at a 45° angle **(photo J).** Drive the chisel into the wood by lightly tapping its butt end with a hammer.

Pry out the waste, pointing the chisel downward at a low angle, with the beveled edge toward the wood **(photo K).** Drive it in, using light hand pressure.

Use a spade bit to bore a latch bolt hole in the center of the mortise. Secure the strike plate to the mortise, using the retaining screws included with the lockset **(photo L).**

Tools: *Tape measure, lockset drill kit (including hole saw and spade bit), drill, chisel, utility knife, hammer.*

Materials: *Security lock.*

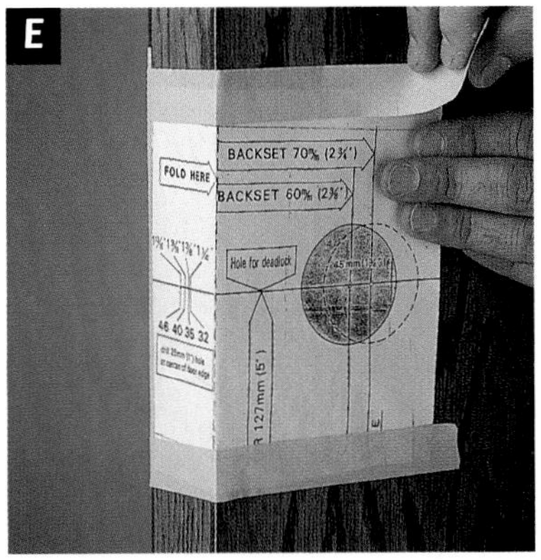

Position the lockset template on the door.

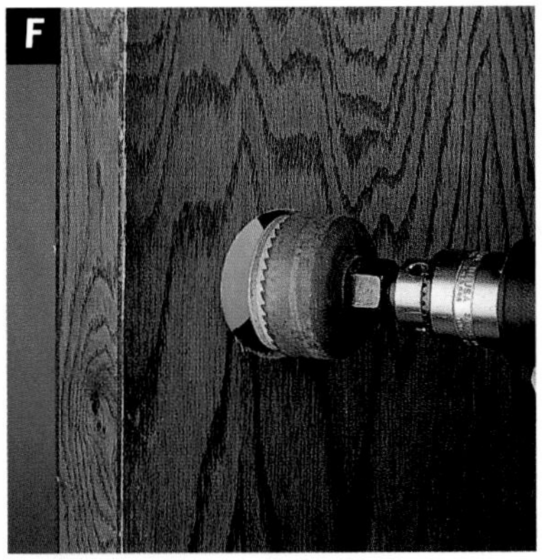

Bore the cylinder hole with a hole saw.

Use a spade bit to bore the latchbolt hole.

Assemble the lock components.

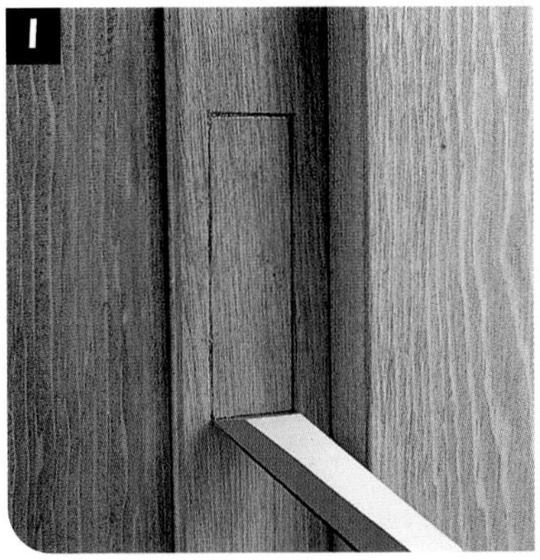

Chisel the outline of the strike plate mortise.

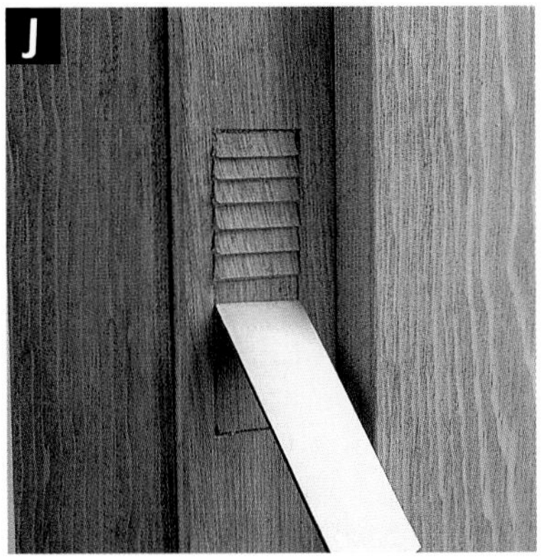

Chisel a series of parallel cuts 1/4" apart.

Point the chisel down to lever out the waste.

Secure the strike plate to the mortise.

Aligning a Latchbolt & Strike Plate

To adjust the alignment of a latchbolt with its strike plate, begin by tightening any loose hinges. Next, fix any minor side-to-side alignment problems by filing the strike plate until the latchbolt fits **(photo A).**

If the latchbolt falls above or below the strike plate, check the door to make sure it fits squarely **(photo B).** If it's badly tilted, remove the door and shim the top or bottom door hinge **(photo C).**

To raise the latchbolt, insert a thin cardboard shim behind the bottom hinge. To lower the latchbolt, place a cardboard shim behind the top hinge.

Tools: *Screwdriver, metal file, ruler.*

Materials: *Cardboard shim.*

To fix a minor problem, file the edges of the strike plate.

Check to see if the door is out of square with its frame.

Raise or lower a latchbolt by placing a shim under a hinge.

Tightening a Loose Hinge

To tighten a loose hinge, begin by removing the door from its hinges, while a helper holds it in place. Use a screwdriver and a hammer to drive the lower hinge pin up and out, and then the upper one. Remove the door and set it aside.

Tighten any loose screws **(photo D).** If you find that the wood behind the hinge won't hold the screws, remove the hinges.

Coat wooden golf tees or dowels with glue and drive them into the worn screw holes as far as you can. Let the glue dry and cut off the excess wood with a utility knife **(photo E).**

Drill pilot holes in the new wood **(photo F).** Rehang the hinge, using the new wood as a base for the screws.

Tools: *Screwdriver, hammer, utility knife, drill.*

Materials: *Sandpaper, wooden golf tees or dowels.*

Tighten any loose screws to see if they're holding.

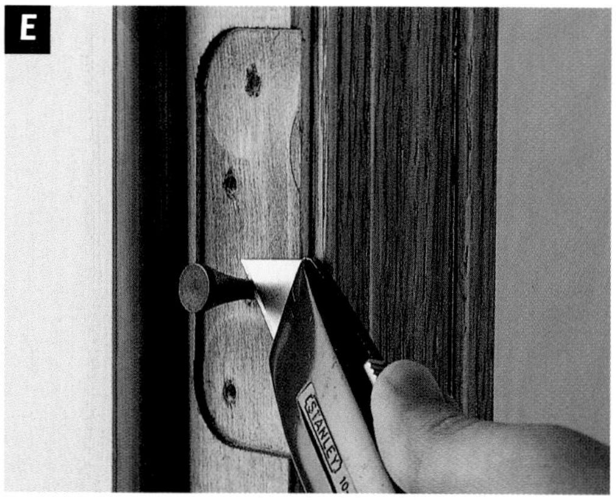

Glue tees or dowels into screw holes.

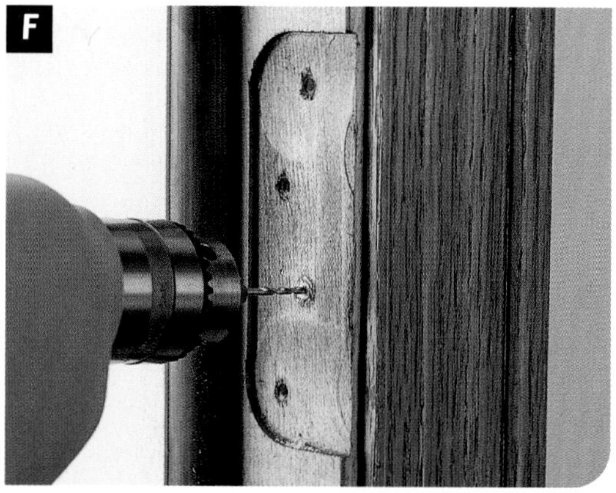

Drill pilot holes in the new wood and rehang the hinge.

Freeing a Sticking Door

To free a sticking door, begin by tightening any loose hinges (page 122). If the door still sticks, mark the areas where it sticks with light pencil lines **(photo G).**

Wait for a spell of dry weather, and remove the door from its hinges. Sand or plane the door at the marked locations **(photo H)** until it fits smoothly into the frame.

Seal the ends and edge of the door with a clear wood sealer. Rehang the door.

If the door only sticks in wet weather, wait for a dry period to sand and seal the edges.

Tools: *Pencil, sanding block or plane, screwdriver, paintbrush.*

Materials: *Sandpaper, clear wood sealer.*

Mark the areas where the door sticks, using light pencil lines.

Sand or plane the marked areas until the door fits smoothly.

Straightening a Warped Door

To straighten a warped door, begin by removing it from its hinges (page 125). Support the top and bottom ends of the door on two sawhorses placed on a level surface.

Put a piece of thin plywood or hardboard on the door to protect its finish. Set heavy weights, such as cinder blocks, centered over the plywood on the bowed part of the door **(photo I).**

Leave the door weighted for several days, or until it flattens out. Check it with a straightedge to make sure the warping is gone.

Apply a clear wood sealer to the ends and edges of the door, to prevent moisture from warping it again **(photo J).** Rehang the door.

Tools: *Screwdriver, straightedge, paintbrush.*

Materials: *Sawhorses, thin plywood or hardboard, cinder blocks, clear wood sealer.*

Set heavy weights, such as cinder blocks, on the protected surface of the door to flatten it out.

To prevent the problem from recurring, reseal all the ends and edges of the door with a clear wood sealer.

Repairing Damaged Wood

It's a good idea periodically to inspect the wood on exterior doors, window sashes, and decks so that you can spot and correct rot or insect damage at a stage where it's still easy to repair. Even durable woods like redwood and cedar may suffer damage, especially if they're left unsealed.

To repair damaged wood, use a two-part wood filler; these products can be easily molded to shape, and they readily accept paint and stain.

If a wood door has suffered damage, remove it from its frame and place it on a steady, level working surface. Wearing goggles or other eye protection, use a chisel to remove all the damaged wood **(photo A).**

If the repair area extends to the edge of the door, create a simple wooden form to establish the boundaries of the area you'll be filling in **(photo B).** Before you tack the forms to the door with brads, coat them with wax or vegetable oil, to keep the filler from sticking to them.

Mix and apply the two-part wood filler, following the manufacturer's instructions. Use a putty knife or trowel to level the filled area and shape it to the original form of the wood **(photo C).** Allow the filler to harden completely before you continue.

Remove the forms. Lightly sand the hardened filler **(photo D).** Don't oversand—this will close the pores in the filler and prevent it from taking a stain properly.

Paint or stain the repaired area to match the existing color. (You may prefer to sand off the remnants of the existing finish and repaint or restain the entire surface.) Finally, remount the door in its frame.

Tools: *Eye protection, chisel, putty knives, sander, tack hammer, painting tools.*

Materials: *Two-part wood filler, sandpaper, wood strips, wire brads, paint or wood stain.*

Begin the repair by removing all the damaged wood with a wood chisel.

Build a simple frame to establish the boundaries of the fill area.

Mix and apply the wood filler; use a putty knife or a trowel to shape it into the proper form.

After the filler has set, lightly sand the repaired area, taking care not to oversand it.

Trimming an Interior Door

Prehung interior doors are sized to allow a 3/8" gap under the bottom of the door. This gap allows the door to swing without binding on the carpeting or floor covering. If you install a new floor, a thicker carpet, or a larger threshold, you may find that you need to trim off the bottom of the door.

Begin by measuring 3/8" up from the top of the threshold or floor covering. Mark the door at that point.

Remove the door from its hinges. While a helper holds it in place, use a screwdriver and a hammer to drive the hinge pins out—first the lower pin, then the upper **(photo E).**

Lay the door on a steady, level surface. Mark the cutting line along the bottom edge of the door by scoring it lightly with a utility knife.

Put a new, sharp blade edge in the utility knife and cut all the way through the door veneer, to prevent it from chipping when you trim the bottom of the door **(photo F).**

Lay the door down on a pair of sawhorses. Clamp a straightedge to the door to use as a cutting guide **(photo G).**

Saw off the bottom of the door **(photo H).** If this exposes the door's hollow core, you'll need to install the original inner frame in the new door bottom. Here's how to do it:

Clamp the cut-off door bottom to hold it steady. Chisel off the veneer from both sides, exposing the inner frame piece **(photo I).**

Apply wood glue to the frame piece and insert it into the hollow bottom of the door **(photo J).** Clamp it down, wipe away any excess glue, and let it dry overnight.

Reseal the bottom edge of the door to prevent warping. Remount the door on its hinges.

Tools: *Circular saw, tape measure, hammer, screwdriver, utility knife, straightedge, chisel, clamps.*

Materials: *Sawhorses, carpenter's glue, clear wood sealer.*

Start by removing the door from its hinges.

Cut through the veneer to prevent it from chipping.

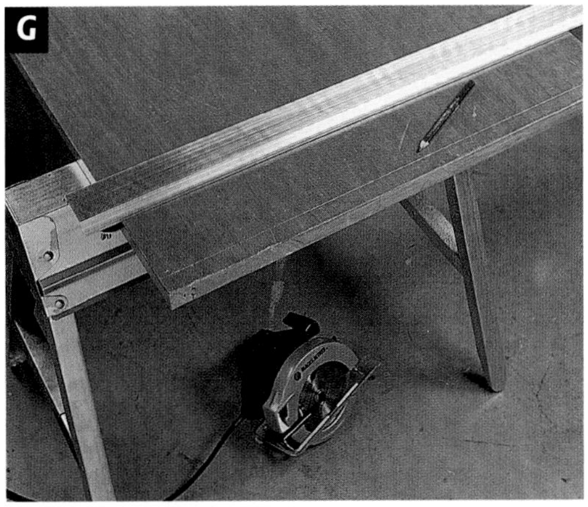

Clamp a straightedge on the door to use as a cutting guide.

Saw off the bottom of the door along the trim line.

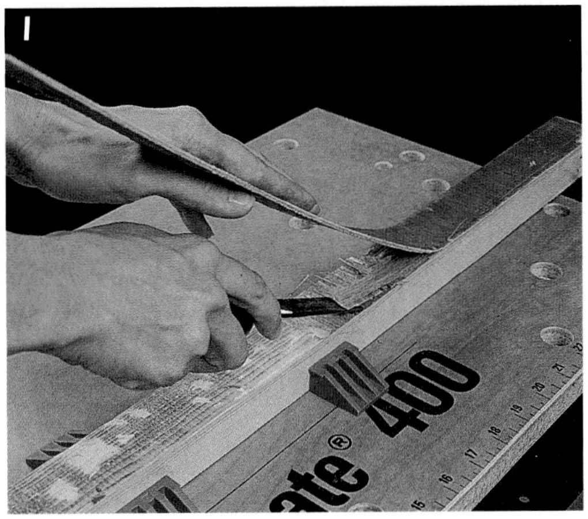

Use a chisel to peel the veneer from the inner frame piece.

Glue the frame piece and insert it into the new door bottom.

Refinishing an Interior Door

Although refinishing woodwork and doors may seem like an overwhelming project, the right techniques can greatly simplify the job. A combination of heat and chemical stripping is the key to making the job easier. Use a heat gun and scraper to remove most of the old paint, and take off the rest by chemically stripping and scraping the wood.

The woodwork in a home is often a combination of different kinds of wood, which can make it challenging to create a uniform color when you refinish it. However, a bit of experimentation can help you find a mixture of stains that produce a uniform color.

Try using a lighter stain for woods that absorb the color well, then mix in a darker hue for woods that are more resistant. If most of your doors and woodwork are one kind of wood and a few pieces are another, establish the base stain color first, then experiment to match that color on the other pieces.

It's also a good idea to scrape the woodwork to find out if the first finish layer is paint. If it is, stripping the wood down to its natural color will be very difficult. You may want to consider another option.

Begin by removing the door from its hinges (page 125) and masking off the work area. Attach plastic to all the door jambs to keep fumes and dust out of the rest of the house **(photo A).**

Next, remove the hinges and all other door hardware, as well as any switchplates and receptacle covers near the work area. When you remove the plates from the switches and

Tools: *Screwdriver, hammer, sawhorses, staple gun, heat gun, paintbrush, broad scrapers, specialty scraper, sander, drill.*

Materials: *Plastic sheeting, abrasive pad, mineral spirits, stainable wood putty, semi-paste chemical stripper, 150- & 220-grit sandpaper, rags, wood stain, varnish or tung oil.*

Staple plastic sheeting to the door jambs to keep fumes and dust out of the rest of the house.

Use a heat gun and a scraper to remove most of the old paint from the large, flat surfaces of the woodwork.

Brush a heavy layer of semi-paste chemical stripper onto the contours and edges of the woodwork.

Remove the chemical sludge and dissolved finish from the trim with a specialty scraper.

receptacles, mask them immediately to avoid the risk of electric shock.

Remove the old finish from the trim, using first heat, then chemical stripping. Before heat stripping, make sure you've scraped off any loose or flaking paint, since a heat gun can ignite paint flakes.

Remove most of the old paint from the large, flat surfaces of the woodwork **(photo B).** Use extra care near the edges to prevent damage to the wood and to the adjoining walls.

A heat gun can quickly scorch intricate surfaces, so use a chemical stripper on any detailed areas. Brush on a heavy layer of semi-paste chemical stripper onto the contours and edges of the woodwork **(photo C).**

Give the stripper time to work, then use a specialty scraper to remove the sludge from the trim **(photo D).**

Once most of the paint is removed, apply a thin layer of stripper to all the woodwork. Scrub it down with an abrasive pad to remove the remaining finish.

Next, strip the doors themselves. Remove all the door hardware and strip off the old finish, following the same sequence used for the woodwork **(photo E).**

Next, clean both the woodwork and the doors by scrubbing all the wood surfaces with an abrasive pad dipped in mineral spirits **(photo F).** This will remove the wax residue left by the chemical stripper, as well as any traces of the old varnish.

Use a stainable wood putty to fill any holes and gouges in the doors and the woodwork **(photo G).** Sand the repair areas and tint the putty with a stain so it matches the color of the surrounding wood.

Sand the woodwork and the doors **(photo H).** Use 150-grit sandpaper to even the surfaces, and 220-grit sandpaper to finish them.

Stain all the wood, using different stains, if necessary, to produce a uniform color throughout. Apply a topcoat, such as varnish or tung oil **(photo I).**

If you wish, chemically strip and clean the door hardware. Remount the hinges and rehang the doors **(photo J).** Reattach the switch and receptacle plates.

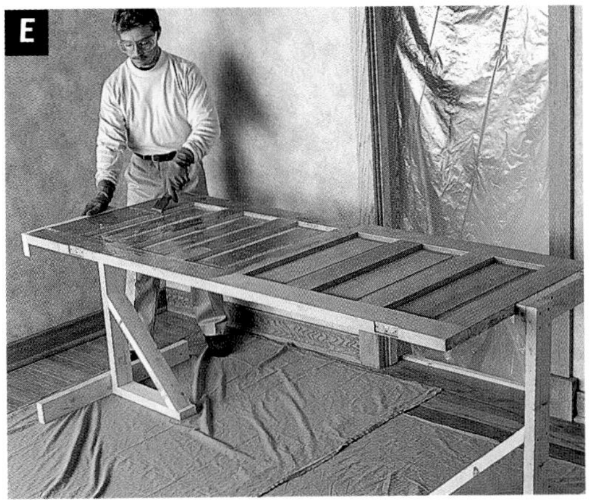

Remove door hardware and strip the finish.

Scrub the woodwork with a pad dipped in mineral spirits.

Fill all holes and gouges with a stainable wood putty.

Smooth the surfaces with 150- and 220-grit sandpaper.

Stain the wood, then apply a topcoat finish.

Clean and reattach the hardware, then rehang the door.

Replacing an Interior Door

Interior passage doors are now available in prehung units that are relatively easy to install.

First, measure the height and width of the existing door. Buy a replacement door that matches the measurements.

To remove the old door, drive out the hinge pins with a hammer and a screwdriver. Use a flat pry bar and a hammer to gently remove the existing door casing **(photo A).** If it's in good condition, you may wish to save it and reattach it after the new door is installed.

Remove the new door from the shipping carton and inspect it for damage. The side jamb will already be attached to one edge of the door (the jamb for the other side will be enclosed separately).

Before installing the unit, paint or stain the door and the casing to the desired color.

Set the prehung door unit into the framed opening. Check it with a level to see if it's plumb **(photo B).**

To plumb the door unit, insert wood shims between the door jamb and the frame on the hinged side of the door. Tap the shims with a hammer until the level shows that the jamb is plumb **(photo C).**

Fill any gaps between the jamb and the framing at the location of the hinges and the locks with more shims. Nail the jamb to the frame, using 6d finish nails driven through the shims **(photo D).**

Cut off the shims, using a handsaw **(photo E).** Hold the saw vertically to avoid damaging either the door jamb or the wall.

Nail the casing to the jambs, using 4d finish nails driven every 16" **(photo F).** Use a nail set to recess the nail heads. Fill the holes with a matching wood putty.

***Tools:** Flat pry bar, hammer, screwdriver, level, nail set, handsaw, tools for painting or staining.*

***Materials:** Prehung door unit, paint or stain, cedar wood shims, finish nails (4d, 6d), wood putty.*

Use a flat pry bar and a hammer to gently remove the trim on the existing door. You can save it to reattach later.

Set the prehung door unit into the framed opening and check for plumb with a level.

To bring the door to a plumb position, insert wood shims on the hinged side between the door jamb and the frame.

Fill any gaps between the jamb and the frame with shims; nail the jamb to the frame with 6d finish nails.

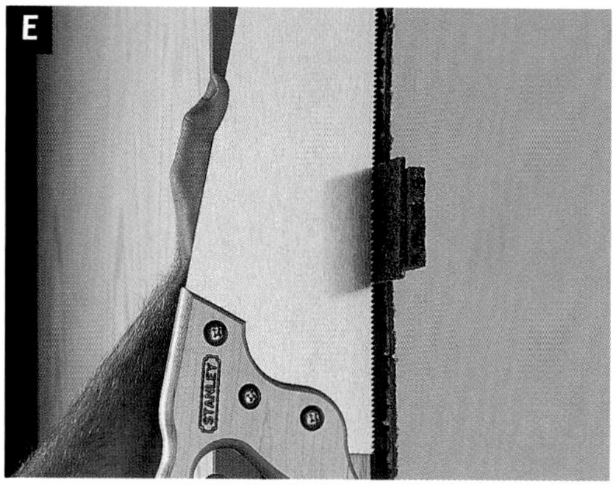

Cut off the shims with a handsaw, holding it vertically to avoid damaging the door jamb or the wall.

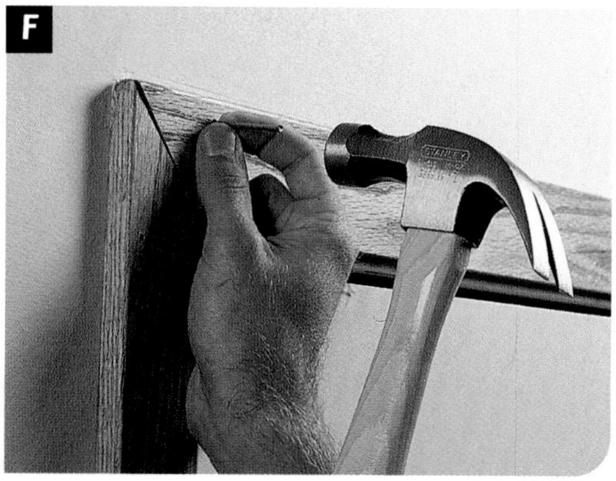

Nail the premitered trim pieces to the jambs with 4d finish nails driven at 16" intervals.

Replacing an Entry Door

Replacing a warped, leaky entry door can be a manageable do-it-yourself project. Like passage doors, energy-efficient entry doors also come prehung with the jambs and all the installation hardware included. The only thing you'll need to buy separately is the lockset.

First, measure the height and width of the existing door. Buy a replacement door that matches the measurements.

To remove the old door, drive out the hinge pins with a hammer and a screwdriver. Use a flat pry bar and a hammer to gently remove the existing casing on the interior side of the door (page 128). If it's in good condition, reuse it on the new door.

Using a utility knife, cut away the old caulk between the exterior siding and the brick molding on the door frame **(photo G).**

Pry away and discard the old door jamb and threshold **(photo H).** Cut off any stubborn nails with a reciprocating saw.

Place the door unit into the rough opening and check the fit. Make sure there's about 3/8" of space all the way around the unit—on both the sides and the top.

Remove the unit from the opening and apply caulk to the new threshold **(photo I).** (This creates a weather seal between the threshold and the floor.) Replace the door unit in the rough opening.

Continued on next page

Tools: *Flat pry bar, utility knife, hammer, screwdriver, reciprocating saw, caulk gun, carpenter's level.*

Materials: *Prehung entry door unit, silicone caulk, cedar wood shims, 16d galvanized casing nails, 6d finish nails, door lockset.*

Replacing Door Casings

When installing a prehung replacement door, you may need to replace a damaged door casing (the interior door trim).

First, take a sample of the old casing to the store and find molding that matches the shape and wood type of the old casing.

To make the mitered ends, cut the casing at a 45° angle, with the flat edge of the casing tight against the horizontal bottom base of the miter box.

Next, either paint or stain the trim to match the rest of the room moldings. You may need to experiment with a variety of stains on a piece of scrap wood (or the back of the trim piece) until you get the right color.

Use a utility knife to cut away the old caulk between the exterior siding and the brick molding on the existing door.

Pry away and discard the old door jamb and threshold, cutting off any stubborn nails with a reciprocating saw.

Apply two bands of caulk to the new threshold to form a weather seal between the threshold and the floor.

Replacing an Entry Door (cont.)

Tap wood shims or filler strips into the gaps between the frame and the jambs, using a level to make sure the unit is plumb. Place the shims at the location of the lockset and all the hinges **(photo J).**

Nail through the jambs and shims into the framing members, using 16d casing nails. After driving each nail, use a level to check to make sure the unit is still plumb **(photo K).**

Drive 16d casing nails through the brick molding into the door frame **(photo L).**

Replace the casing you removed from the interior side of the door jamb **(photo M),** using 6d finish nails.

If the casing wasn't in good condition to begin with, or if it was damaged during removal, miter-cut, finish, and install new casing pieces (page 128).

Install the new door lock. Begin by inserting the latchbolt mechanism through the latchbolt hole in the edge of the door.

Next, insert the lockset tailpieces through the latchbolt. Screw the handles together by tightening the retaining screws **(photo N).**

Screw the strike plate to the door jamb **(photo O).** Adjust the position of the plate to fit the latchbolt.

Finally, recaulk any gaps between the siding and the new door molding. For best results, use a caulk that matches or blends with the color of the siding or the door molding.

Doors in Older Homes

If you're faced with the task of replacing the doors in an older home, measure carefully and expect the unexpected.

Older homes often have nonstandard door frames, and the doors may vary in size.

If the doorways are a nonstandard size, you'll either need to special-order custom doors or to cut down a larger stock door to fit the doorway.

When replacing a door in an older home, also be sure that the new door is suited to the style of the house.

J

Tap wood shims into the gaps between the frame and the jamb at the lockset and all the hinges.

K

After driving each nail, use a level to confirm that the unit remains perfectly vertical.

L

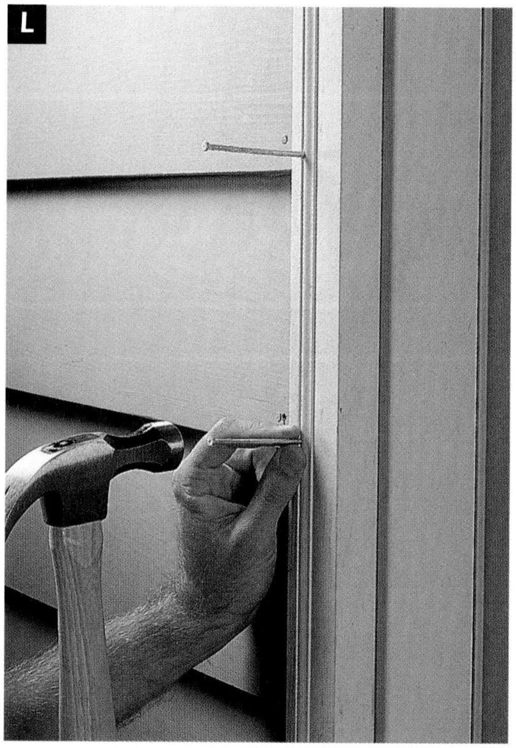

Drive 16d galvanized casing nails through the brick molding into the door frame.

Replace the casing on the interior side of the door jamb. Use the old casing or use the casing that came with the door.

Insert the latchbolt into its hole. Insert the tailpieces through the latchbolt, and tighten the retaining screws.

Screw the strike plate to the door jamb and adjust the position of the plate to fit the latchbolt.

Buying Prehung Doors

Installing a custom door is a fairly difficult job that's best left to a professional with the tools and skills required for very precise work. However, today's prehung doors make replacing or upgrading a door a manageable project for any do-it-yourselfer.

A prehung door unit will include the door itself, the door jamb, and the premitered door casing. The hinges are already mortised and attached, and the holes for the lock and the bolt are already drilled.

With the difficult work already done, installing a door becomes a simple matter of positioning it plumb and square in the opening, shimming and nailing it in place, then finishing it.

When buying a new entry door, remember that most of them must endure heavy use, so it's important not to skimp on quality. Also, since the front entry door gives visitors their first impression of your home, you may want to choose a door that evokes a specific tone, such as informality, elegance, or simplicity.

Before buying any door, you need to find out which way it opens—its "hand." To determine a door's hand, stand facing the inside of the door opening. If the hinge is on your right, it's a right-handed door; if the hinge is on your left, it's a left-handed door.

In addition to these basic considerations, consider the following factors when choosing doors.

Fiberglass entry doors are expensive, but they're strong and have good insulation values. The fiberglass may be pretinted, or you can paint or stain the surface to the desired color.

Insulated heavy-gauge steel entry doors offer good security and protection against the cold, but they're sometimes less inviting than wood doors. Also, if you have a metal threshold, you'll need a "thermal break" to keep the cold metal edges of the door away from the threshold.

Solid wood entry doors are attractive, but they require maintenance and don't insulate as well as fiberglass doors. Core-block doors are less likely to warp than solid-core doors, because the wood grain runs in alternating directions.

Among other features to consider when buying a door is its resistance to sound transmission. Bathrooms and bedrooms, for example, can benefit from passage doors with good soundproofing values.

Weatherizing Entry Doors

Entry doors are a common site for heat loss, and weatherizing your entry door will typically pay off in immediate savings on your heating bills.

This is true even if the doorway has been weatherized in the past—the weatherstripping around entry doors is prone to fail quickly, because it has to endure the stress of constant use. It's important to check every exterior door periodically and replace the weatherstripping whenever it shows signs of wear.

Whenever possible, use tacked-on metal weatherstripping around doors, especially around the jambs—it's much more durable than self-adhesive weatherstripping. If you need a flexible insulator, select a product made from neoprene rubber, rather than foam, for the same reason. Here are some ideas for weatherizing an entry door.

Adjust the door frame to eliminate large gaps between the door and the jamb. Remove the interior casing and drive new shims between the jamb and the framing member on the hinge side of the door **(photo A).** Close the door to test the fit, and adjust as needed. Reattach the casing. (For added security, install plywood spacers between the shims.)

Cut two pieces of metal V-channel to the full height of the door opening. Cut another to the full width of the door opening. Use wire brads to tack the strips to the door jamb and the door header on the interior side of the door stops. Attach metal weatherstripping from the top down, to help prevent buckling. Using a putty knife, flare the strips **(photo B)** so they fill the gaps between the jambs and the door when the door is closed.

Tools: *Putty knife, tack hammer, screwdriver, backsaw, flat pry bar, tape measure, drill.*

Materials: *Metal V-channel, reinforced felt strips, door sweep, wire brads, wood putty.*

The perimeter of an entry door is a typical culprit in the air leakage and energy loss that drive up power bills.

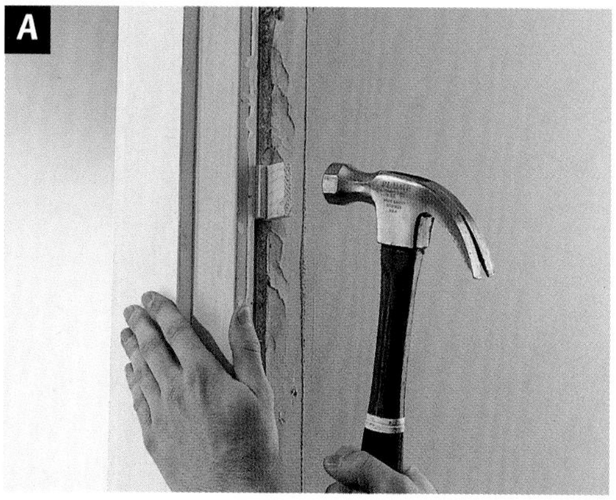

Drive new shims between the jambs and the door frame.

Flare the tension strips with a putty knife to fill air gaps.

Add a reinforced felt strip to the edge of the door stop on the exterior side of the door **(photo C).** When the door is closed, the felt edge should form a close seal with the door.

Attach a new door sweep to the bottom of the door on the interior side **(photo D).** If the floor of the entry is uneven, select a door sweep made of felt or bristle.

Working on the interior side of the door, fill cracks in wooden door panels with tinted wood putty **(photo E).** Sand down and paint or stain to match the door.

Add a reinforced felt strip to the edge of the door stop.

Install a new door sweep at the bottom of the door.

Used tinted wood putty to fill cracks in door panels.

Replacing a Door Threshold

For maximum energy efficiency, it's important to replace old door thresholds or threshold inserts as soon as they begin to show signs of wear.

Before removing the old threshold, determine which side is more steeply beveled, so you can install the new one the same way. Use a backsaw to cut the old threshold in two. Pry out the pieces **(photo F),** and clean any debris from the sill below the threshold.

Measure the opening for the new threshold and trim it to fit, using the pieces of the old threshold as a template. If the profile of the new threshold differs from the old one, trace the new profile onto the bottoms of the door stops. Chisel them to fit **(photo G).**

Apply caulk to the sill. Place the new threshold in position, pressing it down into the caulk. Drive the screws provided with the threshold through the predrilled holes in the center channel and into the sill **(photo H).**

Install the threshold insert, following the manufacturer's instructions.

Tools: *Backsaw, flat pry bar, jig saw, tape measure, chisel, mallet, caulk gun, screw gun.*

Materials: Threshold & insert, caulk.

Cut the old threshold in two and pry out the pieces.

Chisel the profile of the new threshold into the door stops.

Drive screws through the predrilled holes and into the sill.

Storm Doors

Storm doors play an important role in reducing energy loss. A storm door is always used with an inner entry door and can roughly double the insulation value of a doorway, especially if it's properly weatherstripped (pages 132 to 133).

If you live in a cold area of the country, you probably have a wood or aluminum combination door that doubles as a screen door and a storm door. If your storm door is old and leaky, a new insulated model with a continuous hinge and a seamless exterior will add both comfort and savings to your home. However, you can extend the life of any storm door, even a low-maintenance model, by cleaning and maintaining it regularly.

Do an annual inspection in the fall to catch major problems, to add improvements, and to upgrade weatherstripping. At the same time, clean the storm door and touch up any minor problems. Here are some areas to clean, check, and repair:

Vacuum any dirt from the screens. If the surface of the aluminum is becoming oxidized, clean it with car polish.

Check the caulking around the frames of the combination unit. If the caulk is failing, replace it.

Look for any small holes in the screen that insects may be able to fit through. Mend them with a dab of epoxy glue or quick-drying household cement.

If you find a small tear in a metal screen, darn it closed with fine wire or fishing line.

To patch a larger hole in a screen, cut a piece of matching screening to cover the hole. Unravel a few strands, fit the patch over the hole, and bend the strands back over the original screen to secure the patch.

Proper maintenance can maximize the energy efficiency of your combination storm door.

Replacing a Screen

To replace a screen on a wood frame, remove the frame from the door and cut a new piece of screening slightly wider and at least 1 ft. longer than the frame. Staple the top edge in place. Nail the bottom edge to a strip of wood and use wedges to pull it as taut as possible. Staple the screen to the bottom edge, then the sides, then the center rail. Trim off the excess and use small brads to reinstall the moldings. Countersink the brads and cover the holes with wood filler.

To replace a screen on an aluminum frame, remove the frame from the door and pry out the spline. Square up the frame, lay new screening over it, and cut the screen around the outside edge of the frame. Use the convex end of a spline roller to force the screen into the channel in the frame. Use the concave end of the spline roller to push the spline into the channel over the screen.

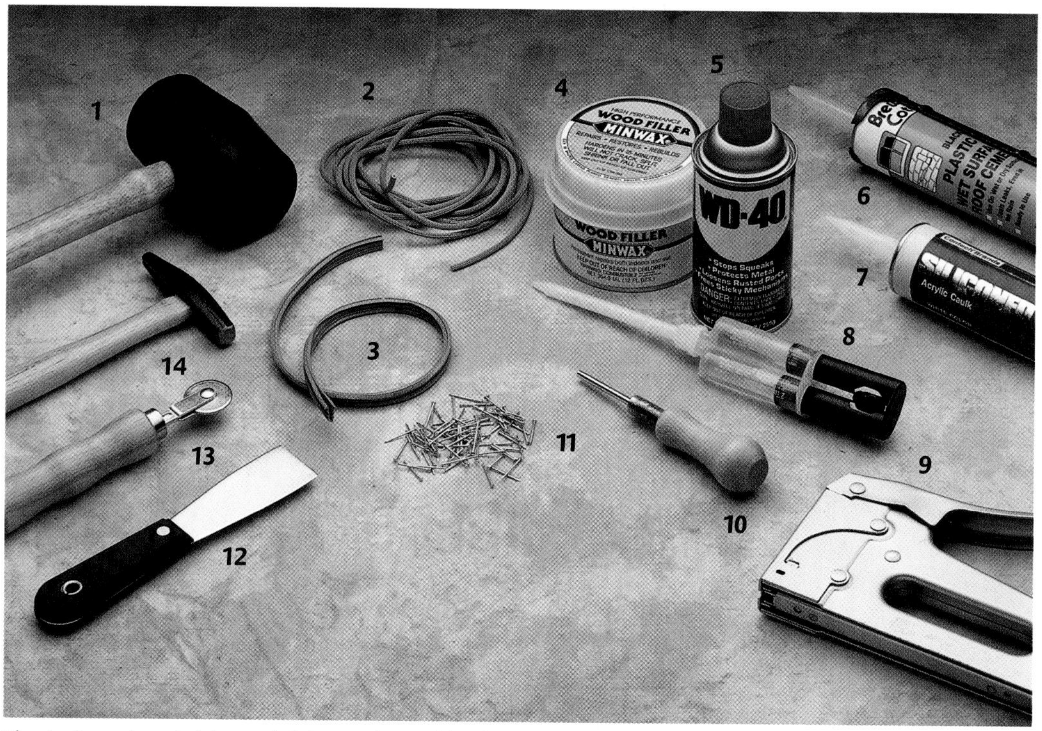

The tools and materials needed to repair combination storm doors include rubber mallet (1), spline cord (2), rubber window gasket (3), two-part wood filler (4), penetrating lubricant (5), roof cement (6), siliconized acrylic caulk (7), epoxy glue (8), staple gun (9), brad pusher (10), wire brads (11), putty knife (12), spline roller (13), and a tack hammer (14).

Maintaining Storm Doors

You'll get the most out of your storm doors if you inspect them annually and maintain them regularly. Here are some tips that will help you keep your storm doors in good working order:

Tighten the latches on storm doors by reattaching any loose screws in the strike plate **(photo A).**

If the latch doesn't catch on the strike plate, loosen the screws on the strike plate, insert thin wood shims between the plate and the jamb, and retighten the screws.

If your storm door doesn't have a wind chain, add one **(photo B).** A wind chain will prevent the door from blowing open too far, which can damage the door hinges or the automatic closer. Set the chain so the door can't open more than 90°.

Adjust the door closer so it has the right amount of tension to close the door securely without slamming **(photo C).** Most door closers have a tension-adjustment screw at the end of the cylinder that's farthest from the hinge side of the door. To maximize the life of your door, replace the automatic closer as soon as it begins to malfunction.

If your storm door includes metal-framed combination storm windows, lubricate the sliding assemblies once a year, using a spray lubricant **(photo D).**

Tools: *Screwdriver.*

Materials: *Thin wood shims, wind chain, spray lubricant.*

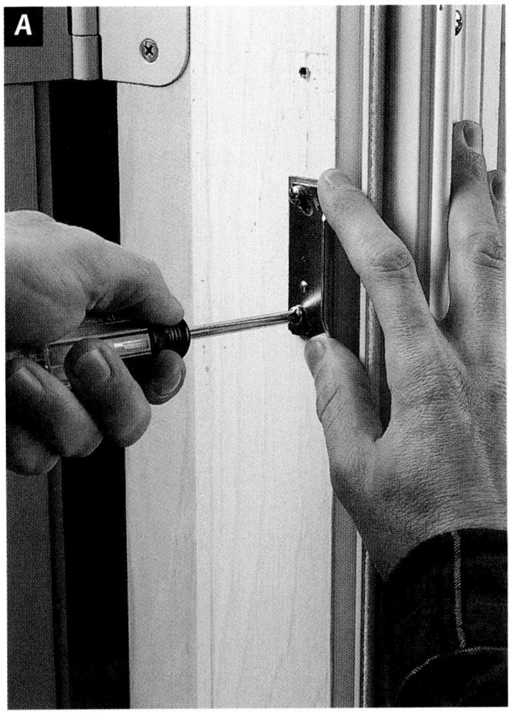

Tighten the latch by driving loose screws on the strike plate.

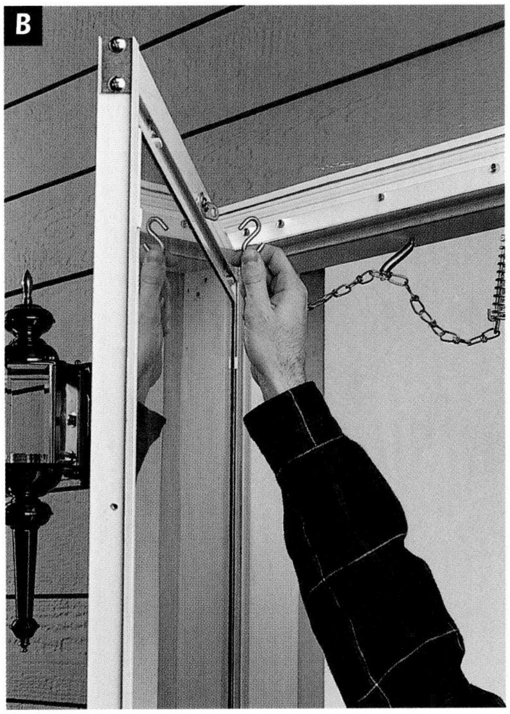

Add a wind chain to prevent the door from opening too far.

Adjust the door closer to secure the door without slamming.

Lubricate a storm door's sliding assembly once each year.

Windows

Windows are your home's eyes to the outside world. They are expected to provide natural light, to open readily when fresh air is called for, and to provide a barricade to insects, intruders, and natural elements. They are also one of the more expensive elements of your home, which is a good reason to keep them in good repair. Properly maintained windows can last 40 years or more.

Windows come in many shapes and sizes—so many that it's almost impossible to catalog them. Many homes, especially older ones that have seen periodic updates over the years, may include as many as four or five different styles of windows. Understanding how each type works can help you identify the likely problems with windows and fix them efficiently.

Double-hung windows are found in many older homes. Double-hung windows have two sashes that move up and down, one behind the other, along tracks in the window opening. Classic double-hungs usually are operated by two sets of pulleys and counterweights that fit into cavities in the walls behind the case moldings. Because they use a single pane of glass, older double-hung windows are often backed up with storm windows to improve the energy efficiency of the window system.

Newer double-hungs may use vinyl tracks and a system of springs to operate them. They're now made so one or both of the sashes tilt forward for easy cleaning. The frames on newer double-hung windows may be wood, or vinyl-clad. Newer double-hungs often use panes of glass with airtight spaces in between, eliminating the need for storm windows.

Single-hung windows resemble double-hungs, but the top sash is fixed in place and doesn't slide.

Casement windows are standard in many newer homes. They are hinged on one side, and are operated by cranks. The window frames are usually wood, or wood clad with vinyl.

Sliding windows resemble double-hung windows placed on their sides. Each window normally includes two sashes that slide to the left and right, one behind the other, along tracks. Because there are no mechanical parts, sliding windows are relatively free of problems, though they can be hard to clean.

Awning windows look like casement windows turned on their sides, with hinges on the top. They're operated by bottom-mounted cranks, and pivot up and down.

Bay windows are multiple window units that angle outward. The side windows are often the operating windows—either casement or double-hung style—while the center window may be fixed.

Picture windows are large, fixed windows designed to provide an open view and plenty of light. Unless the glazing fails, picture windows rarely have problems.

Left and center photos courtesy of Andersen Windows; right photo courtesy of The H-Window Co.

Some examples of window types and styles include (from left): two double-hung windows set in one frame with fixed transom windows above, a bay window unit with individual double-hung windows, and a casement window.

Inspecting Windows & Diagnosing Problems

Problems with windows range from sticking sashes that require you to clean the tracks, to badly rotted frames that require you to replace the entire window. Inspect your windows annually and make repairs promptly to keep minor problems from turning into expensive headaches.

• Look for broken glass. Not only is broken glass dangerous, but it reduces the energy efficiency of the window. Replacing single-pane glass (page 141), such as that found in older double-hung windows, is pretty easy, but double- or triple-glazed window panes must be special-ordered and installed by a professional. Cover cracked glass with tape to keep it from shattering until you can fix it.

• Check the glazing that seals the glass in the window frame. Replace cracked or missing glazing to prevent moisture from infiltrating and rotting the wood. When replacing glazing, use the same process used when replacing glass (page 141).

• Clean and lubricate all mechanical operating parts and sliding surfaces. You can use beeswax or soap to lubricate sliding wood windows and greaseless spray for sliding vinyl windows. Use light oil to keep mechanical parts operating smoothly (page 143).

• Make sure sliding windows are operating smoothly and that they haven't been painted in place. Windows that won't budge may be sealed by paint. You can free them by cutting through the dried paint, then tapping the sash lightly with a block of wood and a hammer (page 138).

With older double-hung windows it's common to find the upper window painted in place—a problem that's so common that some owners of older homes don't even realize that the upper windows are designed to move in their tracks. Opening the top window is the most efficient way to vent hot air from your home, so it's a good idea to fix this problem if you find it.

• Check the seal under each window. A simple way to check the seal is to place a dollar bill under the window, close it, then try to slide the bill out. If the dollar can be pulled out easily, the window fits too loosely and should be weatherstripped (page 142).

• Test double-hung windows to make sure they're operating smoothly. Most older double-hung windows operate with a system of pulleys, counterweights, and sash cords found inside hollow pockets on both sides of the window frame. Inspect and replace the sash cords whenever necessary (page 144).

• Clean and lubricate the tracks, springs, and levers on combination storm windows each year. Use a greaseless silicone spray lubricant rather than a petroleum-based oil.

Tools & Materials for Window Repair

Tools and materials you may need to repair your windows include: a heat gun for loosening glazing, putty knife for glazing windows, paint zipper for breaking paint film around windows, glazier's points for installing new glass in windows, spline roller and vinyl spline for installing new screening in window screens.

In addition to these specialty tools, you'll need some standard household and workshop tools and materials, including: a hammer, screwdrivers, sanding blocks and sandpaper, paintbrushes, primer and paint, lubricants, caulk gun, utility knife, portable vacuum, and flat pry bar.

Helpful Hint

To replace screening in a metal-framed combination storm window, first remove the screen panel. Use a screwdriver to pry the vinyl spline from the grooves around the frame. Stretch new screening fabric tightly over the frame so it overlaps the retaining grooves. (Vinyl screening is the best choice for replacement.) Use a spline roller to press the spline and screen back into the grooves. Cut away the excess screen fabric, using a utility knife.

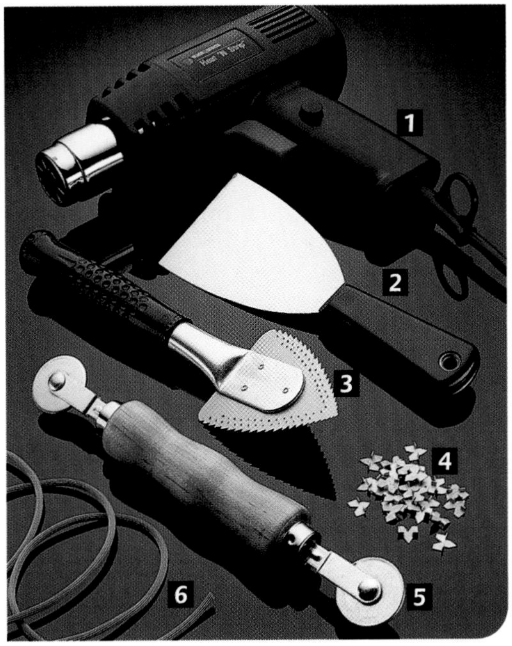

Tools for window repair include: heat gun (1), putty knife (2), paint zipper (3), glazier's points (4), spline roller (5), and vinyl spline (6).

Freeing Stuck Windows

Windows can stick for a variety of reasons, but most commonly it's because the channels or guides need cleaning, or because they've been painted shut. On double-hung windows, it's quite common for the top window to be painted shut.

To loosen a sticky window, begin by using a paint zipper or utility knife to score the crack between the window stock and the window frame **(photo A).** Work slowly to avoid chipping the paint on the window stop and sash. In some cases, the horizontal joint between the front and back window sashes may also be painted shut.

Now, hold a wood block along the window sash and strike it lightly several times with a hammer **(photo B).** Move the block up and down the sashes, then attempt to slide the windows up and down.

If this technique doesn't work, then the window frame may be warped or swollen. One solution for this problem is to remove the window stops and reinstall them so there is a very small but noticeable gap between the stops and the window sashes.

Once the windows are moving freely, clean the running tracks and lubricate them with beeswax or paraffin. The best way to do this is by removing the windows from their tracks. This is also a good time to inspect the sash cords and repair them if necessary (page 144), and to inspect and replace weatherstripping (page 142).

When painting windows, you can prevent sticking problems by following proper painting techniques. Wherever possible, remove the windows when repainting them. If they must be painted while in place, then slide them up and down in their tracks every few minutes while the paint is drying to keep them from becoming frozen in place.

A

Use a paint zipper or utility knife to break the paint seal between the window sashes and the window stops.

B

Use a wood block and hammer to tap lightly around the frame of the window, breaking the seal and freeing the window.

Improving Window Security

There's no question that windows are a weak link when it comes to securing your home against intruders. Fortunately, there are several inexpensive, easy ways to make windows less susceptible to breaking-and-entering.

On double-hung windows, you can pin the sliding sashes together by drilling a hole through the top of the bottom window and into the bottom of the upper window, and inserting a screw eye **(photo C).**

On sliding windows, wedge a thick dowel into the track between the edge of the movable window and the jamb **(photo D).** On the top track, drive a screw to keep intruders from lifting the window sash out of its track **(photo E).**

On ground-level windows, you can install protective bars or gates **(photo F).** Finally, you can remove the handles from casement and awning windows **(photo G).** An intruder breaking the glass will have to climb in across broken glass rather than simply cranking the window open.

Pin double-hung sashes together by drilling a pilot hole, then inserting a screw eye.

Sliding windows can be secured by wedging a thick dowel into the track so the movable window can't be opened when you're not at home.

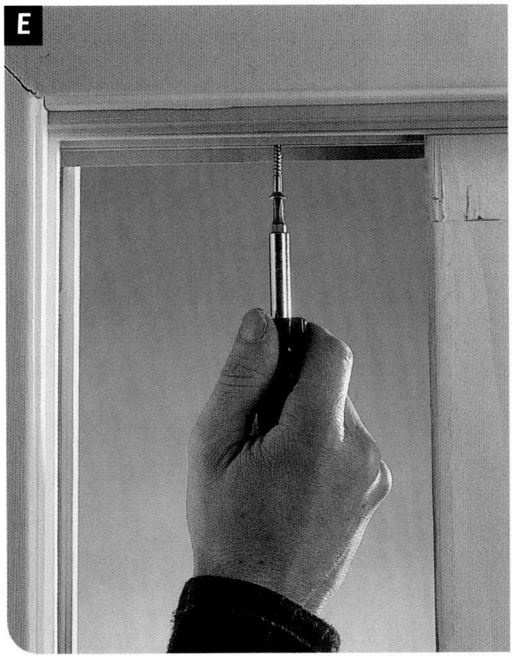

Drive a screw into the top track of a sliding window to keep the sash from being lifted out of its track.

Security bars or gates can be installed in ground-floor windows to prevent intruders from gaining entry to your house.

Removing the handles from casement and awning windows keeps intruders from cranking windows open after breaking the glass.

Cleaning & Lubricating Windows

Keeping the tracks and moving parts of windows clean and well lubricated will prevent many problems. Sliding windows and double-hung windows will operate more smoothly if the tracks are clean and smooth, and keeping the mechanisms on casement and awning windows well lubricated will reduce stress on their cranks and hinges, increasing the lifespans of these components.

Start by choosing a lubricant appropriate for the purpose **(photo A).** Petroleum products are suitable for metal-on-metal mechanisms, but nonpetroleum products, such as graphite powder, wax, or paraffin, are best for lubricating wood surfaces.

Clean the tracks on all types of sliding windows, using a hand vacuum and toothbrush **(photo B).** Dirt buildup is a common problem on double-hung windows, sliding windows, and combination storm windows.

Next, clean window tracks and weatherstripping, using a rag dipped in cleaner or a mild solvent **(photo C).** If you find dried paint in the tracks, use a scraper and paint thinner to remove this residue, which may cause windows to bind. If the weatherstripping is worn or missing, replace it (page 142). NOTE: Never use harsh solvents to clean vinyl-track windows.

Once the tracks are clean, apply a small amount of lubricant to keep them from sticking in the future. Make sure to use a greaseless, nonpetroleum lubricant.

Also clean and lubricate the locking mechanisms on the windows. Clean and lubricate the cranks and hinges on casement windows (page 143).

Tools: *Hand vacuum, toothbrush.*

Materials: *Lubricant, rag, soap, paint solvent (if needed).*

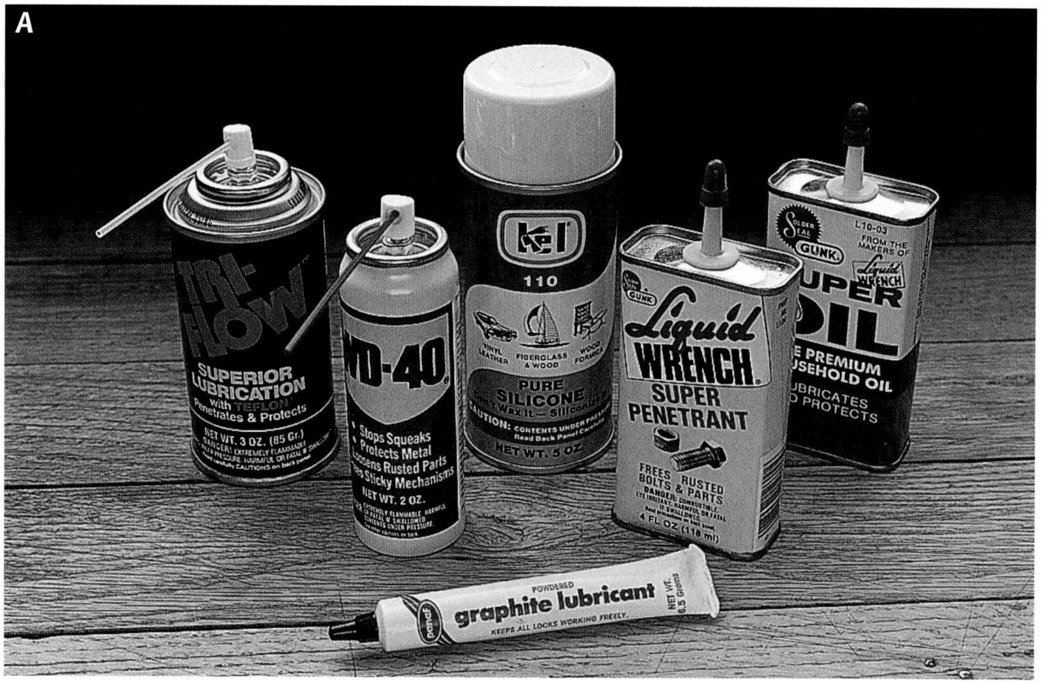

Lubricants include (from left): spray solvent/lubricant, penetrating spray oil, silicone spray, penetrating oils, and powdered graphite (front).

Use a hand vacuum and toothbrush to loosen and remove dirt and grime from the tracks of sliding windows.

Use a rag moistened with cleaner to clean weatherstripping in window tracks. Replace weatherstripping that is worn.

Replacing Window Glass

To replace broken glass, you'll need to remove the glazing putty and glazier's points, then carefully remove the glass. Take the exact measurements of the opening to the hardware store or home center—the replacement glass should measure 1/4" less in each direction than the actual opening. This will provide a 1/8" expansion gap in each edge.

Installing single-glazed glass is an easy do-it-yourself job, but never try to replace double- or triple-glazed glass panels: this is a job for a professional installer.

Start by removing the window from its jambs, if possible. Newer double-hung windows can be removed by depressing the flexible vinyl channels **(photo D);** older double-hungs by removing the stops (page 144).

Next, soften old glazing with a heat gun, being careful not to scorch the wood **(photo E).** Scrape away the softened glazing with a putty knife.

Remove the broken glass and metal glazier's points from the frame, then sand the wood to clean away old paint and putty **(photo F).** Coat the bare wood with sealer, and let dry.

Now, apply a thin layer of glazing compound into the frame recess, then set the new glass into place, pressing lightly to bed it in the glazing. Press in new glazier's points every 10", using the tip of the putty knife **(photo G).**

Apply glazing compound. Some types of glazing are applied with a caulk gun **(photo H),** while others are applied with a putty knife. Smooth the glazing with a wet finger or cloth.

After the glazing sets, paint it. Overlap the paint onto the glass by 1/16" to improve its seal against the weather **(photo I).** Reinstall the window.

Tools: *Heat gun, putty knife, caulk gun, sanding block, paintbrush.*

Materials: *Glazing, glazier's points, wood sealer, paint.*

Remove the window from its jambs, if possible, and lay it on a flat surface. If removal isn't possible, you can replace the glass while the window is in place.

Soften the glazing with a heat gun, then remove the glazing and glazier's points and remove the broken glass.

Clean and sand the wood inside the L-shaped recess, then coat the bare wood with sealer.

Apply a thin layer of glazing compound to the bottom of the recess, then install the new glass panel, pressing lightly to bed it. Install glazier's points to hold the glass in place.

Apply a bead of glazing compound around the glass. Smooth the bead with a wet finger or rag.

After the glazing sets, repaint the window, overlapping the paint onto the glass by 1/16".

Weatherstripping Double-hung Windows

In most climates, weatherstripping is essential to keep windows energy efficient. It prevents heat loss in the winter, heat gain in the summer, and also provides a barrier against moisture and insects.

Start by removing the double-hung window (page 144), and removing any old, worn-out weatherstripping. Clean the tracks thoroughly.

Cut metal V-channel weatherstripping to fit in the channels for the sliding sash **(photo A),** extending at least 2" past the closed position for each sash (don't cover the sash-closing mechanism). Attach the V-channel by driving wire brads with a tack hammer. Drive the fasteners flush with the surface, so the sliding sashes won't catch on them.

Flare out the open end of the V-channels with a putty knife so the channel is slightly wider than the gap between the sash and the track it fits into **(photo B).** Avoid flaring out too much at one time—it's difficult to press the V-channel back together without causing buckling.

Now, wipe down the underside of the bottom window with a damp rag and let it dry. Attach self-adhesive foam or rubber weatherstripping to the underside of the sash **(photo C).**

Seal the gap between the top sash and the bottom sash. Lift the bottom sash and lower the top sash to improve access, then tack metal V-channel weatherstripping to the bottom rail on the top sash **(photo D).** The open end of the V should be pointed down to prevent moisture from infiltrating the joint. Flare out the V-channel, using a putty knife.

Tools: *Hammer, putty knife.*

Materials: *Metal V-channel weatherstripping, self-adhesive foam or rubber weatherstripping.*

Cut and attach metal V-channel weatherstripping to the side channels for the sliding sash. The open side of the V should face the outdoors.

Flare the V-channel open slightly, using a putty knife. This will improve the seal of the weatherstripping.

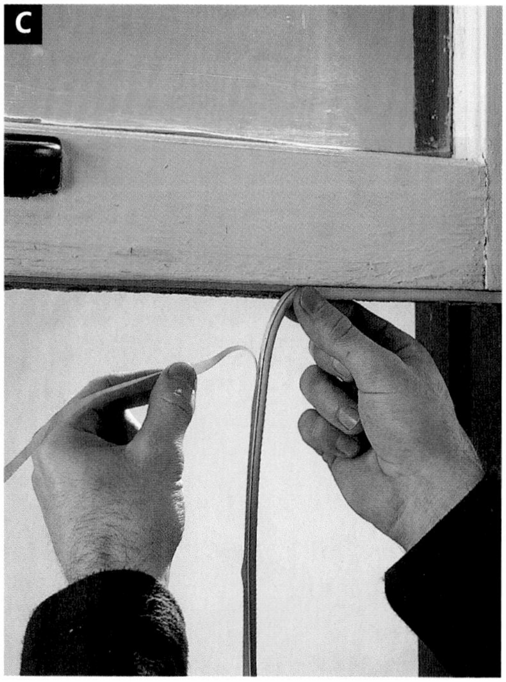

Apply self-adhesive foam or rubber weatherstripping to the underside of the sash.

Apply V-channel weatherstripping to the bottom rail on the rear window.

Weatherstripping Casement & Awning Windows

Casement and awning windows also have weatherstripping that should be inspected periodically and replaced when it becomes cracked or worn.

Start by removing any old weatherstripping and cleaning the surfaces of all dirt and grime. Cut self-adhesive foam or rubber compression strips to fit on the outside edges of the window stops. Peel away the backing, then position the weatherstripping and press it in place. **(photo E).**

Tools: Scissors.

Materials: *Foam or rubber self-adhesive weatherstripping.*

Repairing Casement Windows

When casement windows don't open and close smoothly and easily, it's usually because dirt or grease is preventing the cranks and pivoting arms from operating freely.

Begin by opening the window until the vinyl knob on the extension arm can be pulled free from the track **(photo F).**

Disengage the extension arm from the track **(photo G).** On some windows, you may need to remove a C-clip to get the arm free. Clean the track with stiff-bristled brush.

Use a clean cloth moistened with rubbing alcohol to wipe grime and excess grease from the arm and pivot points **(photo H).** Also clean away dirt and grease from the gears in the crank assembly.

Lubricate the crank, extension arm joints, and track with light machine oil spray. Work the crank by opening and closing the window until the spray has penetrated completely.

Tools: *Rag, stiff-bristled brush.*

Materials: *Rubbing alcohol, light machine oil.*

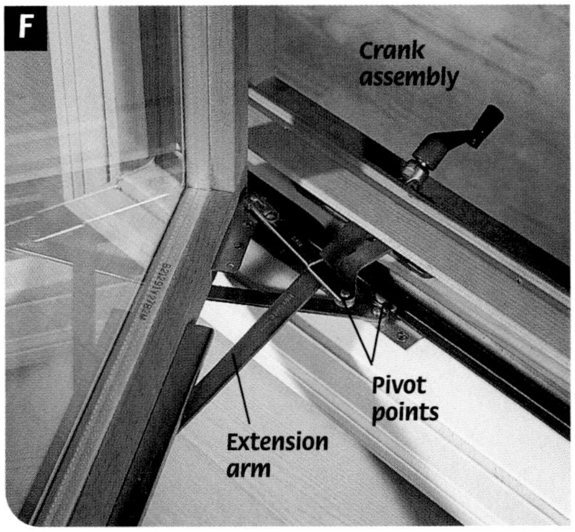

Open the window to align the extension arm channel knob with the slot in the window track.

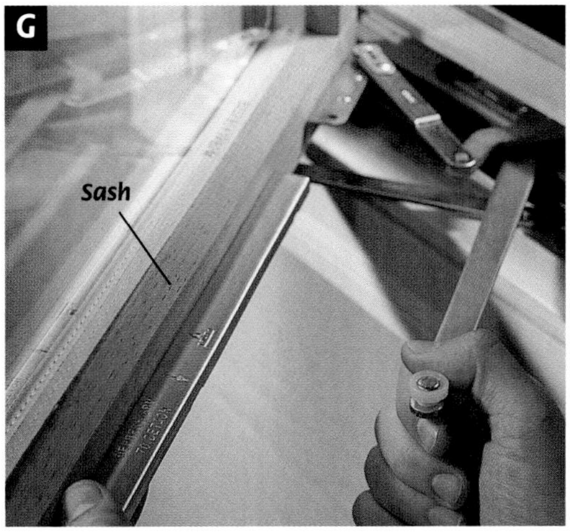

Disengage the extension arm from the track. Clean the track with a stiff-bristled brush.

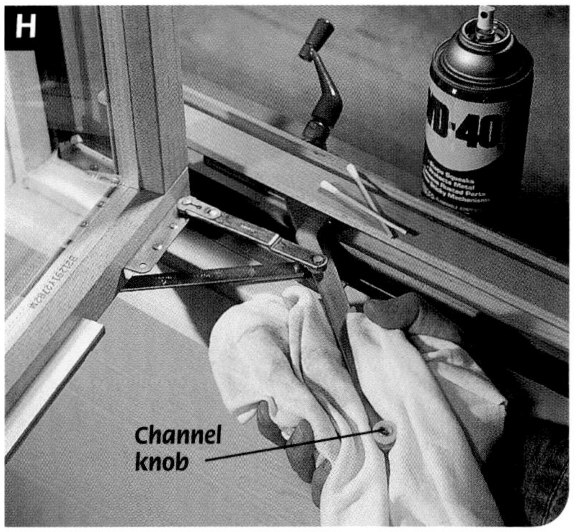

Lubricate the track, joints, and extension arm with light machine oil spray.

Replacing Sash Cords

You don't have to live with a misbehaving double-hung window. Replacing the broken sash cords that operate the window is a surprisingly easy repair.

Start by slicing through the paint film with a utility knife, if the window has been painted shut **(photo A).** Then, use a thin pry bar to carefully pry away the wooden stops that hold the lower, interior window sash in place **(photo B).**

Lift the interior window sash out of the window opening **(photo C),** and remove the knotted cords that fit into holes mortised into the sides of the window frame.

Pry out the parting beads—the narrow vertical strips of wood that separate the two windows. The beads fit into a groove in the side jambs, so be careful. If a parting bead does break, don't panic—they're available at most home centers and lumberyards.

With the parting beads removed, pull the upper, exterior window sash from the window opening. If the window won't budge, it's probably painted in place. Cut through the paint seal around the outside of the sash, using a utility knife. Then, gently tap the sash with a wood block and hammer until it's free from

Tools: *Utility knife, flat pry bar, screwdrivers, hammer, putty knife.*

Materials: *1/4" nylon sash rope, light machine oil, 100-grit sandpaper.*

Cut the paint film on the window stops, using a utility knife.

Remove the windows stops, using a flat pry bar if the stops are nailed, or a screwdriver if they are screwed in place.

Pull the lower, interior sash from the window frame, and detach the sash cords from the sides of the window.

Remove the cover on the cavity holding the sash weights. Remove the parting bead, then remove the top window.

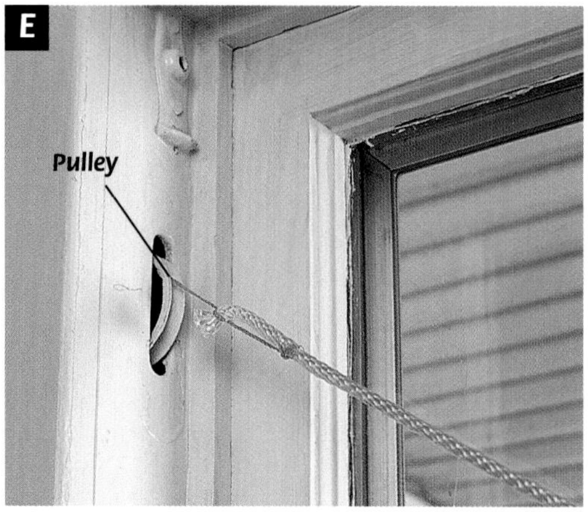

Use a string and small nail to feed new sash cord over the pulleys and down into the wall cavities.

Pull the new sash cord through the cavities and tie the ends to the sash weights.

the frame. Remove any cords that are attached to the window.

Open the small access panel set into each side jamb **(photo D).** In most cases, you'll need to simply remove the nail or screw holding the panel closed. Reach into the wall cavity and pull out the weights.

Untie or cut away the sash cords attached to the weights, and remove the cords from the cavities.

Check the pulleys near the top of each side jamb to make sure they spin freely and aren't clogged with dust, dirt, or paint. Scrape off any dried paint with a putty knife, then apply a few drop of light machine oil to the axles on the pulleys.

To install new 1/4" nylon sash rope, first tie one end of a piece of string to a small nail, and tie the other end to the new sash cord **(photo E).** Feed the new ropes over the pulleys and down into the wall cavities **(photo F).**

Tie the rope ends to the weights, then slip the weights back into the wall cavities **(photo G).**

Scrape off any dried paint and grime from the side jambs. Remove any old weatherstripping. Then, sand these surfaces smooth with 100-grit sandpaper wrapped around a small wood block.

If you want to paint the sashes, do it before you put them back into the frame. Don't paint the vertical edges that slide against the side jambs, however; the finish will make the sash stick and bind.

Apply a coat of wax to the edges of each sash. If you notice any dried paint drips or rough spots on the edges, sand them smooth.

Trim the cords to size for the upper, exterior sash, using the old cords as a reference for length **(photo H).**

Tie knots in the sash cords, and press the knots into the mortises cut into the edges of the sashes. Be sure to locate the knots so the sash can travel freely from fully open to fully closed. If necessary, change the position of the knots to lengthen or shorten the cords. Drive a small nail directly through each knot and into the window frame to hold the rope in place **(photo I).**

Reattach the cover for the access panel. Install new weatherstripping for the rear sash, if you choose (page 142). Push the rear sash into the jambs, then replace the parting bead.

Trim and attach the cords for the lower, interior sash, using the same method.

Reinstall the interior window stops that hold the lower, interior sash in place. The stops should be close enough to the sash to keep it from rattling, but not so close that they bind the sash. Attach the stops with small wood screws or finishing nails just long enough to pass through the stop and into the jamb. (Longer fasteners will protrude into the wall cavities and catch on the sash cords as the weights travel up and down.) Make sure that each sash slides smoothly and closes tightly.

Helpful Hint

Some older double-hung windows may use sash chains rather that ropes. If so, it's best to replace them with nylon ropes rather than to install new chains. Rope is less likely to tangle than metal chain. It's also quieter. Metal chains rattle whenever the window is raised or lowered.

Lift the weights back into the wall cavities.

Measure the length, then cut the new sash cords to length.

Knot the ends of the sash cords and nail them into the mortises cut into the sides of the windows.

Removing & Replacing Windows

If you discover that a window is too deteriorated to repair, you can replace it. Fortunately, the job's not as difficult as it might seem. Make sure to buy a replacement window that matches the rough opening of the window, and wait for a dry day to do the job.

Start by prying off the window aprons, stools, and casings, using a flat pry bar **(photo A).** Save the moldings if you plan to reuse them; some new windows come with their own moldings.

For double-hung windows with sash weights, remove the weights by cutting the cords and pulling the weights from the pockets (page 144).

Cut through the nails holding the window and door frames to the framing members, using a reciprocating saw **(photo B).** From the outside, pull the window from the opening. Make arrangements for help if the window unit is large. Applying masking tape across the panes of glass may prevent the glass from shattering if there is a mishap while you're removing the window **(photo C).**

NOTE: If you can't install the new window immediately, cover the opening temporarily by screwing a scrap piece of plywood to the framing members. Staple plastic sheeting to the outside of the opening to prevent moisture damage.

Test-fit the new window, entering it in the rough opening **(photo D).** Support the window with wood blocks and shims placed under the bottom jamb.

Check the window to make sure it's level and plumb **(photo E).** If necessary, adjust the shims under the low corner of the window,

Tools: *Flat pry bar, utility knife, reciprocating saw, hammer, drill, nail set, handsaw, caulk gun.*

Materials: *Masking tape, wood blocks, wood shims, 8d casing nails, 10d galvanized casing nails, caulk.*

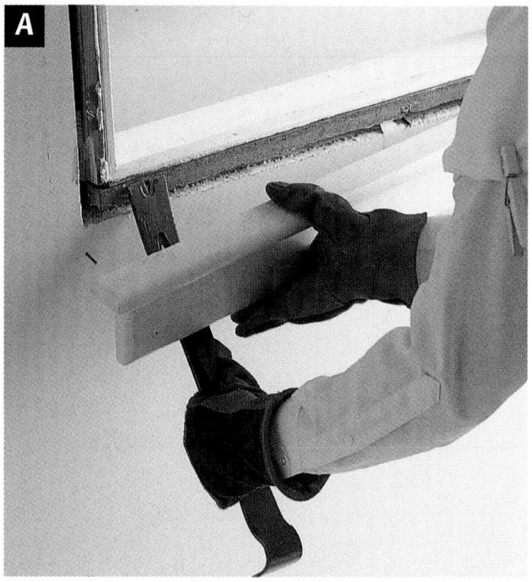

Remove the old window's apron, stool, and case moldings, using a flat pry bar. Save these moldings, if you plan to reuse them with the new window.

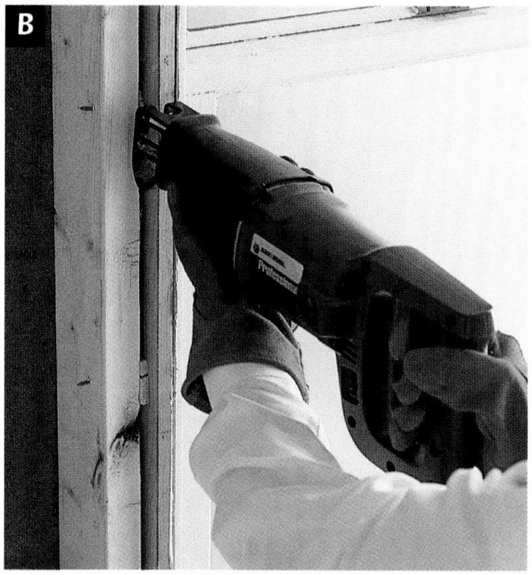

Cut through the nails holding the window to the framing members, using a reciprocating saw equipped with a metal-cutting blade.

With a helper, remove the window from the opening and set it aside. Masking tape placed across the panes of glass can prevent shattering while you're moving the window.

until it's level **(photo F).**

Place pairs of wedge shims together to form flat shims. From inside, insert shims into the gaps between the jambs and framing members, spaced every 12" **(photo G).** Adjust the shims so they're snug, but not so tight that they cause the jambs to bow. Open and close the window to make sure it operates properly. Check again to make sure the window is still level and plumb, adjusting it if necessary.

At each shim location, drill a pilot hole, then drive an 8d casing nail through the jamb and shims and into the framing member **(photo H).** Drive the nail heads below the surface with a nail set.

Fill the gaps between the window jambs and the framing members with loosely packed fiberglass insulation to reduce air infiltration.

Trim off the shims flush with the framing members, using a handsaw.

From outside, drill pilot holes, then drive 10d galvanized casing nails, spaced every 12", through the brick moldings and into the framing members **(photo I).** Recess the nail heads, using a nail set.

Apply silicone caulk around the entire window unit. Fill all nail holes with caulk, then paint the wood trim.

Replace the interior moldings (page 48).

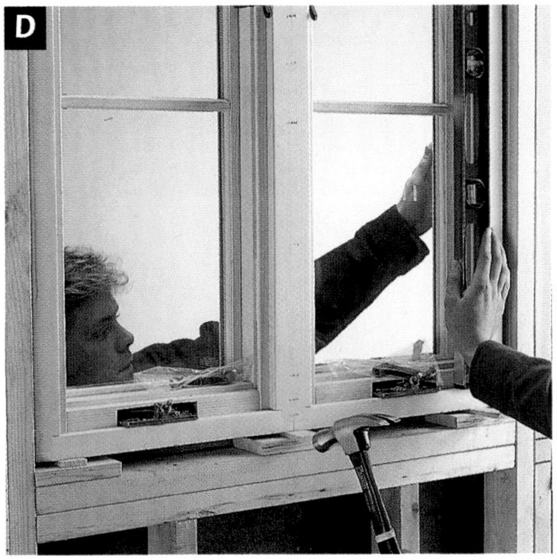

Test-fit the new window in the rough opening.

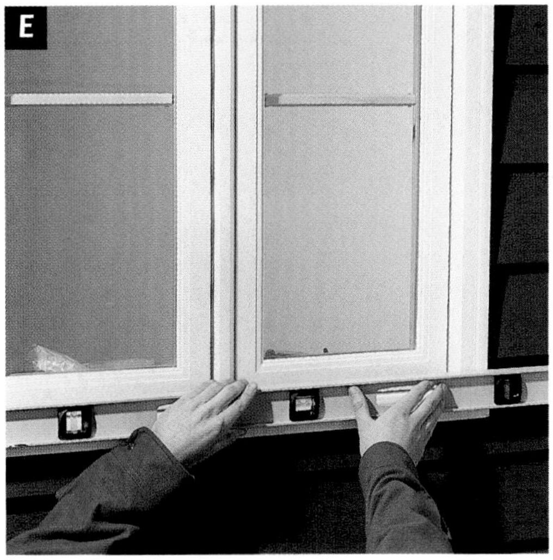

Check the bottom edge of the window for level.

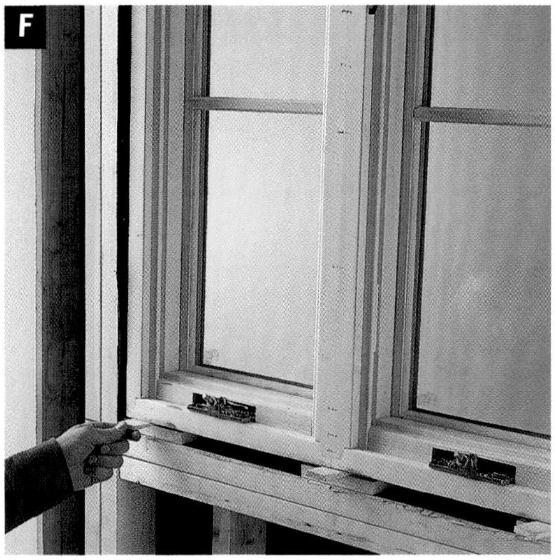

Adjust the window by adjusting the shims under the low edge, if necessary.

Place pairs of shims into the gaps between the jambs and framing members.

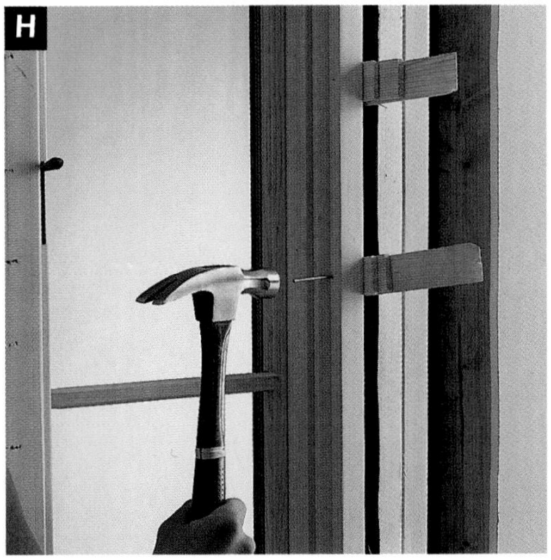

Secure the window with 8d nails driven through the jamb at each shim location.

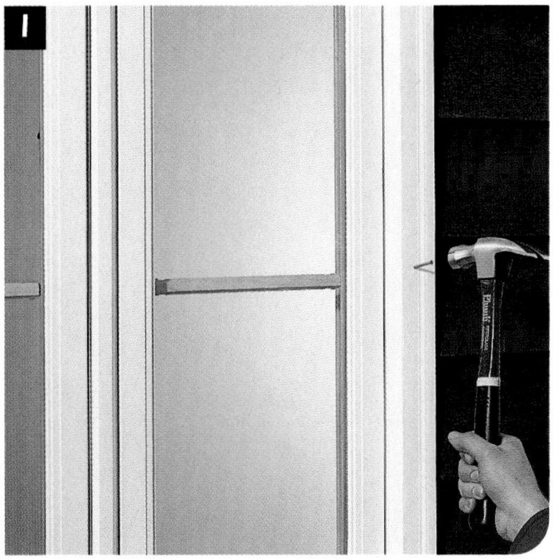

Drive 10d casing nails through the brick molding.

Repairing Storm Windows

Combination storm and screen windows offer more convenience than removable windows, since they don't need to be changed twice a year. They protect the interior of the house from strong winds, create an insulating area of trapped air between the storm window and the permanent window, and can be opened for ventilation at any time.

However, cleaning and maintaining a combination window can be more difficult than cleaning and maintaining a removable window. To address this problem, the newer models incorporate tilt-down designs that make it easier to perform these tasks from inside the house.

Although removable storm and screen windows must be changed with the seasons, they provide excellent insulation in winter and full ventilation in summer. For these reasons, many homeowners still prefer them over combination storm and screen windows, despite the extra effort involved.

The simple wood-sash construction of removable windows and their lack of moving parts make them easy to maintain and repair. The most common repair jobs are replacing screens and glass, tightening loose joints, and applying fresh paint.

Tools: Hammer, screwdriver, putty knife.

Materials: Window-hanging hardware, screw eyes, 2 × 4s, wood putty or toothpicks and epoxy glue, penetrating lubricant spray, glazing compound, glazier's points.

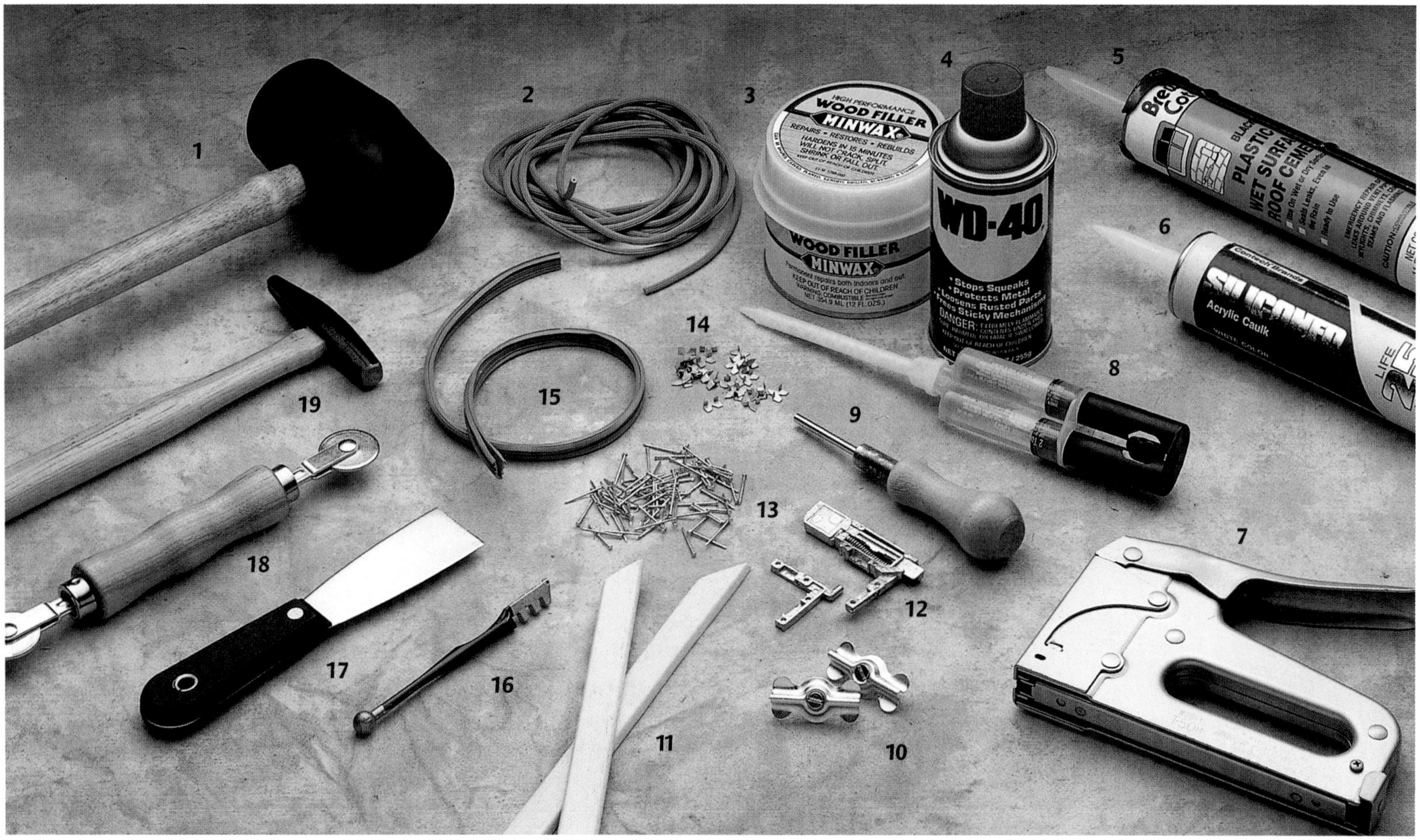

The tools and materials needed for storm window repair include: rubber mallet (1), spline cord for metal sash (2), two-part wood filler (3), penetrating lubricant (4), roofing cement (5), siliconized acrylic caulk (6), staple gun (7), epoxy glue (8), brad pusher (9), turnbuttons (10), retaining strips for wood sash (11), metal sash replacement hardware (12), wire brads (13), glazier's points (14), rubber window gasket for metal sash (15), glass cutter (16), putty knife (17), spline roller (18), tack hammer (19).

Maintaining Storm Windows

Whether you have removable storm windows or combination windows, a few handy tips can greatly simplify the task of maintaining them, extending their life, and improving their performance.

If you have removable screen and storm windows, one of the best ways to prolong their life is to build a storage rack to keep them in good order over the off-season **(photo A).**

If your screen and storm windows don't already have attached window-hanging hardware, begin by securing hangers to the outside top rails of the windows, spacing them 1" in from the ends.

Next, attach a pair of 2 × 4s to the rafters of your garage or the ceiling joists in your basement. Position the lumber to match the spacing between the window-hanging hardware on the windows.

Finally, attach screw eyes to the 2 × 4s in rows that fit the hanging hardware. Install the unused set of storms or screens in the screw eyes.

If your storm windows are loose, it's probably because the turnbuttons or window clips aren't holding them tightly in place. To give the screws a better grip, fill the old screw holes with wood putty, or with toothpicks and epoxy glue (never use regular wood glue for exterior work). Let the filler dry, then reinstall the screws **(photo B).**

To keep the sliding assemblies on metal-frame combination storm windows moving smoothly, lubricate them once a year with a penetrating spray lubricant **(photo C).**

Replace any deteriorated glazing around glass panes in wood-framed windows, using glazing compound and a putty knife **(photo D).** Check first to see if the window is missing any glazier's points, and replace them, if necessary. Renewed glazing will make the windows both more energy efficient and more attractive.

A storage rack will extend the life of removable windows.

Tighten the turnbuttons that hold storm windows in place.

Lubricate sliding assemblies on metal windows every year.

Replace any worn or cracked glazing on wooden windows.

Weatherstripping a Wood Storm Window

Storm windows block heat loss by maintaining a pocket of dead air between the interior and exterior window panes. Air leaks around the panes compromise a storm window's insulating value and drive up your energy bills.

To reduce leaks, seal the edges of the panes **(photo A)** with the appropriate weatherstripping. Create a seal around the outside frame by attaching a foam compression strip to the outside of the storm window stops **(photo B).**

After installing the window, use caulk backer rope to fill any gaps between the exterior window trim and the storm window.

While it's important to limit leaks as much as possible, it's equally important to prevent condensation and frost between the window panes. If you spot moisture buildup between the panes, you'll need to create several small holes, known as *weep holes,* that allow moisture to escape so it won't cause wood rot. Drill one or two weep holes at a slight upward angle through the bottom rail of the storm window **(photo C).**

Tools: Drill.

Materials: *Weatherstripping, foam compression strip, caulk backer rope.*

A

The primary areas of heat loss in windows are located where the edges of the glass panes meet the window frame.

B

Fill the gap between the storm window and the permanent window with caulk backer rope.

C

Drill one or two small holes in the bottom rail of the storm window, to prevent moisture buildup inside the window.

Replacing the Glass in a Wood Storm Window

To replace the glass in a wood storm window, begin by cleaning out the recess in the frame by carefully removing any old glass, glazing compound, and glazier's points. Use an old chisel to scrape the residue from the recess, then apply a coat of primer or sealer to the window frame.

Measuring from the outside shoulders of the recess, determine the full width and height of the opening. Subtract 1/8" from each dimension, and have a new piece of glass cut to fit.

Apply a thin bead of caulk in the recess, to create a bed for the new pane of glass **(photo D).** Press the new pane of glass into the fresh caulk **(photo E).**

Use a putty knife or the blade of a screwdriver to push glazier's points into the frame every 8" to 10" to hold the glass in place.

Roll the glazing compound into 3/8"-dia. "snakes" and press them into the joint between the glass and the frame **(photo F).**

Smooth the compound with a putty knife held at a 45° angle to create a flat surface.

Strip off any excess glazing compound with the edge of the putty knife. Let the compound dry for several days before you paint the window.

Tools: *Old chisel, putty knife, screwdriver, caulk gun.*

Materials: *Caulk, replacement glass, glazier's points, glazing compound.*

Apply a thin bead of caulk to the recess in the frame.

Press the new glass pane into the fresh caulk.

Press glazing compound between the glass and the frame.

Replacing a Screen in a Wood Storm Window

To replace the screen in a wood storm window, begin by cleaning any old screening or retaining strips from the recess. Use an old chisel to scrape the residue from the recess, then apply a coat of primer or sealer to the window frame.

Cut a piece of fiberglass screening at least 3" wider and longer than the opening in the frame **(photo G).** Fiberglass screening is easy to handle, and won't rust or corrode.

Use a staple gun to tack the top edge of the screening into the recess **(photo H).** Stretch the screen tightly toward the bottom of the frame, and tack the bottom of the screen into the recess.

Next, tack one side into the recess. Stretch the screen tightly across the frame, and tack the other side into place.

Attach retaining strips over the edges of the screen. Don't use the old nail holes; drill 1/32"-dia. pilot holes into the retaining strips, then drive wire brads into the holes **(photo I).** Trim the excess screening with a sharp utility knife.

Tools: Old chisel, staple gun, utility knife.

Materials: Fiberglass screening, staples, wire brads.

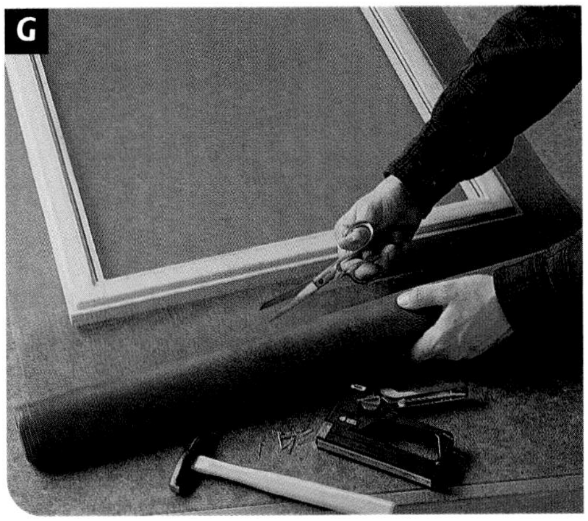

Cut the screen 3" wider and longer than the opening.

Staple the top edge of the screening in place first.

Drive wire brads into new holes in the retaining strips.

Repairing a Loose Joint in a Wood Storm Window

Because removable storm windows are changed, transported, and stored so much, they tend to need regular repair and maintenance. Loose joints are one of the most common problems you may encounter. Fortunately, this problem is easy to repair on most wood storm windows, which typically have butted, lapped, or mortise-and-tenon joints.

Remove the glass pane or screen insert and inspect it. If the pane or insert is damaged, clean and prepare the recess **(photo A),** and plan to replace the glass or screen (pages 150 to 151) after repairing the joint.

Carefully separate the loose joint, using a flat pry bar, if necessary. Use a putty knife to scrape the surfaces of the joint clean.

Use a disposable glue syringe to inject epoxy glue into the joint **(photo B).** Press the joint back together and clamp it into position with a bar clamp. Use a carpenter's square to check the frame for square.

After the glue is dry, reinforce the repair by drilling two 3/16"-dia. holes through the joint. Cut two 3/16"-dia. dowels about 1" longer than the thickness of the frame.

Round over one end of each dowel with sandpaper. Coat the dowels with epoxy glue and drive them through the holes **(photo C).**

After the glue is dry, trim the ends of the dowels with a backsaw, and sand them until they're flush with the sash. Touch up the area with a coat of paint.

Tools: *Flat pry bar, putty knife, disposable glue syringe, bar clamp, carpenter's square, drill, hammer, backsaw, sanding & painting tools.*
Materials: Epoxy glue, 3/16" dowels, sandpaper, paint.

When removing the glass from a wood storm window, it's important to clean and prepare the recess properly (page 150).

Inject epoxy glue into the joint and press it back together.

Drive dowels through the joint to reinforce the repair.

Replacing the Glass in a Metal Storm Window

Repairing a combination metal storm window is more complicated than repairing a removable wood storm window. However, there are some repairs that you can do yourself, as long as you can locate the parts.

When looking for new parts, always bring the originals with you. Go to a hardware store that repairs storm windows, and ask the clerk to help you find the correct replacements. If you can't find the right parts, don't attempt the repair; have a new sash built instead.

The first step is to remove the sash from the window. Align the sash hangers on the ends of the top rail with the notches in the side channels. Press in the release hardware in the lower rail—such as the slide tabs shown here **(photo D)**—and lift out the sash.

Next, remove the broken glass from the sash. Remove any glass fragments as well as the rubber gasket that framed the old glass.

Find the dimensions for the replacement glass by measuring the inside edges of the frame opening, then adding twice the thickness of the rubber gasket to each dimension **(photo E).**

Set the frame on a flat surface and disconnect the top rail **(photo F).** Usually you'll need to remove the retaining screws in the sides of the frame where they join the top rail.

After unfastening the retaining screws, pull the top rail loose, pulling it gently downward to avoid damaging the L-shaped corner keys that join the rail and the stiles.

Wearing gloves, fit the rubber gasket around one edge of the glass pane **(photo G).** At the corners, cut the spline of the gasket partway to bend it around the corner. Continue until all four edges are covered; trim the excess gasket.

Slide the glass into the channels in the stiles and the bottom rail of the sash frame. Insert the corner keys into the top rail, and slip the other ends of the keys into the frame stiles **(photo H).**

Press down on the top rail until the mitered corners are flush with the stiles. Drive in the retaining screws to pull the frame back together.

Tools: *Tape measure, utility knife, screwdriver, gloves.*

Materials: *Replacement rubber gasket, replacement glass, replacement hardware.*

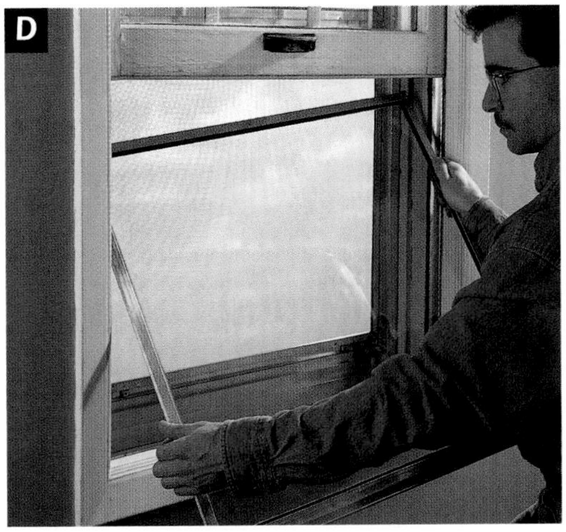

Press the release tabs to remove the sash from the window.

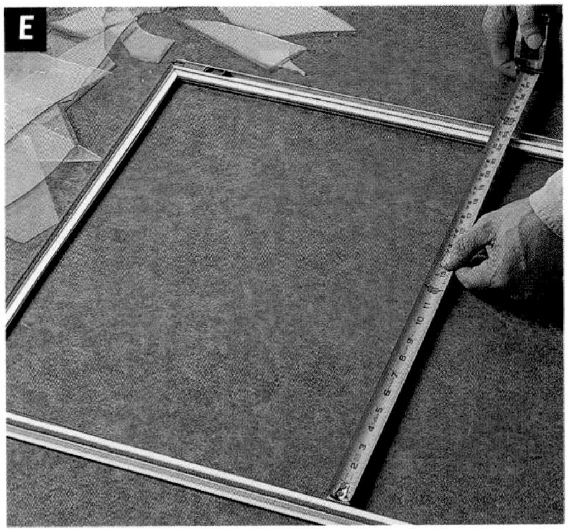

Determine the dimensions of the replacement glass.

Unfasten the retaining screws to disconnect the top rail.

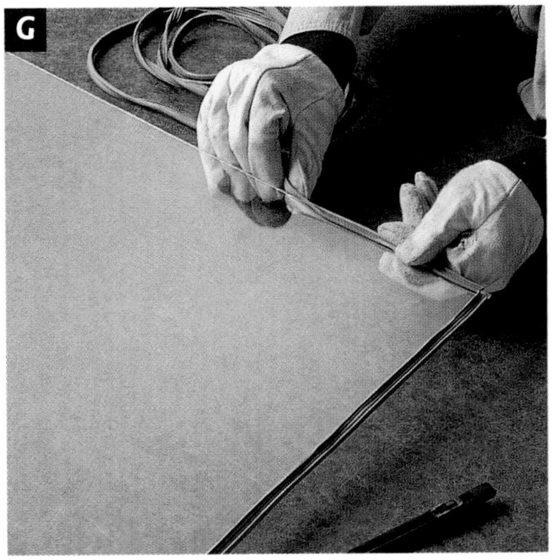

Fit the rubber gasket around the edge of the new glass pane.

Slip the ends of the corner keys into the frame stiles.

Replacing a Screen in a Metal Storm Window

Replacing a screen is one of the simplest repair and maintenance tasks typically required by a metal combination storm window. When replacing a screen, use fiberglass screening, which is easy to handle and doesn't rust or corrode.

Begin by removing the metal sash frame from the window (page 153). Set the sash down on a level working surface.

Use a screwdriver to pry up the spline cord that's holding the damaged screen in the frame **(photo A).** Evaluate the condition of the spline cord and replace it if necessary.

Thoroughly remove any bits of the old screen that may still be clinging to the frame. Clean any debris from the spline-cord tracks in the frame.

Using a utility knife, cut the new screening material, at least 3" wider and longer than the frame opening. Center the screening over the frame **(photo B).**

Lay the spline cord over the screening, roughly aligned with the spline-cord track.

Working at the top edge of the window, use the concave end of the spline roller to press the spline cord down into the spline-cord track. Continue rolling the cord across the top edge of the window. Stretch the screening across the sash frame. Continue rolling the cord all the way around the frame **(photo C).**

Use a utility knife to trim off any remaining spline cord, as well as the excess screening. Replace the metal sash frame in the storm window.

Tools: *Screwdriver, utility knife, spline roller.*
Materials: *Fiberglass screening, replacement spline cord.*

Pry up the spline cord holding the damaged screen in the frame, and check it for wear or damage.

Cut new screening material at least 3" wider and longer than the opening in the sash frame.

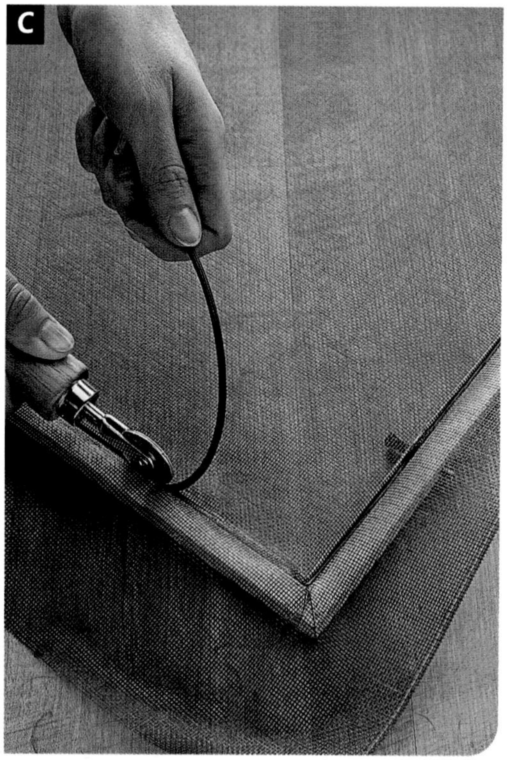

Press the spline cord down into its track, starting at the top edge and continuing all around the frame.

Repairing a Metal Sash Frame

Metal window sashes are held together at the corner joints by corner keys—L-shaped pieces of hardware that fit into the grooves in the sash frame pieces. When a problem develops in a joint, it's usually caused by a broken corner key.

To repair a broken joint, begin by disconnecting the stile and the rail at the corner. Usually there will be a retaining screw driven through the stile that you'll need to remove **(photo D).**

If the frame holds a screen, remove the screen. If the frame holds glass, set it aside so it doesn't get damaged as you work.

The corner keys are secured in the rail slots with crimps that are punched into the metal over the key. To remove the keys, drill through the metal in the crimped area, using a drill bit of the same diameter as the crimp **(photo E).**

Carefully knock all the broken key pieces out of the frame slots, using a screwdriver and a hammer.

Take the broken corner key to the store to locate matching replacement parts, which will usually consist of an assembly of two or three different pieces **(photo F).** There are dozens of different designs, so it's essential to bring the old parts to make sure you get the right style and size.

Insert the replacement corner key assembly into the slot in the rail. Use a nail set as a punch, rapping the point into the metal over the corner key **(photo G).** This creates a new crimp that will hold the replacement corner key in position.

If the frame holds glass, reinsert the glass (surrounded by its rubber gasket) into the slots in the frame **(photo H).** Then reassemble the frame and drive in the retainer screws. If the frame holds a screen, reassemble the frame and the screws first, then reinstall the screening (page 153).

Tools: *Screwdriver, drill, hammer, nail set.*

Materials: *Replacement hardware, replacement fiberglass screening.*

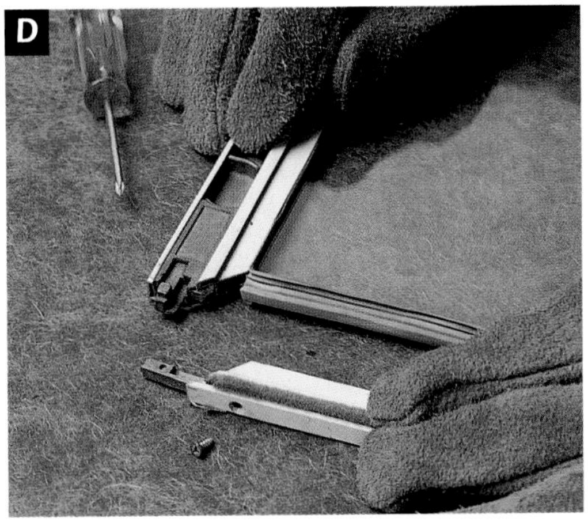

Disassemble the joint by removing the retaining screw from the stile.

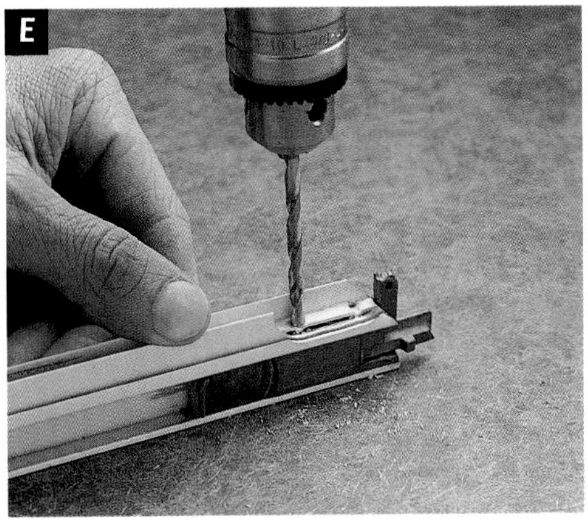

Drill through the metal crimp holding the key in place, and remove the pieces.

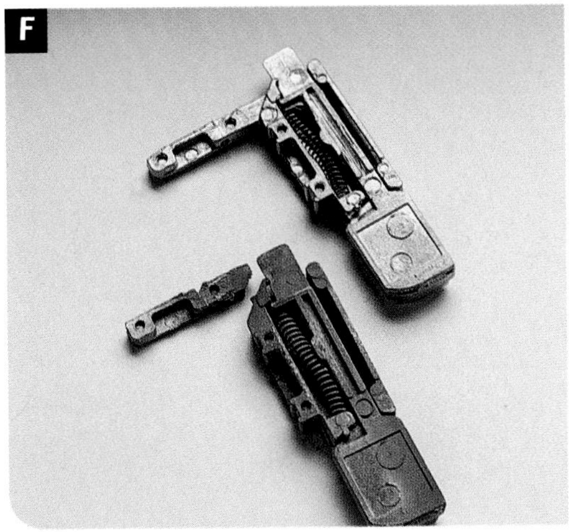

Bring the old corner key with you to the store, and purchase an exact duplicate.

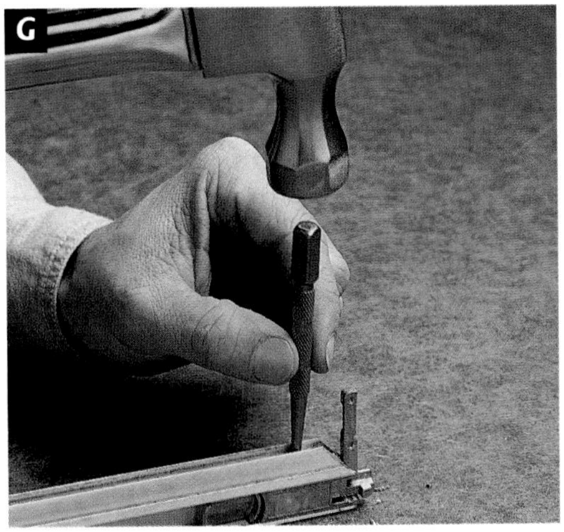

Insert the corner key assembly into the slot in the rail. Use a nail set and hammer to make a new crimp.

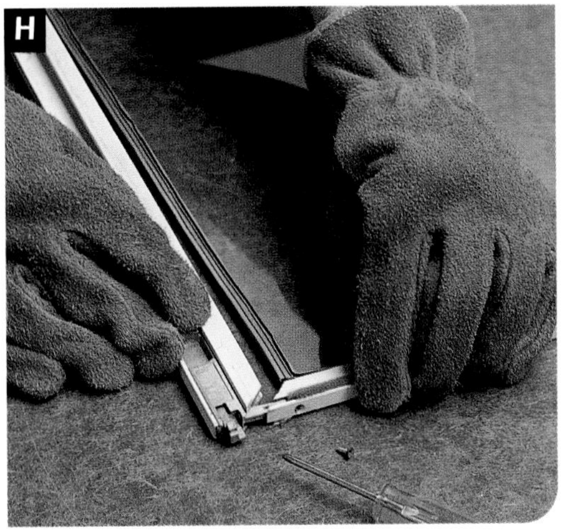

Insert the glass (surrounded by its gasket) into the slots. Reassemble the frame and drive in the retaining screws.

Replacing Storm Windows

As old removable storm windows wear out, many homeowners are choosing to replace them with more convenient combination storm windows, which are designed to mount permanently in the existing opening. These "retrofit" combination storm windows are fairly inexpensive and very easy to install.

Most retrofit storm windows attach to the outside edges of the window stops on the sides and top of the window opening. The window stops are strips of wood that are attached on the outside of the permanent window to hold it into the opening. However, since most windows don't have a bottom stop, the bottom rail of the combination window is secured in place with caulk.

Although building and home centers stock the most common sizes of combination storm windows, you may need to order a custom-made size to fit your windows exactly.

The easiest way to size a combination storm window is to use the dimensions of the old removable storm windows. Otherwise, measure the narrowest point between the side jambs to find the width, and the shortest point from the header to the sill to find the height **(photo A).**

Bring the exact measurements with you when you order the windows. Be prepared, as well, to select a finish color and a style. If you have functioning double-hung windows, choose three-sash windows; this will give you the option of opening the sash on the top storm.

Tools: Screwdriver, drill, tape measure, caulk gun.

Materials: Replacement storm window, exterior-grade panel adhesive or caulk, #4 × 1" sheet-metal screws or other fasteners.

A

Before ordering storm windows, carefully measure the narrowest and the shortest spans of each window.

When your new windows arrive, test-fit all of them in their intended window openings before you begin the installation process. If a window has been incorrectly sized, test-fitting will save you headaches later, and allow you to deal with any problems promptly.

Installing new combination windows is a simple project, although it can become more complicated if your windows are high off the ground or hard to reach.

Begin by applying a bead of exterior-grade panel adhesive or caulk to the outside edges of the window stops around the top and sides of the permanent window **(photo B).**

Drill pilot holes for fasteners in the mounting flanges, spaced 12" apart, making sure they will end up centered over the window stops.

Press the new storm window into the caulked opening. Center it between the side stops; let the bottom rail rest on the windowsill **(photo C).**

Starting on the top edge of the window, drive in the fasteners (#4 × 1" sheet-metal screws work well). Make sure that the window is square in the opening, then install the fasteners on the side stops **(photo D).**

Apply a bead of caulk along the bottom rail. However, be sure to leave a 1/4"-wide gap halfway across the bottom of the window. This will provide a weep hole so that excess moisture doesn't accumulate between the storm window and the permanent window.

Buying Combination Windows

Combination storm windows are a good investment that will pay for themselves quickly in lower energy bills.

However, you do need to watch out for poorer-quality products, which may leak warm air, stick, jam, and break easily.

Storm windows come in double- and triple-track designs. However, only the triple-track designs are truly self-storing. As a rule, the deeper the tracks, the higher the window's insulation value.

Look for windows that have a lapped joint, which is stronger and tighter than a mitered joint.

Don't buy a window if you can see light coming through gaps in the joints.

B

After test-fitting all the windows, apply a bead of exterior-grade panel adhesive or caulk to the outside edges of the window stops at the top and the sides of the window.

C

Press the new storm window into the opening, centering it between the side stops. Allow the bottom rail to rest on the windowsill.

D

Start at the top edge of the window, and drive screws into the window stops. Make sure the window is square, then drive the screws in the sides.

Insulation & Weatherproofing

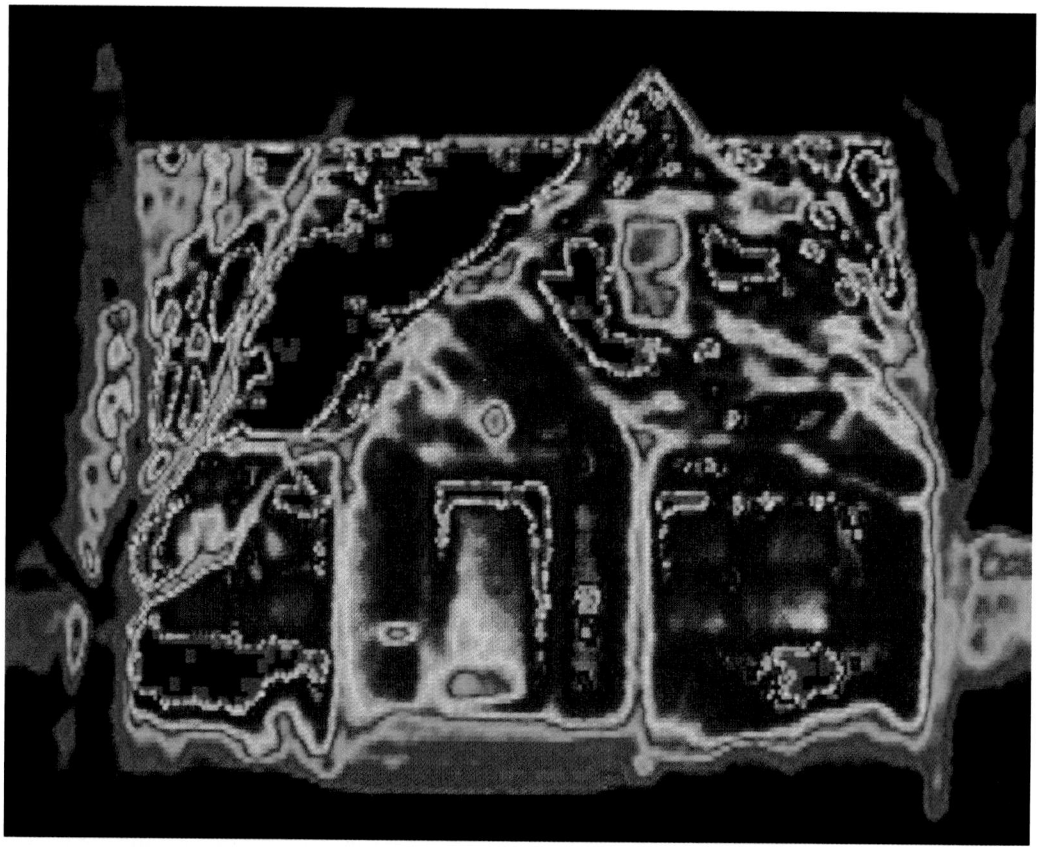

Whether you live in a hot or a cold climate, weatherizing and insulating your home can pay off handsomely. Even in homes with an average amount of insulation, heating and cooling costs account for over half of the total household energy bill.

Since most insulating and weatherstripping projects are relatively inexpensive, you can recover your investment quickly. In fact, in some climates, you can pay back the cost of a weatherproofing project in one heating season.

If you live in a cold climate, you probably already understand the importance of insulation and weatherproofing. The value of keeping warm air inside the house during a cold winter is obvious. From the standpoint of energy efficiency, it's equally important to prevent warm air from entering the house during the summer.

Whether you're concerned about the environment, or just want to spend less on your utility bills, the information in this section can help you recognize and take advantage of opportunities for energy savings.

The average home has many small leaks, which collectively add up to the equivalent of a 2-ft. hole in the wall. The air that leaks through these cracks can account for as much as one-third of your total energy loss.

An infrared photograph can help you identify the areas of energy inefficiency in your home. The owner of the house shown at right had high heating bills. His utility company referred him to an infrared inspection service, which took the above photograph.

The photo clearly shows heat loss (the red and yellow areas) around the entry door and the second-floor window. This information helped the owner make inexpensive weatherstripping improvements that paid off quickly.

An infrared photograph can be a valuable tool for tracking down air leaks and identifying the most important and cost-effective weatherproofing projects for your home.

Common Air Leaks

Gaps around joists, sills, and windows in the foundation wall.

Dryer, bath, and kitchen vents, hoses, dampers, hose outlets, conduits, etc.

Rough openings and poor weatherstripping around doors and windows.

Cracks where chimneys and stacks penetrate ceilings and walls.

Air/vapor barrier breaks at ceiling and wall outlets.

Poorly fitted attic access hatches.

Open chimney dampers.

Detecting Energy Loss

Some of the indications that your home is not energy efficient will be obvious, such as draftiness, fogged or frosted windows, ice dams and high energy bills. However, it can be more difficult to detect problems such as inadequate wall insulation or the loss of warm air around attic vents. Here are some ways to identify where your home may be losing energy:

Measure the temperature in different parts of a room. A difference of more than one or two degrees indicates that the room is poorly sealed. The solution is to update the weather-stripping, especially around the doors and windows (pages 170 to 171).

Check for drafts around doors and windows by holding a tissue next to the jambs on a windy day. If the tissue flutters, the weather-stripping is inadequate. (Another sign is light coming in from the outside around the jambs.)

To locate drafts around attic bypasses, hold a smoking incense stick near the pipes, flues, light fixtures, and any other attic openings. If the smoke drifts due to a draft, caulk or seal the opening. (Although incense doesn't have a flame, be careful when handling it near flammable materials.)

Conduct an energy audit. Most power companies will provide you with an audit kit or conduct an audit for you.

Monitor your energy usage from year to year. If there's a significant increase that can't be explained by variations in the weather, consider hiring a professional to conduct an energy audit.

If you have an unheated attic, measure the depth of the insulation between joists to find out if it meets the recommended standards. To figure the R-value of loose insulation, multiply the number of inches by 3.7. To figure the R-value of fiberglass insulation, multiply the number of inches by 3.1. Compare the result to the recommendations in the chart on page 162.

Condensation or frost buildup on windows is a sign of poor weatherstripping and an inadequate storm window.

The signs of deteriorating weatherstripping and insulation include crumbling foam or rubber.

Some of the energy audits done by power companies use a blower door to measure air flow and detect leaks.

Increased energy usage compared to the previous year may indicate that your weatherstripping or insulation is failing.

Insulating & Weatherizing Materials

A wide range of insulating and weatherizing materials is now available to homeowners. Here are some of the products that can help make your home more energy efficient.

Vapor barriers **(photo A)** can be made of any material that stops the flow of moisture, such as polyethylene film or aluminum foil. In most climates, all exterior walls (whether wood-framed or masonry) should have a vapor barrier between the insulation and the inside wall to keep moist air from migrating into wall spaces, where it can condense.

In cold regions with an average January temperature below 35°F, install the vapor barrier so it faces the warm-in-winter side of the wall. In other climates, practices differ and a vapor barrier may not be necessary; check with local building officials and contractors.

Faced fiberglass insulation **(photo B)** has a paper or foil facing that serves as a vapor barrier. Faced insulation is more expensive than unfaced insulation, but it's especially useful for placing a vapor barrier on the warm-in-winter

A

All exterior walls should have a vapor barrier between the insulation and the inside wall.

B

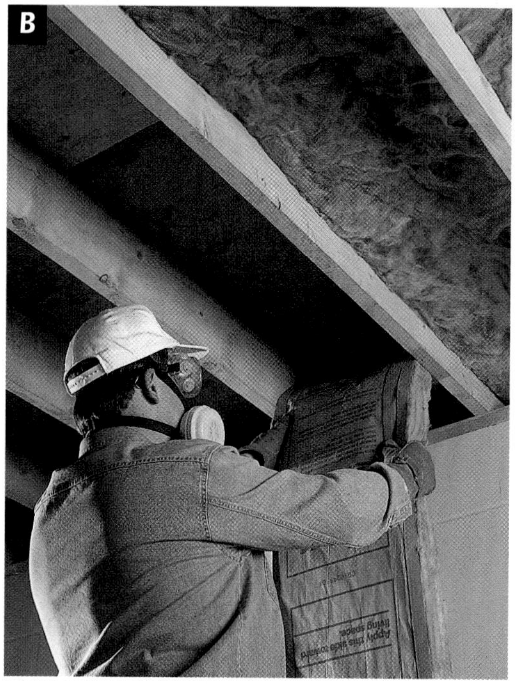

When insulating the floor above an unheated basement, the insulation's facing should be against the floor.

Insulation Safety

Fiberglass insulation can irritate your skin and air passages, so it's best to avoid direct contact with it.

When working with insulation, wear goggles, a respirator or face mask, and protective clothing—long sleeves, heavy pants, boots, and gloves. Consider wearing a disposable coverall over your clothes.

If any fiberglass fibers get on your skin, remove them by gently patting the area with duct tape.

When handling cellulose insulation, remove contact lenses and wear eye protection, such as goggles.

Shower as soon as you finish any insulation project, and immediately wash the clothes you were wearing.

C

Unfaced insulation is sold in rolls and batts to fit in the spaces between studs and joists.

D

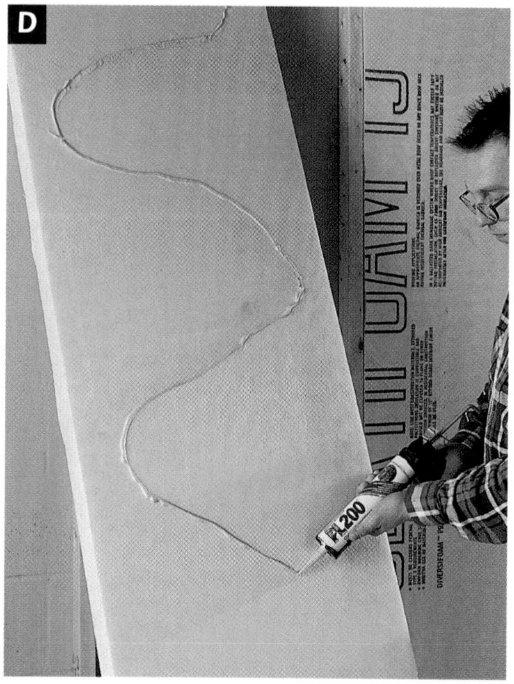

Rigid insulation boards, such as this urethane foam insulation, is a convenient material for insulating basement walls.

sides of the walls, floors, and ceilings.

An attic blanket **(photo C)** is a form of unfaced fiberglass insulation. Unfaced insulation is less expensive than faced insulation, and when used with a solid polyethylene vapor barrier, it provides better protection from moisture. It's sold in rolls and flat batts to fit standard stud and joist cavities.

Baffles are usually made of plastic or polystyrene. They're attached to the rafters at the sill plate in the attic to ensure that insulation doesn't obstruct the air flow across the underside of the roof.

Rigid insulation boards **(photo D)** are available in thicknesses from 1/2" to 2". They're attached directly to basement walls with panel adhesive. Urethane foam boards are strong and insulate well. Open-cell foam boards are less costly, but harder to work with.

A door sweep **(photo E)** attaches to the inside bottom of the door to seal out drafts. A felt or bristle sweep is best if you have an uneven floor or a low threshold. Vinyl and rubber models are also available.

A door bottom fits around the base of the door. Most have a sweep on the interior side and a drip edge on the exterior side, to direct water away from the threshold.

A threshold insert seals the gap between the door and the threshold. These are made from vinyl or rubber, and can be easily replaced.

Switch and receptacle sealers **(photo F)** fit under the coverplates on exterior walls. They block drafts that can cause heat loss.

Self-adhesive foam strips **(photo G)** attach to sashes and frames to seal the air gaps at windows and doors.

Reinforced felt strips **(photo H)** have a metal spine that adds rigidity to high-impact areas, such as doorstops.

Adding caulk is a simple way to fill narrow gaps in interior or exterior surfaces. It's also available in a peelable form, which can be easily removed at the end of the heating season.

When buying caulk, estimate half a cartridge per window or door, four for an average-size foundation sill, and at least one more to close gaps around vents, pipes, and other exterior openings.

A felt door sweep can seal out drafts, even if you have an uneven floor or a low threshold.

Switch and receptacle sealers can block leaks around electrical boxes on exterior walls.

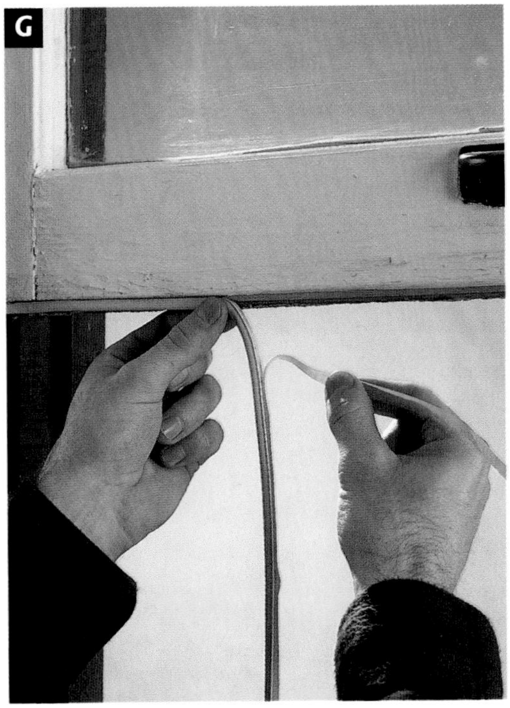

Self-adhesive foam strips are an easy way to seal air gaps around window sashes and door frames.

A reinforced felt strip can add rigidity to high-impact areas, such as doorstops, that tend to develop air gaps.

Improving Insulation

Insulation and weatherproofing create a thermal envelope that improves a home's energy efficiency. The U.S. Department of Energy estimates that average homeowners can save 10 percent on their energy bills simply by updating their insulation and weatherproofing.

Resistance value, or *R-value,* measures how well an insulating material acts as a heat barrier. The charts on this page show the R-value per inch of various types of insulation, the recommended R-values for various climates, and the depth required to produce those values.

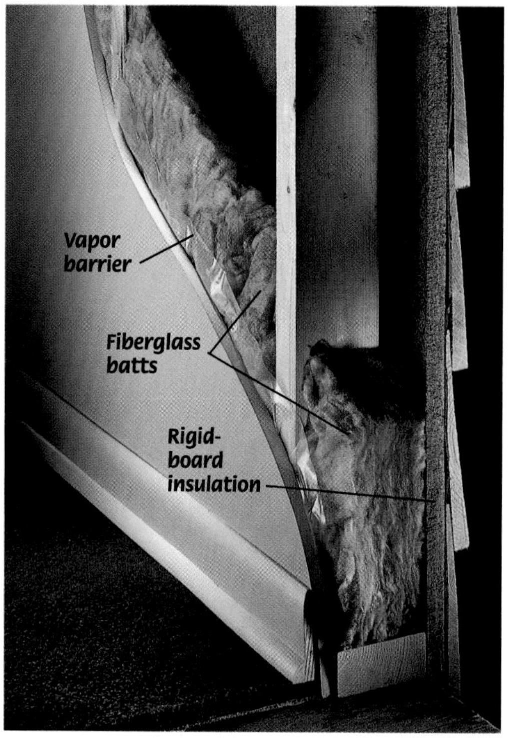

New homes are sheathed with rigid-board insulation, filled with fiberglass batts covered by a plastic vapor barrier.

Older homes are sheathed with wood planks. If the walls are insulated at all, they're usually filled with loose-fill cellulose.

Recommended Insulation Amounts

	Northern ZONE	Temperate ZONE	Southern ZONE
Attic:	R38	R30	R26
Walls:	R19	R19	R19
Floors:	R22	R13	R11

Insulation Comparison

Type of Insulation	R-value per Inch	Cost per R-value per Square Foot	Comments
Fiberglass batts, loose fill	2.9 to 3.2	$.01 to $.019	Easy to work with, but will irritate skin, eyes, and lungs. Nonflammable, except for paper facings.
Loose-fill	3.3	$.019	Uses and precautions similar to fiberglass.
Cellulose	3.2	$.014	Inexpensive. Must be treated with fire-retarding chemicals. Installation labor can be expensive.
Extruded polystyrene panels	5	$.077	Used on exterior foundation walls and under slabs. Cover with fire-rated wallboard when used inside.
Expanded polystyrene panels	4	$.046	Used on foundation walls; not as strong as extruded types. Cover with fire-rated wallboard indoors.
Polyisocyanurate panels	7	$.077	Commonly used on sheathing. R-value may drop over time. CFCs used in manufacturing.
Air Krete	3.9	$.08	Foam applied by trained installer. Prices may depend on availability of trained personnel.

To decide whether you need more insulation, you need to evaluate the current levels. Starting in the attic, measure the depth of the existing insulation. To create a stable surface, lay a sheet of plywood across the joists of the attic floor. As you move around, put your weight only on the joists, not the spaces between.

Other areas that are important to check include basement walls, exterior walls, floors above unheated spaces, and ceilings below unheated spaces.

In an unfinished area, such as an attic or crawl space, it's easy to see the insulation and measure its thickness. It's harder to evaluate insulation in a finished area, but still possible. Here are three methods:

Locate a switch plate along an outer wall. Shut off the proper electrical circuit at the service panel and remove the switch plate. Use a plastic crochet hook to probe around the electrical box, checking the type and depth of insulation in the wall.

Another approach is to use a keyhole or reciprocating saw to cut a 1" to 1½" hole in an exterior wall in a closet or other hidden area. After checking the insulation, repair the wall (pages 34 to 37).

Finally, you can have an energy audit conducted by your utility company or by an energy contractor. To evaluate their services, ask if they use infrared photography, furnace efficiency instruments, or blower door tests.

Refer to the chart on page 162 to determine whether you need to add insulation. Here are some tips for improving insulation:

Install a vapor barrier of 6-mil polyethylene on the warm-in-winter side of your existing insulation **(photo A).**

Insulate the rim joists at the top of the foundation walls by filling them loosely with fiberglass insulation **(photo B).** Pack the insulation just tightly enough to keep it from falling out.

Insulate the walls of an attached garage with faced fiberglass insulation, with the vapor barrier facing into the garage. Cover with a wall covering, such as wallboard **(photo C).**

Never try to compress insulation to fit into a cavity. If the insulation is too thick, trim it to match the depth of the cavity **(photo D).**

Install a vapor barrier of 6-mil polyethylene on the warm-in-winter side of the insulation.

Insulate the rim joists at the top of the foundation walls by filling them loosely with fiberglass insulation.

Insulate an attached garage with faced fiberglass insulation, with the vapor barrier facing into the garage.

Don't compress insulation to fit; it needs air space to work effectively. Instead, trim or tear it to size.

Insulating an Unfinished Attic

In a well-designed attic, vapor barriers, insulation, and vents work together to prevent moisture damage and keep the home comfortable in every season. If you have an unfinished attic that isn't insulated, adding insulation can substantially lower your utility bills and improve the comfort level inside your home. Here's how to proceed:

Before starting, evaluate your existing insulation and calculate how much you need to add, based on the chart on page 162 **(photo A).** Use a piece of plywood to help support your weight on the joists; never step on the spaces between them.

If you're insulating an attic from scratch, use faced fiberglass insulation (in very warm climates, check local Building Codes; the facing may not be necessary). If you're adding to existing insulation, use unfaced batts.

Begin by attaching baffles to the roof sheathing or rafters to keep the insulation from blocking the air flow under the roof **(photo B).** The baffles should extend past the bottoms of the ceiling joists, to provide a free flow of air from the soffit to the attic. Without this gap, moisture can become trapped inside the rafter spaces and cause the roof sheathing, wallboard, or plaster to break down and rot.

Next, locate and seal all thermal bypasses—gaps or cracks around chimneys and plumbing pipes where heat and moisture can rise into the attic from the heated spaces below.

Roll out the insulation, starting at the farthest point from the attic access, and working toward it **(photo C).** If you're using faced

Tools: *Respirator or face mask, gloves, tape measure, utility knife, straightedge, plumb line, insulation board saw, staple gun.*

Materials: *6-mil poly vapor barrier, baffles, insulation, 2 × 2 furring strips, construction adhesive, plywood sheets, panel adhesive.*

Start by evaluating your existing insulation and determining how much you need to add.

Attach baffles to the roof sheathing or rafters to provide proper ventilation under the roof.

Roll out the insulation, starting at the farthest point from the attic access and working toward it.

Leave at least 3" clearance between the insulation and any heat-producing devices, such as metal chimneys.

insulation, install it with the vapor barrier facing down, toward the warm-in-winter side of the ceiling.

Always wear protective clothing (page 160) and work in a well-ventilated area. Use a straightedge and a utility knife to cut insulation to length (page 167).

Place all the long runs first, then cut the pieces for any shorter spaces. If your attic has uneven joist spacing, you may need to trim a few pieces for width as well. Cut the ends of the insulation to fit snugly around any cross bracing.

Leave at least 3" of clearance between the insulation and any heat-producing structures, such as metal chimneys, water heater flues, or recessed lighting fixtures. Build a dam to hold the insulation back **(photo D).**

Some newer recessed lighting fixtures are marked "I.C." ("insulation contact"), which means they're designed for direct contact with insulation. In this case, you can lay the insulation right up to the fixtures.

Although fiberglass insulation itself is noncombustible, the kraft paper or foil used to face the insulation will burn. To prevent fire, always place the faced side of the insulation away from sources of heat, such as chimneys and recessed lighting fixtures.

Adding an Attic Blanket

If you live in a cold climate and you don't use your attic for storage, you can add a second layer of insulation, called an attic blanket, over the tops of the joists. Be sure to use only unfaced insulation for this purpose, as you should never add a second vapor barrier.

Install the second layer of insulation perpendicular to the first **(photo E).** Place the long runs first, then cut the leftover pieces to fill any small spaces.

Extend the second layer to cover the tops of the exterior walls, but don't block the flow of air from the soffit vents. If the attic doesn't have baffles, install them now (page 164).

You can fill the spaces next to a masonry chimney with unfaced insulation **(photo F),** but build a dam to hold the attic blanket at least 3" from other heat-producing devices, such as metal chimneys, water heater flues, or recessed light fixtures **(photo G).**

Some newer recessed light fixtures, which are marked "I.C.," are designed for direct contact with insulation and may be covered with an attic blanket.

But if you have old-style recessed light fixtures, never drape insulation over the tops, and make sure to build a dam that keeps the insulation at least 3" away from the sides of the fixtures. Again, never use faced insulation near a source of heat.

For even more insulation, install an attic blanket—a second layer of insulation placed at a right angle to the first layer.

Use only unfaced insulation next to a masonry chimney or other heat-producing devices.

You can lay the attic blanket over recessed light fixtures that are marked "I.C."

Adding Basement Insulation

In response to growing concerns about energy conservation, many communities require that the foundation walls in new homes be insulated. If your home wasn't built this way, you can add rigid foam insulation to the inside of the foundation walls.

Another effective way to prevent heat loss in a basement is to insulate the rim joists at the top of the foundation walls **(photo A).**

Insulating pipes is another easy basement project that can pay off in big energy savings. Hot water pipes, in particular, tend to lose heat rapidly when left uninsulated in an unheated basement.

Insulating unheated crawl spaces is another essential basement project.

Tools: *Plumb line, utility knife, insulation-board saw, staple gun.*

Materials: *Fiberglass strip insulation, sleeve-type foam pipe insulation, unfaced fiberglass insulation, 2 × 2 furring strips, nails, 2"-thick urethane foam insulation boards, construction adhesive, wallboard, panel adhesive, 6-mil polyethylene sheeting, clear plastic tape.*

A

Insulate the rim joists at the top of your foundation walls by filling them loosely with fiberglass insulation.

Wrapping Pipes

You can save energy and prevent frozen pipes by insulating the pipes that run through unheated parts of the basement.

There are two approaches to insulating pipes—covering them with sleeve-type foam insulation, and wrapping them with strip insulation and waterproof wrap.

The simplest method is to use sleeve-type foam insulation **(photo B).** This is particularly useful in crawl spaces and other areas where the pipes may be difficult to reach.

The second approach is to wrap the pipes with fiberglass strip insulation and waterproof wrap **(photo C).** For the best protection, wrap the pipes loosely, and don't pull the insulation too tight.

It's a good idea to insulate at least the first ten feet of the hot- and cold-water lines coming out of the hot water heater. (Let hot water pipes cool before you work with them.)

If your water heater is in an unheated area, insulate the pipes until they enter the heated part of the house. This will save fuel and money, and reduce the time it takes the water to heat up.

B

To prevent freezing, insulate pipes in crawl spaces with sleeve-type foam insulation.

C

Fiberglass strip insulation and waterproof wrap should be applied loosely around the pipe.

Insulating the Walls

Insulating basement walls with rigid insulation boards is a surprisingly easy project. Begin by marking vertical reference lines for the furring strips, using a plumb line **(photo D).** Space the strips so that the insulation boards fit neatly between them, without gaps (but don't space them more than 24" apart).

If you plan to install wallboard over the furring strips, attach 2 × 2 top and sole plates above and below the furring strips.

Use construction adhesive to attach the furring strips to the foundation walls.

Use an insulation-board saw to cut the boards to the height of the wall (and to fit between the furring strips, if necessary). Make any cutouts needed to fit the boards around receptacles, windows, or other obstructions **(photo E).**

Attach the insulation boards to the wall with panel adhesive **(photo F).** Use an adhesive that's compatible with the insulation.

To create a vapor barrier, staple polyethylene sheeting to the furring strips, and tape the seams with clear plastic tape.

If you wish to finish the wall, install wallboard over the insulation, securing it to the furring strips.

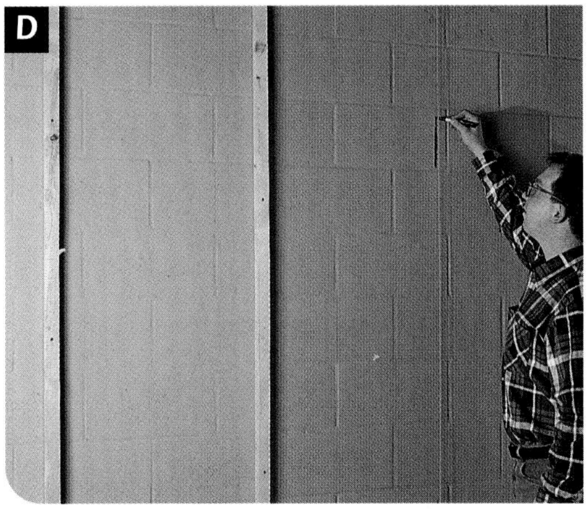

Mark vertical guidelines for attaching the furring strips.

Cut the boards to fit the wall, then cut around obstructions.

Use panel adhesive to secure the boards to the wall.

Working with Insulation

Foam and fiberglass insulation aren't difficult to work with, but there are some helpful hints that can make your insulation projects go more smoothly. (For insulation safety guidelines, see page 160.)

For most insulation projects, you'll need just a few simple tools—a tape measure, a utility knife, and a straightedge or straight 2 × 4.

For more specialized projects, you may also need a lightweight stapler, a portable work light, sheets of plywood (to sit on in an unfinished attic), a pole or rake (to push insulation into out-of-the-way places), and insulation supports (to hold insulation in place between the joists under a floor).

Since fiberglass insulation is significantly compressed for packing, leave the rolls in the original wrapper until you're ready to use them; they'll expand considerably as soon as you open the roll. Once you open the roll, complete the project as soon as possible.

If you accidentally tear the vapor barrier of faced insulation, you can tape the edges together with duct tape. However, this generally isn't necessary unless the rip is large.

To cut fiberglass insulation, lay it on a board with the faced side (if any) on the bottom. Lay a yardstick or a straight 2 × 4 over the cutting line and press it down hard. Cut against the edge with a utility knife.

To cut foam insulation, simply cut or score it with a sharp knife. Seal joints and openings with construction tape.

Don't compress insulation to fit into a shallow space: it requires pockets of trapped air to work effectively.

Insulating a Heated Crawl Space

After attics, crawl spaces are the most important part of a house to insulate, especially if they're unheated.

There are two ways to approach this project: you can either drape rolls of insulation around the perimeter walls, or you can suspend the insulation between the floor joists. The first approach is usually recommended for heated crawl spaces, and the second one for unheated spaces—but there are some exceptions to this.

Draping the walls creates a sealed air chamber, which has a very high insulation value. However, some spaces are built so that the only option is to insulate the floor between the joists.

Also, if you live in an extremely cold area, such as the Northern Plains, don't drape the walls—this method will trap so much heat that it could cause frost heaving and damage your foundation. If you're in doubt about the proper approach for your house, check with local contractors or Building Code.

Wrapping a crawl space isn't hard, as long as there's enough space to get around; however, it is a dirty job. As always when working with insulation, wear protective clothing and a respirator or mask (page 160).

Start by sealing any gaps or air leaks in the crawl space, especially around the band joist. However, don't seal any vents—you'll need them when the weather turns hot and humid.

Start with the small area next to the rim joist. Measure and cut small pieces of insulation, leaving them slightly oversize so they'll fit snugly up against the rim joist between the floor joists **(photo A).**

For the walls of the crawl space itself, place the top end of the insulation roll against the top of the sill plate. Unroll enough insulation to fall down the wall and cover two feet of ground at the bottom of the crawl space.

Tack the insulation in place with long furring strips of 1 × 2 lumber nailed to the sill plate **(photo B).** Try to compress the insulation as little as possible—when you finish, the insulation under the nails should be no less than one-half its original thickness.

After insulating the walls, tape a piece of polyethylene sheeting to the ground under the insulation as a vapor barrier **(photo C).**

Tape the joints between the strips of insulation, or lap them by at least 6". Take care not to puncture the plastic. Weigh down the insulation and the sheeting with bricks or heavy rocks.

Tools: *Tape measure, hammer, utility knife, straightedge.*

Materials: *Gloves, respirator, unfaced fiberglass insulation, 1 × 2 furring strips, nails, 6-mil polyethylene sheeting, clear plastic tape.*

Measure and cut small pieces of insulation, and fit them snugly into the band joists.

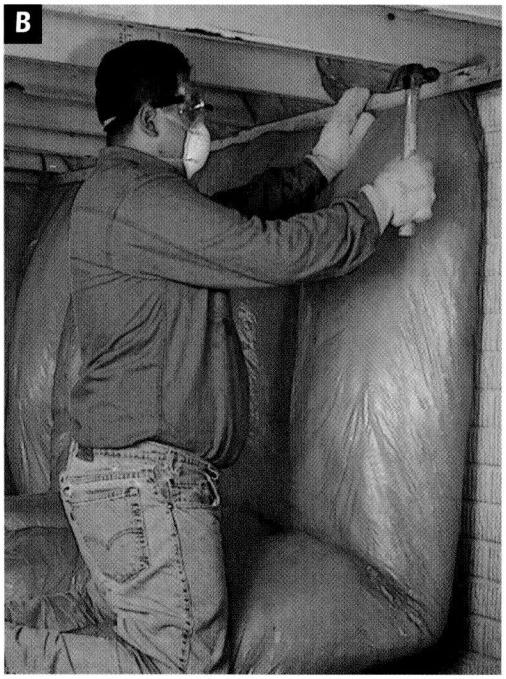

Tack the insulation in place with a furring strip of 1 × 2 lumber nailed to the sill plate.

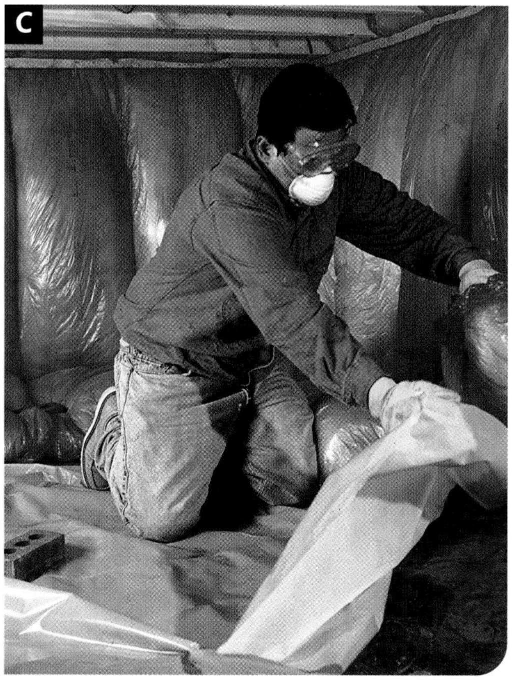

Tape a piece of polyethylene sheeting to the ground under the insulation as a vapor barrier.

Insulating an Unheated Crawl Space

Suspending insulation between the floor joists overhead is the best way to insulate an unheated crawl space, and the only recommended method in very cold climates.

Use faced insulation, unless there's already insulation or a vapor barrier in place. Foil-faced insulation is a good option for this project; it will reflect heat up into the living area above. Install the insulation so the vapor barrier faces upward, toward the warm-in-winter side of the floor **(photo D).**

As you install the insulation, pay particular attention to the joists and headers around the perimeter of the floor. Start the insulation at the end of the joist run so that it touches the rim joist. There's usually a narrower joist run next to the wall; cut a piece of insulation to fit this space **(photo E).**

In a typical crawl space, you'll run into both pipes and wires **(photo F),** and perhaps even a junction box. When working around electrical wiring, take care not to touch any live wires. Cut the insulation to fit around the obstructions, keeping it 3" away from any heat-producing devices.

Insulate water pipes separately (page 166).

Place insulation around any cross braces by cutting it and pushing it up between the braces **(photo G).**

Hold the insulation in place by securing insulation support bands to the joists. Insulation supports may be made of nylon, metal **(photo H),** or 1 × 2 furring strips.

Finally, cover the floor of the crawl space with polyethylene sheeting, to keep ground moisture from seeping up **(photo I).** Use heavy rocks or bricks to hold the sheeting in place.

Tools: *Hammer, utility knife, straightedge.*

Materials: *Gloves, respirator, faced fiberglass insulation, nylon banding or metal insulation supports, 6-mil polyethylene sheeting, clear plastic tape.*

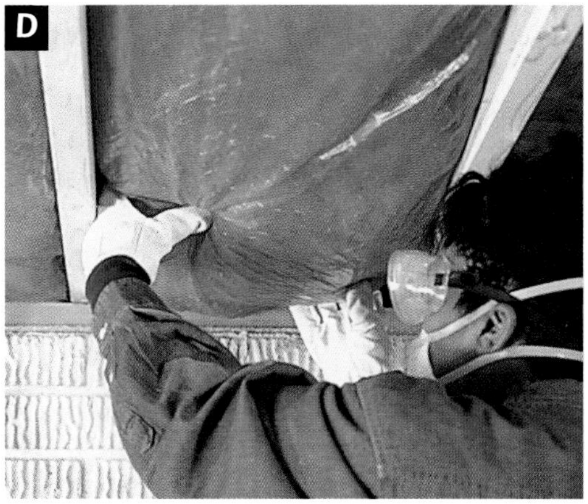

Place the facing against the warm-in-winter side of the floor.

Cut the insulation to fit the narrow joist run next to the wall.

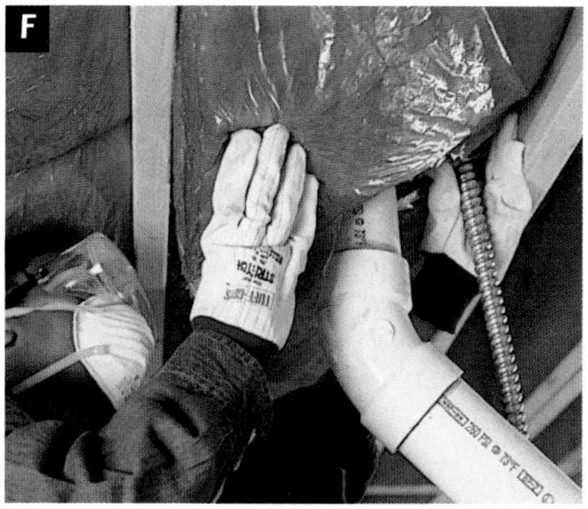

Cut insulation to fit around pipes, wires, and obstructions.

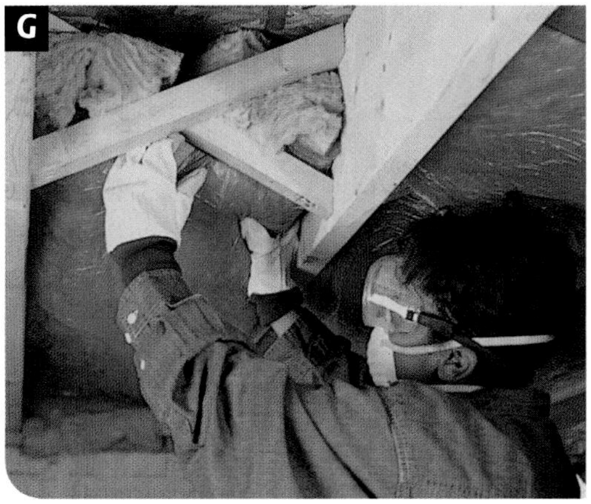

Push insulation up in between any cross braces.

You can support the insulation with nylon or metal banding.

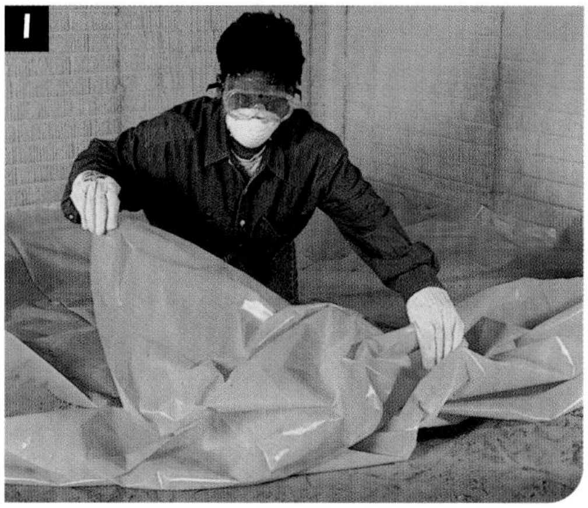

Cover the floor of the crawl space with polyethylene sheeting.

Weatherizing the House

Weatherizing your home is an ideal do-it-yourself project, because it can be done a little at a time, according to your schedule. The best time of the year to weatherize is the fall, just before it turns too cold to work outdoors.

There are many different types of caulk and weatherstripping materials. All are inexpensive and easy to use, but it's important to get the right materials for the job, as most are designed for specific applications.

Generally, metal and metal-reinforced weatherstripping is more durable than products made of plastic, rubber, or foam. However, even plastic, rubber and foam weatherstripping products have a wide range of quality. The best rubber products are those made from neoprene rubber—use this whenever it's available.

Most weatherizing projects deal with windows (pages 150 to 151) and doors (pages 132 to 133), because these are the primary areas of heat loss in most homes. Here are some other weatherizing projects you can do on the exterior of your house:

Caulk around the outside of the window and door frames to seal any gaps **(photo A).** For best results, use a caulk that matches or blends with the color of your siding.

Minimize heat loss from basement window wells by covering them with plastic window well covers **(photo B).** Before buying the covers, measure the widest point on the window well, and note whether the frame is rectangular or semicircular.

Most window well covers have an upper flange designed to slip under the siding. Slip this in place, then fasten the cover to the foundation with masonry anchors, and weigh down the bottom flange with stones. For extra weatherstripping, seal the edges with caulk.

Apply silicone caulk around dryer vents, fan exhaust vents, and any other fittings mounted on the outside of your house **(photo C).**

Seal the gaps around spigots, television cable

Tools: *Screwdriver, drill, caulk gun.*

Materials: *Preformed plastic window well cover, masonry anchors, 1:1 expansion sprayable foam sealant, silicone caulk, 3/8"-dia. plastic or foam caulking backer rope, polyethylene sheeting.*

Use a caulk that matches your siding to seal the window and door frames on the exterior of your house.

Covering a basement window well with a preformed plastic window well cover is an easy way to reduce heat loss in the basement. Before buying the cover, measure the widest point of the window well and note its shape.

jacks, telephone lines, and other exterior entry points with sprayable foam insulation **(photo D).** Take care not to work around or near power cables.

Seal the sill plate gap between the house sill and the siding by stuffing it with 3/8"-dia. plastic or foam caulking backer rope **(photo E).**

Inside the house, it's relatively easy to locate air leaks caused by inadequate weatherstripping. On a cold or windy day, dampen your hand and walk through the house, passing your hand along the baseboards and the window and door frames to detect breezes. Also check all the openings in the exterior walls (such as around electrical boxes and fireplaces) and in the ceilings and floors that separate the heated and unheated parts of the house.

Another way to find leaks is to use a smoking stick of incense and watch how the smoke stream drifts. (Although incense has no flame, take care when using it around flammable materials.)

Wherever you find a breeze, you've located a spot that requires weatherstripping. If you aren't sure if a draft is due to an air leak or to some other factor (such as cold air radiating through a single-pane window), tape a piece of polyethylene over the opening and seal the edges. If the plastic ripples, the spot requires weatherstripping.

Weatherstrip the air leaks around windows and doors (pages 132 to 133 and 150 to 151). Sealing other air leaks on the interior of the house simply involves closing them up with caulk or expandable foam sealant. For example, use silicone caulk to seal the gaps around vents and electrical boxes.

For leaky gaps between baseboards and floorboards, there are two options. The simplest is to seal the edges of the baseboard molding with acrylic caulk.

However, if the gap is large, a more effective option may be to remove the shoe molding and insert 1:1 expansion sprayable foam sealant into the gap so that it spreads out inside the wall **(photo F).** In addition to preventing drafts, this helps keep insects from entering the living areas of your home.

Apply silicone caulk around dryer and fan vents and any other fittings mounted on the outside of your house.

Use sprayable foam insulation to seal the air gaps around spigots and other exterior entry points.

Close up the gap between the house sill and the siding by stuffing it with caulking backer rope.

To seal baseboard leaks, remove the shoe molding and insert expansion sprayable foam sealant into the gap.

Cabinets

Cabinets store our most-used household items, and their appearance affects the look of any room. Keep your cabinets operating smoothly by tightening loose door hinges and drawer pulls. And examine the door hinges—they may have adjustment screws you can use to realign crooked doors.

Cabinets require almost no structural maintenance other than simple repairs to the face frame joints. In fact, cabinets usually go out of style long before they wear out.

You can freshen the look of your cabinets by painting them and installing new hardware (pages 72 to 73). Or, reface your cabinets to freshen a room's appearance without paying the high cost of replacement. Refacing kits include new doors, drawer fronts, and self-adhesive wood veneer for resurfacing cabinet face frames and sides.

Keeping your cabinets in good condition—both functionally and cosmetically—improves the appearance of any room.

Identifying Types of Hinges

Hinges for *framed cabinets* are mounted onto the cabinet frames. One type has a clip that fits over the inside edge of the frame **(photo A).** Other types mount directly to the front face of the frame **(photo B).** *Frameless cabinets* have "invisible" hinges that are screwed to the inside face of the cabinet panel **(photo C).** These may have adjustment screws hidden behind a decorative plastic cover.

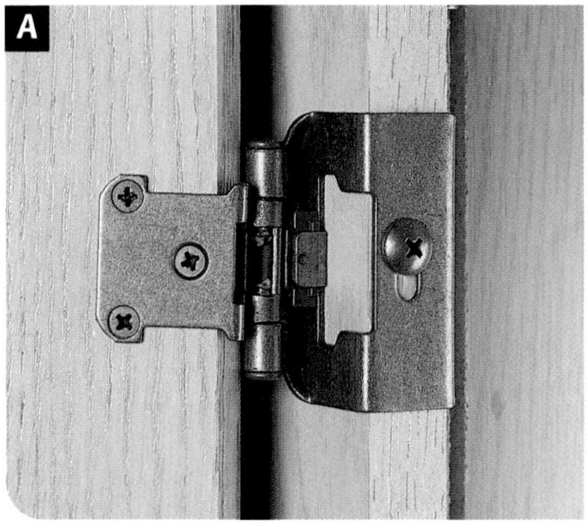

The mounting screw on this hinge can be loosened for realigning the cabinet door.

This face-mounted hinge has no adjustment capabilities.

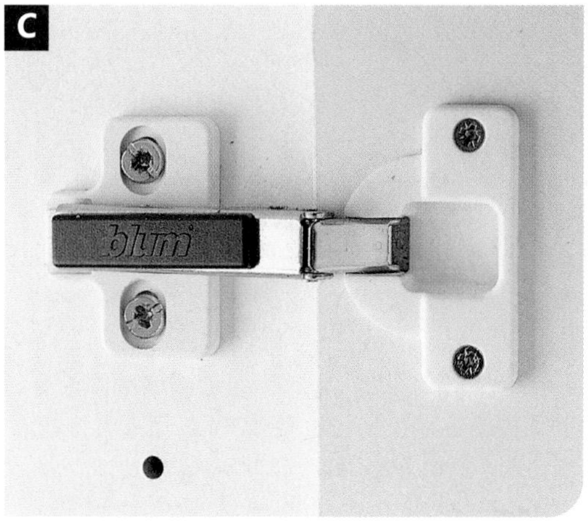

Frameless cabinet hinges cannot be seen when the cabinet doors are shut.

Tightening Loose Hinges

When cabinet doors don't hang straight or open smoothly, tighten the mounting screws on the hinges.

If the screw holes are worn and the wood won't hold the screws tight, remove the cabinet door. Then, unscrew the hinges from the face frame with a screwdriver **(photo D).**

Find a wood dowel with the same diameter as the screw hole—a golf tee often works. Coat the end of the dowel with wood glue and insert it into the screw hole. Then, cut the dowel flush with a utility knife **(photo E).**

When the glue has dried, drill a pilot hole for the screw through the center of the dowel **(photo F).**

Reattach the hinge and door.

You can make the same repair to the screw holes in the door, but take care not to drill through the door.

Tools: *Screwdriver, utility knife, drill.*
Materials: *Dowel, wood glue.*

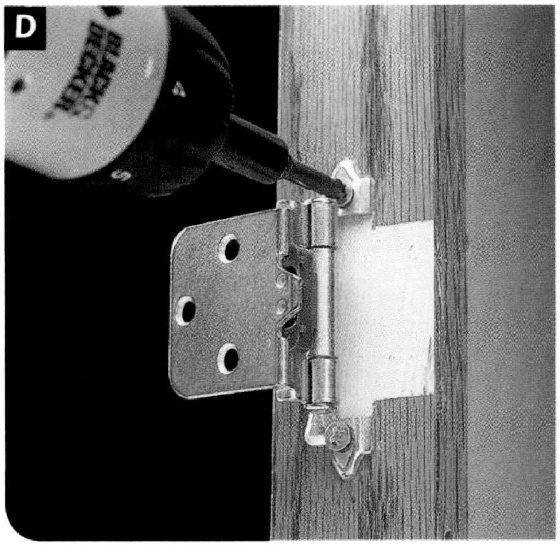

Remove the hinge from the cabinet frame.

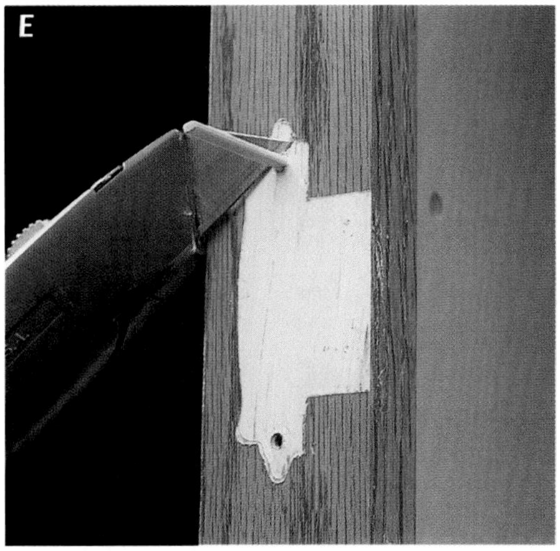

Glue the dowel into the hole, and cut off the excess.

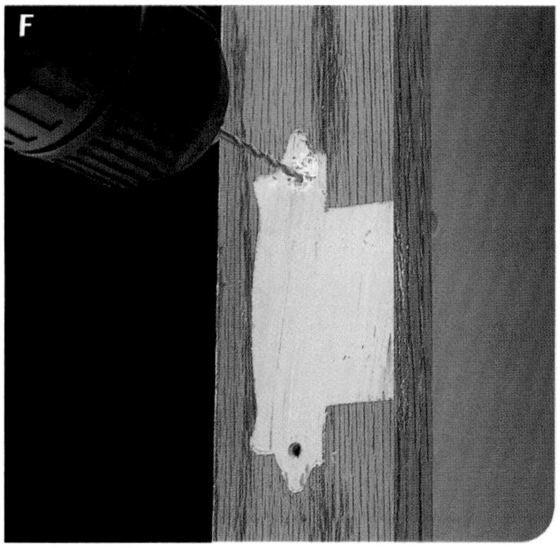

Drill a pilot hole for the screw. Then, reattach the hinge.

Tightening Drawer Pulls

Tighten loose drawer pulls by filling worn screw holes with wood putty. Use a powder-type putty designed for mixing with water just before applying; this type of putty tends to dry harder than most premixed products.

Remove the drawer pull screw, and make sure there's no dust or grime in the screw hole. Mix the putty to the proper consistency, and firmly pack some into the hole with a putty knife **(photo G).** Wipe off excess putty with a damp cloth.

When the putty has dried, drill a pilot hole, and reattach the drawer pull **(photo H).**

Tools: *Screwdriver, putty knife, drill.*
Materials: *Wood putty, cloth.*

Pack the putty into the screw hole, and wipe the surface clean before the putty hardens.

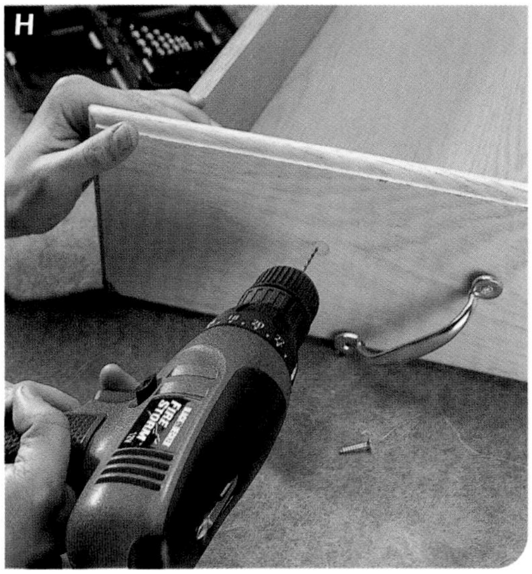

Drill a pilot hole through the center of the hardened putty.

Repairing a Face Frame Joint

Cabinet face frames are assembled with a variety of woodworking joints, but many are simply glued butt joints. Repair separated frame pieces by regluing the joint and securing it with a wood screw.

You'll need to remove the cabinet, so take out any adjustable shelves, and remove the doors if they're in the way. Next, locate all of the mounting screws that anchor the cabinet to the wall. Look around the inside of the cabinet and along the mounting strips at the top and bottom of the cabinet.

A cabinet can be surprisingly heavy; brace large cabinets with temporary supports before removing the mounting hardware.

There should be two or more screws holding adjacent cabinets together along the inside edges of the face frames. Remove these first **(photo A).** Then, remove the mounting screws.

Carefully pull the cabinet from the wall, and lay it on a flat work surface **(photo B).**

Clean the mating surfaces of the joint to remove dirt, grease, and traces of old glue. Use a putty knife or a piece of sandpaper to scrape the inside of the joint.

Gently pull the frame pieces apart to open the joint slightly, and inject wood glue into the joint, using a glue syringe **(photo C).** Clamp the frame together with a bar clamp, using wood blocks to prevent damage to the frame.

Make sure the faces and ends of the frame pieces are flush, and drill a pilot hole through the outside edge of the vertical frame piece and into the end of the horizontal piece **(photo D).** Bore the end of the hole, using a countersink bit, so the screw will be slightly recessed below the surface of the wood. If the screw will be visible after the cabinet is installed, you can cover the screw head with a wood plug that matches the frame pieces.

Drive a wood screw into the pilot hole **(photo E).** Use a brass screw for oak frames, as steel can blacken the wood. Wipe up excess glue with a damp cloth, and let the glue dry.

To reinstall the cabinet, align and attach the frames first. Then, secure the cabinet to the wall with the mounting screws.

Tools: *Drill, screwdriver, putty knife, glue syringe, bar clamp.*

Materials: *Sandpaper, wood glue, wood screws, cloth, wood plugs.*

Remove the face frame screws holding the cabinets together.

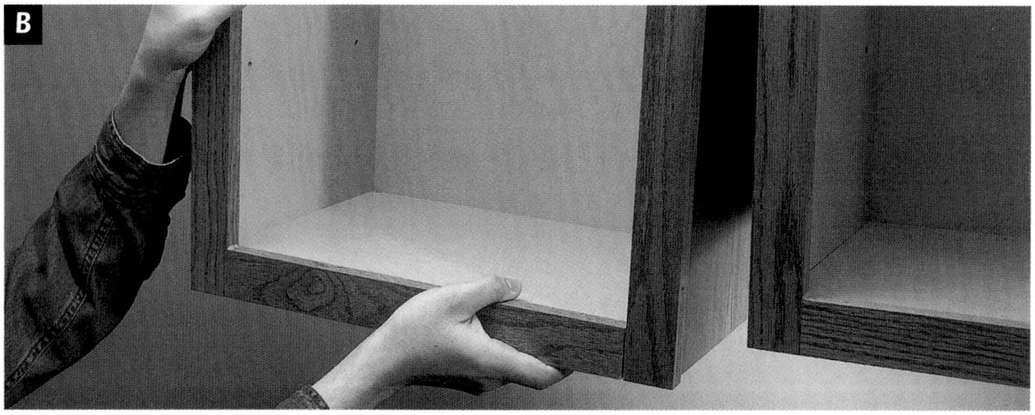

Unscrew the mounting screws that secure the cabinet to the wall, and remove the cabinet.

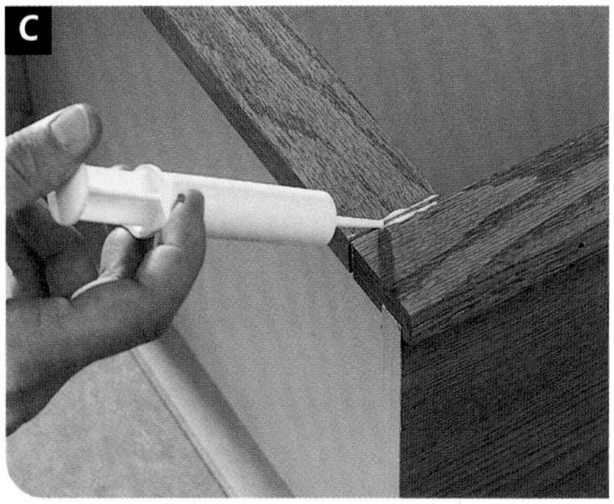

Inject wood glue into the joint, using a glue syringe.

Clamp the frame. Then, drill and counterbore a pilot hole.

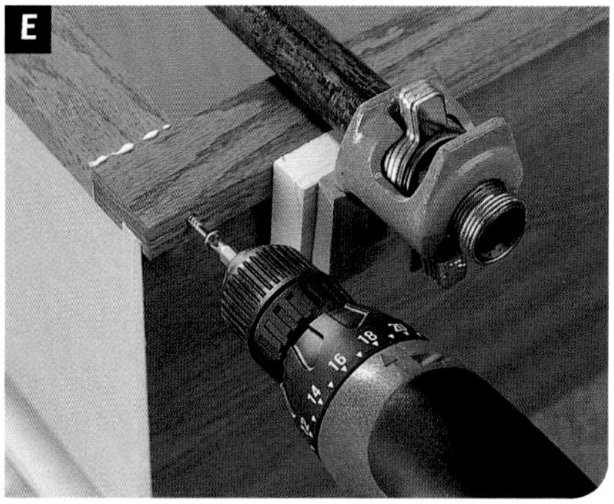

Drive a screw through the joint, and clean up excess glue.

Refacing Cabinets

Cabinet refacing kits come with self-adhesive hardwood veneer, new doors, and drawer fronts.

Repair any loose face frame joints, if necessary (page 174). Remove the old doors, hinges, catches, and other hardware **(photo F).**

Prepare the cabinet surfaces by scraping loose or peeling finish and filling holes and chips with latex wood patch. Lightly sand the cabinets with 150-grit sandpaper.

Lay the veneer sheets flat on a smooth surface. Measure each cabinet surface to be covered, and add 1/4" for overlap. Cut veneer pieces with a utility knife and a straightedge **(photo G).**

First, apply veneer to the vertical face frame members **(photo H).** Peel the backing to expose one corner of the adhesive. Align the veneer, and press lightly to adhere the corner. Gradually remove the backing, and smooth out any air bubbles with your fingertips. Then, bond the veneer by rolling the entire surface with a J-roller. Trim the excess veneer with a utility knife.

Next, apply veneer to the horizontal face frame members, overlapping the inside edges of the veneer on the vertical members. Use a straightedge and utility knife to trim the veneer flush with the inside edge of the vertical frame members.

Apply a finish to doors, drawer fronts, or veneers, if they're unfinished.

Set a combination square at 2", and use it to position the hinges at the top and bottom of each door **(photo I).** Drill pilot holes, and attach the hinges with screws. Install the doors, making sure they overlap the face frames by an equal amount on all sides.

Saw off all overhanging edges of existing solid (one-piece) drawer fronts **(photo J).** If the drawer fronts are the two-piece type, detach the face panels. Attach the new drawer fronts by drilling pilot holes and driving screws through the inside of the drawers.

Attach false drawer fronts on sink cabinets, screwing through wood blocks that span the drawer openings **(photo K).** Install hardware.

Tools: *Screwdriver, utility knife, straightedge, J-roller, combination square, drill, handsaw.*

Materials: *Sandpaper, refacing kit, finishing materials, screws, hardware.*

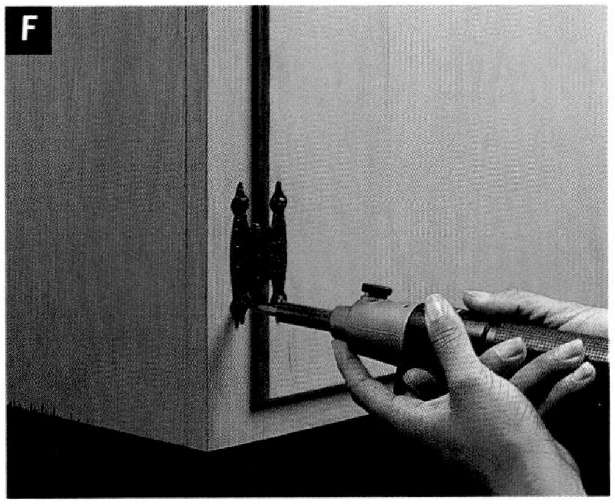

Remove the doors, drawer pulls, and other hardware.

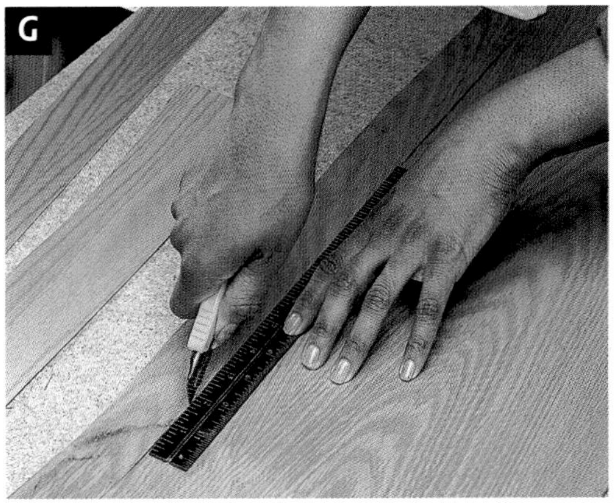

Cut the veneer to size, using a utility knife and straightedge.

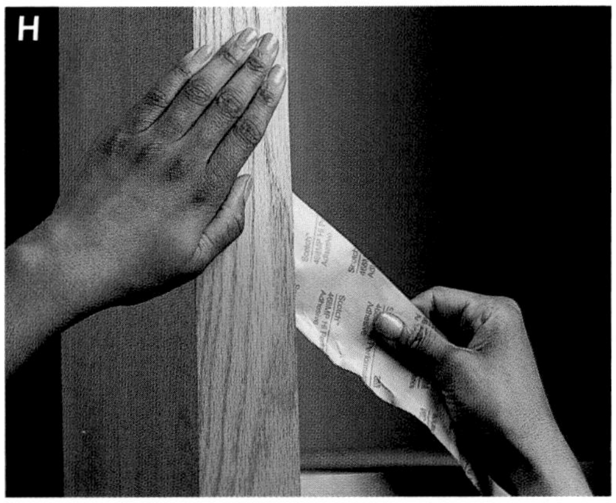

Gradually pull the backing, and press the veneer as you go.

Use a combination square to locate the door hinges.

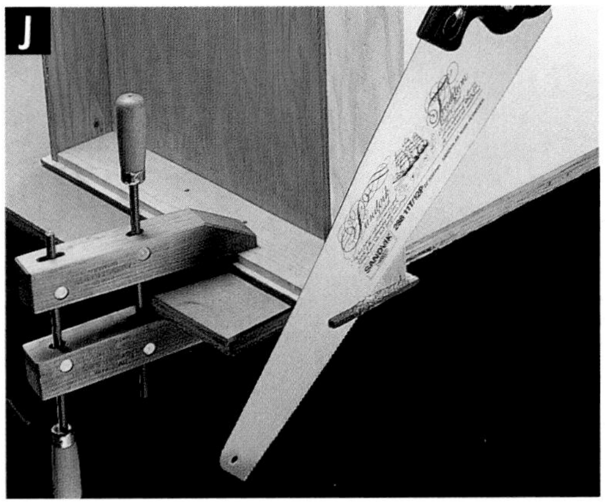

Trim the edges of old drawer fronts, then attach new fronts.

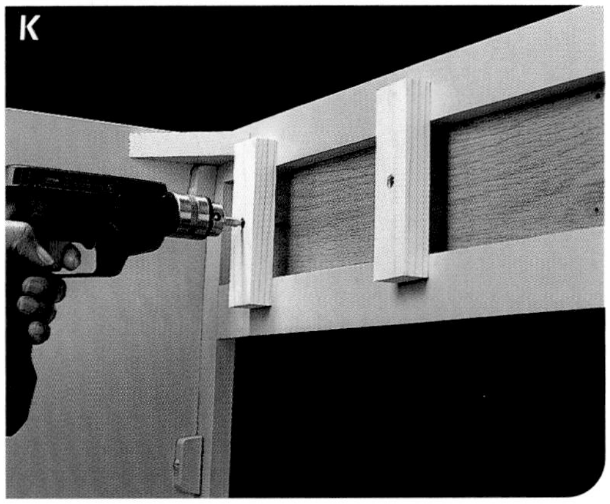

Attach false drawer fronts from inside the cabinets.

Countertops

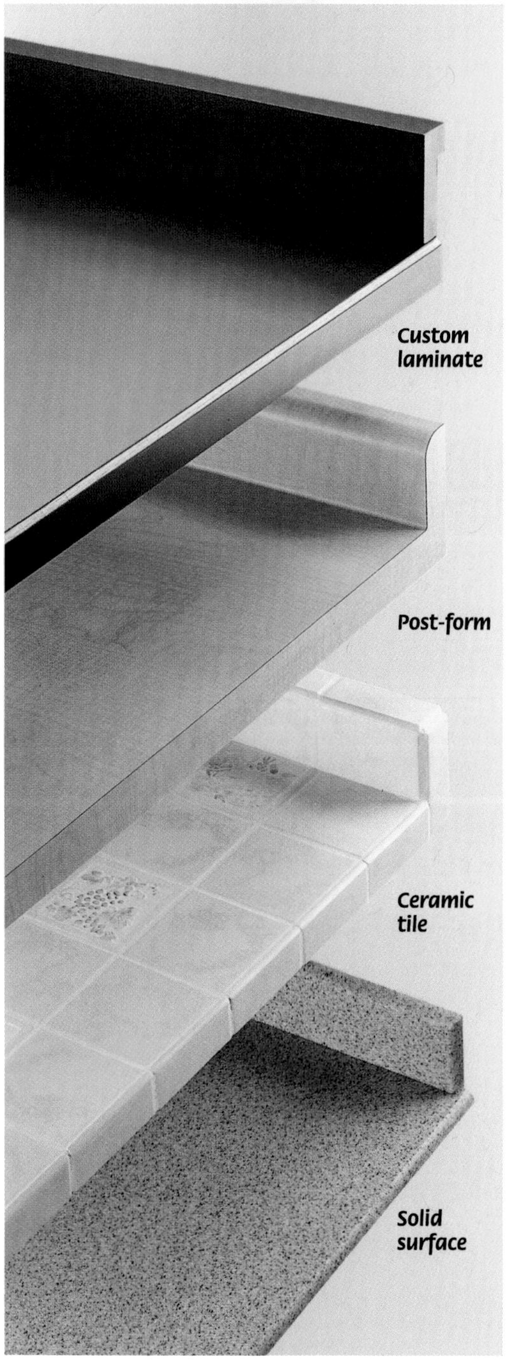

Countertop Basics

Countertops provide the main workspace in a kitchen or bathroom. They must be durable, waterproof, and easy to clean—as well as attractive. Common countertop materials are plastic laminate, ceramic tile, and manufactured "solid surface." Less common materials include natural stone, stainless steel, and wood.

Laminate countertops—by far the most popular—may be custom-made or prefabricated *post-form* type. Made of sheet laminates glued to particleboard, post-form countertops have preattached backsplashes and front edge treatments. They are available in almost any color and are easy to install.

Laminates are durable and stain resistant, but unfortunately, their surfaces are usually impossible to repair.

Ceramic tile countertops offer exceptional durability and a natural look. You can repair damaged tiles following the same methods you would use to repair tiled floors or walls.

Solid-surface countertops are made from acrylic or polyester resins mixed with additives. Superficial repairs are possible on most solid-surface countertops, but new installations and major repairs are best left to a professional.

Repairing Countertops

Like wood furniture, solid-surface countertops develop a mellow luster with use and age. Any repair that removes the surface glow must be blended in to maintain an even appearance.

To remove scratches and stains, try using a mild detergent first, rubbing the area in a circular motion with a wet sponge or cloth. If that doesn't work, switch to a gentle abrasive powder and a plastic scouring pad.

You can remove deep scratches or burns with fine-grit sandpaper **(photo A).** Blend the repaired area by rubbing with a mild abrasive liquid and a sponge or cloth.

Repair ceramic tile countertops by replacing damaged tiles **(photo B).** Carefully remove the grout before breaking out the tile (pages 98 to 99). Protect grout joints by applying a silicone grout sealer about once a year.

Use sandpaper on solid-surface countertops only as a last resort. Consult the manufacturer for care instructions.

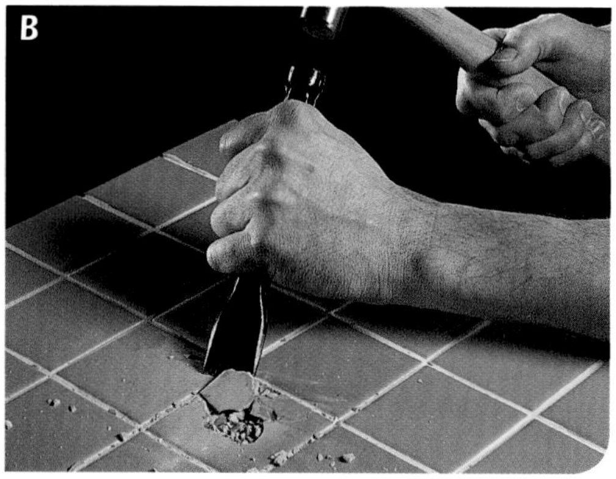

Maintain ceramic tile countertops by sealing grout joints. Remove damaged tiles with a masonry chisel and hammer.

Removing an Old Countertop

First, turn off the water supply to plumbing fixtures and appliances at the shutoff valves. Disconnect electrical and plumbing lines, and remove the sink, fixtures, and appliances.

Countertops typically are fastened to cabinets with screws driven through wood or plastic mounting brackets fixed to the top inside corners of the cabinets **(photo C).** Remove the screws and any other mounting hardware. Unscrew the take-up bolts on the underside of mitered joints.

Use a utility knife to cut caulk beads along the backsplash and the wall. Remove any trim.

Using a flat pry bar, lift the countertop away from the base cabinets **(photo D).**

If you can't pry it up in one piece, cut the countertop into smaller pieces, using a reciprocating saw and a wood-cutting blade **(photo E).** Be careful not to cut into the cabinets.

An old kitchen countertop makes a great workbench surface in your basement or garage. Use a circular saw or a jig saw to cut recycled countertop sections to shape. Cut from the bottom face to prevent chipping.

Tools: *Channel-type pliers, screwdriver, utility knife, flat pry bar, reciprocating saw.*

Remove the mounting screws from inside the cabinets.

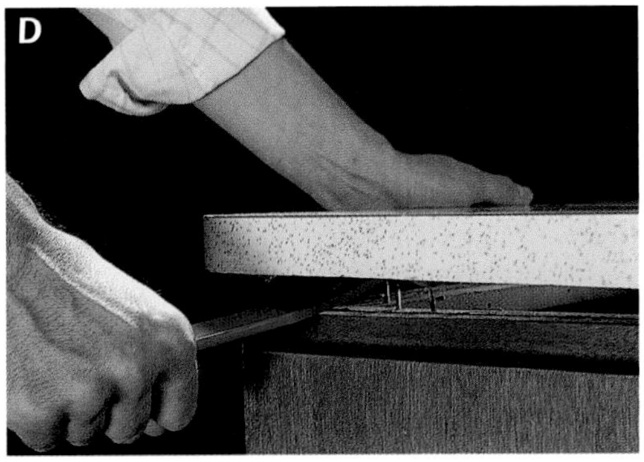

Carefully pry the countertop away from the cabinets.

If necessary, cut out the countertop using a reciprocating saw.

Replacing a Countertop

Post-form laminate countertops come in stock lengths, which you can cut to fit over your cabinets. Countertops are available in straight sections and in mitered sections for installation in a corner. Purchase an end-cap kit for any exposed end of your countertop. The kit includes a wood batten strip and a preshaped strip of matching laminate to cover the end after the section is cut to size.

For a precise fit, trim the backsplash to follow any unevenness in the back wall—a process known as *scribing*.

Start by measuring along the tops of the base cabinets to determine the size of the countertop. Walls are seldom flat or square, so measure at the front and back of the cabinets, and use the longer measurements **(photo F).** Use a framing square to establish a reference line (R) near the middle of the cabinets. Take four measurements (A, B, C, D) from the reference line to the cabinet ends and walls.

Continued on next page

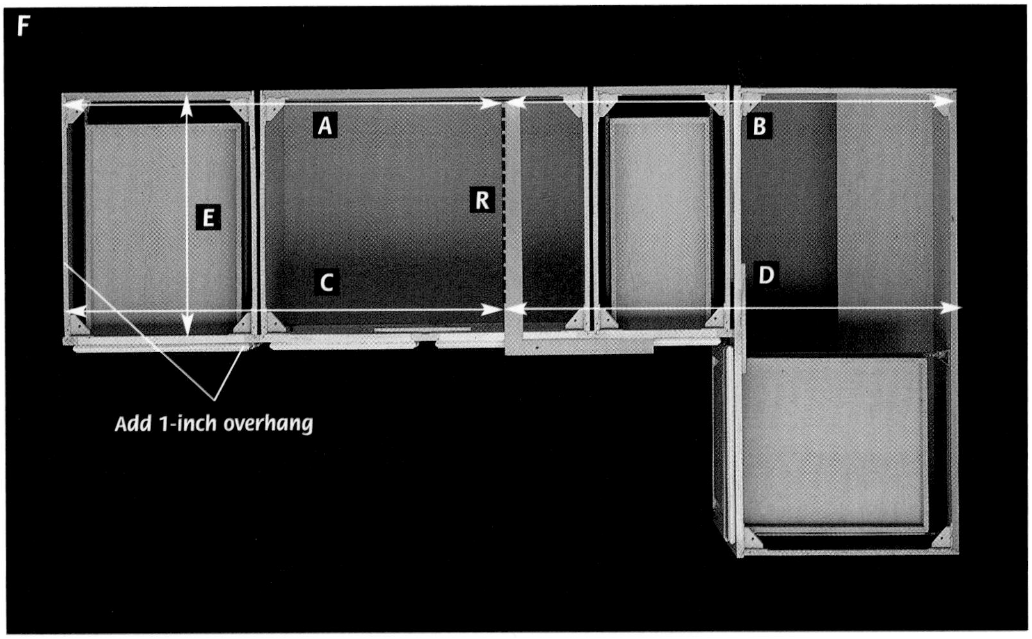

Use a framing square to establish a reference line that is perpendicular to the fronts of the cabinets. Measure on both sides of the line and add the measurements together. Add 1" for overhangs along the fronts and exposed ends of the cabinets.

Replacing a Countertop (cont.)

Allow for overhangs by adding 1" to the length of each exposed end, and 1" to the width (E). Also allow for 1/16" gap where the countertop butts against appliances.

Lay the new countertop facedown on a flat worksurface, and use a jig saw to cut it to length **(photo G).** Clamp a straightedge in place to use as a cutting guide. If the saw chips the laminate surface, switch to a blade with finer teeth.

To finish the exposed ends, attach the batten from the end-cap kit to the underside of the countertop, using waterproof wood glue and small brads **(photo H).** Smooth any unevenness with a belt sander. Then, attach the self-adhesive laminate end cap to the end, slightly overlapping the edges of the countertop. Hold the end cap in place, and press it with a household iron set at medium heat to activate the adhesive. After the end cap cools, use a fine-tooth file to trim the edges flush.

Position the countertop on the cabinets, making sure the front edge is parallel to the cabinet faces. The bottom of the countertop's front edge should be even with the tops of the cabinets. Check the countertop for level **(photo I).** If necessary, use wood shims to level the countertop and to make sure it's evenly supported from underneath.

With the miter joints dry-fitted together and the countertop pieces snug against the back walls, the next step is scribing the backsplash **(photo J).** Post-form countertops have a *scribing strip*, a thin lip of wood and laminate on the end of the backsplash, which makes it easy to shape.

Set the compass arms to match the widest gap between the backsplash and the wall. Then, move the compass along the length of the wall to transfer the outline to the scribing strip. If the laminate is too dark to display your pencil mark, apply masking tape to the top of the backsplash and draw onto the tape.

Use a belt sander with a coarse-grit belt to sand the backsplash to the scribe line **(photo K).** To avoid chipping the laminate, hold the belt sander parallel to the top of the backsplash. Bevel the strip slightly inward from the top surface down. Test-fit the countertop.

Lay out the position of the sink and other elements to be installed in the countertop. To mark the cutout for a self-rimming sink, set the sink upside down on the countertop, and trace the outline with a pencil **(photo L).** Remove the sink, and draw a cutting line 5/8" inside the sink outline. If your sink has a removable frame, position the frame right-side-up on the countertop, and trace around the vertical flange of the frame.

To make the sink cutout, drill a starter hole just inside the cutting line, and use a jig saw with a fine-tooth blade to complete the cut **(photo M).** Support the cutout from below so it doesn't fall and damage the cabinet. Make any other necessary cutouts.

The next step is joining the mitered ends, if you have them. With short countertops, you can do this on a bench, but it's easier to

Tools: *Framing square, straightedge, jig saw, hammer, belt sander, iron, flat file, level, compass, pencil, drill, adjustable wrench, caulk gun.*

Materials: *Post-form countertop, end-cap kit, waterproof wood glue, shims, masking tape, take-up bolts, silicone caulk, wood block, wallboard screws.*

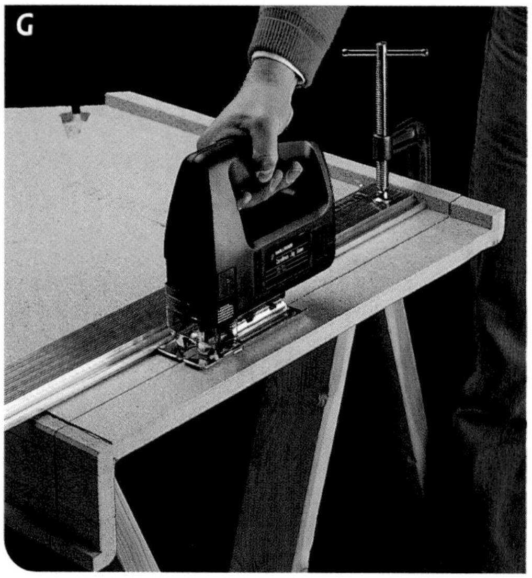

Use a straightedge as a guide for a straight, square cut on the end of the countertop.

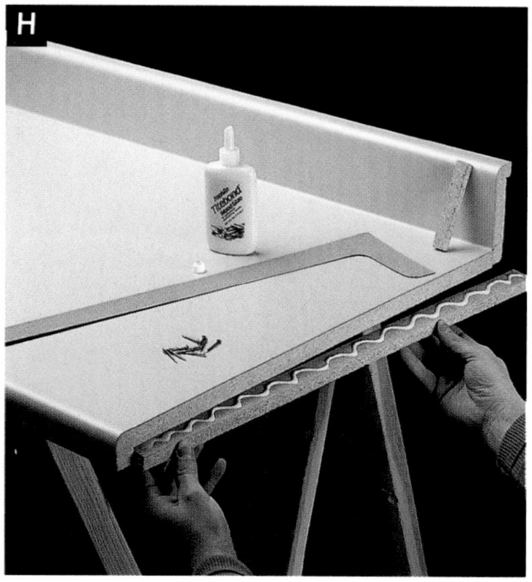

Glue and nail the batten in place. Attach the end cap, using a household iron to activate the adhesive backing.

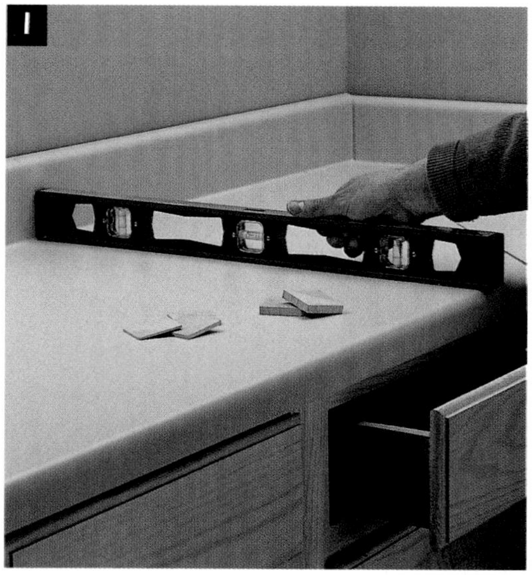

Position the countertop and check it with a level. Use shims to level the countertop and to fill gaps for solid support.

assemble long countertops on top of the cabinets. The miter joints are held together with special take-up bolts that sit in grooves cut into the countertop core.

Apply a bead of silicone caulk to the mating surfaces of the miter joint, and spread the caulk evenly with your finger **(photo N).** Fit the joint together. From inside the cabinet, install the take-up bolts, and tighten them so they are just snug **(photo N, *inset*).**

From above, check the joint to make sure the front edges are flush. Using a wood block and a hammer, tap along the surface of the seam until it is smooth. Then, tighten the take-up bolts.

Position the countertop tightly against the wall, and fasten it to the cabinets by driving wallboard screws up through the mounting brackets and into the countertop core (page 177). Be sure that the screws aren't long enough to puncture the laminate surface.

Run a fine bead of caulk along the joint between the backsplash and wall **(photo O).** Smooth the caulk with a wet fingertip.

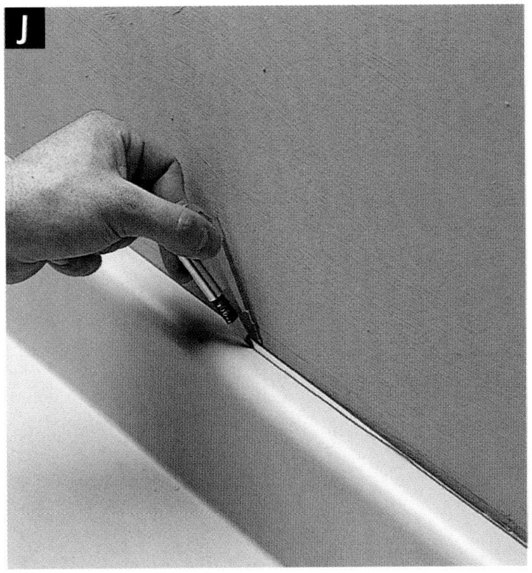

Use a compass to trace the contours of the back wall onto the countertop backsplash.

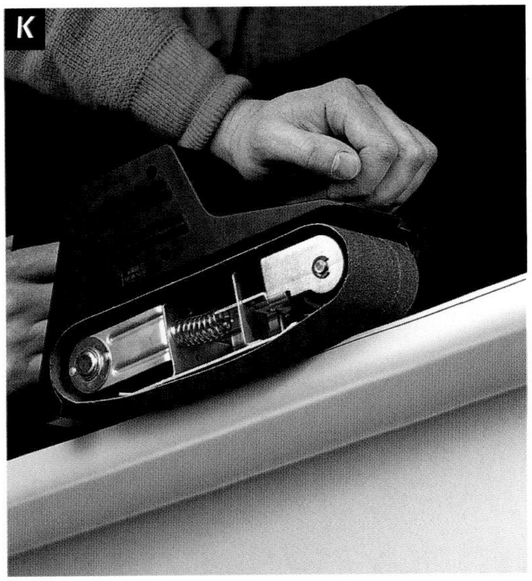

Sand the edge of the scribing strip on the backsplash, using a belt sander.

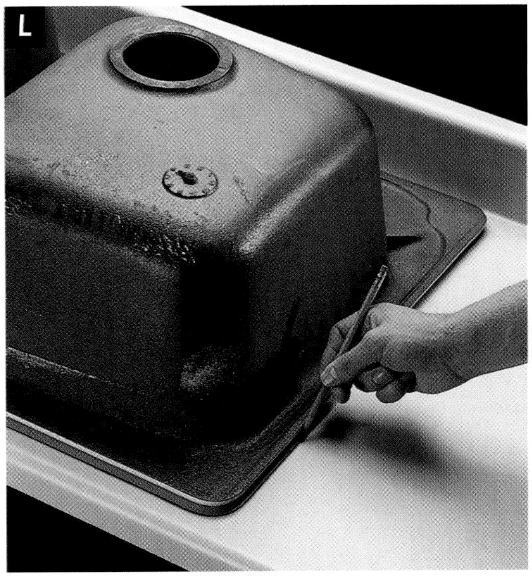

Position your sink upside down on the countertop, and trace the outline. Cut $\frac{5}{8}$" inside of the line.

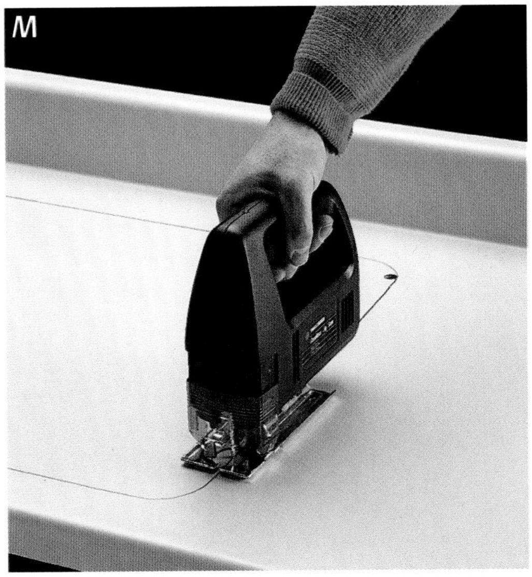

Drill a starter hole on the inside of the sink cutout line, and make the cutout with a jig saw.

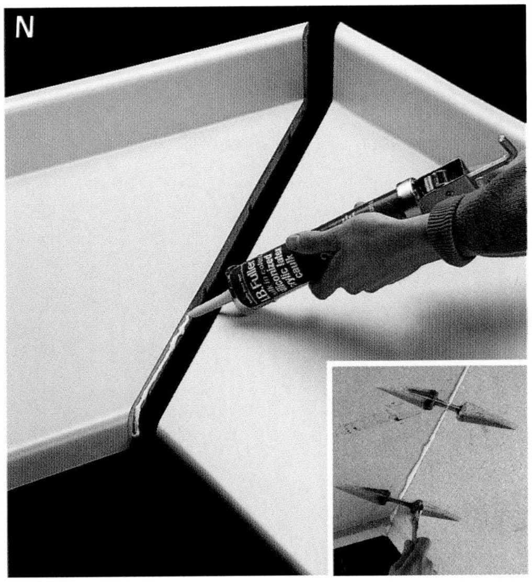

Apply silicone caulk to the mitered ends of the countertop. Secure the joint from below with take-up bolts.

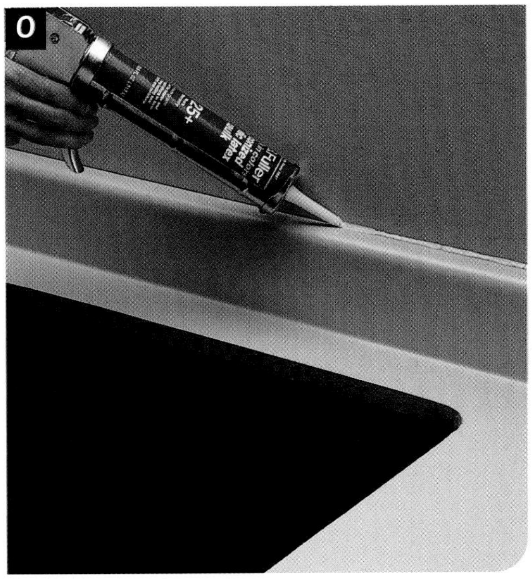

Caulk the joint where the backsplash meets the wall. This seal keeps water away from the wood core of the countertop.

U.S.A.

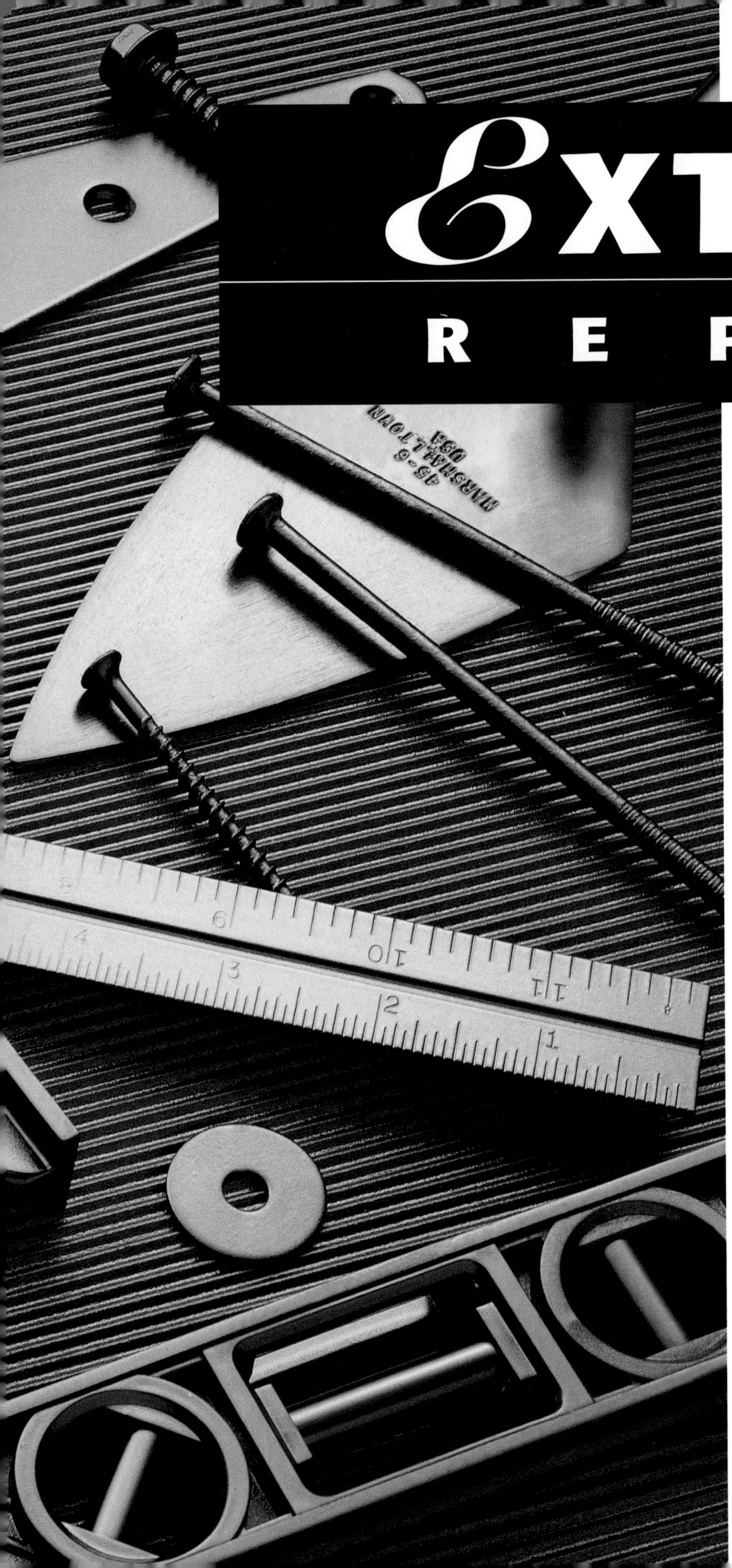

Exterior Repairs

Your home's exterior is more than just the face it presents to the world. Each exterior element is part of a system designed to protect your home's structural integrity. This chapter will help you maintain and repair each part of that system.

Exterior Repairs

A well-maintained home exterior keeps you and your possessions dry and safe from the elements. It can also be a source of personal pride and satisfaction. This section shows you how to maintain, protect, and repair the exterior of your home to keep it both weathertight and attractive. We'll cover roofs, fascia and soffits, gutters, chimneys, walls and siding, walkways, steps, and driveways.

A program of regular inspection and maintenance can alert you to areas of your home's exterior that need attention while the repairs are still relatively simple and affordable. By making small repairs on a regular basis, you'll be increasing your home's curb appeal, protecting the value of your property, and contributing to the attractiveness of your neighborhood.

Working Safely

Repairing the exterior of your house can involve working in a range of weather conditions. In the worst case, an emergency repair may mean facing blistering heat and sweltering humidity or subzero temperatures. Exterior repairs also frequently involve working at heights. A few commonsense precautions will help you perform your exterior repairs safely:

It's not always easy to estimate the amount of time required for a repair. Dress properly for the job and the weather, and take frequent breaks to warm up or cool off, depending on the weather. Extreme weather is a bad time for outdoor repairs. Avoid doing repairs during a storm or high winds.

Work with a helper whenever possible—especially when working at heights. If you

Be careful around the power cables bringing electricity into your house. Carrying 100 amps of electricity or more, these cables are always live unless turned off by the utility company. Never position a ladder near these wires.

Create a tool platform with sawhorses and a piece of plywood. Tools spread on the ground are a safety hazard, and moisture can damage them. It's safer and more efficient to organize your tools so they're dry and easy to find.

must work alone, let a friend or family member know so they can check on you.

Don't use tools or work at heights while under the influence of alcohol. If you take medication, it's important to read the label and follow the recommendations regarding the use of tools and equipment.

The most common ladder for outdoor work is the extension ladder. An extension ladder is made of two interlocking ladders that slide against each other and can be fixed at varying heights. When working with extension ladders, keep the flat tops of the rungs facing up. Adjust the ladder to extend three feet above the roof's edge. This provides greater stability, especially when getting on or off the ladder. When reaching over the side of a ladder, keep your hips between the side rails. Don't exceed the work-load rating for your ladder. Read and follow the load limits and safety recommendations listed on the label.

Helpful Hint

For outdoor work, use a GFCI extension cord for protection against electrical shock. GFCIs (Ground-Fault Circuit-Interrupters) automatically cut power if a short circuit occurs, greatly reducing the risk of serious injury. They are especially important in areas where moisture is present.

Working with Ladders & Scaffolding

Use an extension ladder with an adjustable stabilizer.

Stabilize your ladder with stakes driven into the ground, and level it with blocking.

Make sure that both fly hooks are secure before climbing an extension ladder.

Secure the top of an extension ladder by tying it to a chimney or a securely mounted screw eye.

Use cordless tools to eliminate the hazards of extension cords when working from ladders.

To anchor a ladder, attach a short rope and a block of wood to the top rung; place the block inside a window and close the window.

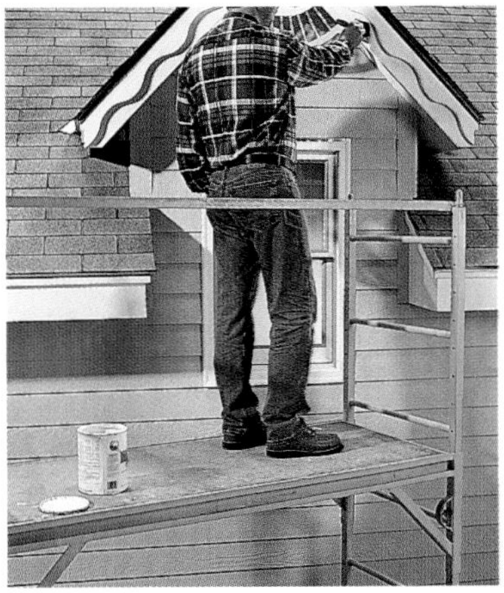

Use scaffolding for projects that require you to work at heights for long periods.

Use plywood blocking to level and stabilize the legs of your scaffolding.

Roofing

Roofing Basics

The roof of your home is your first line of defense against the elements. Its job is to protect your household from the sun, wind, and precipitation of all varieties. The roof structure is overlaid with lapped courses of material that serve the same function as scales on a fish or feathers on a bird.

Other than severe trauma—trees crashing through the house or wind peeling shingles off and dropping them in your yard—most roof problems are caused by water. Either water sneaks in from outside and seeps along hidden roofing members, making its way to the center of your clean, white living room ceiling. Or, it attacks from inside the roof, condensing undetected, bathing rafters and sheathing with moisture, dripping from the tips of protruding roofing nails, lying in wait to cause problems over time.

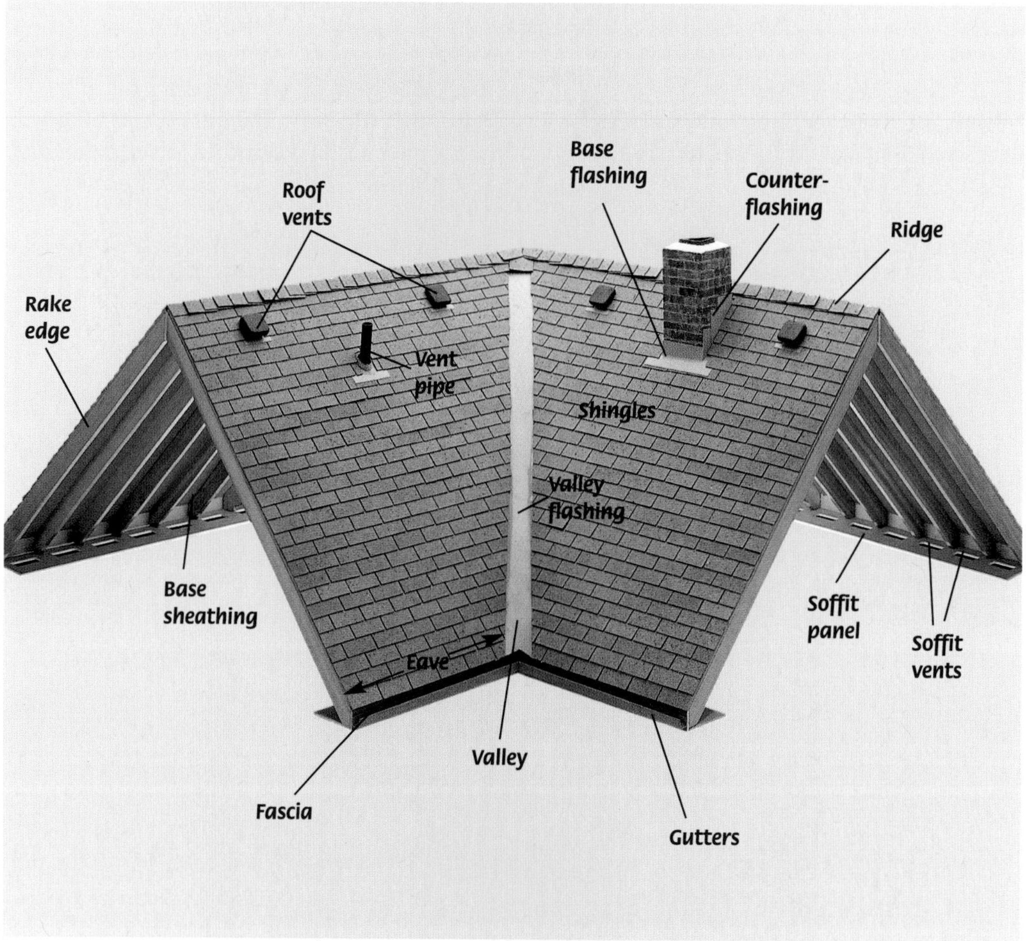

The elements of a roof system work together to provide shelter, drainage, and ventilation. The roof covering is composed of sheathing, building paper, and shingles. Metal flashing is attached in valleys and around chimneys, vent pipes, and other roof elements to seal out water. Soffits cover and protect the eave area below the roof overhang. Fascia, usually attached at the ends of the rafters, supports soffit panels as well as a gutter and downspout system. Soffit vents and roof vents keep fresh air circulating throughout the system.

Types of Roofing

There are several types of roofs commonly used in North America, each with its own distinct set of advantages and disadvantages.

Asphalt shingles **(photo A)** are by far the most common, and are easily installed and repaired by homeowners.

Metal roofs **(photo B)** have been associated in the past with tin-covered storage sheds or copper-domed cathedrals, but today's panels of corrugated aluminum or galvanized steel are practical and attractive options.

Many people admire the beauty of wood shingles **(photo C).** In addition to their beauty, they're durable (especially when treated with a preservative every 3 to 5 years) and easy to install. Shakes are more expensive because they're thicker and made by hand; they're more durable, lasting up to 50 years rather than the 25 years more typical of shingles.

Slate shingles **(photo D)** are made from blocks of slate—often mined in the eastern United States—and split into shingles. Installation is a job best left to professionals, but when maintained regularly, slate shingles are virtually indestructible—Vermont sea-green slate is still in good condition on some 200-year-old houses. Slate roofs are expensive—in addition to requiring professional installation, the material itself is fairly expensive and its weight requires a reinforced roof structure.

Clay tiles **(photo E)** offer virtually the same benefits and drawbacks as slate, but create quite a different appearance. Heavy and relatively expensive, they are also weather-resistant, fireproof, and insect-proof. Clay tiles are available in several different patterns. Clay tiles are generally secured with clips or fasteners, but they may also be held in place by a tie-wire system in which the tiles literally hang from wires suspended from the ridge of the house. Most tile roof repairs require a professional's expertise and equipment.

Built-up roofs **(photo F)** are more commonly found on commercial buildings than homes, but they're well suited to houses with flat roofs. Installation and replacement is best left to professionals, but patches and minor repairs greatly extend the life of the roof, and are easily accomplished by most homeowners.

Asphalt shingles are comprised of roofing felt saturated with asphalt and imbedded with a layer of mineral granules.

Metal roofing has evolved from the terne and copper of days gone by, to the corrugated aluminum or galvanized steel panels most frequently used today. Usually painted, it is attractive, durable, and moderately priced.

Wood shingles are usually made of Western red cedar. They are thinner, smaller, and less expensive than wood shakes.

Slate is a natural stone. Beautiful, durable, and fireproof, the primary drawbacks are its cost and weight.

Clay tiles are fireproof and provide a distinctive appearance. Like slate, the drawbacks are cost and the need to reinforce a roof to bear their weight.

Built-up roofs are made from alternating layers of roofing felt and hot tar, covered with a protective layer of gravel. This construction is suitable for flat roofs or roofs with a slope of less than 3-in-12.

Tools & Materials

Working conditions on a roof can be arduous, so make the job as easy as possible by gathering the right tools and equipment before you begin. Roofing tools include a pneumatic nailer, hooked utility knife, roofing hammer with alignment guides and hatchet-style blade, and a release magnet **(photo A).** If you need to remove shingles, a task referred to as *tear-off*, you'll need a flat pry bar and a slotted roofing shovel.

Safety equipment—including safety glasses, work gloves, roof jacks, a 2 × 6 plank, and knee pads—is essential. Proper shoes are also important for safe rooftop work. High-top boots with rubber soles provide ankle support and traction on sloped roof surfaces. Smooth-soled boots are better for working on an asphalt roof, where lugged soles can damage fragile shingles.

Naturally, you'll also need ladders: a ladder to get up to the roof, and, if your roof has a steep slope, a ladder to use while on the roof. A fiberglass ladder is the best option for an extension ladder, because it's lightweight, sturdy, and won't conduct electricity if it accidentally comes into contact with power lines. Once on the roof, use roof jacks **(photo B),** and a ladder **(photo C)** to ensure you don't slip off. Make sure to follow manufacturer's directions.

Roof flashing protects the roof at the edges, in valleys, and where the roof joins with roofing elements, such as chimneys and vent pipes **(photo D).** Flashing can be cut using aviation snips.

Fasteners are designed specifically for each roofing job **(photo E).** Use aluminum nails for aluminum flashing and rubber-gasket nails for galvanized metal flashing. Purchase two to four nails per foot of flashing. To fasten asphalt shingles, use galvanized roofing nails. Estimate four nails per shingle and 325 nails (about 2½ lbs.) per square of shingles. Hot-dipped galvanized nails offer the best resistance to corrosion at a low price.

Building paper and ice guard membranes protect the roof deck **(photo F).** Roofing cement is used to seal holes or make joints between the flashing and roofing elements.

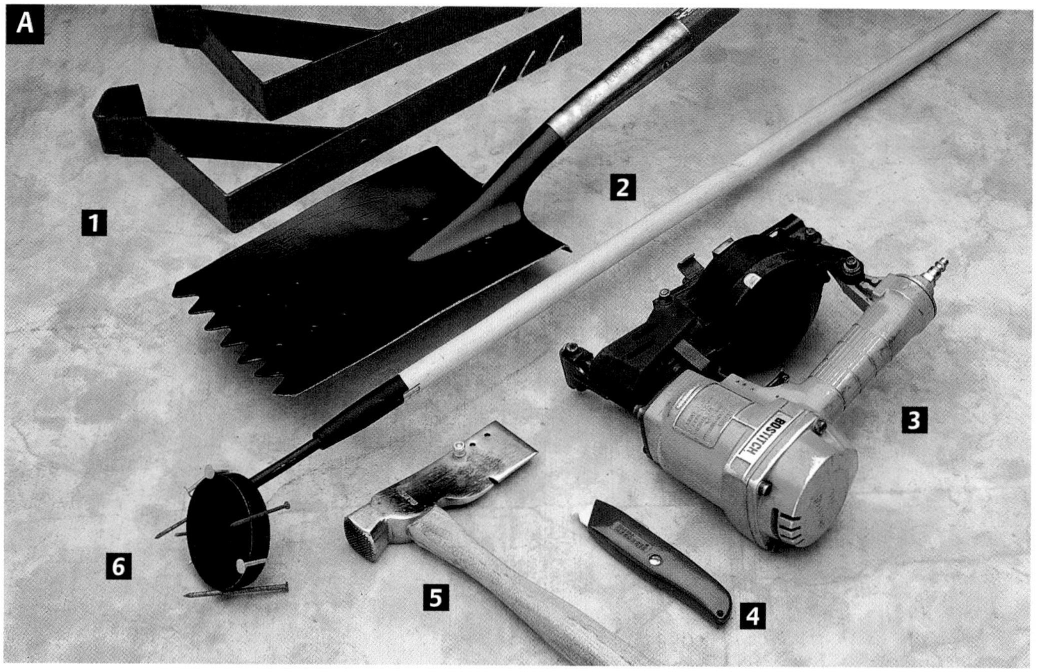

Specialty roofing tools include: roof jacks (1), roofing shovel (2), pneumatic nailer (3), utility knife with hooked blade (4), roofing hammer with alignment guides and hatchet blade (5), and a release magnet for site cleanup (6).

Use roof jacks instead of a ladder. Nail the supports at the fourth or fifth course, and add the widest board the supports will hold.

If you don't like heights, fashion a roofing ladder by nailing strips across a pair of 2 × 4s. Secure the ladder to the roof jacks, and use it to maintain your footing.

Roof flashing can be hand-cut or purchased in preformed shapes and sizes. Long pieces of valley flashing, base flashing, top saddles, and other nonstandard pieces can be cut from rolled flashing material with aviation snips. Step flashing blanks can be bought in standard sizes and bent to fit. Drip edge and vent pipe flashing are available preformed. Skylight flashing usually comes as a kit with the window. Complicated flashings, like chimney crickets, can be custom fabricated by a metalworker.

Helpful Hint

Some types of roofing are more difficult to repair than others. Slate and clay tile, for example, can be damaged just by walking on them—so it's possible that attempting to repair them yourself can actually aggravate the original problem.

If you question your ability to make a repair, meet with a reputable roofing contractor or two. Ask questions and gather information that will help you decide whether to do the work yourself or hire a professional.

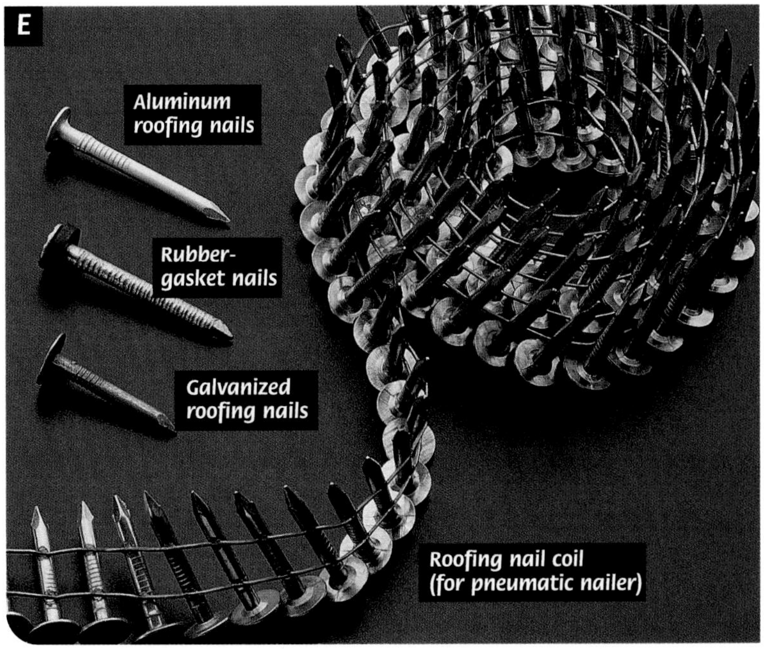

Different fasteners are specially developed for different jobs. Use galvanized roofing nails to hand-nail shingles; use aluminum nails for aluminum flashing; use rubber gasket nails for galvanized metal flashing, and nail coils for pneumatic nailers.

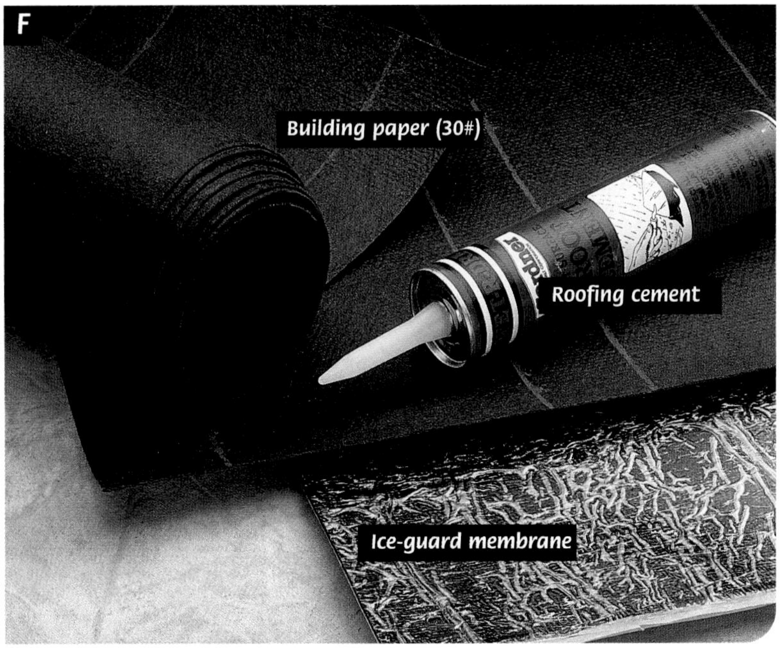

Common roofing materials include 30# building paper for use as underlayment; tubes of roofing cement for sealing small holes, cracks, and joints; and ice-guard membrane.

Inspecting a Roof

A roof system is composed of several elements that work together to provide three basic, essential functions for your home: shelter, drainage, and ventilation. The roof covering and the flashing are designed to shed water, directing it to gutters and downspouts that channel it away from the foundation. Air intake and outtake vents keep fresh air circulating below the roof sheathing, preventing moisture buildup as well as heat buildup.

When your roof system develops problems that compromise its ability to protect your home—cracked shingles, incomplete ventilation, or damaged flashing—damage quickly spreads to other parts of your house. A sound roof system protects your house, and routine inspections are the best way to make sure the roof continues to do its job effectively.

Because of the manner in which roofing problems develop, you need to inspect both the interior and exterior of the roof. From inside the attic, check the rafters and sheathing for signs of water damage. Symptoms will appear in the form of streaking, or discoloration **(photo A).** Of course, a moist or wet area also signals water damage.

While you're in the attic, examine the ventilation system to make sure that air is flowing properly. The flow of air through vents should be adequate and unobstructed. If your attic has vapor barriers, there should be one square foot of venting for every 300 square feet of roof. Without vapor barriers in the attic, you'll need a square foot for 150 square feet of roofing.

When you've completed your inspection of the interior, move to the exterior of the roof. Pay particular attention to the condition of flashing and shingles. Flashing provides flexible, watertight joints between the roof, which expands and contracts, and the intervening roof elements, such as chimneys and vent pipes. Examine the condition of the flashing and the joint compound used to seal its edges. Failed joint compound can easily be replaced, and deteriorated flashing can be patched or replaced.

Torn or missing shingles can also allow moisture to gather and cause further deterioration. Asphalt shingles with too much moisture trapped underneath will often buckle or cup, thereby losing their protective abilities. Once moisture is reduced, buckled shingles may flatten out, but cupped shingles must be replaced.

A

Discoloration on rafters is a symptom of leaks.

Ice Dams & Ventilation Problems

Ice dams occur when melting snow refreezes near the eaves, causing ice to back up under the shingles, where it melts onto the sheathing and seeps into the house **(photo B).**

To reduce damage and prevent further ice backup, melt a channel through the ice with hot water **(photo C).** This allows water to flow off the roof before it freezes. Or call a professional who uses steam equipment.

You can also install an electric roof cable to melt the ice. Lay the cable in the gutters and run it up or down each downspout.

To permanently solve the problem, improve roof ventilation to reduce attic temperatures.

B

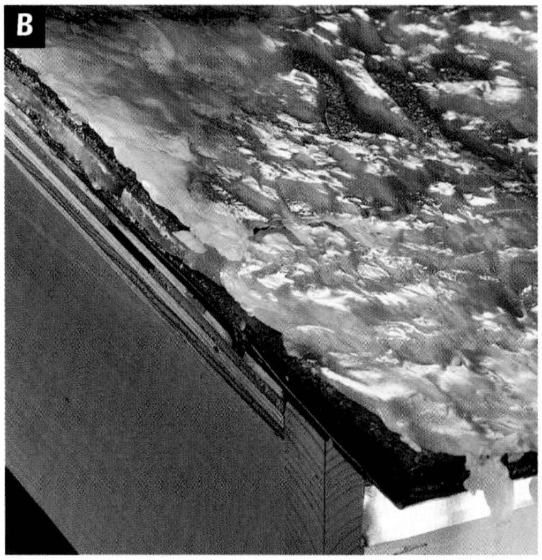

Ice dams are caused by melting snow.

C

Use hot water to melt ice dams.

Inspecting & Maintaining a Roof

You can begin your inspection of the roof's exterior without risking life and limb. With the help of binoculars, you can get a good look from either a neighbor's upper story window or from the yard. Although this is a good start, you're eventually going to need to get up on the roof to do a complete inspection.

Wind, weather, and flying debris can damage shakes and shingles. The areas along valleys and ridges tend to take the most weather-related abuse. Torn, loose, or cracked shingles are quite common in these areas **(photo D).**

Deposits of granules in gutters or at the ends of downspouts are a signal that the protective layer of asphalt shingles is damaged. As deterioration progresses, the shingles begin to lighten in color and curl **(photo E).** At this point, it's time to consider reroofing.

A sagging ridge might be caused by the weight of too many roofing layers **(photo F).** But it might also be the result of a more significant problem, such as a rotting ridge pole or insufficient support for the ridge pole.

Dirt and debris attract moisture and decay, which shorten a roof's life. To protect shingles, carefully wash the roof once a year **(photo G).** Pay particular attention to protected areas where moss and mildew may accumulate.

In damp climates, it's a good idea to nail a zinc strip along the center ridge of a roof **(photo H).** Minute quantities of zinc wash down the roof each time it rains, killing moss and mildew.

Overhanging limbs drop debris and provide shade that encourages moss and mildew. To reduce chances of decay, trim any tree limbs that overhang the roof **(photo I).**

When you're on the roof, carefully feel for any soft spots. A soft spot indicates decay of the sheathing. The shingles around a soft spot will be easy to tear away. If you discover such a problem, replace the sheathing in the area immediately.

The problems common to clay tile and slate shingles are quite minor—generally either cracked or loose pieces, which can quickly be replaced.

Damage or excessive wear become increasingly common as shingles age, become more brittle, and lose their protective mineral surfaces.

Buckled and cupped shingles are usually caused by moisture beneath the shingles. Loosened areas create an entry point for moisture and leave shingles vulnerable to wind damage.

A sagging ridge may be a symptom of major support problems.

Prolong the life of your shingles with an annual or semi-annual cleaning with a pressure washer. Cedar shingles also benefit from a periodic application of wood preservative.

Nail a zinc strip along the center ridge of a shingled roof. When it rains, zinc washes down the roof, killing moss and mildew in its wake.

Cut tree limbs that overhang a roof to increase sunlight and prevent moss and mildew.

Locating & Repairing Leaks

Finding the source of a leak can be a challenge, but the laws of nature work in your favor. Although water often follows a winding path, eventually it always runs downhill.

If you have an unfinished attic, examine the underside of your roof with a strong flashlight on a rainy day. If you find wetness, discoloration, or other signs of moisture, trace the trail up to where the water is making its entrance **(photo A).**

Water that flows down toward a wall can be temporarily diverted to minimize the damage. Nail a small block of wood in the path of the water and place a bucket underneath to catch the drip **(photo B).** Then, on a dry day, drive a nail through the underside of the decking in order to locate and repair the hole.

If there are no obvious signs of wetness, check the insulation between the rafters. Wearing a respirator, long sleeves, and heavy gloves, examine the insulation for mold, discoloration, and dampness. Remove insulation until you find the leak.

If the leak is finding its way to a finished ceiling, take steps to minimize damage until the leak can be repaired. As soon as possible, reduce the accumulation of water behind a ceiling by poking a small hole in the wallboard or plaster and draining the water **(photo C).**

When you find the source of a leak from inside, measure between that spot and a point that will be visible and identifiable from outside the house, such as a chimney, vent pipe, or—if nothing else—the peak of the roof **(photo D).** Next, get up on the roof and use these measurements to locate the leak. While you're there, check for damaged or missing shingles, tiles, or slates; deteriorated flashing; exposed nails; open joints between the roof and siding; damaged chimney masonry; open seams in roofing materials; and missing window or door drip caps.

Check the attic for water on rafters and sheathing. Place a bucket under the leak. Trace its source and mark the location.

If water flows down toward a wall, nail a small block of wood to direct the dripping water into a bucket.

Drive an awl or nail into the center of the water mark and release the water into a bucket.

Using measurements made from inside the house, locate the source of the leak on the roof's exterior.

Making Emergency Repairs

If your roof is severely damaged, the primary goal is to prevent additional damage to your home until permanent repairs can be made. Use a sheet of plywood as emergency cover to keep out the wind and water **(photo E).** Or, cover damage by nailing strips of lath around the edges of a plastic sheet or tarp **(photo F).**

For these temporary measures, use double-headed nails, which easily can be removed when you're ready to make permanent repairs. Mark the locations of the nails as you remove them, and fill the holes with roofing cement when the final repair is complete.

Tools: *Hammer.*

Materials: *Plywood (or wood lath and plastic), double-headed nails.*

Use plywood for an emergency roof cover. When the final repair is complete, fill nail holes with roofing cement.

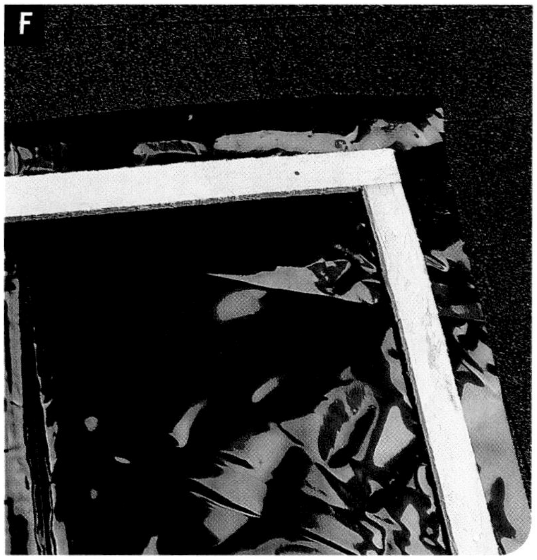

Nail strips of lath around the edges to hold plastic sheeting or a tarp in place as an emergency cover.

Making Spot Repairs with Roofing Cement

Plastic roofing cement and rolled, galvanized flashing can be used for a variety of minor roof repairs. Choose a dry, moderate day to do these repairs. Heat softens the roof's surface while cold makes it brittle, leaving shingles more difficult to work with and more vulnerable to damage. If shingles appear brittle, warm them slightly with a hair dryer to make them easier to handle and less likely to crack.

To reattach a loose shingle **(photo G),** wipe down the building paper and the underside of the shingle. Let each dry, then apply a liberal coat of roofing cement. Press the shingle down to seat it in the bed of cement.

Tack down buckled shingles **(photo H)** by cleaning out below the buckled area, filling with roofing cement, and pressing the shingle into the cement. You can also patch cracks and splits with roofing cement.

Check the joints around flashing, which are common places for roof leaks to occur. Seal gaps by cleaning out and replacing any failed roofing cement **(photo I).**

Reattach loose shingles with roofing cement.

Tack down the edges of buckled shingles by pressing them into roofing cement.

Seal gaps around flashing by removing and replacing failed roofing cement.

Replacing Asphalt Shingles

Replace asphalt shingles by pulling out damaged shingles, starting with the uppermost shingle in the damaged area **(photo A).** Be careful not to damage surrounding shingles that still are in good condition.

Exposed nail heads could puncture new shingles, so remove all the old nails in and above the repair area **(photo B).** Patch damaged building paper with roofing cement.

Install the replacement shingles, beginning with the lowest shingle in the repair area **(photo C).** Nail above the tab slots with 7/8" or 1" roofing nails.

Install all but the top shingle with nails, then apply roofing cement to the underside of the top shingle, above the seal line **(photo D).**

Slip the last shingle into place, under the overlapping shingle. Lift the shingles immediately above the repair area, and nail the top replacement shingles into place **(photo E).**

Tools: Hammer, flat pry bar, caulk gun, utility knife.

Materials: Roofing cement, replacement shingles, roofing nails.

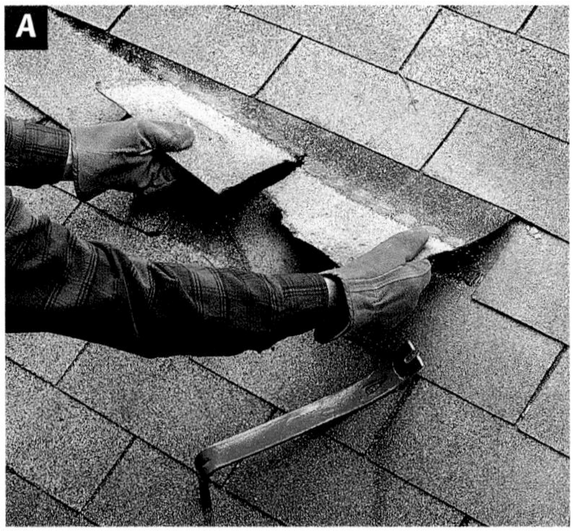

Beginning with the uppermost shingle in the repair area, pull out damaged shingles.

Remove old nails, then patch damaged building paper with roofing cement.

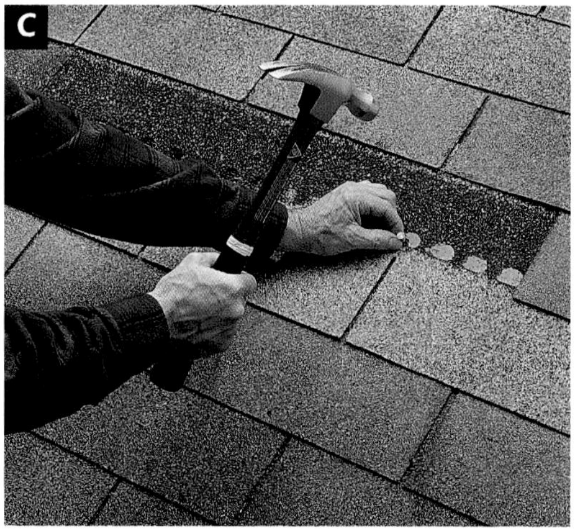

Beginning with the lowest shingle in the repair area, install replacement shingles.

Install all but the top shingle with nails, then apply roofing cement to the underside of the top shingle.

Slip the last shingle into place under the overlapping shingle. Lift the shingle immediately above the repair area to nail down the replacement shingle.

Aging Shakes & Shingles

Almost all shingles change color as they weather. When you make repairs to a roof or install replacement shingles, the replacements often sharply contrast with the older shingles.

Over a few seasons, the new shakes or shingles gradually will begin to blend in with the rest of the roof, but it's not necessary to wait for that. With just a little work, you can make replacement shingles look like the originals so the repair work doesn't resemble a bandage.

To age new wood shakes or shingles to match existing ones, dissolve one pound of baking soda in one gallon of water. Brush the solution onto the shingles, then place them in direct sunlight for four or five hours. Rinse them thoroughly and let them dry. Repeat the process until the color of the new shingles closely matches the originals.

If you have asphalt shingles, use mineral spirits to age them. Dip a white rag in mineral spirits, then wipe the surface of the new shingles to remove some of the granulated material. The granules protect the shingles from the elements, so be conservative as you remove them—remove only enough so that the new shingles resemble the original ones.

Thoroughly rinse the newly aged shingles, and allow them to dry before installing them in the normal manner.

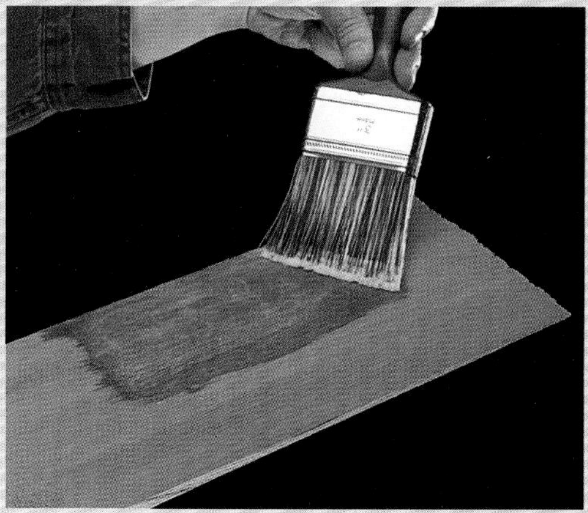

Replacing Wood Shingles & Shakes

Shakes and shingles are attached to the sheathing with nails. Because they are not pliable like asphalt shingles, they must be broken before the nails can be removed.

Begin by splitting the damaged shake or shingle, using a hammer and chisel. Remove the pieces, then slip a hacksaw blade underneath the overlapping shingles **(photo F).** Cut the nails with the hacksaw and pry out the remaining pieces of the shake or shingle.

Gently pry up the shakes or shingles above the repair area. Cut new pieces for the lowest course, leaving about 3/8" on the sides for expansion. Nail replacements in place with ring-shank siding nails **(photo G).** Fill in all but the top course of shingles in the repair area.

Cut the shakes or shingles for the top course. Because the top course can't be nailed down, use roofing cement to fasten the shingles to the sheathing.

Apply a coat of roofing cement where these shingles will sit, then slip them beneath the overlapping shingles. Press down to seat the shingles in the roofing cement **(photo H).**

Use a hacksaw blade to cut the nails underneath the overlapping shingles.

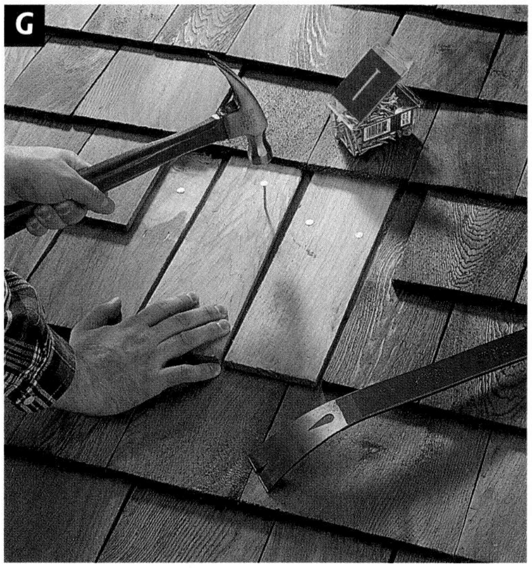

Nail the replacement shakes or shingles in place.

Apply roofing cement to the top course of shingles, and slide them under the overlapping shingles.

Repairing & Replacing Flashing

Flashing protects the joints surrounding roof elements and the seams between roof areas by carrying water off the roof's surface. To maintain a roof's integrity, damaged or deteriorated flashing must be repaired or replaced.

If you're planning a patch or partial replacement, use the same material as the original—aluminum on aluminum, for example. When dissimilar metals are joined, corrosion accelerates. If you're replacing flashing around a chimney or other masonry structure, use copper or galvanized steel flashing—lime from mortar can corrode aluminum.

At first, patches may be obvious, but they will quickly blend in as they discolor.

Wear heavy gloves, and beware of sharp edges when handling flashing.

Tools: *Tape measure, wire brush, aviation snips, trowel, flat pry bar, hammer, utility knife.*

Materials: *Replacement flashing, roofing cement, roofing nails.*

Patching Valley Flashing

When repairing valley flashing, the damaged flashing is not removed, but is instead patched over with pieces of new material.

Measure the damaged area and mark an outline for the patch. The patch should be wide enough to slip under the shingles on both sides of the repair area, and tapered to a point at one end.

Cut the patch with aviation snips **(photo A).** Using a trowel or flat pry bar, carefully break the seal between the damaged flashing and the surrounding shingles.

Scrub the damaged flashing with a wire brush, and wipe it clean.

Apply a heavy bead of roofing cement to the back of the patch **(photo B).**

Cut a slit in the old flashing. Insert the tapered end of the patch into the slit in the old flashing, and slip the side edges under the shingles on each side.

Rest the square end of the patch on top of the old flashing, and press it firmly to seal the roofing cement joint. Add roofing cement to the exposed seams and at the shingle joints.

Using a trowel, feather out the cement to create a smooth path for water flow **(photo C).** Be sure all of the seams are covered.

Cut the metal patch to size, using aviation snips. Make sure the patch is wide enough to fit under the shingles.

Apply a continuous bead of roofing cement along the edges of the patch.

Smooth out the roofing cement to ensure that water flows smoothly and doesn't dam up.

Installing Vent Flashing

Install shingles up to the vent pipe so that the flashing rests on at least one shingle. Apply a heavy double bead of roofing cement along the bottom edges of the flange.

Position the flashing collar so the longer portion of the tapered neck slopes down the roof and the flange lies over the shingles. Nail around the perimeter of the flange with roofing nails **(photo D).**

Cut the shingles to fit around the neck of the flashing so they lie flat against the flange **(photo E).** Apply roofing cement to the shingle and flashing joints, and cover any exposed nails.

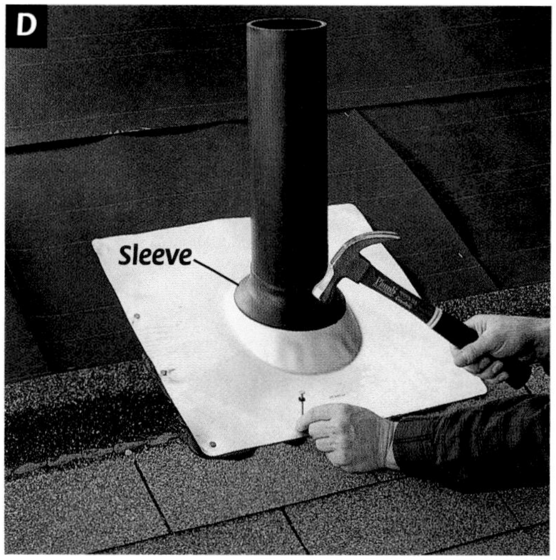

Spread a heavy bead of roofing cement on the bottom of the flashing, then lower it over the vent pipe and nail it in place.

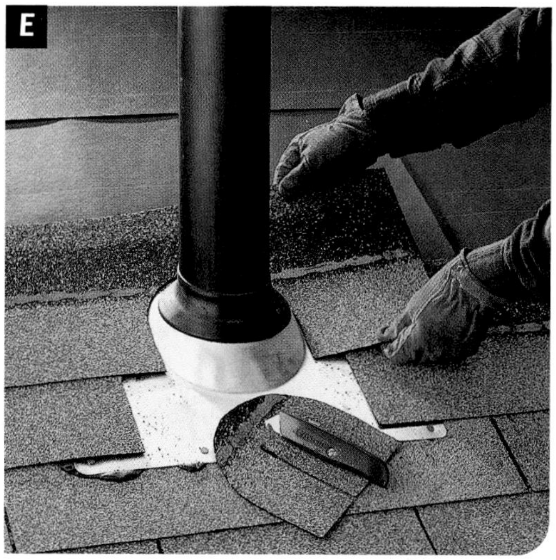

Cut shingles to fit and install them over and around the flashing.

Replacing Step Flashing

To replace a piece of step flashing, carefully bend up the counterflashing or siding covering the damaged flashing. Cut any roofing cement seals, and pull back the shingles.

Use a flat bar to remove the damaged flashing **(photo F).**

Cut the new flashing to fit, and apply roofing cement to all unexposed edges.

Slip the flashing into place, making sure it's overlapped by the flashing above it and that it overlaps the flashing and the shingle below it **(photo G).**

Drive one roofing nail through the flashing, at the bottom corner, and into the roof deck **(photo H).** Do not fasten the flashing to the vertical roof element.

Reposition the shingles and counterflashing, and seal all joints with roofing cement.

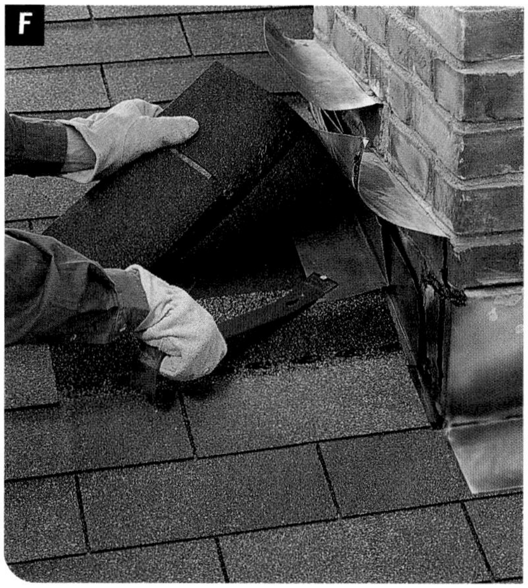

Remove the damaged flashing, using a flat pry bar.

Apply roofing cement, and install the new flashing.

Fasten the flashing to the roof with roofing nails.

Preparing for a New Roof

If your roof has more than one layer of shingles, if the shingles are buckled or cupped, or if the sheathing is buckled, you'll need to remove the old roofing completely. But don't start the project until you've drafted a detailed plan.

Estimate the time your project will require (see chart on the opposite page). Consider the slope of the roof and whether you will need to install roof jacks. The installation and removal of the jacks also takes time. Organizing tasks in a logical sequence and dividing the project into manageable portions that can be completed in a single day saves time and inconvenience. For example, if you plan carefully, you may not need to cover your entire roof every evening.

Measure the square footage of your roof. Shop and compare prices, then make a rough cost estimate for the shingles you select.

Count the number of roof elements, such as vent pipes, vent fans, skylights, dormers, and chimneys, and estimate the amount of flashing needed. If it's necessary to replace the sheathing, include that in your estimate, along with building paper, roofing cement, nails, dumpster rental, and tool purchase or rental. Add 15 percent to your estimate to allow for waste.

Tools: *Aviation snips, broom, caulk gun, flat pry bar, reciprocating saw, release magnet, roofing hammer, roofing shovel, tape measure, trowel.*

Materials: *Exterior-grade plywood, galvanized metal flashing, roofing cement, roofing nails, rubber-gasket nails, scrap wood, screws, vent pipe flashing.*

When working on a roof, wear rubber-soled shoes, knee pads, a nail apron, tool belt, long-sleeved shirt, full-length pants, and work gloves. Wear protective eyewear when working with power tools.

Calculating the Slope of a Roof

Roof slope is defined as the number of inches the roof rises for each 12" of horizontal extension (called the "run"). For example, the roof shown at right has a 5-in-12 slope: it rises 5" in 12" of run. Knowing the slope is important when selecting materials and gauging the difficulty of working on the roof. To ensure safe footing, install temporary roof jacks if the slope is 7-in-12 or steeper. Roofs with a slope of 3-in-12 or less require a fully bonded covering to protect against the effects of pooling water.

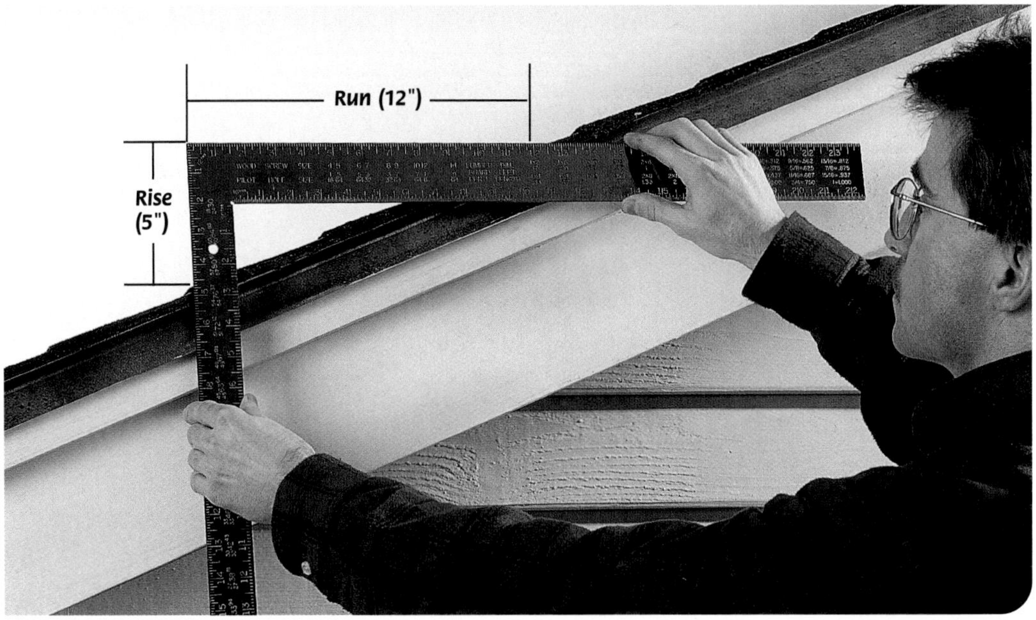

Hold a carpenter's square against the roofline, with the top arm horizontal (check it with a level). Position the square so it intersects the roof at the 12" mark. On the vertical arm, measure down from the top to the point of intersection to find the rise.

Estimating Time Requirements

Task	Time Required ×	Amount =	Total Time
Tear-off	1 hour per square (1 square =100 square feet)		
Install building paper	30 minutes per square		
Apply shingles: Flat run Ridges, hips Dormers	 2 hours per square 30 minutes per 10 feet Add 1 hour each (include area of dormer surface in "flat run" estimate)		
Flashing: Chimneys Vent pipes Valleys Roof vents Skylights Drip edge	 2 hours each 30 minutes each 30 minutes per 10 feet 30 minutes each 2 hours each 30 minutes per 20 feet		
Total Time for Project			

NOTE: All time estimates are based on one worker. Reduce time by 40% if there is a helper.

Installing Roof Jacks

Roof jacks—available at home centers—provide stable footing on a steep slope. When using roof jacks, install the first jack at the fourth or fifth course, driving nails into the overlap, or dead area, where they won't be exposed **(photo A).** Use 16d nails and install one jack every four feet, with a 6" to 12" overhang at the ends. Shingle over the tops of the roof jacks. Then rest a 2 × 8 or 2 × 10 board **(photo B)** on the jacks. Fasten the board with a nail through the hole in the lip of each roof jack. When your project is complete, remove the boards and jacks. Position the end of a flat pry bar over each nail and drive in the nails by rapping the shank with a hammer **(photo C).**

Attach the roof jacks to the roof with 16d nails driven into the dead area, where the nails will not be exposed.

Shingle over the tops of the roof jacks. Rest a 2 x 8 or 2 x 10 on the jacks. Use the widest board the jacks will hold.

Remove the boards and roof jacks and drive in the nails, using a hammer and flat pry bar.

Completing the Tear-off

Removing shingles, commonly referred to in the roofing trade as the *tear-off*, can be done rather quickly. This makes it one of the more satisfying parts of a reshingling project. To work efficiently, have another person deal with the debris on the ground as you work.

If you can't reshingle your entire roof in one day, tear off one section of roofing at a time. Remove the ridge cap with a flat pry bar **(photo A).** Then work downward, tearing off the building paper and old shingles with a roofing shovel or pitchfork **(photo B).** Unless flashing is in exceptional condition, remove it by slicing through the roofing cement that attaches it to the shingles **(photo C).** You may be able to salvage flashing pieces, such as chimney saddles and crickets, and reuse them.

After removing shingles, building paper, and flashing from the entire tear-off section, pry out any remaining nails **(photo D)** and sweep the roof with a broom. At night, cover any unshingled sections using tarps weighted down with shingle bundles **(photo E).**

Remove the ridge cap with a flat pry bar. Then remove the top course of shingles.

Tear off the old shingles and building paper, working from the top down.

Slice through the roofing cement with a flat pry bar. Remove and discard the flashing, unless it is in excellent condition.

Use a roofing shovel or hammer to pull up old nails. On the ground, collect the nails, using a release magnet.

Use tarps weighted down with bundles of shingles to protect unshingled sections overnight.

Dealing with Debris

Roofing produces lots of debris and waste. Taking a few preparatory steps to minimize the amount of work associated with gathering the debris makes cleanup much easier.

First, lay tarps on the ground and lean sheets of plywood against the house to protect shrubbery.

Consider renting a dumpster from a waste disposal company or your local waste management department. If possible, make arrangements for them to haul the debris to a landfill. Then, position the dumpster directly below the roof edge, so the debris can be dumped from the roof.

If it's not practical to rent a dumpster, using wheelbarrows set on tarps is an alternative. However, in the end, you'll be responsible for disposing of the debris, which will probably require several trips to the landfill.

Replacing Sheathing

If you find a soft spot while inspecting your roof after the tear-off, or see a portion of damaged sheathing, it's time to replace it.

Check under the sheathing for wiring. Use a reciprocating saw to cut to the rafters in an area that extends well beyond the damaged area. Pry out the damaged sections **(photo F).**

Attach 2 × 4 nailing strips to the inside edge of the rafters with 3" deck screws **(photo G).**

Use exterior grade plywood to make a patch. Measure the area and cut the patch, allowing for a 1/8" gap on all sides for expansion.

Attach the patch to the rafters and nailing strips, using 2 1/4" decks screws or 8d ring-shank siding nails **(photo H).**

F

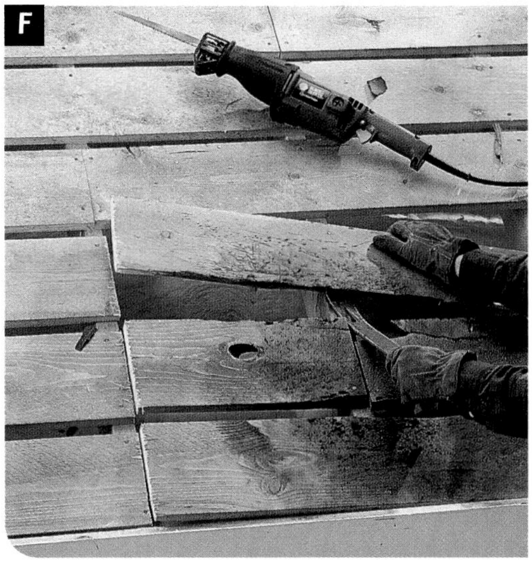

After you've cut out the damaged pieces of sheathing, pry out the pieces.

G

Install 2 × 4 nailing strips to support the sheathing replacement.

H

Attach a patch, 1/8" smaller at every side to allow for expansion, using 2 1/4" deck screws or 8d ring-shank nails.

Installing a New Roof

Installing Building Paper

Building paper is installed on the roof decks as insurance in case leaks develop in shingles or flashing. It is sold in several weights, but 30# paper is a good choice for use under shingles.

In colder climates, Building Codes often require an underlayment called "ice guard" or "ice shield," instead of standard building paper, for the first one or two courses of underlayment. An adhesive membrane, the ice guard bonds with the sheathing to create a barrier to water backing up from ice dams.

Snap a chalk line 35⁵⁄₈" up from the edge of the eaves, so the first course of the 36"-wide membrane will overhang the eaves by ³⁄₈". Install a course of ice guard, using the chalk line as a reference and peeling back the protective backing as you unroll the ice guard **(photo A).** In cold climates, apply as many courses of ice guard as it takes to cover 24" past the roof overhang. In warmer climates, ice guard may not be necessary, so check your local Codes.

Measure up from the eaves' edge to a point 32" above the top of the previous course of underlayment, and snap another chalk line. Roll out the next course of building paper (ice guard, if required), always overlapping the first course by 4". Attach building paper with a hammer stapler, driving a staple every 6" to 12" at the edges and one staple per square foot in the field area **(photo B).** Install building paper up to the ridge—ruled side up—snapping horizontal lines every two or three rows to check alignment. Trim off the courses flush with the rake edge.

Work your way up the roof deck with building paper courses, allowing 4" horizontal overlaps and 12" vertical seams. At valleys, roll building paper across from both sides **(photo C),** overlapping the ends by 36". Overlap hips and ridges by 6".

Tools: *Chalk line, flat pry bar, hammer stapler, roofing knife, tape measure, aviation snips.*

Materials: *30# building paper and/or ice-guard underlayment, drip edge, roofing cement, roofing nails.*

Lay the first course of ice guard or building paper, overhanging the eaves by ³⁄₈".

Fasten with staples every 6" to 12".

Overlap building paper to ensure complete coverage of the roof deck.

Fit building paper patches over obstructions such as vent pipes and roof vents **(photo D).** Apply building paper up to the obstruction. Then resume laying the course on the opposite side (making sure to maintain the line). Cut a patch that overlaps the building paper by 12" on all sides. Make a cross-hatch cutout for the obstruction. Position the patch, staple it in place, then caulk the seams with roofing cement.

At the bottom of dormers and sidewalls, tuck the building paper under the siding **(photo E),** where it intersects with the roof. Also tuck it under counterflashing on chimneys and skylights. Carefully pry up the siding and tuck at least 2" of paper under the siding. Leave the siding or counterflashing unfastened until after you install the step flashing.

Attach the drip edge flashing along the rake edges (below).

Run the building paper up to the edge of any obstructions. Then fit patches over them. Caulk all seams with roofing cement.

Tuck at least 2" of building paper under the siding at the bottom of dormers and sidewalls.

Installing Drip Edge

Drip edge flashing on the eaves is installed *before* the building paper is attached, while drip edge flashing at the rake edges is installed *after* building paper has been attached.

To install drip edge flashing at the eaves, nail a strip of drip edge along the edge of the eaves **(photo F).** Overlap strips by 2" at vertical seams, and nail at 12" intervals. Miter the ends at a 45° angle to make a miter joint with the drip edge on the rake edge. Use galvanized roofing nails to install galvanized or vinyl drip edge; use aluminum nails for aluminum drip edge. Nail at 12" intervals.

To install drip edge flashing at the rakes, start at the bottom, forming a miter joint with the drip edge at the eaves. Work toward the ridge, overlapping pieces of drip edge by 2". Make sure the higher strip is on top at the overlaps **(photo G).**

Drip edge flashing on the eaves is installed before the building paper is attached. Attach a strip of drip edge flashing along the edge of the eaves, nailing it at 12" intervals.

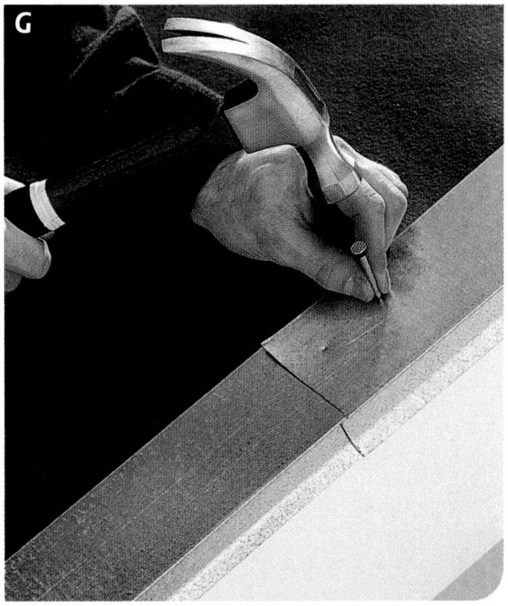

Drip edge flashing at the rake edges is installed after building paper has been attached. Overlap pieces of drip edge flashing on the rake edges by 2".

Installing Flashing

Flashing is a metal or rubber barrier used to protect the seams around roof elements or between adjoining roof surfaces.

Around roof elements, such as chimneys and vent pipes, flashing should be secured to one surface only—usually the roof deck. Use only roofing cement to bond the flashing to the roof elements. Flashing must be able to flex as the roof element and roof deck expand and contract. If the flashing is fastened to both the roof deck and the roof element, it will tear or loosen.

To bend the flashing, first make a bending jig by driving screws into a piece of scrap wood, creating a space one-half the width of the flashing when measured from the edge of the board. Clamp the bending jig to a work-surface. Lay a piece of flashing flat on the board, and bend it over the edge **(photo A).**

Use old flashing as a template for making replacement pieces **(photo B).** This is especially useful for reproducing complicated flashing, such as saddle flashing for chimneys or dormers.

If your roof originally had a cricket to divert water around the chimney, have a metalworker make a new one. Provide the fabricator with either the old cricket to use as a template, or the roof slope and chimney width to use as a guide.

Metal Valley Flashing: Start at the eaves. Set a piece of valley flashing into the valley, so the bottom of the "V" rests in the crease of the valley **(photo C).** Nail the flashing at 12" intervals along each side. Trim the end of the flashing at the eaves so it's flush with the drip edges at each side.

Working toward to the top, add flashing pieces, overlapping each at least 8", until you reach the ridge. Let the top piece of the flashing extend a few inches beyond the ridge **(photo D).** Bend the flashing over the ridge, so it lies flat on the opposite side of the roof. If you're installing preformed flashing, make a small cut in the spine for easier bending. Cover nail heads with roofing cement (unless you're using rubber-gasket nails). Also apply roofing cement along the side edges of the flashing.

Step Flashing: Shingle up to the element that requires flashing so the tops of the reveal areas are within 5" of the element. Install base flashing, using the old base flashing as a template. Bend a piece of step flashing in half and set it next to the lowest corner of the element. Mark a trim line on the flashing, following the vertical edge of the element. Cut and remove the "waste" flashing **(photo E).**

Pry out the lower courses of siding and any trim at the base of the element. Insert spacers to prop the trim or siding away from the work area. Apply roofing cement to the base flashing in the area where the overlap with the step

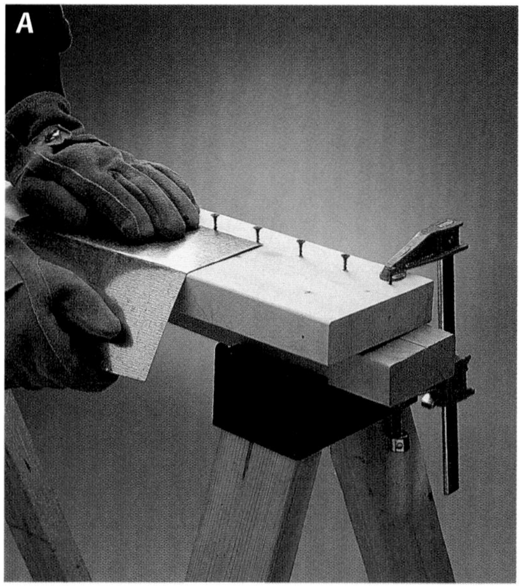

Make a bending jig with screws lined up along a piece of scrap wood. Then bend your own flashing.

Tools: *Aviation snips, caulk gun, flat bar, roofing hammer, tape measure, trowel.*

Materials: *Galvanized metal flashing, roofing cement, roofing nails, rubber-gasket nails, scrap wood, screws, vent pipe flashing.*

Use old flashing as a template for making replacement flashing, especially for complicated pieces.

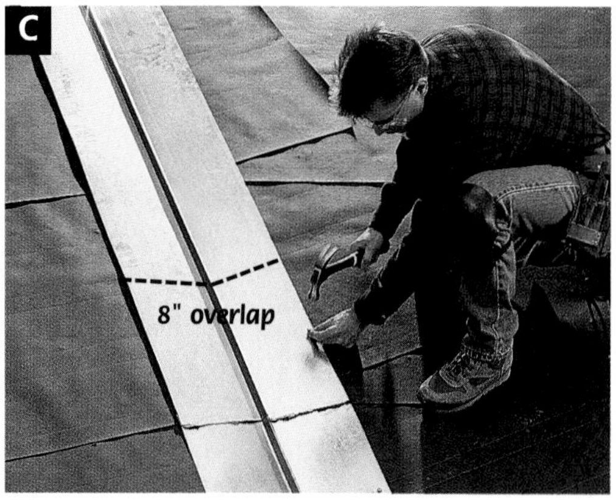

Starting at the eaves, nail the flashing along each side at 12" intervals. Add pieces, overlapping by at least 8", and work up toward the ridge.

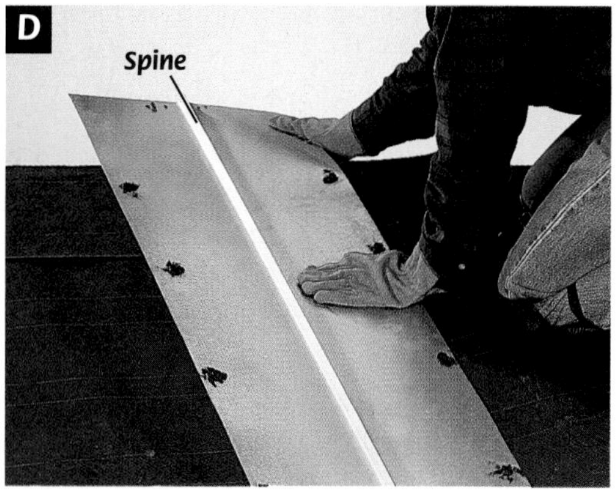

Continue adding overlapping pieces until the flashing reaches a few inches past the ridge. Bend the flashing over the ridge so it lies flat on the opposite side of the roof.

flashing will be formed. Tuck the trimmed piece of step flashing under the propped area, and secure the flashing **(photo F).** Fasten the flashing with one rubber-gasket nail driven near the top, and into the roof deck.

Apply roofing cement to the top side of the first piece of step flashing, where it will be covered by the next shingle course. Install the shingle by pressing it firmly into the roofing cement **(photo G).** Don't nail through the flashing underneath. Tuck another piece of flashing under the trim or siding, overlapping the first piece of step flashing by at least 2". Set the flashing into roofing cement applied on the top of the shingle. Then nail the shingle in place, taking care not to drive nails through the flashing **(photo H).** Continue installing flashing in this manner up to the top of the element. Trim the last piece of the flashing to fit the top corner of the element. Reattach the siding and trim.

Chimney Flashing: Shingle up to the chimney base. Use the old base flashing as a template to cut new flashing. Bend up the counterflashing (pieces anchored in the chimney to cover the step flashing). Apply roofing cement to the base of the chimney and the shingles just below the base. Press the base flashing into the roofing cement and bend the flashing around the edges of the chimney **(photo I).** Drive rubber-gasket nails through the flashing flange into the roof deck.

Install step flashing and shingles, working up the top of the chimney. Fasten flashing to the chimney with roofing cement. Fold down the counterflashing as you go.

Cut and install top flashing (sometimes called a saddle) around the high side of the chimney, overlapping the final piece of flashing along each side, just as the base flashing was installed **(photo J).** Attach the flashing with roofing cement applied to the deck and the chimney, and with rubber-gasket nails driven through the base of the flashing and into the roof deck. Continue shingling past the chimney, using roofing cement (not nails) to attach shingles over the flashing.

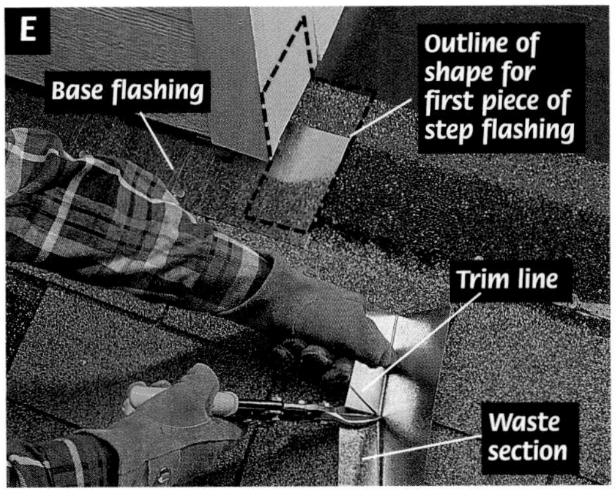

Bend the step flashing in half, set it in place, and trim off the waste, making a starter cut first.

Secure the flashing by pressing it into the roofing cement.

Install the shingle, setting it firmly into the roofing cement.

Secure the flashing to the shingle with roofing cement. Then fasten the shingle in place with nails.

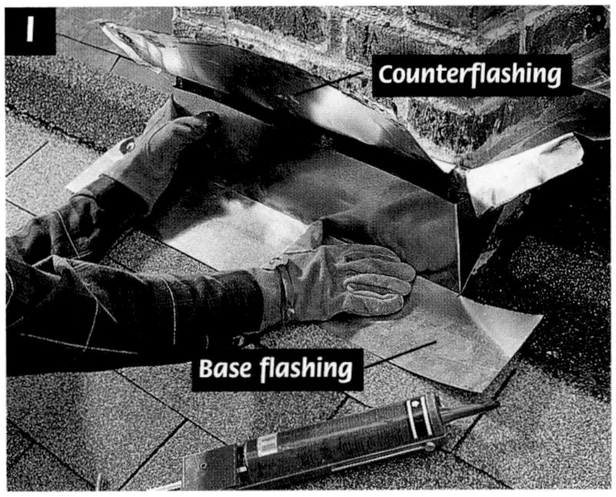

Bend the counterflashing up and slide the base flashing underneath.

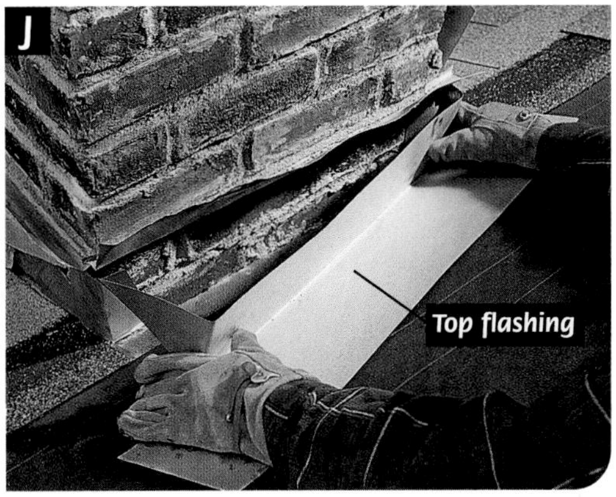

Install top flashing, overlapping the step flashing on the sides, using both roofing cement and rubber-gasket nails.

Shingling

Snap a chalk line onto the first course of building paper or ice guard, 11$\frac{1}{2}$" up from the eaves' edge, to mark the alignment of the starter course **(photo A).** This will result in a $\frac{1}{2}$" shingle overhang for standard 12" shingles. To install the starter row, trim off one-half (6") of an end tab on one shingle. Position the shingle upside down, so the tabs are aligned with the chalk line and the half-tab is flush against the rake edge. Drive $\frac{7}{8}$" roofing nails near each end, about 1" down from each slot between tabs. Butt a full shingle next to the trimmed shingle and nail it. Fill out the row, trimming the last shingle flush with the opposite rake edge **(photo B).**

Apply the first full course of shingles over the starter course, with the tabs pointing down. Begin at the rake edge where you began the starter row. Place the first shingle so it overhangs the rake edge by $\frac{3}{8}$" and the eaves' edge by $\frac{1}{2}$". Make sure the tops of the shingles are flush with the tops of the shingles in the starter course, following the chalk line **(photo C).**

Snap a chalk line from the eaves' edge to the ridge to create a vertical line to align the shingles. Choose an area with no obstructions, as close as possible to the center of the roof. The chalk line should pass through a slot or a shingle edge on the first full shingle course. Use a carpenter's square to establish a line perpendicular to the eaves' edge **(photo D).**

Use the vertical line to establish a shingle pattern with slots that are offset by 6" in succeeding courses. Tack down a shingle 6" to one side of the vertical line to start the second course. The bottom of the shingle should be 5" above the bottoms of the first-course shingles. Tack down shingles for the third and fourth courses, 12" and 18" away from the vertical line. Start the fifth course against the vertical line **(photo E).**

Fill in shingles in the second through fifth courses, working upward from the second course and maintaining a consistent 5" reveal. Slide lower-course shingles under any upper-

To mark the alignment of the starter course, snap a chalk line 11$\frac{1}{2}$" up from the edge of the eaves.

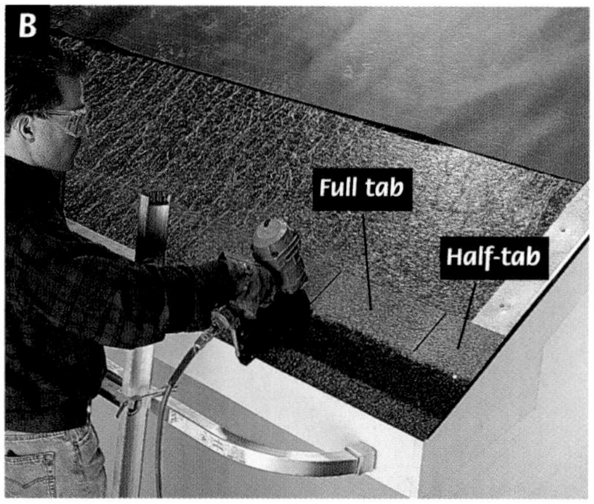

Position the starter course of shingles so the tabs are aligned with the chalk line and the half-tab is even with rake edge.

Tools: *Aviation snips, carpenter's square, chalk line, flat bar, roof jacks, 2 × 10 lumber, roofing hammer, roofing knife, straightedge, tape measure.*

Materials: *Flashing, shingles, nailing cartridges, roofing cement, roofing nails.*

Apply first course over starter course, tabs pointing down.

Snap chalk line from eaves' edge to ridge, near center of roof.

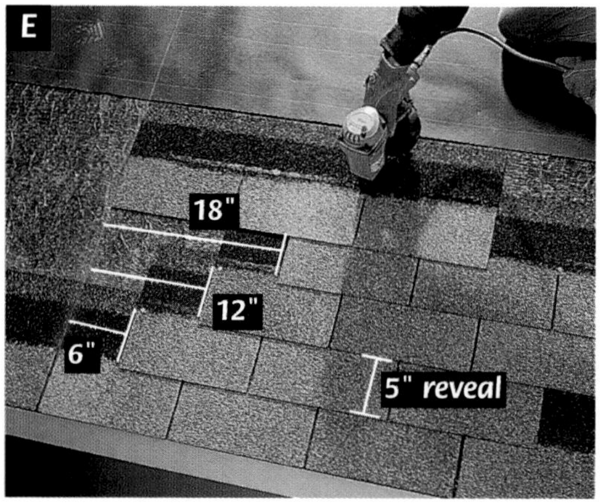

Use the line to make a shingle pattern offsetting slots by 6".

course shingles left partially nailed, and then nail them down **(photo F).** NOTE: Install roof jacks, if needed, after filling out the fifth course.

Check the alignment of your shingles after each 4-course cycle. In several spots on the top course, measure from the bottom edges of the shingles to the nearest building-paper line. If you discover any misalignment, distribute adjustments over the next few rows until it's corrected.

When you reach obstructions, like dormers, shingle a full course above them so you can retain your shingle offset pattern. On the unshingled side of the obstruction, snap another vertical reference line, using the shingles above the obstruction as a guide **(photo G).** Shingle upward from the eaves on this side of the obstruction, using a vertical line as a reference for re-establishing your shingle slot offset pattern **(photo H).** Fill out the shingle courses past the rake edges of the roof, then trim off the excess.

Trim off some of the excess shingle material at the Vs in valley flashing wherever two roof decks join **(photo I).** These edges will be trimmed back farther at a slight taper after both roof decks are shingled. Don't cut into flashing. Install shingles on adjoining roof decks, starting at the bottom edge, using the same offset alignment pattern used on the other roof decks. Install shingles until courses overlap the center of the valley flashing at the joint between roof decks **(photo J).** Trim shingles at both sides of the valley when finished.

When you reach a hip (any peak where two sections of roof meet) or the ridge (the hip at the top of your roof), shingle up the first roof side until the tops of the uppermost reveal areas are within 5" of the hip or ridge. Trim the excess off along the joint at the peak. Overlap the ridge or hip by no more than 5", with the top shingle course on the other side of the peak **(photo K).**

Cut three 12"-square ridge/hip caps from each 3-tab shingle. With the back surface facing up, cut the shingles at the tab lines **(photo L).** Trim the top corners of each square

Continued on next page

F — *As you work upward, leave upper-course shingles partially nailed so you can slide lower-course shingles under them.*

G — *Shingle a full course above obstructions to retain your offset pattern. Then snap a vertical chalk line as a reference.*

H — *Shingle upward on the other side and fill out the shingle courses past the rake edges of the roof, trimming off excess.*

I — *Trim excess material at the dormer valleys.*

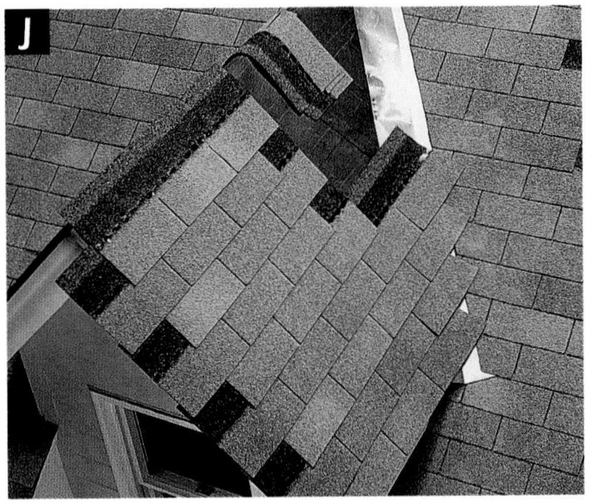

J — *Shingle the decks of the dormer, overlapping the valleys.*

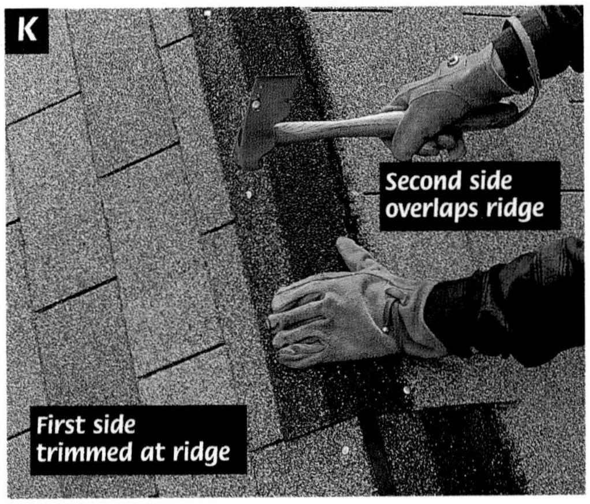

K — *At hips, overlap the shingles from one side.*

Shingling (cont.)

with an angled cut, starting just below the seal strip to avoid overlaps in the reveal area.

Snap a chalk line 6" down from the ridge on one side, parallel to the peak. Begin by attaching cap shingles at one end, aligned with the chalk line. Drive two 1¼" roofing nails per cap, about 1" from each edge, just below the seal strip **(photo M).**

Following the chalk lines, install cap shingles halfway along the ridge, creating a 5" reveal for each cap. Then, starting at the opposite end, install caps over the other half of the ridge to meet the first run in the center.

Cut a 5"-wide section from the reveal area of a shingle tab, and use it as a "closure cap" to cover the joint where the caps meet **(photo N).**

Shingle the hips in the same manner, using a chalk reference line and cap shingles. Start at the bottom of each hip and work to the peak. Where hips join with roof ridges, install a custom shingle cut from the center of a cap shingle. Set the cap at the end of the ridge, and bend the corners so they fit over the hips **(photo O).** Secure each corner with a roofing nail, and cover nail heads with roofing cement.

After all of the shingles are installed, trim them at the valleys to create a gap 3" wide at the ridge that widens at a rate of ⅛" per foot as it moves downward. Use a roofing knife and a straightedge to cut the shingles, and make sure you don't cut through the valley flashing.

At the valleys, seal the undersides and edges of the shingles with roofing cement **(photo P).** Cover exposed nail heads with roofing cement as well.

Mark and trim the shingles at the rake edges of the roof **(photo Q).** Snap a chalk line ⅜" from the edge to make an overhang, then trim the shingles.

Cut three 12"-square ridge/hip caps from each 3-tab shingle. Trim off both top corners.

Snap a chalk line 6" from the hip on one side of hip or ridge and attach cap shingles with two 1¼" roofing nails per cap.

Use a 5"-wide section from the reveal area of a shingle tab as a "closure cap."

Where roof hips join roof ridges, shingle the top of each hip.

Seal the undersides and edges of shingles with roofing cement.

Trim the shingles at the rake edges with a roofing knife.

Shingling Over an Old Roof

NOTE: Read the selection on shingling a roof (pages 204 to 206) before you start.

Cut tabs off shingles and install the remaining strips over the reveal area of the old first course, creating a flat surface for the starter row of new shingles **(photo R).** Use 1$^1/_4$" roofing nails.

Trim the tops of the shingles for the first course. The shingles should be sized to butt against the bottom edges of the old third course, overhanging the roof edge by $^1/_2$". Install shingles so the tab slots don't align with the slots in the old shingles **(photo S).**

Using the old shingles to direct your layout, begin installing the new shingles **(photo T).** Maintain a consistent tab/slot offset (page 204). Shingle up toward the roof ridge, stopping before the final course. Install flashing as you proceed.

Valley flashing that is in good condition does not have to be replaced. However, replace any old flashing as you go. A roof-over is flashed using the same techniques and materials for shingling over building paper, except that you need to trim or fill in shingles around vent pipes and roof vents to create a flat surface for the base flange of the flashing pieces **(photo U).**

Tear off old hip and ridge caps before shingling these areas. Replace after all other shingling has been completed **(photo V).**

Cut tabs off shingles and install strips over reveal area of old course to make a flat surface for the starter row.

Trim the tops off shingles for the first course. Size them to butt against bottom edges of old first course and overhang the roof edge by ½".

Helpful Hint

Most building centers will deliver shingles, building paper, and other materials directly to your roof with a mechanical lift. Try to have at least one section of the old roof torn off, with new building paper and drip edge installed, before the delivery. This will save you time and energy.

Use old shingles to direct your layout. Maintain consistent tab/slot offset.

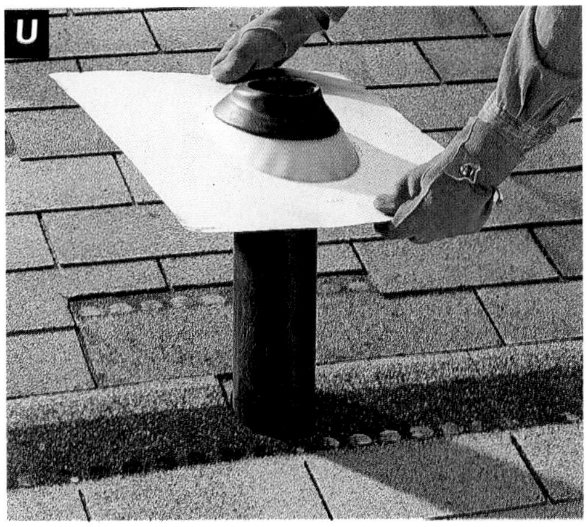

Shingles around roof vents and vent pipes must be cut out to create a flat surface for the base flange of the new flashing pieces.

Tear off hip and ridge caps and replace them after all other shingling is completed.

Fascia & Soffits

Fascia and soffits add a finished look to your roof and promote a healthy roof system. A well-ventilated fascia/soffit system prevents moisture from building up under the roof and in the attic. A secure system keeps pests, like birds and bats, from nesting in the eaves.

Usually fashioned from dimensional lumber, fascia is attached to rafters or rafter lookouts. While enhancing the appearance of your home, fascia also provides a stable surface for hanging gutters.

Most fascia and soffit problems can be corrected by cutting out sections of damaged material and replacing them. Joints between fascia boards are lock-nailed at rafter locations, so you should remove whole sections of fascia to make accurate bevel cuts for patches. Soffits can often be left in place and usually are not removed for repairs.

To ensure better results with soffit and fascia projects, check to see that the rafters, headers, and exterior walls underneath the new or repaired materials are sound and clean.

Tools: *Ladder, circular saw, jig saw, drill, putty knife, hammer, flat pry bar, chisel, nail set, caulk gun.*

Materials: *Replacement materials to match damaged parts, nailing strips, 2" galvanized screws, 4d galvanized casing nails, galvanized common nails, acrylic caulk, primer, paint.*

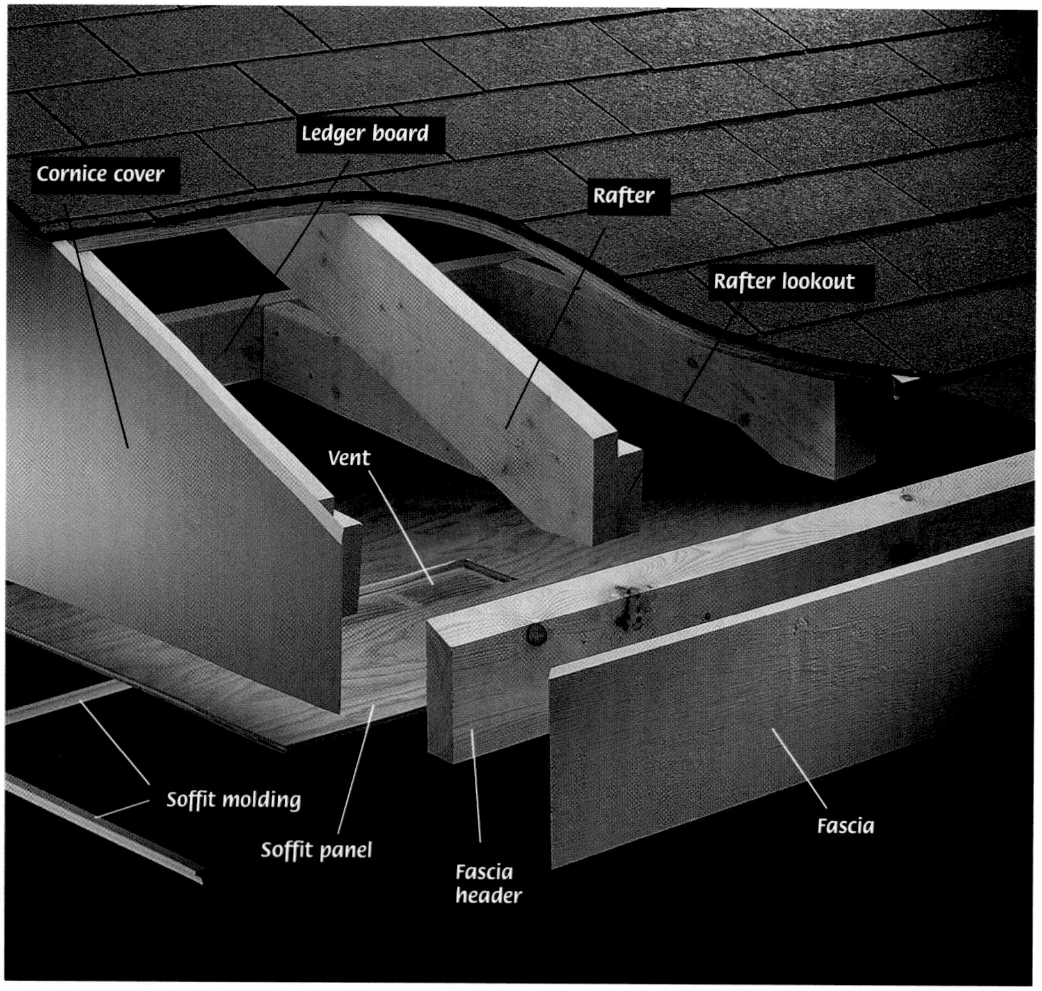

Fascia and soffits close off the eaves area beneath the roof overhang. The fascia covers the ends of rafters and rafter lookouts and provides a surface for attaching gutters. Soffits are protective panels that span the area between the fascia and the side of the house. Some soffit types attach to fascia headers (above), while others fit into grooves cut in the back sides of the fascia. Soffit moldings and ledger boards are used to mount the soffit panels at the side of the house.

Inspecting Soffits

Whenever you begin repairing soffits, take a moment to inspect the vents in the system to make sure they provide sufficient air flow. There should be one square foot of soffit venting for each 150 square feet of unheated attic space.

If your old soffit system has failed, or if pests have infested the open eaves area beneath your roof overhang, consider installing a new soffit system (page 212). A complete soffit system consists of fabricated fascia panels, soffit panels (nonventilated or ventilated), and support channels that hold the panels along the sides of your house.

Most soffit systems sold at building centers are made of aluminum or vinyl. Follow the manufacturer's instructions for installation.

Fascia and soffit materials can be fastened with ring-shank siding nails, or with galvanized deck screws. Nails are easier to work with in some cases, but screws provide more holding power.

Repairing Wood Fascia

Inspect the fascia boards for damage. When you have identified which fascia boards need repair, remove any other items mounted on those boards, such as gutters or shingle moldings **(photo A).** This is also a good time to inspect your gutters to make sure they're in good working condition.

With a flat pry bar, carefully pry off any damaged fascia boards **(photo B).** Remove the entire board and all the old nails.

Find the nail holes on a good section of the fascia board to mark the board for cutting. The nail holes show where the fascia board attaches to a rafter; making the cut here allows you to fasten both the remaining board and the new board securely.

Set your circular saw for a 45° bevel, and saw the old fascia board at a rafter location **(photo C).** Make sure to cut away all damaged wood.

Reattach the original fascia board to the rafters and rafter lookouts, using 2" galvanized deck screws **(photo D).** The screws can be driven in the original nails holes for convenience, or in new holes for greater strength.

With the circular saw still set for a bevel cut, saw a new fascia board long enough to replace the damaged section. When you measure the board, include the angle of the miter cut so that the new board will fit correctly at both ends.

At the rafter where the old and new boards meet, drill pilot holes through both boards and into the rafter. Drive nails into the pilot holes **(photo E).** The nails should pass through the angled ends of both boards and the rafter to create a lock-nail joint.

Replace the shingle moldings and other trim pieces, using 4d galvanized casing nails **(photo F).** Set the nail heads.

Prime and paint the new board to match the original fascia. Reattach the gutter hangers, gutters, and any other trim.

Remove gutters, shingle moldings, and any other material that prevents removal of the damaged section of fascia.

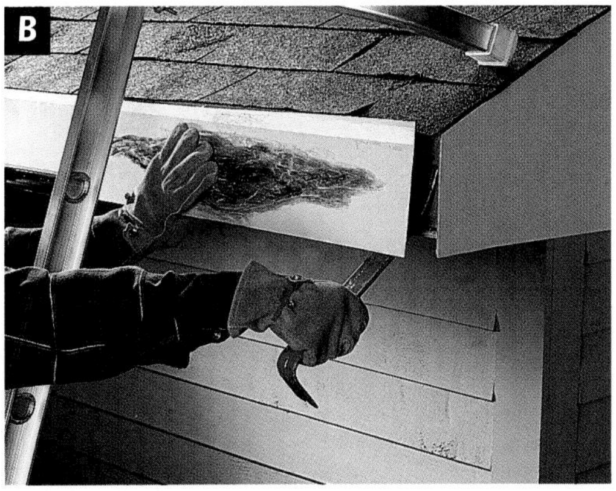

Using a flat pry bar, remove the entire damaged section all the way to the next fascia board. Remove old nails.

Cut off the damaged portion of the fascia board. Bevel-cut at a rafter location (look for nail holes).

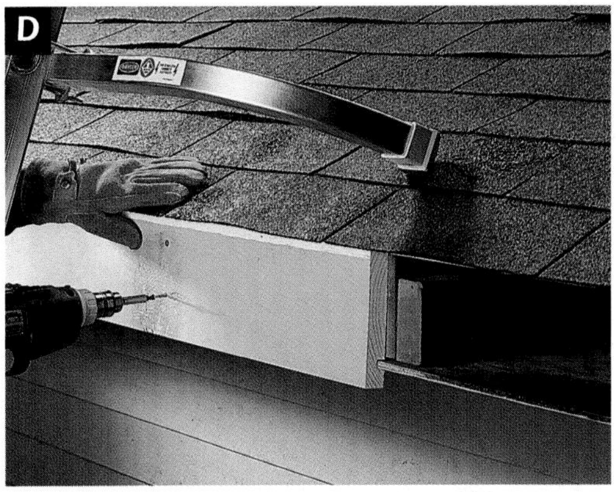

Attach the undamaged original fascia to rafter lookouts or rafters. Bevel-cut a patch board to replace the damaged one.

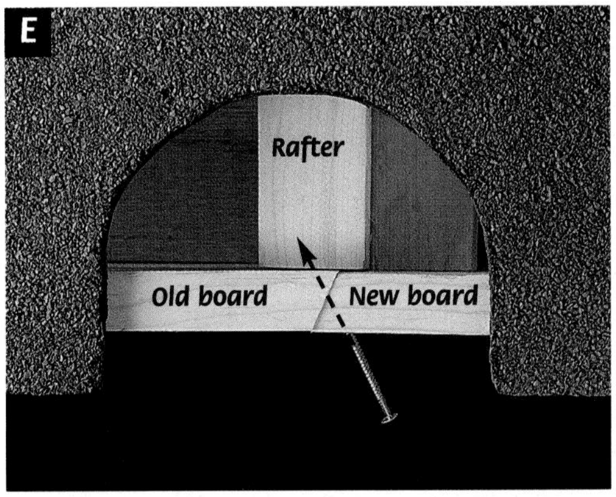

Attach the patch board. Drill pilot holes, and drive nails at an angle through both beveled ends, for a lock-nail joint.

Reattach shingle moldings and trim with 4d galvanized casing nails. Set nail heads. Prime and paint. Reattach gutters.

Repairing Wood-panel Soffits

In the area where soffits are damaged, remove the moldings that hold the soffits in place along the fascia and exterior wall. Set them aside. Drill entry holes, then use a jig saw to cut out the damaged soffit area **(photo A).** Saw as close as you can to the location where the soffit meets the rafters and rafter lookouts. Finish the cuts with a wood chisel, if necessary.

Remove the damaged soffit panels. If they're hard to remove, carefully work them loose with a flat bar **(photo B).** Cut nailing strips to the same length as the exposed area of the rafters. Fasten the nailing strips to the rafters or rafter lookouts at the edges of the opening, so that the replacement soffit panels can be nailed to the strips.

Using soffit material similar to the original panel, make a replacement piece to fit the opening **(photo C).** To allow for expansion, cut it 1/8" smaller than the opening. If the new panel will be vented, cut vent openings.

If you will be painting all the soffits after the repair, you can leave the replacement panels unfinished for now. However, if only the replacement panels need to be primed and painted, do this before mounting the panels.

Holding the replacement soffit panel in place, attach it to the nailing strips or rafter lookouts with 2" galvanized deck screws **(photo D).**

Once the new soffit panel is securely in place, reattach the soffit molding, using 4d galvanized casing nails **(photo E).**

Using siliconized acrylic caulk, fill all remaining nail holes, screw holes, and gaps **(photo F).** Smooth out the caulk with a putty knife or other flat tool until the caulk is even with the surface. If necessary, prime and paint the soffit panels and reinstall the vent covers.

Cut out the damaged soffit, using a jig saw. Saw as close as possible to the rafter or lookout locations.

Remove the damaged section. Cut nailing strips and attach them to the rafters or rafter lookouts.

Cut a soffit patch to fit. Allow 1/8" on all sides for expansion gaps. Make cutouts for soffit vents, if necessary.

Install the soffit patch by driving galvanized deck screws into the nailing strips or rafter lookouts.

Reattach the soffit molding, using 4d galvanized casing nails. Set the nail heads.

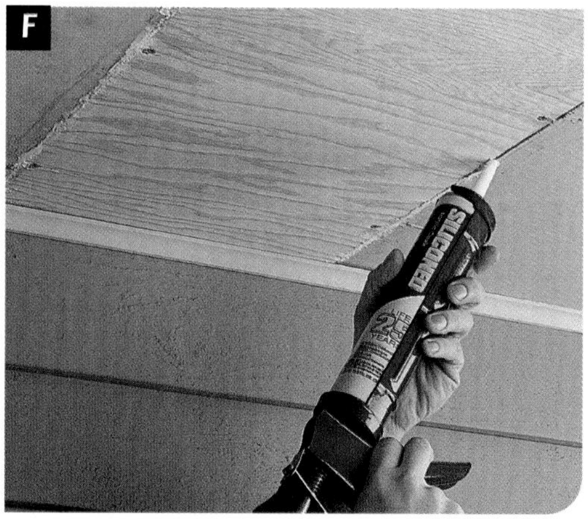

Fill holes and gaps with caulk. Smooth the caulk, then prime and paint the patch. Install vent covers, if needed.

Repairing Tongue-and-groove Soffits

Remove the soffit molding from the area where the soffit is damaged. Find the closest rafter lookout on each side of the damaged area, and drill entry holes for a jig saw near the rafter lookouts.

Using a jig saw, cut out the damaged section, sawing as close as possible to the rafter lookouts. Remove the damaged section **(photo G).**

To remove tongue-and-groove soffits running from the exterior wall to the fascia boards, cut across the ends of boards near the fascia.

Cut 2 × 2 nailing strips to the same length as the exposed area of the rafter lookouts. Using 2" galvanized deck screws, fasten the nailing strips flush with the rafter lookouts at the edges of the opening **(photo H).** These strips provide a surface to which the soffit boards can be nailed.

Using tongue-and-groove stock that matches the original soffits, cut boards to fit the opening. Drill pilot holes through the tongues of the replacement boards where they will meet the nailing strips.

Drive 8d galvanized casing nails through the pilot holes and into the nailing strips **(photo I).** Set the nail heads so that the groove of the next patch board will fit cleanly over the tongue of the first one. Fasten all the replacement boards except the last one.

Trim the top lip from the grooved edge of the last board to be installed. This lets you fit the board in place without breaking the tongue-and-groove pattern.

Position the tongue of the final replacement board in the opening, and slide it into place **(photo J).**

Using 4d casing nails, face-nail the last board to the nailing strips. Prime and paint the replacement boards to match the original soffits. Attach soffit vent covers, if needed.

Cut out the damaged section, cutting as close as possible to the lookout.

Fasten a nailing strip to the rafter lookout at each end of the opening.

Cut patch boards to fit. Nail the boards in place, then set the nails.

Position and nail the final board in place, driving 4d casing nails into the nailing strips.

Installing a New Soffit System

Hidden behind gutters, older soffits and fascia may be weathered or rotted, or may not give adequate air flow. If more than 15 percent of your soffit and fascia boards need repair, your best option is to replace them.

Complete soffit system kits in aluminum or vinyl are available at most building supply centers. Use the guidelines on these pages for installation, and always follow the manufacturer's instructions to get the best results.

Aluminum or vinyl soffit and fascia boards don't need painting, and aren't as vulnerable to harsh weather conditions as wooden boards. They must be attached to clean, smooth surfaces, so be sure that your rafters, frieze boards, and nailing headers (sometimes called subfascia) are in good condition. They provide support for the mounting channels that will hold your new soffit system.

Vinyl and aluminum soffits, fascia, and mounting channels have precut nail slots; to allow the materials to flex as the weather changes, nail in the center of these slots, and leave a small gap under the nail heads so that the materials can move slightly. Don't drive the nails all the way in.

Use vented soffit panels to complement roof or gable vents; this improves air flow underneath the roof, which prevents moisture damage and ice dams. Plan to provide one square foot each of soffit vents for every 150 square feet of unheated attic space. For a consistent appearance, make sure all the fins on the soffit vents are pointed in the same direction.

Most soffit panels cover a span of 16"; if the span of your eaves is more than 16", or if your house is subject to high winds, install nailing strips between the outside wall and the fascia to provide stronger support for the soffits.

Be sure your ladder is secure at both ends. If you plan to work in high places for a long period, use scaffolding instead of ladders. Avoid carrying heavy loads while climbing; use a rope to lift heavy materials once you're safely in place.

Tie back and cover any shrubs and small trees that are close to the foundation; this will protect the plants and give you more room to work.

When cutting vinyl materials with a power saw, use a fine-tooth blade, and mount the blade so the teeth are reversed for smoother cuts; move the saw slowly. If you use a utility knife to cut vinyl, score the cut line and bend the vinyl back and forth until it snaps apart. Aviation snips are best for cutting aluminum.

Before you can install fascia and soffit boards, you will need to remove any gutters, gutter supports, shingle molding, and other trim from the eaves **(photo A).** Next, remove the old soffits and fascia. If the eaves contain debris, such as bird nests or rotted wood, this is a good time to clean them out.

Check the rafters, rafter lookouts, and fascia headers for decay or damage **(photo B).** Repair or replace them as needed.

At the tops of the fascia headers, install a drip edge or shingle molding **(photo C).** Leave a small space, about 1/16", under the shingle molding or drip edge. The fascia boards will slide underneath, to help keep moisture out of the eaves.

Measure from the outside wall of the house to the nailing header at several points. The distance should be the same. If necessary, place shims on the backs of the nailing headers to keep the spaces equal.

Install mounting channels for the soffit panels along the back of the nailing headers and

Tools: *Ladder or scaffolding, flat pry bar, hammer, circular saw with fine-tooth blade, fine-tooth hand saw (for vinyl) or hacksaw (for aluminum), drill, screwdriver, tape measure, aviation snips or utility knife.*

Materials: *Drip edge, mounting channels, soffit panels and fascia boards, galvanized nails (for vinyl) or aluminum nails (for aluminum), nailing strips (if needed).*

Remove gutters, gutter supports, and shingle molding at top of fascia. Remove existing soffit and fascia boards.

Inspect the rafters and rafter headers.

along the outside wall of the house **(photo D).** Follow the manufacturer's instructions.

If the soffit panels must span more than 16", or your house is often subjected to high winds, add nailing strips to provide additional support **(photo E).**

Slide the soffit panels in place. Some panels fit in mounting channels on both sides; others must be nailed to the bottoms of the nailing headers **(photo F).** Also nail the soffit panels to nailing strips, if you've installed them.

Install corner soffit panels and boxed gable returns, following the manufacturer's directions **(photo G).** Fit soffit panels in remaining spaces, cutting them as needed.

Tack the fascia boards to the fascia headers, starting at the center of each fascia board **(photo H).** Align the fascia boards at the corners, then nail them securely. Reinstall the gutter supports, gutters, and downspouts.

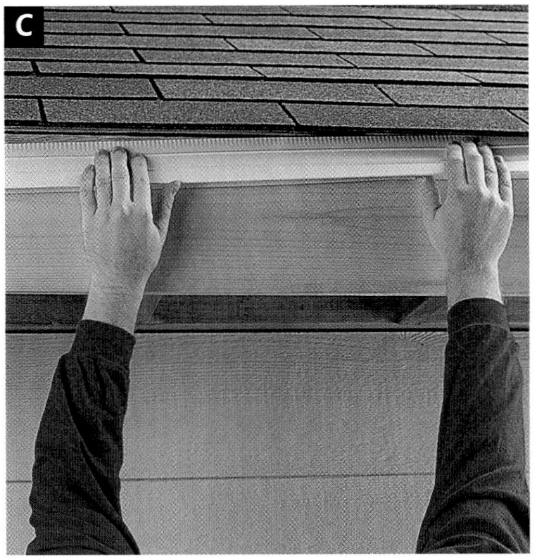

Install a drip edge or shingle molding at the tops of the fascia headers. Leave enough space for the fascia boards.

Install mounting channels along the bottom edges of the fascia headers, and along the outside wall of the house.

Install nailing strips, if needed, to provide additional support.

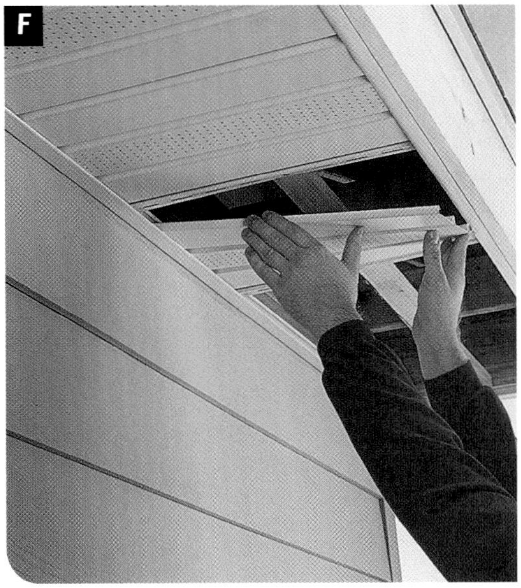

Slide the soffit panels in place, and attach them to the mounting channels.

Fasten the corner soffit panels and boxed gable returns in position.

Tack the fascia boards to the fascia headers. Align them at the corners, then nail them securely.

Gutters

Gutters perform an important task—channeling water away from your home. A good gutter system prevents damage to your siding, foundation, and landscaping, and helps prevent water buildup in your basement.

When gutters fail, you need to evaluate the type and extent of the damage in order to select the best repair method. For metal gutters, you can seal minor leaks with caulk, and patch moderate damage with flashing and roofing cement. For wood gutters, you can fill small holes or rot with epoxy wood filler.

Cleaning Gutters

Keep gutters and downspouts clean so that rain falling on the roof is directed well away from the foundation. Ninety-five percent of all wet basement problems occur because water collects near the foundation, a situation that frequently can be traced to clogged and overflowing gutters and downspouts.

Watch for signs that your gutters or downspouts may be clogged, and clean them as often as necessary to keep the system working efficiently. Use a trowel to remove leaves, twigs, and other debris **(photo A).**

Flush out clogged downspouts with water pressure **(photo B).** Wrap a large rag around a garden hose and insert it in the opening of the downspout. Arrange the rag so it fills the opening of the downspout, containing the water and concentrating its pressure against the clog. Turn on the water full force. When the clog breaks up, water will gush out the bottom of the downspout.

Check the slope of gutters with a level **(photo C),** and adjust hangers, if necessary. Gutters should angle toward the downspouts (page 215) so water travels freely rather than standing in the gutters, promoting rust.

Shield gutters with mesh gutter guards **(photo D)** that match the size and style of your gutters. This will prevent clogs in the future.

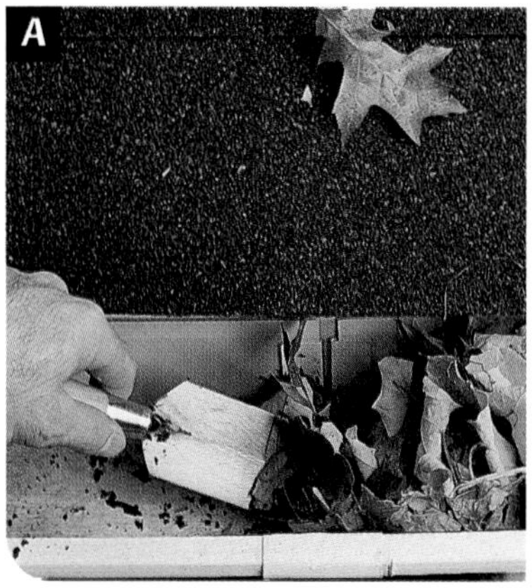

A

Use a trowel to clean leaves, twigs, and other debris out of gutters.

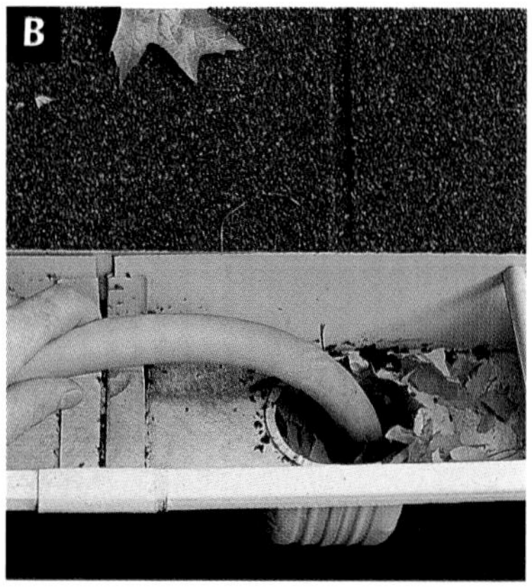

B

Flush debris through the downspout by inserting a hose and turning on the water.

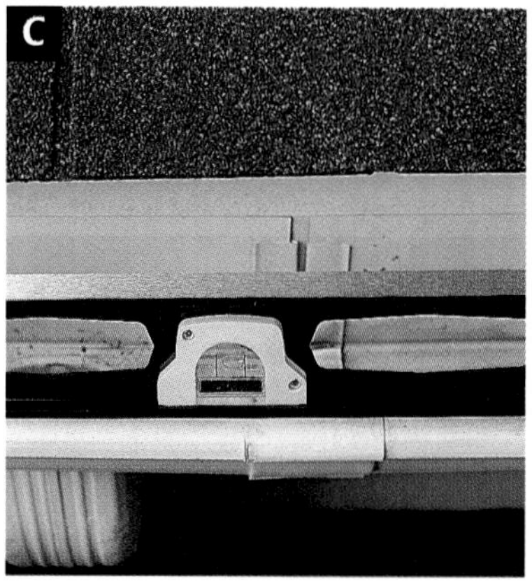

C

Check the slope of your gutters. They should angle slightly toward the downspouts.

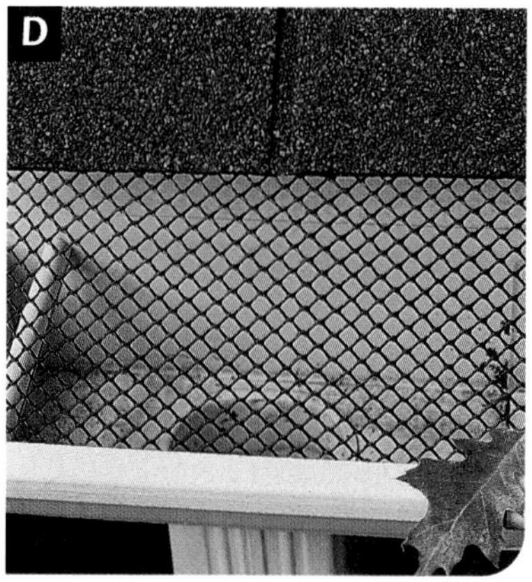

D

Install gutter guards to prevent buildup of debris and clogs in the downspouts.

Rehanging Sagging Gutters & Patching Leaks

Rehanging sagging gutters **(photo E)** is a common gutter repair. Begin by snapping a chalk line that follows the correct slope (usually about $1/4$" per 10 ft. toward the downspouts). Remove the hangers in and near the sag, and lift the gutter until it's flush with the chalk line. Reattach the hangers, replacing them if they're rusty or in poor condition. Shift their location slightly to avoid using the original nail holes. Add hangers, if necessary, to place one at least every 2 ft., and within 12" of every seam.

Now, evaluate the type and extent of gutter damage to select the appropriate repair method. Small leaks and minor damage often can be repaired with easy-to-use gutter repair products. Use gutter caulk to fill small holes and seal minor leaks **(photo F).** Usually made with a butyl-rubber base, gutter caulk is resistant to the elements and flexes without losing its seal.

Use a gutter patching kit to make temporary repairs to gutters with minor damage **(photo G).** Read the manufacturer's recommendations and directions before purchasing and using repair products. For permanent patching methods, see page 216.

Tools: *Utility knife, stiff-bristled or wire brush, steel wool, aviation snips, screwdriver, pry bar, hammer, portable drill, hacksaw, caulk gun.*

Materials: *Gutter caulk, gutter patching kit, roofing cement, flashing material, gutter fasteners.*

To rehang sagging gutters, remove the hangers near the sag and lift the gutter. Replace the hangers, shifting their locations slightly and making new holes. Add hangers, if necessary, to evenly distribute the gutter's weight.

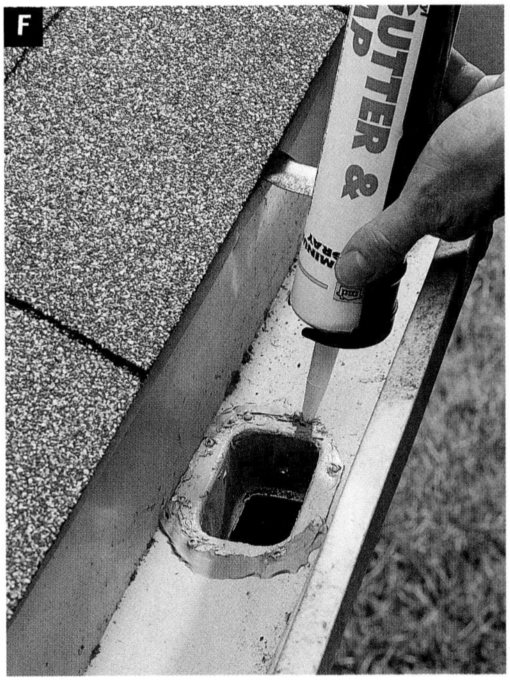

Fill small holes and seal minor leaks with butyl-rubber-based gutter caulk.

Temporarily repair minor damage with a gutter patching kit.

Sealing Leaky Gutters

To seal a leaky gutter joint, disassemble it by drilling out rivets or removing metal screws **(photo A).** When working with downspouts, you may need to take apart the entire downspout to reach the damaged joint.

Scrub both parts of the joint with a stiff-bristled brush. Clean the damaged area with water and allow to dry completely.

Apply caulk to the joining parts **(photo B),** then reassemble and secure the joint with new fasteners.

To prevent corrosion, patch gutters with the same type of metal (usually aluminum or galvanized steel) from which they are made.

To patch a metal gutter, first clean the area around the damage with a stiff-bristled brush **(photo C).** Scrub it with steel wool or an abrasive pad to loosen residue, then rinse it with water.

Apply a 1/8"-thick layer of roofing cement **(photo D)** evenly over the damage, spreading the roofing cement a few inches beyond the damaged area on all sides.

Cut and bend a patch from a piece of flashing and bend it to fit inside the gutter. Bed the patch in the roofing cement, and feather out the cement so it won't cause significant damming **(photo E).**

Tools: *Drill, screwdrivers, caulk gun, stiff-bristled brush, putty knife.*

Materials: *Siliconized acrylic caulk, steel wool, roofing cement, metal flashing.*

A

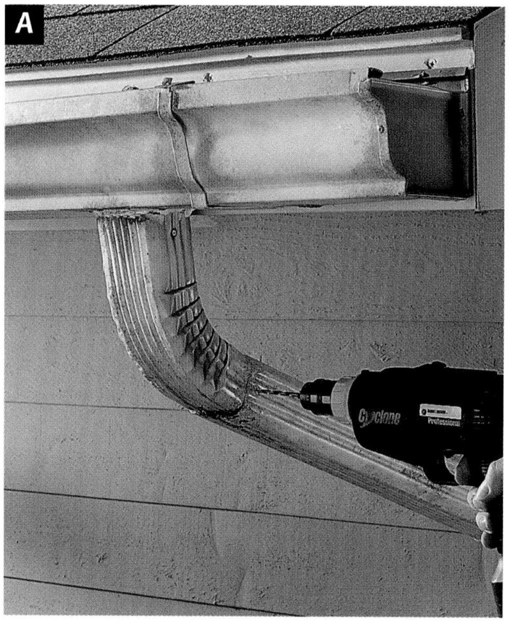

Disassemble the damaged joint and scrub it down.

B

Apply caulk to adjoining parts and reassemble the joint.

C

Use a wire brush and steel wool to clean the damaged area and remove residue.

D

Spread a 1/8" layer of roofing cement a few inches beyond the damaged area.

E

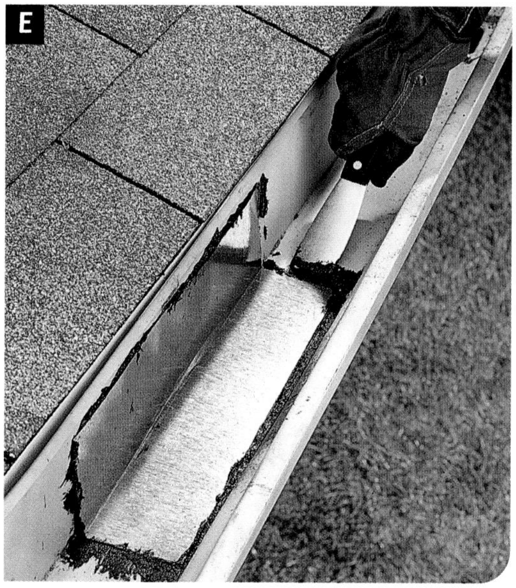

Cut a patch from flashing and bed it in the roofing cement, feathering out the edges to reduce ridges.

Replacing a Section of Metal Gutter

If the damaged area is more than 2 ft. long, replace the entire gutter section with new material. To locate a gutter section, trace the profile of your existing gutters and take it with you to the building center. If your gutters are more than 15 years old, they're probably a little larger than gutters made more recently. You may need to check salvage yards or have a new section custom-bent by a metal fabricator.

Remove gutter hangers in or near the damaged area **(photo F).** Insert wood spacers behind the gutter, near each hanger, before prying against the gutter.

Slip spacers between the gutter and fascia, near each end of the damaged area, so you don't damage the roof when cutting the gutter. Cut out the damaged section with a hacksaw **(photo G).**

Cut a new gutter section at least 4" longer than the damaged section **(photo H).**

Clean the cut ends of the old gutter with a wire brush. Caulk the ends **(photo I),** then center the gutter patch over the damage and press into the caulk.

Secure the gutter patch with pop rivets or sheet-metal screws **(photo J).** Use at least three or four fasteners at each joint. On the inside surfaces of the gutter, caulk over the heads of the fasteners.

Install the gutter hangers **(photo K),** using new hangers, if necessary (don't use old holes). Prime and paint the patch.

Tools: *Flat pry bar, hacksaw, caulk gun, screwdriver or pop rivet gun, hammer.*

Materials: *Wood scraps for spacers, replacement gutter material, caulk, sheet-metal screws or pop rivets, gutter hangers, primer and paint.*

Remove the gutter hangers near the damaged area.

Insert spacers between the gutter and fascia, then use a hacksaw to cut out the damaged area.

Cut a patch from matching gutter material. Make the patch at least 4" longer than the damaged section.

Clean and caulk the ends of the old gutter, then press the patch into the caulk.

Secure the patch with pop rivets or sheet-metal screws. Caulk over the fastener heads on the inside surfaces of the gutter.

Reinstall the gutter hangers, using new holes. Prime and paint the patch to match the existing gutter.

Installing a Vinyl Gutter System

Installing a snap-together vinyl gutter system is a manageable task for most do-it-yourselfers. Before you purchase new gutters, create a detailed plan and cost estimate. Include all the necessary parts, not just the gutter and drain pipe sections; they make up only part of the total system.

Test-fit all the pieces on the ground before you begin the actual installation.

Begin by marking a point at the high end of each gutter run, 1" down from the top of the fascia **(photo A).** Snap chalk lines that slope down toward downspout outlets, 1/4" for each 10 ft. of horizontal run. For runs longer than 35 ft., mark a slope from a high point in the center toward downspouts at each end.

Install downspout outlets **(photo B)** near the ends of gutter runs (at least one outlet for every 35 ft. of run). The tops of the outlets should be flush with the slope line, and they should align with end caps on the corners of

Tools: *chalk line, tape measure, drill, hacksaw.*

Materials: *1¼" deck screws, gutters, drain pipes, connectors, fittings, and hangers.*

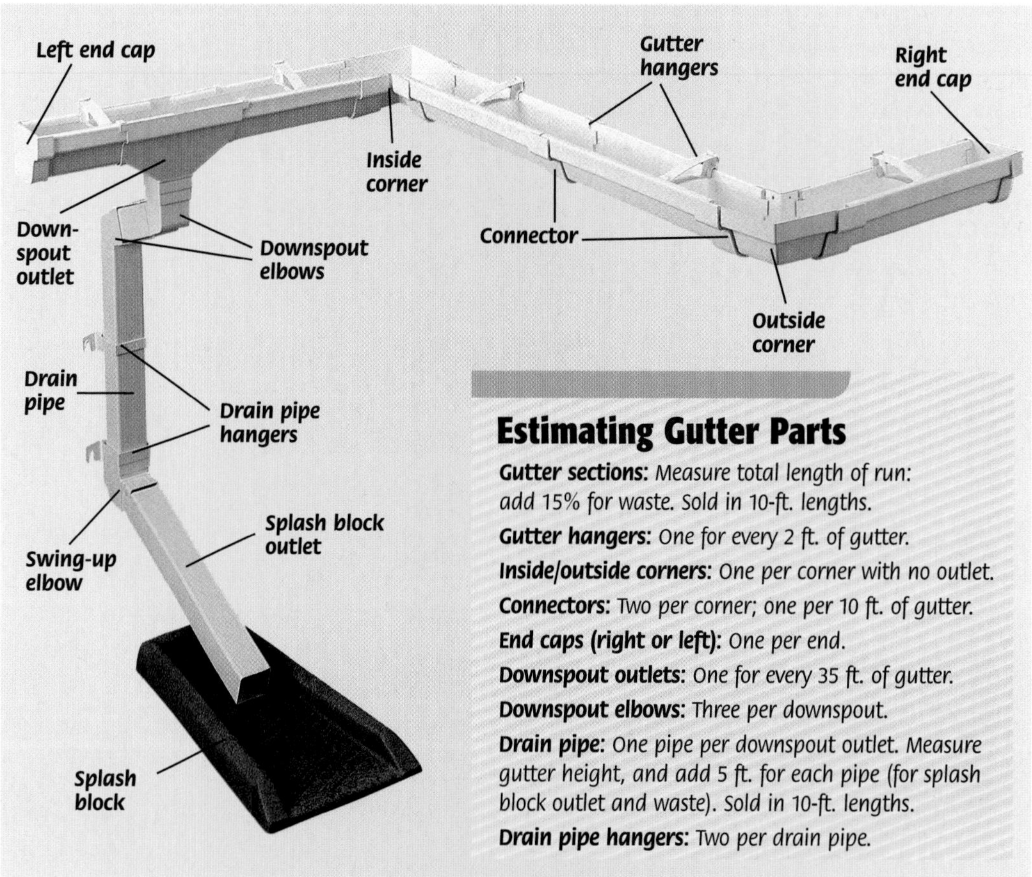

Estimating Gutter Parts

Gutter sections: Measure total length of run: add 15% for waste. Sold in 10-ft. lengths.
Gutter hangers: One for every 2 ft. of gutter.
Inside/outside corners: One per corner with no outlet.
Connectors: Two per corner; one per 10 ft. of gutter.
End caps (right or left): One per end.
Downspout outlets: One for every 35 ft. of gutter.
Downspout elbows: Three per downspout.
Drain pipe: One pipe per downspout outlet. Measure gutter height, and add 5 ft. for each pipe (for splash block outlet and waste). Sold in 10-ft. lengths.
Drain pipe hangers: Two per drain pipe.

Vinyl snap-together gutter systems are becoming increasingly popular. Easy to install and relatively inexpensive, they will not rot or deteriorate. The slip joints allow for expansion and contraction, which contributes to their reliability and longevity.

A

Mark a point at the high end of each gutter run and snap chalk lines toward downspout outlets.

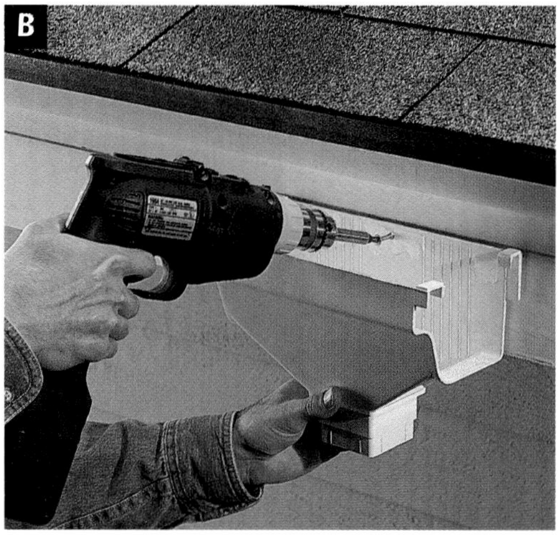

B

Install downspout outlets near the ends of gutter runs, at least one outlet for every 35 ft. of run.

C

Use 1¼" deck screws to attach hangers or support clips for hangers to fascia at 24" intervals.

the house, where drain pipes will be attached.

Following the slope line, attach hangers or support clips for hangers **(photo C)** for a complete run. Attach to fascia at 24" intervals, using deck screws.

Following the slope line, attach outside and inside corners at corner locations that don't have downspout outlets or end caps **(photo D).**

Use a hacksaw to cut gutter sections to fit between outlets and corners. Attach end caps and connect gutter sections to outlet.

Cut and test-fit gutter sections to fit between outlets, allowing for expansion gaps **(photo E).**

On the ground, join the gutter sections together using connectors. Attach gutter hangers to the gutter (for models with support clips mounted on fascia). Hang the gutters, connecting to the outlets **(photo F).**

Cut a section of drain pipe to fit between two downspout elbows—one elbow should fit over the tail of the downspout outlet and the other should fit against the wall. Assemble the parts, slip the top elbow onto the outlet **(photo G),** and secure the other to the siding with a drain pipe hanger.

Cut a piece of drain pipe to fit between the elbow at the top of the wall and the end of the drain pipe run, at least 12" above the ground. Attach an elbow, and secure the pipe to the wall with a drain pipe hanger **(photo H).**

Add accessories **(photo I)** such as swing-up elbows, splash blocks, or extenders.

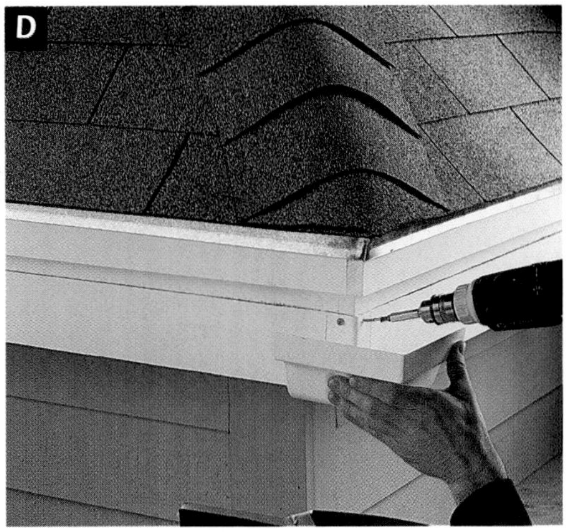

Attach outlets, then attach outside and inside corners. Cut gutter sections to fit between outlets and corners.

Attach end caps and connect gutter sections to outlet. Cut and test-fit sections between outlets.

Attach gutter hangers (for models with support clips mounted on fascia). Hang the gutters, connecting to the outlets.

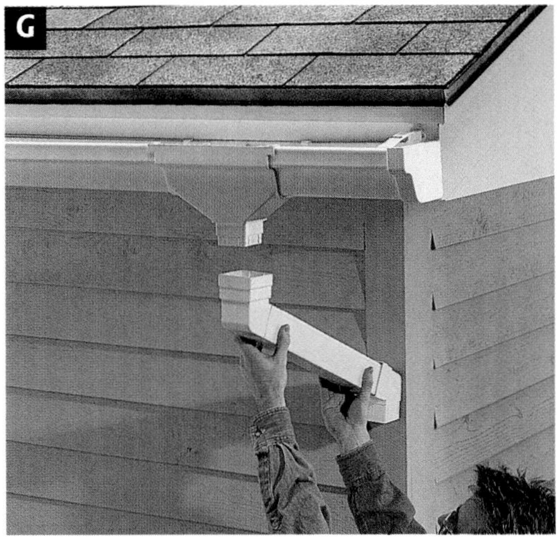

Cut drain pipe and connect one downspout elbow on each end. Slip the top elbow onto the outlet, and secure the other end with a drain pipe hanger.

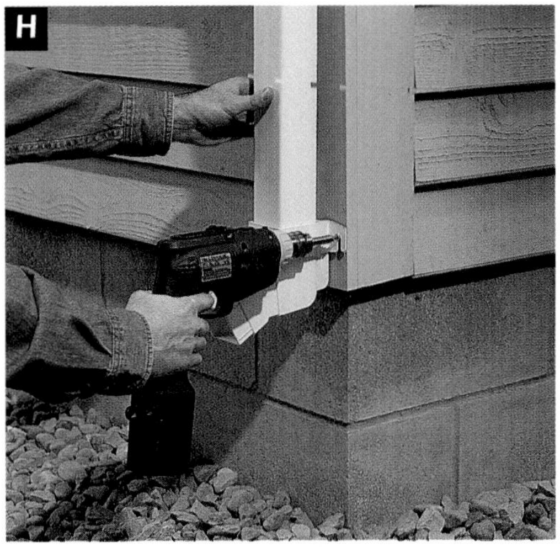

Cut drain pipe to extend the elbow at the top of the wall to a point 12" above the ground. Attach an elbow to the end of this pipe and secure it with a drain-pipe hanger.

Add accessories such as swing-up elbows to allow the outlet pipe to be lifted or splash blocks to help direct runoff away from your house.

Chimneys

Many people equate brick chimneys with fireplaces, but in many homes, the chimney also vents gases from the furnace and water heater.

The major elements of a chimney include the stack, flue, and crown. The *stack* is the visible outer shell of the chimney, usually made of brick, block, or stone. Inside the stack are *flues*, empty spaces or channels that let rising gases escape the house; there is a separate flue for each item being vented. A concrete or steel liner protects the inner walls of a chimney. The chimney *crown*, located at the very top of the chimney, is often made of mortar and seals the space between the edge of the stack and the flues. Crowns are prone to frequent cracking and chipping, due to the extreme temperature fluctuations they must endure. It's important to inspect and repair the crown regularly, filling cracks that might leave the chimney vulnerable to further damage and eventual deterioration.

One of the easiest ways to inspect a chimney without going up on the roof is to use a pair of binoculars. From ground level, take a careful look, checking the chimney for cracks, sags, or other signs of deterioration. You may need to hire professionals to inspect flue liners or do significant masonry repairs, but if working at heights doesn't bother you, it's possible to perform routine chimney maintenance yourself.

The most common locations for chimney problems are the crown, the mortar joints in the stack, and the flue.

Cleaning the Flue

Chimneys should be inspected once a year, according to the National Fire Protection Association. During inspections, check for animal nests or other obstructions, cracks in the flue or masonry, and deposits of creosote (a flammable, tarlike substance created by burning wood).

If the flue needs to be cleaned, rent a chimney brush that fits tightly inside it. Seal the fireplace opening with plastic or an old blanket. Working from the roof, insert the brush into the flue and push down. Gently work the brush up and down the flue, scrubbing hard enough to remove soot but not hard enough to damage the liner or mortar. Add extension handles until the brush reaches the fireplace opening. If the chimney is covered by a nonremovable cap or it's not possible to work from the roof, insert the brush through the fireplace opening and work it up the flue.

Let the dust settle for an hour, then vacuum the fireplace floor with a wet-dry vacuum.

Clean and inspect chimney flues once each year.

Cleaning Bricks

Many brick stains can be removed with water and a scrub brush **(photo A).** Others can be removed with cleaning solvents **(photo B).** Before using cleaning solvents, mask off nonmasonry surfaces, and test the solution on a small, inconspicuous area.

Mix a solvent (see chart at right) with talcum or flour to make a paste for cleaning bricks. To keep cleaning solutions from soaking in too quickly, soak the surface with water before applying them. Apply the paste directly to the stain, let it dry, then scrape it off with a vinyl or plastic scraper. Use nylon scrapers **(photo C),** which are unlikely to damage masonry surfaces. Rinse the entire area thoroughly after cleaning.

Efflorescence, a white powdery substance that appears on masonry, can often be removed with a scrub brush and water or household cleaner.

Clean stained bricks with a paste made of cleaning solvent and talcum powder or flour.

Use a vinyl scraper to removed hardened excess mortar.

Solutions for Brick Stains

Egg splatter: Dissolve oxalic acid crystals in water in a nonmetallic container. Brush onto stained surface.

Efflorescence: Use a stiff-bristled brush to scrub surface with water. Add household cleaning solution if accumulation is heavy.

Iron stains: Dissolve oxalic acid crystals in water. Brush onto stained surface.

Ivy: Cut (do not pull) vines away from the surface. Let remaining stems dry up, then scrub them off with a stiff-bristled brush and household cleaning solution.

Oil: Make a paste of mineral spirits and an inert material, such as sawdust. Spread onto stain and allow to dry.

Paint stains: Remove new paint with a solution of trisodium phosphate (TSP) and water. Old paint usually can be removed with heavy scrubbing or sandblasting.

Plant growth: Apply weed killer according to manufacturer's directions.

Smoke stains: Scrub surface with a household cleanser containing bleach, or with a mixture of ammonia and water.

Tuckpointing a Brick Chimney

Tuckpointing, the process of replacing failed mortar joints with fresh mortar, is the most common brick and block repair. Cracked or missing mortar not only makes a home look unkempt, it also invites moisture into a chimney structure, where it can cause additional damage. Tuckpointing techniques can be used to repair any structure where bricks or blocks are bonded with mortar.

Begin by using a mortar raking tool to clean out loose or deteriorated mortar to a depth of 1/4" to 3/4" **(photo A).** Switch to a masonry chisel and hammer if the mortar is stubborn. Clean away all loose debris, then dampen the surface with water.

Mix the mortar, adding concrete fortifier and, if necessary, pigment to match existing mortar joints. Mix the mortar to a consistency that slides slowly off a trowel. Load the mortar onto a mortar hawk, then push the mortar into the horizontal joints with a joint filler **(photo B).** Apply mortar in 1/4"-thick layers, allowing each layer to dry for 30 minutes before applying the next layer. Fill joints until the mortar is flush with the face of the brick.

Apply the first layer of mortar into the vertical joints by scooping mortar onto the back of a joint filler and pressing it into the joint **(photo C).** Work from the top downward.

After the final layer of mortar is applied, smooth the joints with a jointing tool that matches the profile of the old mortar joints **(photo D),** tooling the horizontal joints first. Brush off the excess mortar with a stiff-bristle brush. To slow down the drying time and strengthen the mortar's bond, periodically mist the repair area with water, or cover it with damp rags for several days.

Tools: *Hammer, joint filler, jointing tool, mason's trowel, mason's chisel, mortar hawk, pointing trowel, mortar raking tool, stiff-bristled brush.*

Materials: Concrete fortifier, mortar mix, mortar pigment (if needed).

Use a mortar raking tool to clean out loose or deteriorated mortar to a depth of 1/4" to 3/4".

Push mortar into the horizontal joints. Apply mortar in 1/4" layers until the mortar is flush with the face of the brick.

Scoop mortar onto the back of a joint filler and press it into the vertical joints. Work from the top downward.

Smooth the joints with a jointing tool. When mortar is dry, brush off the excess with a stiff-bristled brush.

Repairing a Chimney Crown

Once a year, inspect your chimney crown, and patch any minor cracks with fire-rated silicone caulk. If you find widespread damage, use a cold chisel and hammer to break apart deteriorated sections, taking care not to damage the flue as you work. Remove debris, then trowel an even layer of patching compound all the way around the crown.

If the crown is badly damaged, or if cracks recur, consider building and installing a floating chimney crown **(photo E).** This type of crown is less prone to cracking because it's not attached to the chimney, so it can move freely as the temperature changes. It also provides a drip edge that directs runoff and helps protect the mortar and brick from deterioration.

To build a floating chimney cap, measure the chimney stack and flue and build a form from 3/4" plywood **(photo F).** The form, which should be 4 3/4" high in the center and 3 1/2" high at the outside edge, should extend 2" beyond the chimney on all sides. Using 1 1/2" wood screws to connect the parts, attach the form to a plywood base. To form a drip edge, make a frame from 3/8" dowels, then glue it 1" from the edges of the form.

Prepare a stiff (dry) batch of mortar mix and fill the form **(photo G).** Rest a wood float across the edges of the form, and smooth off the cement. Keep angles sharp at the corners. Let the crown cure for at least two days, then carefully disassemble the form.

Chisel away the old crown, and clean the top of the chimney with a wire brush. Set the new crown directly on the chimney. Center it so the overhang is equal on all sides **(photo H).** Adjust the crown so the gap around the flue is even on all sides, then fill that gap with fire-rated rope or mineral wool. Caulk over the fill material with a very heavy bead of fire-rated silicone caulk **(photo I).** Also, caulk the joint underneath the crown. Inspect the caulk every two years and replace it when necessary.

Tools: *Cold chisel, drill, hammer, tape measure, wood float.*

Materials: *Concrete patching compound; mortar mix; ¾"-thick plywood; ¼" dowel; 1½" wood screws; fire-rated rope; fire-rated silicone caulk.*

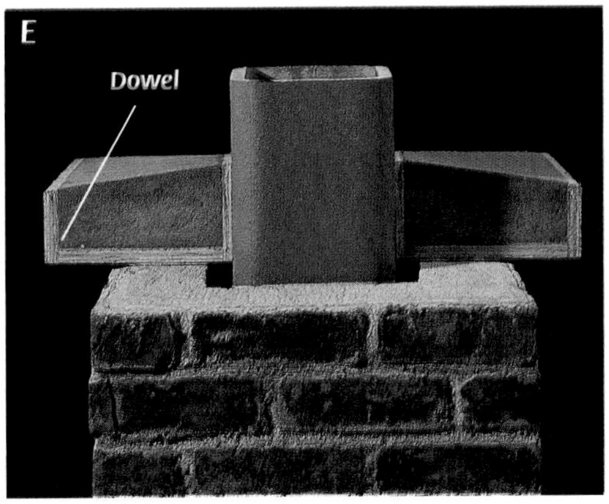

Put an end to annual repairs by building and installing a floating chimney crown.

Measure the chimney and the flue, then build a plywood form for the crown.

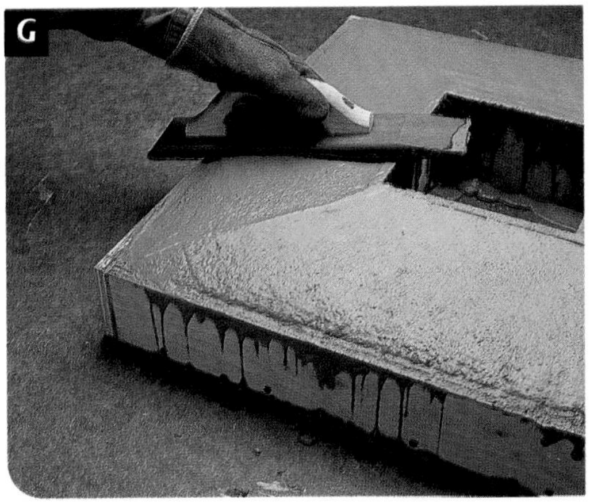

Prepare mortar mix and shape the cement within the form. Let the crown cure for at least two days.

Center the crown onto the chimney so the overhang is equal on all sides.

Fill the gap with fire-rated rope or mineral wood, then caulk it with fire-rated caulk.

Walls & Siding

Siding can be considered a home's skin in much the same way that framing is its skeleton. And in the same way that cuts and scrapes in a person's skin admit dirt and germs, cracks and holes in a home's siding can allow moisture and pests to get in. To avoid such problems, inspect siding twice a year, checking for cracks, holes, paint failure, and signs of deterioration.

Patching the surface without fixing the underlying problem just guarantees that you'll have to repeat the repair in the future. Repair methods depend on the type of siding material, as well as the type and extent of the damage. But in most cases, siding is fairly easy to repair.

If you have to remove siding for repairs, inspect and repair the underlying elements, if necessary. Renail loose sheathing; replace rotted elements; seal around door and window openings; and patch any holes, gaps, or cracks.

Preventive maintenance for siding is simple: wash the walls, caulk joints where different building materials meet, and fill or patch cracks and small holes.

Once a year, treat your home to a bath with a power washer or a long-handled brush and a light detergent solution. As you work, direct the spray at an angle, and avoid spraying directly onto any mortar joints. Pay particular attention to the splash areas below eaves, porches, and any other sheltered locations, which don't weather in the same way as more fully exposed surfaces. For example, exterior paint is formulated to *chalk*, or slowly wear away, with repeated exposure to water. In areas that don't get washed by rain, paint is less likely to chalk, so it needs more careful cleaning. Remember, too, that areas that don't receive direct sunlight are more susceptible to mold and mildew.

Before recaulking utility openings, completely remove the old caulk and thoroughly clean the openings. Reseal the openings with butyl caulk or expandable foam.

Masonry Walls

Masonry repairs are doomed to failure if the underlying causes of the problems aren't addressed. For example, a concrete patch can separate if the structure is still being subjected to the stress that originally caused the damage.

Pinpoint the nature and cause of the problems before you start repairs. Look for obvious clues, such as overgrown tree roots or damaged gutters that let water drain onto masonry surfaces. Also check the slope of the surrounding landscape to see if it needs to be regraded to direct water away from the foundation. After you're sure you've eliminated the problem, you're ready to repair the damage.

Deteriorated mortar joints **(photo A)** are common, and usually are more widespread than surface deterioration of brick. If you find damaged mortar, probe surrounding joints with a screwdriver to determine whether they're sound. Tuckpoint deteriorated joints (below).

Spalling occurs when trapped moisture is exposed to repeated freeze and thaw cycles, exerting enough directional pressure to fracture bricks **(photo B).** If the damage is contained to a fairly small area, you can replace only the affected bricks (page 225); if it's more widespread, the structure may have to be replaced.

Tools: *Electric drill with a masonry-cutting disc, mason's chisel, hammer, wire brush, pointing trowel, masonry trowel, jointing tool.*

Materials: *Mortar mix, concrete fortifier, mortar pigment.*

Tuckpoint joints by removing cracked, damaged mortar and filling the joints with fresh mortar.

Spalling occurs when trapped moisture is exposed to repeated freeze and thaw cycles.

Replacing Damaged Brick

Replacing bricks is appropriate only if the damaged area is small (four or fewer adjacent bricks) and you're dealing with a non-load-bearing wall. For more extensive repairs or repairs to load-bearing walls, consult a professional.

Begin by scoring the damaged brick so it will break apart more easily **(photo C).** Use a power drill with a masonry-cutting disc to score lines on the brick and in the surrounding mortar joints.

Use a mason's chisel and hammer to break apart the brick **(photo D).** When removing several bricks, work from the top down, one row at a time, until all the damaged bricks are removed. As you work, be careful not to damage surrounding bricks.

Chisel out any mortar remaining in the cavity **(photo E),** then brush away dirt and debris with a wire brush. Rinse the area with water.

Mix mortar, adding concrete fortifier and, if necessary, pigment to match the old mortar. Use a pointing trowel to apply a 1"-thick layer of mortar to the bottom and sides of the cavity **(photo F).**

Dampen the replacement brick slightly, then apply mortar to the ends and top **(photo G).** Fit the brick into the cavity and tap it with the handle of the trowel until the face is flush with the surrounding bricks. If the mortar isn't flush with the face of the brick, use the pointing trowel to press a little more mortar into the joints.

Scrape away any excess mortar with a masonry trowel, then smooth joints with a jointing tool that matches the original profile **(photo H).** Let the mortar set until crumbly, then brush away any excess.

Use a power drill with a masonry-cutting disc to score the brick and surrounding joints.

Break the brick apart along the scored lines, using a masonry chisel and hammer.

Chisel out remaining mortar and clean the surface, using a wire brush.

Apply a 1"-thick layer of mortar to the sides and bottom of the cavity, using a pointing trowel.

Apply mortar to the dampened replacement brick, and press it into place.

Scrape away excess mortar. Smooth the joints, using a jointing tool that matches the profile of the surrounding joints.

Stucco Walls

Although stucco siding is very durable, it can be damaged, and over time can crumble or crack. Fill thin cracks with concrete caulk, which remains flexible and prevents further cracking. If cracks are already filled with failed caulk, remove it completely with a wire brush. When the crack is completely clean and dry, fill it with concrete caulk. Overfill it slightly, then smooth the joint, using a disposable paintbrush and denatured alcohol.

Tools: Caulking gun, disposable paintbrush, putty knife or trowel, whisk broom, wire brush.

Materials: Bonding adhesive, concrete caulk, denatured alcohol, metal primer, premixed stucco, masonry paint.

Repair thin cracks in stucco walls with concrete caulk.

Patching a Small Area

This simple repair method works well for damaged areas that are less than two square feet. For more extensive damage, remove the stucco all the way to the wall surface and rebuild it in layers (page 227).

Begin removing loose material with a wire brush **(photo A).** Use the brush to clean rust from any exposed lath, then apply a coat of metal primer. Paint the broken edges of the stucco with bonding adhesive, which will improve the bond between the old stucco and the stucco material of the patch.

Apply premixed stucco with a putty knife or trowel, slightly overfilling the hole **(photo B).** Read manufacturer's directions—drying times vary. Feather the edges until the patch blends into the surrounding surface.

Use a whisk broom or trowel to duplicate the original texture **(photo C).** Let the patch dry for several days, then touch it up with masonry paint, matching the color with the rest of the siding.

A

Remove loose material from the area, using a wire brush.

B

Apply premixed stucco with a putty knife or trowel.

C

Texture the repair area to match the surrounding surface.

Repairing a Large Area

Duplicating stucco textures takes patience, skill, and experience, so it's a good idea to practice before taking on a major repair.

Remove the old stucco by making a starter hole with a drill and masonry bit, then using a masonry chisel and hammer to chip away all the stucco in the repair area. Wear safety glasses and a particle mask or respirator when cutting stucco.

Cut self-furring metal lath and attach it to the sheathing with roofing nails **(photo D).** If it takes more than one width of lath, overlap the pieces by 2". If the patch extends to the base of the wall, attach metal stop bead at the bottom so the stucco can't leak out.

Premixed stucco works well for small jobs, but for large ones, it's more economical to mix your own. Combine three parts sand, two parts portland cement, and one part masonry cement **(photo E).** Add just enough water so the mixture holds its shape when squeezed. Mix only as much as you can use in about an hour.

Apply a 3/8"-thick layer of stucco directly to the metal lath **(photo F).** Push the stucco into the mesh until it fills the gap between the mesh and the sheathing. Score horizontal grooves into the wet surface. Let the stucco dry for two days, misting it with water every two to four hours to help it cure evenly.

Apply a second, smooth layer of stucco **(photo G).** Build up the stucco to within 1/4" of the original surface. Let the patch dry for two days, misting as before.

Combine finish coat stucco mix with just enough water for the mixture to hold its shape. Dampen the patch area, then apply the finish coat to match the original surface **(photo H).** The finish coat pictured here was dabbed on with a whisk broom, then flattened with a trowel. Dampen the patch periodically for a week. Let it dry for several more days before painting it.

Tools: *Aviation snips, masonry chisel, hammer, mortar box, spray bottle, trowel.*

Materials: *Safety glasses, particle mask, self-furring metal lath, roofing nails, metal stop bead, sand, portland cement, masonry cement, finish coat stucco mix.*

Attach self-furring metal lath to the sheathing.

Mix the stucco, adding just enough water that the mixture holds its shape when squeezed.

Apply a layer of stucco directly onto the metal lath, then score grooves into the surface.

Apply the second layer of stucco, smoothing it as much as possible, using a trowel.

Apply the finish coat of stucco, then texture it to match the original surface.

Wood Siding

Damage to wood siding is pretty common, but fortunately it's also easy to repair.

Fill small holes with epoxy wood filler. Repair cracks and splits with epoxy wood glue. Apply glue to both sides of the crack, then press the board together. For best results, position a board under the bottom edge of the damaged piece, pushing it upward to create even pressure until the glue sets. If you're working near the ground, wedge a 2 × 4 under the support board to hold it in place. After the glue sets, drive galvanized deck screws on each side of the crack, and touch up the paint.

Keep in mind that removing boards for repairs creates a great opportunity to add insulation, if necessary. While the siding is off, check the insulation. If you need to increase the R-value, drill holes in the exposed sheathing and blow insulation into the walls. Afterward, seal the holes and proceed with the repairs.

Separated joints can occur in any type of lap siding, but they're most common in wood lap. Fill 1/8" to 1/4"-thick gaps with caulk. If you find gaps that are 3/8" or wider, consult a building inspector—large gaps could be an indication that your house has serious moisture or shifting problems.

Choose specialty siding nails when repairing redwood or other wood sidings. These nails have smaller sinkerheads with waffling to hold finishes. They also have ringed shanks to provide extra holding power and blunt tips to reduce splitting. They're available in double hot-dipped galvanized or stainless steel versions. Select nails that are long enough to penetrate the combined wood sheathing and framing, by a minimum of 1 1/2".

Tools: *Hammer, chisel, trowel, screwdrivers, hacksaw, miter saw or circular saw, jig saw, keyhole saw, flat pry bar, nail set, electronic stud finder, paintbrush.*

Materials: *Epoxy wood filler, epoxy glue, ring-shank siding nails, siliconized acrylic caulk, roofing cement, building paper, sheathing, wood preservative, primer, paint or stain.*

Replacing Lap Siding

First, locate and repair the leak or other source of water damage **(photo A).**

Mark the area of siding that needs to be replaced **(photo B).** Mark the cutout lines over the centers of the framing members of each side of the repair area, staggering the cuts to offset the joints.

Insert spacers beneath the board above the repair area. Make entry cuts at the tops of the cutting lines with a keyhole saw, then saw through the boards **(photo C).** Remove the boards. Pry out any nails or cut off nail heads, using a hacksaw blade. Patch or replace the sheathing and building paper, if necessary.

Use roofing cement to mend small holes or tears in the building paper. If you need to patch a large area, loosen the building paper above the damage, slip the top of the patch

A

Locate and resolve the source of the water damage.

B

Outline the damaged siding that must be replaced.

C

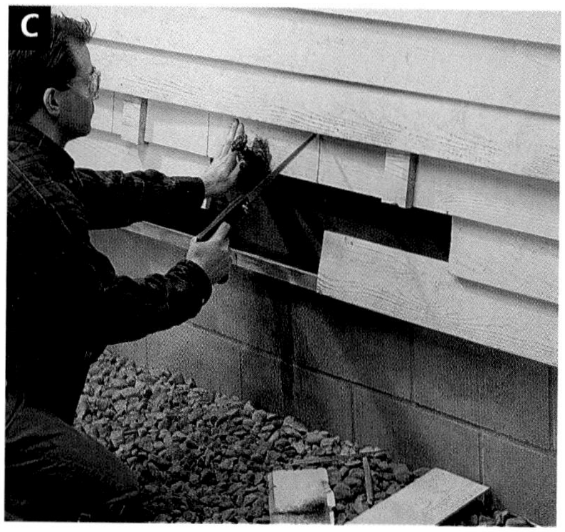

Mark boards for cutting, staggering lines so the vertical joints don't align.

underneath the existing paper, then staple the layers.

If you removed the bottom row of siding, nail a 1 × 2 starter strip along the bottom of the patch area, using 6d siding nails. Leave a 1/4" gap at each joint in the starter strip to allow for expansion.

Measure and cut all replacement boards to fit, leaving an expansion gap of 1/8" at each end **(photo D).** Use the old boards as templates to trace cutouts for fixtures or other openings. Use a jig saw to make the cutouts. Apply wood preservative/sealer or primer to the ends and backs of the boards, and let them dry before installation.

Nail the new boards in place with ring-shank siding nails, starting with the lowest board in the repair area **(photo E).** Drive nails into the framing members using the original nailing pattern (normally at 16" intervals) through the bottom of the new board and the top of the board below.

Fill expansion joints with caulk (use paintable caulk for painted wood or tinted caulk for stained wood), then prime and paint or stain the replacement boards to match the surrounding siding **(photo F).**

Measure and cut replacement boards, allowing for an expansion gap of 1/8" at each end.

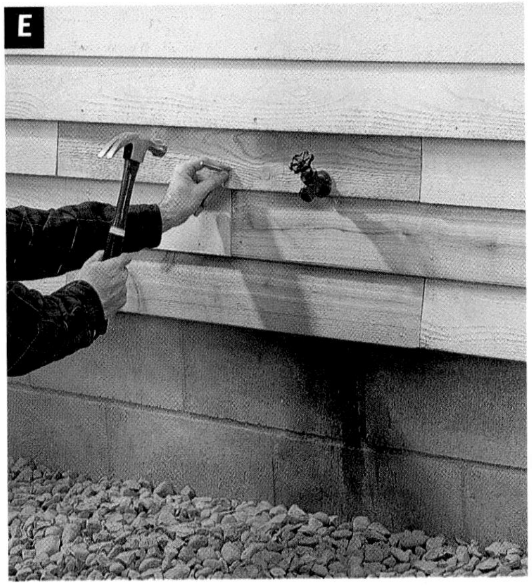

Nail the new boards in place, using original nailing pattern.

Fill expansion joints with caulk, then prime or stain replacement boards.

Replacing Wood Shakes & Shingles

Split damaged shakes or shingles with a hammer and chisel, and remove them. Insert wood spacers under the shakes or shingles above the repair area, then slip a hacksaw blade under the top board to cut off any nail heads remaining from the old shake or shingle **(photo G).**

Cut replacement shakes or shingles to fit, leaving a 1/8" to 1/4"-wide expansion gap at each side. Coat all sides and edges with wood preservative. Starting with the lowest course, slip the patch pieces under the siding above the repair area **(photo H).** Drive ring-shank siding nails near the top of the exposed area on the patch. Cover nail heads with caulk. Remove spacers.

Remove damaged shakes or shingles and cut off old nail heads.

Slip replacement pieces under the siding and attach with ring-shank siding nails.

Replacing Board & Batten Siding

Remove the *battens*, the trim that secures the damaged panels **(photo A).** Pry out the entire damaged panel. Inspect the building paper and patch it if necessary. Cut replacement panels from matching material, allowing a 1/8"-wide gap at side seams **(photo B).** Prime or seal the edges and the back side of the replacement panels, and let them dry.

Nail the new panels in place with ring-shank siding nails **(photo C).** Caulk all seams and expansion joints, then replace the battens and any other trim. Prime and paint or stain the patched area to blend in with the surrounding siding.

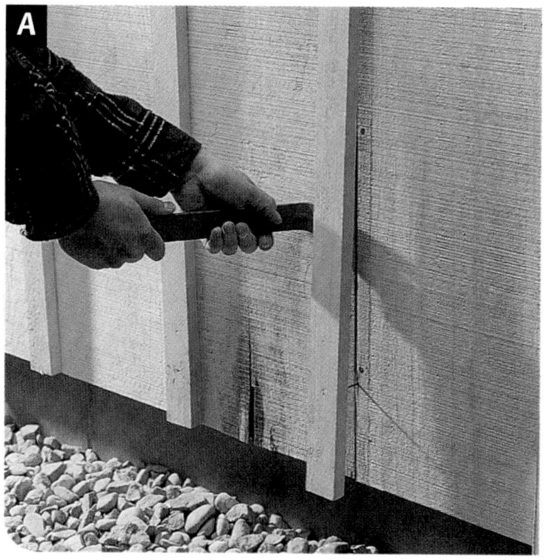

Remove battens or trim, then pry out the damaged panels.

Cut replacement panels from matching material—allow 1/8" gaps at the sides.

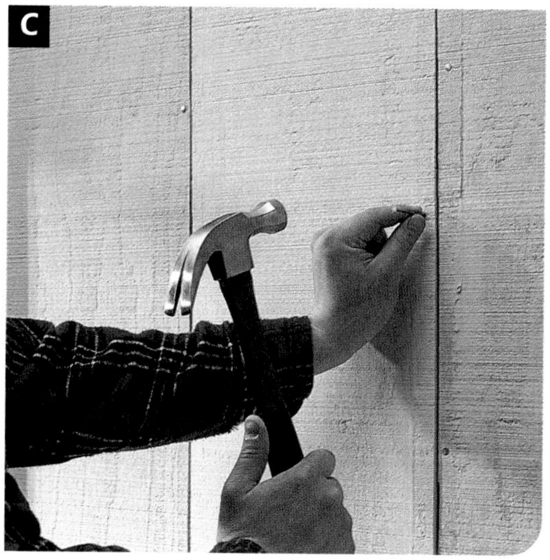

Nail new boards in place. Caulk all seams and joints, then replace trim.

Manufactured Siding

Vinyl and aluminum have joined wood as popular siding materials. Though durable, these materials may sometimes need to be repaired.

Vinyl is reasonably priced, durable, relatively maintenance free, and energy efficient. It's also considered the most forgiving siding material for do-it-yourselfers to install.

Although newer versions are more resistant, older vinyl siding is vulnerable to scratches and abrasions. Some types are also susceptible to damage from UV rays, which can cause faded spots and discoloration. Scratched or discolored pieces of vinyl siding must be patched or replaced.

Vinyl siding can become permanently discolored if exposed to petroleum-based products, such as wasp or bee spray. These stains can't be removed, but it may be possible to lighten them. Dampen a white cloth with naptha or mineral spirits and dab at the stain. Rinse thoroughly with water.

Aluminum siding is relatively inexpensive, easy to install and maintain, and fire-resistant. It's available in a wide variety of styles and colors, with or without an insulation backing.

Aluminum siding can be repainted if scratched, and small dents can be filled with auto-body filler. Larger damage can be patched. If it becomes necessary to replace large sections, you may have trouble finding the original color or pattern. To camouflage repairs, buy the closest possible match, then remove sections from an inconspicuous area. Use the original pieces to repair the more visible location, then install the new pieces in the less visible one, where the mismatch will be less noticeable.

Tools: *Aviation snips, caulk gun, drill, flat pry bar, hammer, straightedge, tape measure, utility knife, zip tool.*

Materials: *Caulk, nails, roofing cement or exterior panel adhesive, trim, siding panels (if needed), end caps.*

Repairing Vinyl Siding

Starting at the seam nearest the damaged area, unlock interlocking joints, using a zip tool. Install spacers, then remove the fasteners in the top piece of damaged siding.

Cut out the damaged area, using aviation snips, then cut a replacement piece 4" longer than the open area. Trim off 2" of the nailing strip from each end of the overlap area. Slide the piece into position **(photo D).** Press ring-shank siding nails in nailing strip, then position the end of a flat bar over each nail head. Drive the nails by rapping on the neck of the pry bar with a hammer **(photo E).** Slip the J-channel over the nailing strip.

Unlock the interlocking joints, then cut out the damaged area. Cut, trim, and insert a replacement piece.

Press ring-shank nails into the nailing strip, then use a pry bar and a hammer to drive them.

Patching Aluminum Siding

Cut out the damaged area with aviation snips **(photo F).** Leave an exposed area on top of the uppermost piece to act as a bonding surface.

Cut a patch 4" wider than the repair area, then remove the nailing strip from the piece. Smooth the edges with metal sandpaper.

Nail the lower patches in place by driving ring-shank siding nails through the nailing strips, starting with the lowest piece. Apply roofing cement to the back of the top piece, then press it into place, slipping the J-channel over the nailing strip below **(photo G).** Caulk the seams.

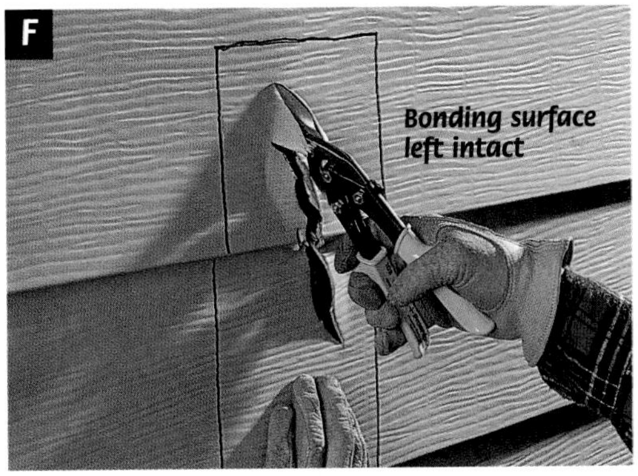

Cut out the damaged area. Cut a patch, then remove the nail strip from the top piece.

Nail the lower patches in place. Apply roofing cement to the top piece and press it into place

Replacing Aluminum End Caps

Remove the damaged end cap. If necessary, pry the bottom loose, then cut along the top with a hacksaw blade **(photo H).**

Starting at the bottom, attach replacement end caps. Drive ring-shank siding nails through the nailing tabs and into the framing members.

Trim the nailing tabs off the top replacement cap, then apply roofing cement to its back **(photo I).** Snap the cap over the J-shaped locking channels of the siding courses. Press the top cap securely in place.

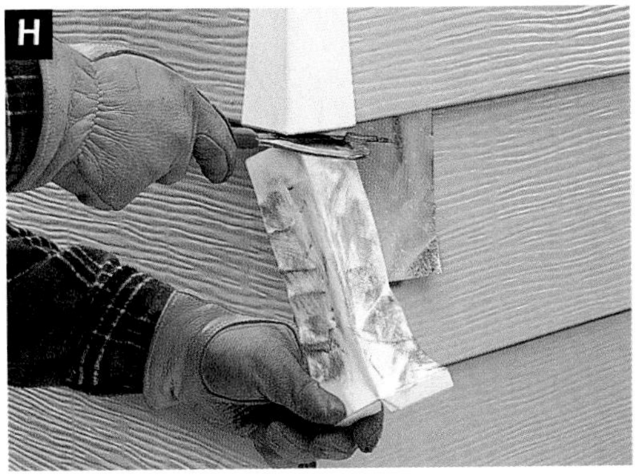

Remove the damaged end cap. Install replacement caps.

Attach the top cap with roofing cement. Press in place.

Exterior Painting

Painting the exterior of a house is a major undertaking, but doing the work yourself substantially reduces the expense of protecting the siding and refreshing your home's appearance. With care and patience, you can create a long-lasting, professional-looking finish.

Painting projects break naturally into two stages: preparation and application. Preparation usually is the more tedious and time-consuming portion of the job, but it's worth the effort—thorough preparation results in a quality finish.

Timing is also a critical element of a painting project. Scraping and sanding exposes siding to the elements. If you leave bare wood exposed for prolonged periods, the pores become plugged, which can keep the paint from bonding properly. For this reason, it's best to address one side of the house at a time, applying primer and paint as soon as the prep work is finished.

Paint can last 10 years or more, especially with regular maintenance. Touching up minor problems can prevent water from building up beneath the surface of the paint. Sand, prime, and paint cracks or alligatoring as soon as they occur. If you don't correct it quickly, deterioration invites mildew to form, which can lead to staining and paint failure. Pressure washing your siding and making minor paint repairs annually are the cornerstones of an exterior maintenance program.

As with any project involving the use of ladders or scaffolding, painting your house requires good safety practices. Read the section on safety (page 186) before you begin.

Identifying Exterior Paint Problems

Evaluate exterior paint every year, starting with sheltered areas **(photo A).** Paint failure in areas that receive little or no direct sunlight may be a warning that similar problems are developing in neighboring areas. It's vital to identify the type of failure before trying to correct it.

Blistering **(photo B),** a term that describes paint with a bubbled surface, results from poor preparation or hurried application of primer or paint. The blisters indicate that trapped moisture is trying to force its way through the surface. Scrape and touch up localized spots. For widespread damage, remove paint down to bare wood, then apply new primer and paint.

Peeling **(photo C)** occurs when paint comes loose and falls away in flakes. Peeling is a sign of persistent moisture problems, generally from a leak or a failed vapor barrier. Here, too, it's important to identify and correct the moisture problem. If the peeling is localized, scrape and sand the damaged areas, and touch up with new primer and paint. If it's widespread, remove the old paint down to bare wood, then apply new primer and paint.

Alligatoring **(photo D),** widespread flaking and cracking, is typically seen on surfaces that have many built-up paint layers. It also can be caused by inadequate surface preparation or by allowing too little drying time between coats

Paint failure will appear first in areas that receive little or no direct sunlight.

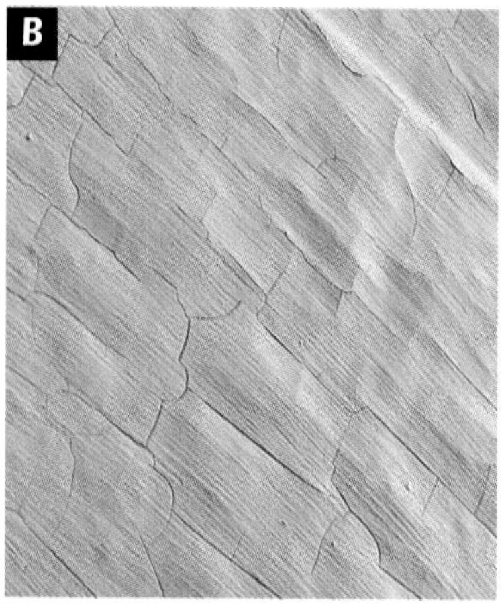

Blistering is early warning sign that more serious problems may be forming.

Peeling occurs when paint falls away from the surface in large flakes.

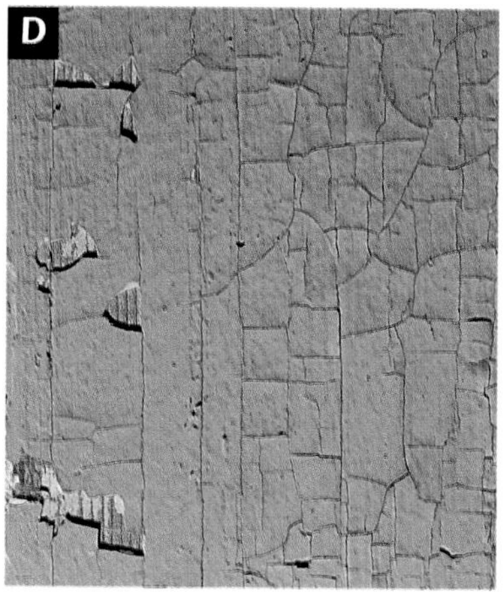

Alligatoring is typically seen on old paint and surfaces with many layers of paint.

of primer and paint. Remove the old paint, then prime and repaint.

Localized blistering and peeling **(photo E)** indicates that moisture, usually from a leaky roof, gutter system, or interior pipe, is trapped under the paint. Find and eliminate the leak, then scrape, prime, and repaint the area.

Clearly defined blistering and peeling **(photo F)** occurs when a humid room has an insufficient vapor barrier. If there is a clear line where an interior wall ends, remove the siding and replace the vapor barrier.

Mildew **(photo G)** forms in cracks and humid areas that receive little sunlight. Wash mildewed areas with a 1:1 solution of household chlorine bleach and water, or with trisodium phosphate (TSP).

Rust **(photo H)** occurs when moisture penetrates paint on iron or steel. Remove the rust and loose paint with a wire brush attachment and portable drill, then prime and repaint.

Bleeding spots **(photo I)** occur when "popped" nails in siding begin to rust. Remove nails, sand out rust, then drive in ring-shank nails. Apply metal primer, then paint to blend.

Use a scrub brush and a muriatic acid solution to remove efflorescence **(photo J)**, a powdery layer that forms when minerals leech through a masonry surface.

Helpful Hint

To determine whether existing paint needs to be removed, try this simple test. With a utility knife, etch a 1" × 1" grid pattern into the paint in several places: scratch six shallow lines $1/8$" apart in each direction. Firmly press a 2"-long piece of masking tape over the center of the grid, then quickly pull it off. If paint comes off with the tape, remove all the old layers and apply a coat of primer before repainting.

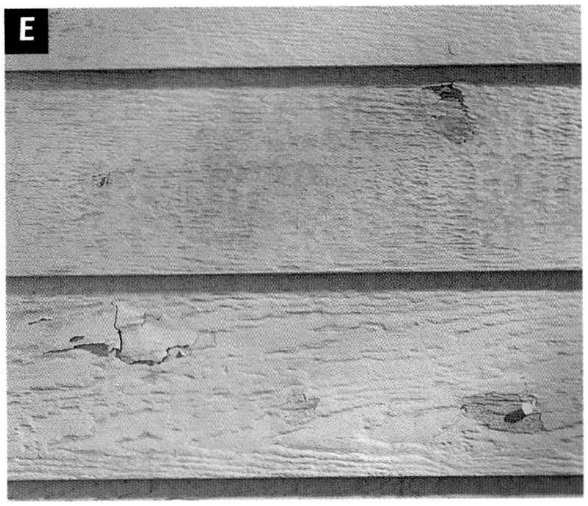

Localized blistering and peeling indicates that moisture is trapped under the paint.

Clearly defined blistering and peeling occurs when a section of vapor barrier is missing or inadequate.

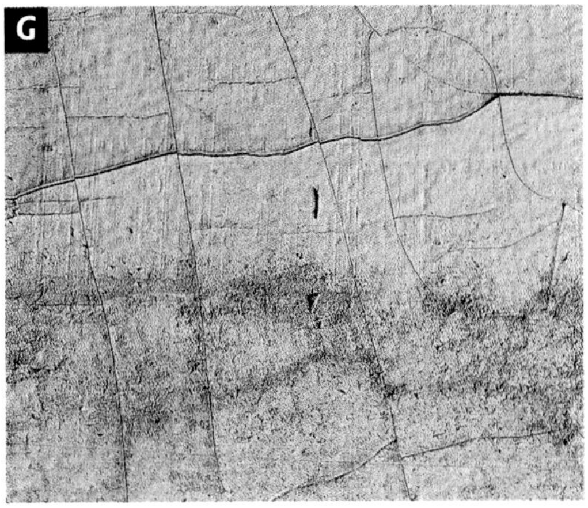

Mildew forms in cracks and humid areas that receive little direct sunlight.

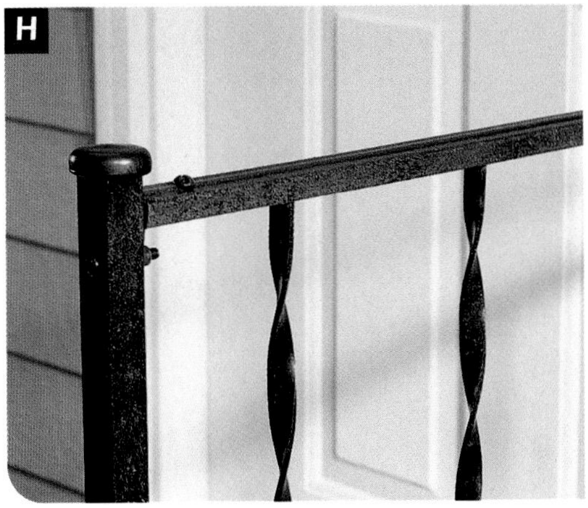

Rust occurs when failed paint on iron or steel allows moisture to penetrate its surface.

Bleeding spots occur when nails in siding pop and turn rusty.

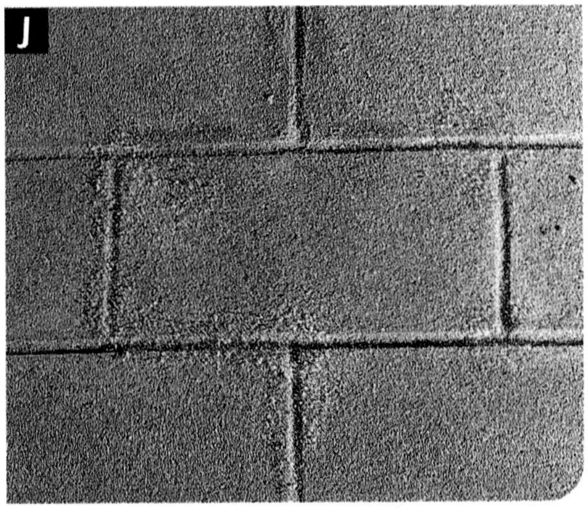

Efflorescence occurs when minerals trapped in the interior leech through to a masonry surface.

Tools & Materials

High-quality painting tools, primers, and paints **(photo A)** usually produce better results with less work than less expensive products. The return on an investment in quality products is a project that goes smoothly and results in an attractive, durable paint job.

As you plan your painting project, make a list of the tools and materials you need. Plan to prime all unpainted surfaces and any surfaces or patches that have been stripped or worn down to bare wood.

Refer to "Estimating Paint" (right) to determine the number of gallons you'll need for one coat of paint, then decide how many coats you plan to apply. For bare wood, the best approach is to apply one primer coat followed by two topcoats. But if the surface was previously painted and the old paint is still good, one coat of new paint will be sufficient.

Traditionally, almost all exterior paint has been oil-based. Oil-based paint does give thinner coats and leaves sharper lines—a definite advantage when you're painting intricate woodwork and trim. However, with increasing concerns about the environment, there's a growing interest in alternative products. Latex-based paints compare well with oil-based products for durability and appearance, and they're less hazardous, less smelly, and easier to dispose of. At one time, an existing coat of oil-based paint meant you couldn't use latex for subsequent coats. But today's acrylic latex paints offer excellent adhesion to oil-based primers and paints.

Although removing layers of old paint can be quite a chore, the proper materials **(photo B)** and tools **(photo C)** can make this task go faster. Removal goes quicker if you use a wire-wheel attachment for a power drill or rent a siding sander with a disc the same width as the reveal of your siding. Buy or rent a heat gun for removing paint from large areas. For

Estimating Paint

To estimate the amount of paint you need for one coat of paint:

Add *up the square footage of the walls (length × height), the square footage of the soffit panels, and a 15% waste allowance.*

Subtract *from this figure the square footage of doors and windows.*

Check *the paint coverage rate listed on the label (350 sq. ft. per gallon is average).*

Divide *the total square footage by the paint coverage rate to determine the number of gallons you need.*

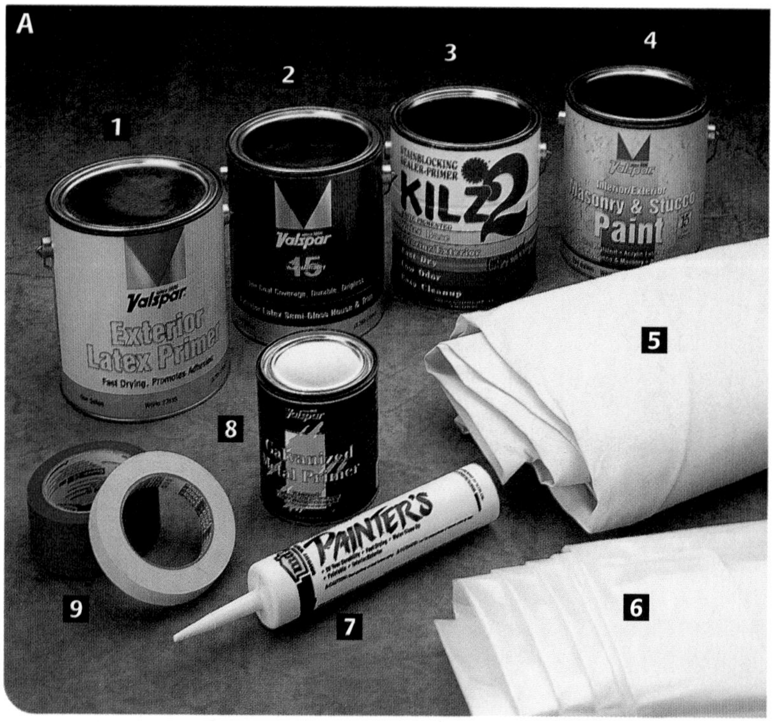

Materials for painting include: primers tinted to match paint color (1), house paint (2), sealer-primer (3), masonry and stucco paint (4), drop cloth (5), plastic sheeting (6), caulk (7) metal primer (8), and masking tape (9).

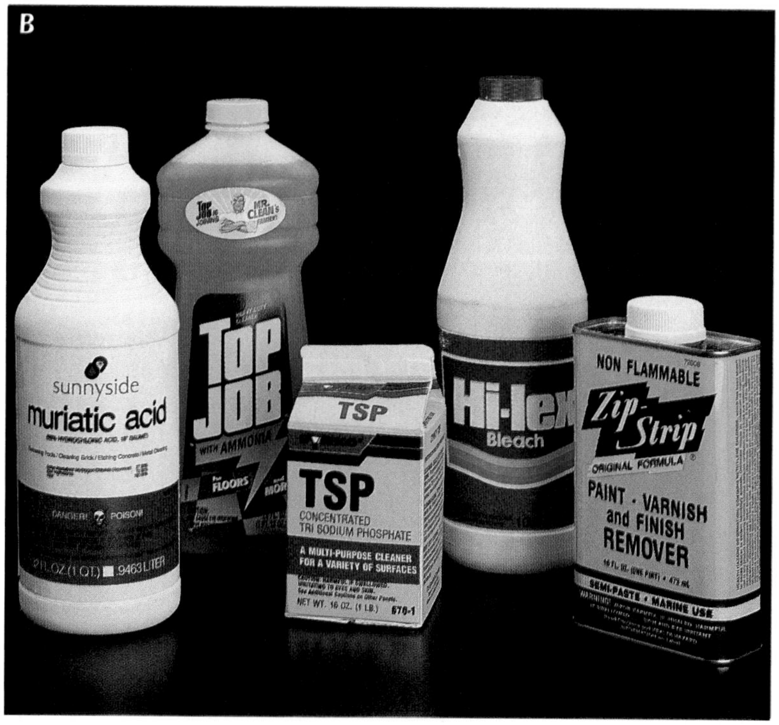

Products for surface preparation and maintenance include (from left): muriatic acid for cleaning rust from metal, detergent, TSP (trisodium phosphate) chlorine bleach for cleaning surfaces, and stripper for removing thick layers of paint from delicate surfaces.

smaller tasks, try a stiff-bristled scrub brush, wire brush, sanding block, putty knife, paint scraper, or detail scraper with interchangeable heads.

Pressure washing will remove loose and flaking paint, but it's no substitute for scraping or sanding. Buy or rent the right unit. One with less than 1200 psi won't do a good job and one with more than 2500 psi could damage your siding **(photo D).** Use a 12- or 25-degree nozzle.

The right tools also simplify paint application **(photo E).** Exterior walls may have a variety of surfaces and shapes, so keep a range of tools on hand, such as: a roller and sleeve with 3/8" nap for smooth and semi-smooth surfaces; a corner roller for corners and trim; a roller with 5/8" nap for rough surfaces; a 4" paintbrush for lap siding; a 3" paintbrush for siding and trim; a 2" sash brush for trim and window frames; and a 3"-wide roller for painting trim. On walls and other flat surfaces, spray-painting equipment can shorten application time **(photo F).**

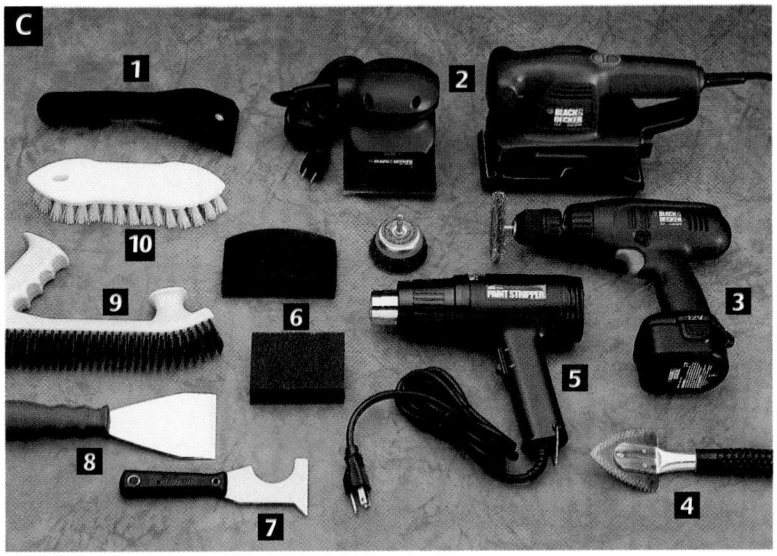

Tools for paint removal: paint scraper (1), 1/4-sheet and 1/3-sheet finishing sanders (2), drill with wire-wheel attachments (3), paint zipper (4), heat gun (5), sanding blocks (6), painter's 5-in-1 tool (7), putty knife (8), double-handle wire brush (9), and stiff-bristled brush (10).

Rent a pressure washer and attachments to clean siding thoroughly and remove loose, flaky paint. A nozzle with an extension pole attaches to the hose from the compressor.

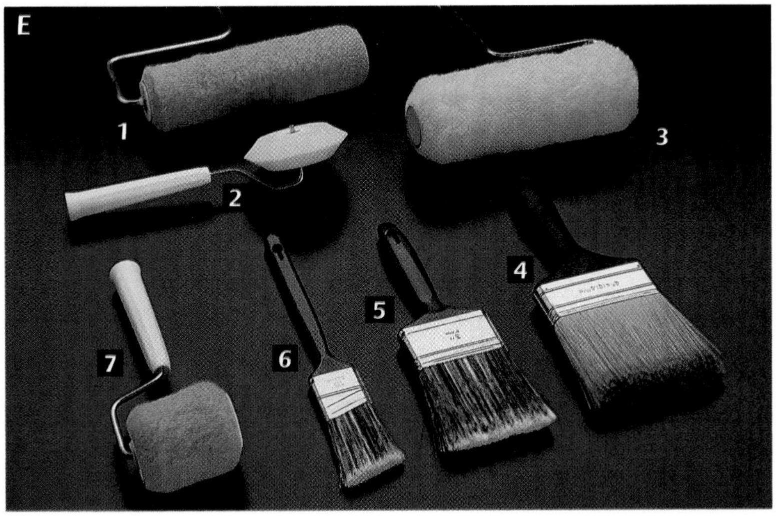

Tools for applying paint include: roller and sleeve with 3/8" nap (1), corner roller (2), roller with 5/8" nap (3), 4" paintbrush (4), 3" paintbrush (5), 2" sash brush (6), 3"-wide roller (7). NOTE: All brushes shown have synthetic bristles, for use with latex-based paint.

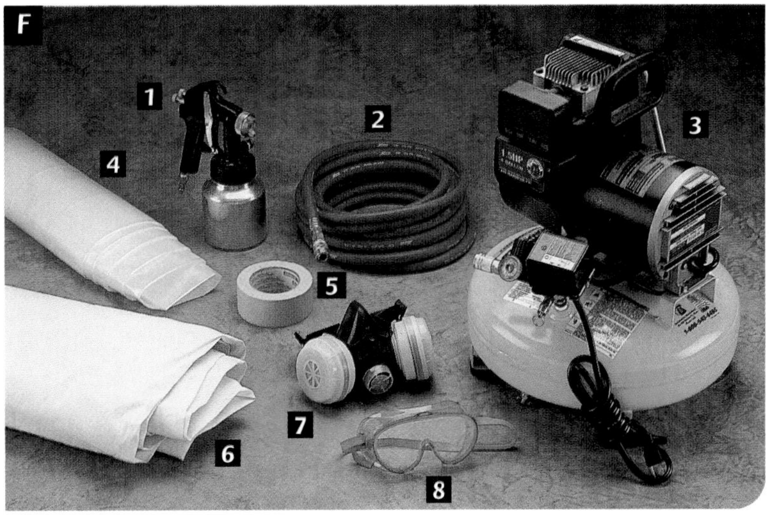

Paint spraying equipment includes a spray gun (1), hose (2), and compressor (3). Proper preparation requires plastic sheeting (4), masking tape (5), and drop cloths (6). Always use the necessary protective devices, including a dual-cartridge respirator (7) and safety goggles (8).

Preparing to Paint

The key to an even paint job is working on a smooth, clean, dry, surface—so preparing the surface is an essential part of a painting job. Generally, the more preparation work you do, the smoother the final finish will be and the longer it will last.

For the smoothest finish, sand all the way down to the bare wood with a power sander. For a less time-consuming (but rougher) finish, scrape off any loose paint, then spot-sand rough areas. You can use pressure washing to remove some of the flaking paint, but by itself, pressure washing won't create a smooth surface for painting.

Before you start painting you need to remove all existing paint that has lost its bond with the surface.

Tools: *Pressure washer (optional), scrapers, sanders, sanding blocks, putty knife, stiff-bristled brush, wire brush, steel wool, coarse abrasive pad, drill, wire-wheel attachment.*

Materials: *80- & 120-grit sandpaper, putty, paintable siliconized caulk, muriatic acid.*

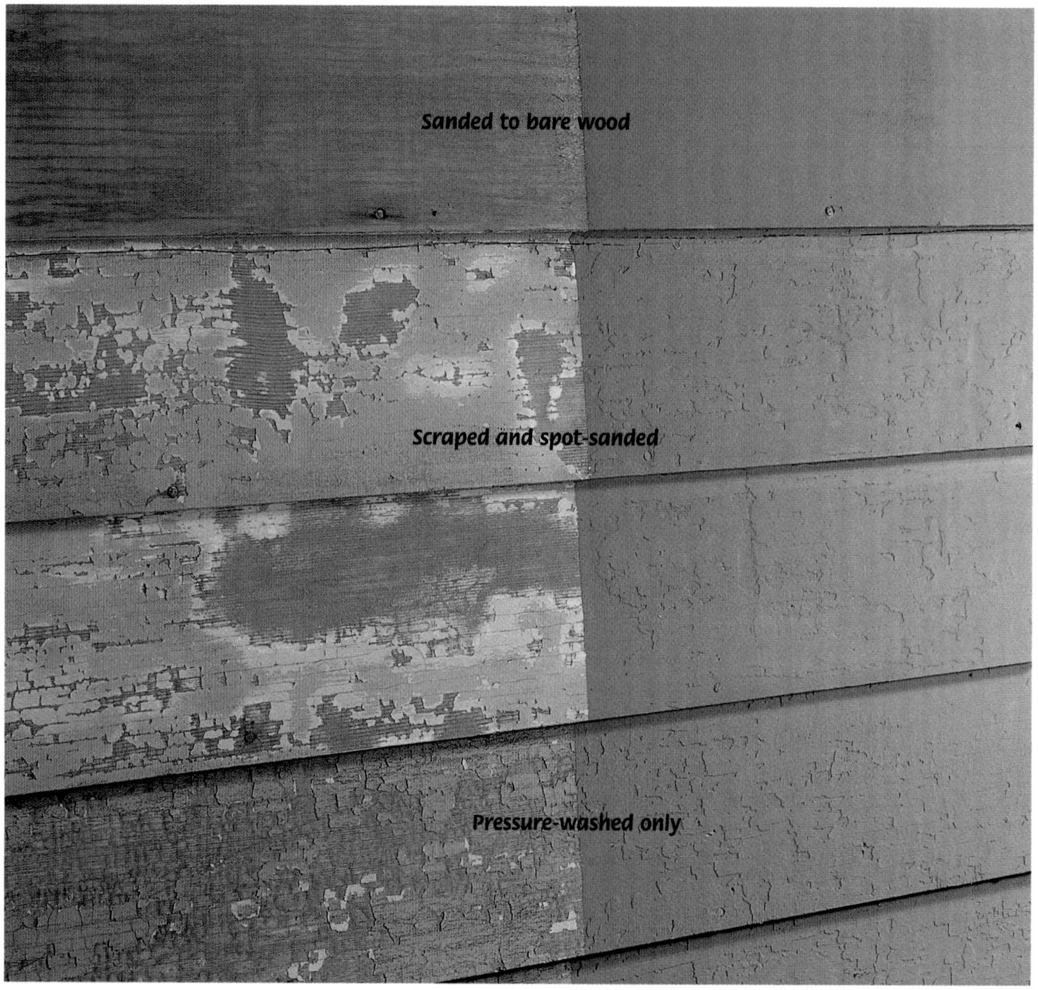

The amount of surface preparation you do will largely determine the final appearance of your paint job. Decide how much sanding and scraping you are willing to do to obtain a finish that you'll be happy with.

Tools for Paint Removal

Removing old paint is a lot easier when you use the right tools for each task.

Use a heat gun to loosen thick layers of old paint **(photo A).** Aim the gun at the surface and scrape the paint as soon as it releases.

To remove large areas of paint on wood lap siding, use a siding sander with a disk that's as wide as the reveal on your siding **(photo B).**

To remove loose paint and rust from metal hardware, use a wire brush. Apply metal primer immediately to prevent new rust.

To scuff metal siding and trim, use medium-coarse steel wool or a coarse abrasive pad. Wash the surface before priming and painting.

When using a heat gun, keep it in constant motion.

Use a siding sander to remove paint from wood lap siding.

Cleaning & Sanding

The first step in preparing to paint is cleaning the surface and removing loose paint. The most efficient method is pressure washing the house **(photo C).** Allow all surfaces to dry thoroughly before continuing with preparation work.

Since pressure washing won't remove all the loose paint, the next step is to scrape the surface with a paint scraper **(photo D).** Be careful not to damage the surface with overly aggressive scraping.

Use detail scrapers to remove loose paint in hard-to-reach areas. Some of these scrapers have interchangeable heads that match common trim profiles **(photo E).**

Smooth out rough paint with a finishing sander and 80-grit sandpaper. Use sanding blocks and 80- to 120-grit sandpaper to sand hard-to-reach areas of trim. Sanding blocks are available in a variety of shapes and sizes, such as a teardrop design **(photo F).** Or, make sanding blocks from dowels, wood scraps, garden hose, or other household materials. Cut old sanding belts into strips to sand small, detailed areas of trim.

Inspect all surfaces for cracks, rot, and other damage. Mark affected areas with colored push pins or tape. Fill holes and cracks with epoxy wood filler **(photo G).**

Use a finishing sander with 120-grit sandpaper to sand down repaired areas, as well as the ridges and hard edges left from the scraping process, creating a smooth surface **(photo H).**

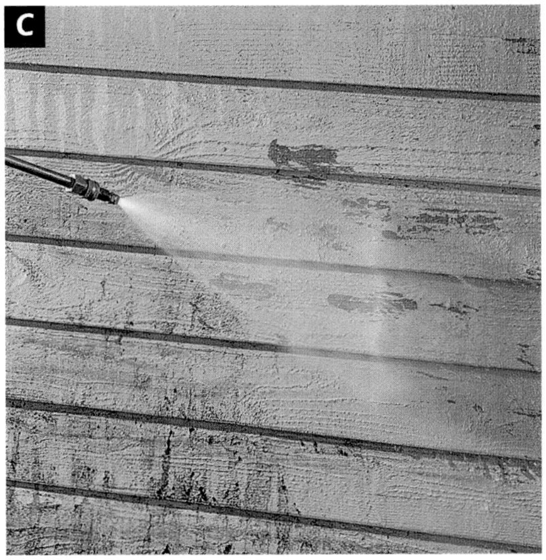

Use a pressure washer to remove paint flakes.

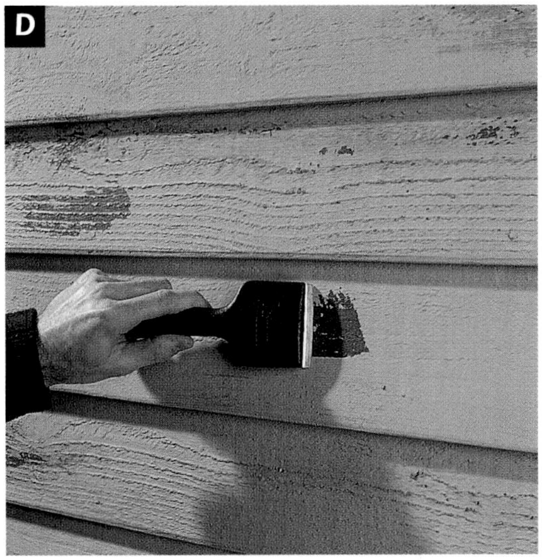

Use a scraper to remove any loose paint.

Use a detail scraper on hard-to-reach areas.

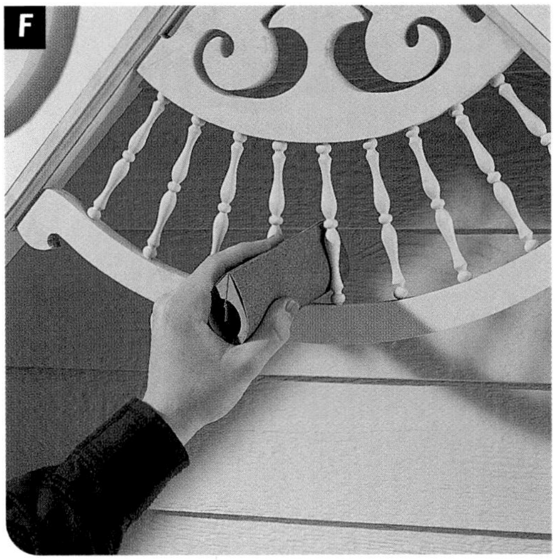

Sand detailed areas with specially shaped blocks.

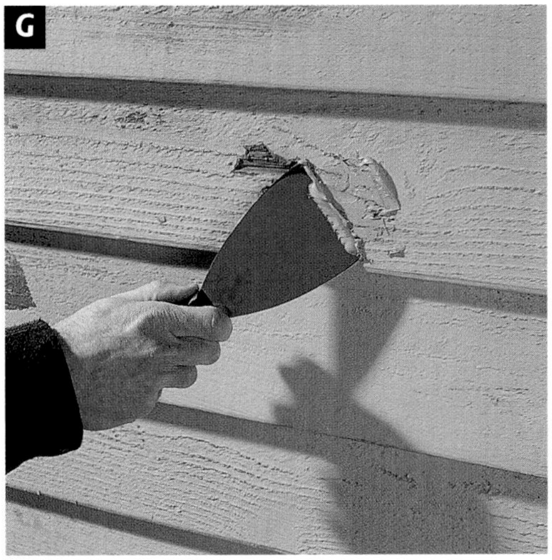

Fill holes and cracks with wood putty.

Sand ridges and repaired areas to smooth the surface.

Pressure Washing

If you decide to pressure-wash your siding, be sure to use the right equipment. For most houses, a pressure washer with 1200 to 2500 psi is best. The nozzle size is also important—a 15- to 25-degree nozzle is best.

As you work, direct the water stream downward **(photo A),** and don't get too close to the surface with the sprayer head; the force of the stream can damage siding and trim.

To clean hard-to-reach areas, such as cornices and soffits, use an extension and a rotating scrub brush attachment **(photo B).**

Direct the water stream at a downward angle when pressure-washing siding.

Add a rotating scrub brush attachment to clean hard-to-reach areas, such as cornices and soffits.

Preparing Trim Surfaces

Scuff-sand glossy surfaces on doors, window casings, and all surfaces painted with enamel paint. Use a coarse abrasive pad or 150-grit sandpaper **(photo C).**

Fill cracks in siding and gaps around window and door trim with paintable siliconized acrylic caulk **(photo D).**

Scuff-sanding glossy surfaces and enamel paint creates a better bonding surface for primer and paint.

Paintable siliconized acrylic caulk makes a tight, long-lasting seal around window and door trim and in cracks.

Removing Clear Finishes

Clear topcoats and sealants can flake and peel, just like paint. Pressure-wash stained or unpainted surfaces that have been treated with a wood preservative or protectant before recoating them with fresh sealant **(photo E).**

Use a stiff-bristled brush to dislodge any flakes of loosened surface coating that weren't removed by pressure washing **(photo F).** Don't use a wire brush on wood surfaces.

Pressure-wash stained or clear-sealed finishes.

Remove flakes of surface coating with a stiff-bristled brush.

Preparing Surfaces

Remove rust and loose paint from metal hardware, such as railings and ornate trim, with a wire brush **(photo G).** Cover the surface with metal primer immediately after brushing to prevent the formation of new rust.

Scuff-sand metal siding and trim with medium-coarse steel wool or a coarse abrasive pad **(photo H).** Wash the surface before priming and painting.

Remove loose mortar, mineral deposits, or paint from mortar lines in masonry surfaces with a drill and wire-wheel attachment **(photo I).** Clean broad, flat surfaces with a wire brush. Correct any minor damage with masonry repair products before repainting.

Dissolve rust on metal hardware with diluted muriatic acid solution **(photo J).** When working with muriatic acid, it's important to wear safety equipment, work in a well-ventilated area, and follow all directions and precautions.

Remove loose paint and rust from metal hardware, such as ornate trim and railings, using a wire brush.

Scuff-sand metal siding and trim with medium-coarse steel wool or a coarse abrasive pad.

Remove loose mortar, mineral deposits, or paint from mortar with a drill and a wire-wheel attachment.

Remove rust from metal hardware by soaking it in a diluted solution of muriatic acid.

Preparing Plants & Yard Structures

Before painting, spread tarps on the ground around the house to collect debris and prevent damage from excess paint. Also cover any delicate plants or shrubs in the area.

Turn off the power to any exterior air-conditioning units, appliances, or structures near the house, and cover them, as well **(photo K).**

Remove exterior shutters and decorative trim to protect them from damage and to provide access to painting areas **(photo L).** Make any necessary repairs to the shutters and trim. Prepare, prime, and paint them, and reinstall after painting is complete.

Use tarps to protect delicate plants and structures.

Take down shutters and decorative trim.

Applying Paint & Primer

Schedule priming and painting tasks so that the primer and paint can be applied within two weeks of each other. If more than two weeks passes, wash the surface with soap and water before applying the next coat.

Check the weather forecast and keep an eye on the sky while you work. Damp weather or rain within two hours of application will ruin a paint job. Don't paint when the temperature is below 50° or above 90°F. Avoid windy days: it's dangerous to be on a ladder in high winds, and wind blows dirt onto the fresh paint.

Plan each day's work so you can follow the shade. It's best to work in the shade or indirect sunlight. Direct sun can dry primers and paints too quickly and trap moisture below the surface, which leads to blistering and peeling. Lap and brush marks also tend to show more when you paint in direct sunlight.

Prepare, prime, and paint one face of the house at a time, and follow a logical painting order. Work from the top of the house down to the foundation, covering an entire section before you move the ladder or scaffolding. Prime and paint vertical surfaces before horizontal ones, so you won't need to touch up splatters or spills.

Here's a good painting sequence to follow: face of fascia; bottom edges of soffit panels; decorative trim near top of the house; gutters and downspouts (from the back to the front); soffit panels and trim; bottom edges of siding; faces of siding (use a shield near corner, window, and door trim if you're not painting it); foundation; doors and windows; inside edges of door and window trim; outside edges of casings and brick moldings; faces of door trim; door thresholds and porch floors.

After the primer or paint dries, return to each section and touch up any unpainted spots or areas that were covered by the pads of the ladder or the ladder stabilizer.

Use the right primer or paint for each job.

Prime and paint vertical surfaces before horizontal ones.

Paint in a logical sequence from the top of the house down.

Apply primer and paint in the shade or in indirect sunlight.

Helpful Hint

Paint color, especially custom-mixed colors, can vary from one can to the next. To avoid problems, it's best to "box," or mix, your paint.

Empty all the paint into a large container and mix it thoroughly. Pour the mixed paint back into the individual cans and seal them carefully. Stir each can thoroughly immediately before you use it.

Selecting Brushes & Rollers

The right paint application tools are another key to creating a professional-looking finish.

Wall brushes—thick, square brushes from 3" to 5" wide—are designed to carry lots of paint and distribute it widely **(photo A).**

Sash brushes, from 1 1/2" to 2 1/2" wide, are good for windows and molding.

Trim brushes, from 2" to 3" wide, are good for doors and trim and cutting in small areas.

It's best to keep a range of clean brushes on hand, including 2 1/2", 3", and 4" flat brushes as well as tapered sash brushes **(photo B).**

You can also use paint rollers to quickly paint smooth surfaces. Use an 8" or 9" roller sleeve for broad surfaces **(photo C)** and a 3" roller **(photo D)** to paint flat-surfaced trim, such as end caps or corner trim.

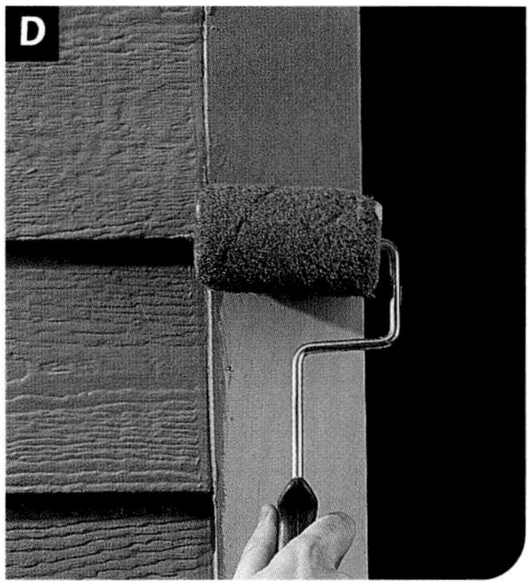

Achieving a Smooth, Even Finish

When you're done painting, the paint layer (primer and all top coats) should be 4 to 5 mils thick—about as thick as a piece of newspaper.

To achieve this kind of smooth, even paint coverage, you need to load your brush with the right amount of paint for the area you're covering. This means dipping only the first third of the brush into the paint, even for full loads of paint.

Use a full load of paint for broad areas, a moderate load for smaller areas and feathering strokes, and a light load when painting or working around trim **(photo E).**

When painting broad, flat areas, hold the brush at a 45-degree angle **(photo F).** Apply just enough downward pressure to flex the bristles and squeeze the paint from the brush.

Helpful Hint

When planning a painting job, use the appropriate primer or paint for each surface you're working on. Use a metal primer with a rust inhibitor on metal surfaces and a masonry primer with an anti-chalking additive on masonry surfaces.

Load your brush with the right amount of paint for the area.

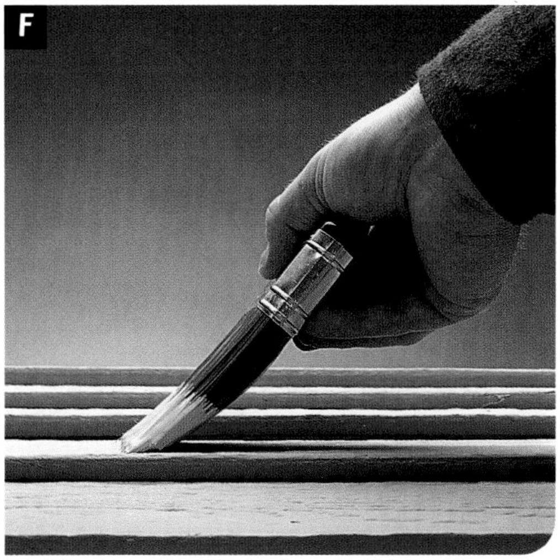

Hold brush at a 45-degree angle and apply gentle pressure.

Brushing Flat Surfaces

Most professional painters agree that brushes provide the best paint coverage. However, to achieve consistently good coverage, you must use good techniques. Load the brush with a full load of paint. Starting at one end of the surface, make a smooth stroke until the paint begins to "feather" out **(photo A).** At the end of the stroke, lift the brush without leaving a definite ending point **(photo B).** If the paint appears uneven or contains heavy brush marks, smooth it out without overbrushing.

Reload the brush and make a stroke from the opposite direction, painting over the feathered end of the first stroke to create a smooth, even surface **(photo C).** If the junction of the two strokes is visible, rebrush with a light coat of paint. Feather out the starting point of the second stroke.

A

Starting at one end, make a long, smooth stroke.

B

Gradually lift the brush. Lightly smooth.

C

Reload the brush and stroke from the opposite direction.

Using Paint Rollers

Before starting to apply latex paint with a roller, wet the roller nap, then squeeze out the excess. Position a roller screen inside a five-gallon bucket. Dip the roller in the paint, then roll it back and forth across the roller screen **(photo D).** The roller sleeve should be full but not dripping when lifted from the bucket.

Start painting by rolling upward, which minimizes dripping. To avoid the waste and mess of excessive splattering, roll smoothly and at an even pace. Make sure the roller rolls rather than slides across the surface. Sliding leaves marks that will be visible when the paint dries. Work paint into cracks and rough textures, finishing each area of paint with vertical strokes **(photo E).**

Use specialty rollers such as cone-shaped rollers for points where two planes intersect **(photo F)** or doughnut-shaped rollers **(photo G)** for painting the edges of lap siding or moldings.

D
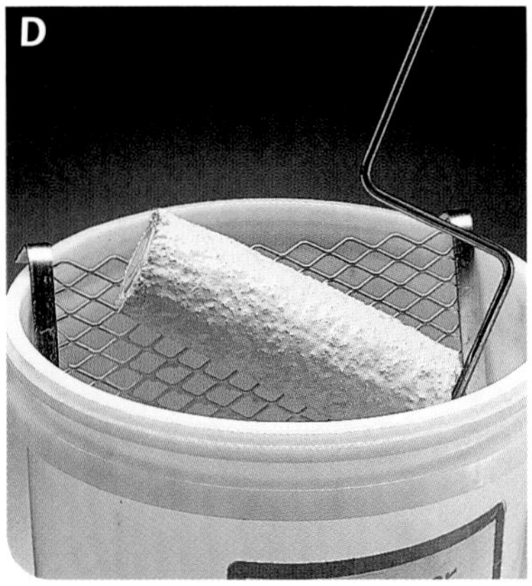
Use a roller screen inside a five-gallon bucket to properly fill a roller sleeve with paint.

E
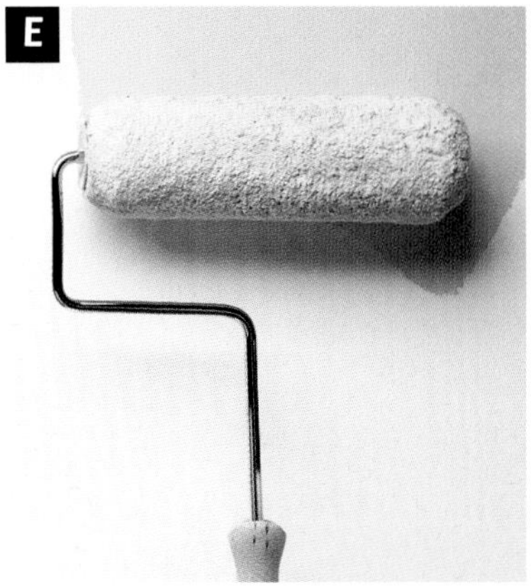
Use standard rollers on wide, flat surfaces, such as board-and-batten siding or stucco.

F
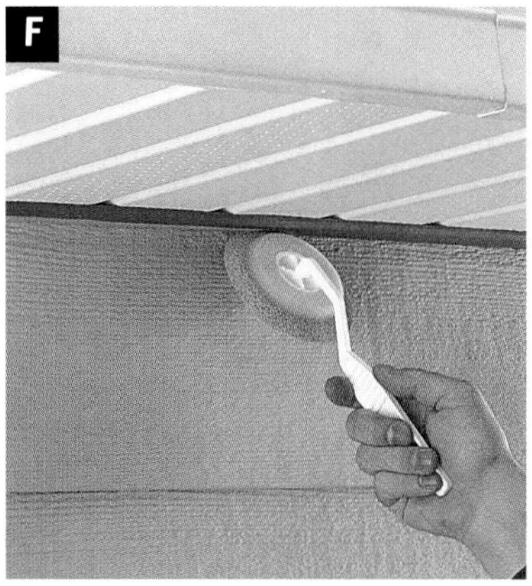
Cone-shaped rollers work well for painting the joints between intersecting surfaces.

G
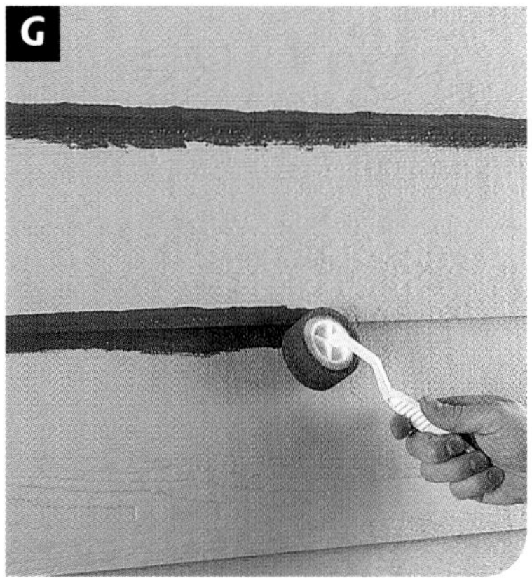
Doughnut-shaped rollers work well for painting the edges of lap siding.

Using Spray Equipment

Spray-paint guns can be purchased or rented at many hardware and home improvement stores. Follow the instructions that accompany the model you've chosen, paying particular attention to the recommendations for paint thickness and the distance the gun should be held from the surface. Maintain the recommended atomizing pressure and paint temperature throughout your project.

Protect any nearby areas that you don't want to paint **(photo H),** and set the sprayer to the desired width. Hold the paint gun perpendicular to the surface, and spray at an angle, making parallel swaths **(photo I).** Overlap each swath.

Use plastic to cover any areas you don't want to paint.

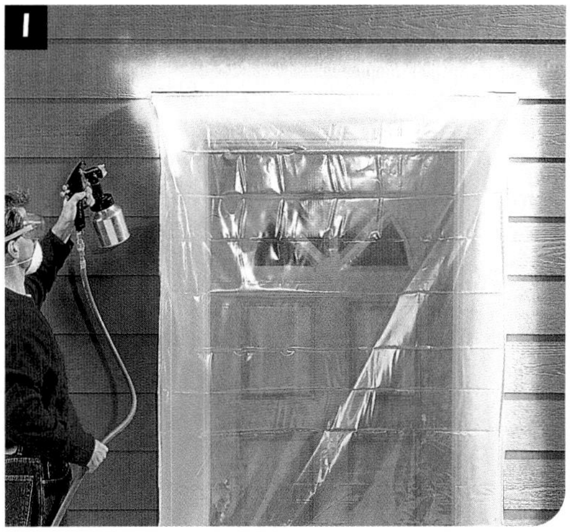

Consistently overlap each spray band to get a quality finish.

Painting Fascia, Trim & Soffits

Prime all surfaces to be painted, allow ample drying time, then apply paint. Don't be concerned if the primer coat shows streaks or shadows—the finish coat will cover them.

Paint the face of the fascia first, then cut in paint at the bottom edges of the soffit panels **(photo J).** NOTE: Fascia and soffits are usually painted the same color as the trim.

After painting the fascia, paint the gutters and downspouts, beginning with the back sides and working toward the front. When painting downspouts, make brush strokes parallel to the direction of the flutes, to avoid drips and splatters.

Paint the soffit panels and trim with a 4" brush **(photo K).** Start by cutting in around the edges of the panels using the narrow edge of the brush, then feather in the broad surfaces of the soffit panels with full loads of paint. Be sure to get good coverage in grooves.

Paint any decorative trim near the top of the house at the same time you paint soffits and fascia. Use a 2½" or 3" paintbrush for broader surfaces, and a sash brush for more intricate trim areas **(photo L).**

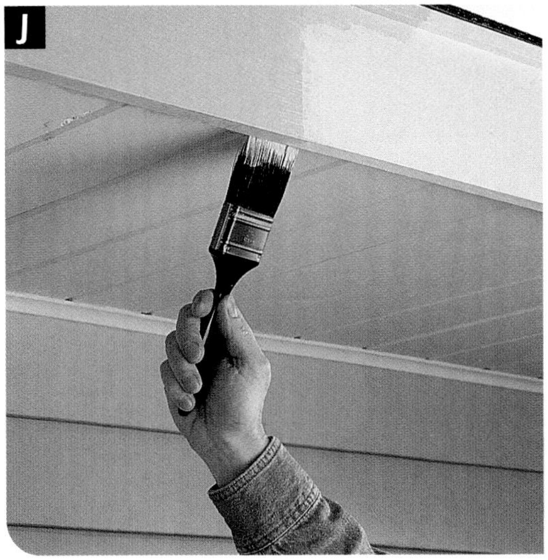

Paint the face of the fascia, then cut in the bottom edges of soffit panels.

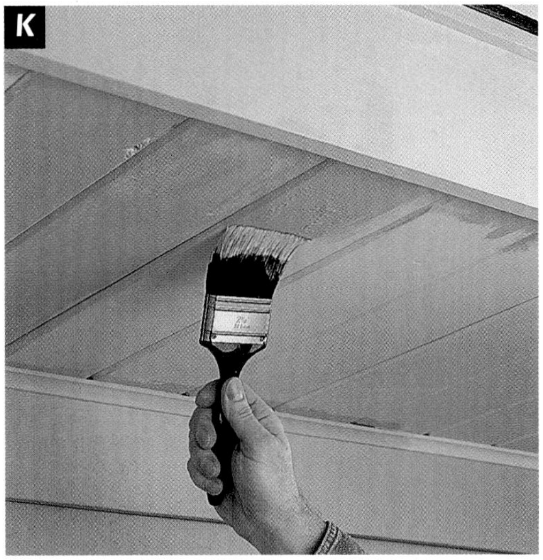

Use a 4" brush to cut in around the edges of soffit panels, then feather in the broad surfaces.

Paint any decorative trim near the top of the house while you're working on soffits and fascia.

Painting Siding

To paint the bottom edges of lap siding, hold the paintbrush flat against the wall **(photo A).** Paint the bottom edges of several siding pieces before returning to paint the faces of the same boards.

Paint the broad faces of the siding boards with a 4" brush **(photo B),** using good painting technique (page 242). Working down from the top of the house, paint as much surface as you can reach without leaning beyond the sides of the ladder.

Paint the siding all the way down to the foundation, working from top to bottom **(photo C).** Shift the ladder or scaffolding, and paint the next section. NOTE: Paint up to the edges of end caps and window or door trim that will be painted later. If you're not planning to paint the trim, mask it off or use a paint shield.

On board-and-batten or any vertical-panel siding, paint the edges of the battens or top boards first **(photo D).** Paint the faces of the battens before the sides dry, then use a roller with a 5/8"-nap sleeve to paint the large, broad surfaces between the battens, feathering in at the edges.

Holding the paintbrush flat against the wall, paint the bottom edges of several pieces of lap siding.

Paint the broad faces of the siding. Paint only an area you can reach without leaning beyond the sides of the ladder.

Paint the siding all the way down to the foundation, then shift the ladder or scaffolding and paint the next section.

On any vertical-panel siding, paint the edges first, then their faces, then the surfaces in between.

Painting Stucco Walls

First, paint the foundation with anti-chalking masonry primer, let it dry, then apply a coat of paint **(photo E).** Scrubbing paint into porous masonry surfaces is hard on paintbrushes, so choose a large, inexpensive one for this task. Start by cutting in the areas around basement windows and doors, then paint the broad surfaces of the foundation.

Apply concrete paint to stucco siding with a paint roller and a 5/8"-nap sleeve **(photo F).** Use a 3" trim roller or a 3" paintbrush for trim.

Start painting the foundation by cutting in around basement windows and doors, then paint the broad surfaces.

Paint stucco with a paint roller and a 5/8"-nap sleeve. Use a 3" trim roller or a 3" paintbrush for trim.

Painting Doors, Windows & Trim

For doors and windows, use a sash brush to paint doors and windows **(photo G).** First, paint the beveled edges of raised door panels, and the insides of frames on windows; before the edges dry, paint the faces of the door panels; next paint the rails (horizontal frame members) on doors and windows; last, paint the faces of the stiles (vertical frame members).

For trim, use a trim brush or sash brush and a moderate load of paint to paint the inside edges of door and window jambs, casings, and brick molding **(photo H).** NOTE: The surfaces on the interior side of the door stop usually should match the color of the interior trim.

Mask off siding—if freshly painted, make sure it's completely dry first. Paint the outside edges of casings and brick molding **(photo I).** Work paint all the way into the corners created by the siding's profile.

Next, paint the faces of door jambs, casings, and brick molding, feathering fresh paint around the previously painted edges **(photo J).**

Finally, paint wood door thresholds and porch floors **(photo K).** Use specially formulated enamel floor paint for maximum durability.

On doors, paint in this sequence: beveled edges (1), panel faces (2), horizontal rails (3), and vertical stiles (4).

Paint the inside edges of door and window jambs, casings, and brick molding.

Mask off the siding and paint the outside edges of casings and brick molding.

Paint the faces of door jambs, casings, and brick molding.

Paint wood door thresholds and porch floors with specially formulated enamel floor paint.

Cleaning Up

Between phases of a painting project, the cleanup required depends upon the length of time that's likely to pass before the next phase begins. For interruptions of an hour or less, simply leave paintbrushes standing with the bristle tips completely immersed in water (for latex paints) or solvent (for oil-based paints). For overnight interruptions, tightly wrap roller covers in plastic wrap or aluminum foil and store them in the refrigerator. When more than a few days will pass between phases, or at the end of a painting project, thoroughly clean paint buckets and trays, roller handles, roller covers, and brushes. Cleaning tools and products **(photo A)** make the process faster and less messy.

A

Cleaning products include, from left: chemical cleaner, spinner tool, cleaner tool for brushes and roller covers.

Remove as much paint as possible before washing tools with solvent or water. When cleaning brushes, start by squeezing out as much paint as possible by hand, then stroking back and forth across a stack of newspapers until the brush is dry. Remove layers of newspaper as necessary to keep a clean surface. To begin cleaning roller covers, use the curved side of a cleaner tool to scrape out paint **(photo B).**

If using oil-based paint, pour solvent into a paint tray and stroke brushes or rollers back and forth until the solvent dripping from them is clear. Remove water-based paints with soap and water, working the bristles or nap until the water runs clear. When brushes and roller covers are clean, use a spinner tool to remove excess solvent or water **(photo C).** Attach the tool to the spinner, hold it inside a cardboard box or five-gallon bucket, and pump the handle to throw liquid out of the roller cover or brush.

Don't stand brushes in containers to soak for extended periods—the bristles will become permanently bent. Comb clean brushes with the spiked side of a cleaner tool to align the bristles so they dry properly **(photo D).**

When brushes are completely dry, return them to their original wrappers **(photo E).** Or, wrap each one in brown wrapping paper, place a rubber band around the ferrule to secure the sheath, and hang it upside down for storage. To avoid flattening the nap, store roller covers on end.

Place used solvent in a sealed container until solid paint sediments settle out **(photo F).** Pour off the clear solvent for later use, then set the solid residue outdoors in a protected location where children and pets can't reach it. When the residue has dried completely, dispose of it in an approved manner.

Check labels before disposing of paint products, and never pour hazardous liquids into a drain system. Make a hazardous waste reminder list and post it above the utility sink. Products rated as environmental hazards by the U.S. Environmental Protection Agency carry one or more of the following terms:

Danger! Toxic, Harmful to Animals and Humans, Harmful Vapors, Poison, Flammable, Combustible, Corrosive, Explosive.

Ordinary vegetable oil removes oil-based paints and stains from skin, safely and inexpensively **(photo G).** Don't use kerosene, mineral spirits, or other solvents to remove paint from skin. These hazardous materials are irritants that can be absorbed by the body.

Save some leftover paint for touch-ups and repairs. Combine partial cans into one container, place plastic wrap over the can, and replace the lid tightly. Rap all the way around the can with a rubber mallet, then store the can upside down for a tight seal. Contact your sanitation department or the Environmental Protection Agency for information about disposal of paint cans and small amounts of leftover paint. Most waste collectors will accept solid, dried latex paint and dried, empty paint cans.

Tools: Cleaner tool, spinner tool, five-gallon bucket.

Materials: Aluminum foil, plastic wrap, newspapers, mineral spirits or other paint solvent, soap.

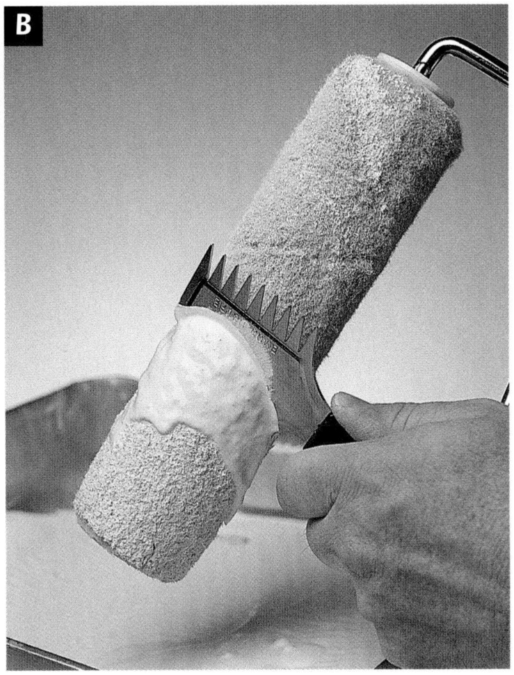

Scrape paint from roller covers with the curved side of a cleaner tool.

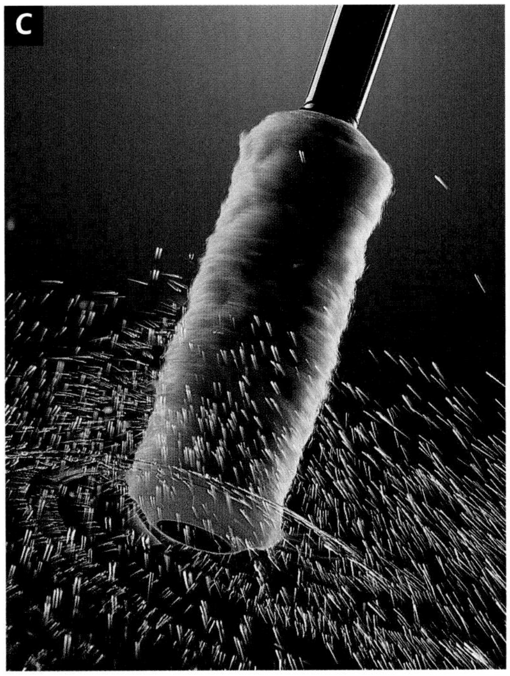

Use a spinner tool to remove paint and solvent from brushes and roller covers.

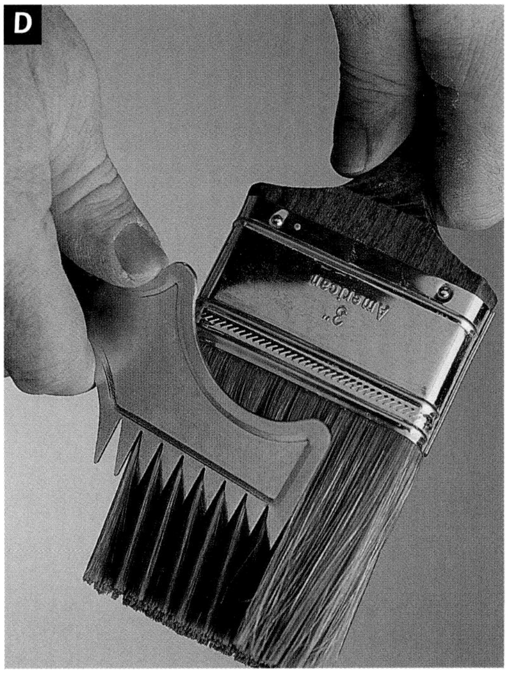

To properly align bristles for drying, comb the brush with the spiked side of a cleaner tool.

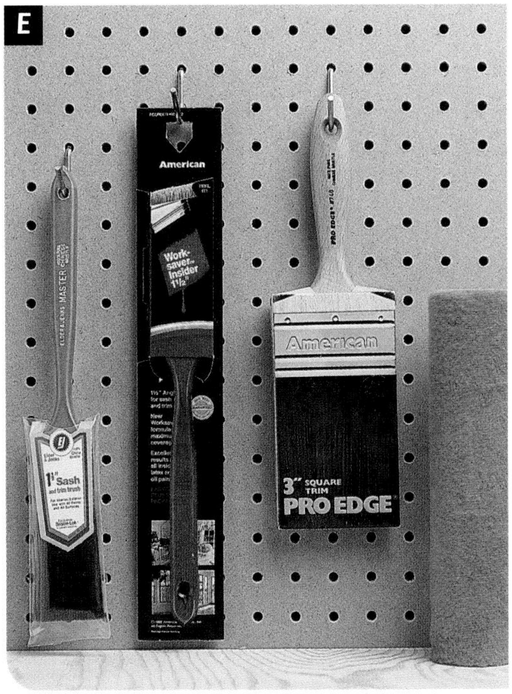

Store brushes in their wrappers or folded inside brown wrapping paper. Store washed roller covers on end.

Remove sediment from used mineral spirits and save the clear solvent for later use.

Clean oil-based paint and stain spills from hands with ordinary vegetable oil.

Concrete & Asphalt

A successful repair can restore both the appearance and the function of a failing concrete structure. However, good preparation and careful work are necessary to produce a well-blended, inconspicuous repair.

Concrete is one of the most durable building materials, but it does require occasional repair and maintenance. Problems can be caused by outside forces, improper finishing techniques, or faulty materials. Whatever the cause, it's best to address concrete problems as soon as you discover them, to prevent further damage that may be difficult or impossible to fix.

Concrete repair projects span a wide range, from sealing a surface to replacing an entire structure. The most common repairs are filling cracks and repairing surface damage. Another option is resurfacing—covering an old surface with fresh concrete. This is a good solution for minor problems (such as spalling, crazing, or popouts) that affect the surface of the concrete more than its structure.

A good surface repair can last for many years, but if there is underlying structural damage, repairing the surface is only a temporary solution. However, the right products, tools, and techniques will help you improve the appearance of the concrete and keep the damage from spreading until you can replace it.

As with any kind of repair, the success of a concrete project will depend largely on proper preparation and using the right supplies for the job. Before buying any repair products, read the manufacturer's instructions carefully to make sure you have all the tools and supplies the job requires.

This section also includes information on patching and resealing asphalt driveways. As with concrete, asphalt is quite susceptible to water damage, and small holes should be fixed promptly to avoid more serious problems in the future.

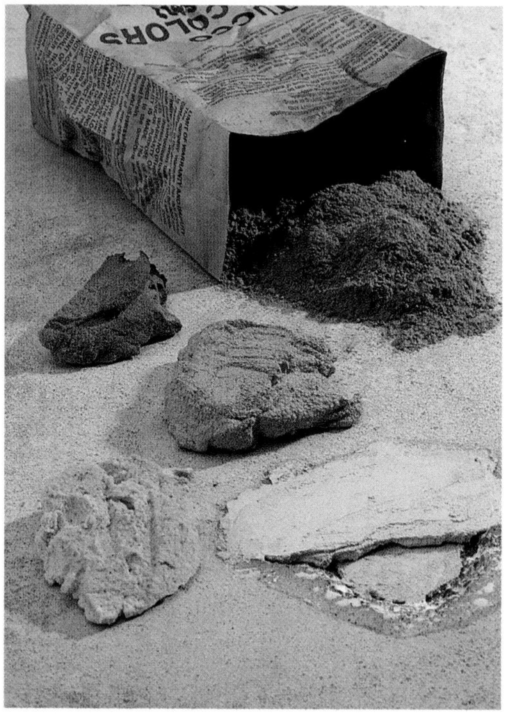

To match the color of the original concrete, mix concrete pigment with concrete patching compound.

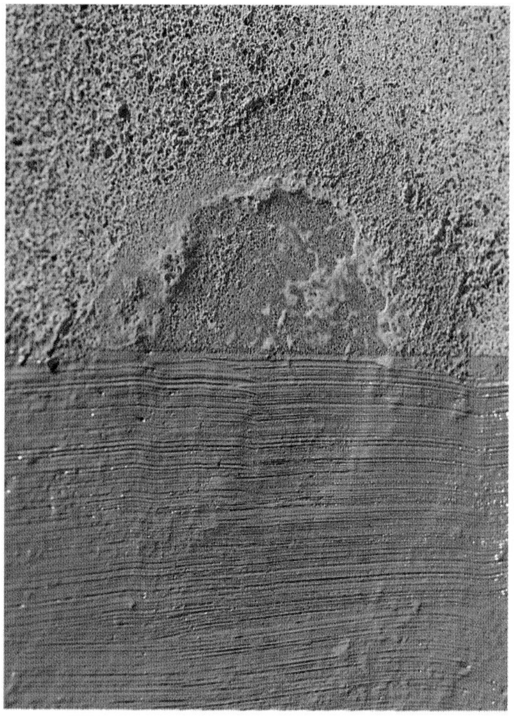

You can use masonry paint to blend a patch with the surrounding area.

Common Problems

There are two general types of concrete problems: structural failure, usually caused by outside forces, such as freezing water; and surface damage, which is usually caused by improper finishing techniques or poorly mixed concrete.

Surface problems can often be permanently repaired, and structural damage can be patched to provide a better appearance and resist further damage. However, the only real solution to a structural problem is to replace the concrete.

Frost heaving is common in cold climates, where the freeze-thaw cycle forces concrete slabs out of the ground **(photo A).** The best solution is to remove the affected sections, repair the subbase, and pour new sections separated by isolation joints (1/2"-thick asphalt-impregnated boards that keep the concrete sections from bonding together).

Sunken concrete is usually caused by erosion of the subbase **(photo B).** Some structures, such as sidewalks, can be raised to repair the subbase and then relaid. However, a better solution is to have a contractor raise the surface by injecting fresh concrete below it.

Isolated cracks are common in concrete **(photo C).** Fill small cracks with concrete caulk or crack-filler, and patch large cracks with a vinyl-reinforced patching product.

Popouts can be caused by freezing moisture or stress **(photo D).** They can also occur in concrete that was improperly floated or cured, as the aggregate near the surface loosens. To repair them, follow the instructions for filling holes (page 252).

Spalling, or general surface deterioration, results from overfloating, which draws too much water to the surface, causing the concrete to weaken and peel **(photo E).** This problem is typically widespread, and calls for resurfacing (page 256).

Crazing—or a network of hairline cracks—is usually caused by overfloating **(photo F).** Cleaning and sealing the surface will help prevent further crazing, but the long-term solution is to resurface the concrete (page 256).

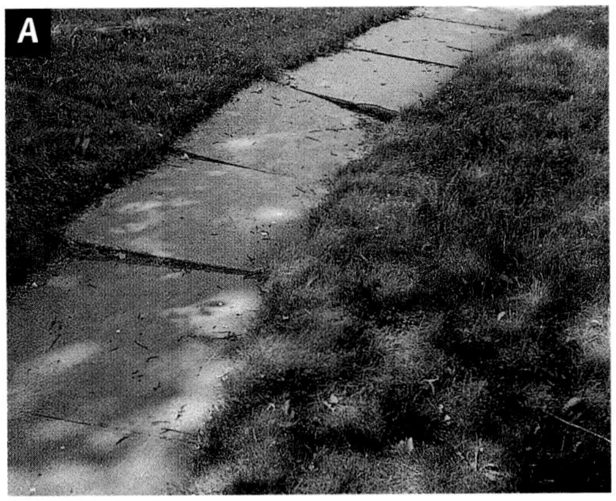

Frost heaving, which causes concrete slabs to pop up, is caused by the freezing and thawing of ground moisture.

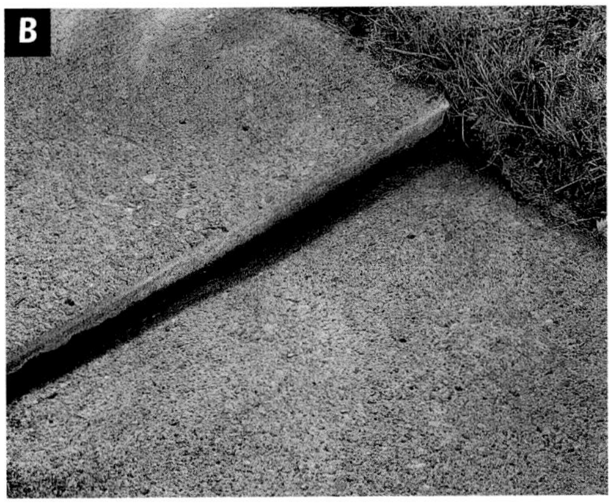

Sinking is usually caused by erosion of the subbase. A mud-jacking contractor can raise the sunken area.

Isolated cracks are common and relatively easy to repair with concrete caulk or patching compound.

Popouts can result from stress, freezing, or improper floating or curing during installation of the concrete.

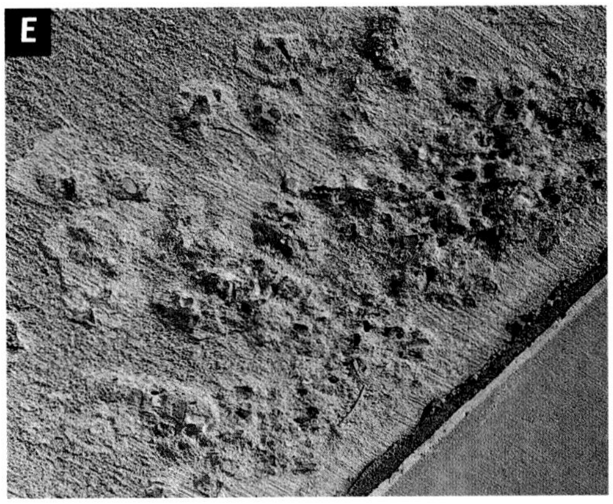

Spalling is caused by overfloating, which draws too much water to the surface, causing it to weaken and peel off.

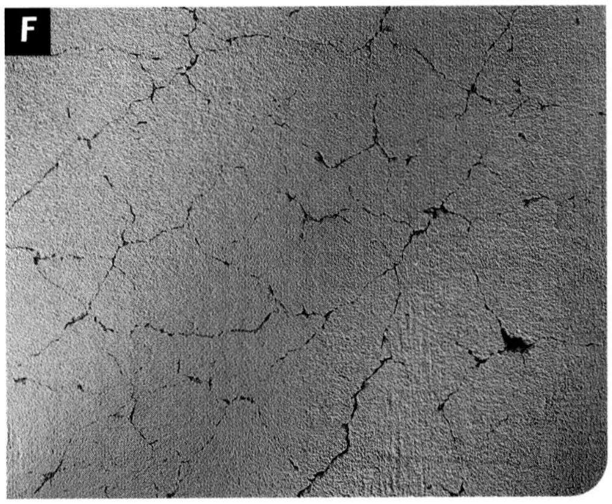

Crazing (hairline cracks) also result from overfloating. To prevent further deterioration, clean and seal the surface.

Masonry Tools & Materials

To work effectively with concrete, brick, block, and other masonry products, you'll need to buy or rent some specialty tools.

The hand tools needed to place, shape, and finish concrete and mortar include trowels, floats, edgers, and jointers. Bricksets and cold chisels are used to cut and fit brick and block. You'll also need to fit your circular saw and power drill with cutting discs and bits designed for use with concrete and brick.

The tools needed to mix concrete and mortar depend on the size of the project. For very small projects and for mixing mortar, you can use a mortar box and masonry hoe. For most other jobs, you'll need a power concrete mixer.

If your project requires more than one cubic yard of concrete (chart, page 254), have it delivered in ready-mix form; this saves you a lot of time and labor, and ensures that the concrete has a uniform consistency for the entire project.

To make the layout phase of the job easier and more accurate, you'll also need to have the proper tools for aligning and measuring.

Concrete, mortar, and masonry tools include: magnesium float (1), wood float (2), groover (3), stair edger (4), edger (5), jointer (6), power drill (7), masonry bits (8), masonry-grinding disc (9), masonry-cutting blade for circular saw (10), masonry trowel (11), pointing trowel (12), brickset (13), cold chisel (14), bricklayer's hammer (15), maul (16).

Removing a Concrete Walk

The best way to remove a concrete walkway is to break it up. Pry up the edge of the walkway with a 2 × 4, then strike the elevated section with a sledgehammer to break it into manageable pieces.

Concrete repair products include: vinyl-reinforced concrete patch (1), hydraulic cement (2), quick-setting cement (3), anchoring cement (4), concrete sealing products (5), concrete recoating product (6), masonry paint (7), joint-filler caulk (8), pour-in crack sealer (9), concrete cleaner (10), concrete fortifier (11), bonding adhesive (12), sand-mix concrete (13).

Sealing & Maintaining Concrete

There are several specialty products available to help you seal, clean, and protect the concrete surfaces around your home.

Regular cleaning is important; it keeps concrete from deteriorating when exposed to oils and deicing salts.

To clean oil stains, dampen sawdust with paint thinner, and apply the sawdust to the stain. The paint thinner will break apart the stain, and the sawdust will absorb the oil. When you're done, sweep up the sawdust with a broom, and reapply as needed **(photo A).**

To paint concrete surfaces, use a waterproof concrete paint **(photo B)** formulated to resist chalking and efflorescence (the dusty film caused by mineral leaching). It's sold in stock colors, but you can also order custom colors.

To fill the control joints in concrete sidewalks and driveways, use concrete repair caulk **(photo C).** The caulk prevents water from accumulating and damaging the concrete.

To keep aggregate from loosening, apply an exposed-aggregate sealer about three weeks after you pour new concrete. First, wash the surface thoroughly and let it dry. Pour the sealer into a roller tray, making a puddle in the corner. Spread the sealer evenly with a paint roller on an extension pole **(photo D).**

To protect concrete that's exposed to traffic or moisture, seal it with a clear concrete sealer, which creates a water-resistant protective layer on the surface **(photo E).** The most popular sealers are acrylic-based and won't attract dirt. Some sealant products will also help the concrete cure more evenly.

To improve appearance of a concrete wall, you can use a masonry recoating product **(photo F).** They're applied like paint, and look like fresh concrete when dry. However, they have little waterproofing value.

Tools: *Paintbrush, paint roller and tray, dust brush and pan, caulk gun, paint pad.*

Materials: *Masonry paint, paint thinner, repair caulk, exposed-aggregate sealer, concrete recoating product.*

Clean oil stains with sawdust dampened in paint thinner to break up the stain and absorb the oil.

Paint concrete surfaces with waterproof concrete paint formulated to resist chalking and efflorescence.

Fill control joints in sidewalks and driveways with concrete repair caulk to prevent water from damaging the concrete.

Apply an exposed-aggregate sealer about three weeks after a new concrete surface is poured.

Use an acrylic-based clear concrete sealer to create a water-resistant seal on a concrete surface.

To improve the surface of a wall, apply a masonry recoating product. When dry, it will look like fresh concrete.

Patching Holes

Use hydraulic or quick-setting cement to repair holes in vertical surfaces (select hydraulic cement if the structure is regularly exposed to moisture). These products set up in just a few minutes, and can be shaped to fill holes without using a form.

Even a well-made concrete structure is subject to wear and tear, which eventually can result in holes or damaged spots. The tools, materials, and techniques required to patch holes in concrete will vary, depending on the severity and location of the damage.

The best product for filling a small hole less than 1/2" deep is a vinyl-reinforced concrete patching compound, which can be applied in layers up to 1/2" thick.

For deeper holes, use sand-mix concrete mixed with an acrylic or latex fortifier, applying it in layers up to 2" thick.

As with cracks, you can make stronger and more durable patches on concrete holes by cleaning the hole first and making a clean, backward-angled cut around the perimeter of the damaged area. This helps the repair material bond to the old concrete, and prevents it from coming loose.

For the extensive cutting required to prepare a large hole for patching, it's faster and more effective to use power tools equipped with masonry blades than to use hand tools. Always wear gloves and eye protection when cutting concrete.

Patching a Small Hole

To prepare a small hole for repair, begin by cutting around the damaged area with a masonry-grinding disc mounted on a drill **(photo A).** If you prefer, you can use a cold chisel and a hand maul instead.

Bevel the cuts about 15° away from the center of the hole. Chisel out any loose material within the repair area.

Using a paintbrush, apply a thin layer of bonding adhesive to the entire patch **(photo B).** This will help create a strong bond.

Fill the damaged area with a layer of vinyl-reinforced patching compound, adding no more than 1/4" to 1/2" at a time **(photo C).** Wait about 30 minutes between each layer to allow the compound to dry before another coat is added.

Continue adding 1/4" to 1/2" layers of the patching compound to the hole until it's filled to a level just above the surface of the surrounding area.

Use the trowel to feather the repair area until it's level with the surrounding surface; allow the patching compound to cure.

Tools: Trowel, drill with masonry-grinding disc, circular saw with masonry-cutting blade, cold chisel, hand maul, paintbrush.

Materials: Gloves, eye protection, concrete bonding adhesive, vinyl-reinforced patching compound.

Prepare a small hole by cutting around it with a masonry-grinding disc mounted on a power drill.

Apply a thin layer of bonding adhesive to ensure a strong bond for the patching compound.

Fill the hole with layers of patching compound, adding no more than 1/2" at a time.

Patching a Large Hole

To prepare a large hole for repair, begin by marking straight cutting lines around the damage. Cut on the lines, using a portable circular saw fitted with a masonry-cutting blade. Set the foot of the saw on a thin board to protect it from the concrete. Bevel the cut away from the damage at a 15° angle **(photo D).**

Chisel out any remaining concrete in the repair area. Brush a thin layer of bonding adhesive onto the patch.

Mix sand-mix concrete with acrylic concrete fortifier. Trowel it into the hole, adding no more than 2" at a time **(photo E).** Allow the concrete to dry between layers. Continue adding concrete until it's just above the level of the surrounding area.

Smooth and feather the repair with a screed board and a wood float until it's level with the surrounding surface **(photo F).**

Re-create any special finish that was used on the original surface (such as brooming), and allow the concrete patch to cure.

Tools: Circular saw with masonry-cutting blade, trowel, hand maul, drill with masonry-cutting disc, mixing box, paintbrush, screed board, wood float.

Materials: Gloves, eye protection, hydraulic cement, concrete bonding adhesive, sand-mix concrete, concrete fortifier.

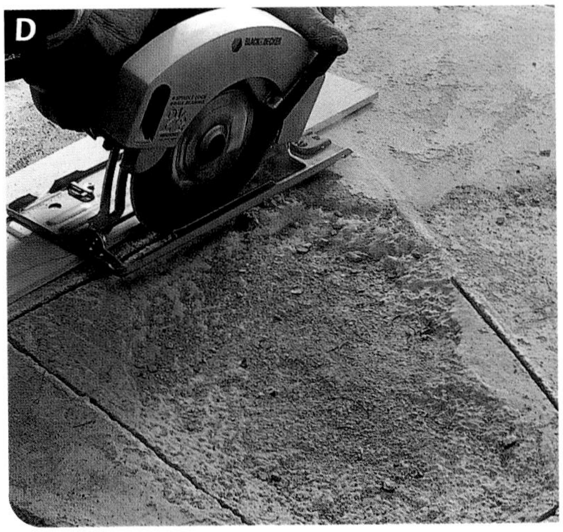

Cut out the area to be patched with a portable circular saw equipped with a masonry-cutting blade.

Fill the damaged area with fortified sand-mix concrete until it's slightly above the surrounding surface.

Using a wood float, smooth and feather the repair area until it's level with the surrounding surface.

Repairing Walkways

Concrete walkways and steps are long-lasting structures that resist damage from traffic and shoveling. However, they can become broken or chipped, stained by rust or oil, or cracked by the effects of water—the greatest enemy of concrete.

To keep water from getting under a slab, keep it well sealed and repair any soil erosion around it.

The tools, techniques, and materials you'll need for concrete repair projects depend on the type of problem you're trying to fix, the magnitude of the problem, and its location.

For example, you'll need to approach a small crack in a step differently than a long sidewalk with a deteriorating surface caused by spalling, crazing, or popouts.

Replacing damaged steps or a deteriorating walkway makes the entrance to your home safer and more attractive.

Tips for Estimating Concrete

The coverage rate of poured concrete depends on the dimensions of the slab. For a given amount of concrete, the thicker the slab, the smaller the overall surface.

To estimate how much concrete you'll need for a replacement project, measure the width, depth, and thickness of the area you're paving, in feet. Multiply these dimensions together to get the cubic footage involved. For example:

3 ft. × 10 ft. × 1/3 ft. = 10 cu. ft.

One cubic yard is equal to twenty-seven cubic feet.

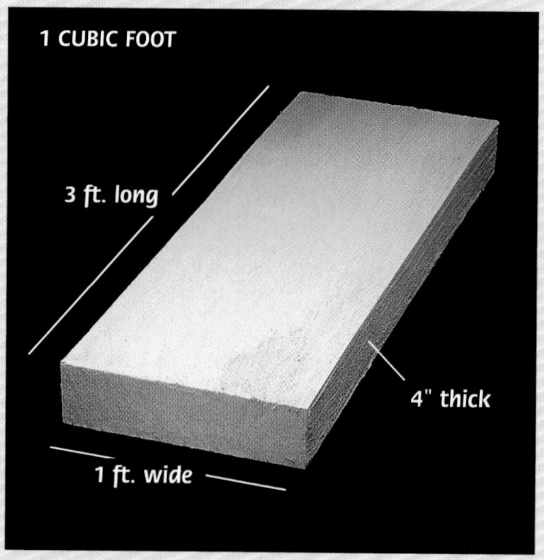

Concrete Coverage

Volume	Thickness	Surface Coverage
1 cu. yd.	2"	160 sq. ft.
1 cu. yd.	3"	100 sq. ft.
1 cu. yd.	4"	80 sq. ft.
1 cu. yd.	5"	65 sq. ft.
1 cu. yd.	6"	55 sq. ft.
1 cu. yd.	8"	40 sq. ft.

Repairing a Crack

To fix a concrete crack, start by preparing the surface. Clean any loose material from the crack with a wire brush or a drill with a wire wheel attachment **(photo A).** Clean the area thoroughly—debris that's left in the crack will result in a poor bond and a weak repair.

To keep the repair material from pushing out of the crack, use a cold chisel and a hand maul to open the crack into a backward-angled cut that's wider at the base **(photo B).**

Next, use a paintbrush to apply a thin layer of bonding adhesive to the area **(photo C).** This also helps keep the repair material from loosening or popping out of the crack.

The materials used to fill a concrete crack depend on the size of the crack. For cracks less than 1/4" wide, you can use concrete caulk for a quick fix, but this is only a short-term solution to prevent further damage. A more permanent solution is to use a vinyl-reinforced patching compound.

To fix a small crack, mix the patching compound and trowel it into the crack. Feather the repair area with the trowel until it's even with the surrounding surface **(photo D).**

For a large crack on a horizontal surface, use sand-mix concrete with a concrete fortifier. First, pour sand into the crack to within 1/2" of the surface. Mix the concrete and the fortifier. Trowel the mixture into the crack and feather until even with the surface **(photo E).**

For a large crack on a vertical surface, use hydraulic or quick-setting cement. Apply the cement in layers no more than 1/2" thick, until the patch is slightly higher than the surrounding area **(photo F).** Feather the patch until the edges are even with the surface.

Tools: *Wire brush or drill with wire-wheel attachment, cold chisel, hand maul, paintbrush, caulk gun, trowel.*

Materials: *Vinyl-reinforced patching compound, concrete caulk, sand, hydraulic or quick-setting cement, sand-mix concrete, concrete fortifier.*

Before starting a crack repair project, clean loose material and debris from the crack.

Chisel out the crack to create a backward-angled cut that's wider at the base than at the surface.

After cleaning and chiseling the crack open, apply a thin layer of bonding adhesive to the entire repair area.

For a small crack, trowel vinyl-reinforced patching compound into the crack and feather it even with the surface.

For a large crack on a horizontal surface, prepare the crack, fill with sand, then trowel sand-mix concrete into it.

For a large crack on a vertical surface, prepare the crack, then trowel a layer of concrete or hydraulic cement into it.

Resurfacing Concrete

A concrete structure that has suffered surface damage but is still structurally sound can be preserved by resurfacing—applying a thin layer of new concrete over the old surface.

Resurfacing is a good solution for concrete that has extensive surface damage, such as spalling or popouts. But, if the old surface has deep cracks or serious damage, use resurfacing only as a short-term fix to fend off more severe deterioration from water penetration, freezing, and erosion.

Because the new surface is so thin (1" to 2"), you need to use a sand-mix concrete for resurfacing. If you have ready-mix concrete delivered by a concrete contractor, make sure they don't include any aggregate larger than 1/2" in the mixture.

The new surface will bond best to the old concrete if it's packed down, so be sure to use a dry, stiff concrete mixture that can be compacted with a shovel. (Bonding adhesive also helps it adhere.)

Begin by cleaning the surface thoroughly. If it's flaking or spalled, scrape it with a spade to dislodge as much loose concrete as you can **(photo A),** then sweep it clean.

Dig a 6"-wide trench around the surface on all sides, for the 2 × 4 forms **(photo B).**

Place the forms in the trench, 1" to 2" above the surface, making sure all the tops are even and level **(photo C).** Drive the stakes into the ground, and screw them to the forms.

Mark the locations of the control joints on

Tools: *Wood float, spade, broom, mixing box or power mixer, circular saw, hand maul, screw gun, paintbrush, paint roller with extension, wheel barrow, shovel, screed board, groover, edger.*

Materials: *Gloves, 2 × 4 forms, 12" stakes, vegetable oil, deck screws, sand-mix concrete, bonding adhesive, plastic sheets.*

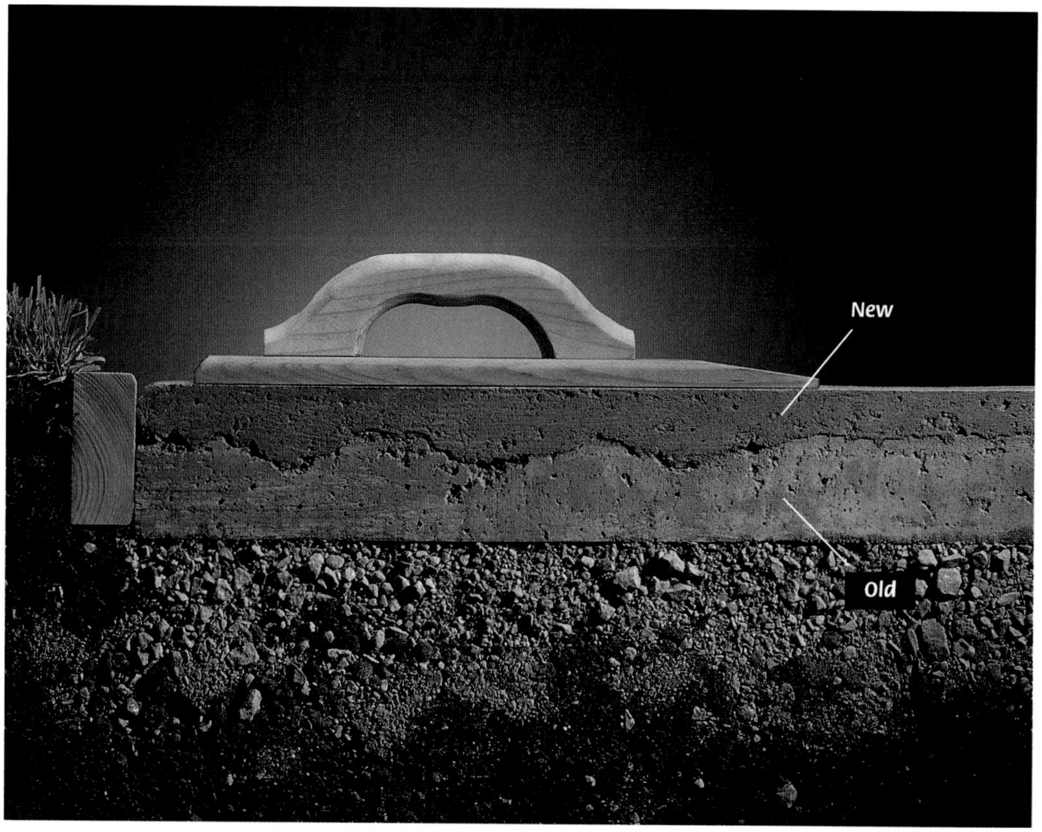

Resurfacing concrete involves applying a thin layer of fresh concrete over an existing surface that has been damaged. This approach can be a less costly alternative to replacing the entire structure.

Begin by cleaning the old surface thoroughly: scrape it with a spade to dislodge any loose concrete and sweep it clean.

Dig a trench around all sides of the area being resurfaced for the 2 × 4 forms that will contain the wet concrete.

the outside of the forms directly above the existing joints. (Control joints prevent damage by controlling the direction of cracking.)

Coat the insides of the forms with vegetable oil. Apply a thin layer of bonding adhesive over the entire area, following the manufacturer's directions **(photo D).**

Mix the sand-mix concrete, making the mixture slightly stiffer (drier) than usual. Spread the concrete and press it down with a shovel or a 2 × 4 to pack it into the forms **(photo E).**

Use a screed board (a straight 2 × 4 resting on opposite forms) to strike off the excess concrete. Move the board in a sawing motion from left to right, keeping it flat as you work. Fill any low spots and repeat the process.

Use a wood float to smooth the surface. Move the tool in a circular motion, tipping its leading edge slightly upward to prevent gouging **(photo F).** Stop floating when the entire surface is smooth and the float leaves no visible marks.

Use an edger to shape the edges next to the forms. If you wish, you can duplicate the texture used on the original surface.

Use a trowel and then a grooving tool to cut the control joints at the marked locations, using a straight piece of lumber as a guide.

Floating will cause puddles of water to form on the surface. Once this water starts to form, finish any tooling as quickly as possible.

For a denser, smoother finish, float the surface with a steel trowel after the surface water has dried, then redo the edges and grooves.

Cover the fresh concrete with plastic and let it cure for one week, then remove the forms.

Place the forms and stake them flush against the sides of the existing concrete slabs, making sure they are all the same height. Mark the location of the control joints on the forms.

To help the new surface adhere to the old one, apply a thin layer of bonding adhesive over the entire surface.

Mix the concrete by hand or with a power mixer. Follow the manufacturer's instructions, but make the mixture drier than normal. Spread the concrete and pack it into the forms.

Float the surface, using a circular motion and tipping the lead edge slightly upward. Work until the entire surface is fairly smooth and the float leaves no visible marks.

Repairing Concrete Steps

Concrete steps tend to require more maintenance and repair than any other concrete structure around the house.

They're especially likely to become damaged at corners and on the front edges of step treads. The corners are prone to erosion and cracking, and the treads experience heavy use, which makes them susceptible to wear and damage.

The horizontal surfaces of steps can be repaired (page 259), and broken step corners can be reattached with patching compound. However, to fix a missing corner or a damaged tread, you need to use quick-setting cement, and shape it to fit the original surface.

Wear and tear on the surfaces and corners of steps can be successfully repaired. Here, a deep popout is being filled. However, step corners and vertical surfaces require the techniques shown below.

Tools: Trowel, wire brush, paintbrush, circular saw with masonry-cutting blade, chisel, wood float, edger.

Materials: Gloves, eye protection, wood form, bonding adhesive, vinyl-reinforced patching compound, quick-setting cement, plastic sheeting.

Repairing a Step Corner

To repair the corner of a step, begin by retrieving the piece that has broken off.

If you can't find the broken piece, rebuild it with quick-setting cement (page 259).

Use a wire brush to clean both the broken piece and its setting on the step. Apply a bonding adhesive to both surfaces **(photo A).**

Spread a heavy layer of fortified patching cement onto the surfaces being joined. Press the broken piece into position on the step corner **(photo B).**

Lean a heavy brick or block against the repair area until the patching compound sets (about 30 minutes).

Protect the repaired corner from traffic for at least one week.

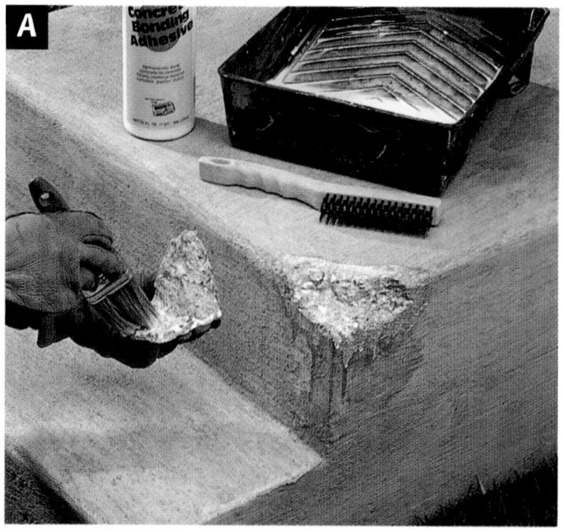

Clean both the corner piece and its setting with a wire brush. Apply a coat of bonding adhesive to both surfaces.

Spread a heavy layer of fortified patching cement onto both surfaces, and press the broken piece into position.

Patching a Step Tread

To patch a broken or damaged step tread, begin by using a portable circular saw fitted with a masonry-cutting blade to cut around the damaged area on the stair tread **(photo C).** Hold the saw so the cut angles toward the back of the step.

Make a horizontal cut into the riser, at a right angle to the first cut. Chisel out any remaining material between the two cuts.

Cut a form board the same height as the step riser. Press it against the riser of the damaged step. Use stakes, nails, or heavy blocks to brace it into position **(photo D).** Make sure that the top of the form is flush with the riser and level with the top of the step tread.

Apply bonding adhesive to the repair area. Use a trowel to press a stiff mixture of quick-setting cement into the repair area **(photo E).**

Smooth the surface of the cement with a wood float, and let it set for a few minutes **(photo F).**

Use an edger to round over the front edge of the nose. Slice off the side of the patch with a trowel, so that it's flush with the side of the steps.

In hot, dry conditions, cover the patch with plastic. Wait at least 24 hours before using the steps.

Use a circular saw fitted with a masonry-cutting blade to make a backward-angled cut into the tread and a straight cut into the riser below it. Chisel out any loose material.

Cut a form board the height of the step riser. Press it flush with the riser, and brace it into position with heavy blocks. Make sure the top of the form is level with the top of the tread.

After applying bonding adhesive to the repair area, use a trowel to press a stiff mixture of quick-setting cement into the damaged area.

Use a wood float to smooth the surface of the cement even with the top of the tread. Round off the front edge of the patch with an edger and the side of the patch with a trowel.

Replacing Concrete Steps

Replacing old or damaged steps with properly designed and built new concrete steps can significantly increase the safety and attractiveness of your entryway.

However, before you demolish the old steps, measure them to see if they meet the step safety guidelines (see box). If they do, you can base the dimensions of the new steps on the old ones. If not, you'll need to redesign the steps from scratch and correct any design errors before you start building.

Designing steps properly requires some math and a bit of trial and error. As you work, sketch out your plan on graph paper.

The goal is to develop a design that fits the space and meets the safety guidelines. In general, wide treads are compatible with a short rise—but you can adjust all the measurements of the steps, as long as you stay within the safety guidelines. However, be sure to make all the risers and treads uniform, with the same dimensions.

Step Safety Guidelines

The landing depth should be at least 12" more than the width of the door.

The step treads should be between 10" and 12" deep.

The step risers should be between 6" and 8" high.

Preparing the Footings & Forms

Start by demolishing the old steps. If they're concrete, use a sledgehammer or a rented chipping gun, and wear protective gear. Set aside the concrete rubble for use as fill material for the new steps.

Dig two 12"-wide trenches for the footings, to the depth required by your local Building Codes. Place the trenches perpendicular to the foundation and spaced so the footings will extend 3" wider than the outside edges of the finished steps. Add steel rebar grids to reinforce the footings **(photo A).** Since they're supporting poured concrete, you don't need any forms.

Mix the concrete and pour the footings. Use a screed board to smooth the concrete at ground level **(photo B).** You don't need to float the surface.

Once the surface water dries, insert 12" sections of rebar 6" into the concrete, spaced 1 ft. apart and centered side to side **(photo C).** Leave 1 ft. of space at each end.

Let the footings cure for two days, then dig out the area between them to 4" deep. Pour in 5" of compactible gravel subbase and tamp until level with the footings **(photo D).**

Tools: *Sledgehammer or chipping gun, screed board, hand tamper.*

Materials: *Gloves, safety glasses, steel rebar grids, 12" rebar sections, compactible gravel.*

A

Install steel rebar grids in the trenches to reinforce the footings.

B

Use a screed board to smooth the concrete, level with the ground.

C

Insert 12" sections of rebar 6" into the concrete, spaced 1 ft. apart.

D

Tamp the compactible gravel subbase until it's level with the top of the footings.

Building the Forms

The next phase in replacing a set of steps is building the forms.

Begin by transferring the measurements for the side forms from your working sketch onto 3/4" exterior-grade plywood **(photo E).** Add a 1/8" per ft. back-to-front slope to the landing area of the form.

Use a jig saw to cut out the side forms along the cutting lines. You can save time by clamping the two pieces of plywood together and cutting both side forms at the same time.

Cut the riser forms from 2 × 8 lumber to fit between the side forms. Bevel the bottom edges of the boards to allow clearance for the float at the back edges of the steps.

Attach the riser forms to the side forms with 2" deck screws **(photo F).**

Cut a 2 × 4 to make a center support for the riser forms. Attach cleats to the riser forms with 2" deck screws, then attach the center support to the cleats **(photo G).**

Check to make sure that all the corners are square and that all the forms are perfectly vertical. Coat the inside surfaces of all the forms with vegetable oil.

Cut an isolation board from asphalt-impregnated fibrous board to cover the back of the project area. Glue it to the house foundation with construction adhesive. The isolation board keeps the concrete from bonding with the house foundation and allows the two structures to move independently, which minimizes the risk of cracking.

Set the assembled forms onto the footings, flush against the isolation board. Check again to make sure that the corners are square and the forms are vertical.

Cut cleats, stakes, and bracing arms for the forms from 2 × 4 lumber. Attach the cleats to the outside surface of the side forms. Attach the 2 × 4 bracing arms to the cleats.

Drive the stakes into the ground and secure the center support and the bracing arms to them **(photo H).**

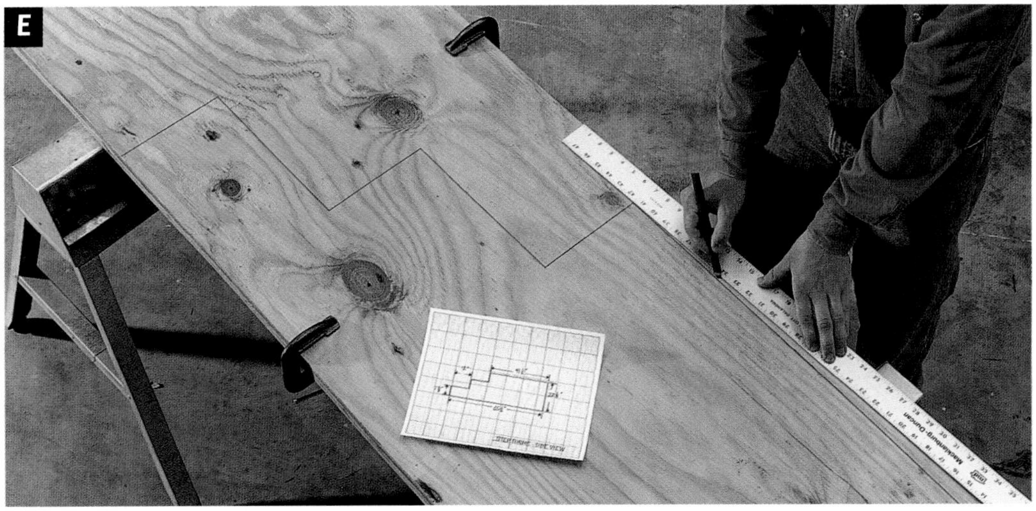

Transfer the measurements of the side forms onto 3/4" exterior-grade plywood, sloping the landing surface 1/8" per foot.

Tools: Pencil, jig saw, clamps, carpenter's square, hand maul, level, caulk gun, screw gun.

Materials: 5-ply 3/4" exterior-grade plywood (side forms), 2 × 4 cleats and stakes, 2 × 8 riser forms, 2" deck screws, vegetable oil, 1/2"-thick asphalt-impregnated fibrous board, construction adhesive.

Attach the riser forms to the side forms, using 2" deck screws.

Attach the center support to the cleats on the riser forms.

Secure the center support and bracing arms to the cleats.

Filling the Forms & Finishing the Steps

The next phase of the construction process is filling in the forms.

Begin by filling the area under the landing with clean fill—broken concrete or concrete rubble. Stack the fill carefully, keeping it 6" away from the sides, back, and top edges of the forms. Shovel smaller fragments onto the pile to fill the empty areas.

Lay pieces of #3 metal rebar on top of the fill pile, spacing them 12" apart. Use wire to attach them to bolsters, so they don't shift when you pour the concrete **(photo A).** Keep the rebar at least 2" below the top of the form.

***Tools:** Shovel or spade, screed board, wood float, wheelbarrow, masonry hoe, hammer, trowel, step edger, stiff-bristled broom.*

***Materials:** Clean fill (broken concrete or concrete rubble), #3 metal rebar, rebar bolsters, wire, general-purpose concrete mix, mixer box or power mixer, J-bolts (optional), plastic sheeting (optional), handrail, concrete sealer.*

Mix the concrete, following the manufacturer's directions. Pour the steps one at a time, beginning with the bottom step.

Don't pour too close to the forms—after each pour, tamp the concrete into the corners. However, don't overwork the concrete or spread it too far; space the batches and work each one just enough to fill the form.

Distribute the concrete evenly with a masonry hoe until the surface is roughly flat, and slightly above the level of the first step.

Settle the concrete by rapping the forms with a hammer or the blade of a shovel. This is especially important, as it creates a smoother surface on the sides of the steps.

Smooth the surface with a screed board. Move it in a sawing motion, keeping it flat as you work. For best results, do this with a helper, with one person on each side of the form. Fill any low spots and repeat.

At this point, press a piece of #3 rebar 1" down into the nose of each tread to reinforce the steps **(photo B).**

Smooth the surface further by doing an initial leveling with a wood float. Move the float in overlapping arcs, then repeat with overlapping straight sideways strokes. Keep the tool's leading edge tipped upward slightly and work its front edge beneath the beveled edge at the bottom of the riser form **(photo C).**

The initial floating will cause puddles of water to form on the surface. Once this water starts to form, finish the initial floating as quickly as possible.

If you're installing a railing that has mounting plates attached to sunken J-bolts, place the J-bolts in the proper position on the step before the concrete sets **(photo D).**

Curing Concrete

To harden properly during curing, a fresh concrete surface needs to stay damp. The danger of overly rapid evaporation is greatest during hot, dry weather.

The easiest way to cure concrete is to cover it with plastic sheeting. Be sure to overlap and tape the seams, then anchor the plastic securely on all sides with 2 × 4s laid flat.

You can also cover the concrete with straw, burlap, or any other water-retaining material, and wet it down as needed.

Lay pieces of rebar on the pile and wire them to rebar bolsters so they don't shift during pouring.

After pouring and floating each step, press a piece of #3 rebar 1" down in the nose of the tread.

Use a wood float to level the surface, working first in overlapping arcs, and then in long, side-to-side strokes.

Pour the concrete in the forms for the remaining steps, one at a time, following the above procedure for each one **(photo E).**

As you work, keep an eye on the steps you've already poured. When the surface water has disappeared and the concrete has lost its sheen, stop to edge and finish the surface.

At this point, shape the edges of the steps and the landing with a step edger. Keep the leading edge of the tool tipped upward slightly **(photo F).**

Next, you can float the edges again to get a smooth final finish **(photo G).** However, for steps that are exposed to a high volume of traffic, a broomed finish is a better alternative, because it produces a nonskid surface.

To create a broomed finish, drag a stiff-bristled broom across the surface of the fresh concrete, always pulling the broom toward you. Avoid overlapping passes, which will destroy the broomed texture and produce a pebbly effect. Finish by redoing the edges.

Cover the surface of the fresh concrete with plastic sheeting to keep it from drying out too quickly. Let the concrete cure for one week before removing the forms.

Check your local Building Codes for the handrail requirements in your area. Install a handrail **(photo H),** if required. Backfill the area around the base of the steps.

If you wish, cover the steps with a concrete sealer. This is a good idea for steps that are exposed to heavy traffic or moisture **(photo I).**

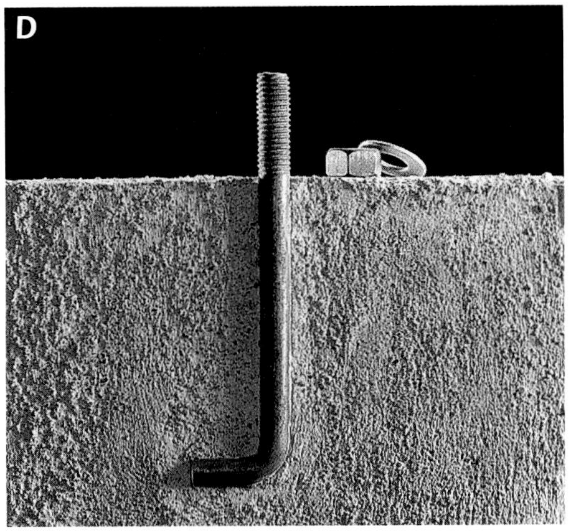

If you'll be installing a railing that's attached to sunken J-bolts, place them in the concrete before it sets.

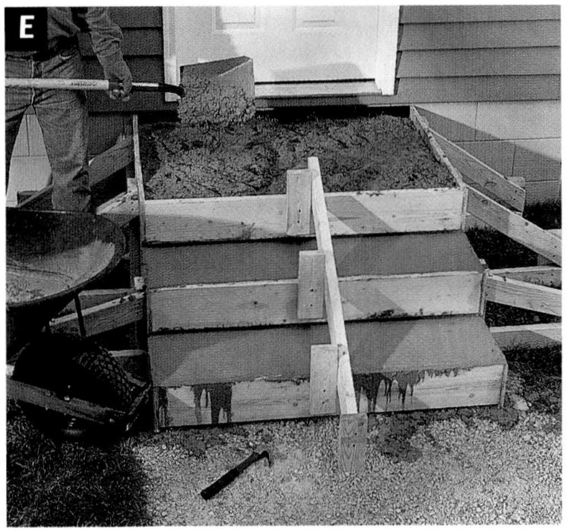

Pour the concrete for each step one at a time, distributing and settling it as you pour.

Use a step edger to shape the edges of the steps and the landing, keeping the leading edge tilted upward.

A final floating will give the surface a smooth finish. For a nonskid finish, use a broomed texture instead.

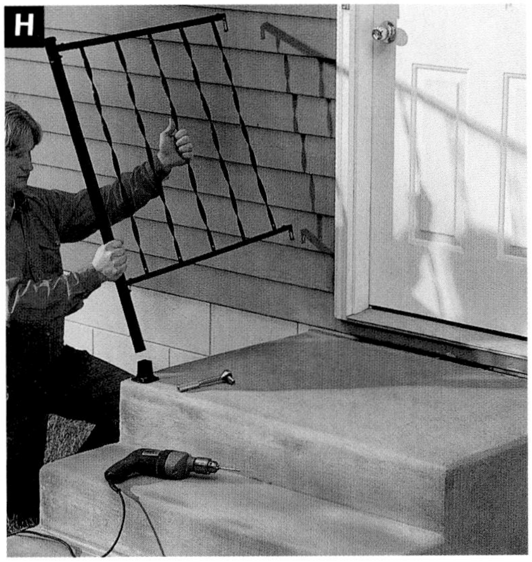

After removing the forms, you can install a handrail and backfill the area around the base of the steps.

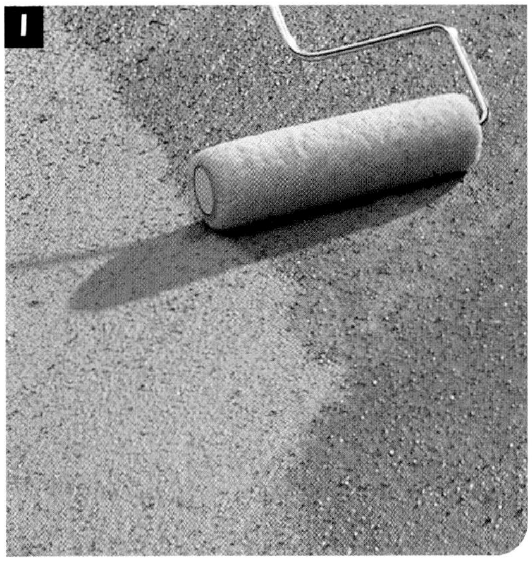

If the steps will be exposed to heavy traffic or constant moisture, apply a coat of concrete sealer.

Repairing Vertical Surfaces

Vertical surfaces usually require different repair materials and techniques than horizontal surfaces. This is true for concrete steps and risers as well as post anchors, contoured cement objects, and the masonry veneer around your home's foundation.

You can adapt the basic repair techniques that follow to just about any vertical concrete surface, including concrete walls. Concrete walls are commonly used as the foundation for many types of structures, as well as for landscaping purposes, such as screens, borders, tree wells, planter walls, or retaining walls.

Although they're strong and durable, concrete walls are prone to the same kinds of damage as other concrete structures, especially the damaging effects of penetration by running water. That's why it's important to repair or fill cracks and holes in a vertical concrete surface as soon as you discover them. Holes and cracks in walls also provide an entry into your home for rodents and insects.

See pages 225 to 227 for additional stucco and masonry repairs.

Repairing Shaped Concrete

Repairing a shaped concrete surface requires careful preparation; you'll need to work quickly. First, use a wire brush or trowel to scrape any loose material from the damaged area **(photo A),** and wipe it down with water.

Mix some quick-setting cement and trowel it onto the damaged area. Work quickly—it will set up within a few minutes. Use a trowel or putty knife to mold the concrete to the form you're repairing **(photo B).** Smooth the concrete as soon as it sets up. After it dries, buff it with emery paper.

Tools: *Putty knife, trowel, wire brush, drill, whisk broom.*

Materials: *Gloves, eye protection, quick-setting cement, emery paper.*

Scrape any loose material or debris from the area to be patched, then wipe it down with water.

Use a putty knife or trowel to mold the concrete into the shape of the object you're repairing.

Repairing Masonry Veneer

Repairing a masonry veneer installed over a metal lath isn't much more difficult than other kinds of concrete repairs.

First, chip off all the crumbled, loose, or deteriorated veneer that remains on the wall, using a cold chisel and a hand maul **(photo C).**

Chisel off the veneer until only good, solid material remains, taking care not to damage the wall behind it. Clean up the repair area with a wire brush.

If the metal lath in the repair area is in good condition, simply clean up any loose chips or debris. If it's in poor condition, cut out the damaged lath with aviation snips. Replace it with new lath, using masonry anchors to attach it to the wall **(photo D).**

Prepare sand-mix concrete with an acrylic concrete fortifier (you can also use specialty concrete blends designed for wall repairs). If you wish, add pigment to the concrete mixture to match the repair area.

Trowel the concrete over the lath until it's even with the surrounding surface **(photo E).**

Smooth the concrete surface and feather until it's even with the surrounding area.

If you wish, duplicate the original surface texture of the veneer in the patched area. In the project shown, we're using a stiff-bristled brush to stipple the surface of the fresh concrete **(photo F).**

You can also paint the repair area after it dries to match the color of the surrounding area.

Tools: Putty knife, trowel, hand maul, chisel, wire brush, aviation snips, drill, mixer box or power mixer, stiff-bristled brush.

Materials: Gloves, eye protection, masonry anchors, quick-setting cement, emery paper, wire lath, acrylic concrete fortifier, sand-mix concrete.

Chisel away the damaged veneer, taking care not to damage the wall or the lath beneath it.

If the original lath is damaged, replace it with new lath secured with masonry anchors.

Trowel the concrete mix over the lath until it's even with the surrounding surface.

Smooth the patched surface and feather it, or use a texturizing tool to duplicate the texture of the surrounding veneer.

Repairing Asphalt

Asphalt blacktop driveways and walkways are prone to damage from various forces, but especially water penetration. If water runs under the blacktop from the side of the slab side or through cracks in the surface, it will undermine the gravel base beneath the slab.

To prevent more serious damage, fill any holes and cracks with an asphalt patching compound and reseal the surface annually. Also, fill any washouts along the edge of the slab to prevent water from running beneath it.

Tools: *Hose with spray nozzle or power washer, shop vacuum, heat gun, trowel, caulk gun, putty knife, scrub brush, squeegee or broom.*

Materials: *Asphalt cleaner, asphalt patching compound, asphalt sealer.*

Asphalt is prone to suffer damage from heavy wear, repeated impacts, and water penetration.

Patching Holes in Asphalt

It's important to tend to holes in asphalt as soon as you find them. If left unattended, a single hole can lead to deterioration of the gravel base and then the asphalt itself. However, a patch can effectively prevent future deterioration and water penetration.

To patch a hole in asphalt, begin by cleaning the hole. Use a shop vacuum to remove all dirt and debris from the area **(photo A).** Flush the hole with a hose fitted with a spray nozzle.

Next, pour asphalt patching material into the hole, overfilling it slightly. Warm it with a heat gun **(photo B).**

Use a trowel to level and smooth the patch. Tamp the patching material with a heavy brick or concrete block until it's firmly packed in the hole and level with the surrounding surface **(photo C).**

A

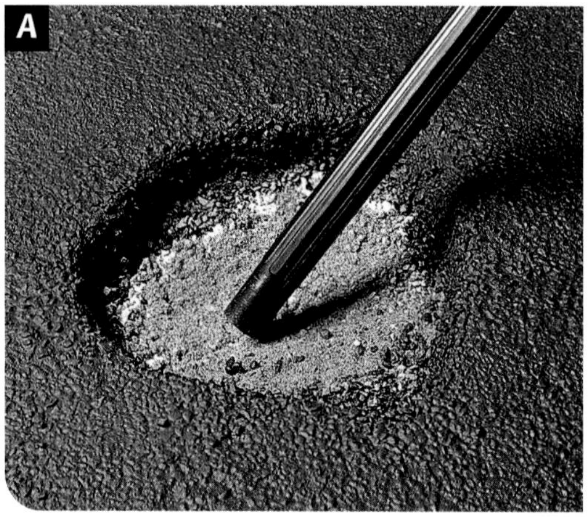

Clean the hole with a shop vacuum, and flush the area with a garden hose fitted with a spray nozzle.

B

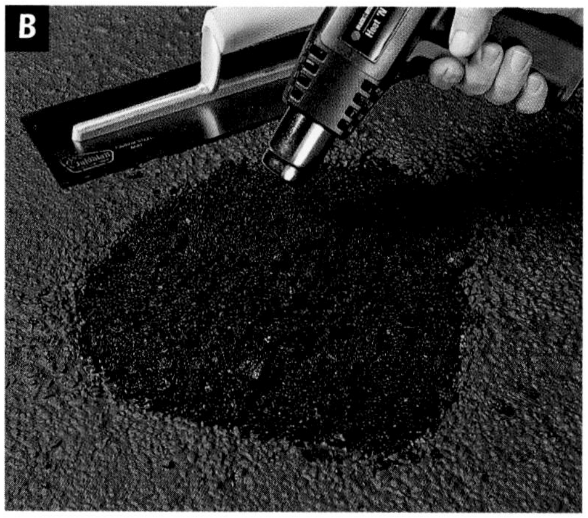

Pour the asphalt patching material into the hole and warm it with a heat gun.

C

Use a heavy brick or concrete block to tamp the area until the patching material is firmly packed into the hole.

Sealing an Asphalt Driveway

An asphalt sealer is an easy way to give an old asphalt driveway a fresh, new appearance.

Before sealing an asphalt driveway, begin by inspecting the surface carefully. Repair any holes (page 266).

Next, use an asphalt cleaning product to clean the slab to remove any oil and dirt from the surface **(photo D).** If the surface isn't heavily soiled, you can use a solution of warm water and a mild detergent.

After cleaning, rinse off the slab with a hose or a power washer.

Use a caulk gun and a tube of asphalt patching compound to patch any cracks in the asphalt surface **(photo E),** slightly overfilling the crack. (Large cracks may require several applications of patching compound to be filled completely.)

Spread and smooth the patching material with a putty knife **(photo F).** To prevent the patcher from sticking to the scraper, dip the scraper in cold water or mineral spirits.

Pour a pool of asphalt sealer onto one corner of the slab. Use a squeegee or a broom to spread it in a thin layer, following the manufacturer's instructions, until the entire surface is coated **(photo G).** Don't apply a layer that's too thick; it won't cure properly. If you'd like a heavier layer of sealer, apply more than one coat.

Allow the sealer to cure thoroughly before you drive or walk on it. While the driveway is drying out, block off the entrance with sawhorses or rope and ladders **(photo H).**

Helpful Hint

The best time to seal an asphalt driveway is a warm, sunny day.

However, if you need to remove an asphalt driveway, choose a cool day. On a hot day, the asphalt will bend when pried up and stick to everything it touches.

D

Clean the driveway thoroughly with an asphalt cleaner or detergent and water.

E

Fill any cracks in the surface with asphalt patching compound applied with a caulk gun.

F

Use a putty knife to smooth the patching compound and press it into the crack.

G

Spread the asphalt sealer in a thin layer, using a squeegee or a broom, until the entire surface is coated.

H

Block off the driveway and don't walk on it until the sealer has thoroughly cured.

№ 350
H

SYSTEMS REPAIRS

The systems in your home basically are delivery and removal systems. This chapter helps you maintain and repair your plumbing, electrical, and heating, ventilation, and air conditioning systems so that water, electricity, and fresh, temperate air are available on demand.

PLUMBING

ELECTRICAL

HVAC

Systems Repairs

Anyone who has experienced a power outage, a water main break near the home, or furnace problems during the winter appreciates the importance of safe, reliable home systems. These include electrical, plumbing and heating, ventilation and air conditioning—or HVAC. Systems Repairs shows you how to maintain, protect, and repair your systems so they are reliable.

Many homeowners assume that these systems must be repaired by professionals. However, most systems repairs are easier than you might think. You can do your own plumbing, electrical, and heating repairs for considerably less than the cost of hiring professionals to do them for you. The investment in tools and materials will be well worth it in the long run.

This section will familiarize you with the required specialty tools and materials for repairing each system. In general, when a specific tool is recommended, don't substitute. Substituting a tool can jeopardize the success of your project (and in some cases may even be dangerous).

Some specialty tools, such as a neon circuit tester, are so inexpensive and essential that they really should be part of every home maintenance toolbox.

Other specialty tools, such as a cast iron snap cutter, are used only for a specific application, and may be hard to justify buying, even for a big project. In this case, your best bet is to rent the tool in question from a hardware store or rental center.

Another reason that homeowners tend to shy away from systems repairs is that changes often require the approval of the local building department, or must comply with local Building Codes.

If you've never dealt with Building Codes, call your local building department to get more information. Also, don't hesitate to contact the building inspector for your city or county: part of the inspector's job is to answer questions about Code compliance. There's no prohibition against homeowners doing their own systems repairs, provided the work is done correctly.

Before you begin any project in this section, be sure to read through the instructions carefully and assess whether you're comfortable with the complexities involved. While some of the repairs (such as installing a dimmer switch) can be managed with little do-it-yourself experience, others (such as replacing a cast-iron pipe) are best attempted once you've had some hands-on experience. (After all, any potential savings from doing the job yourself disappears if you have to call an electrician or a plumber to "fix" your repair in an emergency.)

Finally, since you'll be working in your own home, remember to keep children and pets away from the work area. As always, store ladders, power tools, and toxic substances out of reach of small hands.

The systems covered in this section affect the comfort and convenience of every room of the house.

Working with Plumbing

The Plumbing section covers all of the elements of a standard plumbing system (pipes, fittings, valves, drains, vents, traps, sinks, faucets, tubs and showers, whirlpools, and toilets) and the major appliances that may be connected to your system: food disposers, dishwashers, water heaters, water pumps, and septic systems. When you undertake any plumbing project, follow these basic safety precautions.

Identify the shutoff valves for your plumbing fixtures and label them, so you can easily and quickly shut off the water supply.

Never work on hot water pipes that are still hot. Shut off the supply first and wait for the pipes to cool.

Until recently, new homes often relied on metal plumbing pipes to ground the household electrical system. Replacing metal pipe with plastic pipe could interrupt the grounding of your home's electrical current. Test for ground around your house. You may need to add a jumper cable across the plastic pipe to ensure that ground is not interrupted.

Check with your building inspector to make sure your project is up to Code.

Working with Electricity

The Electrical section covers the standard elements of a home electrical system (service panels, receptacles, wall switches, lighting fixtures, doorbells, and telephones). When you do any of the projects in this section, follow these basic safety precautions.

Before exposing any electrical wiring, go to the main service panel and shut off the circuit that provides power to that area. Then, test the wires with a neon circuit tester to ensure that no current is flowing to the circuit. Leave a note on the panel so no one switches the power on while you're working.

When doing electrical work, wear rubber-soled shoes. Never touch any electrical device with wet hands or while standing in water.

Never touch a metal pipe, faucet, or appliance while working with electricity.

Don't work on the service panel wiring yourself. The wires that bring electricity into your home remain live even when the main power is shut off at the service panel.

Always review plans for new wiring with your local building department before you begin work.

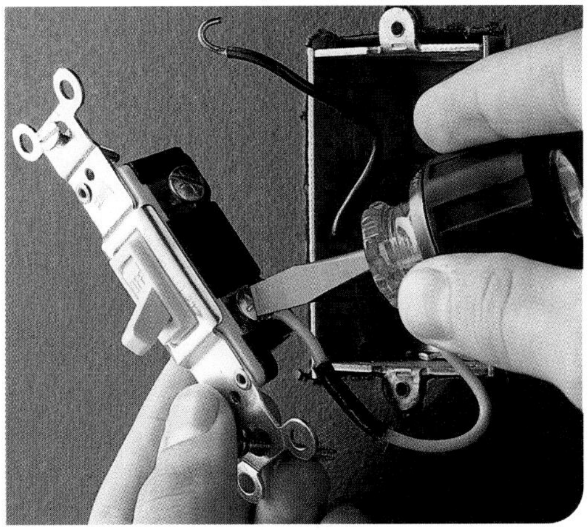

Working with Heating, Ventilation & Air Conditioning

This section covers both major heating components like your furnace or boiler, and supplemental heat sources, such as baseboard heaters and wood stoves. Ventilation includes everything from ceiling and bathroom exhaust fans to household air exchangers that help refresh the air in your home. Cooling includes both central air conditioners and window or wall units, as well as heat pumps and evaporative chillers.

When you do any of the projects in this section, follow these basic safety precautions.

If you smell a persistent gas odor, don't try to light the gas burner pilot. Open the doors and windows, extinguish all cigarettes and open flames, then close the main gas shutoff valve. Quickly leave the house, and call the utility company from a neighbor's home.

Before you work on your furnace, install carbon monoxide monitors in your house.

Ask your fuel company for an annual checkup, including carbon monoxide levels in your house.

Before you install any new heating, venting, or air conditioning units, ask your building department if a permit is required.

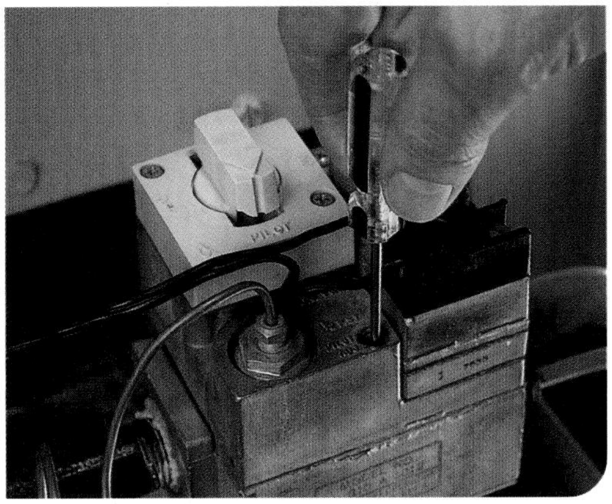

Plumbing

Although a home plumbing system, with its network of pipes and valves, may seem complex and mysterious, it's actually fairly simple and straightforward. Recognizing the major components and understanding the roles they play is the first step to doing repairs or routine maintenance.

A typical home plumbing system includes three fundamental components: the water supply system, the fixtures and appliances, and the drain system. The photograph at right identifies each of these parts.

Fresh water enters a home through a main supply line (1). This fresh water source is provided by either a municipal water company or a private well. If the source is a municipal supplier, the water passes through a meter (2) that registers the amount of water used.

Immediately after the main supply enters the house, the branch line (3) splits off and joins the water heater (4). From the water heater, the hot water line runs parallel to the cold water line to supply water to fixtures and appliances throughout the house.

Once the water becomes waste, it flows into a trap (5) and into the drain system. The drain system works entirely by gravity, allowing waste water to flow downhill through a series of large-diameter drain pipes, attached to a system of vent pipes. Vent pipes (6) allow air to enter the system via a roof vent (7). The fresh air prevents suction that would slow or stop drain water from flowing freely.

All sewage eventually reaches the waste and vent stack (8). The waste water flows into the sewer line (9) that exits the house near the foundation and flows either into a municipal sewer system or a septic system. Meanwhile, sewer gases rise harmlessly through the vent stack to escape the house at the roof vent.

A typical home plumbing system includes three basic parts: a water supply system, fixtures and appliances, and a drain system. The average family of four in America uses about four hundred gallons of water each day.

The Water Supply System

Supply pipes deliver hot and cold water throughout a home's plumbing system. In homes built before 1950, the original supply pipes often are made of galvanized iron; in newer homes supply pipes are often copper, although plastic (CPVC) pipes are gaining acceptance by local plumbing codes in some parts of the country.

Water supply pipes are made to withstand the high pressures of a water supply system. Though small in diameter, usually $1/2$" to 1", water supply pipes are joined with strong, watertight fittings and are meant to withstand high pressures. As they travel throughout a house, water supply pipes are generally located inside wall cavities or strapped to the undersides of floor joists.

Hot and cold water supply pipes are connected to fixtures or appliances. However, some fixtures, such as toilets or hose bibs, are supplied only by cold water. This system reduces the demand volume on the water heater and lowers overall energy costs. Traditionally, hot water supply pipes and faucet handles are positioned on the left-hand side of a fixture, and the cold water is on the right side.

If water is supplied by a municipal water company, a water meter and main shutoff valve are located at the point of entrance. The water meter remains the property of the water company—if it leaks or malfunctions, the water company is responsible for repairing or replacing it.

The Drain-Waste-Vent System

Once used, fresh water becomes waste water and is carried out of the house by the drain-waste-vent (DWV) system. The DWV system takes advantage of gravity, which draws waste water away from fixtures, appliances, and other drains, down through a series of sloped pipes and into a municipal sewer system or septic tank.

Slope is another important factor in the DWV system. Codes assign a degree of slope for each portion of the system, according to the size of pipe and its intended function. This slope allows gravity to do the work of removing the waste water.

Drain pipes usually are plastic (ABS or PVC) or cast iron. Generally drain pipes are larger in diameter than supply pipes, ranging from $1\frac{1}{4}$" to 4", to allow easy passage of waste water through the system. In some older homes, drain pipes may be made of copper or lead. Although lead drain pipes are no longer manufactured for home plumbing systems, they do not pose a health hazard because they are not part of the supply system.

Every drain must have a trap, a curved section of pipe that holds standing water. The standing water in a trap actually is a safety device that prevents sewer gases from backing up through the pipes, out the drain, and into the house. Each time a drain is used, the standing water is flushed away and replaced by new water.

In order for waste water to flow freely, the DWV system needs air. To provide that air, drain pipes are joined to a vent system that allows outdoor air inside the house and lowers the pressure in the pipes, usually through one or more vent stacks that extend through the roof. If a plumbing system is not vented adequately, toilets will not flush completely, and drains will gurgle, choke, or overflow. Inadequately vented lines also can pull water out of traps to allow hazardous sewer gas into your home.

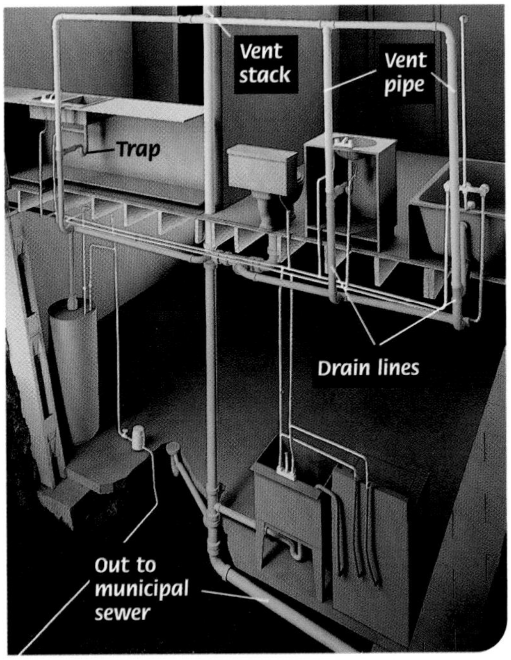

The drain-waste-vent system carries water out of the house. Vent pipes (shown in yellow) provide the air that the drain lines (shown in green) require to function properly.

Basic Plumbing Tools

Many plumbing projects and repairs can be completed with basic hand tools, such as the set of essential tools shown below **(photo A).**

Files are used to smooth metal, wood, and plastic. A round file is used on pipes, while a flat file is used on flat surfaces.

Caulk guns deliver a bead of caulk or glue.

Flashlights are indispensable for inspecting pipes and drain openings.

Screwdrivers include both the slotted type and the Phillips type.

Wooden mallets are used to strike nonmetallic objects.

Levels are used to set appliances and check the slope of drain lines.

Circuit testers are important safety devices that test for live current.

Ratchet wrenches are used to tighten or loosen bolts and nuts. They have interchangeable sockets that can adapt to different sizes of nuts and bolts.

Adjustable wrenches have a movable jaw that allows them to fit a wide variety of bolt heads or nuts.

Hacksaws are used to cut metal objects or plastic pipe.

Utility knives trim plastic pipe and cut a wide variety of materials.

Channel-type pliers have serrated jaws and a movable handle that allows the jaws to be adjusted for maximum gripping strength.

Needlenose pliers have thin jaws that can grip small objects or reach into confined areas.

Wire brushes with soft brass bristles are used to clean metals without damaging them.

Tape measures should have a retractable steel blade at least 16 feet long.

Cold chisels are used with a ball peen hammer to cut ceramic tile, mortar, or hardened metals.

Putty knives scrape away old putty or caulk from appliances and fixtures.

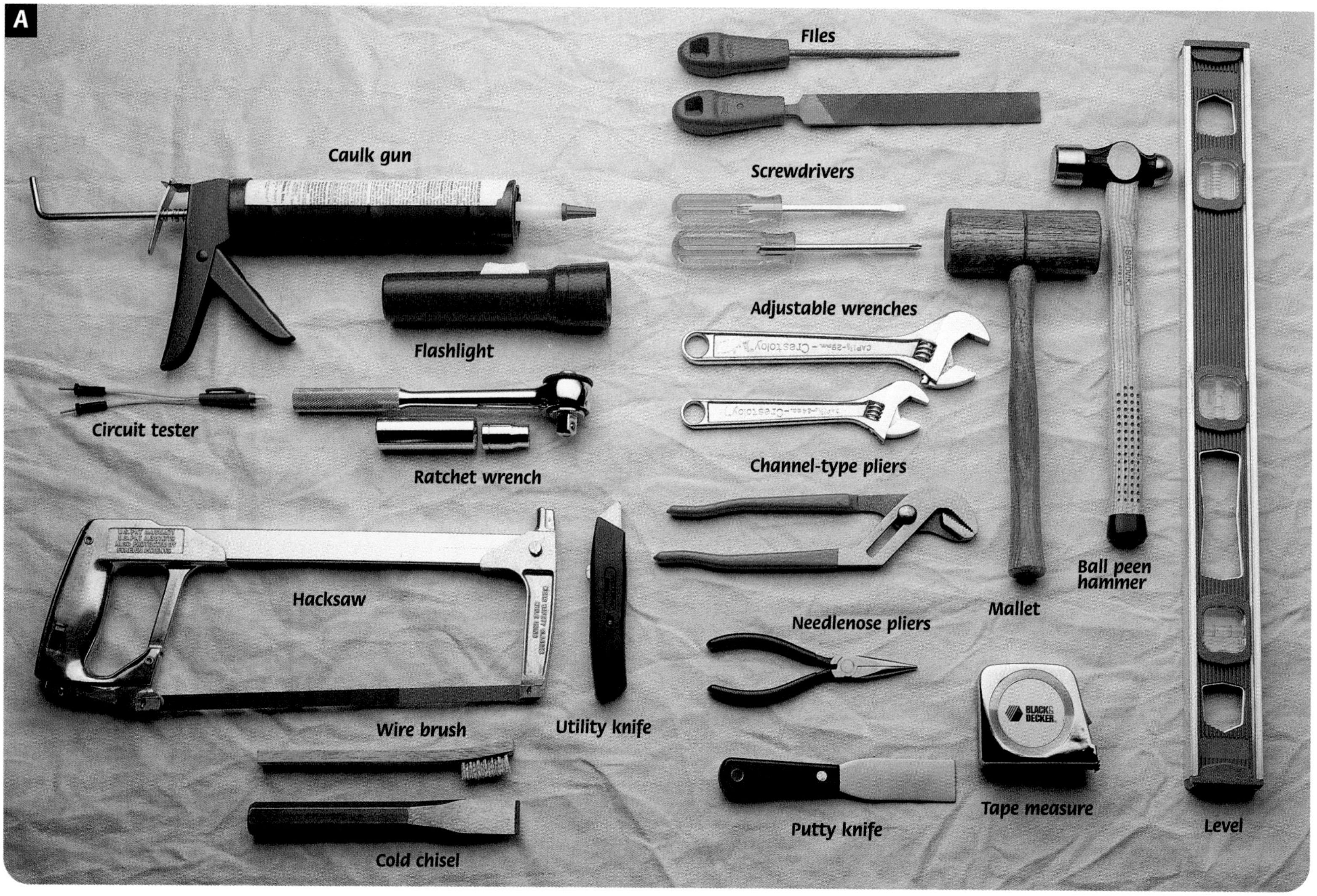

Specialized Plumbing Tools

Other specialty tools can help you complete plumbing projects faster and easier **(photo B).**

A closet auger, a slender tube with a crank handle on one end, clears toilet clogs. A plastic tubing cutter works like pruning shears to quickly cut flexible plastic (PE) pipes. A tubing cutter makes straight, smooth cuts in plastic and copper pipe. It usually has a reaming tip to remove burrs from pipes. A propane torch is used for soldering copper pipe and fittings. A spark lighter starts a torch quickly and safely.

A spud wrench is specially designed for removing or tightening 2"- to 4"-diameter nuts, grabbing onto the lugs of large nuts for increased leverage. A plunger clears drain clogs with air pressure. The flanged plunger (shown) is used for toilet bowls. The flange folds up into the cup for use as a standard plunger to clear clogs in sink, tub, shower, and floor drains. A pipe wrench has a movable jaw that adjusts to fit a variety of pipe diameters. It is used to tighten and loosen pipes, pipe fittings, and large nuts. Two pipe wrenches often are used together to prevent damage to pipes and fittings.

A hand auger, also called a snake, is used to clear clogs in drain lines. A blow bag, also called an expansion nozzle, is used to clear floor drains. When attached to a garden hose, it removes clogs with powerful spurts of water.

Power hand tools can make a job faster and easier **(photo C).** A cordless power ratchet (1) makes it easier to turn small nuts or hex-head bolts. A cordless 3/8" power drill (2) simplifies drilling tasks. A cordless reversible power screwdriver (3) drives screws and fasteners. A reciprocating saw (4) cuts wood, metal, or plastic. A heat gun (5) quickly thaws frozen pipes.

Some plumbing projects may require rental tools **(photo D).** A motorized drain auger (1) clears tree roots from sewer lines. A power miter box (2) makes fast, accurate cuts in many materials. The right-angle drill (3) is useful for drilling holes in hard-to-reach areas. A cast iron snap cutter (4) will cut tough cast-iron pipes. Use an appliance dolly (5) to move heavy objects like water heaters.

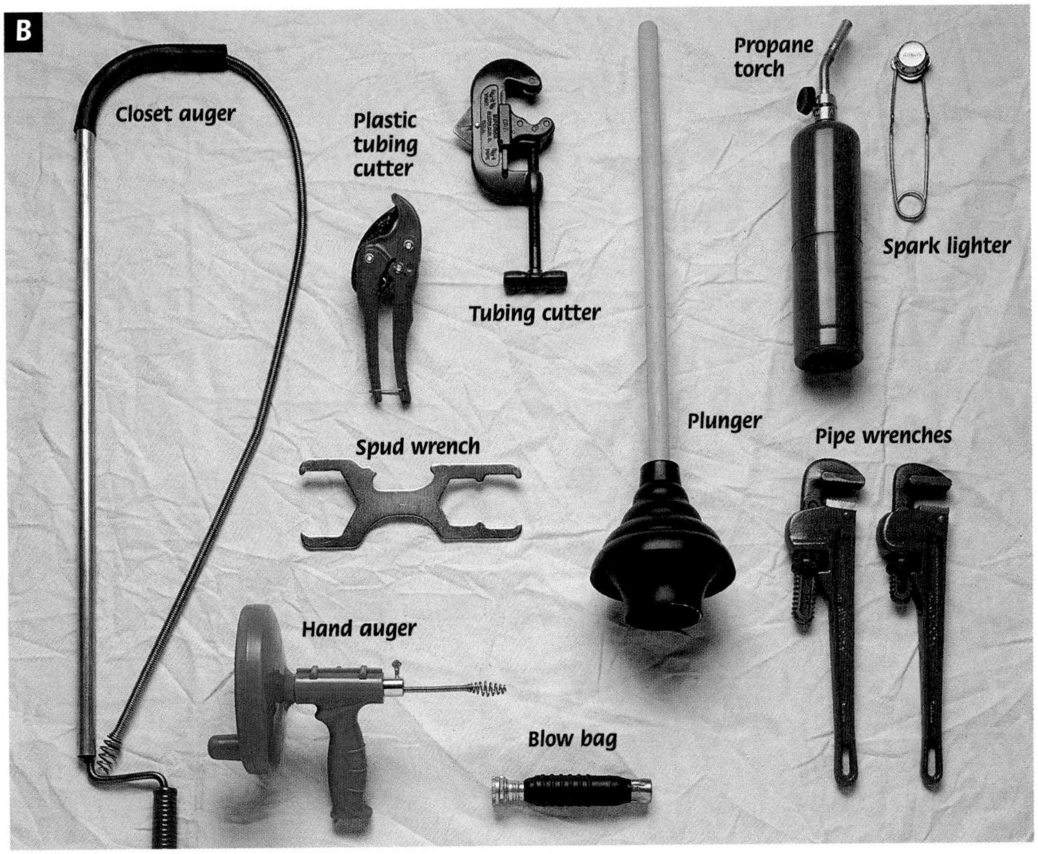

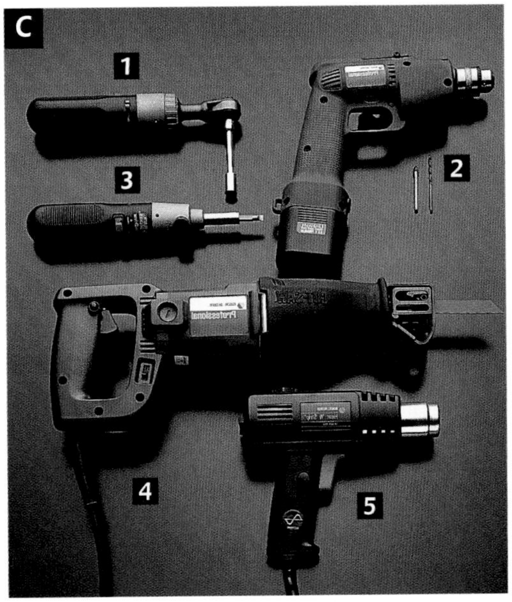

Power hand tools make plumbing jobs faster, easier, and safer. Cordless power tools offer even more convenience.

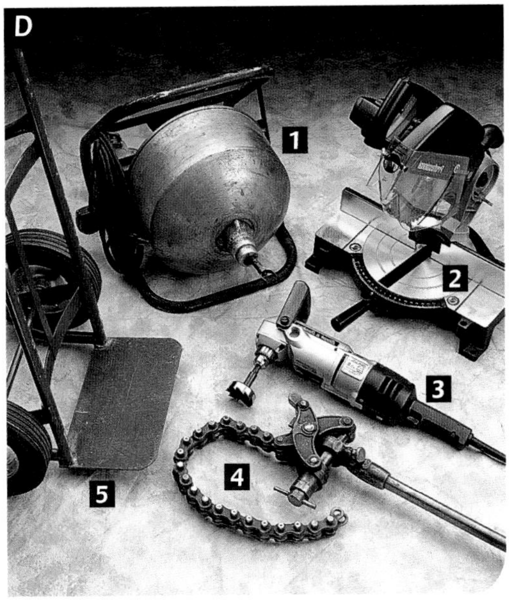

Some jobs may require rental tools. Always follow manufacturer's instructions and safety precautions.

Plumbing Materials

Recognizing different types of piping is important for troubleshooting and crucial when purchasing supplies or making repairs. In many houses the plumbing system includes several different types of pipes and fittings, especially if rooms have been added to the structure or the plumbing has been partially updated through the years.

Each pipe material has advantages and disadvantages, and plumbing contractors often have strong opinions about their use. The materials used in home plumbing systems are closely regulated by Building Codes. The materials shown here and on the following pages are approved for use by the Uniform Plumbing Code at time of publication. However, it is possible that your local Code has other requirements, so check local plumbing regulations before purchasing materials. Approved materials are stamped with one or more product standard codes. Look for these stamps when purchasing pipes and fittings. (In the chart at right, all diameters specified are interior diameters [I.D.].)

Cast iron is commonly used for drain-waste-vent (DWV) purposes. Though it is the strongest piping, it's very heavy, and somewhat difficult to join and install. Its thickness helps contain the noise inherent in drain systems.

Plastic piping is used for water supply pipes in some areas, where local Codes permit it. Plastic piping is quite popular because it is inexpensive, easy to work with, doesn't corrode or rust, and has insulating properties.

Plastic piping is available in four versions, which are commonly referred to by their abbreviations: ABS, PVC, CPVC, and PE. ABS and PVC are used exclusively in home drain systems, though today the use of ABS is not often permitted by Code in new installations. CPVC is suitable for water supply lines, and PE is used exclusively for outdoor water supply pipes.

Brass and chromed brass are durable plumbing materials that are used for drains, valves, and shutoffs. Chromed brass is relatively expensive, but because of its attractive appearance, it is often installed where looks are important or the piping is very visible (e.g., under stand-alone sinks, with bidets, or for older bathtubs).

Galvanized steel is the oldest of the materials shown at right. It was commonly used for plumbing in homes until the 1960s but is rarely used today because it rusts and it's harder to install than copper and plastic. It is suitable for both supply and DWV purposes.

Copper is considered the best choice for water supply lines and is occasionally used in drain-waste-vent systems. It resists scale deposits better than plastic and offers little resistance to water flow, which means that water pressure is better through a copper pipe than a comparably sized steel pipe. Copper is also light, and is easily installed—particularly flexible copper, which bends easily around corners. However, copper is more expensive than plastic.

Helpful Hint

A process called "galvanic action," in which molecules from one type of metal transfer to another type of metal, can lead to premature corrosion and clogging. Keep this in consideration, when joining pipes together. Only like metal should be joined to existing pipes.

Specialized fittings, called "dielectric fittings," make it possible to successfully join dissimilar metals, such as copper and brass. Select brackets and straps made of the same material as the pipes you plan to support, as well. This also prevents the accelerated corrosion caused by galvanic action.

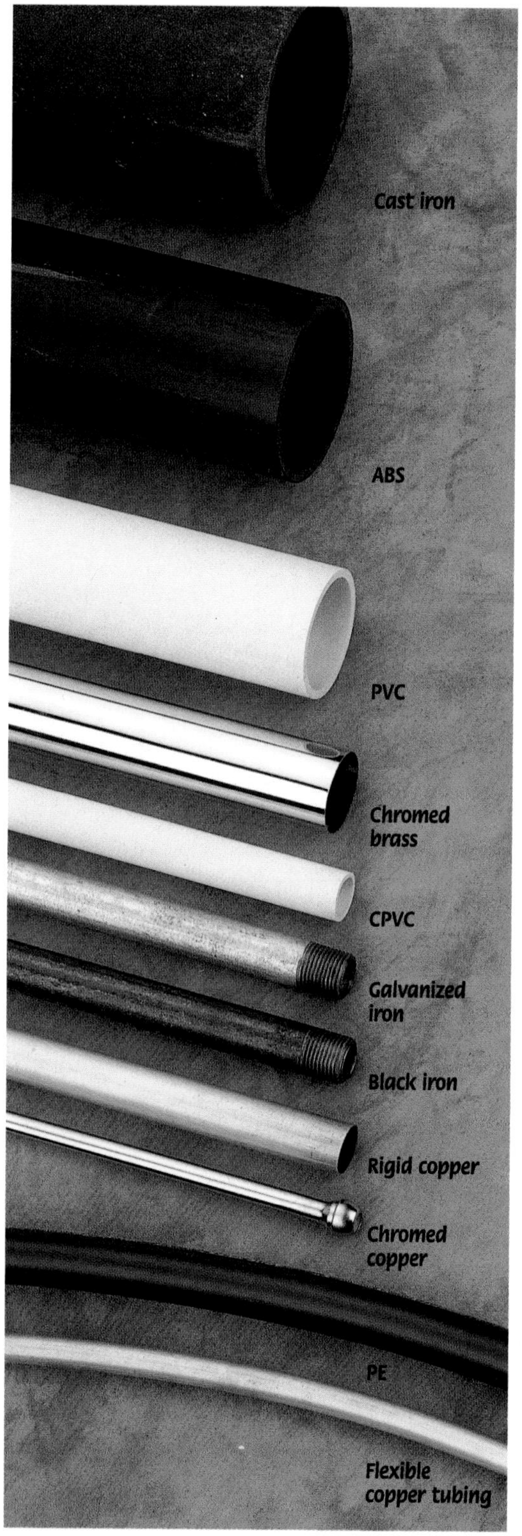

Benefits & Characteristics	Common Uses	Fitting Methods	Tools for Cutting
Cast iron is very strong but is difficult to cut and fit. Repairs and replacements should be made with plastic pipe, if allowed by Code.	Main drain-waste-vent pipes	Joined with hubbed fittings	Cast iron cutter or hacksaw
ABS (Acrylonitrile-Butadiene-Styrene) was the first rigid plastic approved for use in home drain systems. Some local Plumbing Codes now restrict the use of ABS in new installations.	Drain & vent pipes; drain traps	Joined with solvent glue and plastic fittings	Tubing cutter, miter box, or hacksaw
PVC (Poly-Vinyl-Chloride) is a modern rigid plastic that is highly resistant to damage by heat or chemicals. It is the best material for drain-waste-vent pipes.	Drain & vent pipes; drain traps	Joined with solvent glue and plastic fittings	Tubing cutter, miter box, or hacksaw
Chromed brass has an attractive shiny surface and is used for drain traps where appearance is important.	Valves & shutoffs; chromed drain traps	Joined with compression fittings, or with metal solder	Tubing cutter, hacksaw, or reciprocating saw
CPVC (Chlorinated-Poly-Vinyl-Chloride) rigid plastic is chemically formulated to withstand the high temperatures and pressures of water supply systems. Pipes and fittings are inexpensive.	Hot & cold water supply pipes	Joined with solvent glue and plastic fittings, or with grip fittings	Tubing cutter, miter box, or hacksaw
Galvanized iron is very strong but gradually will corrode. Not advised for new installation. Because galvanized iron is difficult to cut and fit, large jobs are best left to a professional.	Drains; hot & cold water supply pipes	Joined with galvanized threaded fittings	Hacksaw or reciprocating saw
Black iron looks much like galvanized iron, but there is an important difference. Black iron is used for gas piping, not for plumbing. Repairs should be handled by professionals.	Gas piping	Joined with black iron threaded fittings	Hacksaw or reciprocating saw
Rigid copper is the best material for water supply pipes. It resists corrosion and has smooth surfaces that provide good water flow. Soldered copper joints are very durable.	Hot & cold water supply pipes	Joined with metal solder or compression fittings	Tubing cutter, hacksaw, or jig saw
Chromed copper has an attractive shiny surface, and is used in areas where appearance is important. Chromed copper is durable and easy to bend and fit.	Supply tubing for plumbing fixtures	Joined with brass compression fittings	Tubing cutter or hacksaw
PE (polyethylene) plastic is a black or bluish flexible pipe sometimes used for main water service lines as well as irrigation systems.	Outdoor cold water supply pipes	Rigid PVC fittings and stainless steel hose clamps	Ratchet-style plastic pipe cutter or miter saw
Flexible copper tubing is easy to shape and will withstand a slight frost without rupturing. Flexible copper bends easily around corners, so it requires fewer fittings than rigid copper.	Gas tubing, hot & cold water supply tubing	Joined with brass flare fittings, compression fittings, or metal solder	Tubing cutter or hacksaw

Pipe & Fittings

Always use fittings made from the same material as your pipes. If unlike materials are to be joined, use a transition fitting.

Fittings come in many sizes, but the basic shapes are standard to all metal and plastic pipes. In general, fittings used to connect drain-waste-vent (DWV) pipes have gradual bends for a smooth flow of waste water from drains. Because water in supply lines is moving under pressure, bends in water supply fittings can be sharper, conserving space within wall cavities.

90° elbows are used to make right-angle bends in a pipe run. DWV elbows are curved so debris doesn't get trapped in the bends.

T-fittings are used to connect branch lines in water supply and DWV systems. A T-fitting used in a DWV system is called a "waste T" or "sanitary T."

Couplings are used to join two straight pipes. Special transition fittings (page 279) are used to join two pipes that are made from different materials.

Reducers connect pipes of different diameters. Reducing T-fittings and elbows are also available.

45° elbows are used to make gradual bends in a pipe run. Elbows are also available with 60° and 72° bends.

Caps close off unused sections of pipe.

Y-fittings are used to join intersecting DWV pipes.

Helpful Hint

When planning a project, buy more than enough DWV and water supply fittings from a reputable retailer with a good return policy. It's much more efficient to return unused materials when a project is complete than to interrupt repairs to run to the store for "just one more" fitting.

Standard Fittings

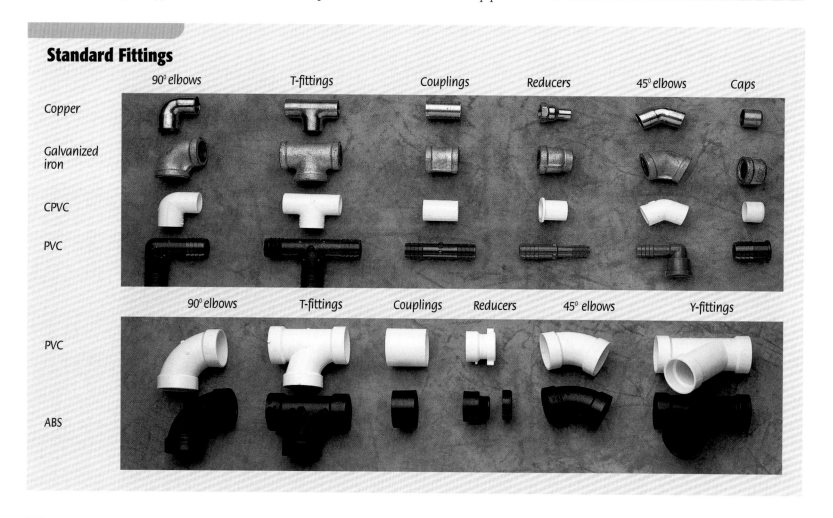

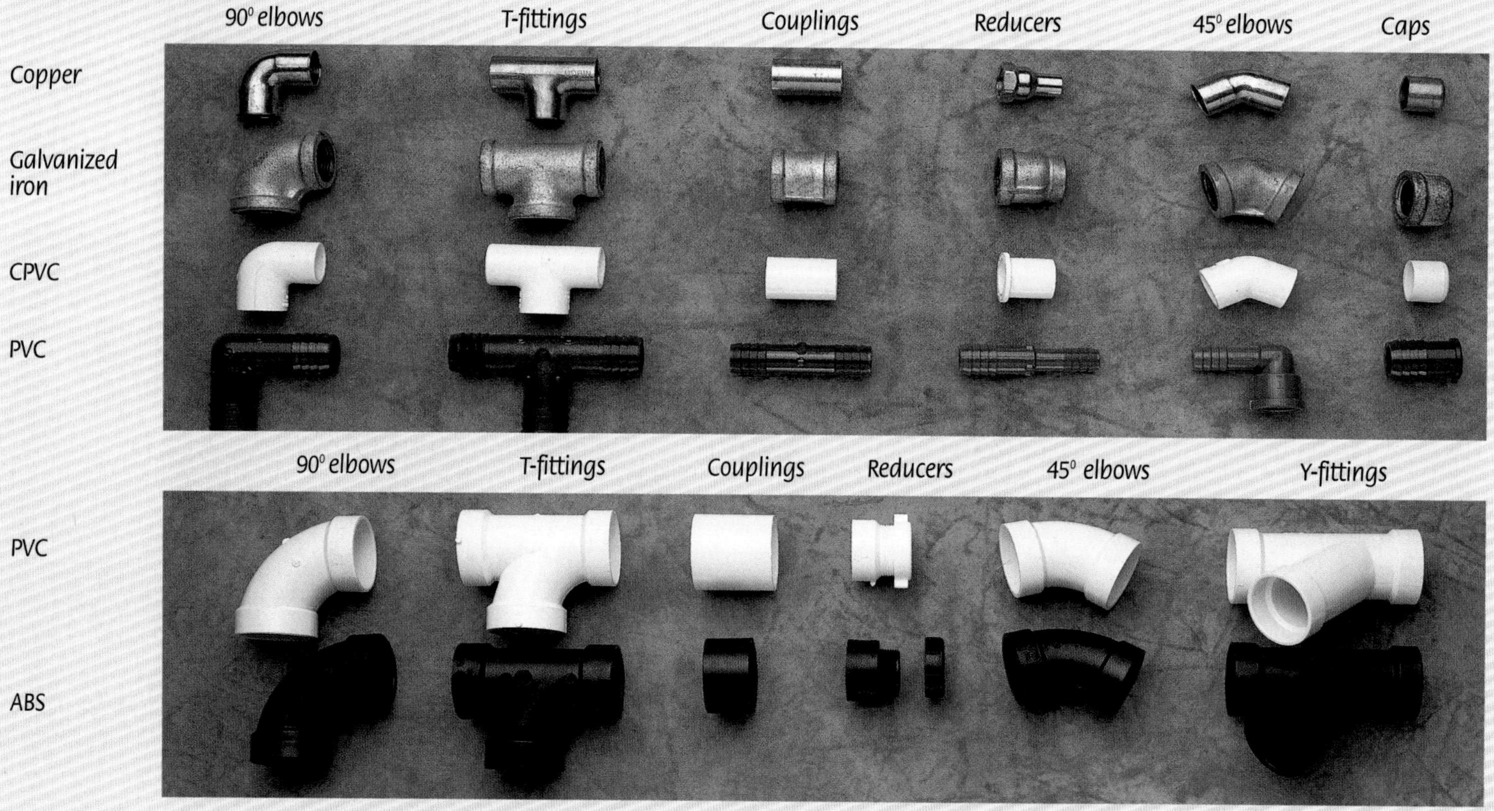

Using Transition Fittings

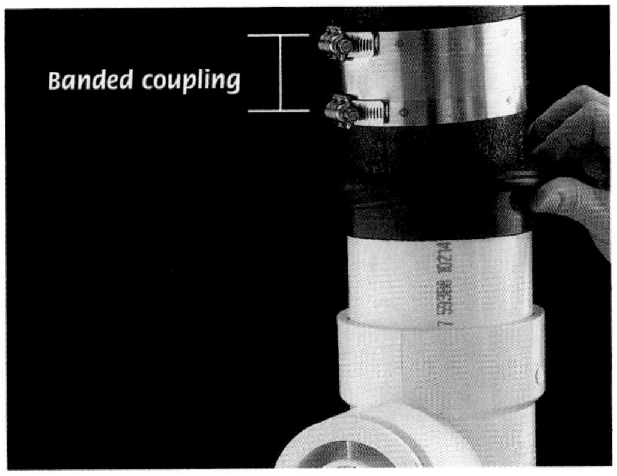

Connect plastic to cast iron with banded couplings. Rubber sleeves cover ends of pipes and ensure a watertight joint.

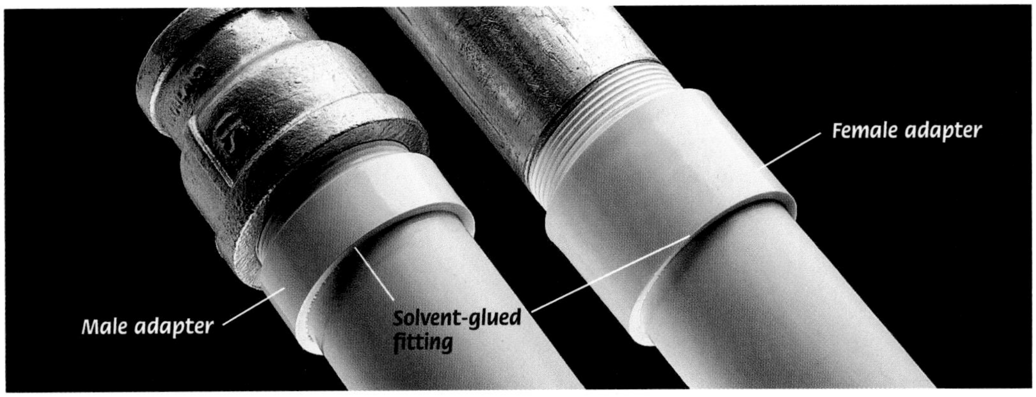

Connect plastic to threaded metal pipes with male and female threaded adapters. Glue a plastic adapter to the plastic pipe with solvent-based glue. Wrap the threads of the pipe with Teflon tape, then screw the metal pipe directly to the adapter.

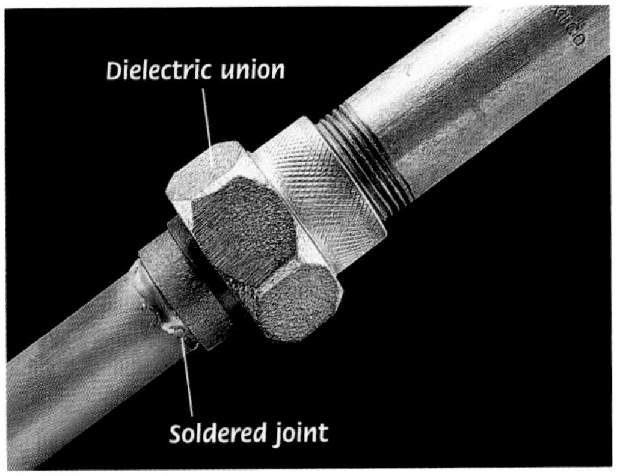

Connect copper to galvanized iron with a dielectric union. Thread the union onto the iron pipe and solder it to the copper pipe.

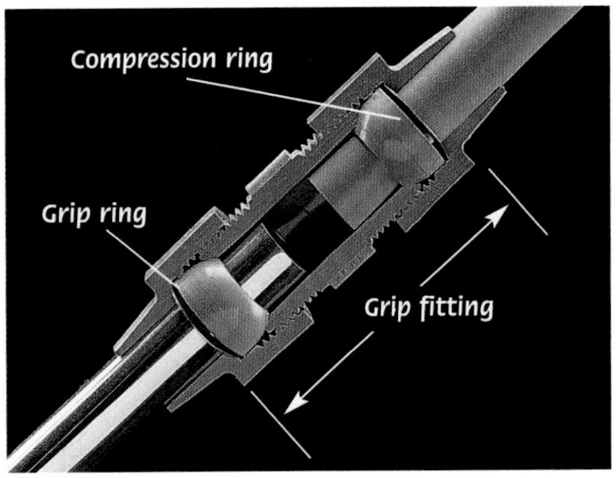

Connect plastic to copper with a grip fitting. Each side of the fitting (shown cutaway) contains a narrow grip ring and plastic compression ring (or rubber O-ring) that form a seal.

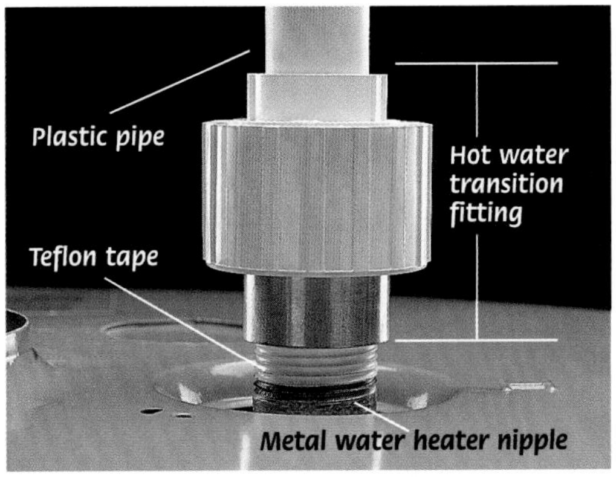

Connect metal hot water pipe to plastic with a hot water transition fitting that prevents leaks caused by different expansion rates of materials.

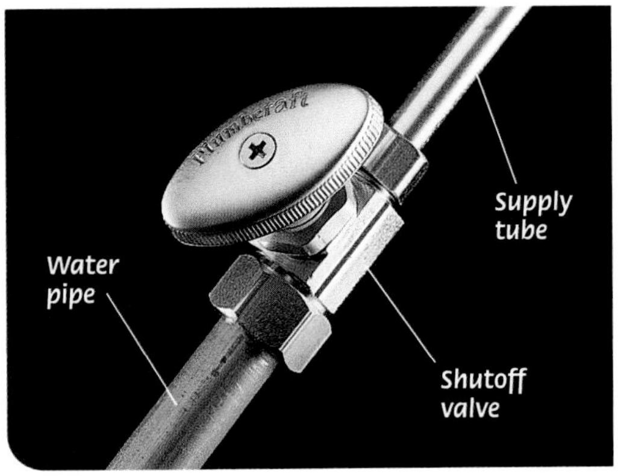

Use a shutoff valve to connect a water pipe to any fixture supply tube.

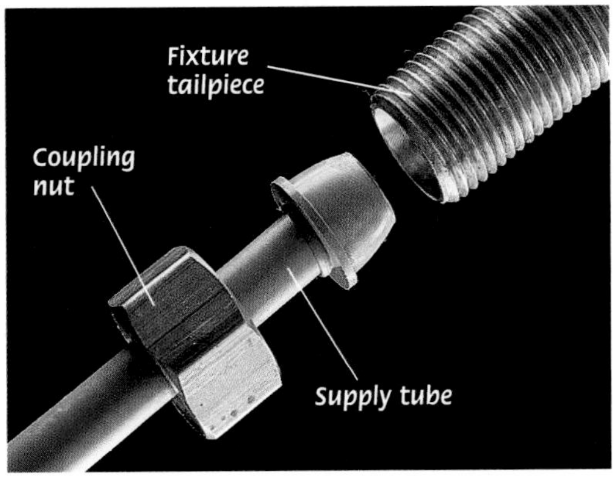

Connect any supply tube to a fixture tailpiece with a coupling nut. A coupling nut seals the bell-shaped end of the supply tube against the fixture tailpiece.

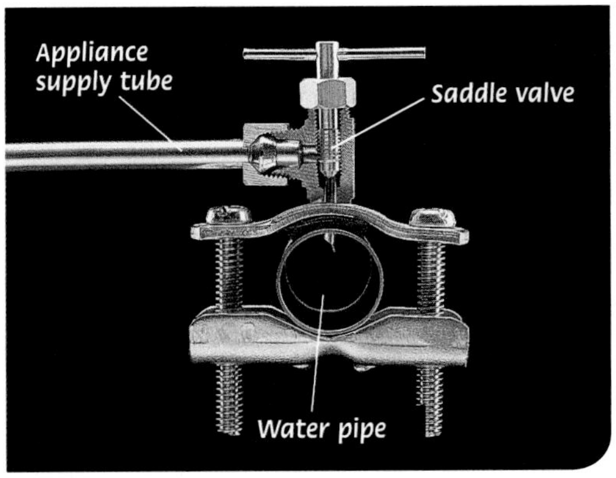

Connect an appliance supply tube to copper water pipe with a saddle valve. Saddle valves (shown cutaway) often are used to connect refrigerator icemakers.

Working with Plastic Pipe

Plastic pipes and fittings are popular because they are lightweight, inexpensive, and easy to use. Local Plumbing Codes increasingly are approving their use for home plumbing.

Plastic pipes are available in rigid and flexible forms. ABS and PVC are used in drain systems. PVC resists chemical damage and heat better than ABS, and is approved for aboveground use by all Plumbing Codes. However, some Codes still require cast-iron pipe for main drains running under concrete slabs.

PE is often used for underground cold water lines, such as those found in sprinkling systems.

CPVC is used for both cold and hot water supply lines. Plastic pipes can be joined to iron or copper pipes with transition fittings, but different types of plastic should not be joined.

PB flexible plastic is no longer considered reliable and isn't widely available. If problems develop with PB pipe or fittings, consult a licensed plumber for advice.

Tools: *Plastic tubing cutter, felt-tipped pen, channel-type pliers, tape measure, utility knife.*

Materials: *Plastic pipe and fittings, emery cloth, petroleum jelly, plastic pipe primer, solvent glue, rags.*

Use PVC or ABS pipe for sink traps and drain pipes. Use CPVC pipe for water supply lines. PVC and ABS pipes for drains usually have an inside diameter of 1¼" to 4". CPVC pipes for water supply usually have an inside diameter of ½" or ¾". For sink traps and drains, choose PVC or ABS pipe with DWV ratings from the National Sanitation Foundation (NSF). For water supply pipes, choose CPVC with PW (pressurized water) ratings. PB pipe is no longer widely available, and may need to be replaced rather than repaired—consult a licensed plumber for advice.

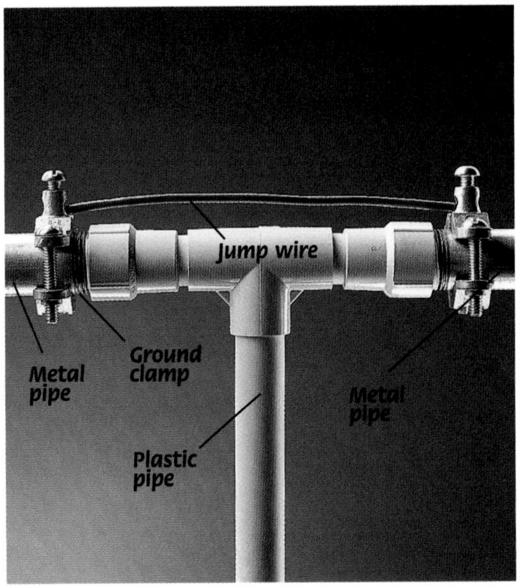

The electrical system often is grounded through metal water pipes. When adding plastic pipes to a metal plumbing system, make sure the electrical ground circuit remains intact.

Solvent-glued fittings are used on rigid plastic pipes. The solvent dissolves a thin layer of plastic and bonds the pipe and fitting together.

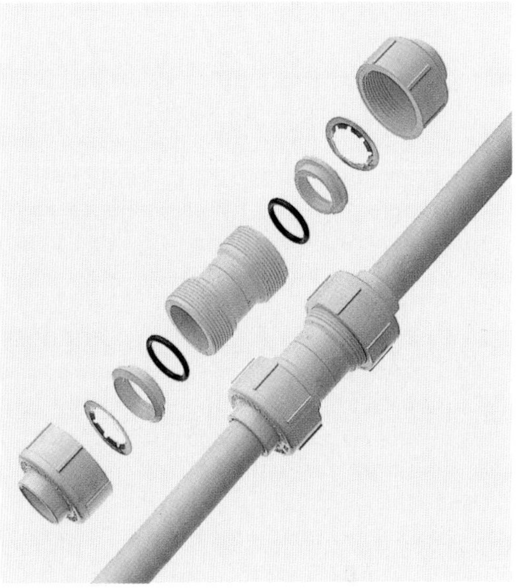

Grip fittings are used to join CPVC pipe. Each fitting has a metal grip ring, plastic compression ring, and rubber O-ring.

Working with PE Pipe

Flexible PE (polyethylene) pipe is commonly used for underground cold water lines.

Connect the PE pipe with drain-and-waste valves, which allow the line to be winterized **(photo A).** Splice in a T-fitting to the copper pipe and attach a drain-and-waste shutoff valve and a female threaded adapter. Screw a barbed PVC male threaded adapter into the copper fitting, then attach the PE pipe.

Use barbed PVC fittings to connect lengths of PE pipe **(photo B).** Slide stainless steel hose clamps over the pipe, then force the ends over the barbed portion of the fitting. Slide the clamps to the ends of the pipe and tighten them.

Winterizing in Cold Climates

To winterize an underground cold water line, such as a sprinkler system, close the valve for the outdoor supply pipe, then remove the cap on the drain nipple. With the faucet on the outdoor spigot open, attach an air compressor to the valve nipple, then blow water from the system, using no more than 50 psi of air pressure. Remove the plugs from the t-fittings in each valve box, and store them for the winter.

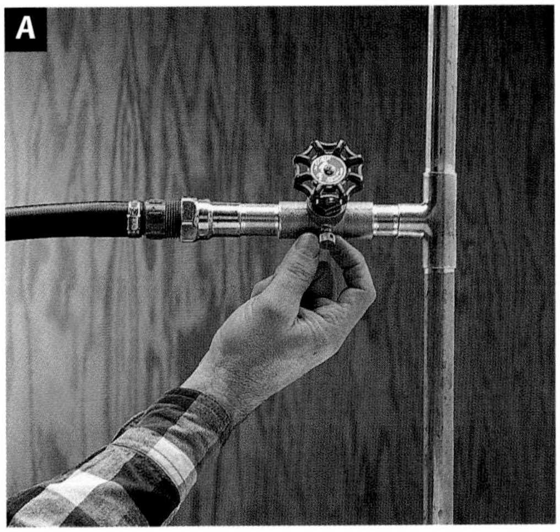

Attaching a shutoff valve and a female threaded adapter makes it possible to drain water from PE lines when winterizing an underground line.

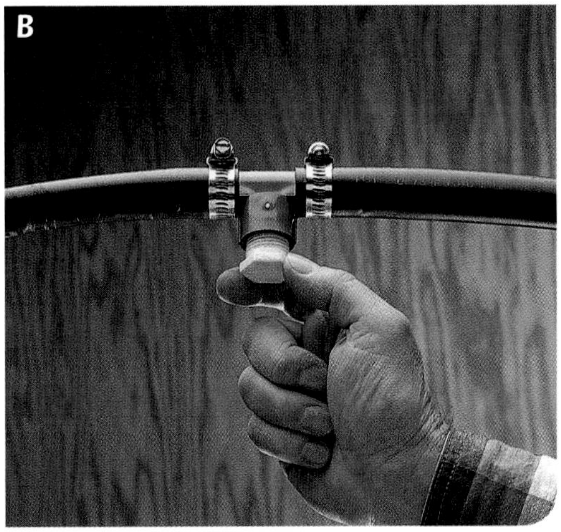

PE pipe is joined with "barbed" rigid PVC fittings and stainless steel hose clamps.

Cutting & Fitting Rigid Plastic Pipe

Cut rigid ABS, PVC, or CPVC plastic pipes with a tubing cutter or saw. Cut flexible PE pipes with a plastic tubing cutter or knife. On all types of pipe, make level, straight cuts to ensure watertight joints.

Determine the length of pipe needed by measuring between the bottoms of the fitting sockets, then marking the pipe with a felt-tipped pen.

Use grip fittings to join rigid plastic pipes to copper pipes.

Connect PE pipe with barbed rigid PVC fittings and stainless steel hose clamps.

Join rigid plastics with plastic fittings and solvent glue specifically made for the pipe material being joined, or select an "all-purpose" or "universal" product.

To join rigid plastic pipe with solvent glue, cut the pipe, then use a utility knife to remove any burrs on the ends **(photo A).**

Test-fit all the pipes and fittings **(photo B).** The pipes should fit tightly against the bottom of the fitting sockets.

Make alignment marks across each joint with a felt-tipped pen **(photo C).** Mark the depth of the fitting sockets on the pipes, then take them apart.

Clean the ends of the pipes and the fitting sockets with emery cloth **(photo D).**

To dull the surface of the pipe and ensure a good seal, apply plastic-pipe primer outside the ends of the pipes **(photo E)** and inside the fitting sockets **(photo F).**

Apply a thick coat of solvent glue to the end of the pipe and a thin coat inside the fitting socket **(photo G).**

Quickly position the pipe and fitting, offsetting the alignment marks by about 2" **(photo H).** Force the pipe into the fitting until the end fits flush against the bottom of the socket. Solvent glue hardens in about 30 seconds, so work quickly.

Twist the pipe until the marks are aligned, then hold it in place for about 20 seconds **(photo I).** Wipe away excess glue, then allow the joint to dry undisturbed for 30 minutes.

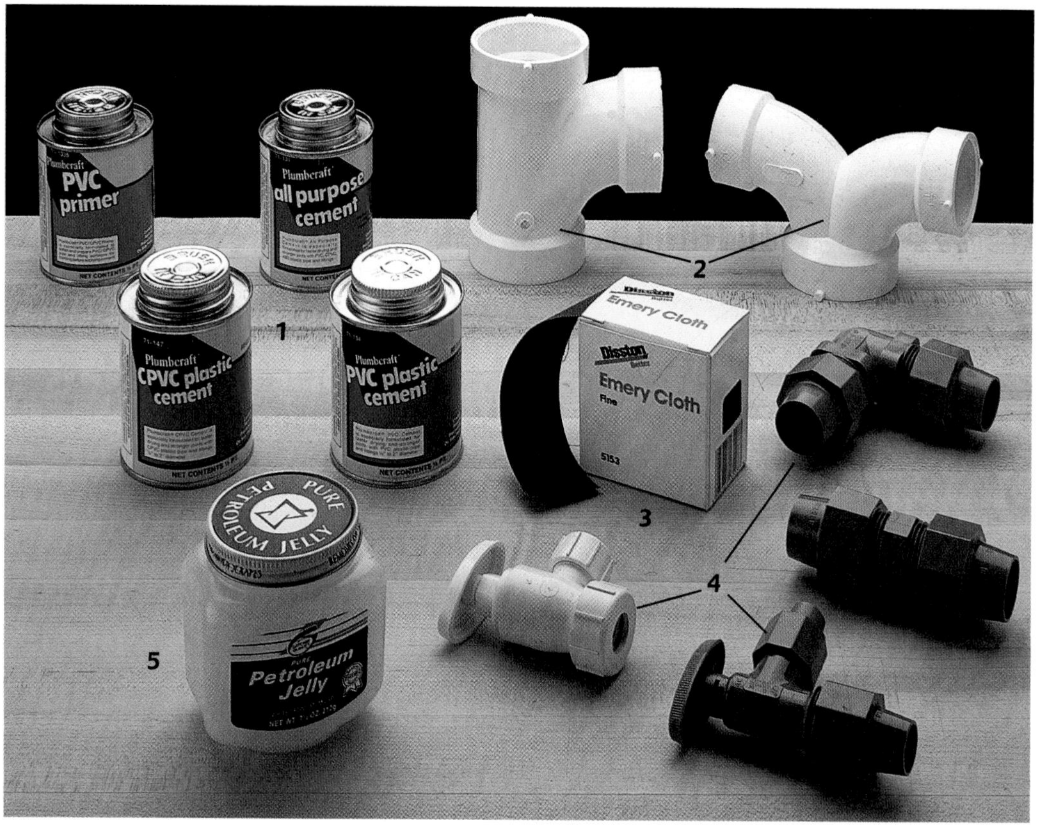

Specialty materials for plastics include solvent glues and primer (1), solvent-glue fittings (2), emery cloth (3), plastic grip fittings (4), and petroleum jelly (5).

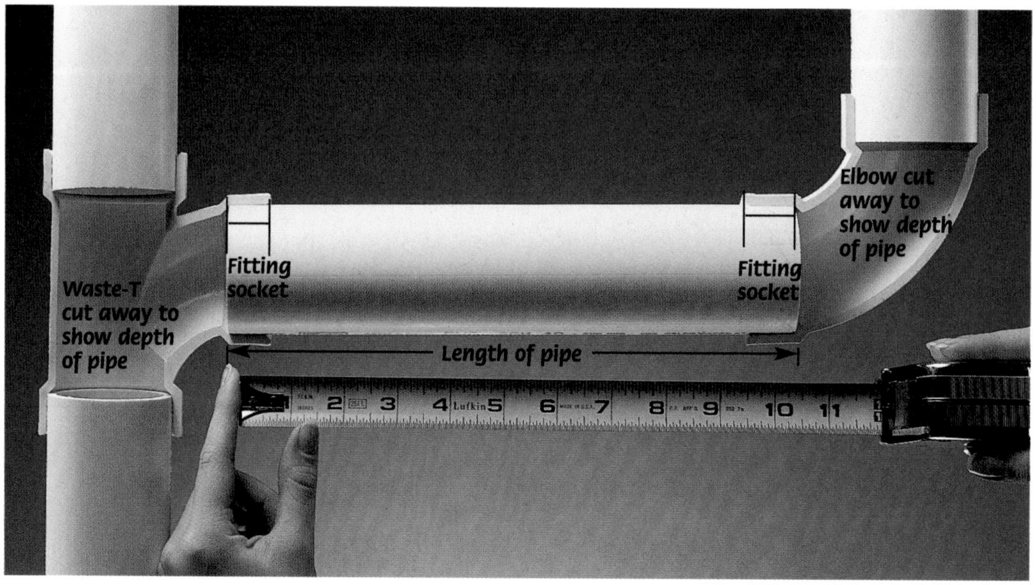

Measure between the bottoms of the fitting sockets (fittings shown in cutaway). Mark the length on the pipe.

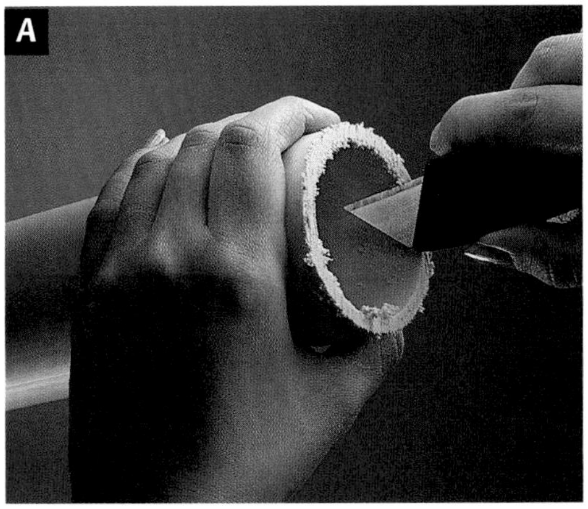

Remove rough burrs on the cut ends of the pipe.

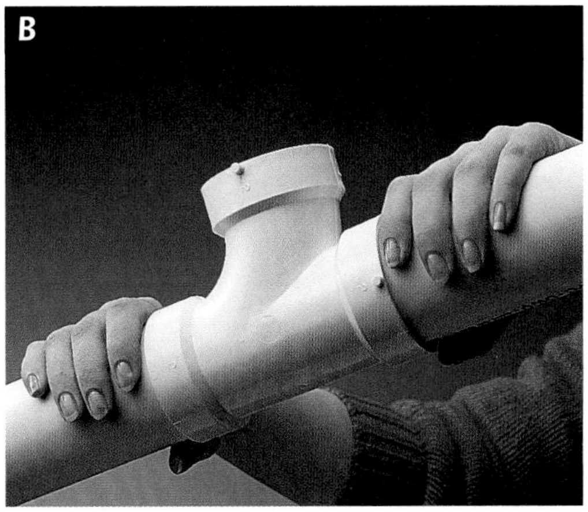

Test-fit all pipes and fittings.

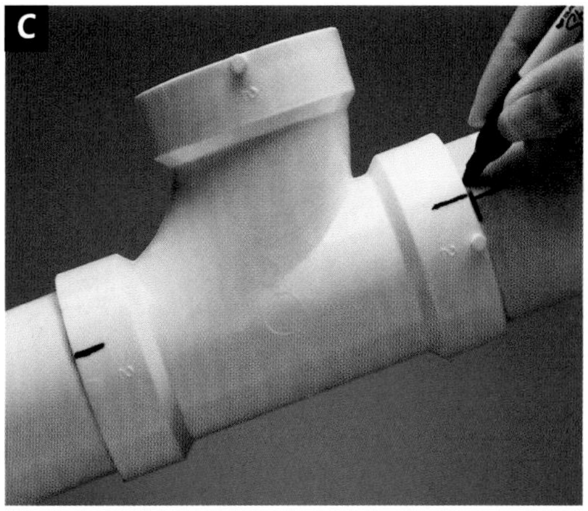

Make alignment marks across each pipe joint using a felt-tipped pen.

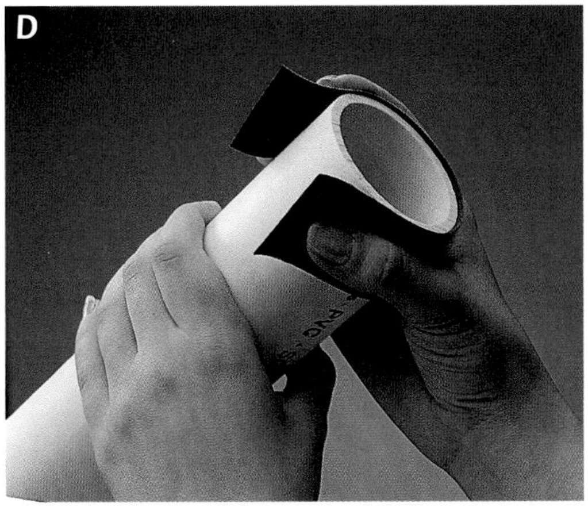

Clean the ends of the pipes and the fitting sockets, using emery cloth.

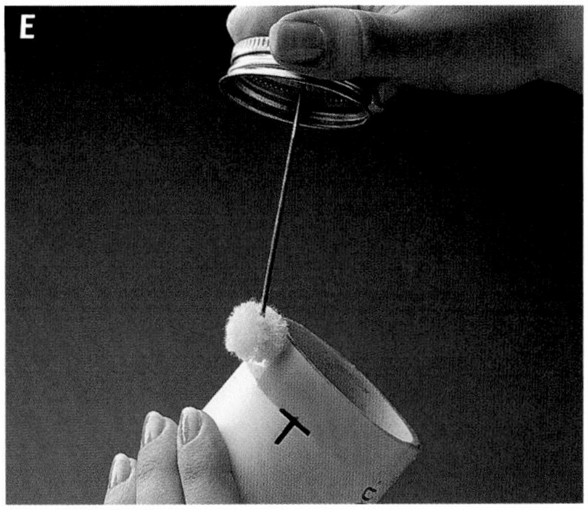

Apply plastic-pipe primer to the ends of the pipes.

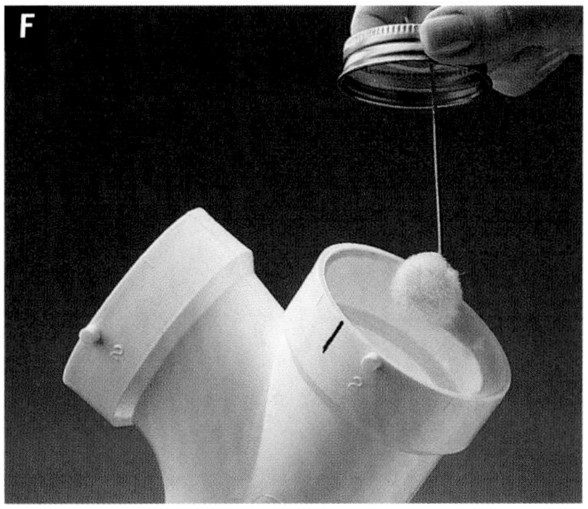

Apply plastic-pipe primer inside the fitting sockets.

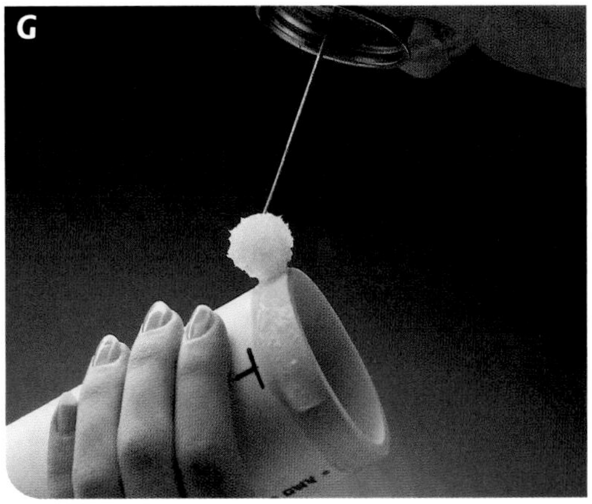

Apply solvent glue to the end of the pipe and inside the fitting socket.

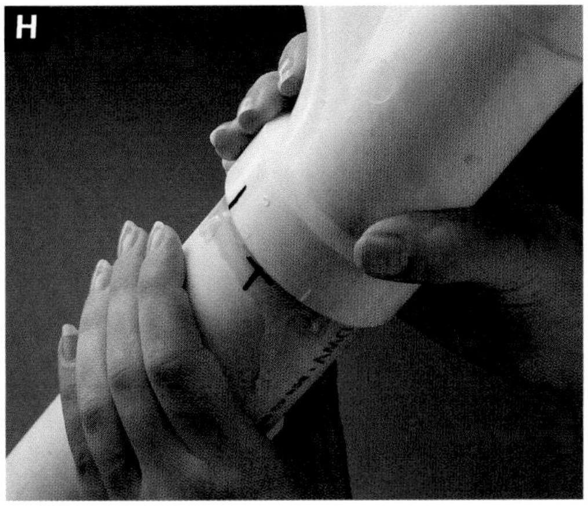

Quickly position pipe and fitting so alignment marks are offset by about 2" and the end fits flush against the fitting.

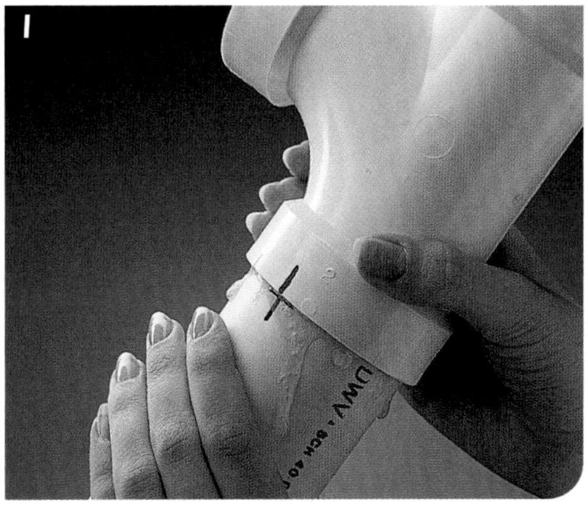

Twist the pipe until marks are aligned. Hold pipe in place for about 20 seconds, then let it dry undisturbed for 30 minutes.

Working with Copper Pipe

Copper is the ideal material for water supply pipes. It resists corrosion and has smooth surfaces that provide good water flow. Copper pipes are available in several diameters, but most home water supply systems use 1/2" or 3/4" pipe. Copper pipe is manufactured in rigid and flexible forms.

Rigid copper, sometimes called hard copper, is approved for home water supply systems by all local Codes. It comes in three wall-thickness grades: Types M, L, and K. Type M is thin and inexpensive, which makes it a good choice for do-it-yourself home plumbing.

Rigid Type L usually is required by Codes for commercial plumbing systems. Because it is strong and solders easily, Type L may be preferred by some professional plumbers, and by do-it-yourselfers for home use. Type K has the heaviest wall thickness, and most often is used for underground water service lines.

Flexible copper, also called soft copper, comes in two wall-thickness grades: Types L and K. Both are approved for most home water supply systems, although flexible Type L copper is used primarily for gas service lines. Because it is bendable and resists mild frosts, Type L may be installed as part of a water supply system in unheated indoor areas, such as crawl spaces. Type K is used for underground water service lines.

A third form of copper, called DWV, is used for drain systems. Because most codes now allow low-cost plastic pipes for drain systems, DWV copper is seldom used.

Copper pipes are usually connected with soldered fittings. Correctly soldered fittings are strong and trouble-free. Copper pipe can also be joined with compression fittings, which are more expensive than soldered joints, but which allow pipes or fixtures to be repaired or replaced readily. Flare fittings are used only with flexible copper pipes, usually as a gas-line fitting. Using flare fittings requires some skill, but it isn't difficult.

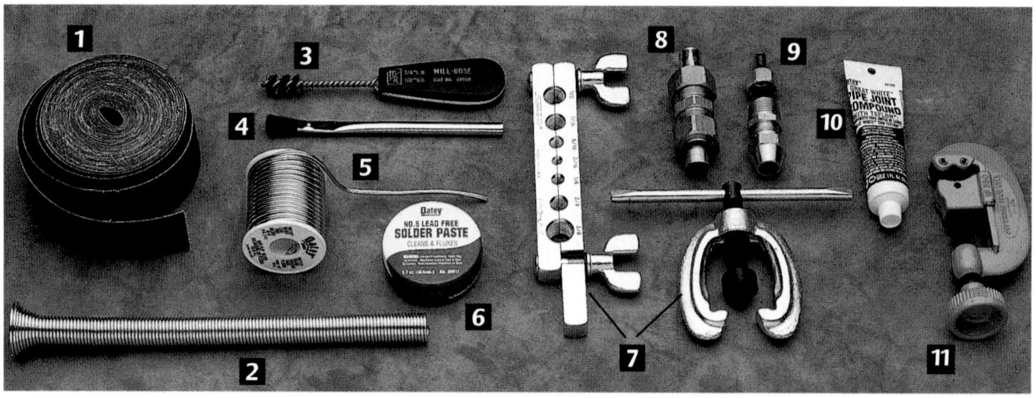

Specialty tools and materials for working with copper include: emery cloth (1), coil-spring tubing bender (2), wire brush (3), flux brush (4), lead-free solder (5), self-cleaning soldering paste (flux) (6), flaring tools (7), flare fitting (8), compression fitting (9), pipe joint compound (10), pipe cutter (11).

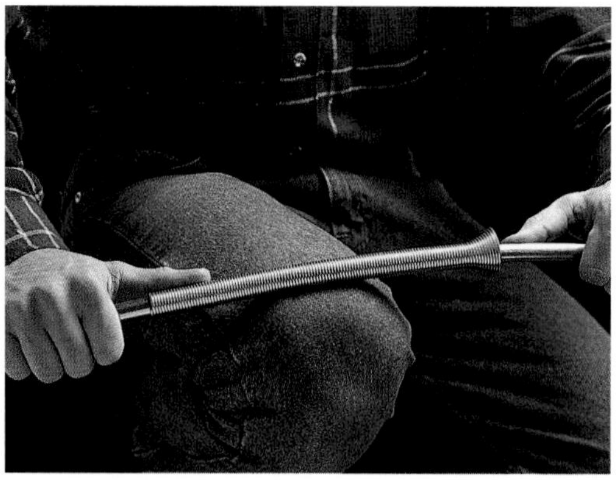

Bend flexible copper pipe with a coil-spring tubing bender to avoid kinks. Select a bender that matches the outside diameter of the pipe.

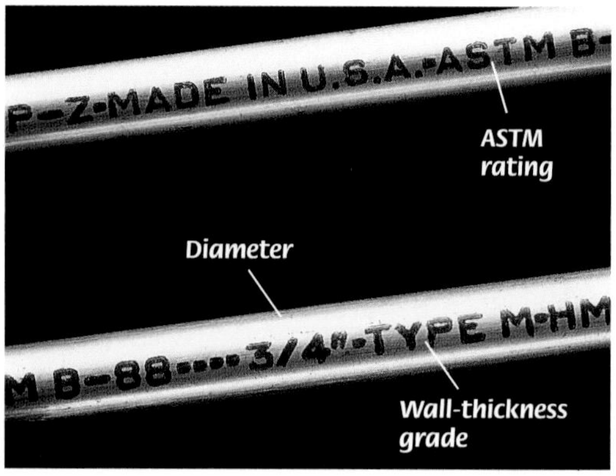

Grade stamp information includes pipe diameter, wall-thickness grade, and a stamp of approval from the American Society for Testing and Materials.

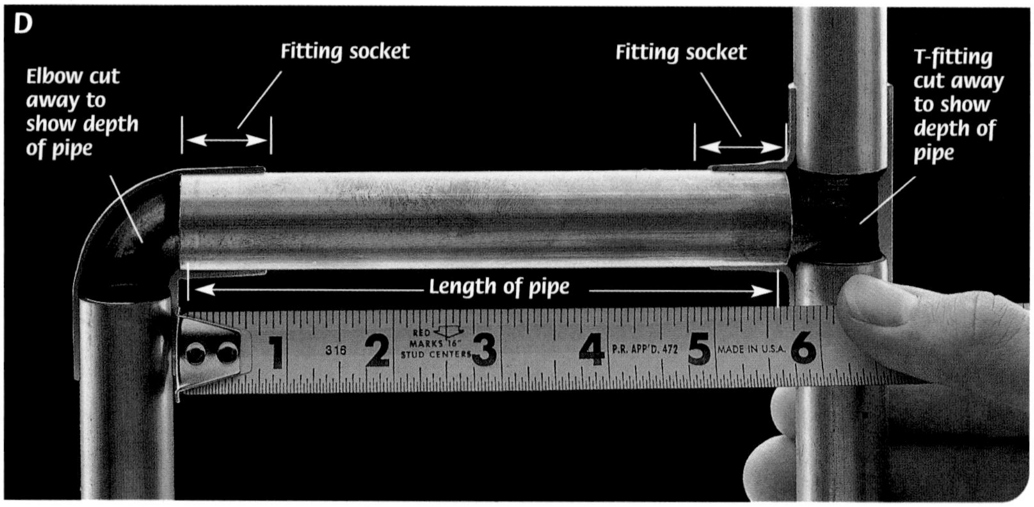

Determine the length of copper pipe needed by measuring between the bottom of the copper fitting sockets (fittings shown in cutaway). Mark the length on the pipe with a felt-tipped pen.

Copper Pipe & Fitting Chart

Fitting Method	Rigid Copper			Flexible Copper		General Comments
	Type M	Type L	Type K	Type L	Type K	
Soldered	yes	yes	yes	yes	yes	Inexpensive, strong, and trouble-free fitting method. Requires some skill.
Compression	yes	not recommended		yes	yes	Easy to use. Allows pipes or fixtures to be repaired or replaced readily. More expensive than solder. Best used on flexible copper.
Flare	no	no	no	yes	yes	Use only with flexible copper pipes. Usually used as a gas-line fitting. Requires some skill.

Taking Apart Soldered Joints

The first step in many plumbing repairs is separating existing joints to remove defective pipes. Though it isn't difficult to take apart soldered joints, it's important to work carefully.

Turn off the water at the main shutoff valve and drain the water in the pipes by opening the highest and lowest faucets in the house.

Light a propane torch and hold the flame tip to the fitting until the solder becomes shiny and begins to melt **(photo A).**

Use channel-type pliers to separate the pipe from the fitting **(photo B).**

Remove the old solder by heating the ends of the pipe with a propane torch. Carefully wipe away the melted solder with a dry rag **(photo C).** Work quickly, but cautiously: **pipes will be hot.**

Allow the pipe to cool for several minutes, then use an emery cloth to polish the ends down to the bare metal **(photo D).** Any residual solder or metal burrs left on the pipe may cause the new joint to leak.

Discard the old fittings—they should not be reused.

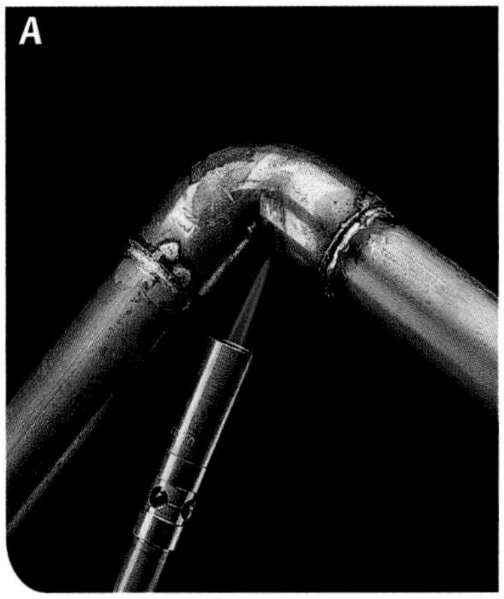

Heat the solder until it becomes shiny and begins to melt.

Separate the pipes from the fitting with a channel-type pliers.

Quickly wipe away melted solder using a clean, dry rag.

Polish the ends of the pipes to bare metal with emery cloth.

Cutting Copper Pipe

Making a smooth, straight cut is the first step in creating a watertight joint. The best way to cut rigid and flexible copper pipe is with a tubing cutter.

Measure the length of pipe to be cut and draw a line with a felt-tipped pen.

Place a tubing cutter over the pipe and tighten the handle until the pipe rests on both rollers and the cutting wheel is centered on the marked line **(photo A).**

Turn the tubing cutter one rotation so the cutting wheel scores a continuous, straight line around the pipe **(photo B).**

Rotate the cutter in the opposite direction, tightening the handle slightly after every two rotations, until cut is complete **(photo C).**

After cutting the pipe, remove metal burrs on the edges with a reaming tool or round file **(photo D).**

Though it's more difficult to make perfectly straight cuts, you can use a hacksaw to cut copper. Again, take care to make a smooth, straight cut and remove all metal burrs. A hacksaw is particularly useful when you're working on installed pipes in tight corners or other areas where a tubing cutter won't fit.

Helpful Hint

If it gradually seems to be taking more effort to cut pipe, the cutting wheel on your tubing cutter may be dull.

Most hardware stores and building centers carry replacements, and changing the cutting wheel is a simple operation that will save you time and trouble in the long run.

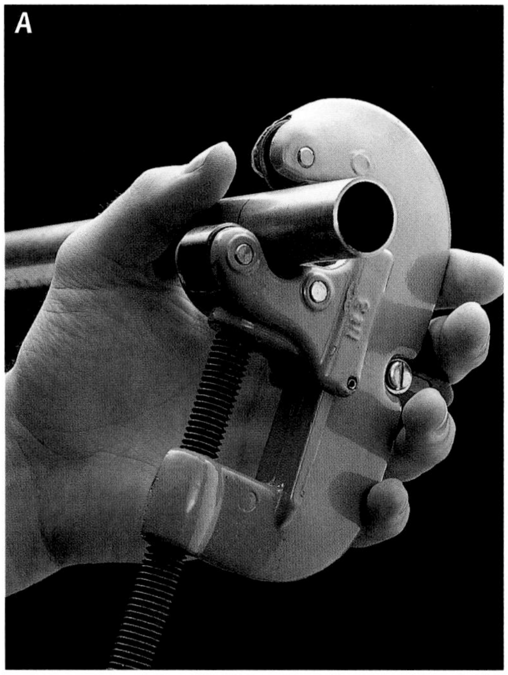

Tighten the handle on a tubing cutter so the cutting wheel rests on the marked line.

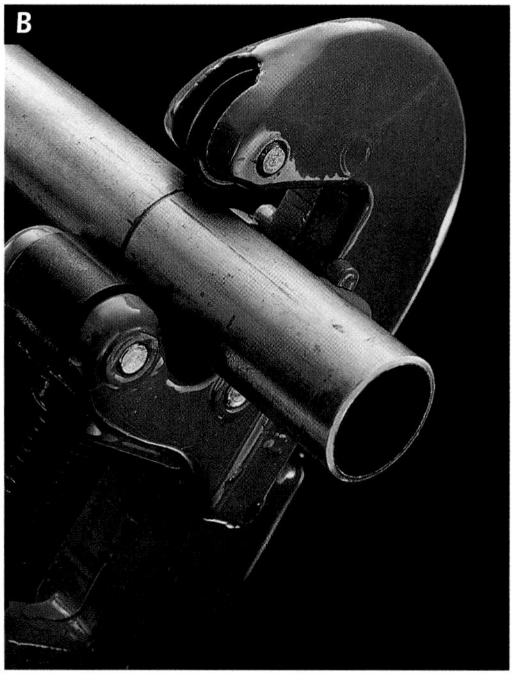

Turn the tubing cutter one rotation to score a continuous straight line around the pipe.

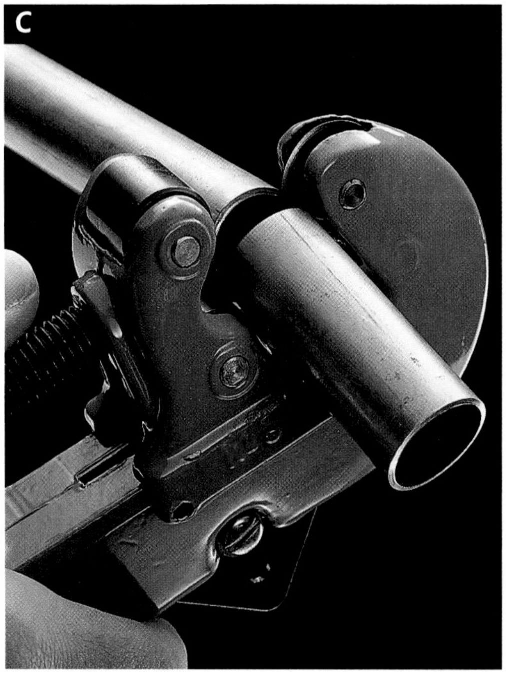

Rotate the cutter in the other direction. After every two rotations, tighten the handle.

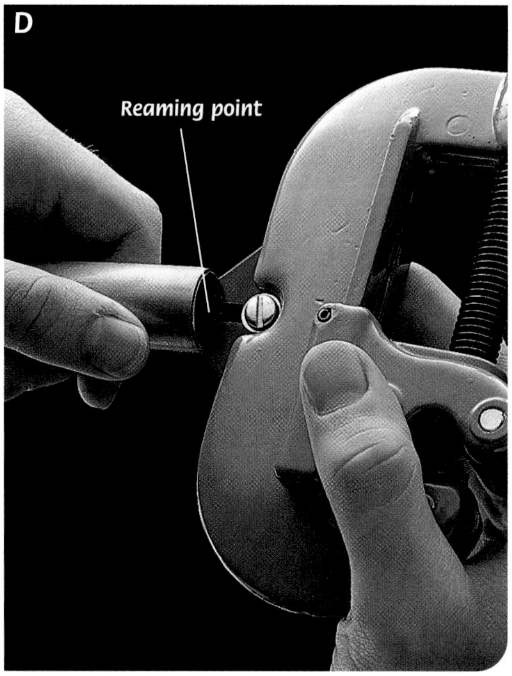

Remove metal burrs from the inside edge of the cut pipe, using the reaming point on the tubing cutter or a round file.

Soldering Copper Pipe

A soldered pipe joint, also called a sweated joint, is made by heating a copper or brass fitting with a propane torch until the fitting is just hot enough to melt the solder. Heat then draws the solder into the gap between the fitting and pipe, forming a watertight seal.

Clean pipes and fittings are essential to successful, watertight joints. Sand the ends of pipes with emery cloth and scour the insides of fittings with a wire brush before beginning to solder. When a joint is soldered, don't touch or disturb the pipes until the solder loses its shiny color.

Using too much heat is the most common mistake made by beginners. To avoid this error, remember that the tip of the torch's inner flame produces the most heat. Direct the flame carefully—solder will flow in the direction heat has traveled. Heat pipe just until the flux sizzles, then remove the flame. Touch the solder to the pipe and let the heated pipe melt the solder.

When soldering joints in place, shield flammable surfaces from the heat of the torch flame. Although heat-absorbent pads are available for this purpose, many experienced plumbers use a double layer of 26-gauge sheet metal. The reflective quality of the sheet metal helps joints heat evenly. Soldering copper pipe and fittings isn't difficult, but it requires some patience and skill. Practice soldering pieces of scrap pipe before taking on repairs or other projects.

Clean, flux, and dry-fit an entire run without soldering any of the joints. When the run is correctly assembled, go back and solder all the joints. After soldering each joint, check for gaps around the edges that could become leaks. Correcting leaks after the water is turned back on requires complete disassembly of the joint—an aggravation best avoided whenever possible.

To form a good seal with solder, the ends of pipes and insides of fittings must be free of dirt and grease. Sand pipes with emery cloth and scour inside each fitting with a wire brush **(photo E).**

Apply a thin layer of water-soluble paste flux to the end of each pipe, using a flux brush **(photo F).** The soldering paste flux should cover about 1" of the pipe end.

Assemble each joint in the run, inserting pipe into fittings until the pipe is tight against the bottom of the fitting sockets **(photo G).** Twist each fitting slightly to spread the flux.

Unwind 8" to 10" of solder from the spool. Bend the first 2" of the wire to a 90° angle **(photo H).** This angle makes it easier to maneuver the solder all the way around a joint, quickly and smoothly.

continued on next page

Tools: *Wire brush, flux brush, propane torch, spark lighter (or matches), adjustable wrench, channel-type pliers.*

Materials: *Copper pipe, copper fittings, emery cloth, soldering paste (flux), lead-free solder, rag.*

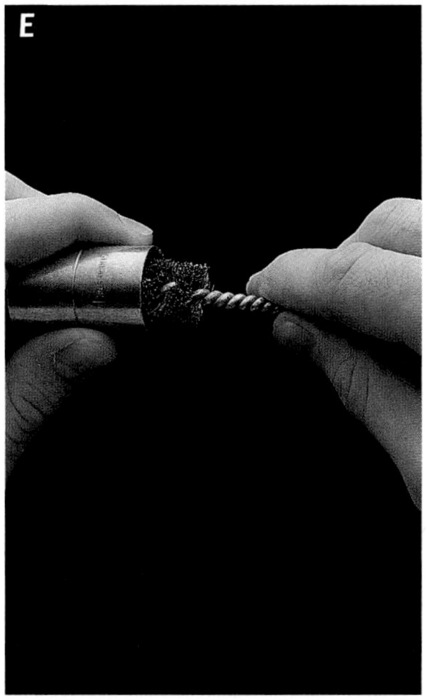

E

Clean inside the fittings with a wire brush.

Brush a thin layer of water-soluble paste flux onto the end of each pipe.

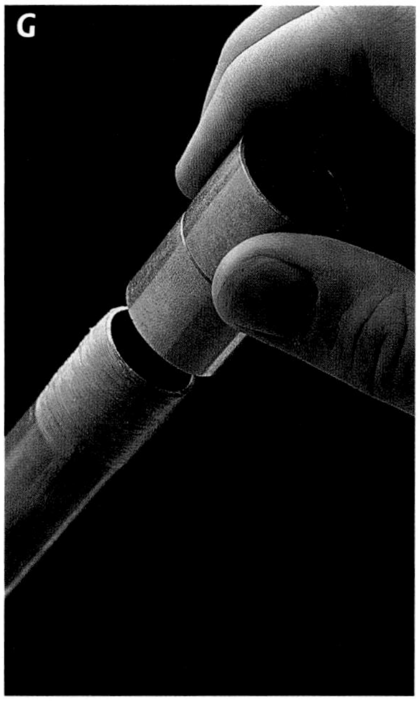

G

Assemble each joint, twisting the fitting to spread the flux.

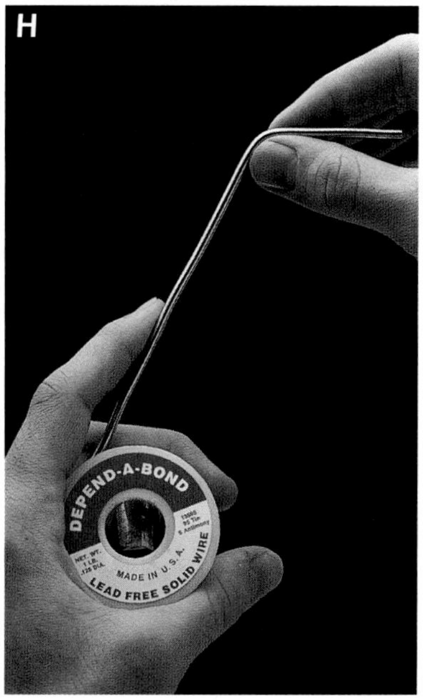

Bend the first 2" of the wire solder to a 90° angle.

Soldering Copper Pipe (cont.)

To light the propane torch, open the valve and strike a spark lighter or match next to the nozzle until the gas ignites **(photo I).** Adjust the torch valve until the inner portion of the flame is 1" to 2" long **(photo J).**

Hold flame tip against the middle of the fitting for 4 to 5 seconds, until the flux begins to sizzle **(photo K).** Heat the other side of the joint, distributing heat evenly **(photo L).** Move the flame around the joint in the direction the solder should flow. Touch the solder to the pipe, just below the fitting. If it melts, the joint is sufficiently hot.

Quickly apply solder along both seams of the fitting, making sure the liquefied solder is being drawn into the fitting **(photo M).** When the joint is filled, solder begins to form droplets on the bottom. A correctly soldered joint shows a thin bead of silver-colored solder around the lip of the fitting. It usually requires about 3/4" of solder wire to fill a 3/4" joint.

If solder pools around the rim rather than filling the joint as it cools, reheat the area until the solder liquifies and draws in slightly.

Let the joint sit undisturbed for at least 20 seconds. When the joint is cool, wipe away excess flux and solder with a dry rag **(photo N).** When all joints have cooled, turn on the water. If any joint leaks, shut off the water and drain pipes. Apply more flux to the rim of the joint, and resolder it.

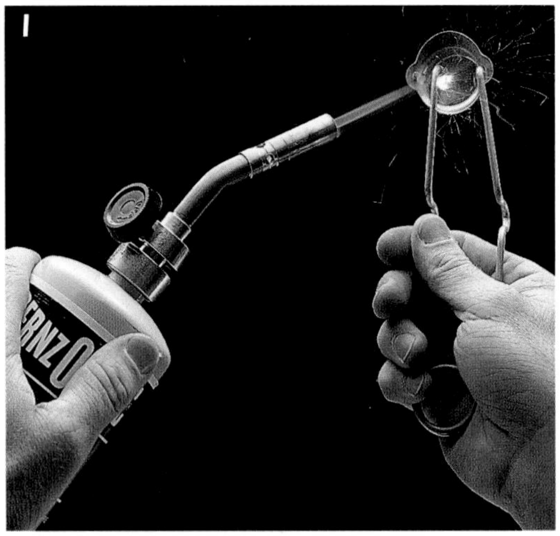

Open the gas valve and strike a spark lighter to light the torch.

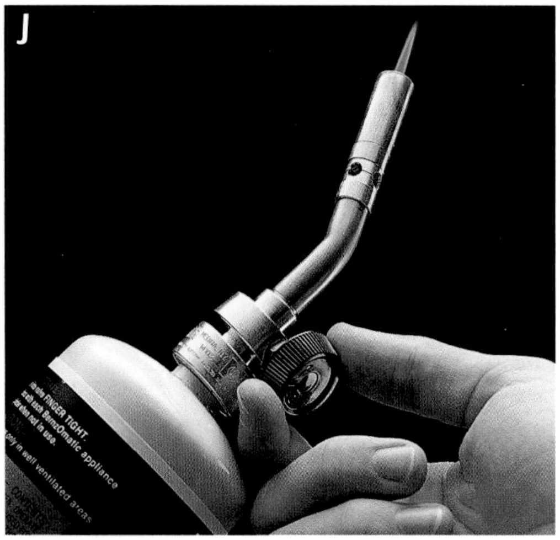

Adjust the valve on the torch until the inner gas flame is 1" to 2" long.

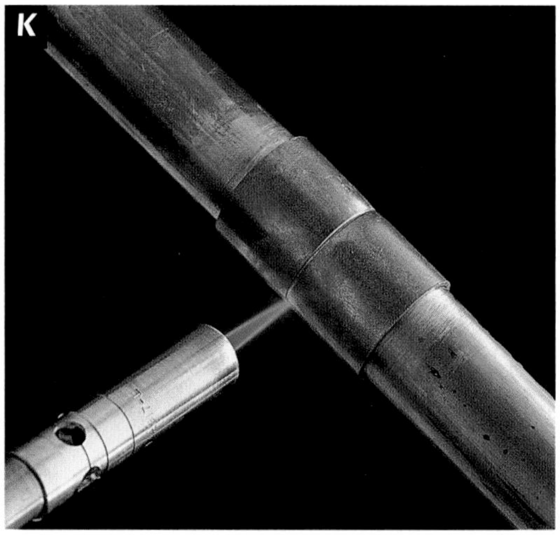

Heat the fitting with the tip of the flame until the flux begins to sizzle.

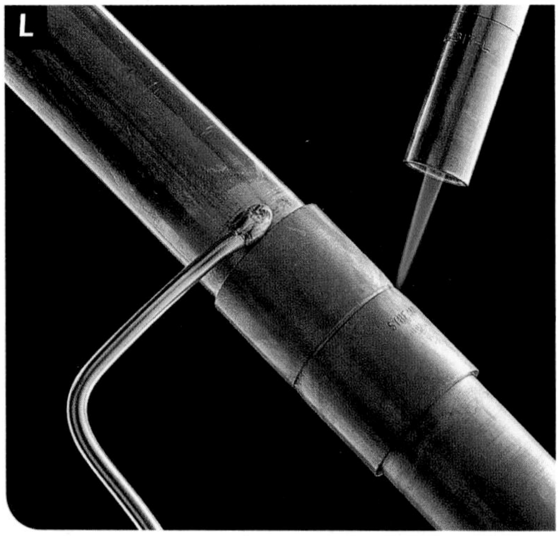

Heat other side of joint, moving the flame in the direction the solder should flow. Test heat by touching solder to pipe.

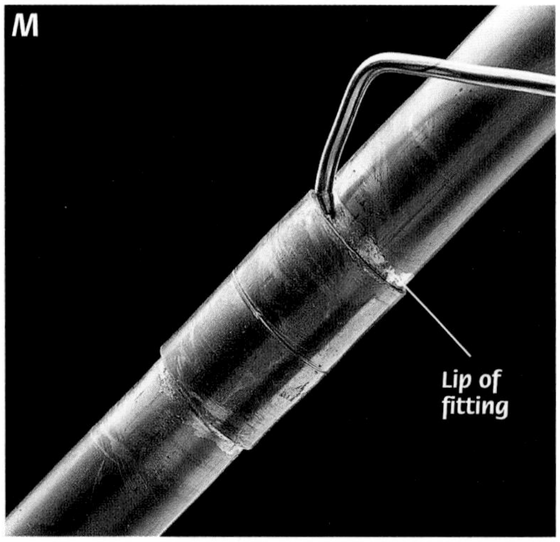

Push ½" to ¾" of solder into each joint, allowing capillary action to draw liquefied solder into the joint.

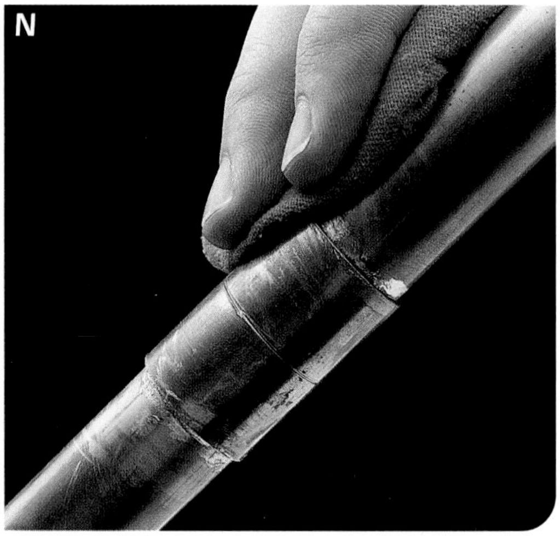

Wipe away excess solder with a dry rag. Be careful: pipes will be hot.

Soldering Tips

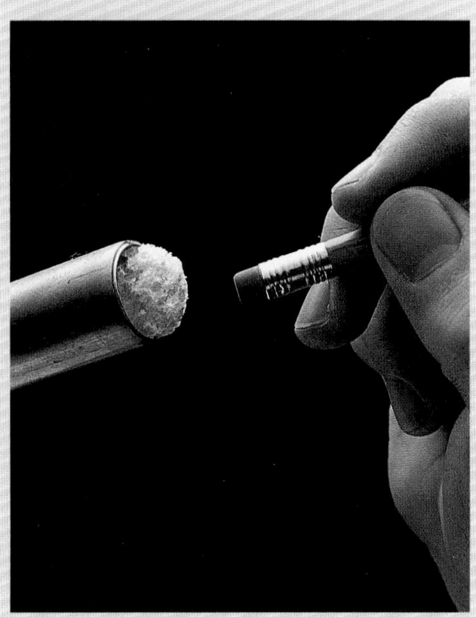

Keep joints dry when soldering existing water pipes by plugging the pipes with bread. The bread absorbs moisture, then dissolves when the water is turned on.

Use caution when soldering copper. Allow pipes and fittings time to cool before handling.

Prevent accidents by shutting off the propane torch immediately after use, making sure the valve is completely closed.

Soldering Brass Valves

Soldering brass is much the same as working with copper, except that brass is denser and takes more time to heat enough to draw solder.

Before beginning to solder, remove the valve stem with an adjustable wrench **(photo A).** This prevents heat damage to rubber or plastic stem parts. Clean and flux the copper pipes, then assemble the joints.

Light the propane torch and heat the body of the valve, distributing the heat evenly **(photo B).** Apply the solder (page 288). Let the metal cool, then reassemble the valve.

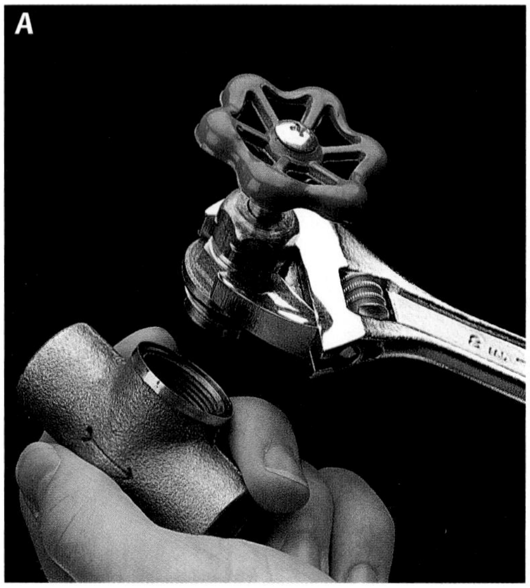

Remove the valve stem with an adjustable wrench.

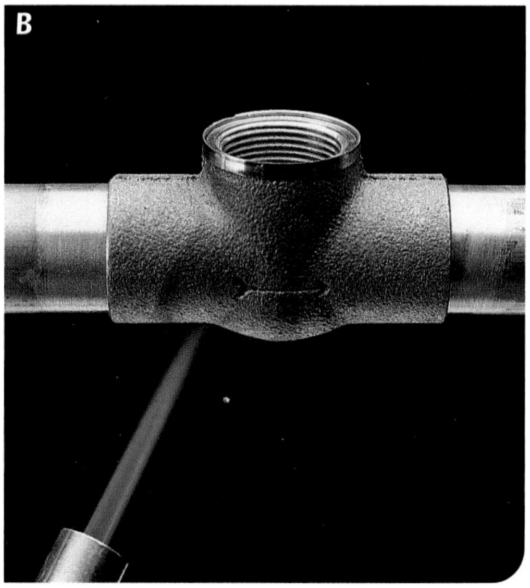

Heat the body of the valve with a propane torch.

Using Compression Fittings

When cramped or poorly ventilated spaces make it difficult or unsafe to solder, compression fittings are a good choice. They're also appropriate for connections that may need to be taken apart at a later date. Because they're easy to disconnect, compression fittings often are used to install supply tubes and fixture shutoff valves.

Compression fittings work well with flexible copper pipe, which is soft enough to allow the compression ring to seat snugly, creating a watertight seal. They are also used to make connections with Type M rigid copper pipe.

When measuring copper tubing to be used with compression fittings, add 1/2" for the length of pipe that must fit inside the valve. As with all plumbing joints, smooth, straight cuts are vital to forming watertight seals with compression fittings. Cut tubing with a tubing cutter or a hacksaw (page 286), and remove any metal burrs on the cut edges, using a reaming tool or round file.

To further ensure a watertight seal, cover compression rings with pipe joint compound before assembling compression fittings.

Tools: *Felt-tipped pen, tubing cutter or hacksaw, adjustable wrenches.*

Materials: *Brass compression fittings, pipe joint compound.*

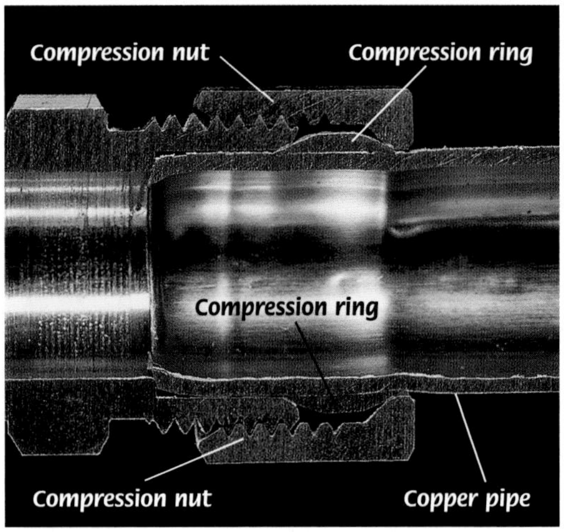

Threaded compression nuts force the compression ring against the copper pipe, forming a seal.

Joining Two Copper Pipes with a Compression Fitting

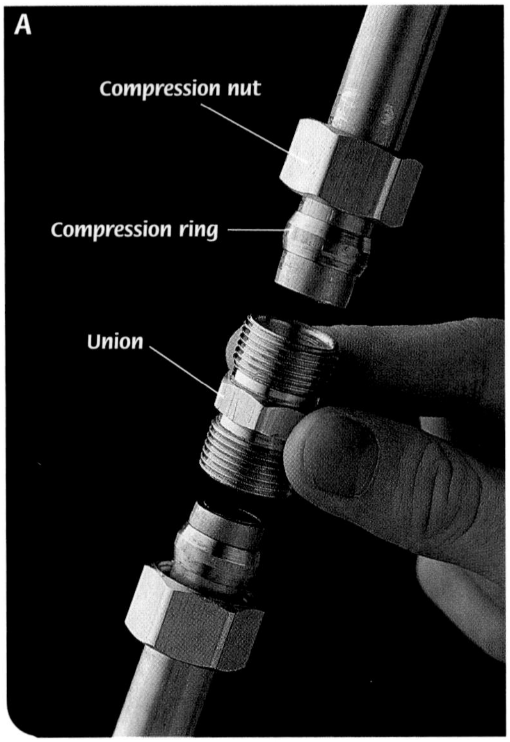

Slide the compression nuts and rings over the ends of the pipes. Place threaded union between pipes.

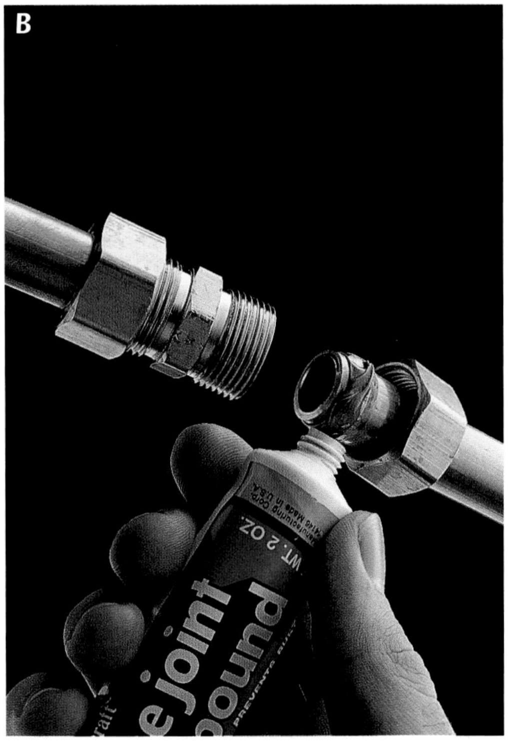

Apply a layer of pipe joint compound to the compression rings, then screw the compression nuts onto the threaded union. Hand-tighten the nuts.

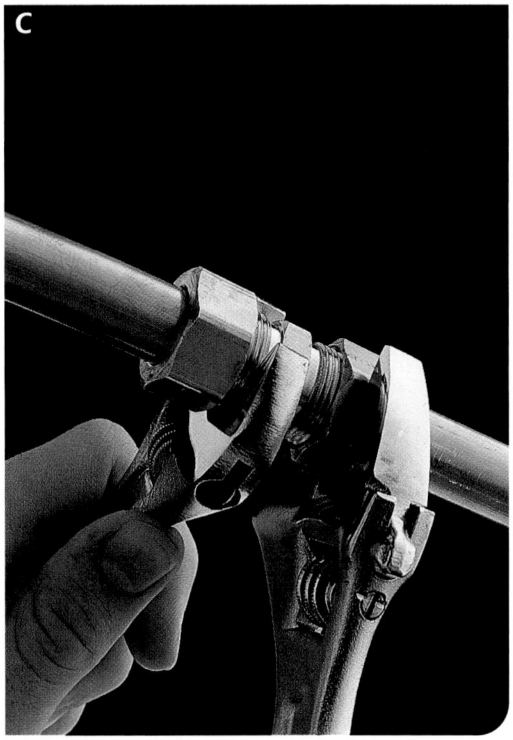

Hold center of union fitting with adjustable wrench. Use another wrench to tighten each compression nut one complete turn. Turn on water. If fitting leaks, gently tighten nuts.

Attaching Supply Tubes to Fixture Shutoff Valves

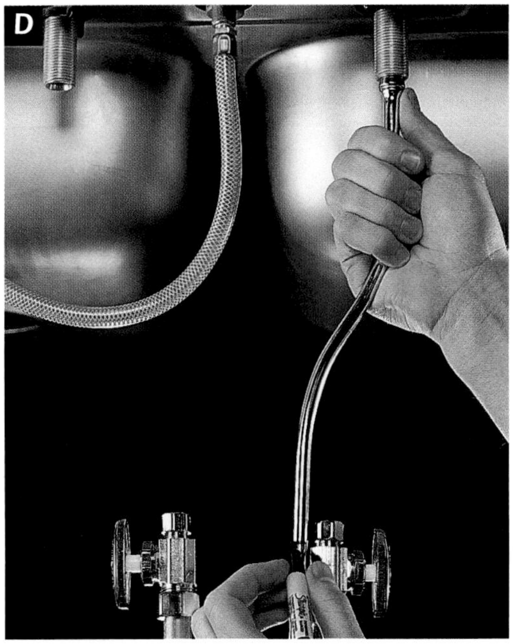

Bend a flexible copper supply tube between the faucet tailpiece and the shutoff valve. Mark the length. Make sure to include the ½" portion that will fit inside the valve.

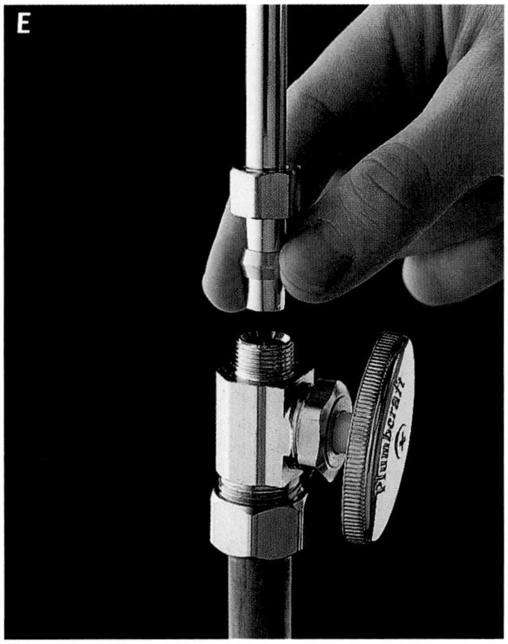

Slide the compression nut over the end of the pipe, with the threads facing the valve. Then slide on the compression ring.

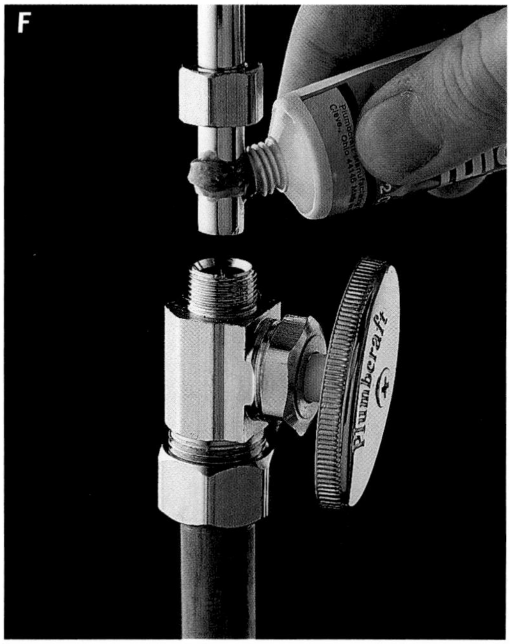

Apply a continuous layer of pipe joint compound over the compression ring.

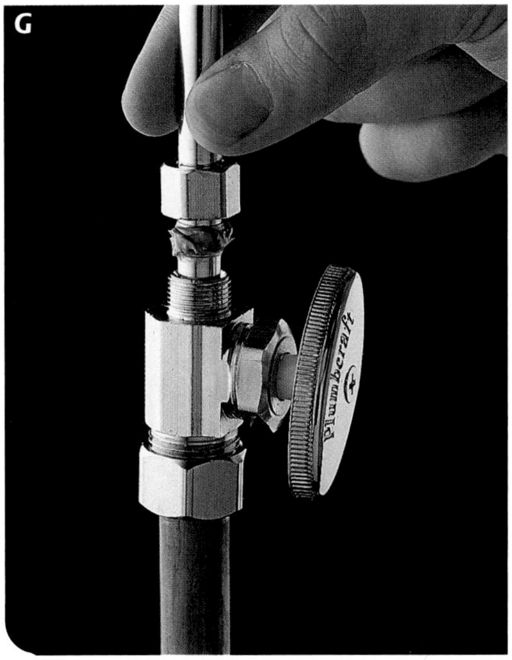

Insert the end of the pipe into the fitting so it sits flush against the bottom.

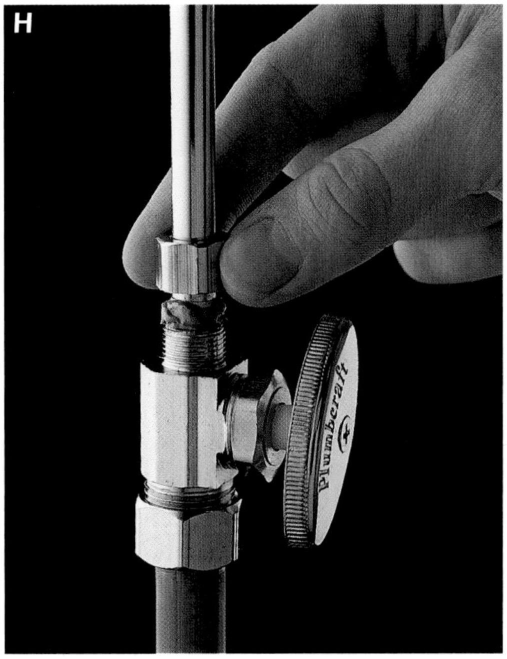

Slide the compression ring and nut against the threads of the valve. Hand-tighten the nut onto the valve.

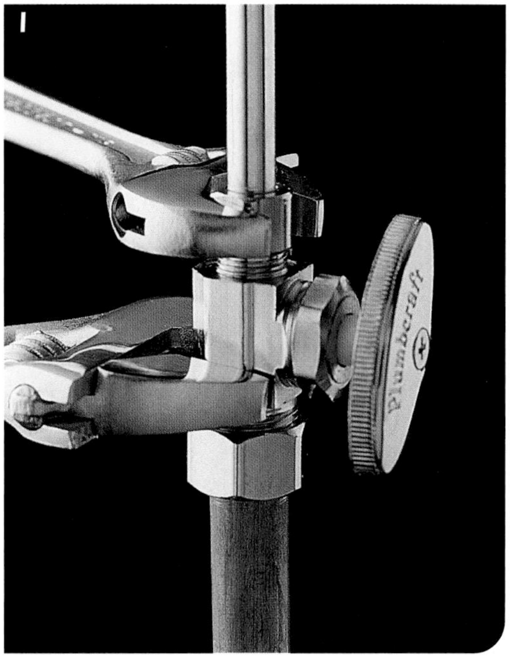

Tighten the compression nut with adjustable wrenches. Do not overtighten. Turn on the water and watch for leaks. If the fitting leaks, gently tighten the nut.

Using Flare Fittings

Flare fittings are used most often for flexible copper gas lines, but are also commonly used with flexible copper water supply pipes. However, they cannot be used when connections will be concealed inside walls. Check local Plumbing Codes regarding their use.

Flare fittings are a natural choice in situations where it's unsafe or difficult to solder, such as in a crawl space or other confined area. They are easy to disconnect, which makes them appropriate for connections that may need to be changed, or moved.

Tools: Two-piece flaring tool, adjustable wrenches.

Materials: Copper pipe, brass flare fittings.

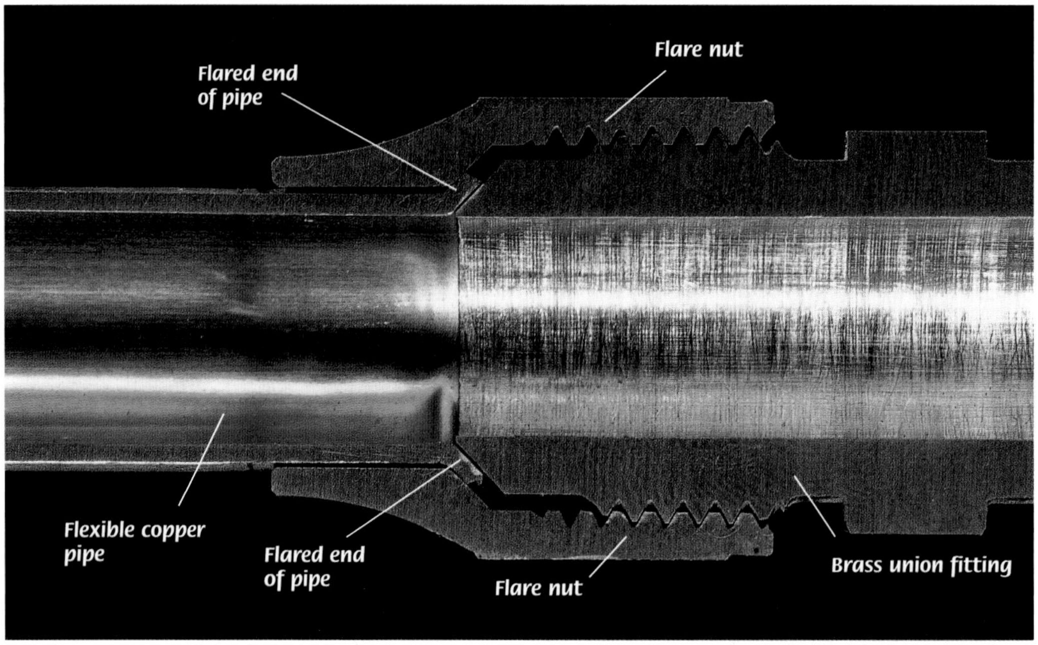

The flared end of flexible copper pipe forms a seal against the head of a brass union fitting, shown here in cutaway.

Joining Copper Pipe with a Flare Union Fitting

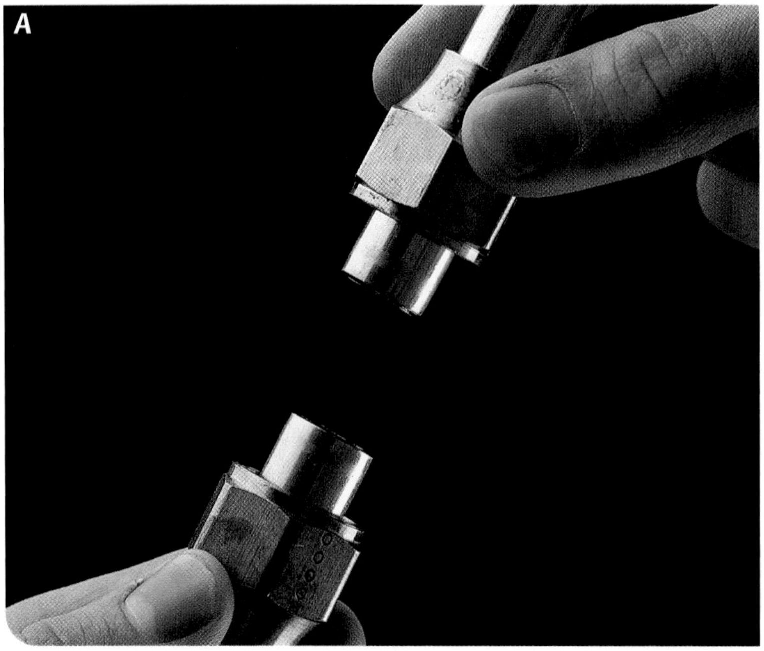

Slide flare nuts onto the ends of the pipes. Nuts must be placed on the pipes before the ends can be flared.

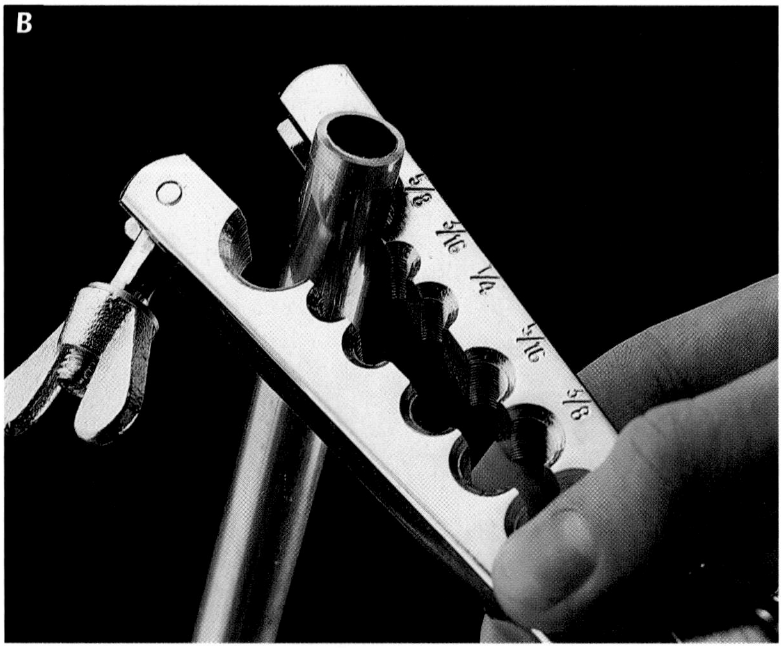

Select the hole in the flaring tool base that matches the outside diameter of the pipe. Open the base and place the end of the pipe inside the hole.

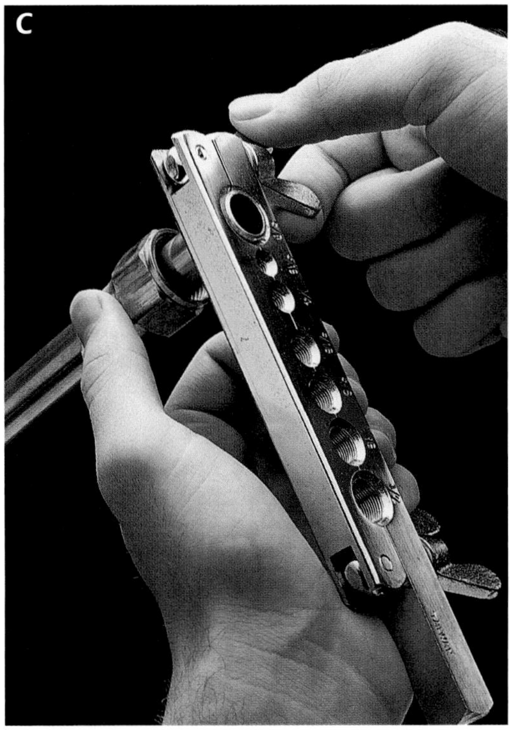

Clamp the pipe inside the flaring tool base. The end of the pipe must be flush with the flat surface of the base.

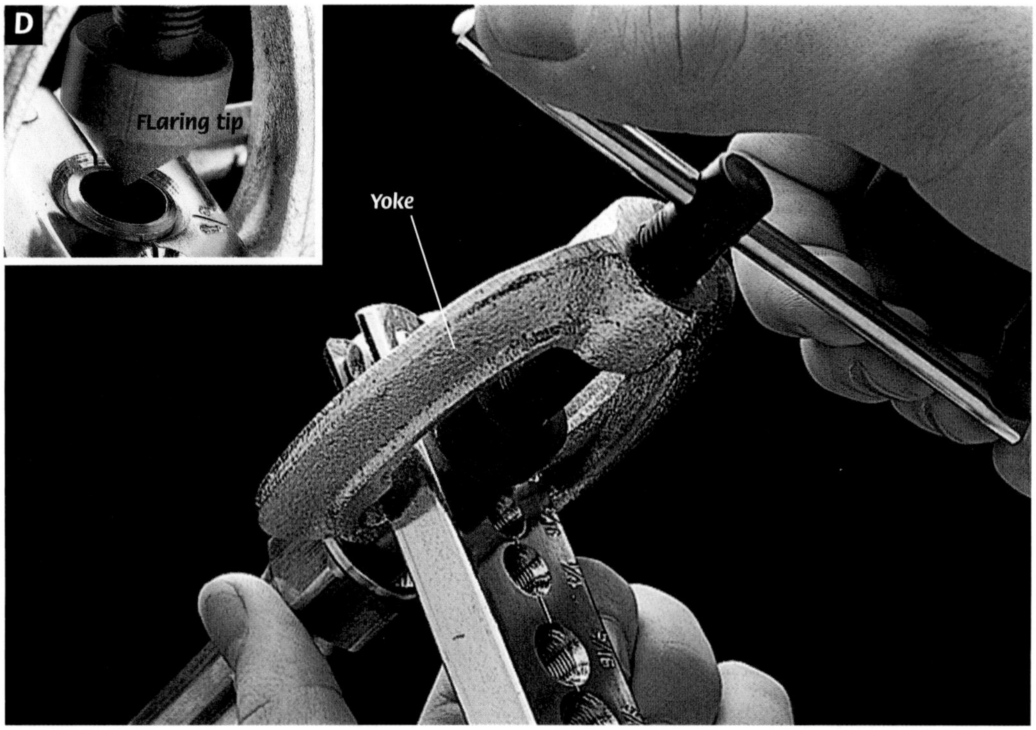

Slip the yoke of the flaring tool around the base. Center the flaring tip of the yoke over end of pipe (inset photo). Tighten the handle of the yoke to shape the end of the pipe. The flare is completed when the handle cannot be turned farther.

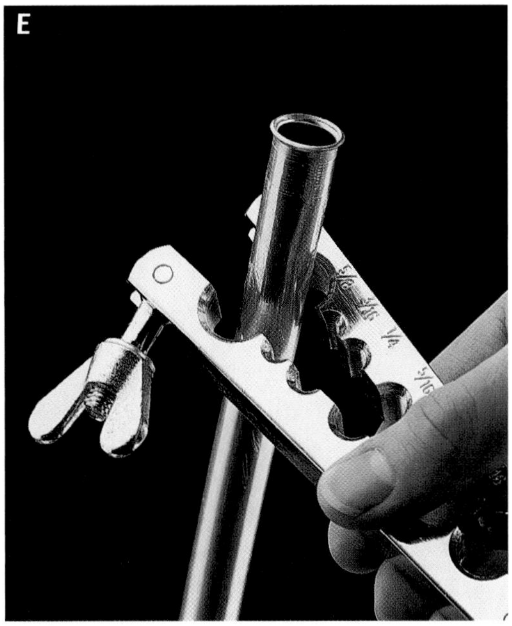

Remove the yoke, then remove the pipe from the base. Repeat this process to flare the other pipe.

Place flare union between flared ends of the pipe and screw flare nuts onto the union. Hand-tighten flare nuts.

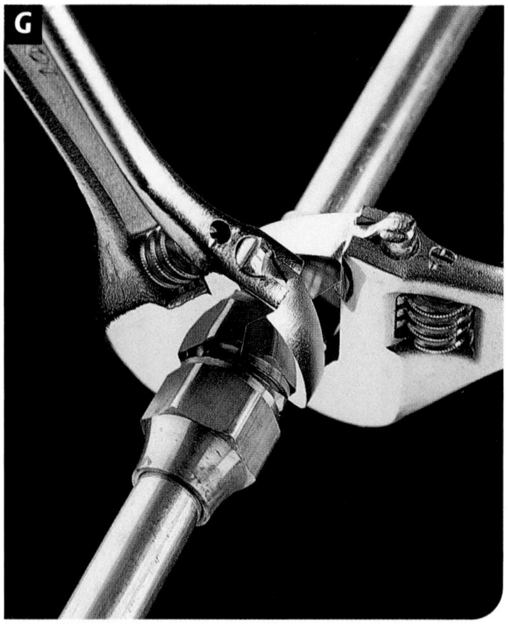

Hold the center of the flare union with an adjustable wrench. Use another wrench to tighten the nuts one turn. Turn on the water, and tighten the nuts if the fitting leaks.

Working with Galvanized Iron Pipe

Galvanized iron pipe often is found in older homes, where it's used for water supply and small drain lines. It can be identified by the zinc coating that gives it a silver color, and by the threaded fittings used to connect the pipes.

Galvanized iron pipes and fittings corrode with age and eventually must be replaced. Low water pressure may be a sign that rust has built up inside galvanized pipes. Blockages usually occur in elbow fittings. Don't try to clean galvanized pipes—replace them instead.

When purchasing galvanized iron pipe and fittings, specify the interior diameter (I.D.). Galvanized iron pipe and fittings can be found at almost any hardware store or home improvement center. Pre-threaded pipes, called *nipples*, are available in lengths from 1" to 1 ft. If a repair requires longer pipes, have a hardware or plumbing supply store cut and thread them to your dimensions.

Old galvanized iron can be difficult to repair. When fittings are rusted in place, what seems like a small job may quickly become a much larger project. Cutting apart a section of pipe often reveals adjacent pipes that also need to be replaced. In the event of extended repairs, you can cap off open lines and restore water to the rest of your house. For this reason, it's a good idea to have an adequate supply of matching nipples and end caps before you begin any repair.

When disassembling a run of pipe and fittings, start at the end of a run and unscrew each piece in turn. Reaching the middle of a run to replace a section of pipe can be a long, tedious job. However, a three-piece fitting, called a *union*, makes it possible to remove a section of pipe or a fitting without taking apart the entire system.

While detaching pipes, use two wrenches, one stationary and one moving. Position the wrenches so the jaws face opposite directions, and move each wrench handle toward the opening of its jaws.

Don't confuse galvanized iron with "black iron," which is available in similar sizes and has similar fittings. Black iron is used only for gas lines.

Tools: *Tape measure, reciprocating saw with metal-cutting blade or a hacksaw, pipe wrenches, propane torch, wire brush.*

Materials: *Nipples, end caps, union fitting, pipe joint compound, replacement fittings (if needed).*

Measure old pipe. Add ½" at each end for the pipe threads inside the fitting. Use this measurement when buying parts.

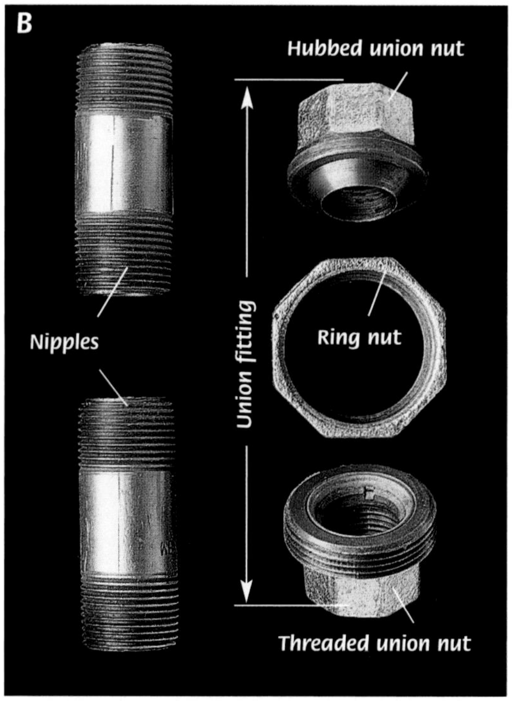

Replace a section of pipe with a union fitting and two threaded pipes (nipples). When assembled, the union and nipples must equal the length of the pipe being replaced.

Removing & Replacing Galvanized Iron Pipe

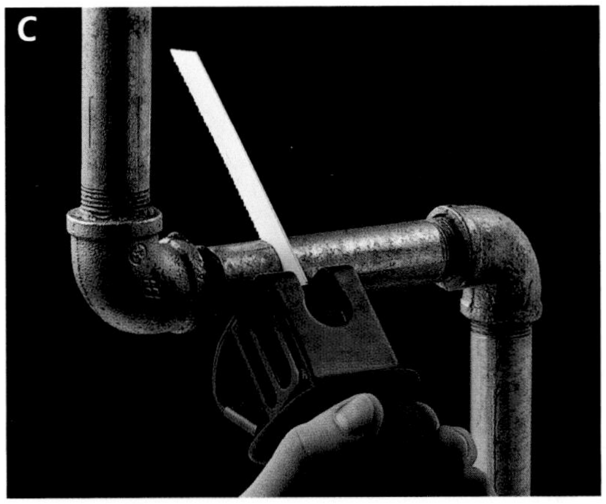

Cut through galvanized iron pipe with a reciprocating saw with a metal-cutting blade, or with a hacksaw.

Hold fitting with a pipe wrench. Use another to twist old pipe, positioning wrenches so jaws face opposite directions.

Remove any corroded fittings using two pipe wrenches. Clean threads with a wire brush.

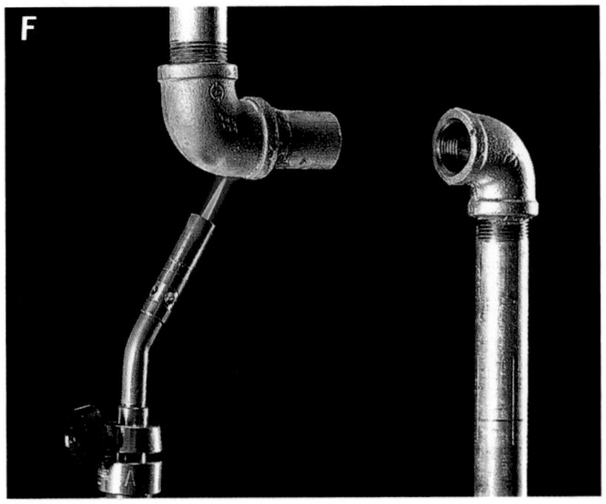

Heat stubborn fittings with a propane torch for easy removal. Shield flammable materials with a double layer of sheet metal, and apply flame for 5 to 10 seconds.

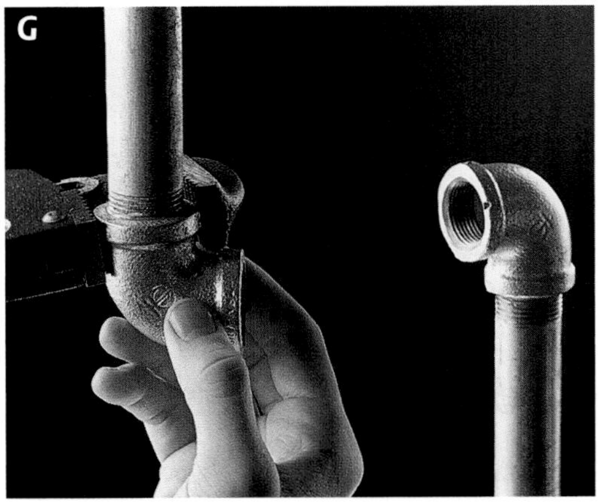

Screw new fittings onto pipe threads. Tighten the fittings with two pipe wrenches, leaving them ⅛ turn out of alignment to allow for the union assembly.

Slide a ring nut onto the nipple, then screw the hubbed union nut onto the nipple and tighten it with pipe wrench.

Screw a second nipple onto the other fitting and tighten it with a pipe wrench.

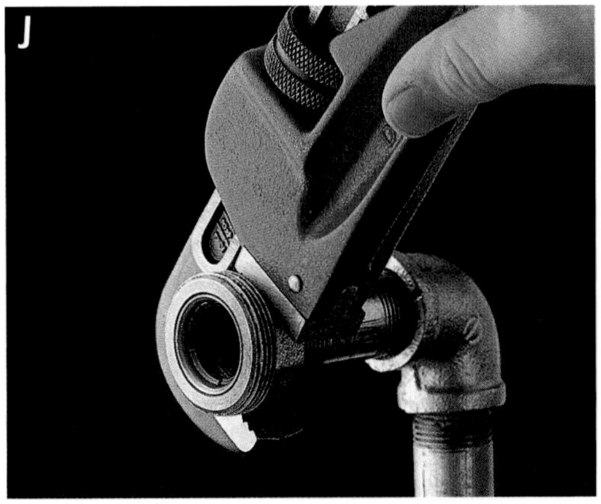

Screw threaded union nut onto second nipple; tighten. Align pipes so lip of hubbed nut fits inside threaded union nut.

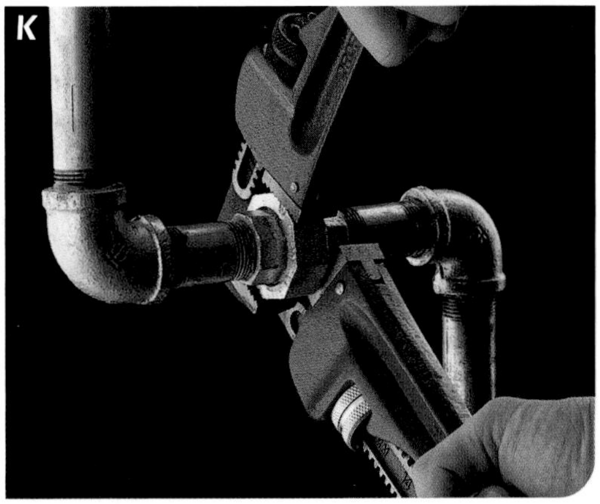

Complete the connection by screwing the ring nut onto the threaded union nut. Tighten the ring nut.

Working with Cast-iron Pipe

Cast-iron pipe is rarely installed these days, but in houses that are more than 30 years old, it's common to encounter cast-iron pipe within the DWV system. Cast-iron pipe can be identified by its dark color, rough surface, and large size. Cast-iron pipes in home drains usually are 3" or more in diameter.

Hubbed fittings may be used to join old cast-iron pipe **(photo A).** Hubbed pipe has a straight end and a flared end. The straight end of one pipe fits inside the hub of the next pipe. Joints are sealed with packing material (oakum) and lead **(photo B).** These hubbed fittings sometimes develop leaks, and pipes can rust through. When pipes or fittings deteriorate, it's necessary to replace them, usually with plastic pipe of the same diameter.

A special fitting called a *banded coupling* is used to connect new plastic pipe to existing cast iron **(photo C).** Banded couplings have a neoprene sleeve that seals the joint, and stainless steel bands and screw clamps that hold the pipes together. These couplings come in several styles, so check your local Plumbing Code to determine the types approved for use in your area.

When installing new plastic DWV pipes, it's sometimes necessary to cut into a cast-iron waste-vent stack in order to connect the new drain and vent pipes. If the iron stack is in poor condition, it often makes sense to replace it entirely with a new plastic waste-vent stack.

Cast iron is heavy and difficult to cut and fit. One 5-ft. section of 4" pipe weighs about 60 pounds, and an iron main waste-vent stack can weigh several hundred pounds. Work with a helper when repairing or replacing cast-iron pipe, and make sure the weight is well supported before cutting into a pipe. Horizontal runs must be supported with strap hangers every 5 feet and at every joint connection. Vertical runs must be supported with riser clamps at every floor level.

Occasionally, a cast-iron waste-vent stack cannot be supported by joists, a situation that might occur in an attic. Before cutting into such a stack, build a 2 × 4 frame to support its weight **(photo below).** Attach blocking across the frame for support, then position clamp risers above and below the section to be cut out.

Fittings & Couplings for Working with Cast Iron

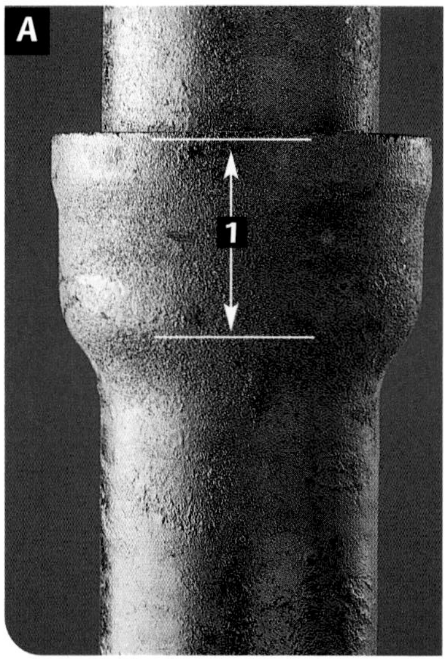

Hubbed fittings **(1)** may be used to join old cast-iron pipe. The straight end of one hubbed pipe fits inside the hub of the next.

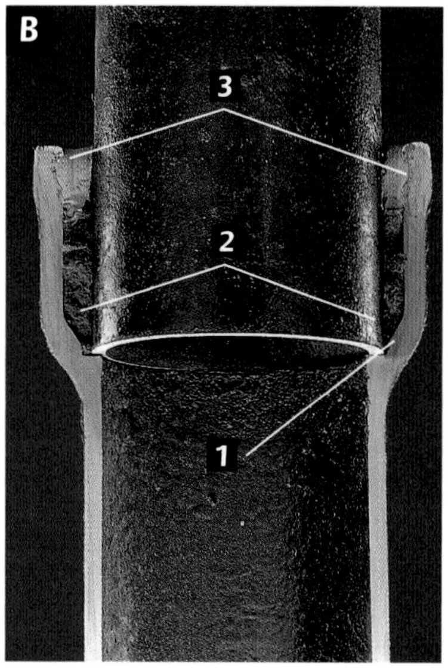

Joints (shown here in cutaway) between the pipe and hub **(1)** are sealed with oakum packing material **(2)** and lead **(3)**.

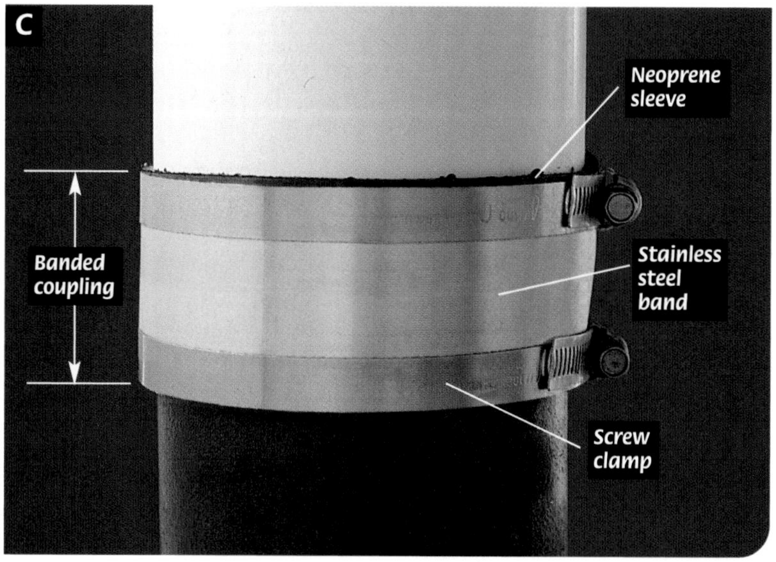

Banded couplings may be used to connect new plastic pipe to remaining cast-iron pipe.

Replacing a Section of Cast-iron Pipe

Cast-iron pipes may rust through or hubbed fittings may leak. If your house is more than thirty years old, you may find it necessary to replace a cast-iron pipe or joint.

The best way to cut cast iron is with a tool called a *snap cutter*, which is available at many rental centers. Designs vary, so ask the rental center for instructions and follow all the manufacturer's precautions. You can also cut cast iron with a hacksaw, though this will be a long, difficult job.

Use chalk to mark two cutting lines on the cast-iron pipe **(photo D).** Plan to remove enough pipe to accommodate the plastic fitting, pipes, and couplings necessary to make the transition. When replacing a hub fitting, measure and mark at least 6" above and below the hub.

Support the lower section of pipe by installing a riser clamp flush against the sole plate of the wall **(photo E).** Tighten the clamp firmly around the pipe.

To support the upper section, attach wood blocks to the wall studs with $2\frac{1}{2}$" wallboard screws **(photo F).** Position these blocks to support riser clamps placed 6" to 12" above the section of pipe to be removed. Install a riser clamp so it rests on top of the blocks. Tighten the clamp securely.

continued on next page

Tools: *Tape measure, chalk, adjustable wrenches, rented cast iron snap cutter, ratchet wrench, screwdriver.*

Materials: *Riser clamps or strap hangers, two wood blocks, $2\frac{1}{2}$" wallboard screws, banded couplings, plastic replacement pipe.*

Helpful Hint

If you don't have access to a snap cutter, you can cut cast-iron pipe by scoring a cutting line with a hacksaw, then tapping along the line with a cold chisel and hammer.

Be sure to wear eye protection when using a hammer and chisel to cut cast-iron pipe. And if you're working in a basement or other enclosed space, wear ear protection as well.

Use chalk to mark cut lines on the cast-iron pipe at least 6" above and below the damaged section.

Support the lower section of pipe by installing a riser clamp flush against the sole plate.

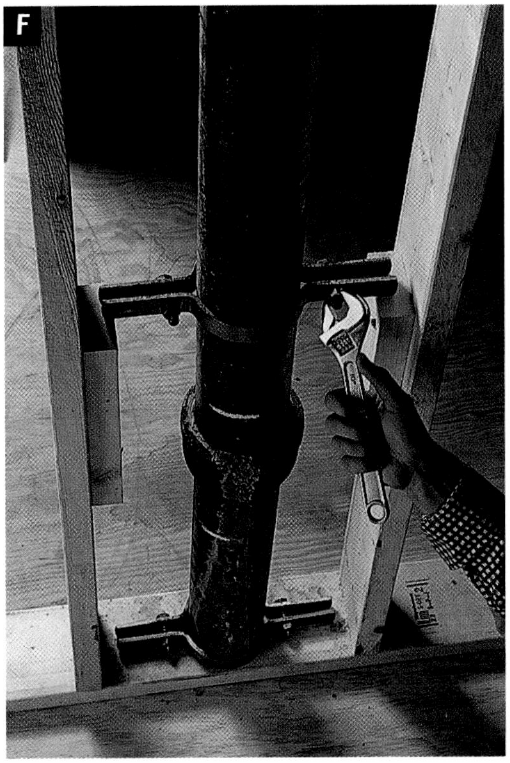

Install a riser clamp 6" to 12" above the section being replaced.

Replacing a Section of Cast-iron Pipe (cont.)

Wrap the chain of the snap cutter around the pipe, aligning the cutting wheels with the upper cutting line **(photo G).**

Following the tool manufacturer's directions, tighten the chain and snap the pipe **(photo H).** Make a second cut at the lower cutting line, then remove the cut section of pipe **(photo I).**

Cut a length of PVC or ABS plastic pipe about 1" shorter than the section of cast-iron pipe being replaced **(photo J).**

Slip a banded coupling and a neoprene sleeve onto each end of the cast-iron pipe **(photo K).** Make sure the cast-iron pipe is seated snugly against the rubber separator ring that is molded into the interior of the sleeve **(photo L).**

Fold back the end of each neoprene sleeve, until the molded separator ring on the inside of the sleeve is visible **(photo M).** Position the new plastic pipe so it is aligned with the cast-iron pipes **(photo N).**

Roll the ends of the neoprene sleeves back down over the ends of the new plastic pipe **(photo O).**

Slide the stainless steel bands and clamps over the neoprene sleeves **(photo P).** Tighten the screw clamps with a ratchet wrench or screwdriver **(photo Q).**

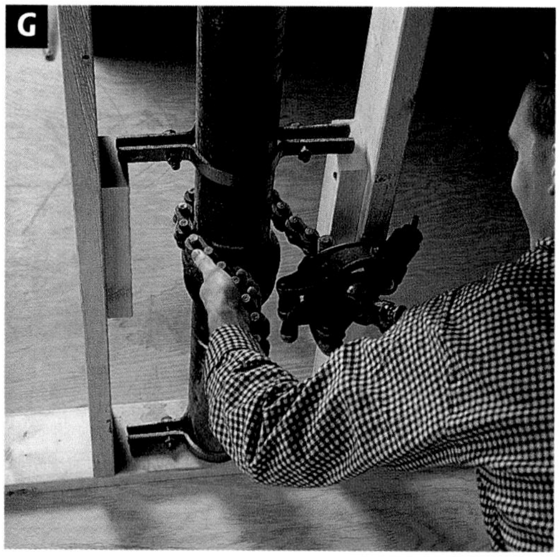

Wrap the chain of a cast iron cutter around the pipe, aligning the cutting wheels with the chalk line.

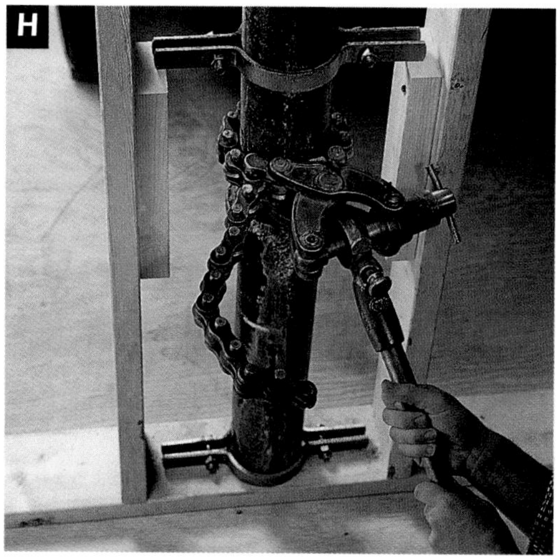

Tighten the chain and then snap the pipe according to the tool manufacturer's directions.

After the cut at the other chalk line has been made, remove the section of pipe.

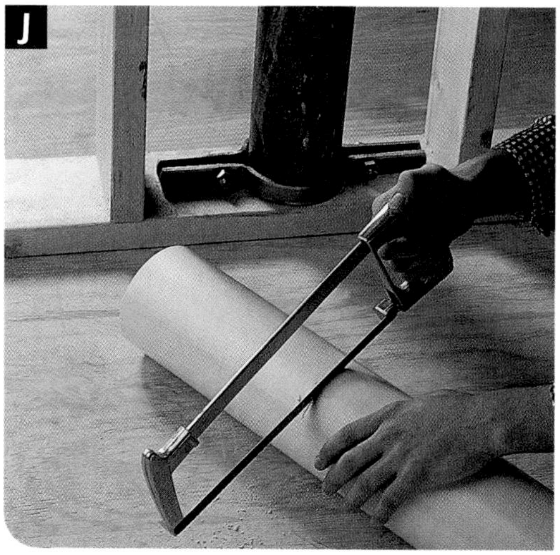

Cut a PVC or ABS plastic pipe section 1" shorter than the section of the old cast-iron pipe.

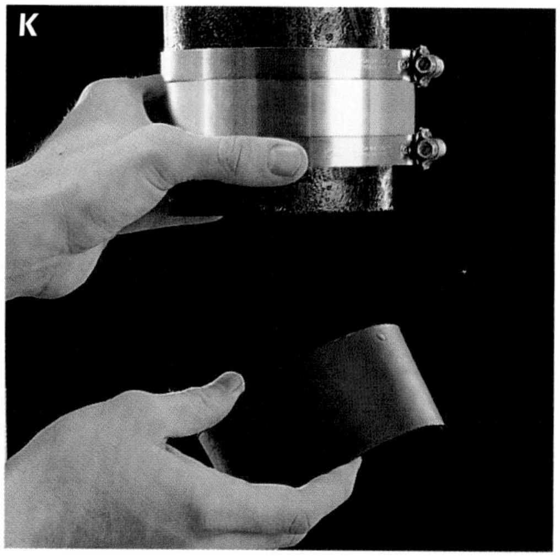

Slip a banded coupling and neoprene sleeve on each end of the cast-iron pipe.

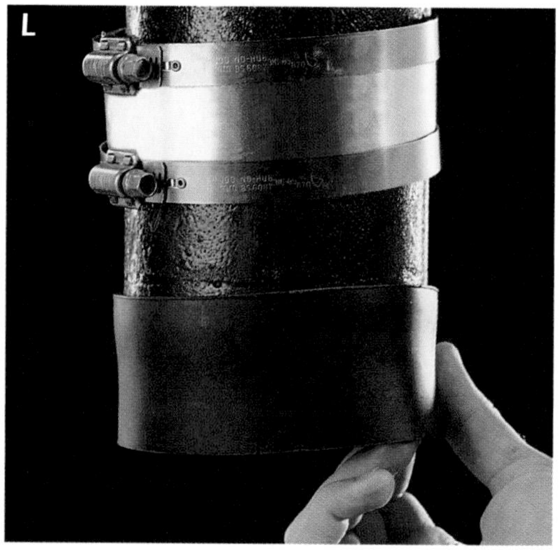

Make sure the cast-iron pipe is seated snugly against the rubber separator ring molded into the interior of the sleeve.

Fold back the ends of the neoprene sleeves to reveal the molded separator ring.

Position the new plastic pipe so it is aligned with the cast-iron pipes.

Roll the ends of the neoprene sleeves over the plastic pipe.

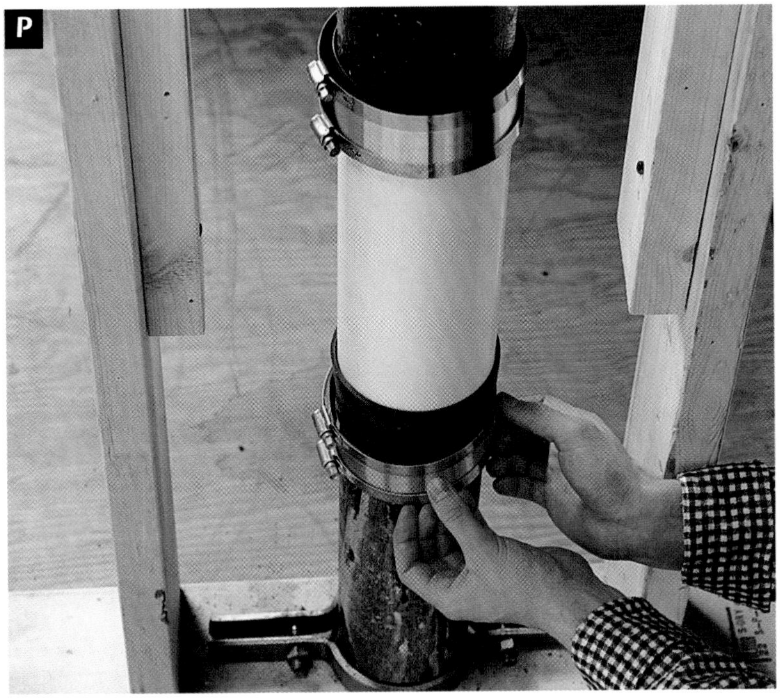

Slide stainless steel bands and clamps over the neoprene sleeves to hold them in place.

Tighten the screw clamps with a ratchet wrench or screwdriver.

Valves

Valves make it possible to shut off water at many points in the system. If a pipe breaks or a plumbing fixture begins to leak, the valve allows you to shut off the water to the damaged area until it's repaired.

Valves leak when washers or seals wear out. Replacement parts are included in the same universal washer kits used to repair compression faucets (page 328). Coat the new washers with heatproof grease to prevent cracking.

Several types of valves are commonly found in homes: globe valves, saddle valves, shutoff valves, gate valves, and hose bibs.

Globe valves (1) have a curved chamber. Repair leaks around the handle by replacing the packing washer. If the valve still leaks when closed, replace the stem washer.

Saddle valves (2) are small fittings often used to connect a refrigerator, icemaker, or sink-mounted water filter to a copper water pipe. They contain a hollow metal spike that punctures the water pipe when the valve is first closed. The fitting is sealed with a rubber gasket. Repair leaks around the handle by replacing the O-ring under the packing nut.

Shutoff valves (3) control water to a single fixture. A shutoff valve has a plastic spindle with a packing washer and a snap-on stem washer. You can usually repair leaks around the handle by replacing the packing washer. If closing the valve doesn't fully stop the flow of water, replace the stem washer.

Gate valves (4) have a movable brass wedge (or "gate") that screws up and down to control the water flow. To repair leaks around the handle, replace the packing washer or packing string beneath the packing nut.

Hose bibs (5) have threaded spouts and are often used to connect rubber utility and appliance hoses.

Tools: *Screwdriver, channel-type pliers, adjustable wrench.*

Materials: *Universal washer kit, heatproof grease.*

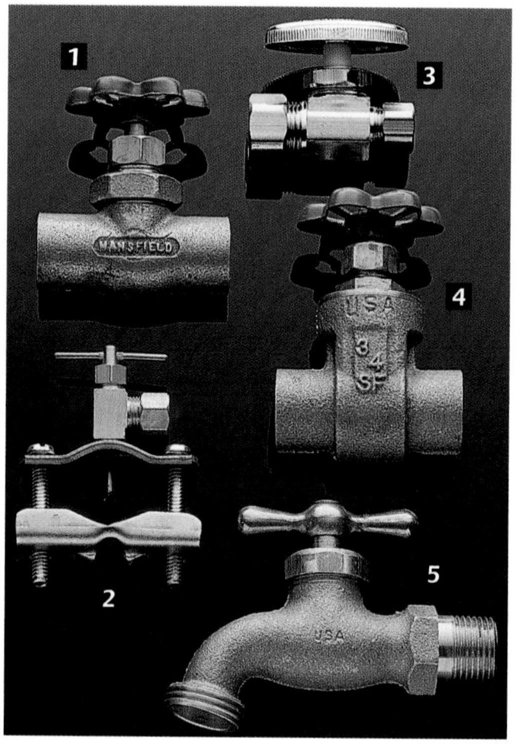

These valve types are found in almost every home.

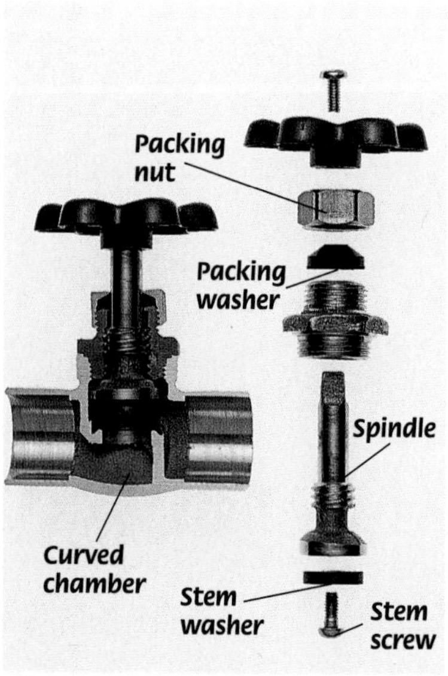

Globe valve: Replace packing washer.

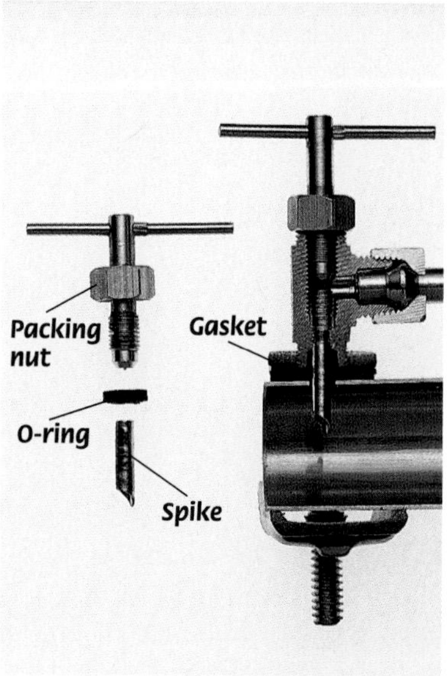

Saddle valve: Replace O-ring.

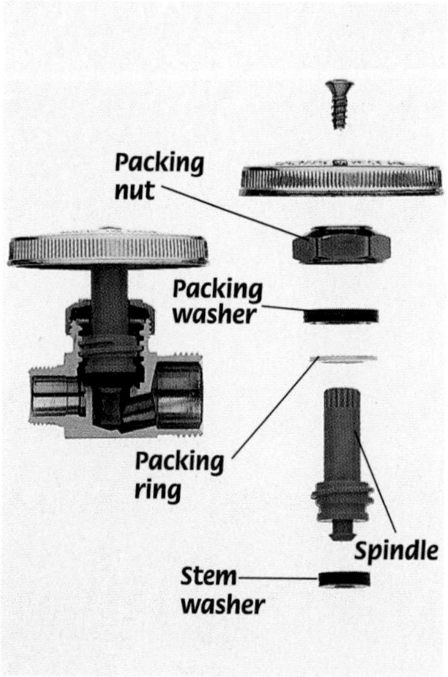

Shutoff valve: Replace packing washer.

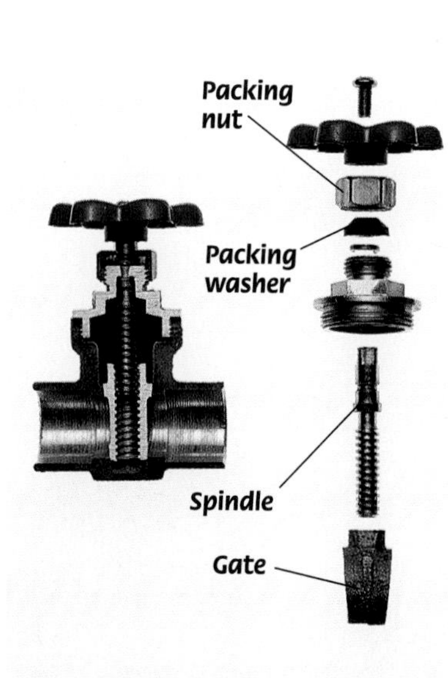

Gate valve: Replace washer or string.

Fixing Hose Bibs

Hose bibs are faucets with a threaded spout, often used to connect rubber utility or appliance hoses. Like valves, hose bibs leak when washers or seals wear out, and replacement parts can be found in universal washer kits.

To repair a leaky hose bib, you need to take it apart. Remove the handle screw and lift off the handle **(photo A).** Unscrew the packing nut, using an adjustable wrench.

Unscrew the spindle and remove it from the valve body **(photo B).** If necessary, use channel-type pliers to unscrew the spindle, but be careful not to scratch the spindle shaft or strip the ridges on the end of the spindle.

Remove the stem screw and the stem washer. Coat the replacement stem washer and packing washer with heatproof grease. Reassemble the valve.

Remove the handle and disassemble the valve.

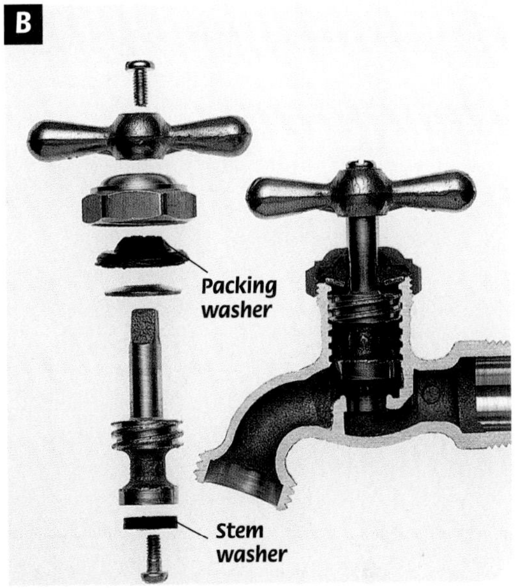

Replace stem and packing washers; reassemble the valve.

Repairing Sillcocks

A sillcock is a faucet attached to the outside of the house **(photo C).** Leaks are usually caused by a faulty stem washer or O-ring.

To repair a leaky sillcock, remove the handle and loosen the retaining nut with a channel-type pliers **(photo D).** Remove the stem. Replace the O-ring on the retaining nut or stem. Remove the brass stem screw at the end of the stem, and replace the washer **(photo E).** Reassemble the sillcock.

Sillcocks can be damaged by frost. Before the cold weather season, take preventative steps: disconnect garden hoses, close indoor shutoff valves, and open sillcocks to drain any trapped water.

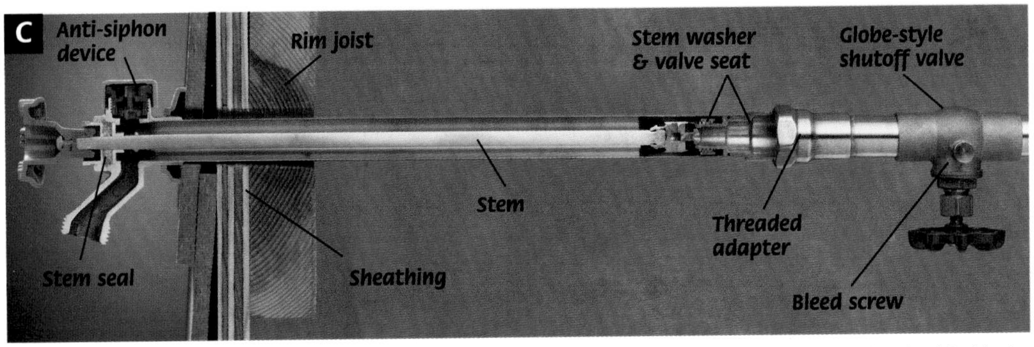

A frostproof sillcock must be mounted against the header joist (sill), with a stem that reaches between 6" and 30" inside the house. Its pipe must angle downward from the shutoff valve, so water is encouraged to drain away.

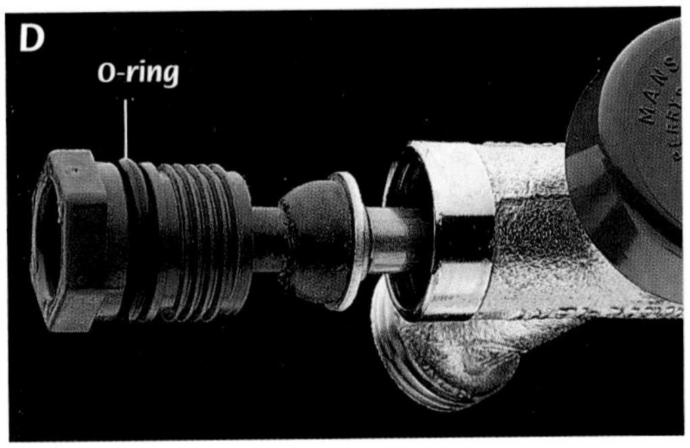

Remove sillcock handle and stem, then replace O-ring.

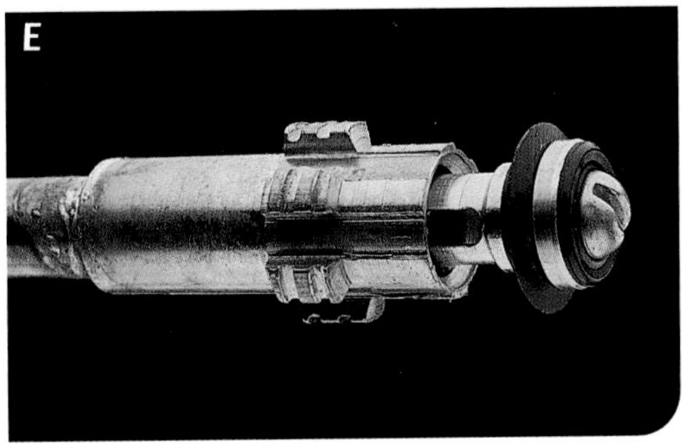

Remove stem screw and replace washer. Reassemble sillcock.

Installing Shutoff Valves & Supply Tubes

Shutoff valves allow you to shut off the water to an individual fixture so it can be repaired. They are made from either durable chromed brass or lightweight plastic and are available in 1/2" and 3/4" diameters to match common water pipe sizes **(photo A).**

Shutoff valves are available in several types. For copper pipes, valves with compression-type fittings (page 219) are easiest to install. For plastic pipes (page 280), use grip-type valves. For galvanized iron pipes, use valves with female threads.

Older plumbing systems often were installed without fixture shutoff valves. When repairing or replacing plumbing fixtures, you may want to install shutoff valves if they are not already present.

Supply tubes are used to connect water pipes to faucets, toilets, and other fixtures. They come in 12", 20" and 30" lengths and a variety of materials **(photo B).** PB plastic and chromed copper tubes are inexpensive. Braided steel and vinyl mesh are more expensive, but easier to install.

Worn-out shutoff valves or supply tubes can cause leaks underneath sinks or other fixtures. If a valve leaks, try tightening the fittings with an adjustable wrench. If tightening the valve doesn't stop the leak, follow the instructions below to replace the shutoff valves and the supply tubes.

Turn off the water at the main shutoff valve (page 273). Remove the old supply pipes. If the pipes are soldered copper, cut them off just below the soldered joint, using a hacksaw or tubing cutter **(photo C),** making sure the cuts are straight. Unscrew the coupling nuts, and dismantle the old pipes.

Tools: *Hacksaw, tubing cutter, adjustable wrench, tubing bender, felt-tipped pen.*

Materials: *Shutoff valves, supply tubes, pipe joint compound.*

Slide a compression nut and compression ring over the copper water pipe **(photo D),** with the threads of the nut facing the end of the pipe. Slide the shutoff valve onto the pipe **(photo E).** Apply a layer of pipe joint compound to the compression ring. Screw the compression nut onto the shutoff valve and tighten with an adjustable wrench.

Bend a chromed copper supply tube to reach from the tailpiece of the fixture to the shutoff

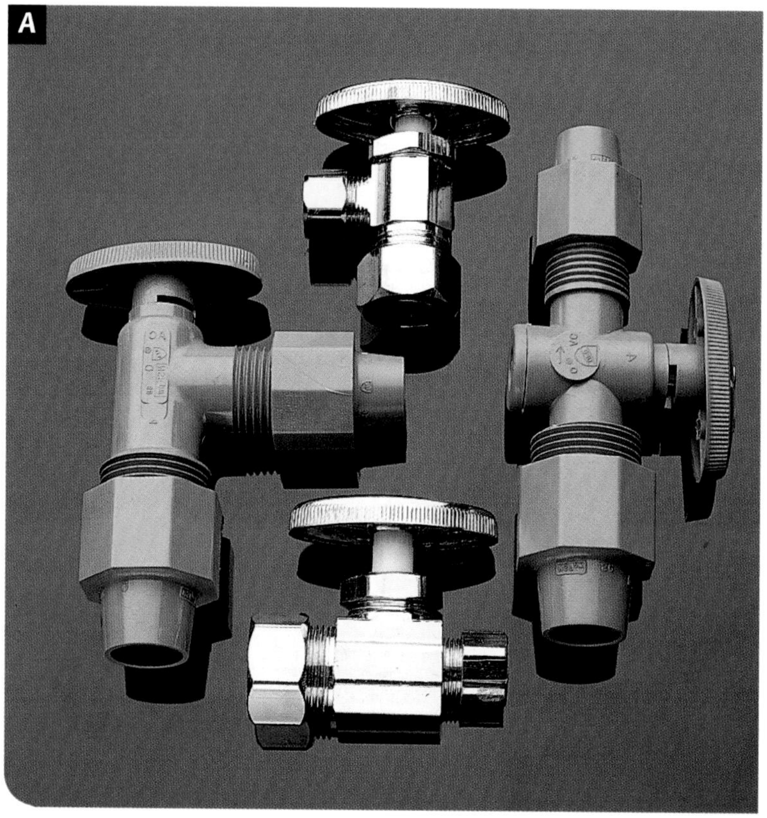

Shutoff valves allow you to shut off the water to an individual fixture so it can be repaired.

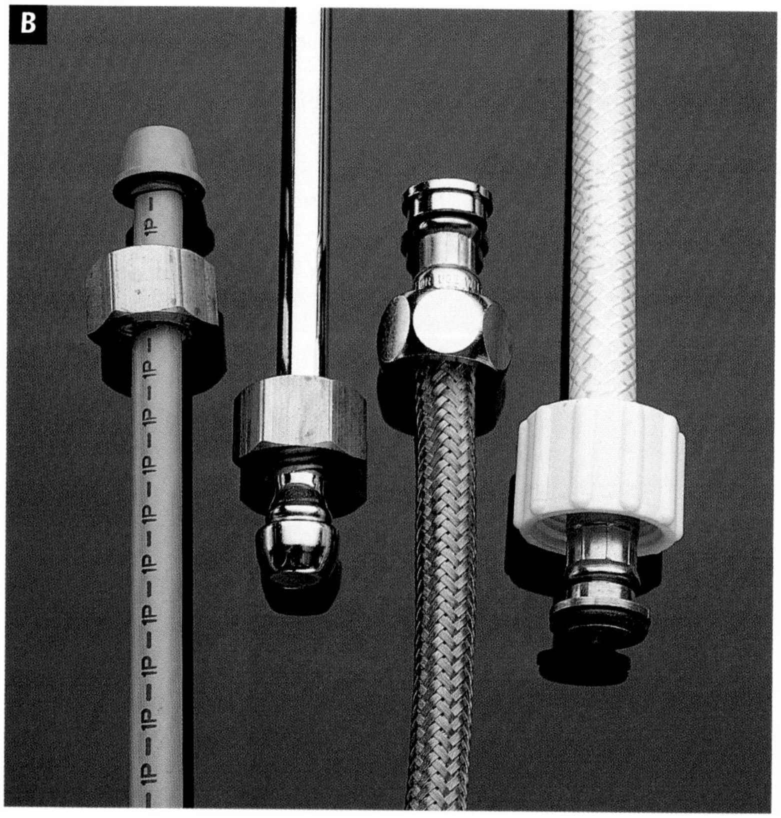

Supply tubes connect pipes to faucets, toilets, and other fixtures. They're available in PB plastic, chromed copper, braided steel, and vinyl mesh.

valve, using a tubing bender **(photo F).**

Position the supply tube between the fixture tailpiece and the shutoff valve. Mark the length of tube necessary to make the connection **(photo G).** Cut the supply tube with a tubing cutter.

Attach the bell-shaped end of the supply tube to the fixture tailpiece with a coupling nut, then attach the other end to the shutoff valve with a compression ring and nut. Tighten all the fittings with an adjustable wrench **(photo H).**

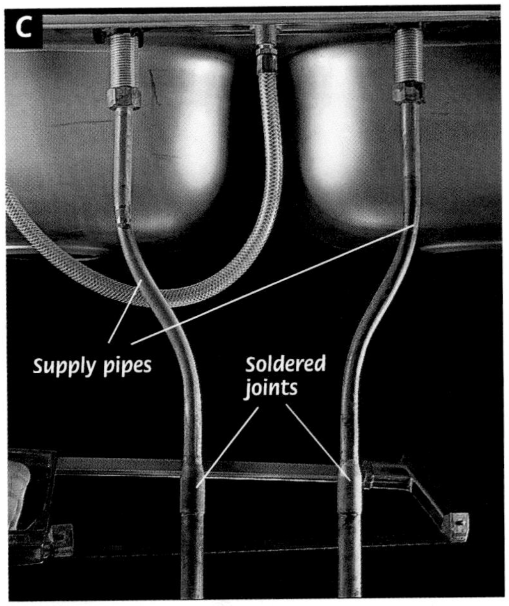

Use a hacksaw or a tubing cutter to cut off old copper supply pipes below the soldered joint.

Slide a compression nut and ring over the copper water pipe. The threads of the nut should face the end of the pipe.

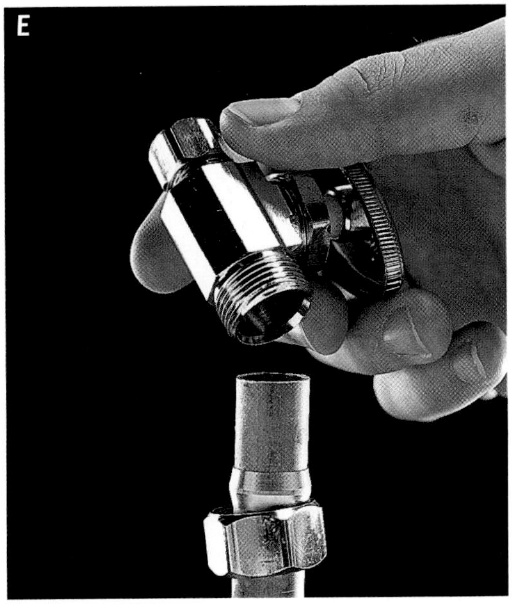

Slide the shutoff valve onto the pipe. Apply pipe joint compound to the ring and screw the nut onto the valve.

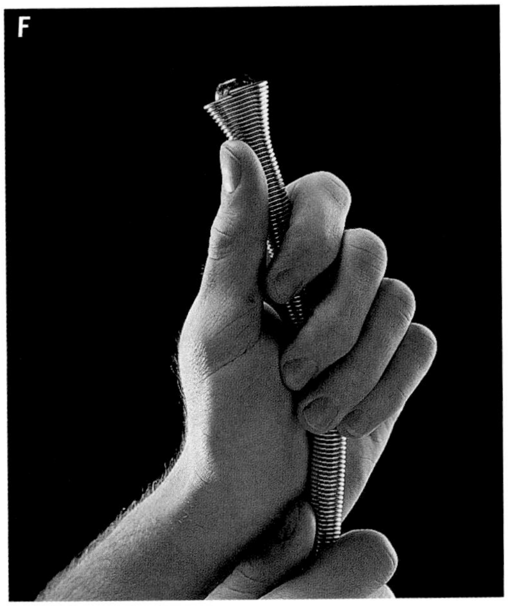

Using a tubing bender, bend a chromed copper supply tube to reach from the fixture tailpiece to the shutoff valve.

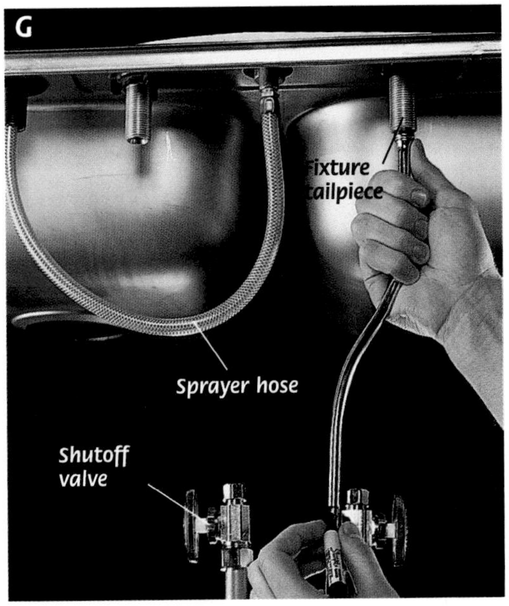

Position the supply tube between the fixture tailpiece and shutoff valve. Mark the tube to length and cut.

Tighten all the fittings with an adjustable wrench.

Drains, Traps & Vents

When a fixture drains slowly or doesn't drain at all, the trap or drain may be blocked. Of course, the clog could also be located farther into the system. However, it's best to check the most obvious possibilities and try the simplest solutions first.

Any time the problem seems to be limited to one fixture, the clog is likely to be in the fixture trap or drain line and should be fairly simple to resolve. But if two or more fixtures are draining slowly or not at all, the clog could be located in a branch drain line or even in the main waste and vent stack. And if fixtures on the upper floor seem to be affected more than the ones on lower levels (basement and first floor), the clog is probably located high within the main waste and vent stack.

Again, it's a good idea to begin with the least invasive methods and use harsher methods as necessary: try plunging, then chemicals, then a hand auger. Although older plumbing systems are particularly susceptible to damage by aggressive clearing methods, it's important to handle plumbing lines carefully no matter how old or new they are.

Clearing drains, traps, and vent stacks is messy, unpleasant work. As a health precaution, make every effort to keep the waste water from getting on your skin. Wear safety goggles, a hat, a dust mask, rubber gloves, long sleeves, and heavy pants as you work. Change clothes and wash your hands with antibacterial soap as soon as you finish; clean your tools thoroughly as well.

If you determine that the sewer lines are clogged and need to be cleared with a power auger, consider hiring a professional sewer cleaning service. If you rent a power auger, ask the rental center for complete instructions for safe and effective operation of the equipment.

Always consult a professional sewer cleaning service if you suspect a collapsed line.

Clearing Branch & Main Drain Lines

If using a plunger or a hand auger doesn't clear a clogged fixture drain, the problem may lie in the branch drain line.

Identify the branch drain line closest to the clogged fixture, and locate the cleanout fitting at the end of the line **(photo A).** Because waste water may be backed up in the drain lines, place a bucket, rags, and newspapers under the opening. Use an adjustable wrench to slowly unscrew the cleanout plug, then open it cautiously. Stand to one side as you work—never position yourself directly under a cleanout opening while unscrewing the plug or cover. Use a hand auger to clear the line.

If using an auger on the branch line doesn't solve the problem, the clog may be located in the main waste and vent stack. To clear the stack, locate the roof vent **(photo B).**

Tools: *Adjustable wrench or pipe wrench, hand auger, cold chisel, ball peen hammer.*

Materials: *Bucket, rags, penetrating oil, replacement cleanout plug (if needed), pipe joint compound.*

Clear a branch drain line by removing the cleanout plug, draining the line, and using a hand auger to clear it.

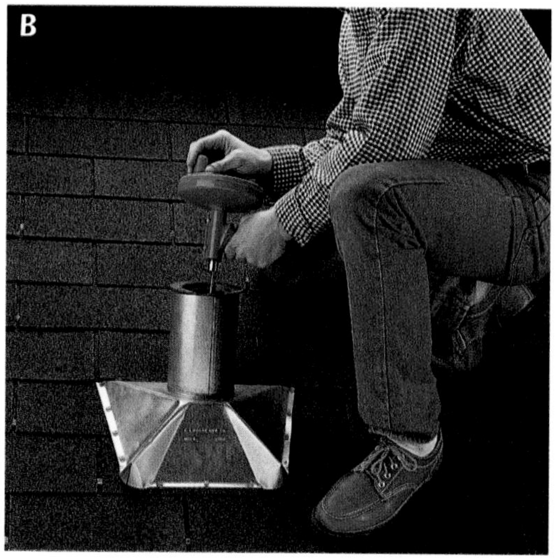

Clear the main waste and vent stack by running the cable of a hand auger down through the roof vent.

Before going up on the roof, make sure your auger cable is long enough to reach the entire length of the stack. Once on the roof, run the cable of the auger all the way down the vent. Always use extreme caution when working on a roof or ladder.

If clearing the main stack doesn't solve the problem, check the sewer service line. Find the main cleanout, which usually is a Y-shaped fitting at the bottom of the main waste and vent stack. Place rags and a bucket under the fitting, and use a large wrench to remove the cleanout plug **(photo C).** If the plug can't be removed, apply penetrating oil around the edge, wait 10 minutes, and try again.

If it still won't come out, try moving it with a hammer and chisel **(photo D).** Place the cutting edge of the chisel on the edge of the plug. Strike the chisel with a ball peen hammer to move the plug counterclockwise. If that fails, chisel out the plug. When all the pieces of the plug have been removed, push the cable of a hand auger into the opening and clear the line.

To replace the old plug, apply pipe joint compound to the threads of a plastic replacement plug and screw it into the fitting **(photo E).** Or use an expandable rubber plug **(photo F),** which has a wing nut that squeezes the rubber core between two metal plates. This causes the rubber to bulge slightly, creating a watertight seal.

Some sewer service lines in older homes have a house trap, a U-shaped fitting at the point where the sewer line exits the house **(photo G).** A house trap can be identified by its two openings, one "street side" and one "house side." Slowly remove only the plug on the street side. If water seeps out of the opening as the plug is removed, the clog is in the sewer line beyond the trap. If no water seeps out, try to clear the trap with a hand auger.

If the auger meets solid resistance in the sewer line, retrieve the cable and inspect the bit. Fine, hairlike roots on the bit indicate that the line is clogged with tree roots, which can be removed with a power auger or by a sewer cleaning service. Dirt on the bit indicates a collapsed line—consult a professional sewer service as soon as possible.

If no clog is present in this trap, replace the street-side plug and remove the house-side plug. Use the auger to clear any clogs located between the house trap and the main stack.

Remove the cleanout plug of the main drain with a large pipe wrench.

Remove stubborn plugs by moving the plug counterclockwise with a chisel and ball peen hammer.

When the drain is clear, replace the old plug with a new plastic one.

Alternate: replace the old plug with an expandable rubber plug, which may be easier to remove in the future.

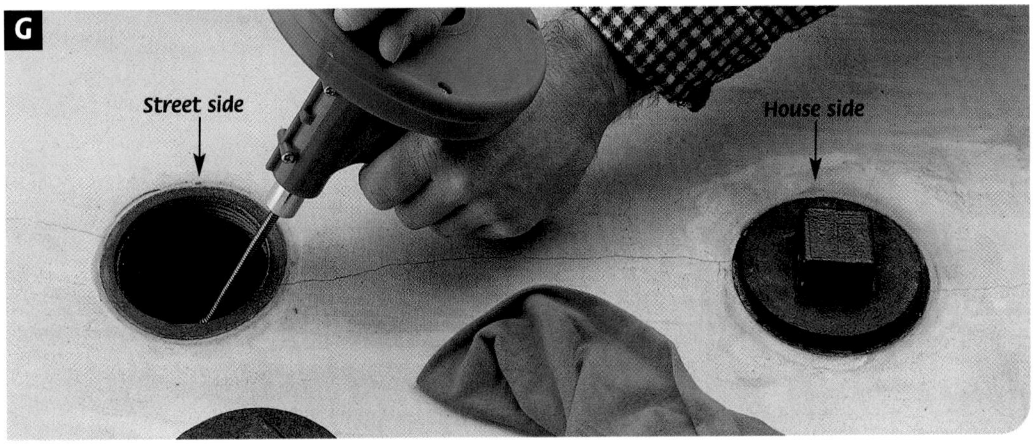

Sewer lines in older homes have a house trap, which has two openings, one on the "street side" and one on the "house side."

Clearing Clogged Floor Drains

When water backs up on the basement floor, there's a clog either in the floor drain line, the drain trap, or the sewer service line.

Clean clogs in the drain line or trap with a hand auger or blow bag.

To clear a floor drain with a hand auger, remove the drain cover with a screwdriver. Use an adjustable wrench to unscrew the cleanout plug in the drain bowl. Push the auger cable through the cleanout opening and directly into the drain line **(photo A).**

A blow bag is especially useful for clearing clogs in floor drain lines. By filling it with a garden hose, you can release a powerful spurt that will dislodge most clogs.

To clear a floor drain with a blow bag, attach it to a garden hose **(photo B).** Connect the hose to a hose bib or a utility faucet. Remove the drain cover and the cleanout plug.

Insert the blow bag completely into the drain and turn on the water **(photo C).** Allow several minutes for the blow bag to work properly.

Tools: *Hand auger, screwdriver, adjustable wrench, blow bag.*

Materials: *Garden hose.*

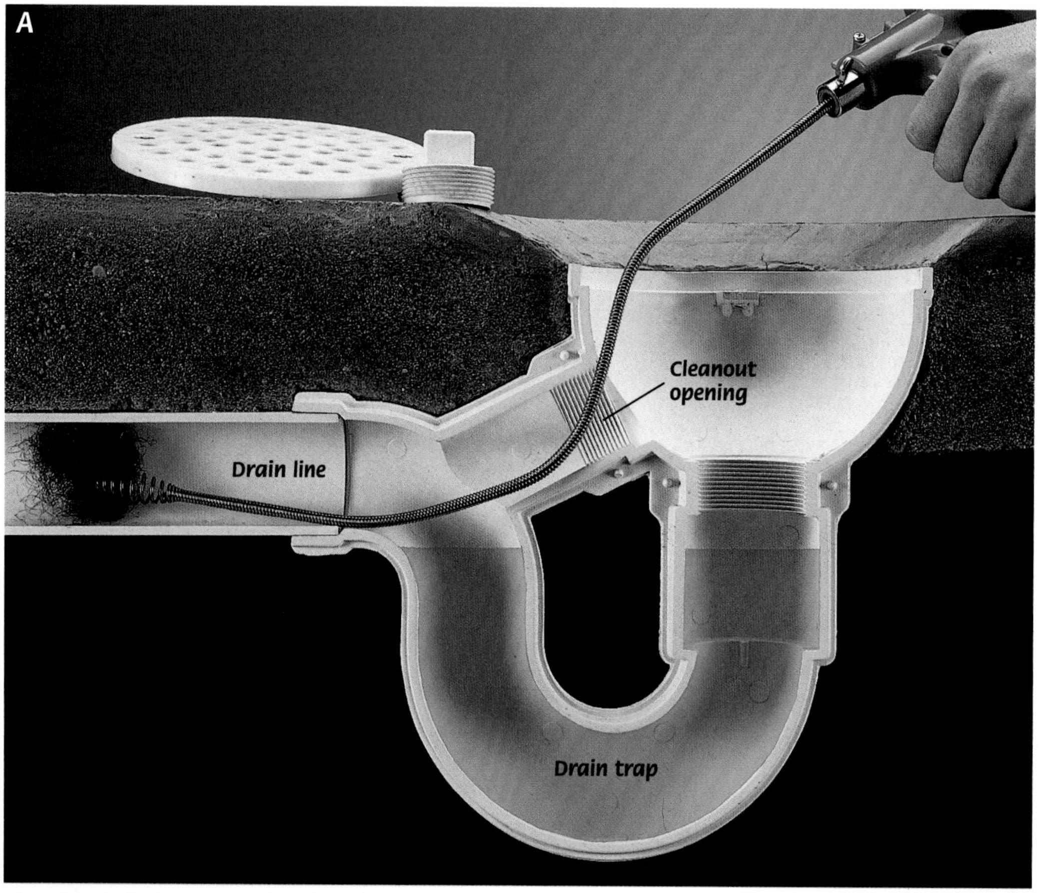

Clear floor drain clogs by removing the drain cleanout plug and feeding an auger cable directly into the drain line.

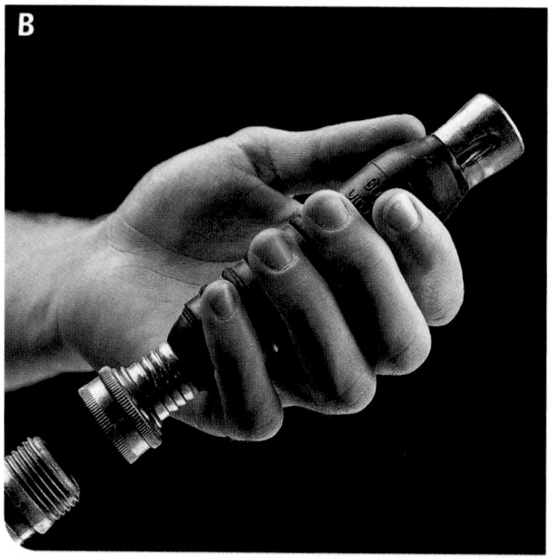

To clear a floor drain clog with a blow bag, first attach the blow bag to a garden hose.

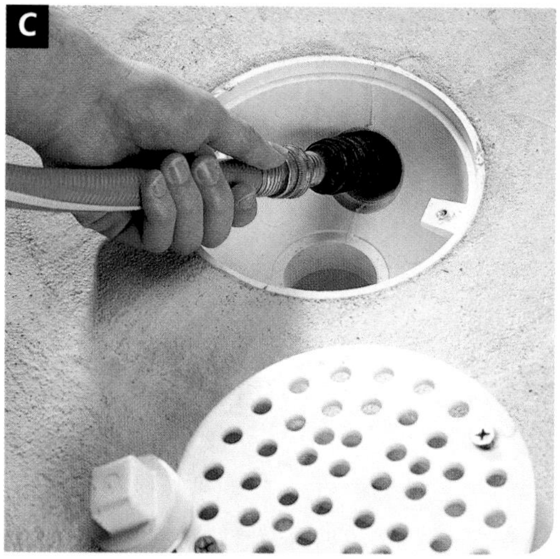

Remove the floor drain plug. Insert the blow bag into the drain, and turn on the water.

Clearing Clogged Drum Traps

In older homes, some drain lines may be connected to drum traps, which usually are located in the floor next to a bathtub **(photo D).** They have flat, screw-in type covers or plugs. Drum traps are sometimes installed upside down under the floor so plugs can be accessed from below.

To clear a drum trap, place rags or towels around the opening **(photo E).**

Carefully remove the trap cover **(photo F).** Older drum traps may be made of lead, which gets brittle with age. If the cover does not unscrew easily, apply penetrating oil.

Use a hand auger to clear the line **(photo G).** Wrap the threads of the cover with Teflon tape and replace it.

Flush all drains with hot water for five minutes to make sure they're clear.

Tools: *Adjustable wrench, hand auger.*

Materials: *Rags or towels, penetrating oil, Teflon tape.*

D

A drum trap is a canister made of lead or cast iron. Usually, more than one fixture drain line is connected to the drum. Drum traps are not vented, so they are no longer approved for new plumbing installations.

E

Place rags or towels around the opening of the drum trap to absorb any water that may be backed up in the lines.

F

Carefully remove the trap cover.

G

Use a hand auger to clear each drain line, then replace the cap. Flush drains with hot water for five minutes.

Clearing Clogged Tub Drains

When water in the tub drains slowly or not at all, remove and clean the drain assembly. Both plunger and pop-up type drain mechanisms catch hair and other debris that cause clogs.

A plunger-type tub drain has a hollow brass plug, called a plunger, that slides up and down inside the overflow drain to seal off the flow of water **(photo A).** The plunger is moved by a trip lever and linkage that runs through the overflow drain.

A pop-up tub drain has a rocker arm that pivots to open or close a metal drain stopper **(photo B).** The rocker arm is moved by a trip lever and linkage that runs through the overflow drain.

Tools: *Plunger, screwdriver, small wire brush, needlenose pliers, hand auger.*

Materials: *Vinegar, heatproof grease, rag.*

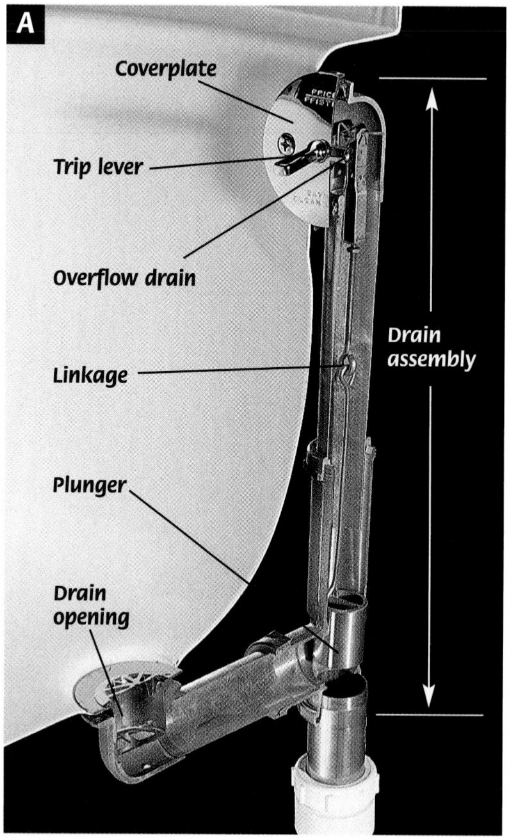

Plunger-type tub drain has a hollow brass plug, called a plunger, inside the overflow drain to seal off the water flow.

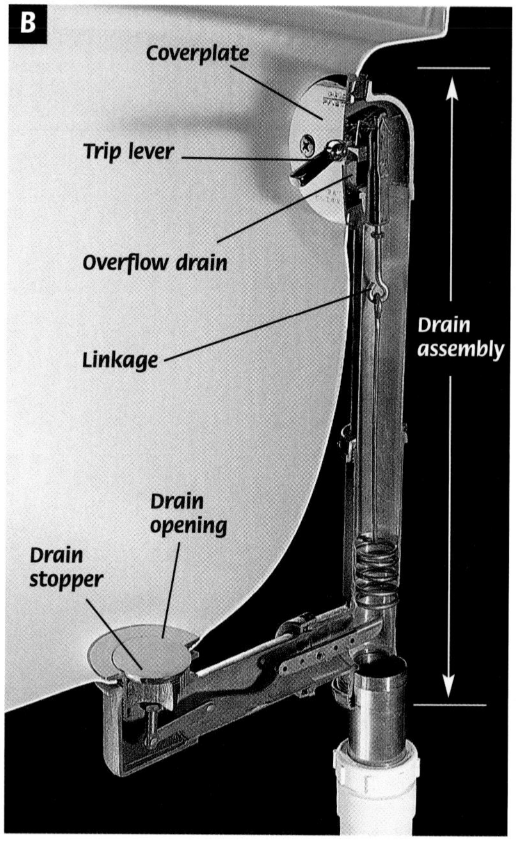

Pop-up tub drain has a rocker arm that pivots to open or close a metal drain stopper.

Cleaning & Adjusting a Plunger-type Tub Drain

To clean and adjust a plunger-type tub drain, remove the screws on the coverplate. Carefully pull the coverplate, linkage, and plunger from the overflow drain opening.

Clean the linkage and plunger with a small wire brush dipped in vinegar **(photo C).** Lubricate the assembly with heatproof grease.

Adjust the drain flow and fix leaks by adjusting the linkage **(photo D).** Unscrew the locknut on the threaded lift rod, using needlenose pliers. Screw the rod down about 1/8". Tighten the locknut and reinstall the entire assembly.

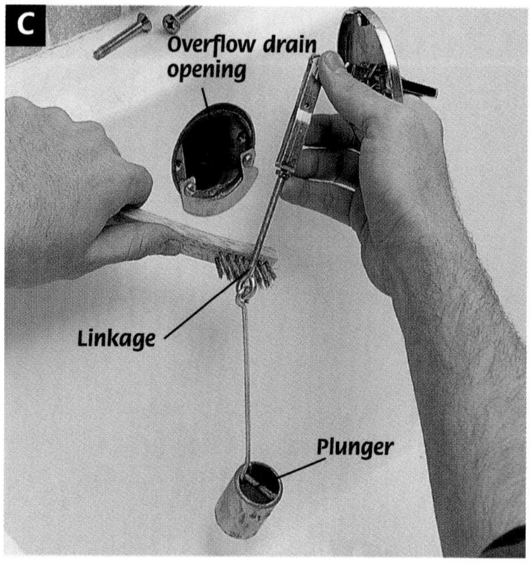

Clean the linkage and plunger, then lubricate the assembly with heatproof grease.

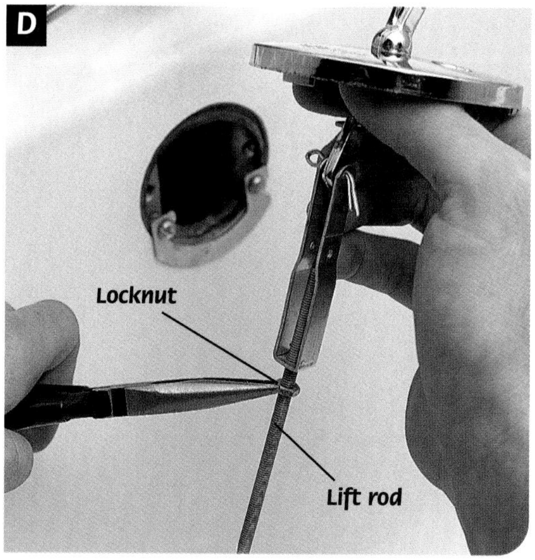

Adjust the drain flow and fix leaks by adjusting the linkage, then reinstall the assembly.

Cleaning & Adjusting a Pop-up Tub Drain

To clean and adjust a pop-up tub drain, raise the trip lever to the full open position. Carefully pull the stopper and rocker arm assembly from the drain opening **(photo E).** Clean hair or debris from the rocker arm with a small wire brush.

Remove the screws from the coverplate. Pull the coverplate, trip lever, and linkage from the overflow drain **(photo F).** Remove any hair and debris. Clean the linkage with a small wire brush dipped in vinegar, then lubricate it with heatproof grease.

Adjust drain flow and fix leaks by adjusting the linkage **(photo G).** Loosen the locknut on the threaded lift rod and screw lift rod up about 1/8". Tighten the locknut and reinstall the entire assembly.

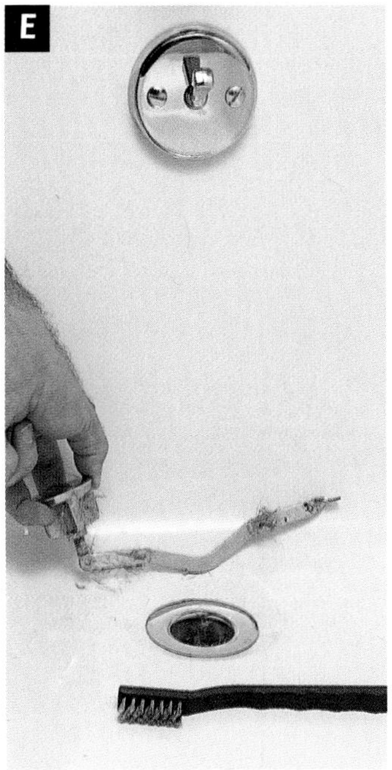

Remove coverplate; pull entire assembly from overflow drain opening.

Clean assembly, then lubricate it with heatproof grease.

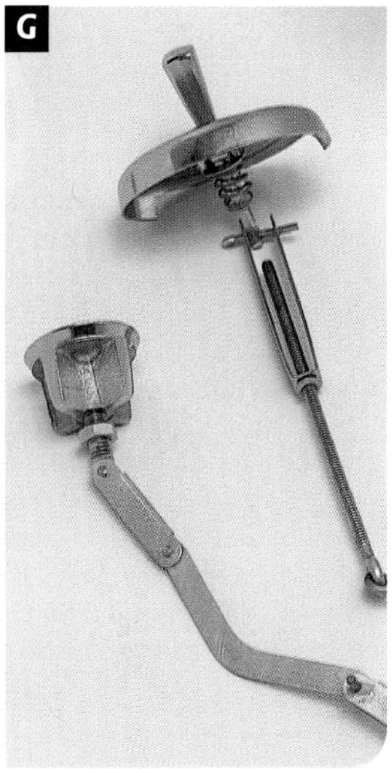

Fix leaks by adjusting linkage. Reinstall entire assembly.

Clearing a Tub Drain Line

If cleaning the drain assembly doesn't resolve the problem, the tub drain line probably is clogged. First, try to clear the line with a plunger. Stuff a wet rag in the overflow drain opening before plunging the drain. The rag prevents air from breaking the suction of the plunger.

If plunging doesn't work, try a hand auger **(photo H).** Remove the coverplate and carefully lift out the drain linkage. Push the auger cable into the opening until it meets resistance. Set the auger lock and crank the handle in a clockwise direction. After using the auger, replace the drain linkage. Open the drain and run hot water through it to flush out any debris.

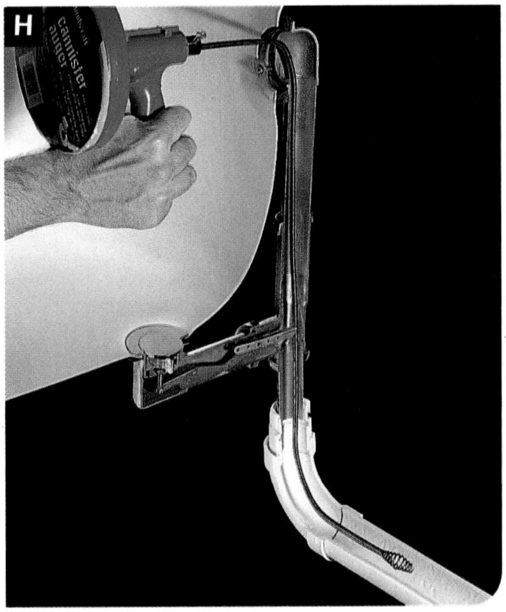

Clear a tub drain by running the auger cable through the overflow opening.

Helpful Hint

To keep drains, including tub drains, running freely, treat them weekly with this nontoxic formula. Combine 1 cup of baking soda, 1 cup of salt, and 1/4 cup of cream of tartar. Pour 1/4 cup of this mixture into each drain in the house, followed by 2 cups of boiling water.

Before resorting to a chemical drain cleaner to clear a clogged drain, try this simple remedy: Pour 1 cup of baking soda into the drain, followed by 1 pint of vinegar. In fifteen minutes, pour 2 or 3 cups of boiling water into the drain, and the clog should be cleared.

Clearing Clogged Sink Drains

Sink clogs usually are caused by buildup in the drain trap or fixture drain line. To remove, use a plunger or hand auger, or disconnect and clean the trap.

To use a plunger to clear a sink, start by removing the stopper. Many sinks have a pop-up stopper that lifts out; others must first be turned counterclockwise. On older sinks, you may need to remove the pivot rod before the stopper can be freed.

Stuff a wet rag in the sink's overflow opening to ensure adequate suction. Place the plunger cup over the drain opening and run the water until it covers the cup. Plunge rapidly up and down. When the line seems clear, run scalding water for two minutes to dissolve any remaining buildup. You can also treat the drain with a noncaustic drain cleaner.

Tools: Plunger, channel-type pliers, small wire brush, screwdriver, spud wrench, hammer, putty knife.

Materials: Rag, bucket, replacement gaskets, plumber's putty, washers, needed replacements parts.

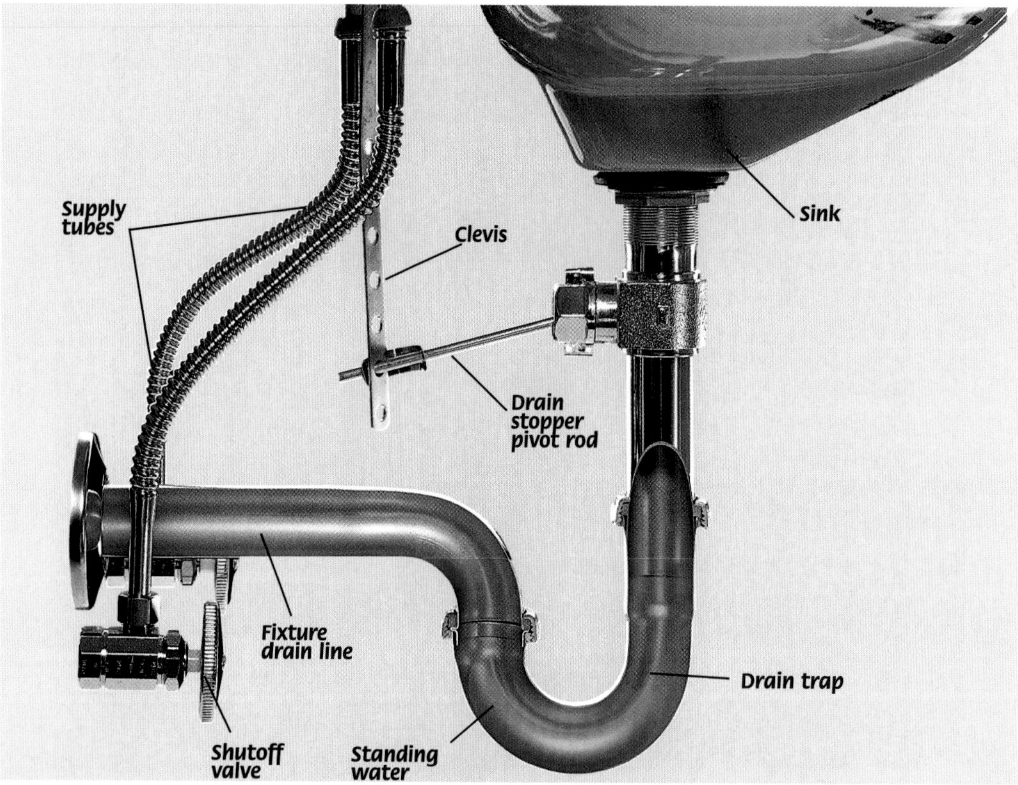

The shape of a drain trap and fixture line may resemble the letter "P," and sink traps are sometimes called P-traps. Sink clogs usually are caused by a buildup of soap and hair in the trap or drain line.

Cleaning & Adjusting a Pop-up Sink Drain Stopper

If a sink will not hold standing water, or if water in the sink drains too slowly, clean and adjust the pop-up stopper.

Raise the stopper lever to full upright (closed) position. Unscrew the retaining nut that holds the pivot rod in position. Pull the pivot rod out of the drain pipe to release the stopper. Remove the stopper and use a small wire brush to clean away debris **(photo A).** Inspect the gasket for wear or damage, and replace it if necessary. Reinstall the stopper.

If the sink still doesn't drain properly, adjust the clevis **(photo B).** Loosen the clevis screw, and slide the clevis up or down on the stopper rod to adjust the position of the stopper. Retighten the clevis screw.

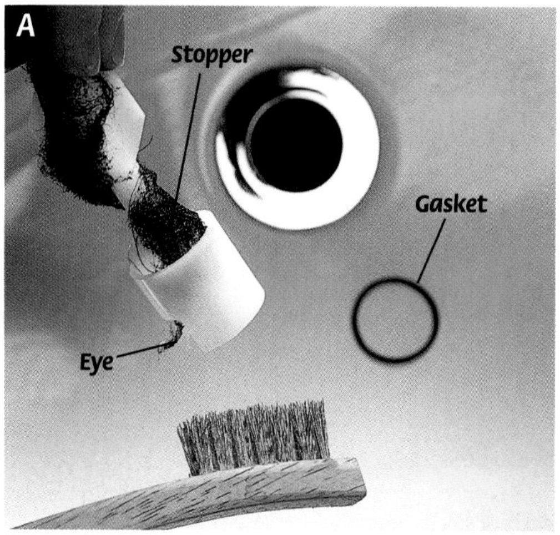

Release, then remove, the stopper. Clean away hair and other debris, then reinstall it.

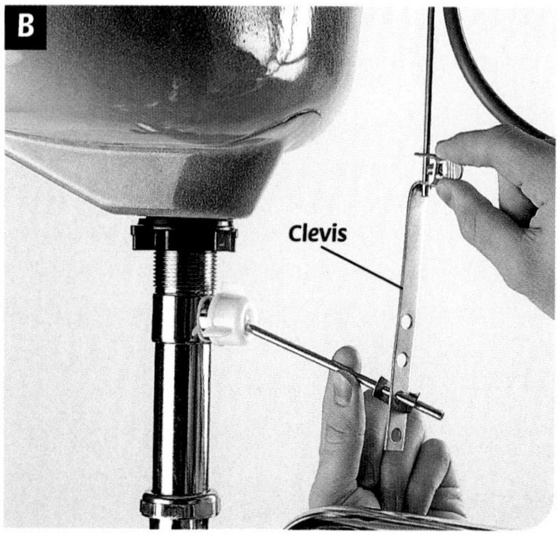

If the sink doesn't hold water properly, adjust the clevis.

Removing & Cleaning a Sink Drain Trap

If neither plunging nor cleaning the drain stopper returns a slow-draining sink to full efficiency, the next step is to remove and clean the sink drain trap. Place a bucket under the trap to catch water and debris, then loosen the slip nuts with channel-type pliers **(photo C).** Unscrew the nuts by hand and slide them away from the connections. Pull off the trap bend. Dump out any debris **(photo D).** Clean the trap bend with a small wire brush. Inspect the slip nut washers for wear, and replace them if necessary. Reinstall the trap bend and retighten the slip nuts.

Loosen the slip nuts and remove the trap bend.

Clean out the trap bend, then reattach it.

Fixing a Leaky Sink Strainer

A leak under a sink may be caused by a strainer body that is not properly sealed to the sink drain opening **(photo E).** Leaks usually can be fixed by removing and cleaning the assembly, and then replacing worn gaskets and deteriorated plumber's putty.

Unscrew the slip nuts from both ends of the tailpiece, using channel-type pliers **(photo F).** Disconnect and remove the tailpiece from the strainer body and trap bend.

Remove the locknut, using a spud wrench **(photo G).** Unscrew the locknut and remove the strainer assembly.

Remove old putty from the drain opening, and from under the flange of the strainer body.

Apply a bead of plumber's putty to the lip of the drain opening. Press the strainer body into the drain opening. From under the sink, place the new rubber gasket, then the metal or fiber friction ring, over the strainer. Reinstall and tighten the locknut, then reinstall the tailpiece.

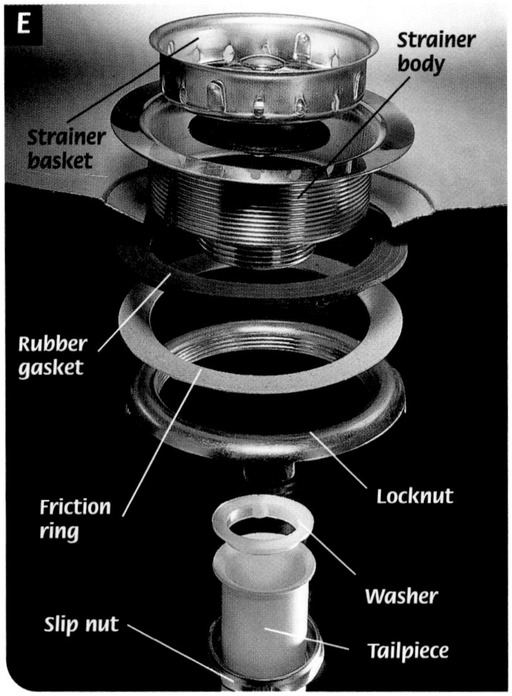

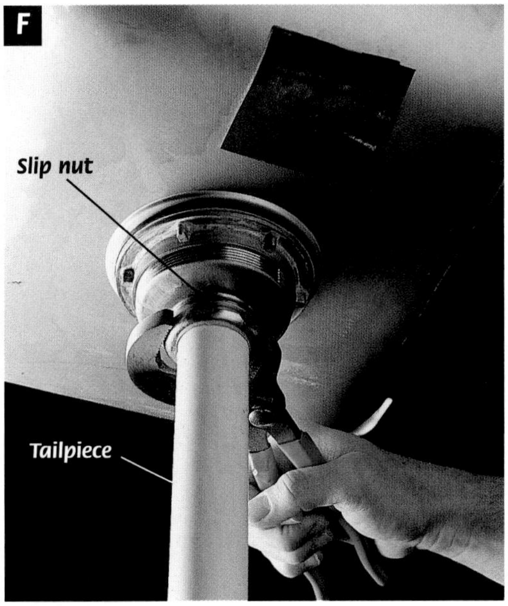

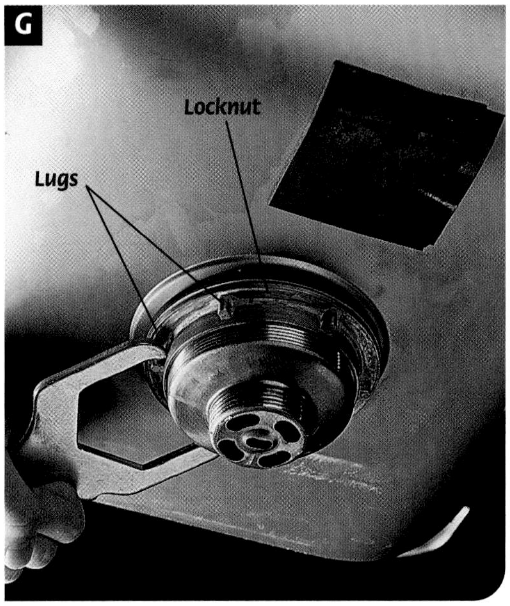

The sink strainer assembly connects a sink to a drain line (left). Leaks can occur where the strainer body seals against the lip of the drain opening. Disconnect the tailpiece from the strainer body and trap bend (center). Remove the locknut and the strainer assembly (right).

Clearing Fixture Drains with a Hand Auger

A hand auger has a flexible steel cable that's pushed into a drain line to loosen clogs. Augers are easy to use, but you need to get a feel for them in order to tell the difference between a soap clog and a bend in the line.

Place a bucket under the trap bend to catch water and debris. Loosen the slip nuts on the trap bend with channel-type pliers. Unscrew the nuts by hand, slide them away from the connections, and pull off the trap bend **(photo A).** Push the end of the auger cable into the drain line opening until the cable meets resistance; this usually indicates the end of the cable has reached a bend in the drain pipe.

Set the auger lock so that at least 6" of cable extends out of the opening **(photo B).** Crank the auger handle clockwise to move the end of the cable past the bend in the drain line.

Release the lock and continue pushing the cable into the opening until it meets firm resistance. Set the auger lock and crank the handle in a clockwise direction. Solid resistance that prevents the cable from advancing indicates a clog, which sometimes can be snagged and retrieved **(photo C).**

To pull an obstruction out of the line, release the auger lock and crank the handle clockwise. If the object cannot be retrieved, reconnect the trap bend and use the auger to clear the nearest branch drain line or main waste and vent stack.

Continuous resistance that allows the cable to advance slowly is probably a soap clog **(photo D).** Bore through the clog by cranking the auger handle clockwise while applying steady pressure on the hand grip of the auger. Repeat the procedure two or three times, then retrieve the cable. Reconnect the trap bend and flush the system with hot tap water to remove debris.

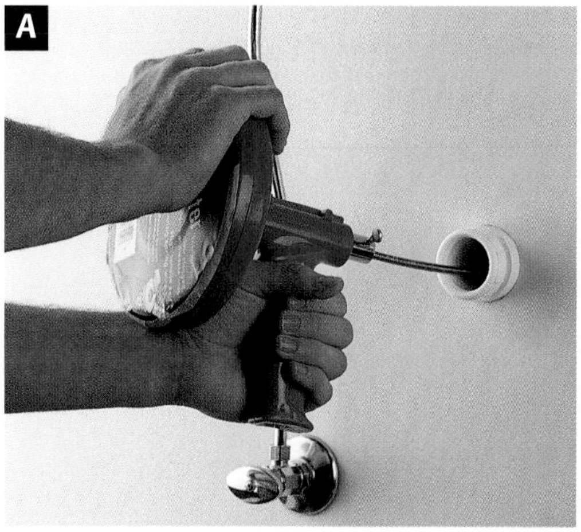

Remove the trap bend and feed the auger cable into the drain line. When the cable end first meets resistance, it has probably reached a bend in the pipe.

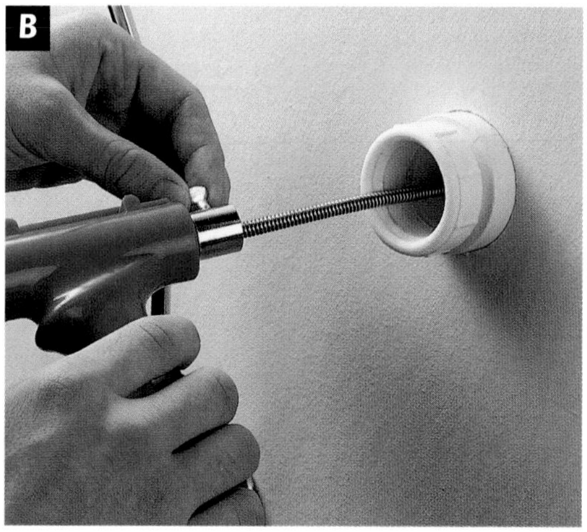

With at least 6" of cable extending from the drain opening, tighten the auger lock and crank the handle on the auger.

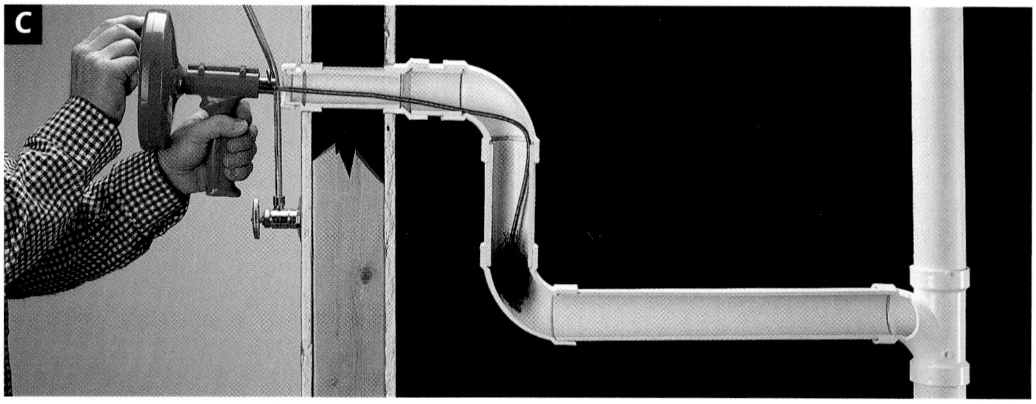

Solid resistance indicates a clog. Snag and retrieve the obstruction by releasing the auger lock and cranking the handle clockwise. If retrieval fails, use the auger to clear the nearest branch drain line or main waste and vent stack.

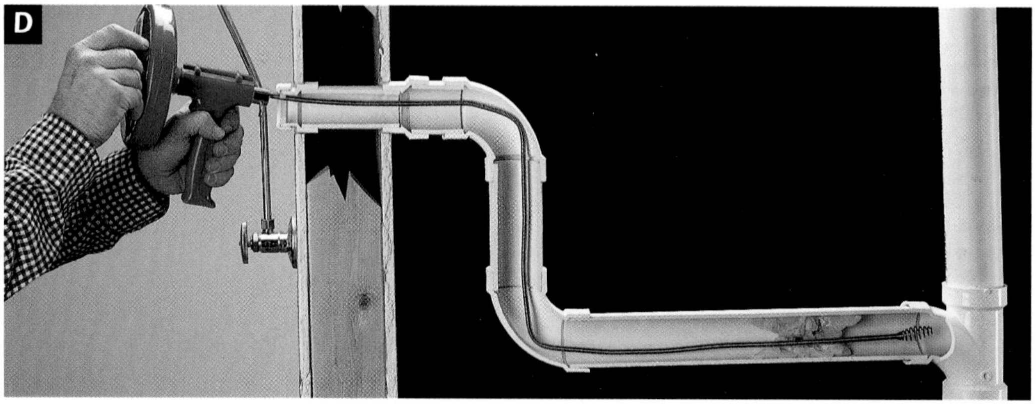

Continuous resistance with some cable movement indicates a soap clog. Clear the clog by repeatedly boring through it with the auger bit. Crank the auger handle clockwise, using the hand grip to maintain pressure on the cable. Reconnect the trap bend and flush the system with hot water.

Clearing Clogged Toilets

The toilet drain system has a drain outlet at the bottom of the bowl and a built-in trap. The toilet drain is connected to a drain line and a main waste and vent stack.

Most toilet clogs occur because an object is stuck inside the toilet trap. A toilet that is sluggish during the flush cycle may be partially blocked. Use a flanged plunger or a closet auger to remove the clog.

Plungers create pressure to dislodge clogs. A few inches of water in the bowl helps seal the plunger against the bowl, increasing its effectiveness.

Place the cup of the plunger over the drain outlet opening and rapidly plunge up and down, 15 to 20 times **(photo E).** Pour a bucket of water into the bowl to flush debris through the drain. If plunging doesn't clear the clog, push the plunger down over the drain outlet opening to create a vacuum, then quickly pull it up, which may suck the clog free. If the toilet still doesn't drain properly, try a closet auger.

To clear a toilet with a closet auger, place the auger bend in the bottom of the drain opening and push the auger cable into the trap **(photo F).** Crank the auger handle in a clockwise direction to snag any obstructions. Continue cranking while retrieving the cable to pull the obstruction out of the trap.

If neither plunging nor using a closet auger returns the toilet's flushing action to normal, the problem may not be with the toilet itself. Occasionally, a sluggish toilet flush indicates a blocked waste and vent stack. Clearing the stack (page 304) will resolve the problem.

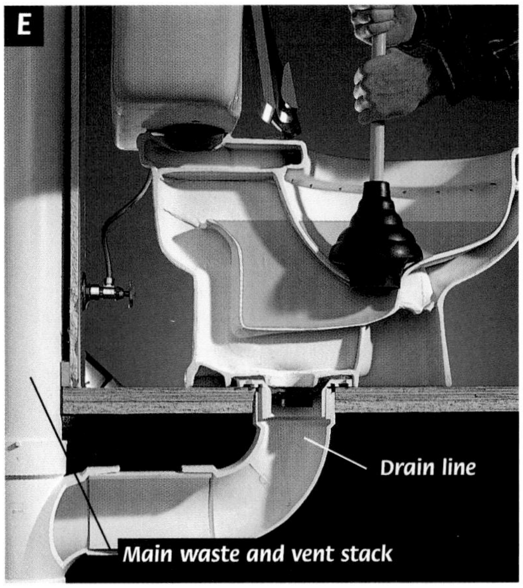

First, try plunging. Use a flanged plunger to force the clog through the drain lines.

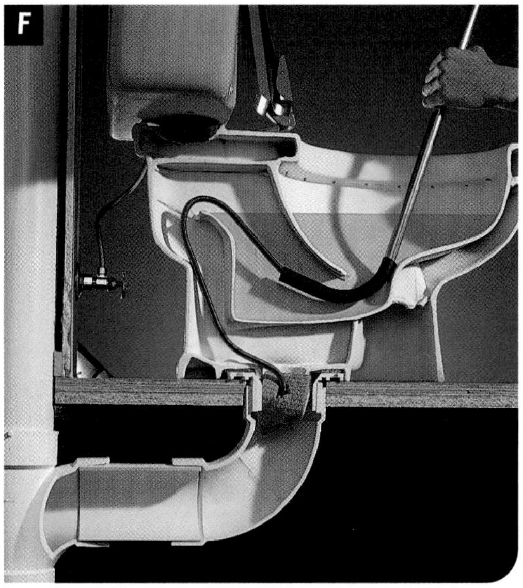

Use a closet auger to retrieve obstructions from the toilet trap or to clear stubborn clogs.

Clearing Clogged Shower Drains

A shower drain system has a sloped floor, a drain opening, a trap, and a drain line that connects to a branch drain line and waste and vent stack.

Shower drain clogs usually are caused by hair. These clogs often can be removed with a piece of wire, but others sometimes require more aggressive efforts.

Pry up the strainer cover with a screwdriver. Shine a flashlight into the opening and check for hair or other clogs near the opening. Use a piece of stiff wire to retrieve obstructions.

If you can't reach the obstruction, try plunging. Place the rubber cup of the plunger over the drain opening, then pour enough water into the shower floor to cover the lip of the cup. Move the plunger handle up and down rapidly.

Clear stubborn clogs with a hand auger **(photo G).** Feed a hand auger into the drain and rotate it in a clockwise direction to snag and retrieve the clog.

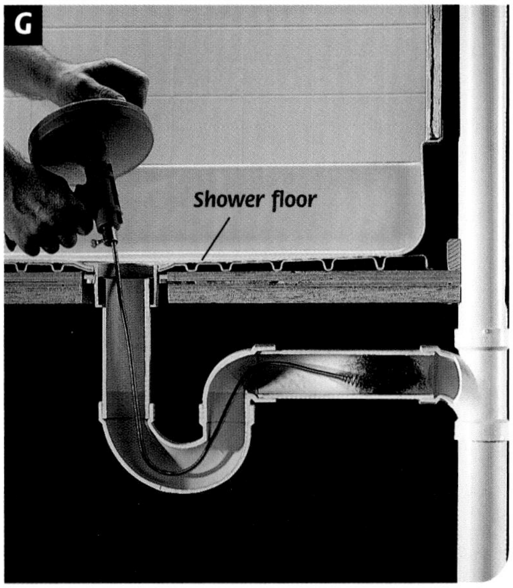

Sinks

Although sinks generally last for many years, their finishes get worn and they can crack or chip. When it's time to replace a damaged sink, it may be easier than you imagined.

Buy the new sink before you take out the old one. If you're planning to use the same countertop and faucet, measure the countertop opening and the perimeter of the old sink, as well as the faucet openings. Look at the underside of the sink to find the configuration of the faucet openings, as well as the distance between them.

Kitchen sinks for do-it-yourself installation are made from cast iron coated with enamel, stainless steel, or enameled steel. Kitchen sinks made from solid-surface material or porcelain usually are installed by professionals.

Bathroom sinks suitable for do-it-yourself installation include cultured marble, porcelain, solid-surface, stainless steel, enameled cast iron, enameled steel, and tempered glass.

Cast-iron sinks are durable and relatively easy to install. Most cast-iron sinks are frameless, requiring no mounting hardware.

Stainless steel and enameled steel sinks may require a metal frame and mounting brackets. A good stainless steel sink is made of heavy 18- or 20-gauge nickel steel. Steel designated by numbers higher than 20 dents too easily.

Integral (one-piece) sink-countertop units made from cultured marble or other solid-surface materials are very popular, partly because they're very simple to install. Porcelain sinks, usually self-rimming, are also easy to install. Installing undermounted and flush-mounted sinks may prove more challenging.

Tools: *Basin wrench, pencil, hacksaw, utility knife, channel-type pliers, ratchet wrench.*

Materials: *Bucket, plumber's putty, tub & tile caulk, silicone caulk.*

Disconnecting & Removing a Kitchen Sink

Before you begin working, turn off the water, either at the shutoff valves or the main supply valve located near the water meter.

Use a basin wrench to remove the coupling nuts connecting the supply tube to the faucet tailpieces **(photo A).** If the supply tubes are soldered, use a hacksaw to cut them off *above* the shutoff valves.

If the sink is connected to a disposal and dishwasher, disconnect them (see pages 356 to 359, 361 to 364).

Place a bucket beneath the P-trap, loosen the slip nuts at both ends, and remove the trap **(photo B).** If you can't turn the nuts, use a hacksaw to cut out the trap.

Use a utility knife to cut through any caulk or sealant between the sink rim and the countertop **(photo C).** Carefully lift the sink off the countertop and set it aside. If you plan to reuse the faucet, remove it from the sink now.

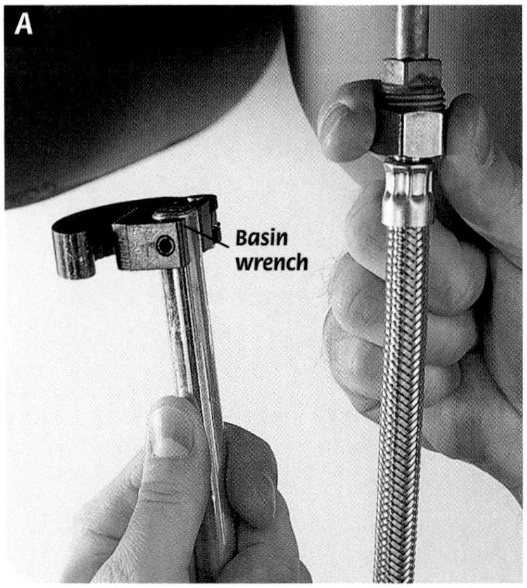

Disconnect the supply tubes from the faucet tailpieces.

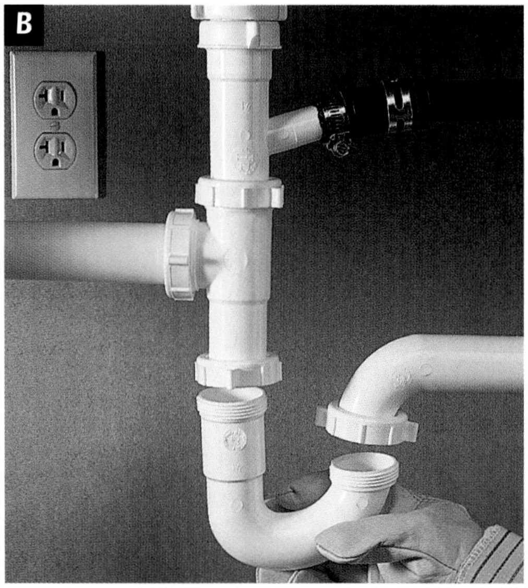

Loosen the slip nuts at both ends of the P-trap; remove it.

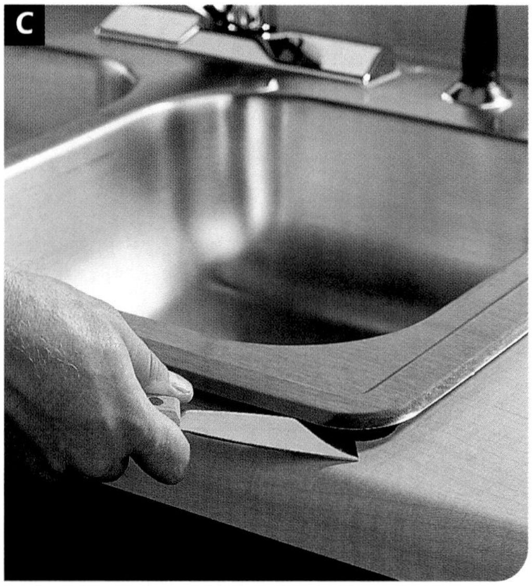

Cut through the caulk or sealant under the sink rim.

Disconnecting & Removing a Bathroom Sink

Replacing a damaged or unattractive sink is quick, relatively inexpensive, and fairly simple.

In all cases, the first steps are to turn off the water supply and disconnect the plumbing **(photos D, E).** If there are shutoff valves, close them. If the supply tubes are soldered, cut them above the shutoff valves. If no shutoff valves exist, turn off the water at the main supply valve, and add shutoff valves when installing the new sink.

Methods of removal vary slightly for different styles of sinks (for specifics, see photos below).

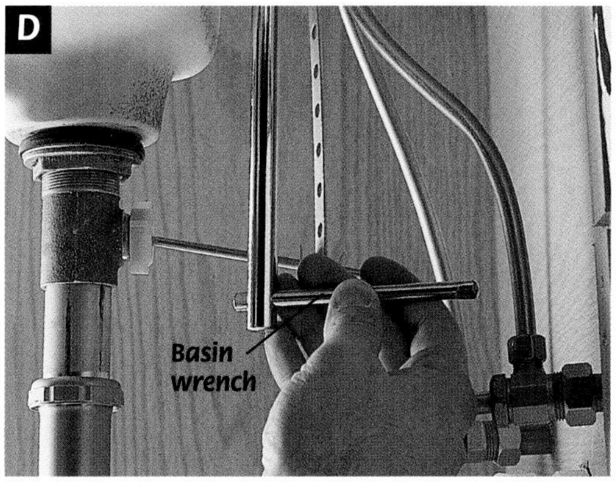

Turn off the water, then use a basin wrench to remove the coupling nuts that connect the supply tubes to the faucet tailpieces.

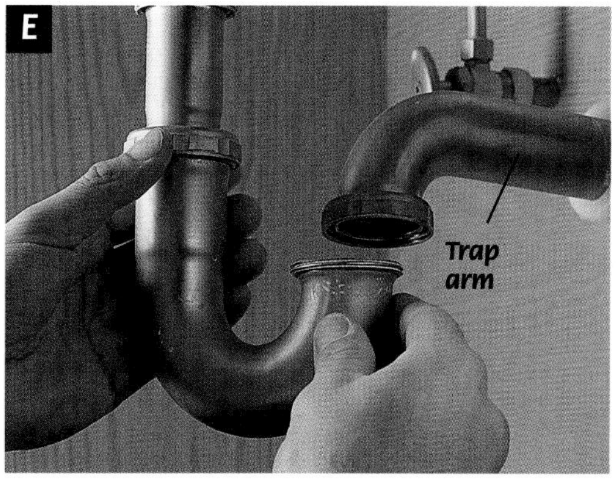

Set a bucket beneath, then loosen the slip nuts at both ends of the P-trap. If they won't turn, cut out the trap with a hacksaw, taking care not to damage the trap arm.

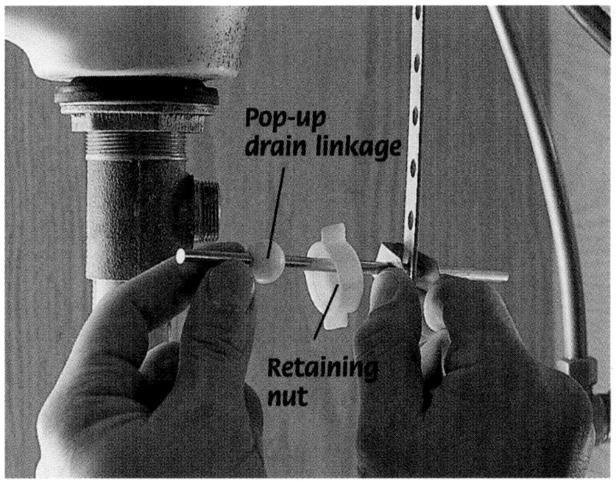

Sinks with countertop-mounted faucet: Disconnect the pop-up drain linkage from the tailpiece of the sink drain by unscrewing the retaining nut.

Wall-mounted sinks: Slice through caulk or sealant, then lift sink off wall brackets. If attached with lag screws, wedge a 2 × 4 between the sink and the floor while removing them.

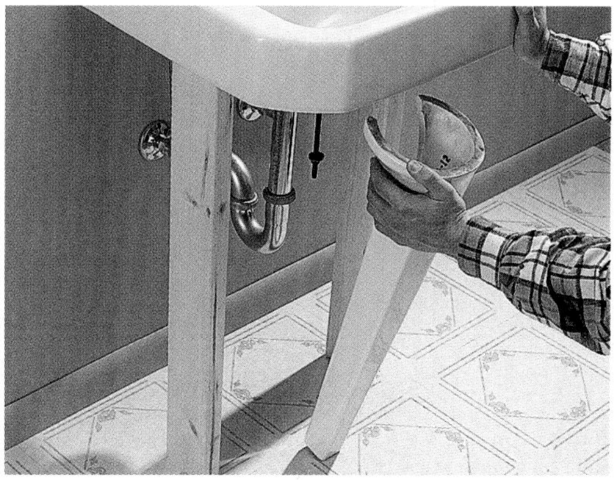

Pedestal sinks: If the sink and pedestal are connected, remove the bolts. Support the sink from below with 2 × 4s. Remove pedestal, then lift the sink off the wall brackets.

Integral sinks: Detach mounting hardware beneath countertop. Cut caulk or sealant between countertop and wall and between countertop and vanity, then lift sink off vanity.

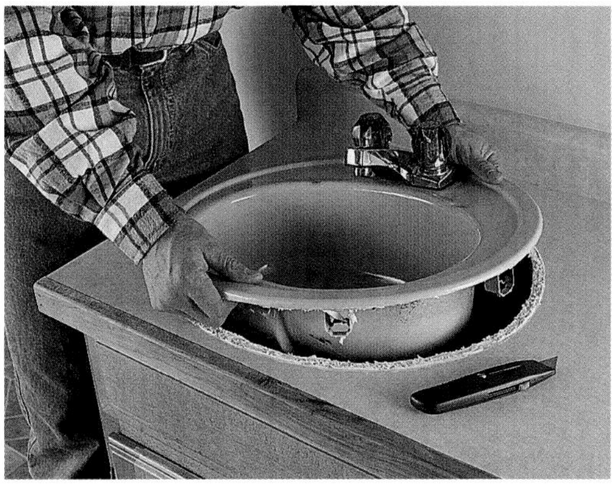

Self-rimming sinks: Slice through any caulk or sealant between the sink rim and the countertop. Lift the sink off the countertop.

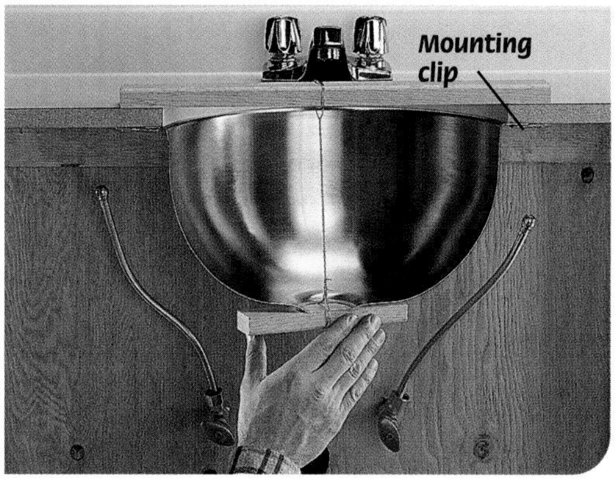

Rimless sinks: Tie wire to a wood scrap; thread through drain hole and twist around another wood scrap until taut. Remove mounting clips. Slice caulk, loosen wire, and remove sink.

Installing a Drop-in Sink

Measure the existing countertop cutout and purchase a sink that fits or is slightly larger than the current opening. If the opening must be enlarged, or if the countertop is being replaced along with the sink, draw and cut out a cardboard template 1/2" narrower than the sink rim.

To make or enlarge the cutout, drill a 3/8" starter hole, then use a jig saw to cut around the template.

Apply a ring of plumber's putty around the cutout **(photo A).** Attach the faucet body to the sink or countertop, depending on the sink style. Install the drainpiece, the drain flange, and the pop-up drain assembly.

Set the sink into the opening and embed it in the plumber's putty **(photo B).** Connect the drain and water supply fittings, then caulk around the rim.

Apply plumber's putty around the edge of the opening, then position the faucet body and install the drain piece assembly.

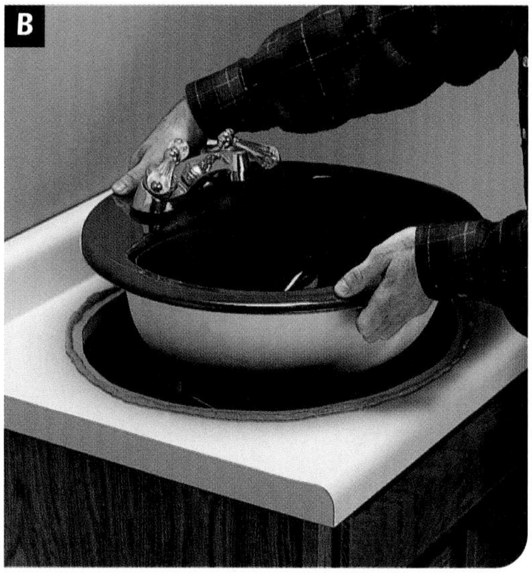

Set the sink into the cutout, pressing the rim into the putty. Hook up the drain and supply fittings, then caulk the rim.

Installing a Wall-mounted Sink

If you're installing a wall-mounted sink in a new location, you'll need to provide additional wall support. To provide this support, cut away the wallboard and endnail a 2 × 8 between the studs. Position the 2 × 8 directly behind the location where you plan to attach the hanger bracket. Most people find a height between 30" and 38" from the floor to be most comfortable. Replace the wallboard and finish its surface.

Attach the hanger bracket **(photo C)**, following manufacturer's directions.

Attach the drain flange and faucet to the sink and lower the fixture onto the bracket **(photo D).** Check the sink for level and make any adjustments that are necessary. Secure any additional fasteners that were provided with the sink.

Connect supply lines to the faucet by tightening the coupling nuts (page 303). Attach the drain flange to the trap and drain lines with channel-type pliers (page 311). Connect the drain stopper and pivot rod to the clevis (page 310). Apply tub and tile caulk along the joint between the sink and the wall.

Attach the hanger bracket to the wall; make sure it's level.

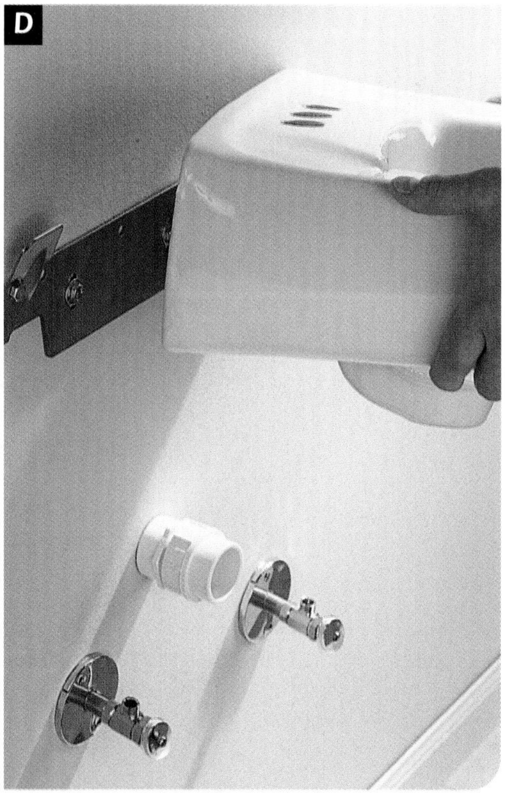

Lower the sink onto the hanger, then make the connections.

Installing a Self-rimming Sink

Apply a ¼" bead of silicone caulk or plumber's putty around the underside of the sink flange.

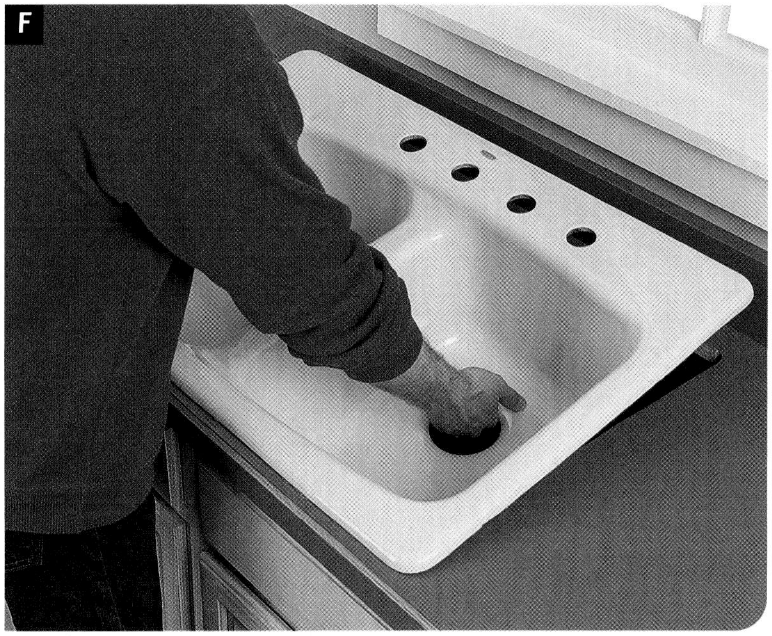

Holding the drain openings, position the front of the sink in the countertop cutout. Carefully lower the sink into position. Press down to create a tight seal; wipe away any excess caulk.

Installing a Framed Sink

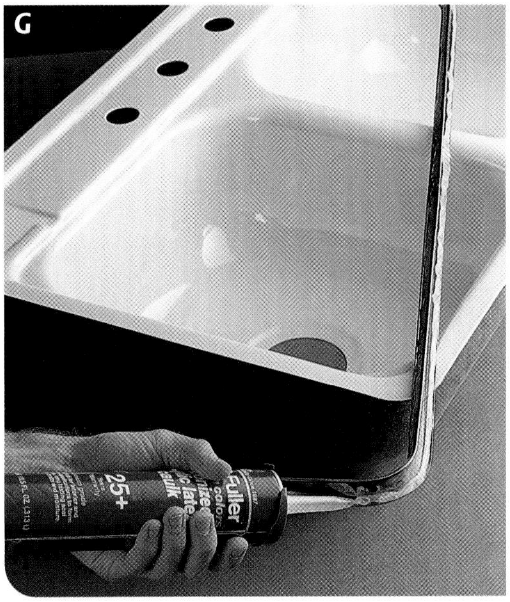

Turn the sink frame upside down. Apply a ¼" bead of silicone caulk or plumber's putty around both sides of the vertical flange.

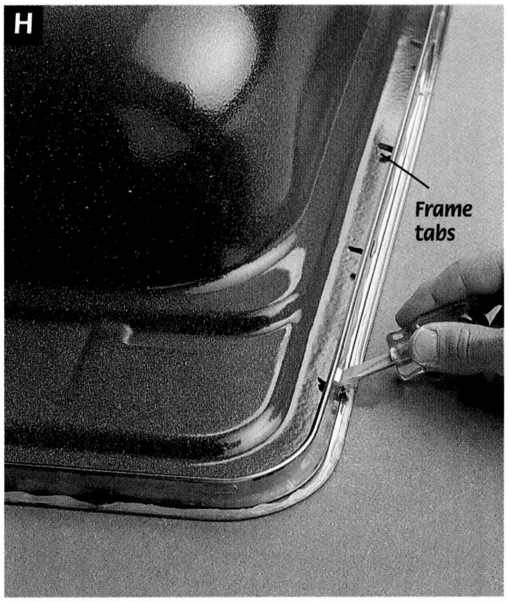

Set the sink upside down inside the frame. Bend the frame tabs to hold the sink. Carefully set the sink into the countertop cutout and press down to create a tight seal.

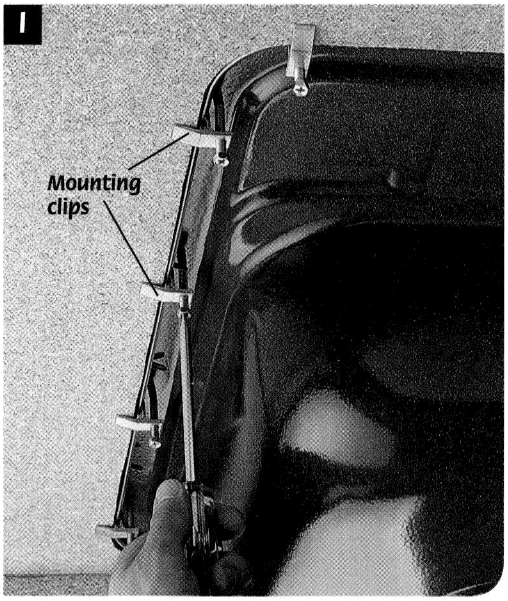

Hook mounting clips every 6" to 8" around the frame from underneath the countertop. Tighten the mounting screws. Wipe any excess caulk away from the frame.

Installing a Pedestal Sink

Installing a pedestal sink is quite simple if the unit you're replacing was also a pedestal-style sink.

If the pedestal sink is a new installation or replacing another type of sink, you'll need to cut away the wallboard and install 2 × 4 blocking about 34" above the floor. Once this is done, cover the wall with water-resistant wallboard and repaint the area.

If the previous sink was a pedestal style, make sure the profile and configuration of the new sink matches the old mounting holes.

Set the basin and pedestal in position, bracing the basin in place with 2 × 4s **(photo A).**

Outline the top of the basin on the wall, and mark the base of the pedestal on the floor.

Mark reference points on the wall and floor through the mounting holes found on the back of the sink and the bottom of the pedestal.

Set aside the basin and pedestal. Drill pilot holes in the wall and floor at the reference points.

Reposition the pedestal, and anchor it to the floor with lag screws **(photo B).**

Attach the faucet (pages 334 to 335), then set the sink on the pedestal. Align the mounting holes on the back of the sink with the pilot holes drilled in the wall. Drive lag screws and washers into the wall brace, using a ratchet wrench **(photo C).** Be careful not to overtighten the lag screws.

Connect the drain fittings (page 311 and opposite page) **(photo D),** and the water supply fittings (page 303).

When all the fittings are connected, seal the joint between the back of the sink and the wall, using silicone caulk.

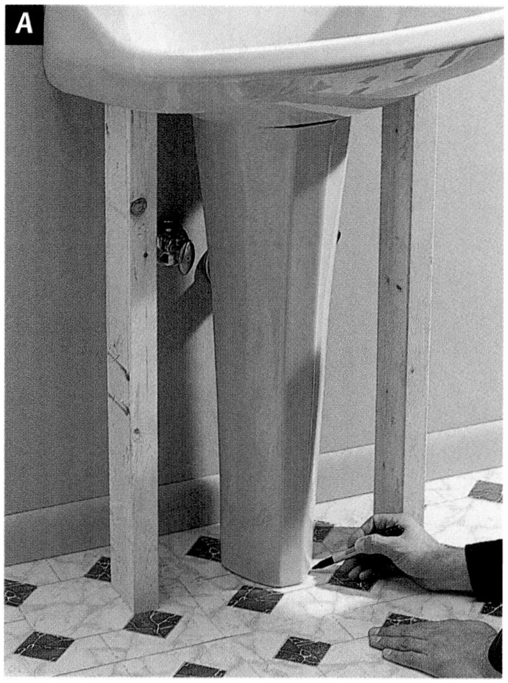

Brace the basin in place. Outline the top of the basin and the base of the pedestal on the wall.

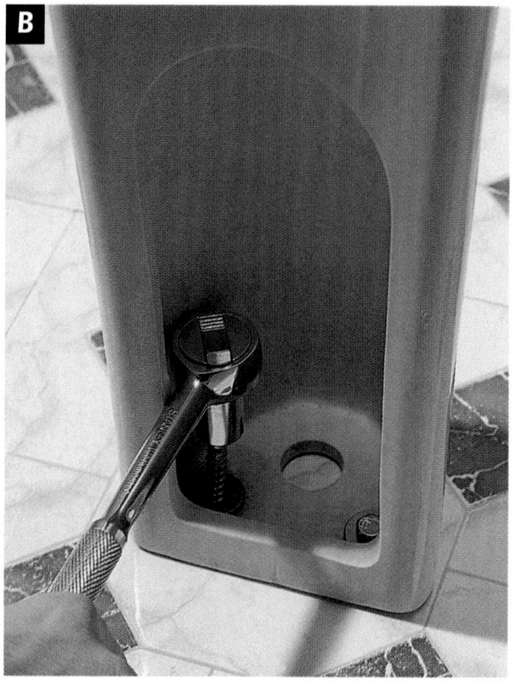

Drill pilot holes at reference points, then anchor the pedestal to the floor with lag screws.

Attach the faucet, then place the basin on the pedestal. Drive lag screws through mounting holes into the wall brace.

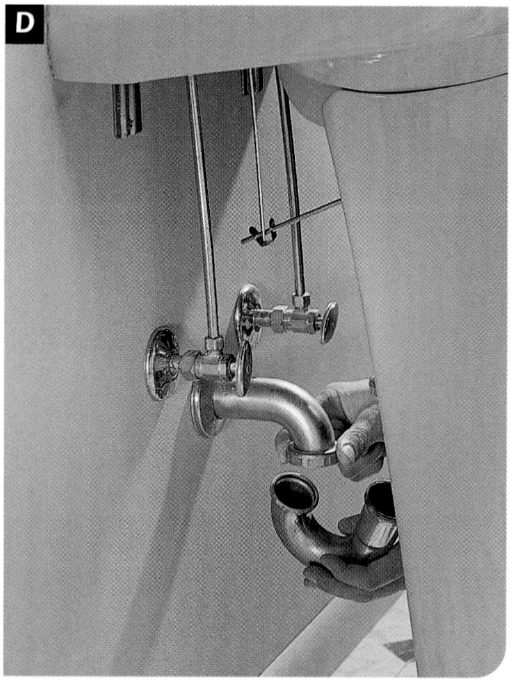

Hook up drain and supply fittings, then caulk between the sink and the wall.

Attaching Drain Lines to a Sink

After replacing or installing a new sink, you'll need to connect it to the drain lines.

If the drain hookups are being replaced, use plastic piping if your local Code allows it. Plastic is not only inexpensive and easy to install, it's available in a wide variety of extensions and angle fittings to accommodate almost any sink configuration. In addition, manufacturers offer kits containing all the fittings necessary to attach food disposers or dishwashers to kitchen sink drain systems.

Start by installing a sink strainer in each sink drain opening. Apply a 1/4" bead of plumber's putty around the bottom of the strainer flange. Then, insert the strainer into the drain opening. Place the rubber and fiber washers over the neck of the strainer. Screw a locknut onto the strainer neck **(photo E)** and tighten it with channel-type pliers.

Next, attach the drain tailpiece to the strainer. Begin by checking the length of the tailpiece. If necessary, you can cut it to length, using a hacksaw. Slide a slipnut onto the tailpiece so the threads face the flanged side of the tailpiece. Place an insert washer in the flared end of the tailpiece. Attach the tailpiece by screwing the slip nut onto the sink strainer by hand **(photo F)**.

If your sink has two basins, next you'll need to attach a continuous waste T-fitting **(photo G)**. The continuous waste T-fitting joins the tailpieces for each basin and funnels the drain water to a single trap arm. Position a slip nut and slip washer on the end of each tailpiece, so the beveled side of the washer faces down, then attach the T-fitting by screwing the slip nut down onto it.

Now, attach the trap arm to the drain stubout, using a slip nut and washer **(photo H)**. Again, slide a slip nut and beveled washer onto the arm, then insert the arm into the drain stubout and tighten the slip nut down onto it. If necessary, use a hacksaw to cut the trap arm to fit.

Finally, attach the trap bend, using slip nuts and washers **(photo I)**. Tighten all the nuts with channel-type pliers, then run water to check for leaks.

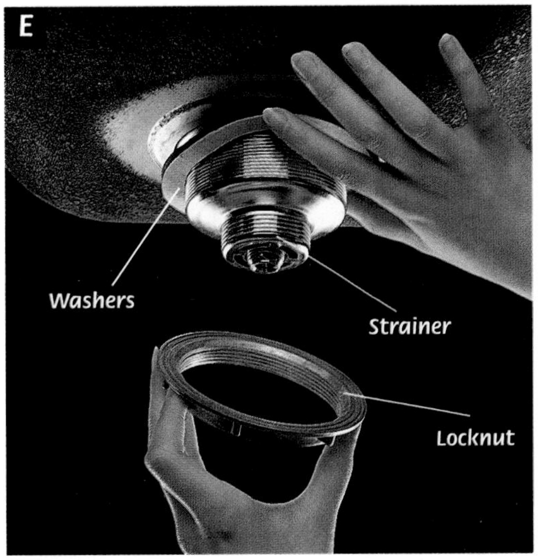

Install a sink strainer in each sink drain opening.

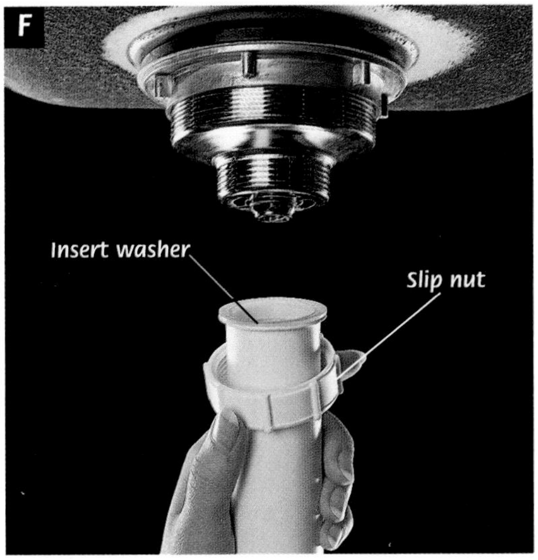

Attach a tailpiece to the sink strainer.

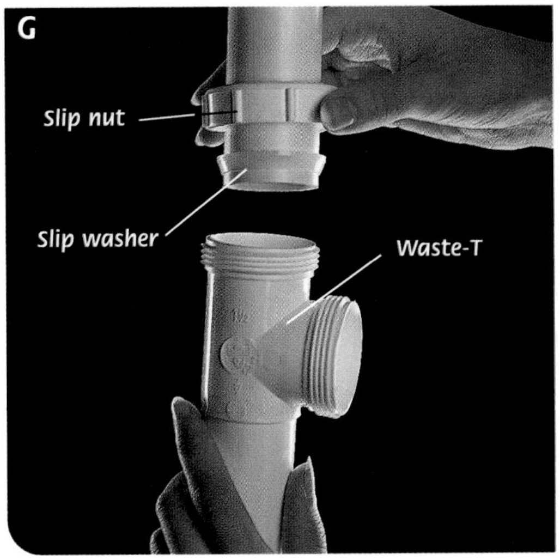

On two-basin sinks, use a continuous waste T-fitting to join the two tailpieces.

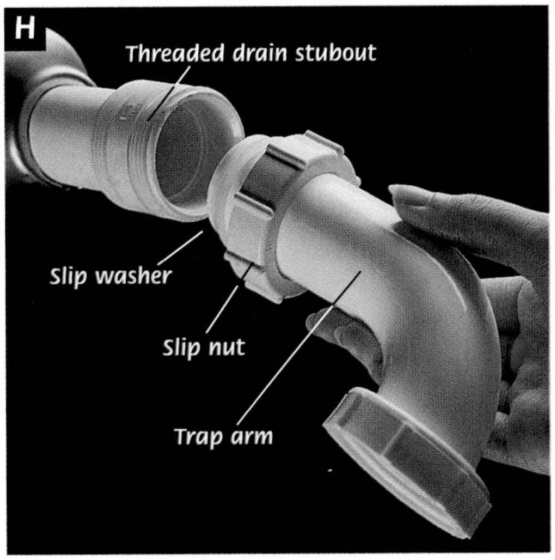

Connect the trap arm to the drain stubout, using an insert washer and slip nut.

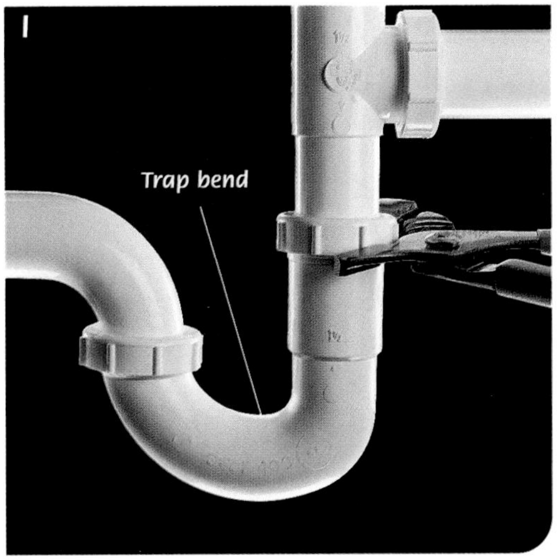

Connect the trap bend to the trap arm, using washers and slip nuts.

Faucets

A leaky faucet is the most common home plumbing problem. Most faucet problems are easy to fix, and you can save time and money by fixing them yourself. Leaks generally occur when washers, O-rings, or seals inside the faucet become dirty or worn. Fixing most leaks is a matter of cleaning or replacing one of these parts.

It's important to fix a leak as soon as possible. Although the trickle or drip from your faucet may not seem like much, it can quickly make an impact on your water bill. And if left unrepaired, a leak can also cut a channel in the metal faucet seat, which may require that the entire faucet be replaced.

The typical faucet has a single handle attached to a hollow cartridge that controls the flow of hot and cold water from the supply tubes into a mixing chamber. From there, water is forced out of the spout and the aerator. When repairs are needed, replace the entire cartridge.

If a faucet continues to leak after repairs have been made, it's time to replace the whole thing. In less than an hour, you can install a new model that will provide years of trouble-free service.

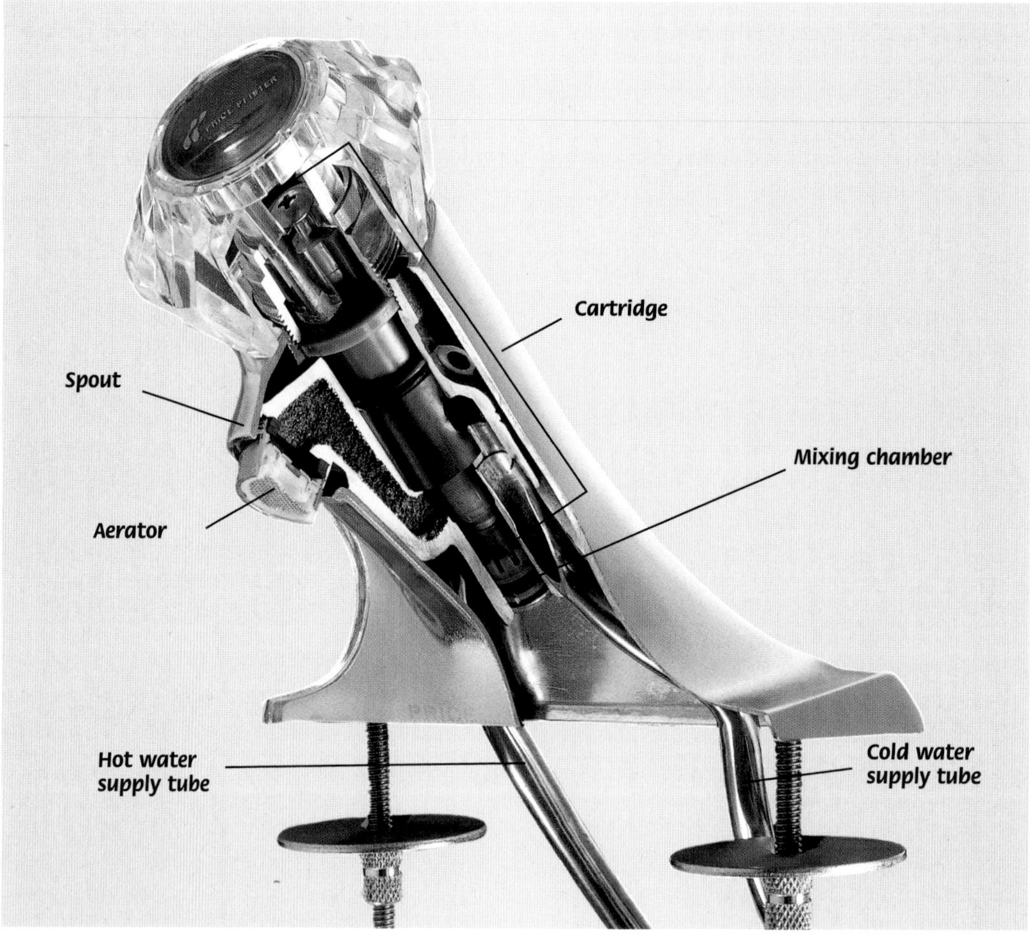

The anatomy of a typical single-handled faucet.

Tools & Materials for Faucet Repairs

Having the right tools for the task is important for any home improvement project, but it's particularly important when working with faucets. Without tools such as a seat wrench or a handle puller, you'll be unable to fix some types of faucets, and may even destroy the faucet as well as your tools.

When purchasing tools, always select quality products, even if they may cost a bit more. Well-made tools last longer and are easier to work with, which saves you time, money, and frustration.

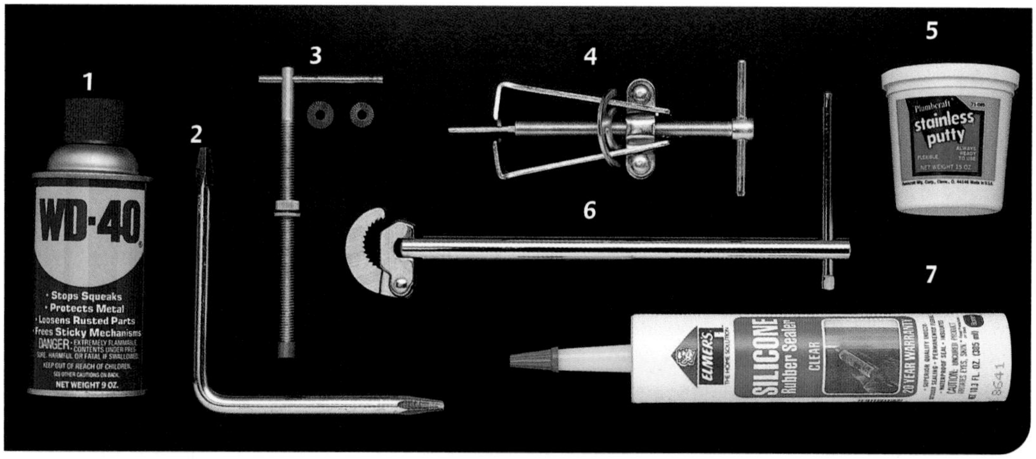

Specialty tools and materials for faucet repairs include: penetrating oil (1), seat wrench (2), seat-dressing (reamer) tool (3), handle puller (4), plumber's putty (5), basin wrench (6), silicone caulk (7).

Faucet Problems & Repairs

Problems	Repairs
Faucet drips from the end of the spout, or leaks around the base.	Identify the faucet design, then install replacement parts.
Old, worn-out faucet continues to leak after repairs are made.	Replace the old faucet (page 332).
Water pressure at spout seems low, or water flow is partially blocked.	1. Clean faucet aerator (page 330). 2. Remove corroded galvanized pipes (page 295) and replace with copper.
Water pressure from sprayer seems low, or sprayer leaks from handle.	1. Clean sprayer head (page 330). 2. Fix diverter valve (page 331).
Water leaks onto floor underneath faucet.	1. Replace cracked sprayer hose (page 331). 2. Tighten water connections, or replace supply tubes and shutoff valves (page 302).
Hose bib or valve drips from spout or leaks around handle.	Take valve apart and replace washers or O-rings (page 301).

Identifying Faucet Designs

There are four basic types of faucet designs: *ball, cartridge, disc,* and *compression*. Some faucet models can be easily identified by their appearance; others must be taken apart for identification.

The compression design is mostly used in double-handled faucets **(photo A).** The two handles compress against rubber washers or seals to control the flow of water. The washers or seals eventually wear out and must be replaced. However, the replacement parts are inexpensive, and the repairs are easy to do.

Ball, cartridge, and disc faucets are all known as "washerless" faucets **(photos B to D).** Many washerless faucets are controlled with a single handle, although some cartridge models use two handles. Washerless faucets are more trouble-free than compression faucets, and are designed for quick repair.

When purchasing new faucet parts, select replacements that match the original parts. Parts are identified both by brand name and model number.

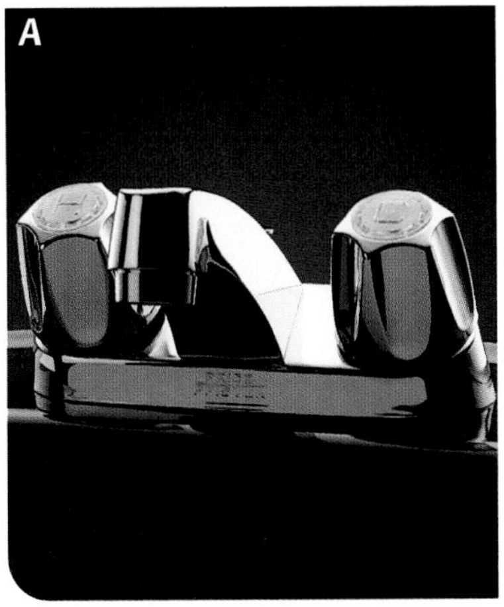

Compression faucets use washers or seals to control the flow of water (page 328).

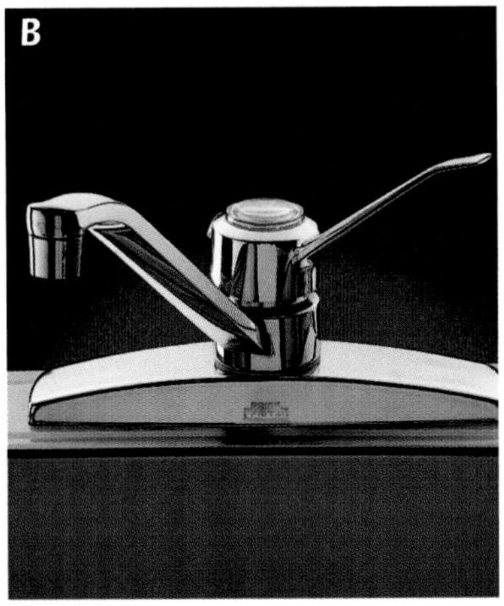

Cartridge faucets come in single- or double-handle models (page 324).

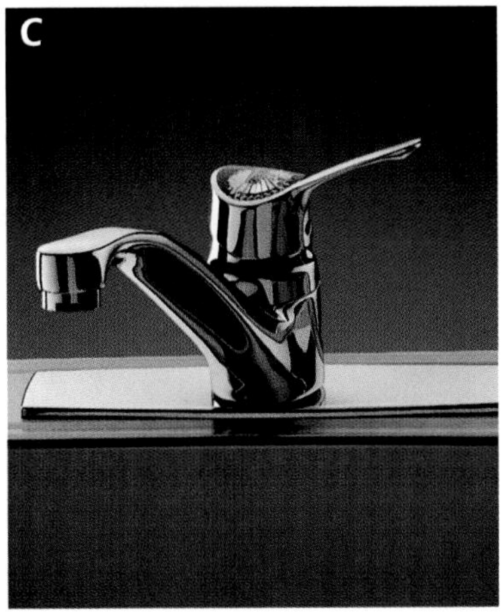

Disc faucets have a single handle and a solid chrome body (page 326).

Ball faucets have a single handle over a dome-shaped cap (page 322).

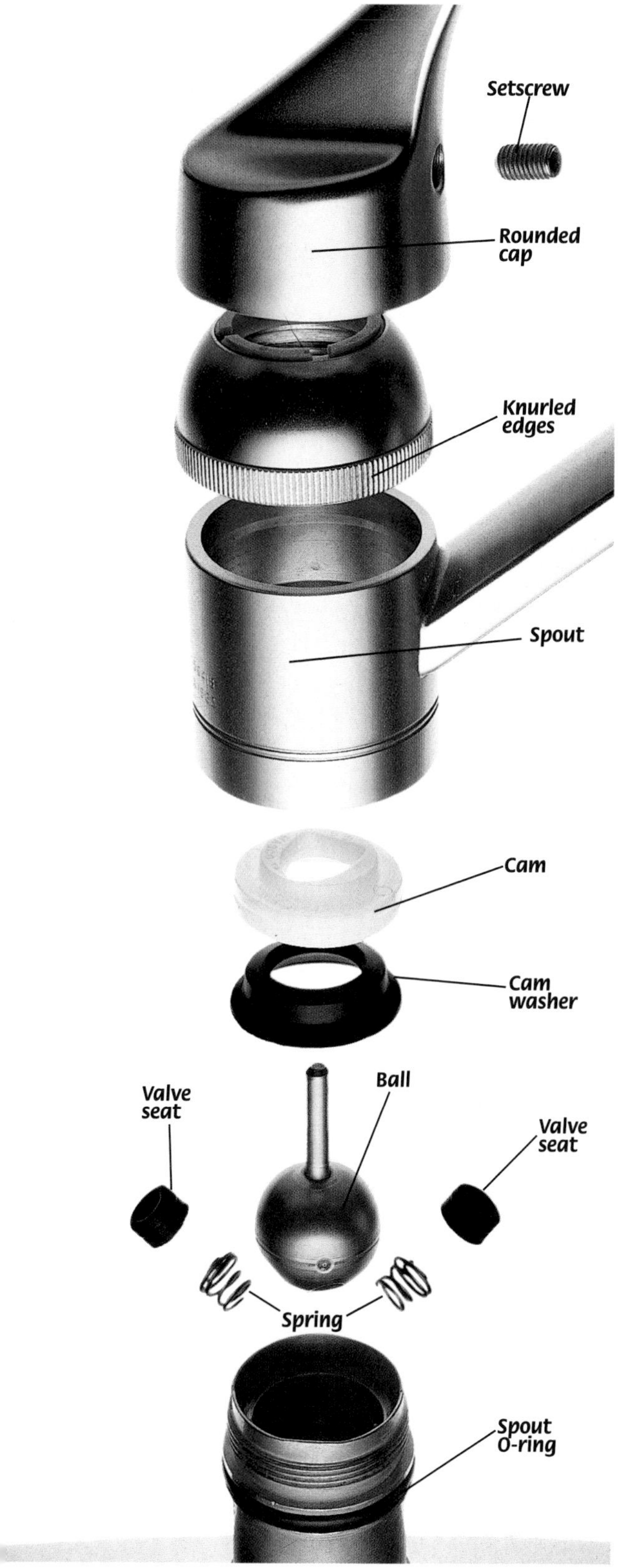

Ball Faucets

Ball faucets have a single handle and can be identified by a hollow metal or plastic ball inside the faucet body. This rotating ball controls the temperature and flow of water into the faucet. Many ball-type faucets have a rounded cap with knurled edges located under the handle.

If a faucet with this type of cap leaks from the spout, try tightening the cap with channel-type pliers. If this doesn't fix the leak, take the faucet apart and inspect it. Look for worn-out valve seats, springs, or a damaged ball; any of these can cause spout drips. Leaks around the base of the faucet are usually caused by worn O-rings.

Faucet manufacturers offer several types of replacement kits for ball faucets **(photo A).** Some kits contain only the springs and neoprene valve seats. The best kits also include the cam and the cam washer.

Replace the rotating ball only if it's obviously worn or scratched. Replacement balls are available in metal and plastic. Metal replacement balls are slightly more expensive than the plastic ones, but they're more durable.

Tools: *Channel-type pliers, Allen wrench, screwdriver, utility knife.*

Materials: *Ball-type faucet repair kit, new rotating ball (if needed), masking tape, O-rings, heatproof grease.*

A

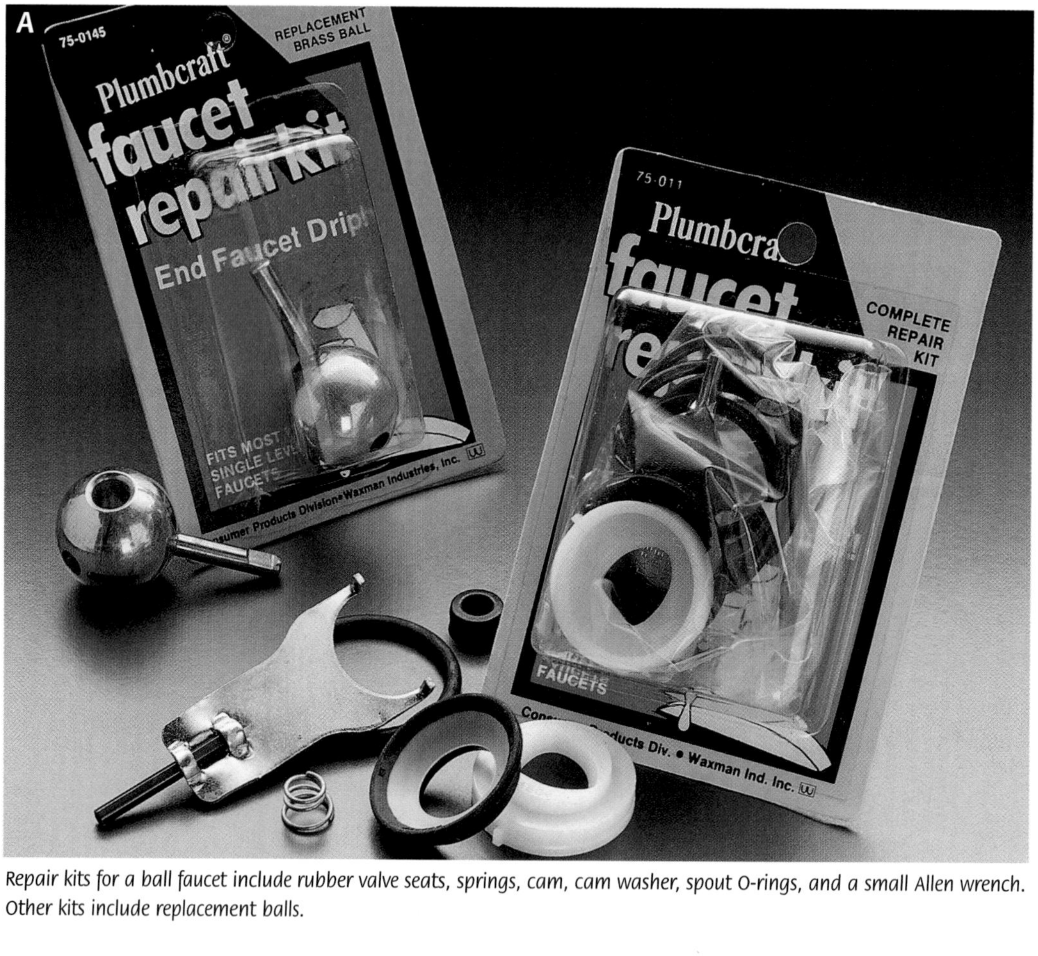

Repair kits for a ball faucet include rubber valve seats, springs, cam, cam washer, spout O-rings, and a small Allen wrench. Other kits include replacement balls.

Fixing a Ball Faucet

Turn off the water at the shutoff valves or the main supply valve near the water meter. Loosen the handle setscrew with an Allen wrench **(photo B).** Remove the handle, exposing the faucet cap.

Remove the faucet cap with channel-type pliers **(photo C).** Lift out the faucet cam, cam washer, and the ball **(photo D).** Check the ball for signs of wear.

Reach into the faucet with a screwdriver and remove the old springs and neoprene valve seats **(photo E).** Remove the spout by twisting it upward, then cut off old O-rings **(photo F).** Coat the new O-rings with heatproof grease and install them. Reattach spout, pressing downward until the collar rests on the plastic slip ring. Install new springs and valve seats.

Insert the ball, the new cam washer and cam **(photo G).** Fit the small lug on the cam into the notch on the faucet body. Screw the cap back onto the faucet and reattach the handle.

Turn the faucet on. Slowly open the shutoff valves to restore the water supply. Check for leaks and tighten connections as needed.

Helpful Hint

To keep your channel-type pliers from scratching the finish when you take a faucet apart for repair, wrap masking tape around the jaws of the pliers.

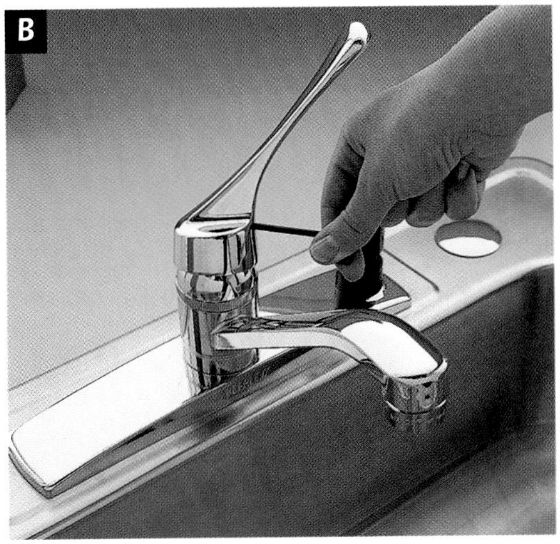

Loosen the setscrew and remove the faucet handle.

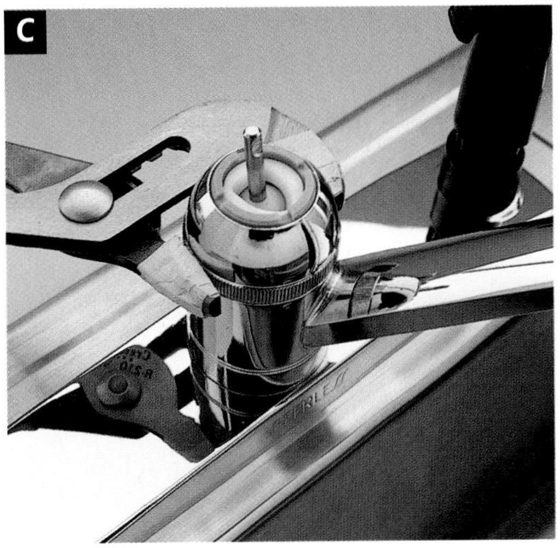

Remove the faucet cap, using channel-type pliers.

Remove the faucet cam, cam washer, and the rotating ball.

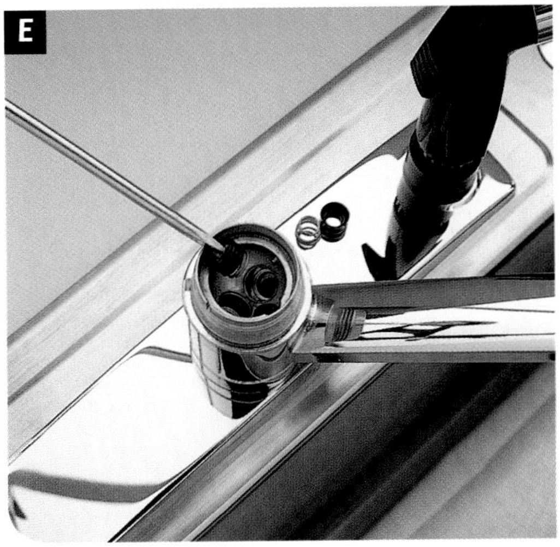

Take out the old springs and neoprene valve seats.

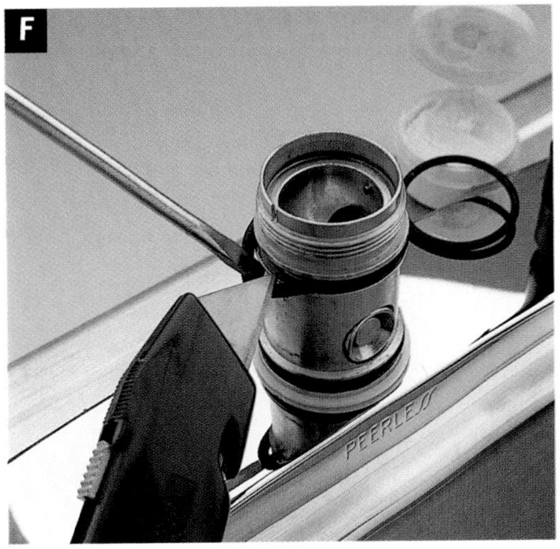

Replace O-rings, then install new springs and valve seats.

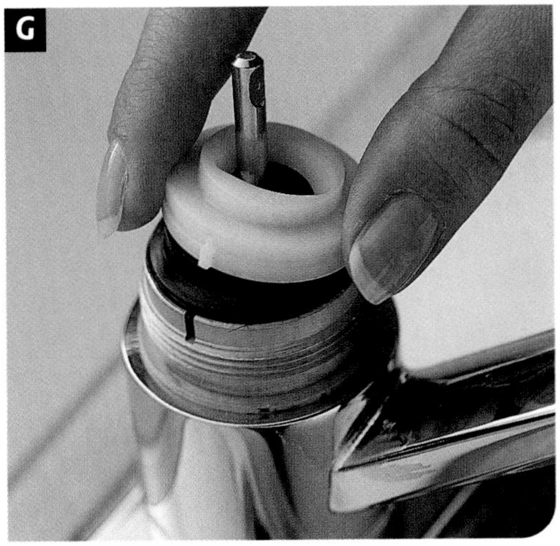

Install ball, cam washer, and cam. Replace cap and handle.

Cartridge Faucets

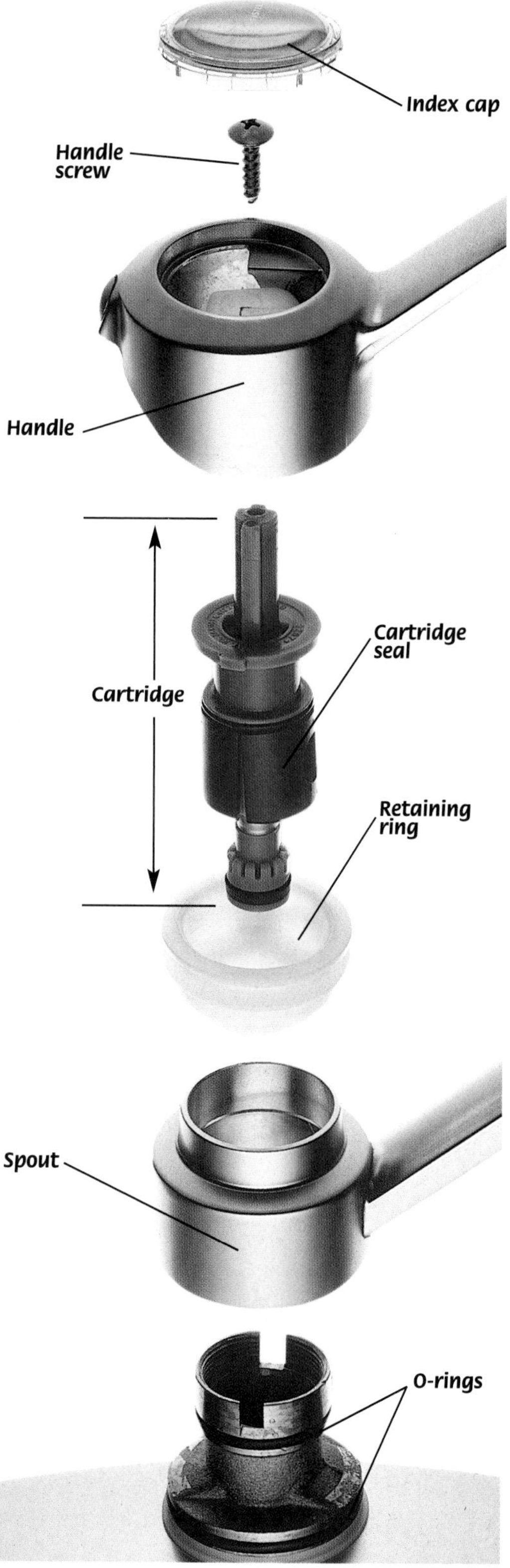

Cartridge faucets can be identified by a cylindrical metal or plastic cartridge inside the faucet body. The cartridge holds a movable stem that's controlled by lifting the handle. When the stem rises, its holes align with the cartridge holes, allowing hot and cold water to mix. Rotating the handle adjusts the mix of hot and cold water. Most cartridge designs are single-handle faucets.

Leaks around the base of a cartridge faucet are typically caused by worn O-rings, and can be fixed by replacing them. Spout drips are generally caused by worn cartridge seals, and can be solved by replacing the cartridge. Other problems, such as a decrease in water flow, may be caused by clogs in the cartridge holes or a corroded cartridge. If a cartridge appears to be corroded or worn, replace it.

Before you remove the cartridge, make note of its alignment. Look for the tabs (or "ears") on the top of the cartridge housing that fit into the notches in the rim of the faucet body. When you insert the new cartridge, align it in the same position as the old one. If the cartridge isn't aligned correctly, the hot and cold water controls may be reversed. If that happens, just take the faucet apart and rotate the cartridge 180°. Cartridges come in many styles—bring yours along for comparison when shopping for a new one **(photo A).**

Tools: *Screwdriver, channel-type pliers, utility knife.*

Materials: *Replacement cartridge, O-rings, heatproof grease.*

Replacement cartridges for popular faucet brands (from left): Price Pfister, Moen, Kohler. O-rings may be sold separately.

Fixing a Cartridge Faucet

Before starting, turn off the water at the shutoff valves or the main supply valve near the water meter. Pry off the index cap on top of the faucet and remove the handle screw underneath the cap **(photo B).**

Remove the faucet handle by lifting it up and tilting it backward **(photo C).** Remove the threaded retaining ring, using channel-type pliers **(photo D).** Remove any retaining clip holding the cartridge in place.

Grip the top of the cartridge with channel-type pliers **(photo E).** Pull straight up to remove the cartridge. Install the replacement cartridge in the same position as the old one.

Remove the spout by pulling up and twisting **(photo F).** Use a utility knife to cut off the old O-rings. Coat the new O-rings with heatproof grease and install. Reattach the spout **(photo G).** Screw the retaining ring onto the faucet and tighten with channel-type pliers. Attach the handle, handle screw, and index cap.

Turn the faucet on. Slowly open the shutoff valves to restore the water. Check for leaks and tighten connections as needed.

Helpful Hint

Close the sink drain before disassembling the faucet. Then, if parts fall as you work, they'll stay in the sink rather than falling down the drain and into the trap.

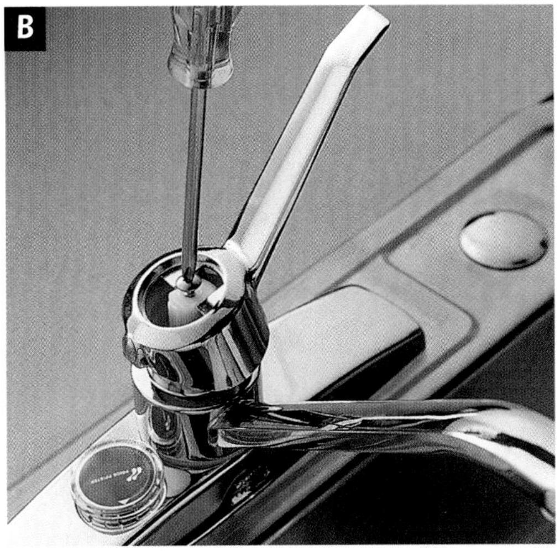

Pry off the index cap and remove the handle screw.

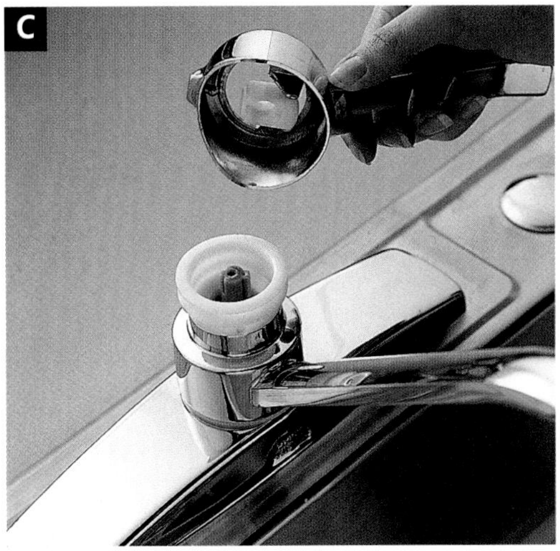

Remove the faucet handle.

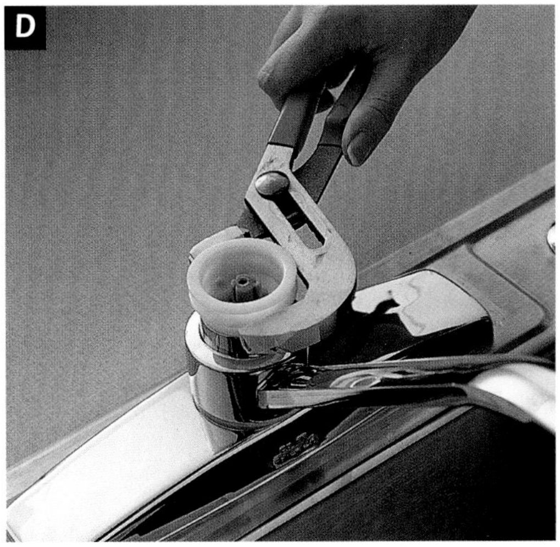

Remove the retaining ring and retaining clip, if present.

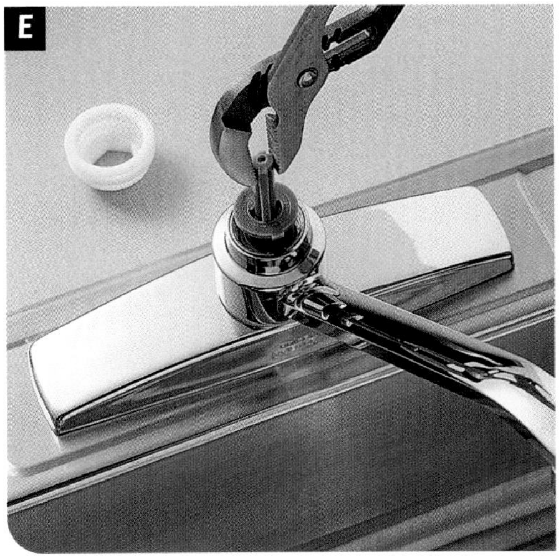

Insert a new cartridge in the same position as the old one.

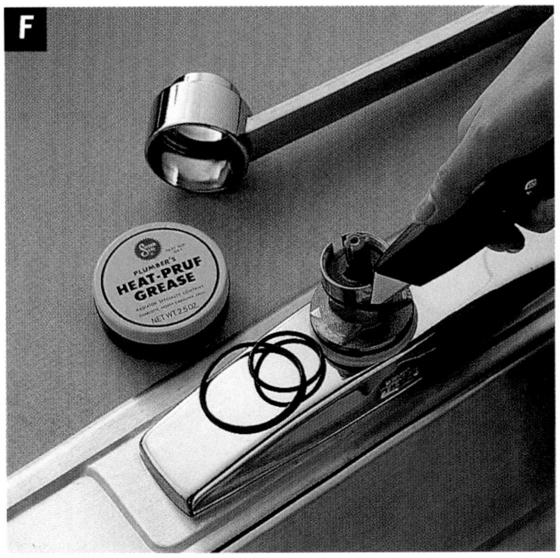

Remove the spout. Remove and replace the O-rings.

Reattach the spout, handle, handle screw, and index cap.

Disc Faucets

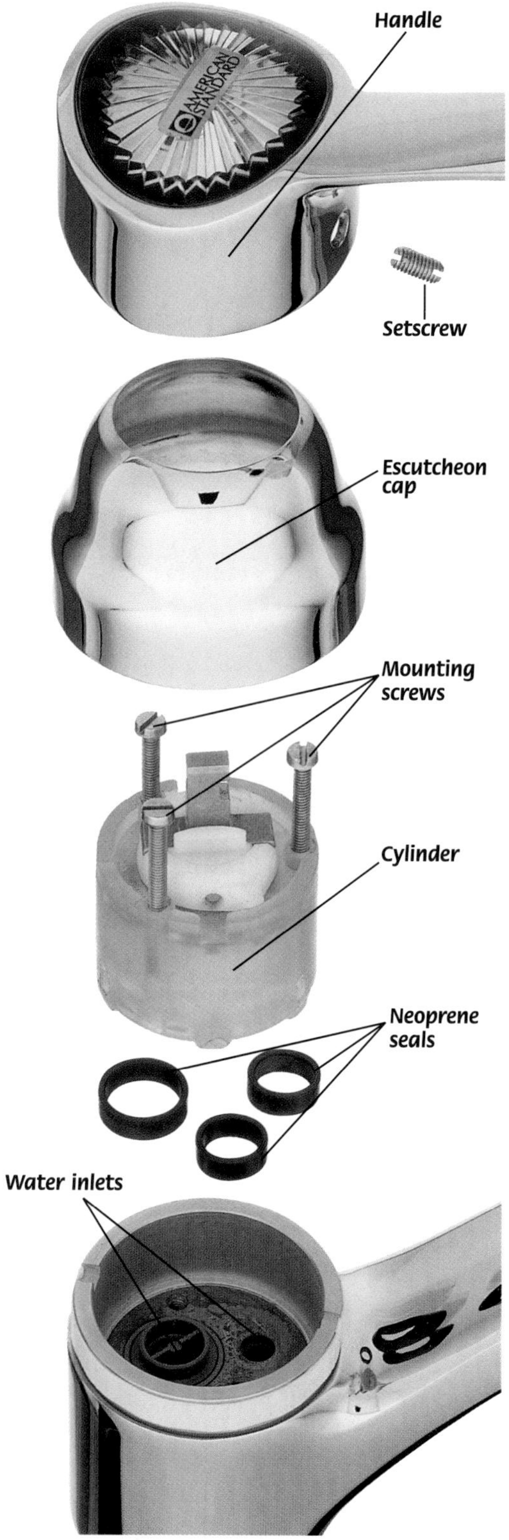

A disc faucet has a single handle and can be identified by a wide cylinder inside the faucet body. The cartridge contains two tight-fitting ceramic discs. The discs have inlet holes for hot and cold water and an outlet hole to the spout. Lifting the handle causes the upper disc to slide across the lower disc. This aligns their holes, allowing water to flow into a mixing chamber and through the outlet to the spout.

A ceramic disc faucet is a top-quality fixture that's easy to repair. The discs are durable and rarely need replacement. Most disc faucet problems are caused by dirty neoprene seals or cylinder openings. Leaks at the spout or around the faucet body usually can be fixed by cleaning the seals and the cylinder openings.

Never use a sharp tool, such as a wire or the tip of a screwdriver, to clean cylinder openings—you may scratch or chip the smooth surface of the discs. Inspect the inlet holes for mineral deposits that may be restricting water flow; remove them with an abrasive pad.

If a disc faucet continues to leak after you've cleaned it thoroughly, replace the cylinder **(photo A).** A continuous leak indicates that a ceramic disc may be cracked or scratched, or that a particle has become lodged between the discs, breaking the tight seal.

When buying a replacement cylinder, note the faucet's make and model, or bring the old one for comparison when shopping.

When installing a cylinder, be sure to line up the holes in the cylinder with the correct inlet and outlet holes in the faucet body.

Tools: *Screwdriver.*

Materials: *Abrasive pad, replacement cylinder (if needed).*

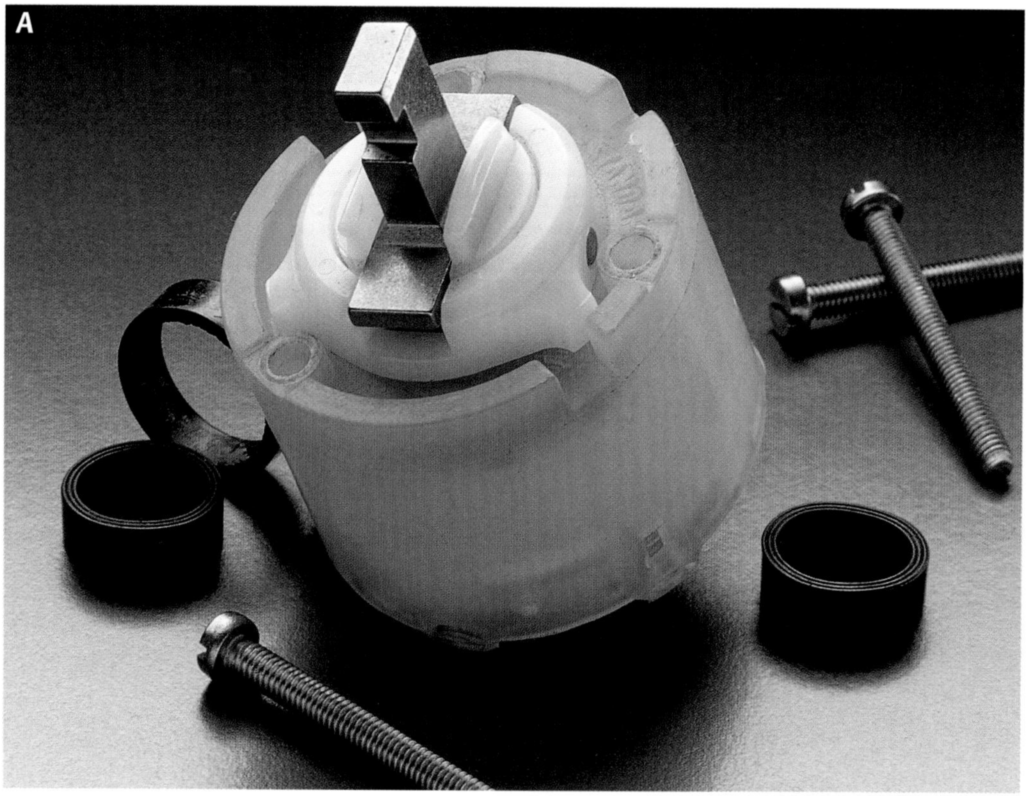

A replacement cylinder kit for a ceramic disc faucet includes all mounting screws and seals.

Fixing a Disc Faucet

Turn off the water at the shutoff valves or the main supply valve near the water meter. Rotate the faucet spout to the side, then raise the handle **(photo B).** Remove the setscrew and lift off the handle.

Remove the escutcheon cap **(photo C).** Remove the cylinder mounting screws and lift the cylinder out. Remove the neoprene seals from the cylinder openings **(photo D).** Be careful not to scratch the ceramic discs.

Clean the cylinder openings and the neoprene seals with an abrasive pad **(photo E).** Rinse the cylinder with clear water. If necessary, clean the inlet holes in the faucet body, using an abrasive pad. Return the seals to the cylinder openings, and reassemble the faucet **(photo F).**

Move the handle to the ON position, then open the shutoff valves very slowly. Once the water runs steadily, close the faucet.

If the faucet continues to leak after cleaning, install a new cylinder **(photo G).**

Helpful Hint

Be very careful when you turn the water back on after repairing a disc faucet. Ceramic discs can be cracked by air rushing through the faucet when the water is restored. After making repairs, place the handle in the ON position, and then very gradually open the shutoff valves. Don't turn the faucet off until the water runs steadily, without bursts of air.

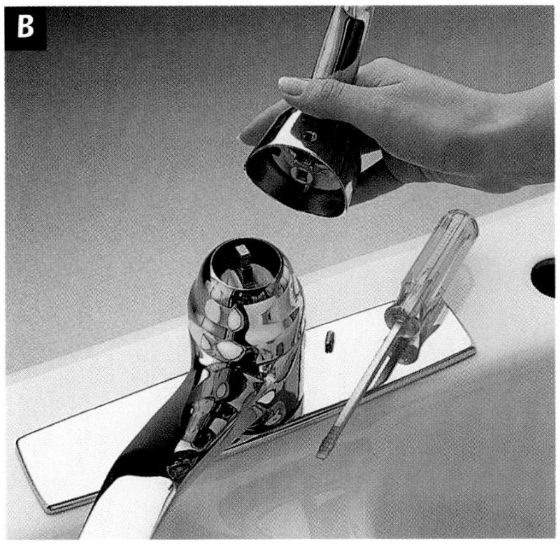

Remove the setscrew and lift off the handle.

Remove the escutcheon cap, mounting screws, and cylinder.

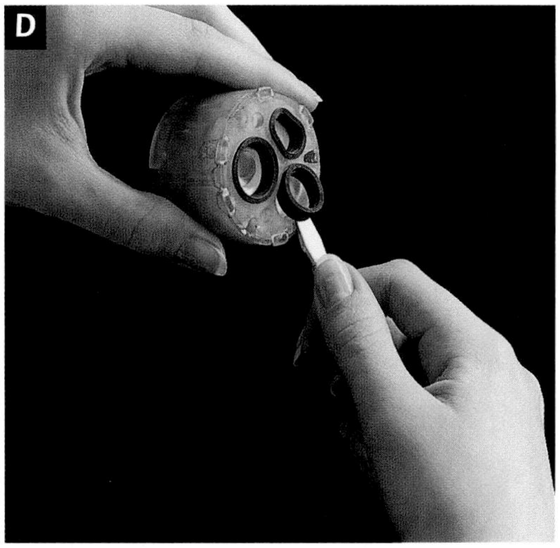

Remove and clean neoprene seals.

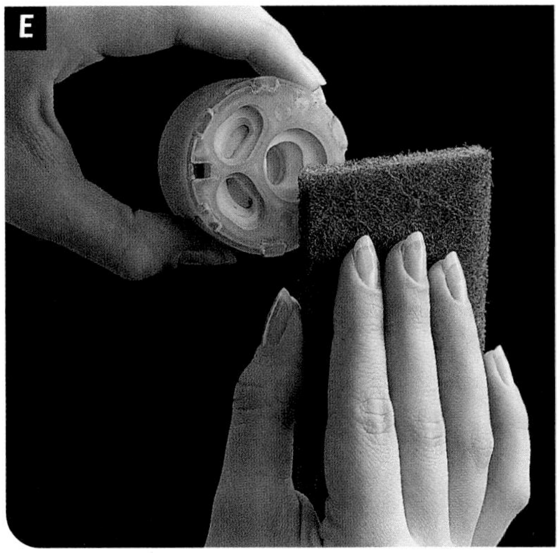

Clean the cylinder openings with an abrasive pad.

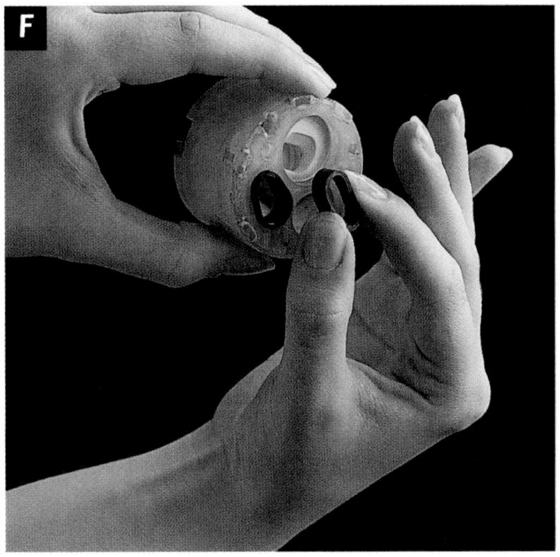

Return the seals to cylinder openings and reassemble faucet.

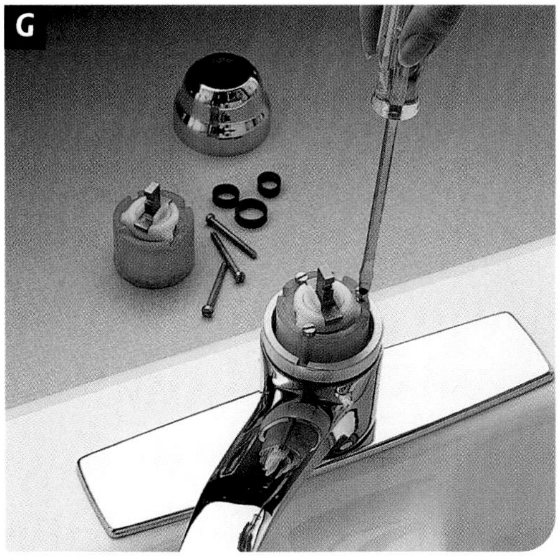

If the faucet continues to leak, replace the cylinder.

Compression Faucets

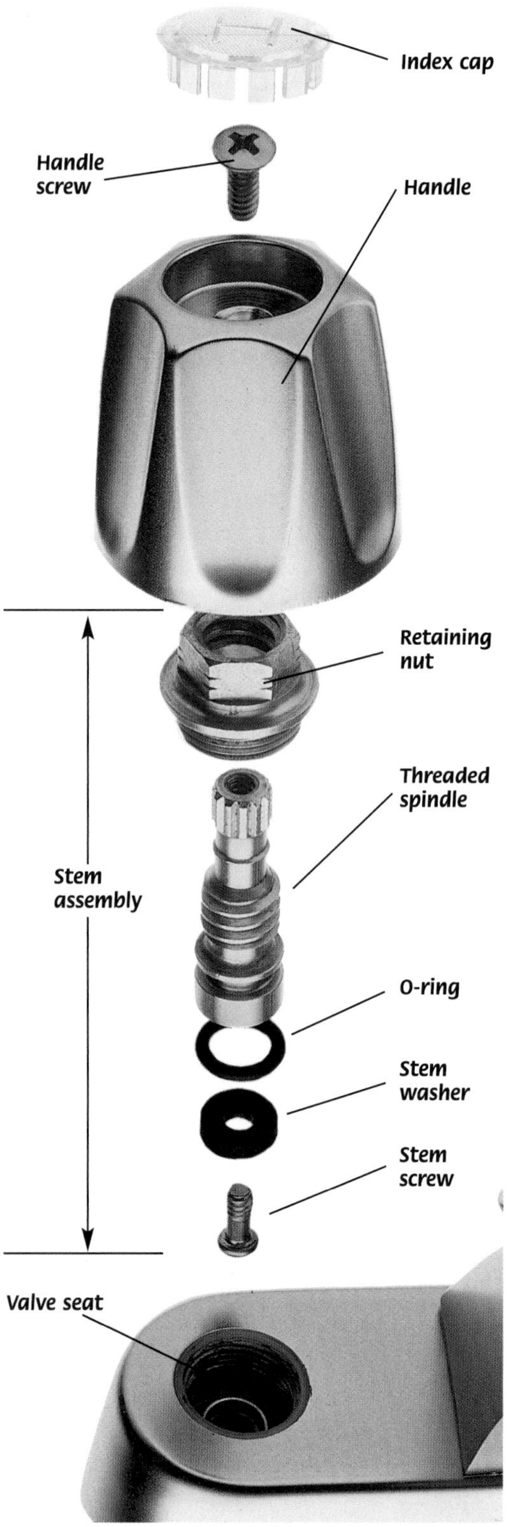

Compression faucets have separate handles for hot and cold water, and can be identified by a threaded stem assembly inside the faucet body. The stems come in many styles, but all styles use neoprene washers or seals to control the flow of water. The stem shown at left has a retaining nut, threaded spindle, O-ring, stem washer, and stem screw. Spout drips are usually caused by worn stem washers, and leaks around the handle typically are caused by worn O-rings.

When replacing washers, check the metal valve seats inside the faucet body. If they're rough, replace or resurface them (page 330).

Tools: *Screwdriver, handle puller (opt.), channel-type pliers, utility knife, seat wrench or seat dressing tool (if needed).*

Materials: *Universal washer kit, packing string, heatproof grease, replacement valve seats (if needed).*

A universal washer kit includes a variety of washers, O-rings, and screws.

Common Types of Compression Stems

Standard stem: brass stem screw holds neoprene washer to end of spindle. Replace worn washer and stem screws.

Tophat stem: snap-on neoprene diaphragm instead of a standard washer. Replace the diaphragm.

Reverse-pressure stem: beveled washer at end of spindle. Unscrew spindle to replace washer.

Fixing a Compression Faucet

Turn off the water at the shutoff valves or the main supply valve. Remove the index cap from the top of the handle and unfasten the screw.

Remove the handle by pulling straight up. If a handle won't pull free, clamp the side bars of a handle puller under the handle. Thread the puller into the faucet stem, and tighten until the handle comes free **(photo A).**

Unscrew the stem assembly from the body of the faucet, using channel-type pliers **(photo B).** Inspect the valve seat for wear and replace or resurface it, if necessary. If the faucet body or stems are badly worn, replace the entire faucet. Remove the brass stem screw from the stem **(photo C).** Remove the worn stem washer. Unscrew the threaded spindle from the retaining nut **(photo D).**

Cut off and replace the O-ring with an exact duplicate **(photo E).** If the faucet has packing string rather than an O-ring, wrap new packing string around the stem, just beneath the packing or retaining nut **(photo F).** Install a new washer and stem screw. Coat all parts with heatproof grease. Reassemble the faucet.

Helpful Hint

If your compression faucet is an older model, it will likely need frequent repairs. In this case, it's probably better to replace the faucet.

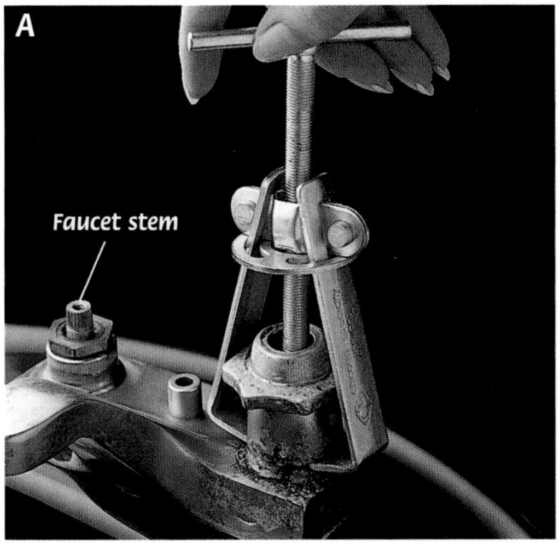

Use a handle puller to remove corroded handles.

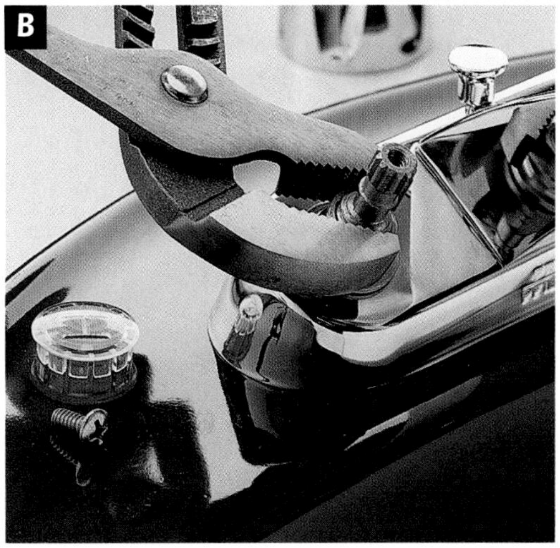

Unscrew the stem assembly and inspect valve seats for wear.

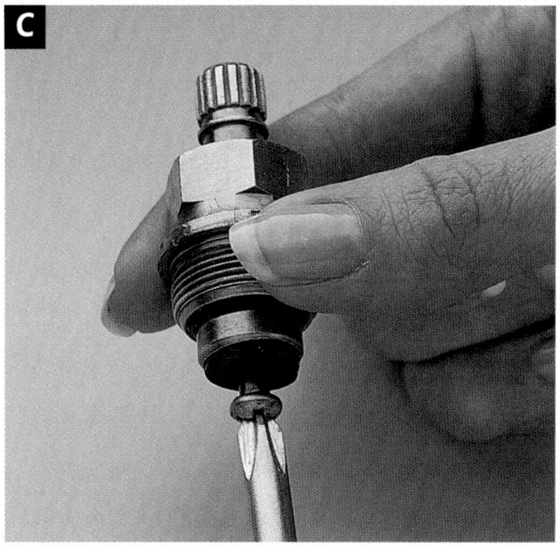

Remove brass stem screw and stem washer from assembly.

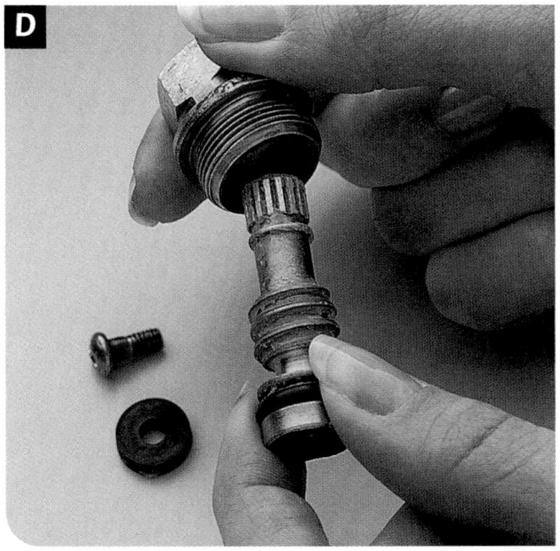

Unscrew the threaded spindle from the retaining nut.

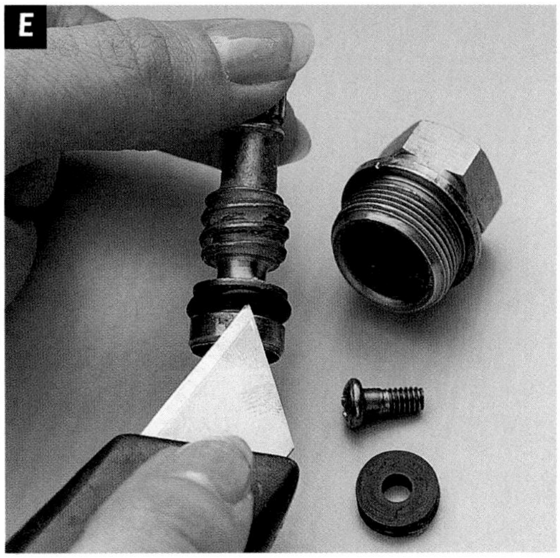

Cut off and replace the O-ring with the same kind.

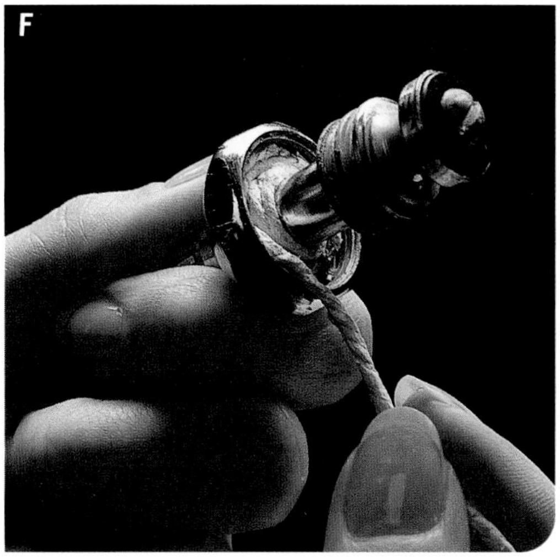

Install a new washer and packing string.

Replacing Compression Valve Seats

When fixing a compression faucet, check the valve seat for damage by running your fingertip around its rim **(photo A).** If the seat feels rough, replace it.

Remove the valve seat, using a seat wrench **(photo B).** Select the end of the wrench that fits the seat, and insert it into the faucet. Turn counterclockwise to remove the seat, then install an exact duplicate.

If the seat can't be removed, resurface it with a seat-dressing tool (reamer), as shown below.

Check the valve seat for damage or roughness.

Remove the valve seat and replace it with an exact duplicate.

Resurfacing Compression Valve Seats

To resurface the valve seat of a compression faucet, select a cutter that fits the inside diameter of the retaining nut **(photo C).** Slide the retaining nut over the threaded shaft of the seat-dressing tool, then attach the locknut and cutter head to the shaft.

Loosely screw the retaining nut into the faucet body **(photo D).** Press the tool down lightly and turn the tool handle clockwise for two or three rotations. Reassemble the faucet.

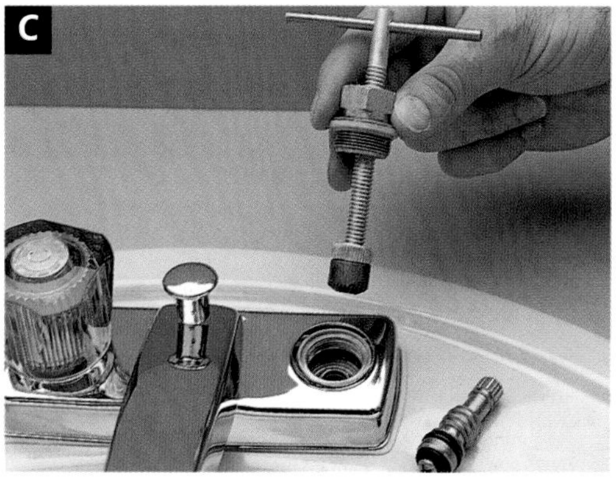

Attach a cutter head to the seat-dressing tool.

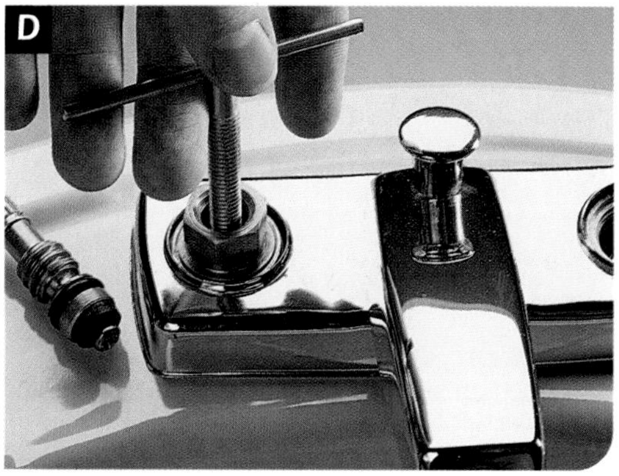

Turn the tool handle clockwise, two or three rotations.

Fixing Spout & Sprayer Pressure Problems

If the water pressure from a faucet spout seems low or blocked, it's usually because mineral buildup has filled the small holes in the aerator, a screw-on attachment with a small metal screen that mixes tiny air bubbles into the water flow. To fix the problem, take the aerator apart and clean it with a small brush dipped in vinegar **(photo E).**

If the water pressure from a sink sprayer seems low, or if water leaks from its handle, it's usually because mineral buildup is blocking the openings inside the sprayer head. Take the sprayer head apart and clean the parts in the same way. If cleaning doesn't help, the problem may be a faulty diverter valve (page 331).

If you have galvanized iron water pipes and the water pressure seems low throughout the house, the pipes may be corroded. Your best option is to replace them with copper pipes.

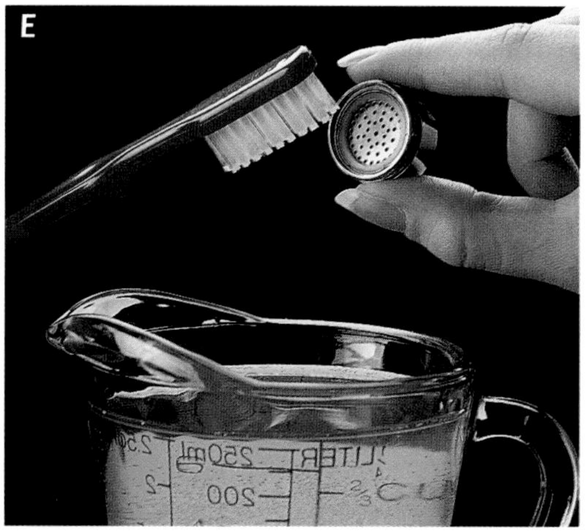

Cleaning aerators and sprayers may restore water pressure.

Fixing a Diverter Valve

The diverter valve inside the faucet body shifts, or diverts, the water flow from the faucet spout to the sprayer when you press the sprayer handle. If water pressure problems persist after cleaning the sprayer head, the answer may be to clean or replace the diverter valve.

Turn off the water at the shutoff valves or the main supply valve near the water meter. Remove the faucet handle and the spout **(photo F).**

Pull the diverter valve from the faucet body with needlenose pliers **(photo G).** Use a small brush dipped in vinegar to clean mineral buildup and debris from the valve.

Replace any worn O-rings or washers, if possible. Coat the new parts with heatproof grease **(photo H).** Reinstall the diverter valve and reassemble the faucet.

Remove the faucet handle and spout.

Remove and clean the diverter valve.

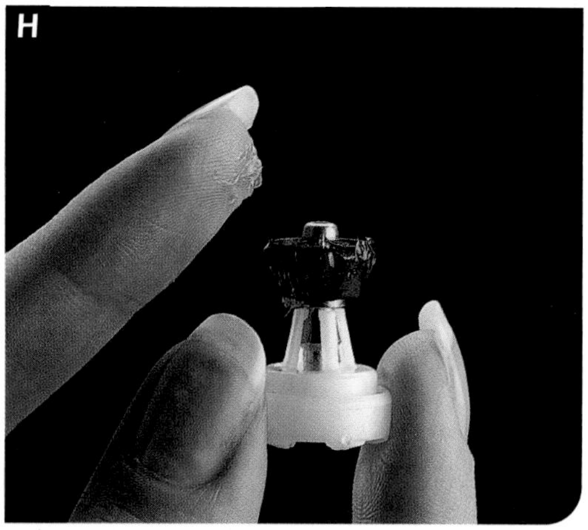

Replace O-rings and washers, then reinstall the diverter valve.

Replacing a Sprayer Hose

Turn off the water at the shutoff valves or the main supply valve near the water meter. Unscrew the hose from the sprayer nipple on the bottom of the faucet, using channel-type pliers **(photo I).** Pull the hose through the sink opening, then check it for kinks or cracks. If it's worn or damaged, replace it.

Unscrew the sprayer head from the handle mount **(photo J).** Remove the washer to expose the retaining clip. Remove the retaining clip with needlenose pliers, and slide off the handle mount from the end of the sprayer hose **(photo K).** Discard the old hose.

Attach the handle mount, retaining clip, washer, and sprayer head to the new hose. Attach the sprayer hose to the faucet sprayer nipple on the faucet.

Unscrew the hose from faucet sprayer nipple.

Remove sprayer head and washer from the handle mount.

Remove the retaining clip and the handle mount.

Replacing a Faucet

If a faucet requires constant repairs, or if nothing you do seems to permanently stop the drips or leaks, the time has come to replace it. You'll find that replacing a faucet is an easy project that takes about an hour. The first step is measuring the diameter of the sink openings and the distance between the centers of the openings **(photo A).** Choose a new faucet that matches the size and configuration of the sink openings.

When shopping for a new faucet, choose a model made by a reputable manufacturer. One advantage of purchasing a well-known brand is that replacement parts will be easier to find when you need them. Faucets with solid brass bodies are very durable and easy to install.

Install new supply tubes when replacing a faucet. Some faucets are sold without supply tubes, which means you need to purchase them separately **(photo B).** Supply tubes are available in braided steel or vinyl mesh and chromed copper. Other faucets are sold with preattached copper supply tubing ready to be connected with compression fittings directly to the shutoff valves **(photo C).**

If the sink's supply pipes don't have attached shutoff valves, install them before you install the faucet.

Tools: *Basin wrench or channel-type pliers, putty knife, caulk gun, adjustable wrenches.*

Materials: Penetrating oil, silicone caulk or plumber's putty, replacement faucet, two flexible supply tubes, shutoff valves (if needed).

A

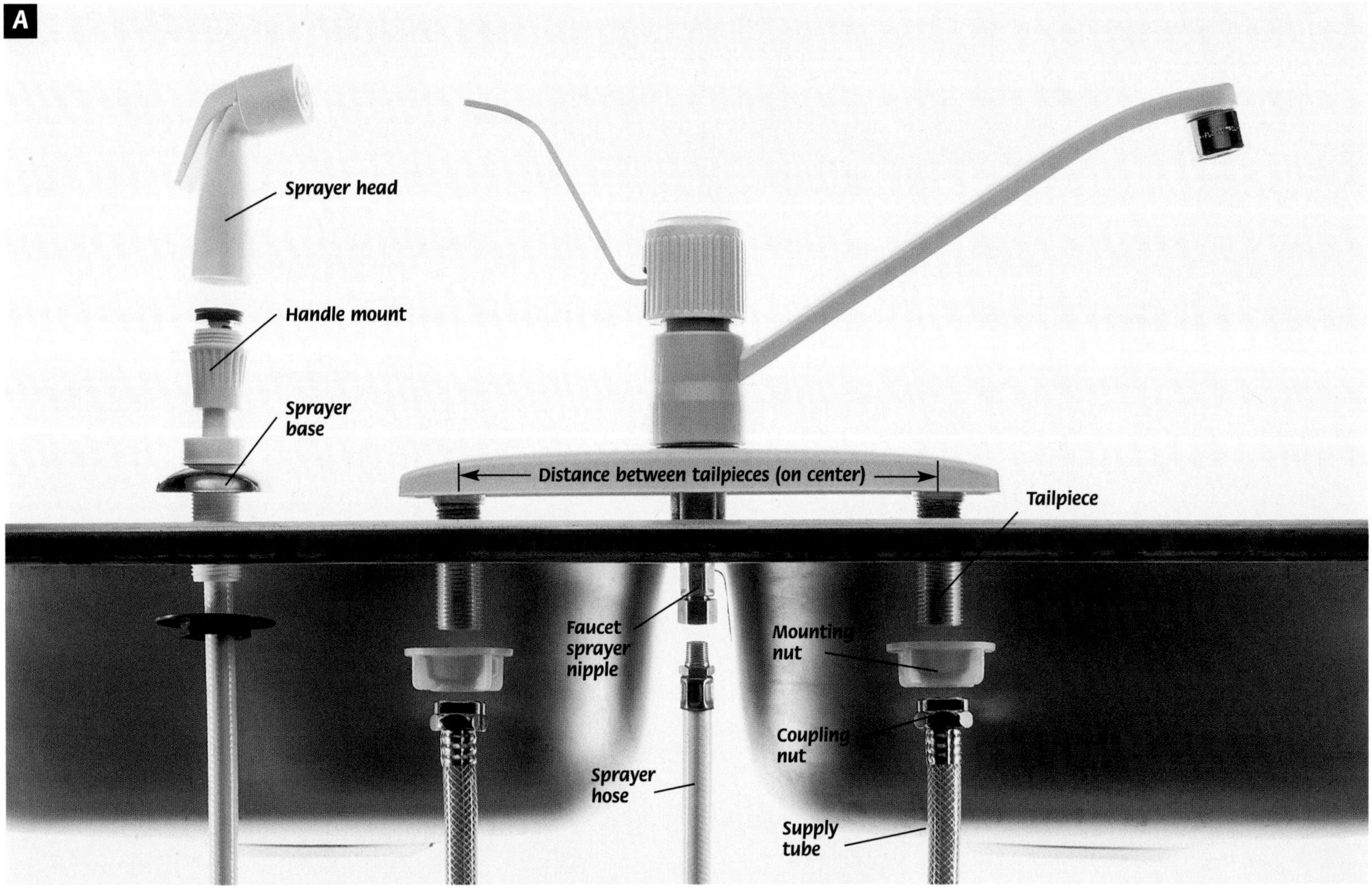

Before buying a replacement, study the configuration of the sink openings and measure the distance between tailpieces.

Faucet Hookup Variations

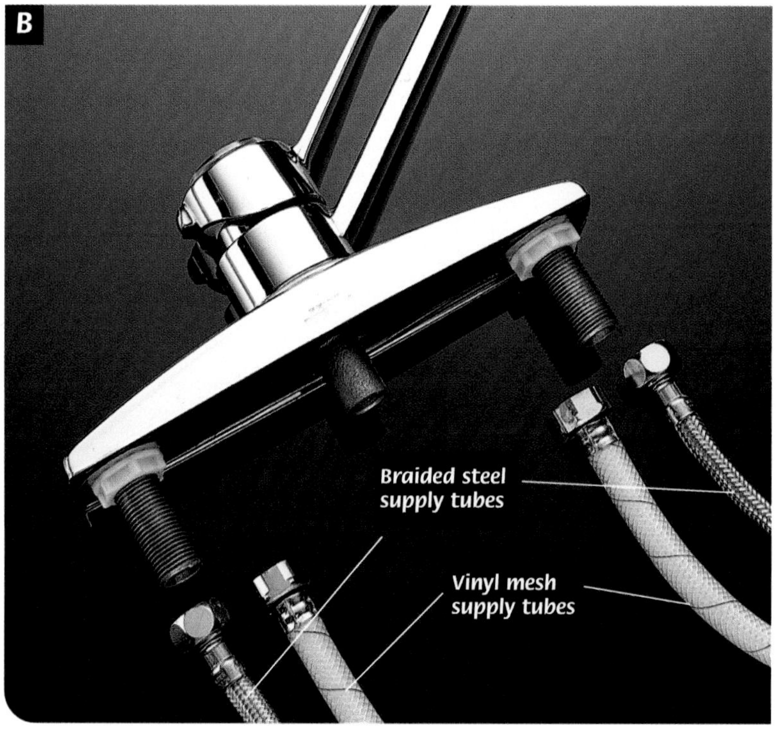

Some faucets require you to buy supply tubes.

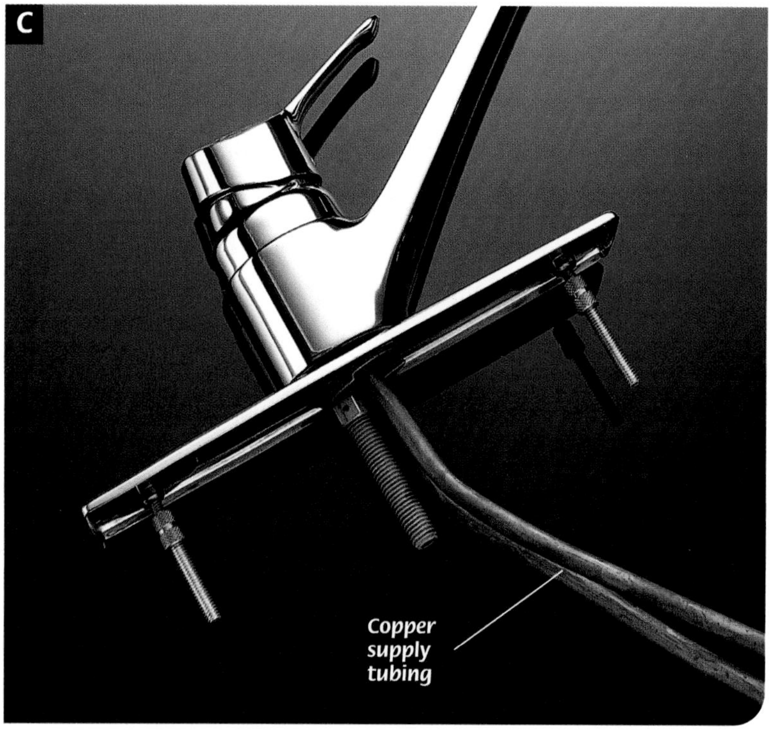

Other faucets come with preattached copper supply tubes.

Removing a Faucet

Turn off the water at the main shutoff, located near the water meter.

Spray penetrating oil on the tailpiece mounting nuts and supply tube coupling nuts **(photo D).** Wait 5 to 10 minutes, then remove the coupling nuts with a basin wrench or channel-type pliers.

Remove the tailpiece mounting nuts, using a basin wrench or channel-type pliers. The tailpiece mounting nuts often are located in small, tight spaces. It's not essential to have a basin wrench to loosen them, but the long handle of a basin wrench makes the job easier.

Pull the faucet from the sink openings **(photo E).** Use a putty knife to clean away the old putty from the surface of the sink.

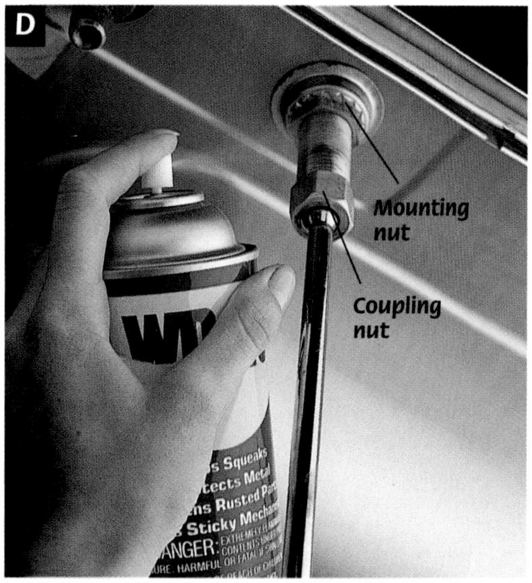

Spray penetrating oil on the supply tube coupling nuts and tailpiece mounting nuts. Remove nuts, using a basin wrench or channel-type pliers.

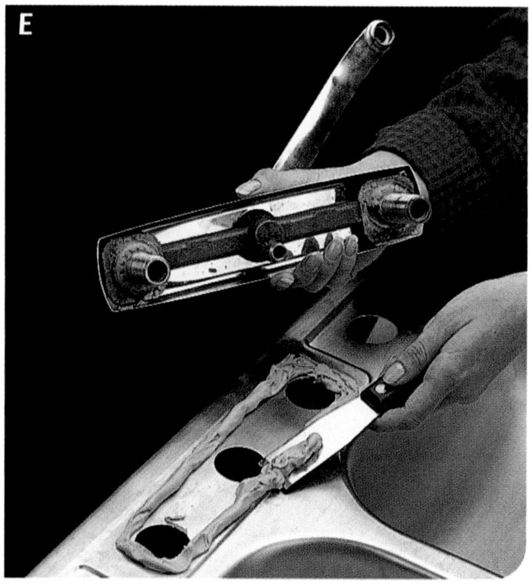

Remove the faucet and clean away the old putty from the sink, using a putty knife.

Installing a New Faucet

Apply a 1/4" bead of silicone caulk or plumber's putty around the base of the faucet **(photo A).** Insert the faucet tailpieces into the sink openings. Position the faucet so the base is parallel to the back of the sink, then press it down to make sure the caulk forms a good seal.

Screw the metal friction washers and the mounting nuts onto the tailpieces **(photo B)**, then tighten them with a basin wrench or channel-type pliers. Wipe away excess caulk from around the base of the faucet.

Connect the flexible supply tubes to the faucet tailpieces **(photo C).** Tighten the coupling nuts with a basin wrench or channel-type pliers.

Attach the supply tubes to the shutoff valves, using compression fittings (page 291). Hand-tighten the nuts, then use adjustable wrenches to tighten them another 1/4 turn **(photo D).**

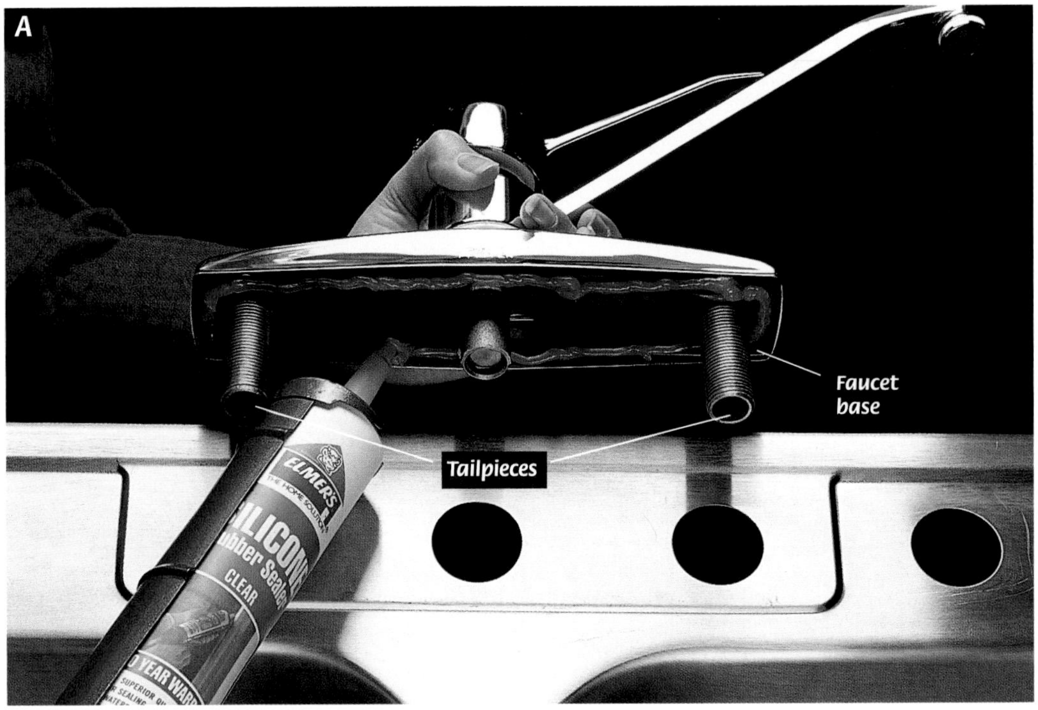

Line up the tailpieces with the sink opening, positioning the base so it's parallel to the back of the sink.

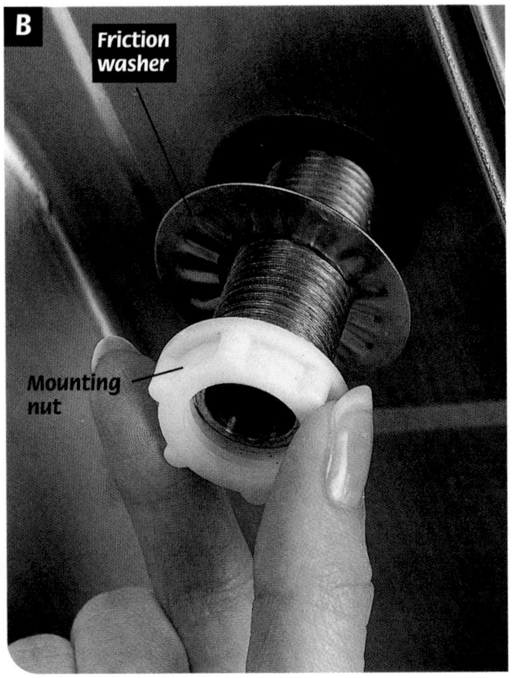

Install the metal friction washers and the mounting nuts onto the faucet tailpieces.

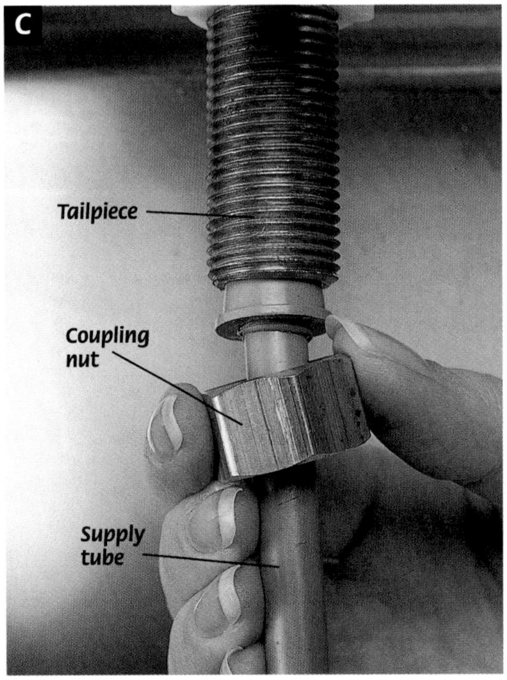

Connect the flexible supply tubes to the tailpieces and tighten the coupling nuts.

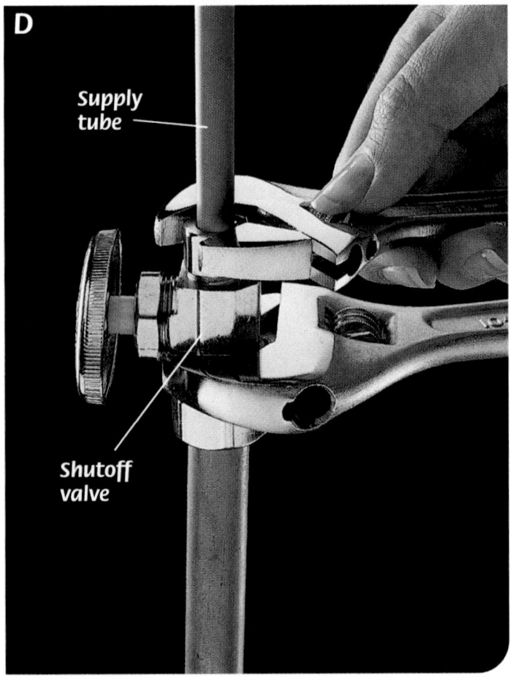

When tightening the compression fittings, hold the valve with one wrench while gently tightening with another.

Connecting a Faucet with Preattached Supply Tubing

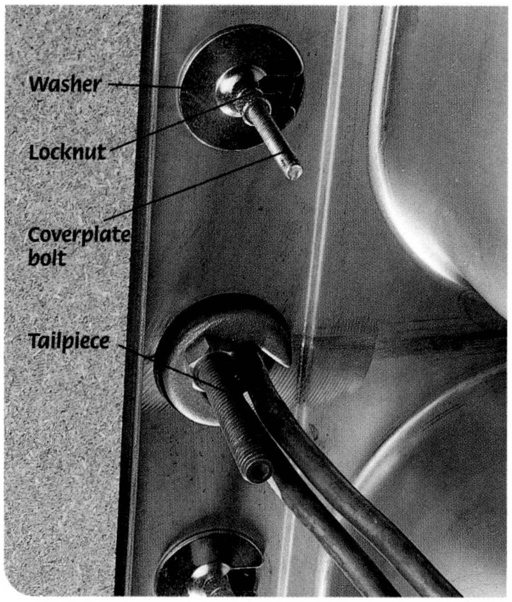

For a faucet with preattached supply tubing, apply caulk or plumber's putty and position the faucet as described on page 334. If the faucet has a decorative coverplate, screw its washers and locknuts onto the coverplate bolts.

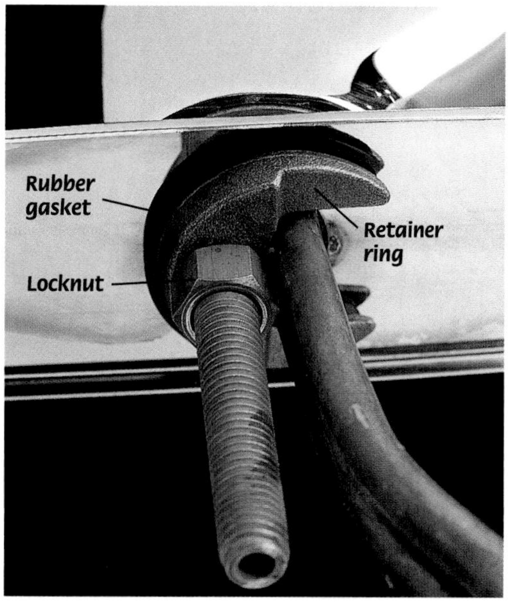

Attach the faucet to the sink by placing the rubber gasket, retainer ring, and locknut onto the threaded tailpiece. Tighten the locknut.

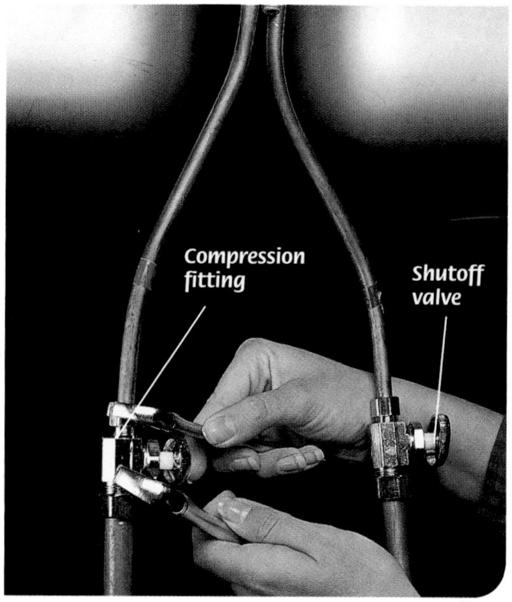

Connect the preattached supply tubing to the shutoff valves with compression fittings (page 291). Attach the red-coded tube to the hot water pipe and the blue-coded tube to the cold water pipe.

Attaching a Sink Sprayer

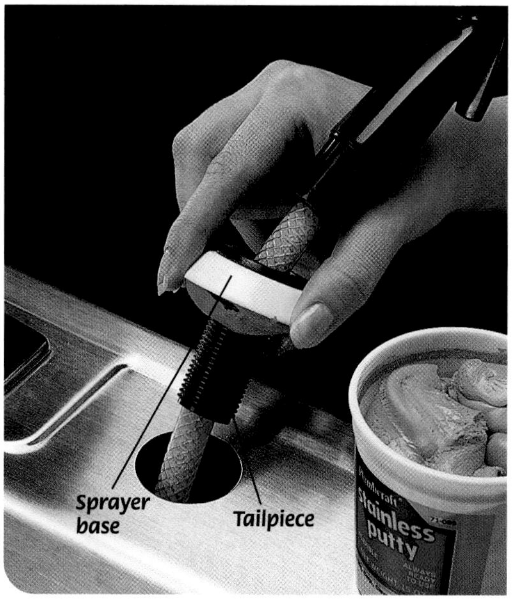

Apply a 1/4" bead of plumber's putty or silicone caulk to the bottom edge of the sprayer base. Insert the tailpiece of the sprayer base into the sink opening.

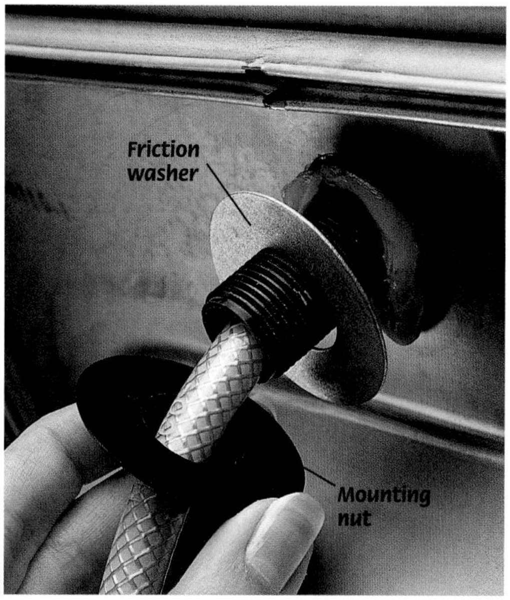

Place a friction washer over the tailpiece. Screw the mounting nut onto the tailpiece and tighten it with a basin wrench or channel-type pliers. Wipe away excess putty.

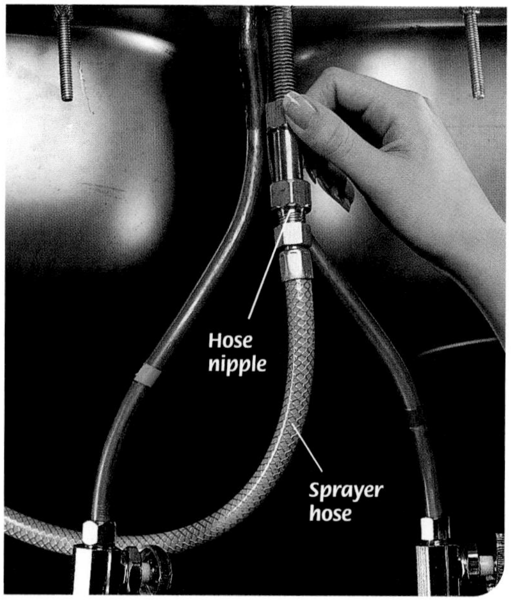

Screw the sprayer hose onto the hose nipple on the bottom of the faucet. Tighten 1/4 turn with a basin wrench or channel-type pliers.

Tubs, Showers & Whirlpools

Bathtubs are connected to the drain system via a drain-waste-overflow assembly. Risers with individual shutoff valves connect the faucets to the hot and cold water lines. Many bathtubs allow you to divert water from the tub to a showerhead with the flip of a lever.

A tub-shower is usually contained by a stall lined with ceramic tile or a prefabricated fiberglass shower surround and base. The "wet wall" that contains the shower supply pipes has a removable panel that provides access to the shutoff valves and connections.

Whirlpools are large bathtubs that pump water through jets in the body of the tub. The pumps create a massaging effect that can relieve stress and muscle pain. In addition to general tub repairs, a whirlpool may require specialized repairs to its jets and pumps.

Tub and shower faucets come in the same four basic designs as sink faucets, and the repair techniques are the same as described on pages 320 to 329. To identify the design, you may need to disassemble the faucet.

When a tub and shower are combined, the shower head and the tub spout share the same hot and cold water supply lines and handles. Combination faucets are available in three-handle, two-handle, or single-handle designs **(photos A to C).**

When tub-shower faucets and diverter valves are set inside wall cavities, removing them may require a deep-set ratchet wrench.

Single-handle tub and shower faucets feature a cartridge, ball-type, or disc valve design.

Two-handle tub and shower faucets use either a compression or cartridge valve design.

Three-handle tub and shower faucets have either a compression or cartridge valve design.

Fixing Single-handle Tub & Shower Faucets

A single-handle tub and shower faucet has one valve that controls both the water flow and the temperature. The water flow is directed to either the tub spout or the shower head by a gate diverter. Gate diverters seldom need repair, although occasionally the lever may break, come loose, or refuse to stay up. If a diverter fails, replace the tub spout (page 338).

Single-handle faucets may feature ball, cartridge, or disc designs. Use the repair techniques described on page 322 for ball faucets, and page 326 for disc faucets.

To repair a single-handle cartridge tub and shower faucet, start by using a screwdriver to remove the handle screw, then remove the handle and escutcheon **(photo D).**

Turn off the water supply. Some faucets have built-in shutoff valves **(photo E).** Or, you can shut off the water at standard shutoff valves attached to risers, or at the main shutoff valve near the water meter.

Unscrew and remove the retaining ring or bonnet nut, using an adjustable wrench **(photo F).**

Remove the cartridge assembly by grasping the end of the valve with channel-type pliers and pulling gently **(photo G).**

Flush the valve body with clean water to remove sediment. Replace any worn O-rings, reinstall the cartridge, and test the valve.

If the faucet still doesn't work correctly, disassemble it again and replace the cartridge.

Tools: *Screwdriver, adjustable wrench, channel-type pliers.*

Materials: *O-rings, replacement cartridge (if needed).*

Remove the handle and escutcheon, using a screwdriver.

Turn off the water supply at the shutoff valves.

Unscrew and remove the retaining ring or bonnet nut.

Remove the cartridge assembly.

Fixing Two-handle Tub & Shower Faucets

Tub and shower faucets with two handles may have either a cartridge or a compression design. Use the repair techniques described on page 324 for cartridge faucets, and page 328 for compression faucets.

Two-handle tub and shower faucets have one handle that controls hot water and one that controls cold water flowing into a mixing chamber and through the spout.

A gate diverter, a simple mechanism in the tub spout, directs the flow of water to either the tub spout or shower head.

Gate diverters seldom need repair, although occasionally the lever will break, come loose, or refuse to stay in the up position. If the diverter fails, replace the entire tub spout (below).

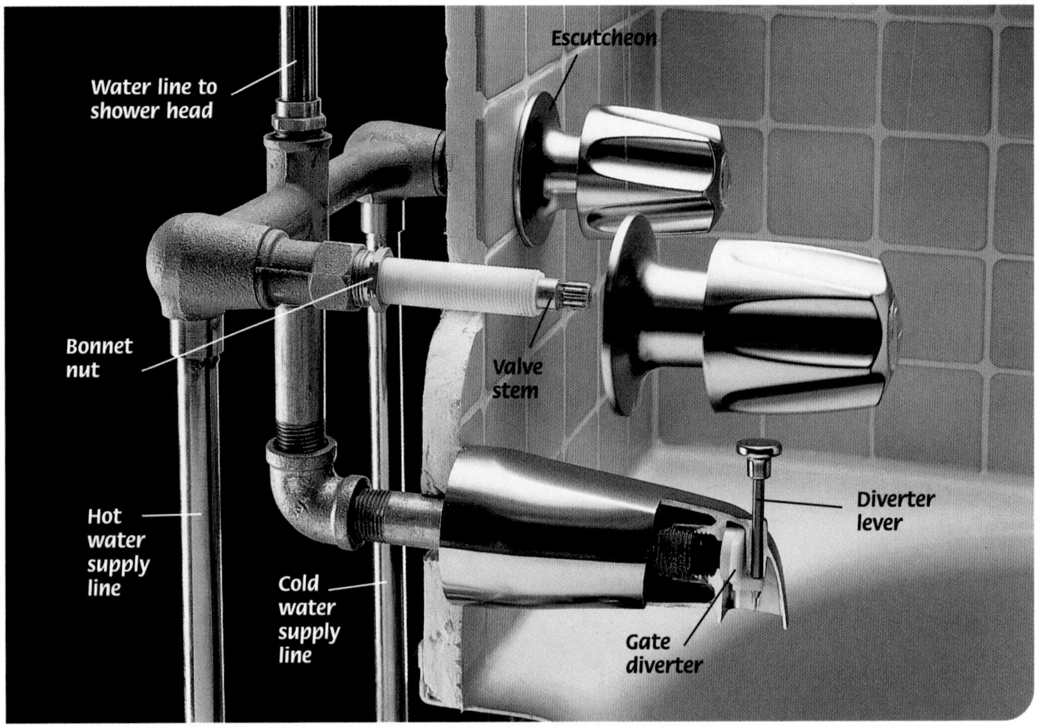

In two-handle tub and shower faucets, a gate diverter in the tub spout directs the water to the tub spout or the shower head.

Replacing a Tub Spout

Begin by removing the old spout. Check under the spout for a small access slot, which indicates that it's held in place by an Allen screw **(photo A).** If it has one, use an Allen wrench to remove the screw, then slide the spout off.

If there's no access slot, unscrew the spout itself **(photo B).** Use a pipe wrench, or insert a large screwdriver, hammer handle, or 2" dowel into the spout and turn counterclockwise. If you use a wrench, make sure to wrap the jaws with masking tape or fold a cloth around the spout to avoid scratching the finish.

Spread pipe joint compound on the threads of the spout nipple and attach the new spout.

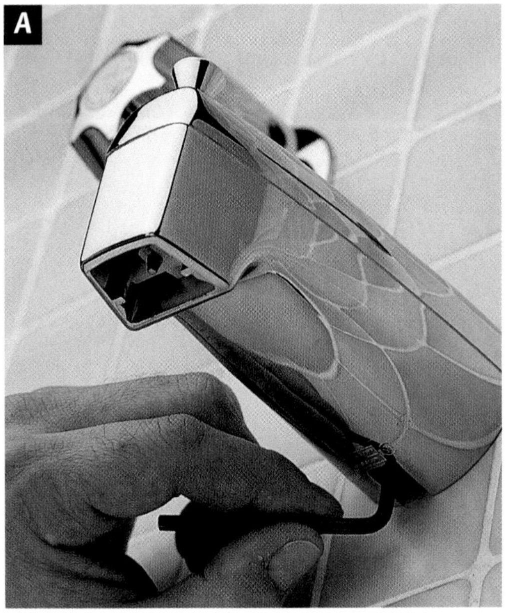

Some spouts are removed by loosening an Allen screw.

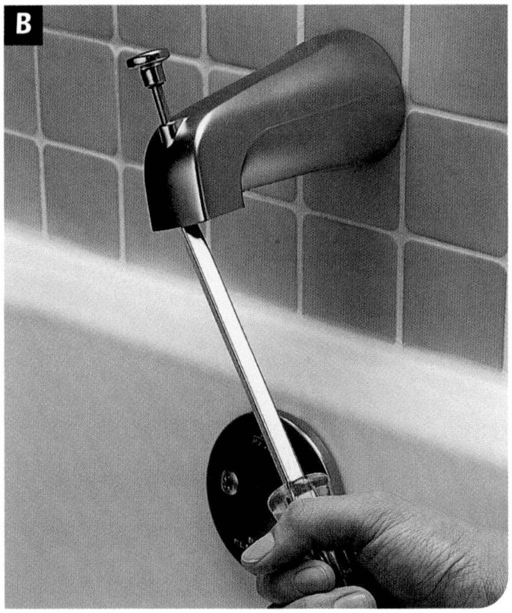

On other styles, unscrew the spout by rotating it counterclockwise.

Fixing Three-handle Tub & Shower Faucets

Three-handle tub and shower faucets have one handle for hot water, another for cold water, and a third handle for the diverter valve, which directs the flow of water to either the tub spout or the shower head.

As with sink faucets, separate hot and cold handles indicate that a tub-shower faucet uses either a cartridge or compression design. For repair techniques, see page 324 for a cartridge design and page 328 for a compression design.

If a diverter valve sticks, the water flow is weak, or the water comes out of the tub spout when it's supposed to come out of the shower head, the diverter needs to be repaired or replaced.

Most diverter valves are similar in design to compression or cartridge faucet valves. Compression-type diverters can be repaired, but defective cartridge types must be replaced.

Before starting to repair a compression-type diverter, turn off the water supply at the built-in shutoff valves or at the main shutoff valve near the water meter.

Remove the diverter valve handle with a screwdriver **(photo C)** and unscrew or pry off the escutcheon.

Remove the bonnet nut with an adjustable wrench or channel-type pliers **(photo D).**

Unscrew the stem assembly, using a deep-set ratchet wrench **(photo E).** If necessary, chip away any mortar surrounding the bonnet nut. Remove the brass stem screw **(photo F).**

continued on next page

Tools: *Screwdriver, adjustable wrench or channel-type pliers, deep-set ratchet wrench, small wire brush.*

Materials: *Replacement diverter cartridge or universal washer kit, heatproof grease, vinegar.*

Remove the diverter valve handle, then pry off or unscrew the escutcheon cap covering the diverter valve.

Remove the bonnet nut that secures the diverter valve, using an adjustable wrench or channel-type pliers. If the faucet is a cartridge-type, replace the cartridge.

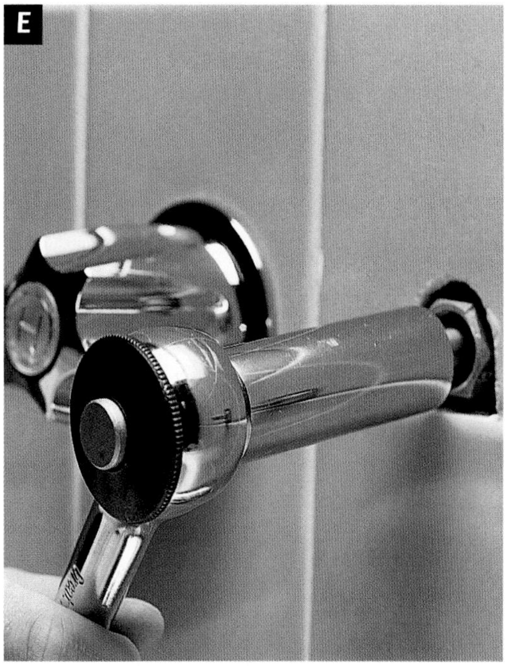

Unscrew the stem assembly if the faucet is a compression style, using a deep-set ratchet wrench.

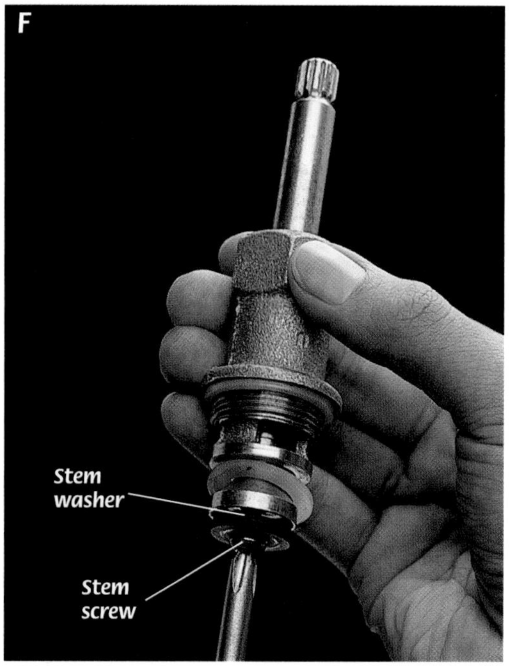

Remove the brass stem screw and replace the stem washer.

Fixing Three-handle Tub & Shower Faucets (cont.)

Replace the stem washer with an exact duplicate (page 329). If the stem screw appears worn, replace it as well.

Unscrew the threaded spindle from the retaining nut **(photo G).** Using a small wire brush dipped in vinegar, clean any sediment or buildup from the nut **(photo H).**

When the nut is clean and dry, coat all the parts with heatproof grease and reassemble the diverter valve. Reattach the escutcheon and handle.

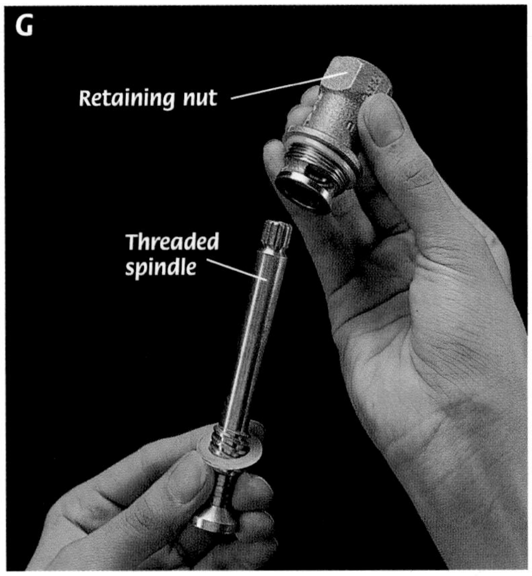

Unscrew the threaded spindle from the retaining nut.

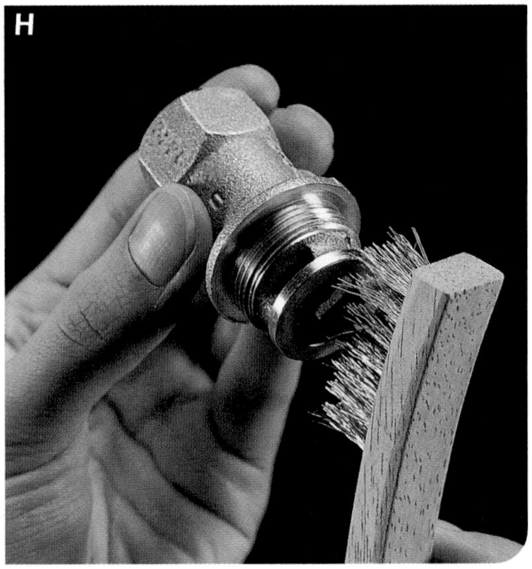

Clean sediment and mineral buildup from the nut, using a wire brush.

Removing a Deep-set Faucet Valve

The valves of some tub and shower faucets are set inside the wall cavity. Removing these valves requires a little finesse and a deep-set ratchet wrench.

First, remove the handle **(photo A).** Use channel-type pliers to unscrew the escutcheon. (Wrap masking tape around the jaws of the pliers so they don't scratch it.)

Working as gently as possible, use a ball peen hammer and a small cold chisel to chip away any mortar around the bonnet nut **(photo B).** Unscrew the bonnet nut with a deep-set ratchet wrench **(photo C).** Remove the bonnet nut and stem from the faucet body.

Tools: Channel-type pliers, ball peen hammer, small cold chisel, deep-set ratchet wrench.

Materials: Masking tape.

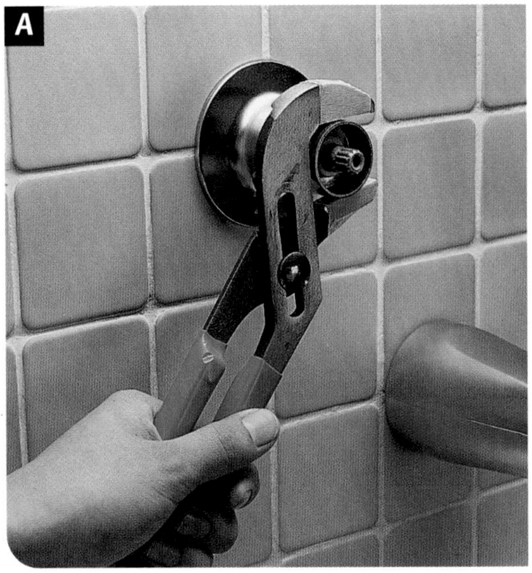

Remove the handle and unscrew the escutcheon.

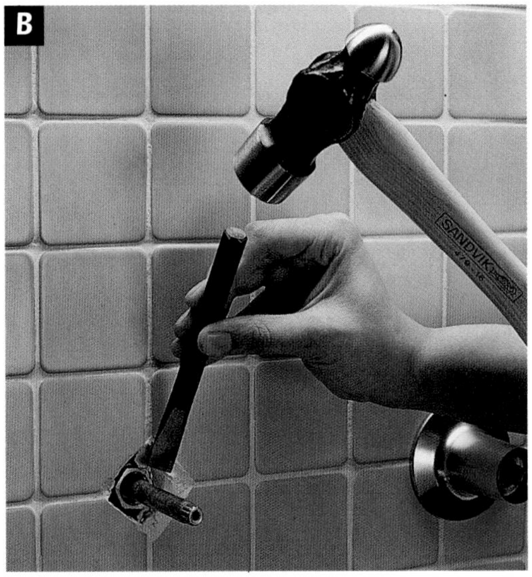

Chip away any mortar surrounding the bonnet nut.

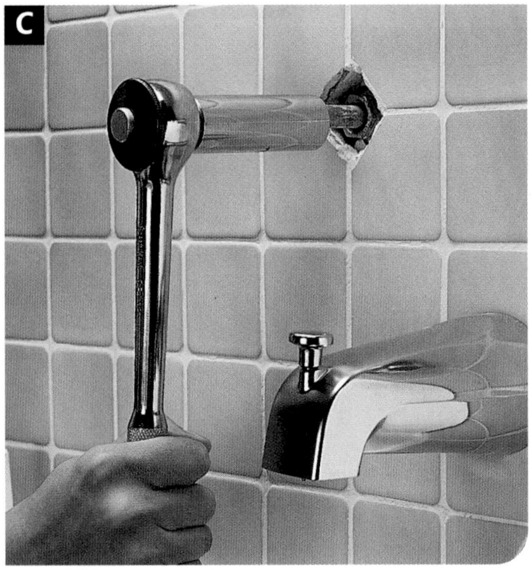

Use a ratchet wrench to unscrew the bonnet nut.

Cleaning & Repairing a Shower Head

The typical shower head is easy to disassemble for cleaning and repair. But before starting to repair a shower head, you need to turn off the water supply, either at the built-in shutoff valves or at the main shutoff valve located near the water meter.

Some shower heads, such as the one shown at right **(photo D),** include a spray adjustment cam lever that is used to change the force of the spray.

The most common problems with shower heads are clogged outlet holes or problems with the pivot head.

The outlet or inlet holes in the shower head tend to get clogged with mineral deposits, a problem indicated when the water from the shower head starts to spray off to the side.

Disassemble the shower head to clean it. Wrap the jaws of an adjustable wrench or channel-type pliers with masking tape, then use it to unscrew the swivel ball nut **(photo E).** Next, unscrew the collar nut. Clean the outlet and inlet holes of the shower head with a thin wire, such as a straightened paper clip **(photo F).** Flush the head with clean water.

Some shower heads have pivot heads designed to rotate into different positions. If a pivoting shower head won't stay in position, or if it leaks, check the O-ring that seals the pivot head against the swivel ball. If this O-ring is worn, replace it **(photo G).** Before installing the new O-ring, lubricate it with heatproof grease.

Tools: *Adjustable wrench or channel-type pliers.*

Materials: *Masking tape, thin wire (paper clip), heatproof grease, replacement O-rings (if needed).*

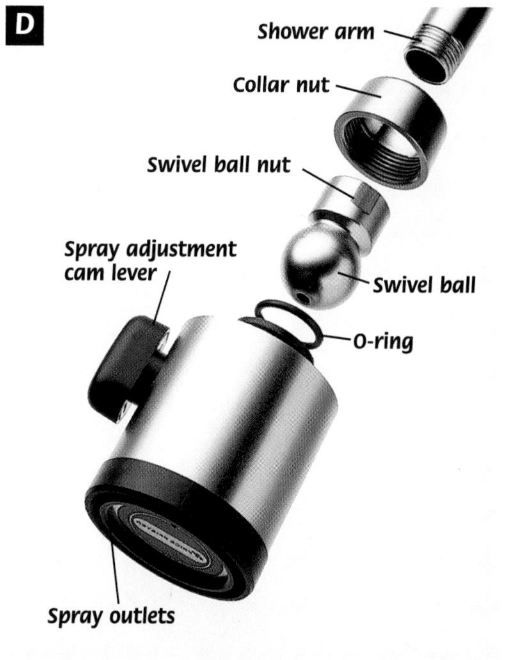

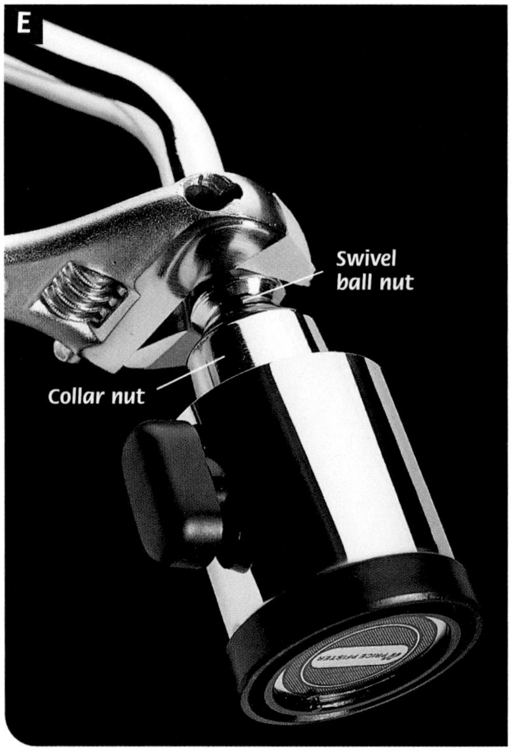

Unscrew the swivel ball nut, using an adjustable wrench or channel-type pliers. Then unscrew the collar nut.

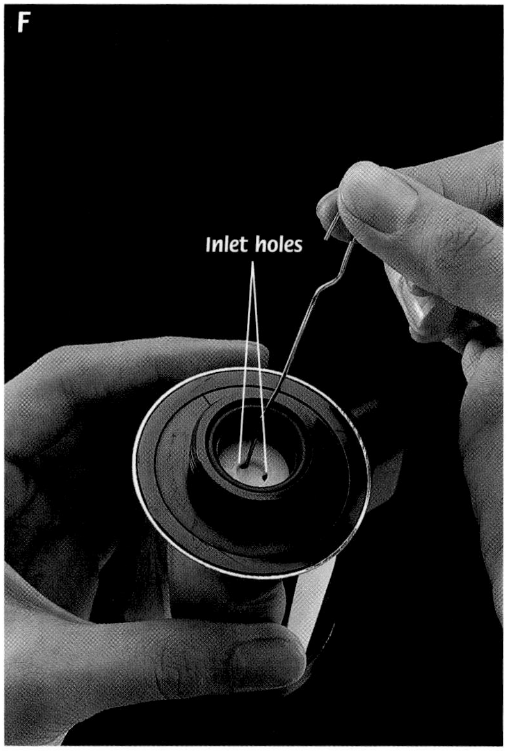

Clean the outlet and inlet holes of the shower head, then flush the head with clean water.

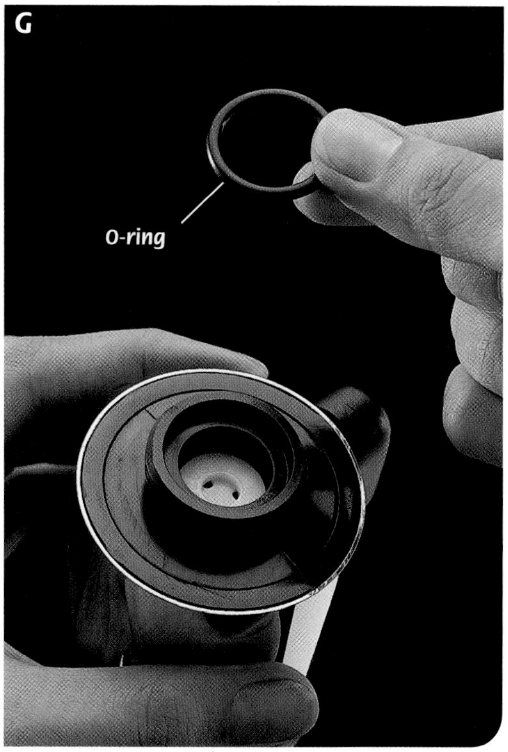

Check the O-ring, and replace it if it's worn. Before installing, lubricate the new O-ring with heatproof grease.

Maintaining & Fixing a Whirlpool Tub

The hot water and massaging jets of a whirlpool tub can be a great way to relieve stress and tension. However, this stress-reliever occasionally suffers stress of its own and needs repair. Most of the common problems associated with whirlpools are easy to repair.

Whirlpools are simply enhanced bathtubs. Air and water circulate through pump-powered jets to create a massaging effect. Some systems also have a timer and an in-line water heater to maintain the temperature.

The size and shape of whirlpools vary widely, from standard bathtub size to fixtures large enough to accommodate two bathers at a time. Cast iron, porcelain-enameled steel, gel-coated fiberglass, and fiberglass-backed acrylic are the most common materials used in whirlpools.

Since whirlpools are drained after each use, they don't require the water sanitation or pH level testing needed to maintain a hot tub.

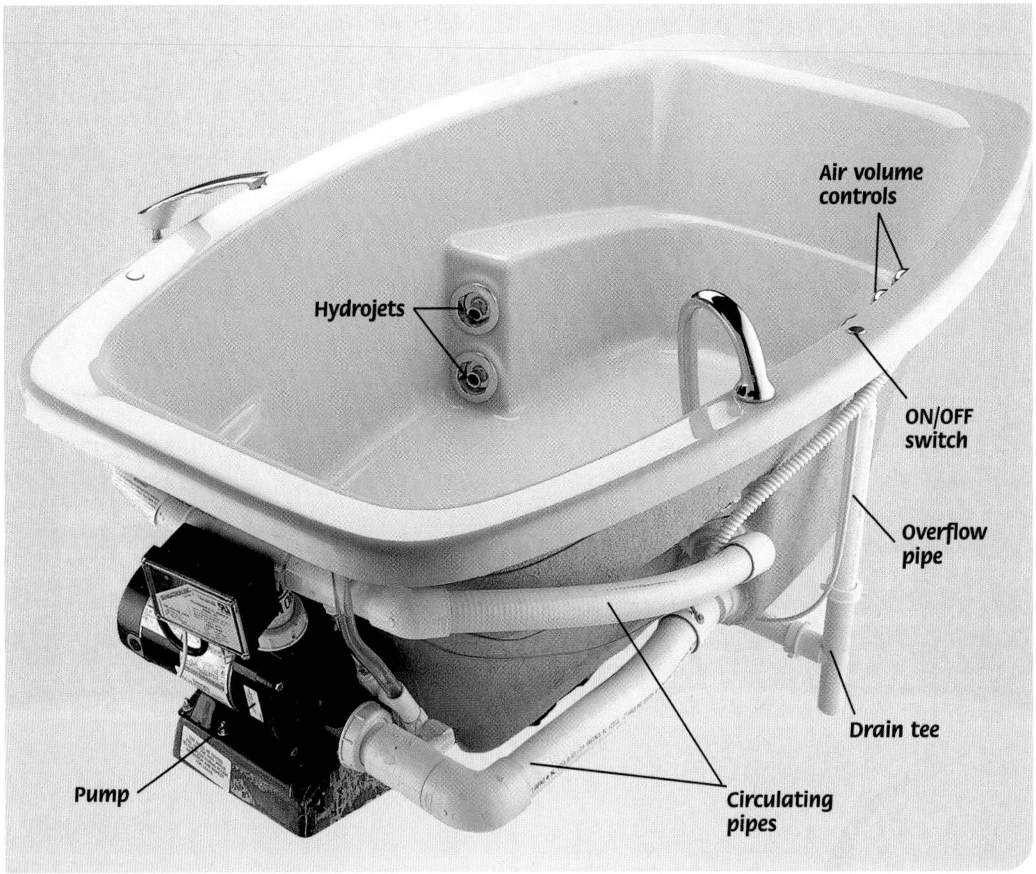

Cleaning a Whirlpool

Regular cleaning with water and a nonabrasive cleanser will prolong the life of your whirlpool by removing the soap residue, oils, and mineral deposits that remain after bathing.

Never clean a whirlpool with abrasive cleansers, which can mar the finish. Remove tough stains by dabbing rubbing alcohol or paint thinner onto the affected spots.

Never use liquid chemical drain openers to clear a whirlpool drain. They can damage both the pump and the tub surface.

Many systems should be flushed out monthly (check your owner's manual for specific recommendations). This procedure will clean out the hydrojets and the water lines.

To flush a whirlpool, fill the tub with warm water and add automatic dishwasher detergent. Use two tablespoons of liquid detergent or two teaspoons of dry crystals. Run the system for 10 to 20 minutes. Drain the water and rinse the whirlpool by filling the tub with cold water and running the pump for ten more minutes.

Some manufacturers recommend using 1/2 cup of bleach, instead of soap, on alternate monthly cleanings. Bleach will help to dry out and remove bacteria in the system.

You can polish and protect the whirlpool's finish by cleaning the surface with a mild detergent and applying a car wax, or other product recommended by the manufacturer **(photo A)**. To remove minor scratches, apply a rubbing compound before waxing.

Clean the tub surface to remove scuffs and soap deposits, then apply a car wax and buff to restore the original shine.

Servicing a Whirlpool Pump

Excessive noise or problems with water circulation indicate that a whirlpool pump is malfunctioning.

Make sure that all the hydrojet nozzles are directed away from the intake screens. An improperly aimed hydrojet can hinder the system's operation by sending air into the pump.

Remove each intake screen and clean it with a mild detergent **(photo B).** Some models are equipped with an intake filter installed behind the intake screen. Check the manufacturer's instructions for directions on removing and cleaning the intake filter. Reinstall the filter (if equipped), then reattach the intake screen.

Make sure that all of the pipe connections to the pump are tight. Tighten the connections by hand **(photo C);** overtightening them will break the seals. You should be able to reach most of the connections with little difficulty.

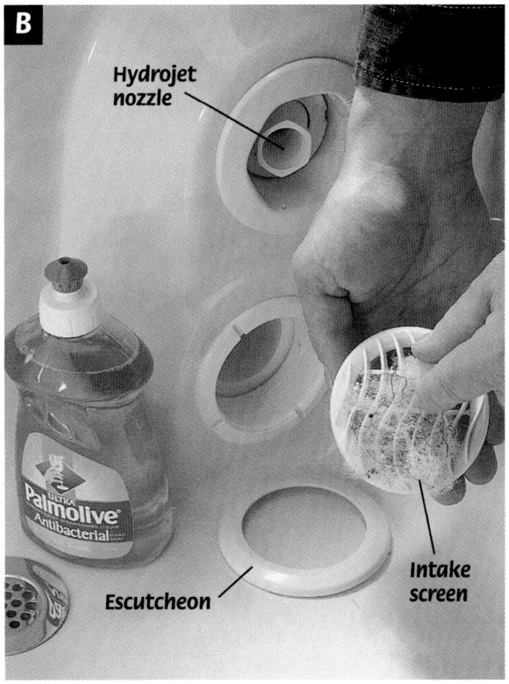

Clean the intake screen with mild detergent and water.

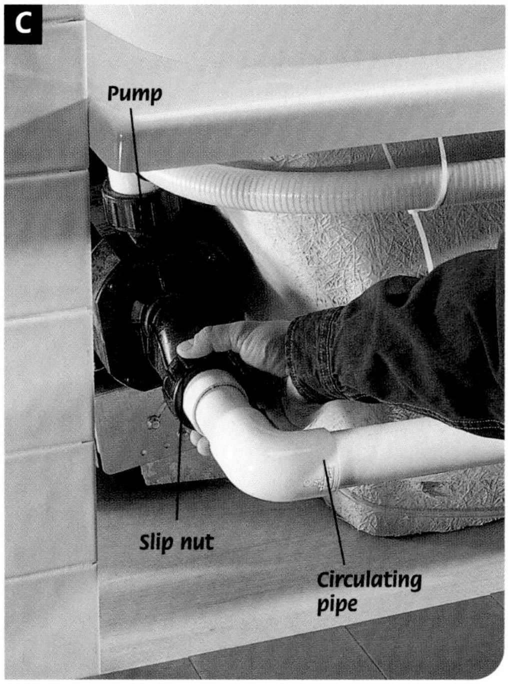

Tighten the slip nut by hand.

Cleaning Whirlpool Hydrojets

If one of the hydrojets on the whirlpool isn't blowing, it's probably blocked with hair, soap scum, and oils, any of which can build up and restrict the passage of water through the hydrojet nozzles.

To unblock a hydrojet nozzle, unscrew it by hand until it's completely removed from the whirlpool wall **(photo D).**

Remove any debris lodged in the jet body. Clean the jet, using a mild detergent and a cloth or a soft brush.

Lubricate the O-rings with heatproof grease.

Reinstall the hydrojet, and point the nozzle in the desired direction. Be sure to position the jet so the stream is directed away from the intake screen.

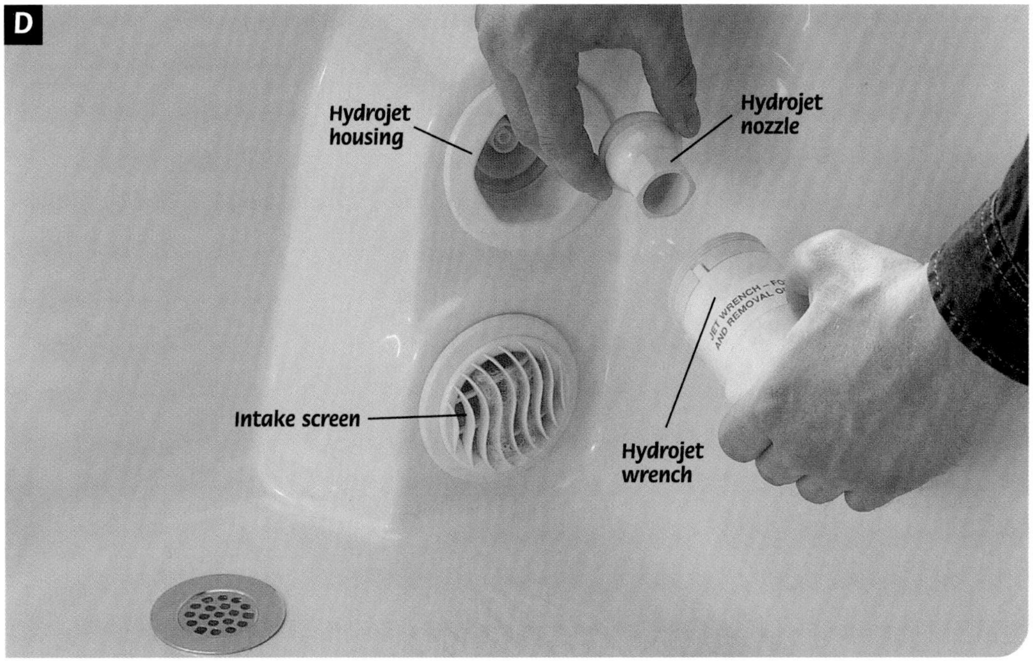

Unscrew the hydrojet, then clean and reinstall it with the nozzle pointing away from the intake screen.

Toilets

A standard toilet is a simple device, and only minor adjustments are needed to resolve most common problems.

The first step in toilet repair is recognizing the parts and knowing how they work together.

When you push the *handle*, the *lift chain* or *lift wire* raises a rubber seal, which is called either a *flapper* or a *tank ball*. Water in the tank rushes down through the *flush valve* opening, in the bottom of the tank, into the *toilet bowl*.

Waste water in the bowl is forced through the *trap* into the *main drain*.

When the toilet tank is empty, the flapper seals the tank, and a water supply valve, called a *ballcock*, refills the toilet tank. The ballcock is controlled by a *float ball* that rides on the surface of the water.

When the tank is full, the float ball automatically shuts off the ballcock.

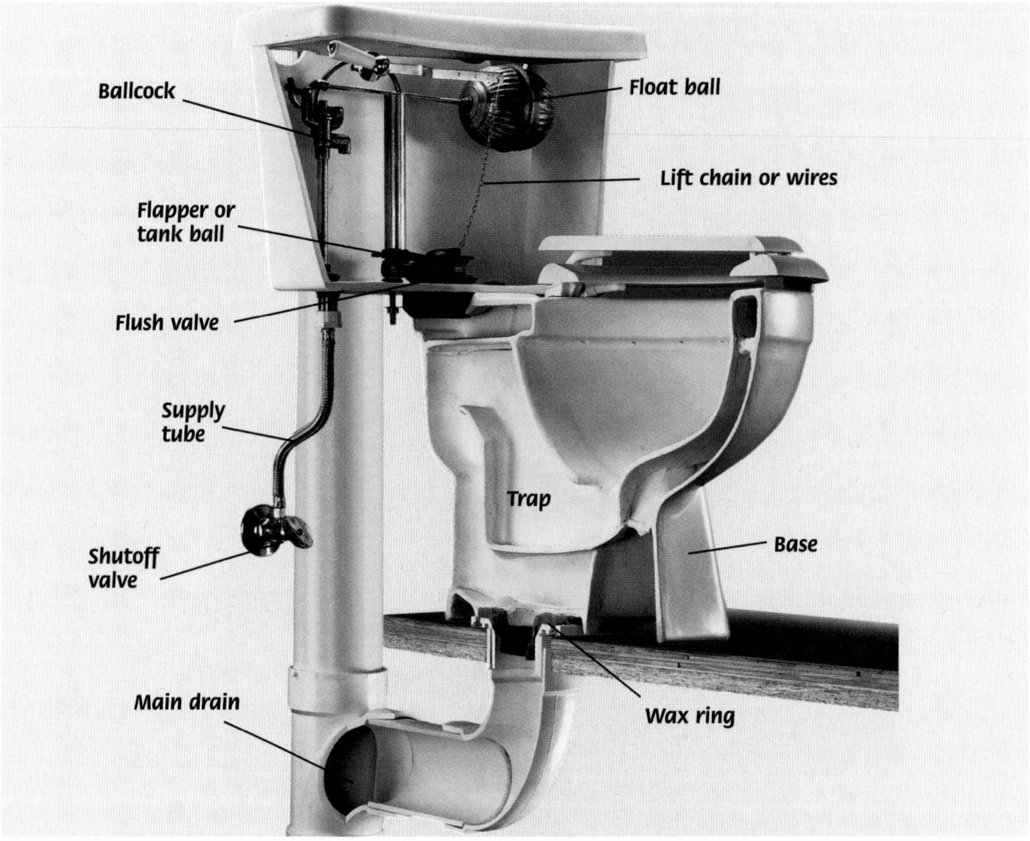

Toilet Problems & Repairs

Problems	Repairs
Toilet handle sticks, or is hard to push.	1. Adjust lift wires (page 345). 2. Clean & adjust handle (page 345).
Handle is loose.	1. Adjust handle (page 345). 2. Reattach lift chain or lift wires to lever (page 345).
Toilet will not flush at all.	1. Make sure water is turned on. 2. Adjust lift chain or lift wires (page 345).
Toilet overflows, or flushes sluggishly.	1. Clear clogged toilet (page 313). 2. Clear clogged main waste and vent stack (page 304).
Toilet runs continuously.	1. Adjust lift wires or lift chain (page 345). 2. Replace leaky float ball (page 346). 3. Adjust water level in tank (page 346). 4. Adjust & clean flush valve (page 349). 5. Replace flush valve (page 349). 6. Repair or replace ballcock (page 348).
Water on floor around toilet.	1. Tighten tank bolts and water connections (page 350). 2. Insulate tank to prevent condensation (page 350). 3. Replace wax ring (page 351). 4. Replace cracked tank or bowl (page 352).

Repairing a Running Toilet

If the sound of running water continues after you have adjusted the float ball and the lift wires, check the overflow pipe.

If water is flowing into the overflow pipe, adjust the ballcock to lower the water level in the tank (page 346). If the problem persists, repair or replace the ballcock (page 348).

If water is not flowing into the overflow pipe, check the tank ball or flapper for wear, and replace it, if necessary. If the problem persists, replace the flush valve (page 349).

Tools: *Small wire brush, screwdrivers, adjustable wrench, channel-type pliers, spud wrench, utility knife, ratchet wrench, sponge, putty knife.*

Materials: *Vinegar, emery paper, replacement washers and O-rings, replacement toilet parts, tank liner kit, wax ring, spud washer.*

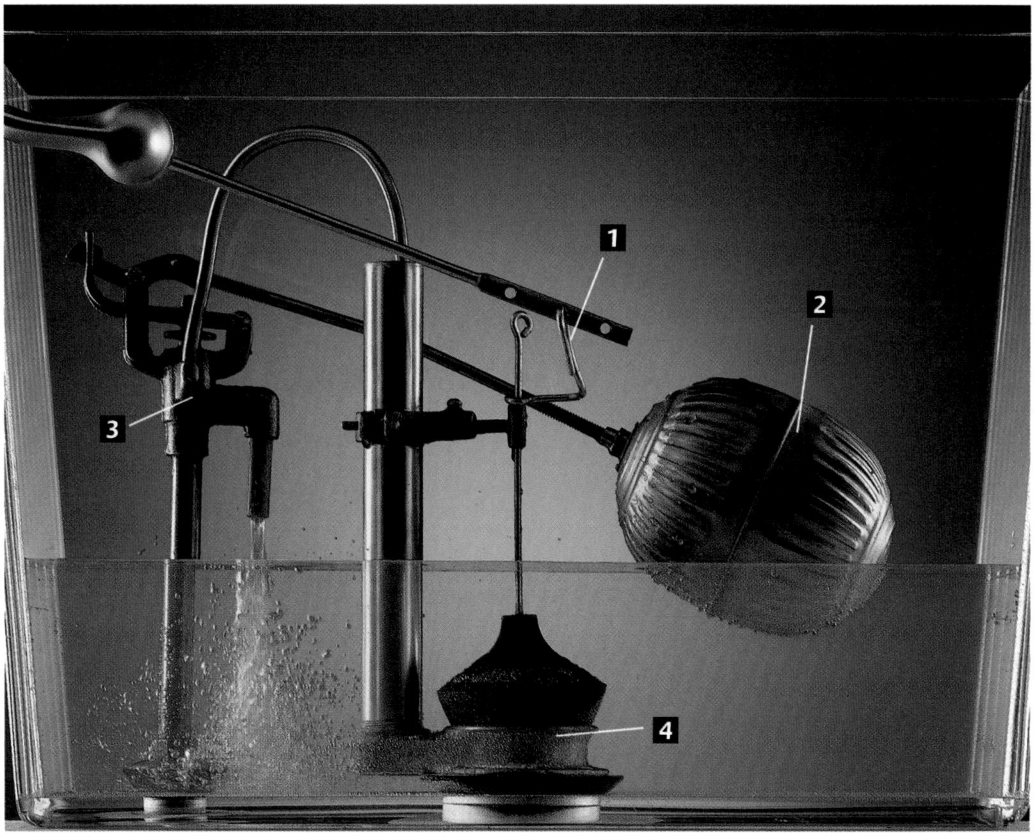

If a toilet runs continuously, check out possible causes in this order: Is the lift chain or lift wire (1) bent or kinked? Is the float ball (2) rubbing against the side of the tank or leaking? Is a faulty ballcock (3) failing to shut off the flow of fresh water after the bowl fills? Is the flush valve (4) allowing water to leak down into the toilet bowl?

Adjusting a Handle & the Lift Chain or Wires

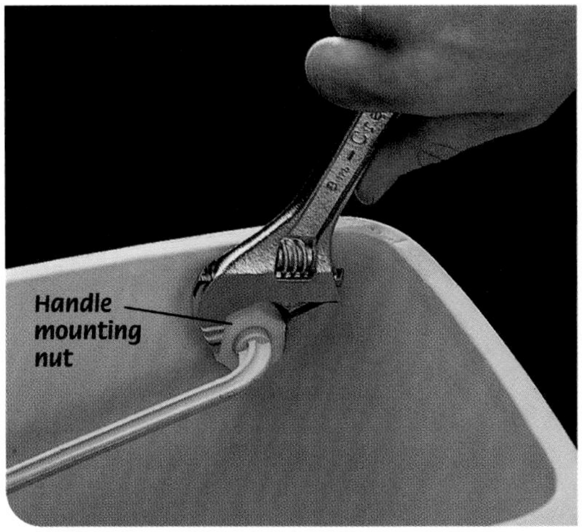

If a handle sticks, clean its mounting nut, which has reversed threads. Loosen it by turning clockwise. Remove lime buildup by scrubbing the parts with a brush dipped in vinegar.

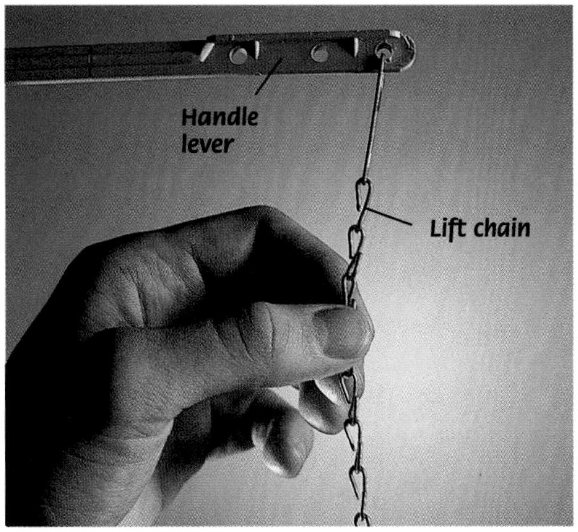

If a toilet won't flush or doesn't flush completely, the lift chain may have too much slack or may be broken. Replace it or adjust it so it hangs straight with about 1/2" of slack.

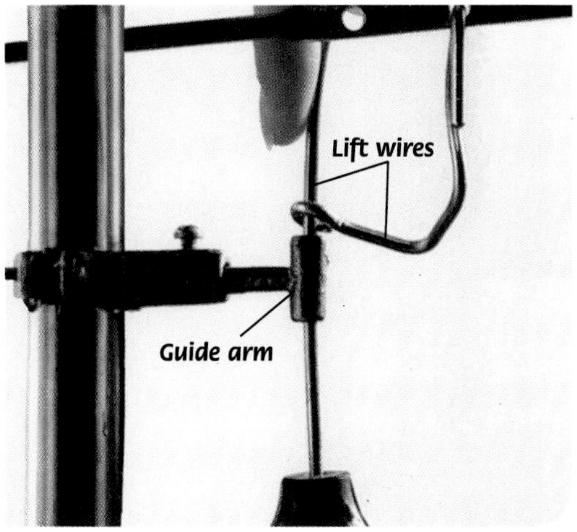

On toilets with lift wires instead of chains, a bent lift wire can cause the handle to stick. Straighten the wires so they operate smoothly.

Fixing a Leaky Tank Ball or Flapper

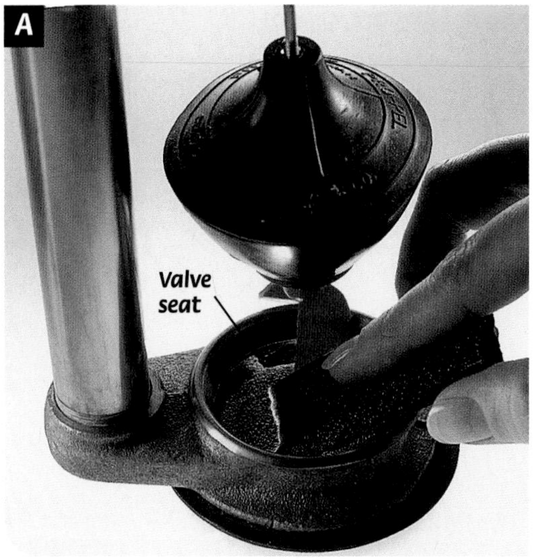

Turn off the water supply and flush the toilet to empty the tank. Lift the tank ball or unhook the flapper. Gently scrub the inside of the valve seat and rim, using emery paper.

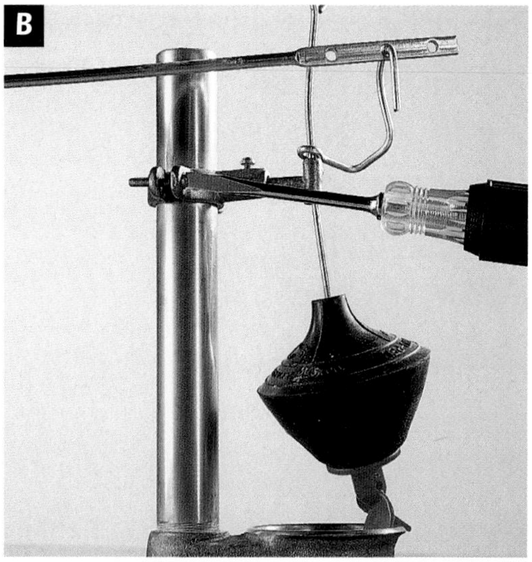

Line up the tank ball. Loosen the screws holding the guide arm, and position the arm directly over the valve seat. If the flapper or tank ball is soft or cracked, replace it.

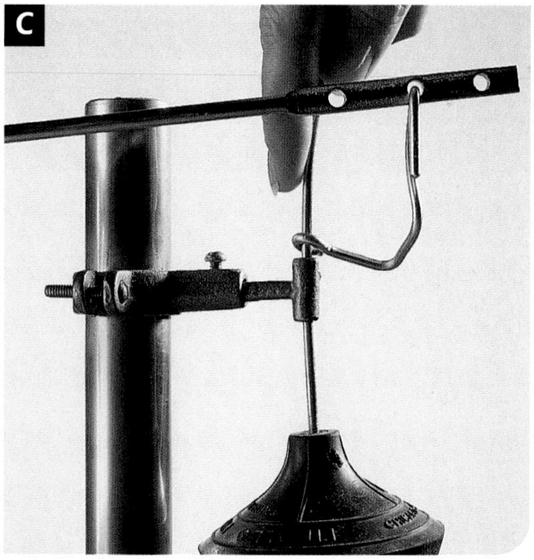

Straighten the vertical lift wire on the tank ball assembly. The ball should rise and fall smoothly when you trip the lever. Turn on the water, let the tank refill, and test by flushing.

Adjusting a Ballcock

Adjusting the ballcock allows you to raise or lower the water level in the tank. There are four ballcock styles and adjustment methods.

A *traditional plunger-valve ballcock* controls the flow of water with a brass plunger attached to the float arm and ball **(photo D).** To raise the water level, bend the float arm up. To lower it, bend the float arm down slightly.

A *diaphragm ballcock* is usually made of plastic and has a wide bonnet with a rubber diaphragm **(photo E).** To raise the water level, bend the float arm up. To lower it, bend the float arm down slightly.

A *float cup ballcock* is also made of plastic and is easy to adjust **(photo F).** To raise the water level, pinch the spring clip on the pull rod, and move the float cup upward on the ballcock shank. To lower the water level, move the cup downward.

A *floatless ballcock* controls the water level with a pressure-sensing device **(photo G).** To raise the water level, turn the adjustment screw clockwise, 1/2 turn at a time. To lower it, turn the screw counterclockwise.

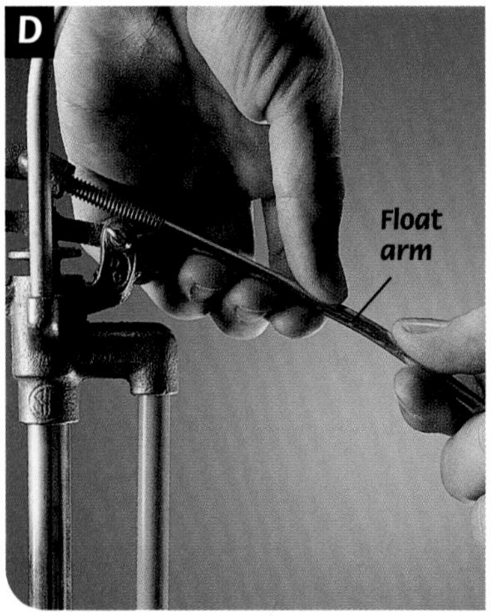

Adjusting a plunger-valve ballcock.

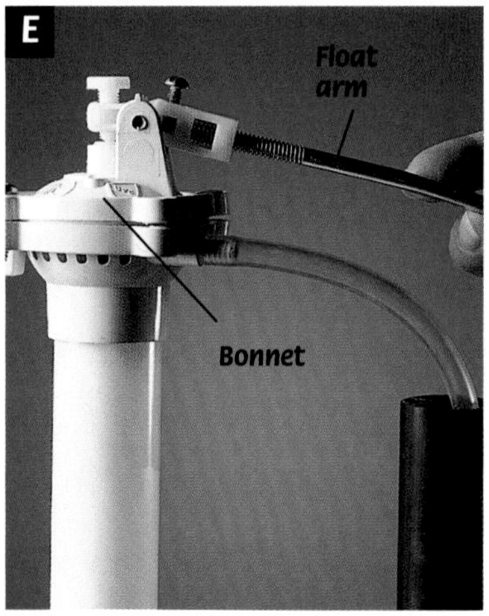

Adjusting a diaphragm ballcock.

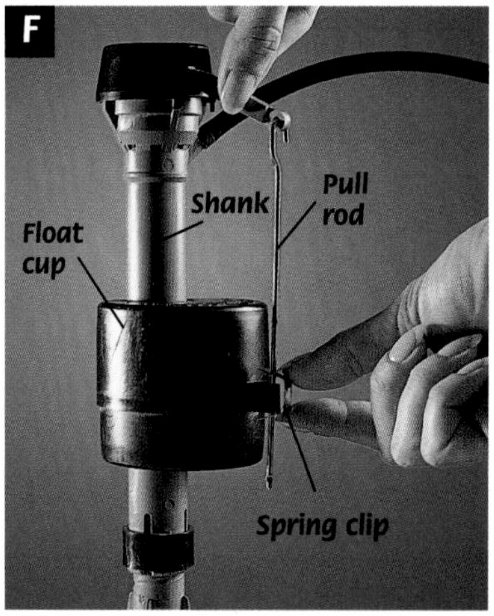

Adjusting a float cup ballcock.

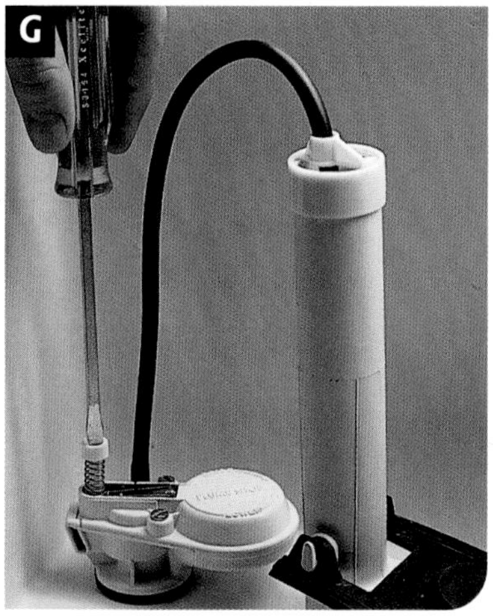

Adjusting a floatless ballcock.

Repairing a Plunger-valve Ballcock

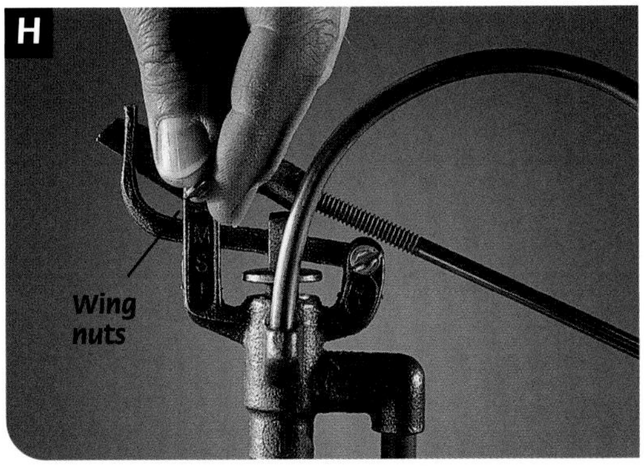

Shut off the water and flush to empty the tank. Remove the wing nuts on the ballcock. Slip out the float arm.

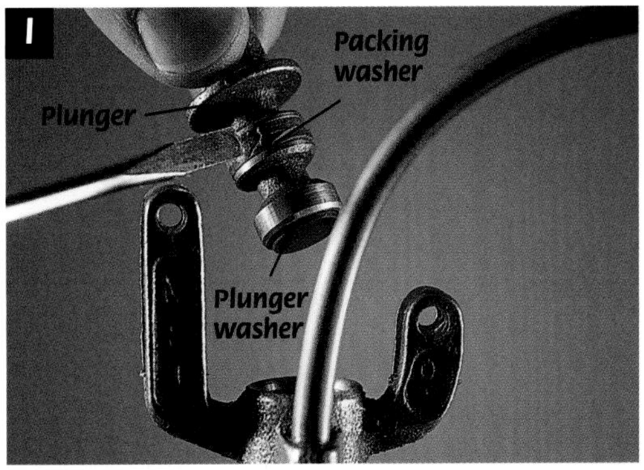

Remove the plunger. Pry out the packing washer or O-ring. Pry out the plunger washer to remove the stem screw.

Install replacement washers. Using a wire brush, clean sediment from inside the ballcock, then reassemble it.

Repairing a Diaphragm Ballcock

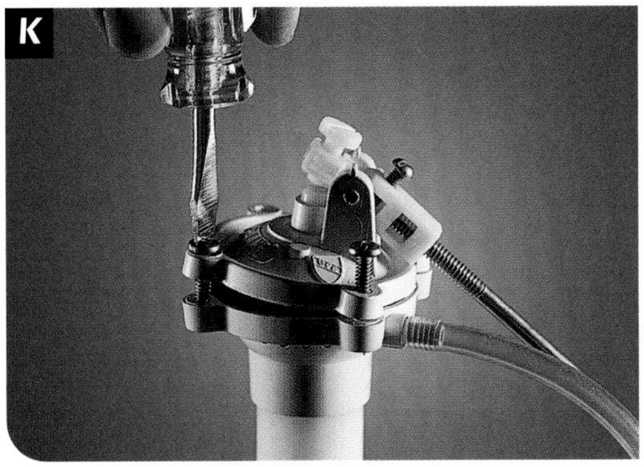

Shut off the water and flush to empty the tank. Remove the screws from the bonnet of the ballcock.

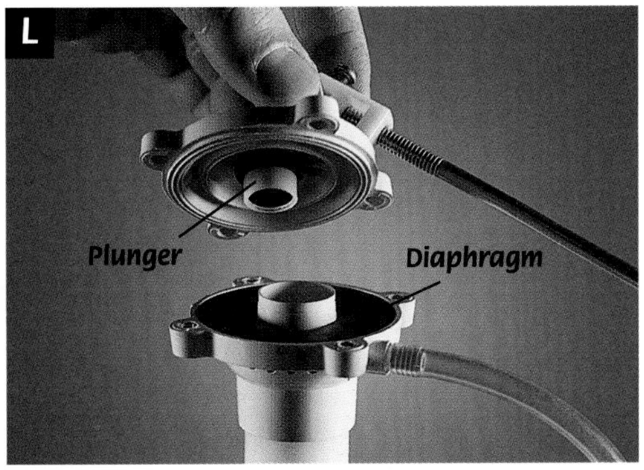

Lift off float arm with the bonnet attached. Check the diaphragm and plunger for wear.

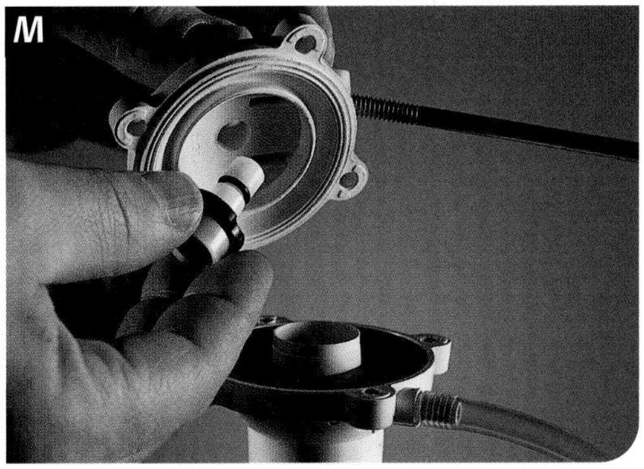

Replace any stiff or cracked parts. If assembly is badly worn, replace the entire ballcock (page 348).

Repairing a Float Cup Ballcock

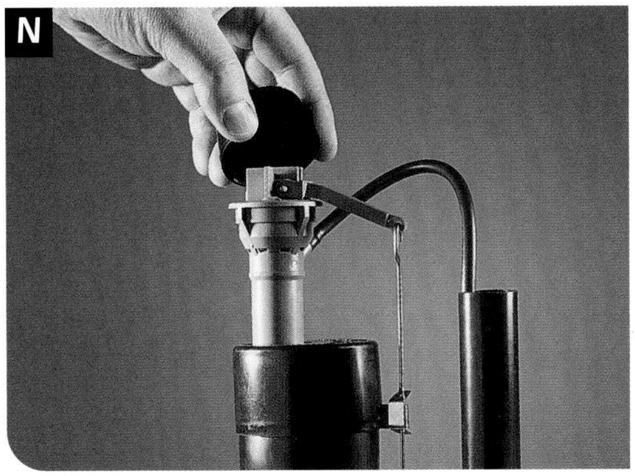

Shut off the water, and flush to empty the tank. Remove the ballcock cap.

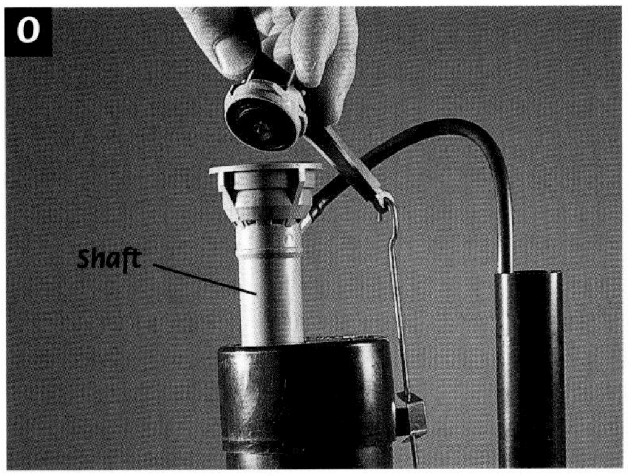

Push the ballcock shaft down and turn counterclockwise to remove it. Clean away any sediment with a wire brush.

Replace the ballcock seal. If the assembly is badly worn, replace the ballcock (page 348).

Replacing a Ballcock

If water continues to run into the overflow pipe after you've adjusted the ballcock, or if the ballcock is badly worn, it's time to install a new one. Begin by shutting off the water and flushing the toilet to empty the tank. Remove any remaining water with a sponge.

Disconnect the supply tube coupling nut and the ballcock mounting nut, using an adjustable wrench **(photo A).** Remove the old ballcock.

Attach a cone washer to the new ballcock tailpiece and insert the tailpiece into the tank opening **(photo B).**

Line up the float arm socket so the float arm passes behind the overflow pipe. Screw the float arm onto the ballcock. Screw the float ball onto the float arm **(photo C).**

Bend or clip the refill tube so the tip is inside the overflow pipe **(photo D).**

Screw the mounting nut and supply tube coupling nut onto the ballcock tailpiece, then tighten them, using an adjustable wrench **(photo E).** Turn on the water and check for leaks.

Adjust the water level in the tank by adjusting the ballcock (page 346). The water level should be about 1/2" below the overflow pipe **(photo F).**

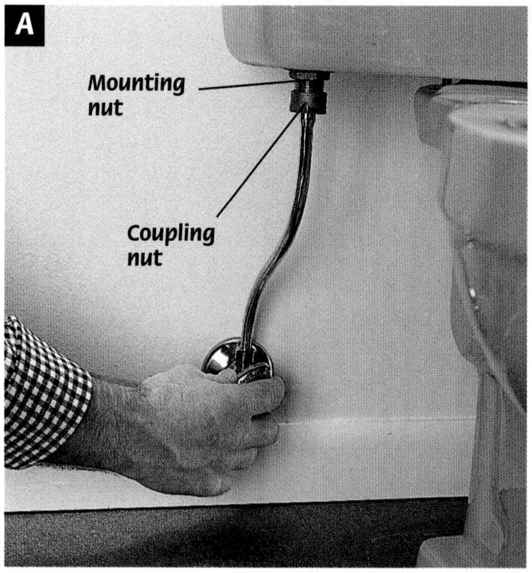

Disconnect the connecting nuts and remove the old ballcock.

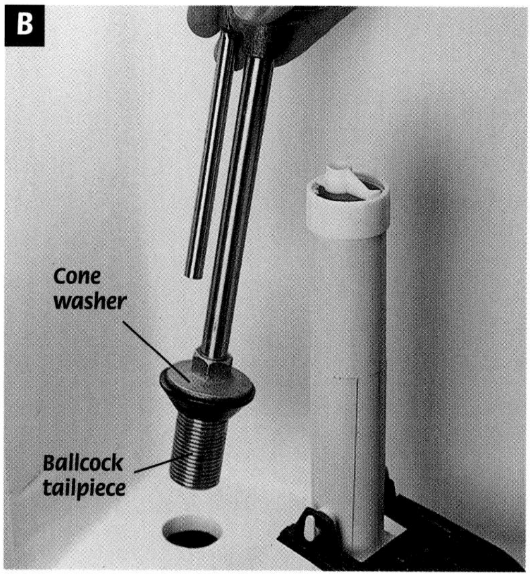

Install the new ballcock, securing it with the mounting nut.

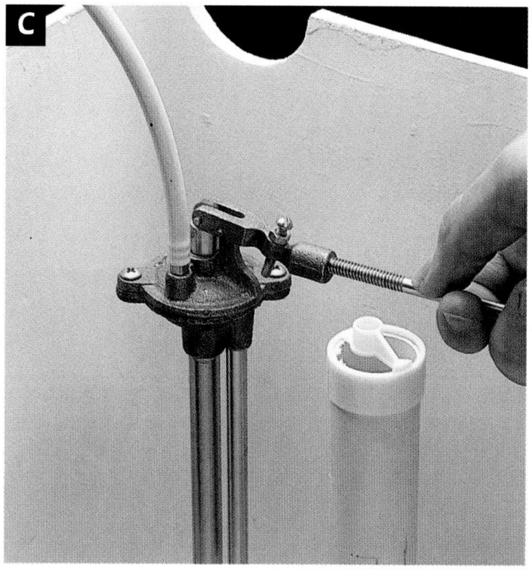

Screw float arm onto ballcock. Attach float ball to float arm.

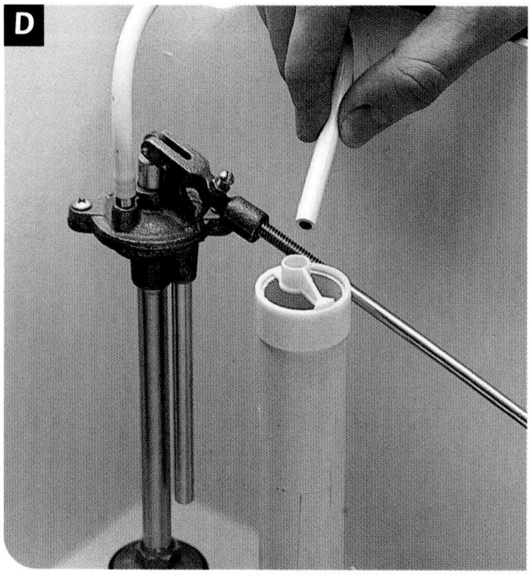

Position the refill tube inside the overflow pipe.

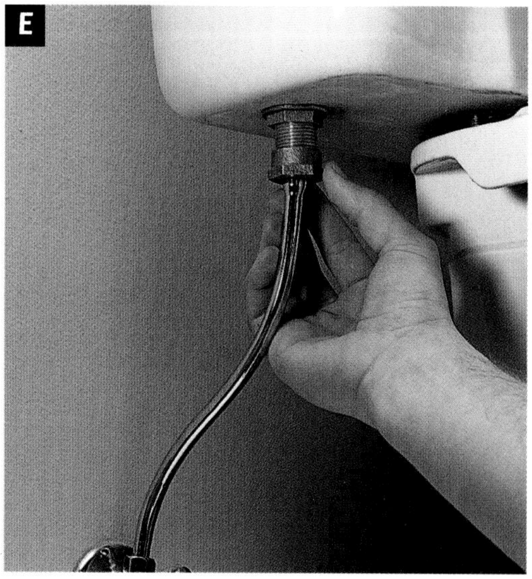

Screw the coupling nuts onto the ballcock tailpiece.

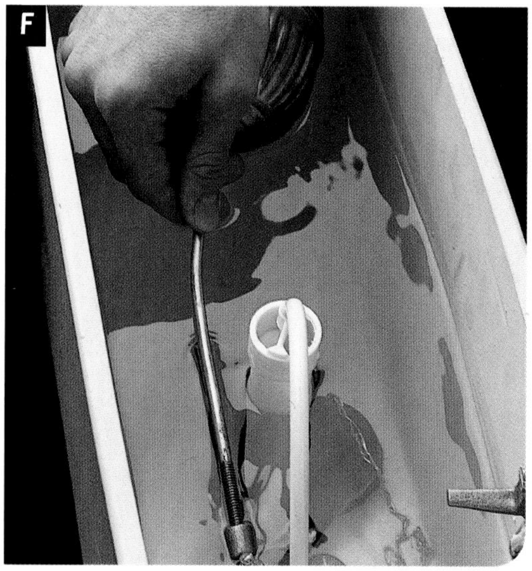

Adjust the ballcock to set the correct water level.

Adjusting & Cleaning a Flush Valve

If adjusting the float ball and lift wires isn't enough to stop a running toilet, and the water level isn't so high that water flows into the overflow pipe, the next step is to clean and adjust the flush valve.

First, remove the tank ball or flapper, and clean the flush valve opening **(photo G)**, using emery cloth for a brass valve, or a nonscratch abrasive pad for plastic.

Next, loosen the guide arm and reposition the tank ball (or flapper) so it's directly over the flush valve **(photo H).**

Inspect the tank ball or flapper, and replace it if it's worn. Install the tank ball or flapper, adjusting so it's directly over the flush valve opening.

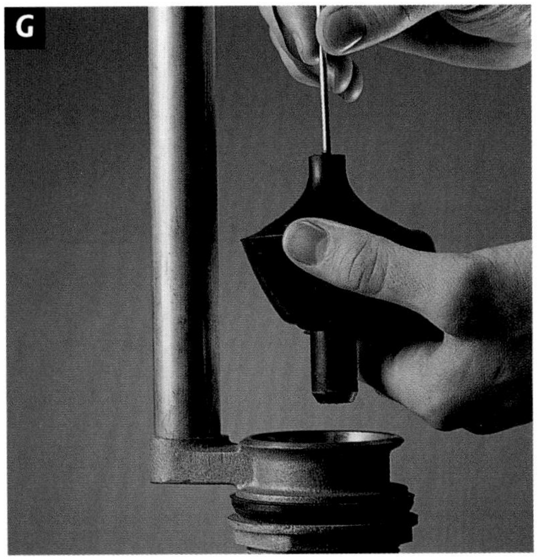

Remove the ball, then clean the opening of the flush valve.

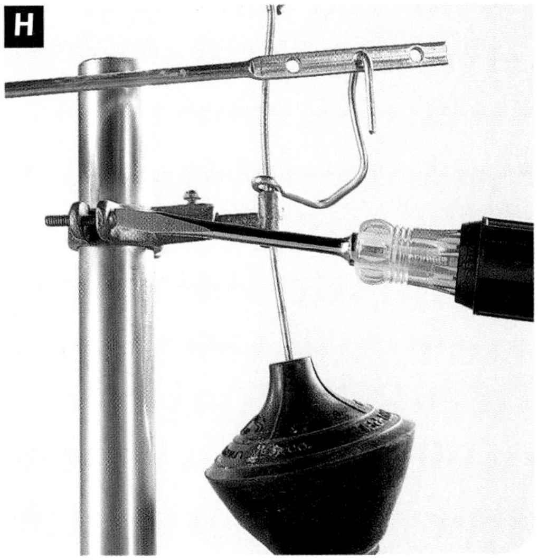

Adjust the tank ball so it's directly over the flush valve.

Replacing a Flush Valve

If you've tried all the adjustments described so far, and the water is still running, try replacing the flush valve. First, shut off the water and disconnect the ballcock (page 348). Detach the tank from the bowl by loosening the tank mounting bolts (page 351), and turn the tank upside down.

Remove the old flush valve by unscrewing the spud nut with a spud wrench or channel-type pliers **(photo I).**

Slide the cone washer onto the tailpiece of the new flush valve, with the beveled side of the cone washer facing the end of the tailpiece **(photo J).** Insert the flush valve into the tank opening so that the overflow pipe faces the ballcock.

Screw the spud nut onto the tailpiece of the flush valve, and tighten with a spud wrench or channel-type pliers **(photo K).** Place the spud washer over the tailpiece, and reinstall the tank.

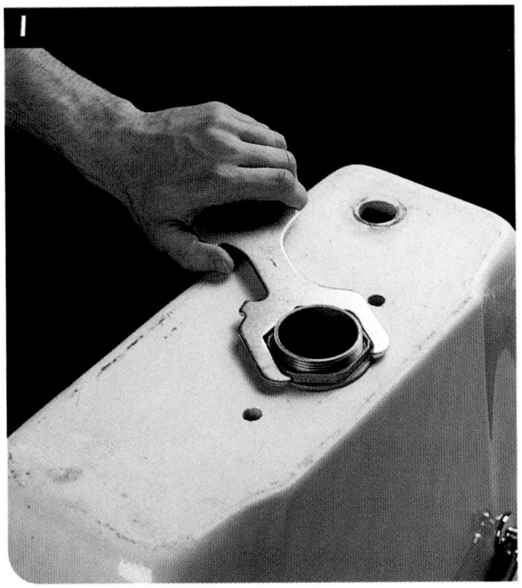

Remove the old flush valve by unscrewing the spud nut.

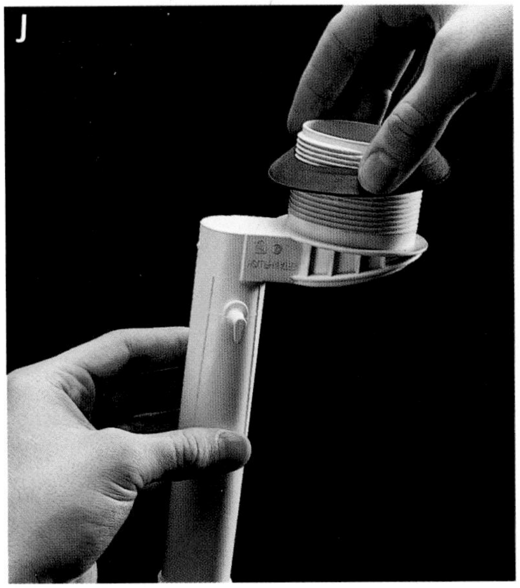

Slide the cone washer onto the flush valve tailpiece.

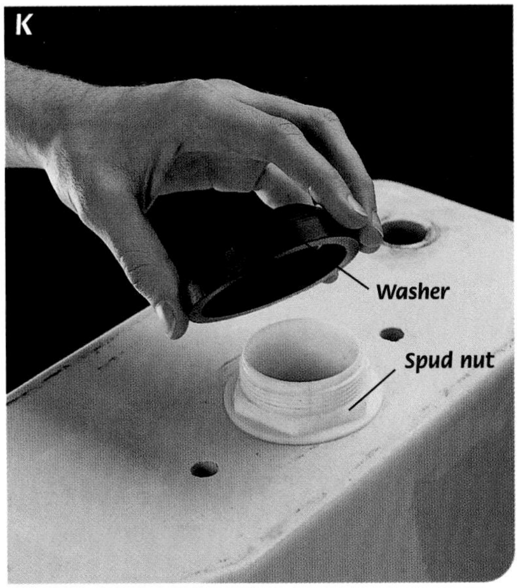

Screw spud nut and soft spud washer onto the flush valve.

Repairing a Leaky Toilet

When a toilet leaks, you need to find and resolve the source of the problem as soon as possible. Over time, standing water will penetrate the layers of the floor, damaging the subfloor and even the floor joists **(photo A).** As you look for the source of the problem, start with the simplest possibilities.

First, check all connections and make sure they're watertight. Use a ratchet wrench to tighten the tank bolts, and an adjustable wrench to tighten the ballcock mounting nut and the supply tube coupling nut, and the tank bolts **(photo B).** Never overtighten the tank bolts; this can crack the toilet tank.

If moisture drips from the tank during humid weather, condensation may be forming on the exterior of the tank. To stop this "sweating," you need to insulate the inside of the tank with a tank liner kit.

Shut off the water, drain the tank, and clean the inside with an abrasive cleanser. Use a utility knife to cut the foam liner panels to fit the bottom, sides, front, and back of the tank. Attach the panels to the tank with waterproof adhesive. Let the adhesive cure as directed, then turn on the water and refill the tank **(photo C).**

If water seems to be seeping out from around the base of the toilet, especially during or just after a flush, the wax ring may be worn or broken. To find out, add a few drops of food coloring to the water in the tank and flush. If colored water appears on the floor, you can be fairly sure that's the problem. In this case, you need to remove and replace the wax ring (page 351).

Check the tank and the toilet base for cracks, which can cause leaks. A cracked tank or base can't be repaired and must be replaced as soon as possible (page 352).

When buying a new toilet, consider a water-saver design, which can be twice as efficient as a standard toilet. Some new toilets are sold with the flush valves and ballcocks already installed, while others don't include these parts. If they aren't included, you'll need to buy them separately.

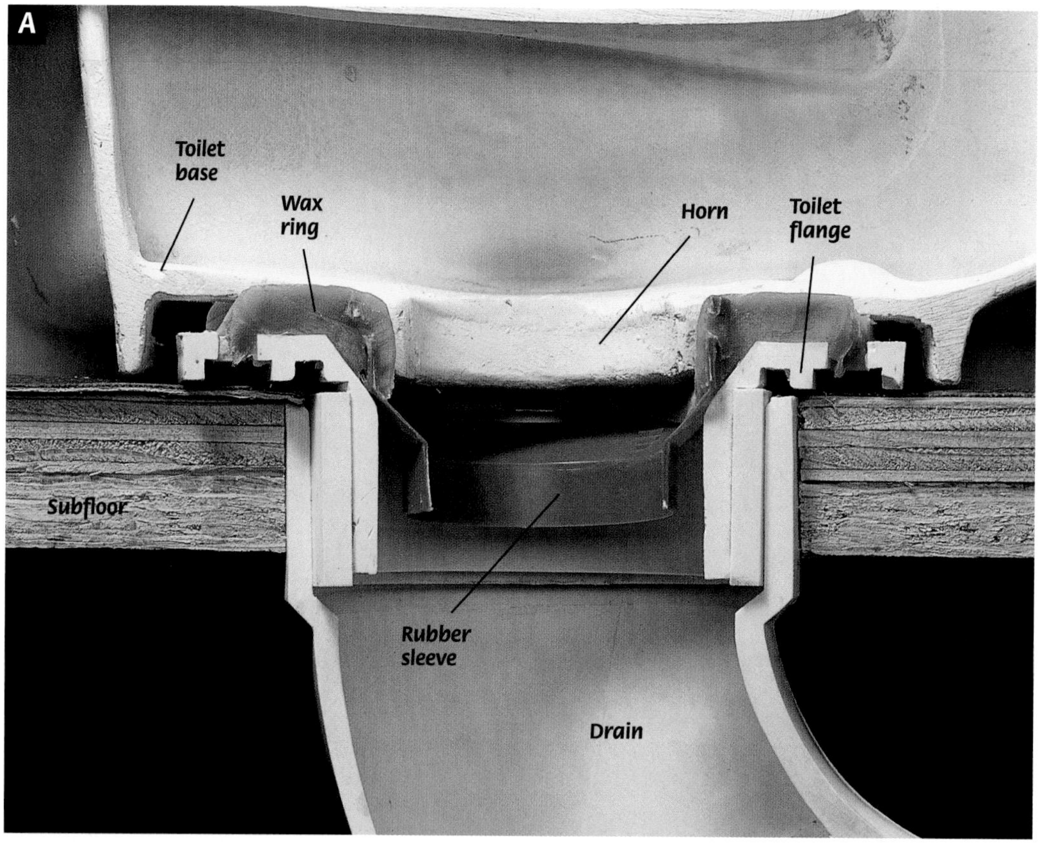

Fix a leaky toilet as soon as possible. Standing water can damage the surrounding subfloor and framing members.

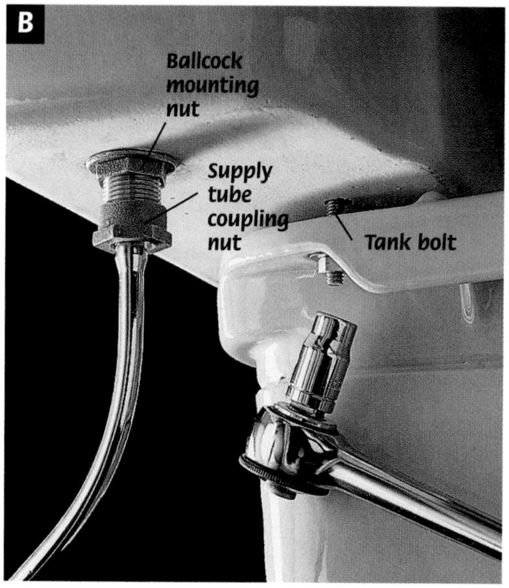

To eliminate leaks, start by tightening all connections.

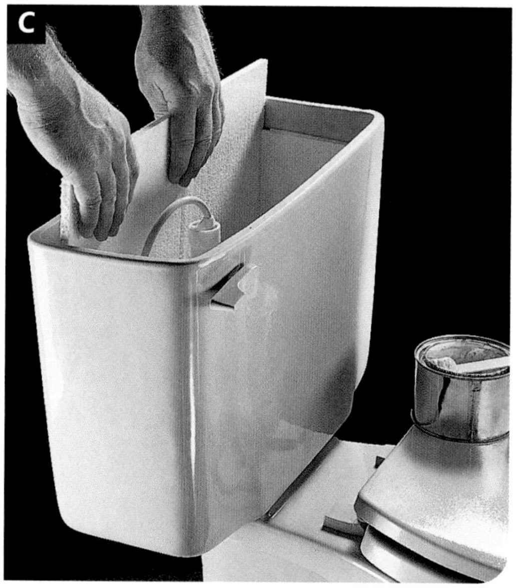

Insulate the toilet tank to prevent condensation.

Removing a Toilet & Wax Ring

The connection between the toilet and the floor drain is sealed with a thick ring of wax. As the wax ages, it can dry out, crumble, or crack, which can break the seal and cause leaks. If a wax ring leaks, you can remove and replace it. This job isn't complicated or difficult, but it can be messy; you'll want to have plenty of rags on hand.

Turn off the water at the shut-off valve and flush the toilet to empty the tank. Use a sponge to soak up any water remaining in the tank and bowl. Disconnect the supply tube, using an adjustable wrench **(photo D).**

Remove the nuts from the tank bolts, using a ratchet wrench **(photo E).**

Carefully remove the tank and set it aside. If you intend to reinstall it, treat it with care; most toilet tanks are porcelain, which is easily damaged.

Pry off the floor bolt trim caps at the base of the toilet, using a screwdriver. Use an adjustable wrench to remove the nuts from the floor bolts **(photo F).**

Straddle the toilet and rock the bowl from side to side, until the seal breaks **(photo G).**

Carefully lift the toilet off the floor bolts and set it on its side. This is the messy part; water may spill from the toilet trap as you remove the toilet. Wear rubber gloves while cleaning up this water and cleaning the toilet and flange.

Scrape the old wax from the toilet flange in the floor, using a putty knife **(photo H).**

Plug the drain opening with a damp rag so that sewer gas doesn't escape from the drainpipe into the house.

If you're reinstalling the old toilet, clean the old wax and plumber's putty from around the horn and base of the toilet **(photo I).**

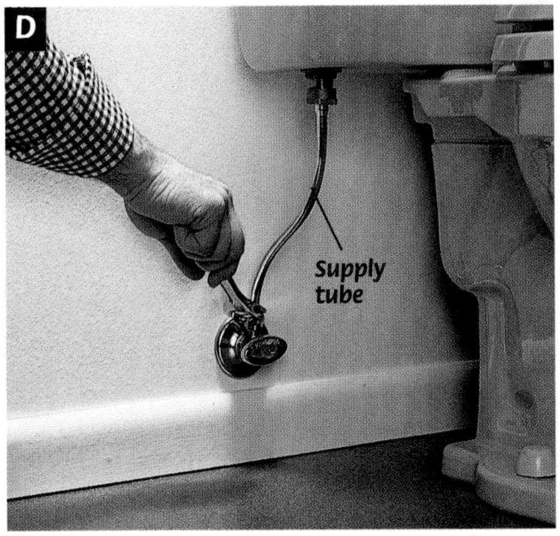

Disconnect the supply tube, using an adjustable wrench.

Remove the nuts from the tank bolts and remove the tank.

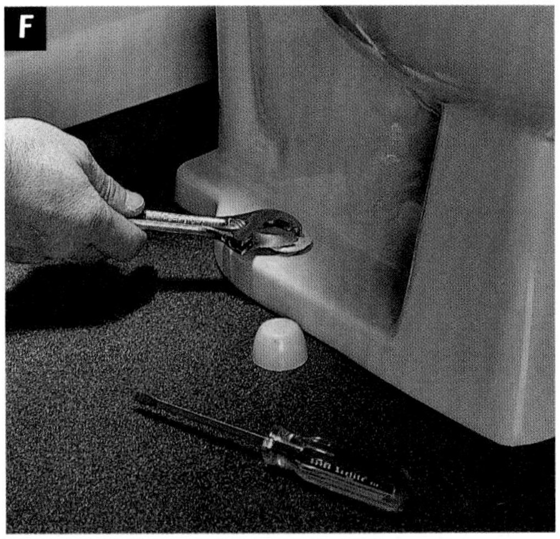

Remove the floor bolt nuts with an adjustable wrench.

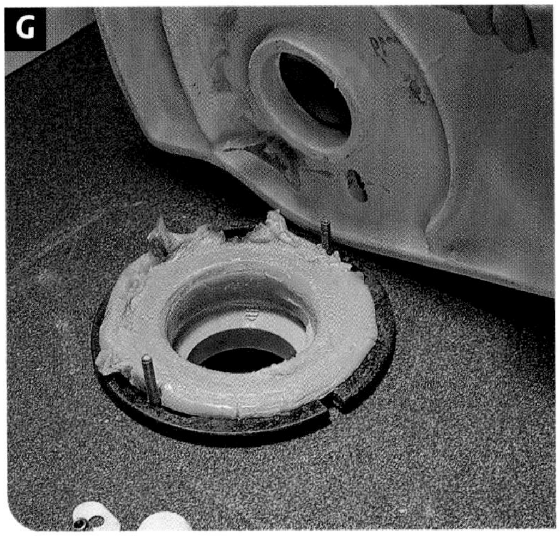

Break the seal and lift the toilet off the floor bolts.

Scrape the old wax from the toilet flange.

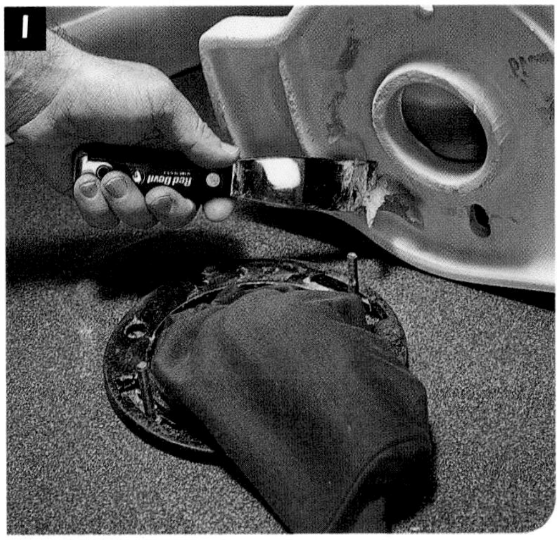

Clean wax and putty from the horn and base of the toilet.

Installing a Toilet & Wax Ring

Turn the toilet base upside down, and place a new wax ring over the drain horn **(photo A).** If you're reinstalling the old toilet, make sure you've removed the old wax and plumber's putty first.

If the ring has a rubber or plastic sleeve, position it so that it faces away from the toilet. Apply a bead of plumber's putty to the bottom edge of the toilet base. Position the toilet over the drain so that the floor bolts are aligned with the openings in the base of the toilet **(photo B).**

Press down on the toilet base, rocking it gently from side to side, to compress the wax and putty **(photo C).**

Thread the washers and nuts onto the floor bolts. Tighten them with an adjustable wrench just until they're snug.

Caution: Do not overtighten these nuts; this can cause the toilet base to crack.

Wipe away any excess putty from around the outside edge of the base. Cover the nuts with the trim caps.

The next step is to prepare the new tank for installation. If you're reinstalling the old tank, or if you're installing a new tank that has the flush valve and ballcock already installed, you can move on to the next step.

Otherwise, install a handle, ballcock (page 348), and flush valve (page 349).

Once those items are in place, carefully turn the tank upside down and place a soft spud washer over the flush valve tailpiece **(photo D).**

Turn the tank right side up and position it on the rear of the toilet base, so that the spud washer is centered over the water inlet opening **(photo E).**

Line up the tank bolt holes with the holes in the base of the toilet. Slide the rubber washers onto the tank bolts and insert the bolts into the holes **(photo F).**

Working from underneath the tank, thread washers and nuts onto the bolts.Tighten the nuts with a ratchet wrench until the tank is snug **(photo G).**

Use caution when tightening the nuts; most toilet tanks rest on the spud washer rather than directly on the toilet base.

Attach the water supply tube to the ballcock tailpiece, with an adjustable wrench **(photo H).**

Turn on the water and test the toilet. Check for leaks around the tank bolts and water connections. Tighten any leaky connections, if necessary.

To replace the toilet seat, insert the seat bolts into the mounting holes in the toilet. Screw the mounting nuts onto the seat bolts, and tighten them **(photo I).**

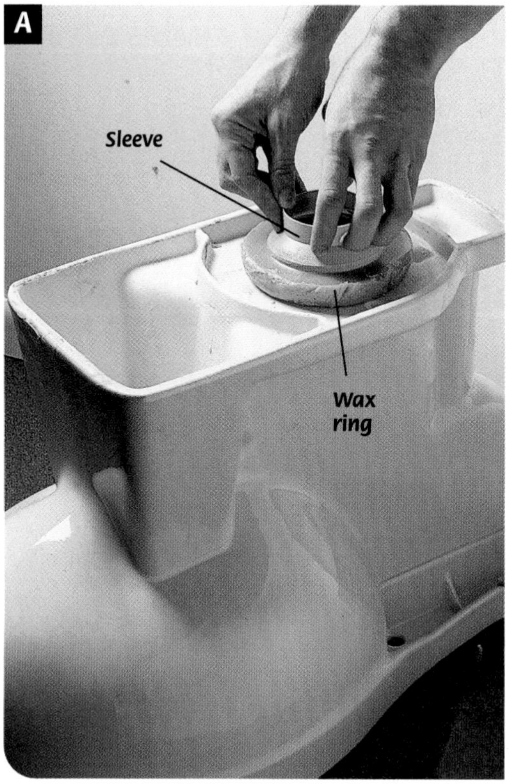

Place new wax ring over drain horn.

Align the floor bolts with the openings in the toilet base.

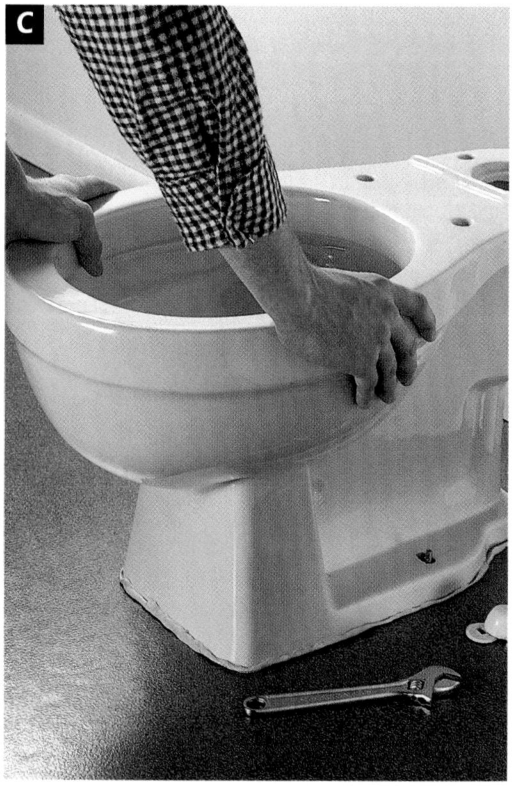

Press down on the toilet base to compress the wax and putty.

Place a soft spud washer over the flush valve tailpiece.

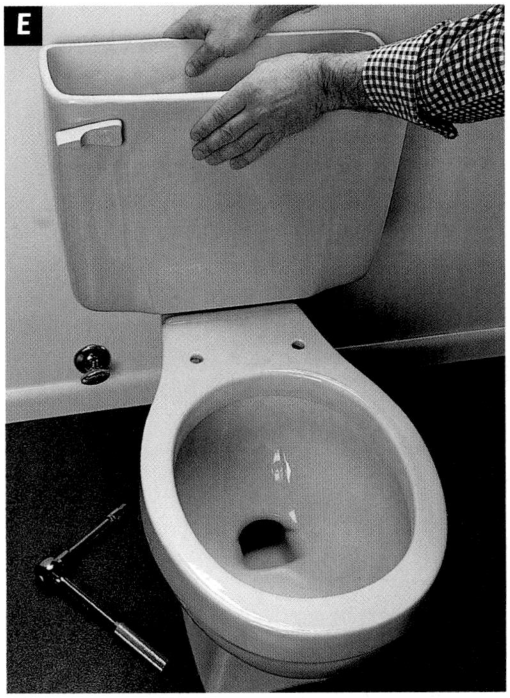

Carefully position the tank on the toilet base.

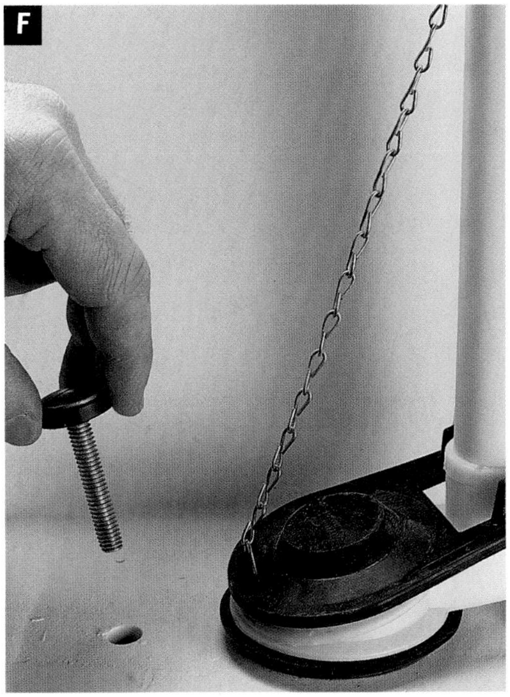

Place the tank bolts in holes and install washers and nuts.

Gently tighten the nuts until the tank is snug.

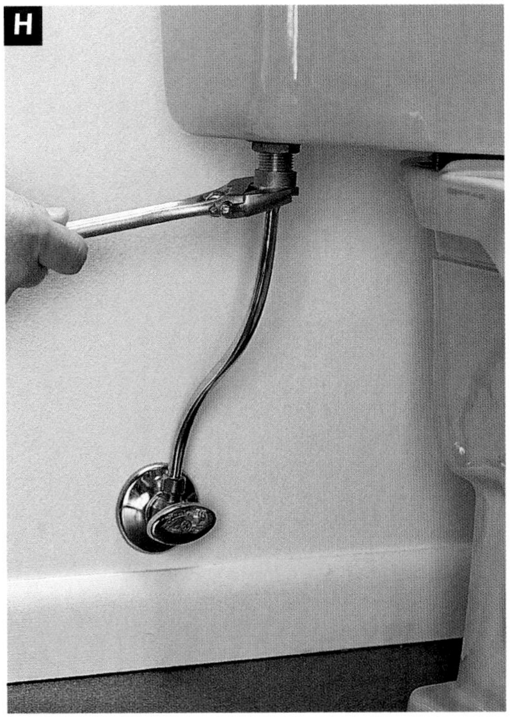

Connect the water supply tube to the ballcock tailpiece.

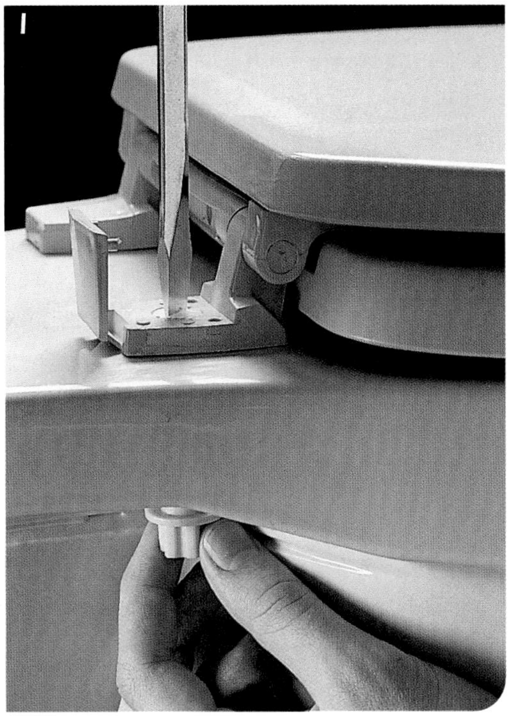

Insert the seat bolts into the mounting holes and secure them with nuts.

Repairing Pressure-assisted Toilets

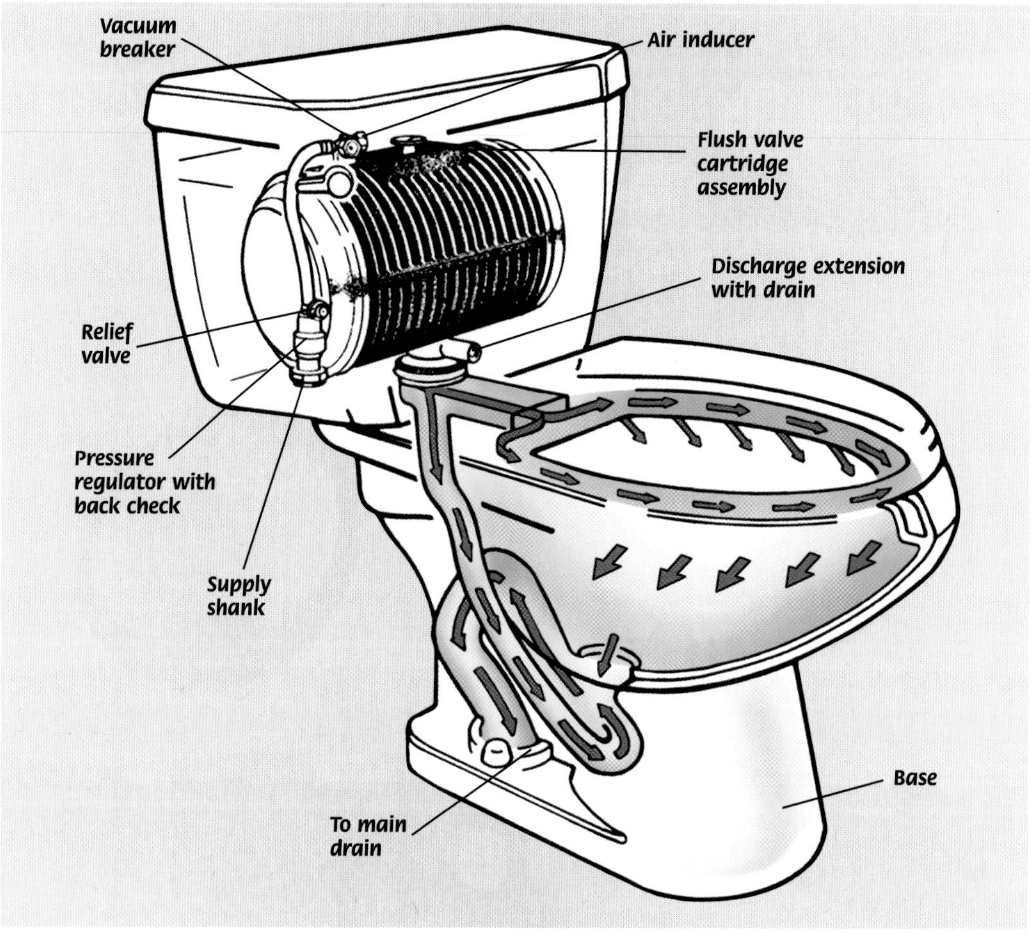

Pressure-assisted toilets rely on either compressed air or water pumps to boost their flushing power. This increased flushing velocity results in fewer backups and greater efficiency.

Because of their advanced technology, pressure-assisted toilets are more expensive than standard toilets, and their additional moving parts make them more susceptible to failure.

On the other hand, toilets are one of the most water-hungry devices in your house, and a pressure-assisted toilet can reduce your water usage significantly. Also, in many areas they are now required in new construction.

Because of these requirements and their benefits of greater power and lower water usage, pressure-assisted toilets are becoming increasingly common.

Measuring Water Pressure

If you have a problem with a pressure-assisted toilet, the first step is to check the water pressure. Insufficient water supply can cause many problems in a pressure-assisted toilet—it may run constantly, have a weak flush, or not flush at all.

For a pressure-assisted toilet to work properly, the constant pressure should be between 20 and 80 pounds per square inch (PSI).

To check a toilet's water pressure, begin by turning off the water supply at the fixture's shutoff valve.

Place a five-gallon bucket under the end of the supply tube. Disconnect the supply tube and place the tube inside the bucket.

Turn on fixture water supply and let water fill the bucket for 30 seconds **(photo A).**

Shut off the water and measure the water that has accumulated in the bucket. For the toilet to operate properly, you should have more than a gallon of water.

If you determine that the water pressure is too low, possible solutions include increasing the size of the supply tubing that connects to the ballcock (a job you can do yourself), or replumbing to install larger supply pipes (a job for a professional).

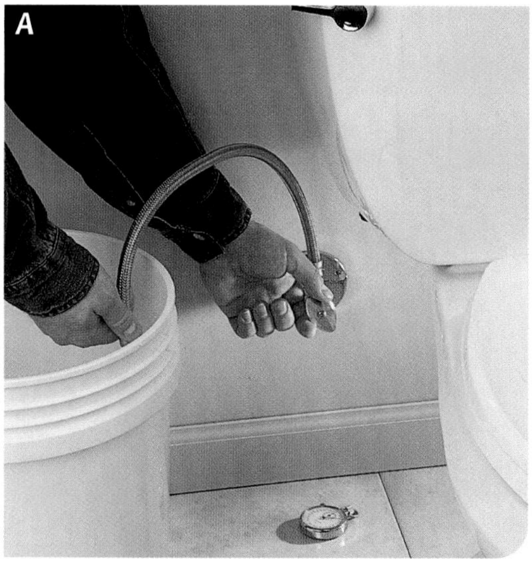

Fixing a Pressure-assisted Toilet

If the water pressure is satisfactory, but the toilet is running constantly, follow these steps: Turn off the fixture shut-off valve and inspect the shank screen **(photo B).** If you find any obstructions that may be hampering the flow, remove them.

Next, remove the cover and check the actuator adjustment. The rod shouldn't interfere with the flush. Empty the system by flushing the toilet. Remove the rod and the flush valve cartridge. Inspect the O-rings for wear **(photo C).** If needed, replace the cartridge.

Set the flush valve cartridge in the grooves by rotating it two turns counterclockwise. Screw it clockwise until it fits tightly, but don't overtighten. Turn on the water supply and allow the tank to refill.

If water continues to run beyond the refill, depress the actuator. If this stops the flow, tighten the valve cartridge in quarter turns until the water flow stops. If the water flow continues, loosen the cartridge in quarter turns until the flow stops.

If the water pressure is satisfactory, but the toilet has a weak flush, follow these steps: Remove the cover and flush the system by operating the actuator. Raise the actuator as the unit flushes to remove any debris in the supply lines and pressure tank **(photo D).** A minute-long flush should clear away any debris.

To test the air regulator, remove the muffler cap on the air regulator and flush the toilet **(photo E).** You should be able to hear air being drawn into the pressure tank as the valve retracts during the refill. If you don't hear any air being drawn, remove the cap and clean it thoroughly.

Finally, turn off the water supply and drain the pressure tank by operating the actuator. Pour water onto the cartridge housing and turn on the water supply.

If you see a stream of bubbles emanating from the center of the cartridge, it means that the cartridge has a leak and must be replaced.

Inspect the shank screen; remove any obstructions.

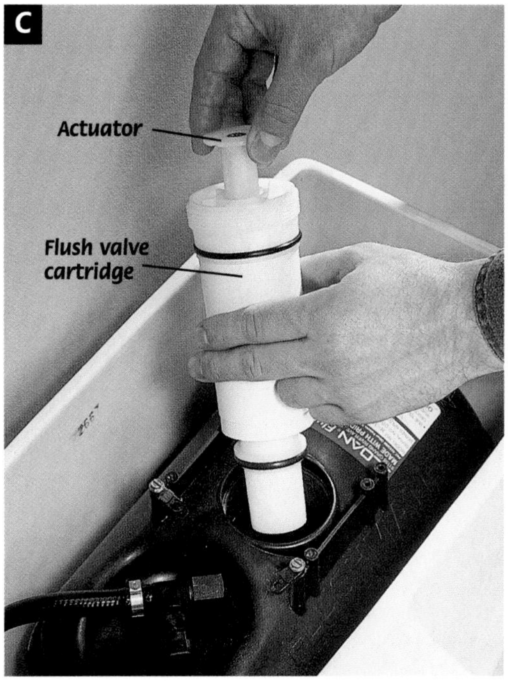

Check the O-rings on the cartridge for signs of wear.

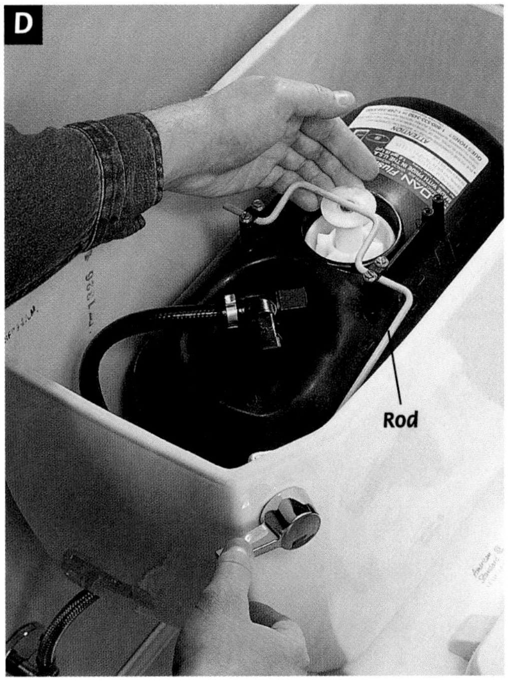

Raise the actuator while flushing to remove debris.

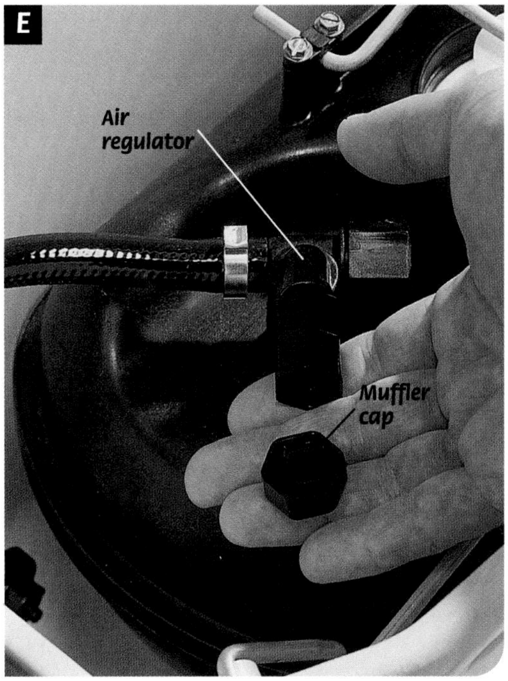

Detach the muffler cap on the air regulator.

Food Disposers

Food disposers grind food waste so it can be flushed down the sink drain. They are convenient, but significantly increase the load handled by the sewage system—as much as adding another person to the household.

To prevent problems, choose a food disposer with at least a 1/2 horsepower motor, and a self-reversing feature to prevent jamming. Also look for foam sound insulation, a cast-iron grinding ring, and overload protection that resets the motor if it overheats.

To keep the disposer smelling clean, periodically grind up lemon or lime rinds. To clean the assembly, grind up ice cubes.

If the disposer won't run and doesn't hum when you turn it on, push the reset button on the bottom of the unit **(photo A).** If that doesn't work, check the circuit breaker or fuse.

If the disposer won't run, but hums when you turn it on, it's probably jammed. In this case, you may be able to free it by turning the impeller assembly. Some models even come with a wrench to turn the assembly from the bottom of the unit. First, turn off the electricity to the unit at the service panel. Then find the slot, insert the wrench, and turn clockwise **(photo B).** Restore the electricity, push the reset button, and test the disposer to see if it's working.

Another way to free a jammed disposer is to use a wood handle, such as a broomstick, to turn it from the top. First, turn off the electricity to the unit. Then insert the broom handle into the disposer and try to rotate the impeller assembly. Once the impeller seems to be free, restore the electricity, push the reset button, and test the disposer.

If all these measures fail, install a new disposer (page 358).

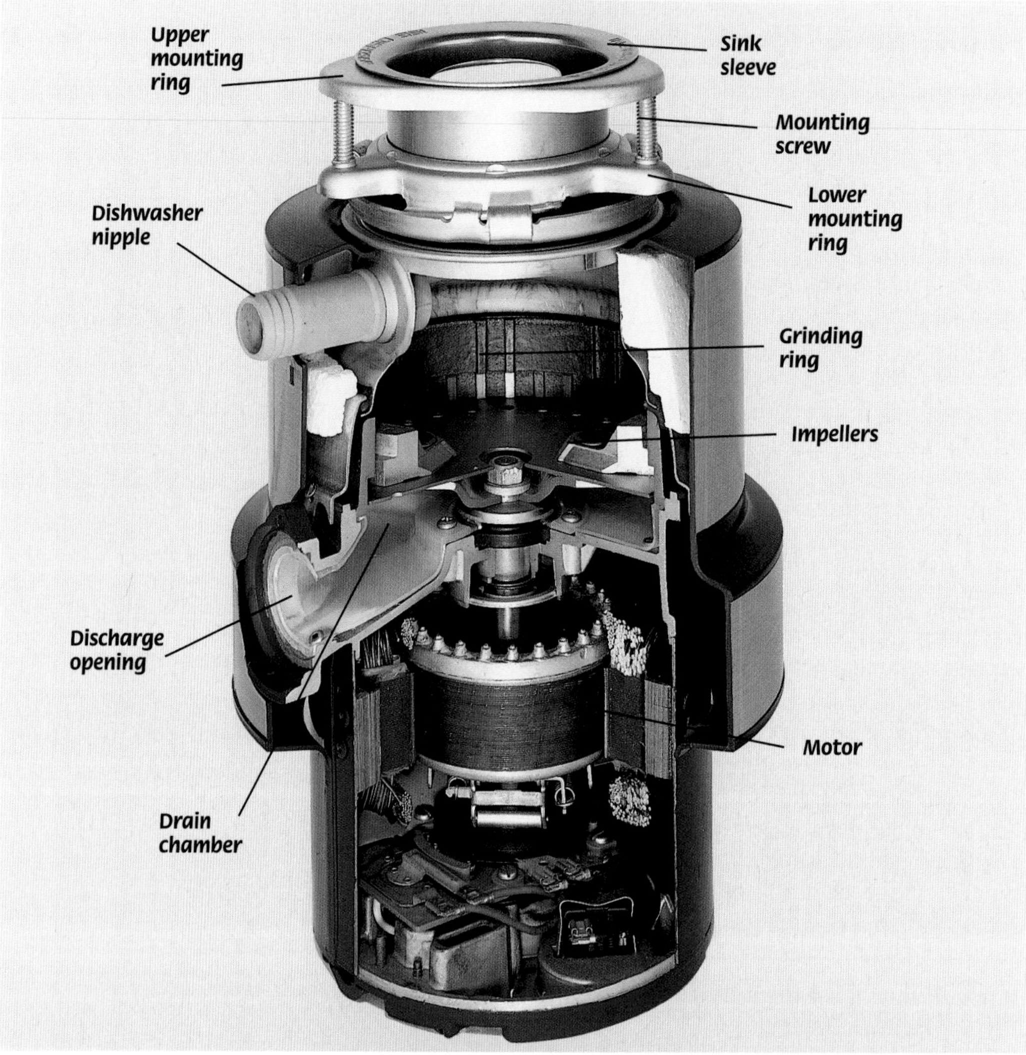

Food disposers grind food scraps and kitchen waste so they can be flushed away through the sink drain system.

To free a disposer jam, press the reset button.

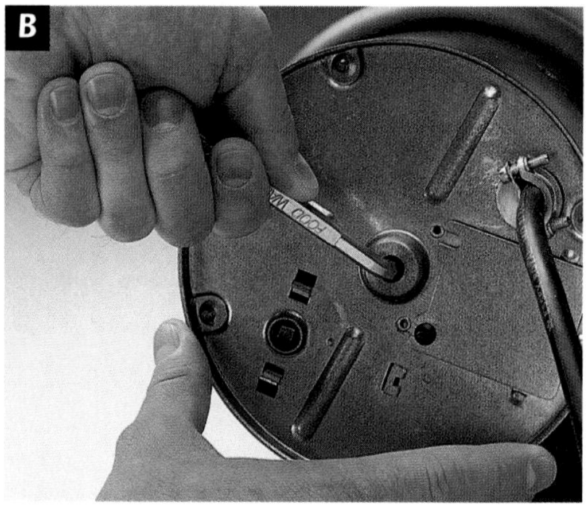

Or, insert a wrench into the slot and turn the impellers.

Removing a Food Disposer

Removing the old food disposer is the first step if you're installing a new disposer or if you're replacing a sink. When replacing a disposer, bear in mind that both removal and installation will be easier if you replace the unit with another of the same make and model, since some parts can remain in place. However, if you end up buying a different model, you can still do the work yourself. The extra steps aren't difficult.

Using a screwdriver, loosen the screw on the hose clamp, then remove the dishwasher drain hose from the dishwasher nipple **(photo C)**.

Place a bucket under the pipe. Use an adjustable wrench to loosen the slip nut connecting the continuous waste pipe and the discharge tube. Disconnect the pipe from the tube **(photo D).** If the slip nuts are stuck in place, use a hacksaw to cut the pipe loose, just past the elbow.

Insert a screwdriver or the disposer wrench into a mounting lug on the lower mounting ring. Turn counterclockwise until the mounting ears are unlocked **(photo E).**

If the mounting assembly in place is compatible with the new unit, you're done with the removal phase of the project. If it isn't, use a screwdriver to loosen the three mounting screws, then remove the mounting assembly **(photo F).**

Pry off the fiber gasket, the sink sleeve, and flange **(photo G).**

Scrape away the plumber's putty, using a putty knife and an abrasive pad. Thoroughly clean the sleeve, flange, and sink opening.

Tools: *Screwdriver, adjustable wrench, hacksaw (if needed), putty knife.*

Materials: *Bucket, abrasive pad.*

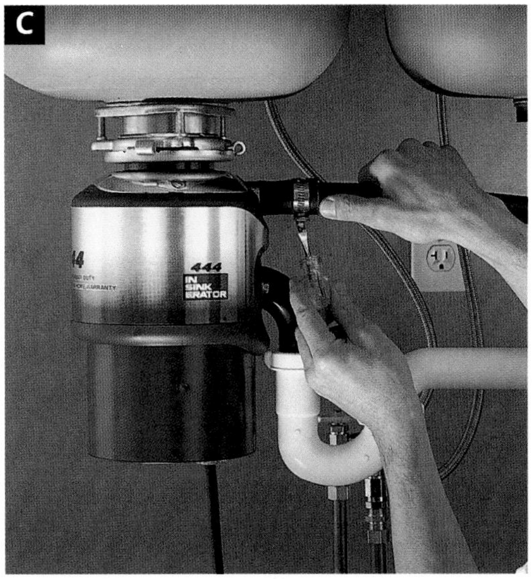

Loosen the screw holding the clamp. Remove the drain hose.

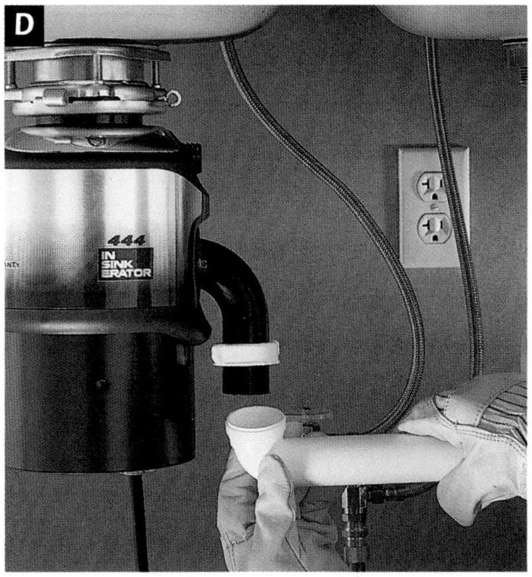

Disconnect the continuous waste pipe from discharge tube.

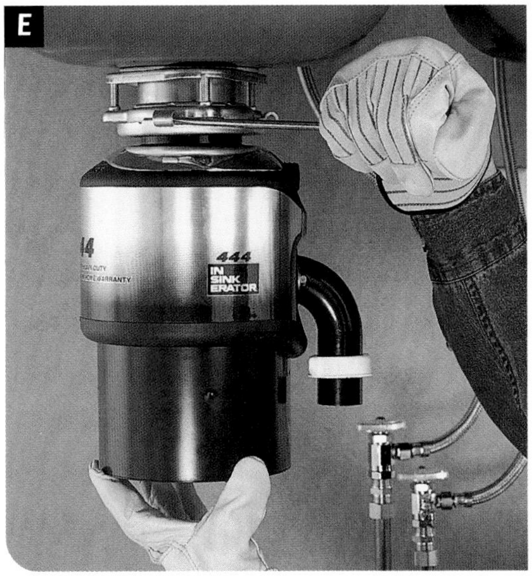

Insert screwdriver into the lug and turn counterclockwise.

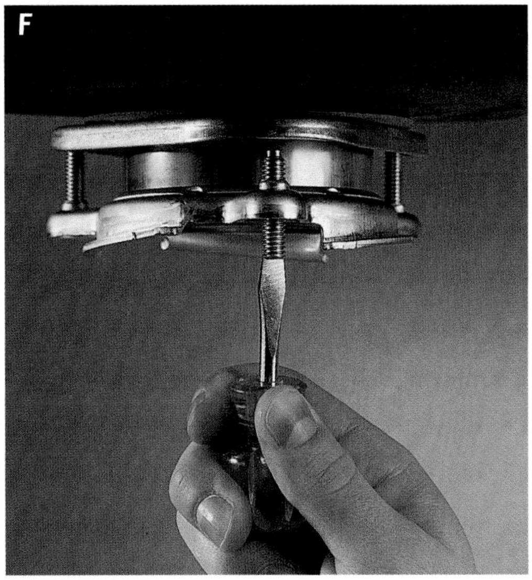

Loosen mounting screws and remove mounting assembly.

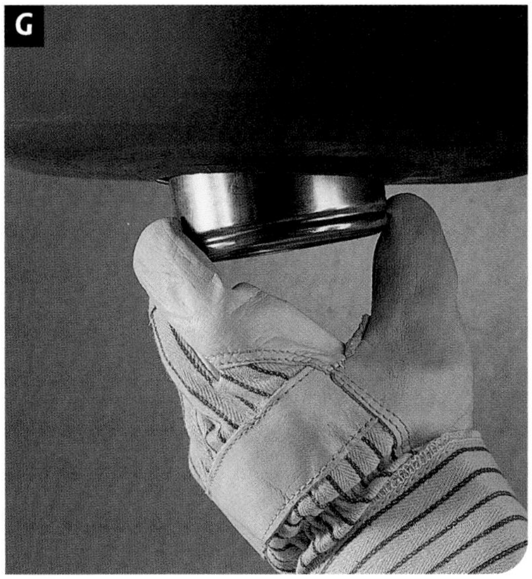

Remove the sink sleeve by pushing up from the bottom.

Installing a Food Disposer

Before installing a new food disposer, you need to wire an appliance cord to the disposer unit. Strip about 1/2" of insulation from each wire, using a combination tool.

Remove the plate on the bottom of the unit **(photo A).** Feed the appliance cord into the wire connection compartment. Using wire connectors, connect the white wires, then the black wires. Attach the green insulated wire to the unit's green ground screw. Gently push the wires into the compartment. Replace the plate.

If you're replacing an old disposer with one of the same make and model and the old mounting assembly is in place, you should be able to reuse the existing mounting rings. In that case, skip the next step.

If you're installing the disposer on a new sink, or have removed the mounting assembly because it wasn't compatible with the new disposer, install the mounting ring assembly as follows:

Apply a 1/4" bead of plumber's putty under the flange of the disposer sink sleeve.

Insert the sleeve in the drain opening, and slip the fiber gasket and the backup ring onto the sleeve. Place the upper mounting ring on the sleeve and slide the snap ring into the groove **(photo B).**

Tighten the three mounting screws on the upper mounting ring until the sleeve is tight against the sink opening **(photo C).**

Hold the disposer against the upper mounting ring, so that the mounting lugs on the lower mounting ring are directly under the mounting screws.

Turn the lower mounting ring clockwise until the disposer is fully supported by the mounting assembly.

Attach the discharge tube to the discharge opening on the side of the disposer, using the rubber washer and the metal flange **(photo D).**

If you plan to attach a dishwasher, knock out the plug in the dishwasher nipple, using a screwdriver. Attach the dishwasher drain hose

Tools: *Combination tool, screwdriver, adjustable wrench, hacksaw (if needed), channel-type pliers.*

Materials: *Replacement food disposer, 12-gauge appliance cord with grounded plug, wire connectors, plumber's putty.*

Connect the appliance cord to the disposer wires with wire connectors.

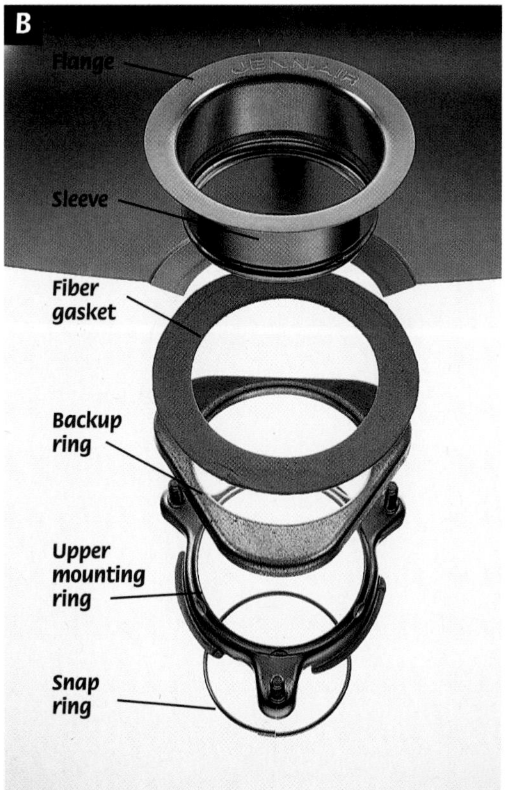

Attach the fiber gasket, backup ring, and upper mounting ring onto the sleeve. Slide the snap ring into place on the sleeve.

Position the disposer so the lower mounting ring fits into the upper mounting ring, then turn the lower mounting ring clockwise until it locks in place.

to the nipple with a hose clamp **(photo E).**

Attach the discharge tube to the continuous waste pipe with a slip washer and nut **(photo F).**

If the discharge tube is too long, cut it with a hacksaw or tubing cutter. If you had to cut the continuous waste pipe to remove a previous disposer, add an elbow and fittings as necessary to reconfigure the pipe. To lock the disposer in place **(photo G),** insert a screwdriver or the disposer wrench into a mounting lug on the lower mounting ring. Turn clockwise until the mounting ears are locked.

Tighten all drain slip nuts with channel-type pliers. Run the water, then turn on the disposer and check for leaks.

Helpful Hint

In some communities where the sewer capacity is strained to its limit, food disposers are no longer allowed by Code. And a food disposer isn't advised if you have a septic system, since too much food waste can interfere with the normal decomposition of septic waste.

Attach discharge tube and dishwasher hose, if the disposer will be connected to a dishwasher.

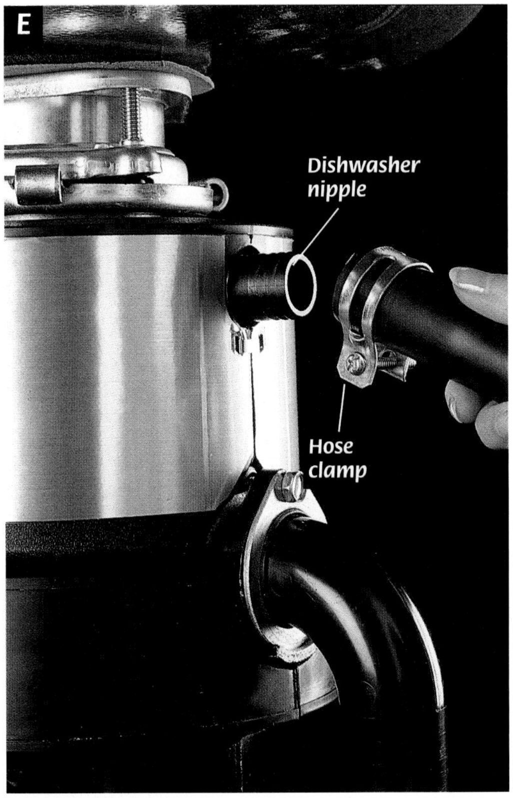

Attach discharge tube and dishwasher hose, if the disposer will be connected to a dishwasher.

Attach the discharge tube to the continuous waste pipe. If necessary, cut the discharge pipe to length, using a hacksaw or tubing cutter.

Insert a screwdriver into a mounting lug on the lower mounting ring and turn until it locks in place.

Dishwashers

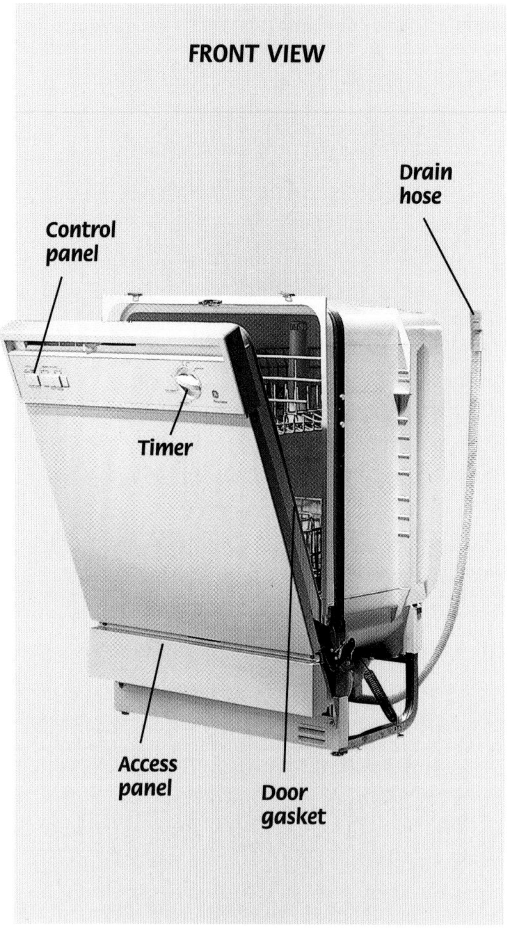

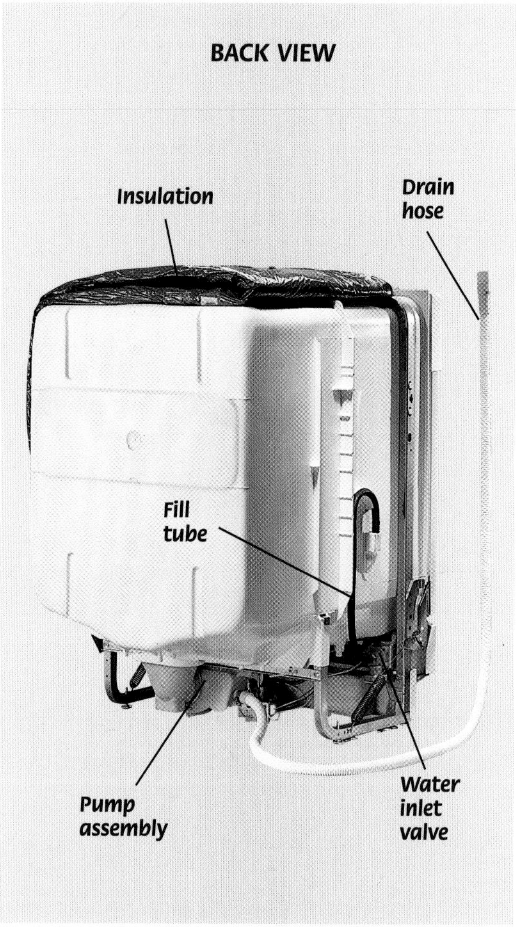

A standard dishwasher is a slide-in appliance that can be pulled out from the cabinet when repairs are necessary.

Dishwashers are designed for durability, which means that they're relatively low-maintenance appliances. The few problems that do occur can be solved relatively easily.

Replacing defective door gaskets typically eliminates leaks. Relocating water or waste lines that are resting against the dishwasher usually reduces excessive noise levels.

Clogged water lines can present more serious problems. A clogged filter or defective solenoid can keep the dishwasher from filling correctly. You can clean the inlet valve, which may solve the problem, but solenoid repair requires professional attention.

Tools: Pliers, screwdriver, continuity tester.

Materials: *Replacement drain hose, clamps, replacement gasket, replacement valve screen.*

Replacing a Drain Hose

If your dishwasher won't drain properly, inspect the drain hose. If you find that it's damaged or has a kink that can't be straightened, it's time for a new hose.

Start by turning off both the water supply and the electrical power. Remove the lower panel of the dishwasher. Depending on the model, it will be held in place by either clips or retaining screws.

Place a baking pan or bowl beneath the pump to catch any water that may be trapped in the hose. Loosen the drain hose clamp with pliers or a screwdriver. Remove the drain hose from the pump **(photo A).**

Working underneath the sink, detach the other end of the drain hose from the drain or garbage disposer.

Install the new drain hose, using new clamps.

Restore the electrical power and the water supply to the dishwasher.

Test the unit to make sure that it drains properly and that there are no leaks in the new hose.

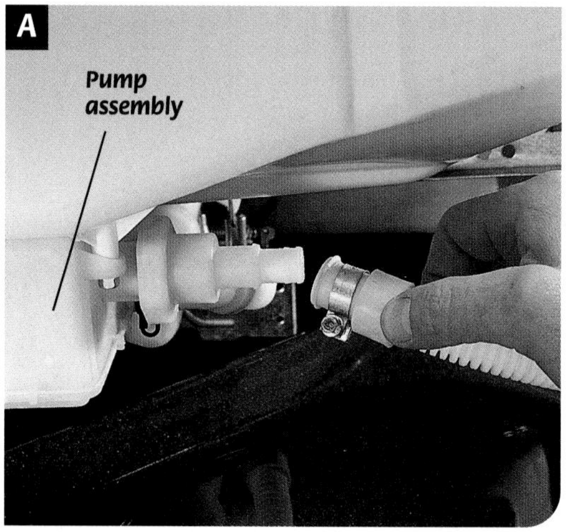

Loosen the hose clamps and remove the drain hose.

Replacing a Door Gasket

If a dishwasher starts to leak around the door, inspect the gasket—the rubber strip that extends around the inside edge of the door. If the gasket appears to be in good condition, adjusting the door catch may solve the problem. Loosen the retaining screws on the door catch, reposition it, and tighten the screws.

If the gasket is cracked or damaged, however, replace it. Buy a replacement gasket that's identical to the old one.

Disconnect the electrical power at the main service panel. Pull out the bottom dish rack.

Remove the old gasket, using a screwdriver to pry up the tabs or loosen the retaining screws that hold it in place.

Soak the new gasket in warm soapy water to make it more pliable and to lubricate it.

Install the new gasket, pressing or sliding it into its track. If your gasket has screws or clips, refasten as you go **(photo B).** Work from the center of the door to the ends.

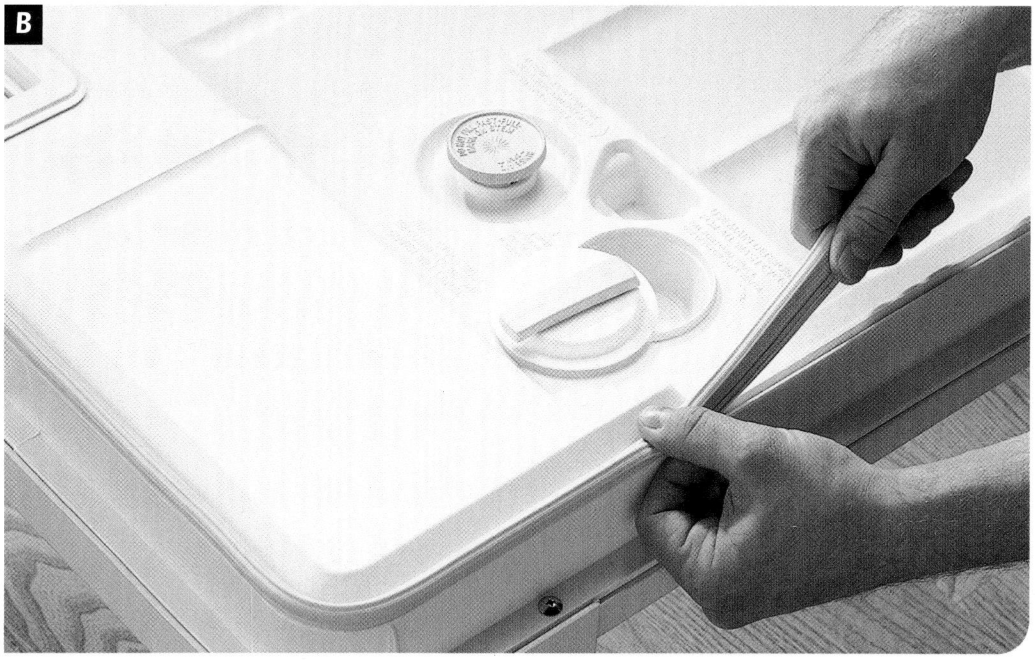

Install the replacement gasket, working from the middle to the ends.

Testing an Inlet Valve & Replacing the Valve Screen

If the dishwasher won't fill, or won't stop filling, check the water inlet valve solenoid.

Turn off the power at the service panel and shut off the water supply to the dishwasher. Remove the access panel and locate the water supply connection.

Disconnect the wires from the terminals on the valve. Attach the clip of a continuity tester to one terminal and touch the probe to the other. If the tester does not glow, the solenoid is faulty and should be replaced.

Some inlet valves have a screen or filter which can become clogged, restricting water flow. To replace the screen, place a shallow pan beneath the inlet valve.

Release the clamp on the fill tube and pull the tube from the valve outlet **(photo C).**

Disconnect the water supply tube. Loosen the valve bracket screws and remove the valve.

Remove the screen, using a small screwdriver **(photo D).** Replace the screen with a new one and reinstall the valve.

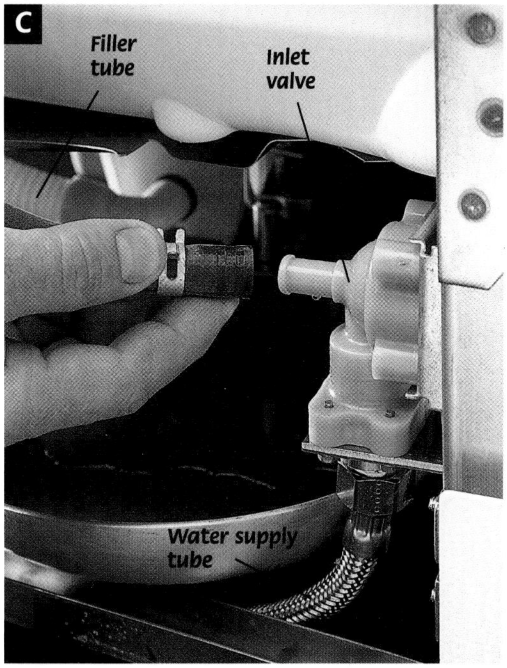

Position a pan to catch draining water, then remove the fill tube from the inlet valve.

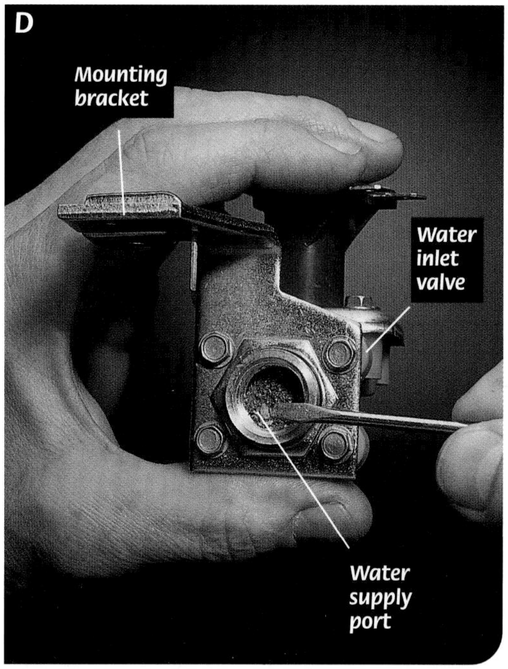

Remove the water inlet valve screen with a screwdriver, and install a new one.

Replacing a Dishwasher

When replacing a dishwasher, make sure the existing plumbing and wiring service is sufficient for the new dishwasher. Code now requires a dedicated 20-amp circuit. You can wire this circuit into half of a split duplex receptacle, and use the other half of the receptacle to power a food disposer. Code may also require an air gap, a device designed to keep drain water from back-siphoning into the dishwasher and contaminating clean dishes.

To remove the old dishwasher, shut off the power to the appliance at the main service panel and the water supply at the shutoff valve.

Disconnect the drain hose at the garbage disposal or the sink waste-T tailpiece. Remove the access panel below the dishwasher door.

Remove the metal cover on the electrical box. Disconnect the black and white wires at the wire nut connections and detach the green wire from the ground screw.

Place a shallow pan beneath the water inlet valve, and detach the water supply tube at the L-fitting with channel-type pliers. Remove any screws or brackets holding the dishwasher in place. Pull the dishwasher from the cabinet.

If you need an air gap, install one in a predrilled sink opening, or bore a new hole into the sink or countertop with a drill and hole saw **(photo A).**

Drill holes for electrical and plumbing lines into the sink base cabinet **(photo B).** Check the manufacturer's specifications for the sizes of holes. Enlarge existing holes, if necessary.

Tools: *Drill, hole saw, channel-type pliers, level, screwdriver, utility knife, combination tool.*

Materials: *Air gap, drain hose, waste-T tailpiece (if needed), rubber hose, hose clamps, braided steel supply tube, brass L-fitting, 12-gauge power supply cord, wire connectors.*

Slide the new dishwasher into place, feeding the rubber drain hose through the hole in the cabinet. Level the dishwasher by adjusting the threaded feet, and test the door for smooth operation. Make sure the dishwasher's mounting brackets are aligned with the underside of the countertop and cabinets.

Make the plumbing connections inside the sink cabinet. Attach the dishwasher drain hose to the small nipple on the air gap. If your dishwasher will drain into a food disposer, connect a hose between the large air gap nipple and the disposer drain nipple **(photo C).** Otherwise, run a hose from the air gap to the nipple on the waste-T tailpiece in the sink drain line **(photo D).**

Note: If you do not use an air gap, create a high bend in the drain hose by attaching the hose to the underside of the cabinet top. Elevating the hose will help prevent sewage from entering the dishwasher if the sink drain backs up. Use wire or a plastic strap to fasten the hose.

Connect the dishwasher water supply tube to the hot water shutoff valve, using channel-type pliers **(photo E).**

Remove the access panel on the dishwasher. Connect a brass L-fitting to the threaded outlet on the dishwasher's water inlet valve and tighten with channel-type pliers **(photo F).** Be careful not to overtighten the water connections. Connect the water supply tube to the L-fitting **(photo G).**

Remove the metal cover on the dishwasher's electrical box. Feed a 12-gauge power cord into the electrical box. Strip 1/2" of insulation from each wire, using a combination tool.

Using wire connectors, connect the black wires together, then the white wires **(photo H).** Connect the green ground wire to the ground screw. Replace the electrical box cover and the dishwasher access panel.

Anchor the dishwasher to the countertop or cabinet, using the mounting brackets.

Restore the power and water supply, then run a test cycle. Check for leaks and tighten plumbing connections, if necessary.

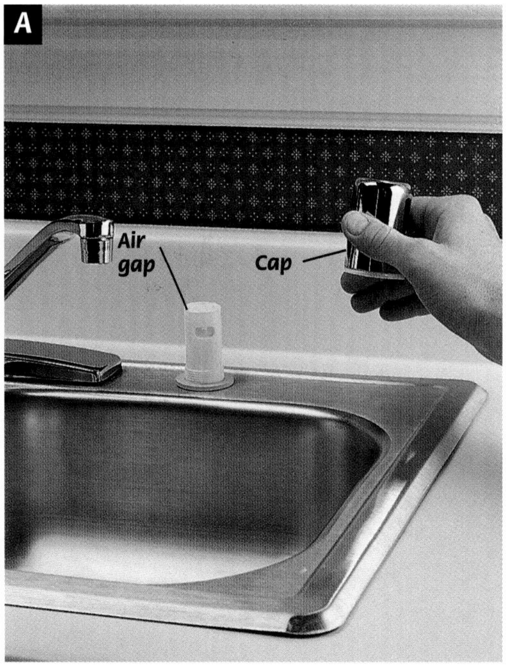

Mount air gap into sink opening, or drill a new hole.

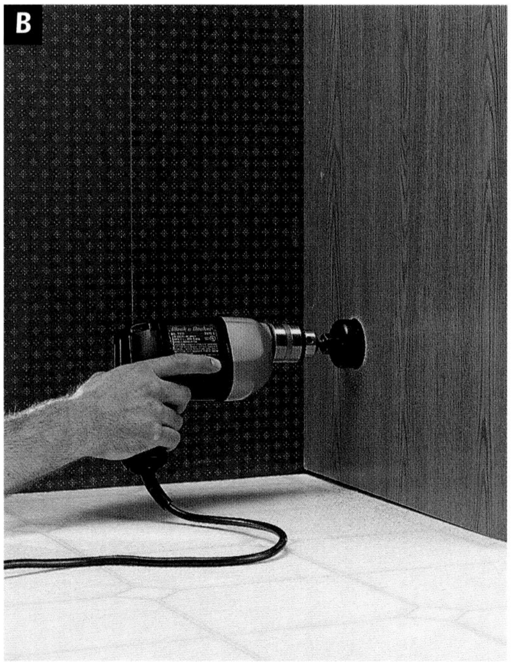

Drill holes for electrical and plumbing lines.

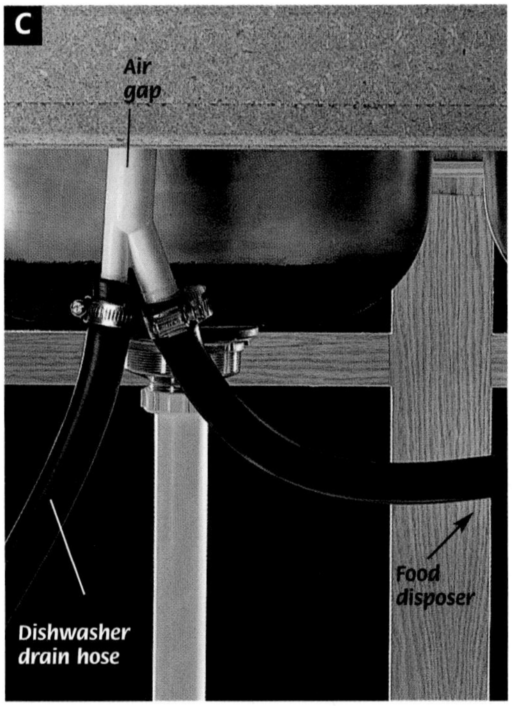

Connect an air gap to the drain nipple on the food disposer.

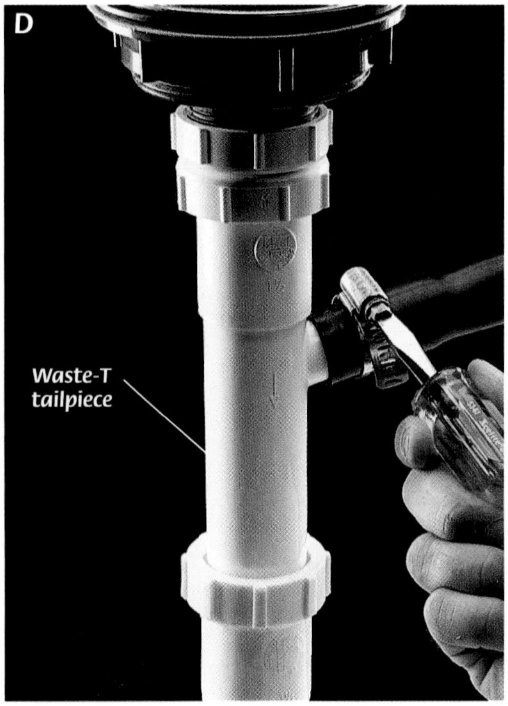

On sinks without a disposer, connect the dishwasher drain hose to the waste-T nipple.

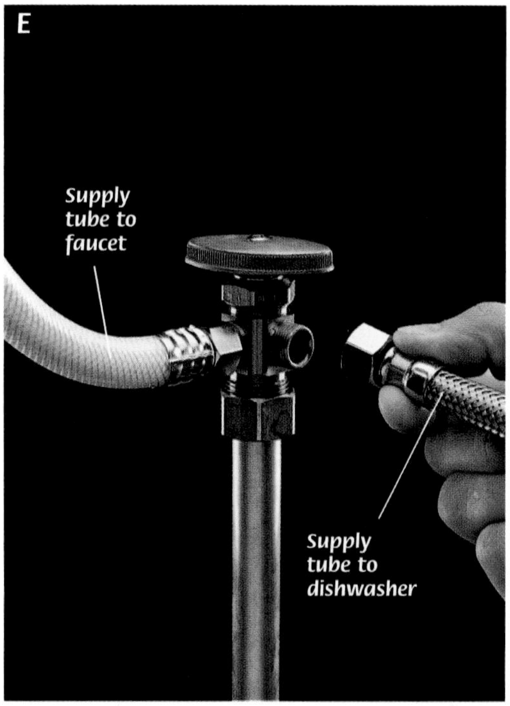

Connect the dishwasher supply tube to the hot water shutoff valve.

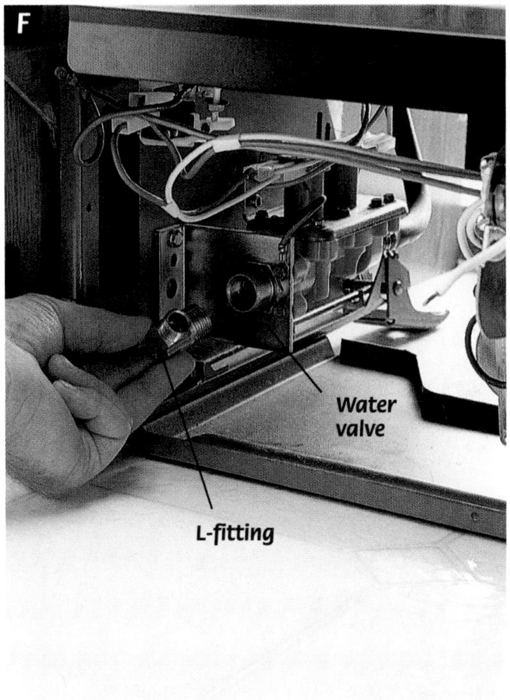

Remove the access panel, and connect a brass L-fitting to the dishwasher's water inlet valve.

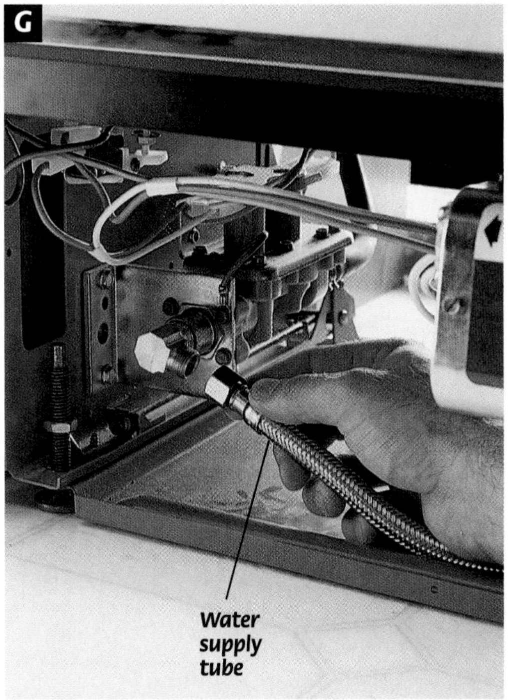

Attach the water supply tube to the L-fitting, using channel-type pliers.

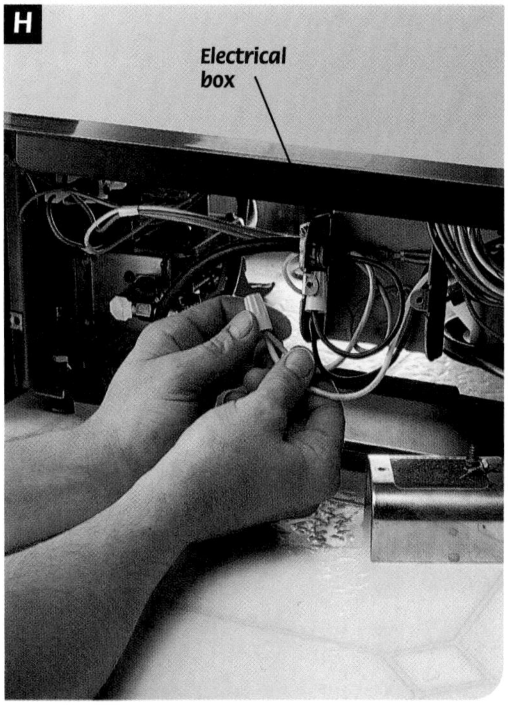

Use wire connectors to join wires of matching colors. Attach the ground wire to the ground screw.

Water Heaters

Most water heaters are fueled by either gas or electricity. Gas models, which are most common, use a single burner to heat up to 65 gallons of water. They're simple devices and are easy to maintain and repair.

Hot water leaves the tank through the *hot water outlet* and cold water enters through the *dip tube*. As the water temperature drops, the *thermostat* opens the gas valve, and the pilot flame lights the *gas burner*. Exhaust gases are vented through the *flue*.

When the water reaches a preset temperature, the thermostat closes the gas valve, shutting off the burner. The *thermocouple* protects against gas leaks by shutting off the gas if the pilot flame goes out. The *anode rod* creates a reverse electron flow, which prevents pinholes from developing in the tank lining. The *pressure-relief valve* guards the tank against rupture from steam buildup.

A plate on the side lists the tank capacity, insulation R-value, and working pressure (pounds-per-square-inch). On an electric heater, it also lists the voltage and wattage of the heating elements and thermostats.

When a water heater leaks, replace it immediately—this means that the inner tank has rusted through; if it gives way, the resulting flood of scalding hot water could cause serious injury and property damage.

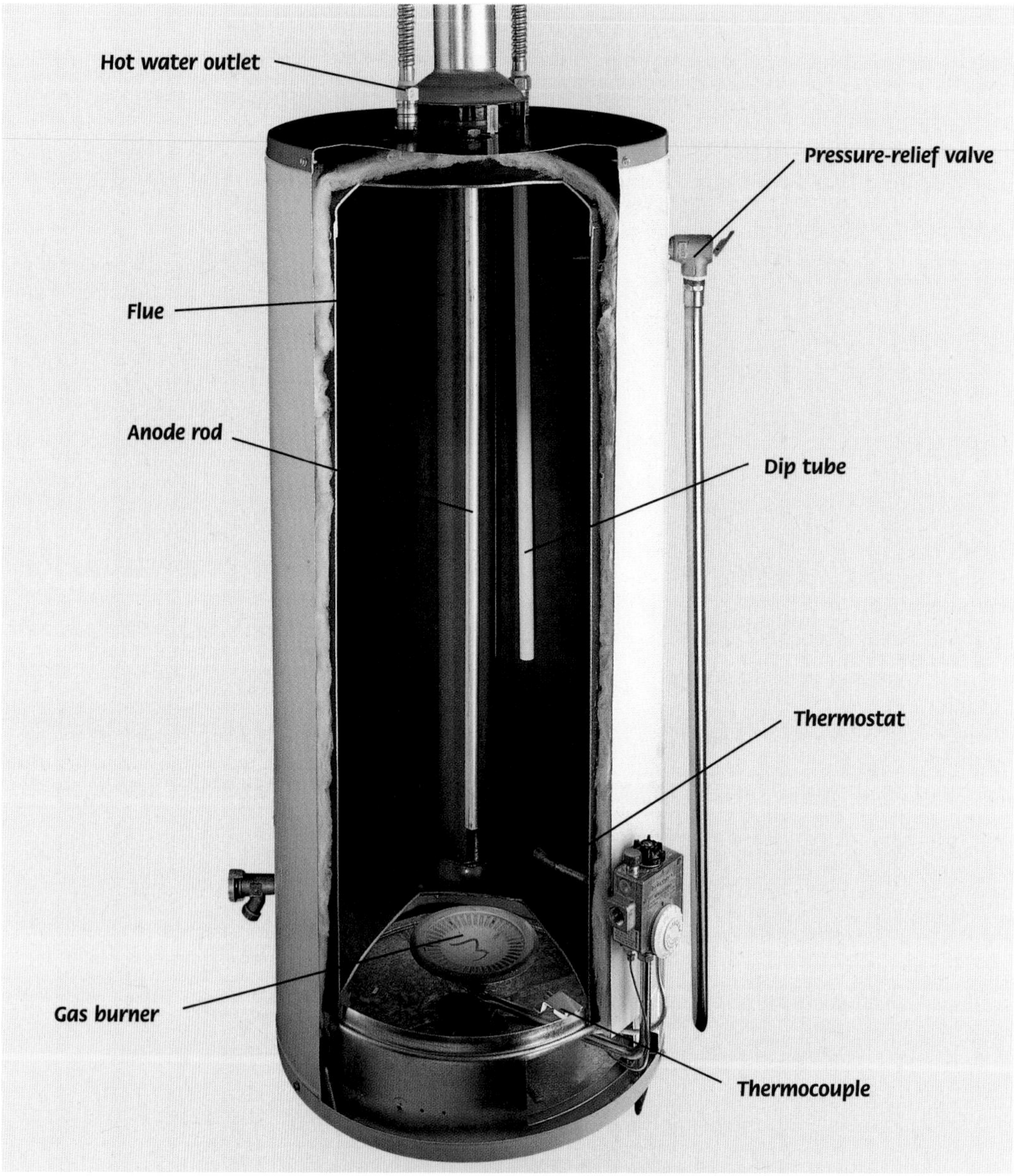

The elements of a typical gas water heater. With regular maintenance, a water heater can last 20 years or more.

Water Heater Safety

Don't set a water heater thermostat so high that tap water reaches an unsafe temperature. Children and the elderly are especially likely to be injured by hot tap water. The best setting for a water heater thermostat is 120° or 125°F (L or Low). To check the temperature, let the water run for a few minutes, then check its temperature with a thermometer.

It's essential to ventilate a gas water heater properly. If you smell smoke or gas around the heater, turn it off immediately, close the gas valve, and ventilate the area. Make sure the flue is clear and the exhaust duct isn't rusted out or clogged. If you can't fix the problem, call a professional.

Dust and dirt are quite combustible, so keep the burner area of the heater clean. Store any flammable materials well away from it.

Don't add an insulation blanket to a gas water heater. Insulation can block the air supply or interfere with ventilation of exhaust.

Before adding an insulation blanket to an electric water heater, check the caution labels. Some newer water heaters have so much insulation that it isn't advisable to add any more.

Water Heater Problems & Repairs

Problems	Repairs
No hot water, or not enough hot water.	1. Gas heater: Make sure gas is on, then relight pilot flame (page 373). Electric heater: Make sure power is on, then reset thermostat (page 368). 2. Flush water heater to remove sediment in tank (below). 3. Insulate hot water pipes to reduce heat loss (page 166). 4. Gas heater: Clean gas burner & replace thermocouple (page 366). Electric heater: Replace heating element or thermostat (page 368). 5. Raise temperature setting of thermostat.
Pressure-relief valve leaks.	1. Lower the temperature setting (below). 2. Install a new pressure-relief valve (page 371).
Pilot flame will not stay lighted.	Clean gas burner & replace the thermocouple (page 366).
Water heater leaks around base of tank.	Replace the water heater immediately (gas: page 370, electric: page 374).

Maintaining a Water Heater

Standard water heaters are designed for easy maintenance, with removable access panels that allow you to easily remove and replace worn-out parts. Buy only parts that match the make and model of your water heater. Most units have a nameplate with the information you'll need, including the pressure rating of the tank and the voltage and wattage ratings of heating elements if the water heater is an electric model.

On average, water heaters last about 10 years, but with regular maintenance, they can last far longer, up to 20 years. To get longer life from your water heater, perform the following maintenance steps:

1. Lower the thermostat setting to 120°F **(photo A).** Lower temperatures minimize tank damage from overheating and reduce energy consumption.

2. Once a year, test the pressure-relief valve **(photo B).** Lift up on the lever and let it snap back. The valve should allow a burst of water into the drain pipe. If it doesn't, install a new valve (page 371).

3. Once a year, flush the water heater by draining several gallons of water from the tank **(photo C).** This annual flushing removes the sediment that can cause corrosion and reduce efficiency.

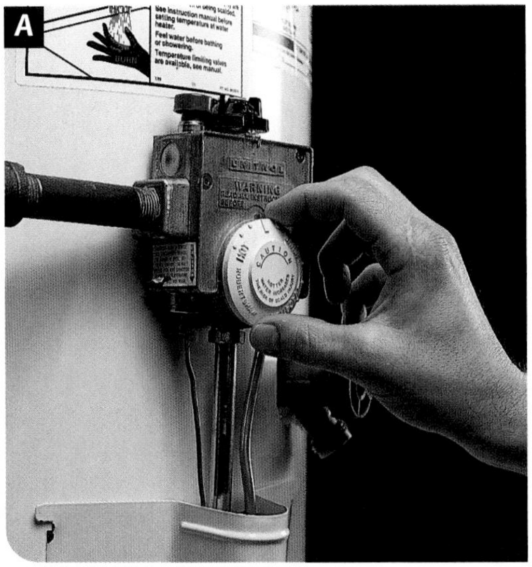

Lower the thermostat setting to 120°F.

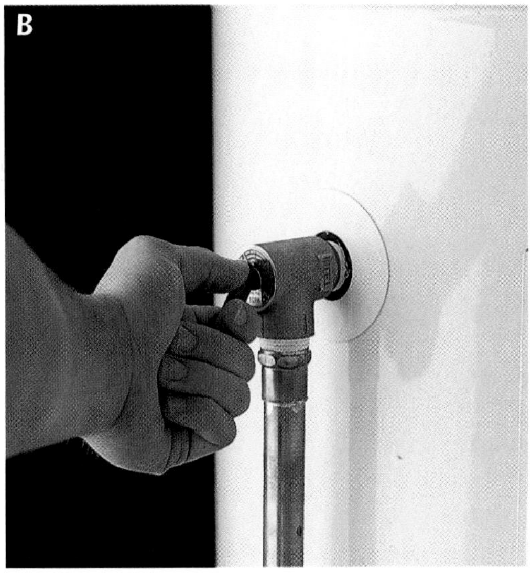

Test the pressure-relief valve and replace it, if necessary.

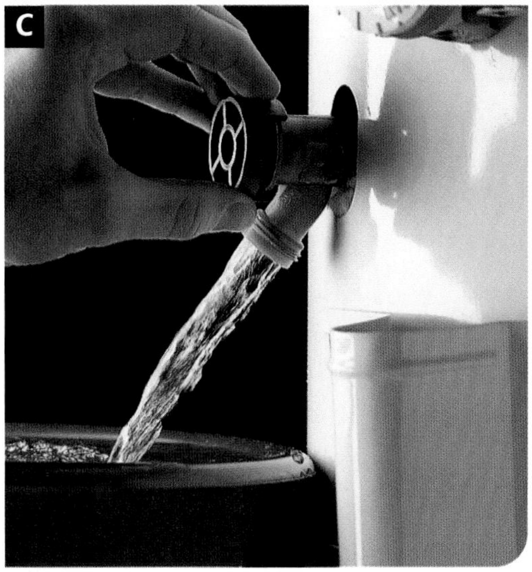

Flush the system by draining water from the tank.

Servicing a Gas Water Heater

If a gas water heater isn't heating water, check the pilot light. Remove the outer and inner access panels to make sure the pilot is lighted. If not, relight it (page 373). Replace both the inner and outer access panels, and keep them in position—operating the water heater without the panels can allow air drafts to extinguish the pilot light.

If the pilot light is lit but the burner won't light, or if the gas is burning with a yellow, smoky flame, clean the burner and the pilot gas tube.

If you can't get the pilot light lit, the thermocouple may be worn out. The thermocouple, a thin copper wire running from the control box to the gas burner, is a safety device designed to automatically shut off the gas if the pilot light goes out. New thermocouples are inexpensive and can be installed in a few minutes. When you replace a thermocouple, it's a good idea to clean the burner and gas tube at the same time.

Start by shutting off the gas by turning the gas cock on top of the control box to the OFF position **(photo A).** Wait 10 minutes for the gas to dissipate.

Disconnect the pilot gas tube, the burner gas tube, and the thermocouple from the bottom of the control box **(photo B).**

Remove the outer and inner access panels covering the burner chamber **(photo C).**

Pull down slightly on the pilot gas tube, the burner gas tube, and the thermocouple wire to free them from the control box **(photo D).** Tilt the burner unit slightly and remove it from the burner chamber.

Unscrew the burner from the burner gas tube nipple **(photo E).** Clean the small opening in the nipple, using a piece of thin wire. Vacuum out the burner jets and the burner chamber.

Clean the pilot gas tube with a piece of wire **(photo F).** Vacuum out any loose particles. Screw the burner onto the gas tube nipple.

Pull back the old thermocouple from the bracket **(photo G).** Install a new thermocouple by pushing its tip into the bracket until it snaps into place.

Insert the burner unit into the chamber **(photo H).** Fit the flat tab at the end of the burner into the slotted opening in the mounting bracket at the bottom of the chamber.

Reconnect the gas tubes and the thermocouple to the control box. Turn on the gas and test for leaks; light the pilot light (page 373).

Make sure the flame of the pilot light wraps around the tip of the thermocouple **(photo I).** If it doesn't, use a pair of needlenose pliers to adjust the thermocouple until the tip is surrounded by flame. Reattach the inner and outer access panels.

Tools: *Adjustable wrench, vacuum cleaner, needlenose pliers.*

Materials: *Thin wire, replacement thermocouple.*

Turn off the gas. Wait 10 minutes to let gas dissipate before you start working.

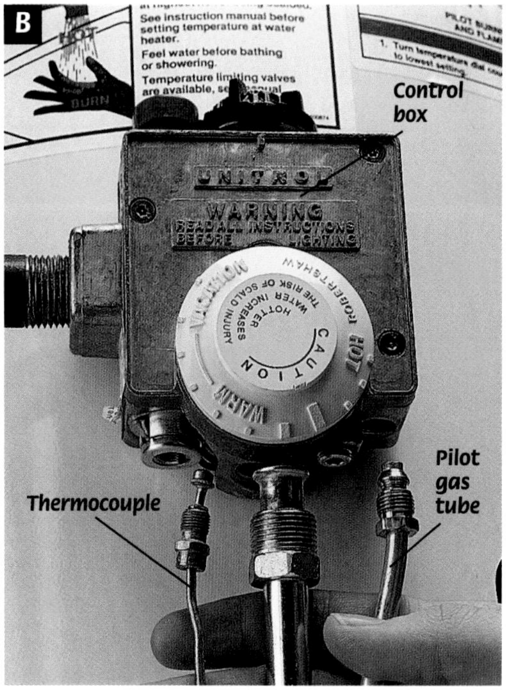

Disconnect the pilot gas tube, the burner gas tube, and the thermocouple.

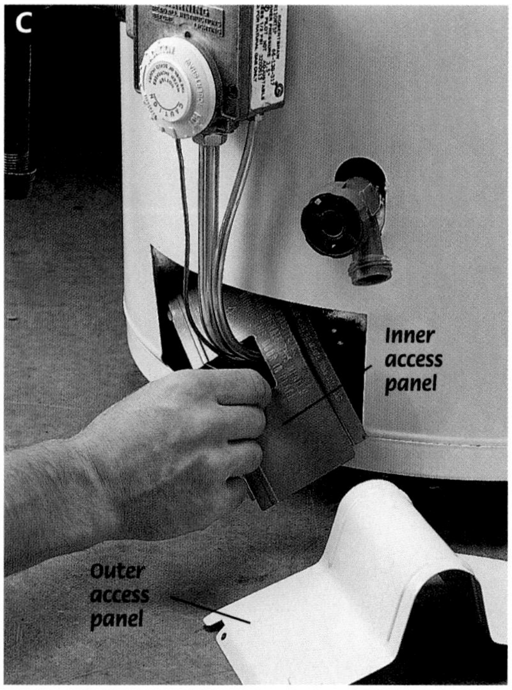

Remove the burner chamber's outer access panel, then the inner panel.

Free the pilot gas tube, burner gas tube, and thermocouple wire from the control box. Remove the burner through the access opening.

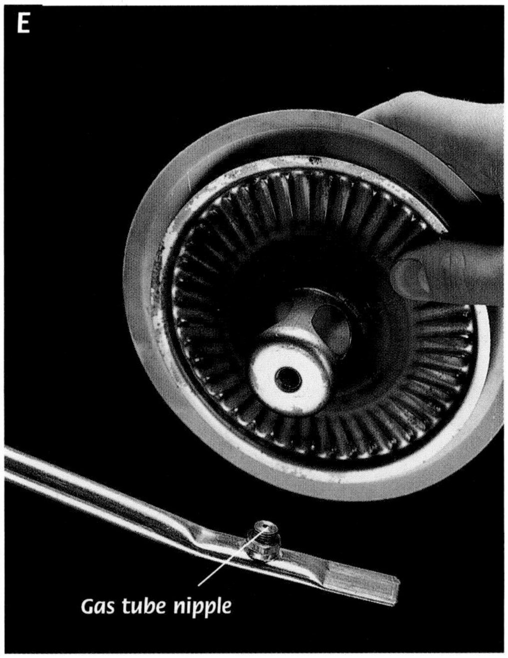

Unscrew the burner from the burner gas tube nipple and clean both using a piece of wire. Vacuum out the burner jets and burner chamber.

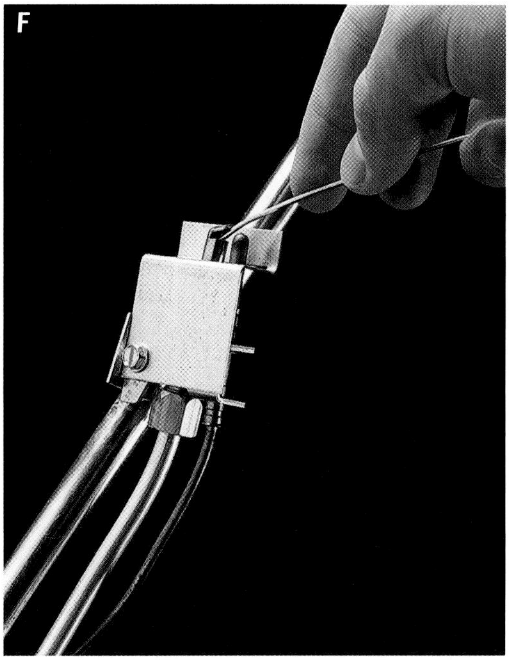

Clean the pilot gas tube, using a piece of thin wire. Vacuum out any loose particles. Screw the burner onto the gas tube nipple.

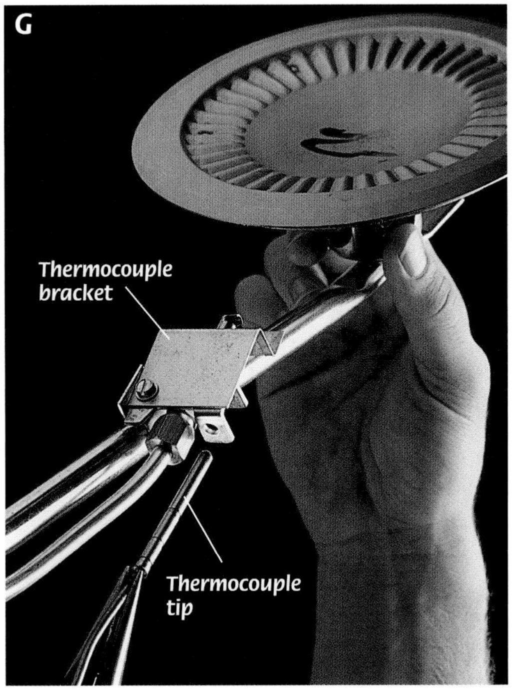

Remove the old thermocouple from the bracket. Install a new thermocouple by pushing its tip into the bracket.

Reinstall the burner unit, fitting the flat tab at the end of the burner into the slotted opening in the mounting bracket at the bottom of the chamber.

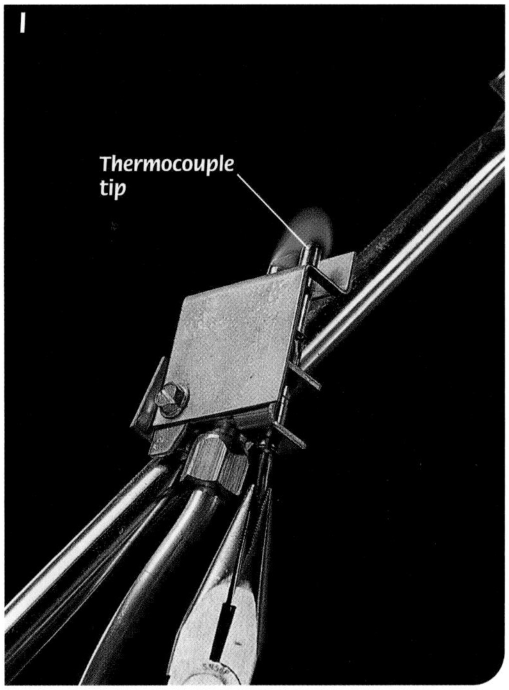

Adjust the pilot flame so it surrounds the thermocouple tip, using needlenose pliers.

Diagnosing Problems with an Electric Water Heater

The most common problem with electric water heaters is a burned-out heating element. Every heater has one or two heating elements mounted in the side wall.

To determine which element has failed, check the hot water at a faucet. If the faucet delivers water that's warm, but not hot at any setting, replace the top heating element. If it delivers a small amount of very hot water, followed by cold water, replace the bottom heating element.

If replacing the heating element doesn't solve the problem, replace the thermostat, which is located under the access panel on the side of the water heater.

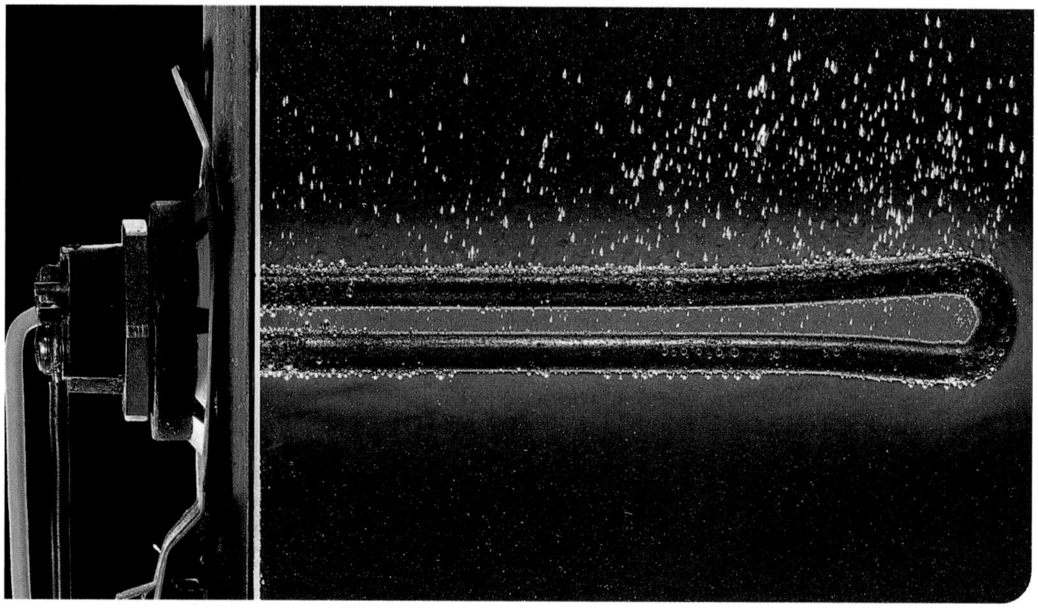

Select a replacement heating element or thermostat with the same voltage and wattage rating listed on the nameplate.

Replacing an Electric Thermostat

Turn off the power at the main service panel. Remove the access panel on the side of the heater, and test for current by touching the probes of a neon circuit tester to the top pair of terminal screws on the thermostat (page 374).

Label the connections with masking tape, then disconnect the thermostat wires **(photo A).** Pull the old thermostat out of its mounting clips. Snap the new thermostat in place, and reconnect the wires.

Press the thermostat reset button, then use a screwdriver to set the thermostat to the desired temperature, between 120° and 125°F **(photo B).** Replace the insulation and access panel. Restore power to the water heater.

Tools: *Screwdriver, neon circuit tester.*
Materials: *Replacement thermostat.*

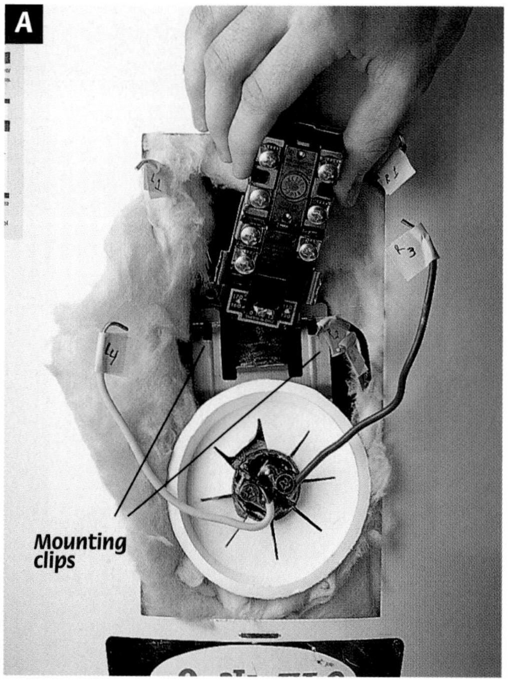

Label wires for connection locations, then disconnect them. Remove the old thermostat and place a new one into the mounting clips. Reconnect the wires.

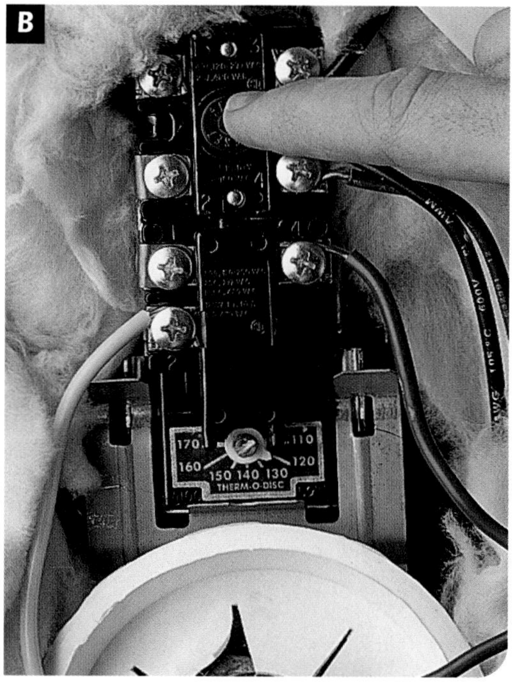

Press thermostat reset button. Set thermostat temperature, using a screwdriver. Replace insulation and access panel, then turn on power.

Replacing an Electric Heating Element

When replacing a heating element, begin by closing the shutoff valves, draining the tank (page 370), and shutting off the power to the water heater.

When these steps are complete, remove the access panel on the side of the unit **(photo C).**

Put on protective gloves and carefully move the insulation aside **(photo D).** Test for power (page 374). When you're sure there is no power to the unit, disconnect the wires from the heating element. Remove the protective collar.

Unscrew the heating element, using channel-type pliers **(photo E).** Remove the old gasket from around the water heater opening. Coat both sides of the new gasket with pipe joint compound.

Slide the new gasket over the heating element, and screw the element into the tank **(photo F).** Tighten the element with channel-type pliers.

Replace the protective collar, and reconnect all the wires **(photo G).** Open the hot water faucets throughout the house, then open the water heater shutoff valves. When water runs steadily from all the taps, close the faucets.

Use a screwdriver to set the thermostat between 120° and 125°F **(photo H).** Press the thermostat reset buttons. Wearing gloves, fold the insulation over the thermostat. Replace the access panel, then restore the power.

Tools: *Screwdriver, gloves, neon circuit tester, channel-type pliers.*

Materials: *Masking tape, replacement heating element or thermostat, replacement gasket, pipe joint compound.*

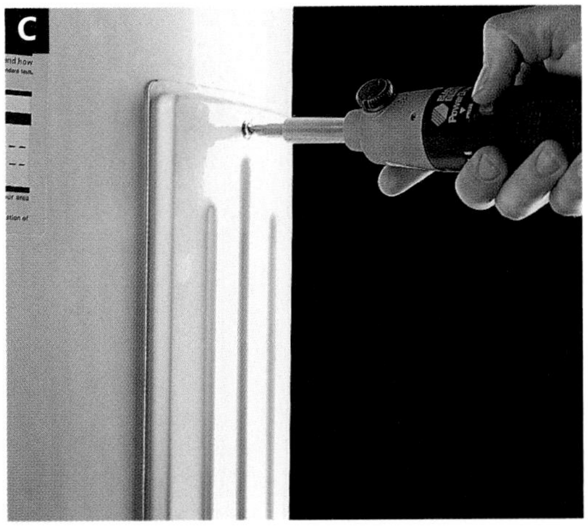

Shut off the power, drain the tank, then remove the access panel.

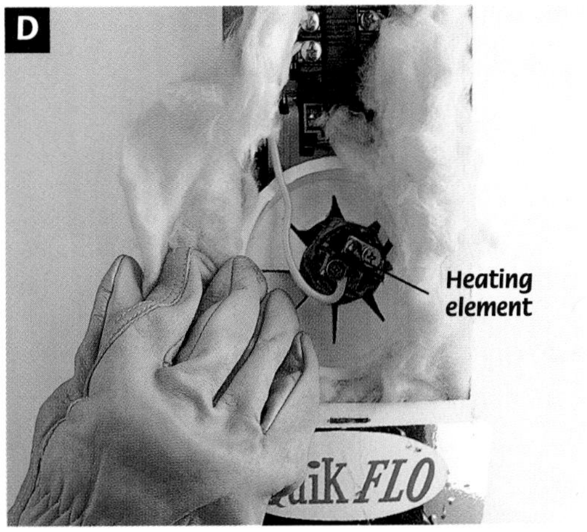

Test for current, then disconnect wires to the heating element.

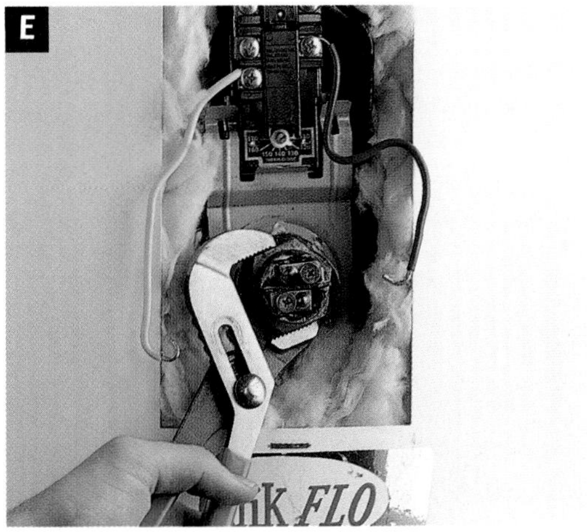

Unscrew and remove the heating element.

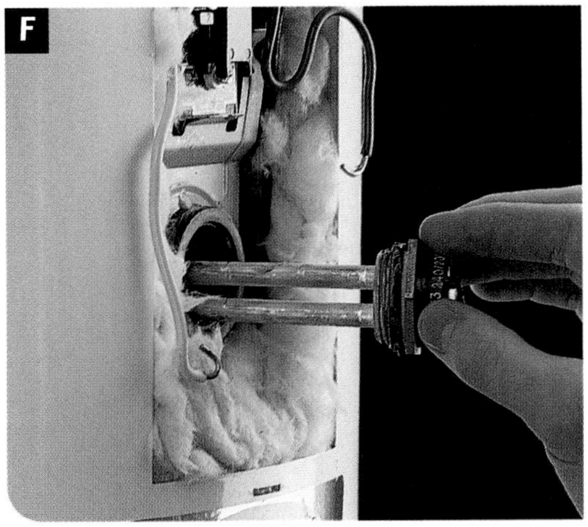

Screw the element into the tank, using channel-type pliers.

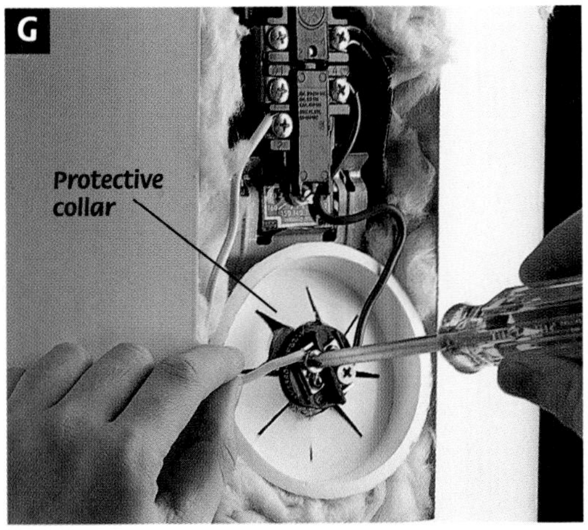

Replace the protective collar, reconnect the wires, and restore water to the unit.

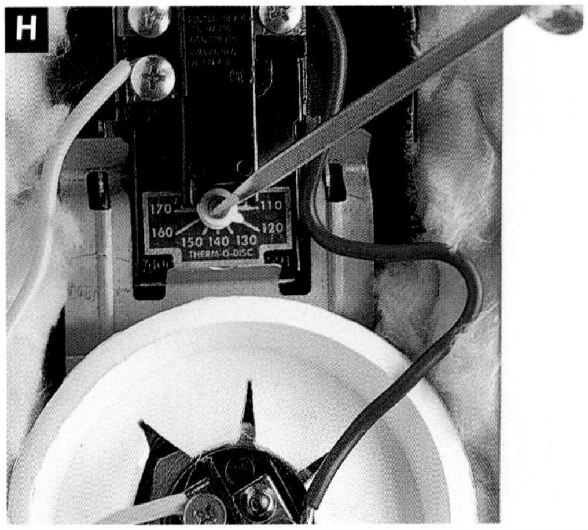

Set the temperature, and reset the thermostat.

Replacing a Gas Water Heater

When you buy a new water heater, remember that an energy-efficient model may be more expensive than a lower quality model, but over the life of the unit, it may cost less to own. Also, keep in mind that pressure-relief valves usually must be purchased separately from the water heater. Make sure you purchase a valve that matches the *working pressure* rating of the tank you purchase.

Shut off the gas by turning the handle of the in-line valve until it's perpendicular to the gas line **(photo A).** Wait 10 minutes for the gas to dissipate. Shut off the water supply at the shutoff valves.

Disconnect the gas line at the union fitting or at the flare fitting below the shutoff valve, using pipe wrenches **(photo B).** Disassemble the pipes and fittings and set them aside for later use.

Open the hose bib on the side of the tank to empty the tank **(photo C).** Drain the water into buckets or attach a hose and run it to a floor drain.

Disconnect the hot and cold water pipes above the water heater **(photo D).** If the pipes are soldered copper, use a hacksaw or tubing

Tools: Pipe wrenches, hacksaw or tubing cutter, screwdriver, hammer, appliance dolly, level, small wire brush, propane torch, adjustable wrench.

Materials: Bucket or garden hose, wood shims, #4 gauge $\frac{3}{8}$" sheetmetal screws, pressure-relief valve, threaded male pipe adapters, lead-free solder, two heat-saver nipples, Teflon tape, flexible water connectors, $\frac{3}{4}$" copper pipe, pipe joint compound, sponge, masking tape.

Shut off the gas and wait 10 minutes. Shut off the water at the shutoff valves.

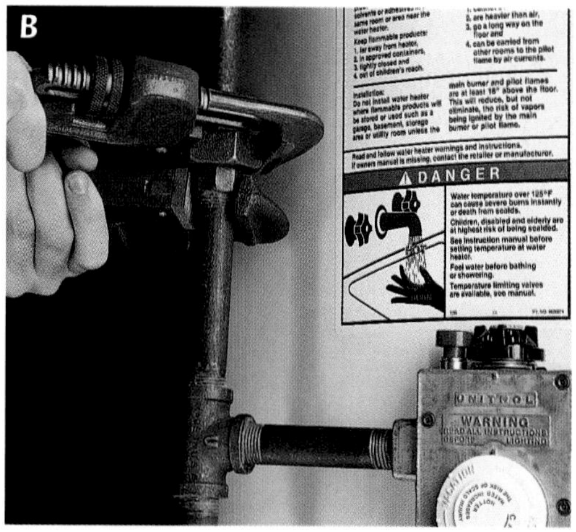

Disconnect the gas line, then disassemble the pipes and fittings.

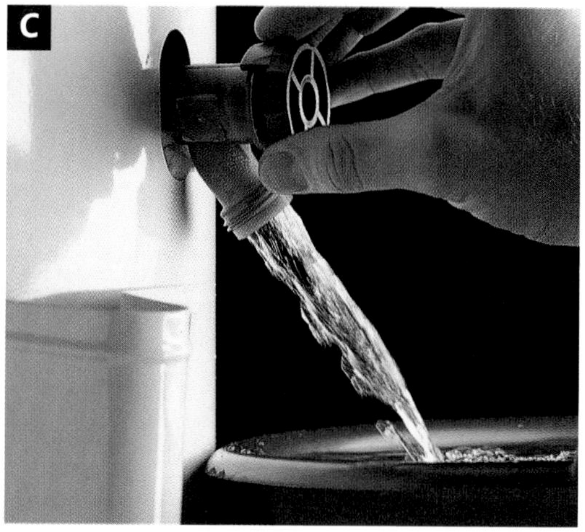

Drain the water from the water heater's tank.

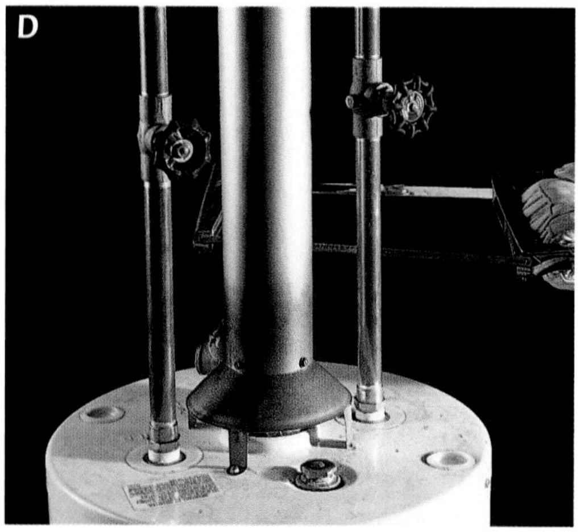

Disconnect the hot and cold water pipes above the water heater.

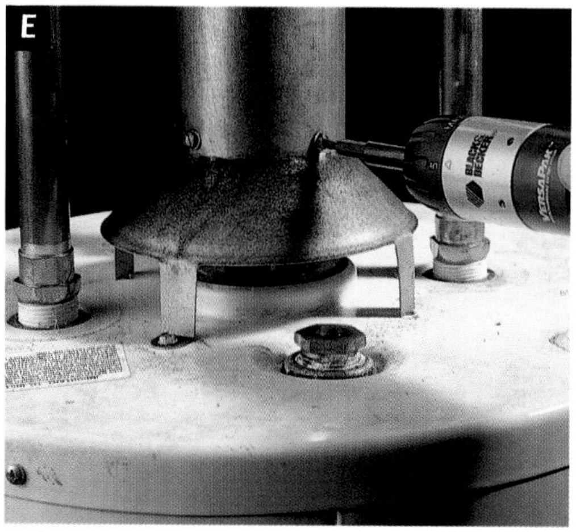

Remove the sheetmetal screws and disengage the exhaust duct, then remove the old water heater.

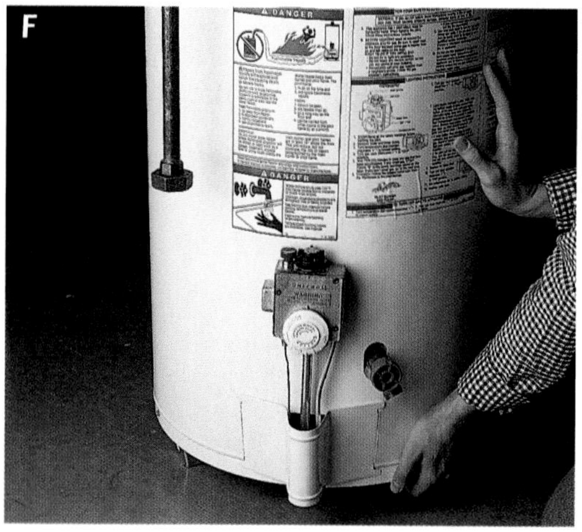

Position with the control box close to the gas line, the access panel accessible, and adequate clearance around the unit.

cutter to cut through them, just below the shutoff valves. It's important to make straight cuts so the fittings will be watertight when you connect the new water heater.

Disconnect the exhaust duct by removing the sheetmetal screws **(photo E).** Remove the old water heater with an appliance dolly. Use the appliance dolly to put the new water heater in place, positioning it so the control box is close to the gas line **(photo F).** Maintain 6" or more clearance around the unit for ventilation, and make sure the access panel for the burner chamber isn't obstructed.

Check the side of the tank with a level **(photo G).** If necessary, place wood shims under the legs to level the unit.

Position the flue hat so its legs fit into the slots on the water heater, then slip the exhaust duct onto the flue hat. Using a level, check the horizontal duct for the proper slope—it should slope upward 1/4" per foot to keep fumes from backing up into the house **(photo H).**

Attach the flue hat to the exhaust duct, driving #4 gauge 3/8" sheetmetal screws every 4" around the duct **(photo I).**

Wrap the threads of a new pressure-relief valve with Teflon tape **(photo J).** Use a pipe wrench to screw the valve into the tank opening.

Measure the distance between the pressure-relief valve and the floor **(photo K).** Cut a length of copper or CPVC drain pipe that will reach to within 3" of the floor. Attach the pipe to the pressure-relief valve, using a threaded male adapter.

Solder a threaded male adapter to each of the water supply pipes **(photo L).** Let the pipes cool, then wrap Teflon tape around the threads of the adapters.

Wrap Teflon tape around the threads of two

continued on next page

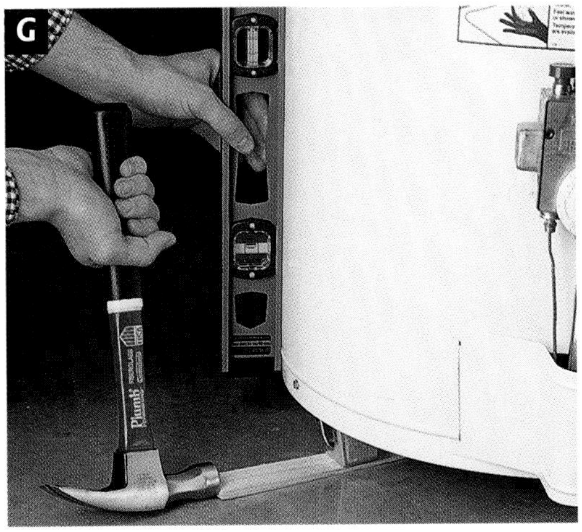

Check the unit with a level, and shim, if necessary.

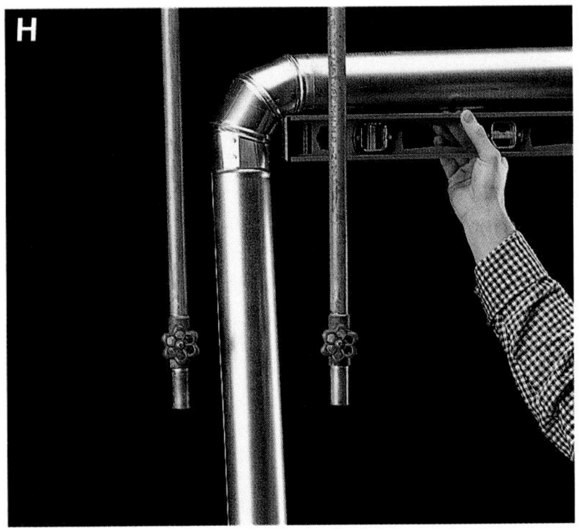

Put in place the flue hat, then the exhaust duct. Make sure the horizontal duct hangs at the correct slope.

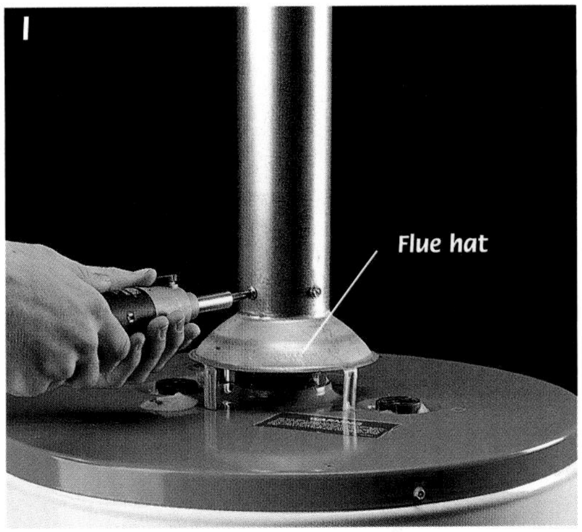

Drive one sheetmetal screw every 4" to attach the flue hat to the exhaust duct.

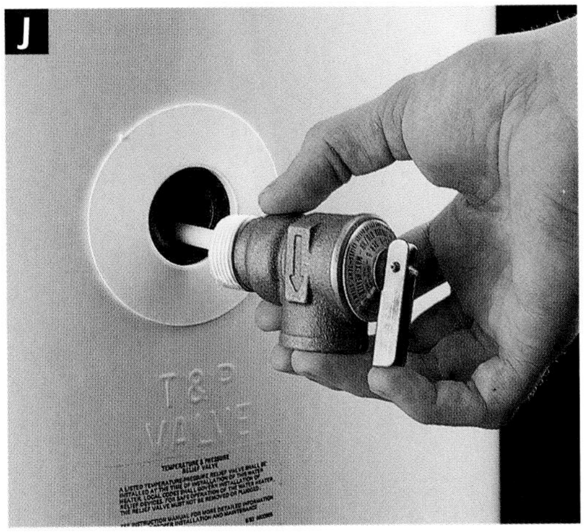

Install the pressure-relief valve.

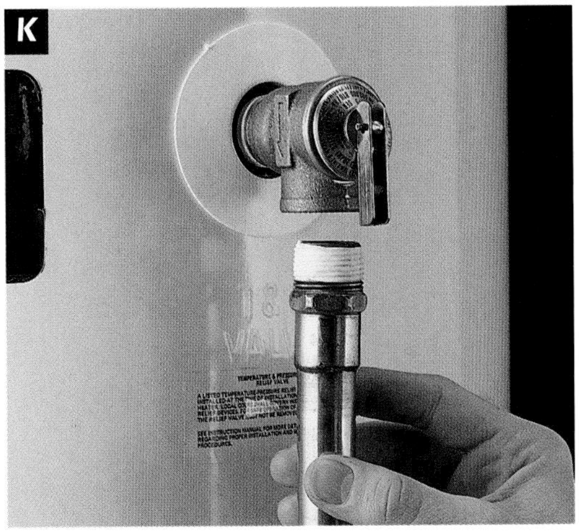

Attach a copper or CPVC drain pipe to the pressure-relief valve.

Solder a threaded male adapter to each water supply pipe.

Replacing a Gas Water Heater (cont.)

heat-saver nipples **(photo M).** Look closely at the nipples—they're color coded and have directional arrows to help you install them properly.

Attach the blue-coded nipple fitting to the cold water inlet and the red-coded fitting to the hot water outlet, using a pipe wrench **(photo N).** Install the cold water nipple with the water direction arrow facing down; install the hot water nipple with the arrow facing up.

Connect the water supply pipes to the heat-saver nipples with flexible water connectors **(photo O).** Tighten the fittings, using an adjustable wrench or channel-type pliers.

Gather the gas pipes and fittings that you removed from the old water heater, and test-fit them for the new unit **(photo P).** You may need one or two new black-iron nipples if the new water heater is taller or shorter than the old one. The capped nipple, called a *drip leg,* protects the gas burner by catching dirt particles. (**Note**: always use black iron, **not** galvanized iron, for gas lines.)

Use a small wire brush to clean the pipe threads, then coat them with pipe joint compound **(photo Q).** Assemble the gas line fittings in the following order: control box nipple (1), T-fitting (2), vertical nipple (3), union fitting (4), vertical nipple (5), cap (6). Black iron is fitted with the same methods used for galvanized iron (page 295).

If the gas line is made of flexible copper, use a flare fitting to connect the gas line to the water heater **(photo R).** Remember to use the proper techniques for flare fittings (page 292).

To restore the water supply, open the hot water taps at faucets throughout the house, then open the water heater inlet and outlet shutoff valves **(photo S).** When the water runs

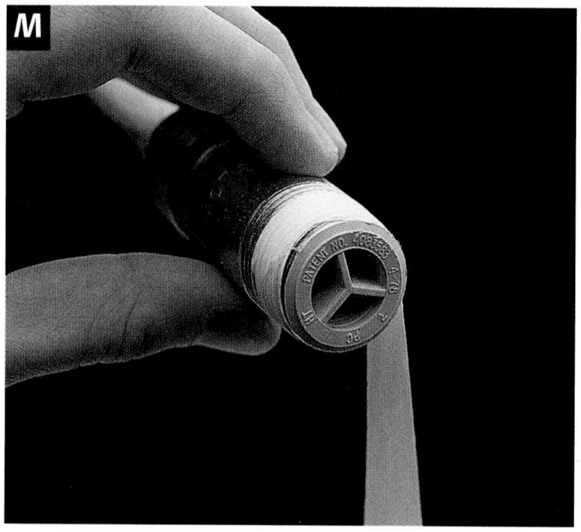

M

Wrap Teflon tape around the threads of two heat-saver nipples.

Attach the blue-coded nipple to the cold water inlet and the red-coded nipple to the hot water outlet.

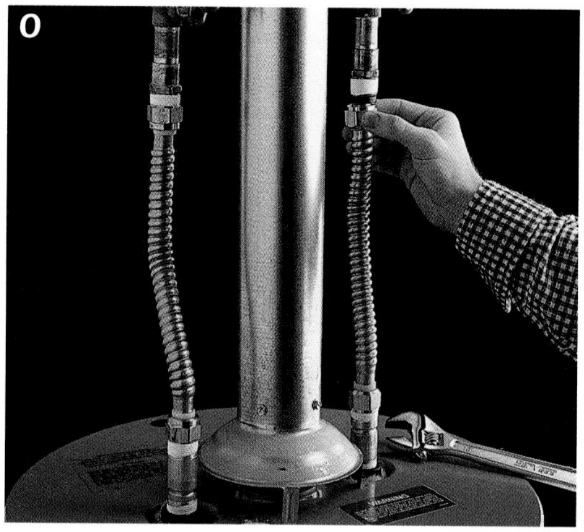

O

Connect the water lines to the heat-saver nipples with flexible water connectors.

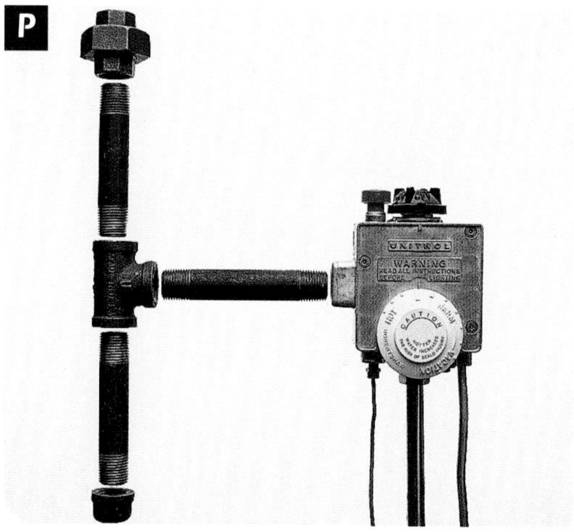

Test-fit the old gas pipes and fittings, adding fittings as necessary to adapt to the size and position of the new unit.

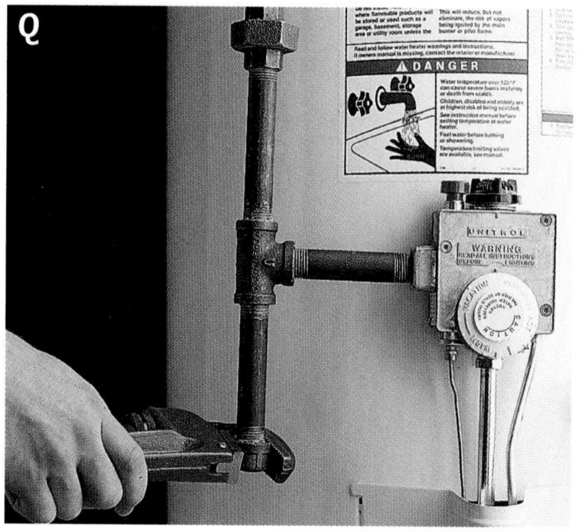

Clean the pipe threads, then coat them with pipe joint compound. Assemble and tighten the fittings.

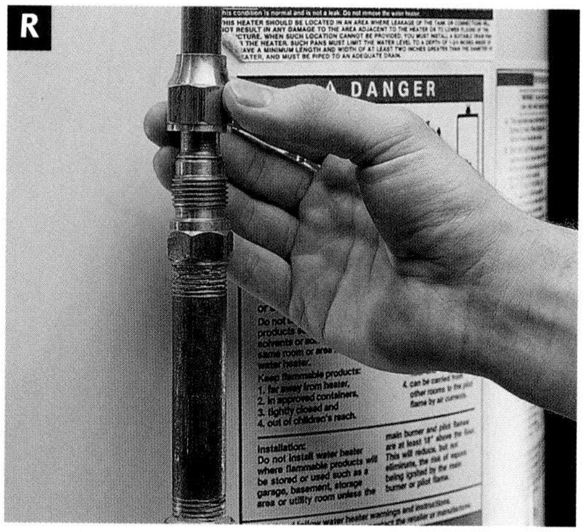

Alternate: If the gas line is flexible copper, use a flare fitting to connect it to the water heater.

steadily from all the faucets, close them.

Open the in-line valve on the gas line. To test for leaks, dab soapy water on each joint **(photo T).** If the fittings leak, the water will bubble noticeably. Use a pipe wrench to tighten any leaking joints.

Turn the gas cock on top of the control box to the PILOT position **(photo U).** Set the temperature control on the front of the box to the desired temperature, between 120° and 125°F.

Remove the outer and inner access panels covering the burner chamber **(photo V).** Light a match, and hold the flame next to the end of the pilot gas tube inside the burner chamber **(photo W).**

While holding the match next to the end of the pilot gas tube, press the reset button on top of the control box **(photo X).** When the pilot flame lights, continue to hold the reset button for one minute. Turn the gas cock to the ON position, and reattach the inner and outer access panels.

Helpful Hint

If local Plumbing Codes do not allow the use of flexible water connectors, connect the water lines to the heat-saver nipples with rigid copper pipe and fittings. Measure and cut pipe to fit the distance between the heat-saver nipples and one of the water supply lines. Sweat a fitting to the pipe, then to the supply line. Repeat this process with the other supply line.

Restore water supply to the water heater.

Open the valve on the gas line, then test fittings for leaks.

Turn the gas cock to the PILOT position, then set the temperature contol to the desired temperature.

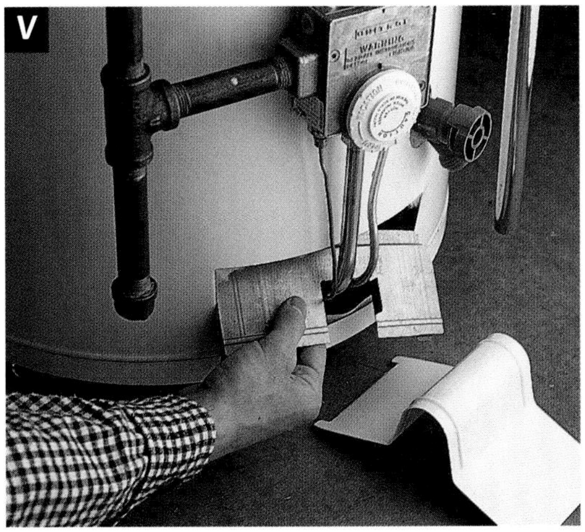

Remove the outer and inner access panels covering the burner chamber.

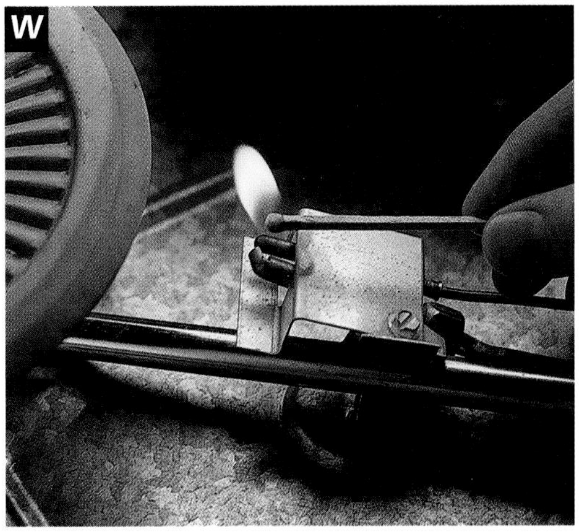

Hold a lighted match next to the pilot gas tube.

Press the reset button on top of the control box, and hold it for one minute after the pilot flame lights.

Replacing an Electric Water Heater

When you buy a new electric water heater, choose one with the same voltage as the old model, and remember that pressure-relief valves usually must be purchased separately. Make sure the valve you buy matches the *working pressure* rating of the tank. Water heaters are available with tank sizes ranging from 30 to 65 gallons. A 40-gallon tank typically is large enough for a family of four.

Turn off the power to the water heater by switching off the circuit breaker (or removing the fuse) at the main service panel **(photo A).**

Remove one of the access panels on the side of the tank **(photo B).** Wearing protective gloves, fold back the insulation to expose the thermostat **(photo C). Do not touch the bare wires until you have tested them for current.**

To make sure there is no power to the unit, test for current by touching the probes of a neon circuit tester to the top pair of terminal screws on the thermostat **(photo D).** If the tester lights, the wires are not safe to work on; turn off the main power switch and retest for current.

Open the hose bib on the side of the tank to empty the tank. Drain the water into buckets or attach a hose and run it to a floor drain.

Disconnect the hot and cold water pipes above the water heater. If the pipes are soldered copper, use a hacksaw or tubing cutter to cut through them, just below the shutoff valves. It's important to make straight cuts so the fittings will be watertight when you connect the new water heater.

Remove the coverplate on the electrical box, located at the side or top of the water heater **(photo E).** Label all wires with masking tape for reference, then disconnect them. Loosen the cable clamp, then remove the wires by pulling them through the clamp. Using an appliance dolly, remove the old unit, then put the new one in place.

Wrap Teflon tape around the threads of a new pressure-relief valve (page 371). Using a pipe wrench, screw the new valve into the

Tools: *Pipe wrenches, hacksaw or tubing cutter, screwdriver, hammer, appliance dolly, level, adjustable wrench, neon circuit tester, propane torch.*

Materials: *Bucket or garden hose, wood shims, pressure-relief valve, masking tape, lead-free solder.*

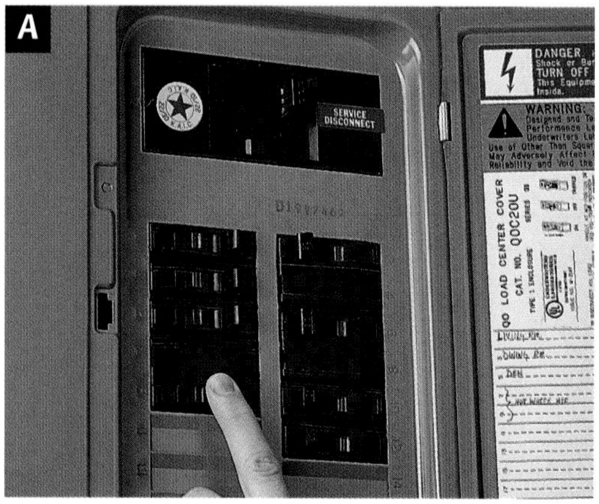

Switch off the appropriate circuit breaker or remove the fuse to turn off power to the water heater.

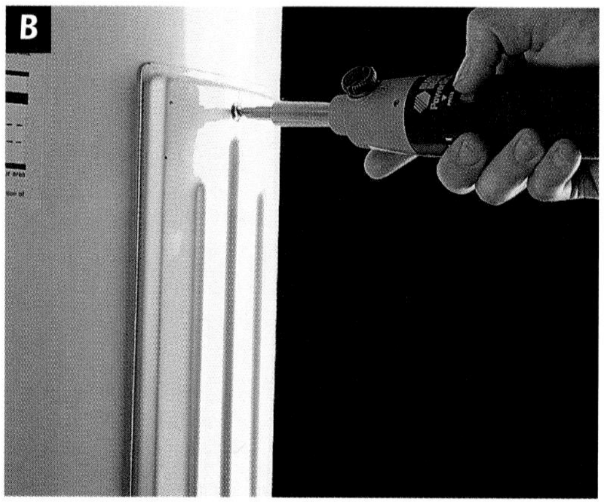

Unscrew the retaining screws on one of the heating element access panels of the water heater.

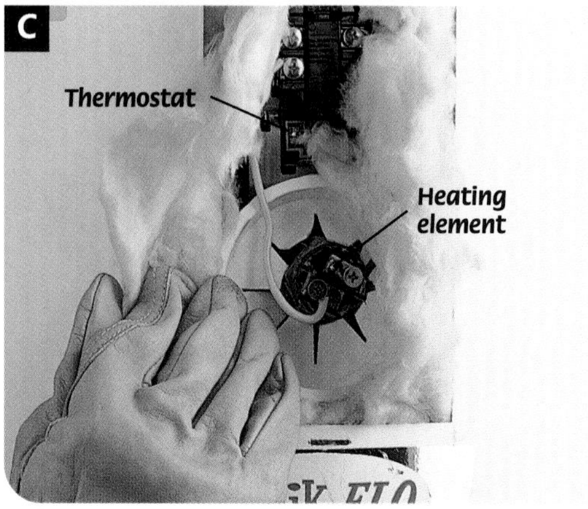

Wearing protective gloves, fold back the insulation. Caution: Do not touch bare wires until they have been tested.

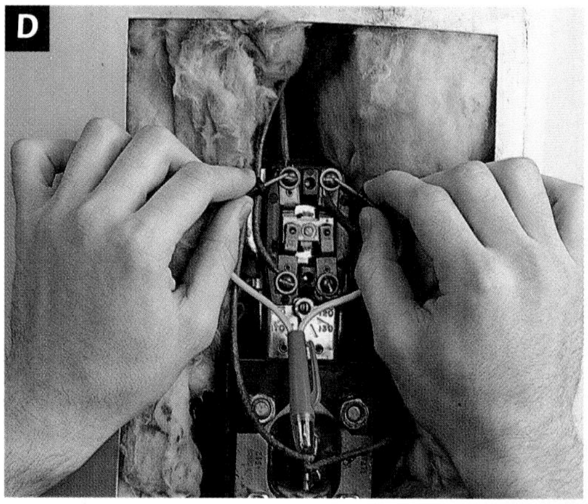

Touch the probes to the top pair of terminal screws. If the tester lights, turn off main power switch and retest.

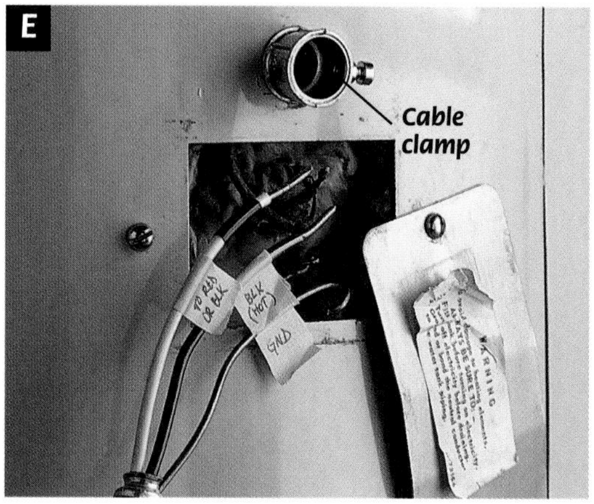

Disconnect wires and release the cable from the clamp. Remove the old heater, then position and level the new one.

tank opening.

Measure the distance between the pressure-relief valve and the floor. Cut a length of copper or CPVC drain pipe that will reach to within 3" of the floor. Attach the pipe to the pressure-relief valve, using a threaded male adapter (page 371).

Solder a threaded male adapter to each of the water supply pipes (page 371). Let the pipes cool, then wrap Teflon tape around the threads of the adapters.

Wrap Teflon tape around the threads of the two heat-saver nipples (page 372). Look closely at the nipples—they're color coded and have directional arrows to help you install them properly.

Attach the blue-coded nipple fitting to the cold water inlet and the red-coded fitting to the hot water outlet, using a pipe wrench. Install the cold water nipple with the water direction arrow facing down; install the hot water nipple with the arrow facing up.

Connect the water supply pipes to the heat-saver nipples with flexible water connectors **(photo F).** Tighten the fittings with an adjustable wrench. To restore the water supply, open the hot water taps at faucets throughout the house, then open the water heater inlet and outlet shutoff valves. When the water runs steadily from all the faucets, close them.

Remove the electrical box coverplate on the new water heater **(photo G).** Thread the circuit wires through the clamp, then through the cable opening on top of the water heater. Attach the clamp to the water heater.

Connect the circuit wires to the water heater wires, using wire connectors **(photo H).**

Attach the bare copper or ground wire to the ground screw on the unit **(photo I).** Replace the coverplate.

Use a screwdriver to set the thermostat to the desired water temperature, 120° to 125°F **(photo J).** If the unit has two elements, set both thermostats.

Press the reset button on each thermostat **(photo K).** Replace the insulation and access panels, and restore power to the unit.

Connect water pipes and pressure-relief valve. Restore water supply.

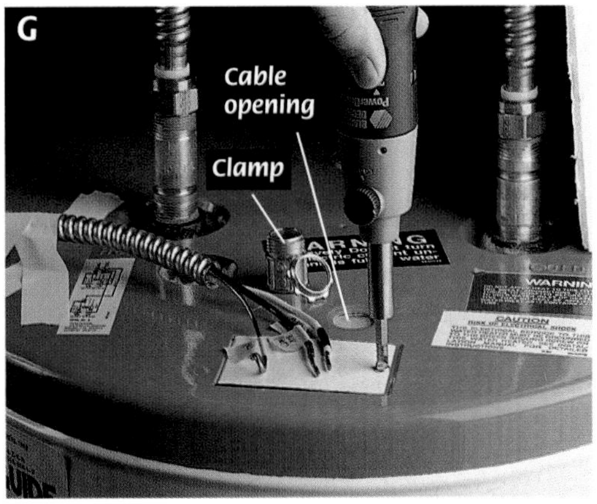

Thread the circuit wires through the clamp, then through the cable opening. Connect the clamp to the unit.

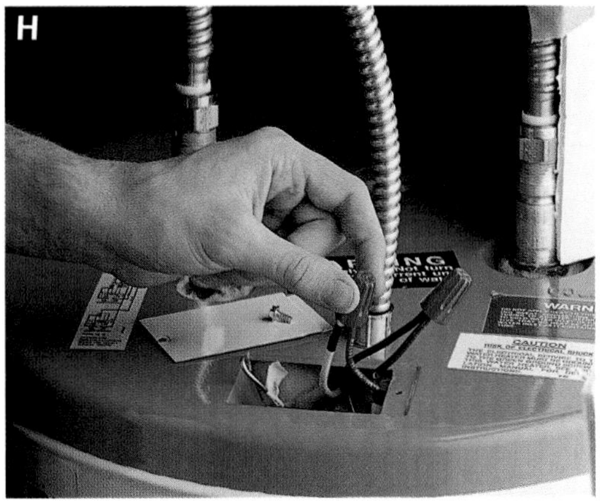

Connect the circuit wires to the water heater wires.

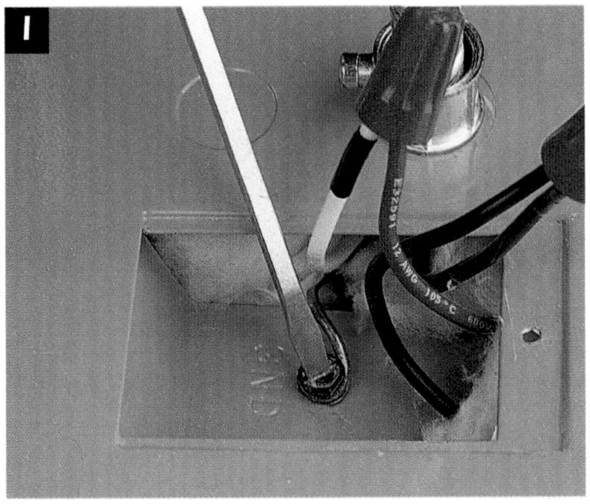

Attach the ground wire to the ground screw.

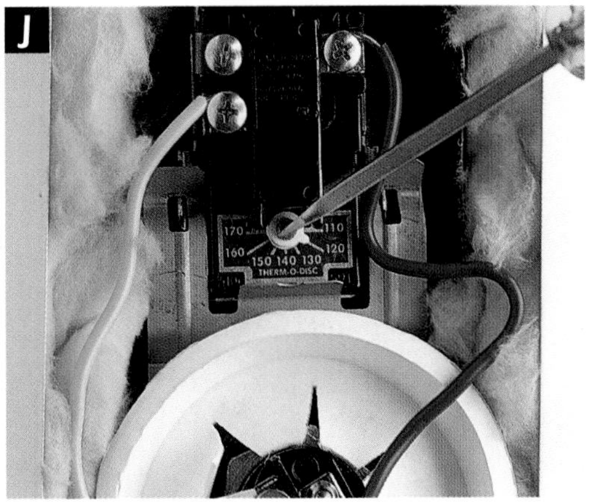

Set thermostats to desired water temperature.

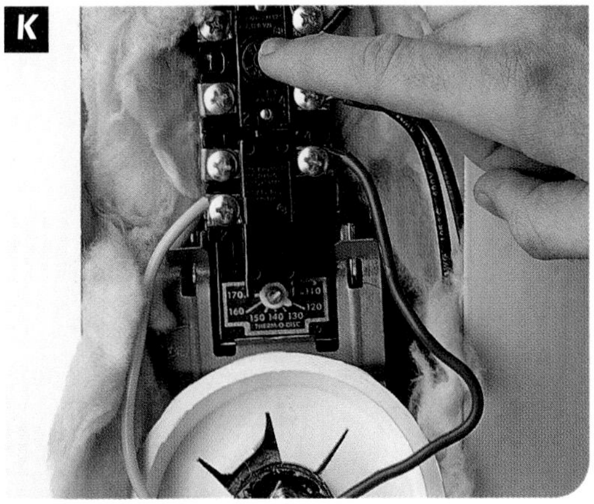

Press reset buttons on thermostats. Replace insulation and access panels, then restore power.

Water Softeners

A water softener is a fairly simple appliance that lowers the content of "hard" minerals in water—magnesium and calcium—and replaces them with sodium or potassium. Removing hard minerals can prolong the life of pipes and appliances.

The actual softening process takes place in the resin tank, which is filled with plastic beads containing sodium. The brine tank contains salt or potassium pellets and is designed to recharge the sodium in the mineral tank when the plastic beads become depleted.

A water softener has just a few mechanical parts—valves to control water flow in and out of the tank, and a timer, which regulates the regeneration process during which the mineral tank is recharged by the brine tank.

If your water becomes hard, it may be because the brine tank needs additional salt or potassium pellets. Depending on usage, pellets need to be replaced every couple of months. Because household demands vary, check your supply every week until you can determine roughly how often your salt or potassium supply should be replenished.

Hard water can also be the result of an improperly set timer. Adjusting the timer to run more frequently may be all that's needed to ensure a constant supply of soft water. Iron content also is a cause of hard water. From time to time, the iron content of your water supply should be measured. Adding a water filter can prevent problems by reducing the iron flowing into the water softener.

Repair problems generally arise either in the brine line or in the control unit. The brine line can be inspected and cleaned (opposite page). If the control unit needs servicing, remove it and bring it to your nearest dealer. Removal instructions for your particular unit should accompany your owner's manual.

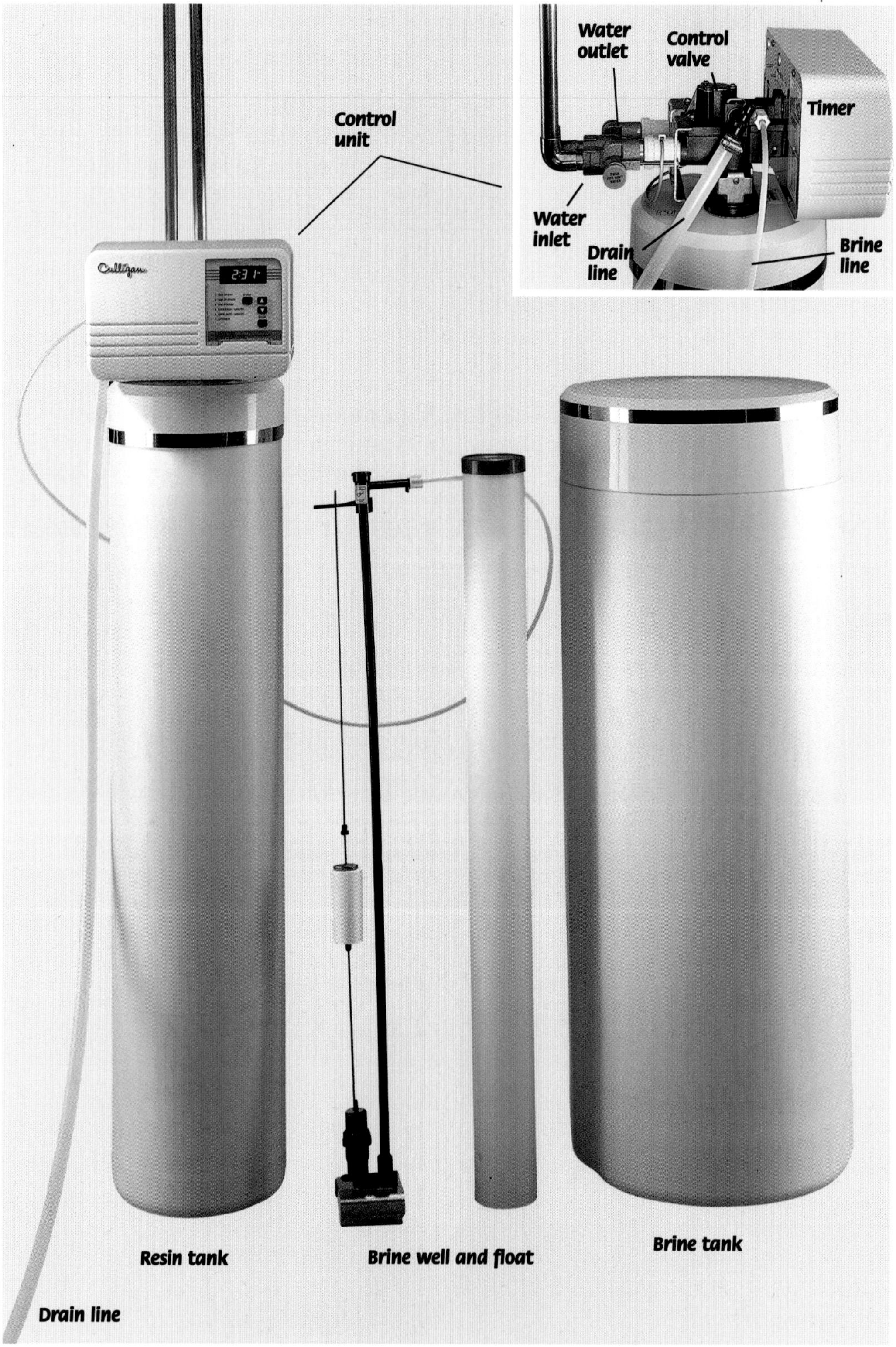

A water softener includes two tanks: a mineral tank (left) and a brine tank (right). Inside the brine tank is the brine well and float (center).

Inspecting & Cleaning Brine Connections

The brine line can be blocked by the buildup of sediment from the water supply or by foreign particles in the salt or potassium. As the line becomes restricted, the movement of brine into the resin tank slows down. When the brine water can't reach the resin tank, calcium and magnesium accumulate, hindering the ability of the salt or potassium to soften the water. For this reason, it's a good idea to inspect the brine line every two years.

Begin by unplugging the softener. To divert the water supply, turn the bypass valve or close the inlet valve and turn on the nearest faucet. Turn the timer dial to BACKWASH.

With needlenose pliers, remove the compression nut that connects the brine line to the control unit. Inspect the line for obstructions **(photo A).**

Remove particles or residue from the line, using a small screwdriver (**photo B).** Then flush the line with warm water—a funnel or kitchen baster is useful for this task—then reattach the brine line.

Next, inspect the brine injector. Don't reconnect the power or make any changes to the supply or control dial. To gain access to the brine injector, which is often directly below the brine line connection, use a screwdriver to remove the cover. Unscrew the injector from the housing **(photo C).**

Pull off the injector filter screen that covers the injector **(photo D).** Wash the screen with soap and water. Clean the injector by blowing into it or wiping it out with a soft cloth. Don't use a sharp object that might scratch the metal and damage the injector.

Reattach the screen and screw the injector back into the water softener. Attach the cover.

Return the bypass valve to its original position (or open the inlet valve and turn off the faucet). Reset the control dial and plug in the water softener.

Tools: *Needlenose pliers, screwdriver, kitchen baster.*

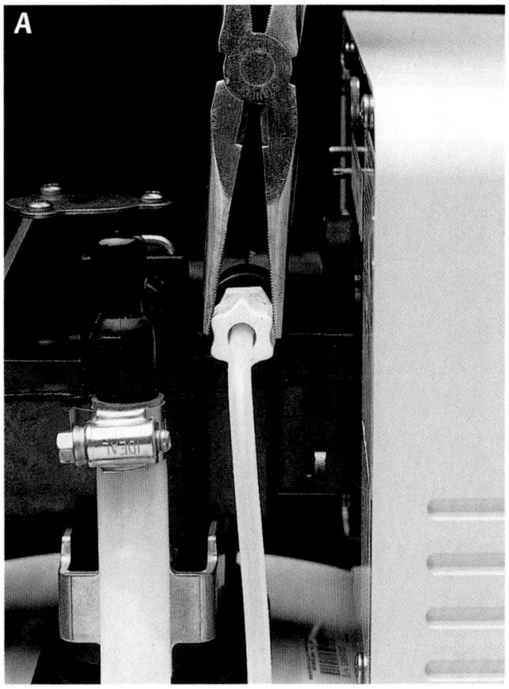

Remove the brine line to inspect it for any obstructions.

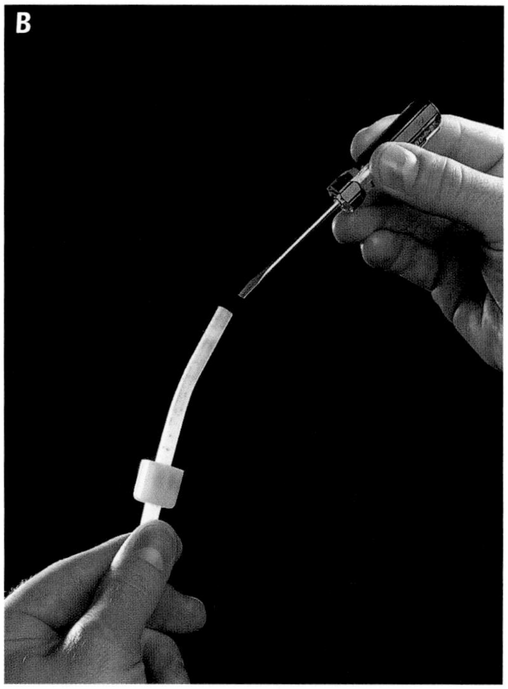

Scrape particles or residue from the end of the line, using a small screwdriver, then flush the line with water.

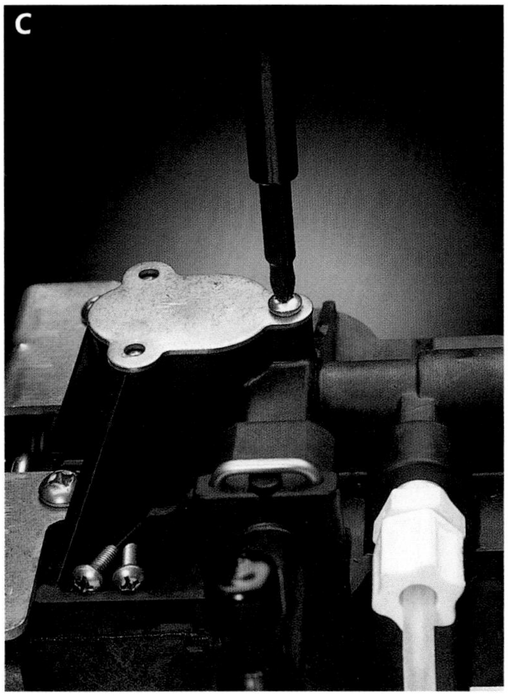

Unscrew the injector and remove it from the housing.

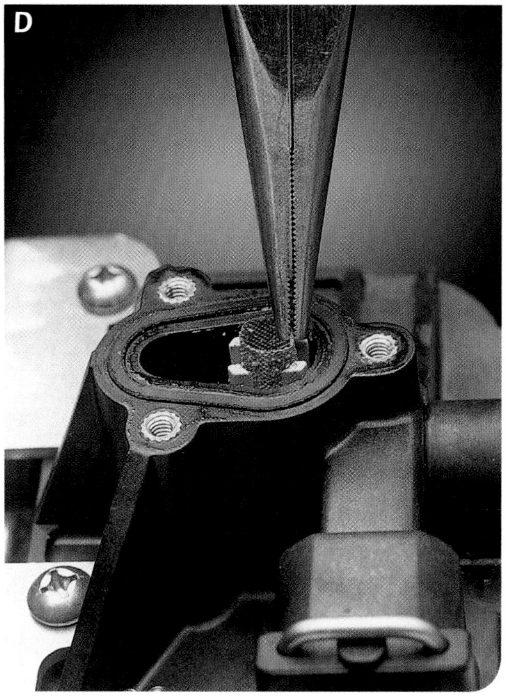

Pull off the injector filter screen and wash it with warm soapy water.

Water Pumps

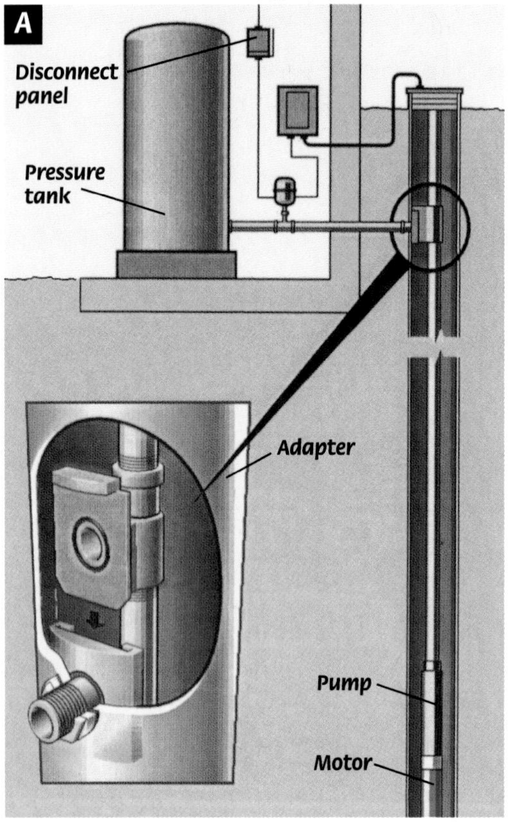

A submersible pump is a single unit that is submerged in the bottom of the well and uses a series of stacked impellers to drive water to the surface

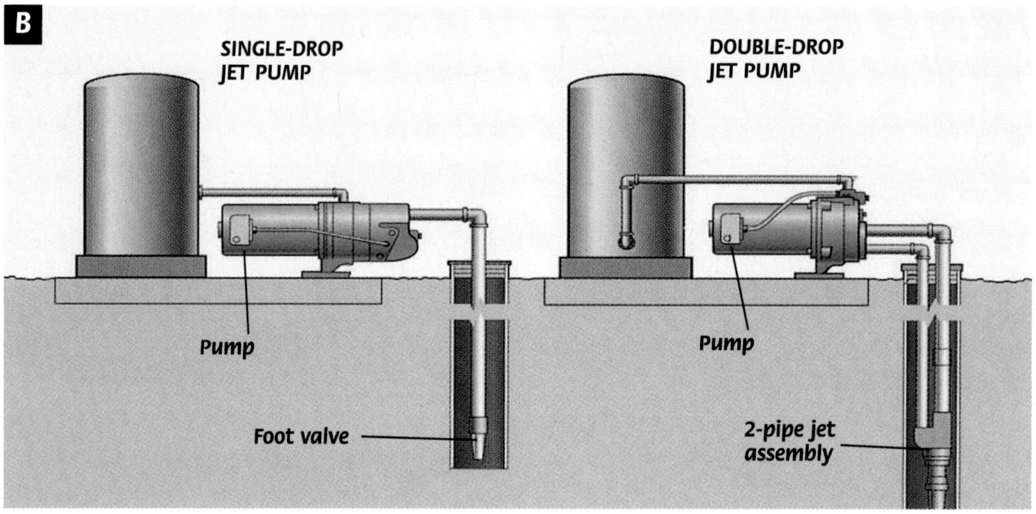

Jet pumps are located on the surface.

Well water systems use a pump to extract water from the underground aquifer, sending it up through the well pipe and storing it in a pressurized tank. There are two types of pumps used in most residential wells: the submersible pump and the jet pump.

Submersible pumps are popular today because they are more reliable for everyday use and require less maintenance than jet pumps. A submersible pump is a single unit that is submerged in the bottom of the well and uses a series of stacked impellers to drive water to the surface **(photo A).** Submersible pump motors can operate trouble-free for more than 20 years. But repairing or replacing the pump requires a truck-mounted derrick .

Jet pumps are typically used with shallow wells or with wells used seasonally, such as at summer cabins. The jet pump mechanism combines the forces of a centrifugal pump and a jet nozzle to suck water up to the surface.

A single-drop jet pump is used for wells with a depth of up to 30 feet, at average elevations **(photo B).** In deeper wells, where pressure must be greater to extract the same amount of water, a double-drop jet pump is used. This is similar to the single-drop pump but includes a surface impeller that directs a portion of the water back down the well. The water exits through an ejector at the bottom of the well, creating pressure to aid the pumping process.

As the pump draws the water from the well, it deposits it into a galvanized steel water tank, usually located in the basement of the house. As the tank fills, the air pressure inside the tank increases until it trips a pressure switch, which turns off the pump. The compressed air in the tank provides the pressure to supply the faucets. As water is drawn from the tank, the air pressure drops until the pressure gauge restarts the pump.

Standard storage tanks are subject to a problem called "waterlogging." This occurs when water in the tank absorbs the air, disrupting the balance between the water level and the pressurized air cushion. When the pressure system has little "give," slight changes in the water level cause the tank pressure to drop, and the pump turns on. This places stress on the pump, and should be corrected as soon as possible.

Some newer storage tanks have a rubber diaphragm that separates the water and air, preventing the absorption of the air into the water.

Another common problem with pump systems is low water pressure in the house supply system. Often, this can be corrected by adjusting the pressure gauge on the pump.

Maintaining Water Pump Systems

If you have low pressure problems with your well system, you may simply need to adjust the pressure setting on your pump.

Your pump's maximum pressure rating should be listed near the gauge, but it may also be in your owner's manual. If you can't locate the maximum ratings for your pump, contact the manufacturer.

If your pump's maximum setting is higher than the current setting, adjustments are easy.

Turn off the power to the pump and remove the cover on the pressure switch to access the adjusting nut on the tall spring **(photo C).**

Raise the pressure incrementally by turning the nut clockwise—one and a half turns raises the pressure by about 3 pounds. Cover the pressure switch and turn on the power. To make sure your adjustments have not increased the pressure above the maximum rating, watch the gauge as the pump runs through an entire cycle.

If the pump starts and stops frequently, the tank may be waterlogged. To correct this, drain the tank and allow it to fill with air passively.

First, close the supply valve between the pump and the water tank **(photo D).** Turn on a cold-water faucet in the house to prevent a vacuum in the piping system.

Open the drain valve near the tank and allow the tank to drain completely. Wait a few minutes, then turn off the house faucet and close the drain valve.

Open the valve between the pump and the tank. As the tank fills, the water will pressurize the air cushion.

If this doesn't solve the problem, the pressure switch or air volume control may need to be serviced by an expert.

C

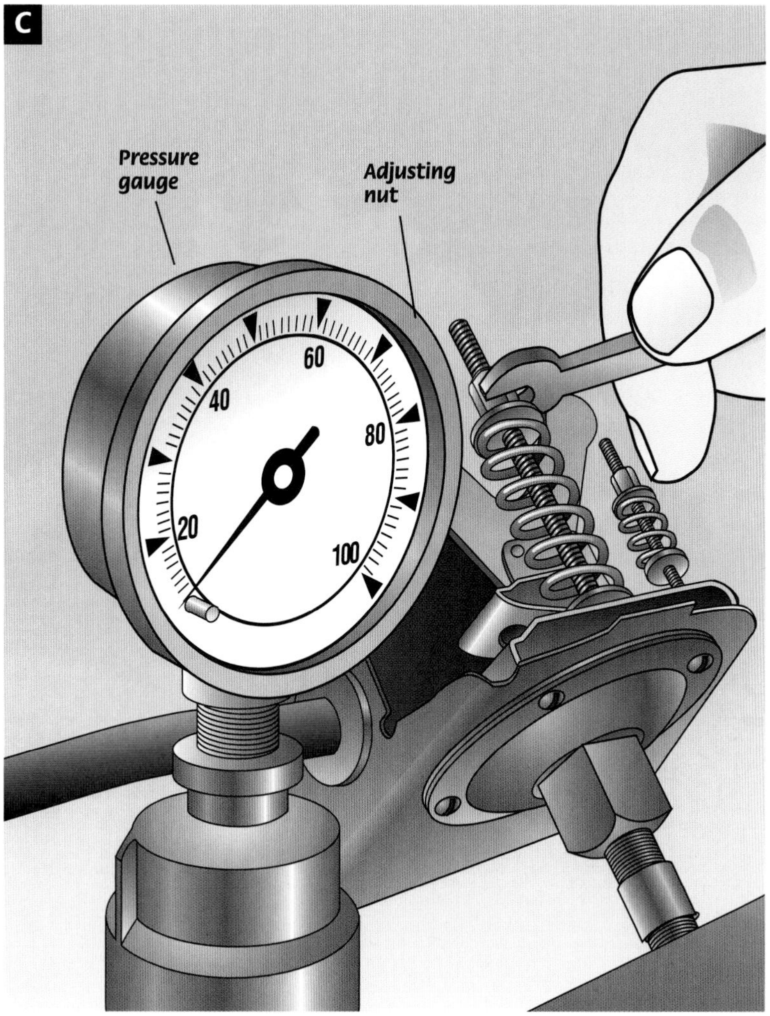

Tighten or loosen the adjusting nut in small increments to increase or decrease the pressure in the tank.

D

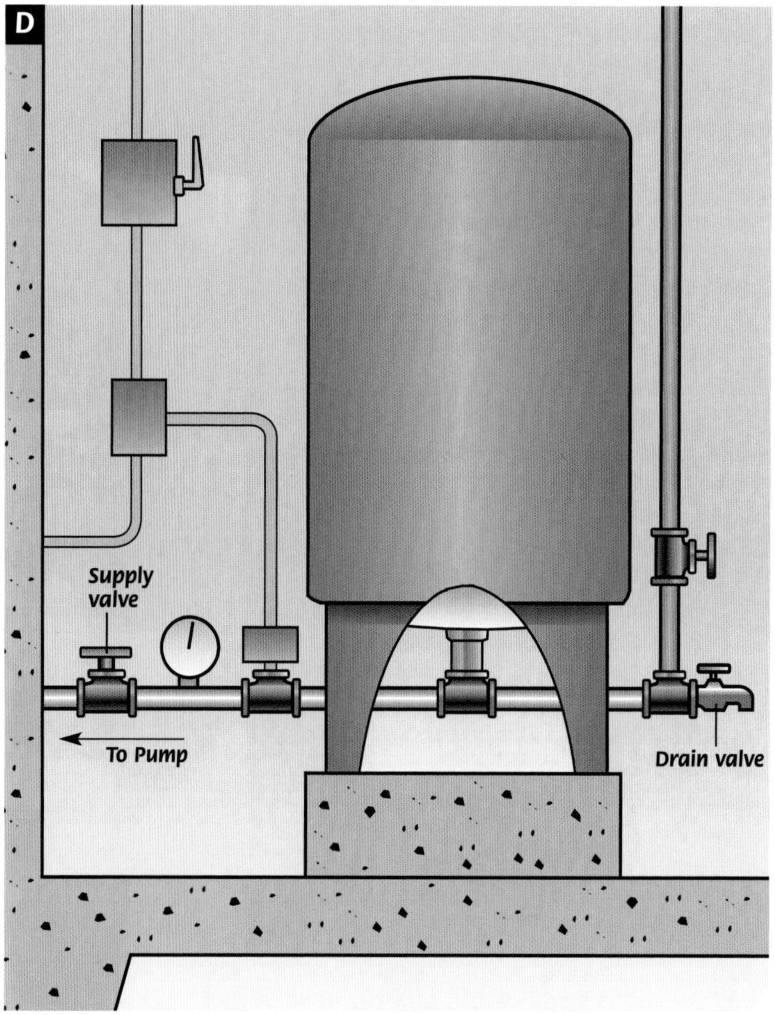

A waterlogged tank can be fixed by shutting the supply valve, opening the drain valve, and running cold water in the house while the tank fills with air.

Septic Systems

About 15 percent of homes in the U.S. are not hooked up to a municipal sewer service. In these homes, the household waste is usually managed by a private septic system.

Private septic systems consist of an underground holding tank that feeds a network of pipes fanning out into a drainage field. Sewage from the house is directed through the DWV system and into the septic tank. Once in the tank, the solid wastes separate from the liquid and settle to the bottom, where they're decomposed by microorganisms.

The breakdown of the wastes creates a liquid effluent that exits the tank and travels through a pipe to a sealed junction box. The junction distributes the effluent among several perforated pipes lying on a bed of gravel or other loose-fill material. Seeping through holes in the pipes, the effluent is purified as it filters through layers of soil and rock on its return to the water table.

The storage and breakdown of sewage in the septic tank produces methane gas. Like a DWV system in a house with municipal sewer service, a septic system must have a vent pipe for the gases to escape at the roof of the house. Without this vent, the pressure in the tank would quickly increase to dangerous levels.

Undecomposed solids accumulate in the bottom of the tank, forming a growing layer of sludge. Over time, the tank reaches its capacity and the sludge must be pumped out. Most septic tanks need to be pumped out every one to three years, depending on tank capacity and the number of people who live in the home.

When neglected septic tanks become overfilled, the solid wastes do not separate from the liquid and instead pass through the tank and into the drainage field. There they clog the loose-fill material, barring the passage of effluent. When this happens, the field must be dug up and the loose-fill material replaced.

Septic systems rely on a natural process of decomposition; like most natural systems, they work best when left alone. Give your system time to do its job and don't try to help it along by adding yeasts or other biological additives.

Regular tank maintenance and careful waste disposal should keep your septic system healthy for 20 years, or more. However, if the system has been neglected for many years, it's possible you'll need to have the entire drainage field replaced or enlarged by a professional.

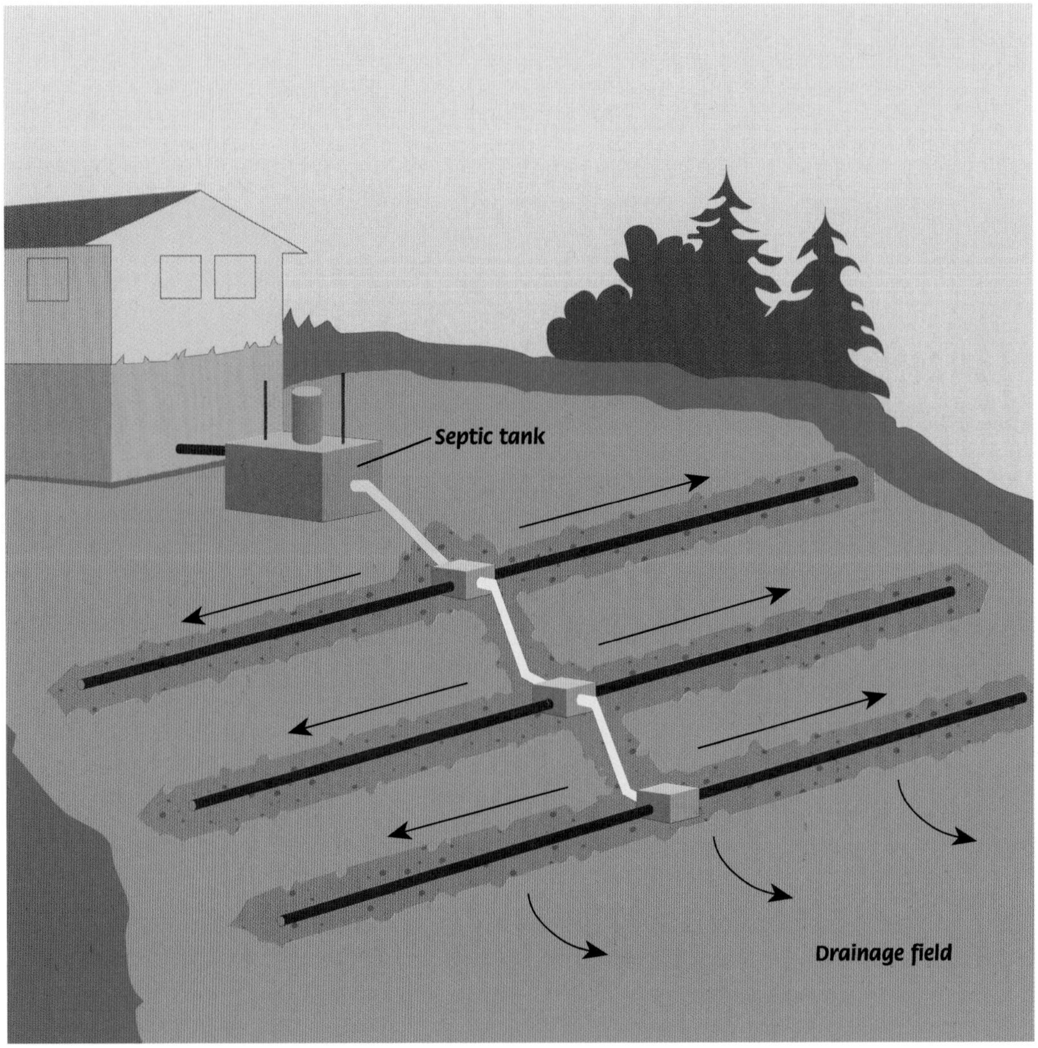

A properly maintained septic system feeds waste water into pipes that fan out into the drainage field. The remaining solid waste settles in the tank, and must be pumped out every few years for disposal.

Maintaining Your Septic System

Have your tank inspected and emptied regularly.	*A neglected tank will cause your system to fail, resulting in sewage backup and posing a serious risk to your family's health.* *Experts recommend pumping a septic tank every one to two years.*
Avoid using chemicals.	*Harsh chemicals and antibacterial agents kill the bacteria your system depends on.* *Keep these chemicals out of your toilets and house drains:* *Drain cleaner* *Paint and paint thinner* *Chemical cleaners* *Chlorine – including toilet bowl flush-cleaners* *Antibacterial soft-soaps*
Limit kitchen wastes.	*Grease and fat from food hinder the septic process by coating drain pipes, interfering with bacterial breakdown in the tank, and clogging the loose-fill material in the drain field.* *Food disposers overload your system with solid food particles, sometimes doubling the rate of sludge accumulation in the tank.* *Throw cooking grease and food scraps in the garbage or compost heap.*
Limit water inflow. *Repair leaky plumbing fixtures as soon as possible.* *Route roof drains out of the house drain system.* *Don't drain a swimming pool or hot tub into the house drain.*	*Excess water speeds up the flow through the septic system. The natural bacteria can't do its job, allowing too many solids to pass into the drain field.*
Never use additives.	*Biological additives designed to stimulate bacterial growth often harm more than they help. These additives agitate the anaerobic bacteria in the septic tank, and the increased activity forces undissolved solids into the drain field.*

Troubleshooting Your Septic System

Once problems arise within a septic system, there isn't much a homeowner can do, but being able to identify signs of trouble may prolong the life of your system and will probably save you some money.

If your drains are working slowly, or not draining at all, there may be a clog in the main house drain, or the septic system may be backed up. Check for clogs first. Use a motorized auger (photo, right) to clear the main drain. Never use chemical drain cleaners.

If the house drain isn't clogged, the problem may be a clogged drain field, an absence of bacteria in the system, or a full septic tank.

In addition to slow drainage, common signs of trouble include the presence of dark-colored water on the surface of the drain field and a sewage odor in or around the home.

Any of these symptoms may indicate a serious problem. Human sewage is considered a hazardous waste, and there are strict regulations governing its removal. Servicing a septic system isn't something you should try to do yourself.

Septic tanks produce explosive methane gas and may contain deadly viruses. Contact a licensed sewer service to have your septic system inspected and serviced.

Electrical

If you plan to make electrical repairs around the house, it's important to begin with a basic understanding of your home's electrical system. Make sure you recognize the various elements and understand the part each one plays in carrying electricity or safeguarding the system and your family.

Electrical current is delivered to a house by buried or overhead lines that run to a post called the *service head.* Most homes built after 1950 have three wires running to the service head: two power lines, each carrying 120 volts of current, and a grounded neutral wire. The power from the two 120-volt lines can be combined at the service panel to supply current to 240-volt appliances, such as clothes dryers and electric water heaters.

Some older homes have only two wires running to the service head: one 120-volt line and a grounded neutral wire. Two-wire service cannot support large numbers of heavy appliances, computers and other electrical devices common in today's homes. If you still have two-wire service, contact an electrical contractor and your utility company for an upgrade.

After arriving at the house, incoming power passes through an *electric meter*, which measures the home's power consumption in watts. From the meter, power travels to a *service panel.* The panel contains either fuses or circuit breakers that shut off the power in the event of a short circuit or overload.

The service panel distributes current to *circuits*—the wire pathways designed to deliver power to fixtures, switches, and receptacles. Most circuits service a number of locations or devices, but one circuit may be dedicated to a high-wattage appliance, such as a washing machine or refrigerator.

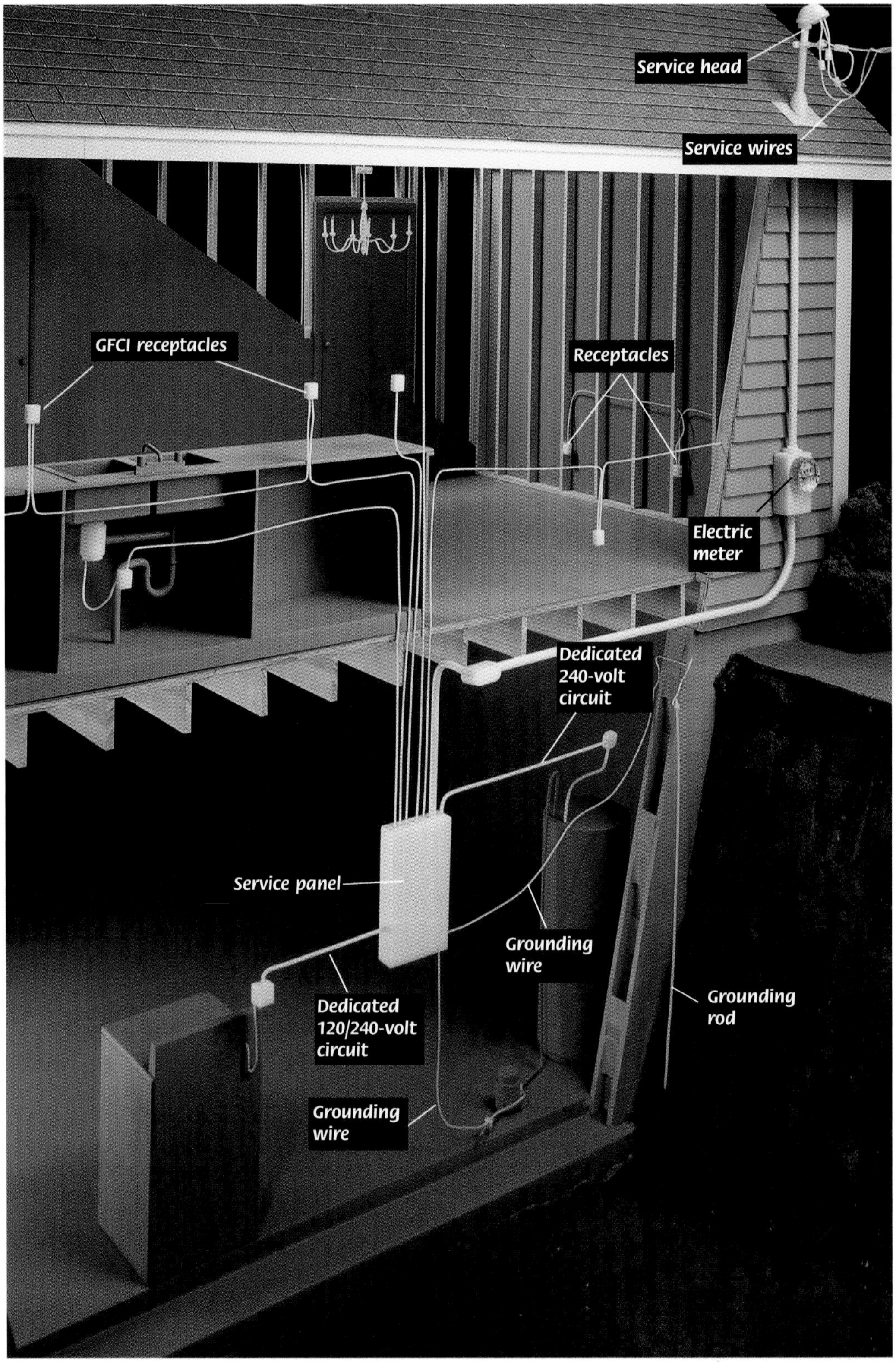

A home electrical system consists of several elements that work together to deliver electricity safely for everyday use.

The Electrical System

To function correctly, electricity must always complete a circuit. As you work with your electrical system, you'll find that problems often result from interruptions in the current's circular path. The photos below show some of the places your electrical system could fail.

The *service head*, or weather head, anchors the power supplied by overhead service wires to your house. Standard 240-volt service is delivered by three wires: two wires of 120-volt current and a grounded neutral wire **(photo A).**

The *electric meter* measures every watt of power consumed by your electrical system. It's usually attached to the side of the house, and is connected to the service head or buried power lines. A thin metal disc inside the meter rotates whenever power is in use **(photo B).**

The *service panel,* also called the breaker box or fuse box, distributes power to individual circuits. The fuse or circuit breaker is designed to close down the circuit in the event of an overload or a short circuit **(photo C).**

NOTE: The wires to the service head, electric meter, and service panel are always live unless the utility company turns them off. Never attempt to inspect or repair any of these devices. If you suspect a problem with them, contact the utility company.

Electrical boxes enclose wire connections. The National Electrical Code requires that every wire connection and splice be entirely contained within a plastic or metal electrical box **(photo D).**

Receptacles, or outlets, provide plug-in access to power. A 125-volt, 15-amp receptacle with a grounding hole is most typical in wiring systems installed after 1965 **(photo E).**

Switches control the current passing through circuit wires to light fixtures, ceiling fans, appliances, and receptacles **(photo F).**

Light fixtures are wired directly into the electrical system and usually controlled by wall switches **(photo G).**

The *grounding wire* connects the entire system to the earth through a metal water pipe or grounding rod. In the case of an overload or short circuit, it should channel excess electrical current harmlessly into the earth **(photo H).**

The utility company's service lines are connected to the house at the service head.

The electric meter measures the amount of power used by the household.

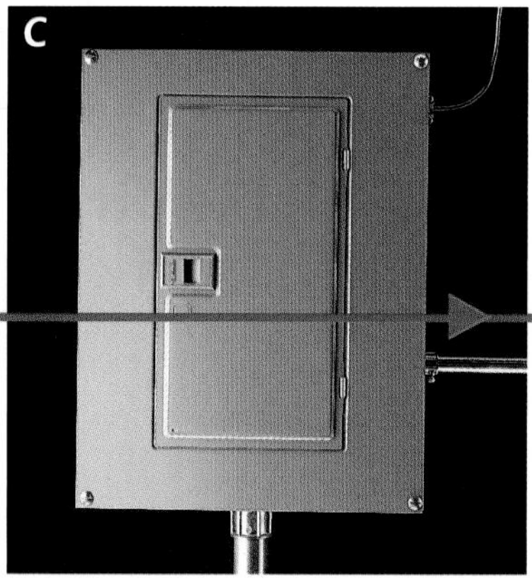

The service panel distributes the current to the individual circuits.

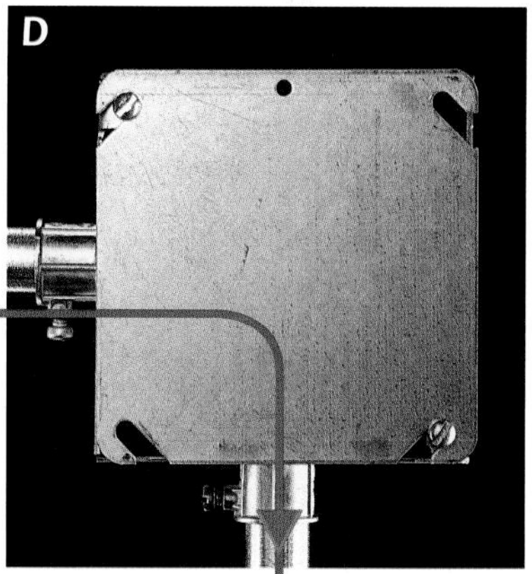

Throughout the house, electrical boxes enclose the wire connections.

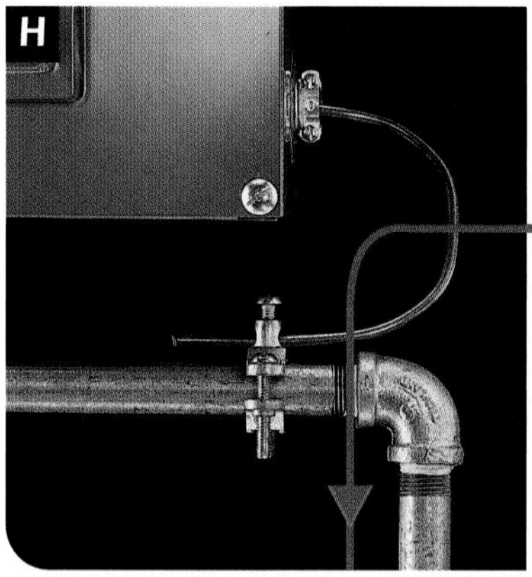

The grounding wire connects to a cold water pipe or a metal grounding rod.

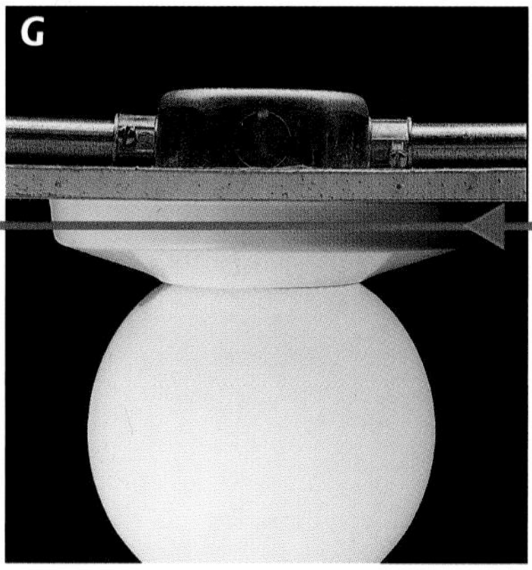

Light fixtures are wired directly into the system.

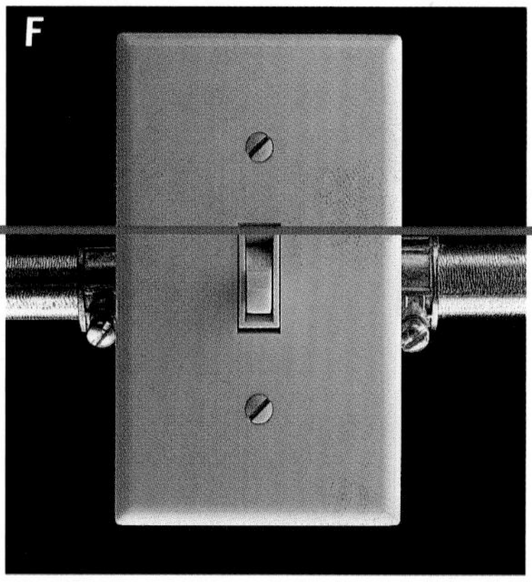

Switches control the current passing through a circuit.

Receptacles, or outlets, provide plug-in access to power.

Understanding Circuits

If you look up the word *circuit* in the dictionary, you'll find the definition: "a regular tour around an assigned territory." As this indicates, household circuits carry electricity along a regular route from the main service panel, through the house, and back to the service panel. For the circuit to function properly, this loop must remain uninterrupted.

Current travels outward to electrical devices on hot wires and returns along neutral wires. The two kinds of wires are color coded: hot wires are black or red, and neutral wires are white or light gray.

For safety, most circuits also include a bare copper or green insulated grounding wire. The grounding wire helps reduce the chance of electrical shock and carries any excess current in the case of a short circuit or overload.

Circuits are rated according to the amount of power they can carry without overheating. If the devices on a circuit try to draw more power than that amount, the fuse or circuit breaker is triggered and automatically shuts down the circuit.

Usually, several switches, receptacles, fixtures, or appliances are connected to each circuit, and a loose connection at any device can cause a short, or break, in the circuit. The resulting reduction in resistance triggers the circuit breaker or fuse, and the circuit shuts down.

After passing through the electrical devices, current returns to the service panel along a neutral circuit wire. There it merges with a main circuit wire and leaves the house on a neutral service line that returns it to the transformer on the utility pole.

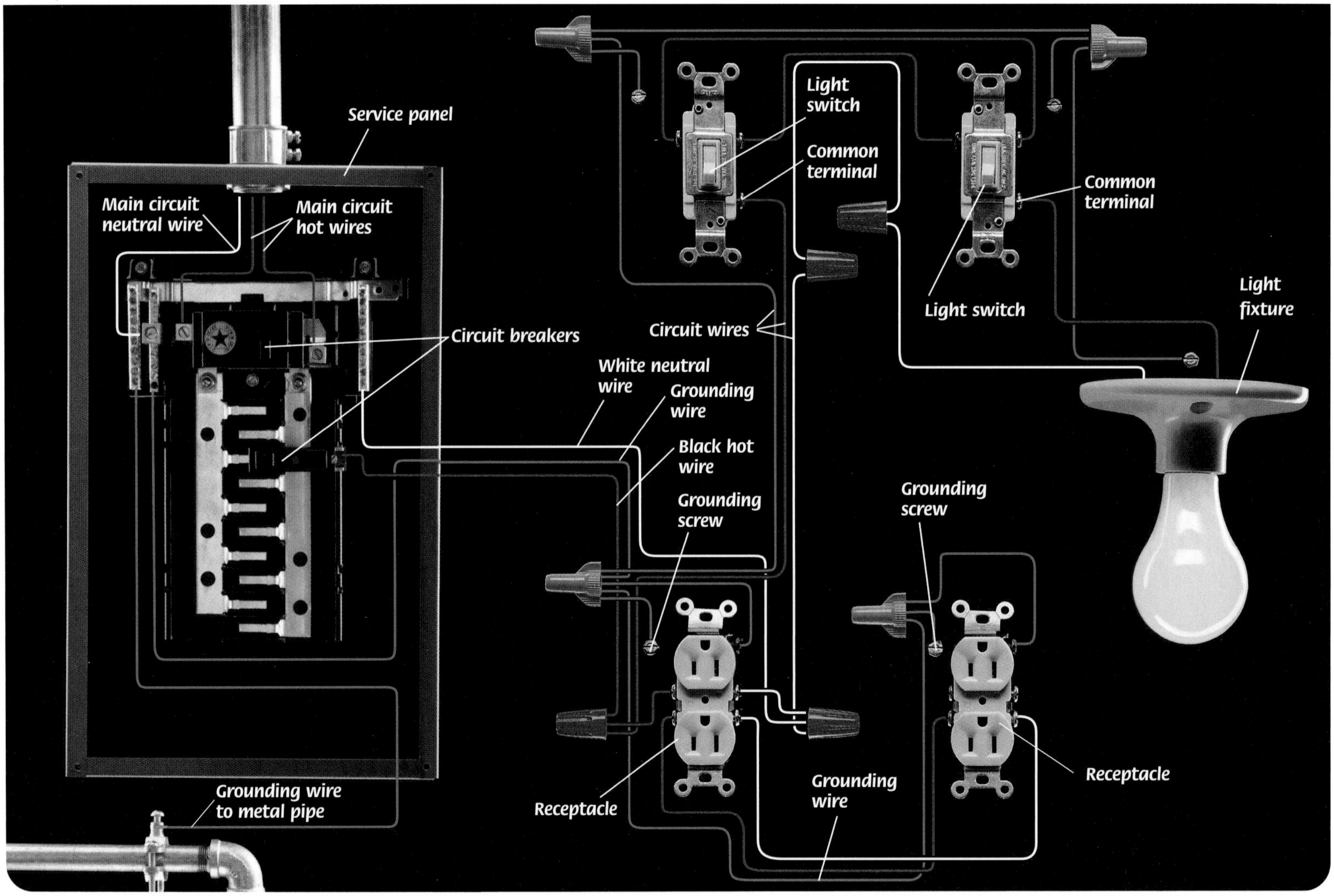

Household circuits carry electrical current through the house in a continuous loop. Power enters the system on hot wires (red) and returns along neutral wires (white). The system also includes grounding wires for safety (green).

Grounding & Polarization

Electricity always tries to return to its source and complete a continuous circuit. In a household wiring system, the return path is provided by neutral wires (usually coded white), that return the current to the main service panel.

When working with wiring, remember that electric current always seeks the path of least resistance. When you touch a device, tool, or appliance that has a short circuit, the current may attempt to return to its source by passing through your body.

Grounding wires are designed to minimize this danger by providing a safe, easy path for the current to follow back to its source. If you touch a short-circuited device that has a properly installed grounding wire, your chance of receiving a severe shock is greatly reduced.

Most electrical systems installed since 1920 also have another safety measure—receptacles that accept polarized plugs. While it's not a true grounding method, polarization is designed to keep the current flowing along the proper wires within the circuit.

In the 1940s, armored cable (also called BX cable) was installed in many homes. Armored cable has a metal sheath that, when connected to a metal junction box, provides a true grounding path back to the service panel.

Most wiring systems installed since 1965 contain NM (nonmetallic) cable that has a bare or green insulated copper wire that serves as a continuous grounding path for excess current. These circuits are usually equipped with three-slot receptacles, which have direct connections to the circuit grounding wire. This protects appliances, tools, and people from short circuits.

If a two-slot receptacle is connected to a grounded electrical box, you can plug three-prong plugs into it by using a receptacle adapter. To connect the adapter to the grounded metal electrical box, attach the short grounding wires or wire loops on the adapter to the receptacle's cover plate mounting screw.

Another safety precaution is the use of double-insulated tools. These devices have nonconductive plastic bodies that prevent shocks caused by short circuits. Because of these features, double-insulated tools can be used safely with two-slot receptacles.

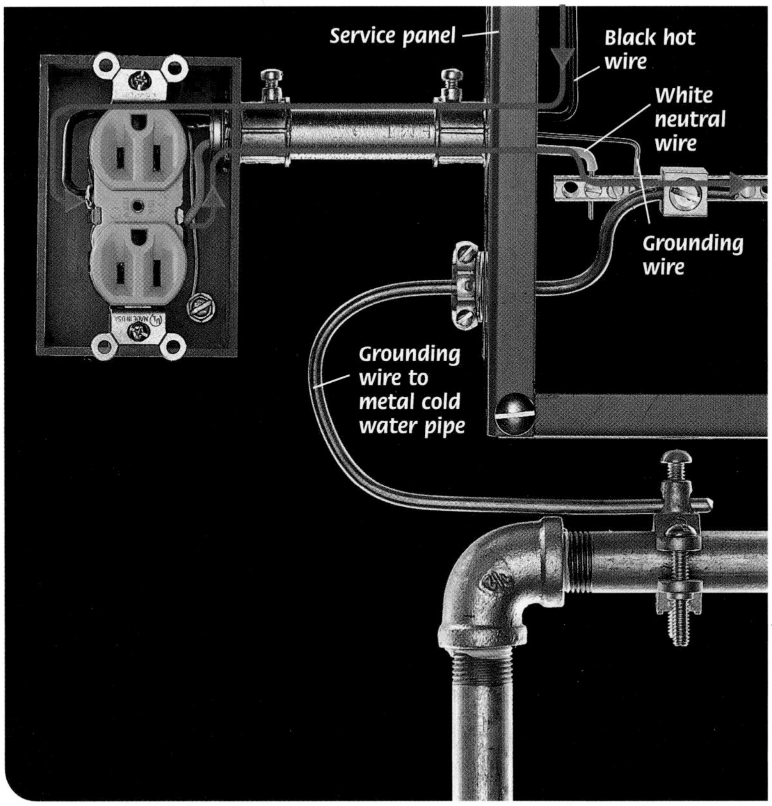

Normal current flow: Current enters the electrical box along a black hot wire, then returns to the service panel along a white neutral wire. Any excess current passes into the earth via a grounding wire attached to a metal water pipe or grounding rod.

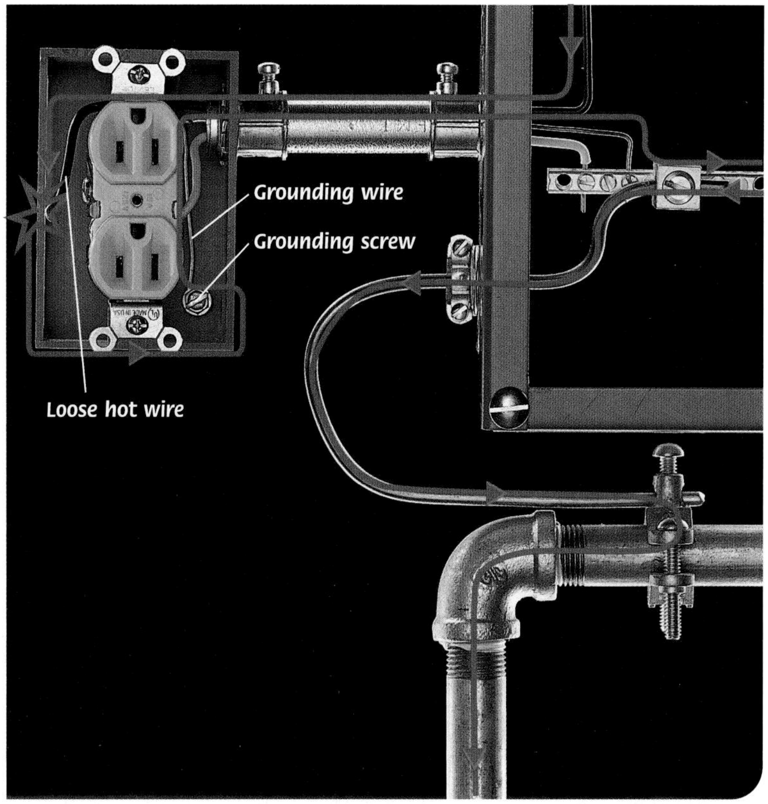

Short circuit: Current is detoured by a loose wire in contact with the metal box. The grounding wire picks it up and channels it safely back to the main service panel. There, it returns to its source along a neutral service cable or enters the earth via the grounding system.

Service Panels

Every home has a main service panel that distributes electrical current to the individual circuits. It's usually located in the basement, garage, or utility area and can be identified by its gray metal casing. Before making any repairs to your electrical system, shut off the power to the appropriate circuits at the main service panel. Mapping the circuits or indexing the panel (page 390) will make it easy to identify the circuits.

Service panels use either fuses or circuit breakers to control the circuits and protect them from overloads. Service panels installed before 1965 generally have fuses, while newer service panels have circuit breakers.

Service panels vary in number of circuits and amperage. Very old wiring may have 30-amp service with only two circuits, while new homes may have 200-amp service with 30 or more circuits. The amperage rating of your panel is printed on the main fuse block or circuit breaker.

Your electrical system may also include a subpanel that controls other circuits in your home. Subpanels, which have their own fuses or breakers, are used to increase capacity by adding circuits to an existing wiring system. A subpanel resembles the main service panel, but it's usually smaller. It may be located near the main panel, or in the new area that it serves, such as a garage or attic.

When handling fuses or circuit breakers, make sure that the area around the service panel is dry. Keep that space clean and uncluttered. Never store or pile anything against the service panel, and keep children away from it at all times.

The first step in doing any electrical work is to shut off the power to the circuit. To shut off a circuit, identify the fuse or circuit breaker that controls it. (This is where a circuit map or index saves time.) Once you've identified the circuit, unscrew its fuse or move its breaker to the OFF position. As an added precaution, close the panel door and post a note telling others that you're working on the circuit.

Before you start working on a circuit, test it to make sure the power is really off, using a neon circuit tester (page 395). If you removed the correct fuse or closed the right circuit breaker, there won't be any power in the circuit, and the circuit tester won't light up. If the tester lights, it means that power is still reaching the circuit. Continue shutting off fuses and breakers and testing until you're sure the power is off and it's safe to touch the wires.

A 30-amp Fuse Panel

Thirty-amp service panels are common in systems installed before 1950. They have a ceramic fuse holder containing two plug fuses and a "knife-blade" switch lever. The fuse holder is sometimes contained in a black metal box mounted in an entryway or basement.

Since 30-amp service panels provide only 120 volts of power, they are now considered inadequate and should be upgraded. Most home loan programs, such as the Federal Housing Administration (FHA), require that 30-amp service be updated to 100 amps or more before a home can qualify for mortgage financing.

To shut off the power to an individual circuit, carefully unscrew the appropriate plug fuse, touching only the insulated rim of the fuse.

To shut off the power to the entire house, open the knife-blade switch. Be careful not to touch the metal contacts on the switch.

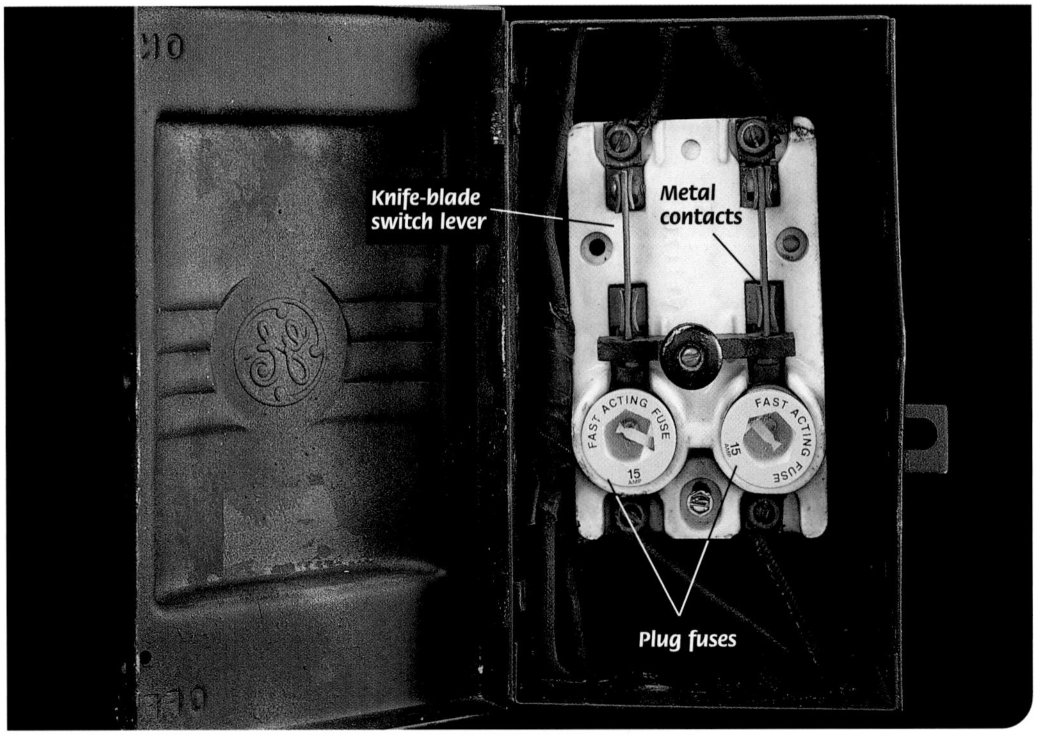

A 30-amp service panel has a ceramic fuse holder with two plug fuses and a knife-blade switch lever. These panels are inadequate and should be upgraded as soon as practical.

A 60-amp Fuse Panel

Sixty-amp fuse panels are common in wiring systems installed between 1950 and 1965. They're usually housed in a gray metal cabinet that holds four plug fuses and one or two pull-out fuse blocks for cartridge fuses.

A 60-amp fuse panel is adequate for small homes (up to 1100 sq. ft.) that have no more than one 240-volt appliance. However, you should consider updating to at least 100 amps so that more circuits can be added to the system. In some cases, home loan programs may require that 60-amp service be updated before a home can qualify for financing.

To shut off the power to an individual circuit, carefully unscrew the appropriate fuse, touching only its insulated rim.

To shut off the power to the entire house, grasp the handle of the main fuse block and pull sharply to remove it. If there is a second cartridge fuse block for the major appliance circuit, you can shut off that circuit separately by removing its fuse block.

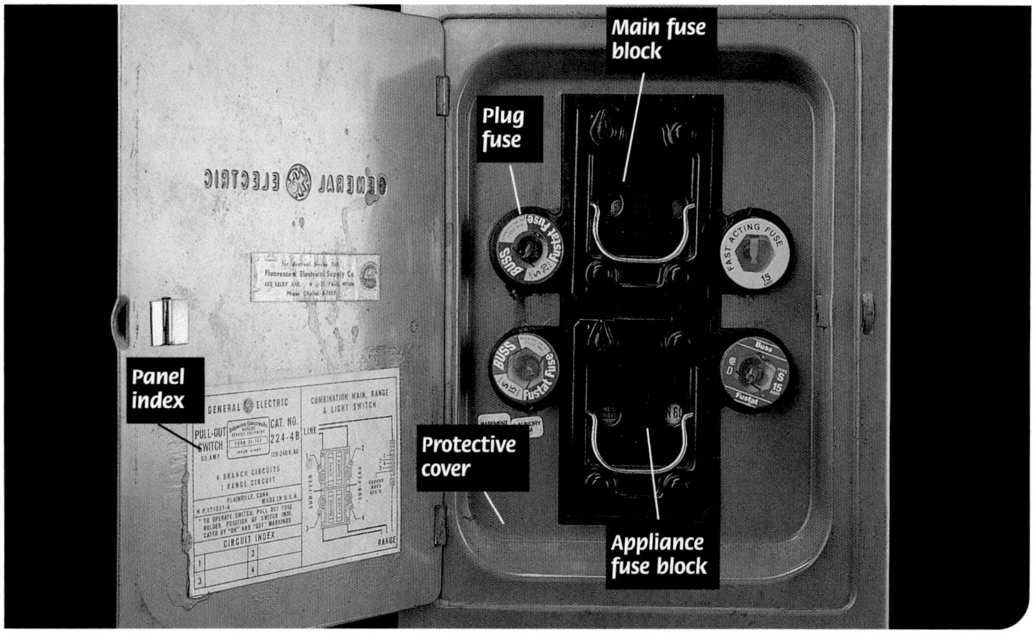

A 60-amp fuse panel holds four plug fuses plus one or two pull-out fuse blocks. This panel is adequate for a small home that has no more than one 240-volt appliance.

A Circuit Breaker Panel

Circuit breaker panels that provide 100 amps of power or more are common in wiring systems installed since the 1960s. They're usually housed in a gray metal cabinet that holds two rows of circuit breakers. The size of the service can be identified by reading the amperage rating of the main circuit breaker, which is located at the top of the main service panel.

A 100-amp service panel is now the standard minimum for new home construction. This is considered adequate for medium-sized homes with up to three major electric appliances. Larger homes with more major appliances require a service panel that provides 150 amps or more.

To shut off the power to an individual circuit, flip the lever on the appropriate circuit breaker to the OFF position. To shut off the power to the entire house, flip the lever on the main circuit breaker to the OFF position.

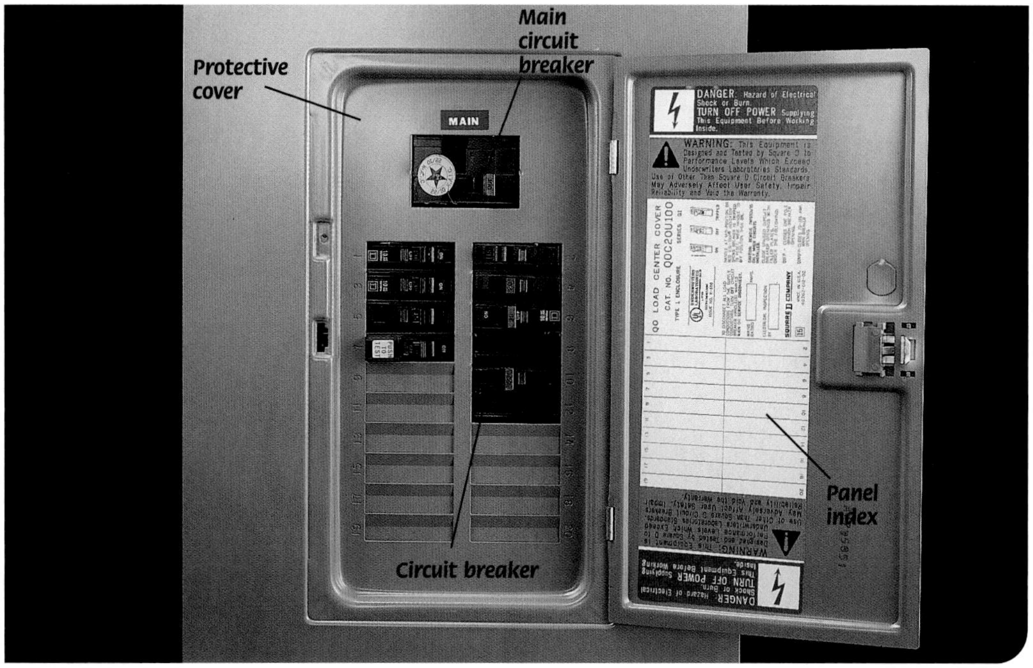

A circuit breaker panel of 100 amps or more holds two rows of individual circuit breakers. The size of the service is indicated on the main circuit breaker.

Evaluating Fuses & Circuit Breakers

The fuses and circuit breakers on the main service panel are safety devices that control the circuits and protect the electrical system from short circuits and overloads.

Fuses **(photo A)** contain a current-carrying metal alloy ribbon. Excessive voltage causes the ribbon to melt, which stops the flow of power. The capacity of a fuse must always match the capacity of the circuit—never replace a fuse with one that has a larger amperage rating.

Screw-in plug fuses (1) control the 120-volt circuits that power lights and receptacles. They're rated for 15, 20, or 30 amps.

Tamper-proof plug fuses (2) have threads that fit only matching sockets, so you can't install the wrong fuse in a circuit.

Time-delay fuses (3) can temporarily absorb heavy power loads.

Cartridge fuses (4) control the 240-volt circuits used by major appliances. They can range from 30 to 100 amps.

Circuit breakers **(photo B)** have a metal strip that heats up and bends when voltage passes through it. Excessive voltage causes the strip to bend, tripping the switch and stopping the flow of power. Worn circuit breakers may trip frequently, without any apparent cause, and should be replaced by an electrician.

Single-pole breakers (5) control 120-volt circuits and usually are rated for 15 or 20 amps.

Double-pole breakers (6) control 240-volt circuits and are rated for 20 to 50 amps.

GFCI breakers (7) provide shock protection for an entire circuit. Their amperage ratings range from 15 to 100 amps.

When a fuse blows or a circuit breaker trips, it's usually because there are too many fixtures and appliances drawing power on the circuit. Move some of them to another circuit, then replace the fuse or reset the breaker. If the circuit shuts down again immediately, there may be a short circuit in the system. If you suspect that you have a short, call a licensed electrician.

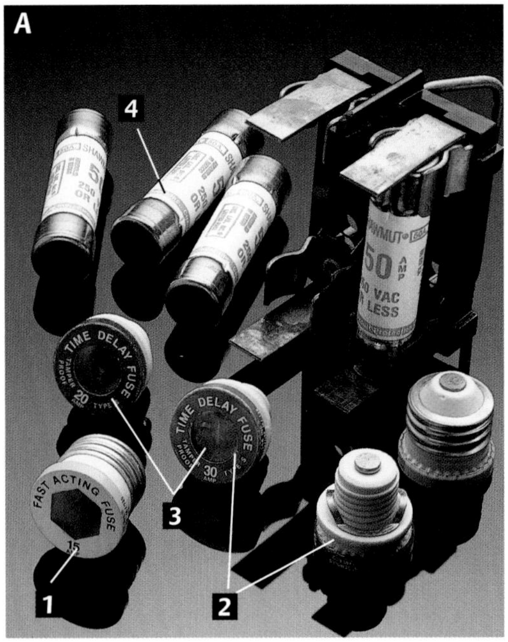

Fuses are found primarily in older service panels.

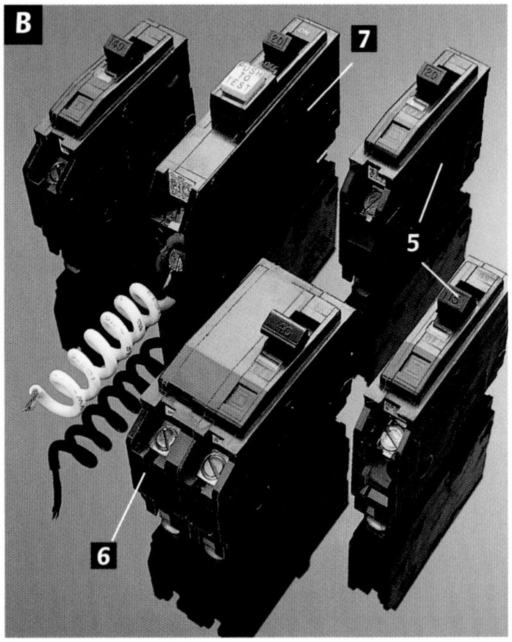

Circuit breakers are found in newer service panels.

Removing & Replacing Plug Fuses

When a screw-in plug fuse blows, go to the main service panel and locate the blown fuse. Examine the metal alloy ribbon inside each fuse. The fuse that has blown will look different from the others.

If the circuit has overloaded, the ribbon inside the fuse will have melted. If the circuit has shorted out, the window of the fuse will be darkened **(photo C).** Find and repair the short circuit before replacing the fuse.

To remove the fuse, unscrew it, touching only its insulated rim **(photo D).** Replace the fuse with a new one that has the same amperage rating as the circuit.

A short (left) will be dark; an overload (right) will be melted.

When unscrewing a fuse, touch only the rim.

Replacing Cartridge Fuses

When a cartridge fuse blows, go to the main service panel and remove the fuse block by grasping its handle and pulling out sharply **(photo E).** Use a fuse puller to remove the cartridges from the block **(photo F).**

To find out which fuse needs to be replaced, test both with a continuity tester **(photo G).** Touch the clip to one end of the fuse and the probe to the other. If the light in the tester goes on, the fuse is good.

If both fuses are good, the problem lies elsewhere in the system. If the light doesn't go on with either fuse, replace them both with new fuses that have the same amperage rating.

Tools: *Fuse puller (for cartridge fuses only), continuity tester.*

Materials: *Replacement fuses.*

Grasp the handle of the fuse block and pull it out.

Remove the cartridge fuses from the block with a fuse puller.

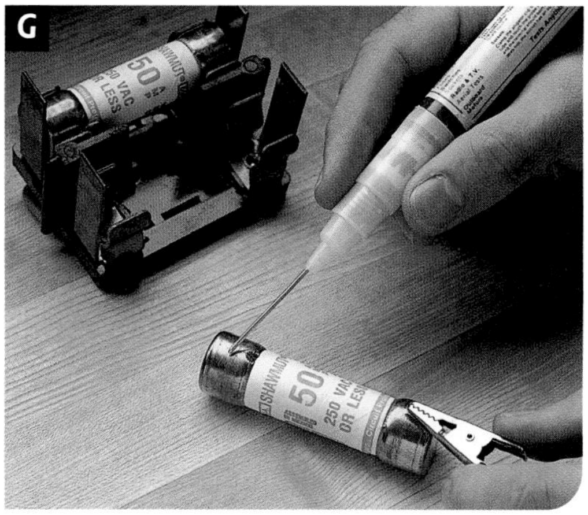

If the tester doesn't glow, replace the fuse.

Resetting a Circuit Breaker

When a circuit breaker trips, go to the main service panel and locate the tripped breaker. Its lever will have moved to the OFF position, or to a position between ON and OFF. On many panels it's easy to spot a tripped breaker because the breakers have a red tab that becomes visible when the lever flips **(photo H).**

To reset the circuit breaker, push its lever all the way to the OFF position, then back to the ON position (**photo I).**

GFCI circuit breakers should be periodically tested. To do so, simply push the TEST button **(photo J).** The breaker should trip to the OFF position. If it doesn't, it's faulty and must be replaced by a licensed electrician.

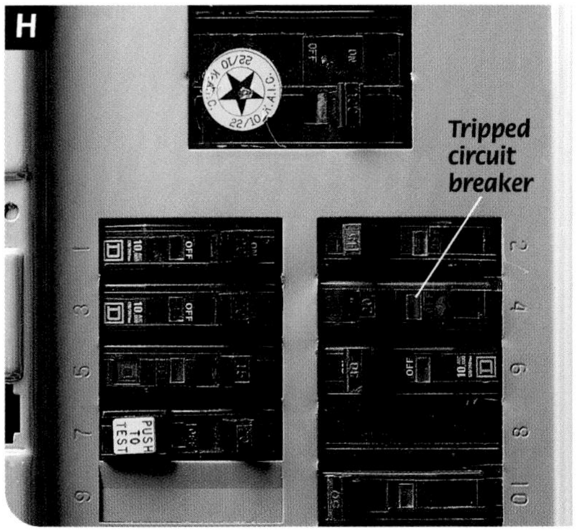

Locate the tripped breaker on the service panel.

Push the lever all the way to OFF, then back to ON.

Periodically test GFCI circuit breakers on the service panel.

Mapping Circuits & Indexing a Service Panel

Electrical repairs will be easier and safer if you have an up-to-date map of your circuits. A circuit map shows all the lights, appliances, switches, and receptacles connected to each circuit. It also allows you to index the main service panel so that the correct circuit can be shut off when repairs are needed.

A circuit map can also help you evaluate the demand on each circuit, which can help determine if your wiring needs to be updated.

Mapping circuits and indexing the service panel usually takes about four to six hours. Even if the service panel was indexed by a previous owner, it's best to make your own map. If any circuits have been added or changed, the old map will be outdated.

The easiest way to map circuits is to turn on one circuit at a time and check to see which fixtures, receptacles, and appliances are affected. To do this, all electrical devices must be in good working condition.

Start by making a sketch of every room in the house on graph paper **(photo A).** Include the hallways, basement, attic, and all utility areas. (You can use a blueprint of your home, if you have one.) Also sketch the exterior of the house, the garage, and any other structures that are wired for electricity.

On each sketch, indicate the location of all electrical devices, including receptacles, light fixtures, switches, appliances, doorbells, thermostats, heaters, fans, and air conditioners.

At the main service panel, number each circuit breaker or fuse **(photo B).** Turn off all the circuit breakers or loosen all the fuses, but leave the main shutoff in the ON position.

Turn on one circuit at a time by flipping its circuit breaker lever or tightening the fuse. Note the amperage rating printed on the circuit breaker lever or the rim of the fuse.

Turn on each switch, light, and appliance in the house one at a time, and identify the ones powered by the circuit, using masking tape **(photo C).**

Test all receptacles for power, using a neon circuit tester. Check both halves of the receptacle **(photo D),** and indicate which circuit supplies power to each receptacle **(photo E).** Although it's uncommon, receptacles can be wired so that each half of the receptacle is powered by a different circuit.

To check the furnace for power, set the thermostat to its highest temperature setting **(photo F).** Furnaces and their low-voltage thermostats are on the same circuit. If the circuit is on, the furnace will begin running. Use the lowest thermostat setting to check the central air conditioner.

Check the electric water heater for power by setting its thermostat to the highest temperature. If the circuit is on, it will begin to heat.

Check the doorbell system for power by ringing all the doorbells.

On the circuit maps, indicate the circuit number, voltage, and amperage rating of each receptacle, switch, light fixture, and appliance **(photo G).**

Tape the completed index to the door of the main service panel. Include a brief summary of all fixtures and appliances powered by each circuit (**photo H).** Tape the completed circuit maps to the main service panel. Restore the power to all circuits.

Tools: Neon circuit tester.

Materials: Paper, pencils, masking tape.

Sketch the house for easy reference when mapping circuits. On the sketch, show the location of all receptacles, light fixtures, switches, appliances, doorbells, and thermostats.

At the main service panel, label each circuit with masking tape. Turn off all the circuits, then turn on one circuit at a time. Note the amperage of each circuit.

Turn on each switch, light, and appliance throughout the house one at a time to identify those that are powered by the circuit.

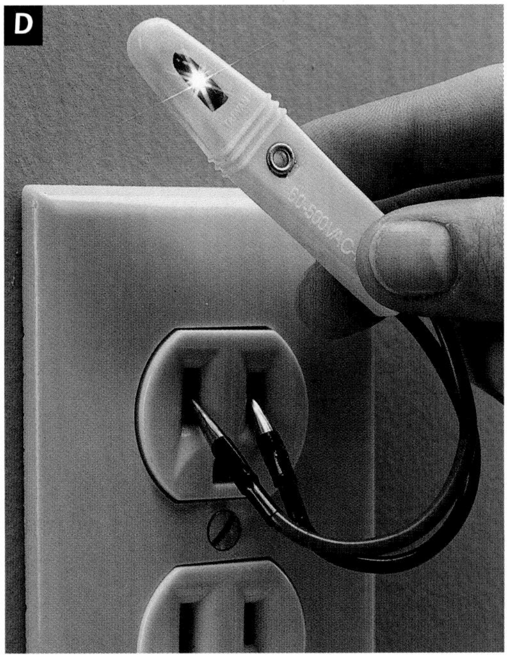

Test receptacles for power, using a neon circuit tester. To test, stick one probe of the circuit tester in each slot of the receptacle. Check both halves of each receptacle.

Label the receptacle to show which circuit supplies it with power and the circuit's amperage rating. The two halves of the receptacle may be on different circuits.

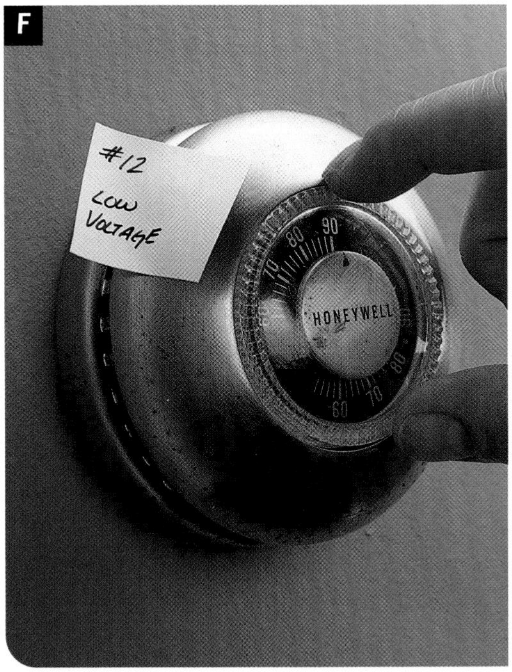

To check for power to the furnace, turn the thermostat up to the highest setting. To check for power to the central air conditioner, turn the power down to the lowest setting.

On the circuit map, record the number of the circuit, and the voltage and amperage rating of every switch, receptacle, light fixture, and appliance.

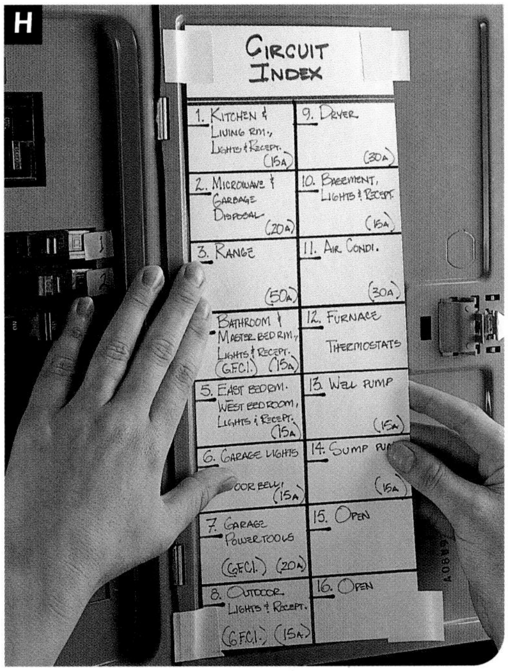

Summarize all the fixtures, appliances, and receptacles that are powered by each circuit. Tape the finished index to the door of the service panel. Turn all the circuits back on.

Tools for Electrical Repair

Unlike some other kinds of repair work, the tools required for home electrical repairs are simple, inexpensive, and widely available.

The set shown below includes everything you'll need for the repair projects that follow. Tools for electrical repair include:

Combination tools cut cables and wires, measure wire gauges, and strip insulation from wires. Their insulated handles ensure safety when working with electrical wires.

Needlenose pliers bend and shape wires, especially for screw terminal connections. Some have cutting jaws for clipping wires.

Continuity testers check switches, lighting fixtures, and other devices for faults. A continuity tester has a battery that generates current and a wire loop that creates a miniature electrical circuit.

Fuse pullers remove cartridge-type fuses from fuse blocks.

Cable rippers remove the outer sheath from nonmetallic (NM) cable.

Insulated screwdrivers have rubber-coated handles to reduce the risk of shock.

Neon circuit testers check circuit wires for power.

Cordless screwdrivers quickly drive screws and fasteners when the electrical circuits are switched off.

Multi-testers measure voltages and test continuity in switches, fixtures, and other devices.

As in purchasing any tool, it's important to invest in high-quality electrical tools and to care for them well. Here are some tips for maintaining electrical repair tools:

Keep all electrical repair tools clean and dry, and store them securely.

Periodically resharpen cutting tools, such as needlenose pliers and combination tools.

Regularly check and replace the batteries in electrical testing devices, such as circuit testers, continuity testers, and multi-testers.

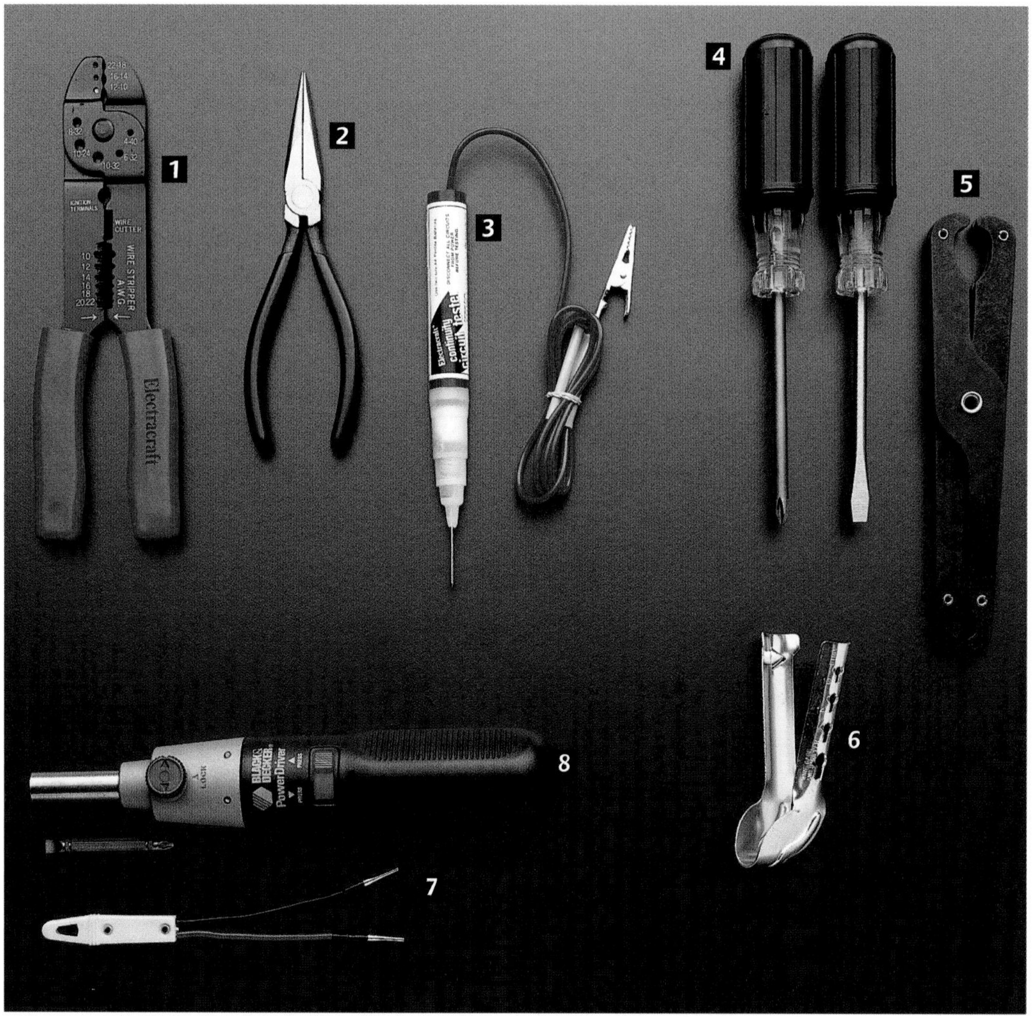

(left) A basic set of electrical tools includes (clockwise from top left): combination tool (1), needlenose pliers (2), continuity tester (3), insulated screwdrivers (4), fuse puller (5), cable ripper (6), neon circuit tester (7), cordless screwdriver (8).

(below) A multi-tester is a versatile, battery-operated tool that measures voltages and continuity in switches, light fixtures, and other electrical devices. It has an adjustable control to measure current ranging from 1 to 1000 volts.

Materials for Electrical Repair

The most basic material for wiring projects is electrical wire. Modern wire is solid copper, which is the best conductor of electricity. The individual wires are insulated with rubber or plastic, except for a bare copper grounding wire, which doesn't need to be insulated. The color of the insulation identifies the wire as hot (black or red), neutral (white or gray), or grounding (green or bare).

In the past, some wire was made from aluminum or aluminum covered with a thin layer of copper—known as *copper-coated* or *copper-clad.* Replacing devices on a circuit with wires that contain aluminum requires special tools that are available only to licensed electricians. If your electrical system has aluminum wires, contact an electrician for repairs.

Electrical wires must be large enough for the amperage rating of the circuit. Other electrical materials, such as receptacles, boxes, and connectors, also carry size ratings. You'll need receptacles that match the amperage of the circuit, and wire connectors designed for the size and number of wires you'll be connecting.

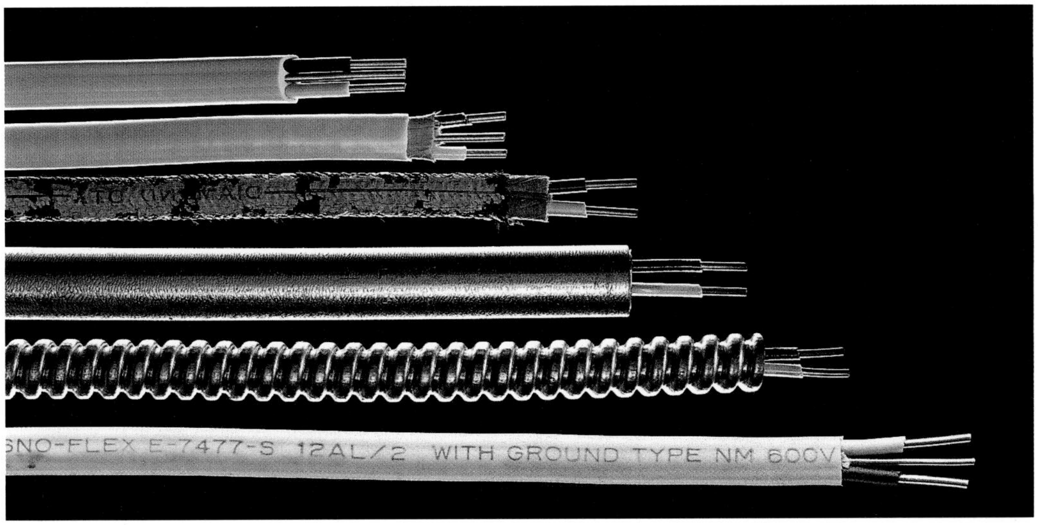

Cables used in home wiring include (from top): UF (underground feeder) cable, modern NM (nonmetallic) cable, early NM (nonmetallic) cable, metal conduit, flexible armored cable, and aluminum wire.

Wire Color Chart

Wire Color	Function
White	Neutral wire carrying current at zero voltage.
Black	Hot wire carrying current at full voltage.
Red	Hot wire carrying current at full voltage.
White, black markings	Hot wire carrying current at full voltage.
Green	Serves as a grounding pathway.
Bare copper	Serves as a grounding pathway.

Electrical supplies are available at almost any hardware store or home center. Plastics now play a large role in home wiring.

Stripping Nonmetallic Cable

Modern nonmetallic (NM) cable has a sheathing that's labeled with the number of wires it contains (excluding the bare grounding wire). A cable marked *14/2 G* or *14/2 with ground*, has two insulated 14-gauge wires plus a bare copper grounding wire. Cable marked *14/3 G* or *14/3 with ground* has three wires plus a ground. Inside the sheathing is a strip of paper, and the individual wires also have their own protective sheathings.

When working with NM cable, you often need to strip the cable, paper, and sheathing. Here's how to do it:

Measure and mark the cable 8" to 10" from the end. Slide a cable ripper onto the cable, line up the cutting points with the mark, and squeeze the tool firmly to force the cutting point through the plastic sheathing **(photo A).**

Grip the cable tightly with one hand, and pull the cable ripper toward the end of the cable, cutting open the plastic sheathing **(photo B).**

Peel back the plastic sheathing and the paper from the individual wires **(photo C).**

Cut away the excess plastic sheathing and paper wrapping, using the cutting jaws of a combination tool **(photo D).** Strip the individual wires, using the combination tool **(photo E).**

Tools: *Cable ripper, combination tool.*

Materials: *NM cable.*

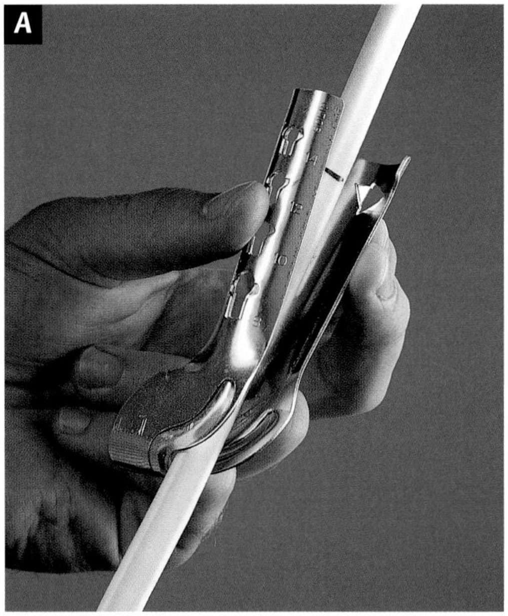

Squeeze the cable ripper tool to pierce the plastic sheathing.

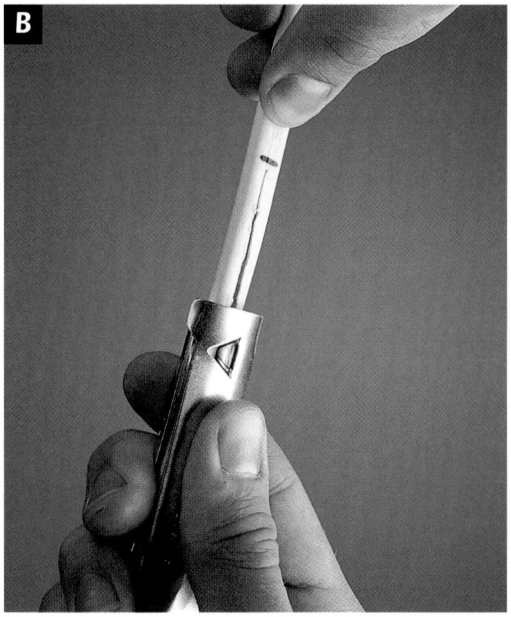

Hold the cable firmly and pull the ripper along the cable.

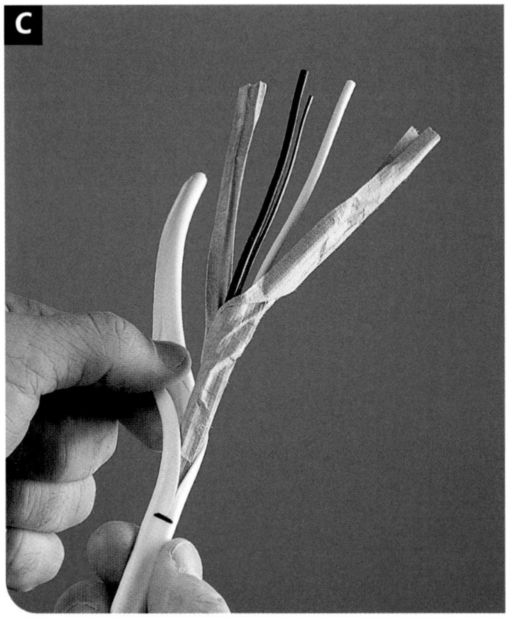

Peel back the paper and plastic sheathing from the wires.

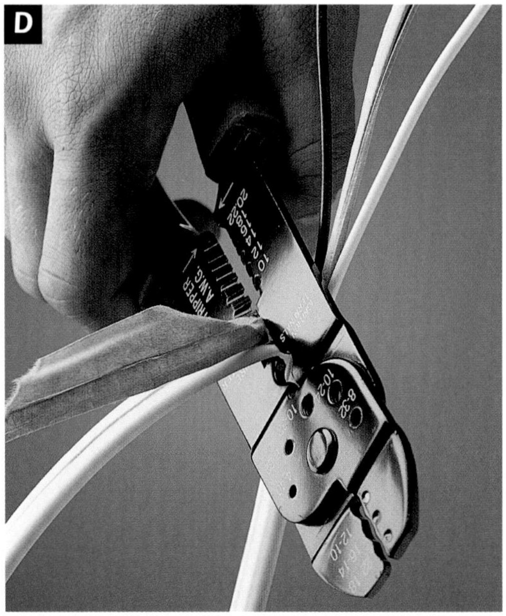

Cut away the excess plastic sheathing and paper wrapping.

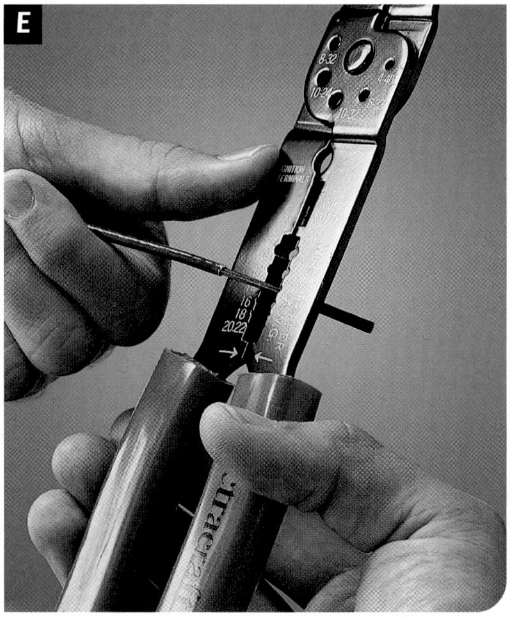

Strip insulation from each wire, using stripper openings.

The Rules of Electrical Safety

When working with electricity, safety is always a primary concern. An electric current follows its own rules. As long as you respect those rules and take a few commonsense precautions, you should be safe.

The first rule is to turn off power to the area you're working on. In the service panel, remove the fuse or shut off the breaker that controls the circuit involved **(photo F).** A circuit map will help you find the right one quickly. Leave a note on the service panel so that no one turns on the power while you're working **(photo G).**

Use a neon circuit tester to check that the power is off **(photo H).** Don't begin work until you're absolutely sure. Restore power only when your project is done.

Use fiberglass or wood ladders when making routine household repairs near the service head. These wires are always live **(photo I).**

Wear rubber-soled shoes for electrical work. If the floor is damp, stand on a rubber mat or dry wooden boards. Never touch any electrical device while standing in water.

Don't touch metal pipes, faucets, or fixtures while working with electricity. The metal could provide a grounding path that allows the current to flow through your body **(photo J).**

Don't drill into walls or ceilings without shutting off electrical power to any circuits that may be hidden **(photo K).**

Use only UL approved electrical parts or devices (they have been tested for safety).

Use the correct fuses or breakers in the main service panel. Never install a fuse or breaker with a higher amperage than the circuit.

Turn off the power at the service panel before you start work.

Post a sign to keep others from turning the power on.

Make sure the power is off before you touch any wires.

Call a professional contractor for any repairs near the service head. Never attempt repairs in the area yourself.

Don't touch metal pipes, faucets, or fixtures during repairs.

Don't drill into walls or ceilings without shutting off power.

Receptacles

A typical home will have several types of electrical receptacles. Each one is designed to accept certain kinds of plugs and fulfill a specific purpose.

Household receptacles provide either standard or high voltage. Standard receptacles should be rated for 110, 115, 120, or 125 volts. For replacement purposes, these voltages can be considered the same. High-voltage receptacles are rated for 220, 240, or 250 volts, and again, can all be considered the same.

When replacing a receptacle, check the amperage rating of the circuit and use a receptacle with the correct rating.

If you have older receptacles that won't accept modern plugs, never modify the plugs to fit. Replace the older receptacles with modern polarized, grounded receptacles.

Modern Standard Receptacles

Standard three-slot receptacle with a U-shaped grounding hole. 15 amps, 125 volts.

Polarized two-slot receptacle common before 1960. 15 amps, 125 volts.

Grounded three-slot receptacle for large appliances or tools. 20 amps, 125 volts.

Modern High-voltage Receptacles

High-voltage receptacles are used to provide power to large appliances, such as clothes dryers, water heaters, and air conditioners. Their slots have distinctive shapes that will not accept a plug rated for 125 volts.

A high-voltage receptacle can be wired in one of two ways. In a standard high-voltage receptacle, the voltage is brought to the receptacle with two hot wires, each carrying a maximum of 125 volts. A grounding wire is also attached to the receptacle and to its metal receptacle box.

However, a clothes dryer or range may also require normal current (125 volts) for lights, timers and clocks. In this case, a white neutral wire is attached to the receptacle, and the appliance itself splits the incoming current into a 125-volt circuit and a 250-volt circuit.

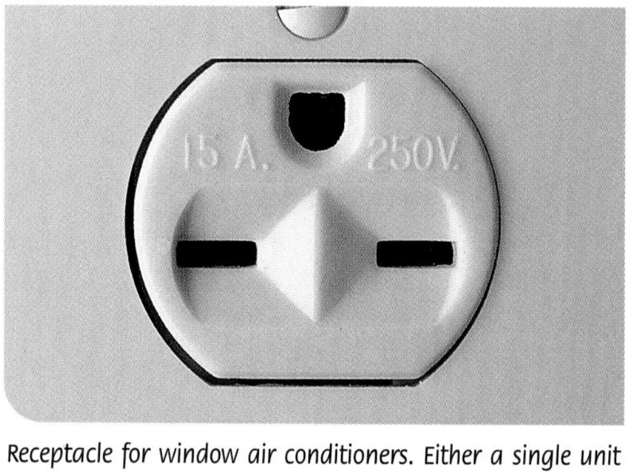

Receptacle for window air conditioners. Either a single unit or half a duplex receptacle. 15 amps, 250 volts.

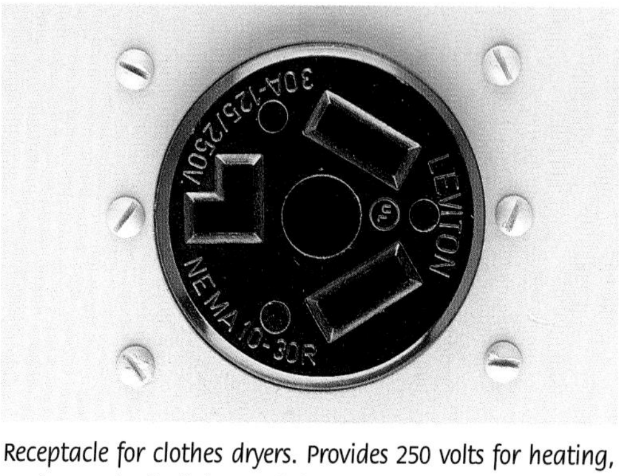

Receptacle for clothes dryers. Provides 250 volts for heating, and 125 volts for lights and timers. 30 amps, 125/250 volts.

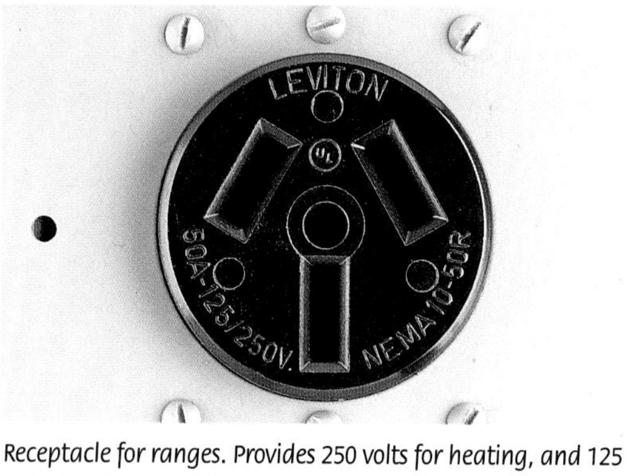

Receptacle for ranges. Provides 250 volts for heating, and 125 volts for clocks and lights. 50 amps, 125/250 volts.

Older Receptacles

Unpolarized receptacles won't accept modern polarized plugs.

Surface-mounted receptacles (1940s and 1950s) are often ungrounded.

Ceramic duplex receptacles (1930s) are polarized but ungrounded.

Twist-lock receptacles are designed for use with old plugs that are inserted and rotated.

GFCI Receptacles

The ground-fault circuit-interrupter (GFCI) receptacle is a safety device that protects against electrical shock caused by a faulty appliance or a worn cord or plug. It senses small changes in the current flow and can shut off power in as little as 1/40 of a second.

When updating wiring, installing new circuits, or replacing receptacles, bear in mind that GFCIs are now required in bathrooms, kitchens, garages, crawl spaces, unfinished basements, and outdoor locations. They can be easily installed as safety replacements for any standard duplex receptacle. Consult your local Building Codes for any requirements regarding the installation of GFCI receptacles.

The GFCI receptacle may be wired to protect only itself (a single location), or to protect all receptacles, switches, and light fixtures from the GFCI "forward" to the end of the circuit (multiple locations). It cannot protect devices that exist between the GFCI and the main service panel.

Because a GFCI is so sensitive, it's most effective when wired to protect a single location. The more receptacles any one GFCI protects, the more susceptible it is to "phantom tripping"—shutting off power because of tiny, normal fluctuations in current flow.

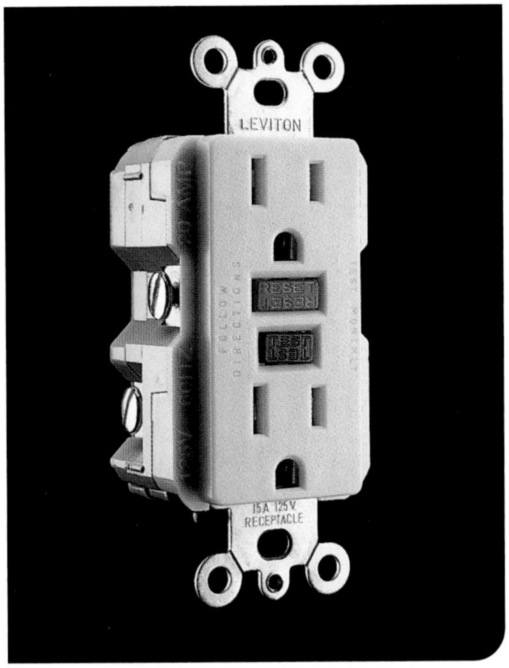

Common Receptacle Problems

Household receptacles have no moving parts to wear out and they'll usually last for many years without servicing. Most of the problems associated with receptacles are actually caused by faulty lamps and appliances or by plugs and cords. However, plugging and unplugging appliances constantly can wear out the metal contacts inside a receptacle. If a receptacle no longer holds plugs firmly, you can easily replace it.

Loose wire connections are another possible problem. A loose connection can send out sparks, trip a circuit breaker, or cause potentially dangerous heat buildup in the receptacle box.

Wires can come loose for many reasons. The vibrations caused by walking across the floor or by street traffic can shake a connection loose. In addition, wires heat and cool with normal use, and the ends of the wires expand and contract slightly. These tiny movements can loosen receptacle connections.

Other problems may be caused by an old receptacle that's in poor condition or that lacks grounding. If your home has old two-slot, unpolarized receptacles, replace them with three-slot polarized receptacles. If no grounding is available at the receptacle box, install a GFCI.

Receptacles are easy to repair and replace. Repairs can be as simple as reconnecting a loose wire or cleaning the inside of the box. Replacing a receptacle only takes a few minutes. Before starting, always turn off the power at the service panel and use a circuit tester to confirm that there is no power to the receptacle (page 402).

When testing or working with receptacles, take the opportunity to inspect them, making sure that all the wires are intact and properly connected.

A problem at one receptacle may affect others in the same circuit. If the cause of a faulty receptacle is not readily apparent, check the other receptacles in the circuit.

Receptacle Problems & Repairs

Problems	Repairs
Circuit breaker trips repeatedly or fuse burns out immediately after being replaced.	*1. Repair or replace worn or damaged lamp or appliance cord.* *2. Move lamps or appliances to other circuits to prevent overloads.* *3. Tighten any loose wire connections (page 406).* *4. Clean dirty or oxidized wire ends (page 406).*
Lamp or appliance does not work.	*1. Make sure lamp or appliance is plugged in.* *2. Replace burned-out bulbs.* *3. Repair or replace worn or damaged lamp or appliance cord.* *4. Tighten any loose wire connections (page 406).* *5. Clean dirty or oxidized wire ends (page 406).* *6. Repair or replace any faulty receptacle (page 407).*
Receptacle does not hold plugs firmly.	*1. Repair or replace worn or damaged plugs.* *2. Replace faulty receptacle (page 407).*
Receptacle is warm to the touch; buzzes or sparks when plugs are inserted or removed.	*1. Move lamps or appliances to other circuits to prevent overloads.* *2. Tighten any loose wire connections (page 406).* *3. Clean dirty or oxidized wire ends (page 406).* *4. Replace faulty receptacle (page 407).*

Inspecting Receptacles & Checking Wire Connections

Problem: Two or more wires are attached to a single screw terminal. This is outdated wiring that is now prohibited by the National Electrical Code.

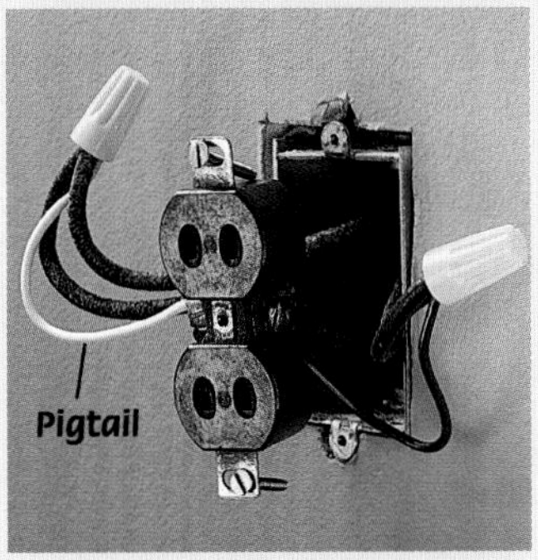

Solution: Disconnect the wires from the screw terminal. Join them with a short length of wire (a pigtail) using a wire connector. Connect the other end of the pigtail to the screw terminal.

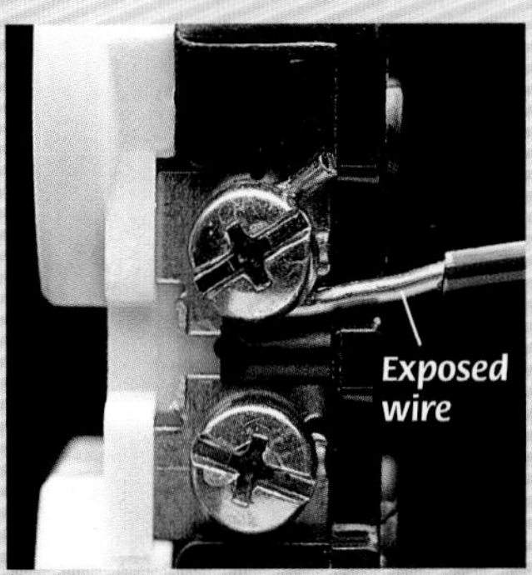

Problem: Bare wire extends past a screw terminal. Exposed wire can cause a short circuit if it comes into contact with the metal box or another circuit wire.

Solution: Clip the wire and reconnect it to the screw terminal. The bare wire should wrap completely around the screw terminal, and the plastic insulation should just touch the screw head.

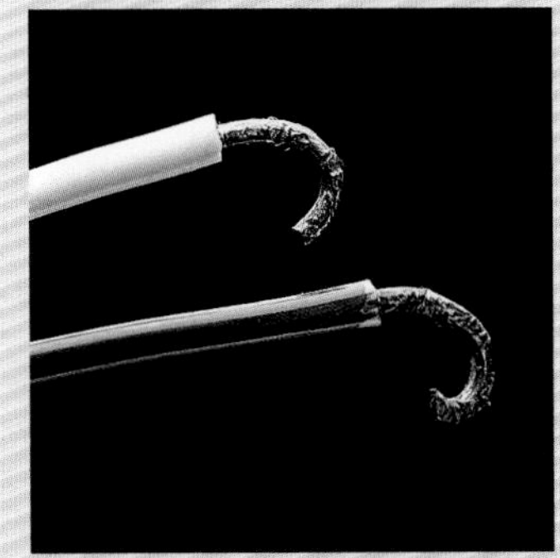

Problem: Nicks and scratches in bare wires interfere with the flow of the current. This can eventually cause the wires to overheat.

Solution: Clip away the damaged section of the wire, then restrip about 3/4" of the wire insulation and reconnect the wire to the screw terminal.

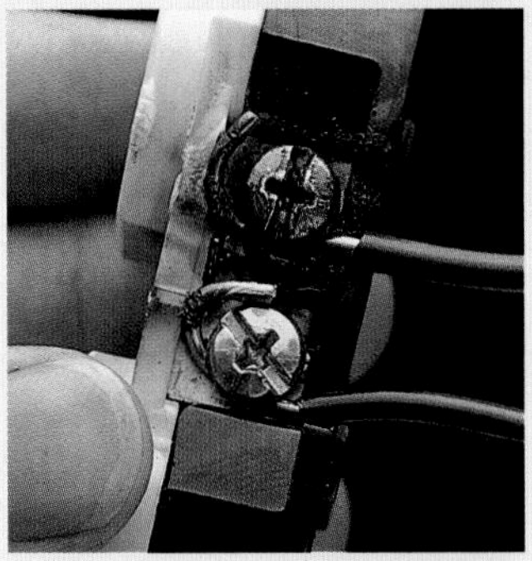

Problem: Scorch marks near screw terminals indicate that electrical arcing has occurred. Arcing is usually caused by loose wire connections.

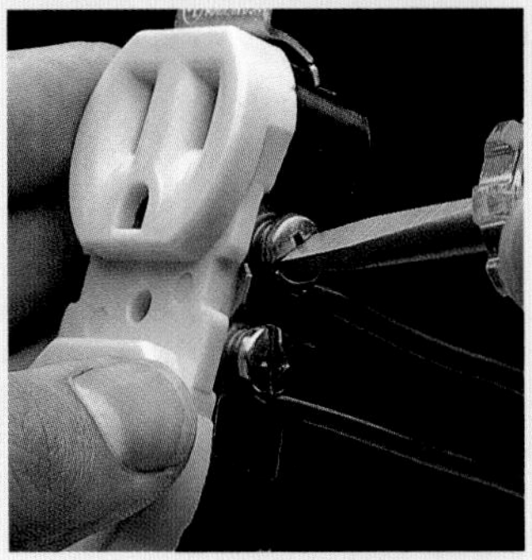

Solution: Clean the wires with fine sandpaper, and replace the receptacle if it's badly damaged. Make sure the wires are connected securely to the screw terminals.

Standard Receptacle Wiring

A standard duplex receptacle has two halves that receive plugs **(photo A).** Each half has a long (neutral) slot, a short (hot) slot, and a U-shaped grounding hole. The three slots fit the wide prong, the narrow prong, and the grounding prong of a three-prong plug. This ensures that the connection will be polarized and grounded for safety.

The wires are attached to screw terminals or push-in fittings, and a connecting tab joins the terminals, to allow for different wiring configurations **(photo B).** Receptacles are attached to electrical boxes with mounting straps.

The marks "UL" or "UND LAB INC LIST" on the front or back of the receptacle indicate that it meets strict safety standards.

Receptacles are marked for maximum volt and amp ratings and wire compatibility. The most common receptacles are 15A, 125V. Receptacles marked "CU" or "COPPER" are for use with solid copper wire. Those marked "CU-CLAD ONLY" are for copper-coated aluminum wire and should not be used with solid copper wiring. Code now forbids the use of receptacles marked AL/CU on any type of wire. If you have aluminum wiring, only a licensed electrician can replace receptacles in your home (page 393).

A 125-volt duplex receptacle can be wired several ways. The most common configurations are shown here. Before disconnecting the old switch, make sure to label each wire according to its location on the screw terminals.

Receptacles are wired either as *end-of-run* or *middle-of-run*, which you can identify by the number of cables that enter the receptacle box. End-of-run wiring has only one cable, because the circuit ends there **(photo C).** Middle-of-run wiring has two cables, because the circuit continues to other receptacles, switches, or fixtures **(photo D).**

In a *split-circuit receptacle,* each half of the receptacle is wired to a separate circuit, so it can accommodate two high-wattage appliances without overloading the circuit **(photo E).** In this configuration, both 125-volt circuits are controlled by one 250-volt circuit breaker.

A *switch-controlled receptacle* is wired in a similar way (page 421). Switch-controlled receptacles are required in rooms that don't have a built-in light fixture operated by a wall switch.

Split-circuit and switch-controlled receptacles are connected to two hot wires. Be especially careful when doing repairs on them, and make sure the connecting tab between the hot screw terminals is removed.

Two-slot receptacles are common in older homes **(photo F).** They have no grounding screw, but the box may be grounded through metal cable or conduit.

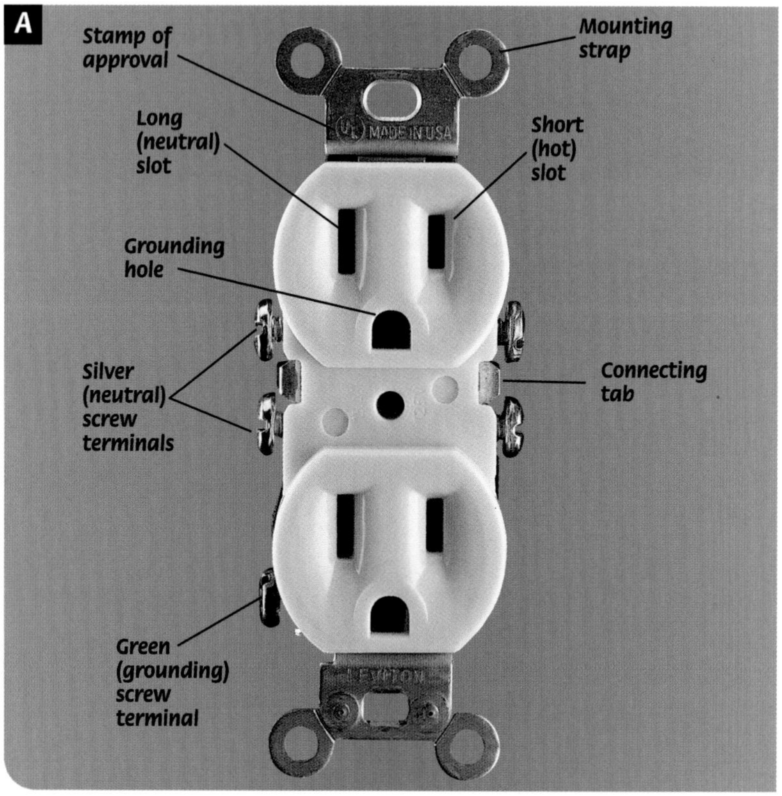

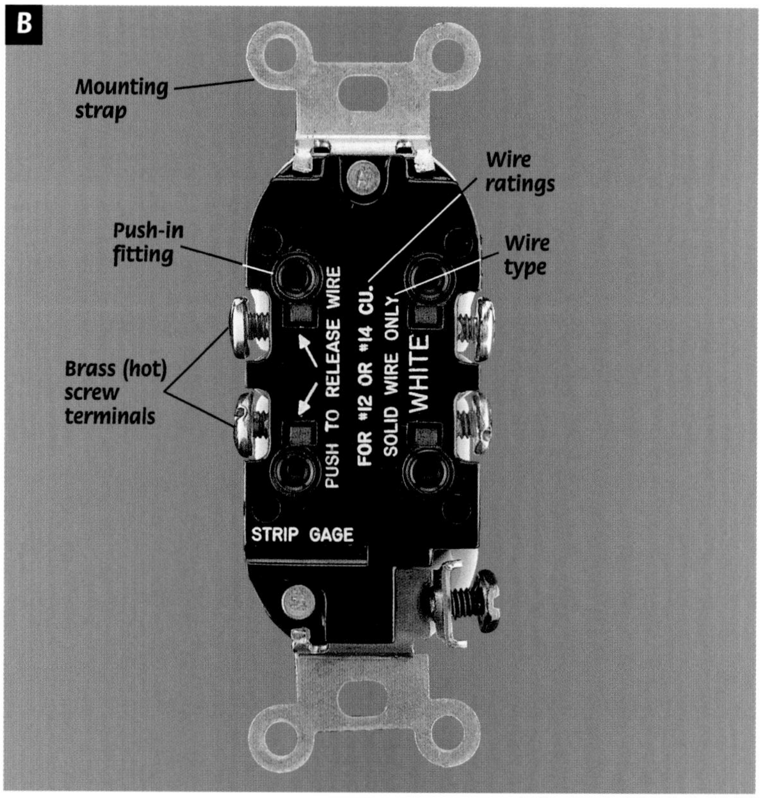

Standard receptacles have two slots, one long and one short, and a grounding hole. Wires can be attached to the receptacle at either the screw terminals or the push-in fittings.

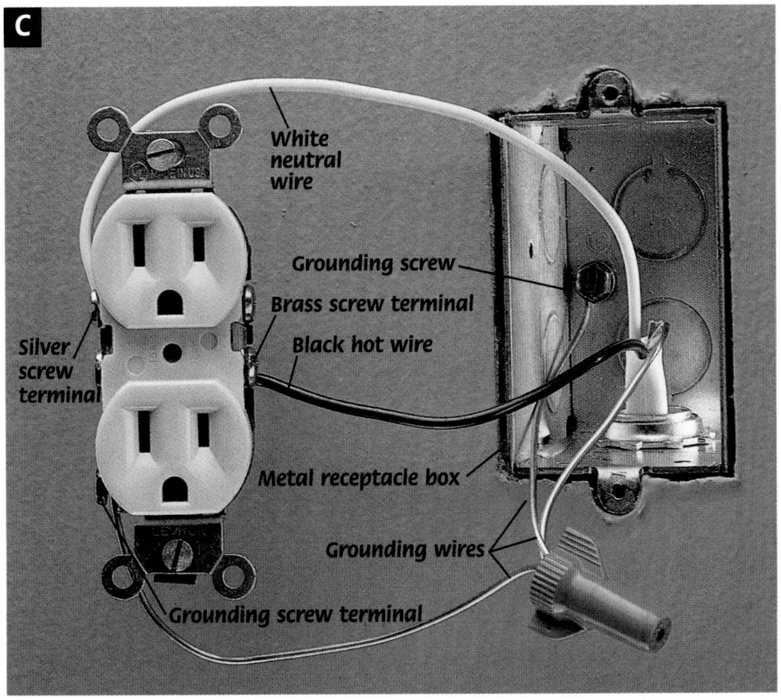

End-of-run wiring includes one black hot wire and one white neutral wire. The grounding wires are pigtailed to the metal box.

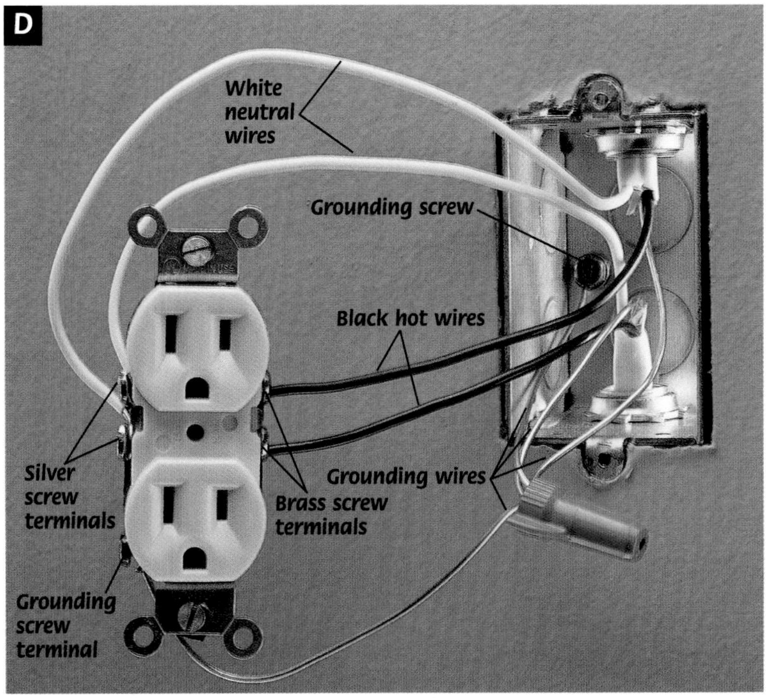

Middle-of-run wiring has two black hot wires and two white neutral wires. Both sets of screw terminals are usually used.

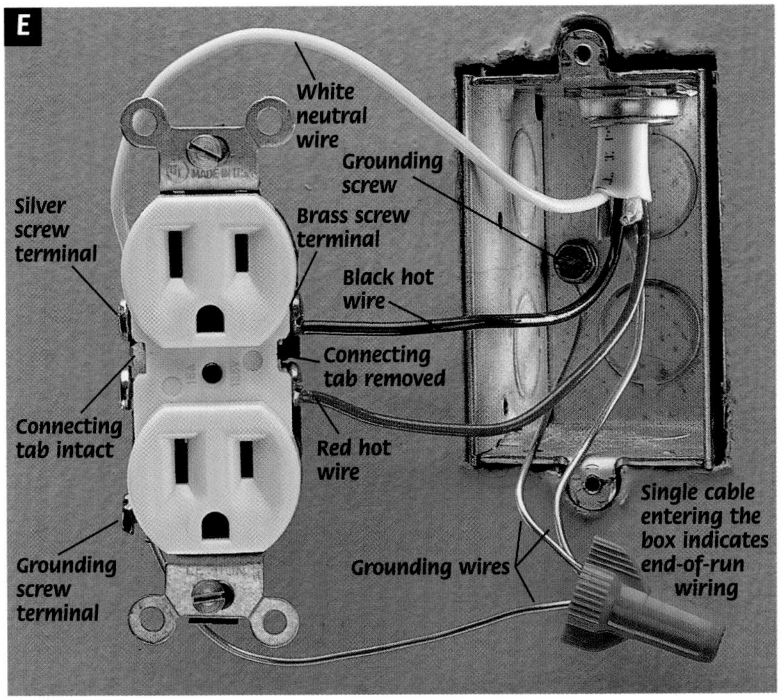

Split-circuit receptacles are attached to a black hot wire, a red hot wire, a white neutral wire, and a grounding wire. The connecting tab between the hot screw terminals is broken.

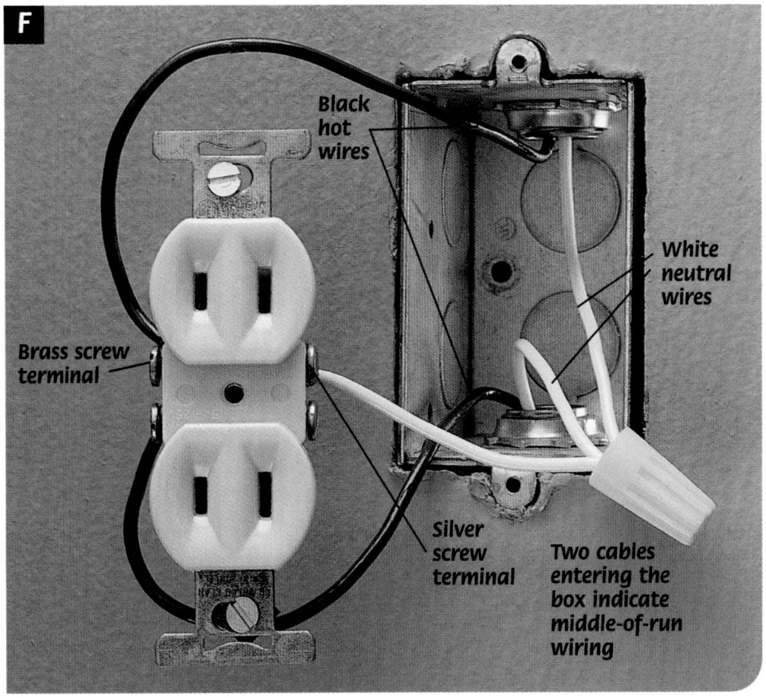

Two-slot receptacles have no grounding wire. They can be replaced with three-slot grounded receptacles, provided the metal box is grounded.

Testing Receptacles

During repair or replacement work, you'll often need to test receptacles for various reasons. For example, before starting to work you always need to test a receptacle to make sure that no live voltage is reaching it.

Before you replace a receptacle, you'll need to test it to see if it's grounded. This test will indicate whether you need to replace it with a two-slot polarized receptacle, a grounded three-slot receptacle, or a GFCI. If the test indicates that the wires are reversed, install the wires correctly on the replacement receptacle. The test for hot wires confirms which wire is carrying the live voltage.

All these tests are done with an inexpensive neon circuit tester, which has a small bulb that glows when electrical power passes through it.

However, the tester only glows when it's part of a complete circuit. For example, if you touch one probe to a hot wire and don't touch anything with the other probe, the tester won't glow, even though the hot wire is carrying power. When using a tester, take care not to touch the metal probes.

When testing for power or grounding, always confirm any negative results (tester does not glow) by removing the coverplate and examining the receptacle to make sure all wires are intact and properly connected. Never touch any wires without first turning off the power at the main service panel.

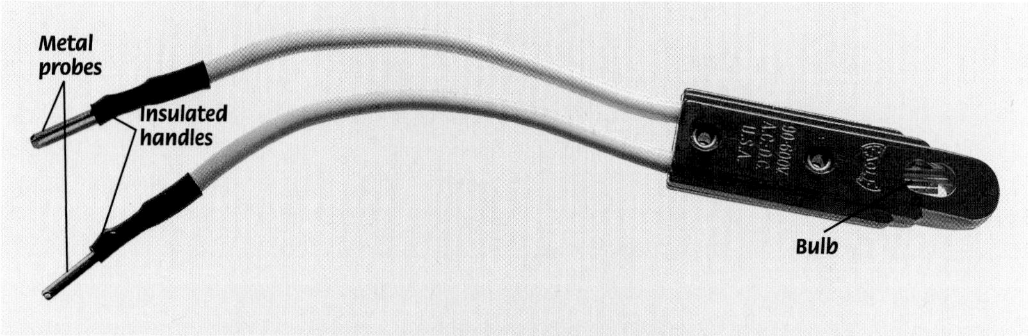

A neon circuit tester, which has two wire leads and a small light bulb, can be used for a variety of tests.

Testing for Power

Testing for power is the same process, whether you're testing a two-slot or a three-slot receptacle. To do a preliminary test, start by turning off the power at the main service panel. Place one probe of the tester in each slot of the receptacle. (For a duplex receptacle, test both receptacles.) The tester should not glow **(photo A).** If it does glow, go back to the service panel and turn off the correct circuit.

This is just a preliminary test; to confirm that there is no power to the receptacle, you need to test the receptacle wires. Remove the coverplate and loosen the mounting screws. Without touching any of the wires, pull the receptacle from its box.

Touch one probe of the tester to a brass screw terminal, and one to the silver screw terminal directly across from it **(photo B).** If there are wires connected to both sets of terminals, test both sets.

If the tester glows, there is power in the receptacle and you need to shut off the correct circuit at the service panel.

To do a preliminary test for power, place one probe in each slot. If the tester glows, return to the service panel and shut off the right circuit. If it doesn't glow, go on to the next step.

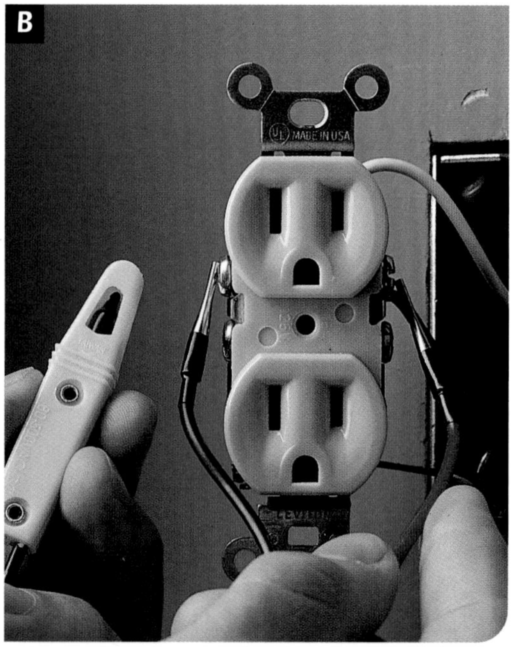

Remove the coverplate and pull the receptacle from the box without touching the wires. Touch one probe to the brass screw terminal and the other to the silver screw terminal.

Testing for Grounding

To test a three-slot receptacle for grounding: With the power on, place one probe of the tester in the short (hot) slot, and the other in the U-shaped grounding hole. The tester should glow. If it doesn't glow, place a probe in the long (neutral) slot and one in the grounding hole. If the tester glows, the hot and neutral wires are reversed **(photo C).** If the tester doesn't glow in either position, the receptacle isn't grounded.

To test a two-slot receptacle for grounding: With the power on, place one probe of the tester in each slot. The tester should glow **(photo D).** If it doesn't glow, there is no power to the receptacle.

Place one probe of the tester in the short (hot) slot, and touch the other probe to the coverplate screw **(photo E).** The screw head must be free of paint, dirt, and grease. If the tester glows, the receptacle box is grounded. If it does not glow, place one probe of the tester in the long (neutral) slot, and touch the other to the coverplate screw **(photo F).** If the tester glows, the receptacle box is grounded but the hot and neutral wires are reversed. If the tester doesn't glow, the box is not grounded.

Test a three-slot receptacle for grounding by inserting one probe into the hot slot, and the other into the neutral.

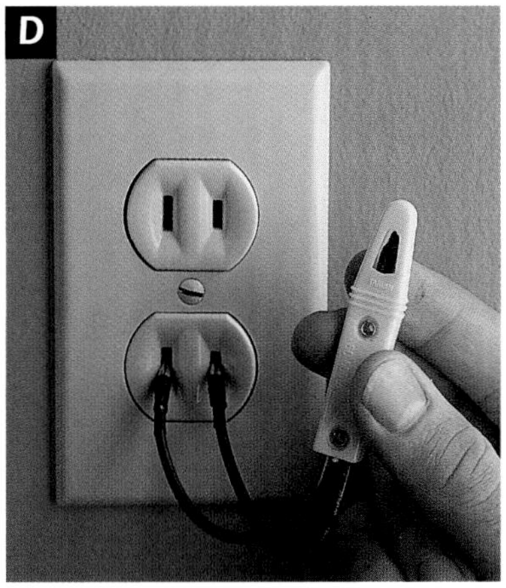

To check a two-slot receptacle for grounding, begin by testing both slots together.

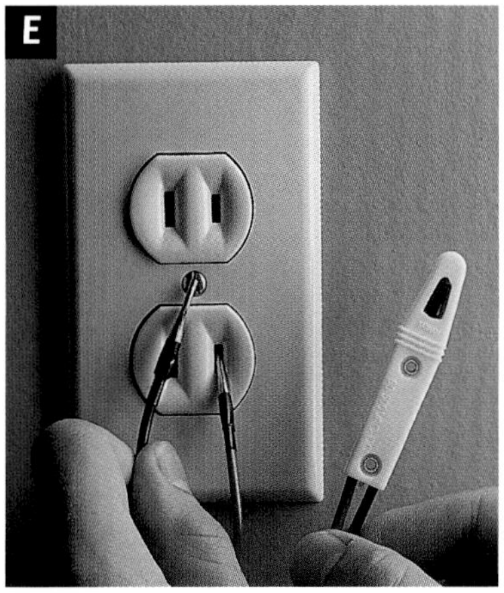

Test the short slot and the grounding screw. If the tester glows, the receptacle box is grounded.

Test the long slot and the grounding screw. If the tester glows, the hot and neutral wires are reversed.

Testing for a Hot Wire

Occasionally you may need to determine which wire in a receptacle is hot. Begin by turning off the power at the main service panel. Next, carefully separate the ends of all the wires and spread them out so that they aren't touching each other or anything else.

Restore the power to the circuit at the main service panel. Touch one probe of the tester to the bare grounding wire or grounded metal box, and the other probe to the ends of each of the wires. In this manner, check each wire in turn **(photo G).**

If the tester glows, it means that a wire is hot. Take note of the hot wire and continue testing.

Turn off the power at the service panel again before continuing to work.

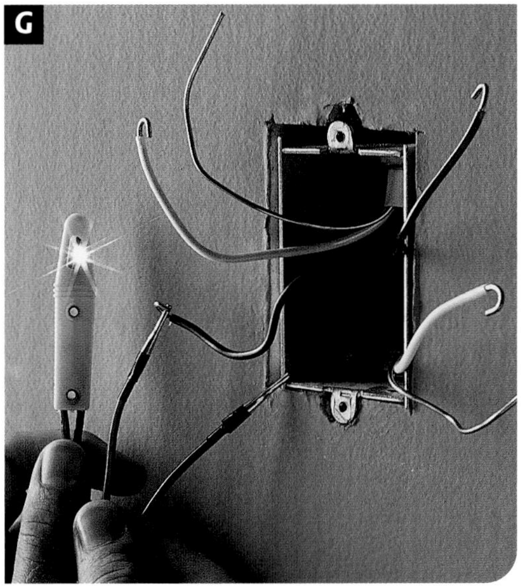

With the wires isolated, touch one of the probes to each of the wires while holding the other probe on the grounded metal box or to a grounding wire entering the box from the source. If the tester glows, the wire is hot.

Connecting Wires to Screw Terminals

With a combination tool, strip about 3/4" of insulation from each wire (page 394). Find the opening that matches the wire gauge, clamp the wire and pull it firmly to remove its insulation.

Form each wire into a C-shaped loop, using needlenose pliers **(photo A).** The wire should have no scratches or nicks.

Hook each wire around the screw terminal so it forms a clockwise loop **(photo B).** Tighten the screws firmly. The insulation should just touch the head of the screw.

Never place the ends of two wires under a single screw terminal. Instead, pigtail them (page 405).

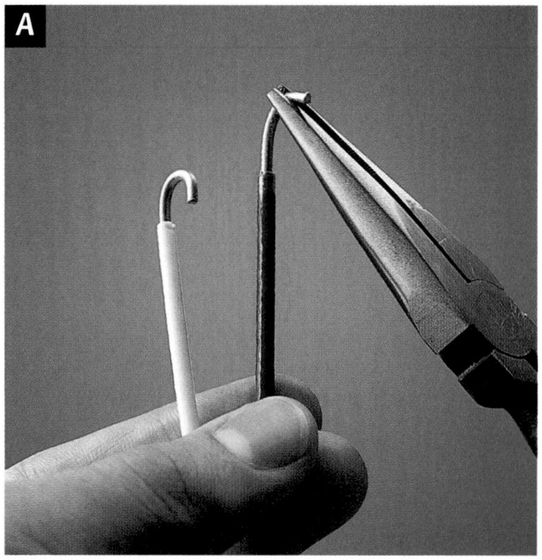

Form a C-shaped loop in the end of each wire, using needlenose pliers. The wire should be free of scratches and nicks.

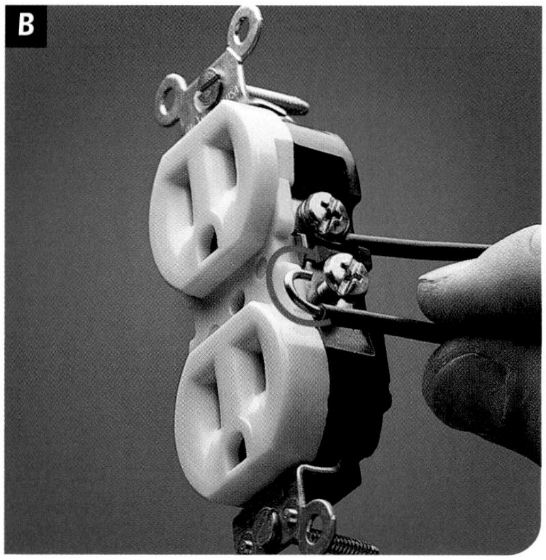

Hook the wires around the screw terminals in clockwise loops. Tighten connections with a screwdriver.

Connecting Wires to Push-in Fittings

Mark the amount of insulation you need to strip from each wire, using the strip gauge on the back of the switch or receptacle **(photo C).** Strip the wires, using a combination tool (page 394).

Insert the bare copper wires firmly into the push-in fittings on the back of the switch or receptacle **(photo D).** When inserted, no bare copper should be visible.

To remove a wire from a push-in fitting, insert a small nail or screwdriver in the release opening next to the wire **(photo E).** The wire can then be pulled out easily.

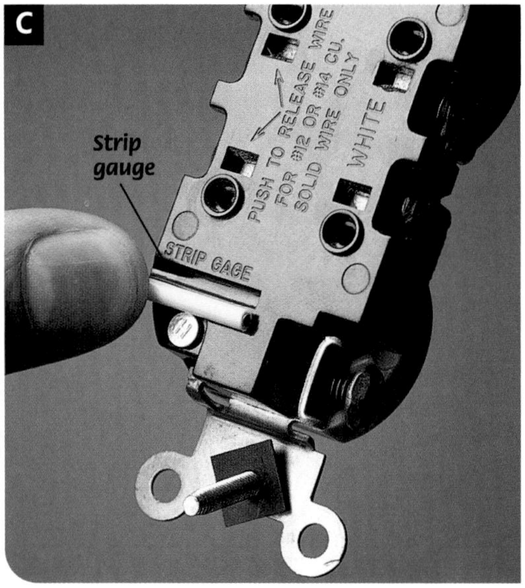

Use the strip gauge on the back of the receptacle or switch to mark the amount of insulation you need to strip.

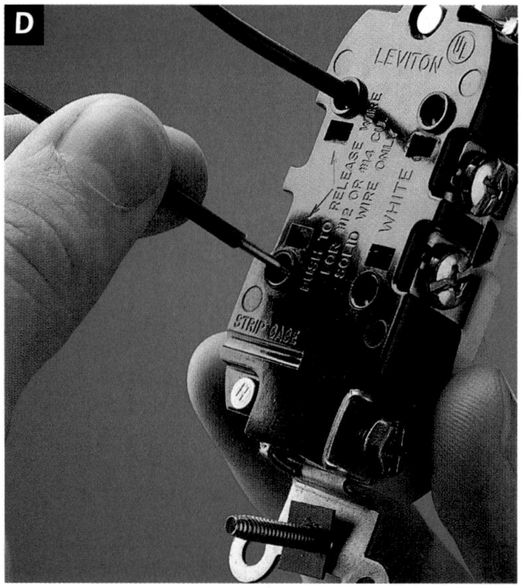

Insert the stripped wires into the push-in fittings. When fully inserted, no bare copper should be visible.

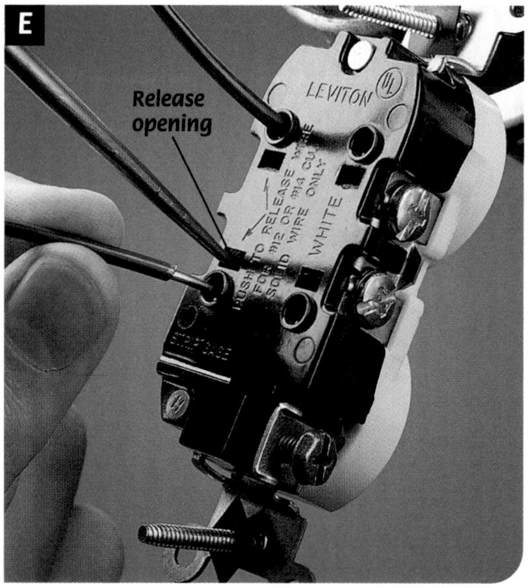

To remove a wire, push a small nail or a screwdriver in the release opening next to the wire, and pull out the wire.

Using Wire Connectors

Wire connectors are the most effective device for connecting two or more wires, and they're far easier to use than electrical tape.

First, strip about ½" of insulation from each wire. Hold the stripped portions of the wires so they're parallel, and cut the ends even. Insert the wires in a wire connector and screw the connector clockwise until it's snug **(photo F).** Tug gently on each wire to make sure it's secure, then inspect the connection to make sure no bare wire is visible outside the wire connector.

With wire connectors, there's no need to twist wires together with pliers. The wire connector creates a very effective connection, provided you use the right size for the job. Select wire connectors that are rated for the gauge and number of wires you're working with, using the chart on the package **(photo G)** as a guide.

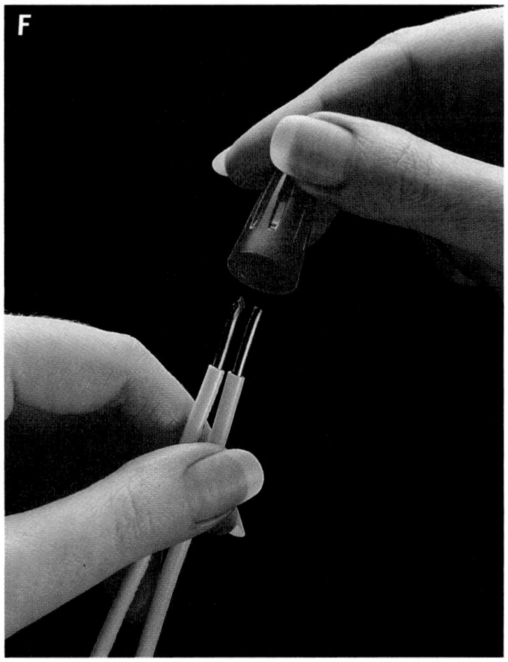

Hold the wires parallel and screw a wire connector clockwise until it's snug.

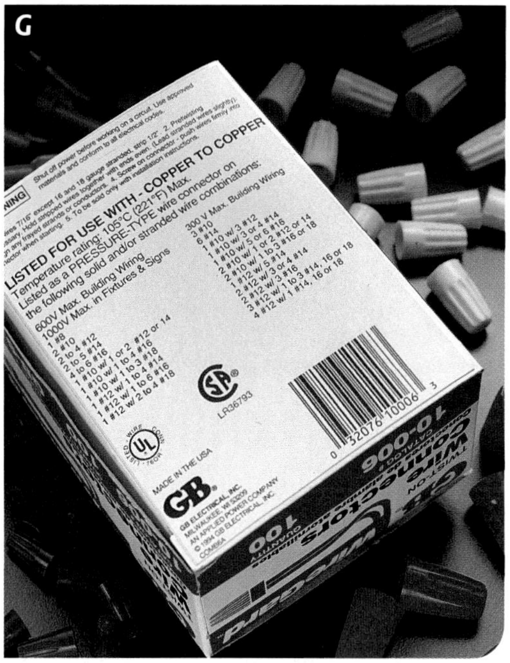

Check the chart on the package to determine the wire gauge and the number of wires each connector can hold.

Pigtailing Wires

A pigtail is a short piece of wire that's used to connect two or more wires to a single screw terminal. A pigtail can be cut from scrap wire, but it should be the same gauge and color as the circuit wires.

One end of the pigtail wire is connected to the screw terminal and the other is connected to the circuit wires with a wire connector **(photo H).**

Pigtails can also be used to lengthen circuit wires that are too short. Short wires are difficult to handle, and the National Electrical Code requires that every wire in an electrical box have at least 6" of workable length.

Grounding pigtails have green insulation and are available with a preattached grounding screw that you attach to the grounded metal box. Attach the other end of the pigtail wire to the bare copper grounding wires with a green wire connector **(photo I).**

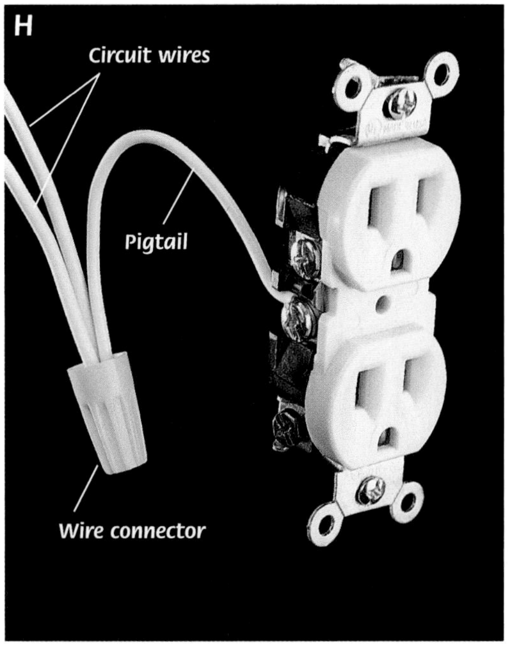

Use a pigtail to connect two or more wires to a single screw terminal. Pigtails can also lengthen wires that are too short.

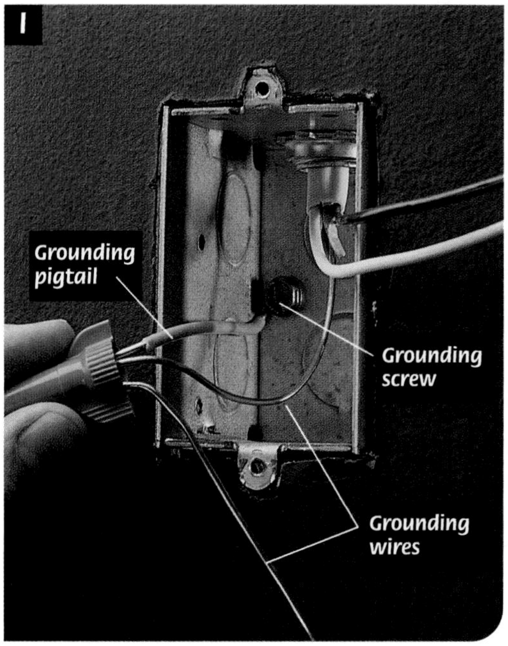

A grounding pigtail connects two or more grounding wires to a grounded metal screw in an electrical box.

Repairing a Standard Receptacle

Turn off the power at the main service panel. Before inspecting the receptacle, use a neon circuit tester to test for power (page 402). If you're working on a duplex receptacle, test both ends.

Remove the coverplate and the receptacle mounting screws. Carefully pull the receptacle from its box, without touching any bare wires. Confirm that the power is off **(photo A).** If there are wires attached to both sets of screw terminals, test them both. If the tester glows, return to the service panel and turn off the correct circuit.

Inspect the wires. If they're darkened or dirty, disconnect them one at a time, and clean them with fine sandpaper **(photo B).**

Reconnect the wires, and tighten all the connections **(photo C).** Be careful not to over-tighten or strip the screws.

Check the receptacle box for dirt or dust. If necessary, clean the box with the narrow nozzle attachment of a vacuum cleaner **(photo D).**

Reinstall the receptacle, and restore the power at the main service panel. Test the receptacle for power. If it doesn't work, check the other receptacles in the circuit before replacing it.

Tools: *Neon circuit tester, vacuum (if needed).*

Materials: *Fine sandpaper.*

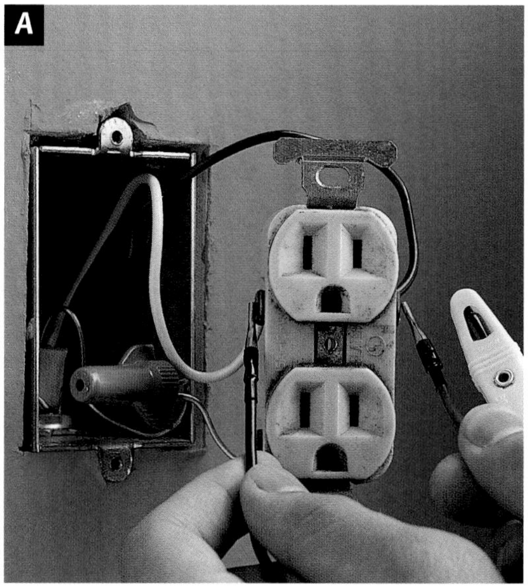

Test the receptacle for power at the screw terminals.

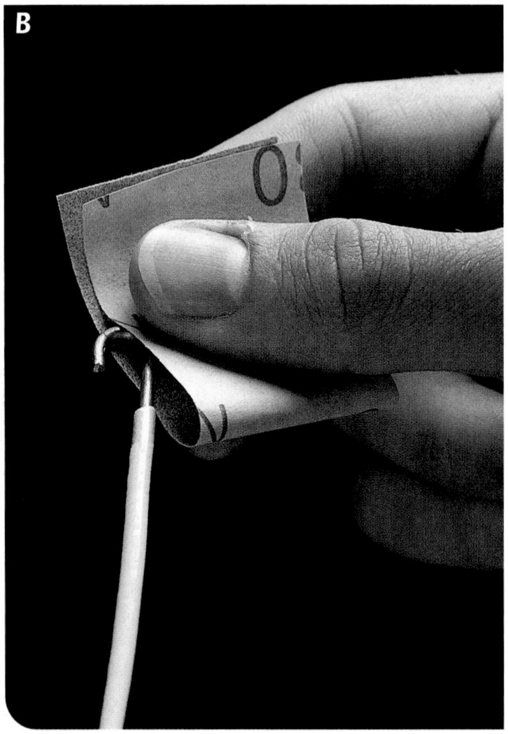

Disconnect the wires, then clean the ends of the wires with fine sandpaper.

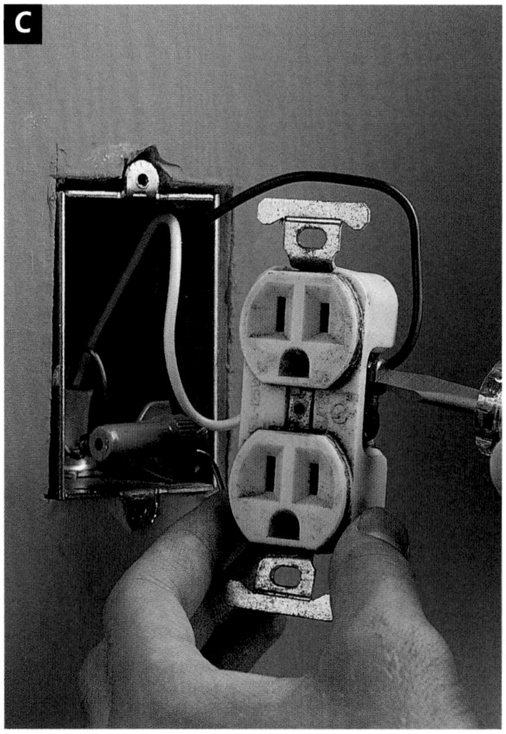

Reattach the wires and carefully tighten the connections.

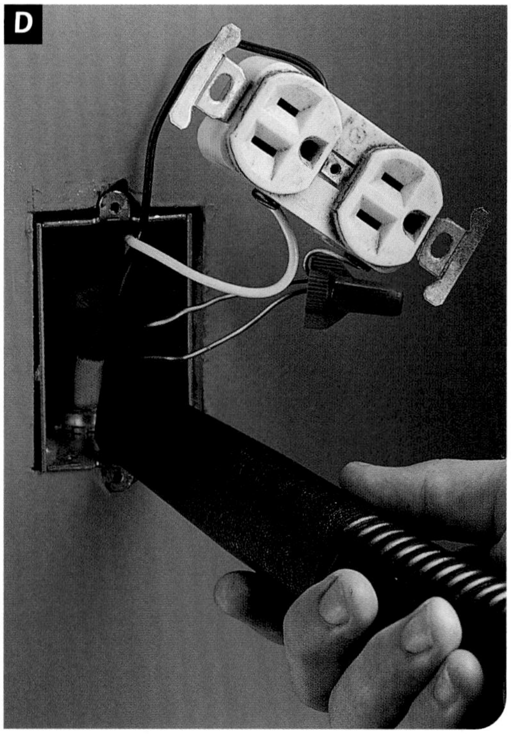

Use a vacuum cleaner to remove dirt and dust from the box. Reinstall the receptacle and turn on the power.

Replacing a Standard Receptacle

Test for grounding (page 403) to find out how the existing receptacle is wired and whether the replacement should be a two-slot polarized receptacle, a grounded three-slot receptacle, or a GFCI receptacle.

Check the amperage rating for the circuit at the main service panel, and buy a replacement receptacle with the correct amperage rating.

If the test indicates that the hot and neutral wires are reversed, be sure to install the wires correctly for the replacement receptacle.

Consult an electrician if you need to install a three-slot receptacle where there is no grounding or if you want to replace a two-slot ungrounded receptacle with a receptacle of another type.

Turn off the power at the main service panel. Before removing the old receptacle, test for power (page 402). Be sure to test both ends of a duplex receptacle. Remove the coverplate, using a screwdriver.

Remove the mounting screws that hold the receptacle to the box. Carefully pull the receptacle from the box. Confirm that the power to the receptacle is off (page 402), using a neon circuit tester.

With the power off, label each wire for its location on the receptacle screw terminals, using masking tape and a marking pen **(photo E).**

When all the wires are labeled, disconnect all of them and detach the receptacle **(photo F).**

Replace the receptacle with one that's rated for the correct amperage and voltage. Connect each wire to its respective screw terminal on the new receptacle **(photo G).** Tighten all the screw connections with a screwdriver. Take care not to overtighten or strip the screws.

Carefully tuck the wires back into the box and mount the new receptacle, using the mounting screws.

Reattach the coverplate, and turn on the power. Test the receptacle with a neon circuit tester.

Tools: *Neon circuit tester, screwdriver.*

Materials: *Masking tape, marking pen.*

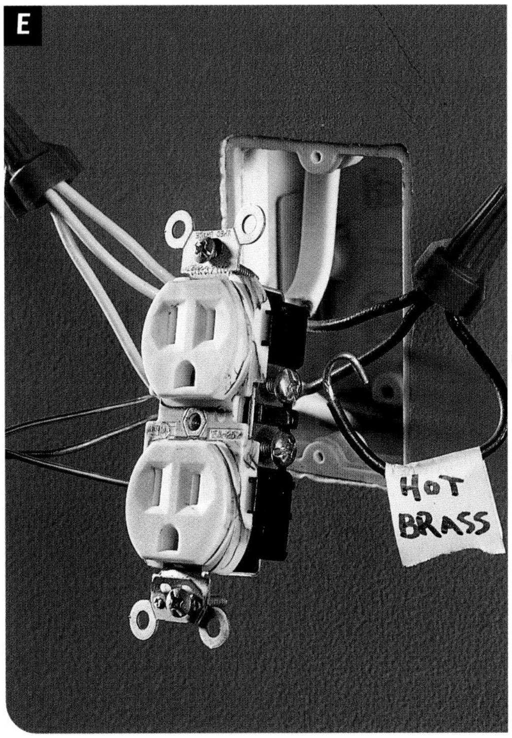

With the power off, label each circuit wire with masking tape to identify its location on the receptacle.

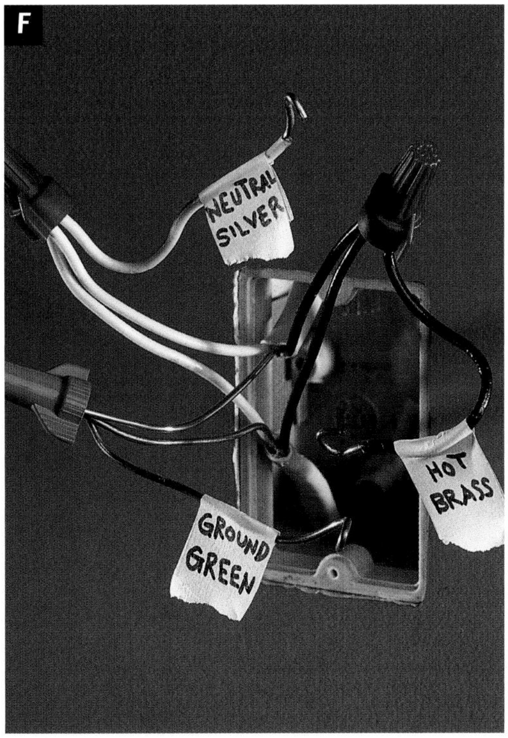

Disconnect all wires and remove the receptacle. Buy a new receptacle that matches the amp and voltage rating of the circuit.

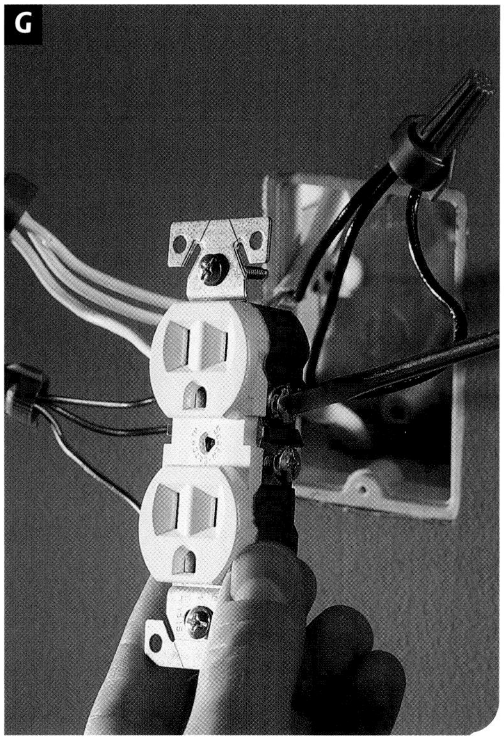

Connect each wire to the proper screw terminal. Tuck the wires into the box, then mount the receptacle and coverplate.

GFCI Receptacles

A ground-fault circuit-interrupter (GFCI) receptacle protects against electrical shock caused by a faulty appliance or a worn or wet cord or plug. In circuits that aren't grounded, a GFCI can be installed in place of a standard duplex receptacle to improve safety.

A GFCI can be wired to protect only itself (single-location) or to protect itself and all receptacles, switches, and fixtures beyond it in the circuit (multi-location). A GFCI wired for a single location will have hot and neutral wires connected only to the terminals marked *line* **(photo A).** A GFCI wired for multiple locations will have wires connected to both the *line* and the *load* terminals **(photo B).**

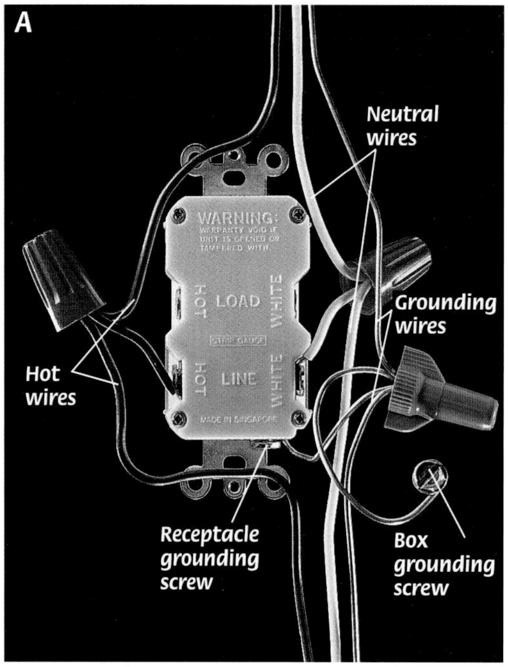

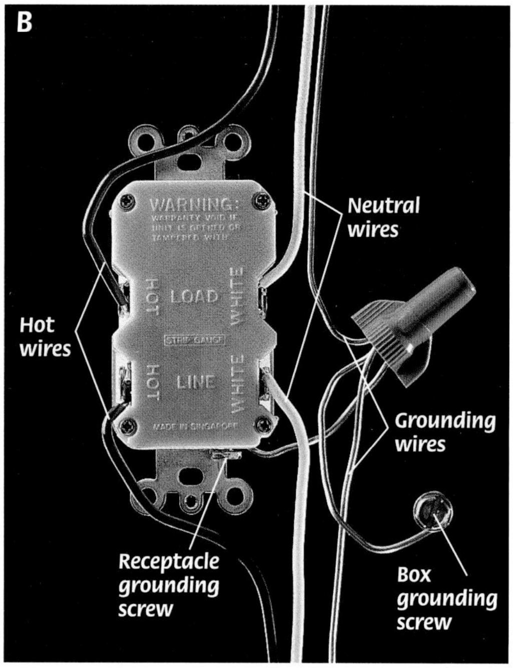

Installing a Single-location GFCI

Turn off the power at the service panel. Remove the coverplate and mounting screws, and pull out the receptacle without touching any bare wires. Use a circuit tester to confirm that the power is off (page 402).

Disconnect the white neutral wires from the silver screw terminals on the old receptacle. Pigtail the white wires and connect the pigtail to the *white line* terminal on the GFCI **(photo C).** Disconnect the black hot wires from the brass screw terminals on the old receptacle. Pigtail them and connect the pigtail to the *hot line* terminal on the GFCI **(photo D).**

If there is a grounding wire, disconnect it and attach it to the green grounding screw terminal on the GFCI **(photo E).** If there is no grounding wire, the GFCI will function properly. However, ask your building inspector about local restrictions.

Mount the GFCI in the receptacle box and reattach the coverplate. Restore the power and test the GFCI.

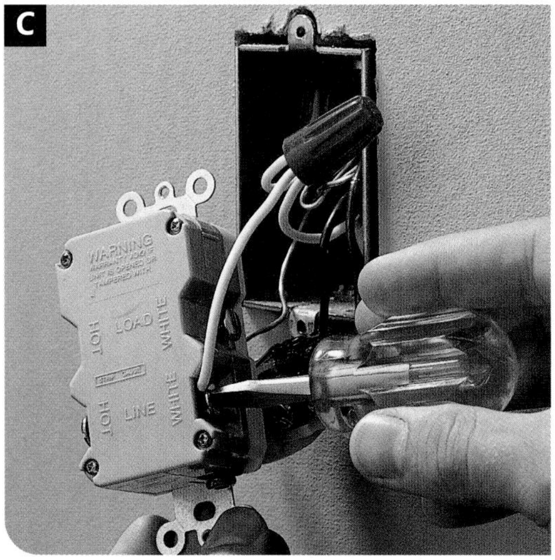

Pigtail the white neutral wires to the WHITE LINE terminal.

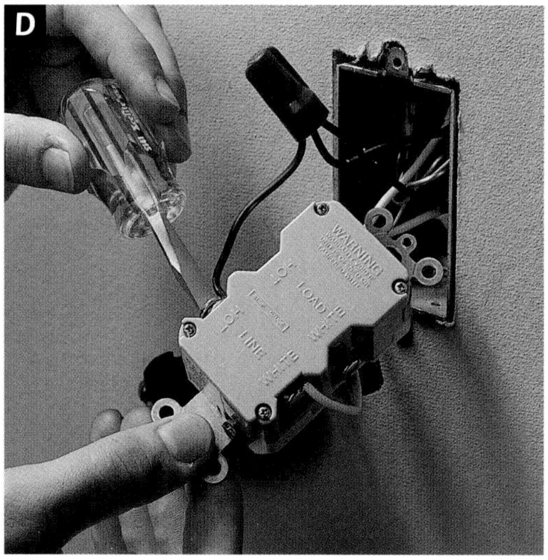

Pigtail the black hot wires to the HOT LINE terminal.

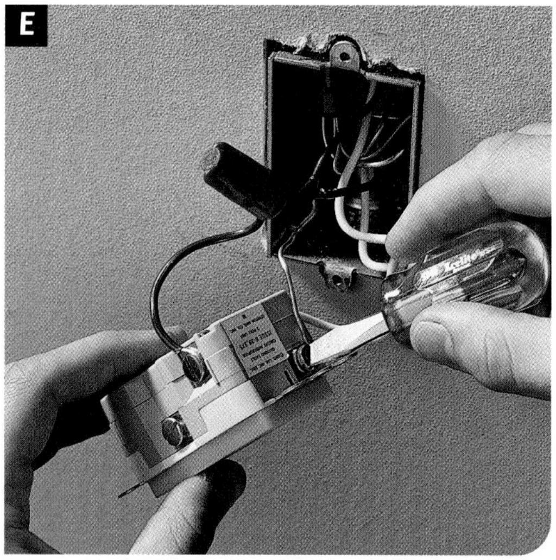

Connect the grounding wire to the grounding screw.

Installing a Multi-location GFCI

Turn off the power and test the receptacle for current (page 402). Carefully pull the old receptacle from its box and test for power at the screw terminals.

Disconnect the black hot wires and separate them. Restore power to the receptacle and use a neon circuit tester to find the black "feed" wire (page 403). Touch one probe of the tester to the receptacle box and the other probe to the ends of each of the black wires. The tester will glow to indicate that you have identified the feed wire.

Turn off the power and test for current. Use masking tape to label the feed wire **(photo F).**

Disconnect the white neutral wires and label the white feed wire, which shares the same cable as the black feed wire **(photo G).**

Disconnect the grounding wire from the old receptacle and connect it to the GFCI grounding terminal **(photo H).**

Connect the white feed wire to the GFCI terminal marked *white line* and the black one to the terminal marked *hot line* **(photo I).** Connect the other white wire to the GFCI terminal marked *white load* **(photo J).** Connect the other black wire to the terminal marked *hot load* **(photo K).**

Carefully tuck all wires into the box. Mount the GFCI in the box and restore power to the circuit. Test the GFCI according to the manufacturer's instructions.

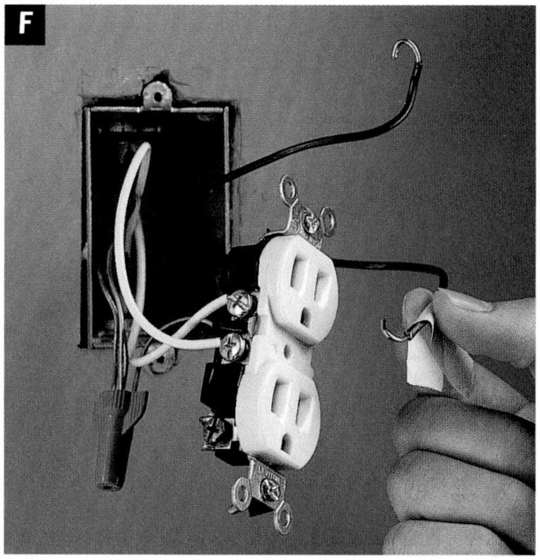

Shut off the power and label the black feed wire.

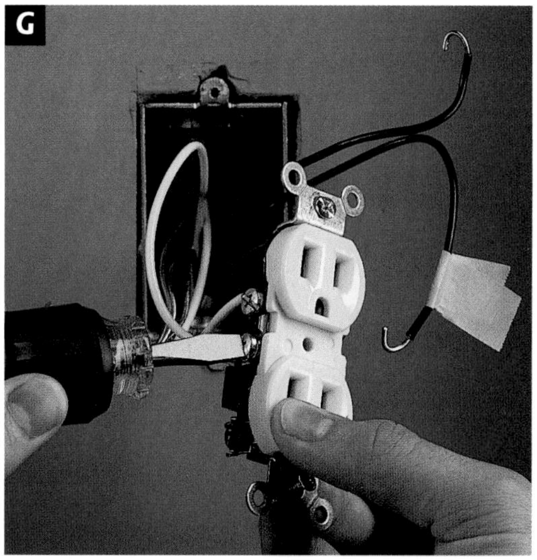

Disconnect the white wires and label the white feed wire.

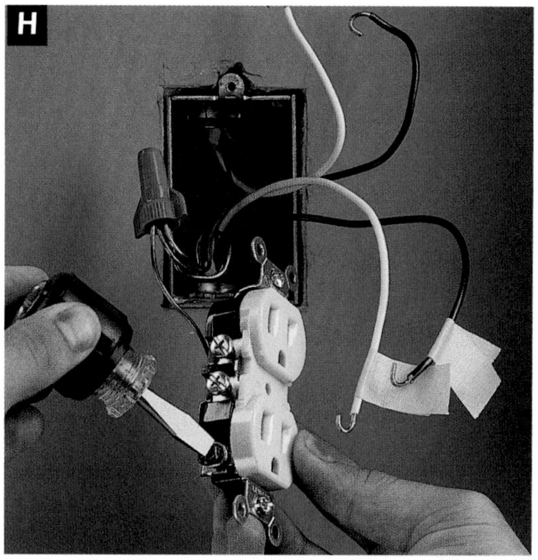

Disconnect the grounding wire from the old receptacle.

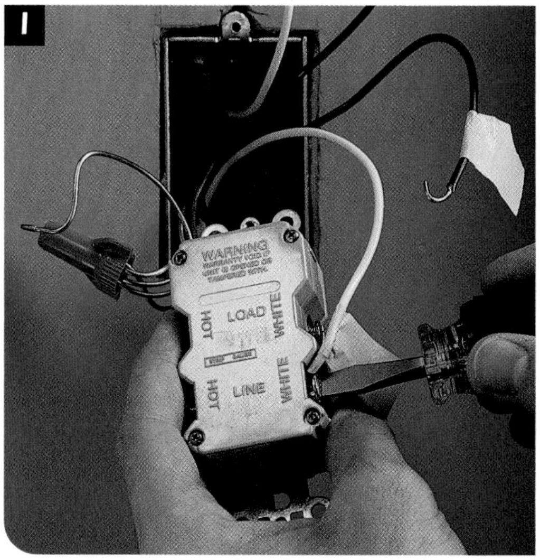

Connect the feed wires to the proper "line" GFCI terminals.

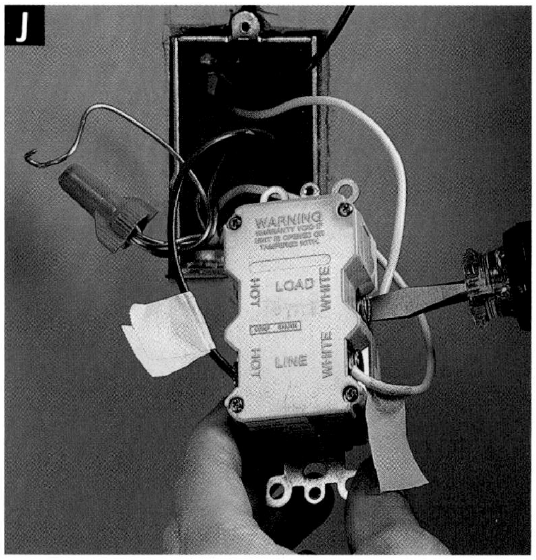

Connect the other white wire to the "white load" terminal.

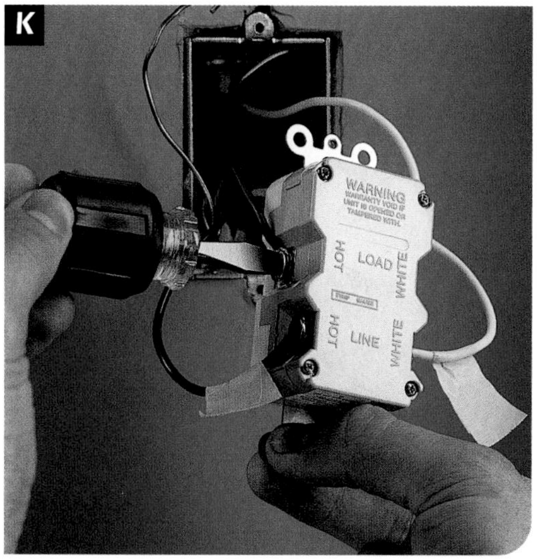

Connect the other black wire to the "hot load" terminal.

Replacing an Electrical Box

It's important to replace any electrical box that's too small for the number of wires it contains. Forcing wires into an undersized box can damage the wires and disturb their connections, creating a potential fire hazard.

You're likely to find boxes that are too small when repairing or replacing switches, receptacles, or fixtures. If a box is so small that it's hard to fit the wires inside, replace it with a larger box.

Metal and plastic retrofit electrical boxes are available in a variety of styles and sizes, and can be found at hardware stores and home centers. Most can be installed without cutting into the wall.

To replace an electrical box, start by shutting off the power to the circuit at the service panel. Test for power with a circuit tester (switches, page 415; receptacles, page 402; fixtures, page 429). Disconnect and remove the device from the existing box **(photo A).**

Examine the box to determine how it was installed. Most older metal boxes are attached to framing members with nails, and the nail heads are visible inside the box **(photo B).**

Cut through the mounting nails by slipping the metal cutting blade of a reciprocating saw between the box and the framing member **(photo C).** Be careful not to damage the circuit wires.

If there are no mounting nails visible in the box, the box is mounted with straps as in the cutaway **(photo D).** Remove the box by cutting through the straps, using a reciprocating saw and a metal-cutting blade **(photo E).** Take care not to damage the wires.

Tools: *Screwdriver, neon circuit tester, reciprocating saw, hammer, needlenose pliers.*

Materials: *String, electrical tape, retrofit electrical box with flexible brackets, grounding screw.*

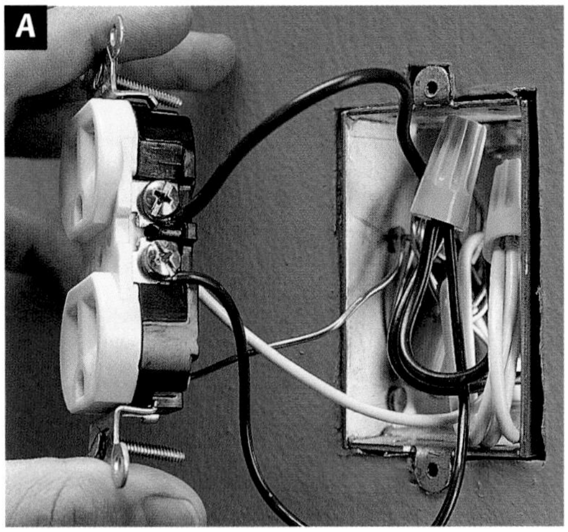

Shut off the power and test for current. Disconnect and remove the receptacle, switch, or fixture from the box.

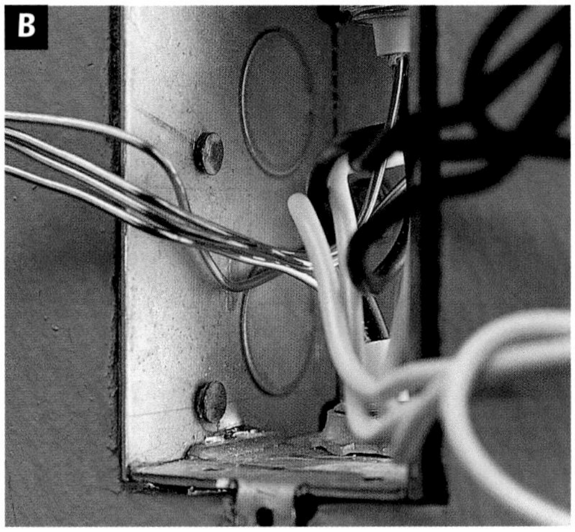

Determine how the box was installed. Boxes may be attached with nails, screws, or straps.

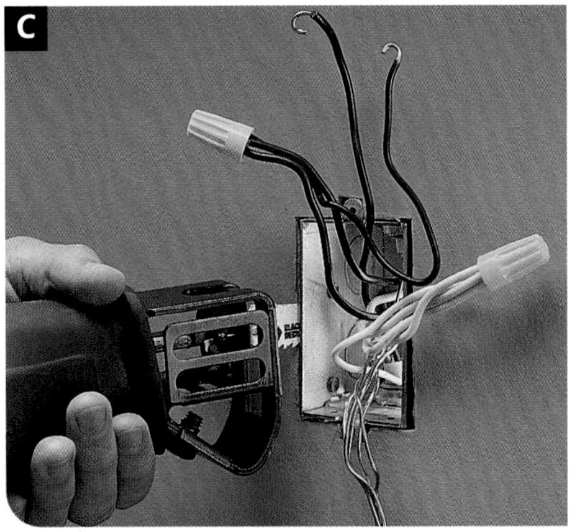

Cut through the mounting nails with the metal-cutting blade of a reciprocating saw. Take care not to cut the wires.

If the box is attached with straps, refer to this cutaway view to see where straps are located above and below the box.

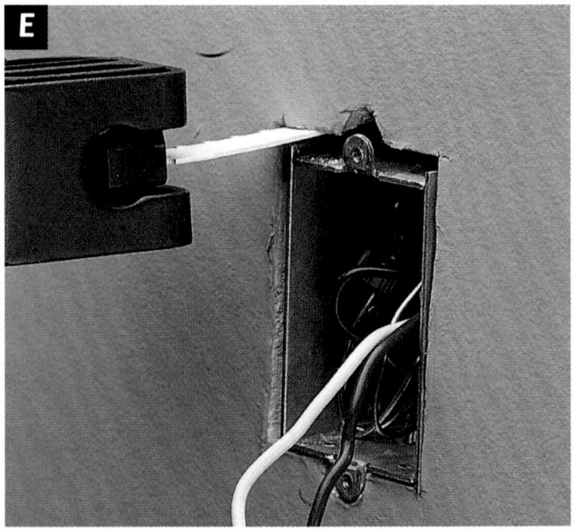

Cut through straps with the metal-cutting blade of a reciprocating saw. Take care not to cut the circuit wires.

To prevent wires from falling into the wall cavity, gather the wires from each cable and tie them together with a piece of string. Secure the string to the wires with a piece of electrical tape **(photo F).**

Disconnect the internal clamps or locknuts that hold the circuit cables to the box **(photo G).**

Pull the old electrical box from the wall, taking care not to damage the insulation on the circuit wires, and holding the string to make sure the wires don't fall inside the wall cavity **(photo H).**

Securely tape the wires to the edge of the wall cutout **(photo I).**

With a screwdriver and hammer, punch out one knockout hole for each cable that will enter the new retrofit electrical box **(photo J).**

Thread the cables into the new electrical box. Slide the box into the wall opening **(photo K).** Tighten the internal clamps or locknuts that hold the circuit cables to the electrical box. Remove the strings.

Insert flexible brackets into the wall on each side of the electrical box **(photo L).** Pull out the bracket arms until the inside tab is tight against the inside of the wall.

Bend the bracket arms around the walls of the box, using needlenose pliers **(photo M).** Reinstall the switch, receptacle, or fixture, and turn on the power to the circuit at the main service panel.

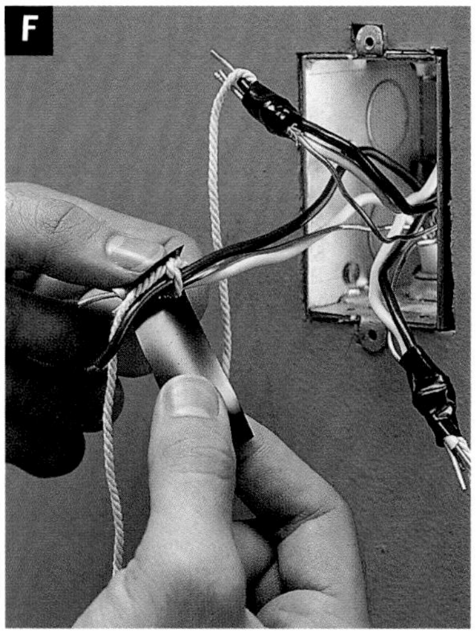

Tie wires with string and secure them with electrical tape.

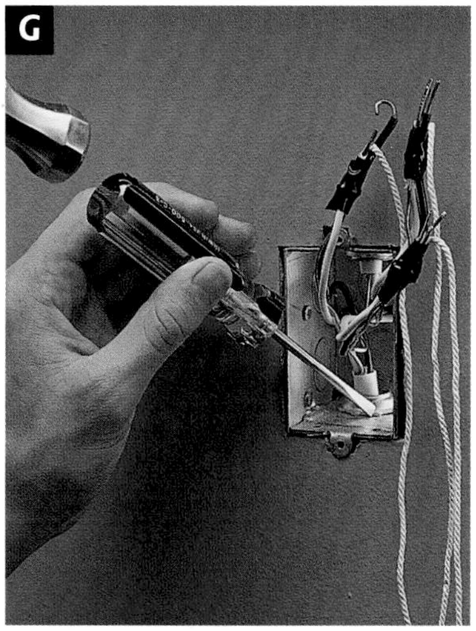

Disconnect the locknuts or clamps that hold the cables to the box.

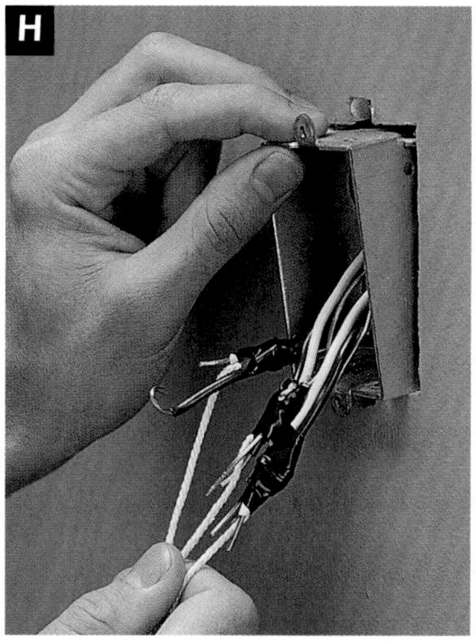

Remove the electrical box while holding the strings so the wires don't slip into the wall.

Securely tape the wires to the edge of the wall cutout.

Open up one knockout for each cable that will enter the box.

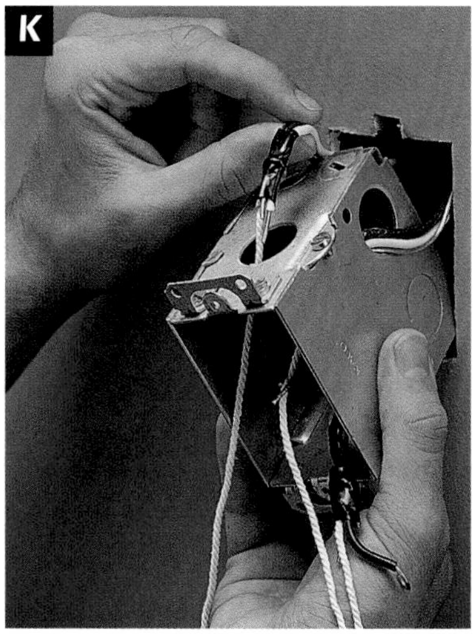

Feed the cables through the knockouts and into the electrical box.

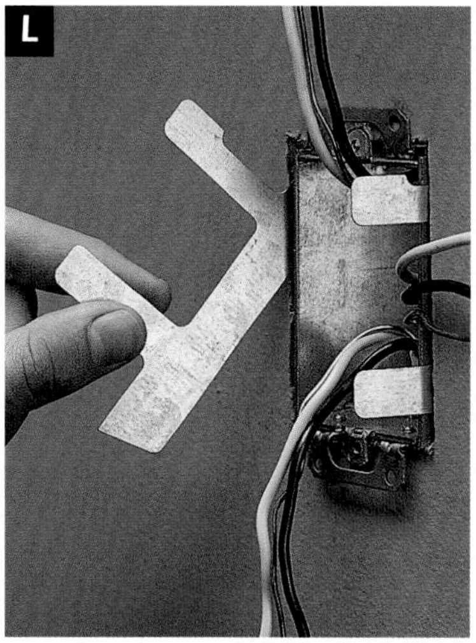

Install flexible brackets on each side of the electrical box.

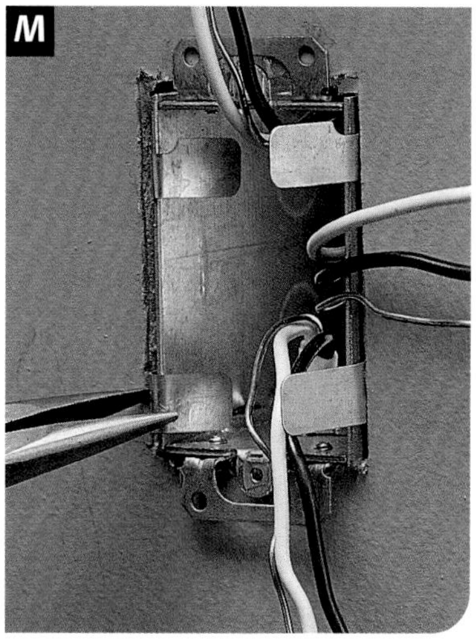

To secure the box, use needlenose pliers to bend the bracket arms around the box.

Wall Switches

There are three kinds of wall switches: *Single-pole switches* control lights from one location. *Three-way switches* control lights from two locations. *Four-way switches,* combined with a pair of three-way switches, control lights from three or more locations.

Before repairing a switch, identify its type by counting the number of screw terminals. Single-pole switches have two terminals; three-way and four-way switches have three and four terminals, respectively.

Some switches also have a green grounding screw terminal that can provide added protection against shock. Most Building Codes require grounded switches in the bathroom, kitchen, and basement.

When replacing a switch, use a replacement with the same number of screw terminals as the old switch. (The location of the screws may vary, but this doesn't affect how a switch works.) Standard switches are rated 15A, 125V, but voltage ratings of 110, 120, and 125 are interchangeable for replacement purposes.

The switch body is attached to a metal mounting strap. Newer switches have push-in fittings in addition to screw terminals. Some specialty switches have wire leads instead of screw terminals and are connected with wires and wire connectors. The screw terminals and push-in fittings are located on the back of the switch.

The switch may also have a stamped strip gauge that tells how much insulation must be stripped from the wires to connect them.

For standard wall switch installations, choose a switch with a wire gauge of #12 or #14. For wire systems with solid copper wiring, use only switches marked "Copper" or "CU."

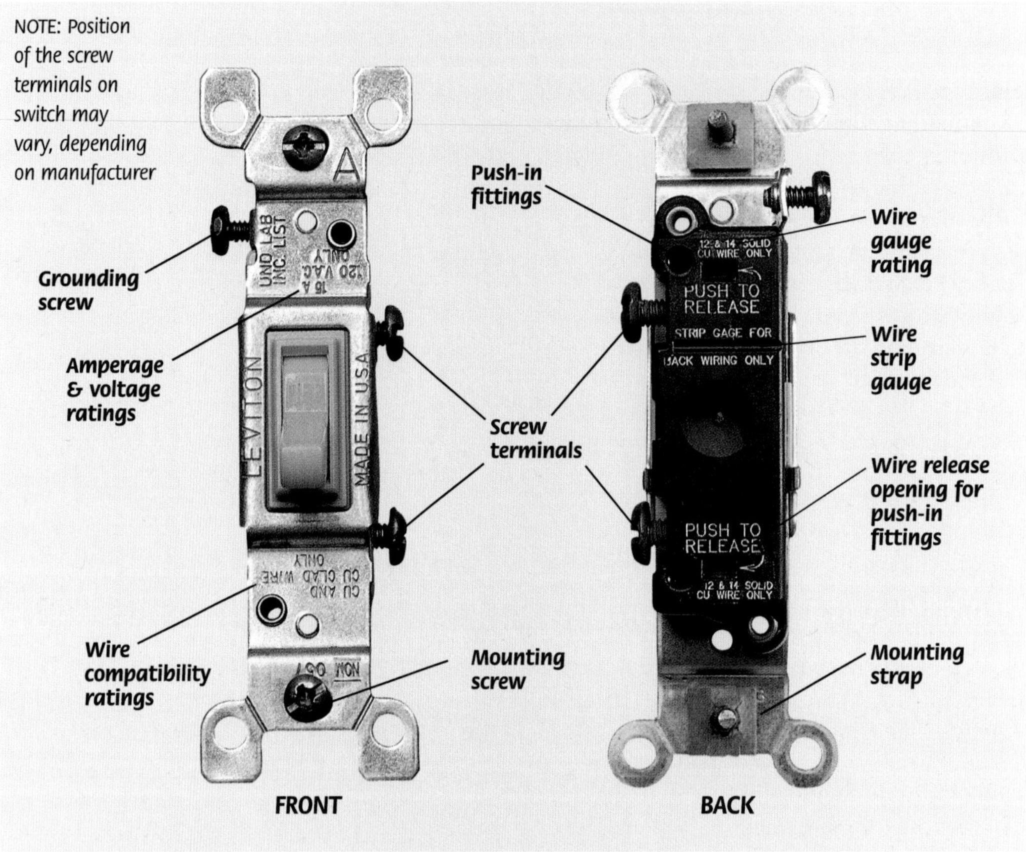

Wall Switch Problems & Repairs

Problems	Repairs
Fuse burns out or circuit breaker trips when the switch is turned on.	1. Tighten any loose wire connections on switch (page 415). 2. Move lamps or plug-in appliances to other circuits to prevent overloads. 3. Test switch and replace, if needed (page 415). 4. Repair or replace faulty fixture (pages 428 to 440) or faulty appliance.
Light fixture or permanently installed appliance does not work.	1. Replace burned-out light bulb. 2. Check for blown fuse or tripped circuit breaker to make sure circuit is operating (page 395). 3. Check for loose wire connections on switch (page 413). 4. Test switch and replace, if needed (page 415). 5. Repair or replace light fixture (pages 428 to 440) or appliance.
Light fixture flickers.	1. Tighten light bulb in the socket. 2. Check for loose wire connections on switch (page 413). 3. Repair or replace light fixture (page 428) or switch (page 415).
Switch buzzes or is warm to the touch.	1. Check for loose wire connections on switch (page 413). 2. Test switch and replace, if needed (page 415). 3. Move lamps or appliances to other circuits to reduce demand.

Common Wall Switch Problems & Repairs

Since the average wall switch is turned on and off more than 1,000 times a year, it's not surprising that the wire connections tend to loosen and the parts tend to wear out. It's just surprising that it doesn't happen more often. The replacement or repair method depends on the type of switch. The following pages explain how to repair and replace the three most common types of switches.

If you're replacing an ordinary wall switch with a specialty switch, such as a timer or an electronic switch, make sure the new switch is compatible with the wiring configuration of the switch box. Follow the removal instructions for the old switch and the steps for installing the specialty switch (page 428).

Troubleshooting switches requires a continuity tester, which detects any break in the metal pathway in the switch. The battery in the tester generates a small current that illuminates a bulb when it detects a complete circuit. (There are a few specialty switches, such as dimmers and automatic switches, that can't be tested for continuity.) Never use a continuity tester on wires that may be carrying power. Before working on a switch, always shut off the power and disconnect the switch.

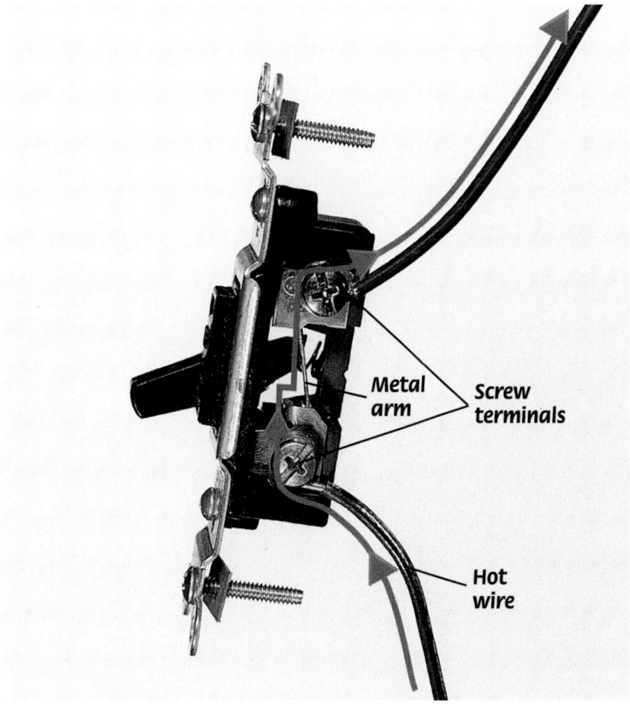

A typical wall switch has a movable metal arm that opens and closes the electrical circuit. When it's in the ON position, the arm completes the circuit between screw terminals and power passes through the black hot wire to the light fixture. Problems can occur if the screw terminals aren't tight, or if the metal arm inside the switch wears out.

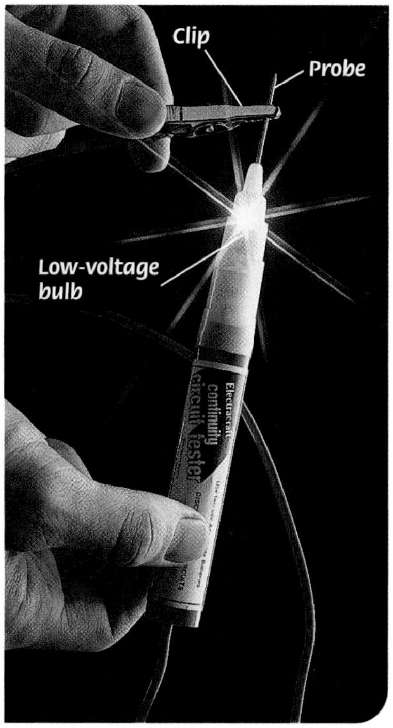

A continuity tester is essential for switch repairs. Always test it before each use by contacting the tester clip to the metal probe. If the tester doesn't signal a connection, the battery or the bulb needs to be replaced.

Common Wall Switch Designs

Toggle switches such as this early design were first introduced in the 1930s.

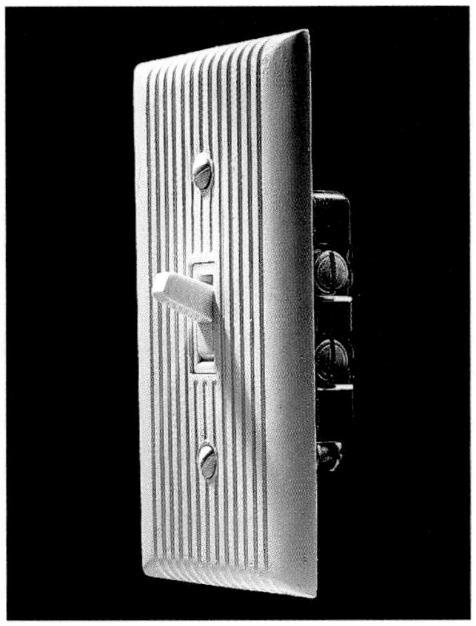

Toggle switches were improved in the 1950s, to include a sealed plastic housing.

Mercury switches (1950s) offer more durability; some are guaranteed for 50 years.

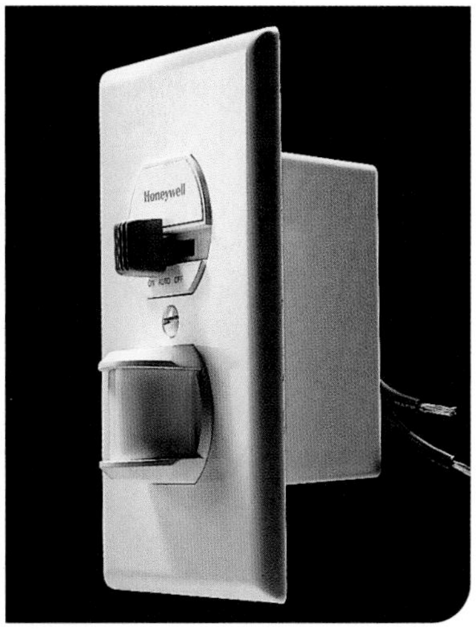

Electronic motion-sensor switches automatically turn lights on when you enter a room.

Single-pole Switches

Single-pole switches are the most common type of wall switch. They usually have ON and OFF markings on the switch lever and are used to control a light fixture, an appliance, or a receptacle from a single location. These switches have two screw terminals and may also have a grounding screw.

Most problems with single-pole switches are caused by loose wire connections. If a fuse blows or a circuit breaker trips when the switch is turned to the ON position, a loose wire may be touching the metal box. Other symptoms of this kind of problem include overheating or buzzing in the switch box.

These switches may also fail when the internal parts wear out. To check for wear, remove the switch entirely and check it for continuity.

When installing a single-pole switch, make sure the ON marking shows when the switch lever is in the up position.

In a correctly wired single-pole switch, a hot circuit wire is attached to each screw terminal. However, the color and number of wires inside the switch box will vary, depending on the location of the switch on the electrical circuit.

If you find that the wires inside a switch have less than 6" of workable length, lengthen them by connecting them to short pigtail wires with wire connectors (page 405).

Tools: *Screwdriver, circuit tester, combination tool, continuity tester.*

Materials: *Pigtail wires, wire connectors, sandpaper, masking tape.*

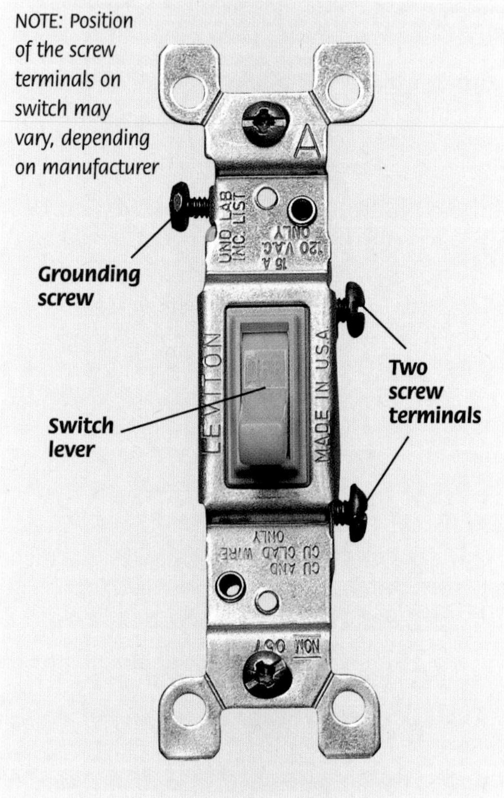

Typical Single-pole Switch Installations

When a switch is located in the middle of a circuit, two cables enter the box **(photo A).** Each cable has a white and a black insulated wire, plus a bare copper grounding wire. The black wires are hot and are connected to the screw terminals on the switch. The white wires are neutral and are joined together with a wire connector. Grounding wires are pigtailed to the grounded box.

When a switch is located at the end of a circuit, one cable enters the box **(photo B).** The cable has a white and a black insulated wire plus a bare copper grounding wire. In this kind of installation, both the insulated wires are hot. The white wire should be labeled with black tape to identify it as a hot wire. The grounding wire is connected to the grounded metal box.

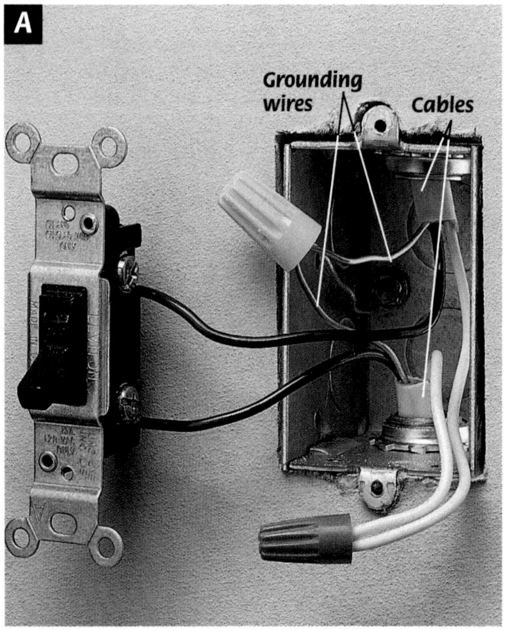

Installation of a single-pole switch in the middle of a circuit.

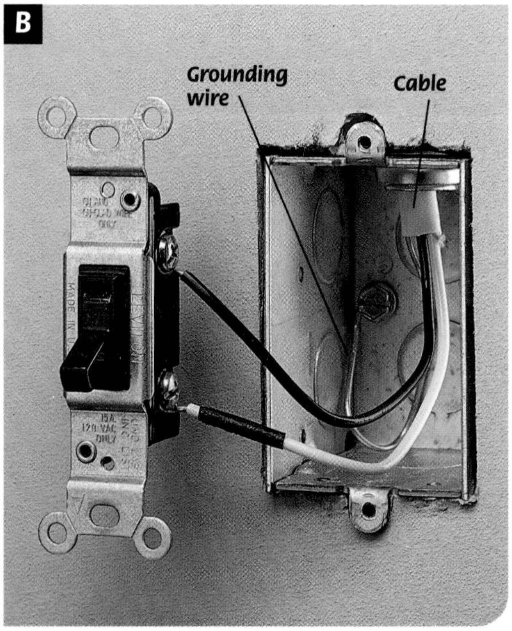

Installation of a single-pole switch at the end of a circuit.

Repairing a Single-pole Switch

Turn off the power to the switch at the service panel. Remove the switch coverplate and mounting screws. Holding the mounting straps carefully, pull the switch from the box **(photo C)**. Don't touch any bare wires or screw terminals until you've tested for power.

To test for power, touch one probe of a circuit tester to the grounded metal box or the bare copper grounding wire; touch the other probe to each screw terminal. The tester shouldn't glow at any point. If it does, turn off the correct circuit at the circuit panel.

When you're sure the power is off, disconnect the circuit wires and remove the switch **(photo D)**.

Check the wires: if they're nicked, use a combination tool to clip and strip about 3/4" of wire. If the ends look darkened or dirty, clean them with fine sandpaper **(photo E).**

Test the switch for continuity: attach the clip of a continuity tester to one screw terminal and touch its probe to the other screw terminal **(photo F).** Flip the switch lever on and off. The tester should glow only when the lever is in the ON position. If the switch is faulty, replace it.

Connect the wires to the screw terminals on the switch **(photo G).** Tighten the screws firmly, but don't overtighten them or strip the screw threads.

Remount the switch, carefully tucking the wires into the box **(photo H).** Reattach the switch coverplate.

Restore the power to the switch at the service panel.

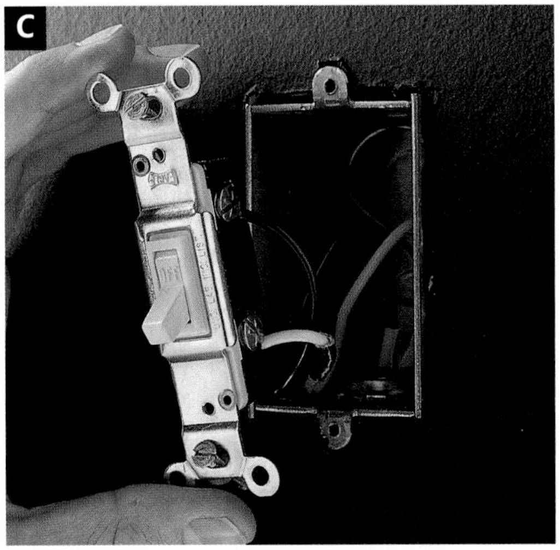

Pull the switch from the box, then test for power.

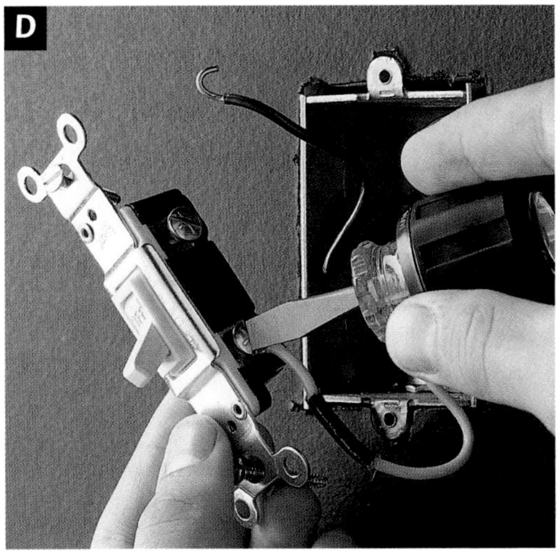

Remove the switch and inspect the wires.

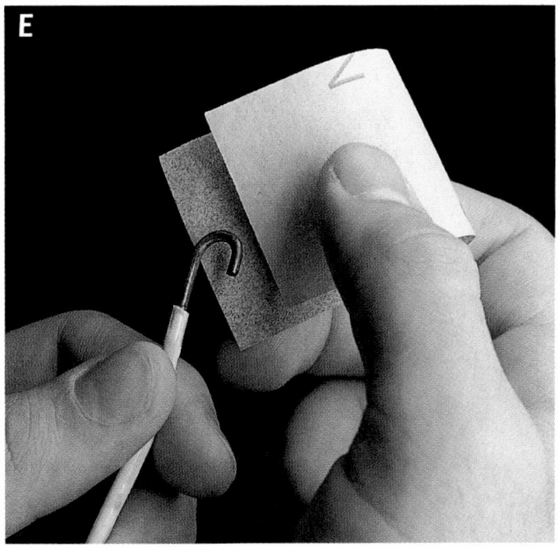

Sand wires to improve their connection with the terminals.

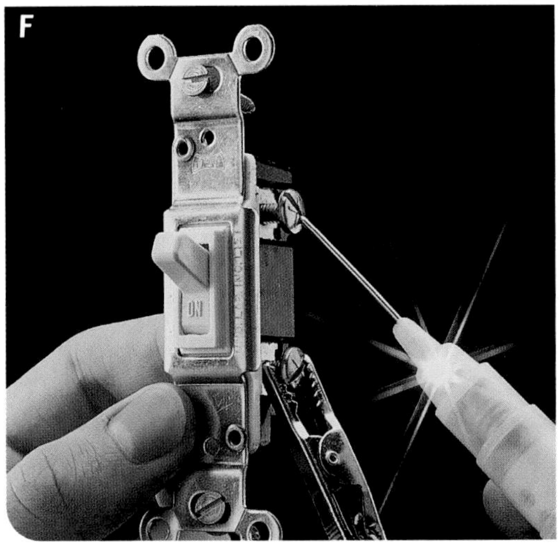

Test the switch, using a continuity tester.

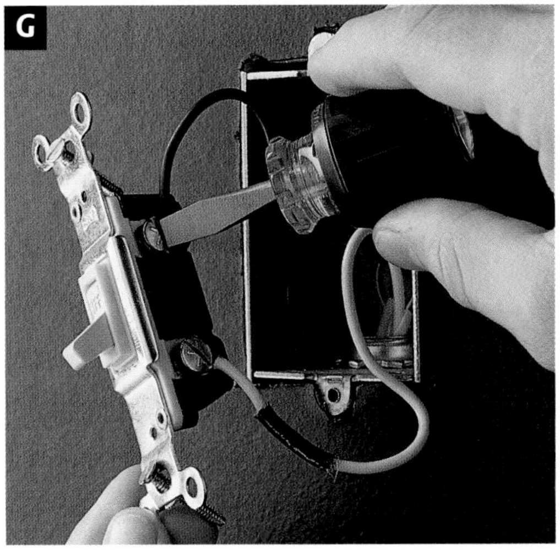

Connect the wires to the switch; don't overtighten.

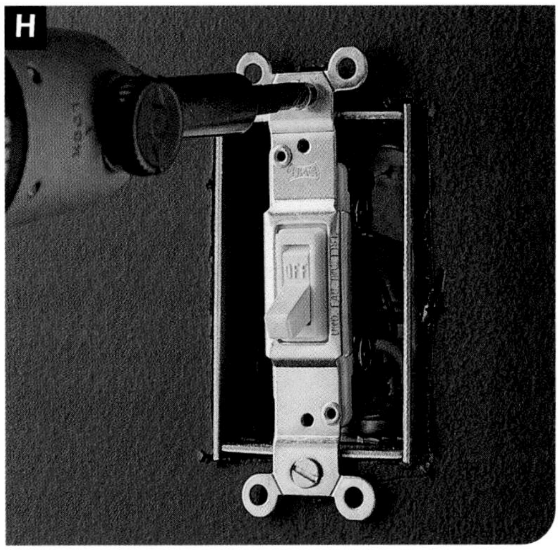

Remount the switch, and reattach the coverplate.

Three-way Switches

Three-way switches have three screw terminals, and don't have ON/OFF markings. They're always installed in pairs, and are used to control a light fixture from two locations.

One of the screw terminals on a three-way switch is darker than the others. This is the common screw terminal. Its position on the switch body will vary, depending on the manufacturer. Before disconnecting a three-way switch, always label the wire that's connected to the common screw terminal. It must be reconnected to the common screw terminal on the new switch.

The two lighter-colored screw terminals are called the *traveler screw terminals*. The traveler terminals are interchangeable, so there's no need to label the wires attached to them.

Since three-way switches are installed in pairs, when there is a problem it can be difficult to tell which of the two switches is the cause. The switch that gets the most use is more likely to fail, but you may need to inspect both switches to find the source of the problem.

Most problems with three-way switches are caused by loose wire connections. If a fuse blows or a circuit breaker trips when the switch is turned on, a loose wire may be touching the metal box. Other symptoms of this kind of problem include overheating or buzzing in the switch box.

These switches may also fail when the internal parts wear out. To check for wear, remove the switch entirely and check it for continuity.

Tools: Screwdriver, circuit tester, combination tool, continuity tester.

Materials: Pigtail wires, wire connectors, sandpaper, masking tape.

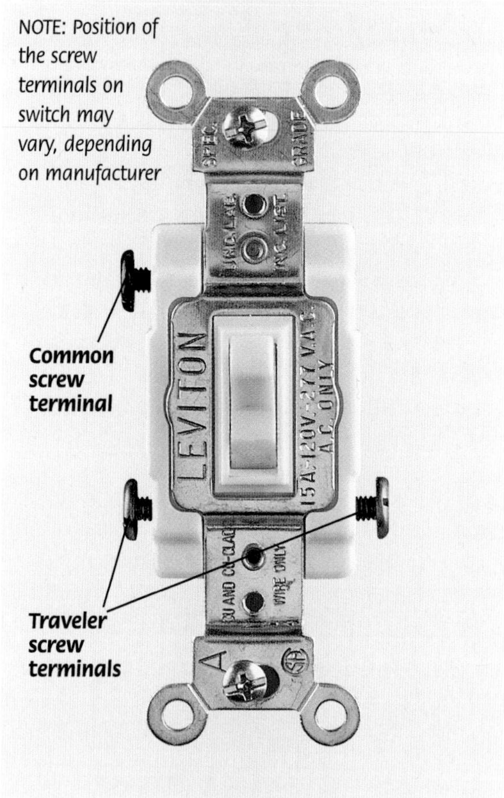

Typical Three-way Switch Installations

When the switch lies in the middle of a circuit, two cables enter the box **(photo A).** One cable has two wires plus a bare copper grounding wire. The other cable has three wires plus a ground.

Connect the black wire from the two-wire cable to the dark common screw terminal. Connect the red and black wires from the three-wire cable to the traveler screw terminals. Join the white neutral wires together with a wire connector, and pigtail the grounding wires to the grounded metal box.

When the switch lies at the end of the circuit, one cable enters the box **(photo B).** The cable has a black wire, red wire, and white wire, plus a bare copper grounding wire.

Connect the black wire to the dark common screw terminal. Connect the white and red wires to the two traveler screw terminals and the bare copper grounding wire to the grounded metal box.

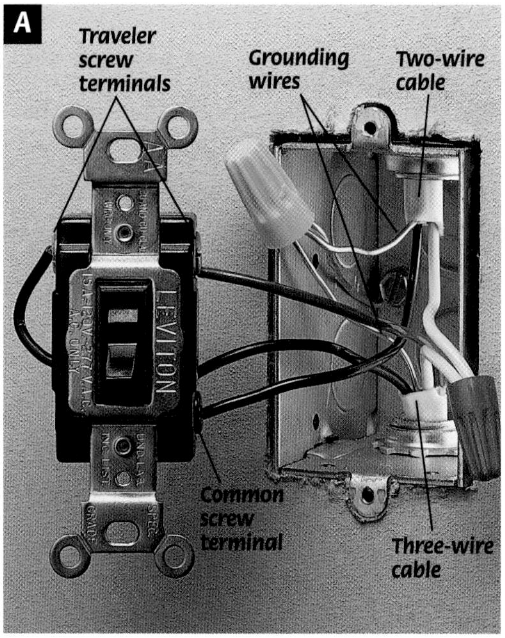

Installation of a three-way switch in the middle of a circuit.

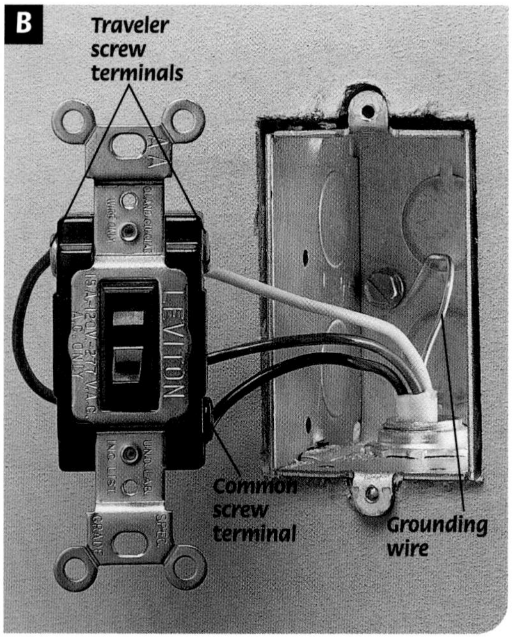

Installation of a three-way switch at the end of a circuit.

Repairing Three-way Switches

Turn off the power to the switch at the service panel. Remove the switch coverplate and mounting screws. Holding the mounting straps carefully, pull the switch from the box **(photo C).** Don't touch any bare wires or screw terminals until you've tested for power.

Test for power: touch one probe of a circuit tester to the grounded metal box or the bare copper grounding wire, and the other probe to each screw terminal **(photo D).** The tester shouldn't glow at any point. If it does, turn off the correct circuit at the service panel.

Locate the dark common screw terminal. It's usually copper, or may be labeled common. Label the common wire attached to this screw with masking tape **(photo E).** Disconnect the wires and remove the switch.

Check the wires; if they're nicked, use a combination tool to clip and strip about 3/4" of clean bare wire. If the ends look darkened or dirty, clean them with fine sandpaper.

Test for continuity: attach the clip of a continuity tester to the common screw terminal and touch its probe to one of the other screw terminals **(photo F).** Flip the switch lever on and off. The tester should glow only when the lever is in the ON position. Touch the probe to the other screw terminals, and repeat. If the switch is faulty, replace it.

Connect the common wire to the common screw terminal **(photo G).** Connect the remaining wires to the other screw terminals **(photo H).** Remount the switch, carefully tucking the wires into the box. Reattach the coverplate. Restore the power to the switch.

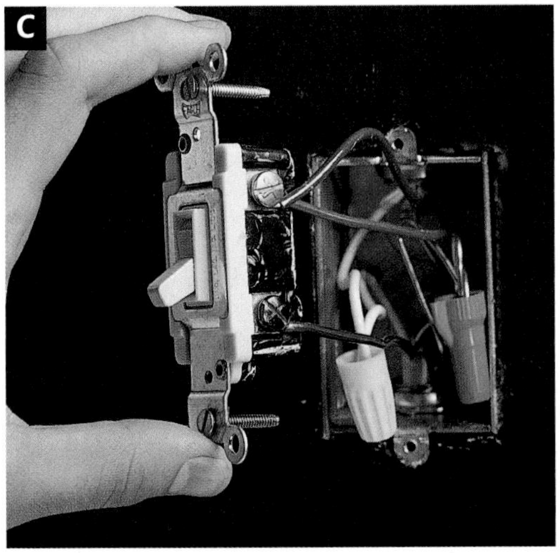

Pull the switch from the box, then test for power.

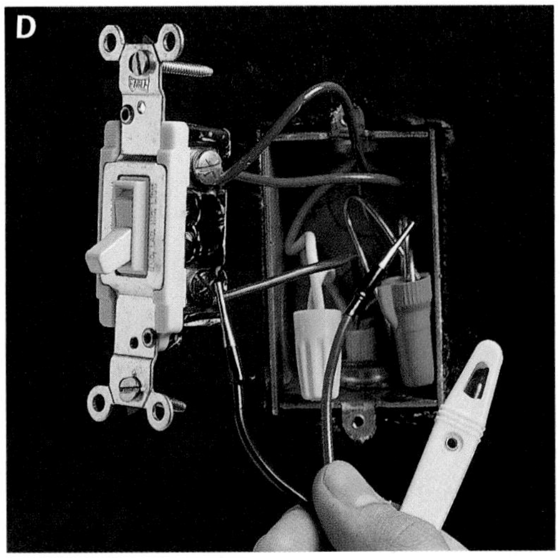

Test the three-way switch for power, using a circuit tester.

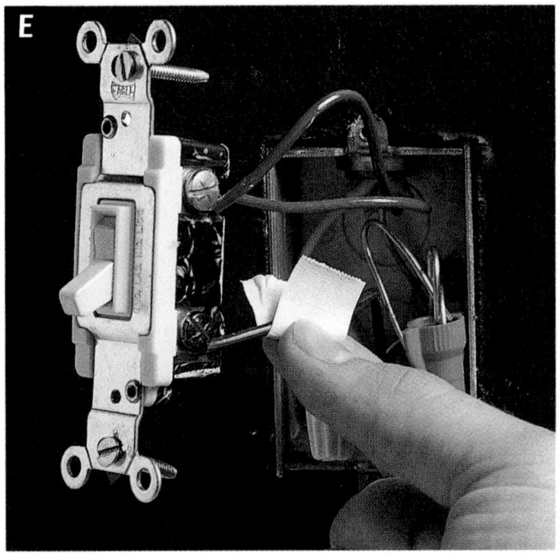

Label the common wire with masking tape.

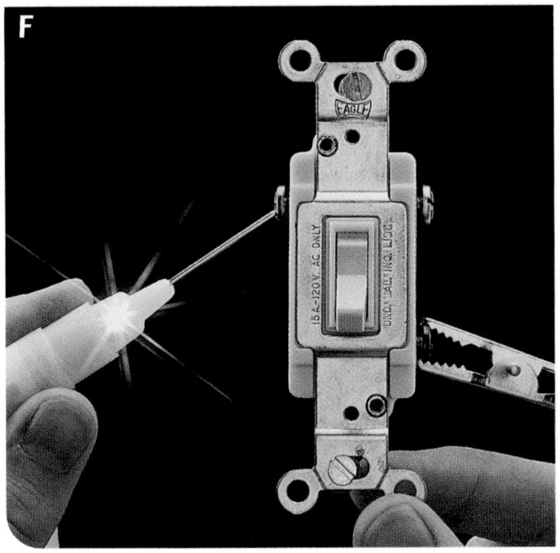

Test a three-way switch, using a continuity tester.

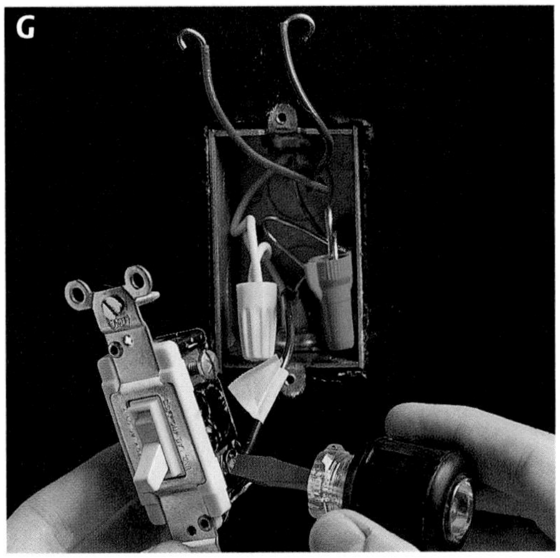

Connect the common wire to the common screw terminal.

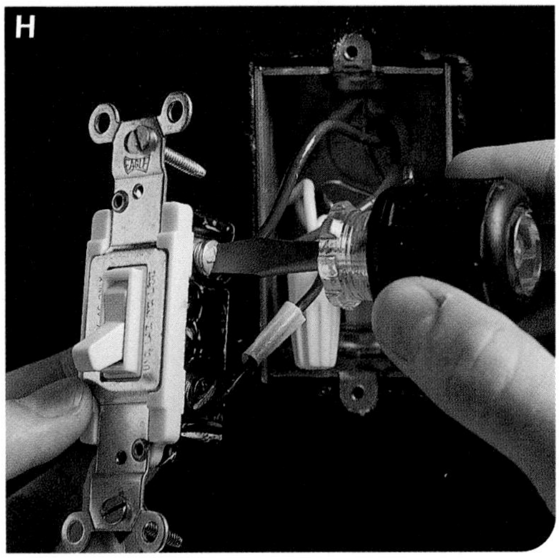

Connect the remaining wires to any of the traveler terminals.

Four-way Switches

Four-way switches have four screw terminals, and they don't have ON and OFF markings. They're installed between a pair of three-way switches to make it possible to control a light fixture from three or more locations. Four-way switches aren't common, but may be found in large rooms or long hallways.

Switch problems in a four-way installation can occur either in the four-way switch or in one of the three-way switches (page 416).

In a typical installation, two pairs of color-matched wires are connected to the four-way switch. Newer four-way switches have screw terminals that are paired by color. One pair is usually copper and the other brass.

When installing the switch, match the wires to the screw terminals by color. For example, if you connect a red wire to one of the brass screw terminals, make sure the other red wire is connected to the other brass screw terminal.

Most problems with four-way switches are caused by loose wire connections. If a fuse blows or a circuit breaker trips when the switch is turned on, a loose wire may be touching the metal box. Other symptoms of this kind of problem include overheating or buzzing in the switch box.

These switches may also fail when the internal parts wear out. To check for wear, remove the switch entirely and check it for continuity.

Tools: *Screwdriver, circuit tester, combination tool, continuity tester.*

Materials: *Pigtail wires, wire connectors, sandpaper.*

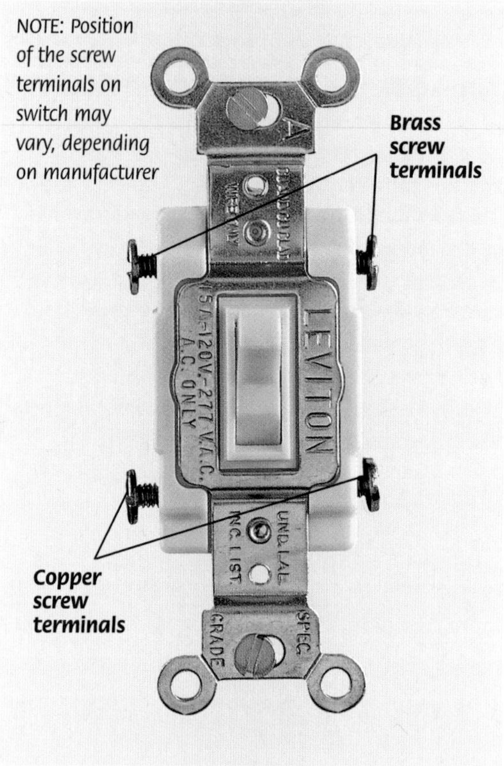

Typical Four-way Switch Installations

Since four-way switches are always installed between a pair of three-way switches, they're always installed in the middle of a circuit.

Four wires are attached to a four-way switch **(photo A).** One pair of same-color wires is connected to the copper screw terminals, and the other pair of same-color wires to the brass screw terminals.

The third pair of wires inside the box is joined with a wire connector. The two bare copper grounding wires are pigtailed to the grounded metal box.

Some four-way switches have a wiring guide stamped on the back to help simplify installation **(photo B).** On the switch shown, one pair of color-matched circuit wires will be connected to the screw terminals marked LINE 1, and the other pair of wires will be attached to the screw terminals marked LINE 2.

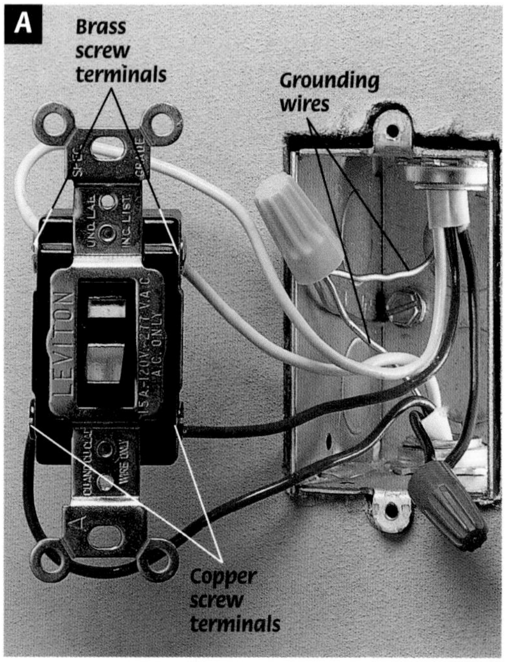

Typical installation of a three-way switch.

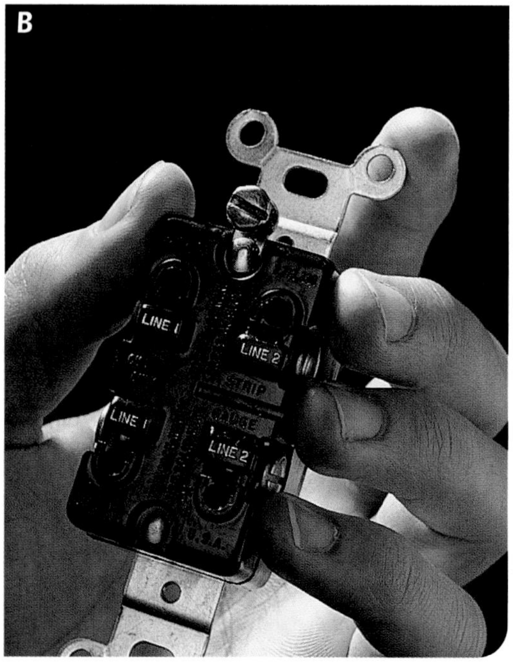

Some have a wire guide on the back for easier installation.

Repairing Four-way Switches

Turn off the power to the switch at the service panel. Remove the switch coverplate and mounting screws. Holding the mounting straps carefully, pull the switch from the box. Don't touch any bare wires or screw terminals until you've tested for power.

Test for power: touch one probe of a circuit tester to the grounded metal box or the bare copper grounding wire, and the other probe to each screw terminal **(photo C).** The tester shouldn't glow at any point. If it does, turn off the correct circuit at the service panel.

Disconnect the wires and remove the switch **(photo D).** Check the wires; if they're nicked, use a combination tool to clip and strip about 3/4" of clean bare wire. If the ends look darkened or dirty, clean them with fine sandpaper.

Test for continuity: touch the clip and the probe of a continuity tester to each pair of screw terminals (A-B, C-D, A-D, B-C, A-C, B-D). Flip the lever to the opposite position, and retest **(photo E).**

If the switch is good, the test will show a total of four continuous pathways for each lever position. If it doesn't, the switch is faulty and must be replaced. The arrangement of the pathways may differ, depending on the switch manufacturer **(photo F).**

Connect two wires of the same color to the brass screw terminals **(photo G).**

Attach the remaining wires to the copper screw terminals **(photo H).** Remount the switch, carefully tucking the wires inside the switch box. Reattach the coverplate. Restore the power at the main service panel.

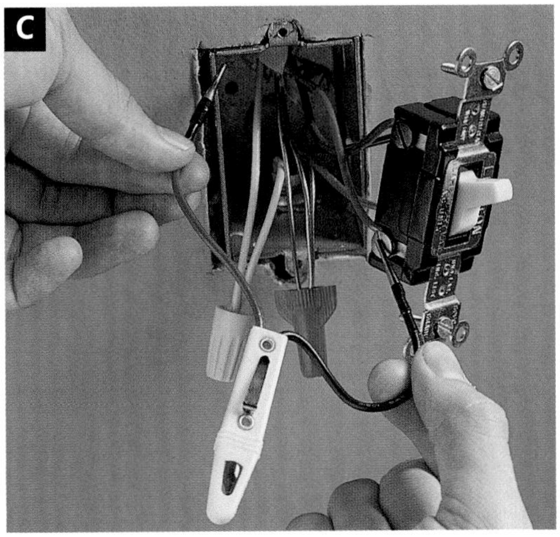

Test the switch for power, using a neon circuit tester.

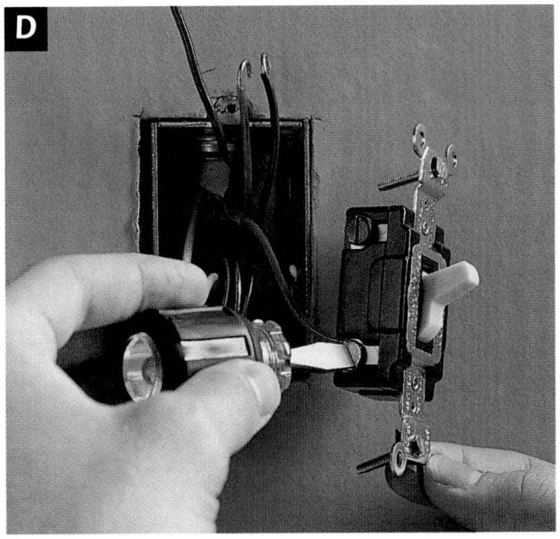

Disconnect the wires and inspect them for damage.

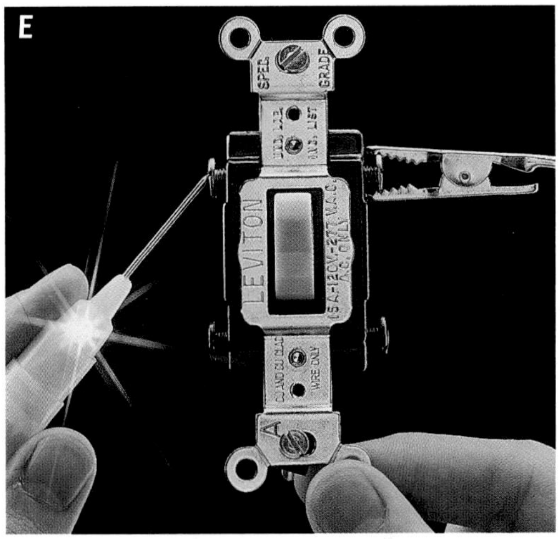

Test the switch, using a continuity tester.

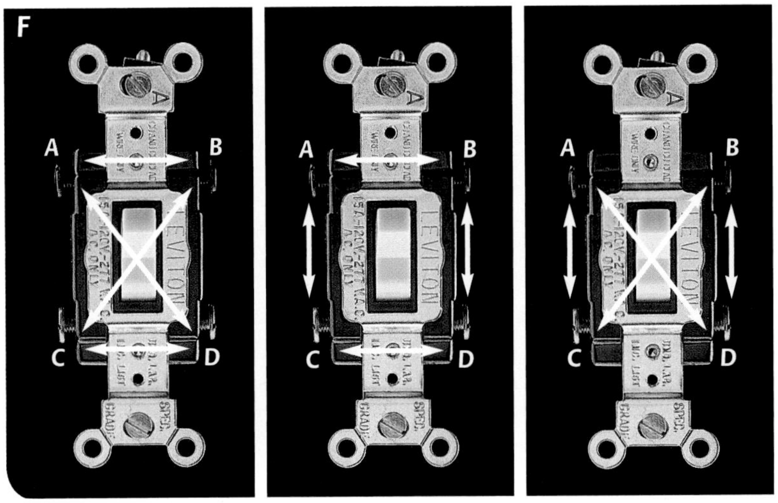

Three possible pathway arrangements are shown here.

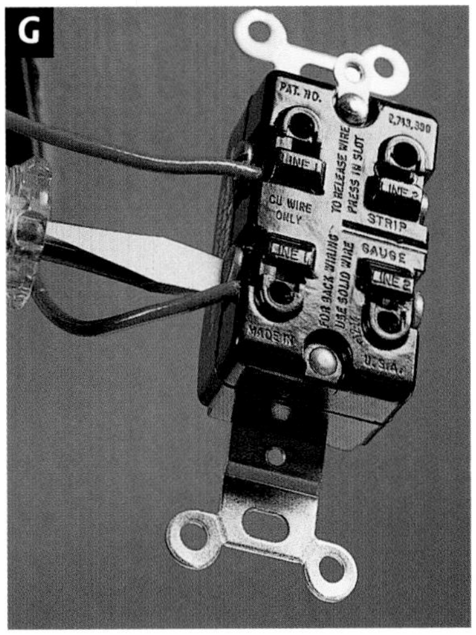

Connect two wires of the same color to the brass terminals.

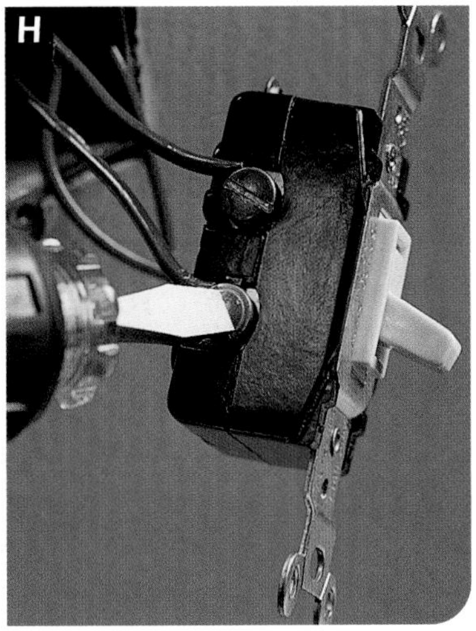

Fasten the remaining wires to the copper screw terminals.

Double Switches

A double switch contains two switch levers in a single housing so that two light fixtures, appliances, or light/appliance combinations can be controlled from one switch box.

Use a continuity tester to test a double switch for current problems. Test each half of the switch by clipping the tester to one screw terminal and touching the probe to the opposite side **(photo A).**

Flip the switch lever ON and OFF. The tester should glow only in the ON position. Repeat with the remaining pair of terminals. If either half of the switch fails, replace the unit.

In most installations, both halves of the switch are powered by the same circuit. For this single-circuit installation **(photo B)**, connect three wires to the switch, as follows.

First, connect the black feed wire that brings power into the box to the side of the switch that has a metal connecting tab joining two of the screw terminals. This tab supplies power to both halves of the switch.

Connect the wires that carry power out to the light fixtures or appliances to the other side of the switch.

Join the white neutral wires together with a wire connector.

Occasionally you may find a double switch in which each half of the switch is powered by a different circuit. For this double-circuit installation **(photo C),** attach four black wires to the switch, as follows.

First, connect the two feed wires from the power source to the side of the switch with the metal connecting tab.

Next, remove the connecting tab with needlenose pliers or a screwdriver **(photo D).**

Connect the other two wires (which carry power to the light fixtures or appliances) to the other side of the switch.

Connect the white neutral wires together, using a wire connector.

Tools: *Screwdriver or needlenose pliers, circuit tester, combination tool, continuity tester.*

Materials: *Pigtail wires, wire connectors.*

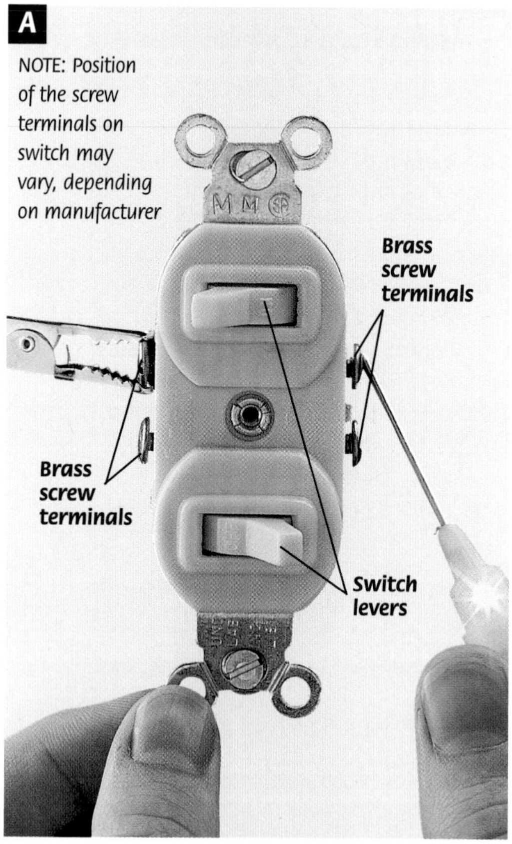

Use a continuity tester to check a double switch for current problems. If either half of the switch fails, replace the unit.

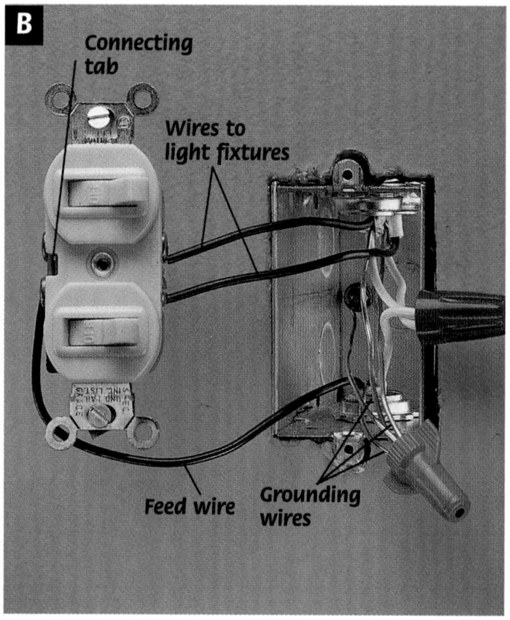

In this typical single-circuit wiring of a double switch, three wires are connected to the switch.

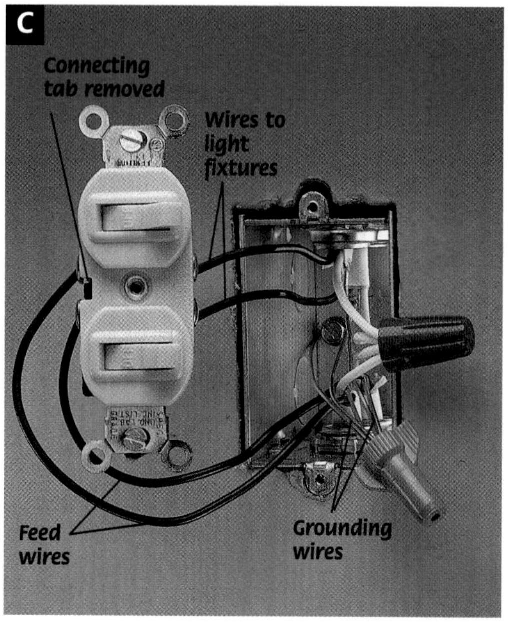

In this typical double-circuit wiring of a double switch, four black wires are attached to the switch.

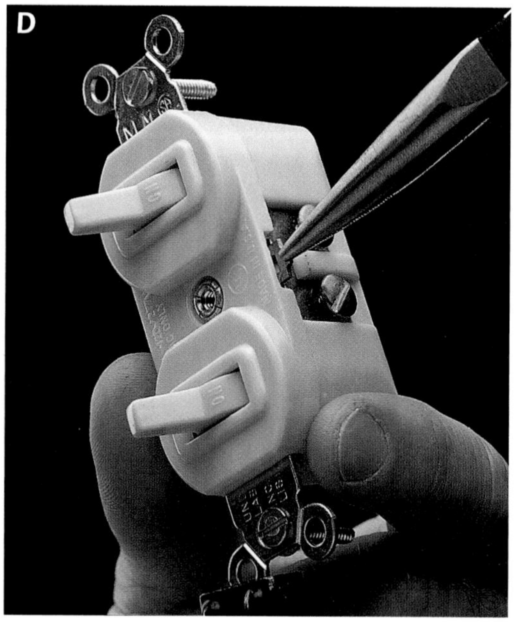

For a double circuit, you need to remove the connecting tab.

Pilot-light Switches

Pilot-light switches have built-in bulbs that glow when power flows through them to a fixture or appliance. These switches are often used when a device isn't visible from its switch. Since they require a neutral wire, they can't be placed in a switch box that has only one two-wire cable.

Connect the three wires to the switch, as follows **(photo E).** Connect the black feed wire to the brass screw on the side of the switch opposite the connecting tab. Connect the other black wire to the brass screw next to the connecting tab. Pigtail the white neutral wires to the neutral screw terminal.

If the pilot light doesn't glow when the device is on, it's defective. To test the switch for continuity, first remove the unit. Attach the clip of the continuity tester to one of the top screw terminals. Touch the tester's probe to the top screw terminal on the other side **(photo F).** Flip the switch on and off. If the switch is working correctly, the tester will glow only when the switch lever is in the ON position.

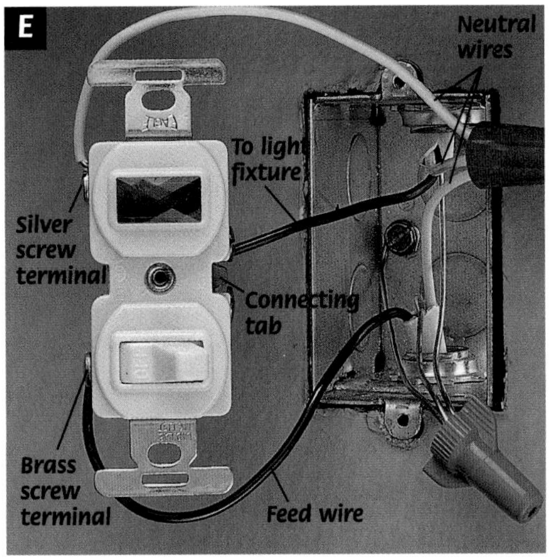

Three wires are connected to a pilot-light switch.

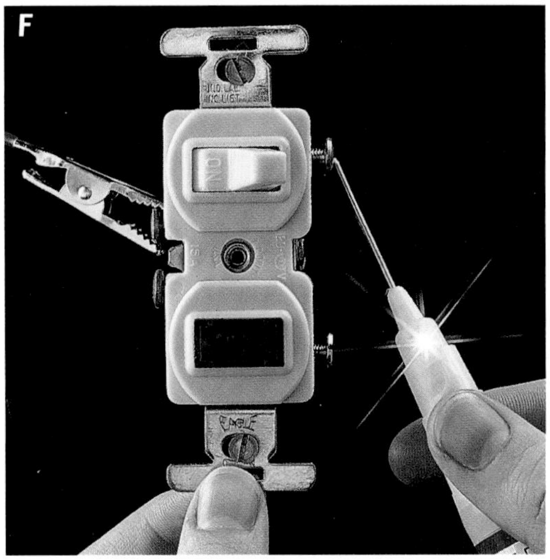

Use a continuity tester to check the switch.

Switch/Receptacles

Switch/receptacles combine a grounded receptacle with a single-pole wall switch. If a room doesn't have enough receptacles, it may be a good idea to replace a single-pole switch with a switch/receptacle. Switch/receptacles require a neutral wire.

Usually the receptacle is wired so that it's hot even when the switch is off **(photo G).** The hot feed wire is connected to the brass screw on the side with the connecting tab, and the other black wire is attached to the other brass screw. The white neutral wires are pigtailed to the silver neutral screw. But it can be wired so the switch controls the receptacle. To do this, simply reverse the hot wires and attach the feed wire to the brass screw terminal on the side without a connecting tab.

To test the switch for continuity, attach the clip of the continuity tester to one of the top screw terminals. Touch the tester's probe to the top screw terminal on the other side **(photo H).**

Flip the switch on and off. If the switch is working correctly, the tester will glow only when the switch lever is in the ON position.

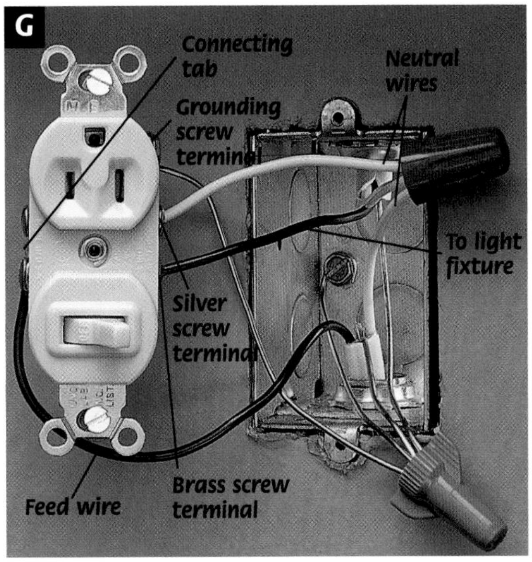

The most common wiring for a switch/receptacle.

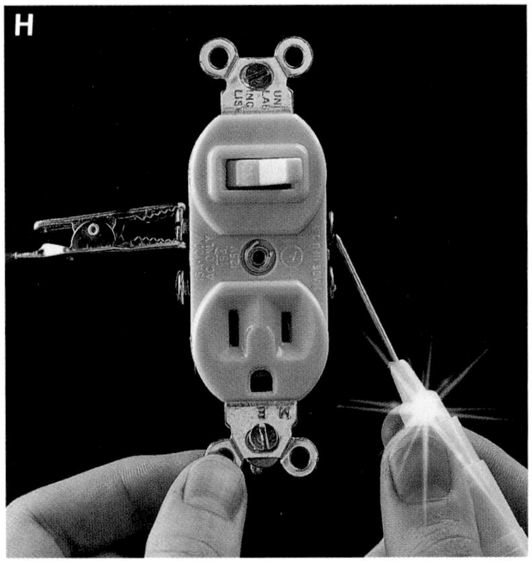

Use a continuity tester to check the switch.

Dimmer Switches

A dimmer switch allows you to vary the brightness of a light fixture. Any standard single-pole switch can be replaced with a dimmer if the switch box is large enough and isn't already cluttered with wires. Dimmer switches are large and generate heat that needs plenty of room to dissipate. Follow the manufacturer's instructions and check the dimmer's wattage rating. The wattage of light bulbs controlled by the dimmer should total no more than 80 percent of the dimmer's rating to keep the dimmer from overheating.

In lighting configurations that use three-way switches (page 416), one of the three-way switches can be replaced with a special three-way dimmer. In this arrangement, all the switches will turn the light fixture on and off, but the light intensity can only be controlled by the dimmer switch.

Dimmer switches are available in several styles. All have wire leads instead of screw terminals and are connected to circuit wires with wire connectors. Some have a green grounding lead that's connected to the grounded metal box or the bare copper grounding wires.

Toggle-type dimmers **(photo A)** look like standard switches and are available in single-pole and three-way designs.

Dial-type dimmers **(photo B)** use a dial to adjust the light intensity.

Slide-action dimmers **(photo C)** are easy to find because they're illuminated in the dark.

Automatic dimmers **(photo D)** can also be operated manually. On the automatic setting, an electronic sensor adjusts the light fixture to compensate for changes in the natural light.

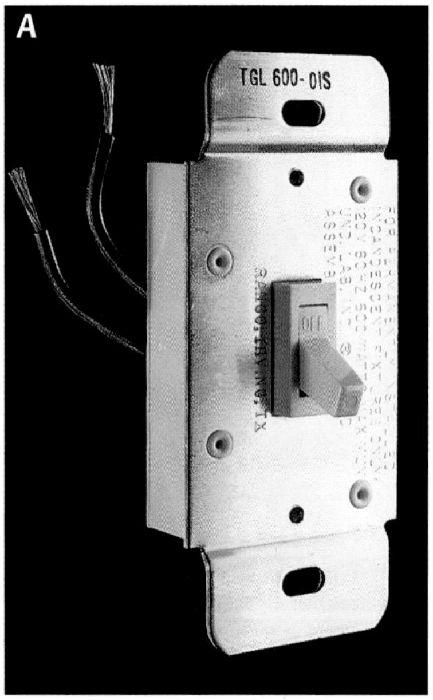

Toggle-type dimmers look like standard switches.

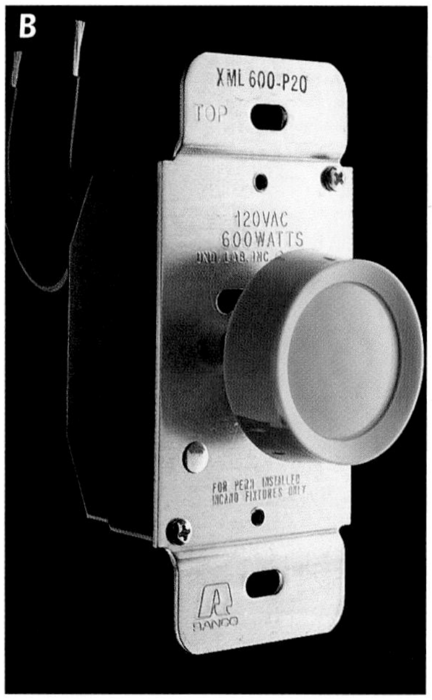

Dial-type dimmers are the most common form of dimmers.

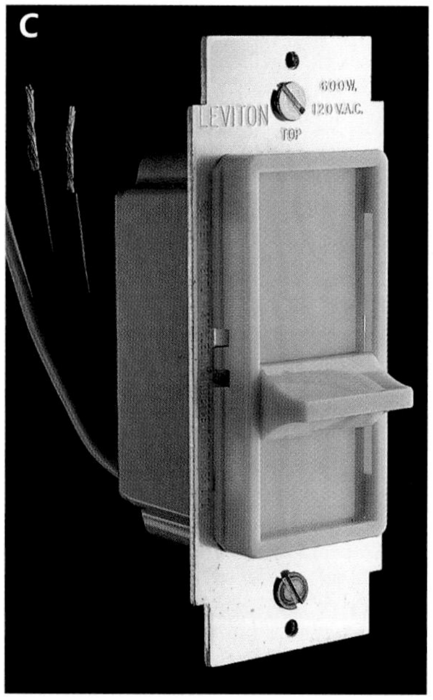

Slide-action dimmers have an illuminated face that shines in the dark.

Automatic dimmers are designed to compensate for changes in natural light.

Replacing a Switch with a Dimmer

Replacing a regular switch with a dimmer is an easy electrical project that can add convenience to any room.

Before starting, turn off the power to the switch at the main service panel. Remove the coverplate and mounting screws.

Holding the mounting straps carefully, pull the switch from the box **(photo E).** Be careful not to touch any of the bare wires or screw terminals until you've tested them for power.

Next, test for power: touch one probe of the neon circuit tester to the grounded metal box or the bare copper grounding wires. Touch the other probe to each screw terminal **(photo F).** If the tester glows, return to the service panel and shut off the correct circuit.

Tools: *Screwdriver, neon circuit tester, needlenose pliers.*

Materials: *Wire connectors, masking tape.*

If you're replacing an old dimmer, test for power by touching one probe to the grounded metal box or copper grounding wire, and inserting the other probe into each wire connector **(photo G).**

If the tester glows, power is still reaching the switch. Return to the service panel and shut off the correct circuit.

Disconnect the circuit wires and remove the switch. Straighten the circuit wires, and clip the ends, leaving about 1/2" of bare wire exposed **(photo H).**

Connect the wire leads on the dimmer switch to the circuit wires, using wire connectors **(photo I).** The switch leads are interchangeable, and can be attached to either of the two circuit wires.

A three-way dimmer has an additional wire lead, called a *common wire.* Attach it to the wire that was attached to the darkest screw terminal **(photo J).**

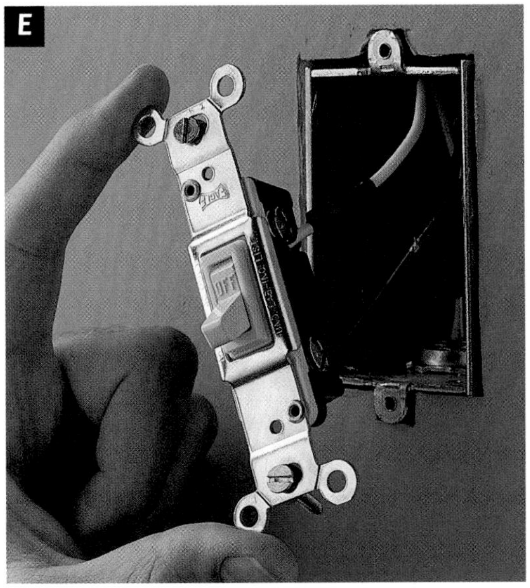

Remove the coverplate and mounting screws. Pull the switch from the box, holding the mounting strips carefully.

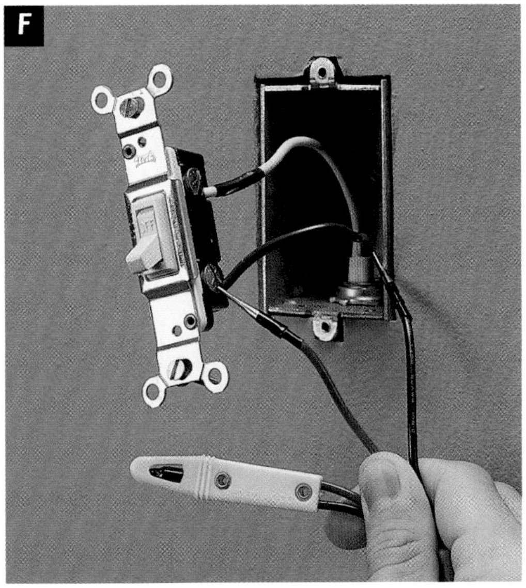

Use a neon circuit tester to test the connection to make sure the power is off.

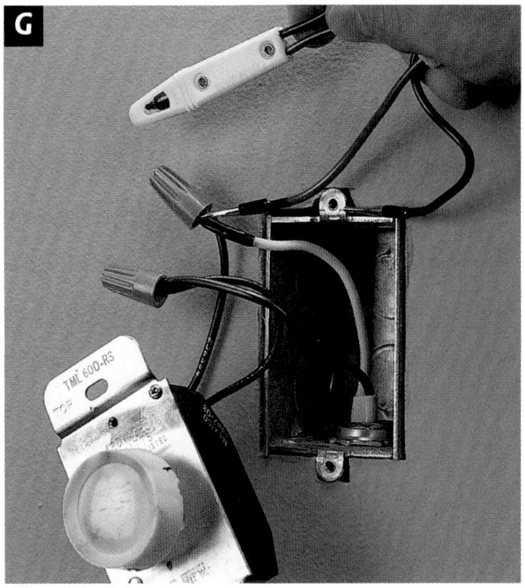

To test a dimmer, insert one probe into each wire connector while holding the other to the grounding wire or connector.

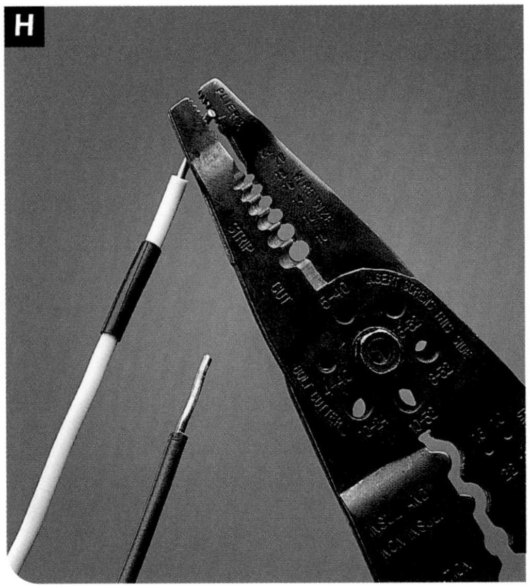

Disconnect the circuit wires and remove the switch. Straighten the circuit wires, and clip the ends.

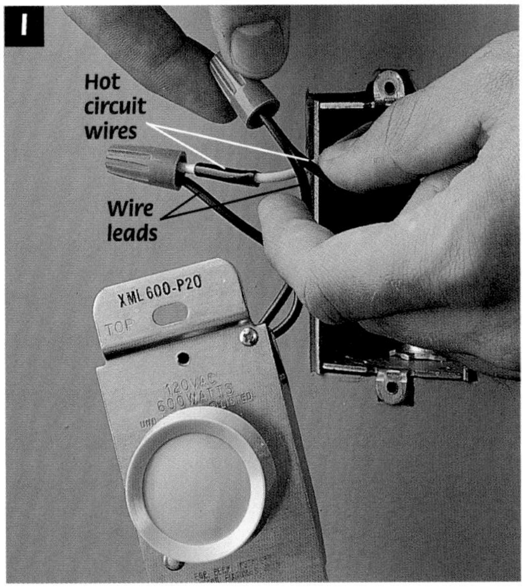

Connect the wire leads on the dimmer switch to the circuit wires, using wire connectors.

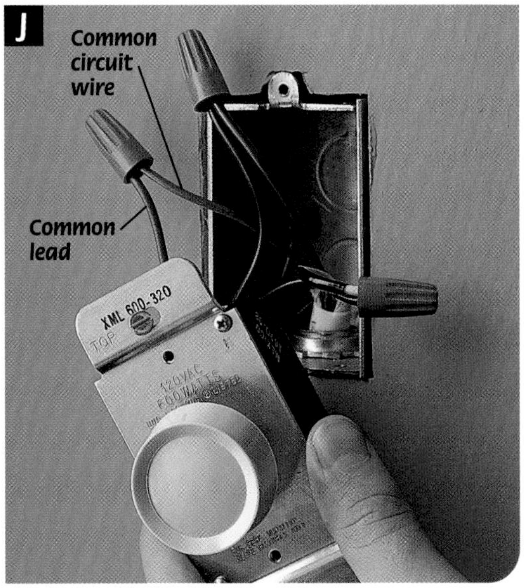

The common lead is attached to the wire that was attached to the darkest screw terminal on the old switch.

Specialty Switches

In addition to regular and dimmer switches, there are many specialty switches that are easy to install in place of a single-pole switch. These devices are an easy way to add convenience and security to your home.

Specialty switches usually have preattached wire leads that you connect to circuit wires with wire connectors. Some motor-driven timer switches require a neutral wire connection, and can't be installed in switch boxes that have only one cable with two hot wires.

If a specialty switch isn't working correctly, you may be able to check it with a continuity tester. Timer and time delay switches can be tested for continuity, but dimmer switches can't. In general, manual switches can be tested and those with automatic features can't.

To remove a specialty switch, turn off the power to the switch at the service panel. Remove the switch coverplate and mounting screws. Pull the switch from the box, while holding the mounting strap carefully. Take care not to touch any bare wires or screw terminals until you've tested them for power.

To test for power, touch one probe of a circuit tester to the grounded metal box or the bare grounding wire, and the other probe to each of the other screw terminals. The tester should not glow. If it does, return to the service panel and turn off the correct circuit.

Time-delay Switches

A time-delay switch has a dial that you set to turn off a fixture after one to sixty minutes. These switches are typically used for exhaust fans, electric space heaters, and heat lamps. Since they don't need a neutral wire, they can be placed in boxes that have one or two cables.

To install one, connect the black wire leads on the switch to the hot circuit wires. If the box has white neutral wires, join them with a wire connector. Pigtail the bare copper grounding wires to the grounded metal box.

To test for continuity, attach the clip to one of the wire leads, and touch the probe to the other one. Set the timer for one minute. The tester should glow until the time expires.

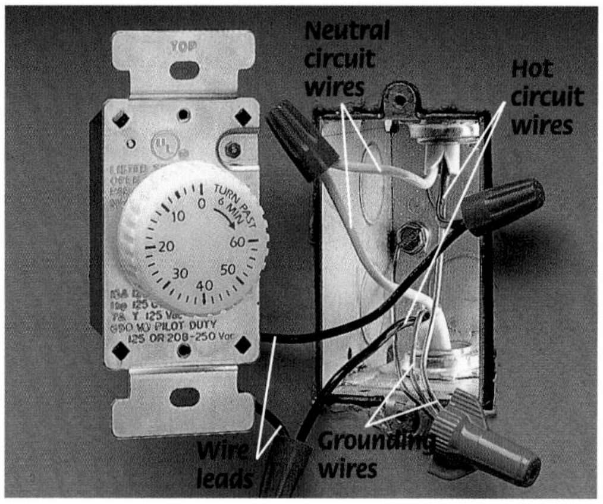

A time-delay switch has a spring-driven dial that you wind by hand to turn off a fixture after one to sixty minutes.

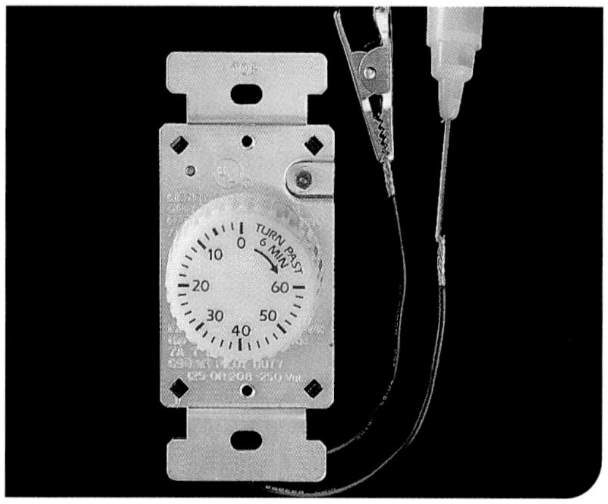
To test, attach the tester clip to one lead and the probe to the other. Set the timer; it should glow until the time expires.

Timer Switches

A timer switch has a dial that can be set to turn fixtures on and off automatically at a preset time of day. These switches need a neutral wire, and can't be placed in a box that has one cable.

Timer switches have three preattached wire leads. To install one, connect the black lead to the hot feed wire, and the red lead to the wire that carries power to the light fixture. Connect the remaining lead to the neutral circuit wires.

To test for continuity, attach the clip to the red lead, and the probe to the black lead. Rotate the dial clockwise until the ON tab passes the arrow; the tester should glow. Rotate the dial clockwise until the OFF tab passes the arrow; the tester shouldn't glow.

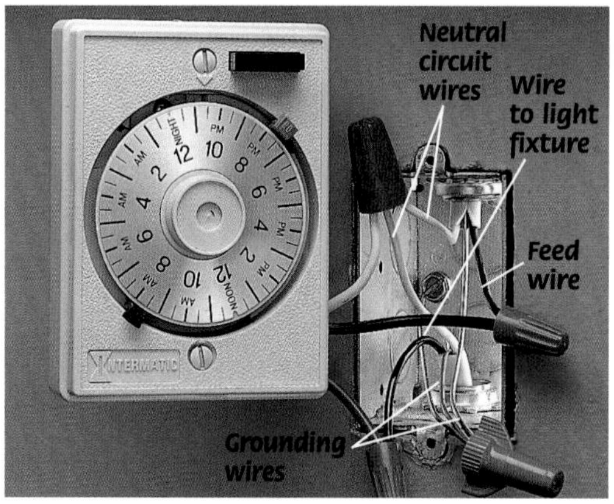

A timer switch has an electrically powered control dial that must be reset after a power failure.

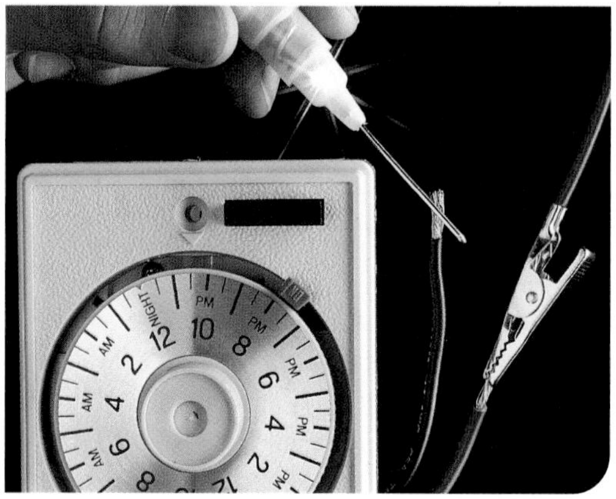
To test, attach the tester clip to the red wire lead and the probe to the black lead. Rotate the dial.

Automatic Switches

An automatic switch has a narrow infrared beam that detects nearby movement (such as a passing hand) and signals the switch to turn on or off. Some also have a manual dimmer. These switches don't need a neutral wire.

To install one, connect the wire leads on the switch to the hot circuit wires with wire connectors.

To test the manual controls for continuity, clip the tester to one lead and touch the probe to the other one. Flip the manual switch lever from ON to OFF. The tester should glow only when the lever is in the ON position.

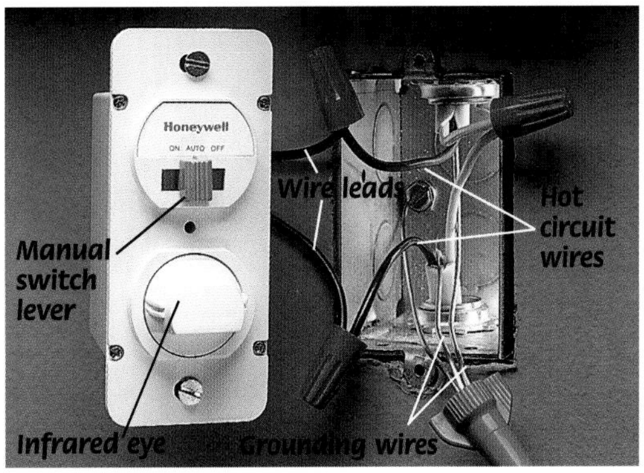

Automatic switches are especially convenient for children and the handicapped. This model has a manual dimmer.

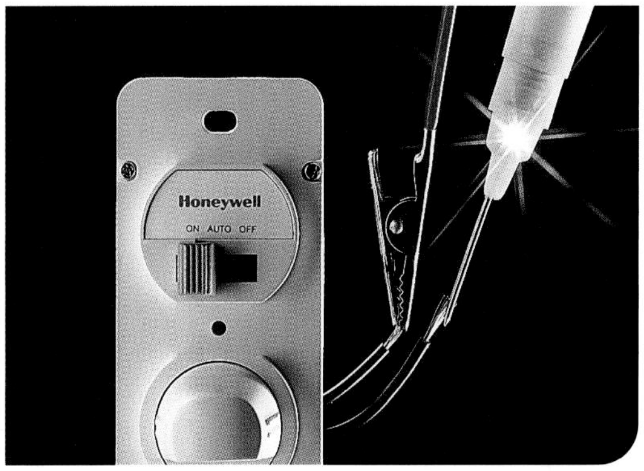

To test, attach the clip to one lead and the probe to the other. The tester should glow only when the switch is on.

Motion-sensing Switches

A motion-sensing switch has a wide-angle infrared beam that detects movement over a large area and turns on a fixture in response. Most have a manual override, and some have a sensitivity control and time-delay shutoff.

These switches don't need a neutral wire. To install one, connect the wire leads on the switch to the hot circuit wires with wire connectors.

To test the manual controls for continuity, clip the tester to one lead and touch the probe to the other one. Flip the manual switch lever from ON to OFF. The tester should glow only when the lever is in the ON position.

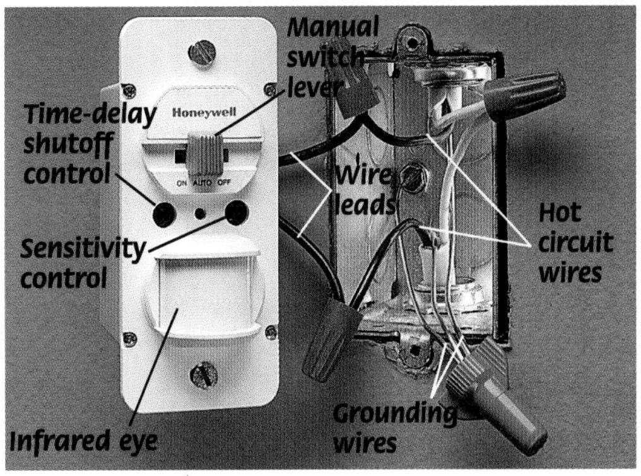

Motion-sensors have a time-delay feature that turns the lights off after the movement stops.

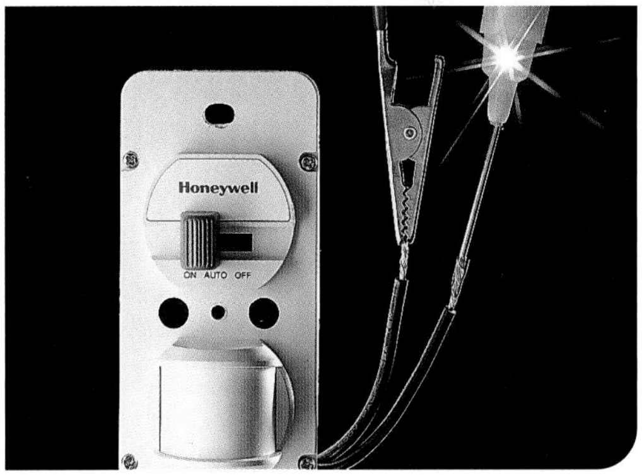

To test, attach the clip to one lead and the probe to the other. The tester should glow only when the switch is on.

Programmable Switches

A programmable switch has digital controls and can remember up to four on-off cycles per day. This switch typically is used when a homeowner is gone, and to provide the best security, it should be set to a random on-off pattern.

These switches don't need a neutral wire. To install one, connect the wire leads on the switch to the hot circuit wires with wire connectors.

To test the manual controls for continuity, clip the tester to one lead and touch the probe to the other one. Flip the manual switch lever from ON to OFF. The tester should glow only when the lever is in the ON position.

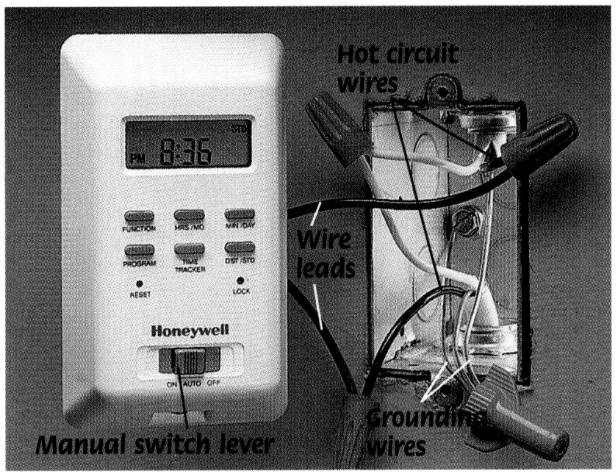

Programmable switches represent the latest in switch design and the greatest flexibility in automatic controls.

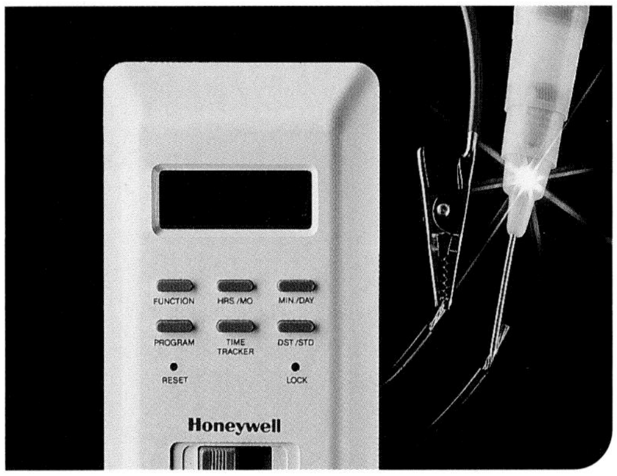

To test, attach the clip to one lead and the probe to the other. The tester should glow only when the switch is on.

Lighting Fixtures

Lighting can have a tremendous impact on the overall atmosphere of your home, and the many lighting fixtures available today allow you to create a wide range of lighting effects.

Each room in your home may call for a different combination of light fixtures. The typical home light fixture uses incandescent bulbs and is mounted to the wall or ceiling. However, fluorescent lights are gaining in popularity for home use, due to their better energy efficiency. Specialty home light fixtures include recessed lighting, track lighting, and chandeliers.

You'll be able to make better choices among the many kinds of light fixtures if you understand how they work and how to repair them when something goes wrong.

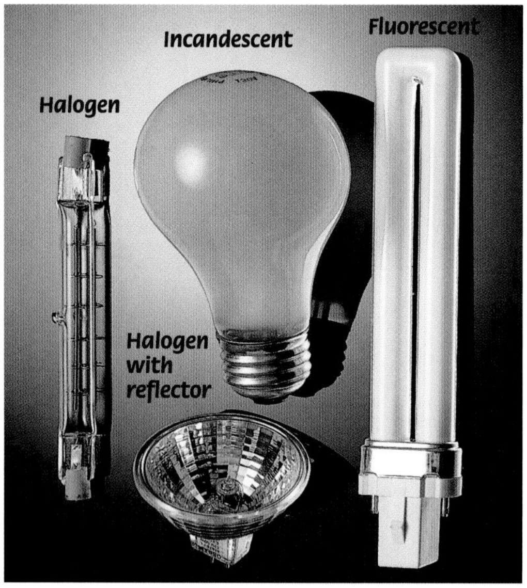

A variety of bulbs are now used in home lighting fixtures.

Photo courtesy of Crystal Cabinets

Incandescent lamps can be wall- or ceiling-mounted.

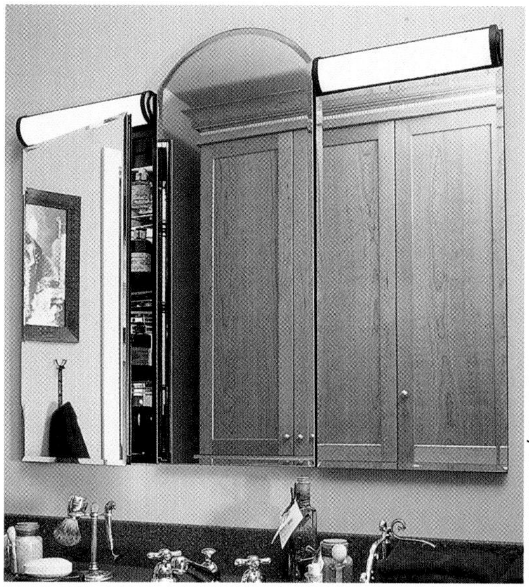

Photo courtesy of PL Bath Products

Fluorescent fixtures are energy efficient

Photo courtesy of Cooper Lighting

Recessed lights are well suited for modern-style rooms.

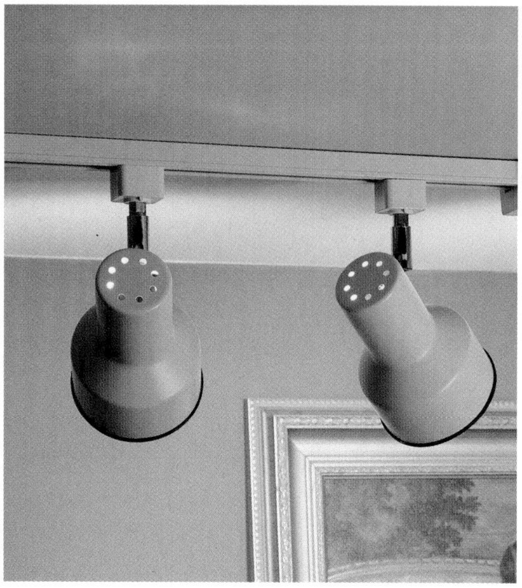

Track lighting fixtures can be aimed in any direction.

Photo courtesy of PL Bath Products

Chandeliers offer some of the most dramatic lighting effects.

Incandescent Mounted Light Fixtures

Household incandescent light fixtures are permanently attached to a wall or ceiling. They come in a wide range of styles, including wall-mounted sconces, ceiling-mounted globe fixtures, pendant (hanging) lights, recessed lights, and chandeliers. See page 432 for information on recessed lighting and page 434 for information on chandeliers.

The tools needed to repair and replace mounted light fixtures generally include a neon circuit tester, a continuity tester, screwdrivers, a combination tool, and replacement parts as needed.

Since wall and ceiling fixtures are permanently attached to walls or ceilings, repairing them requires that you work in tight spaces. This means that you have to be especially careful to follow all the safety rules and precautions involved in working with electricity (page 395). Make sure the power to the circuit is shut off before you begin.

In a typical incandescent light fixture **(photo A),** a black hot wire is connected to a black wire lead or brass screw terminal. The power flows to a small tab at the bottom of the metal socket and through a metal filament inside the bulb, heating the filament and making it glow. The current then flows back through the socket and the white neutral wire back to the main service panel.

Before 1959, incandescent light fixtures were mounted directly to an electrical box **(photo B)** or to plaster lath. Codes now require that fixtures be attached to mounting straps that are anchored to the electrical box as shown in photo A. If you have a fixture attached to plaster lath, install an approved electrical box with a mounting strap to support the fixture.

Tools: *Screwdrivers, neon tester, continuity tester.*

Materials: *Wire connectors, replacement parts as needed.*

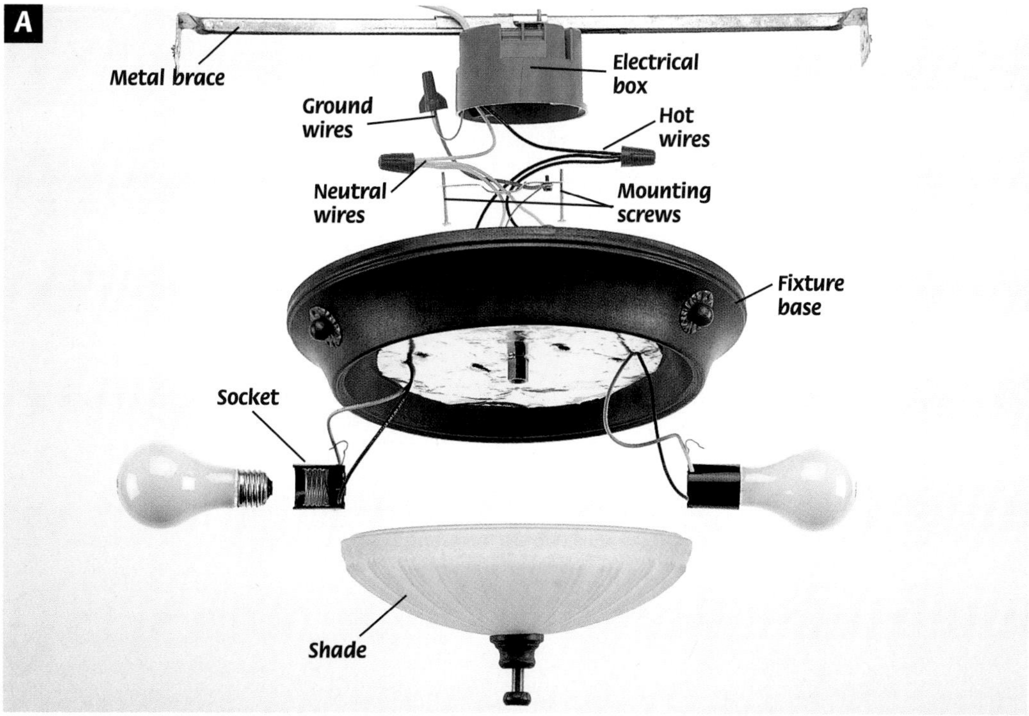

Correct configuration for a typical incandescent light fixture includes the components shown here.

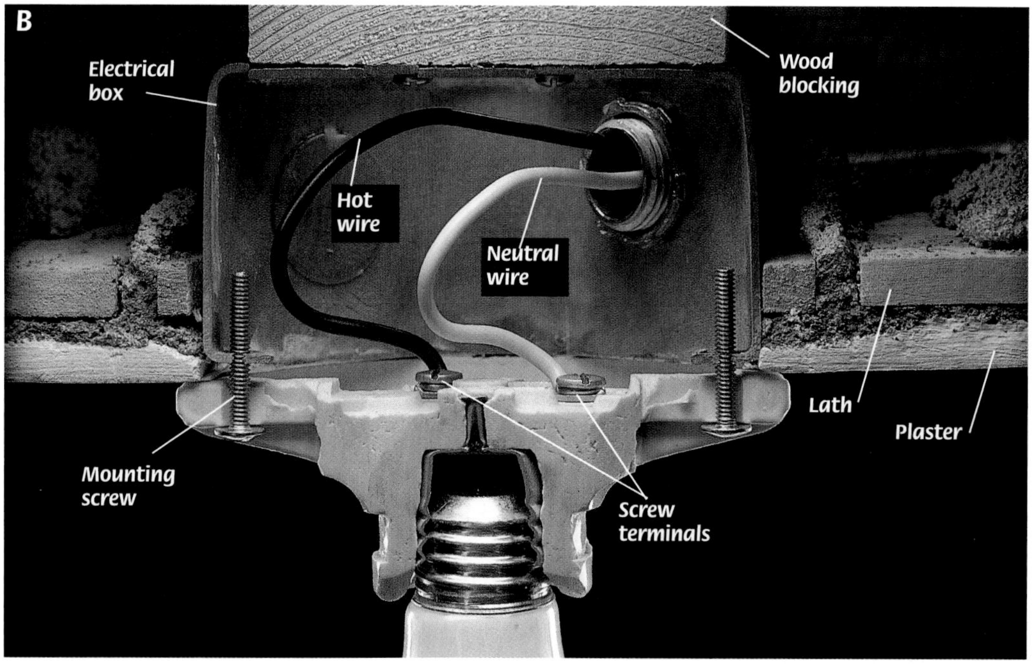

Typical mounting of an incandescent light fixture before 1959. This installation should be replaced with an electrical box equipped with a metal mounting strap to support the fixture.

Diagnosing Fixture Problems

If a fixture doesn't light when it's switched on, it's usually because the bulb is burned out. If the fixture is controlled by a wall switch, the switch may also be the source of the problem.

Light fixtures can also fail when sockets or built-in switches wear out. Some fixtures have sockets that can be removed for repair; others are joined permanently to the base. When they fail, you need to install a new fixture.

Damage often occurs when people install light bulbs that have a wattage that's too high for the fixture. You can prevent this problem by using only bulbs that match the rating printed on the fixture.

Helpful Hint

Compact fluorescent bulbs use less wattage to produce the same light as incandescent bulbs. Use these guidelines to select compact fluorescent equivalents.

13W to 16W fluorescent = 60W incandescent.

20W fluorescent = 75W incandescent.

23W to 28W fluorescent = 100W incandescent.

Common Light Fixture Problems & Repairs

Problems	Repairs
Wall- or ceiling-mounted fixture flickers or does not light.	*1. Check for faulty light bulb.* *2. Check wall switch, and repair or replace, if needed (pages 412 to 425).* *3. Check for loose wire connections in electrical box.* *4. Test socket (below), and replace if needed (page 430).* *5. Replace light fixture (pages 431 to 441).*
Built-in switch on fixture does not work.	*1. Check for faulty light bulb.* *2. Check for loose wire connections on switch.* *3. Replace switch (page 430).* *4. Replace light fixture (page 441).*
Chandelier flickers or does not light.	*1. Check for faulty light bulb.* *2. Check wall switch, and repair or replace, if needed (pages 412 to 425).* *3. Check for loose wire connections in electrical box.* *4. Test sockets (below) and fixture wires, and replace, if needed (page 437).*
Recessed fixture flickers or does not light.	*1. Check for faulty light bulb.* *2. Check wall switch, and repair or replace, if needed (pages 412 to 425).* *3. Check for loose wire connections in electrical box.* *4. Test fixture, and replace, if needed (pages 432 to 433).*

Removing a Standard Fixture & Testing the Socket

If a light continues to fail even after the bulb has been replaced and you've determined that the switch isn't the source of the problem, remove the fixture and test the socket.

Before starting, turn off the power to the light fixture at the main service panel. Remove the light bulb and the shade or globe.

Remove the mounting screws that hold the fixture base to the electrical box or mounting strap **(photo A).** Carefully pull the fixture base away from the box.

Test for power: touch one probe of a circuit tester to the green grounding screw, then insert the other probe into each wire connector **(photo B).** The tester should not glow. If it does, return to the service panel and turn off the power to the correct circuit.

Disconnect the light fixture base by loosening the screw terminals **(photo C).** If the fixture has wire leads instead of screw terminals, remove the light fixture base by unscrewing the wire connectors.

Adjust the metal tab at the bottom of the fixture socket by prying it up slightly with a small screwdriver **(photo D).** This will improve the contact between the socket and the light bulb.

Test the socket by attaching the clip of a continuity tester to the hot screw terminal (or black wire lead) and touching the probe to the metal tab in the bottom of socket **(photo E).** The tester should glow. If it doesn't, the socket is faulty and should be replaced (page 430).

Attach the tester clip to the neutral screw terminal (or white wire lead), and touch the probe to the threaded portion of socket **(photo F).** The tester should glow. If it doesn't, the socket is faulty and should be replaced.

Remove the mounting screws that secure the fixture.

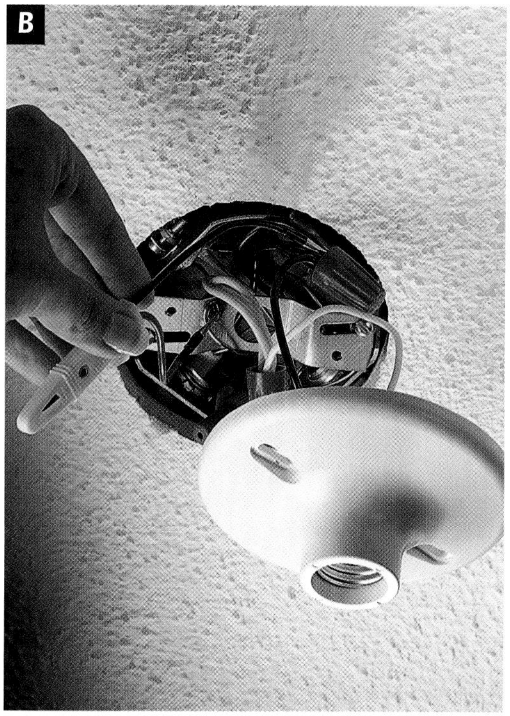

Test for power in the electrical box.

Disconnect the light fixture base.

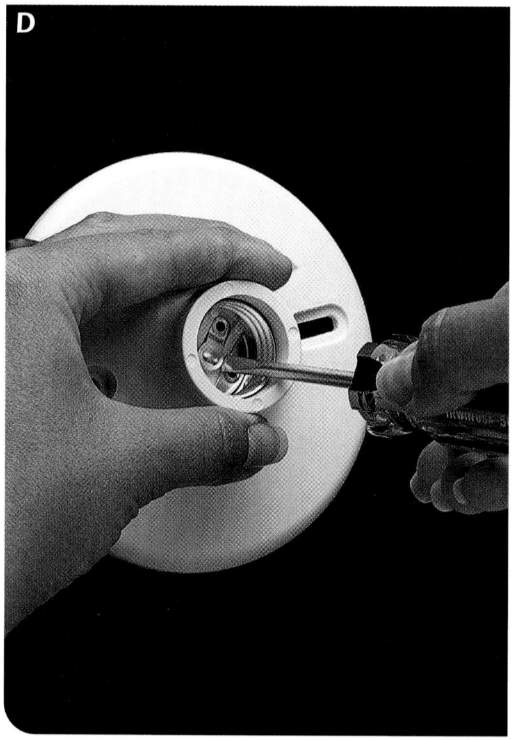

Pry up the metal tab slightly with a screwdriver.

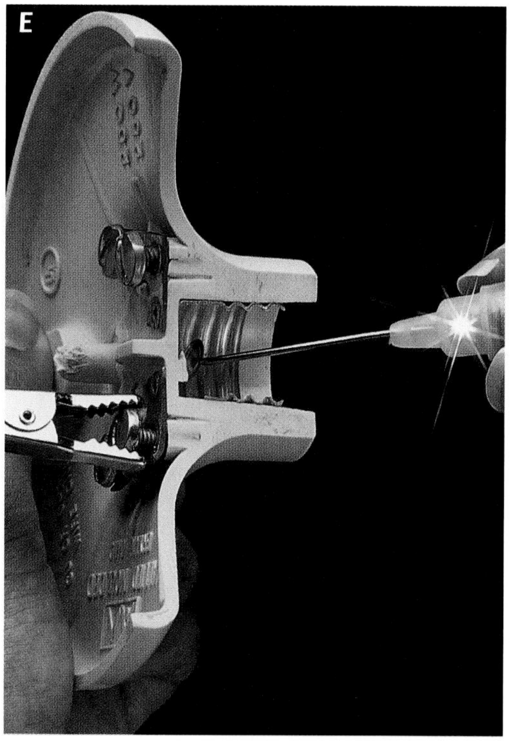

Check the hot screw terminal or wires for continuity.

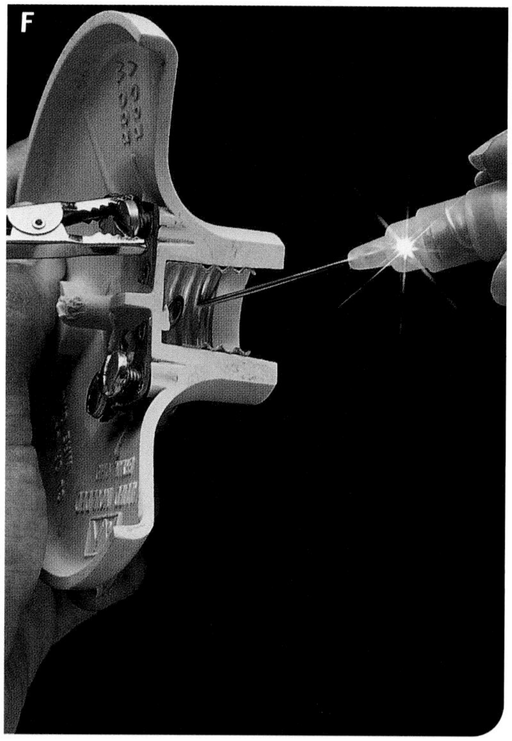

Check the neutral screw terminal or wires for continuity.

Replacing a Socket

Before starting, make sure the power to the circuit you will be working on is shut off (page 395). Test for power before touching any wires (page 428).

Remove the light fixture (page 428), then remove the socket from the fixture. The socket may be held in place by a screw, clip, or retaining ring. Disconnect the wires attached to the socket **(photo A).**

Buy an identical replacement socket. Connect the white circuit wire to the silver screw terminal on the socket, and the black circuit wire to the brass screw terminal **(photo B).**

Attach the socket to the fixture base and reinstall the fixture.

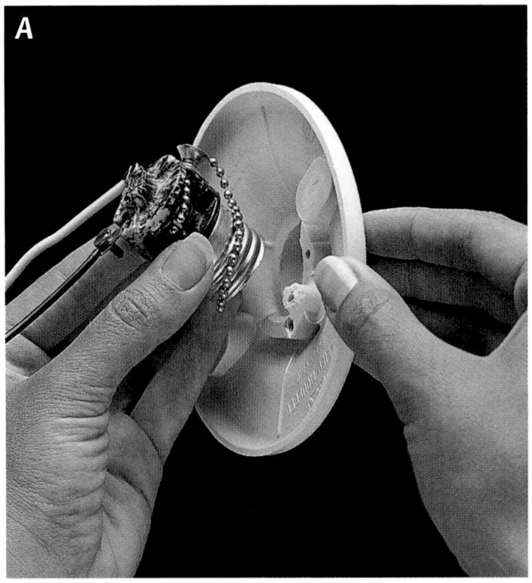

Remove the socket from the light fixture and disconnect the wires.

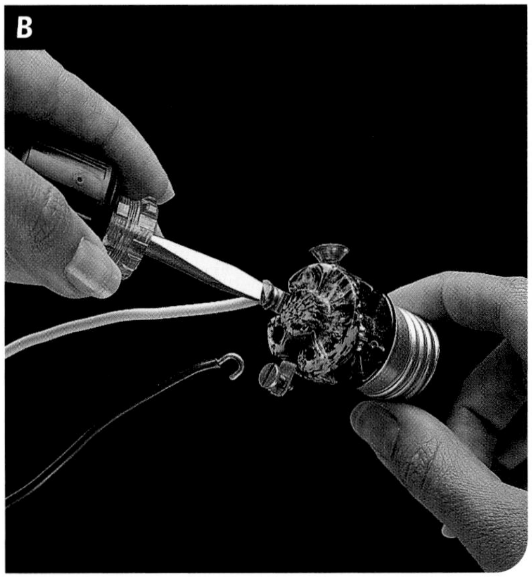

Connect the circuit wires to the screw terminals.

Testing & Replacing a Built-in Light Switch

Turn off the power to the circuit and test the switch for power (page 395). Remove the light fixture (page 428). Unscrew the retaining ring that holds the switch in place **(photo C).**

Label the wires connected to the switch leads **(photo D).** Disconnect the switch leads and remove the switch.

Test the switch for continuity: attach the clip of a continuity tester to one of the switch leads, and touch the probe to the other lead **(photo E).**

Operate the switch control. If the switch is good, the tester will glow when the switch is in one position, but not both.

If the switch is faulty, replace it with an exact duplicate **(photo F).**

Remount the light fixture, and restore the power at the main service panel.

Unscrew the retaining ring.

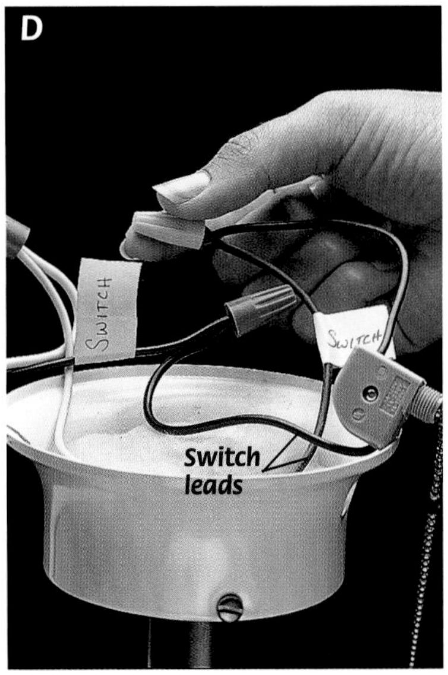

Label the wires to the switch leads.

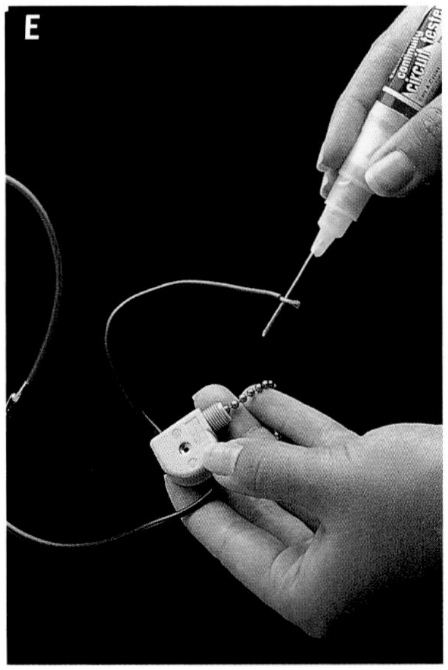

Test the switch for continuity.

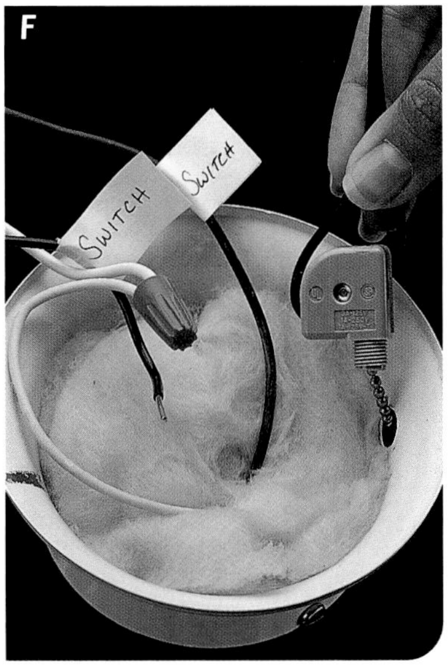

If necessary, replace the switch.

Replacing a Ceiling-mounted Light Fixture

Before starting, make sure the power to the circuit you will be working on is shut off (page 395). Test for power before touching any wires (page 428).

Remove the globe, the bulb, and the old light fixture **(photo G)**, following the directions for standard light fixtures (page 428) or chandeliers (page 435).

Attach a mounting strap to the electrical box, if the box doesn't already have one **(photo H).** The mounting strap, which is included with the new light fixture, will have a preinstalled grounding screw. Some fixtures have a threaded mounting rod that screws into an opening in the mounting strap.

Connect the circuit wires to the base of the new fixture, using wire connectors. Connect the white wire lead to the white circuit wire, and the black wire lead to the black circuit wire **(photo I).**

Attach the circuit grounding wire to the green grounding screw on the mounting strap. If there is more than one grounding wire—or if the fixture has a grounding lead—use a pigtail to connect the grounding wires to the grounding screw.

Attach the light fixture base to the mounting strap, using mounting screws **(photo J)** or mounting nut.

Install a light bulb with a wattage rating that is the same as or lower than the rating indicated on the fixture. Attach the globe.

Restore the power at the main service panel.

Helpful Hint

If the replacement fixture is substantially heavier than the old fixture, make sure the electrical box is firmly secured to ceiling joists or cross-blocking before you hang the new fixture.

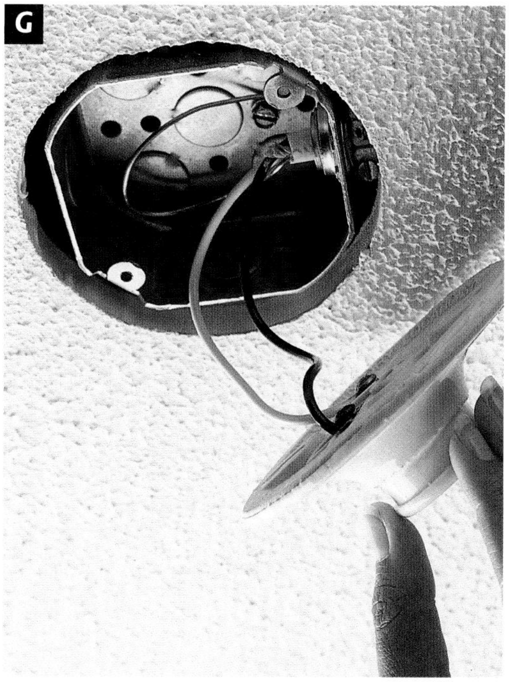

Turn off the power to the circuit, then disconnect the wires and remove the old light fixture.

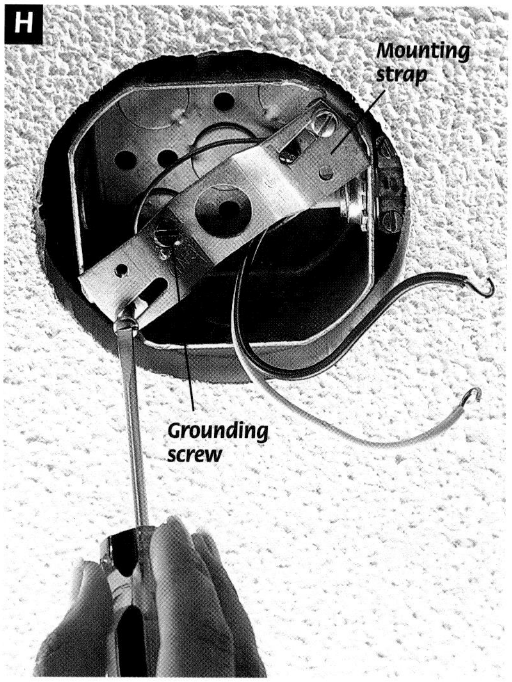

Fasten the mounting strap for the new fixture to the electrical box.

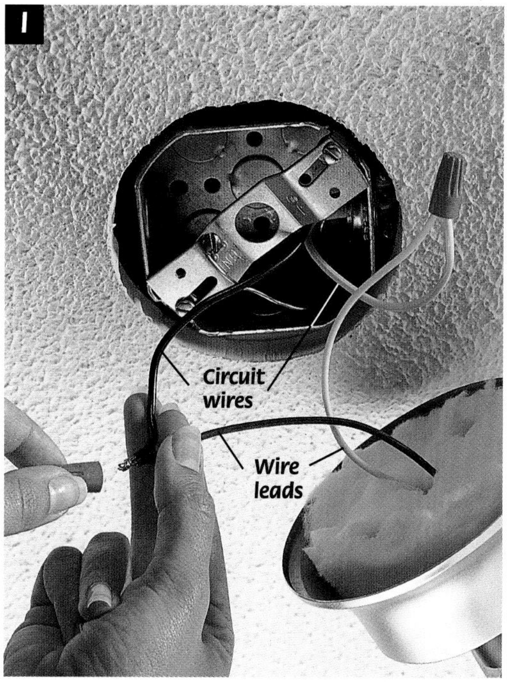

Connect the circuit wires to wire leads attached to the base of the new fixture.

Attach the light fixture base to the mounting strap, using the mounting screws or nut included with the fixture.

Recessed Light Fixtures

Most problems with recessed light fixtures occur when heat builds up inside the metal canister and melts the insulation on the socket wires. On some recessed fixtures, sockets with damaged wires can be removed and replaced. However, most newer fixtures have non-removable sockets; when the wires are damaged you need to buy a new fixture.

Choose a replacement fixture that matches the old one. Install the new fixture in the metal mounting frame that's already in place.

Unless the fixture is rated *IC* (insulation covered), make sure that any insulation is at least 3" away from the metal canister.

Tools: Screwdriver, circuit tester, continuity tester.

Materials: Replacement light fixture, wire connectors.

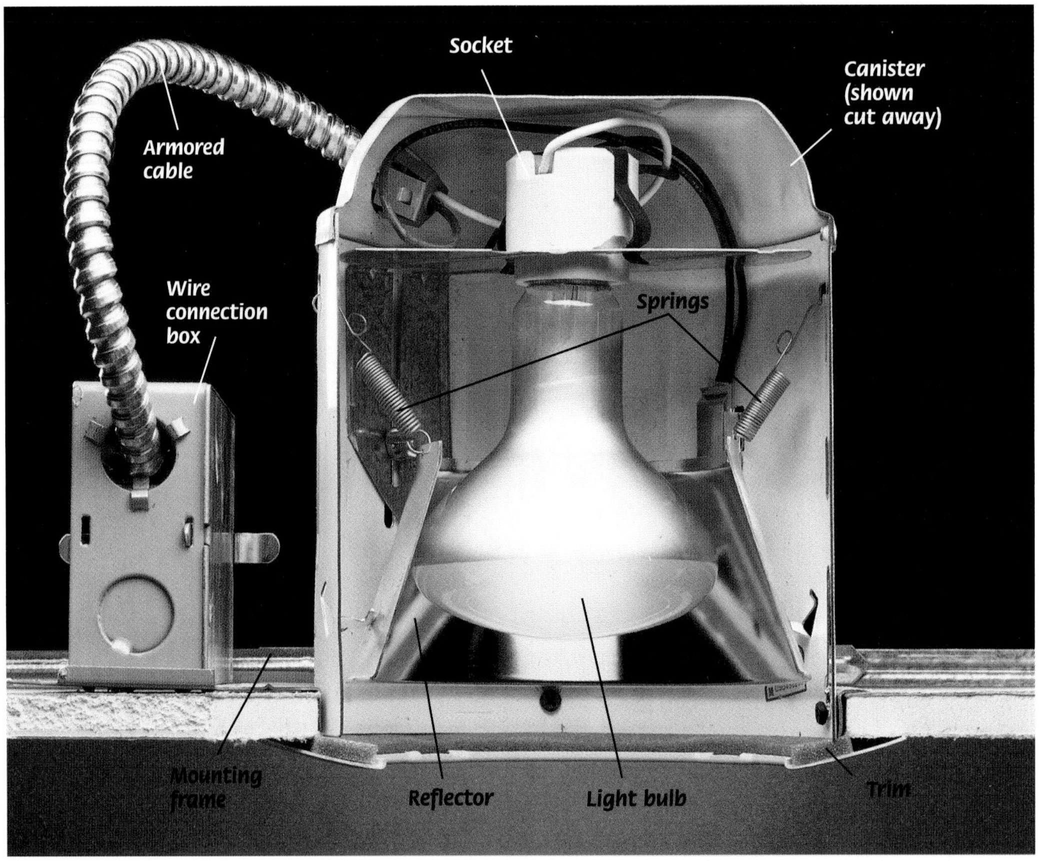

A typical recessed lighting fixture has a metal mounting frame that holds the fixture in place between framing members.

Removing & Testing a Recessed Light Fixture

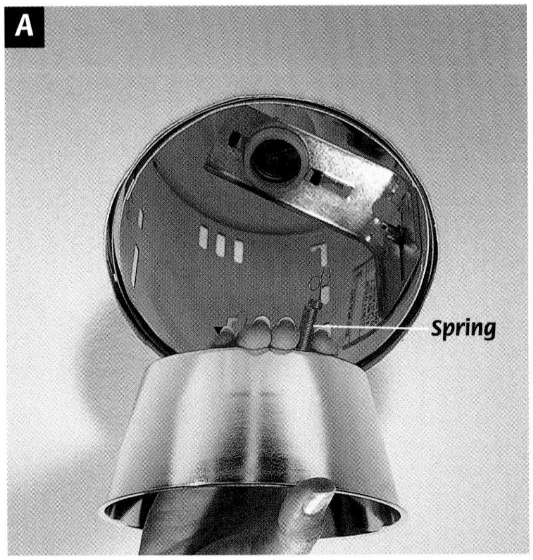

Turn off the power to the fixture (page 395). Remove the trim, the bulb, and the reflector, which is held in place by springs or mounting clips.

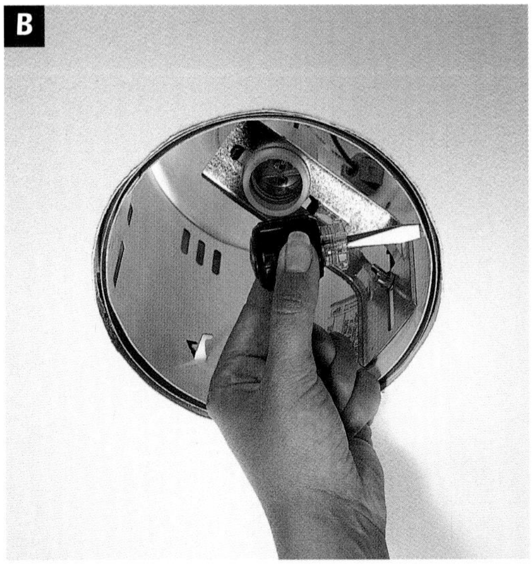

Loosen the screws or clips that hold the canister to the mounting frame. Carefully raise the canister and set it aside inside the ceiling cavity.

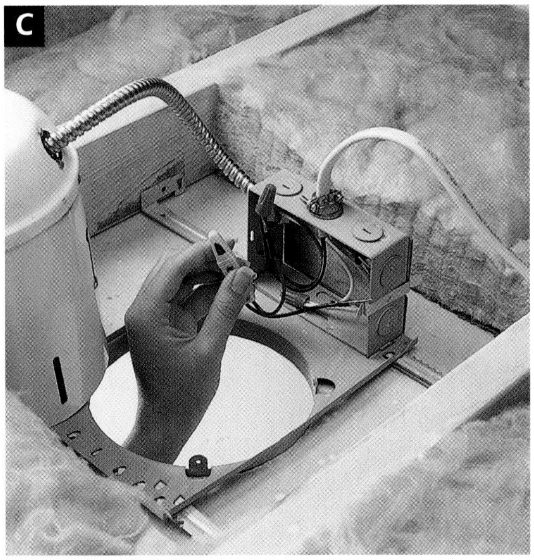

Remove the coverplate and test for power: touch one probe of a circuit tester to the grounded wire connection box, and insert the other one into each wire connector.

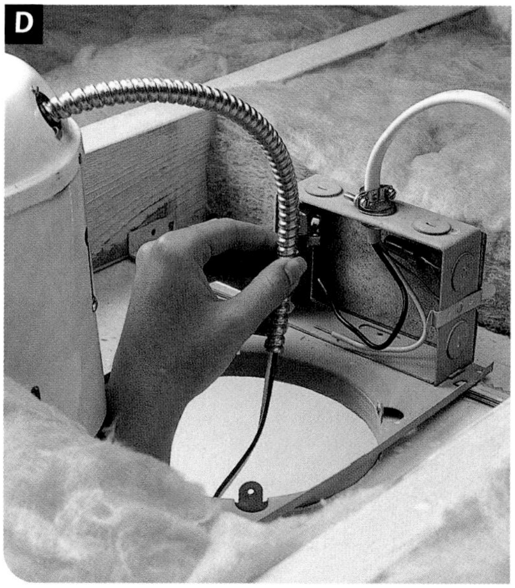

After ensuring that the power is off, disconnect the black and white circuit wires by removing the wire connectors. Pull the armored cable from the wire connection box. Remove the canister through the frame opening.

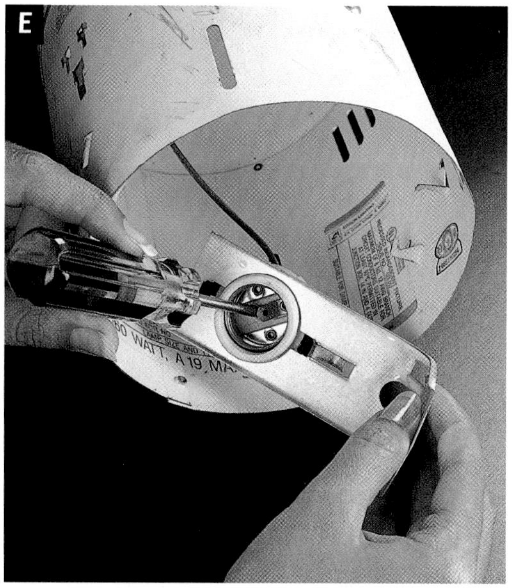

Lift out the socket and adjust the metal tab at the bottom of the fixture by prying it up slightly with a small screwdriver. This will improve its contact with the light bulb.

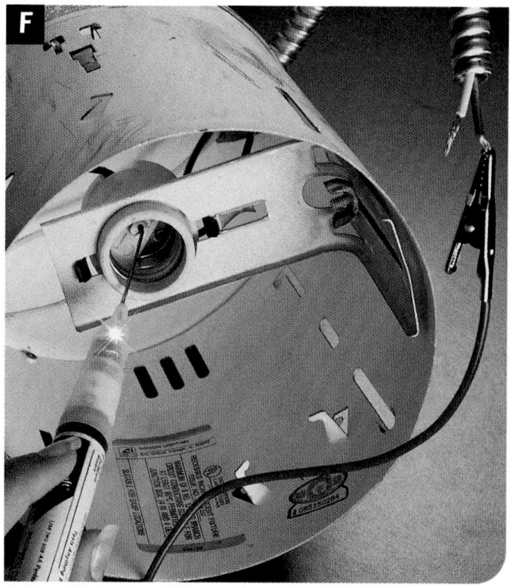

Test the socket with a continuity tester: Place the clip on the black wire and touch the probe to the metal tab. Then clip the white wire and touch the threaded metal socket. The tester should glow for both tests. If not, install a new fixture.

Installing a Recessed Light Fixture

Remove the old fixture (above). Set the new canister inside the ceiling hole, and thread its wires through the hole in the wire connection box. Push the armored cable into the wire connection box to secure it.

Connect the white fixture wire to the white circuit wire and the black fixture wire to the black circuit wire with wire connectors. Attach the coverplate to the wire connection box. Place insulation at least 3" away from the canister and box.

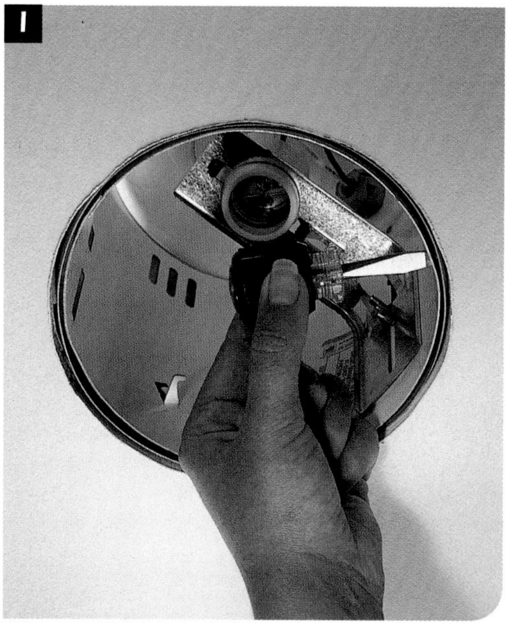

Position the canister inside the mounting frame, and attach the mounting screws or clips. Attach the reflector and trim. Install a light bulb with a wattage no higher than the rating on the fixture. Restore power to the fixture.

Chandeliers

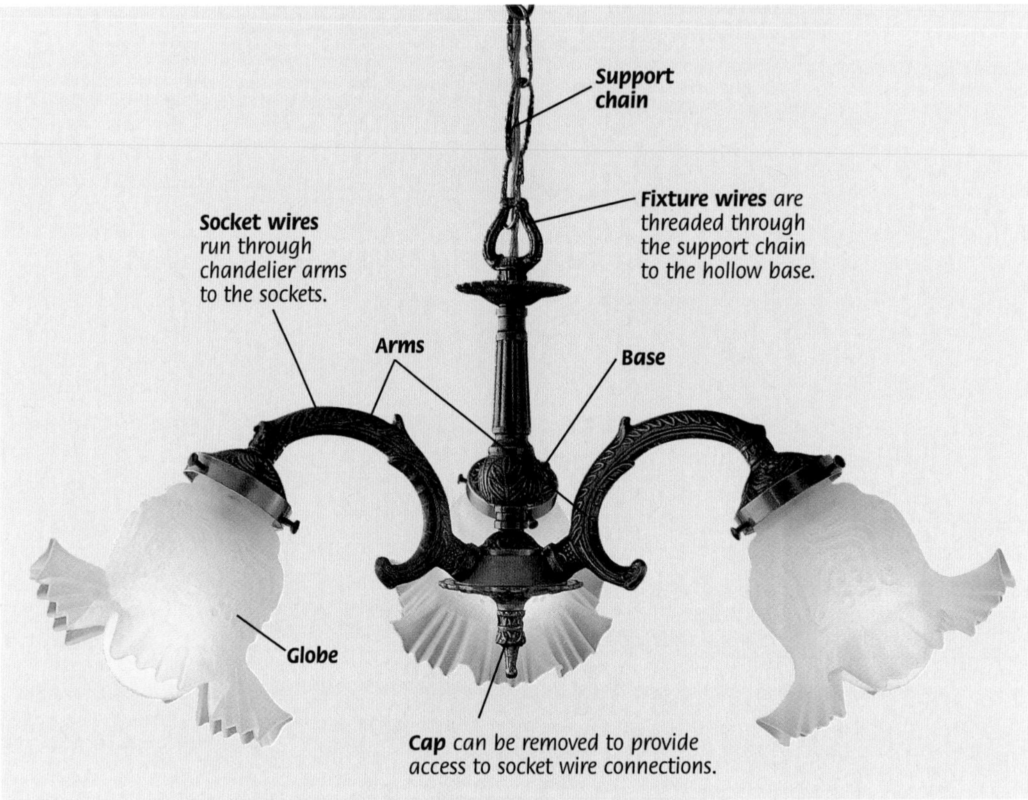

Support chain
Fixture wires *are threaded through the support chain to the hollow base.*
Socket wires *run through chandelier arms to the sockets.*
Arms
Base
Globe
Cap *can be removed to provide access to socket wire connections.*

Repairing chandeliers requires special care, since they tend to be quite heavy and bulky, as well as expensive. For these reasons, it's best to have a helper when removing a chandelier. As you work, support the chandelier so that its weight doesn't pull against the electrical wires.

Many older chandeliers have two fixture wires that are threaded through the support chain from the electrical box to the hollow chandelier base, where they connect with the socket wires. The fixture wires are marked. Look for lettering or a colored stripe on one of them; this is the neutral wire that's connected to the white circuit and socket wires. The unmarked wire is hot and is connected to the black wires.

Some new chandeliers also have a grounding wire that runs through the support chain to the electrical box. Connect this wire to the grounding wires in the electrical box.

Repairing Chandeliers

Before starting, label any sockets that aren't in good working order, using masking tape **(photo A).**

Identify which fixture wire is hot and which is neutral. Look over the wires closely for lettering or a colored stripe. The marked wire is the neutral wire that's connected to the white circuit and socket wires. The unmarked fixture wire is the hot wire that's connected to the black wires.

At the main service panel, shut off the power to the circuit (page 395).

Remove all the light bulbs and all shades or globes. Unscrew the retaining nut and lower the decorative coverplate away from the electrical box **(photo B).** Most chandeliers are supported by a threaded nipple attached to a mounting strap. However, some don't have a threaded nipple and are supported only by the coverplate, which is bolted to the mounting strap in the electrical box **(photo C).**

Test for power: touch one probe of the circuit tester to the green grounding screw, and insert the other probe into each wire connector **(photo D).** The tester shouldn't glow. If it does, return to the service panel and turn off the power to the correct circuit.

Disconnect the fixture wires by removing the wire connectors. Unscrew the threaded nipple **(photo E).** Carefully remove the chandelier and place it on a flat surface. Remove the cap at the bottom of the chandelier, exposing the wire connections inside the base.

Disconnect the black socket wires from the unmarked fixture wire, and the white socket wires from the marked fixture wire, by removing the wire connectors **(photo F).**

Test each suspect socket by attaching the clip of the continuity tester to the black socket wire and touching the probe to the metal tab in the bottom of the socket **(photo G).** Repeat the test with the threaded part of the socket and the white socket wire. The tester should glow for both tests. If not, replace the socket.

Remove a faulty socket by loosening any mounting screws or clips and pulling the socket and the socket wires out of the fixture arm **(photo H).** Buy and install a new chandelier socket, threading the socket wires through the fixture arm.

Test each fixture wire by attaching the clip of a continuity tester to one end of the wire and the probe to the other end **(photo I).** If the tester doesn't glow, the wire is faulty and needs to be replaced.

Install new wires, if needed. Reassemble and rehang the chandelier.

Tools: *Screwdrivers, circuit tester, continuity tester.*

Materials: *Masking tape, replacement parts.*

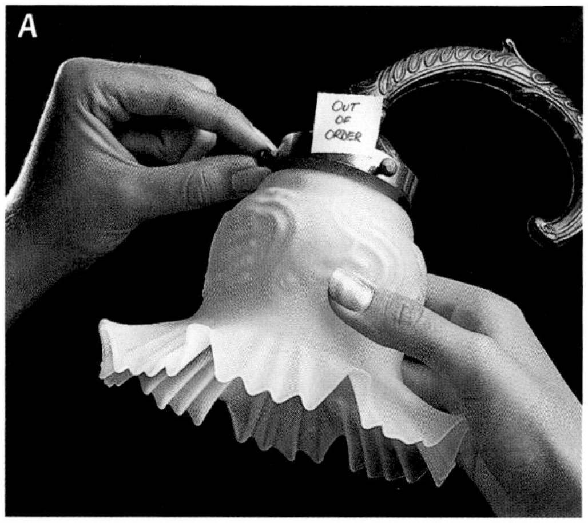

Label any sockets that aren't in good working order.

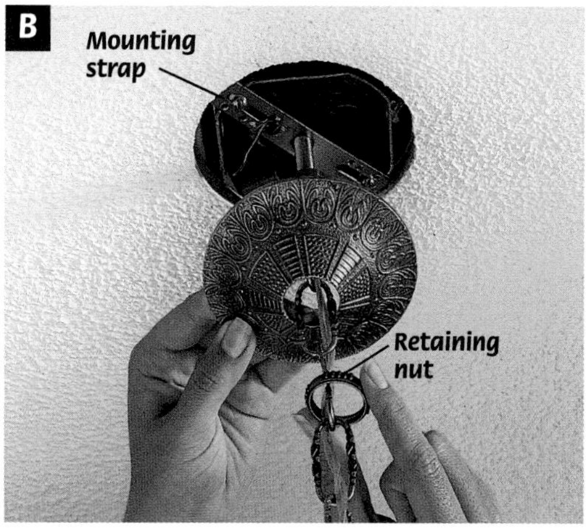

Unscrew the retaining nut and lower the coverplate.

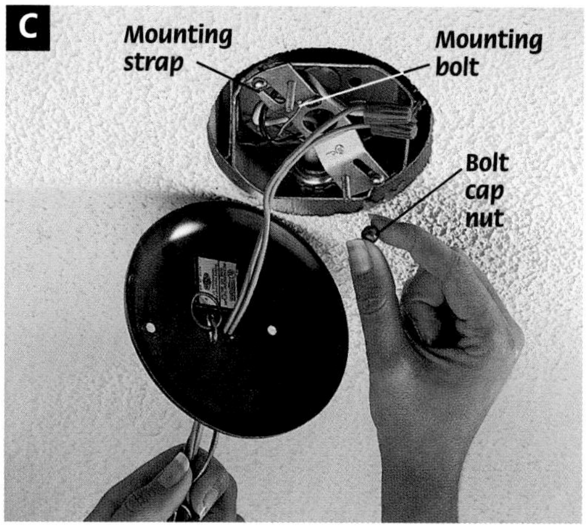

Mounting variation: chandeliers without a threaded nipple.

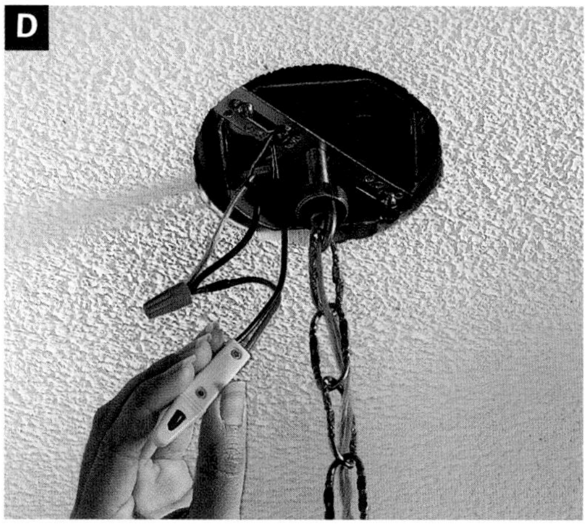

Test the circuit wires for power, using a circuit tester.

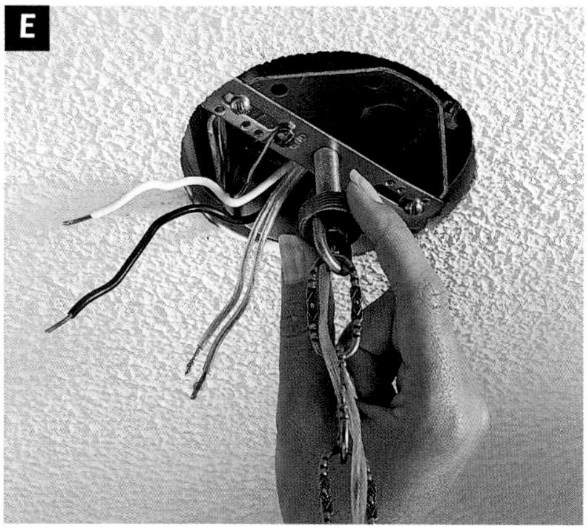

Disconnect the fixture wires and remove the chandelier.

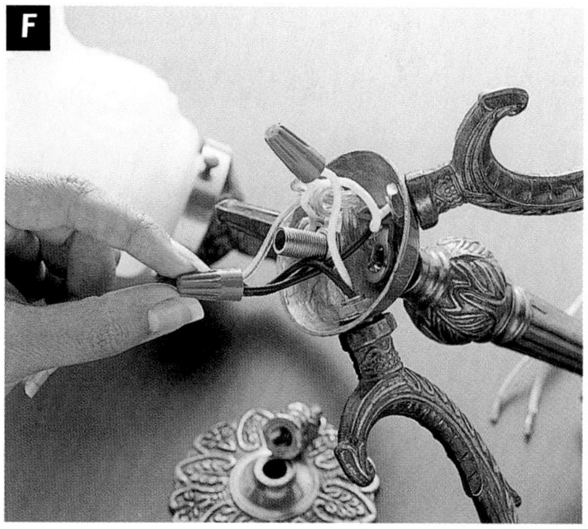

Remove the cap from the bottom of the chandelier.

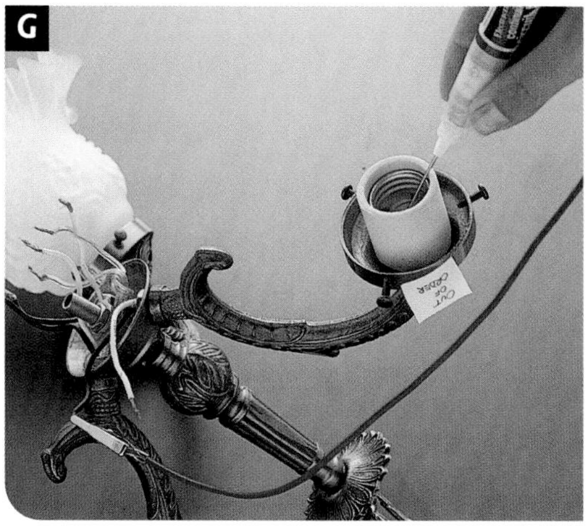

Test suspect sockets, using a continuity tester.

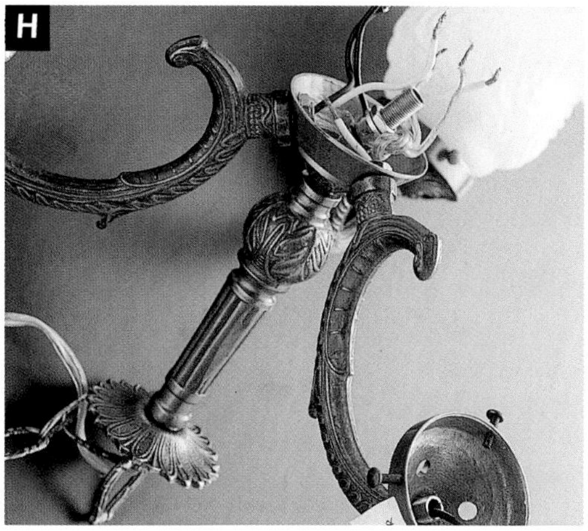

Remove any faulty sockets and replace them.

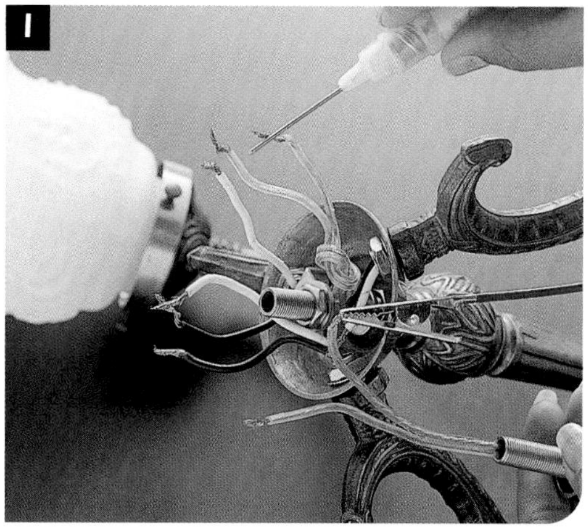

Test each fixture wire for continuity.

Track Lighting

A track lighting system consists of one or more modular fixtures attached to a metal track. This arrangement offers great flexibility to add, remove, or reposition light fixtures.

The system begins with a connector that's mounted to an electrical box in the ceiling. The connector is attached to a metal channel, or track, either at the middle or at one end. Inside the track are two metal power strips that provide power the individual light fixtures, and a lever is used to secure each fixture's stem assembly to the track.

The stem of the light fixture pivots to turn the light in the desired direction. An insulating sleeve protects the wires inside the fixture from heat buildup. For further heat protection, the bulbs may be coated with a reflective finish that directs the light beam downward.

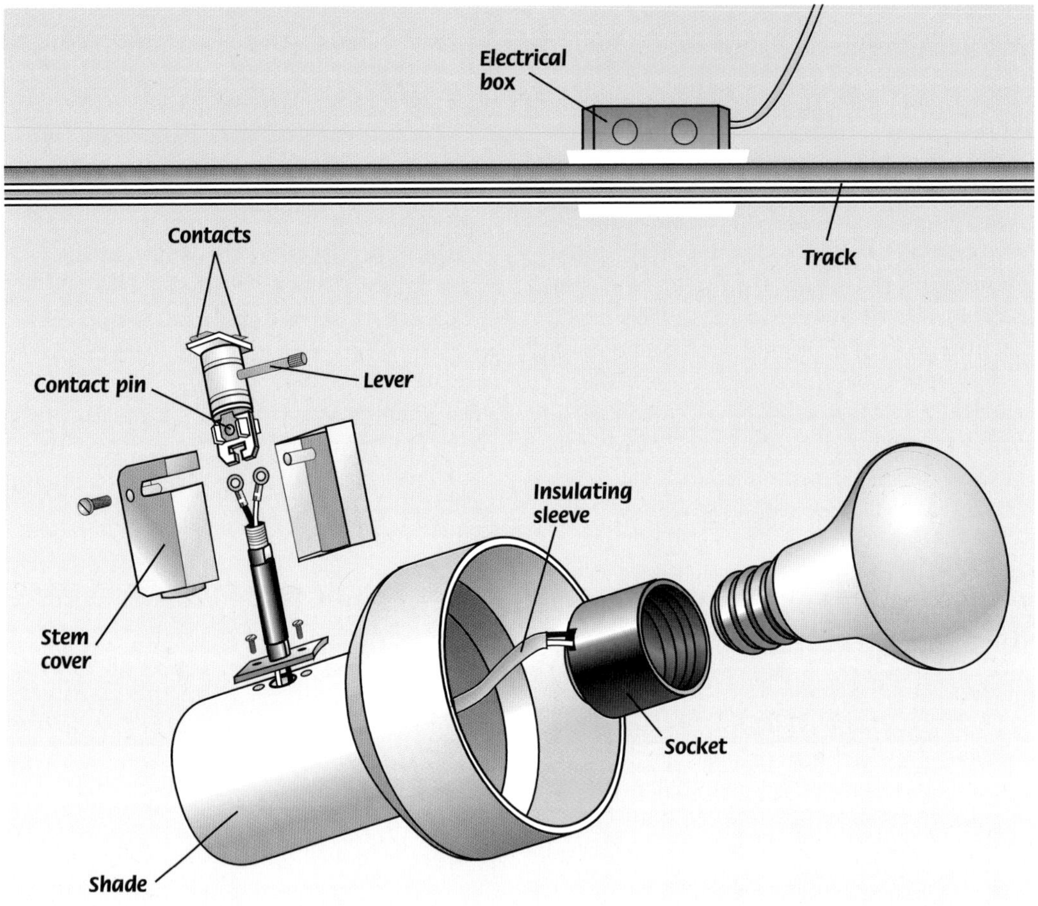

Tools: *Screwdriver, continuity tester, combination tool.*

Materials: *Fine sandpaper, replacement socket and crimp-style wire connectors (if needed).*

Cleaning Track Light Contacts

When a track light fails, tighten or replace the bulb. If that doesn't work, clean the track and contacts. Turn off the power to the circuit at the main service panel (page 395). Let the fixture cool, then release the fixture from the track **(photo A).** Use fine sandpaper to clean the power strips in the track in the general area where the fixture hangs. Sand the fixture contacts clean, then bend them up slightly with a screwdriver **(photo B).**

Remove the bulb. Scrape any corrosion from the socket contact tab. Pry it up slightly to improve its contact with the bulb. Reinstall the bulb and fixture, then restore the power. If the bulb still doesn't light, test the socket (page 428), and replace it if necessary.

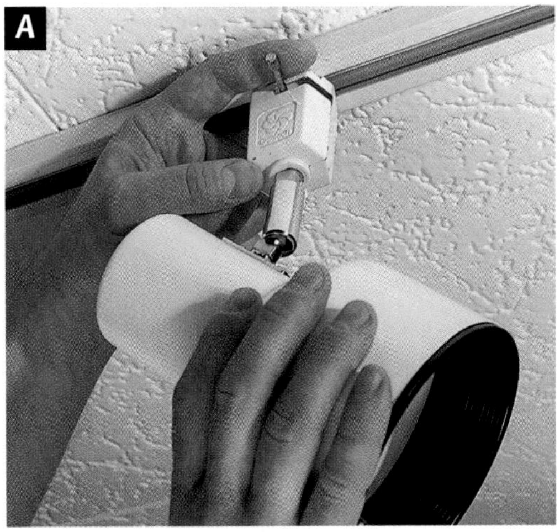

Shift the lever to release the fixture from the track.

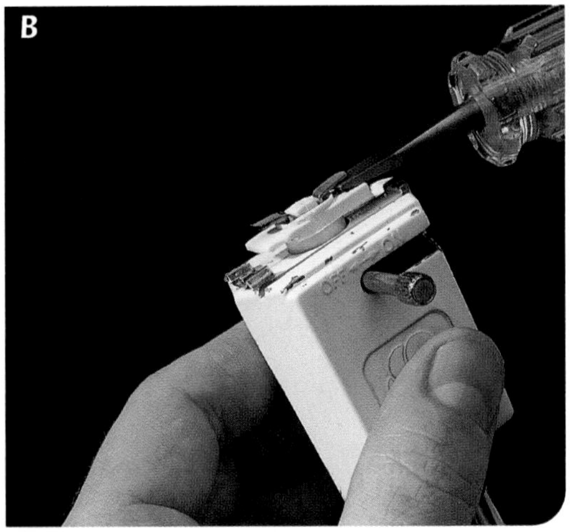

Clean the track contacts and pry them up slightly.

Testing & Replacing a Socket

To test a malfunctioning track light socket, begin by turning off the power to the track at the main service panel (page 395).

Take the fixture down. Unscrew the lever by hand to provide slack at the socket. Loosen the stem screws with a screwdriver. Take the stem apart **(photo C).**

Remove the screws that attach the shade to the socket. Pull the socket from its mounting.

To test the socket, attach the clip on a continuity tester to the brass track contact and touch the probe to the black wire connection at the socket terminal **(photo D).**

Repeat the test, attaching the clip to the silver track contact and touching the probe to the white wire connection. The tester should light in both tests. If it doesn't, replace the socket.

To remove the old socket, begin by loosening the terminal screws and removing the wires from the contact pins **(photo E).**

Pull the socket from the shade, along with its wires **(photo F).** If the wires are held in an insulating sleeve, remove it and set it aside.

To install the new socket, slip the insulating sleeve (if equipped) over the new wires. Thread the wires through the hole in the shade and both parts of the stem.

Strip $^{1}/_{4}$" from the wire ends; twist each one so the strands are tight, feed it into a crimp connector, and crimp the connector with a combination tool. Attach the black wire to the brass contact pin and the white wire to the silver contact pin and tighten the terminal screws **(photo G).**

Fit the socket in the shade and secure it by tightening the screws. Reattach the lever to the stem assembly **(photo H).** Place the stem in the track and give the lever a quarter turn, (without touching any wires in the track). Replace the bulb and restore the power to the track.

C
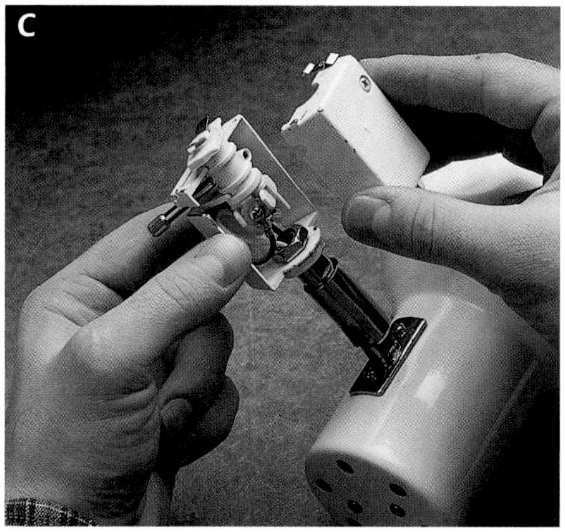

Loosen the stem screws and disassemble the stem.

D
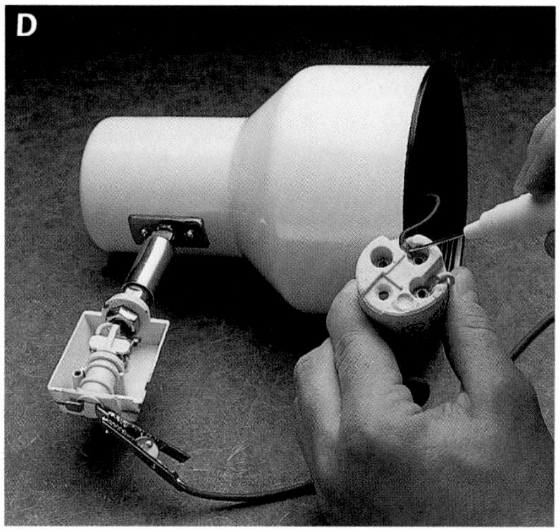

Test the socket with a continuity tester.

E
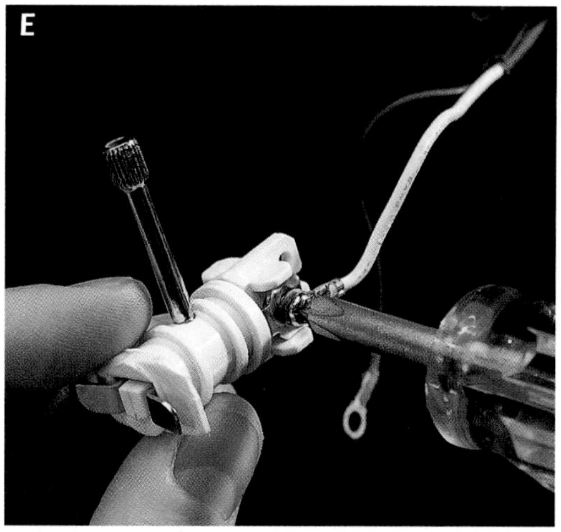

Disconnect the wires from the contact pins.

F
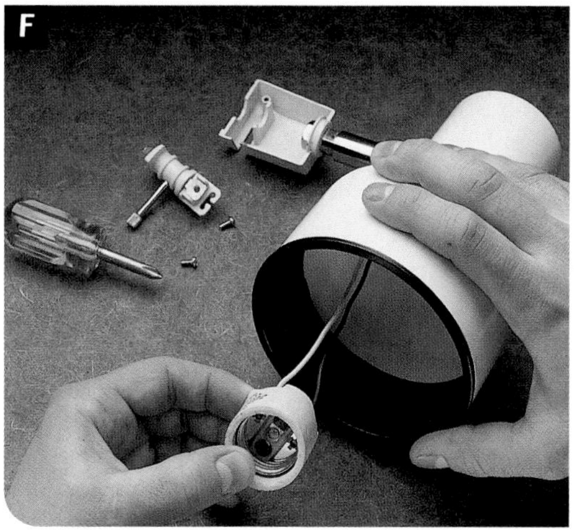

Pull the socket and wires through the shade.

G
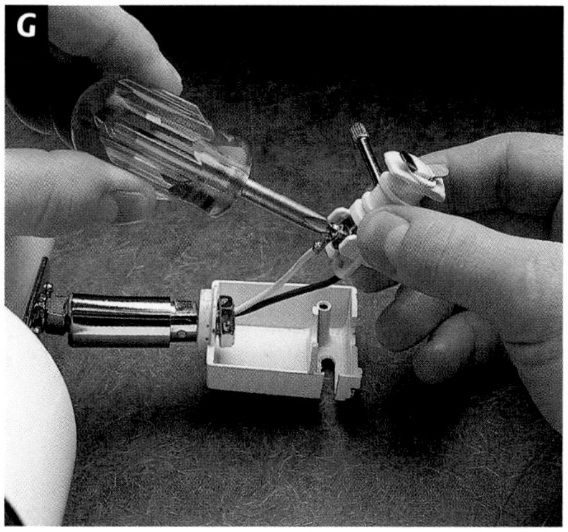

Attach the wires for the new fixture to the contact pins.

H
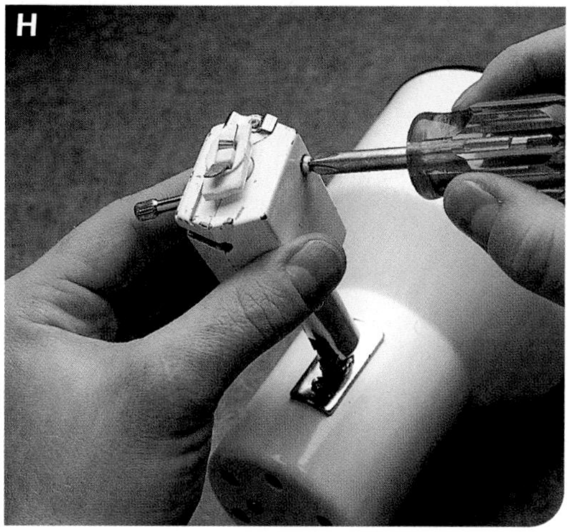

Screw the stem back together before remounting the fixture.

Fluorescent Lights

Fluorescent lights pass electrical current through a gas-filled tube that glows when energized. A translucent diffuser protects the tube and softens its light. A coverplate protects the transformer, or *ballast*, which regulates the current to the sockets. The sockets transfer power to metal pins that extend into the tube.

Fluorescent fixtures are relatively trouble-free, and the tubes typically last about three years. A worn-out tube will be signaled by flickering or partial lighting.

Older fluorescent fixtures may have a small cylindrical device, called a *starter*, near one of the sockets. When a tube wears out, you need to replace both the tube and the starter. Turn off the power, then remove the starter by pushing it slightly and turning it counterclockwise **(inset).**

Since fluorescent tubes contain a small amount of mercury, always dispose of them properly, and never break them. Contact your local environmental agency for instructions.

Tools: Screwdriver, neon circuit tester, combination tool.

Materials: Wire connectors, replacement parts as needed (ballast, sockets, tubes, or entire fixture).

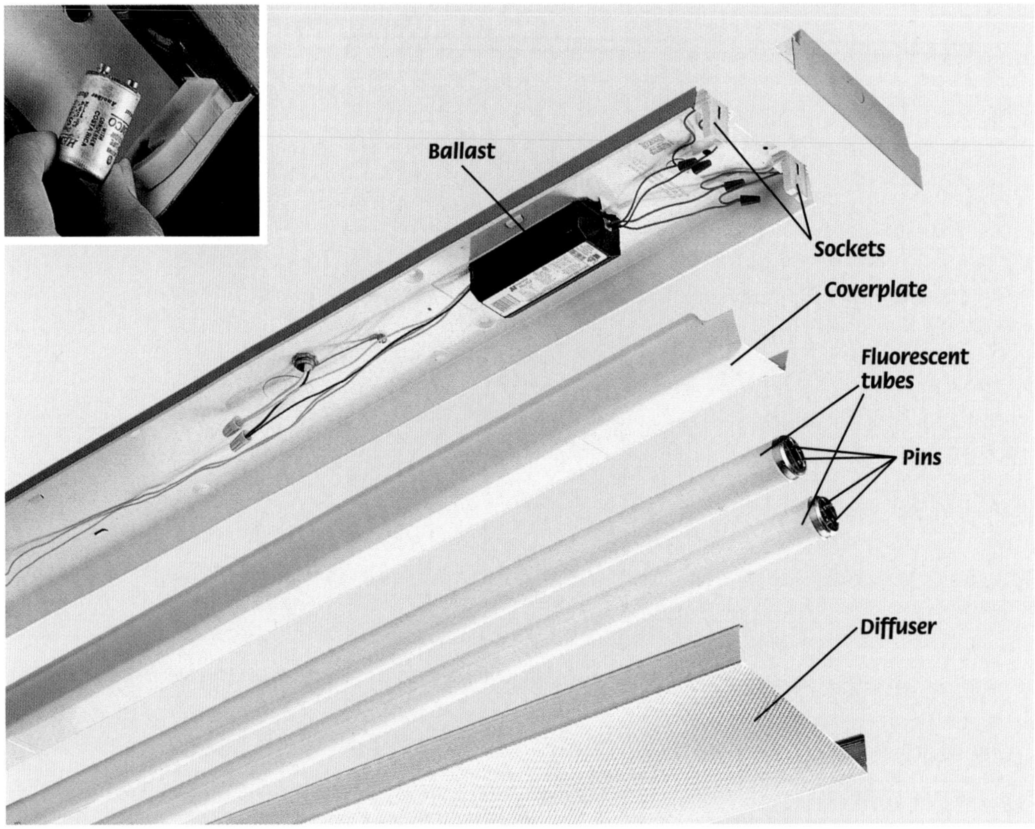

Common Fluorescent Light Problems & Repairs

Problems	Repairs
Tube flickers, or lights partially.	1. Rotate tube to make sure it is seated properly in the sockets. 2. Replace tube (page 439) and the starter (where present) if tube is discolored or if pins are bent or broken. 3. Replace the ballast (page 439) if replacement cost is reasonable. Otherwise, replace the entire fixture (page 441).
Tube does not light.	1. Check wall switch, and repair or replace, if needed (page 415). 2. Rotate the tube to make sure it is seated properly in sockets. 3. Replace tube (page 439) and the starter (where present) if tube is discolored or if pins are bent or broken. 4. Replace sockets if they are chipped, or if tube does not seat properly (page 440).
Noticeable black substance around ballast.	Replace ballast (page 439) if replacement cost is reasonable. Otherwise, replace the entire fixture (page 441).
Fixture hums.	Replace ballast (page 439) if replacement cost is reasonable. Otherwise, replace the entire fixture (page 441).

Replacing a Fluorescent Tube

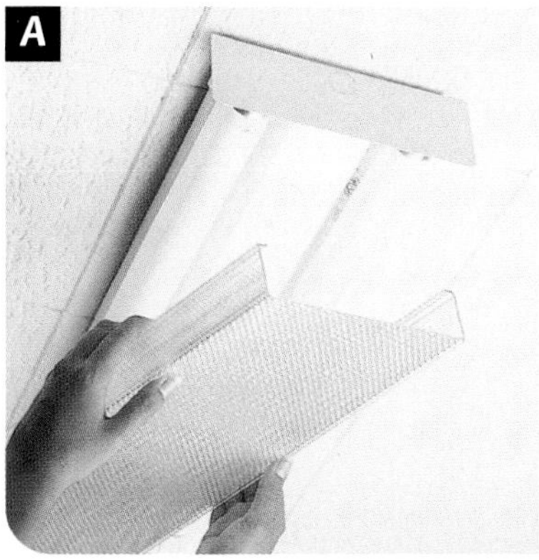

A. Turn off the power to the light fixture at the main service panel. Remove the diffuser to expose the fluorescent tube(s).

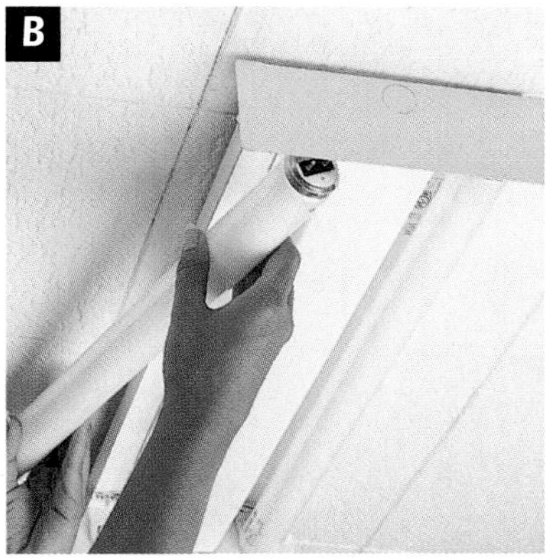

B. Remove the tube by rotating it $1/4$ turn in either direction and sliding it out of the sockets. Inspect the pins at the ends. If they're bent or broken, replace the tube.

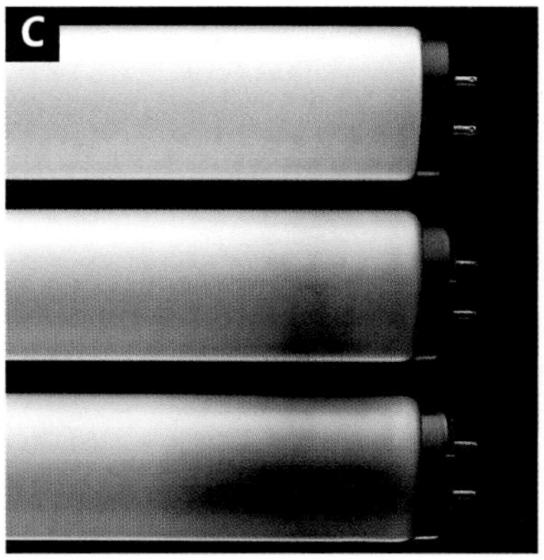

C. The ends of a new tube (top) have no discoloration. The ends of a working tube (middle) may be starting to darken. The ends of a worn-out tube (bottom) are dark gray.

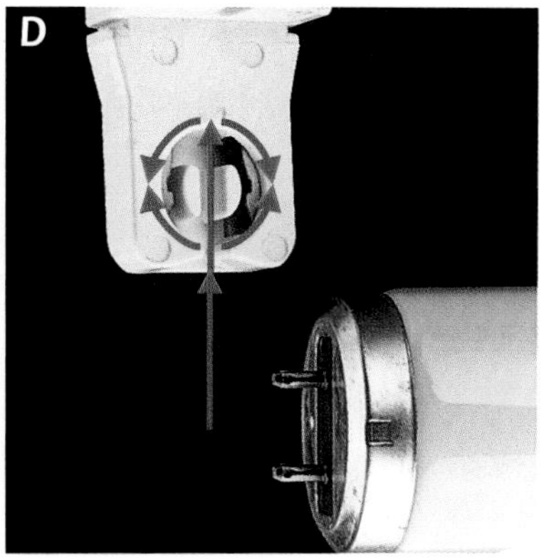

D. Insert the new tube so that the pins slide fully into the sockets, then twist it $1/4$ turn in either direction until it's securely locked. Reattach the diffuser and restore the power.

Replacing a Fluorescent Ballast

Although the most common problem with fluorescent fixtures is a worn-out tube, problems can also be caused by other parts of the fixture. If the fixture still doesn't work after the tube and the sockets have been replaced, the problem is most likely due to a defective ballast. A faulty ballast may leak a black, oily substance and can cause a fixture to make a loud humming sound.

Ballasts can be replaced, but always compare prices before buying a new one. It may be cheaper to buy a new fixture than to replace the ballast in an old one.

E. Turn off the power to the fixture. Remove the diffuser, tube, and coverplate. Test for power (page 440). Remove the sockets by sliding them out or by removing their mounting screws and lifting them out.

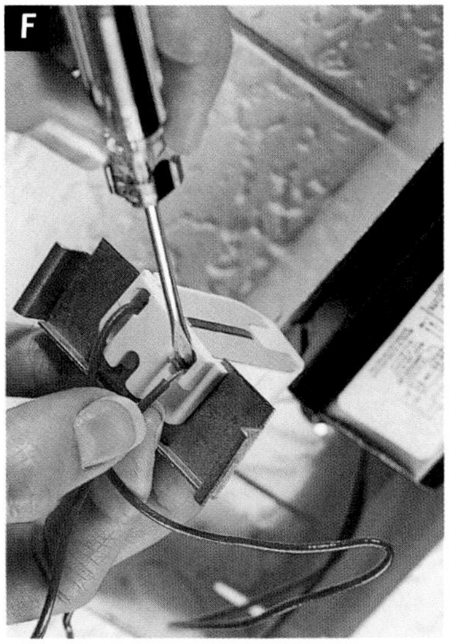

F. Disconnect the wires attached to the sockets in one of the following ways: 1) pushing a screwdriver into the release openings, 2) loosening the screw terminals, or 3) cutting the wires to within 2" of the sockets.

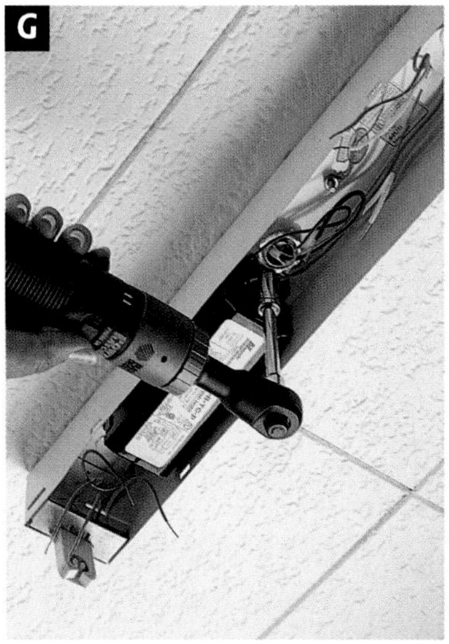

G. Remove the old ballast, using a ratchet wrench or a screwdriver. Take care to support the ballast as it comes loose so it doesn't fall. Install a new ballast that has the same ratings as the old one.

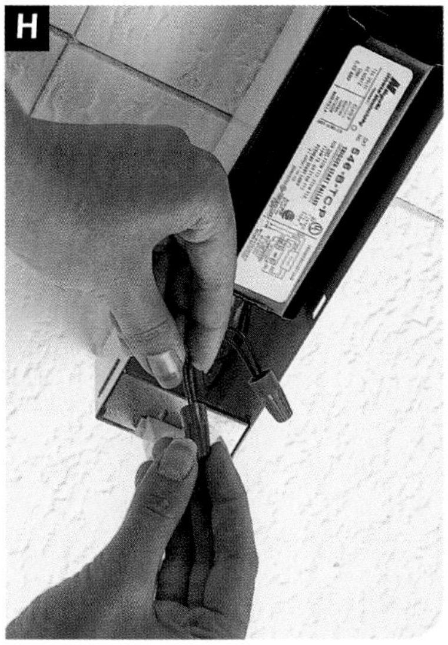

H. Attach the ballast wires to the socket wires, using wire connectors, screw terminal connections, or push-in fittings. Reinstall the coverplate, tube, and diffuser. Restore power to the fixture at the main service panel.

Replacing a Fluorescent Socket

When a socket becomes chipped or a tube no longer seats properly, it's time to replace the socket. Bring the old socket with you to a home center or hardware store to find an identical replacement.

Before starting, turn off the power to the circuit at the main service panel (page 395). Remove the diffuser, tube, and coverplate **(photo A).**

Before removing the socket, test for power: touch one probe of a circuit tester to the grounding screw, and insert the other probe into each wire connector **(photo B).** The tester should not glow. If it does, return to the service panel and turn off the correct circuit.

Remove the faulty socket from the fixture housing **(photo C).** Some sockets slide out; others must be unscrewed.

Disconnect the wires attached to the socket. For push-in fitting, remove the wires by inserting a small screwdriver into the release openings. Some sockets have screw terminal connections, and others have permanent wires that must be cut before the socket can be removed **(photo D).**

Install the new socket. If the socket has permanent wire leads, connect the leads to the ballast wires with wire connectors **(photo E).**

Replace the coverplate, taking care to avoid pinching any wires. Replace the fluorescent tube, making sure that it seats properly. Replace the diffuser. Restore power to the fixture at the main service panel.

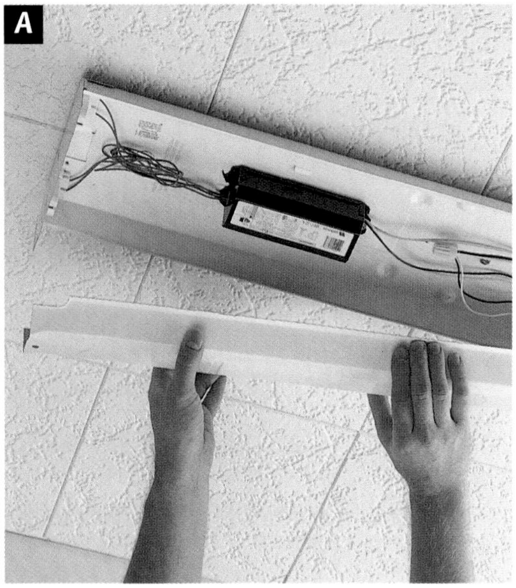

Remove the diffuser, tube, and coverplate.

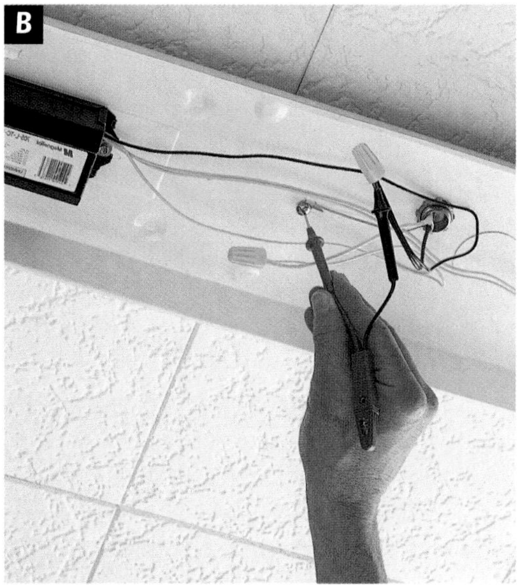

Use a circuit tester to check the wires for power.

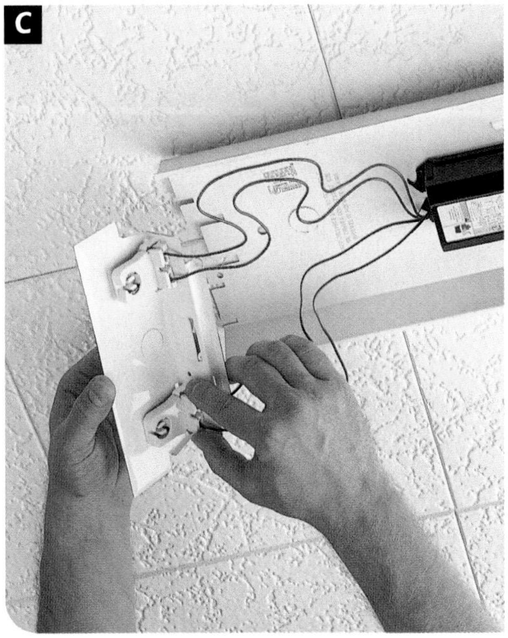

Remove the faulty socket from the fixture housing.

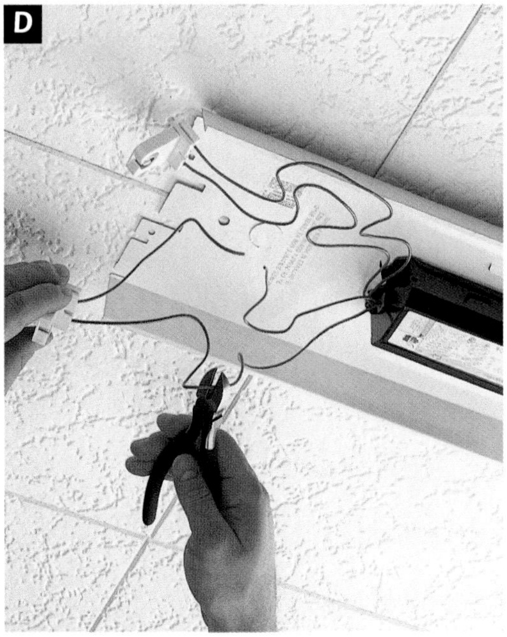

Disconnect the wires attached to the socket.

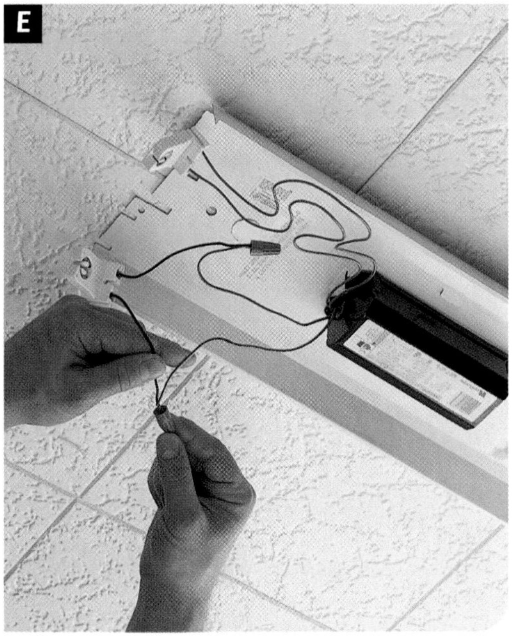

Install a new socket, joining the wires with wire connectors.

Replacing a Fluorescent Light Fixture

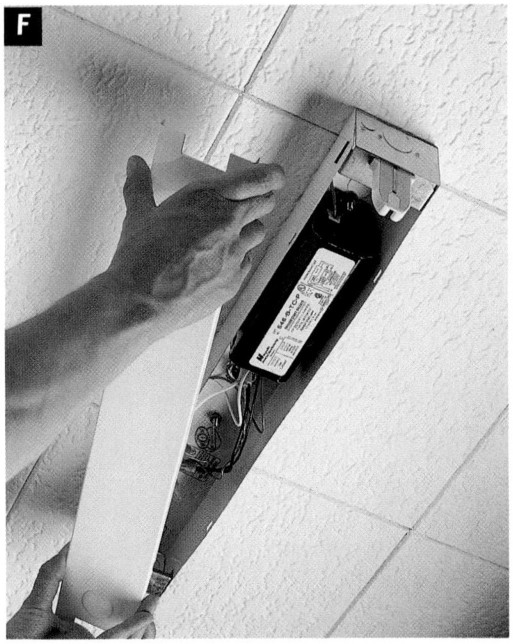

Turn off the power to the light fixture at the main service panel. Remove the diffuser, tube, and coverplate. Test for power, using a neon circuit tester (page 440).

Disconnect the insulated circuit wires and the bare copper grounding wire from the light fixture. Loosen the cable clamp that holds the circuit wires.

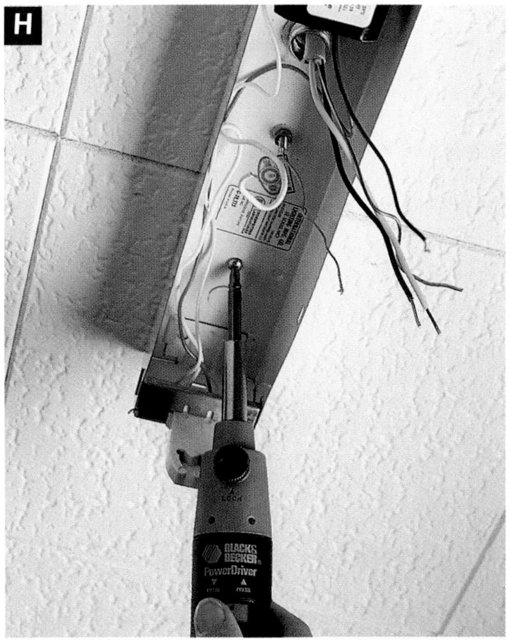

Unscrew the fixture from the wall or ceiling, and carefully remove it. Take care to support the fixture as it comes loose.

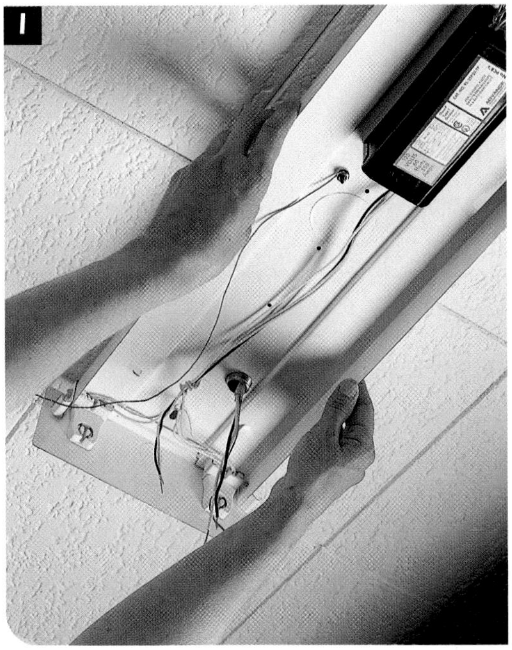

Position the new fixture, threading the circuit wires through the knockout opening in the back of the fixture. Screw the fixture in place so it's firmly anchored to the framing members.

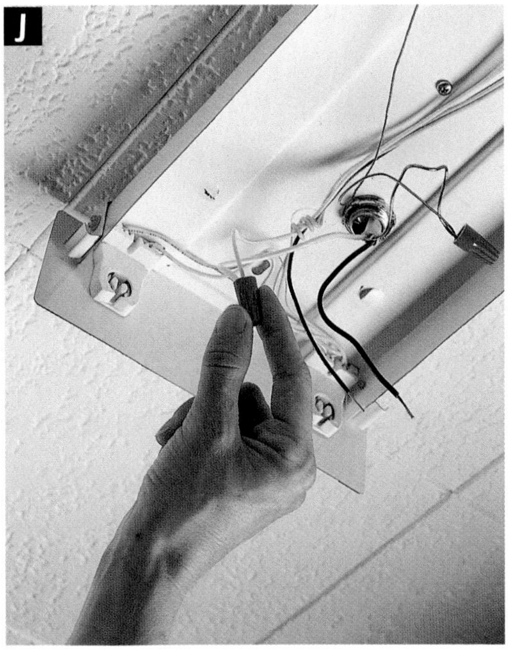

Connect the circuit wires to the fixture wires, using wire connectors. Follow the wiring diagram included with the new fixture. Tighten the cable clamp that holds the circuit wires.

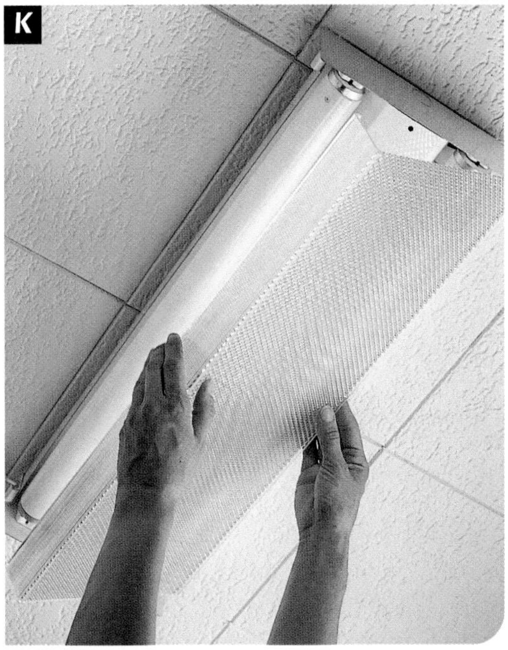

Attach the coverplate of the new fixture. Install the fluorescent tube(s) and attach the diffuser. Restore power to the fixture at the main service panel.

Doorbells

Doorbell systems are powered by transformers that reduce 120-volt current to a low-voltage current of 20 volts or less. The current flows from the transformer to one or more push-button doorbell switches. These switches activate a magnetic coil inside the chime unit, causing a plunger to strike a musical tuning bar.

Most doorbell problems are caused by loose connections or faulty switches. Other causes may be a burned-out transformer or a dirty or worn chime unit. A breakage in the low-voltage wiring can also cause a system failure.

Tools: *Screwdriver, continuity tester, needlenose pliers, multi-tester, neon circuit tester, marking pen.*

Materials: *Masking tape, cotton swab, rubbing alcohol, replacement parts (as needed).*

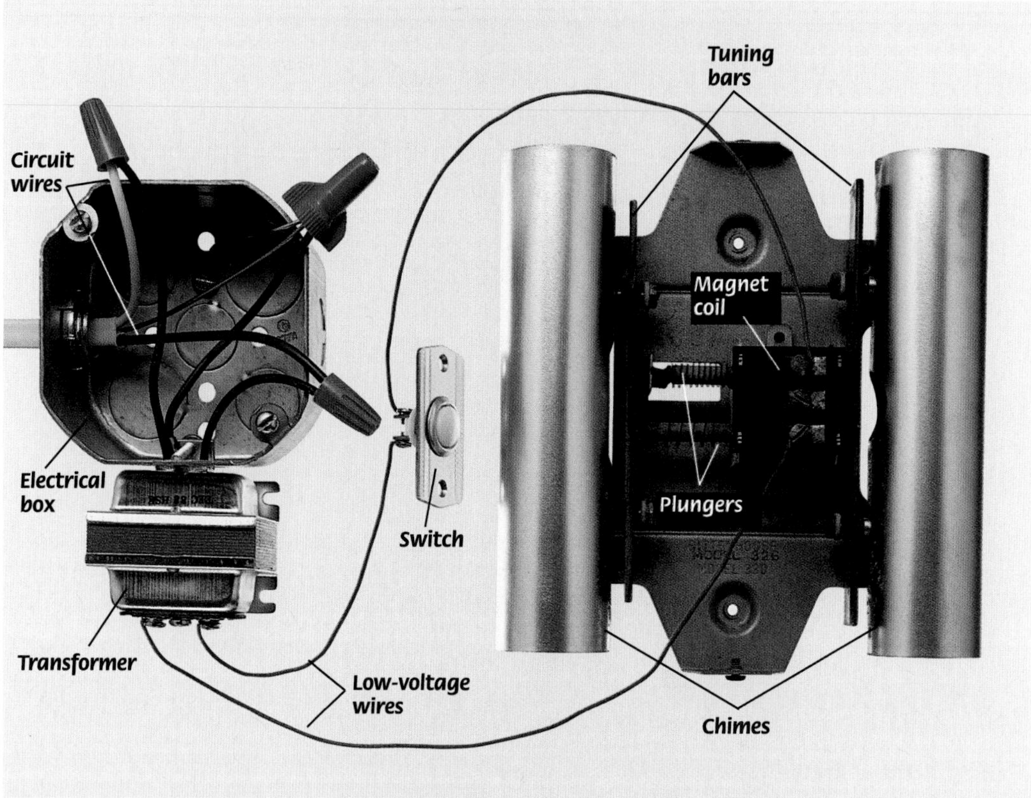

Testing & Replacing a Doorbell Switch

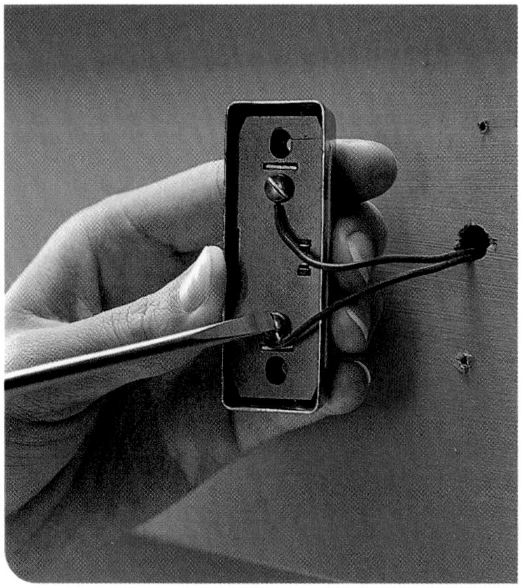

Remove the screws that hold the switch to the wall. Carefully detach the switch. Check the low-voltage wire connections. Reattach any loose wires to the screw terminals and tighten them with a screwdriver.

Push the switch button. If the doorbell still doesn't work, you need to test for continuity. Start by disconnecting the switch wires. Tape them to the wall to keep them from slipping into the wall cavity.

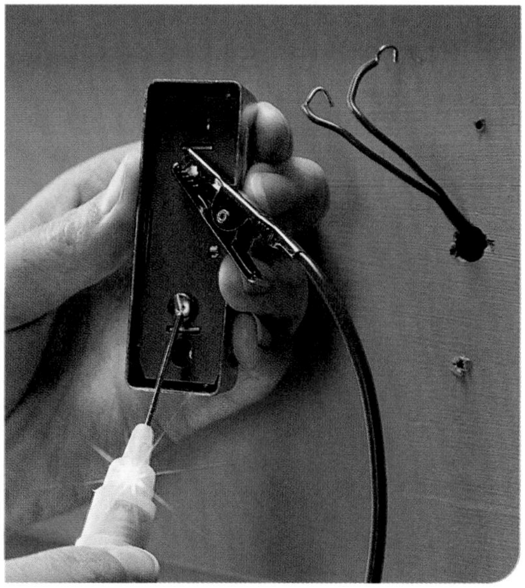

Attach the clip of a continuity tester to one screw terminal and touch the probe to the other one. Push the switch. If the tester doesn't glow, install a new switch: Connect the wires to either terminal and screw the switch to the wall.

Testing a Low-voltage Transformer

Once you've ruled out the switch as the source of a doorbell problem, test the doorbell transformer, which can usually be found near the main service panel **(photo A).**

The transformer for the doorbell will be rated for 20 volts or less **(photo B),** while the transformers for a furnace and other devices will carry higher voltage ratings.

Turn off the power to the transformer at the service panel (page 395). Remove the coverplate from the electrical box. Carefully remove the wire connector that joins the black circuit wire to the transformer lead. Don't touch any bare wires.

Touch one probe of the circuit tester to the grounded metal box and the other one to the wire ends **(photo C).** Repeat the test on the white wires. If the tester glows either time, it means the power is still on. Turn off the correct circuit at the service panel.

Reconnect the loose wires. If any of the connections were made with electrical tape, replace them with wire connectors **(photo D).** Reattach the coverplate.

Inspect the low-voltage wire connections. Reconnect loose wires, and tighten terminal connections with needlenose pliers **(photo E).** Restore power to the transformer.

Test the current with a multi-tester set to the 50-volt (AC) range. Touch the tester probes to the transformer screw terminals **(photo F).**

The multi-tester should detect a current within 2 volts of the transformer's rating. If it doesn't, the transformer must be replaced with a new one of the same voltage (page 444).

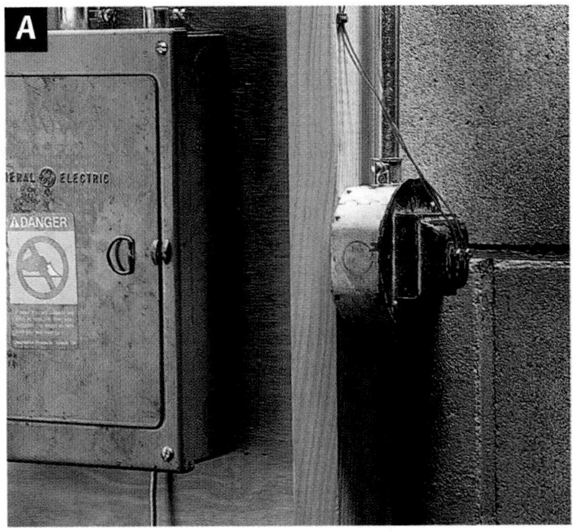

The doorbell transformer may be attached directly to the side of the service panel or to an electrical box.

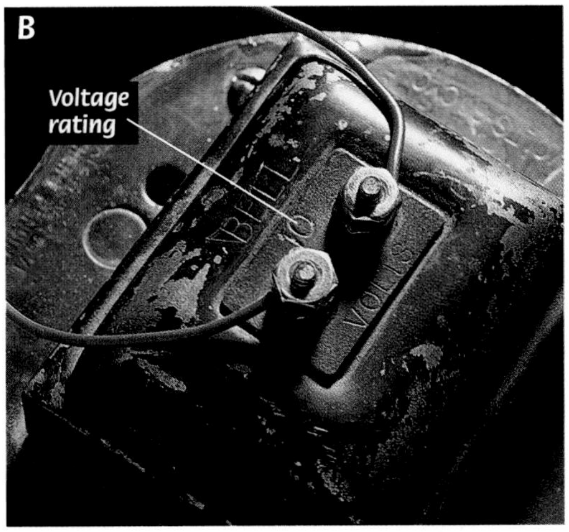

Identify the doorbell transformer by its voltage rating, which will be 20 volts or less.

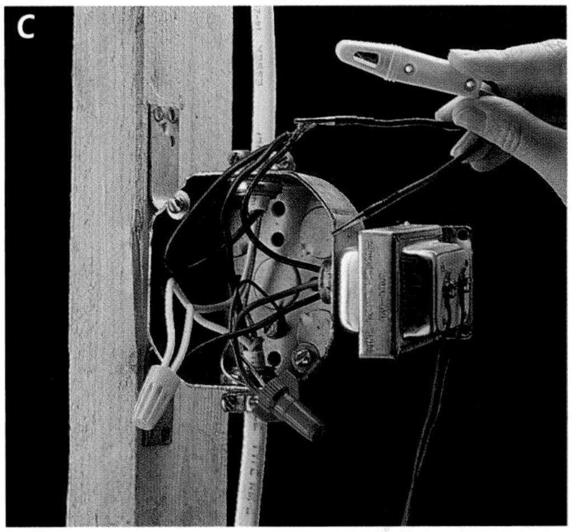

Use a circuit tester to check for power. Test the black wires first, then the white wires.

Check the wire connections and replace any taped connections with wire connectors.

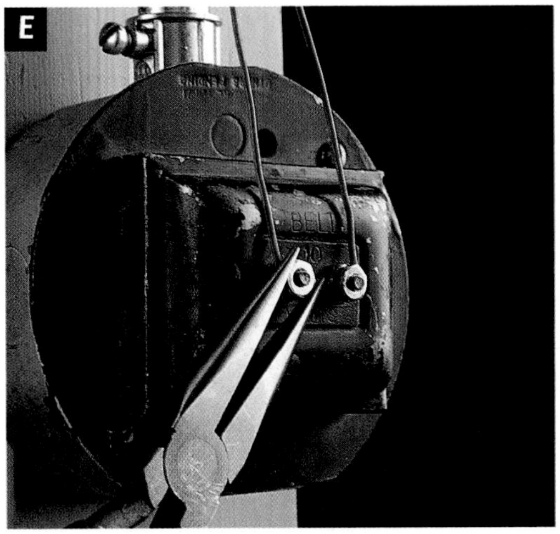

Check low-voltage wire connections on the face of the transformer. Reconnect loose wires, using needlenose pliers.

Touch the probes of a multi-tester to the low-voltage screw terminals on the transformer.

Replacing a Low-voltage Transformer

Before starting, turn off the power to the transformer at the service panel (page 395). Remove the coverplate from the electrical box.

Carefully remove the wire connector that joins the black circuit wire to the transformer lead **(photo A).** Don't touch any bare wires.

Touch one probe of a circuit tester to the grounded metal box and the other one to the wire ends. Repeat the test on the white wires. If the tester glows either time, there is still power to the box. Turn off the correct circuit at the service panel.

Disconnect the grounding wires inside the box, then the low-voltage wires from the transformer screw terminals **(photo B).**

Unscrew the transformer mounting bracket inside the box and remove the transformer.

Attach the new transformer to the electrical box. Connect the circuit wires to the transformer leads and the circuit grounding wires to the transformer grounding lead **(photo C).**

Connect the low-voltage wires to the transformer screw terminals. Replace the coverplate and restore power to the transformer.

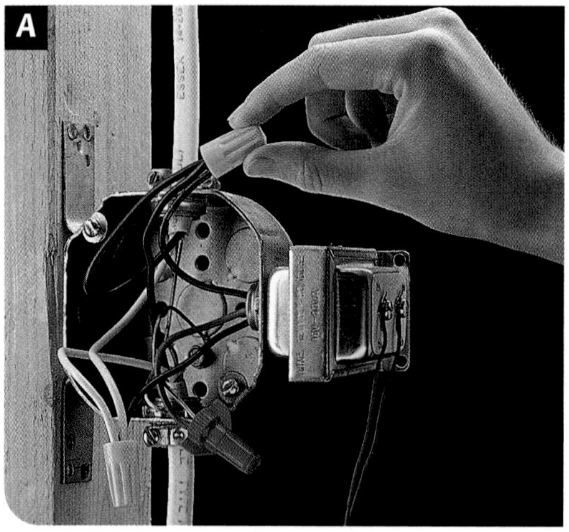

Remove the connector that joins the black wires.

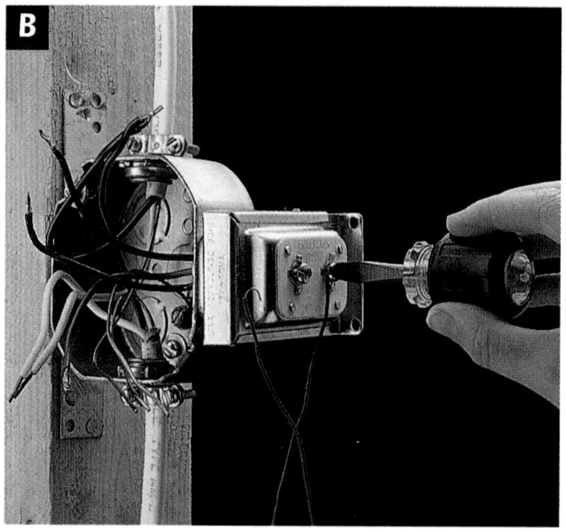

Disconnect all wires leading to the transformer.

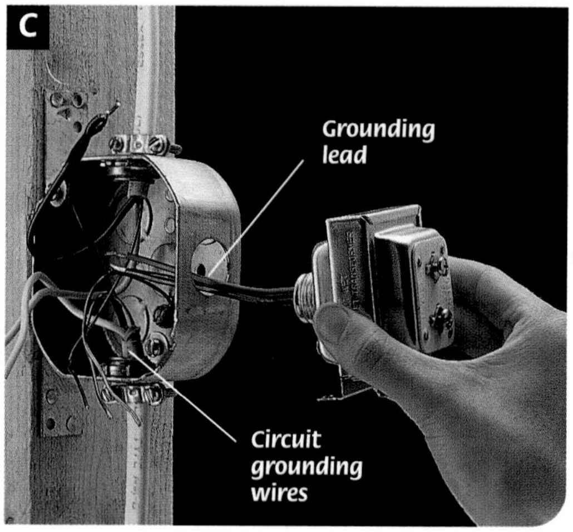

Connect the circuit wires and grounding wires.

Testing & Replacing a Chime Unit

If you find that the switches and the transformer are in good working order, but the doorbell still doesn't work, the problem must lie in the chime or in the low-voltage wires that lead to it.

Remove the decorative coverplate from the chime. Inspect its low-voltage wire connections and reconnect any loose wires **(photo D).**

Test the current with a multi-tester set to the 50-volt (AC) range. Touch one tester probe to the screw terminal marked TRANS or TRANSFORMER and the other to the terminal marked FRONT **(photo E).**

The multi-tester should detect a current within 2 volts of the transformer's rating. If it registers less power, there's a break in the low-voltage wiring. Repeat this test for the rear doorbell switch, moving the black probe to the REAR terminal.

Use the test results to determine if there is a breakage between the switches and the chime unit or between the chime unit and the transformer. Replace any broken wires.

If the current is reaching the chime unit but the doorbell won't ring, the chime plungers may be gummed up with lint and dirt. Clean them, using a cotton swab dipped in rubbing alcohol **(photo F).** Don't oil the plungers.

Test the unit by pushing one of the doorbell switches. If it still doesn't work, replace the chime unit with a new one that has the same voltage rating.

To replace the chime unit, turn off the power to the doorbell system at the main service panel (page 395).

Using masking tape, label the low-voltage wires to identify their screw terminal locations on the doorbell unit **(photo G).** Disconnect the wires.

Unscrew the mounting screws and remove the old chime unit **(photo H).**

Temporarily secure the low-voltage wires to the wall with masking tape to prevent them from slipping into the wall cavity **(photo I).**

Thread the low-voltage wires through the openings in the base of the new chime unit **(photo J).**

Attach the new chime unit to the wall, using the mounting screws and wall anchors included in the installation kit **(photo K).**

Connect the wires to the proper screw terminals with a screwdriver **(photo L).**

Attach the decorative coverplate to the new chime unit. Restore the power at the main service panel and test the operation of the doorbell.

Check wire connections. Reconnect loose wires to terminals.

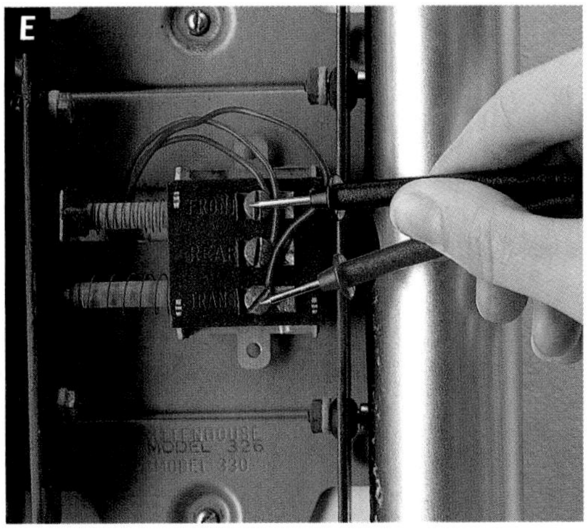

Test for current by holding multi-tester probes to terminals.

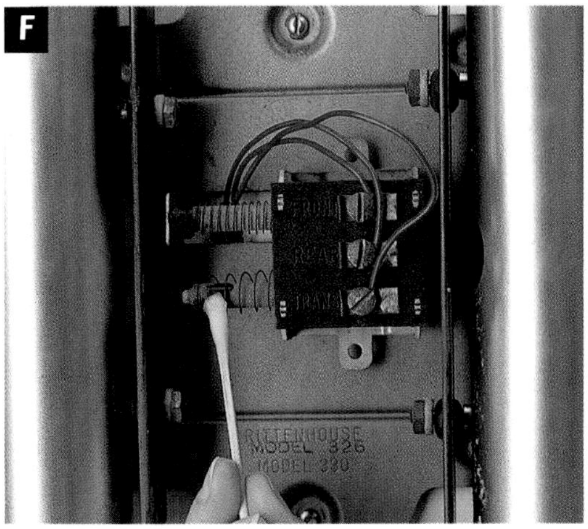

Clean chime plungers by swabbing with rubbing alcohol.

Label the low-voltage wires before disconnecting them.

Unscrew mounting screws and remove the old chime unit.

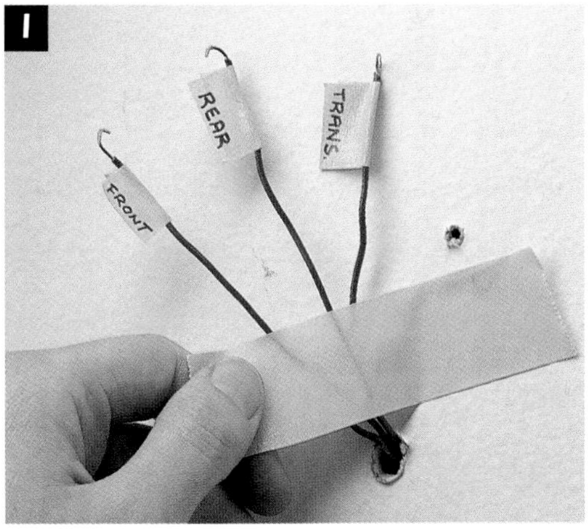

Tape wires to the wall so they won't slip into the wall cavity.

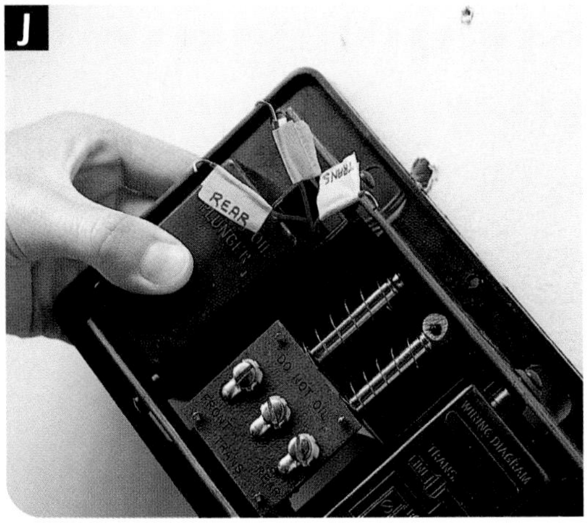

Thread the wires through hole in base of the new unit.

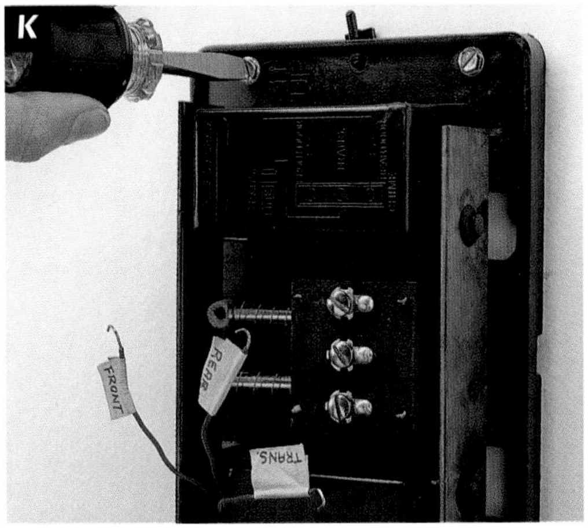

Anchor the unit base to the wall with mounting screws.

Connect the low-voltage wires to the proper screw terminals.

Telephones

Although the telephone company owns the wires that bring telephone service to your house, you're allowed to repair or add wiring for any part of the telephone system that extends past the company's *demarcation jack.* The demarcation jack is usually located in a basement or utility area, although it may also be mounted on a baseboard in a home's living quarters **(photo A).**

Because the voltage running through telephone wires is very low, there's little danger of shock when working on the wiring. Still, it's best not to work in wet conditions when repairing any wiring. Also, don't work on your phone system if you wear a cardiac pacemaker, because the mild electrical currents in phone lines can interfere with the device.

Common telephone repairs you can do yourself include replacing a loose or broken modular connector, installing a modular jack in place of an outdated jack, and installing a junction box that will let you run additional phone extensions anywhere in the house.

You can plug a phone directly into the demarcation jack to find out if a problem lies in the house wiring or in the phone company's wires and equipment. If you get no dial tone at the demarcation jack, the problem lies outside your home and should be fixed by the phone company. If you do get a dial tone, however, this means that any problem lies inside the house.

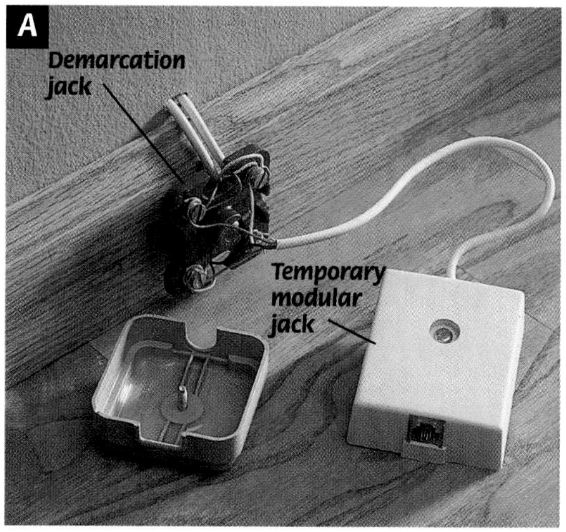

Connecting a modular jack to your home's demarcation jack allows you to diagnose the source of a line problem.

A Home Telephone System

This diagram shows the typical layout of a household telephone system. Your telephone company owns and maintains the wires entering your house up to the demarcation jack. The wiring and telephone outlets installed beyond this point throughout the house are your responsibility.

If your phone system is relatively new, there will probably be a wire distribution hub, or junction box, that feeds individual lines running to the various phone jacks in your house. This method of wiring phones is sometimes called the *home run* method. It's the best way to wire phones, because if one line becomes damaged, the other jacks will still operate. If your system has a junction box, you can easily add a new jack by running new wires from this junction box.

Older phone systems sometimes use a *continuous loop* method, in which the various phone jacks are installed along a single loop of wire running through the house. Although it's easier to install, a continuous loop system is less reliable, since a single problem in the wire can render all the jacks inoperable.

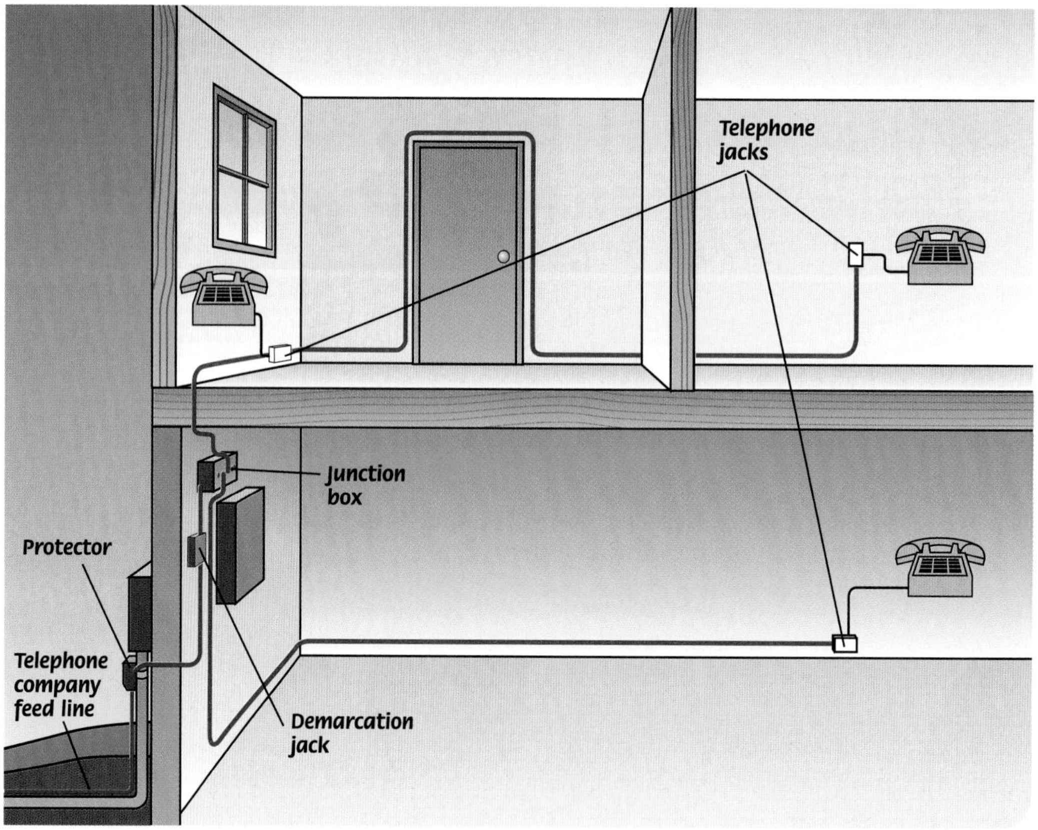

Troubleshooting Phone Problems

Problems	Possible Causes	Solutions
Dead air; no sound on line.	Wires may be crossed.	Make sure bare copper wires inside jack aren't touching.
Static on line.	Wires may be wet. Wire connections may be loose.	Check for moisture in phone jacks. Check all connections.
Buzzing on line.	Wires may be touching metal. Wires may be connected to wrong terminals.	Check all wires and connections. Check color coding of connections.

Replacing a Modular Connector

Over time, the modular connectors that join a telephone to the wall jack can become loose and worn. To replace the snap-in modular connectors on a telephone, you'll need a crimper tool and a package of inexpensive plastic connectors.

Remove the telephone cord from the wall jack and telephone. Use wire cutters to snip off the cord just below the connector you're replacing **(photo B).** Make sure to trim the cord at a straight angle.

Insert the cord into the stripper section of the tool, then squeeze the handle to sever the outer insulation. Tug on the cord to pull the wires free of the insulation **(photo C).** Make sure not to cut the inner insulation on the individual wires.

Push the individual wires into a plastic connector until they're flush with the tip of the connector and touching the metal contacts. It's important to insert the wires so the sequence is opposite from that at the connectors for the opposite end of the cord.

Insert the modular connector and cord into the matching slot on the crimper tool, then squeeze the handles of the tool and hold them in place for a few seconds to secure the connector to the wires **(photo D).**

Tools: Crimper tool, wire cutters.

Materials: Modular phone connectors.

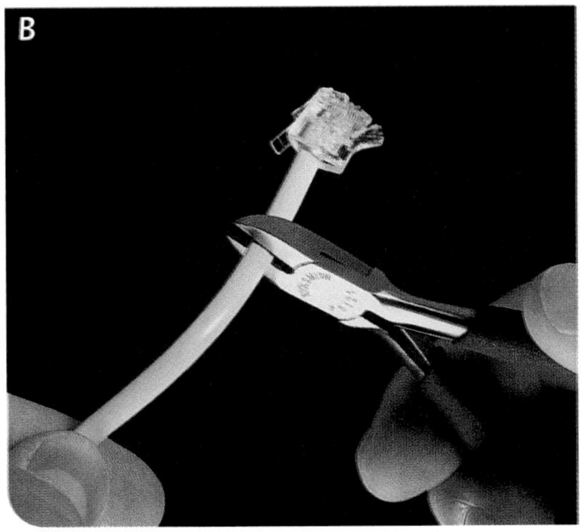

Remove the telephone cord from the phone line. Clip the end of the cord, using wire cutters.

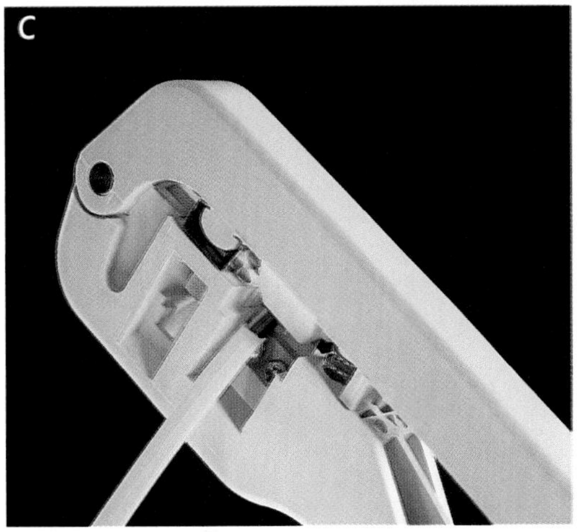

Insert the end of the cord into the stripper section of the crimper, and strip the outer sheathing from the cord.

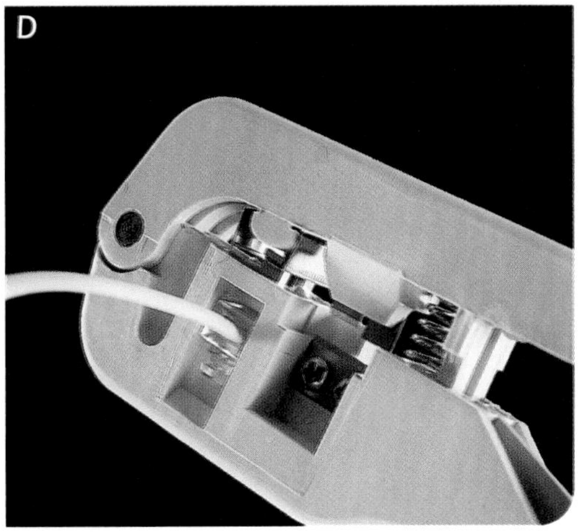

Insert the stripped end into a connector fitting and place it in the matching slot on the crimper. Squeeze the handle.

Installing a Modular Jack

Modern phone systems use snap-in modular jacks to make it easy to relocate telephones, answering machines, and modems. But, modular jacks can wear out and require replacement. Also, if your telephone wiring is old, you may have outdated jacks that won't accept modular cords, and it's a good idea to replace old jacks with modular jacks.

To install a modular jack, start by disconnecting the phone cord from the jack. Unscrew the phone jack from the wall or baseboard, using a screwdriver. Gently pull the jack away from the wall **(photo A).**

Disconnect the individual wires from the terminals on the jack. Clip off the bare copper ends of the wire, using wire cutters **(photo B).**

Remove the casing from the connection block on the new modular jack and feed the phone cables through the back of the base piece. Force each colored wire into one of the metal slots on the terminal block that has a wire of the same color **(photo C).** About 1/2" of wire should extend through the slot.

Most phone cords have four wires: red, green, yellow, and black, but there are two other possible color schemes. Use the following as a guide to connecting the wires:

The red terminal will accept:
- a red wire
- a blue wire
- a blue wire with white stripe

The green terminal will accept:
- a green wire
- a white wire with blue stripe

The yellow terminal will accept:
- a yellow wire
- an orange wire
- an orange wire with white stripe

The black terminal will accept:
- a black wire
- a white wire with orange stripe

If there are extra wires in the cord (usually these will be green and white), they can be tucked into the jack and left unconnected. The phone company will use these wires to connect additional phone lines if you should ever need them.

Screw the connection block to the wall with the screw included with the jack, and snap the coverplate in place **(photo D).** Attach a phone to the new jack and test to make sure it works.

Tools: *Crimper tool, wire cutters.*
Materials: *Modular jack.*

Helpful Hint

This is a good time to add new jacks and extend your phone line. Just attach additional jacks where you want them, then run cable between them and connect the wires as you did on the first jack.

A
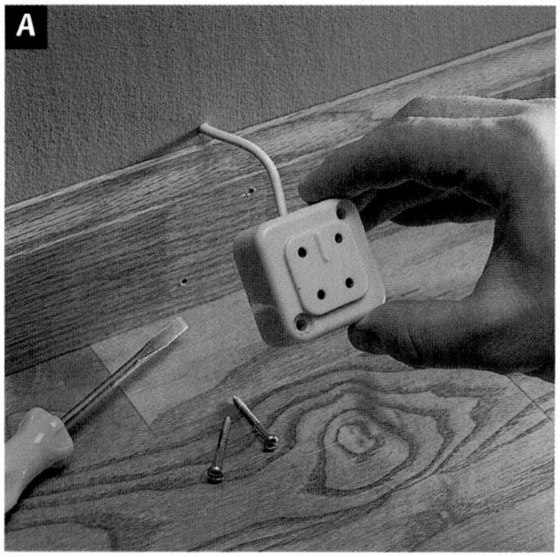
Remove the coverplate from the old phone jack and unscrew the jack from the wall.

B
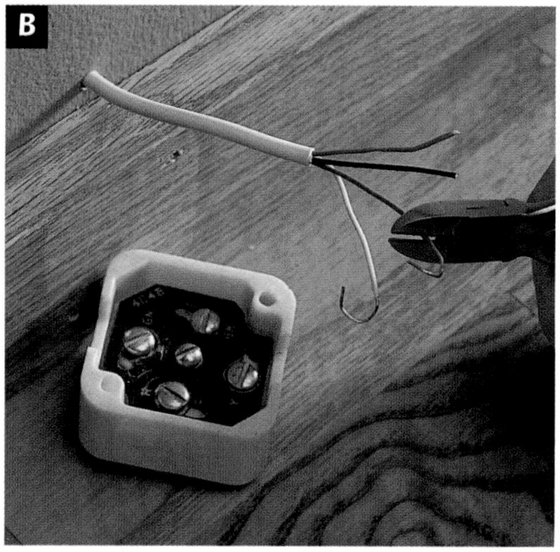
Disconnect the wires from the jack. Clip the bare copper ends of the wires, using a crimper tool or wire cutter.

C
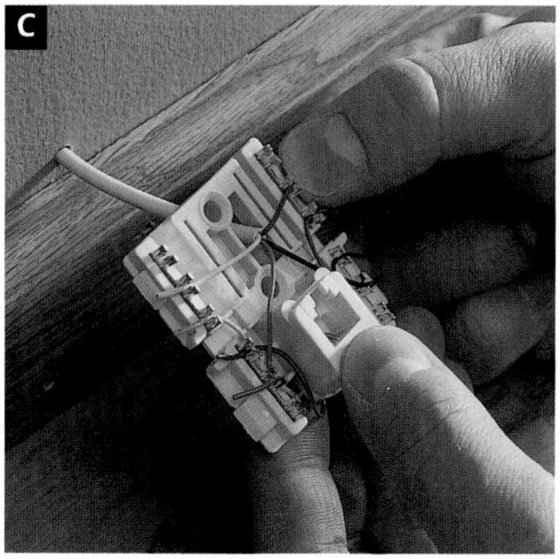
Feed the phone cables through the back of the jack. Force each colored wire into one of the slots on the terminal block.

D
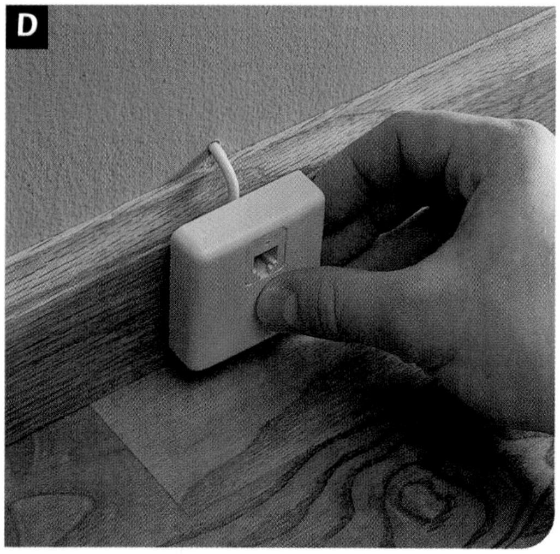
Screw the connection block to the wall. Snap the cover onto the new jack, and test to make sure it's working.

Installing a Telephone Junction Box

If your phone system doesn't already have a junction box, adding one will make it much easier to rewire the system or add phone extensions in the future.

The best place to connect a junction box is directly to the demarcation jack, usually located near the point where the phone wires enter the home. Sometimes the demarcation jack is on an outside wall of the house, but usually it's located in a basement or utility area.

Start by selecting a location that's close enough to the demarcation jack to be reached by the cable for the junction box. Snap off the cover of the junction box. Attach the box to a wall, baseboard, or framing member, using the mounting screws that are included with it **(photo E).**

Run telephone cable to the demarcation jack, securing it to the wall or framing members with staples every 2 ft. NOTE: Some junction boxes have an attached cord with a modular connector that can be plugged directly into a demarcation jack.

Trim off all but 5" of the cable at the demarcation jack end, and strip off 3" of the outer insulation from the cable, using a crimper. Strip away 1" of inner insulation from each of the four individual wires, using a utility knife. Loop the bare copper wires in a clockwise direction around the demarcation jack screw terminals coded for the matching color. Tighten the screws.

At the the junction box end of the cable, strip 3" of outer insulation from the cable, using a crimper tool. Take care not to strip or damage the insulation on the individual wires.

Loosen one terminal screw on each of the four color-coded sections of the junction box. Insert each wire into a slot in the corresponding section. About 1/2" of wire should extend through the slot **(photo F).**

For each phone extension line, attach the cable to the junction box **(photo G)** following the same procedure used for the cable running to the demarcation jack. Screw the terminals down tight, then bend the wires upright so they don't touch each other. Snap the cover back on the junction box.

***Tools:** Crimper tool, utility knife, screwdriver.*

***Materials:** Junction box with mounting screws, telephone cable, wire staples.*

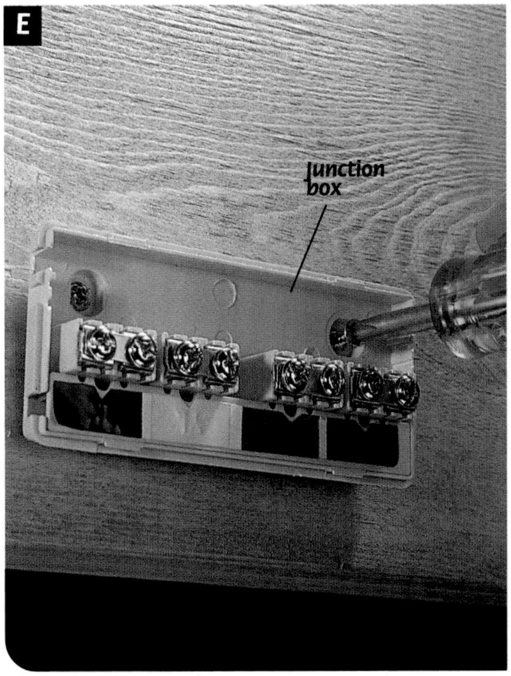

Attach the junction box to a wall or framing member within easy reach of the demarcation jack.

Strip the wires on the junction box and attach them to the screw terminals on the demarcation jack.

Connect the cables for each phone extension to the slotted terminals in the junction box.

Heating, Ventilation & Air Conditioning

Heating, ventilation, and air conditioning (HVAC) comprise one of the fundamental systems that make a house livable. If some rooms in your house are too hot or too cold or have humidity problems, you are likely to spend much of your time in other rooms. A well-maintained HVAC system keeps the temperature and humidity at comfortable levels throughout the house, regardless of outside weather changes.

In most houses, heating begins at a furnace or boiler, where heat is released from burning fuel and transferred to air or water. The air or water is then circulated through a series of ducts or pipes to registers, radiators, or convectors that warm the individual rooms.

Ventilation ensures a supply of fresh air in the house and can help regulate both temperature and humidity. Without proper ventilation, a house can feel stale, and gases such as radon and carbon monoxide can rise to dangerous levels.

Central air-conditioning systems lower the temperature by capturing heat in a refrigerant and transferring it outside the house while circulating cooled air through the furnace ducts to the rooms. Window air conditioners function the same way for an individual room or area. A heat pump operates on the same principle as an air conditioner, with the advantage that it can act as either a cooling unit or a heating unit, extracting heat from cool outdoor air during cold weather, and removing heat from indoor air during hot weather. The following pages offer instructions on basic maintenance procedures and essential HVAC repairs.

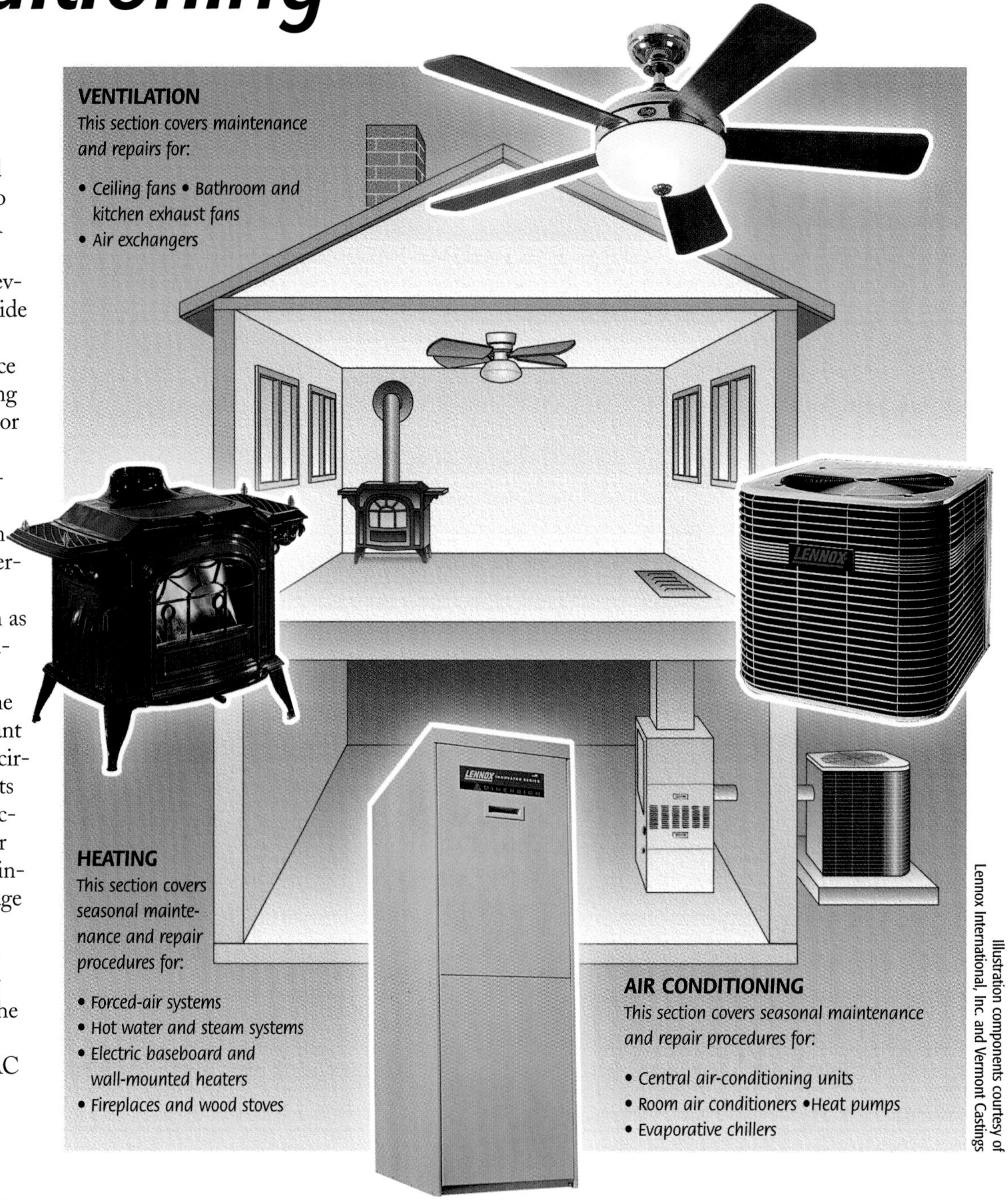

VENTILATION
This section covers maintenance and repairs for:
- *Ceiling fans • Bathroom and kitchen exhaust fans*
- *Air exchangers*

HEATING
This section covers seasonal maintenance and repair procedures for:
- *Forced-air systems*
- *Hot water and steam systems*
- *Electric baseboard and wall-mounted heaters*
- *Fireplaces and wood stoves*

AIR CONDITIONING
This section covers seasonal maintenance and repair procedures for:
- *Central air-conditioning units*
- *Room air conditioners • Heat pumps*
- *Evaporative chillers*

Illustration components courtesy of Lennox International, Inc. and Vermont Castings

HVAC Health & Safety Issues

Public health studies have shown that some of the worst air pollution we encounter is inside our own homes. Because you probably spend far more time indoors than out, you should be aware of the way your heating and cooling systems can affect your health.

A familiar hazard associated with heating systems is asbestos, which was used to insulate heating pipes and ducts **(photo A)** for many years. Asbestos was also used in wallboard, joint compound, shingles, floor tiles, chimney flues, and many other fire-resistant surfaces. When asbestos is stable, it poses no threat to health. But when disrupted, it's apt to release microscopic fibers that can cause skin irritation or respiratory problems, including lung cancer. If you're concerned about the presence of asbestos in your house, ask a certified asbestos abatement specialist to inspect it.

For several years, building materials—from particleboard and insulation to carpeting, paneling, and furniture—contained formaldehyde.

Radon gas, which is odorless and colorless, occurs naturally in some areas. Radon can penetrate basement floors and walls, and its presence can only be reduced, not eliminated. Kits **(photo B)** are available that allow you to test for radon. The most common means of reducing radon is to seal basement floors and walls, and ventilate crawl spaces.

Pollens, viruses, bacteria, and other respiratory and skin irritants may not seem related to heating and cooling systems. But some microorganisms grow in areas that are poorly ventilated or insulated. Many of these organic hazards can be reduced with the use of an electrostatic furnace filter or an air exchanger **(photo C).**

Carbon monoxide (CO), a by-product of combustion, is a common health hazard. CO poisoning can be fatal. Often, the first signs are dizziness, headache, nausea, and drowsiness. Leaks in exhaust flues, chimneys, gas ranges, wood stoves, and fireplaces are potential sources of CO **(photo D).** To minimize your chances of being exposed to unsafe levels, have your furnace or boiler inspected every two years, and use a UL-approved CO detector **(photo E).**

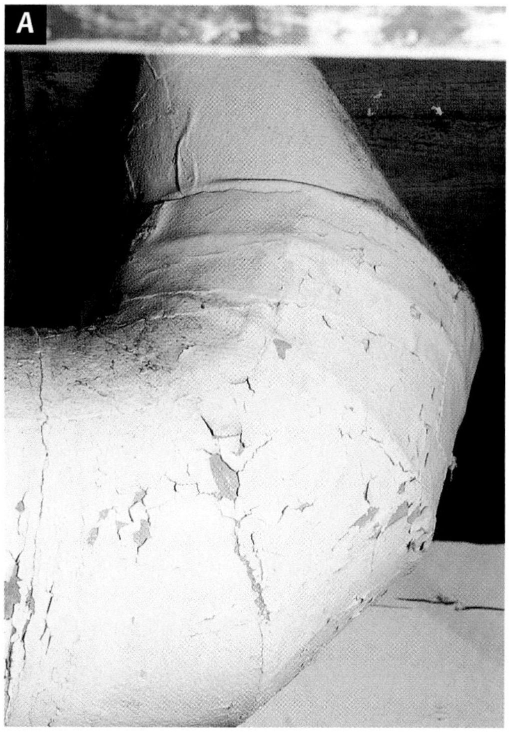

Avoid handling materials that contain asbestos, and call an asbestos abatement specialist if the material has been disturbed or appears to be loose or crumbling.

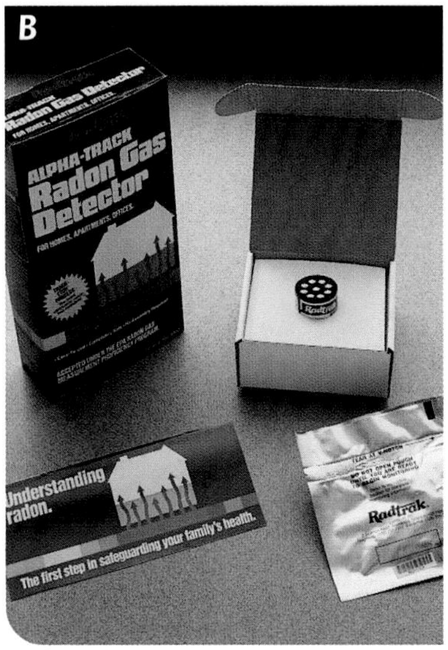

Radon gas can be detected with a home detection kit available at home centers. An abatement specialist can show you ways to reduce radon's presence to tolerable levels.

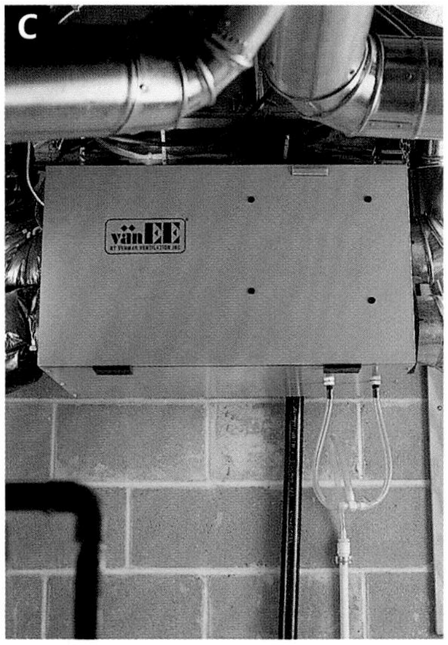

An air exchanger supplies fresh air with minimal heat loss. It can eliminate many of the airborne irritants and pollutants common in superinsulated homes.

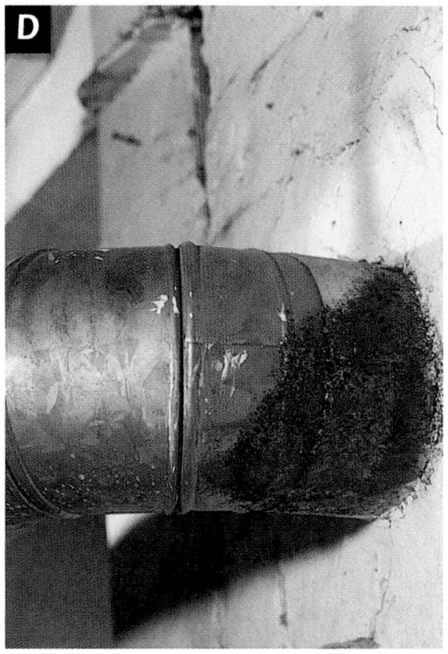

A damaged flue is a likely source of carbon monoxide in the home. Replace the damaged section and seal it well.

Use an approved CO detector, and have your heating system checked every two years for carbon monoxide levels.

Heating

Heating your home would be extremely costly and inefficient if your heating system was always heating cold outdoor air. To avoid this, modern heating systems recycle the water or air that is used to heat your home. Previously warmed air or water can then be reheated to compensate for the gradual cooling that occurs as it is circulated throughout your home. The illustration (right) shows the basic cycle of a common heating system. A furnace burns fuel supplied from a storage tank or utility line to heat air or water. Exhaust from the combustion process is carried away through a chimney or vent. A delivery system, made up of air ducts or pipes, carries warm air, hot water, or steam to most rooms in the house. Room registers, radiators, or convectors circulate the air or water in each room. They also provide a means for cooled air or water to return to the furnace, where it can be reheated and recycled.

Although some modern heating systems use high-tech materials and elaborate delivery methods—radiant heat, for example, relies on a labyrinth of thermoplastic tubes or electric heating cable installed in the floor or ceiling—such systems are seldom easy for homeowners to reach or repair. Most homes in the United States use furnaces or boilers that burn natural gas, liquid propane, or oil, and deliver heat through ductwork or pipes.

To keep your heating system functioning as it should, and to avoid inconvenient or expensive failures, make preventive maintenance a seasonal practice. A clean thermocouple and burner tubes will add greatly to the efficiency of a gas furnace. An oil burner that is clean and well oiled will give you years of reliable service.

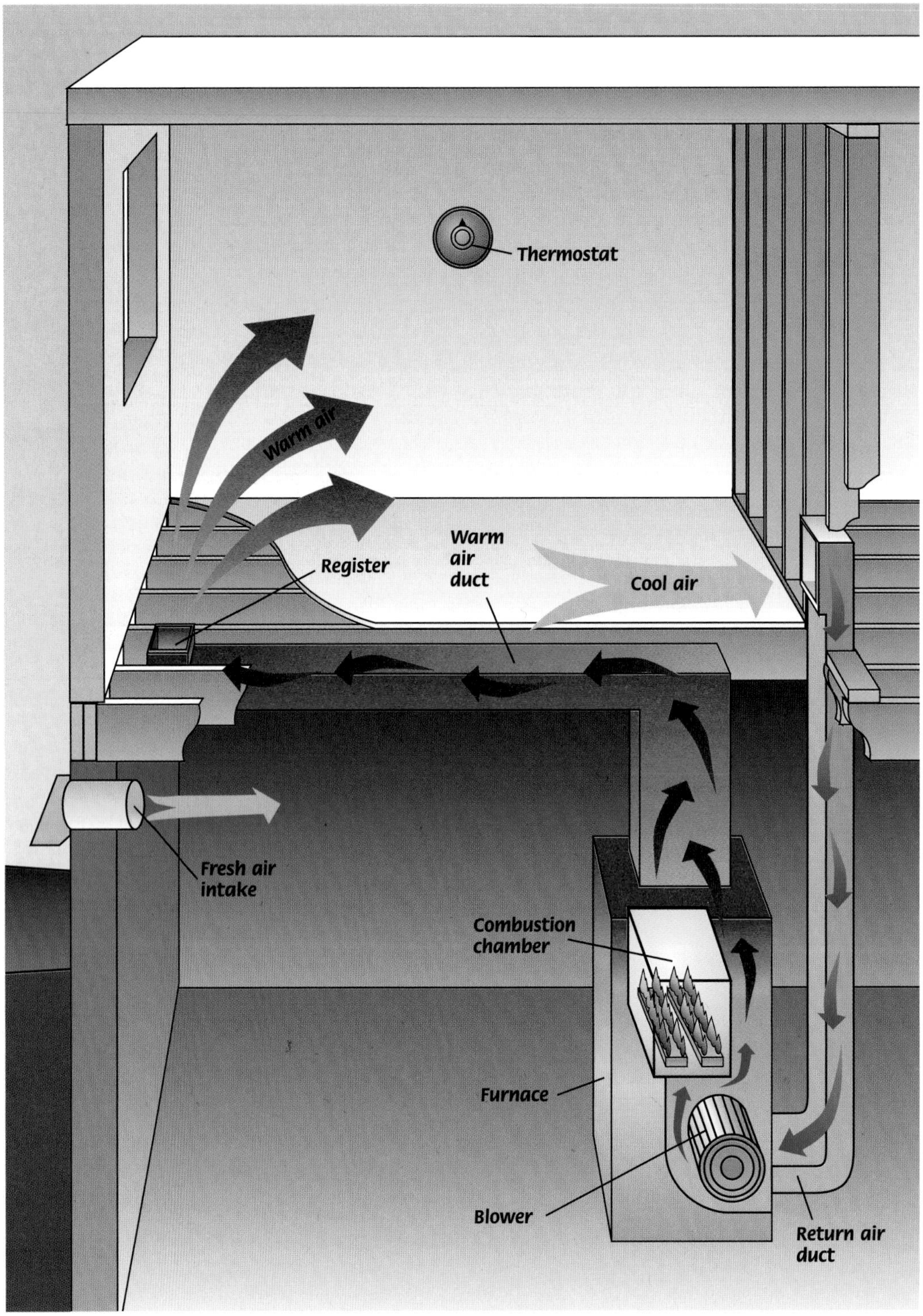

Modern heating systems recirculate heated air or water. Many use a fresh air intake to ensure an adequate supply of fresh air in the home.

Tools & Materials

Tools for heating repairs include refractory furnace cement for sealing furnace leaks (1); circuit tester (2); funnel, for pouring rust inhibitor and other liquids (3); multitester, for testing electrical devices for continuity (4); pipe wrench, for tightening large fittings (5); light machine oil, for lubricating moving parts (6); utility bucket, for draining a boiler and bleeding radiators and convectors (7); garden hose, for flushing a heating system (8); nut drivers, ratchet wrenches, open-end wrenches, and screwdrivers, for tightening nuts, bolts, and screws on furnaces, flues, dampers, and small appliances (9); pocket thermometer, for checking duct temperature (10); fin comb, for straightening fins on a heat pump or air conditioner (11); chisel, for removing humidifier deposits (12); broad-billed pliers, for straightening convector fins (13); and pilot jet tool, for clearing a thermocouple tip (14).

Common Heating Systems

The most common method of home heating is the use of air warmed by a furnace and forced through ducts that carry it to the rooms in the house. This method is known as forced air heat (pages 454 to 463). It is one of three major heating methods (forced air, hot water and steam, and electric) covered in this book. Forced air is, by far, the most common form of home heat, because it uses natural gas or liquid propane, which are generally more affordable than other fuels.

Hot water and steam heat, although rarely installed today, are still found in many older homes (pages 464 to 469). They rely on a boiler-type furnace that typically burns natural gas or oil and delivers hot water or steam to room radiators or convectors.

Electricity is used as a primary method of home heating, mainly in regions with very mild winters. In cold climates, electric heat may be a supplemental heat source (pages 470 to 475). Electric baseboard or wall-mounted heaters are often used to heat room additions or small areas that do not receive adequate heat from the furnace or boiler.

Wood is an inexpensive and widely available heating fuel (pages 476 to 477). With proper maintenance, today's wood stoves and fireplaces burn far more cleanly and efficiently than older models.

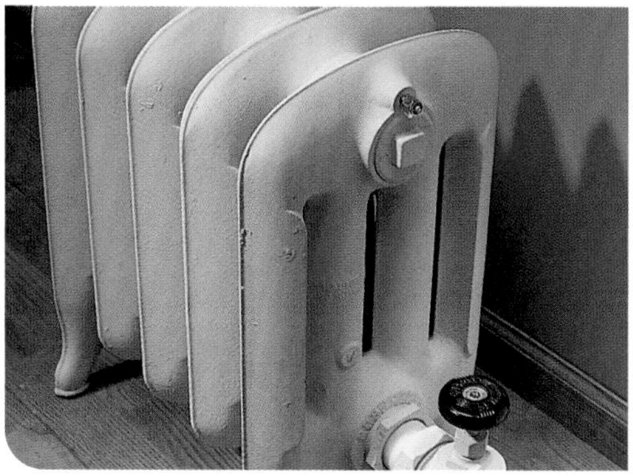

Hot water and steam radiators require little maintenance other than occasional bleeding to release trapped air.

Room registers that circulate warm air from the furnace work best if they're removed and cleaned seasonally.

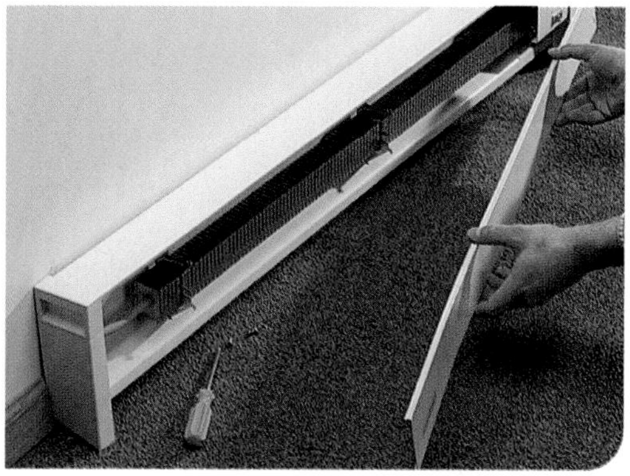

Baseboard electric heaters should be cleaned at the start of the heating season to remove dust from the heating element.

Gas Forced-air Systems

Gas forced-air systems are widely used in cool climates worldwide. A gas forced-air furnace—running on natural gas or liquid propane (LP)—draws in surrounding air, channels it across a set of heated plates, known as a *heat exchanger,* and then uses a blower to circulate the air throughout the house **(illustration).** A chamber on top of the furnace, known as a *plenum,* leads the warmed air from the furnace to a network of ducts **(photo A)** that carry the warm air to heat registers or vents mounted on walls or ceilings. To keep the cycle going, *return ducts* carry cooled air from each room back to the furnace so it can be reheated and recirculated. Older systems use gravity to carry warm air throughout the house and cool air back to the furnace.

Advances in home design have required some changes in today's forced-air systems. Conventional forced-air heat operates by recycling indoor air. In drafty older homes, this worked well since fresh air trickled in from outdoors. Problems arise in newer, superinsulated homes, where air contaminants can be constantly recirculated, causing respiratory ailments and other health problems. Many Building Codes now require a fresh air intake in new construction to reduce such hazards. Some homes use a heat recovery ventilator, which improves air quality without significant heat loss by drawing prewarmed outdoor air into the system.

Builders have also begun installing high-velocity (HV) forced-air systems. These systems increase living space by using small-diameter tubes that require far less space in ceilings and walls than sheet-metal ducts.

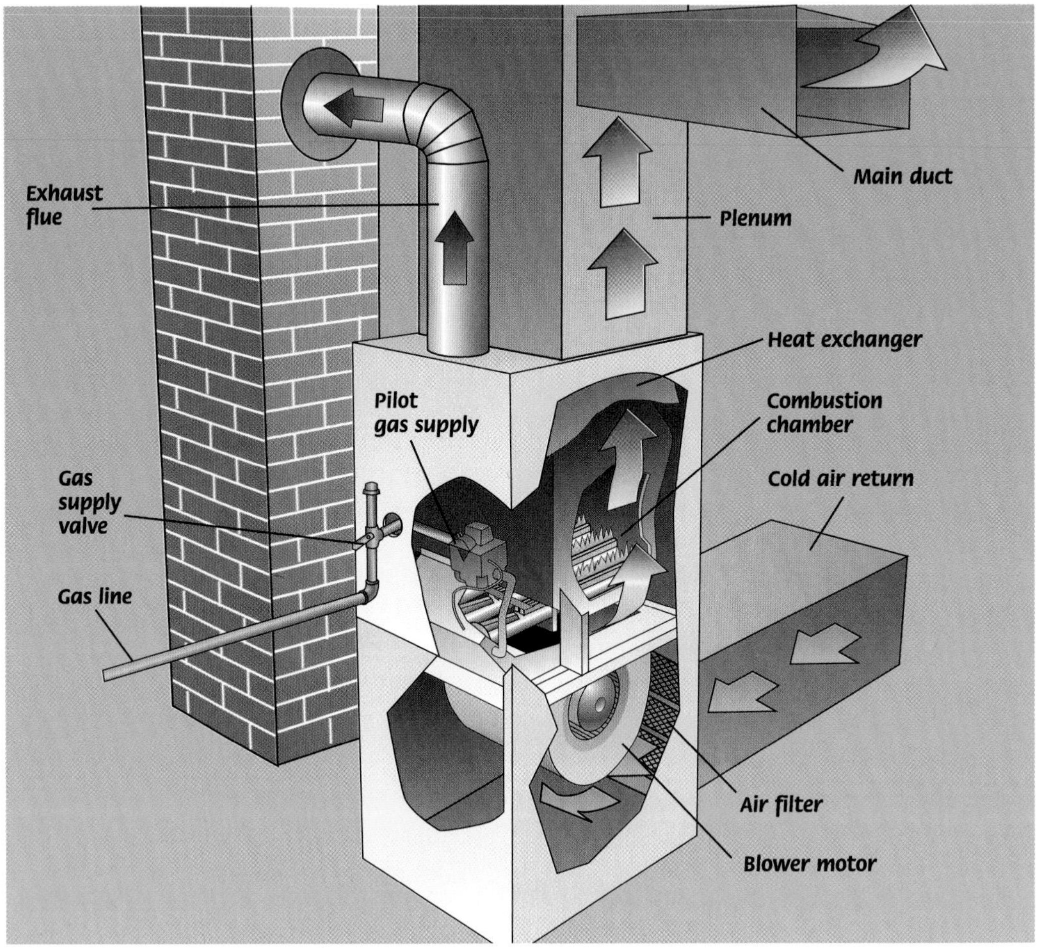

Identifying the plenum and cold air return, as well as the main duct leading to the rooms in your home, is a good way to begin familiarizing yourself with your forced-air system.

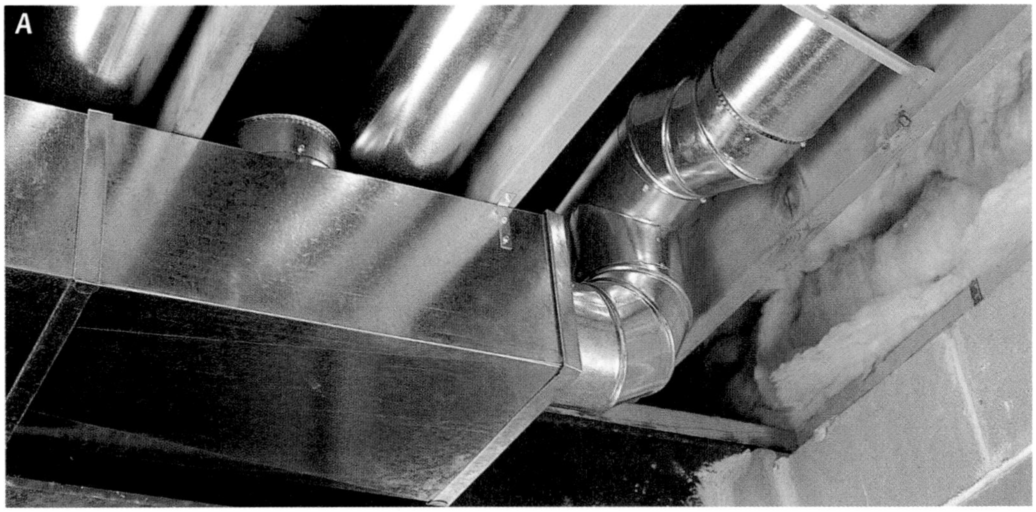

Most modern homes use a forced-air heating system that includes either ductwork (above) or space-saving high velocity tubes. Many systems also include a built-in humidifier and air conditioner that rely on the same delivery network.

Balancing a Forced-air System

Most forced-air systems have dampers within the ducts that let you control how much air flows to various parts of the house. These are separate from the registers used to manage airflow within each room. Adjusting the dampers one at a time ensures that rooms farthest from the furnace receive enough warm air, and that rooms closest to the furnace don't get too hot. This is called *balancing* the system.

Balancing a forced-air system is relatively easy, but it takes time—often several days—to fine-tune your adjustments. Start by locating the dampers **(illustration).** When a damper handle or wing nut is parallel to the duct, it is wide open, allowing maximum airflow. When the handle is perpendicular to the duct, it is closed **(photo B),** restricting air flow as much as possible. If your system has no dampers, or needs more dampers than it has, you can make and install them yourself or hire a professional to do it.

To balance your system, start by setting the thermostat as you would for the times when you're at home. Close the dampers that lead to the room with the thermostat. Wait a few hours, and go to the rooms that are farthest from the furnace. If those rooms are too warm, leave them until later, when more dampers are open; if they're too cold, ask an HVAC professional to increase the blower speed on the furnace. Check the other rooms for comfort. After each damper adjustment, wait a few hours for the air temperature to stabilize.

Once you're satisfied with the amount of air and heat each room receives, use a permanent marker on each duct to indicate the correct setting for each damper **(photo C).** Repeat the process in the summer for air conditioning, making a second set of marks to indicate the correct damper settings for cooling.

Open or close the damper by inserting a standard screwdriver in the damper handle or by turning the damper wing nut.

Mark damper positions for summer and winter on the side of each duct, and indicate which room is affected by the settings.

Maintaining a Forced-air System

You can handle most routine furnace maintenance yourself. Generally, the newer the furnace, the simpler the maintenance, since a number of heavy-maintenance components have been eliminated on newer models.

Most furnaces installed since the 1980s do not have a thermocouple-controlled pilot light. In fact, the standing pilot light found on older furnaces has been eliminated completely. In most cases, it's been replaced with either an intermittent pilot light that's lit only when there's a call for heat from the thermostat, or a glowing element, known as a *hot-surface igniter.* An intermittent pilot light must be repaired by a professional technician, should it fail. You can replace a hot-surface igniter yourself.

Use this section to identify and complete the maintenance procedures that apply to the furnace in your home.

Before doing any maintenance, always turn off the furnace's main gas supply and the pilot gas supply, if your furnace has a separate one. Then, switch off the furnace's main power switch and the power to the furnace at the main service panel. Check your owner's manual for any warnings or special instructions concerning your furnace. Then, clear the area, so you have a safe work space.

Start with the most important and simplest furnace maintenance procedure—inspecting the air filter. There are many types of filters. Read the section below to find out how to clean yours and how often it must be changed.

Tools: *Standard screwdriver, ratchet wrench, nut driver, open-end wrench set, straightedge, channel-type pliers, pilot jet tool, parts brush.*

Materials: *Mild liquid detergent, light machine oil.*

Replacing the Air Filter

The air filter on your forced-air furnace is designed to capture dust, pollen, and other airborne particles that would otherwise recirculate whenever the furnace blower is on. The filter must be cleaned regularly, according to the manufacturer's specifications, and should be inspected once a month. Locate the filter compartment and remove the access cover **(photo A).** The location of the compartment depends on the furnace type and the style of filter. Many filters fit in a slot between the return air duct and blower. A few styles are located inside the main furnace compartment. An electrostatic filter is installed in a separate unit attached to the furnace.

Slide the filter out of its compartment, taking care not to catch it on the sides of the blower housing. Hold the filter up to a light **(photo B).** If the filter blocks much of the light, replace it. Electrostatic filters can be reused after cleaning. Always read the manufacturer's instructions for your filter.

A

Many filters are located between the return air duct and the blower, and rest in a slot or bracket.

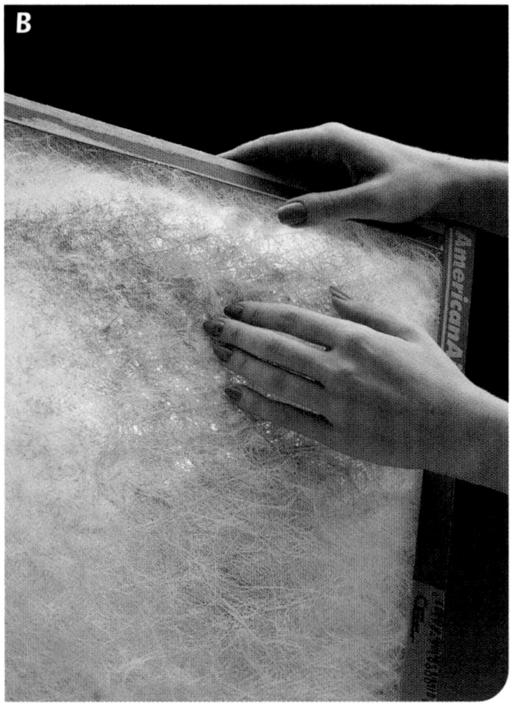

B

Hold the filter up to a bright light for inspection.

Maintaining the Blower Motor

Inspect the blower motor before the start of the heating season. Inspect it again before the start of the cooling season if your central air conditioning uses the same blower.

Turn off the power to the furnace. Remove the access panel to the blower housing and inspect the motor **(photo C).** Some motors have oil ports and an adjustable, replaceable drive belt. Others are self-lubricating and have a direct-drive mechanism. Wipe the motor clean with a damp cloth and check for oil fill ports. The access panel may include a diagram indicating their location. Remove the covers to the ports (if equipped) and add a few drops of light machine oil **(photo D).** Place the covers on the ports.

With the power still off, inspect the drive belt. If it is cracked, worn, glazed, or brittle, replace it. Check the belt tension by pushing down gently midway between the motor pulley and blower pulley **(photo E).** The belt should flex about an inch. To tighten or loosen the belt, locate the pulley tension adjustment nut on the blower motor **(photo F).** Loosen the locknut, and turn the adjustment nut slightly. Check the belt tension, and readjust as required until the tension is correct.

If the belt is out of alignment or the bearings are worn, adjusting the belt tension will not solve the problem. With the power off, hold a straightedge so it's flush with the edge of both pulleys **(photo G).** To align the belt, locate the motor mounting bolts on the motor's sliding bracket **(photo H).** Loosen the bolts, and move the motor carefully until the pulleys are aligned. Tighten the bolts and check the belt tension and alignment again. Repeat until the pulley is aligned and the tension is adjusted. Replace the furnace access panels that have been removed. Restore power at the main service panel and switch on the furnace.

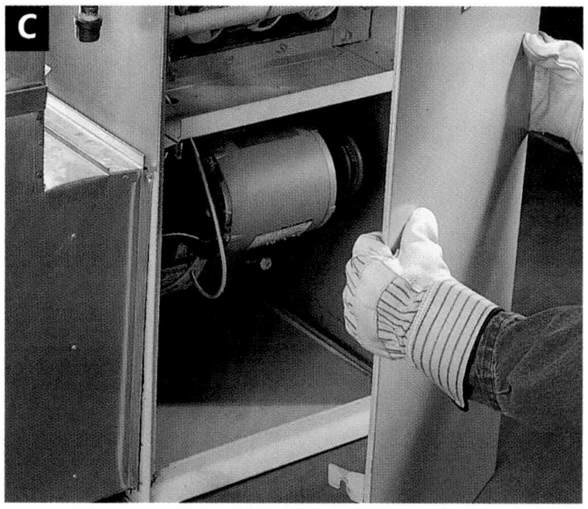
C

Remove the access panel to the blower housing and inspect the motor.

D

Remove the covers to the oil ports and add a few drops to each port.

E

Check the tension by pushing down on the middle of the belt.

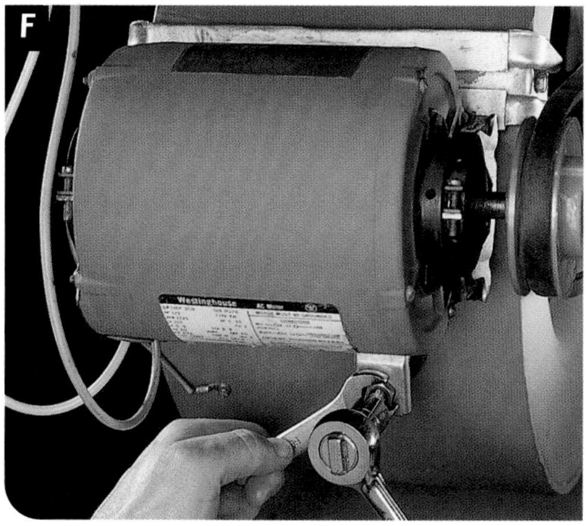
F

Loosen the pulley tension adjustment nut slightly to tighten the belt.

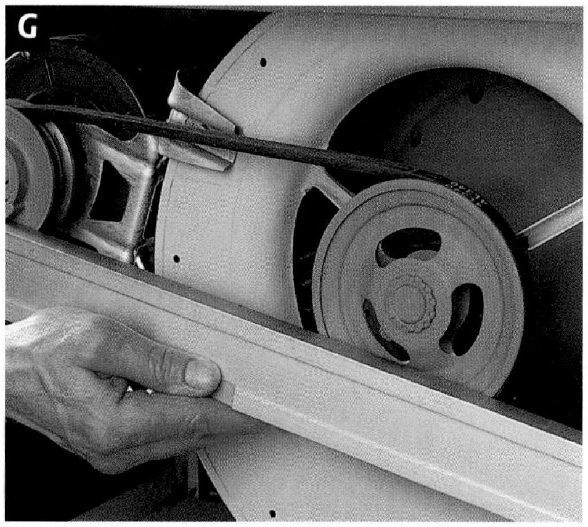
G

Check the pulley alignment, using a straightedge.

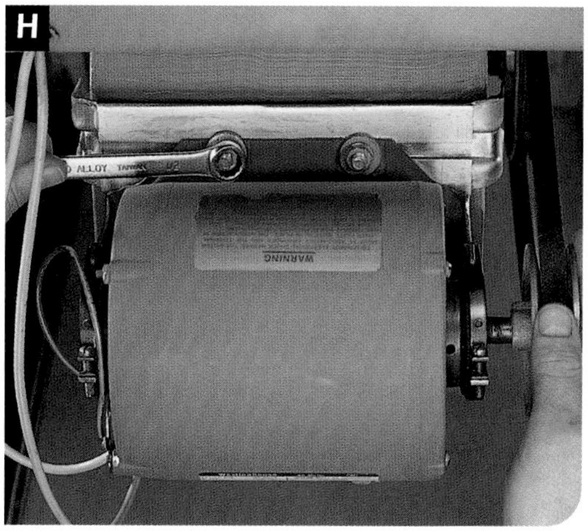
H

Loosen the bolts that hold the motor on its sliding bracket, and move the motor carefully until the pulleys are aligned.

Inspecting the Pilot & Thermocouple

Every part of the heating system depends on a correct pilot light setting. The pilot light (it's actually a flame used to ignite gas flowing through the burners) plays a large role in the efficiency of the entire system, and a clean-burning pilot saves money, improves indoor air quality, and extends furnace life.

If your furnace has a standing pilot light, always check the flame before the start of the heating season to ensure that it's burning cleanly and with the proper mix of air and fuel. Start by removing the main furnace access panel. If you can't see the pilot flame clearly, turn off the gas supply **(photo A)** and the pilot gas shutoff switch (if equipped). Wait 10 minutes for the pilot to cool, and remove the pilot cover. Relight the pilot, following the instructions on the control housing or access cover. If the pilot won't stay lit, shut off the gas supply once again and inspect the thermocouple.

Once the pilot is burning, inspect the flame **(photo B).** If the flame is too weak (left flame), it will be blue and may barely touch the thermocouple. If the flame is too strong (center flame), it will also be blue, but may be noisy and lift off the pilot. A well-adjusted flame (right flame) will be blue with a yellow tip, and cover 1/2" at the end of the thermocouple. Turn the pilot adjustment screw **(photo C)** on the control housing or gas valve to reduce the gas pressure. If it's weak, turn the screw in the other direction to increase the gas pressure. If the flame appears weak and yellow even after adjustment, remove the pilot jet and clean the orifice (page 459).

The thermocouple creates an electrical charge from the heat of the pilot flame. If the pilot in your furnace or boiler goes out quickly, and you have made sure the gas supply is sufficient, you may need to replace the thermocouple. Turn off the gas supply. Using an open-end wrench, loosen the thermocouple tube fitting from the control housing or gas valve. Unscrew the thermocouple from the pilot housing and install a new one **(photo D).** Tighten it with a wrench just until it's snug.

Turn off the main gas supply and the pilot gas supply (if your furnace has a separate one).

Adjust the flame so it is steady, has a yellow tip, and covers the thermocouple's tip (right).

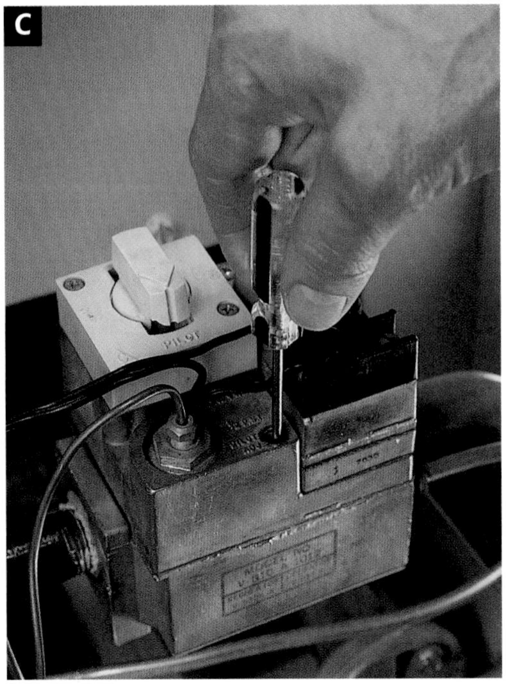

Turn the screw to adjust the height of the flame so it covers the top of the thermocouple.

Remove the thermocouple from the control housing and install a new one.

Cleaning & Adjusting the Pilot Light

If the thermocouple and burners in your furnace or boiler appear to be working correctly, but the pilot flame is inconsistent or weak, remove the pilot jet and clean or replace it. Turn off the power and close the gas supply, including the gas supply to the pilot if your unit has a separate one. Wait at least 30 minutes for the parts to cool. Disconnect the pilot gas line and thermocouple from the control housing (page 458), holding each line steady to avoid damaging it. You may find that a pair of open-end wrenches or a wrench and a pliers are best for this task.

Unscrew and remove the pilot bracket where it is mounted near the burner tubes. Carefully remove the pilot gas line and thermocouple from the bracket **(photo E).**

Clean the outside of the pilot jet with a parts brush, and carefully clean the inside with a pilot jet tool **(photo F)**. Take care not to scratch the inside of the jet or enlarge the orifice. If the pilot jet is severely corroded or difficult to clean, replace it.

Taking care to avoid damaging the thermocouple and pilot gas line, reattach them at both ends, then reattach the pilot bracket to the furnace. Reopen the gas supply and turn the power back on, then light the pilot.

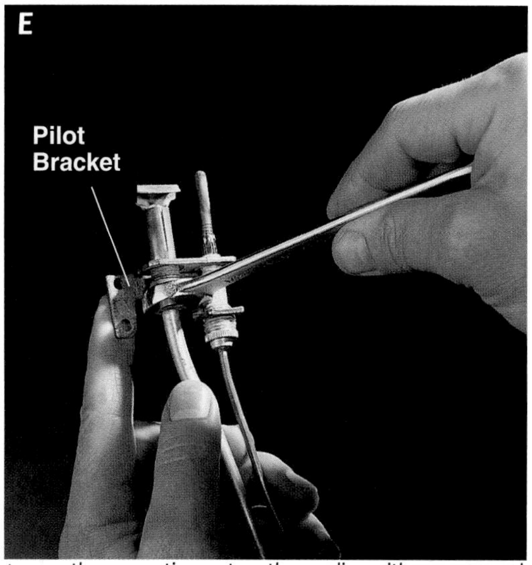

Loosen the connecting nut on the gas line with an open-end wrench.

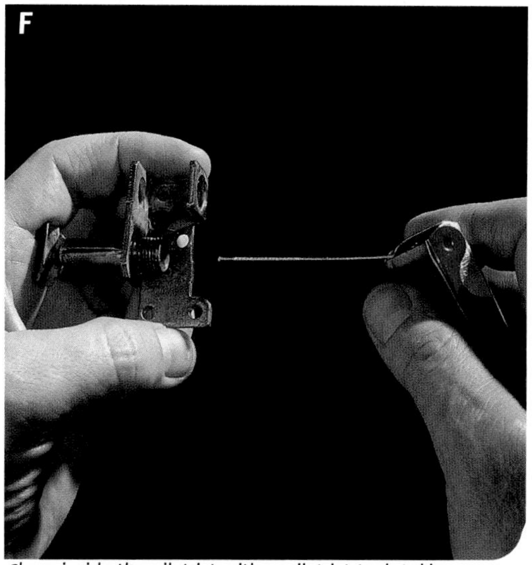

Clean inside the pilot jet with a pilot jet tool, taking care to avoid scratching the inside surface.

Inspecting the Burner Flame

Once you've set the pilot flame, check the burner flame. Its color will tell you whether the furnace is providing the right mixture of gas and air. The burner flame should be blue, with a bluish green flame at the center and occasional streaks of yellow **(photo G).** If it appears too blue or too yellow, adjust the air shutter at the end of the burner tube **(photo H).**

Start by setting the thermostat high so that the furnace continues to burn. Wearing protective gloves, loosen the air shutter locking screw. Open the shutter wide, then close it slowly until the flame color is right. Retighten the locking screw. Repeat the procedure for each remaining burner. Reset the thermostat.

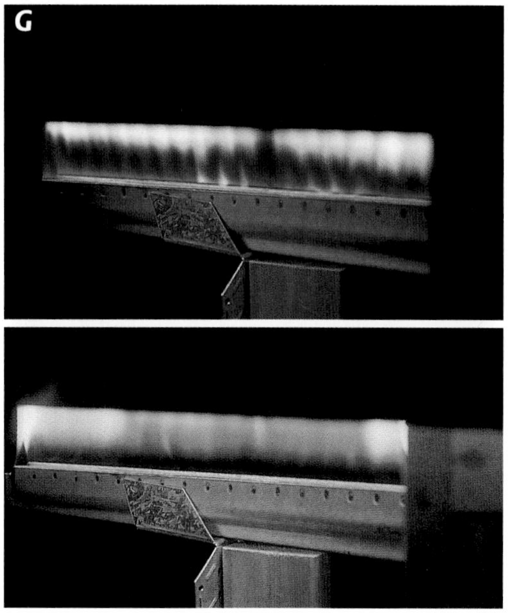

Compare your burner flame with the two above. Yours should be blue-green, with streaks of yellow (top).

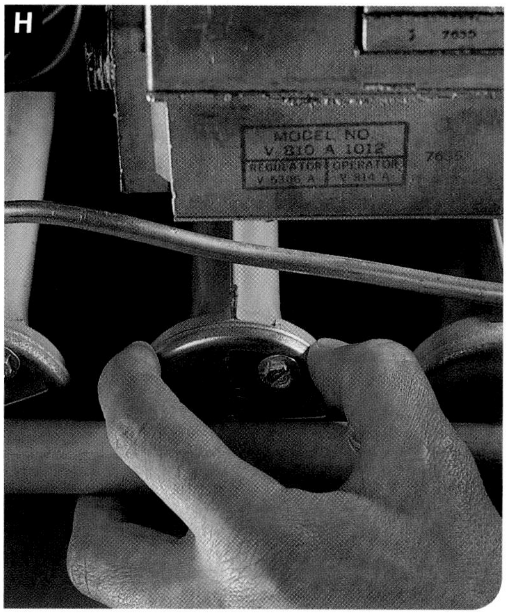

If the shutters are adjustable, you can set them yourself. Otherwise, call a professional for service.

Cleaning the Burners

Burners work by mixing together gas and air that is then ignited by a pilot flame or a heated element. Gas is delivered by a *manifold* and enters each burner tube through a small orifice, known as a *spud.* Burners and spuds gradually become encrusted with soot and other products of the combustion process and must be cleaned occasionally to keep them working efficiently.

To clean the burners, turn off the furnace's main shutoff, and switch off the power to the furnace at the main service panel. Shut off the gas supply, including the pilot gas supply if your unit has a separate one. Wait at least 30 minutes for the parts to cool. Remove the burner tubes by unscrewing them from their retaining brackets **(photo A),** by pulling out the metal pan that holds them, or by loosening the screws that attach the gas manifold to the furnace. On some furnaces, you need to remove the pilot housing to reach the burners.

Twist each burner carefully to remove it from its spud **(photo B).** Fill a laundry tub with water and soak the burners. Carefully clean the outside of the burner tubes and the burner ports with a soft-bristled brush. Replace any tubes that are cracked, bent, or severely corroded.

Inspect the spuds: clean burners won't work effectively if the spuds are dirty or damaged. Use a ratchet wrench to loosen and remove each spud **(photo C).** Clean the outside of each spud with a soft-bristled brush. Then, use a pilot jet tool to clean the inside of each spud **(photo D).** The tool is designed for cleaning small orifices, but take special care to avoid scratching or enlarging a spud's opening. Reinstall the spuds in the manifold. Tighten them just until they're snug. Once the burner tubes are dry, install them on the spuds, and attach them to the burner tube brackets or burner pan. Connect the pilot housing, if equipped. Turn the power and gas supply back on. On furnaces with a standing pilot, relight the pilot flame.

Remove the screws holding the burners to their brackets or to a slide-out pan.

If a burner is difficult to remove, twist it carefully from side to side while lifting and pulling.

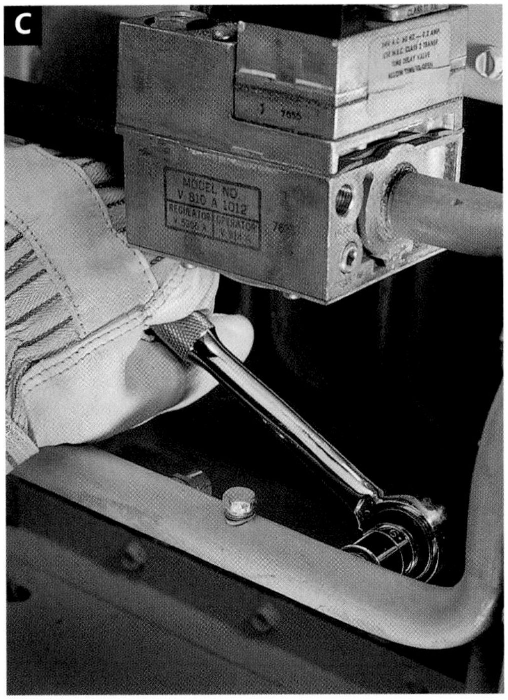

To avoid bending or damaging the spud threads, hold the manifold steady with one hand as you remove each spud.

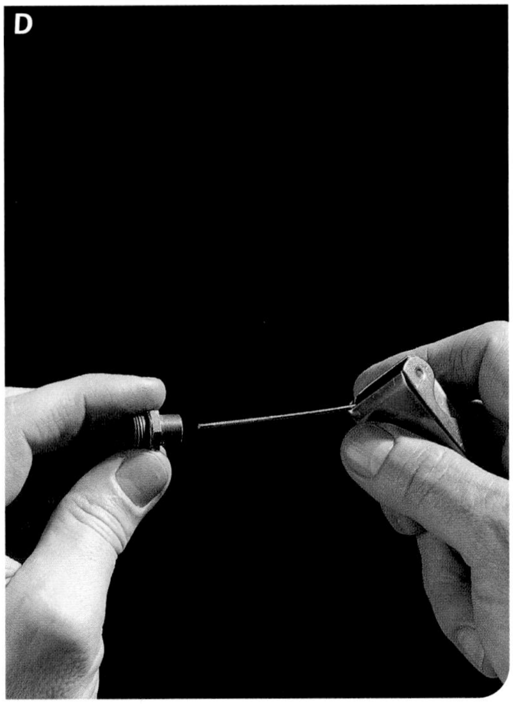

Clean each spud orifice carefully with a pilot jet tool, taking care not to scratch or enlarge the orifice.

Servicing Electronic Ignition Furnaces

Newer furnaces include an intermittent pilot light or hot-surface igniter as well as an electronic control center, which monitors furnace safety and has warning lights to help you recognize problems.

Newer furnaces also require specific types of maintenance. On some models, the temperature difference between the supply and return ducts needs to be within a narrow range to avoid damaging the *heat exchanger.* To find out whether this applies to your furnace, check the information plate on the burner compartment—it may include an indication of the acceptable range.

Each season, check the differential by slipping the probe of a pocket thermometer into a slit in an expansion joint in the supply duct **(photo E).** Record the reading and compare it with the temperature in the return air duct. Call a professional technician if the difference between the two numbers falls outside the recommended range.

Your furnace may contain an *intermittent pilot,* which is lighted with a spark when signaled by the thermostat. An intermittent pilot consumes gas only when necessary, reducing home fuel costs. If the electronic ignition fails to spark, call a technician for service.

Some furnace models ignite the gas with a glowing element, known as a *hot-surface igniter.* If the igniter fails, replace it. Remove the main furnace panel and locate the igniter just beyond the ignition end of the burner tubes. Disconnect the igniter plug and remove the nut on the mounting bracket with a nut driver or ratchet wrench **(photo F).** Replace the igniter.

If the igniter still doesn't function properly, check with the manufacturer: you may need to replace the control center. Detach the wires from the old control center one at a time and attach them to the replacement **(photo G).** Then, disconnect the old control center, using a screwdriver, and connect the new one **(photo H).**

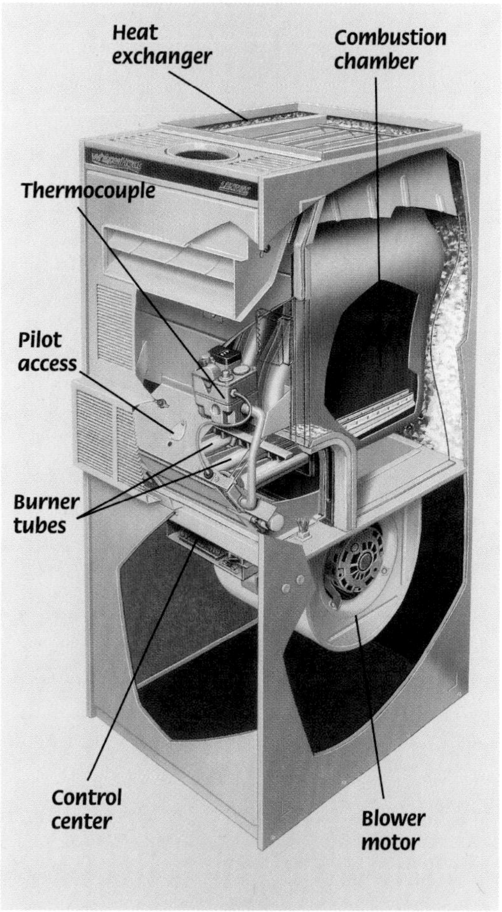

Newer furnaces contain either an electronic "intermittent" pilot (above) or a hot-surface igniter. A control center monitors furnace operation and aids with diagnostics.

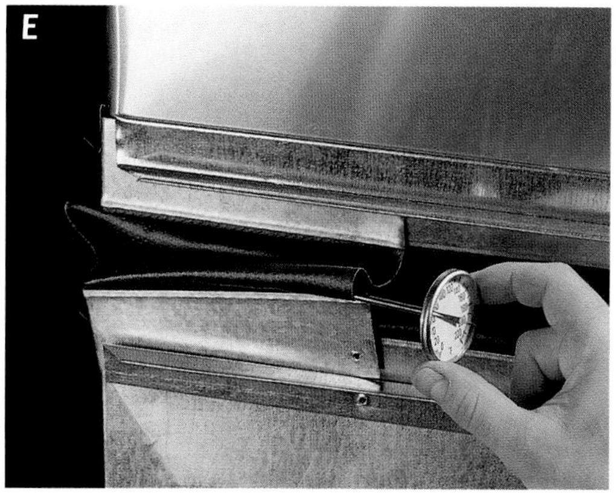

Check the temperature inside the supply duct and compare it with the temperature in the return duct.

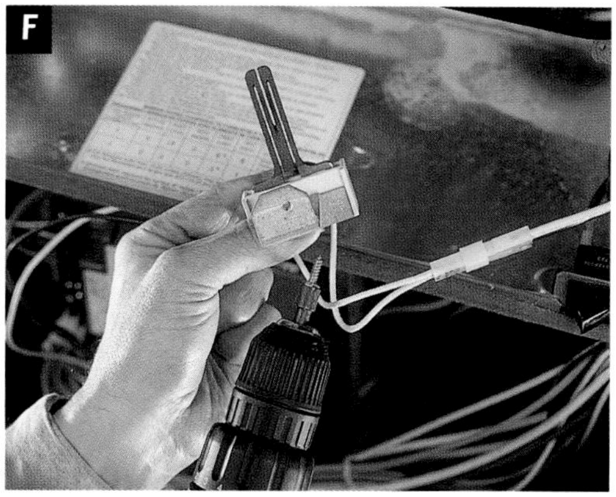

Disconnect the faulty hot-surface igniter from the mounting bracket.

Remove the control center wires one at a time and switch them over to the new control center.

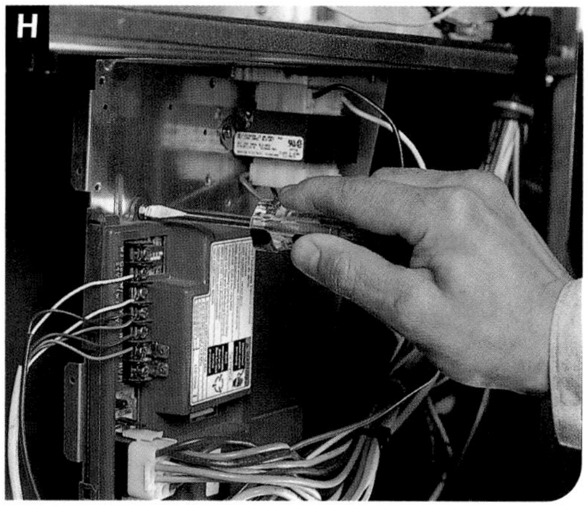

Unscrew the control center's mounting screws and install the replacement unit.

Maintaining a Furnace Humidifier

Furnace humidifiers are an effective means of increasing the humidity in your home. There are two types of furnace humidifiers, drum-style and drip-style. They attach to the furnace's warm air or return air duct.

A drum-style humidifier **(photo A)** picks up water from a reservoir or pan, using a rotating drum covered with an absorbent pad. Air flows through the pad and the water evaporates, raising the humidity level. In a drip-style humidifier, water drips into a stationary evaporator pad through which the air passes.

Drip-style humidifiers typically consume more water, since excess water runs off the bottom of the pad and into a drain. However, they stay cleaner and require far less maintenance, because the flow of water greatly reduces scum buildup. Drum-style humidifiers must be cleaned more often to keep mold from growing in the standing water.

Tools: *Tape measure, open-end wrench set, chisel, putty knife.*

Materials: *Vinegar, replacement evaporator pad (if required).*

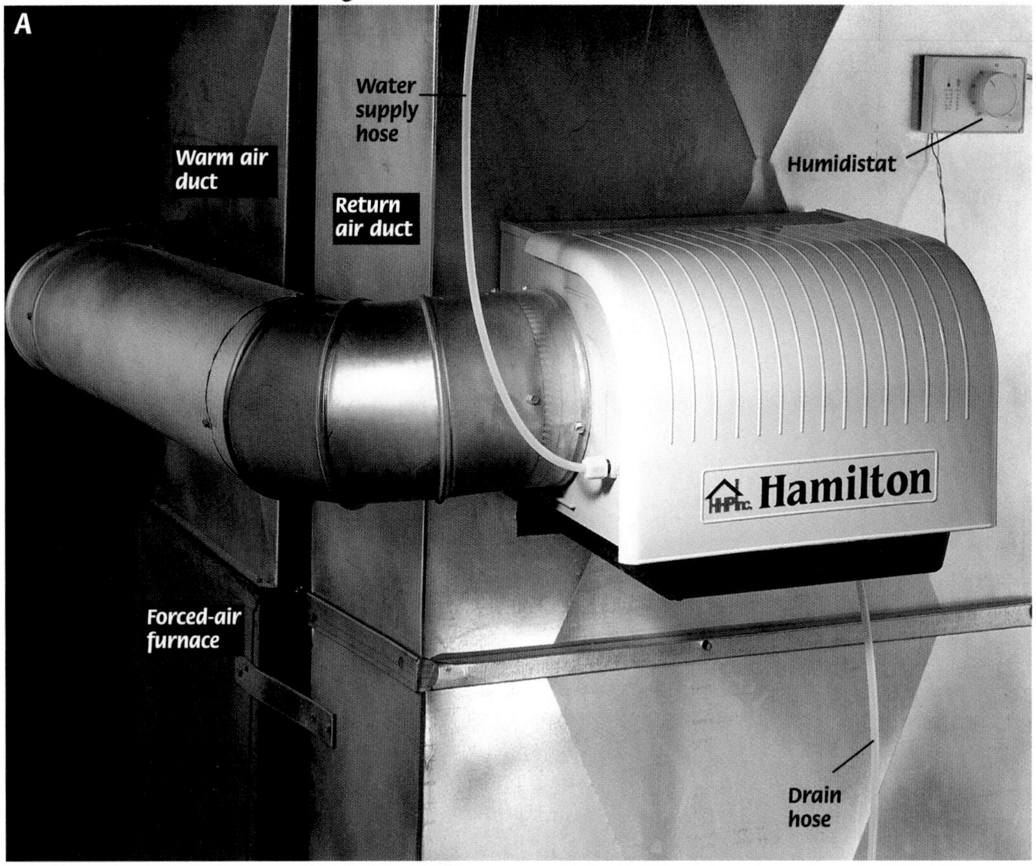

Maintaining a Drum-style Humidifier

Drum-style evaporator pads should be cleaned monthly and replaced at the end of each heating season. Turn off the power to the heating and cooling system and the water at the water supply valve. Then, loosen the nuts or release the clips that hold the humidifier cover in place, and remove the cover.

Lift out the drum-style evaporator, by holding both ends **(photo B).** If the pad is hard, clean or replace it.

Separate the pad from the drum shaft by removing the clip on the center spindle and pulling apart the two parts of the drum shaft **(photo C).**

Soak the pad in a 1:3 mixture of water and vinegar. Squeeze the pad to rinse it. If the pad remains hard or appears damaged, replace it.

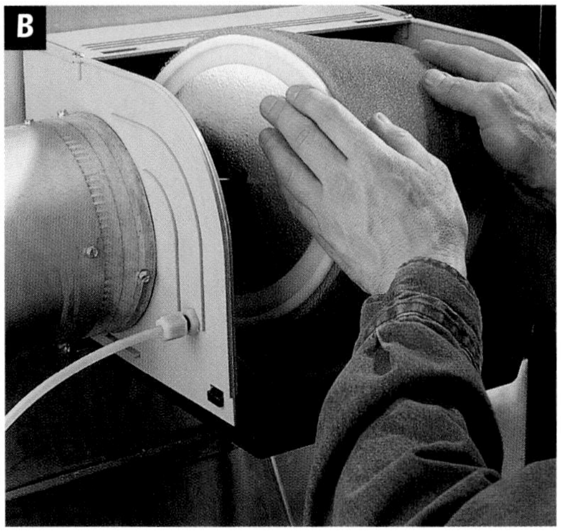

Remove the drum-style evaporator by lifting it from its slots.

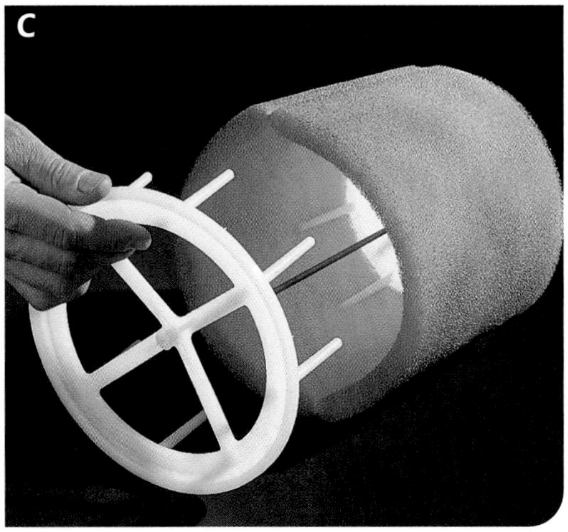

Separate the two parts of the drum shaft by removing the clip and pulling the two pieces apart.

With the pad in place, use a tape measure to check the depth of the water in the pan **(photo D).** Your owner's manual may indicate the correct water depth. If not, see if the pad dips into the water in each rotation and comes up wet, and whether there is a mineral line on the side of the tray wall, indicating where the water level should be.

To adjust the water level either up or down, loosen the screw on the float mount **(photo E).** To raise the water level, raise the float height and then tighten the screw. To lower the level, lower the float, then tighten the screw. Wait 30 minutes and check the water level and evaporator pad again. If water leaks from the supply tube fitting, tighten the nut with an open-end wrench **(photo F).**

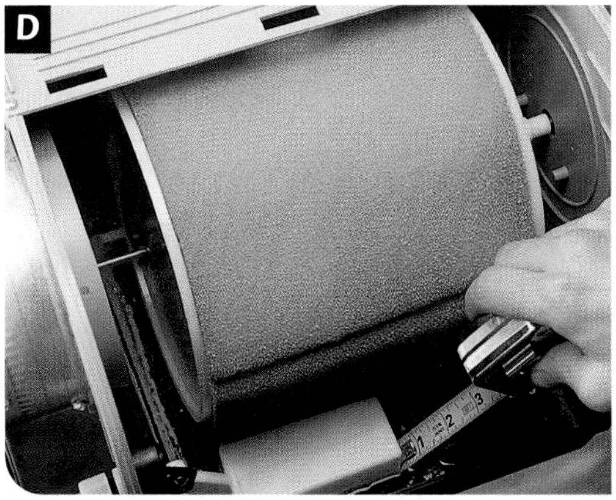

Make sure the pad soaks in the water. Mineral deposits left on the wall will indicate the original water level.

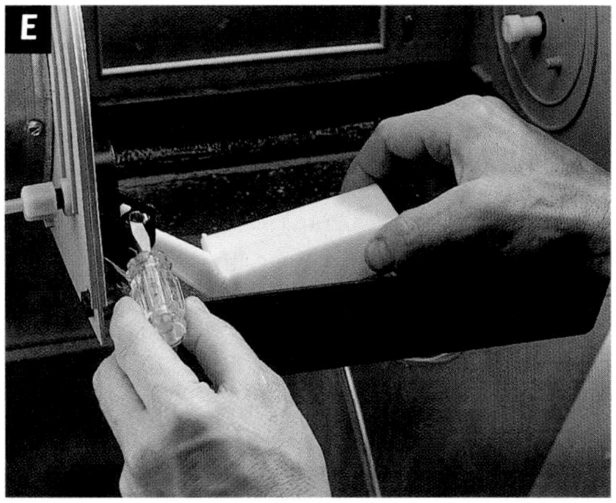

Loosen the locknut on the water line with an open-end wrench.

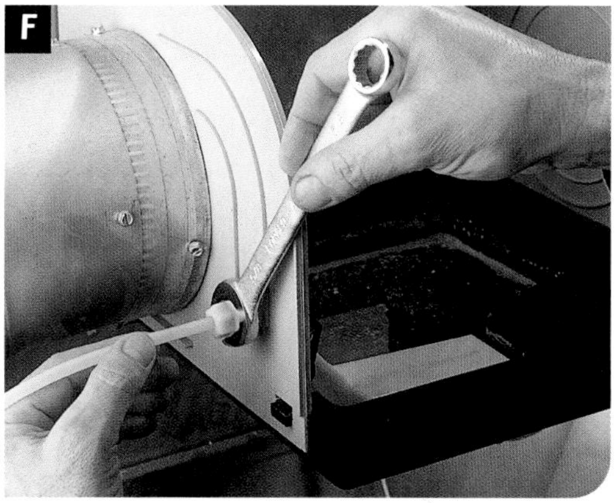

Adjust the float height and retighten the locknut.

Maintaining a Drip-style Humidifier

A drip-style humidifier should be inspected monthly. The evaporator pad should be replaced at the end of every heating season.

To service a drip-style humidifier, shut off the power at the main service panel, and turn off the water supply. Slide your finger under the plastic water outlet and lift up to pop off the outlet. Remove the distribution tray from the assembly by pushing down on the tray while pushing out on the plastic frame **(photo G).** Use a chisel to scrape out any mineral deposits from the V-notches on the tray **(photo H).**

Slide the evaporator pad from the frame **(photo I).** Twist and flex the evaporator pad to loosen the deposits, using a putty knife to scrape them away, if necessary. If the pad itself crumbles, replace it.

Disconnect the drain hose. Flex it, then flush it with cold water **(photo J).** Reassemble the humidifier and attach the drain hose. Turn on the electricity and the water supply.

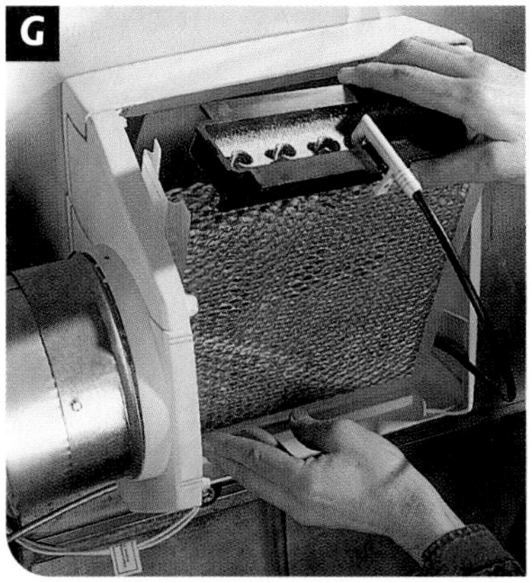

Remove the distribution tray from the humidifier.

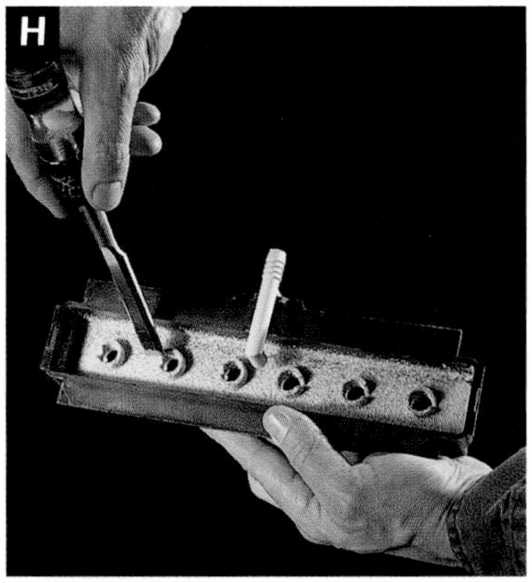

Use a chisel to scrape mineral deposits from the V-notches.

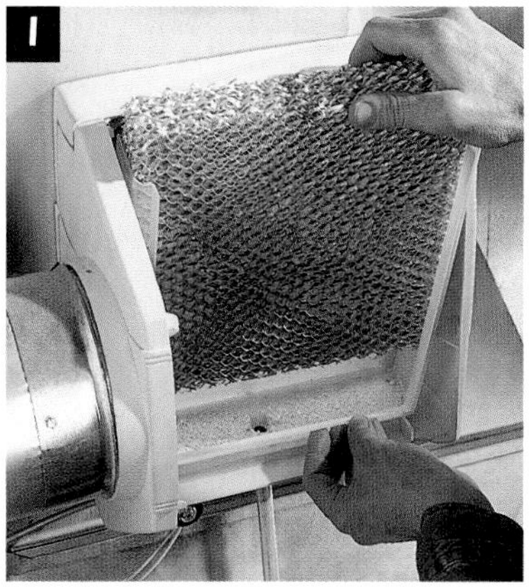

Remove the evaporator pad from the frame.

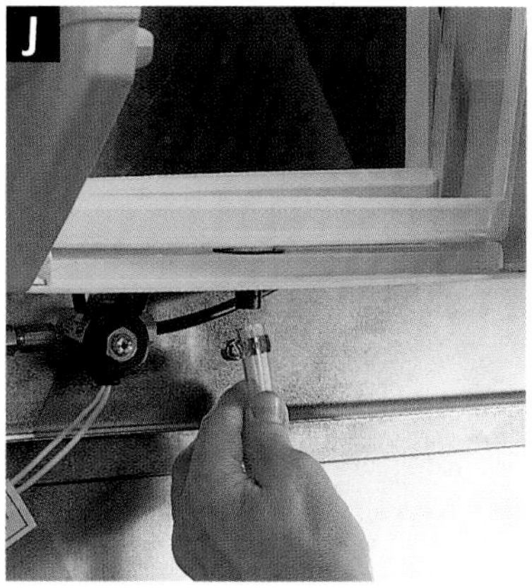

Disconnect the drain hose and flush it with cold water.

Hot Water & Steam Systems

Hot water and steam systems, also known as *hydronic systems,* feature a boiler that heats water and circulates it through a closed network of pipes to a set of radiators or convectors. Because water expands and contracts as it heats and cools, these systems include expansion tanks to ensure a constant volume of water circulating through the pipes.

Hot water and steam systems warm the surrounding air through a process called *convection.* Hot water radiators **(photo A)** are linked to the system by pipes connected near the bottom of the radiator. As water cools inside the radiator, it is drawn back to the boiler for reheating. The radiators in steam systems **(photo B)** have pipes connected near the top of the radiator. These radiators can be very hot to the touch. Convectors **(photo C)** are smaller and lighter and may be used to replace hot water radiators, or to extend an existing hot water system.

Although the delivery of hot water or steam to the rooms in your house is considered a closed system, some air will make its way into the system. Steam radiators have an automatic release valve that periodically releases hot, moist air. Hot water radiators contain a bleed valve that must periodically be opened to release trapped air. It is usually necessary to bleed convector systems using a valve near the boiler.

Today's hot water and steam systems are often fueled by natural gas. Older systems may use fuel oil. Fuel oil systems require more frequent maintenance of the filter (page 465) and blower (page 466).

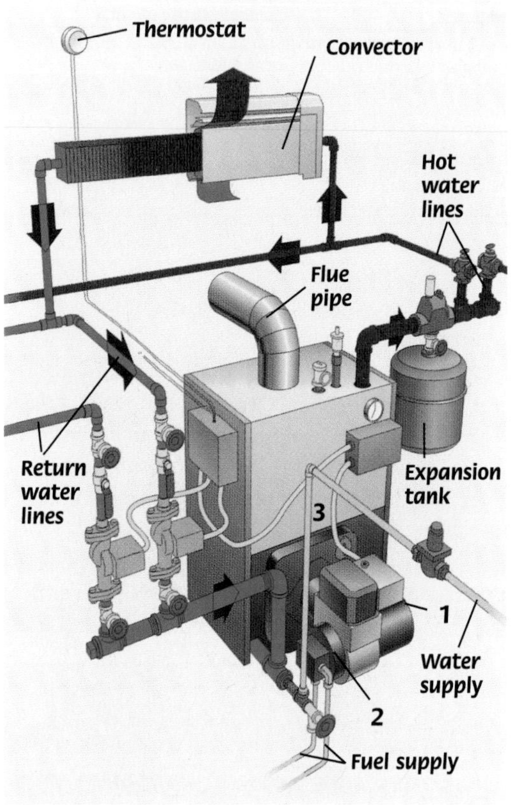

A blower draws in air through the air intake (1) while a fuel pump (2) maintains a constant supply of fuel oil. The mixture is ignited by a high-voltage spark as it enters the combustion chamber (3) and heats water.

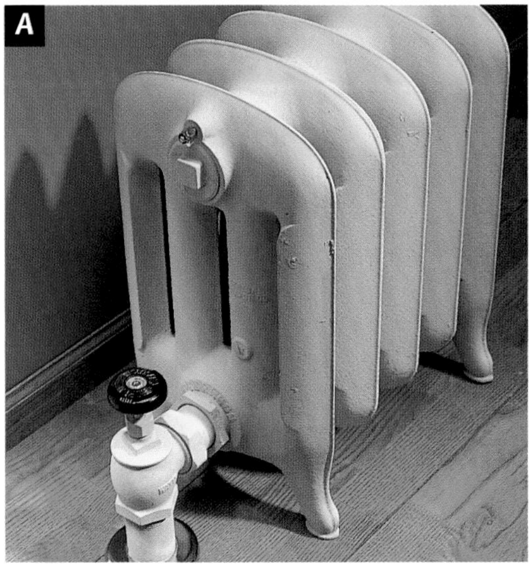

Hot-water radiators circulate heated water through pipes. As it cools, water is drawn back to the boiler for reheating.

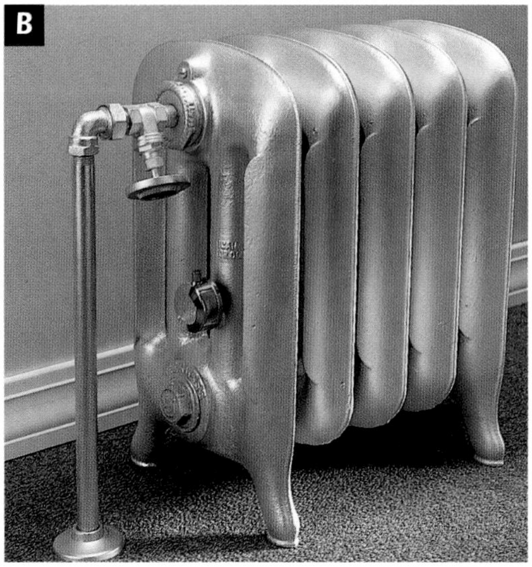

Steam radiators operate at a higher temperature. Steam cools in the radiators, returns to a liquid state, and then flows back to the boiler.

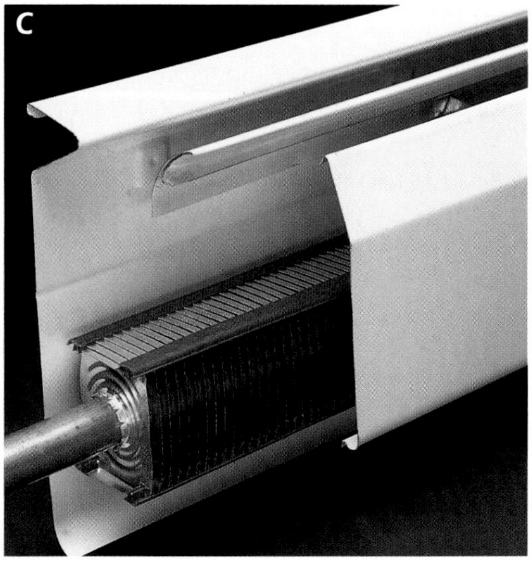

Space-saving hot water convectors work on the same principle as radiators, but use thin sheet-metal fins to transfer heat to the air.

Maintaining Hot Water & Steam Systems

Servicing the Oil Filter & Strainer

Replacing the oil filter is the best routine maintenance you can do for your hot water or steam heating system. The oil filter captures impurities that would otherwise damage the boiler.

Surround the base of the boiler with a drop cloth and newspaper. Shut off the power to the boiler at the main service panel and at the boiler shutoff switch, usually located near the boiler. Then, close the fuel line supply valve and wait 30 minutes for all parts to cool.

Wearing disposable gloves, unscrew the top of the filter cartridge **(photo D).** Remove the cartridge with a twisting motion and turn it over to dump the old filter into a plastic bag **(photo E).** Remove the gasket from the cartridge and wipe out the inside, first with a cloth dipped in solvent, then with a dry cloth. Install a new filter and gasket **(photo F).** Position the cartridge under the cover and screw it back in place.

Use an open-end wrench to remove the bolts from the pump cover **(photo G).** Leave the oil line attached, and remove the gasket and mesh strainer from the cover **(photo H).** Clean the strainer with solvent and a parts brush. If it's badly worn or damaged, replace it. Wipe the cover with a clean cloth. Place the clean strainer or replacement strainer in the cover and install a new gasket. Fasten the cover bolts in place. Restart the boiler.

Tools: *Open-end wrench set, parts brush.*

Materials: *Gloves, drop cloth, solvent, replacement oil filter and cartridge gasket, strainer gasket, cloth.*

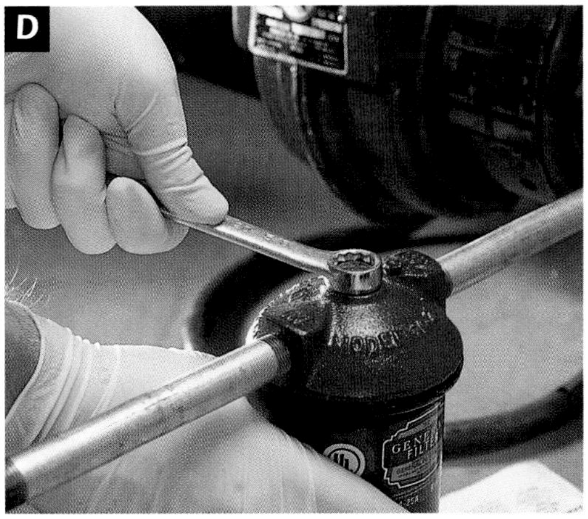

Have a disposable plastic bag ready, and unscrew the top of the filter cartridge.

Twist the cartridge to remove it from the oil supply line. Ask your waste removal company for disposal instructions.

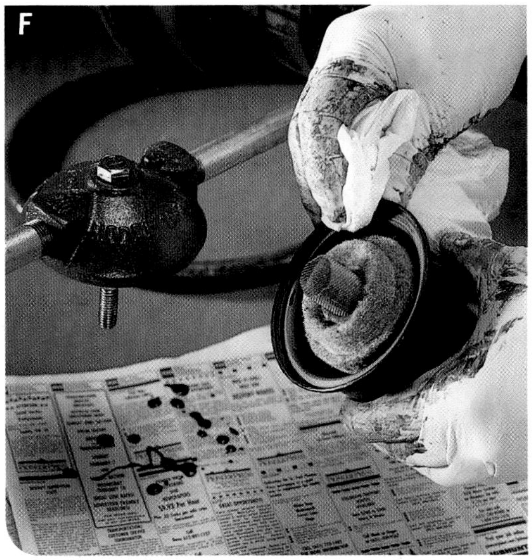

Wipe the edge of the cartridge, first with a solvent-dipped rag and then with a dry rag.

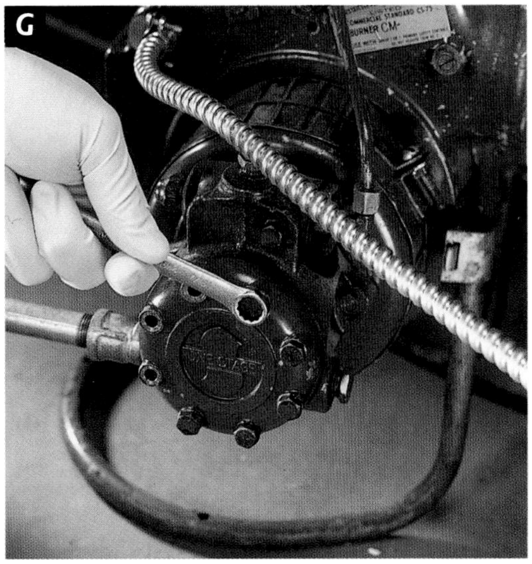

Leave the pump cover attached to the fuel line when you remove it.

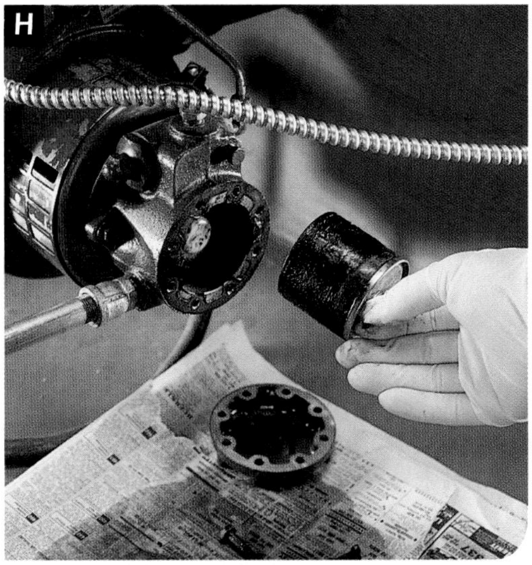

Remove the mesh strainer carefully. Even a heavily soiled one can often be reused after a good cleaning.

Cleaning & Lubricating the Blower

Clean fuel and a reliable air supply are critical to your boiler's performance. Clean the air intake on your boiler every month and lubricate the motor every two months during the heating season.

Turn off the power to the boiler. Brush any dust and debris from the air intake with a narrow, medium-bristle brush **(photo A).** Use an open-end wrench or screwdriver, as required, to loosen the transformer. With the transformer still attached, move it aside to reach the blower fan **(photo B).** Use the brush and a damp cloth to remove dirt and debris from the fan blades **(photo C).**

Most boiler blowers have a port on top or cups at each end for adding lubricating oil. Check your owner's manual or consult the manufacturer on the best lubricating oil for your blower. Before removing the plugs or opening the cups, clean the outside of the motor with a damp cloth **(photo D)** to keep dirt and debris from getting into the motor. Remove the plug from the opening or the lid from each cup, using a wrench or screwdriver, as required. Add a few drops of lubricating oil **(photo E).**

If the motor doesn't have oil ports or cups, it's probably a self-lubricating type **(photo F).** Check your owner's manual to be sure.

Tools: *Open-end wrench set, screwdrivers (standard and Phillips), medium-bristle brush.*

Materials: *Drop cloth, boiler lubricating oil, cloth.*

A

To clean the air intake, use a brush designed for cleaning the condensing coils on a refrigerator.

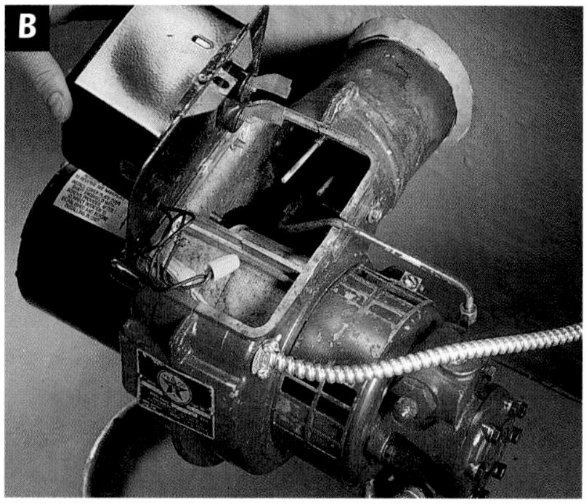

B

If the transformer attaches to the blower housing with a hinge, simply swing it out of the way. If it comes loose, be careful not to strain the wire connections.

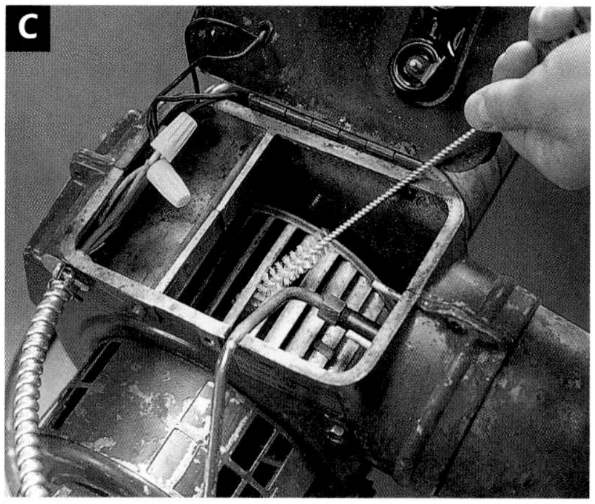

C

The blades on most blower fans are thin and hard to reach, so use a long brush carefully: a bent fan blade makes much more noise than a dirty one.

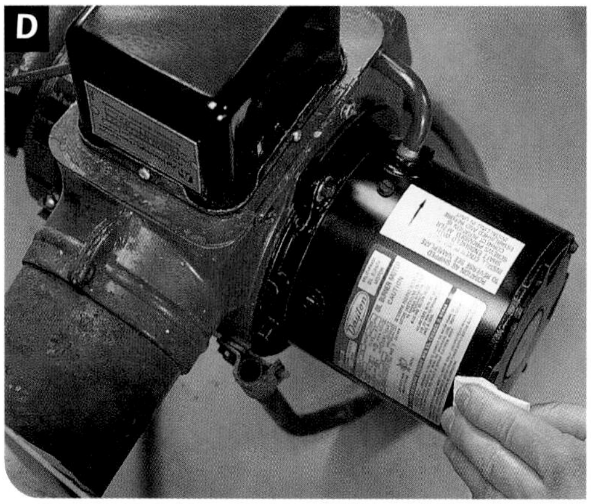

D

To prevent dust or dirt from getting in the motor while you add oil, clean off the surface with a damp cloth before opening the ports or cups.

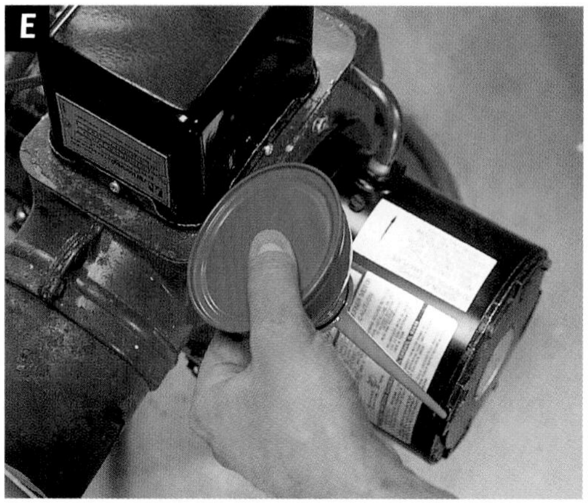

E

Add lubricating oil to the ports or cups. The motor housing may indicate what kind of oil to use.

F

If the motor doesn't have cups or openings for adding lubricating oil, it's probably sealed and may not need extra lubrication.

Draining & Filling a System

Sediment gradually accumulates in any water-based system, reducing the system's efficiency and damaging internal parts. Draining the boiler every season reduces the accumulation of sediment. Be aware that draining the system can take a long time, and the water often has an unpleasant odor. This doesn't indicate a problem. Drain the system during warm weather, and open the windows and run a fan to reduce any odor.

Start by shutting off the boiler and allowing an hour or two for a hot system to cool. Attach a garden hose to the drain at the bottom of the boiler **(photo G),** and place the other end in a floor drain or utility sink. Open the drain valve, then open a bleed valve on the highest radiator in the house (page 468).

When water stops draining, open a bleed valve on a radiator closer to the boiler. When the flow stops, locate the valve or gauge on top of the boiler, and remove it with a wrench **(photo H).** Many boilers have two nuts, so you'll need a pair of wrenches for the task.

Make sure the system is cool before you add water. Close the drain valve on the boiler. Insert a funnel into the gauge fitting and add rust inhibitor, available from heating supply dealers **(photo I).** Check the container for special instructions. If necessary, install a temporary elbow onto the gauge fitting. Reinstall the valve or gauge. Close all radiator bleed valves, and slowly reopen the water supply to the boiler.

When the water pressure gauge reads 5 psi, bleed the air from the radiators on the first floor, then do the same on the upper floors. Let the boiler reach 20 psi before you turn the power on **(photo J).** Allow 12 hours for water to circulate fully, then bleed the radiators again.

Tools: *Open-end wrench set, pipe wrenches, garden hose, funnel, plastic bucket.*

Materials: *Drop cloth, boiler rust inhibitor.*

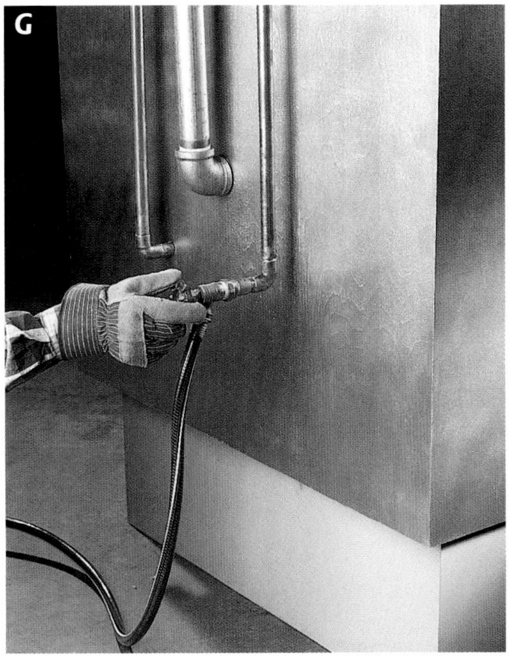

Use a garden hose to drain water from the boiler. Keep the drain end of the hose lower than the drain cock on the boiler.

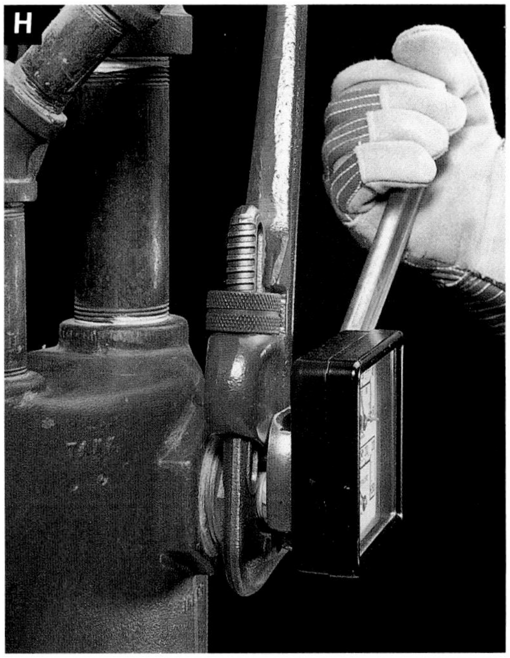

If the valve or gauge on top of the boiler is attached to a separate fitting, hold the fitting still with one wrench while removing the valve or gauge with another.

Using a funnel, add a recommended rust inhibitor to the boiler through the valve or gauge fitting.

The boiler should reach a pressure of 20 psi before you turn the power back on.

Bleeding Radiators

Hot water systems operate more quietly and efficiently if you bleed them each year before the start of the heating season. Bleeding reduces noise by releasing trapped air from the system. During the heating season, bleed individual radiators again if they remain cold when the boiler is running.

To bleed a hot-water system, the boiler must be on. Start with the radiator that's highest in the house and farthest from the boiler. Place a cloth under the bleed valve, and open the valve slowly **(photo A).** Close it as soon as water squirts out. Some bleed valves have knobs, which open with a half turn; others must be opened with a screwdriver or a valve key, available at hardware stores.

Steam radiators have automatic bleed valves. To clear a clogged bleed valve, first close the shut off valve at the radiator, and let the unit cool. Unscrew and remove the bleed valve and clear the valve orifice with a fine wire or needle **(photo B).**

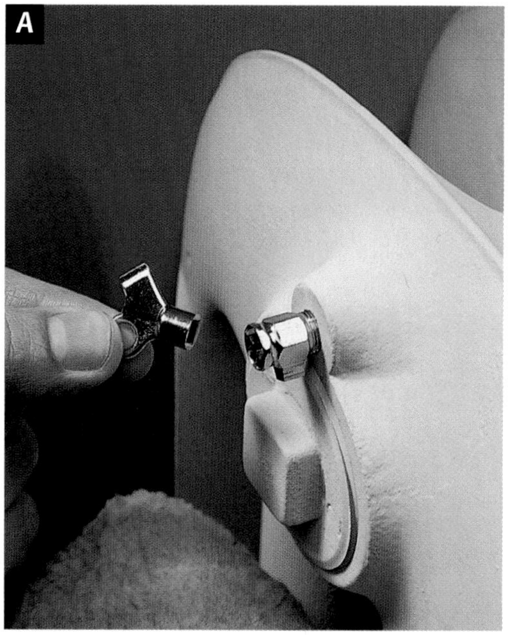

If you can't find the valve key for your radiators, a local hardware store or home center may have a replacement.

If a steam radiator isn't heating, clear the bleed-valve orifice with a fine wire or needle.

Bleeding Convectors

Older hot water convector systems may have bleed valves on or near the convectors. You can bleed these convectors as you would radiators. Most convector systems today don't contain bleed valves, but you can bleed the entire system by attaching a hose at the boiler.

Locate the return water line and shut it off near the boiler. Locate the hot water main that delivers water to the convectors and shut that off near the boiler as well. Check that the main water supply valve, usually the smallest pipe in the system, is open. Finally, locate the hose bib at the base of the boiler **(photo C).** Attach a short section of hose to the hose bib and immerse the other end in a bucket half filled with water. Open the hose bib so any air in the boiler is flushed out, producing bubbles in the bucket. When no more air bubbles appear, open the valve on the return water line to bleed any remaining air, then quickly close the hose bib. Reopen the hot water main before restarting the boiler.

A convector-based heating system is usually bled at the boiler by holding a hose underwater and flushing the system until there are no more air bubbles coming from the hose.

Identifying & Repairing Exhaust Leaks

Leaks in the exhaust flue, around the burner mounting flange, combustion chamber cover plate, or fire door are potential sources of carbon monoxide. Any leak that might allow carbon monoxide to enter your home should be repaired immediately.

Holes and rusted portions are visible signs of a damaged flue. Smaller leaks can be found by turning on the burner and holding a lighted candle along the joints in the flue and the seams of the burner mounting flange, combustion chamber cover plate, and fire door **(photo D).** The flame is drawn toward the joint or seam when there is a leak.

Tools: Wire brush, putty knife, long candle, power drill/screwdriver.

Materials: Replacement flue sections, refractory furnace cement.

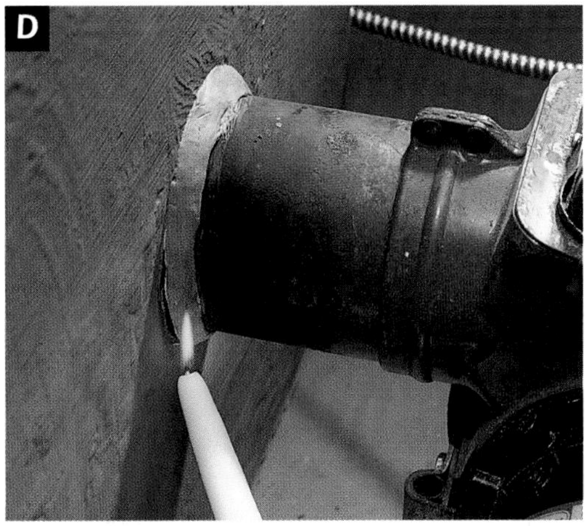

Hold a lighted candle to the joints on the flue and seams around the burner to find leaks.

Repairing a Damaged Flue

If there is a leak at a flue joint, seal the joint, following the instructions for sealing a furnace leak (below). Damaged sections of flue must be replaced. Before doing this, shut off the burner and make sure the area around your boiler is well ventilated.

Remove the retaining screws on the damaged section, and lift away the flue **(photo E).** Install a replacement section of flue from your local home center or HVAC dealer **(photo F).** Tighten the screws, then seal the joints with refractory furnace cement.

Remove the damaged section of flue pipe.

Attach the retaining screws on the replacement section. Then, seal the joints with furnace cement.

Sealing an Exhaust Leak

To seal a leak at a seam, turn off the burner and let the boiler cool. Then, use a wire brush to remove any dirt or rust that has accumulated around the leak **(photo G).**

Seal the leak by applying refractory furnace cement with a putty knife **(photo H).** To stop a mounting flange leak, loosen the retaining bolts located at the edges of the flange. Scrape away the decayed gasket and apply refractory furnace cement at the edge. Then, tighten the bolts.

To test your repair, turn on the boiler and hold a lighted candle to the repair area. The candle flame should not flicker or waver.

Use a wire brush to clean off any rust or dirt deposits that have accumulated on the surface.

With a putty knife, apply refractory furnace cement to seal the leak.

Supplemental Heating Systems

Supplemental heating systems—including baseboard heaters, wall-mounted heaters, and fireplaces or wood stoves—are not often used as primary heating sources, since they're either too expensive to operate (electrical units) or inconvenient to run (wood-burning systems). But your home may have a supplemental system installed in a room addition, or in an uninsulated porch or garage that has been converted to living space. Since supplemental systems are relatively inexpensive to install, they're often used in spaces that can't easily be served by existing central heating systems. A fireplace or wood stove can also add to your home's charm and resale value.

Though supplemental systems aren't as complicated as gas-fired air or hot-water systems, they do require regular maintenance and occasional repair. Equipped with some basic knowledge and a few tools, you can make many of these repairs quickly and easily.

Since these systems are often installed by homeowners rather than professionals, it's important to be particularly aware of health and safety issues. A wood stove or fireplace that is improperly installed or poorly maintained can cause a fire or introduce deadly carbon monoxide into your home. Electric heaters can cause short circuits and should never be touched with wet hands. They should always be installed out of reach of children and in locations where no one is likely to brush against their hot surfaces.

Electric Baseboard Heaters

Baseboard heaters are simple units consisting of a heating element, with metal fins for transferring heat, and a *limit control*–a switch that prevents overheating. To control the temperature, some models have a built-in thermostat; others are controlled by a *line voltage* thermostat on the wall (page 488).

Most baseboard heaters are wired to a 240-volt circuit, which means both the black and white circuit wires are "hot" and carry voltage. Others use 120-volts and are wired directly to a circuit or are plugged into a standard receptacle. The tests for all three types are nearly the same.

If your baseboard heater is wired to a household circuit, shut off the power at the main service panel, then check the wires for power before making any tests or repairs (page 471). **Note:** Wiring for heaters and thermostats may vary. For the best–and safest–results, check the manufacturer's wiring instructions, and label all wires before you disconnect them.

Tools: *Screwdrivers, circuit tester, needlenose pliers, multi-tester, soft-bristled brush, vacuum cleaner.*

Materials: Cloth.

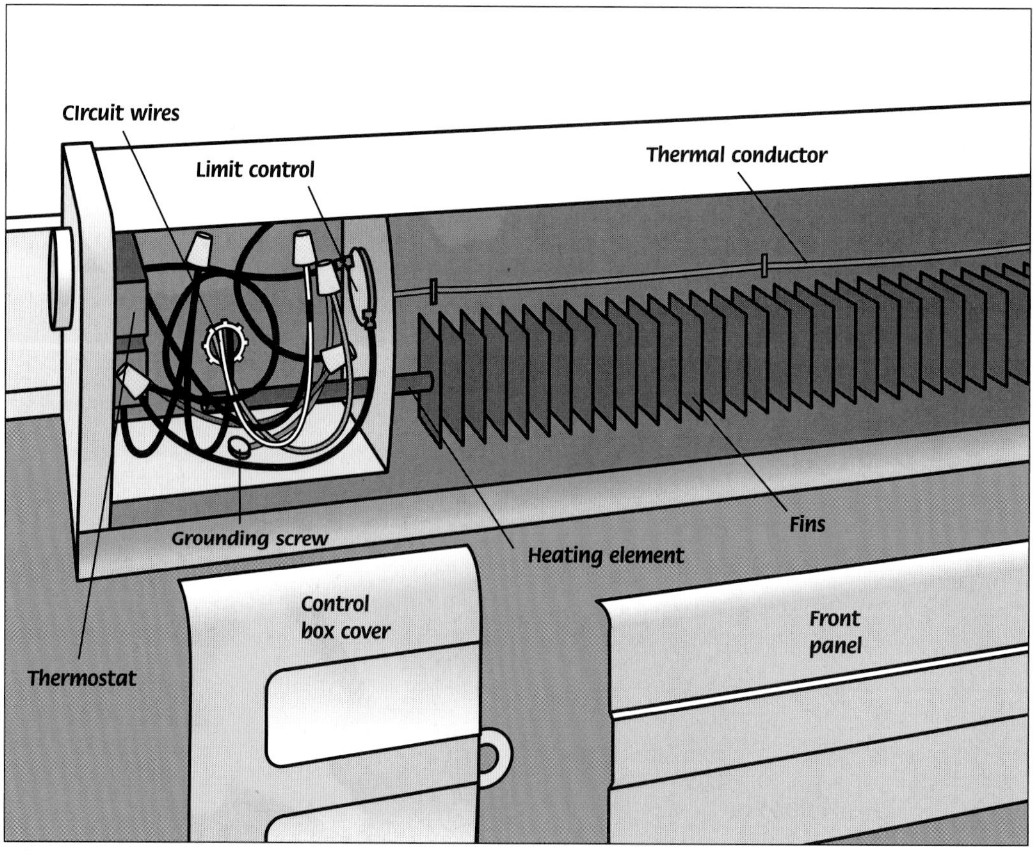

Electric baseboard heaters require little maintenance and are easy to repair once you've taken a few basic precautions.

Using a Multi-tester

Testing for continuity with a multi-tester is the best way to check for faulty components in an electric baseboard or wall-mounted heater. Always test the multi-tester first, by setting it to test for continuity (look for the Ω symbol and a marking such as X1, X10, or XK1, sometimes preceded by an R). Touch the probes or alligator clips to each other. The tester's needle should swing across the scale to ZERO, indicating a completed circuit. A digital multi-tester should read 00.0 and may also beep to indicate continuity.

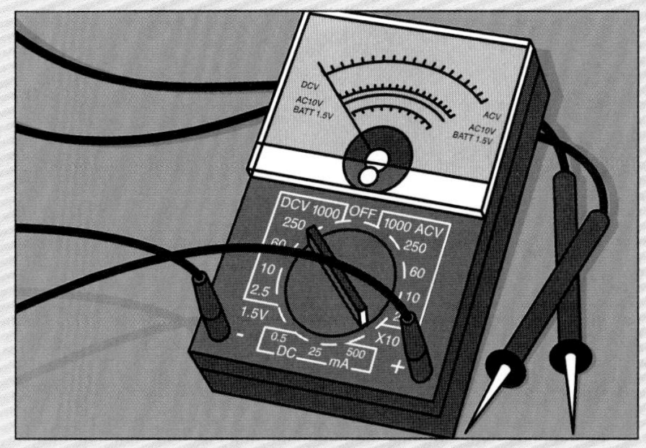

Checking for Power

Baseboard heaters are either wired directly to the household electrical system or plugged into a wall receptacle. If the heater is plugged into a receptacle, you can safely inspect or repair the unit after unplugging the cord and waiting until the unit is cold. If no cord is visible, the heater is probably connected directly to household wiring. In that case, conduct the following tests before disassembling the unit.

Turn off the power to the heater at your home's main service panel. Remove the heater's control box cover, and label the black hot circuit wire leading from the cable in the wall. Insert one probe of a neon circuit tester into the wire connector at the end of the circuit wire, and touch the other probe to the grounding screw on the heater casing. Then, label the other circuit wire (with a 240-volt heater, this wire will also carry voltage). Insert the tester probe into its wire connector, and touch the other probe to the grounding screw **(Illustration A).** Finally, insert one probe of the tester into each of the wire connectors you've just tested. If the tester glows for any of the tests, the power is still on. Return to the service panel and shut off the correct circuit.

Repeat the tests to confirm that the power to the unit is off.

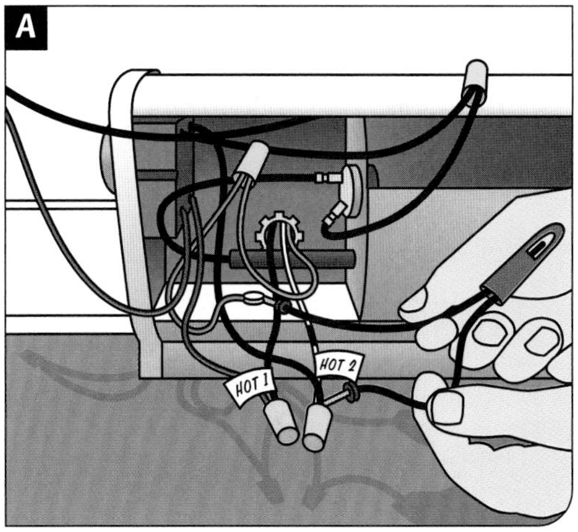

Use a circuit tester to make sure the power to the unit is off.

Servicing the Fins

Baseboard heater fins often become clogged with dust and debris, which restrict air flow through the fins and decrease the heater's output. To clean the fins, shut off the power to the heater at the main service panel, then use a circuit tester to confirm that the power is off (above).

Remove the front panel from the heater **(Illustration B).** Clean dust and dirt from the element with a dry rag and a dry, soft-bristled brush, or use a vacuum cleaner and a nozzle attachment **(Illustration C).**

Straighten badly bent fins, using needlenose pliers. Don't worry if the some fins are slightly bent; it won't affect the heater's operation.

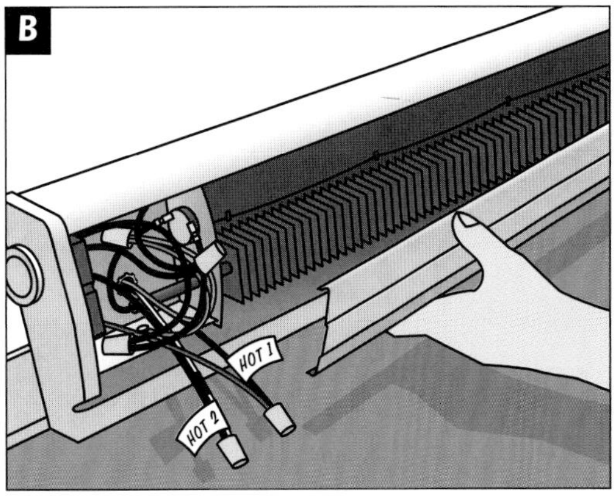

Remove the front panel after checking that the power is off.

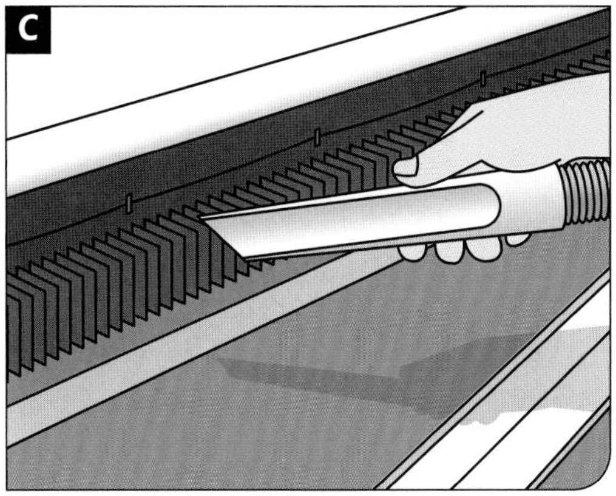

Clean away dirt and debris, taking care not to bend the fins.

Testing & Replacing a Limit Control

The limit control contains a switch designed to shut off the heater if it overheats. Overheating can occur simply due to a dirty heating element. If you have inspected the fins and still detect a burning smell and the heater doesn't shut itself off, you'll need to test the limit control with a multi-tester to determine whether it's faulty (page 471).

Shut off the power to the heater at the main service panel, and confirm that the power is off (page 471). Pull one of the limit control leads from its terminal. Set the multi-tester to test for continuity, and touch one probe to each limit control terminal **(Illustration A).** The tester needle should move to ZERO, indicating continuity; if not, the limit control is faulty.

To replace the limit control, disconnect the other limit control lead from its wire connector. Remove the screws or bend out the tabs securing the limit control to the unit. Remove the front panel and pull the thermal conductor from each of its mounting clips. Slide the limit control assembly out of the heater and replace it with an identical part from the manufacturer **(Illustration B).** Reconnect the wire leads, then reattach the covers and panel.

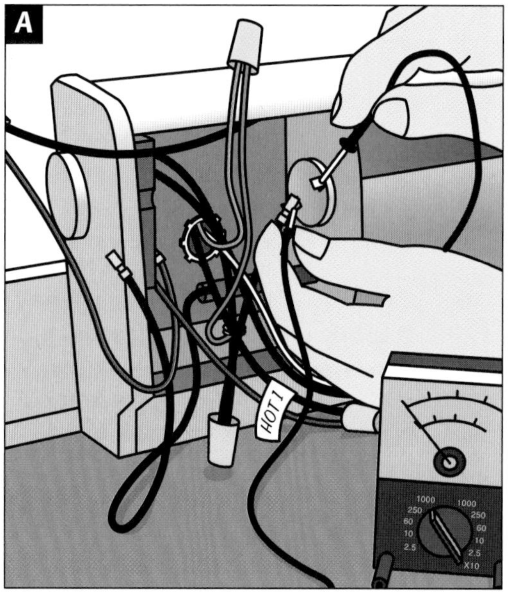

Use a multi-tester to check for continuity in the limit control.

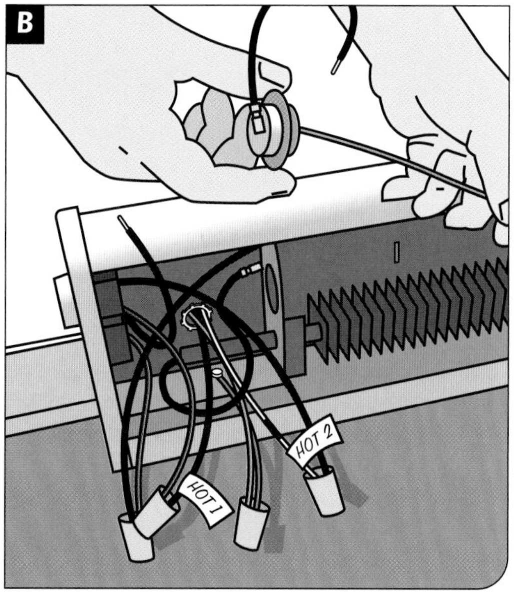

Replace a faulty limit control with an exact duplicate part.

Testing & Replacing a Thermostat

Test the thermostat if the heater doesn't respond when you adjust the knob and you're sure the limit control is operating. Shut off power at the main service panel, and confirm that the power is off (page 471).

Label each thermostat lead and the wire connected to it, giving both wires the same "name." Designate the circuit wires and their respective leads as "HOT," and designate the heater wires and their respective leads as "UNIT" **(Illustration C).** Unscrew the wire connectors and separate the wires.

Remove the thermostat from the heater unit. Set a multi-tester to test for continuity (page 471). Turn the thermostat dial to the highest (hottest) setting. Touch one tester probe to a "HOT" wire lead, and touch the other probe to each of the "UNIT" leads **(Illustration D).** During one of the connections, the tester needle should move to ZERO, indicating continuity.

Next, touch one probe to the other "HOT" wire lead, and touch the other probe to each of the "UNIT" leads. Again, there should be continuity with one of the connections. If the thermostat fails either test, replace it with a duplicate part from the manufacturer.

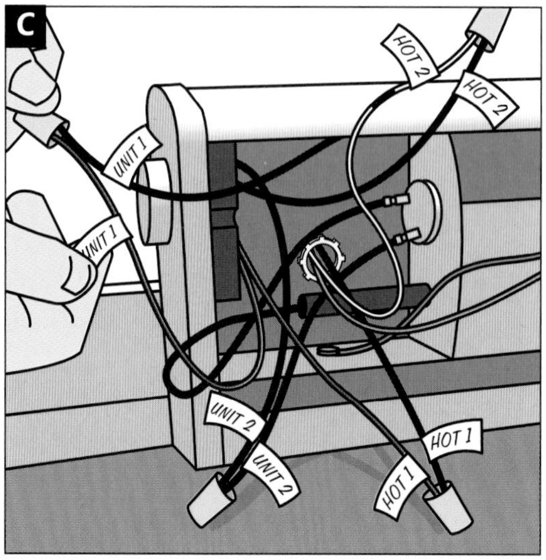

Label each thermostat lead with respect to the wire it is connected to.

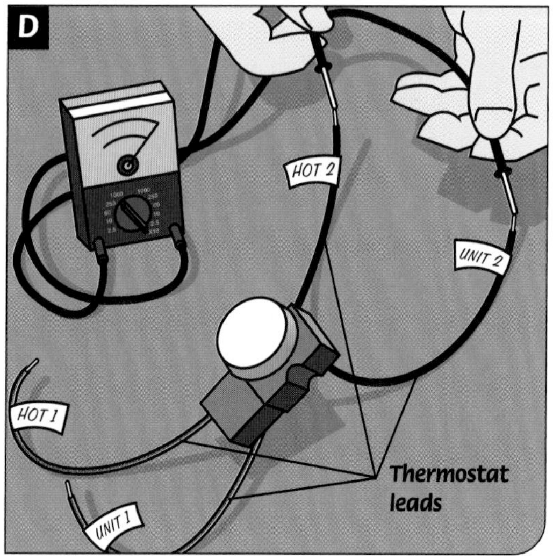

Test the thermostat for continuity, using a multi-tester.

Testing the Heating Element

If the heater doesn't generate heat even though the thermostat and limit control appear to be functioning, the heating element may be the problem. Shut off the power to the heater at the main service panel, and confirm that the power is off (page 471).

Find the heating element wire that is connected to one of the thermostat leads (This wire will probably be coming from the far end of the heating element. Unscrew the wire connector and separate the wires **(Illustration E).**

Set a multi-tester to test for continuity (page 471). Touch one tester probe to the free heating element wire, and touch the other probe to the wire running from the limit control to the other end of the element **(Illustration F).** The tester needle should move to ZERO, indicating continuity. If so, the heating element is sound, and the problem may lie in the circuit. If not, the element is bad, and you should replace the entire unit.

E

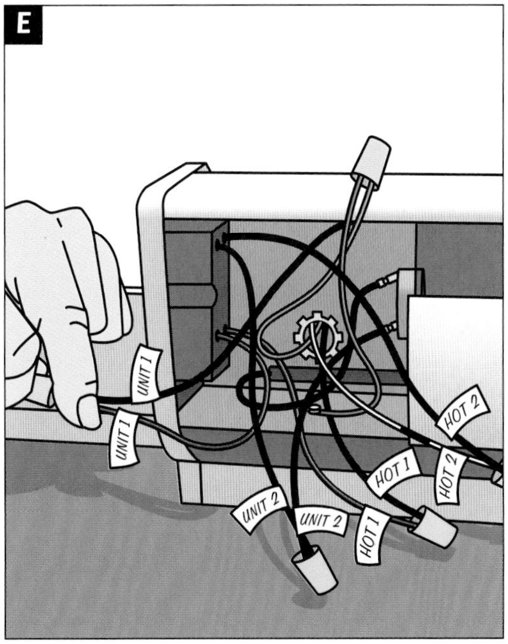

Disconnect a heating element wire from the thermostat lead.

F

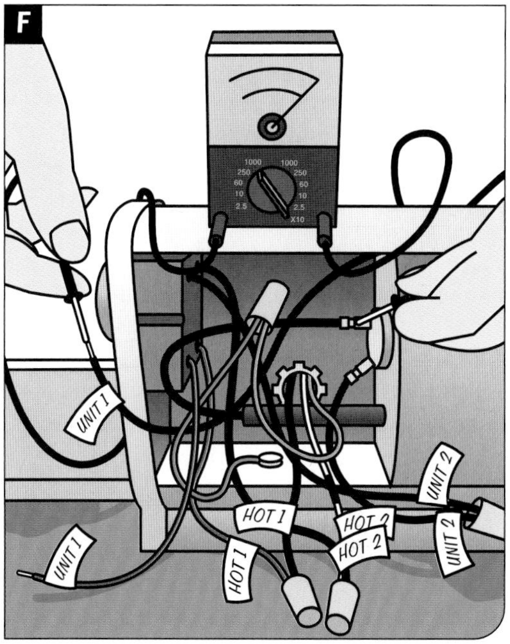

Use the multi-tester to check for a faulty heating element.

Replacing a Baseboard Heater

Shut off the power to the heater at the main service panel, and confirm that the power is off (page 471). Unscrew the wire connectors and disconnect all of the wires entering the heater from the circuit cable. This includes two hot wires (if the heater is 240-volt) or one hot and one neutral wire (120-volt heater), plus a bare copper or green ground wire. Loosen the main mounting screws securing the heater to the wall. **(Illustration G).**

Gently lift the heater away from the wall **(Illustration H).** If the heater is stuck to the wall, a tug may damage the wall surface: use a putty knife or wallboard knife to pry it away from the wall. Loosen the nut or clamp holding the circuit cable to the back of the heater.

Install a new heater that has the same wattage and voltage ratings as the old one. Feed the circuit wires into the heater's control box and attach them to the heater leads or thermostat leads, using wire connectors. Reconnect the circuit ground wire to the grounding screw in the control box.

G

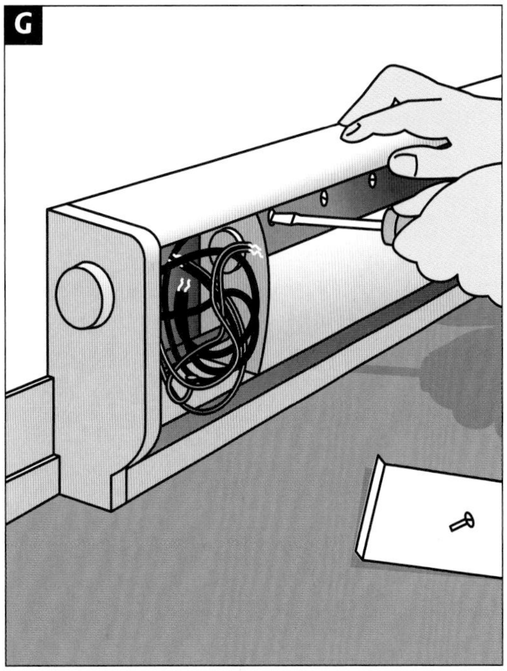

With the power off, disconnect the circuit wires, then remove the mounting screws from the wall.

H

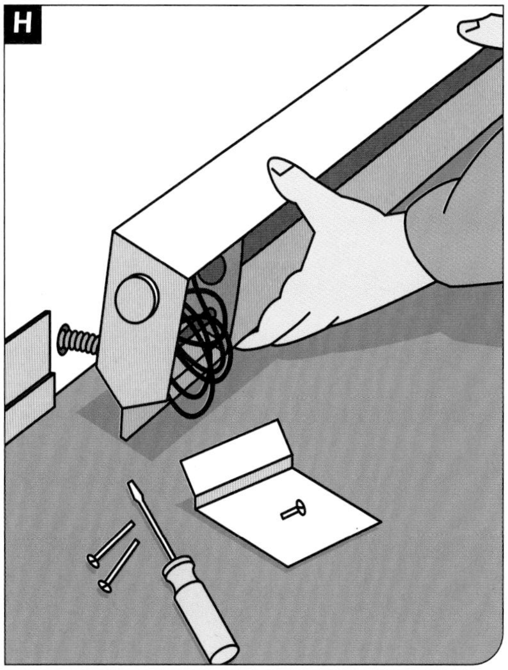

Gently lift the heater away from the wall and disconnect the circuit cable from the back of the heater.

Wall-mounted Electric Heaters

Wall-mounted electric heaters are installed between the studs in an interior wall of your home. They are typically installed in small areas, such as entryways or bathroom additions, where no other heat source is available. Wall-mounted heaters work on the same principles as electric baseboard heaters (pages 470 to 473), generating heat by running electrical current through a heating element. Like some baseboard heaters, most wall-mounted heaters have a built-in thermostat that can be adjusted with a control knob. Since they usually generate less heat than a baseboard unit, however, wall-mounted heaters often contain a fan to help distribute heat to the room. If your wall-mounted heater won't turn on or shut off when the room temperature changes or when you turn the control knob, minor repairs may solve the problem.

Tools: *Screwdrivers (standard and Phillips), circuit tester, needlenose pliers, multi-tester, soft-bristled brush.*

Materials: *Cloth.*

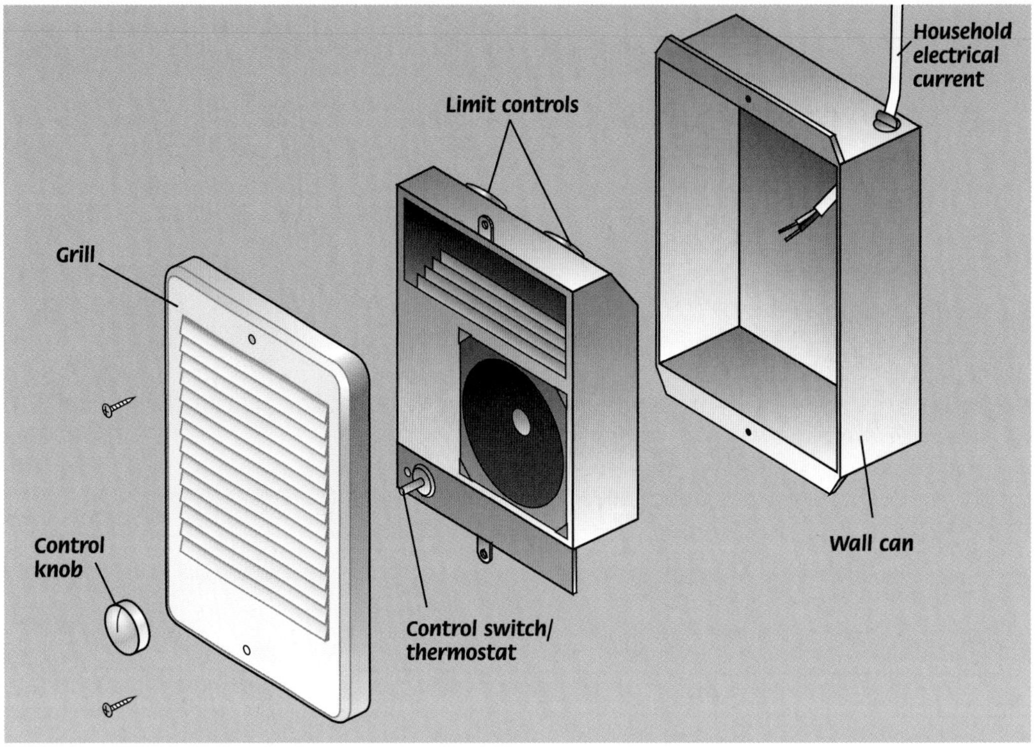

Inspect a wall-mounted heater before the start of the heating season. Dirt and dust can build up around the heating element, resulting in a burning smell when the heater is back in service. A careful cleaning with a soft-bristled brush is important for safe, reliable use.

Removing the Heater & Checking for Power

A wall-mounted heater is installed in a protective metal can that's permanently mounted between the studs in the wall. To remove and test the heater, shut off the power to the heater at the main service panel. Remove the control knob. Loosen the mounting screws on the grill and slide the heater out of the wall can **(photo A).** Lift the top out first, disengaging the tabs at the base. Insert one end of a neon circuit tester into the wire connector holding the black circuit wire, and touch the other end of the probe to the grounding screw **(photo B).** Now insert one end of the circuit tester into the wire connector holding the white circuit wire and touch the other probe to the grounding screw. Finally, insert the probes of the circuit tester into the wire connectors, one probe into each connector. The tester should not glow for any of these tests. If it does, find the correct circuit breaker on the main service panel and shut it off. Repeat the tests until the tester does not glow.

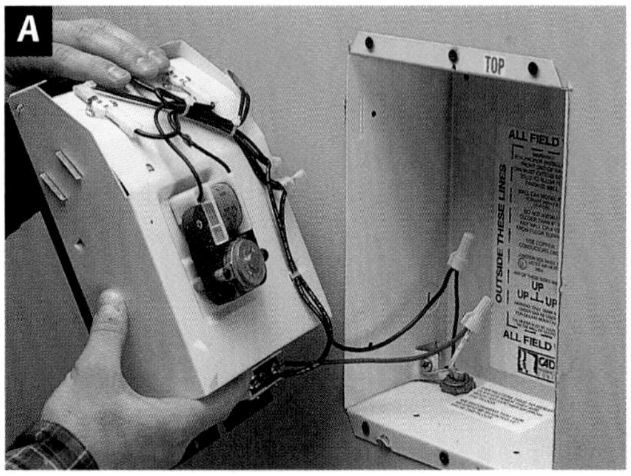

Loosen the mounting screws on the heater's grill and remove the heater.

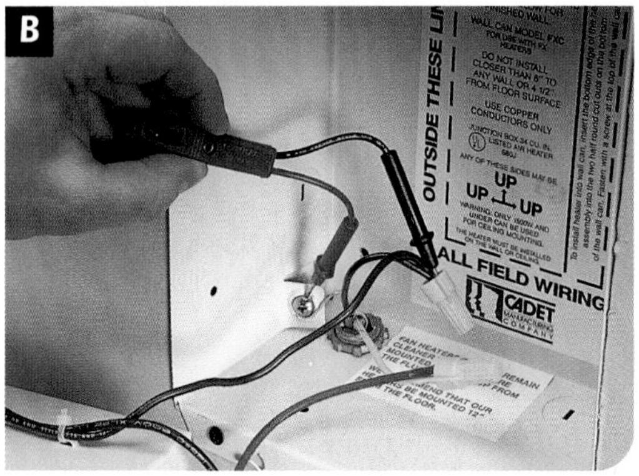

Test for power, using a neon circuit tester.

Testing & Replacing a Limit Control

Your heater may have one or two limit controls near the heating element. They are designed to shut off the heater if it overheats. If you detect a burning smell and the heater doesn't shut itself off, one or both limit controls may be faulty. Shut off the power to the heater at the main service panel and check for power (page 474). Use needlenose pliers to remove a single limit control lead from its terminal on the back of the heater and test for continuity with a multi-tester (page 471). Touch one probe of the multi-tester to each limit control terminal **(photo C).** Repeat the test for the other limit control. If the tester doesn't indicate continuity, remove the limit control and thermal conductor assembly from the heater **(photo D).** When purchasing a replacement, bring the old limit control with you for identification. Install the new limit control and reassemble the heater.

Helpful Hint

The delicate wires in the heating element can become covered with dust, dirt, and cobwebs, especially during warm weather when the heater isn't used for extended periods. Remove the grill, and clean the element by holding a vacuum hose in front of the wires. To remove stubborn dirt and debris, gently clean the wires with a soft-bristled brush or cloth.

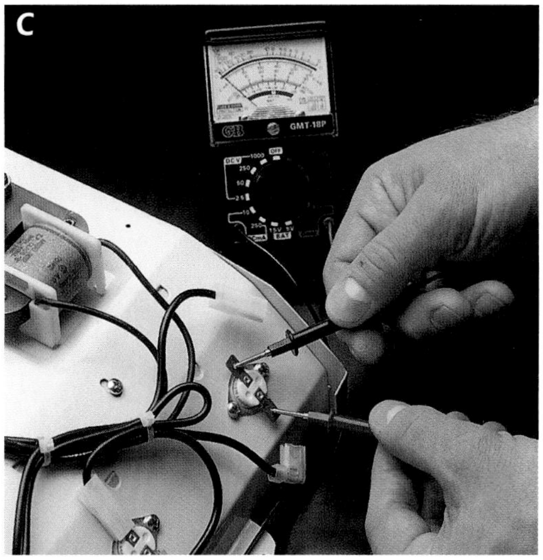

Set your multi-tester to test for continuity (page 471).

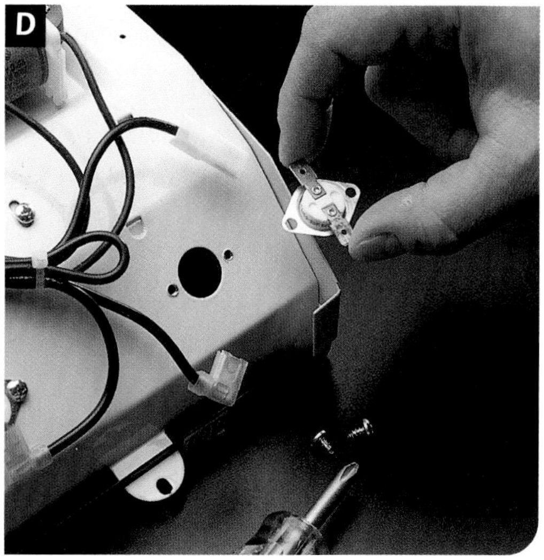

Replace a faulty limit control with an identical replacement.

Testing & Replacing a Thermostat

If your wall-mounted heater doesn't respond when you adjust the control knob, the thermostat may be faulty. Shut off the power to the heater at the main service panel and check for power (page 474). Turn the thermostat knob, starting at OFF, and listen for a click. If the unit doesn't click, test the thermostat for continuity, using a multi-tester (page 471). Disconnect one lead from the back of the control switch/thermostat unit by prying it loose with needlenose pliers or unscrewing it. With the multi-tester set to test for continuity, place one probe on each terminal **(photo E).** If the multi-tester doesn't indicate continuity, remove the other lead and unscrew the control switch/thermostat unit from the base of the heater **(photo F).** Install an identical replacement unit.

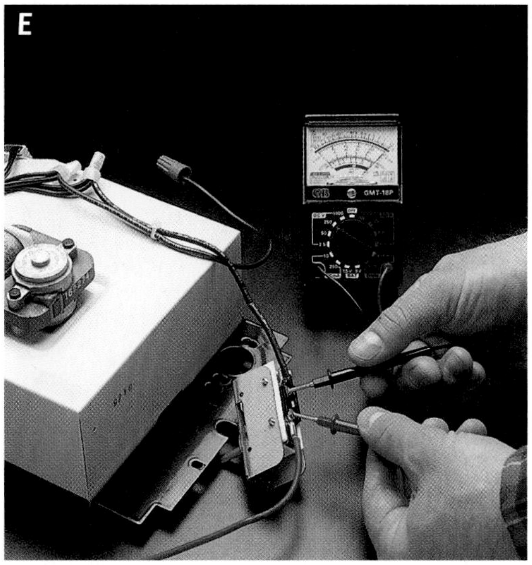

Test the thermostat for continuity to find out if it's faulty.

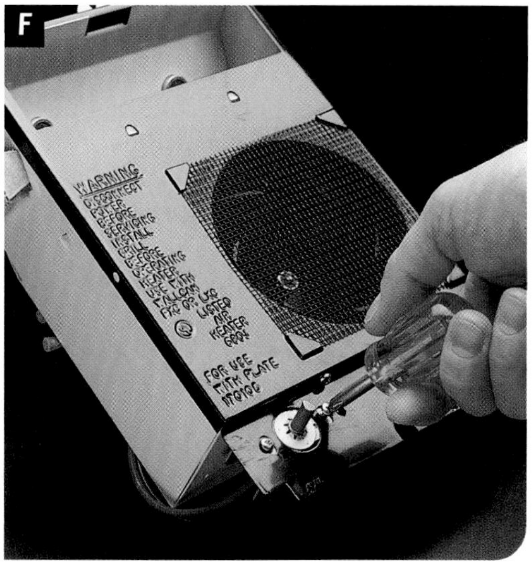

If the thermostat is faulty, remove the mounting screws and replace the control switch/thermostat unit.

Fireplaces & Wood Stoves

Although wood serves as the primary heat source in only about 2 percent of all homes, a great many homes include fireplaces or wood stoves as a supplemental heat source. These units are often chosen as much for decorative purposes as for their ability to provide a source of heat. The older your fireplace or wood stove, the more likely it is to need repair.

If you depend on wood heat, make sure you have a clean-burning wood stove or fireplace. A newer unit can quickly pay for itself in cost savings and reduce the amount of maintenance required.

Tools: Ash scoop, whisk broom, stiff-bristled brush, spray bottle, flashlight, mirror, masonry chisel, bricklayer's trowel, jointing tool.

Materials: Drop cloth, muriatic acid, fire bricks, fire brick-rated mortar.

Photo courtesy of Vermont Castings

A newer high-efficiency wood stove can pay for itself in one season by providing more heat from the same fuel, and less harmful exhaust.

Photo courtesy of Walter Moberg, Firespaces, Inc. (Portland, OR)

A fireplace can be an economical source of supplemental heat if it draws air for combustion from outdoors and has a damper and a set of doors that close securely. It can also be an enjoyable part of your living space.

Cleaning the Ash Pit

To get the best and safest results from your fireplace, take a few hours before the start of each heating season to make sure the fireplace is ready for use.

It can be a messy chore, but your fireplace will work best if the ash pit is cleaned out once every two years, more often if you use your fireplace regularly. Locate the cleanout door, which is usually in the basement or on an outside wall.

Wear clothing you don't mind getting dirty, and place newspaper or a drop cloth around your work area. Open the cleanout door and scoop the ashes into a nonporous container **(photo A).** You may want to mist the ash pit with a spray bottle to avoid creating a dust cloud as you clean out the soot. Sweep out small amounts of stubborn debris with a whisk broom or wire brush, and seal the container. NOTE: You can put small amounts of ash in your compost heap. If you have large quantities to throw away, ask your waste removal contractor for advice on proper disposal.

Scoop the ashes into a nonporous container.

Inspecting the Flue & Damper

Soot and creosote deposits, bird nests, and other obstructions in a chimney can create a serious hazard when you light a fire. To inspect the chimney, open the flue damper and peer up through the flue. You should see a shaft of light from above. If the firebox is too small for a clear view, use a bright light and a mirror for the inspection **(photo B).** Routine cleaning is a job you can handle yourself (page 221). However, if the flue is blocked or hasn't been cleaned in a few years, have it serviced by a professional. An inspection by a professional can give you peace of mind, knowing that the chimney is safe to use.

Once you know the flue is clear, make sure the damper seals tightly **(photo C).** When the fireplace is in use, the damper helps control the draft—how fast air goes up the chimney—and determines the rate at which the fire burns. If left open when the fireplace is not in use, a damper can allow 10 to 15 percent of a home's heat to escape. Test the lever or chain that controls the damper; you should be able to tell when the damper is open or closed all the way. If the damper doesn't open or close completely, open it as far as you can and clear the area around its edges on all sides with a stiff-bristled brush. Remove any debris that may have fallen from the chimney, and try closing the damper again.

Use a mirror and a shop light to inspect the chimney easily from below.

Make sure the damper seals tightly, moves freely, and is free of dirt and debris.

Inspecting & Repairing the Firebox

Using a bright flashlight, examine the bricks and mortar in the firebox **(photo D).** If the soot is too heavy for you to see clearly, clean the firebox with a 9:1 solution of water and muriatic acid. NOTE: Always add acid to water, not water to acid, and protect your hands, skin, and eyes when working with acid.

Remove any faulty bricks and mortar with a masonry chisel **(photo E).** Using a stiff-bristled brush, clean the edges of the remaining bricks so that new ones will fit neatly. Apply water to the existing bricks to keep the new mortar from drying too quickly. With a bricklayer's trowel, apply mortar to the new bricks and to the surfaces where they will fit **(photo F).** Use only mortar that is rated for use with fire brick. Slide the bricks in place gently until they are flush with the existing wall. Scrape off any extra mortar and let the area dry for a few minutes. Then, use a jointing tool to smooth the mortar.

Check for loose mortar in the firebox.

Chisel out loose mortar and remove faulty bricks.

"Butter" the new bricks with mortar before positioning them.

Ventilation

Good ventilation is key to a healthy, comfortable home. It prevents indoor air from becoming stale, dusty, and too dry or too humid. But it's not just a matter of how the air "feels." A constant supply of fresh air reduces susceptibility—especially among children—to viruses, chronic respiratory ailments, and the effects of carbon monoxide.

Poor ventilation reduces the efficiency of your heating and cooling systems. The problem is magnified in superinsulated homes. Some Building Codes have addressed this issue by requiring a fresh air intake near the furnace or boiler. The intake draws air from outside and ensures an adequate oxygen supply for heating. A popular option is the air exchanger (page 479), an intake device that is highly effective at supplying fresh air, without adding significantly to your heating costs.

In addition to drawing fresh air into your home, good ventilation keeps air circulating throughout your home and vents home appliances, such as the kitchen fan (page 480) and fireplace and wood stove (pages 476 to 477), to the outside. Effective maintenance of your home's ventilation systems can improve your health, reduce heating and cooling costs, and enhance the comfort of your home.

Tools: *Hammer, screwdrivers (standard and Phillips), neon circuit tester, tape measure.*

Materials: *1½" wallboard screws, ceiling fan balancing kit and silencer band (as required).*

Don't underestimate the importance of a clean, reliable kitchen vent hood. In a year, the fan may release as much as 200 pounds of moisture to the outdoors. Clean the filter regularly and replace it if it won't come clean.

Common Problems

Home ventilation includes everything from cross ventilation through open windows, to breezes from electric fans, and fresh air from an air exchanger. Keeping each of these elements working smoothly contributes to your overall health and comfort. A wobbly ceiling fan **(photo A)** loses some of its ability to circulate air throughout your home. Whether you rely on the fan to distribute heat evenly in the winter or to cool air in the summer, it will do the job more effectively if you reduce the wobble (page 481).

It's easy and inexpensive to repair or replace a faulty bathroom fan (page 480). Failure to do so can result in moisture buildup on the bathroom walls and ceiling and even in adjacent areas of the house. If they persist, such conditions can lead to extensive mildew **(photo B)** or—even more costly—wood rot.

Newer superinsulated homes often suffer from inadequate ventilation. Evaluate your home's ventilation if people in your home suffer from allergies or asthma, or if you notice stale air or sweaty windows during the heating season when windows are closed **(photo C).** Installing exhaust fans is one solution. Installing a household air exchanger (below) is far more expensive, but also far more effective. Instead of relying on the circulation of stale indoor air, the air exchanger provides a constant supply of fresh air from outside, warming it with the heat from stale air being discharged from your home.

Loose blades can cause a ceiling fan to wobble, reducing the effectiveness of the unit.

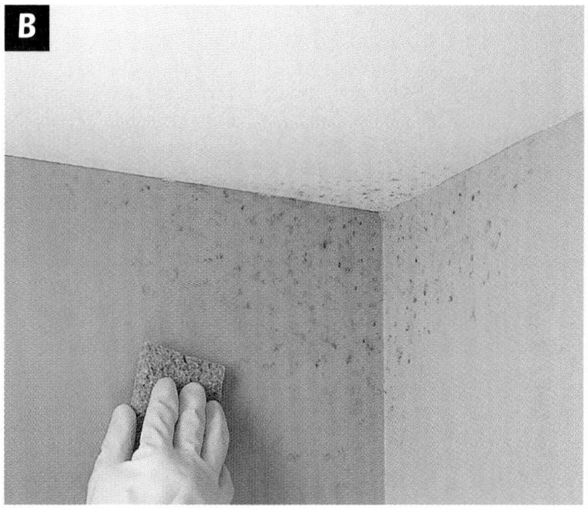

A poorly ventilated space manifests itself as condensation in winter and mildew in the warmer seasons.

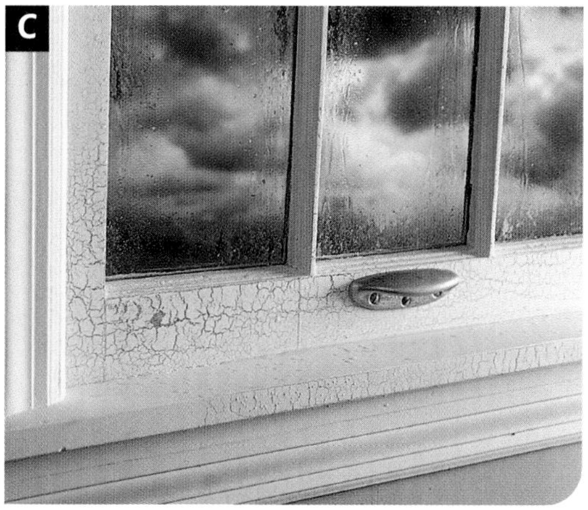

Sweaty windows are an indication of poor ventilation in your home.

Servicing an Air Exchanger

Air exchangers, also known as heat-recovery ventilators, replace stale indoor air with fresh air from outside at little cost **(illustration).** In the process, the stale indoor air passes through a heat exchanger, where it warms the colder fresh air, minimizing additional heating costs.

Air exchangers also filter the fresh air as it enters the system. The filter should be inspected and cleaned monthly during the heating season. Start by shutting off the power to the exchanger at the main service panel. Remove the filter cover and filter. If the filter is damaged, replace it. Otherwise, soak it in a 3:1 mixture of vinegar and water. Allow the filter to dry before reinstalling it and switching on the power.

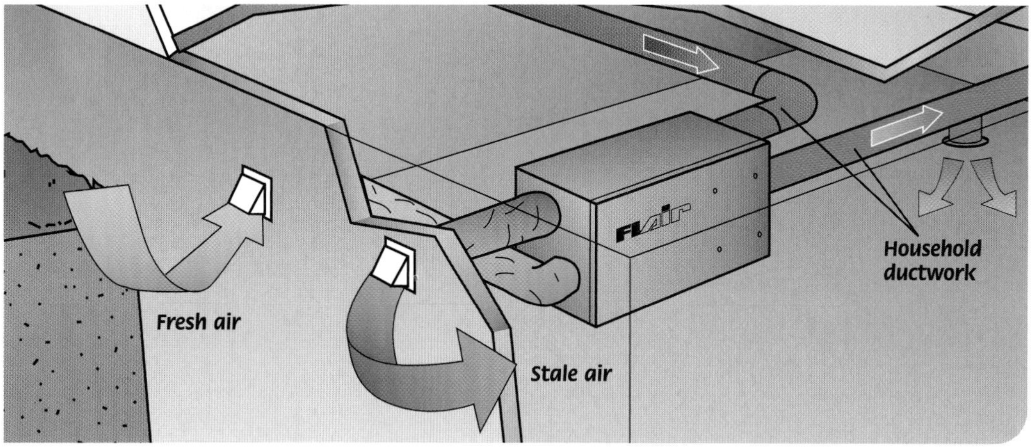

Air exchangers introduce fresh air to your home while removing stale air. A filter removes airborne particles before air enters the heating system. Clean the filter monthly throughout the heating season.

Replacing an Exhaust Fan

A bathroom exhaust fan should remove as many cubic feet of air per minute as the room has square feet of floor space. If your fan is not venting fast enough to control moisture buildup, replace it with a more powerful unit.

Shut off the power to the circuit at the main service panel, remove the fan grill, and test the unit for power with a circuit tester. Taking care not to touch bare wires, insert one probe of the tester into a wire connector so it touches the bare wires. Place the other probe on the grounding screw on the fan's metal housing. Repeat the test for each wire connector in the assembly. If the tester glows in any of the tests, return to the service panel and switch off the correct circuit. Repeat the tests until the tester does not glow.

Remove the fan's mounting screws so you can pull the fan out of the ceiling or wall cavity and access the vent hose and wiring that are connected at the back. Loosen the hose clamp over the vent hose and remove the hose from the exhaust port. Locate the household wiring and disconnect it from the fan leads, then remove the fan.

Measure the size of the opening in the wall or ceiling. Also, measure the square footage of the room. Then, take the old fan assembly to your local home center so you can purchase a fan that has the same size exhaust port and meets the needs of your bath.

From the other side of the wall or ceiling, attach the flange of the new fan housing to the stud or joist **(photo A).** Avoid using the original nail holes, if possible. Test the circuit wires for power. Then, make the electrical connections according to the manufacturer's instructions. Connect the exhaust port of the fan to the vent hose. Install the cover and switch on the power at the main service panel.

Screw or nail the fan box to an adjacent stud or joist with the fan's faceplate flush with the wall or ceiling.

Servicing a Kitchen Fan

A kitchen fan lasts longer if the filter is kept clean. Remove the grill and filter **(photo B)** and clean the filter with lots of warm water and liquid detergent.

If the fan motor fails, install a manufacturer's replacement motor. Switch off the power to the fan at the main service panel. Remove the grill and filter. Loosen the mounting screws and disconnect the mounting bracket from the fan box and motor **(photo C).** On most models, the motor has a plug that fits in a receptacle inside the unit. Disconnect the plug, and slide the motor from the housing. If the motor is wired directly to household wiring, check for power and then disconnect the wires.

Attach the replacement motor to the mounting bracket with screws. Reconnect the motor to the household wiring or to the built-in receptacle and screw the bracket to the fan housing. Attach the filter and grill, and restore power at the service panel.

Remove the grill and filter to gain access to the fan motor.

Unscrew the mounting bracket to remove the fan and motor from the housing.

Maintaining a Ceiling Fan

Wobbling fan blades reduce a ceiling fan's efficiency and shorten the life of the fixture. Balancing blades is a relatively simple process that takes just a few minutes.

To balance the blades, shut the fixture off and tighten the screws holding the blades to the blade brackets. Compare the blade angles by holding a tape measure vertically from the ceiling and measuring the distance from the end of one blade to the ceiling **(photo D).** Then, without moving the tape measure, rotate the fan and measure the distances between the other blades and the ceiling. To make a correction, gently bend the blade brackets, as required, until the end of each blade is the same distance from the ceiling.

If this doesn't correct the wobble, place counterweights on the blades. Purchase a blade balancing kit at a hardware store or home center. Attach the clip to the middle of the rear edge of a blade, turn the fan on, and note whether the wobble increases or decreases. Remove the clip, and try it on each of the remaining blades, watching for changes in the wobble. Attach the clip to the blade that wobbles the most. Adjust the clip's position until the wobble is gone. Affix a weight along the centerline on the top side of the blade, in line with the clip **(photo E)** and remove the clip.

Check the blade angles by measuring each blade's distance from the ceiling.

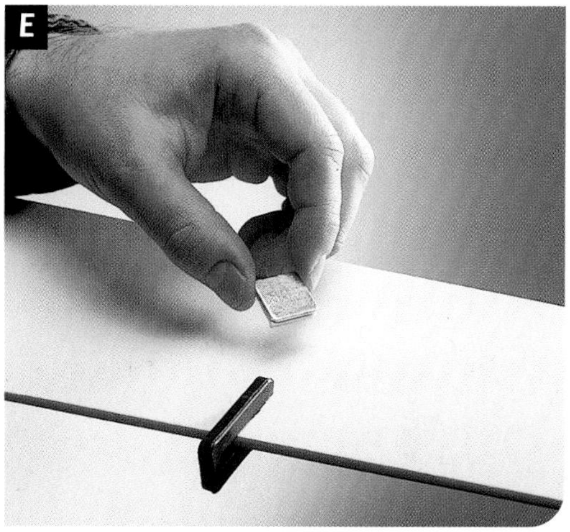

Use the clip to find the blade that requires extra weight. Remove the clip after affixing the weight to the blade.

Reducing Ceiling Fan Noise

The popularity of ceiling fans lies not only in their aesthetic appeal, but also in the comfort they provide. By circulating the air throughout a room, ceiling fans reduce heating and cooling costs and make room temperatures more uniform.

Most fans require occasional adjustment. If your fan is noisy, it may not be operating at its highest efficiency. Often, you can correct this by simply tightening the screws that have loosened due to normal vibration.

To eliminate the noise, begin by shutting off the fan. Make sure the canopy doesn't touch the ceiling. If it does, adjust it. Tighten all of the screws in the motor housing. Then, check the screws holding the fan blade bracket to the motor hub **(photo F).** On models with lights, tighten the screws securing the globe and light fixture.

If this doesn't quiet the noise, the problem may stem from glass globes rattling against their mounting screws. Buy a light silencer band at your local hardware store or home improvement center. To install, slip the silencer band—essentially a rubber band—over the neck of the globe. Then, tighten the screws in the lamp holder.

Helpful Hint

You can stay comfortable while using less heat and air conditioning if you make full use of your ceiling fan. In the summer, set the fan to draw warm air up. In the winter, set the fan to force warm air down. You'll save 4 to 8 percent on cooling costs for every degree you raise the thermostat in hot weather, and 1 to 2 percent on heating costs for every degree you lower the thermostat in cold weather.

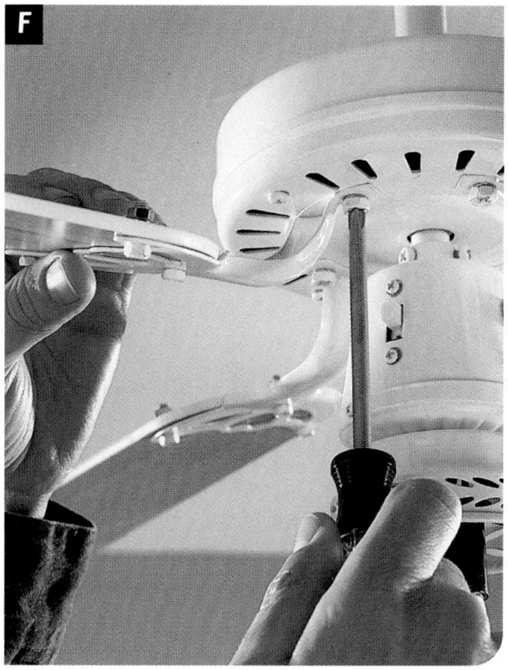

Tighten the screws to reduce vibration noise.

Air Conditioning

Air conditioning, a term often associated with cooling systems, is used in this book to refer to the role of heat pumps as well as conventional air conditioners. This is because air conditioners and heat pumps operate in much the same way. In simple terms, they circulate refrigerant through an indoor coil, the *evaporator coil,* that absorbs heat from the air. The refrigerant flows outside to the *condensor coil,* where heat is released. The refrigerant returns to liquid, and the cycle repeats.

Heat pumps have one major advantage over air conditioners: they run in reverse during the winter, drawing heat out of moderately cool outdoor air and using it to heat a home.

Since air conditioners and heat pumps operate on the same basic principles, most of their maintenance and repair needs are the same. When parts are dirty, fan blades or fins are bent or broken, or filters are clogged, performance suffers. Regular cleanings and inspections produce better results and reduce long-term maintenance and repair costs.

You can do the routine maintenance yourself. Repairs that involve discharging a capacitor, checking refrigerant levels, and adding refrigerant should be made by a repair technician.

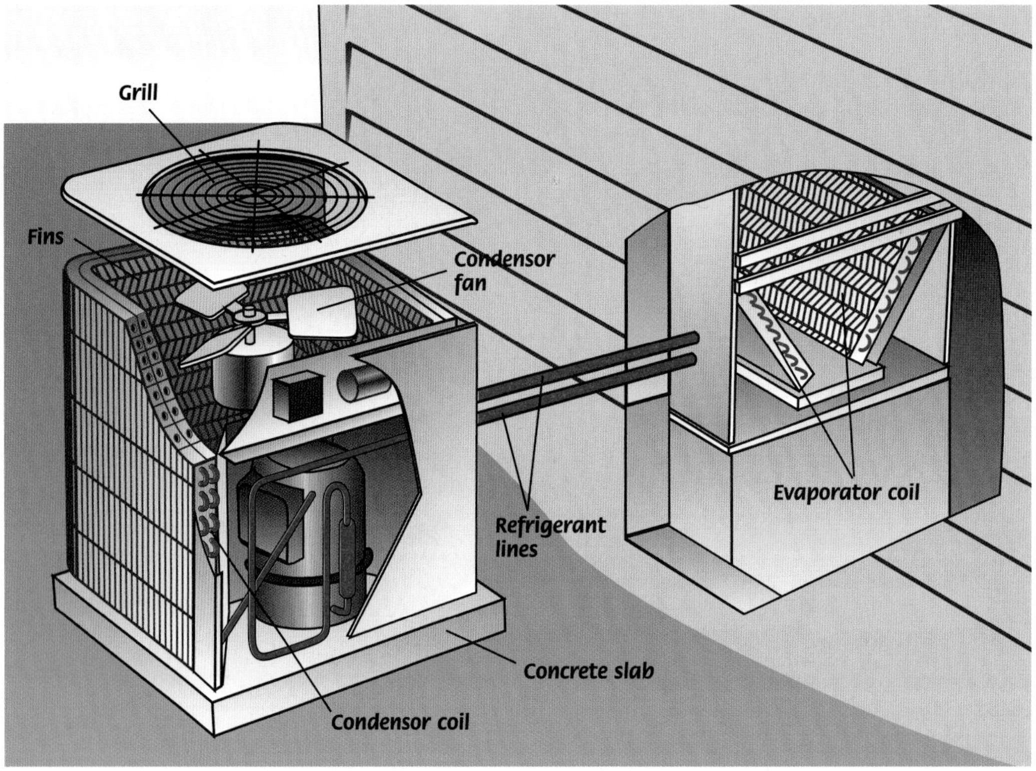

Refrigerant is pressurized and pumped through a condensor coil where it releases heat. It then flows to the evaporator coil. Air from the furnace blower is cooled as it crosses the evaporator. The refrigerant is then pumped back outdoors to be cooled once again. A heat pump operates much the same as an air conditioner during the summer. During the winter, a solenoid is used to reverse the heat pump's operation so that refrigerant extracts heat from outdoor air and releases the heat indoors. As a heating system, a heat pump is effective down to about 32°F.

Common Problems

Air conditioners and heat pumps can operate for many years with relatively few problems as long as they are regularly maintained and repairs are performed routinely.

Most systems, for example, will still function with a slightly bent fan blade **(photo A).** But they'll suffer damage in the long run and eventually break down due to the added strain on the system. The end result is a far larger and more expensive repair that requires the services of a licensed professional.

A bent blade often results when a blade has become loose to the point of wobbling, and then strikes one of the unit's outside panels. Fan blades are shaped to move air efficiently. When they become bent, they can't do the job as effectively. The extra strain can ruin the motor.

If you notice that a blade is bent, don't try to fix it. A blade that has been weakened from being realigned may break, causing further damage. Instead, replace the entire blade assembly. To avoid the problem in the future, make sure that all of the blades are tight and that the fan rotates smoothly, both when you spin it by hand and when the unit is operating.

Bent fan blades are not the only problem

you may confront. A close look is likely to reveal debris that has collected inside the condensor coil **(photo B).** Twigs, leaves, and rubbish are often sucked inside the unit by the fan. Regular cleaning keeps debris from building up and reducing the air flow across the condensor coil. When obstructed, the fan works harder to draw in sufficient air. This increases the cost of operating the unit, and, again, the added strain shortens the life of the fan motor.

An outdoor condensor should be adjusted so it is level (page 485). However, the slab under the condensor or heat pump unit should slope slightly away from the house to provide proper drainage for condensation **(photo C).** If the slab has shifted due to frost heave and no longer slopes away from the house, call a mudjack professional to adjust it before water from the unit drains into your basement. Also make sure the grade in your yard slopes away from the house, to discourage run-off from flowing toward the foundation.

Replace the fan assembly if a blade is bent. Don't try to bend a blade back into shape.

Remove dirt and debris with a brush and a garden hose to reduce interference with airflow across the coil.

An outdoor compressor won't drain properly if it's not level. Hire a masonry professional to lift the slab and add concrete to achieve the proper angle.

Maintaining Central Air Conditioners & Heat Pumps

The outdoor portion of a central air conditioner or heat pump has to endure the weather all year—not just when it's in use. Rain, cold, wind, and sun can eventually hurt the performance of your system. To keep it in peak operating condition, clean the condenser fins and coils before the start of each cooling season, and whenever they become dirty or clogged (page 484). If you use your air conditioner just a few weeks out of the year, you can get by with one round of thorough cleaning and maintenance each spring. If you use your air conditioner more than a few months each year, or if you use a heat pump for both heating and cooling, inspect the filter monthly to keep dirt and debris from putting an unnecessary strain on the equipment. You should also check once a month to make sure that the condensor is not obstructed by leaves or other debris. Always inspect the condensor unit after a heavy rain or a wind storm.

Annual maintenance includes lubricating the fan motor (page 484), removing dirt and debris from the unit, and inspecting the fan carefully for alignment.

CAUTION: Air conditioners and heat pumps contain capacitors that store electricity. Wait five minutes after shutting off your unit. This discharges the capacitors, making it safe to conduct maintenance and repairs inside.

Tools: Screwdrivers (standard and Phillips), open-end wrench set, level, fin comb, soft-bristled brush, garden hose, vacuum cleaner.

Materials: Cloth, all-purpose oil, heavy gloves.

Cleaning the Coils & Fins

Shut off the power at the unit's disconnect switch **(photo A),** and switch off the power to the unit at the main service panel. Remove the screws from the top access panel and lift the panel **(photo B).** Remove the screws from the side panel, which surrounds the condenser coils, and carefully pull the panel away from the condenser. Remove any debris from around the condenser coil, fan, and motor.

With a soft brush, remove dust from the fins and coils. Hire a professional to remove stubborn dirt and debris.

Straighten bent fins carefully with a fin comb **(photo C).** Most fin combs have three or more sides with different tooth widths and spacing. Before you try to pull the comb through the fins, match the teeth to the fins by holding one side of the comb at a time up to the fins.

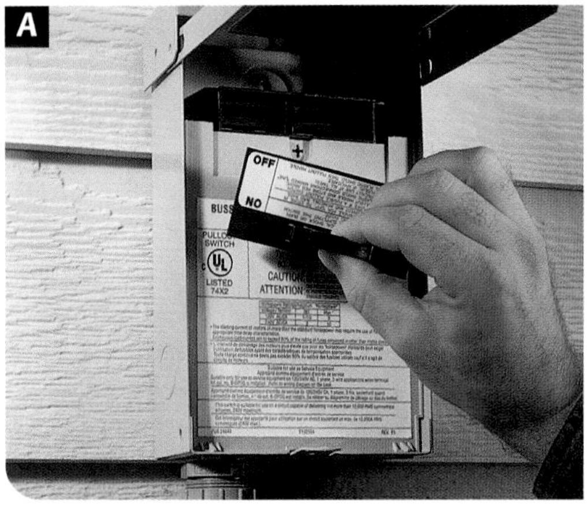

Shut off the power at the unit's disconnect switch.

Raise the top panel and remove any debris from inside the condenser coil.

Use a fin comb to straighten bent fins.

Lubricating the Fan Motor

Switch off the air conditioner or heat pump disconnect switch and shut off the power to the system at the main service panel. Remove the retaining screws from the top access panel and lift the panel.

Locate the oil ports. If the fan is attached to the top panel, the oil ports will be located above the fan blades. If the fan is separate from the panel, first loosen the setscrew on the fan blade assembly **(photo D).** Wearing heavy gloves, remove the assembly. Pry out the rubber oil plugs and add three drops of all-purpose oil to each port **(photo E).**

Reattach the fan blades, securing them so the assembly rests 1" above the motor.

Then, make sure the fan blades spin freely. Adjust the setscrew that holds the fan to the motor shaft until the fan rotates smoothly.

Next, inspect the blades. If a blade is bent, replace the entire fan blade assembly.

To install the fan blade assembly, line up the setscrew with the flat side of the motor shaft. Slide the assembly onto the shaft until it rests 1" from the motor. Tighten the setscrew.

Secure the top panel by fastening the retaining screws. Turn on the power to the system at the disconnect switch and the main service panel. Set the thermostat so the condensor unit will run and inspect the fan blade assembly. Reinspect the condensor unit. If you notice the fan blade assembly wobbling or hear unusual noise, shut off the power again and check for interference, debris, or a loose fan blade assembly.

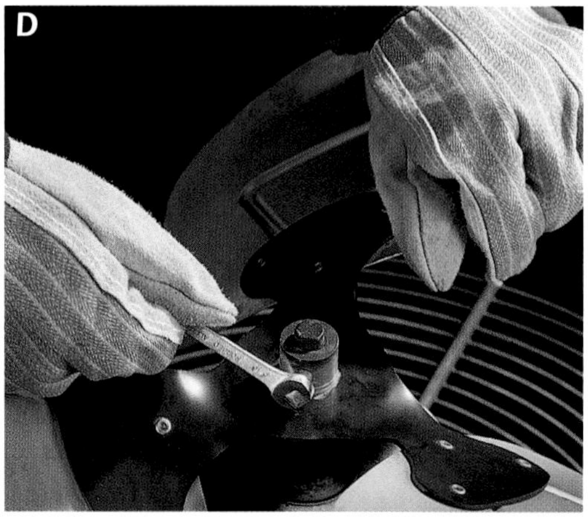

Loosen the setscrew and remove the fan blade assembly.

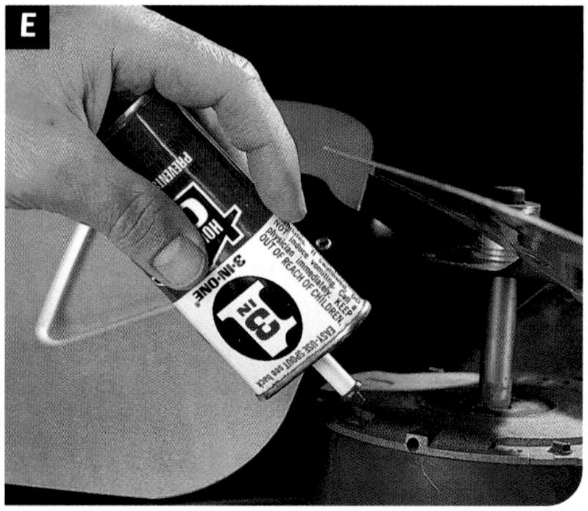

Add three drops of oil to each port on the fan motor.

Checking a Condensor for Level

A condensing unit must always be level to operate properly and to reduce wear on the motor. Place a level lengthwise across the top of the unit **(photo F),** then widthwise. If the unit is not level in either direction, inspect the bottom of the unit; it may have adjustable feet designed for leveling the unit. You can also make slight adjustments by placing wood shims under the feet. If leveling requires a major adjustment, you will need to repair or replace the slab (page 483).

To ensure proper airflow and more efficient operation, cut any vegetation that's less than 2 ft. from the condensor coils.

Concrete provides the strongest, most stable surface for a condenser unit. Whether your condenser rests on concrete, bare ground, or any other surface, you need to check it for level each spring.

Inspecting a Heat Pump Reversing Valve

A heat pump relies on a solenoid attached to a coil to reverse its operation for heating and cooling. If your heat pump generates hot air in the summer or cold air in the winter, check for a faulty solenoid.

Switch off the heat pump's disconnect switch (page 484) and shut off the power to the system at the main service panel. CAUTION: After shutting off the power, wait five minutes before opening the unit, to allow the capacitors to discharge (page 483). Remove the rear access panel. Disconnect the plug from the solenoid **(illustration G).** Set a multi-tester to test for continuity (page 471). Place one tester probe on each of the contacts on the solenoid **(illustration H).** A value other than 0 indicates a faulty solenoid. To replace the solenoid, remove the locknut. Slip off the bracket cover and solenoid **(illustration I)** and install a replacement solenoid from the manufacturer. Reattach the access panel and restore power.

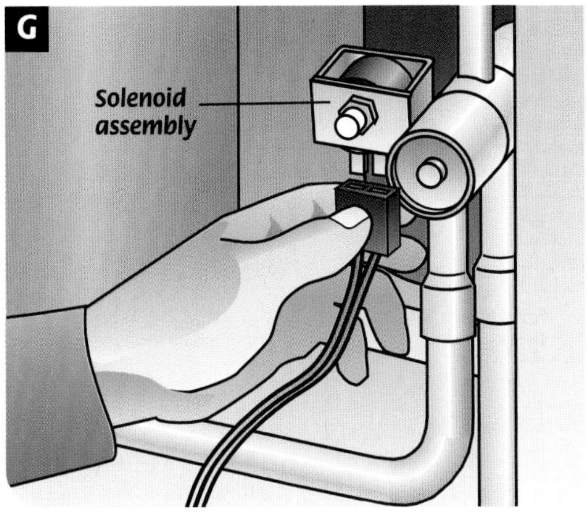

Disconnect the plug leading to the solenoid.

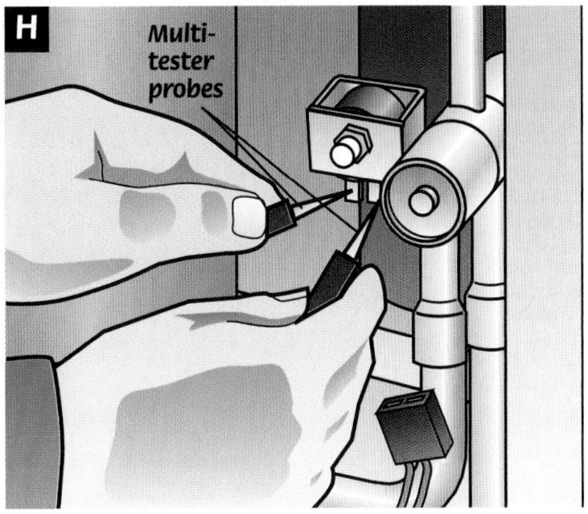

Use a multi-tester to test the solenoid for continuity.

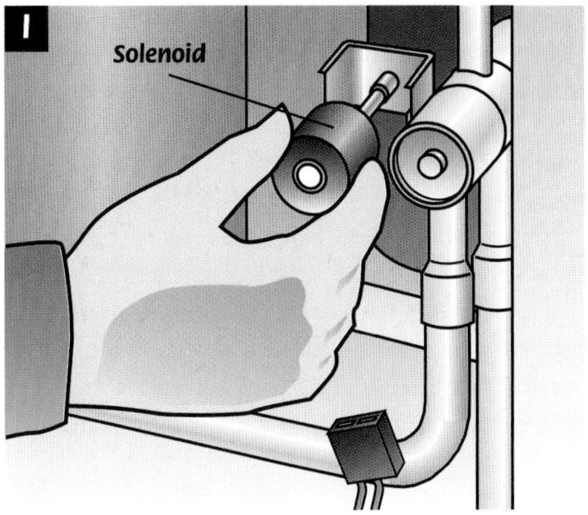

Loosen the locknut and remove the bracket and solenoid.

Maintaining a Room Air Conditioner

Room air conditioners require little regular maintenance. But it's important to clean the air filter frequently to reduce the strain on the motor caused by dirt buildup. Each season, you should also inspect the fins and clear the drains on the unit.

Clean the filter once a month during the cooling season. Switch off the power and unplug the unit. Remove the retaining clips or screws and lift off the front access cover **(photo A).** Remove the filter and inspect it. If it's damaged, install a replacement. You can reuse most filters by washing them with mild detergent; check the label on the filter for directions. Lay the filter on a towel and pat it dry **(photo B).** Let it dry completely before reinstalling it.

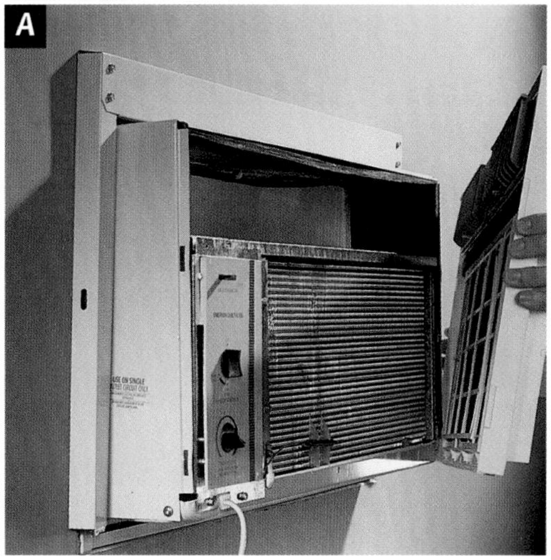

Detach the front cover, then remove the air filter by releasing the clips or tabs and sliding it out.

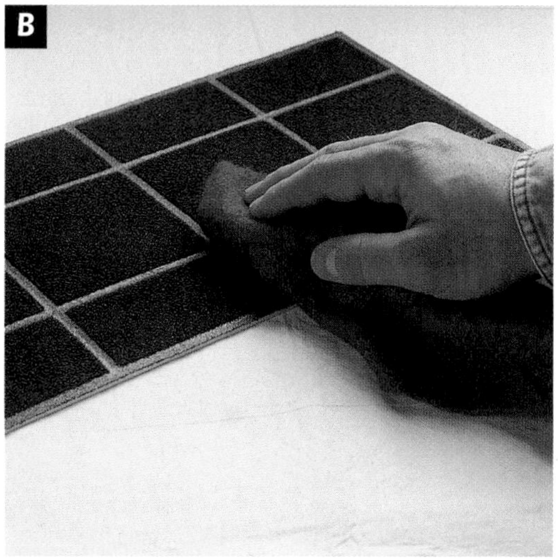

To dry the filter, lay it on a soft, clean surface and pat it with a clean cloth.

Straightening Fins & Clearing Drains

With the air conditioner removed from its window or wall sleeve, loosen the retaining screws and remove the back panel. You may first need to remove the unit's outer cover. Gently clean the condenser fins, using the soft brush attachment on a vacuum. Straighten any bent fins, using a fin comb **(photo C).**

Air conditioners need to drain away the moisture that condenses around the coils. The drain hole on a room unit is located on the outside, with a drain pan usually found just below the condenser coils. If the pan contains water, soak it up with a rag or sponge. Inspect the drain hole to make sure it's clear, and remove any blockage by wiping the area with a clean cloth **(photo D).** Hard-to-reach areas can be cleaned by gently wiping the area with a screwdriver tip covered with cloth. Remove and wash the drain pan, if possible. Otherwise, flush it with a 1:1 solution of bleach and water to discourage algae growth.

Find the proper comb teeth for your air conditioner before pulling the comb through the fins.

Remove dirt, grease, and debris from the drain hole, to ensure proper drainage.

Evaporative Chillers

In addition to fresh-air ventilation and refrigerant cooling, evaporative chillers—also known as evaporative coolers—are popular in hot, dry regions **(illustration E).** These units cool and moisten the air by means of evaporation. As dry outdoor air passes through an evaporative chiller's wet paper or cellulose pad, the air is cooled. The effect is much the same as the one experienced when a breeze or fan blows air across wet skin. Evaporative chillers reduce the temperature of outdoor air by as much as 40°F before blowing it into your home.

The cool air supplied by an evaporative chiller can enter the house through a central duct or in conjunction with the ducts of another heating or cooling system.

Evaporative chillers cost a bit more to operate than whole-house fans, but far less than air conditioners designed to cool the same amount of space. They supply a constant flow of fresh air instead of sealing the house off from the outside world. Chillers are also less expensive to install and maintain than air conditioners, and don't require the use of environmentally hazardous refrigerants. Because they depend on evaporation and increase the humidity of indoor air, chillers are best suited to dry climates.

A two-stage chiller **(illustration F),** which uses a heat exchanger to cool and dry incoming air before it passes through the pad, can reduce air temperatures by an additional 5° to 15°F.

Traditionally, evaporative chillers were mounted on rooftops and vented directly into the house from above. Most chillers are large and unattractive, however, so this works best on flat roofs or where appearance is less important. While rooftop placement is still common, newer models can be installed in the attic, or on the ground next to the house. Ground-based units are easiest to reach for maintenance and repairs.

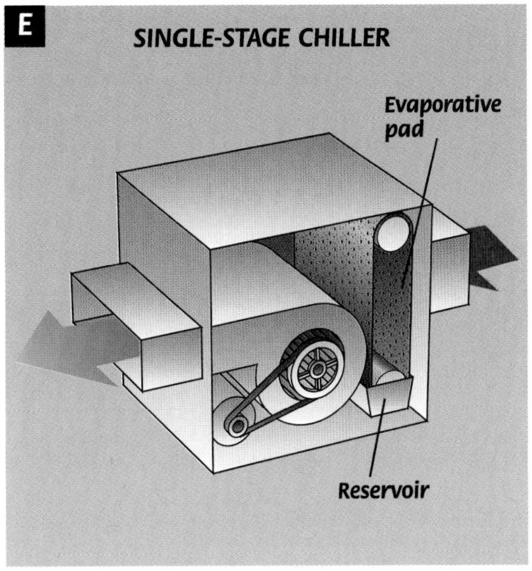

Evaporative chillers, also called swamp coolers, consume about 25 percent of the energy of air conditioners with comparable cooling power.

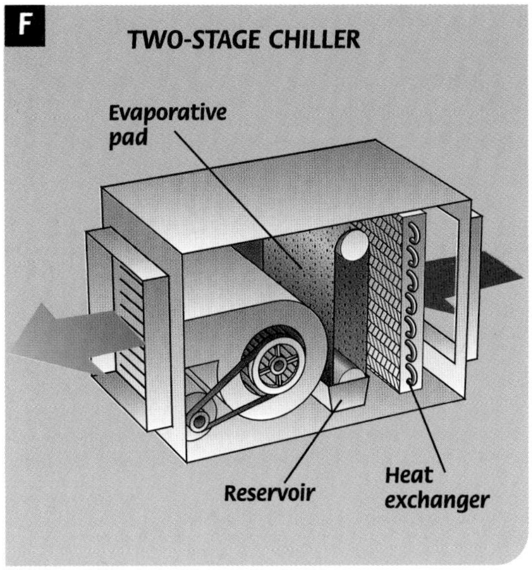

In two-stage chillers, a heat exchanger mounted ahead of the evaporative chiller makes the incoming air cooler and drier.

Maintaining an Evaporative Chiller

Chillers are mechanically simple and seldom need repair. But they do require careful maintenance. During the cooling season, check the filters, pads, reservoir, and pump twice a month. Replace the pads once a year—twice a year if you live in an area with hard water.

You'll need to start your maintenance by draining the reservoir. Switch off the power at the main service panel and shut off the water supply to the chiller. Attach a garden hose to the drain fitting on the lower edge or bottom of the chiller cabinet **(illustration G).** Unscrew the overflow tube inside the reservoir, and allow all the water to run out. Once the reservoir is drained, reinstall the overflow tube and remove the garden hose from the drain fitting.

Check the fan blades and louvers for dirt or grease buildup, and clean them with a mild detergent, if necessary. Make sure the water supply holes above the pad are clear so that water flows freely. Check the intake of the water pump and remove any deposits or obstructions. As you turn the water supply back on, watch the float valve, if necessary, checking for leaks. Restore power to the evaporative chiller.

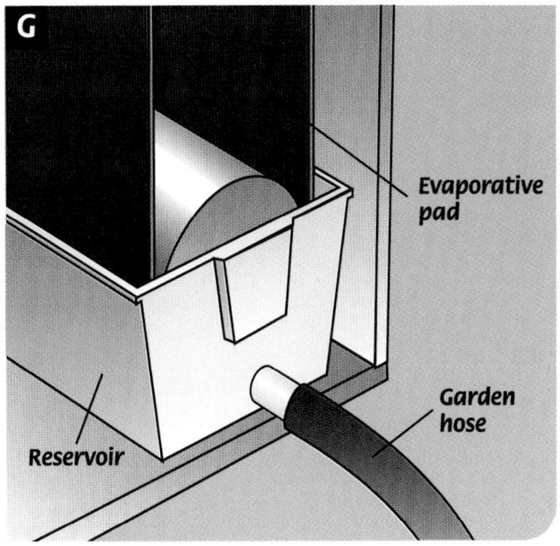

Attach a garden hose and let the reservoir drain completely.

Thermostats

Most thermostats have few parts and the parts seldom need repair or replacement. But wires can occasionally come loose, contacts can corrode, and dust can interfere with operation.

A faulty thermostat can create an uncomfortable home environment and raise heating and cooling costs, so it's a good idea to check yours at least once a year to make sure it's working properly.

Most thermostats are either low-voltage, line-voltage, or electronic. Low-voltage thermostats receive power from a transformer that converts 120-volt household current to 24 volts. Line-voltage thermostats use the same power source as the electric heaters they control. Most electronic thermostats operate on a low-voltage circuit. They're convenient to use and can easily replace older low-voltage units.

A simple low-voltage thermostat **(photo A)** switches a heating or cooling system on and off. Other models have separate controls for a forced-air fan and a cooling system. The thermostat contains a bi-metal coil that expands and contracts as the temperature changes. At the end of the coil is a glass bulb that holds a mercury ball and two electrical contacts. When the coil turns far enough to tip the bulb, the mercury ball rolls onto the two contacts, closing a circuit and switching on the system. The controls determine the temperature at which the circuit will close.

A line-voltage thermostat **(photo B)** is linked to an electric heater, and uses the same current as the heater. This current may be either 120 or 240 volts, either of which can cause a severe shock. Line-voltage thermostats may be connected directly to a baseboard or wall-mounted heater or to a wall nearby. You can test a wall-mounted thermostat using the same techniques as for a unit-mounted thermostat (page 472). If you plan to dismantle and inspect or repair a line-voltage thermostat, shut off the circuit at the main service panel and check for power first.

An electronic thermostat **(photo C)** uses the same connections as a low-voltage thermostat to control a heating system or other component, such as an air conditioner or humidifier. You can install an electronic thermostat in place of a low-voltage thermostat quite easily, with no modifications to the wiring. Electronic thermostats can be programmed to adjust the temperature automatically. By keeping temperatures low when you are away or asleep, these thermostats conserve energy. Reduced heating or cooling costs will quickly pay for the new thermostat.

Tools: Fine-bristled brush, needlenose pliers, circuit tester, screwdrivers (standard and Phillips).

Materials: Masking tape.

Low-voltage thermostats rarely fail, but are most reliable when inspected seasonally for dust and loose wiring.

Line-voltage thermostats operate on 120-volt or 240-volt current. Make sure power to the thermostat is shut off at the main circuit panel before attempting any repairs.

Electronic thermostats for central heating systems run on a low-voltage line and require little maintenance.

Inspecting & Replacing a Low-voltage Thermostat

If too much dust or grime accumulates on a thermostat's bi-metal coil, it won't work correctly. To clean the coil, turn off the power to the thermostat, remove the cover, and place the thermostat at its lowest setting. Clean the coil with a soft brush **(photo D),** adjust the thermostat to its highest setting, clean the coil again, and reset the thermostat.

If your low-voltage thermostat fails, first make sure that the wires inside are secure. Tighten any loose screw terminals just until they are snug. Use needlenose pliers to place loose wires back on their terminals **(photo E),** then tighten the screws.

Locate the low-voltage transformer that powers the thermostat. You'll probably find it near the heating/air conditioning system, or inside a furnace access panel. Tighten any loose wire connections on the transformer.

Set the control dial of a multi-tester to the 50-volt (AC) range. Turn on the power to the thermostat, then touch one probe of the multi-tester to each of the screw terminals on the transformer **(photo F).** If the tester doesn't detect current, the transformer is defective, and you'll need to replace it, using the same technique used for a doorbell transformer (page 444).

Now, set the thermostat to AUTO and HEAT. Strip 1/2" from each end of a short piece of insulated wire. Touch one end of the wire to the terminal marked W and the other end to the terminal marked R **(photo G).** If the heating system begins to run, then the thermostat is faulty and must be replaced.

A faulty low-voltage thermostat is easily replaced with a new electronic type. With the power to the thermostat turned off, disconnect the old thermostat and label the wires to indicate their screw-terminal connections. Remove the thermostat, making sure the wires don't fall into the wall cavity. Thread the wires through the base of the new thermostat and mount the thermostat to the wall **(photo H).** Connect the wires to the screw terminal on the base of the new thermostat, using the manufacturer's connection chart as a guide **(photo I).**

Remove the cover and inspect the coil, contacts, and wiring connections.

Twist loose wires around the terminals with needlenose pliers and tighten the screws.

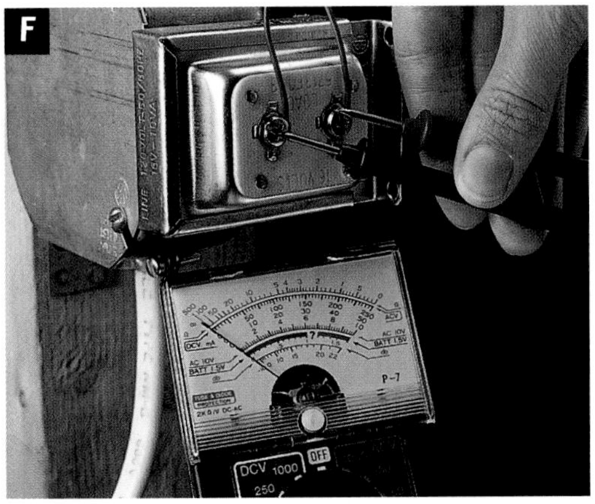

Use a multi-tester to test whether the low-voltage transformer is functioning correctly.

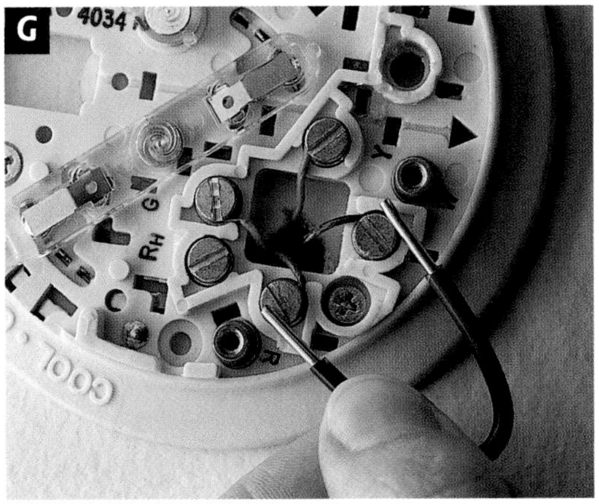

Use a short length of wire to create a connection between the R and W terminals.

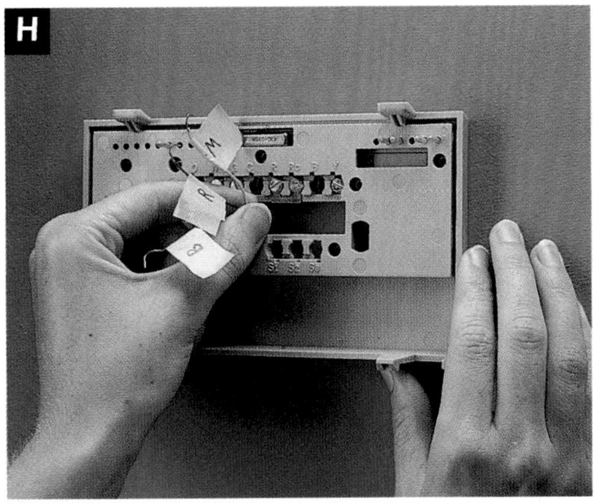

Thread the low-voltage wires into the base, attach the thermostat to the wall, and connect the wires.

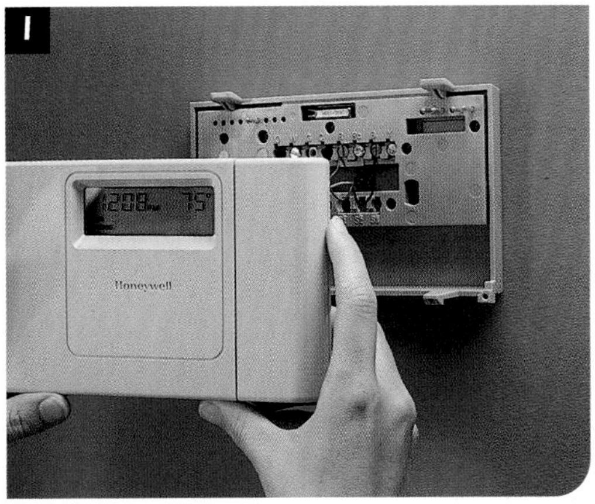

Secure the low-voltage wires to their designated screw terminals, then reattach the cover.

MAINTENANCE SCHEDULE

The best way to keep your home in prime condition is to perform routine maintenance inspections throughout the year. The checklists below are designed to help you remember the elements of your home that need to be inspected regularly. For convenience, the checklist includes monthly and seasonal inspections (Spring, Summer, Fall, and Winter), as well as a separate section for Additional Maintenance Items particular to your home. Record the dates and details of your inspections and repairs in the Notes column, so you'll have a reliable maintenance and repair history for future reference, which will prove invaluable as a home maintenance record, should you decide to sell your home.

Items that you should inspect monthly include air filters and the batteries in your smoke and carbon monoxide detectors. You may not need to clean or replace these items every time you inspect them, but frequent checks will draw your attention to problems before they become serious.

Seasonal inspections and repairs are designed to address typical wear and tear, as well as damage due to freeze and thaw cycles, summer heat and other weather conditions.

Make each of your inspections as soon as weather permits. You'll be glad to have them completed, and you'll avoid working outdoors or in attics and other semi-exposed areas in harsh weather.

MONTHLY

ITEM	PROJECT	NOTES
Smoke/carbon monoxide detectors	Test units for power by depressing the test button and waiting for the alarm to sound.	
Fire extinguishers	Check the tank pressure. If the pressure is low, replace the extinguisher or have it recharged.	
Clothes dryer	Clean the flexible ventilation duct at the back of the dryer to remove accumulated lint.	
Bathroom	Check grout and caulk joints for cracks, crumbling, and mold (pages 40, 42).	
House drains	Inspect plumbing fixtures and appliance drains for leaky connections (page 272).	
Water supply lines	Inspect hoses, pipes, and tubes supplying water to appliances and plumbing fixtures.	
Whirlpool	Flush the water pump system to remove mineral deposits, oils, and bacteria (page 342).	
GFCI receptacles	Test the trip mechanism by pushing the black TEST button (page 408).	
Furnace filter	Inspect the filter for buildup of particles. Clean a soiled filter or replace it, according to the manufacturer's instructions (page 456).	
Boiler	Remove dust and debris from the air intake fan. Lubricate the blower motor every two months (page 466).	
Air exchanger	Inspect and clean or replace the filter (page 479).	
Air conditioner/ Heat pump	Check the condenser unit for level, and remove leaves, branches, and other debris from the fan and coils (page 483).	

SPRING

ITEM	PROJECT	NOTES
Basement	Check for moisture on foundation walls (pages 24 to 25). Inspect beams, posts, floor joists, and sill plates for water or stress damage (pages 76, 82).	
Weatherstripping	Inspect weatherstripping around doors and windows for wear. Feel for drafts (pages 132 and 137).	
Insulation	Add insulation in areas where existing protection proved insufficient during the winter months (page 158).	
Attic	Check rafters and roof sheathing for signs of moisture. Feel around vents to check for air flow (page 188).	
Roof	Inspect the roof for damaged or missing shingles. Check flashing and joint compound for wear and cracking (page 188).	
Gutters	Clean gutters and downspouts. Check for loose connectors and leaky joints. Make sure that long runs are straight and sloped properly (page 214).	
Chimney	Inspect the masonry and flashing. Clean the flue to remove creosote buildup (page 220).	
Dampers	Open or close dampers to balance the flow of forced air for the season (page 455).	
Boiler (oil-burning type only)	Replace the oil filter (page 465).	
Furnace filter	Inspect the filter for buildup of particles and clean it or replace it, according to the manufacturer's instructions (page 456).	
Air conditioner/ Heat pump	Ask a professional to inspect the refrigerant level. Clean the condenser fins and coils. Check the fan blades and lubricate the motor (page 484).	
Thermostat	Inspect the wires and remove dust and grime from the bi-metal coil. Check the unit for level (page 489).	
Exhaust and bath fans	Clean filters, grills, or blades to maximize air flow (page 480).	

SUMMER

ITEM	PROJECT	NOTES
Foundation	Inspect outside walls for deterioration. Seal and repaint where needed. If necessary, regrade the soil to redirect water drainage (page 24).	
Windows	Check for leaks, wood rot, and moisture buildup.	
Masonry walls and structures	Check for cracks, deterioration, and spalling. Repair mortar joints and replace damaged bricks. Caulk or patch stucco walls (page 224).	
Roof/ Exterior walls	Pressure-wash the surfaces to remove dirt and debris.	
Exterior siding	Repair damaged areas and touch up chipped or peeling paint (page 228).	
Walkways, driveways and concrete surfaces	Inspect for cracking, crumbling, frost heave and other common problems (page 248).	

SUMMER CONT.

ITEM	PROJECT	NOTES
Septic tank	Ask a professional to inspect the tank and pump it, if necessary (page 380).	
Dampers	Open or close dampers to balance the flow of forced air for the season (page 455).	
Boiler	Drain the system to flush accumulated sediment (page 467).	
Room air conditioner	Clean the filter and clear the drains monthly (page 486).	
Evaporative chiller	Replace the pads. Drain the reservoir and check the filter, pads, and pump twice a month (page 487).	

FALL

ITEM	PROJECT	NOTES
Weatherstripping	Inspect materials around doors and windows for wear. Feel for drafts (pages 132 and 137).	
Storm windows	Repair damaged windows. Tighten and lubricate fastening hardware (page 148).	
Gutters	Clean gutters and downspouts. Check for loose connectors and leaky joints. Make sure long runs are straight and sloped properly (page 214).	
Water heater	Drain the tank to remove accumulated sediment. Test the pressure relief valve (page 365).	
Heat registers	Clean register to maximize air flow (page 453).	
Dampers	Adjust the flow of forced air to accommodate specific rooms for the season (page 455).	
Furnace	Clean and lubricate the blower motor (page 457). Inspect the drive belt, pilot light, and burner flame (page 458).	
Furnace humidifier	Clean the evaporator pad and distribution tray. Check the water level (page 462).	
Baseboard heater	Clean the element to increase heating efficiency and prevent burning odors (page 471).	
Radiators/ Convectors	Bleed air from the system (page 468).	
Fireplace/ Wood stove	Inspect the flue, damper, and firebox. Clean the ash pit every two years (page 476).	
Exhaust and bath fans	Clean filters, grills, or blades to maximize air flow (page 478).	
Heat pump	Clean the condensor fins and coils. Check the fan and lubricate the motor (page 484).	
Sillcock	Remove garden hoses, close indoor shutoff valves, and open the sillcock to drain trapped water (page 301).	

WINTER

ITEM	PROJECT	NOTES
Smoke/Carbon monoxide detectors	Replace batteries on battery-operated and battery-backup units.	
Emergency supplies	Check emergency items, such as a radio, batteries, flashlights, stored water and food, candles, and matches. Stock the first-aid kit (page 6).	
Home air quality	Check windows for moisture buildup and bathroom ceilings for mold and mildew.	
Windows/ Doors	Check for drafts during cold or windy periods.	
Roof	Check for ice dams and record their locations (page 188).	
Water softener	Inspect the brine line and injector screen for sediment buildup every two years (page 377).	
Dampers	Adjust the flow of forced air to accommodate specific rooms for the season (page 455).	

ADDITIONAL MAINTENANCE ITEMS

ITEM	PROJECT	NOTES

GLOSSARY

ABS – acrylonitrile butadiene styrene; rigid plastic piping commonly used for drain, waste, and vent plumbing lines in home construction.

Air exchanger – also known as a heat-recovery ventilator; a device that draws fresh air into a forced-air heating/cooling system, warming the air as it enters the system by passing it across metal tubes containing warm air.

Alkyd – a synthetic resin used in oil-based paints. "Alkyd" paint is another name for oil-based paint.

Amperage – a measure of the pressure with which electricity is forced into a circuit. Amperes = watts ÷ voltage.

Ash pit – collection area for ash dumped through the grate in a fireplace.

Ballast – a device, similar to a transformer, in fluorescent light fixtures that regulates the flow of electricity to the light-producing cathodes.

Ballcock – a valve that controls the water supply entering a toilet tank.

Baseboard – a wide trim molding, typically made of wood, fastened along the bottom of interior walls.

Base shoe – a strip of wood trim with two flat sides and a curved front that is typically installed along flooring in front of a baseboard.

Batt insulation – insulation, typically fiberglass, supplied in rolls and often used as a household insulation material.

Bleed valve – a valve on a room radiator or convector used to release air from a hot water heating system.

Blocking – a piece of solid lumber spanning a cavity between framing members to add strength or retard the spread of fire.

Building Code – the set of formal regulations used to dictate construction standards in a community.

Carbon monoxide – an odorless, tasteless gas produced during fuel combustion that can cause dizziness, headaches, and death.

Caulk – a mastic substance, usually containing silicone, used to seal joints. Caulk is waterproof and flexible when dry and adheres to most dry surfaces.

Cement – also called portland cement; the component that hardens masonry mixtures when mixed with water; a blend of lime, silica, alumina, iron, and gypsum.

Concrete – a mixture of portland cement, gravel, and sand. Concrete structures may be reinforced internally with iron bars or mesh.

Condensor – a component of an air-conditioning or heat pump system that condenses a refrigerant to a liquid state, causing it to cool as it releases heat to the air.

Continuity – the uninterrupted flow of electrons from one point to another in an electrical circuit or appliance.

Cope – to cut the profile of one molding piece into the end of another so the two can be joined at a right angle. Done with a coping saw.

CPVC – chlorinated polyvinyl chloride; rigid plastic material used for high-quality water supply pipe products.

Crazing – fine cracking in the finish coat of paint or on the surface of concrete, caused by uneven shrinkage during the drying process.

Crown – the convex edge of a lumber board that has warped during the drying process. When set on edge, a "crowned" board has an arched shape.

Damper – a device installed on most forced-air and hot water systems as a means of controlling the flow of water or air to various parts of the system.

Diverter – a valve that stops the supply of water to one fixture and redirects it to another fixture. Commonly found in sink fixtures with a sprayer attachment or bathtub fixtures with a shower attachment.

Downspout – the vertical tubing of a gutter system, which extends from the gutter to the ground.

Drip edge – a metal strip that protects the edges of the lowest roof shingles and helps divert water away from the house.

Eaves – the portion of the lower end of a roof that overhangs the exterior walls.

Element – a fine metal coil used in electric furnaces and heaters to generate heat by creating resistance to the flow of electrons.

Escutcheon – a decorative metal cover plate used to conceal the entry point of a pipe in a wall or floor surface.

Evaporative chiller – a type of air cooler, found mainly in hot, dry regions, that uses evaporation of water to dampen and cool the air.

Evaporator – a component of an air conditioner or heat pump that cools air by blowing it across a coil through which a chilled refrigerant flows.

Faced insulation – batt insulation (see Batt) with an outer layer, often made of kraft paper or foil, that serves as a vapor barrier.

Facing – any material used as a veneer to cover an inferior surface and improve appearance.

Fascia – a wide board nailed across the ends of the roof rafters. The fascia holds the outside edge of the soffit.

Fin – one of a series of plates in a convector or electric heater that disperses heat to the surrounding air.

Firebox – the area of a fireplace where fire is contained.

Flapper – a rubber seal in a toilet that controls the flow of water from the tank to the bowl.

Flashing – aluminum or galvanized steel sheeting cut and bent into various sizes and shapes. Used to keep water from entering joints between roof elements and to direct water away from structural elements.

Four-way switch – a switch installed between a pair of three-way switches. Four-way switches do not have ON-OFF markings and make it possible to control a single fixture or set of lights from three or more locations.

Framing member – a common term for a single structural element of a construction framework, such as a stud, joist, truss, beam, or rafter.

Frost heave – the upward movement of structural footings caused by the expansion of the ground as it freezes.

Frost line – the depth to which frost penetrates the ground in winter. The depth differs depending on the climate of the region.

Furring strip – narrow strips of wood or other material attached to a solid surface to create a flat or level foundation for a finish surface.

GFCI – see Ground-Fault Circuit-Interrupter.

Ground – a pathway for conducting electricity between the earth and an electrical circuit or device. On a switch, receptacle, or electrical box, the screw or terminal to which a ground wire (usually green or uninsulated) normally is connected.

Ground-Fault Circuit-Interrupter – a safety device designed to detect minute changes in current—as in a short circuit—and to interrupt the flow by shutting off power before the short can cause injury. GFCI receptacles are required by Code in many parts of the house.

Grounding rod – a metal rod buried deep in the earth and connected to household wiring to provide a safe outlet for electricity in the event of a short circuit.

Grout – a fluid cement product used to fill spaces between ceramic tiles or other crevices.

Heat exchanger – the area of a furnace where heated gases are used to heat air that will circulate throughout the house.

Heat pump – a reversible air-conditioning system that extracts heat from the air for heating or cooling purposes.

High-voltage circuit – a 240-volt circuit (see Voltage).

Hot – carrying live voltage, as in an electrical circuit. In NM cable, the "hot" wires are usually black or red.

Impeller – the grinding mechanism in a food disposer, consisting of two metal teeth fixed to a rotating metal disk powered by the motor.

Jack – the female part of an electrical connection that receives a probe or plug to complete a circuit.

Joist – horizontal framing member secured to beams or wall frames to support floor and ceiling surfaces. Ceiling joists are smaller than floor joists.

Jumper wire – a wire used to bypass the water meter and ensure an uninterrupted grounding pathway.

Limit control – a heating element that switches an electric heater off if it reaches too high a temperature.

Line voltage – the voltage that comes directly from a household circuit without being reduced by a transformer.

Low voltage – voltage produced by a transformer that reduces standard household current to about 24 volts to power doorbells, telephones, and many thermostats.

Miter – an angled end-cut for fitting two pieces together at an angle. Doorway trim is often mitered at 45 degrees.

Molding – a strip of wood or other material used to cover construction joints or decorate functional elements of a building.

Mortar – a mixture of portland cement, lime, and sand used to bond the bricks or blocks of a masonry wall.

Mortise-and-tenon – a common woodworking joint in which a protrusion cut from the end of one board fits into a matching cavity cut into another board.

Neutral – a wire or terminal in an electrical circuit that is designed to return current to its source. A neutral wire is usually coated with white insulation.

Newel post – the vertical post supporting the handrail of a staircase. Starting and landing newels stand at the foot and landing of a staircase, respectively.

NM cable – standard modern-day cable for indoor use, with either two or three individually wrapped wires (plus a bare copper ground) encased inside.

Nonmetallic cable – see NM cable.

On center – a construction layout term used to describe the measurement or spacing from the center of one member to the center of another member.

Pilot light – a flame on an oven, furnace, or other heating device, used to ignite fuel when there is a call for heat.

Plenum – a central duct exiting a furnace and leading to branch ducts that extend to various sections of a home.

Plumb – a carpentry term meaning perfectly vertical. The outer bubble gauges of a level are used to inspect for plumb.

Polarized plug – a type of plug with a long and a short slot designed to keep electrical current directed along the proper wires for safety.

PVC – polyvinyl chloride; rigid plastic material that is highly resistant to heat and chemicals. Used for drain-waste and vent piping.

Radon – a tasteless, odorless, naturally occurring gas that can produce illnesses.

Ridge – the horizontal line along the high point of a peaked roof. The ridge is created by the ridge beam, which joins the top ends of the rafters.

Saddle valve – a plumbing fitting that is clamped to copper supply pipe, with a hollow spike that closes the pipe to divert water to another supply line.

Sash – the frame that encases the glass panes of a window.

Sash cord – a rope connecting the window sash to a weight inside the window frame. The cord travels on a pulley that rotates as the window is opened or closed.

Scribing – the technique of tracing the contour of one surface onto another for custom cutting. Usually done using a compass.

Service panel – a panel of fuses or circuit breakers from which electrical current is directed to various household circuits.

Shake – a hand-split cedar roofing shingle.

Sheathing – a layer of plywood or other sheet goods covering the wall or roof framing of a house. Also: the protective outer layer of nonmetallic electrical cable, made of plastic or woven fibers.

Sheet vinyl – a flooring material made from vinyl and other plastics in the form of sheets that are 6 ft. or 12 ft. wide and approximately 1/8 in. thick.

Single-pole switch – a switch designed to serve as the exclusive switch for a light or fixture. The labels ON and OFF are marked on the switch.

Soffit – the covering that attaches to the fascia and exterior wall to enclose the underside of the roof eaves.

Solenoid – a switch that uses electricity passing through coiled wires to create a magnetic field that moves a metal cylinder into position to complete a circuit.

Sole plate – a 2 × 4 or 2 × 6 board nailed flat on the floor to support the bottom ends of wall studs.

Spalling – chipping or flaking of a brick or block surface, caused by weather changes, freezing water, or other forces.

Spline – a flexible rubber cord used to hold screening in a frame. Also: a narrow piece of wood or metal used for strengthening joints.

Spud – the orifice at the end of a fuel supply tube in a forced-air furnace that releases heating fuel for combustion.

Stack – the main vertical drain line in a home plumbing system, designed to carry waste from the branch drains to a sewer line.

Strike plate – a metal plate with a curled front edge that is fastened to a door jamb to receive the live-action bolt of a doorknob mechanism.

Stringers – the structural members of a staircase that extend diagonally from one floor to another and support the stair treads and risers.

Stucco – a cement-based plaster used to cover exterior walls. Installed in three layers over strips of wood lath or metal mesh.

Stud – a vertical framing member of a wall. In house construction, studs are typically 2 × 4 boards spaced 16 in. apart.

Subfloor – plywood or 1-in. lumber decking nailed across the tops of the floor joists to create the foundation of the floor surface.

Thermocouple – a safety device found in gas appliances that automatically shuts off the gas supply if the pilot light goes out.

Three-way switch – a switch used in applications in which two switches control the same fixture or set of lights. Three-way switches are always installed in pairs and do not have ON-OFF markings.

Transformer – a device that receives the line voltage in a household circuit and reduces it to a specific low-voltage rating.

Trap – also called a P-trap, a curved section of pipe used in most household drains. The trap holds standing water that prevents sewer gases from backing up into the house.

Tread – the horizontal platform of each step in a set of stairs. Treads are supported from below or at the ends by stringers.

Trim – any decorative molding used for ornamentation or to conceal construction seams.

Tuckpointing – the process of repairing a brick or block surface by cleaning out failed mortar joints and filling them with fresh mortar.

Underlayment – a layer of plywood or other material laid over the subfloor to create a smooth surface for a floor finish.

Valley – the junction between two sloping roof surfaces.

Voltage – a measure of the pressure with which electrons are forced through a wire or cable. In the United States and Canada, most household circuits are 120-volt circuits. Heavy appliances may require a 240-volt circuit. Voltage = wattage ÷ amperes.

Wallboard – also called drywall or Sheetrock; flat 4 × 8 panels made of gypsum covered with several layers of paper. Used for most interior wall and ceiling surfaces.

Waste vent – an open-ended pipe that ventilates a plumbing drain line, allowing waste water to travel through the drain system without getting stopped by trapped air.

Wattage – a measure of the rate at which electricity is consumed. Wattage = voltage × amperes.

INDEX

A

B

C

D

E

P

Q

R

S

T

U

Look for these other fine Black & Decker books from Creative Publishing international. They are available at all fine booksellers.

The Complete Guide to Home Masonry

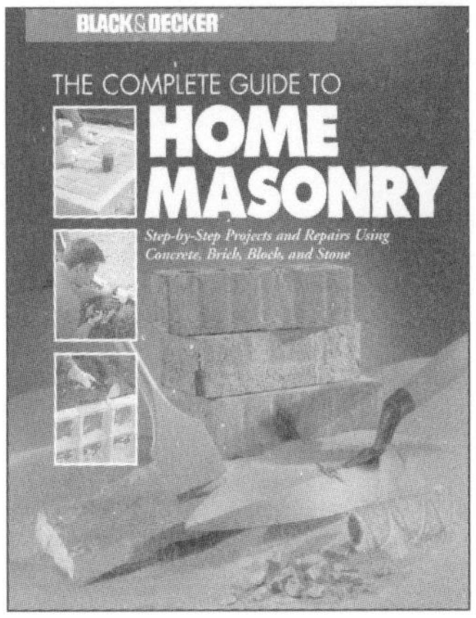

Contains more than 50 original projects, a complete maintenance and repair section, and an extensive "basic techniques" section for the major types of masonry (concrete, brick, block, and stone), as well as specialty materials, including stucco, tile, and hypertufa. From laying a foundation for a wall to placing the keystone in an arch, *The Complete Guide to Home Masonry* shows every step of your project with clarity and simplicity—using the most up-to-date information and products.

Building Garden Ornaments

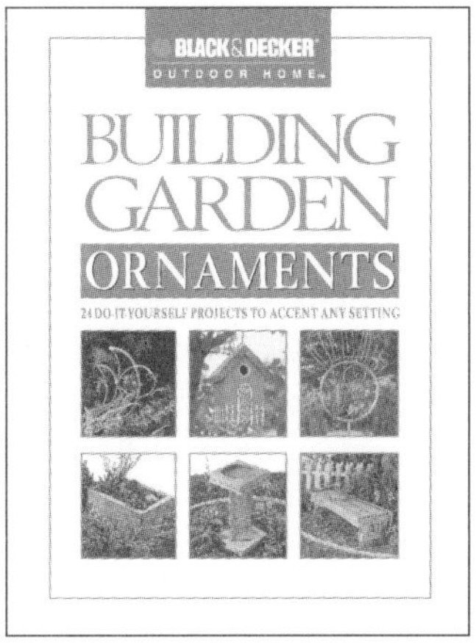

Ornaments transform a garden into a reflection of personal style and reinforce the impression that the gardener loves his or her work, down to the smallest detail. Until now, the prices of some popular ornaments have put them out of reach for many people. But with *Building Garden Ornaments,* anyone can build dozens of stylish garden ornaments—easily and inexpensively. Each project uses simple construction methods and inexpensive, readily-available materials. Clear step-by-step instructions guide you through the process, and tips and variations let you achieve truly unique results.

Home Improvement

The New Everyday Home Repairs
Decorating with Paint & Wallcovering
Remodeling Kitchens
Building Decks
Basic Wiring & Electrical Repairs
Advanced Home Wiring
Carpentry: Remodeling
Bathroom Remodeling
Built-in Projects for the Home
Refinishing & Finishing Wood
Exterior Home Repairs & Improvements
Home Masonry Repairs & Projects
Building Porches & Patios
Flooring Projects & Techniques
Great Decks & Furnishings
Advanced Deck Building
Advanced Home Plumbing
The Complete Guide to Wiring
The Complete Guide to Plumbing
The Complete Guide to Painting & Decorating
The Complete Guide to Decks

Outdoor

Landscape Design & Construction
Designing Your Outdoor Home
Building Your Outdoor Home
Vegetable Gardening: Your Ultimate Guide
Annuals
Shade Gardening
Lawns
Container Gardening

Saw Blades

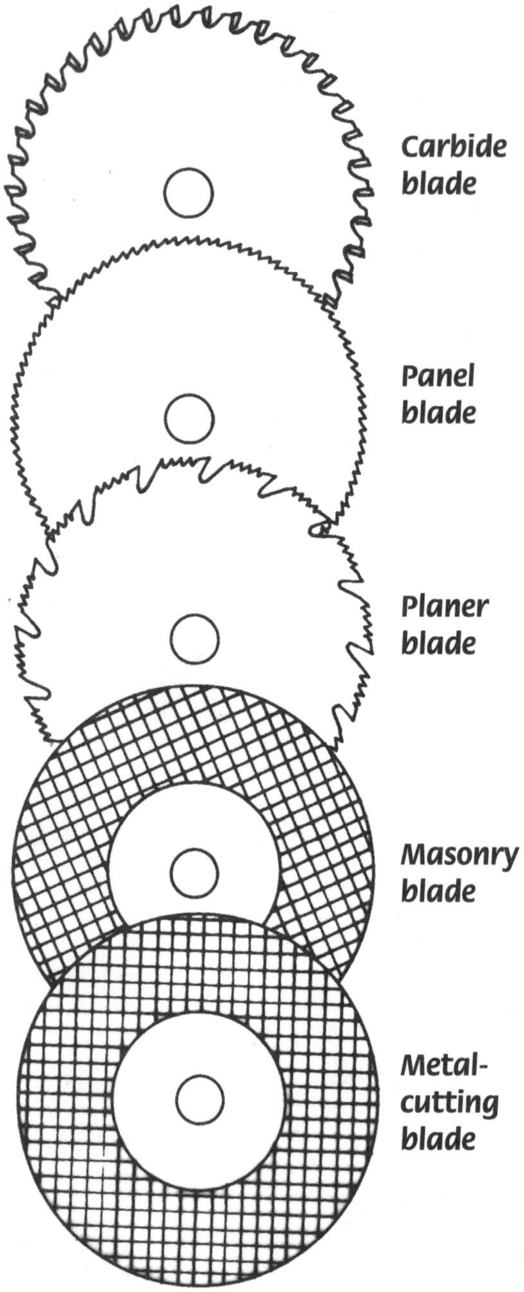

Adhesives

TYPE	CHARACTERISTICS	USES
WHITE GLUE	**Strength:** moderate; rigid bond **Drying time:** several hours **Resistance to heat:** poor **Resistance to moisture:** poor **Hazards:** none **Cleanup/solvent:** soap and water	**Porous surfaces:** Wood (indoors) Paper Cloth
YELLOW GLUE (carpenter's glue)	**Strength:** moderate to good; rigid bond **Drying time:** several hours; faster than white glue **Resistance to heat:** moderate **Resistance to moisture:** moderate **Hazards:** none **Cleanup/solvent:** soap and water	**Porous surfaces:** Wood (indoors) Paper Cloth
TWO-PART EPOXY	**Strength:** excellent; strongest of all adhesives **Drying time:** varies, depending on manufacturer **Resistance to heat:** excellent **Resistance to moisture:** excellent **Hazards:** fumes are toxic and flammable **Cleanup/solvent:** acetone will dissolve some types	**Smooth & porous surfaces:** Wood (indoors & outdoors) Metal Masonry Glass Fiberglass
HOT GLUE	**Strength:** depends on type **Drying time:** less than 60 seconds **Resistance to heat:** fair **Resistance to moisture:** good **Hazards:** hot glue can cause burns **Cleanup/solvent:** heat will loosen bond	**Smooth & porous surfaces:** Glass Plastics Wood
CYANOACRYLATE (instant glue)	**Strength:** excellent, but with little flexibility **Drying time:** a few seconds **Resistance to heat:** excellent **Resistance to moisture:** excellent **Hazards:** can bond skin instantly; toxic, flammable **Cleanup/solvent:** acetone	**Smooth surfaces:** Glass Ceramics Plastics Metal
CONSTRUCTION ADHESIVE	**Strength:** good to excellent; very durable **Drying time:** 24 hours **Resistance to heat:** good **Resistance to moisture:** excellent **Hazards:** may irritate skin and eyes **Cleanup/solvent:** soap and water (while still wet)	**Porous surfaces:** Framing lumber Plywood and paneling Wallboard Foam panels Masonry
WATER-BASE CONTACT CEMENT	**Strength:** good **Drying time:** bonds instantly; dries fully in 30 minutes **Resistance to heat:** excellent **Resistance to moisture:** good **Hazards:** may irritate skin and eyes **Cleanup/solvent:** soap and water (while still wet)	**Porous surfaces:** Plastic laminates Plywood Flooring Cloth
SILICONE SEALANT (caulk)	**Strength:** fair to good; very flexible bond **Drying time:** 24 hours **Resistance to heat:** good **Resistance to moisture:** excellent **Hazards:** may irritate skin and eyes **Cleanup/solvent:** acetone	**Smooth & porous surfaces:** Wood Ceramics Fiberglass Plastics Glass

Abrasive Paper Grits - (Aluminum Oxide)

VERY COARSE	COARSE	MEDIUM	FINE	VERY FINE
12 - 36	40 - 60	80 - 120	150 - 180	220 - 600